ISBN 978-1-5310-1736-1
eISBN 978-1-5310-1737-8
LCCN 2020946569

Carolina Academic Press
700 Kent Street
Durham, North Carolina 27701
Telephone (919) 489-7486
Fax (919) 493-5668
www.cap-press.com

Printed in the United States of America

Contents

Online Materials

Additional content for *Criminal Law* (second edition) is available on Carolina Academic Press's *Core Knowledge for Lawyers* (CKL) website.

Core Knowledge for Lawyers is an online teaching and testing platform that hosts practice questions and additional content for both instructors and students.

To learn more, please visit:

coreknowledgeforlawyers.com

Instructors may request complimentary access through the "Faculty & Instructors" link.

Table of Cases

Acknowledgments

I give special thanks to Michael Dimino, Russell Covey, B.J. Priester, Michael Whiteman, and my colleague Mike Benza for their generosity in providing me with insightful comments and suggestions on various iterations of the manuscript. I'm pleased to welcome Dan Medwed as a coauthor on the book and am grateful for his insights, suggestions, and contributions. I would also like to acknowledge the many students in my criminal law classes who have helped shape my thinking about teaching criminal law. Their insights, comments, and questions in large measure shaped this book.

Daniel Medwed would like to thank Kevin McMunigal, whose work he has long admired from afar, for inviting him to work closely on this book. He is also grateful to the legions of his criminal law students over the years who have offered feedback about the book, and planted seeds that have borne fruit in this edition. Finally, he would like to thank his wife Sharissa Jones and their daughters Clementine and Mili for their willingness to endure his occasional criminal law war stories and his (more frequent) dad jokes.

We would also like to thank the authors, publishers, and copyright holders listed below for giving permission to reprint excerpts from their materials.

The American Law Institute, THE MODEL PENAL CODE, Copyright 1985 by the American Law Institute. Reprinted with permission. All rights reserved.

Breyer, Stephen, *On the Uses of Legislative History in Interpreting Statutes*, 65 Southern California Law Review, 845–890 (1992). Reprinted with the permission of the Southern California Law Review.

Buchandler-Raphael, Michal, *Fear-Based Provocation*, 67 Am. L. Rev. 1719 (2018). Reprinted with permission of the author.

Buel, Sarah, *Violence Against Women: How to Improve the Legal Services' Response*, Nov. 18, 1991 (cited in Defending Our Lives, Study and Resource Guide 13, 19). Reprinted with permission of the author.

Crump, David & Susan Waite Crump, *In Defense of the Felony Murder Doctrine*, 8 Harv. J. L. & Pub. Pol'y 359, 362–68, 370–71, 374–75 (Spr. 1985). Reprinted with permission of the authors.

Denno, Deborah W., *Crime and Consciousness: Science and Involuntary Acts*, 87 Minn. L. Rev. 269, 269–72, 274–75, 361, 369 (2002). Reprinted with permission of the author.

DiIulio, Jr., John J., *Help Wanted: Economists, Crime and Public Policy*, 10 Journal of Economic Perspectives 3–24 (Winter 1996). Reprinted with permission of the author.

Eskridge, Jr., William N., *Dynamic Statutory Interpretation*, 135 Univ. Pa. L. Rev. 1479, 1479–1480, 1482–1484, 1496–1497, 1498, 1506–1507 (1987). C1987 by the University of Pennsylvania Law Review.). Reprinted with permission of the author.

Harrington, Matthew P., *The Law-Finding Function of the American Jury*, 1999 WISCONSIN LAW REVIEW 377, 377–380. Reprinted with permission of the author.

Kahan, Dan M., *Three Conceptions of Federal Criminal-Lawmaking*, 1 BUFF. CRIM. L. R. 5, 5–18 (1997). Reprinted with permission of the author.

Kitrosser, Heidi, *Meaningful Consent: Toward a New Generation of Statutory Rape Laws*, 4 Va. J. of Soc. Pol'y and L. 287, 322–326 (1997). Reprinted with permission of the author.

Lee, Evan Tsen, *Cancelling Crime*, 30 Conn. L. Rev. 117 (1997). Reprinted with permission of the author.

Roth, Nelson E., & Sundby, Scott E., *The Felony-Murder Rule: A Doctrine at Constitutional Crossroads*, 70 Cornell L. Rev. 446 (1985). Reprinted with permission of the authors.

Scalia, Antonin, *A Matter of Interpretation* 16-37. Copyright 1997 by Princeton University Press. Reprinted with permission of Princeton University Press.

Some materials and ideas in this book, *Criminal Law: Problems, Statutes, and Cases*, are drawn from an original 2005 book entitled, *Criminal Law: A Contemporary Approach*, co-authored by Kate E. Bloch and Kevin C. McMunigal. The author of *Criminal Law: Problems, Statutes, and Cases*, Kevin C. McMunigal, is indebted to Kate E. Bloch for her innovative and thoughtful scholarship as reflected in the original work. Although the current text may draw upon that scholarship, because Kate E. Bloch did not prepare the materials for *Criminal Law: Problems, Statutes, and Cases*, Kate E. Bloch bears no responsibility for *Criminal Law: Problems, Statutes, and Cases*, including no responsibility for the selection or use in *Criminal Law: Problems, Statutes, and Cases* of any ideas or materials from the original work.

Diagramming Crimes

By Kevin C. McMunigal

In my criminal law class, I routinely "diagram" crimes to help students grasp their elements and master the skill of legal analysis. The technique is reminiscent of diagramming sentences, once a staple of elementary school English classes. Criminal offense diagrams don't look like sentence diagrams. But each is useful in breaking something down, whether a sentence or a criminal statute, to identify and understand its component parts.

A word of caution at the outset. Diagramming is a tool to help extract from a statute or an opinion and clearly state the elements of an offense. It is not alchemy. It cannot, for example, transform an ambiguous statute into a clear one. But it can help students spot ambiguity in the definition of an offense and respond by developing and deploying statutory interpretation skills.

Diagramming Basics

Each offense element gets a box. The boxes are stacked in two adjacent columns with the non-mental elements on the right and the mental elements on the left. For reasons revealed below, it makes sense to start with the non-mental elements. I typically place the conduct element at the top and put other non-mental elements, such as a result or circumstance, directly below the conduct box. The non-mental column for a hypothetical statute penalizing the transportation of stolen archaeological artifacts would look like this:

Non-Mental Elements

Transport
Stolen
Artifacts

The mental state boxes come next. I draw an empty box to the immediate left of each non-mental element box:

Mental Elements	Non-Mental Elements
	Transport
	Stolen
	Artifacts

Each empty box provides space for filling in any required mental state regarding the non-mental element to its immediate right.

Understanding Mental States

Simply drawing a column of empty mental state boxes helps one grasp several important points about mental state. First, it helps in distinguishing mental from non-mental elements. Second, it demonstrates that criminal statutes may and often do require more than one mental state for conviction. The stolen artifacts statute, for example, might require *purpose* to transport, *knowledge* that the objects are stolen, but only *recklessness* that the objects are archaeological artifacts. These mental states would be reflected in an offense diagram as follows:

Mental Elements	Non-Mental Elements
Purpose →	Transport
Knowledge →	Stolen
Recklessness →	Artifacts

Failure to distinguish clearly among mental states is a common problem in the criminal law's treatment of mental state.

Diagramming also reveals that mental state is relational. A person at any one time has many mental states regarding many different things. In order to speak and think clearly about mental state, it helps to clarify the reference point for the mental state in question. If we were to ask, for example, "What was the mental state of the defendant?" in a case arising under our stolen artifacts statute, it would be impossible to answer the question clearly without specifying the reference point for the mental state—the act of transporting the artifacts, their status as stolen, or their status as artifacts. That a crime may require and a criminal may possess more than one mental state make it critical to specify a reference point for a mental state to avoid confusion.

Because mental state is relational, it helps to begin an offense diagram by constructing the non-mental element boxes *before* constructing the mental state boxes to clarify the reference points for the mental states.

Once one is familiar with Model Penal Code mental state terminology, one can use a "P" for purpose, "K" for knowledge, "R" for recklessness, and "N" for negligence. If a statute is written or interpreted as doing away with mental state regarding a particular non-mental element, I indicate that by putting "SL" for strict liability in the mental box next to that element. Adding an arrow to the mental state boxes as shown here helps emphasize the relational nature of mental states:

Mental Elements	Non-Mental Elements
P	Transport
K	Stolen
R	Artifacts

Some mental state boxes are easy to fill in. With negligent homicide, for example, negligence is the required mental state regarding the resulting death. Some statutes provide for alternative mental states. Pennsylvania, for example, includes both reckless and grossly negligent killings under manslaughter.[1] Many jurisdictions provide that murder can be based on purpose, knowledge, or extreme recklessness regarding the death. Diagrams of such manslaughter and murder statutes look like this:

Mental Elements	Non-Mental Elements
P	Conduct
R or N	Death

Mental Elements	Non-Mental Elements
P	Conduct
P or K or ER	Death

Figuring out what mental states a statute requires for conviction, though, can be difficult. One routine ambiguity pertaining to mental state that diagramming helps illustrate is what I refer to as a mental state "carryover" problem. Sometimes a statute sets out a mental state without clearly indicating the non-mental element or elements

---

1. *See* 18 Pennsylvania Consolidated Statutes Section 2504.

to which the mental state applies. Assume, for example, that the stolen artifacts statute made it a crime to "knowingly transport stolen archeological artifacts." What sort of knowledge is required for conviction? Knowledge that one is engaged in the act of transporting? Knowledge that the item transported is stolen? Knowledge that the item transported is an archaeological artifact? All of these?

Diagramming is a great way to illustrate this interpretive issue by putting a "K" next to the non-mental element to which "knowingly" is closest in the statute and question marks in the mental state boxes next to the other non-mental elements.

The Model Penal Code has a rule to resolve this interpretation dilemma. Section 2.02 (4) states that a prescribed mental state applies to *all* material elements "unless a contrary purpose plainly appears." Diagramming demonstrates the usefulness of this Model Penal Code provision. In a Model Penal Code jurisdiction, I would replace each question mark with a "K" and use arrows to show that the mental state carries over from one non-mental element to the others.

Sometimes a statute requires proof of a mental state beyond those pertaining to its non-mental elements. Burglary statutes, for example, often require intent to commit a felony inside a building. One can easily incorporate such an additional mental state by adding a mental state box at the bottom of the mental state column. There would be no non-mental element box to the right of such a mental state box, as in the following diagram.

Mental Elements		Non-Mental Elements
P	$\longrightarrow$	Enter
K	$\longrightarrow$	Dwelling
K	$\longrightarrow$	At Night
P to Commit a Felony		

Statutory Interpretation

If a statute or a case found its way into a criminal law case book, there is a good chance that ambiguity will be found in the statutory language defining the crime at issue. Just as a map often facilitates following written directions when finding one's way to an unfamiliar location, using a diagram to chart the extraction of elements from a statute aids in performing that extraction process. Diagramming represents and clarifies the process of analyzing a statute, something that can become quite murky using language alone.

Diagramming helps isolate and spotlight the ambiguity that gives rise to the need for interpretation. Statutes that are silent on mental state, for example, are regular sources of ambiguity. Should the silence be interpreted as legislative approval of strict liability? Or did the legislature intend to require some mental state without stating it in the text of the statute? If so, what mental state? Just putting a question mark in the mental state box next to a particular element can be a great way to illustrate and focus on the statutory interpretation question such a statute poses.

Criminal Law

Chapter 1

Overview of the Criminal Justice System

The subject of this book and the course you are starting is criminal law. Law professors and other lawyers often refer to this subject as substantive criminal law to distinguish it from criminal procedure. Both substantive criminal law and criminal procedure have an impact on criminal investigations and prosecutions. Substantive criminal law creates and defines criminal offenses such as murder, robbery, and assault, for which people may be tried, convicted, and punished. Substantive criminal law determines what evidence the police need to gather for trial, such as evidence of premeditation in a case of first-degree murder. Criminal procedure, in contrast, creates and defines the rules and processes for enforcing criminal offenses, those regulating investigations and those regulating adjudication. For example, criminal procedure governs the manner in which the police conduct searches and question suspects and how a jury is selected for trial. Criminal procedure is the subject of courses you may take later in your law school career.

Because you will read many opinions dealing with cases that were investigated and tried, it will be helpful for you to have a general grasp of how the criminal justice system operates. This chapter serves that purpose.

A. The Start of a Criminal Case

Criminal cases start with events outside a courthouse. An event, such as a theft of property or an assault, occurs and it catches the attention of law enforcement officials. Sometimes the news arrives through reports from others and sometimes through firsthand observations by the police. Once officers receive news of potential criminal activity, they exercise discretion in deciding whether and how to investigate. Police typically react to crimes such as homicide and robbery after their occurrence. In contrast, police are sometimes proactive in investigating possible crimes such as drug and white-collar offenses. Exercises of discretion pervade the criminal justice system.

Various considerations influence this early exercise of discretion. They include police policy, legal boundaries, the information available about the case, social and cultural perceptions, the gravity of the harm (or threatened harm), any criminal history of the accused, and resources. If law enforcement officials decide to proceed, they may conduct minimal or extensive investigation. Police investigations can employ a host of tools, including search warrants, forensics, sting operations, and surveillance. A typical petty theft from a local retail store involves minimal investigation. The investigation of a theft of computer trade secrets may involve months or years. Sometimes prosecutors supervise investigations. Other times the police investigate a case without involving the prosecutor and simply turn over the results of their investigation once it has been concluded. Is prosecutorial involvement in an investigation a good idea?

When the police exercise discretion in ways that coincide with public attitudes and constitutional norms, it rarely generates comment. For example, we generally applaud police pursuit of a hit-and-run driver or investigation of a kidnapping. We find relief in learning that police succeeded in apprehending an individual wanted in connection with a serious crime or that they have responded promptly to a panicked 911 call.

Sometimes, however, police practices generate concern and criticism. The New York Police Department's use of aggressive stop-and-frisk tactics, for example, has been the subject of much public controversy, as well as federal litigation challenging its constitutionality. We provide two more examples below. The first involved a law enforcement approach to domestic violence. The second involved the question of police targeting of homosexual men as potential offenders.

Research shows that almost one in three women and approximately one in four men report that they have been physically and/or sexually assaulted or stalked by an intimate on at least one occasion.[1] In light of these statistics, consider the following analysis of police responses to domestic violence:

> For many years, societal responses to domestic violence excluded legal intervention.... [M]any police departments had "hands off" policies prior to the 1970s, and police training manuals actually specified that arrest was to be avoided whenever possible in responding to domestic disputes.[2]

In the 1970s, 80s, and 90s, scrutiny of and challenges to the lack of police response, in addition to enhanced public understanding of domestic violence and the availability of new legal tools, produced substantial change. From "hands off" as described above, Professor Cheryl Hanna explains the near-complete reversal in approach to preferred or mandatory arrest policy for domestic violence crimes:

> In 1984, the United States Attorney General recommended arrest as the standard police response to domestic violence. This recommendation resulted from a landmark Minneapolis study that compared the deterrent effects of

---

1. Michele C. Black et al., National Center for Injury Prevention and Control, Centers for Disease Control and Prevention, THE NATIONAL INTIMATE PARTNER AND SEXUAL VIOLENCE SURVEY: 2010 SUMMARY REPORT (2011), *available at* http://www.cdc.gov/violenceprevention/pdf/nisvs_report2010-a.pdf.
2. Jeffrey Fagan, National Institute of Justice, THE CRIMINALIZATION OF DOMESTIC VIOLENCE: PROMISES AND LIMITS 4, 8 (January 1996) (citations omitted) [hereinafter Fagan].

arresting the suspect, mediating the dispute, and requiring the batterer to leave the house for eight hours. The study found that arrest more effectively deterred subsequent violence than did the other courses of action. This study, followed by the Attorney General's recommendation, provided the foundation for nationwide legal reform.... All fifty states now provide for warrantless misdemeanor arrests in domestic violence cases.

Since arrest statutes have been broadened, many jurisdictions have moved toward mandatory and pro-arrest policies. Under these policies, an arrest is either required or preferred if there is probable cause to believe that a domestic battery has taken place.[3]

Some challenges to police discretion focus on categories of crime, such as domestic violence. Other challenges question police discretion in targeting particular offenders. In one case, a group of defendants challenged their arrests, alleging that the:

police who arrested them engaged in a pattern of discriminatory arrest and prosecution of homosexuals.... In support of their [challenge], defendants presented 10 arrest reports spanning a 2-year period. The reports described decoy officers' arrests of men in and outside an adult bookstore [for soliciting a lewd act to be performed in a public place.] ... The arrests involved a decoy officer who had engaged a person in small talk ... [using a] modus operandi ... typical of a 'cruising' pattern of homosexual men and that it invited homosexual men to make contact with the decoy officer.... The [trial] court concluded that the operation was focused solely on persons who had a proclivity to engage in homosexual conduct.... [The trial court determined] that there was discrimination ... evidenced by the officers' method of operation; that their method of operation was designed to ferret out homosexuals or those who were likely to engage in homosexual acts, and that it did so without any relationship to the alleged problems at that location for which the citizen complaint had been initially lodged.[4]

As these examples illustrate, police discretion and control play key roles at the outset of a criminal case.

B. Charging: The Prosecutor's Office

If, after investigating, police decide that a case warrants prosecution, they contact a prosecutor's office. Geographic boundaries and the nature of the case play a role in determining the jurisdictions of local, state, and federal prosecutors. Sometimes their jurisdictions overlap. State courts, those in which local and state prosecutors

---

3. Cheryl Hanna, *No Right to Choose: Mandated Victim Participation in Domestic Violence Prosecutions*, 109 HARV. L. REV. 1849, 1859–60 (1996) (citations omitted) [hereinafter Hanna].

4. *Baluyut v. Superior Court*, 12 Cal.4th 826, 830–31 (1996).

file their cases, hear more than 95 percent of criminal cases.[5] Of these, local prosecutors at the county level usually handle the overwhelming majority. Prosecutors working for the state's Attorney General's office tend to specialize in particular types of offenses or relieve local prosecutors when they have a conflict of interest. Federal jurisdiction arises in a variety of circumstances. For instance, state and local agencies may lack jurisdiction over a crime that occurred on federal land, or a federal statute may authorize federal prosecution of cases that raise a particular federal concern. For example, federal, rather than state or local, agencies commonly prosecute the robbery of banks, which are insured by the federal government.

1. The Charging Decision

Charging a crime affects people's lives. Charging alone can subject the accused to ridicule, shame, alienation, poverty, and imprisonment. The impact on victims and witnesses can also be enormous. Like decisions surrounding investigation, charging decisions also involve exercises of discretion, typically by prosecutors. To guide the exercise of prosecutorial discretion, prosecutorial organizations, state bar associations, and legislatures have adopted rules, standards, and statutes.

For example, state legal ethics rules routinely require that a prosecutor not institute criminal charges when the prosecutor knows or should know that the charges are not supported by probable cause. In this context, probable cause may be understood as "a state of facts [that] would lead a [person] ... of ordinary caution or prudence to believe and conscientiously entertain a strong suspicion of the guilt of the accused."[6] This probable cause standard is equivalent to the standard police must meet in exercising discretion to arrest someone. In the range of legal standards, probable cause is not very demanding and requires much less than the "beyond a reasonable doubt" standard for conviction.

Much to the dismay of many, the fact that police and prosecutors have limited time and resources can also play a substantial role in charging decisions. Prosecutorial perspectives often change over time, in response to shifting political and social dynamics, new research, education, or information. After the 9/11 attacks, for example, the FBI shifted resources away from drug cases and into investigating threats of terrorism. In the early 1990s, California police arrested and prosecutors charged and tried individuals who provided clean needles to addicts for the misdemeanor crime of possessing or distributing syringes without a prescription. In contrast, in 2002 a local San Francisco Bay Area newspaper reported:

> [i]nstead of arresting people for helping drug addicts get access to clean needles, [one of those California counties] ... just might start paying for it ... Many, especially people in law enforcement, used to view such programs as encouraging drug use.... There is now substantial research indicating that needle exchange programs significantly help decrease the rate of HIV and

---

5. Administrative Office of the U.S. Courts, Court Statistics Project, EXAMINING THE WORK OF STATE COURTS 3 (2010).

6. *People v. Uhlemann*, 9 Cal.3d 662, 667 (1973).

hepatitis C infection without promoting drug use, [said County Health Officer Dr. Scott Morrow.][7]

In recent years, more than two dozen women and men often referred to as "progressive prosecutors" have been elected in cities throughout the United States.[8] Examples include Rachael Rollins in Boston, Larry Krasner in Philadelphia, and Eric Gonzalez in Brooklyn. These prosecutors have chosen to exercise their discretion to address multiple problems in the criminal justice system. Common themes include the elimination of bail as a condition of pretrial release to help poor defendants, treatment rather than punishment for low level drug offenses, sensitivity to the impact of the criminal justice system on the poor and racial minorities, reducing incarceration, and dealing more effectively with police misconduct. Rachael Rollins, for example, has pledged to focus limited police and prosecutorial resources on more serious crimes and not prosecute certain low level offenses. Eric Gonzalez publicly announced a list of police officers his office would no longer call as sole witnesses in cases because of the officers' past credibility problems. Larry Krasner is supporting the establishment of a safe drug injection site in Philadelphia.

Progressive city prosecutors, though, have encountered resistance from some police unions as well as some conservative governors and state legislators.[9] Under the Trump administration, the United States Department of Justice has sought to challenge some of the progressive prosecutors' initiatives. For example, the federal government brought suit to stop the creation of the safe injection site District Attorney Larry Krasner supports in Philadelphia on the ground that it would violate federal drug laws. In late 2019, a federal district court judge in Philadelphia ruled against the Department of Justice and in support of the safe injection site.[10]

In the area of domestic violence, prosecutorial policies have undergone substantial modification. The change from a policy designed to avoid arrest to a preferred or mandatory arrest policy encouraged collection of evidence and referral to prosecutors. Following years in which "[p]rosecutors failed to actively pursue cases where victims and offenders had intimate relationships...,"[11] "many offices now have pro-prosecution or 'no-drop' policies."[12] Although the specifics vary, "no-drop" policies encourage or require prosecutors to proceed with cases, sometimes even in the face of adamant victim noncooperation.

Professor Cheryl Hanna discusses some of the initial data on the no-drop policies:

Early data indicate that aggressive prosecution policies can reduce homicides. In San Diego, homicides related to domestic violence fell from thirty in 1985

---

7. Sara Zaske, *County May Fund Needle Exchange*, The Independent, May 18, 2002, at 1A.

8. Mark Berman, *These Prosecutors Won Office Vowing to Fight the System. Now, the System Is Fighting Back*, The Washington Post (November 9, 2019); Emily Bazelon, *Charged: The New Movement to Transform American Prosecution and End Mass Incarceration* (2019).

9. *Id.*

10. *United States v. Safehouse*, 408 F. Supp. 3d 583 (E.D. Pa. 2019).

11. Fagan, *supra* note 2, at 4.

12. Hanna, *supra* note 3, at 1861–1862.

to seven in 1994, after successful implementation of its … no-drop program. Additionally, evaluations suggest that jurisdictions that commit significant resources to domestic violence improve prosecution rates, lower recidivism rates, and communicate a stronger message that domestic violence will not be tolerated.[13]

The proper methods for police and prosecutors to use in addressing domestic violence remain subject to debate. What is clear is that the discretion once exercised to limit, or exclude, domestic violence from criminal dockets is now being exercised to emphasize recognition of domestic violence as serious criminal conduct.

A number of factors coalesced to trigger changes in how police and prosecutors address domestic violence. Research showing the widespread nature of domestic abuse, its subsequent effect on children, and the unique socioeconomic and psychological obstacles that victims of domestic abuse face influenced shifts in policy. Changing social attitudes toward domestic violence and the success of lawsuits against law enforcement officers who failed to effectively police abuse also had an impact.

Some types of conduct can result in both civil and criminal liability. For example, while assault and battery are crimes, they are also civil wrongs, called torts. A prosecutor may or may not choose to proceed criminally with such cases. An important factor distinguishing criminal cases from civil cases, such as those involving torts and contracts, is that the plaintiff in a criminal action is the government, either state or federal, as the captions of the criminal cases you will read in this book demonstrate. So when the relevant conduct constitutes a tort, an aggrieved private party can sue the perpetrator civilly regardless of the prosecutor's choice.

A prosecutor's decision not to prosecute a case is virtually unreviewable. But a prosecutor's affirmative decision to charge a criminal case is subject to challenges at a variety of stages.

2. The Applicable Law

A key component of any charging decision is whether a criminal law was broken. Our criminal law originated in decisions that English and American judges made in particular cases. Their accumulated decisions, developed over the course of centuries, were known as the "common law." Today, in contrast to common law, virtually all crimes are created by legislatures through statutes. In fact, Professor Michael Moore contends that "the science of legislation has reached its highest form in criminal legislation."[14] As a consequence, prosecutors turn to statutes to ascertain the law. Federal

---

13. *Id.* at 1864.

14. Michael S. Moore, Act and Crime: The Philosophy of Action and Its Implications for Criminal Law 1 (Clarendon Press, Oxford 1993).

prosecutors charge violations of federal statutes. State and local prosecutors charge violations of state statutes or local laws or ordinances.

A collection of statutes devoted to a particular topic is often called a code. In the 1950s, amidst widespread dissatisfaction with existing criminal codes, a group of criminal law scholars assembled and drafted a detailed new criminal code, the Model Penal Code (often referred to simply as the "MPC"), to be used as a guide for legislators reforming their states' criminal laws. The Model Penal Code has had, and continues to have, a substantial influence on the statutes to which prosecutors turn in determining the appropriate charge. The Model Penal Code functions as a guide for legislators, but it does not become the law in any jurisdiction unless the legislature of that jurisdiction adopts its provisions. A number of jurisdictions have, however, revised their penal codes to reflect or incorporate portions, sometimes substantial portions, of the Model Penal Code. You will encounter and study Model Penal Code provisions throughout this course.

Once a prosecutor decides that someone has violated a criminal statute and the case merits prosecution, she must follow the jurisdiction's charging procedures.

3. Grand Jury versus Prosecutorial Charging and Preliminary Hearing

Two procedures dominate charging in the United States. The first, used by the federal government and some states, involves citizens of the community convened as a grand jury. These citizens determine whether a prosecutor can file charges in court. In the second, the prosecutor alone decides whether to charge and files the charges directly with the court, but the court then conducts a hearing in which it reviews the prosecutor's decision to charge. Each of these two charging procedures constrains prosecutorial discretion. The grand jury or judge serves a screening function and acts as a check on the validity of the police and prosecutor's evaluation of the case.

a. Grand Jury

A grand jury has two functions. One is to investigate crime through its power to subpoena witnesses, documents, and other evidence. The second is to determine whether there is probable cause that a crime was committed and that the proposed defendant committed it. During a grand jury hearing, the prosecutor brings witnesses to testify before a group of citizens who have been sworn as grand jurors. This group of jurors is distinct from the jury that acts as the factfinder at a trial, sometimes referred to as a "petit jury" because it is routinely composed of a smaller number of jurors than a grand jury. The grand jurors decide whether the prosecution has produced adequate proof of the proposed charges. If the grand jurors find the standard met as to any or all of the charges, they issue what is referred to as a "true bill of indictment" as to those charges. The resulting charging document is typically captioned and referred to thereafter simply as an indictment. Grand jurors regularly follow the recommendations of the presenting prosecutor. For some jurisdictions, this is the only form of charging available for serious cases. Grand jury proceedings are closed and confidential. The target of the proceedings, unless called by or permitted by the prosecutor to testify, is barred from attendance.

b. Preliminary Hearing

In some jurisdictions, prosecutors file charges directly without relying on a grand jury. Issued charges appear on a formal charging document, sometimes called a complaint or information. When the charges in the complaint involve serious offenses, they are usually subject to preliminary testing in what is termed a preliminary hearing. At the preliminary hearing, the prosecution produces evidence to prove the charges in the complaint. The prosecution must meet at this early stage is much lower than the standard used at trial, and is commonly a probable cause standard. Unlike grand jury proceedings, preliminary hearings occur in open court in front of a judge or magistrate. Defense counsel may cross-examine witnesses and sometimes presents witnesses. At the conclusion of the evidentiary portion of the hearing, counsel can present arguments. Ultimately, the judge or magistrate determines whether the prosecution's evidence meets the probable cause standard. If the judge finds probable cause, the case moves forward. In some jurisdictions, prosecutors may select between the grand jury or direct charging process for a serious case.

It is useful to grasp at the very outset of your study of law the distinction between *burden of proof* and *standard of proof*. Burden of proof deals with who is assigned the task of bringing forth evidence. In a criminal case, the prosecution bears the burden of proof and in a civil case the plaintiff does so. Standard of proof, in contrast, deals with the strength of the evidence a party assigned the burden of proof must produce at various stages of a case in order to proceed. The prosecution bears the burden of proof at a preliminary hearing, before a grand jury, and at the trial of a criminal case. But in these settings, different standards of proof apply. At trial, as discussed below, the prosecution must prove a defendant's guilt *beyond reasonable doubt*. The beyond reasonable doubt standard of proof is the most demanding in our legal system. At a preliminary hearing, though, as discussed above, the prosecution needs to meet the less demanding *probable cause* standard of proof. The probable cause standard also applies to the prosecution when presenting evidence to a grand jury.

C. In the Courthouse

1. Arraignment, Counsel, and Settings

Once the grand jury indicts or the prosecution files a charging document in court, the court arraigns the accused, who then is formally labeled "the defendant" in court papers. Arraignment has several functions. The first is to determine whether the defendant has counsel, would like counsel, or wishes to represent himself (known as proceeding *pro se, in propria persona,* or simply *in pro per*). If the defendant has funds and wishes to hire counsel, the court will usually grant the defendant a short continuance to arrange representation unless the attorney is already present at the arraignment. For those without adequate funds, the Constitution guarantees counsel to indigent persons accused of serious crimes and to those accused of many types of less serious ones, particularly when incarceration is possible. Some jurisdictions fund an office of attorneys, called public defenders, who represent indigent clients. In other areas, courts appoint or contract with private attorneys to handle such cases. Securing representation is often most problematic for defendants whose income is small, but too large to qualify for publicly funded representation. The Constitution also guarantees a defendant the right to represent herself, though trial judges typically discourage individuals from representing themselves.

At arraignment, the court also informs the defendant of the charges and inquires whether the defendant wishes to enter a plea of guilty or not guilty. The judge also decides whether the defendant will be held in custody pending trial or allowed to remain free on certain conditions. Often, the court sets the case for further proceedings, which may consist of pretrial conferences, motions, or even the trial itself.

2. Plea Negotiations

Most criminal cases are not resolved through a trial. Commonly, more than 90 percent of both state and federal convictions in criminal cases are based on defendants' pleas of guilty. Plea negotiations can even begin before charges are filed. Efforts to dissuade or influence prosecutorial decision making in the pre-charging phase are especially common in white-collar cases, where potential defendants often engage defense lawyers long before the final charging decision. Of course, the luxury of contacting prosecutors at this early stage is often reserved for those who can afford private counsel because some jurisdictions do not appoint public defenders until court appearances on a formal charging document begin. Consequently, most plea negotiations begin after the formal filing of charges.

It is worth noting that in this book we avoid the term "plea bargain." The word "bargain" is at times used to describe something that results from a process of negotiation reflecting reciprocal give and take. Most, if not all, guilty pleas are "bargains" in this sense since they are preceded by and reflect a process of negotiation. But the word "bargain" also is frequently used to describe something that involves a discount, often a steep or even inappropriately large discount. Thus use of the phrase "plea bargain" suggests that a defendant who enters one is "getting off easy." Negotiated guilty pleas may at times lead to the imposition of an inappropriately steep discount in punishment. But this is not necessarily or typically the case. Many defendants who enter negotiated guilty pleas expose themselves to and receive severe punishments. For example, someone charged with murder in a state that uses the death penalty may enter a negotiated guilty plea to life imprisonment without the possibility of parole in exchange for the prosecution's agreement not to seek the death penalty.

Prosecutors and defense counsel may engage in protracted and complex discussions, or the exchange may last but a moment, especially when the prosecutor's office has established a standard offer for certain criminal conduct. Frequently, plea negotiations involve a series of brief conversations as a case progresses toward trial, in which offers change based upon the latest ruling in the case or the perceived strength of the evidence and availability of witnesses. Occasionally, cases even settle while jurors are deliberating. To competently advise a client whether to accept a plea offer, defense counsel sometimes need expertise in domains outside criminal law, criminal procedure, and evidence. For example, defense counsel may need to explore the immigration consequences of accepting a plea.

Judges actively participate in plea negotiations in some courts and not at all in others. When a judge is actively involved, she may undercut a prosecutor's offer or refuse to accept a guilty plea based on terms the prosecutor and defense counsel have agreed to. Due to the high volume of criminal cases in some urban areas, plea negotiations sometimes receive only a brief discussion.

Substantive criminal law, as well as rules and standards, cabin the discretion exercised by prosecutors during plea negotiations. For example, in some jurisdictions, mandatory minimum sentences influence both the tenor of discussions and limit specific offers. Ethical and constitutional rules also affect the negotiation process. Defense counsel must abide by a client's decision to accept an offer or to refuse and go to trial. Similarly, ethical rules require defense attorneys to communicate offers to their clients, even if, in particular cases, they strongly encourage a client to refuse the offer. Still, commentators regularly criticize the paucity of regulations on negotiation tactics.

Consider the following perspectives on the institution of plea bargaining:

> A criminal defense bar which denies defendants their day in court is a failure. A bar that conducts fewer and fewer jury trials does not protect the innocent, and a bar which pleads clients guilty within days of arrest does not fulfill its constitutional role of checking the power of government. It is a shocking, but statistically undeniable fact that the American legal system is in the midst of a dramatic and dangerous shift on the part of defense attorneys from an adversarial to an accommodational approach.... The number of jury trials conducted in criminal cases in the California superior courts has declined to the point of insignificance. In 1980, 12.4 percent of the cases were heard by juries. Today that figure is a miserly 3.9 percent. The percentage of felony convictions has risen sharply. In 1980, 79.3 percent of felony cases resulted in convictions. Today it is an astonishing 93 percent.[15]

* * *

In California, justice isn't colorblind. As more and more cases are decided by plea bargain, whites as a group get significantly better deals than Hispanics

---

15. Jeff Brown, *Dealing Away the Defense*, The Recorder, August 5, 1991.

or blacks who are accused of similar crimes and who have similar criminal backgrounds, a *Mercury News* analysis of nearly 700,000 cases shows.... At virtually every stage of pre-trial negotiation, whites are more successful than non-whites. They do better at getting charges dropped. They're better able to get charges reduced to lesser offenses. They draw more lenient sentences and go to prison less often. They get more chances to wipe their records clean.[16]

3. Discovery

Between the formal filing of charges and trial, the prosecution, and sometimes the defense, provide information about the case to the opposing side. This process of disclosure and the items disclosed are called "discovery." The United States Supreme Court has determined that the Constitution requires that the prosecution disclose exculpatory information to the defense.[17] Ethical rules and statutes in some jurisdictions expand that discovery obligation. In some, statutes mandate reciprocal discovery by requiring defense counsel to disclose certain types of information to the prosecution. Statutes or court rules often govern the timing of required disclosures. Failure to disclose or failure to do so in a timely manner are the focus of numerous trial court proceedings and appeals.

4. Trial

If counsel do not settle a case and the prosecution does not dismiss the charge, the case proceeds to trial. Recall that only a small percentage of criminal cases result in trial, perhaps five percent to 10 percent. For serious criminal charges and many less serious ones, the Constitution mandates that jurisdictions provide the opportunity for a jury trial. Defendants can waive their right to a jury trial and have, instead, a bench or court trial. In a bench trial, a judge or magistrate acts as both the fact-finder and decision maker on legal issues. Jurisdictions differ in the number of jurors required for a jury trial, generally ranging from 6 to 12. They usually require that jurors in criminal cases achieve unanimity to reach a verdict of guilty or not guilty. Failure to unanimously agree produces a hung jury. To obtain a conviction, prosecutors must convince jurors of the truth of the charge "beyond a reasonable doubt." The task of furnishing an appropriate definition for this term of art has plagued jurists and legal scholars. However defined, it represents the highest legal standard, exceeding other legal standards such as "probable cause," "preponderance of evidence," and "clear and convincing evidence."

A trial consists of several segments. Following discussions or motions in the trial court out of the presence of prospective jurors, jury selection begins. This process is

---

16. Christopher H. Schmitt, *Plea Bargaining Favors Whites as Blacks, Hispanics Pay Price*, San Jose Mercury News, December 8, 1991, at 1A.3.

17. Brady v. Maryland, 373 U.S. 83, 87 (1963).

called *voir dire*. The court and, to varying extent, counsel, question jurors about their ability to serve in the case. Counsel may excuse jurors from service through challenges for cause and peremptory challenges. To prevail on a challenge for cause, counsel must demonstrate to the court that the juror is unlikely to be able to serve impartially. Courts generally allow an unlimited number of challenges for cause while statutes usually assign a fixed number of peremptory challenges based upon the type of case. Counsel using a peremptory challenge need not make any showing to the court of cause, such as juror bias, and may simply excuse a juror without articulating a reason. However, peremptory challenges are subject to attack if based upon an illegal reason. For example, attorneys cannot exclude African-Americans from a jury because of their race or men because of their gender.

Following the selection and formal swearing-in of the jury, the prosecution gives an opening statement which describes the evidence the prosecution will rely on. The defense may address the jury immediately after the prosecutor or wait until the start of the defendant's case. After opening statements, the prosecutor introduces evidence of the crimes alleged in the charging document. Witnesses, both lay and expert, are sworn and testify. The prosecutor guides the witnesses through direct examination and the defense attorney cross-examines the prosecution's witnesses. The prosecution may also present physical evidence, such as a gun, a threatening note used in a bank robbery, or items of stolen property. The prosecution also often offers diagrams and other demonstrative evidence. At the conclusion of the prosecution's evidence, the prosecution rests. At this stage, the defense may choose to rest by declining to present evidence, or the defense may present its own evidence. The Constitution reserves for the defendant the decision whether to testify or exercise her Fifth Amendment right to remain silent.

Ethical rules also govern this portion of the proceedings. For example, both sides are forbidden to present testimony that they know to be perjurious. Occasionally, the defendant's right to testify conflicts with counsel's duty to avoid presenting perjured testimony. This conflict has spawned extended discussion in both the scholarly literature and court opinions.

Prosecutors can respond to the defense's presentation by furnishing rebuttal evidence and the defense can respond to that with what is called surrebuttal evidence. After the conclusion of the evidentiary portion of the trial, the judge instructs the jurors on the law to apply to the case and each side concludes with closing argument. Because the prosecution carries the burden of proof, the prosecutor argues first and last. After the initial prosecution argument, defense counsel has an opportunity to respond. Following the defense response, prosecutors may make a final closing argument. Judges determine whether arguments precede or follow the judge's instructions to the jury.

One of the most important instructions the trial judge gives a jury in a criminal case is that the prosecution must prove each element of the charged offense *beyond a reasonable doubt*. This is to be contrasted with the standard of proof used in civil cases, such as those dealing with torts and contracts, which requires the plaintiff to prove the elements of his or her cause of action by a *preponderance of the evidence.* Here is a typical criminal jury instruction explaining the standard of proof the prosecution must meet.

Maryland Criminal Jury Instructions and Commentary § 5.51(C)

Your task now is to determine whether the State has proven beyond a reasonable doubt the allegations ... _____ (insert name of defendant) is not required to persuade you that the allegations have not been proven. A reasonable doubt is a doubt founded upon reason.

Proof beyond a reasonable doubt requires such proof as would convince you of the truth of a fact to the extent that you would be willing to act upon such a belief, without reservation, in an important matter in your own business or personal affairs. However, if you are not satisfied of the proof of the allegation to that extent, then reasonable doubt exists and you must find that the allegation has not been proven.

* * *

After being instructed, the jury retires to deliberate. If the jury reaches a verdict, the foreperson of the jury or clerk of the court announces the verdict. If jurors acquit on the charges, the case ends. The double jeopardy clause of the Constitution prohibits prosecution by the same sovereign twice for the same offense. As the case involving the officers who beat Rodney King illustrates, state courts and federal courts are separate sovereignties. There, local police officers repeatedly assaulted Rodney King. State prosecutors tried the officers for the assault and the jury acquitted. Following the acquittal, which triggered extensive rioting, the federal government charged the same officers with federal crimes based on the same conduct. The jury in the federal case convicted. As separate sovereignties, both the state and federal courts could prosecute the officers without violating the double jeopardy clause.

In a small number of cases in which jurors find the defendant guilty, such as those involving the death penalty, jurors participate in the sentencing process. In others, the court excuses jurors before undertaking sentencing.

5. Post-Trial: Sentencing and Probation

If the jury finds the defendant guilty, then the judge will generally order the preparation of a report by the department of probation and set a date for sentencing..For the report, the probation department examines a host of issues that can affect the sentencing decision. Reports commonly include background material on the defendant, the crime, and a proposed sentence. Often judges also have reports prepared when there was a plea agreement. Sentencing procedures vary, both from jurisdiction to jurisdiction and case to case. They may be informal or involve a lengthy hearing with testimony. Criticism reflecting a lack of attention to the needs and treatment of victims in the criminal justice process has resulted in various statutory reforms. As a result of these reforms, in many jurisdictions victims may participate in the sentencing process.

Two types of sentencing schemes are common. A determinate sentencing scheme prescribes penalties on a relatively detailed level, sometimes imposing severe limitations on a judge's discretion. For example, a sentencing scheme might provide a base term for the offense and very limited ranges to increase or decrease a defendant's sentence based upon specific and limited criteria.

In contrast, an indeterminate sentencing scheme gives the judge much greater discretion. For example, under such a scheme the potential sentence for armed bank robbery might range between straight probation to up to 25 years imprisonment. Once a certain percentage of the sentence has been served, a parole board will determine whether to release the defendant or continue to confine her. If you have seen the movie *The Shawshank Redemption,* you've seen the work of a parole board vividly dramatized.

D. Participants

As the description of the process illustrates, many participants can play a role in and influence the life cycle of a criminal case. In this section, we concentrate briefly on the role of nine of them: (1) prosecutor, (2) defense counsel, (3) judge, (4) defendant, (5) victim, (6) court personnel, (7) jurors, (8) probation officers, and (9) media.

Prosecutors represent the government. They are entrusted with seeking justice, not only convictions. Their role encompasses decision making on a case from its initial presentation through disposition—dismissal, plea agreement or trial, sentencing, and sometimes appeal, if a conviction results. Prosecutors wield tremendous power over the lives of others. Most prosecutors strive to apply that power fairly and with integrity.[18] But prosecutors have often been criticized in recent decades as being overly harsh in their charging and sentencing practices, contributing to the mass incarceration that currently exists in the United States. Prosecutors are fallible and often lack resources, particularly on the state and local levels. Even the best-intentioned prosecutors can

---

18. Consider, however, the results of a CHICAGO TRIBUNE national investigation on prosecutorial misconduct, collated and reprinted in THE VERDICT: DISHONOR, by Ken Armstrong and Maurice Possley, from articles originally published Jan. 10, 1999–Jan. 14, 1999:

In the first study of its kind, a *Chicago Tribune* analysis of thousands of court records, appellate rulings, and lawyer disciplinary records from across the United States has found:
- Since a 1962 U.S. Supreme Court ruling designed to curb misconduct by prosecutors, at least 381 defendants nationally have had a homicide conviction thrown out because prosecutors concealed evidence suggesting innocence or presented evidence they knew to be false. Of all the ways that prosecutors can cheat, those two are considered the worst by the courts. And that number represents only a fraction of how often such cheating occurs....
- Of the 381 defendants, 67 had been sentenced to death....
- Nearly 30 of those 67 Death Row inmates—about half of those whose cases have been resolved—were subsequently freed. But almost all spent at least five years in prison. One served 26 years before his conviction was reversed and the charges dropped.

A CHICAGO TRIBUNE *Reprint* p. 3.

make mistakes and can succumb to the pressures of a high volume of cases. For example, busy prosecutors may fail to adequately investigate a case or neglect to consult crime victims regarding the proposed disposition of a criminal case.

In addition, because some prosecutorial offices unwisely rely on the number of cases that a prosecutor has tried, and, of those, the number that resulted in jury convictions to determine advancement, prosecutors must reconcile their personal and professional desire to "win" cases in order to advance their careers with their overarching mandate to seek justice. For example, prosecutors must guard against both reluctance to go to trial on difficult cases and the inclination to try "easy" cases in which jurors are highly likely to convict but that should have settled before trial. On some days, a prosecutor enjoys the satisfaction of helping those who have been criminally victimized or dismissing a case against someone wrongfully accused. On others, the work can prove frustrating, when, for example, witnesses fail to appear for court or when cases that have involved many hours of preparation are repeatedly postponed.

Defense counsel represent the accused, the guilty as well as the innocent. Their successes take many forms. They can succeed when they thoroughly test the prosecution's case, exposing deficiencies of proof and forcing the prosecution to prove the charges beyond a reasonable doubt. They can succeed when gaining a dismissal of the charges or when negotiating a favorable plea disposition for a client. They can succeed in some cases by convincing the prosecutor and the judge to agree to what is often called "diversion" by placing a client in rehabilitation rather than in prison to help the client conquer an addiction.

As with prosecutorial work, defense lawyers face many challenges. Often caseloads are large and resources limited. While prosecutors may look to larger institutional issues when handling individual cases, defense counsel must zealously represent each client. Thus, they must resist the temptations that arise from being a repeat player in the system. Even within sizable urban areas, the number of attorneys who regularly practice in the criminal bar may be relatively small. The norm of reciprocity and the give-and-take of daily practice with the same prosecutors and judges can tempt counsel to lose sight of their responsibilities to individual clients. Defense counsel, especially those whose practices involve a high volume of cases, must juggle the needs of, and responsibilities to, many clients simultaneously.

Judges preside over criminal proceedings, but their roles vary with different proceedings and different assignments. They determine legal issues, both procedural and substantive. They may actively facilitate settlement or decline to participate in negotiations. They may serve as fact finders in motions or trials without juries. Many judicial tasks, such as some sentencing decisions, involve the exercise of discretion. As is true for prosecutors and defense counsel, ethical standards govern the conduct of judges. They must maintain their impartiality in deciding matters before them. The standards demand that they avoid conflicts of interest and even the appearance of impropriety. Holding judicial office can prove prestigious and engaging, but it can also isolate the individual judge who often must confront weighty decisions alone or with very limited outside assistance.

Defendants are the center of a criminal case. The federal Constitution entrusts them with the right to decide whether to settle a case or proceed to trial, as well as whether to testify or remain silent. In practice, defendants often follow the advice of their attorneys in most, if not all, major case-related decisions.

Victims, in cases in which identifiable individuals suffer harm, at times play crucial, and at other times peripheral, roles in the criminal justice system. With some exceptions, prosecutors, rather than victims, control the pursuit of a criminal case. Victims, though, may furnish information, testify, and express their views on the outcome of cases. To increase the attention and dignity afforded victims, most have enacted statutes affording victims certain rights.

Court personnel play a vital role in the criminal justice system. They, too, exercise discretion and make choices. Clerks handle the administrative business of the courts. Clerks may control the courtroom to which a case is sent or the scheduling of various procedures in a case. Bailiffs control security in the courtroom. Court reporters transcribe the proceedings, producing verbatim accounts of the verbal interactions. Wise attorneys recognize court personnel as individuals whose discretion can affect each criminal case.

Jurors are typically the fact-finders in a criminal case that goes to trial, though some defendants choose to waive their right to a jury trial and have the trial judge act as the finder of fact. Their judgment of acquittal frees the accused from those charges and bars further criminal proceedings on them. Their verdict of guilt permits the sovereignty to proceed in holding an accused accountable. A jury that fails to reach a verdict is often referred to as a "hung jury." The consequence of a hung jury varies. In some cases, often those involving serious felonies, the prosecution will retry the case to a second jury. In others, the result induces the prosecution to offer guilty plea terms more favorable to the defendant or to dismiss the charge altogether. Although only a small percentage of cases actually arrive for jury consideration, the impact of jury verdicts pervades the system. In particular, guilty plea offers depend upon the likely response of a jury to the case. Jurisdictions often develop reputations as having jurors who tend to lean strongly toward the prosecution or defense. These perceived leanings also permeate guilty plea negotiations.

Probation is the most common criminal sentence.[19] As a result, probation officers are busy serving a multitude of functions. They research and draft probation reports for judges to review in sentencing offenders. Within those reports, they generally recommend sentencing terms. In some jurisdictions, they advise judges on appropriate settlements. They supervise and monitor persons on probation, conducting interviews, searches, and drug checks, as well as facilitating employment and education. They also participate in hearings and revocations of probation.

From investigation through appeal, the media may influence criminal proceedings. Media publicity can provoke outrage at a prosecutor's failure to charge and offers

19. Pew Center on the States, One in 31: The Long Reach of American Corrections 4 (2009).

one of the few checks on a prosecutor's otherwise unreviewable discretion to decline to pursue a case. But media attention can also taint the jury pool, resulting in the need to move a trial to a different location. In these and many other ways, the media exert power over the criminal justice system.

E. Problems with the Criminal Justice System

An overview of the criminal justice system would not be complete without acknowledging and describing at least some of its many problems. One of the most pervasive is lack of adequate resources. All lawyers have an ethical duty of competence, which requires them to adequately investigate and otherwise prepare a case. But in many of the state courts in which most criminal cases are prosecuted, public defenders and prosecutors often have overwhelming caseloads that make it difficult, if not impossible, for them to meet this obligation. Lack of resources resulting in such large caseloads also creates an enormous and unhealthy pressure on both prosecutors and defense counsel to resolve too many cases through negotiated guilty pleas rather than trials.

In recent decades, lawyers working with the original Innocence Project in New York and related projects in many states have won the release of a significant number of wrongly convicted people serving long prison terms. These exonerations have revealed many of the factors that undermine the accuracy and fairness of our criminal justice system. One of these is poor representation by defense counsel who, because of limited resources, conduct little investigation. Another is police inducement of false confessions from suspects in custody through interrogation tactics that include both psychological pressure and deceit. Erroneous eyewitness identifications are also a significant factor, as is the misapplication of forensic science, either bad science or good science badly applied. Finally, government misconduct also was found to have occurred in a significant percentage of wrongful conviction cases, such as police perjury and the failure of prosecutors to turn over to the defense evidence that tended to prove the defendant's innocence.

Critics of the criminal justice system have urged a wide variety of reforms to help remediate the corrosive effect of these factors. One example is video recording of custodial police interrogations. Another is the adoption of more reliable eyewitness identification methods. Yet another is devoting greater resources to defense representation. Some states have heeded these calls for reform, but many have resisted them.

For a look at our criminal justice system and some of its problems, watch the documentary film *Murder on a Sunday Morning*, chosen as Best Documentary Feature at the 2002 Academy Awards. Your school's library may have a copy or you can find it online. It reveals a cross-racial misidentification by a crime victim, a shoddy and unethical police investigation, a false confession, and police perjury, all of which result in an innocent 15-year-old, Brenton Butler, being falsely accused, charged, and tried for murder. In the film highly effective defense representation by hard-working public defenders reveal the inadequacies of the prosecution's case at trial and win an acquittal for the defendant. The same public defenders also figure out who did kill the victim in the case and uncover key evidence proving this person's guilt.

The 2019 film *Just Mercy*, based on the real life work of attorney Bryan Stephenson, focuses on the challenges that face a convicted defendant in obtaining a new trial based on a claim of actual innocence. It highlights two particularly problematic practices often associated with wrongful convictions, the use of a jailhouse informant and prosecutorial failure to turn over exculpatory evidence.

Problems

1.1 Catherine Sweeney, an Irish schoolteacher, visited the United States. She was driving on a coastal highway and stopped her car at the side of the road to observe birds with her three-year-old daughter. "When she resumed the trip, Sweeney, in the habit of driving on the left side of the road, drove into the wrong lane, [came around a curve and struck a motorcyclist in his own lane, causing his death.] ... Sweeney remained at the scene of the crash, and investigators determined she showed no signs of intoxication. No blood samples were taken ... [Ms. Sweeney] teaches third- and fourth-graders. Her supporters describe her as a peaceful vegetarian so respectful of life that when a bee once strayed into her classroom, she captured and released it because she did not want to teach the children to kill a living thing."[20]

"Nick Calder, a native Londoner and friend of the Sweeneys, said it is commonplace for expatriates and international travelers to get momentarily confused about which side of the road to use. And in Sweeney's case, he said, the hilly terrain and winding roads of [the area in which she was driving] are similar to the geography of Ireland and the United Kingdom."[21]

Assume that the following definitions apply:

Felony Vehicular Manslaughter is defined as "driving a vehicle in the commission of an unlawful act, not amounting to felony, and with gross negligence."

Misdemeanor Vehicular Manslaughter is defined as "driving a vehicle in the commission of an unlawful act, not amounting to felony, without gross negligence."

---

20. Gary Klien, *Teacher Guilty in Fatal Crash*, MARIN INDEPENDENT JOURNAL, October 5, 2001, at A1, A9.
21. *Id.*

Ordinary negligence "is the doing of something which a reasonably prudent person would not do, or the failure to do something which a reasonably prudent person would do, under similar circumstances.... Ordinary or reasonable care is that care which persons of ordinary prudence would use in order to avoid injury to themselves or others under similar circumstances."[22]

Gross negligence "means conduct which is more than ordinary negligence.... [It] refers to a negligent act which is aggravated, reckless or flagrant and which is such a departure from the conduct of an ordinarily prudent, careful person under the same circumstances as to be contrary to a proper regard for human life or to constitute indifference to the consequences of those acts. The facts must be such that the consequences of the negligent acts could reasonably have been foreseen and it must appear that the death was not the result of inattention, mistaken judgment or misadventure but the natural and probable result of an aggravated, reckless or flagrantly negligent act."[23]

If you were the prosecutor, would you charge Ms. Sweeney with vehicular manslaughter? If you decide to exercise discretion to charge Ms. Sweeney, should you charge the crime as a felony or misdemeanor? If you were Ms. Sweeney's lawyer, what arguments could you make to the prosecutor to try to persuade her to exercise her discretion not to charge Ms. Sweeney?

1.2 You are a defense attorney. The prosecution has charged your client with robbery. When you interview your client, she confirms that she committed the offense as detailed in the police report. Your investigation produces nothing to dispute the account in the police report. Your client does not want a felony on her record and would prefer to go to trial and take her chances. She does not plan to testify. She believes that the victim will be too scared to testify or that jurors will feel sorry for her and acquit. Having read the police reports and witness interviews, you are convinced that a jury would convict your client. Your client, though, insists on going to trial. What should you do?

1.3 You are the elected chief prosecutor in a large city that has been suffering in recent decades from the national opioid crisis. Growing addiction to prescription pain medications such as oxycodone and addiction to heroin have resulted in a dramatic increase in deaths from drug overdoses. In 2017, approximately 72,000 people across the country died of drug overdoses.[24] In your city, drug overdose has now become the leading cause of the death for people under the age of fifty. A non-profit organization, Prevention Point, has proposed creating a safe injection site in a neighborhood of your city that has

22. California Jury Instructions-Criminal (CALJIC) 8.91 (West 2003).
23. CALJIC 3.36 (West 2003).
24. Farida B. Ahmad et al., *Provisional Drug Overdose Death Counts* (2018), https://www.cdc.gov/nchs/vsrr/drug-overdose-data.htm.

been particularly plagued by both drug use and overdose deaths. Such safe injection sites have been used for years in Canada and Europe. Prevention Point plans to model its site closely on one that has been particularly successful in Vancouver, Canada, called Insite. A safe injection site provides drug users with a place where they can consume drugs without fear of being arrested by the police or assaulted or robbed by others. The Prevention Point site would:

- provide clean needles and require anyone entering the site to exchange needles they bring with them for clean needles to prevent the spread of disease through contaminated needles;

- provide medical supervision, monitoring, and, in case of an overdose, naloxone, an effective treatment for a drug overdose;

- encourage those using the site to enter drug rehabilitation and help them to obtain placement in a rehabilitation program;

- provide testing for heroin to identify the presence of the powerful and dangerous synthetic opioid fentanyl, which has contributed to many deaths.

The proposed site would not distribute any illegal drugs. In order for Prevention Point to operate its site, it needs your support and your agreement not to prosecute anyone inside, entering, or leaving the site's premises for possessing or using illegal drugs or anyone on the site's staff for assisting in the use of illegal drugs. Would you agree to support the site that Prevention Point proposes? What are the arguments Prevention Point's advocates are likely to make in favor of such a site? What are the arguments opponents of such a site are likely to make?

Chapter 2

Punishment

In this chapter, you will study a range of issues related to punishment. First, we consider the meaning of the term "punishment." The government, can confine individuals against their will if they suffer from mental illness and are dangerous to themselves or others. Is this punishment? If not, what distinguishes this governmental restriction of individual freedom from punishment? Once we have explored what constitutes punishment, we will turn to why the state punishes and examine several rationales society relies on to justify punishment. The final section deals with how much punishment should be imposed on an offender.

A. What Is Punishment?

In 1994, Kansas enacted the following legislation dealing with sexual offenders:

Kansas Statutes Annotated

§ 59-29a01

The legislature finds that a small but extremely dangerous group of sexually violent predators exist who do not have a mental disease or defect that renders them appropriate for involuntary treatment pursuant to the treatment act for mentally ill persons defined in K.S.A. 59-2901 et seq. and amendments thereto, which is intended to provide short-term treatment to individuals with serious mental disorders and then return them to the community. In contrast to persons appropriate for civil commitment under K.S.A. 59-2901 et seq. and amendments thereto, sexually violent predators generally have antisocial personality features which are unamenable to existing mental illness treatment modalities and those features render them likely to engage in sexually violent behavior. The legislature further finds that sexually violent predators' likelihood of engaging in repeat acts of predatory sexual violence is high. The existing involuntary commitment procedure pursuant to the treatment act for mentally ill persons defined in K.S.A. 59-2901 et seq. and amendments thereto is inadequate to address the risk these sexually violent predators pose to society. The legislature further finds that the prognosis for rehabilitating sexually violent predators in a prison setting is poor, the treatment needs of this population are very long term and the treatment modalities for this population are very different than the traditional treatment modalities for people appropriate for commitment under the treatment act for mentally ill persons defined in K.S.A. 59-2901 et seq. and amendments thereto, therefore a civil commitment procedure for the long-term care and treatment of the sexually violent predator is found to be necessary by the legislature.

§ 59-29a02

As used in this act: (a) "Sexually violent predator" means any person who has been convicted of or charged with a sexually violent offense and who suffers from a mental abnormality or personality disorder which makes the person likely to engage in the predatory acts of sexual violence.

§ 59-29a05

Upon filing of a petition [by the attorney general], the judge shall determine whether probable cause exists to believe that the person named in the petition is a sexually violent predator. If such determination is made, the judge shall direct that person be taken into custody and the person shall be transferred to an appropriate facility for an evaluation as to whether the person is a sexually violent predator....

§ 59-29a06

Within 45 days after the filing of a petition [by the attorney general], the court shall conduct a trial to determine whether the person is a sexually violent predator. At all stages of the proceedings under this act, any person subject to this act shall be entitled to the assistance of counsel, and if the person is indigent, the court shall appoint counsel to assist such person.... The person, the county or district attorney or attorney general, or the judge shall have the right to demand that the trial be before a jury.

§ 59-29a07

The court or jury shall determine whether, beyond a reasonable doubt, the person is a sexually violent predator. If such determination that the person is a sexually violent predator is made by a jury, such determination shall be by unanimous verdict of such jury. Such determination may be appealed. If the court or jury determines that the person is a sexually violent predator, the person shall be committed to the custody of the secretary of social and rehabilitation services for control, care, and treatment until such time as the person's mental abnormality or personality disorder has so changed that the person is safe to be at large.

* * *

Leroy Hendricks was the first person committed under these provisions. Hendricks challenged his commitment and ultimately sought review of it before the United States Supreme Court.

Kansas v. Hendricks

521 U.S. 346 (1997)
United States Supreme Court

Thomas, J. In 1994, Kansas enacted the Sexually Violent Predator Act, which establishes procedures for the civil commitment of persons who, due to a "mental abnormality" or a "personality disorder," are likely to engage in "predatory acts of sexual violence." The State invoked the Act for the first time to commit Leroy Hendricks, an inmate who had a long history of sexually molesting children, and who was scheduled for release from prison shortly after the Act became law....

During the trial, Hendricks' own testimony revealed a chilling history of repeated child sexual molestation and abuse, beginning in 1955.... [After convictions for several sex offenses involving children ranging from indecent exposure to molestation, Hendricks was sent to prison. After release on parole he was rearrested for another sex offense involving a young child.] Attempts were made to treat him for his sexual deviance, and in 1965 he was considered "safe to be at large," and was discharged from a state psychiatric hospital.

Shortly thereafter, however, Hendricks sexually assaulted another young boy and girl.... He was again imprisoned in 1967, but he refused to participate in a sex offender program, and thus remained incarcerated until his parole in 1972. Diagnosed as a pedophile, Hendricks entered into and then abandoned, a treatment program. He testified that despite having received professional help for his pedophilia, he continued to harbor sexual desires for children. Indeed, soon after his 1972 parole, Hendricks [was convicted of sex offenses involving] his own stepdaughter and stepson. As a result of that conviction, he was once again imprisoned, and was serving that sentence when he reached his conditional release date in September 1994.

Hendricks admitted that he had repeatedly abused children whenever he was not confined. He explained that when he "gets stressed out," he "can't control the urge" to molest children. Although Hendricks recognized that his behavior harms children, and he hoped he would not sexually molest children again, he stated that the only sure way he could keep from sexually abusing children in the future was "to die." The jury unanimously found beyond a reasonable doubt that Hendricks was a sexually violent predator. The trial court subsequently determined, as a matter of state law, that pedophilia qualifies as a "mental abnormality" as defined by the Act, and thus ordered Hendricks committed to the Secretary's custody.

The thrust of Hendricks' argument is that the Act establishes criminal proceedings; hence confinement under it necessarily constitutes punishment. He contends that where, as here, newly enacted "punishment" is predicated upon past conduct for which he has already been convicted and forced to serve a prison sentence, the Constitution's Double Jeopardy and Ex Post Facto Clauses are violated. We are unpersuaded by Hendricks' argument that Kansas has established criminal proceedings.

The categorization of a particular proceeding as civil or criminal "is first of all a question of statutory construction." We must initially ascertain whether the legislature meant the statute to establish "civil" proceedings. If so, we ordinarily defer to the legislature's stated intent. Here, Kansas's objective to create a civil proceeding is evidenced by its placement of the Sexually Violent Predator Act within the Kansas probate code, instead of the criminal code, as well as its description of the Act as creating a "civil commitment procedure." Kan. Stat. Ann., Article 29 (1994) ("Care and Treatment for Mentally Ill Persons"), section 59-29a01. Nothing on the face of the statute suggests that the legislature sought to create anything other than a civil commitment scheme designed to protect the public from harm.

Although we recognize that a "civil label is not always dispositive," we will reject the legislature's manifest intent only where a party challenging the statute provides "the clearest proof" that "the statutory scheme is so punitive either in purpose or effect as to negate the State's intention" to deem it "civil." In those limited circumstances, we will consider the statute to have established criminal proceedings for constitutional purposes. Hendricks, however, has failed to satisfy this heavy burden.

As a threshold matter, commitment under the Act does not implicate either of the two primary objectives of criminal punishment: retribution or deterrence. The Act's purpose is not retributive because it does not affix culpability for prior criminal conduct. Instead such conduct is used solely for evidentiary purposes, either to demonstrate that a "mental abnormality" exists or to support a finding of future dangerousness.

Moreover, unlike a criminal statute, no finding of scienter is required to commit an individual who is found to be a sexually violent predator; instead, the commitment determination is made based on a "mental abnormality" or "personality disorder" rather than on one's criminal intent. The existence of a scienter requirement is customarily an important element in distinguishing criminal from civil statutes. The absence of such a requirement here is evidence that confinement under the statute is not intended to be retributive.

Nor can it be said that the legislature intended the Act to function as a deterrent. Those persons committed under the Act are, by definition, suffering from a "mental abnormality" or a "personality disorder" that prevents them from exercising adequate control over their behavior. Such persons are unlikely to be deterred by the threat of confinement.

Discussion Questions

1. How would you define punishment? What criteria does the Court in *Hendricks* use to define it? What role does the definition of punishment play in resolving *Hendricks's* constitutional arguments?

2. Section 59-29a01 of the Kansas Sexually Violent Predator Act describes the Act as a "civil commitment procedure for the long-term care and treatment of the sexually violent predator." What if Kansas failed in fact to provide any treatment to a person committed as a sexually violent predator? Would such failure transform that person's commitment into punishment?

Problems

2.1 Geoffrey is arrested and charged with a violent carjacking. The evidence in the case is strong and the grand jury returns an indictment. Geoffrey asks the trial judge to release him on bail prior to and during his trial, but the trial judge denies Geoffrey bail and he is held in the county jail for three and a half months prior to and during his trial. Does his pretrial incarceration constitute punishment? What if the reason for the denial was risk of flight? What if the denial was based on the danger of him committing another carjacking or other violent crime? If Geoffrey is convicted, should he receive credit against his carjacking sentence for the three and a half months he spent incarcerated prior to being convicted?

2.2 Part (a) Shannan is a 26-year-old single mother of two children, ages two and five. She works as a driver for a private van service and is going to school part-time to become a medical biller. She has no prior criminal record. Shannan has a younger sister who suffers from a variety of mental illnesses. One day, Shannan has a heated verbal disagreement with her sister. Afterward, her sister phones the police and accuses Shannan of having struck her during the argument. The next day, the police arrest Shannan and take her to the police station, where she is fingerprinted, photographed, and interviewed. During the interview, Shannan strenuously denies ever having struck her sister. Shannan is then taken to court where she is charged with assault, a felony. The judge sets Shannan's bail at $35,000 dollars. Shannan does not have $35,000 to pay the bail, so she remains in jail for five days until she and her family manage to pay a non-refundable $350 fee to a private bail bond agent, who pledges to pay Shannan's $35,000 bail if she fails to appear for any of her court dates. While in jail, Shannan misses four days of work and loses the pay she would have earned. She also misses a week's worth of classes she had paid for. Six weeks later the public defender appointed to represent Shannan succeeds in having the charge against Shannan dismissed after her sister admits that her accusation against Shannan was false. Do the five days Shannan spent in jail before she could pay the bail bond agent constitute punishment? How about the $350 fee she and her family paid the bail bond agent, for which neither Shannan nor her family were reimbursed?

Part (b) Same facts as Part (a), but assume that Shannan's bail is set at $100,000 and that she and her family cannot afford to pay the $1,500 fee the bail bond agent charges to pledge to pay $100,000 in bail. As a result, Shannan remains in jail for six weeks before her lawyer succeeds in having the charge against her dismissed. Do the six weeks Shannan spent in jail before the charge against her was dismissed constitute punishment?

2.3 Deborah is a 28-year-old married woman who is six months pregnant with her first child. Deborah became addicted to heroin in her late teenage years, went through drug treatment when she was 24 and did not use drugs for several years. Recently, Deborah's husband, Wayne, began to suspect that she had begun using heroin again when he found various items of drug paraphernalia hidden in the basement of their house. Wayne confronted Deborah, who admitted that she was using heroin again and had been doing so for the past three months. Wayne tries to convince Deborah to stop using heroin and again seek treatment, but Deborah refuses. A statute in the state in which Deborah and Wayne live allows a person's spouse, guardian, or physician to petition a court to commit a person who "is pregnant and abusing alcohol or drugs." Wayne hires a lawyer and files a petition to have Deborah committed until she gives birth to their child. After holding a hearing, a judge commits Deborah to state custody and she remains in custody for three months before giving birth. Do the three months Deborah spent in state custody constitute punishment?

B. Why Punish?

In this section you will learn about a number of reasons used to justify punishment. These include retribution, deterrence, incapacitation, and rehabilitation. These purposes of punishment will serve as guideposts throughout your study of criminal law. As you will see in this chapter, they play important roles in deciding whether a particular person should be punished and, if so, how severely that person should be punished. These justifications will also help you to understand the contours of many of the crimes you will encounter later in the course, such as murder, manslaughter, attempt, and conspiracy.

1. The Purposes of Punishment: An Overview

What justifies the imposition of punishment? The rationales that most readily come to mind are likely those aimed at increasing public safety by preventing or reducing crime. One such rationale is *deterrence*. Deterrence is the notion of reducing crime through the fear of punishment, the "intimidation or terror of the law."[1] The words *deterrence* and *terror* derive from the same Latin verb meaning "to frighten or terrify." The deterrence argument in favor of the death penalty, for example, claims that fear of being executed scares potential offenders from committing crimes such as murder, the crime most likely to trigger the death penalty.

Specific or *special deterrence* is the use of punishment to frighten the person actually punished away from reoffending. A five-year prison term imposed on a bank robber for specific deterrence attempts to intimidate the bank robber from robbing another bank after release from prison. *General deterrence* aims at frightening potential offenders other than the person punished. At the same time that the bank robber's five-year sentence may specifically deter her from a repeat offense, it may also deter others who learn of her sentence from robbing banks. Under general deterrence, the bank robber's punishment in essence becomes an object lesson to others considering following in the bank robber's footsteps. While the five-year sentence cannot specifically deter the bank robber from robbing another bank until after release from prison, its

---

1. Jeremy Bentham, *Principles of Penal Law* 396 in Vol. 1, THE WORKS OF JEREMY BENTHAM (John Bowring ed. 1843).

general deterrent effect in theory operates on other potential offenders as soon as it is publicly imposed.

Another rationale for punishment that, like deterrence, aims to increase public safety is *incapacitation*. Incapacitation seeks to reduce future crime, but operates differently from deterrence. Incapacitation aims to deprive the criminal of the ability or opportunity to commit crime. An incapacitation argument for the death penalty, again by way of example, would point out that a defendant who is executed is no longer capable of committing future offenses. While a deterrence rationale assumes its target has the ability and opportunity to commit crime and tries to influence the criminal's choice whether to do so, incapacitation, if successful, denies or restricts the offender's ability or opportunity to choose to commit a crime. Our hypothetical bank robber's five-year jail sentence should incapacitate the robber in regard to robbing banks while the robber is in prison, because presumably the robber will have no opportunity to rob a bank while in prison. Note that a prison sentence would not incapacitate the robber from committing other crimes while in prison, such as drug offenses or assault. Once the robber is released from prison and again has the opportunity to rob a bank, the incapacitating effect of imprisonment ends and its specific deterrent effect hopefully begins.

Rehabilitation is another classic justification often offered for punishment. Like deterrence and incapacitation, it aims to increase public safety by reducing crime. But rather than intimidating a potential offender, as deterrence seeks to do, or disabling an offender, as incapacitation seeks to do, rehabilitation adopts a strategy of reshaping or remolding a defendant's attitude or character so the defendant no longer is disposed to commit crime. If rehabilitation is successful, the criminal no longer needs to be deterred or incapacitated.

A fourth classic justification for punishment is *retribution*. Unlike deterrence, incapacitation, and rehabilitation, retribution is not grounded in concerns about future public safety or crime prevention. Rather, retribution reflects the view that punishment is justified because and only because a particular defendant deserves to be punished because the defendant has done something blameworthy. Accordingly, it is often referred to as the "just deserts" theory. As expressed by one of its leading proponents, Immanuel Kant:

> Judicial punishment can never be used merely as a means to promote some other good for the criminal himself or for civil society, but instead must in all cases be imposed on him only on the ground that he has committed a crime; for a human being can never be manipulated merely as a means to the purposes of someone else.... He must be found deserving of punishment before any consideration is given to the utility of this punishment for himself or for fellow citizens.[2]

---

2. Immanuel Kant, Metaphysical Elements of Justice 138 (Hackett; Trans. John Ladd, 2d ed.1999).

In order for a criminal to receive his just deserts, Kant demanded an "equality" or "sameness of kind" between the crime and the punishment. If, for example, the criminal "has committed murder, he must die."[3] A retributive argument for imposition of the death penalty in a first-degree murder case, for example, would rest on the claim that because the defendant took the life of another person with premeditation and deliberation she deserves to forfeit her own life.

Deterrence, incapacitation, and rehabilitation have several common features. Each is future-oriented in focusing on what follows from punishment, the *consequences* of its imposition. Each seeks to make punishment *useful* to society by reducing crime. Accordingly, each of these theories is properly described as consequentialist and utilitarian. Jeremy Bentham, the famous nineteenth-century philosopher, legal reformer, and originator of modern utilitarianism, for example, proposed preventing a criminal from reoffending "[b]y taking from him the physical power of offending ... taking away the desire of offending ... [and] making him afraid of offending."[4] Phrased in modern terminology, this quote from Bentham relies on incapacitation, rehabilitation, and specific deterrence—in that order.

Retribution differs from deterrence, incapacitation, and rehabilitation in several ways. Rather than looking to the future, retribution has a retrospective orientation in that it looks back at the criminal's past acts, mental state, and harm done to assess the criminal's just deserts. Second, retribution is not concerned with the consequences or usefulness of punishment, but with the criminal's blameworthiness. Third, where deterrence, incapacitation, and rehabilitation seek to advance society's collective welfare, retribution focuses narrowly on the blameworthiness of the individual criminal.

The four purposes of punishment described above can, at times, work in harmony. Some offenders, for example, are both very blameworthy and very dangerous. The imposition of a lengthy prison term on such an offender may be justified on grounds of retribution, incapacitation, and specific deterrence. At other times, one or more of these purposes of punishment may be at odds with other purposes.

Some theorists advance what is called a "mixed" theory of punishment that blends the use of different purposes of punishment. One such mixed theory "asserts that punishment is justified if and only if it achieves a net social gain and is given to offenders who deserve it."[5] Do you think this or some other form of mixed theory makes sense?

Discussion Questions

1. How are specific deterrence and incapacitation similar? How do they differ?

2. Does prison incapacitate criminals? What crimes does someone in prison retain the capacity to commit?

---

3. *Id.*

4. *Id.*

5. Michael S. Moore, A Taxonomy of Purposes of Punishment, Law and Psychiatry: Rethinking the Relationship 239 (1984).

3. Reconsider *Kansas v. Hendricks*. What difference would it have made if the Court had determined that incapacitation is a primary purpose of punishment?

* * *

Which purposes of punishment are reflected in the following statutes?

California Penal Code § 1170(a)(1)

The Legislature finds and declares that the purpose of imprisonment for crime is punishment. This purpose is best served by terms proportionate to the seriousness of the offense with provision for uniformity in the sentences of offenders committing the same offense under similar circumstances. The Legislature further finds and declares that the elimination of disparity and the provision of uniformity of sentences can best be achieved by determinate sentences fixed by statute in proportion to the seriousness of the offense as determined by the Legislature to be imposed by the court with specified discretion.

A System of Penal Law for the United States of America 2 (1828)
Edward Livingston

Vengeance is unknown to the law. The only object of punishment is to prevent the commission of offenses: it should be calculated to operate,

First, on the delinquent, so as by seclusion to deprive him of the present means, and by habits of industry and temperance, of any future desire to repeat the offence.

Second, on the rest of the community, so as to deter them by the example, from a like contravention of the laws. No punishments, greater than are necessary to effect these ends, ought to be inflicted.

Alaska Code of Criminal Procedure § 12.55.65.005 Declaration of Purpose

The purpose of this chapter is to provide the means for determining the appropriate sentence to be imposed upon conviction of an offense. The legislature finds that the elimination of unjustified disparity in sentences and the attainment of reasonable uniformity in sentences can best be achieved through a sentencing framework fixed by statute as provided in this chapter. In imposing sentence, the court shall consider

(1) the seriousness of the defendant's present offense in relation to other offenses;

(2) the prior criminal history of the defendant and the likelihood of rehabilitation;

(3) the need to confine the defendant to prevent further harm to the public;

(4) the circumstances of the offense and the extent to which the offense harmed the victim or endangered the public safety or order;

(5) the effect of the sentence to be imposed in deterring the defendant or other members of society from future criminal conduct;

(6) the effect of the sentence to be imposed as a community condemnation of the criminal act and as a reaffirmation of societal norms; and

(7) the restoration of the victim and the community.

* * *

Apply the purposes of punishment described above in analyzing the following problems.

Problems

2.4 In August 2005, 20-year-old Andrew, wearing a ski mask and brandishing a BB gun, robbed a fast food restaurant and obtained $550 in cash. The restaurant manager wrote down the license plate number on Andrew's car as he drove away and he was soon caught and charged with armed robbery. Andrew pled guilty and in October 2005, the trial judge sentenced Andrew, who had no prior criminal record, to 13 years in prison. Because of overcrowded conditions in the state's prisons, the judge instructed Andrew, who was free on bail, to go home and await instructions from the state Bureau of Prisons about where and when he should report to begin serving his sentence. Andrew waited, but the Bureau of Prisons never contacted him and Andrew never reported. In the intervening years, Andrew did not flee, change his name, or try to hide. He regularly paid property and income taxes and kept a driver's license showing his real name and address.

The experience of being convicted of a serious crime motivated Andrew to turn his life around. He became a skilled carpenter and started several small businesses that focus on redeveloping abandoned inner-city properties. He is active in the community and spends a substantial amount of time doing carpentry work for Habitat for Humanity. He is married and has two children.

Recently the Bureau of Prisons finally discovered its mistake. The police sent a SWAT team to arrest Andrew at his home, where they found him feeding his three-year-old daughter breakfast and getting his eight-year-old son ready for school. Andrew is now in custody. Based on the purposes of punishment, what punishment is now appropriate for Andrew? Should he be required to serve his original 13-year sentence? Should his punishment be altered? Should it be eliminated? Why?

2.5 June is convicted of the premeditated murder of her husband. June was having an affair and killed her husband to collect on a large insurance policy and remove him as an obstacle to her being able to marry her lover. The jurisdiction has a death penalty and the prosecutor concludes that June is an appropriate candidate for it. But June's lawyer approaches the prosecutor with an offer. If the prosecutor foregoes the death penalty, June will agree to life imprisonment. She will also volunteer to be a subject for a dangerous medical experiment the results of which could save hundreds of lives. The experiment is so dangerous that medical researchers have so far been unable to find a human subject. Based on the theories of punishment, should the prosecutor accept June's offer?

2.6 Kenny killed a man for a $5,000 bounty offered by the leader of a local drug gang. Kenny is 13 years old. He is enrolled in the seventh grade but rarely attends school. Kenny grew up in a poor neighborhood rife with crime, drug addiction, and trafficking. Kenny's father abandoned him, his mother, and his older brother when Kenny was an infant. His mother is unemployed and addicted to heroin, which she started taking after Kenny's older brother was shot and killed in an exchange of gunfire between local drug gangs. Kenny lives with his mother in an abandoned apartment building with no electricity or running water. A local drug gang recruited Kenny when he was 10 years old and started paying him to be a lookout on a corner where the drug gang sells heroin. When he was 11, Kenny was promoted to being a "runner" delivering drugs to customers so older gang members could avoid touching the drugs, making it harder for police to charge them. By the time Kenny was 13, the gang had supplied him with a handgun and employed him to guard a street corner stash of drugs and money.

The victim of Kenny's crime was a man named Lemar, who made his living by "ripping and running," street slang for robbing drug dealers of money and drugs. The leader of the gang with which Kenny is affiliated offered $5,000 to anyone who killed Lemar. One day, Kenny saw Lemar walk into a corner store to buy cigarettes. Kenny followed him in and shot him once at close range in the back of the head. Kenny then dropped the gun and ran. The convenience store's video camera provided a clear image of Kenny shooting Lemar. A few weeks after the shooting, police matched Kenny's fingerprints to fingerprints found on the gun and arrested Kenny. At the time of arrest, Kenny was under the influence of heroin, which he started using almost immediately after killing Lemar. What punishment should be imposed on Kenny? Should he be treated as a juvenile and placed for a few years in a facility focused primarily on rehabilitation and treatment? Or should he be treated as an adult and given an adult prison sentence? If treated as an adult, how long a term of imprisonment is appropriate for Kenny?

2.7 Ronnie has been homeless for the past six months. He recently went through a supermarket checkout line and paid $1.25 for a loaf of bread. When he went through the checkout line, though, he had $4.70 worth of cheese and sausage he did not pay for hidden in one of his coat pockets. Ronnie was detained by supermarket security officers as he was leaving the supermarket and later arrested by police for attempted theft of the cheese and sausage. The $1.25 Ronnie paid for the bread was the last of the money he had. He had not eaten for three days prior to the attempted theft. Should Ronnie be punished for attempted theft? If so, what punishment would you impose?

2.8 Robert was recently released on parole after serving 10 years of a 15-year sentence for having robbed someone to obtain money to buy drugs. During those 10 years, Robert became acclimated to prison and did not want to leave it. Under the state's parole system, a prisoner is eligible to be paroled after having served one-third of a sentence and must be paroled after serving two-thirds of that sentence. Robert has been a model prisoner but he declined to seek parole when he was first eligible after having served five years. Robert, though, was mandatorily paroled after serving 10 years. After his release, Robert struggled to find a job and a place to live. He lost touch with his family and soon was out of money. He started living under a freeway overpass with a group of other homeless people.

About six months after his release, Robert walks into a bank and hands a teller a note that says "Give me all your money or else." The teller hands Robert a marked packet of bills from her drawer and triggers a silent alarm that alerts police. After receiving the money, Robert sits down in a chair in the bank's lobby and waits for the police. When they arrive, he hands them the robbery money, waives his *Miranda* rights, and confesses his crime. Robert tells the police he robbed the bank because he wants to return to prison and that he chose to rob the bank without a gun so no one would get hurt. He also tells them he is willing to plead guilty and accept the maximum penalty in order to be sent back to prison as soon as possible. Robert eventually does plead guilty to one count of unarmed bank robbery, which carries a maximum 20-year prison sentence. What punishment is appropriate for Robert?

2.9 Section 154 of the Imperial Code, enacted by the Inter-Galactic Empire in the year 2041, provides:

> Any adult convicted of possession or sale of a controlled substance is guilty of a felony punishable with between 10 to 20 years imprisonment on a correctional planet doing hard labor.

Controlled substances are defined elsewhere in the Code to include such items as cocaine, heroin, alcohol, and tobacco. The Code also makes clear that the term of imprisonment imposed for violation of the statute is not to be served by the offender, but by a member of the offender's family, such as a spouse, child, or parent. Criteria for choosing the family member to serve the sentence are supplied in the Code with the aim of selecting the person in the offender's family, imprisonment of whom will cause the most grief and suffering to the offender. Can this sentencing provision be justified in terms of the purposes of punishment?

2.10 From 2011 to 2019, William ran a corrupt scheme helping the children of wealthy parents be admitted to elite universities. After an FBI investigation named Operation Varsity Blues uncovered evidence of the scheme, William pled guilty and cooperated by revealing whom he had helped and how he had helped them. Two of William's methods were: (1) bribing testing officials to alter SAT admission scores and (2) bribing university coaches to falsely tell their universities that certain children were elite athletic recruits.

Part (a) Felicia paid William $15,000 dollars to bribe a testing official to falsely inflate her daughter's SAT admission test score. Her daughter was then admitted to a university which is very selective. Confronted with the evidence against her, Felicia admitted what she did and pled guilty to engaging in a conspiracy to defraud the universities to which her daughter had applied. She has acknowledged what she did was wrong, shown remorse, and publicly apologized. She was in tears and her voice frequently broke as she addressed the judge at her sentencing hearing acknowledging the wrongfulness of her conduct. Felicia is fifty-seven years old and has no prior criminal record. She is a successful actress whose career has been stalled by the publicity regarding her participation in the college admissions scandal. What punishment should Felicia receive? Why? Should she receive some term of imprisonment?

Part (b) David used William's illicit services more often and over a longer period of time than any other parent implicated in the conspiracy, from 2011 through 2019. He relied on a different sort of scheme than the one involved in Felicia's case. He and William created false athletic credentials for four of his children, two in tennis, and one each in soccer and football. David paid bribes totaling $325,000 dollars to a coach at one school and $525,000 to two coaches at another school. All four children were admitted to the universities whose coaches David bribed. Admission to both schools is very selective. None of the four children played or were capable of playing on the sports teams to which the coaches had designated them as elite recruits. When evidence of William's scheme came to light, the FBI claimed that David had paid an additional bribe for a fifth child to be admitted to a different university. David claims that this payment was a legitimate charitable contribution to the university. David has pled guilty, like Felicia, to a single count of conspiracy to defraud. He has no prior record and has expressed remorse for his actions. He is a wealthy retired businessman and philanthropist who has legitimately donated $30 million to a number of charities, including charter schools and a Cambodian orphanage. What punishment should David receive? Why? Should he receive some term of imprisonment?

Part (c) David and his lawyers have argued that his children were unaware of their father's illicit efforts on their behalf, but some of the evidence strongly suggests some level of awareness on the part of the children. Assume for purposes of this part that David's children did know about some aspects of their father's efforts and participated in some, such as misleading university officials about their athletic qualifications and interests. All four clearly benefitted from the scheme. Assuming these facts have been established, do you think David's children should be punished criminally or not? Punished in some other way? If so, how?

2.11 A man was convicted in Lahore, Pakistan, of killing 100 children, then mutilating and disposing of their corpses in vats of acid. After conviction, the trial judge announced: "The sentence is that he should be strangled 100 times.... His body should be cut in 100 pieces and put in acid, as he did with his victims." Pakistan's Interior Minister expressed doubt the sentence would actually be carried out because it would offend various international conventions on human rights to which Pakistan is a signatory.[6] What theory or theories of punishment might have motivated the judge to impose such a sentence?

The following two cases, *Graham v. Florida* and *United States v. Bergman*, address and apply the four purposes of punishment discussed above. The first case is from the United States Supreme Court and the second is from a United States District Court, a federal trial court.

In 2005, the Supreme Court in the landmark case of *Roper v. Simmons* held that it is unconstitutional to impose the death penalty for a crime committed by someone under 18. Five years later, in *Graham v. Florida*, the first case below, the Supreme Court held that it is also unconstitutional to impose life imprisonment without the possibility of parole for a crime other than homicide committed by someone under 18. The majority opinions in both *Roper* and *Graham* rely on a variety of rationales, including application of the four purposes of punishment described at the outset of this section—retribution, deterrence, incapacitation, and rehabilitation. The excerpt below from Justice Kennedy's majority opinion in *Graham* contains the Court's analysis and application of these four purposes of punishment.

Graham v. Florida
560 U.S. 48 (2010)
United States Supreme Court

Justice Kennedy delivered the opinion of the Court.

The issue before the Court is whether the Constitution permits a juvenile offender to be sentenced to life in prison without parole for a nonhomicide crime. The sentence was imposed by the State of Florida. Petitioner challenges the sentence under the Eighth Amendment's Cruel and Unusual Punishments Clause....

Roper established that because juveniles have lessened culpability they are less deserving of the most severe punishments. As compared to adults, juveniles have a " 'lack of maturity and an underdeveloped sense of responsibility' "; they "are more vulnerable or susceptible to negative influences and outside pressures, including peer pressure"; and their characters are "not as well formed." These salient characteristics mean that "[i]t is difficult even for expert psychologists to differentiate between the juvenile offender whose crime reflects unfortunate yet transient immaturity, and the rare juvenile offender whose crime reflects irreparable corruption." Accordingly, "juvenile offenders cannot with reliability be classified among the worst offenders." A juvenile is not absolved of responsibility for his actions, but his transgression "is not as morally reprehensible as that of an adult."

---

6. *For Killing 100 Children: To Be Cut in 100 Pieces*, N.Y. Times, March 17, 2000, at A10.

No recent data provide reason to reconsider the Court's observations in *Roper* about the nature of juveniles. As petitioner's *amici* point out, developments in psychology and brain science continue to show fundamental differences between juvenile and adult minds. For example, parts of the brain involved in behavior control continue to mature through late adolescence. Juveniles are more capable of change than are adults, and their actions are less likely to be evidence of "irretrievably depraved character" than are the actions of adults. It remains true that "[f]rom a moral standpoint it would be misguided to equate the failings of a minor with those of an adult, for a greater possibility exists that a minor's character deficiencies will be reformed." These matters relate to the status of the offenders in question; and it is relevant to consider next the nature of the offenses to which this harsh penalty might apply.

The Court has recognized that defendants who do not kill, intend to kill, or foresee that life will be taken are categorically less deserving of the most serious forms of punishment than are murderers. There is a line "between homicide and other serious violent offenses against the individual." Serious nonhomicide crimes "may be devastating in their harm ... but 'in terms of moral depravity and of the injury to the person and to the public,' ... they cannot be compared to murder in their 'severity and irrevocability.'" This is because "[l]ife is over for the victim of the murderer," but for the victim of even a very serious nonhomicide crime, "life ... is not over and normally is not beyond repair." Although an offense like robbery or rape is "a serious crime deserving serious punishment," those crimes differ from homicide crimes in a moral sense.

It follows that, when compared to an adult murderer, a juvenile offender who did not kill or intend to kill has a twice diminished moral culpability. The age of the offender and the nature of the crime each bear on the analysis....

The penological justifications for the sentencing practice are also relevant to the analysis.... With respect to life without parole for juvenile nonhomicide offenders, none of the goals of penal sanctions that have been recognized as legitimate—retribution, deterrence, incapacitation, and rehabilitation—provides an adequate justification.

Retribution is a legitimate reason to punish, but it cannot support the sentence at issue here. Society is entitled to impose severe sanctions on a juvenile nonhomicide offender to express its condemnation of the crime and to seek restoration of the moral imbalance caused by the offense. But "[t]he heart of the retribution rationale is that a criminal sentence must be directly related to the personal culpability of the criminal offender." And as *Roper* observed, "[w]hether viewed as an attempt to express the community's moral outrage or as an attempt to right the balance for the wrong to the victim, the case for retribution is not as strong with a minor as with an adult." The case becomes even weaker with respect to a juvenile who did not commit homicide. *Roper* found that "[r]etribution is not proportional if the law's most severe penalty is imposed" on the juvenile murderer. The considerations underlying that holding support as well the conclusion that retribution does not justify imposing the second most severe penalty on the less culpable juvenile nonhomicide offender.

Deterrence does not suffice to justify the sentence either. *Roper* noted that "the same characteristics that render juveniles less culpable than adults suggest ... that juveniles will be less susceptible to deterrence." Because juveniles' "lack of maturity and underdeveloped sense of responsibility ... often result in impetuous and ill-considered actions and decisions," they are less likely to take a possible punishment into consideration when making decisions. This is particularly so when that punishment is rarely imposed. That the sentence deters in a few cases is perhaps plausible, but "[t]his argument does not overcome other objections." Even if the punishment has some connection to a valid penological goal, it must be shown that the punishment is not grossly disproportionate in light of the justification offered. Here, in light of juvenile nonhomicide offenders' diminished moral responsibility, any limited deterrent effect provided by life without parole is not enough to justify the sentence.

Incapacitation, a third legitimate reason for imprisonment, does not justify the life without parole sentence in question here. Recidivism is a serious risk to public safety, and so incapacitation is an important goal. But while incapacitation may be a legitimate penological goal sufficient to justify life without parole in other contexts, it is inadequate to justify that punishment for juveniles who did not commit homicide. To justify life without parole on the assumption that the juvenile offender forever will be a danger to society requires the sentencer to make a judgment that the juvenile is incorrigible. The characteristics of juveniles make that judgment questionable. "It is difficult even for expert psychologists to differentiate between the juvenile offender whose crime reflects unfortunate yet transient immaturity, and the rare juvenile offender whose crime reflects irreparable corruption." As one court concluded in a challenge to a life without parole sentence for a 14-year-old, "incorrigibility is inconsistent with youth." ... A life without parole sentence improperly denies the juvenile offender a chance to demonstrate growth and maturity. Incapacitation cannot override all other considerations, lest the Eighth Amendment's rule against disproportionate sentences be a nullity.

Finally there is rehabilitation, a penological goal that forms the basis of parole systems. The concept of rehabilitation is imprecise; and its utility and proper implementation are the subject of a substantial, dynamic field of inquiry and dialogue. It is for legislatures to determine what rehabilitative techniques are appropriate and effective.

A sentence of life imprisonment without parole, however, cannot be justified by the goal of rehabilitation. The penalty forswears altogether the rehabilitative ideal. By denying the defendant the right to reenter the community, the State makes an irrevocable judgment about that person's value and place in society. This judgment is not appropriate in light of a juvenile nonhomicide offender's capacity for change and limited moral culpability. A State's rejection of rehabilitation, moreover, goes beyond a mere expressive judgment. As one *amicus* notes, defendants serving life without parole sentences are often denied access to vocational training and other rehabilitative services that are available to other inmates. For juvenile offenders, who are most in need of and receptive to rehabilitation, the absence of rehabilitative opportunities or treatment makes the disproportionality of the sentence all the more evident.

In sum, penological theory is not adequate to justify life without parole for juvenile nonhomicide offenders.

Discussion Questions

1. According to the *Roper* and *Graham* opinions:

- juveniles have an underdeveloped sense of responsibility that often results in impetuous and ill-considered actions and decisions;
- juveniles are susceptible to negative influences;
- the parts of the human brain involved in behavior control are not fully developed in juveniles; and
- juveniles are less susceptible than adults to deterrence.

If all these are true, what are the implications in terms of the need to incapacitate juveniles?

2. In recent decades, many states have treated an increasing number of juvenile offenders who have committed serious offenses as adults. These juveniles are prosecuted in adult courts and given sentences similar to those given adult criminals. What do you think explains such treatment?

3. Justice Kennedy identifies four penological goals as legitimate: retribution, deterrence, incapacitation, and rehabilitation. Recall that Justice Thomas in the *Hendricks* case said there were only two "primary objectives of criminal punishment: retribution and deterrence." Should Justice Thomas in *Hendricks* have considered the other two purposes stated by Justice Kennedy? What impact might that have had on Justice Thomas's analysis?

* * *

In the opinion that follows, a particularly able and thoughtful trial judge, United States District Court Judge Marvin Frankel, applies the same four justifications of punishment Justice Kennedy uses in *Graham*. Unlike Justice Kennedy, though, Judge Frankel does not use the purposes of punishment to decide the constitutionality of a particular punishment. Instead, he uses them to decide the appropriate sentence to impose on the defendant in the case, Bernard Bergman. Judge Frankel points out that using these purposes to decide precisely what punishment to impose in a particular case is not an easy task. You may have reached the same conclusion while working on the problems that appear in this section.

It is worth noting that the *Bergman* case is unlike many of the other cases you will encounter in this course. First, Judge Frankel was a *federal* judge. Most of the opinions you will read in this course were written by *state* judges or justices. This is so because the vast majority of criminal cases are prosecuted by state authorities under state criminal laws in state rather than federal courts. Second, Judge Frankel was a *trial* court judge. Most of the opinions you will read in this course, as well as in your other law school courses, will be from intermediate *appellate* and *supreme* courts because those courts are the primary sources of judicial opinions. Finally, the *Bergman* case is unlike the typical case in this book because the defendant in *Bergman* chose to waive his right to a jury trial and enter a *guilty plea*. More than 90 percent of defendants in both state and federal courts waive the right to trial and plead guilty, just as Bergman did. But most of the cases you will read about in this book were resolved through a *trial* rather than a guilty plea. The reason for this is that a case that ends in a guilty plea typically does not go up on appeal and thus does not usually produce an appellate opinion discussing the sort of criminal law issues you will study in this course.

United States v. Bergman

416 F. Supp. 496 (S.D.N.Y. 1976)
United States District Court

Frankel, District Judge.

Defendant is being sentenced upon his plea of guilty to two counts of an 11-count indictment. The sentencing proceeding is unusual in some respects. It has been the subject of more extensive submissions, written and oral, than this court has ever received upon such an occasion. The court has studied some hundreds of pages of memoranda and exhibits, plus scores of volunteered letters. A broad array of issues has been addressed. Imaginative suggestions of law and penology have been tendered.... It seems fitting now to report in writing the reasons upon which the court concludes that defendant must be sentenced to a term of four months in prison.

Defendant and His Crimes

Defendant appeared until the last couple of years to be a man of unimpeachably high character, attainments, and distinction. A doctor of divinity and an ordained rabbi, people around the world have acclaimed him for his works of public philanthropy, private charity, and leadership in educational enterprises. Scores of letters have come to the court from across this and other countries reporting debts of personal gratitude to him for numerous acts of extraordinary generosity. (The court has also received a kind of petition, with fifty-odd signatures, in which the signers, based upon learning acquired as newspaper readers, denounce the defendant and urge a severe sentence. Unlike the pleas for mercy, which appear to reflect unquestioned facts inviting compassion, this document should and will be disregarded.) In addition to his good works, defendant has managed to amass considerable wealth in the ownership and operation of nursing homes, in real estate ventures, and in a course of substantial investments.

Beginning about two years ago, investigations of nursing homes in this area, including questions of fraudulent claims for Medicaid funds, drew to a focus upon this defendant among several others. The results that concern us were the present indictment and two state indictments. After extensive pretrial proceedings, defendant embarked upon elaborate plea negotiations with both state and federal prosecutors. A state guilty plea and the instant plea were entered in March of this year....

For purposes of the sentence now imposed, the precise details of the charges, and of defendant's carefully phrased admissions of guilt, are not matters of prime importance. Suffice it to say that the plea on Count One (carrying a maximum of five years in prison and $10,000 fine) confesses defendant's knowing and willful participation in a scheme to defraud the United States in various ways, including the presentation of wrongfully padded claims for payments under the Medicaid program to defendant's nursing homes. Count Three, for which the guilty plea carries a theoretical maximum of three more years in prison and another $5,000 fine, is a somewhat more "technical" charge. Here, defendant admits to having participated in the filing of a partnership return that was false and fraudulent in failing to list people who had bought partnership interests from him in one of his nursing homes, had paid for such interests, and have made certain capital withdrawals.

The conspiracy to defraud, as defendant has admitted it, is by no means the worst of its kind; it is by no means as flagrant or extensive as has been portrayed in the press; it is evidently less grave than other nursing-home wrongs for which others have been convicted or publicized. At the same time, the sentence, as defendant has acknowledged, is imposed for two federal felonies including, as the more important, a knowing and purposeful conspiracy to mislead and defraud the Federal Government.

The Guiding Principles of Sentencing

Proceeding through the short list of the supposed justifications for criminal sanctions, defense counsel urge that no licit purpose could be served by defendant's incarceration. Some of these arguments are plainly sound; others are not.

The court agrees that this defendant should not be sent to prison for "rehabilitation." Apart from the patent inappositeness of the concept to this individual, this court shares the growing understanding that no one should ever be sent to prison for rehabilitation. That is to say, nobody who would not otherwise be locked up should suffer that fate on the incongruous premise that it will be good for him or her. Imprisonment is punishment. Facing the simple reality should help us to be civilized. It is less agreeable to confine someone when we deem it an affliction rather than a benefaction. If someone must be imprisoned—for other, valid reasons—we should seek to make rehabilitative resources available to him or her. But the goal of rehabilitation cannot fairly serve in itself as grounds for the sentence to confinement....

Equally clearly, this defendant should not be confined to incapacitate him. He is not dangerous. It is most improbable that he will commit similar, or any, offenses in the future. There is no need for "specific deterrence."

Contrary to counsel's submissions, however, two sentencing considerations demand a prison sentence in this case: First, the aim of general deterrence, the effort to discourage similar wrongdoing by others through a reminder that the law's warnings are real and that the grim consequence of imprisonment is likely to follow from crimes of deception for gain like those defendant has admitted. Second, the related, but not identical, concern that any lesser penalty would, in the words of the Model Penal Code, § 7.01 (1) (c), "depreciate the seriousness of the defendant's crime."

Resisting the first of these propositions, defense counsel invoke Immanuel Kant's axiom that "one man ought never to be dealt with merely as a means subservient to the purposes of another." In a more novel, but equally futile, effort, counsel urge that a sentence for general deterrence "would violate the Eighth Amendment proscription against cruel and unusual punishment." Treating the latter point first, because it is a short subject, it may be observed simply that if general deterrence as a sentencing purpose were now to be outlawed, as against a near unanimity of views among state and federal jurists, the bolt would have to come from a place higher than this.

As for Dr. Kant, it may well be that defense counsel mistake his meaning in the present context. Whether or not that is so, and without pretending to authority on that score, we take the widely accepted stance that a criminal punished in the interest of general deterrence is not being employed "merely as a means * * *." Reading Kant to mean that every man must be deemed more than the instrument of others, and must "always be treated as an end in himself," the humane principle is not offended here. Each of us is served by the enforcement of the law—not least a person like the defendant in this case, whose wealth and privileges, so long enjoyed, are so much founded upon law. More broadly, we are driven regularly in our ultimate interests as members of the community to use each other, and ourselves in war and in peace, for social ends. One who has transgressed against the criminal laws is certainly among the more fitting candidates for a role of this nature. This is no arbitrary selection. Warned in advance of the prospect, the transgressor has chosen, in the law's premises, "between keeping the law required for society's protection or paying the penalty."

But the whole business, defendant argues further, is guesswork; we are by no means certain that deterrence "works." The position is somewhat overstated; there is, in fact, some reasonably "scientific" evidence for the efficacy of criminal sanctions as deterrents, at least as against some kinds of crimes. Moreover, the time is not yet here when all we can "know" must be quantifiable and digestible by computers. The shared wisdom of generations teaches meaningfully, if somewhat amorphously, that the utilitarians have a point; we do, indeed, lapse often into rationality and act to seek pleasure and avoid pain. It would be better, to be sure, if we had more certainty and precision. Lacking these comforts, we continue to include among our working hypotheses a belief (with some concrete evidence in its support) that crimes like those in this case—deliberate, purposeful, continuing, non-impulsive, and committed for profit—are among those most likely to be generally deterrable by sanctions most shunned by those exposed to temptation.

The idea of avoiding depreciation of the seriousness of the offense implicates two or three thoughts, not always perfectly clear or universally agreed upon, beyond the idea of deterrence. It should be proclaimed by the court's judgment that the offenses are grave, not minor or purely technical. Some attention must be paid to the demand for equal justice; it will not do to leave the penalty of imprisonment a dead letter as against "privileged" violators while it is employed regularly, and with vigor, against others. There probably is in these conceptions an element of retributiveness, as counsel urge. And retribution, so denominated, is in some disfavor as a reason for punishment. It remains a factor, however, as Holmes perceived, and as is known to anyone who talks to judges, lawyers, defendants, or people generally. It may become more palatable, and probably more humanely understood, under the rubric of "deserts" or "just desserts." However the concept is formulated, we have not yet reached a state, supposing we ever should, in which the infliction of punishments for crime may be divorced generally from ideas of blame-worthiness, recompense, and proportionality.

An Alternative, "Behavioral Sanction"

Resisting prison above all else, defense counsel included in their thorough memorandum on sentencing two proposals for what they call a "constructive," and therefore a "preferable" form of "behavioral sanction." One is a plan for Dr. Bergman to create and run a program of Jewish vocational and religious high school training. The other is for him to take charge of a "Committee on Holocaust Studies," again concerned with education at the secondary school level.

A third suggestion was made orally at yesterday's sentencing hearing. It was proposed that Dr. Bergman might be ordered to work as a volunteer in some established agency as a visitor and aide to the sick and the otherwise incapacitated. The proposal was that he could read, provide various forms of physical assistance, and otherwise give comfort to afflicted people.

No one can doubt either the worthiness of these proposals or Dr. Bergman's ability to make successes of them. But both of the carefully formulated "sanctions" in the memorandum involve work of an honorific nature, not unlike that done in other projects to which the defendant has devoted himself in the past. It is difficult to conceive of them as "punishments" at all. The more recent proposal is somewhat more suitable in character, but it is still an insufficient penalty. The seriousness of the crimes to which Dr. Bergman has pled guilty demands something more than "requiring" him to lend his talents and efforts to further philanthropic enterprises. It remains open to him, of course, to pursue the interesting suggestions later on as a matter of unforced personal choice.

"Measuring" the Sentence

In cases like this one, the decision of greatest moment is whether to imprison or not. As reflected in the eloquent submissions for defendant, the prospect of the closing prison doors is the most appalling concern; the feeling is that the length of the sojourn is a lesser question once that threshold is passed. Nevertheless, the setting of a term remains to be accomplished. And in some respects it is a subject even more perplexing, unregulated, and unprincipled.

Days and months and years are countable with a sound of exactitude. But there can be no exactitude in the deliberations from which a number emerges. Without pretending to a nonexistent precision, the court notes at least the major factors.

The criminal behavior, as has been noted, is blatant in character and unmitigated by any suggestion of necessitous circumstance or other pressures difficult to resist. However metaphysicians may conjure with issues about free will, it is a fundamental premise of our efforts to do criminal justice that competent people, possessed of their faculties, make choices and are accountable for them. In this sometimes harsh light, the case of the present defendant is among the clearest and least relieved. Viewed against the maxima Congress ordained, and against the run of sentences in other federal criminal cases, it calls for more than a token sentence.

On the other side are factors that take longer to enumerate. Defendant's illustrious public life and works are in his favor, though diminished, of course, by what this case discloses. This is a first, probably a last, conviction. Defendant is 64 years old and in imperfect health, though by no means so ill, from what the court is told, that he could be expected to suffer inordinately more than many others of advanced years who go to prison.

Defendant invokes an understandable, but somewhat unworkable, notion of "disparity." He says others involved in recent nursing home fraud cases have received relatively light sentences for behavior more culpable than his. He lays special emphasis upon one defendant whose frauds appear indeed to have involved larger amounts and who was sentenced to a maximum of six months' incarceration, to be confined for that time only on week nights, not on week days or weekends. This court has examined the minutes of that sentencing proceeding and finds the case distinguishable in material respects. But even if there were a threat of such disparity as defendant warns against, it could not be a major weight on the scales.

Our sentencing system, deeply flawed, is characterized by disparity. We are to seek to "individualize" sentences, but no clear or clearly agreed standards govern the individualization. The lack of meaningful criteria does indeed leave sentencing judges far too much at large. But the result, with its nagging burdens on conscience, cannot be meaningfully alleviated by allowing any handful of sentences in a short series to fetter later judgments. The point is easy, of course, where Sentence No. 1 or Sentences 1–5 are notably harsh. It cannot be that a later judge, disposed to more leniencies, should feel in any degree "bound." The converse is not identical, but it is not totally different. The net of this is that this court has considered and has given some weight to the trend of the other cited sentences (though strict logic might call for none), but without treating them as forceful "precedents" in any familiar sense.

How, then, the particular sentence adjudged in this case? As has been mentioned, the case calls for a sentence that is more than nominal. Given the other circumstances, however — including that this is a first offense, by a man no longer young and not perfectly well, where danger of recidivism is not a concern — it verges on cruelty to think of confinement for a term of years. We sit, to be sure, in a nation where prison sentences of extravagant length are more common than they are almost anywhere else. By that light, the term imposed today is not notably long. For this sentencing court, however, for a nonviolent first offense involving no direct assaults or invasions of others' security (as in bank robbery, narcotics, etc.), it is a stern sentence. For people like Dr. Bergman, who might be disposed to engage in similar wrongdoing, it should be sufficiently frightening to serve the major end of general deterrence. For all but the profoundly vengeful, it should not depreciate the seriousness of his offenses.

Punishment in or for the Media

Much of defendant's sentencing memorandum is devoted to the extensive barrage of hostile publicity to which he has been subjected during the years before and since his indictment. He argues, and it appears to be undisputed, that the media (and people desiring to be featured in the media) have vilified him for many kinds of evil-doing of which he has in fact been innocent. Two main points are made on this score with respect to the problem of sentencing.

First, as has been mentioned, counsel expressed the concern that the court may be pressured toward severity by the force of the seeming public outcry. That the court should not allow itself to be affected in this way is clear beyond discussion. Nevertheless, it is not merely permissible, but entirely wholesome and responsible, for counsel to bring the expressed concern out in the open. Whatever our ideals and mixed images about judges, it would be naïve to doubt that judges have sometimes been swept by a sense of popular demand toward draconian sentencing decisions. It cannot hurt for the sentencing judge to be reminded of this and cautioned about it. There can be no guarantees. The sentencer must confront and regulate himself. But it bears reaffirmance that the court must seek to discount utterly the fact of notoriety in passing its judgment upon the defendant. Defense counsel cite reported opinions of this court reflecting what happens in a large number of unreported cases, by the present sentencer and many others, in which "unknown" defendants have received prison sentences, longer or shorter than today's, for white-collar or comparable non-violent crimes. The overall run of cases with all their individual variations, will reflect, it is hoped, earnest efforts to hew to the principle of equal treatment, with or without publicity.

Defendant's second point about his public humiliation is the frequently heard contention that he should not be incarcerated because he "has been punished enough." The thought is not without some initial appeal. If punishment were wholly or mainly retributive, it might be a weighty factor. In the end, however, it must be a matter of little or no force. Defendant's notoriety should not in the last analysis serve to lighten, any more than it may be permitted to aggravate, his sentence. The fact that he has been pilloried by journalists is essentially a consequence of the prestige and privileges he enjoyed before he was exposed as a wrongdoer. The long fall from grace was possible only because of the height he had reached. The suffering from loss of public esteem reflects a body of opinion that the esteem had been, in at least some measure, wrongly bestowed and enjoyed. It is not possible to justify the notion that this mode of non-judicial punishment should be an occasion for leniency not given to a defendant who never basked in such an admiring light at all. The quest for both the appearance and the substance of humiliation serves the function of imprisonment.

Writing, as judges rarely do, about a particular sentence concentrates the mind with possibly special force upon the experience of the sentencer as well as the person sentenced. Consigning someone to prison, this defendant or any other, "is a sad necessity." There are impulses of avoidance from time to time—toward a personally gratifying lenience or toward an opposite extreme. But there is, obviously, no place for private impulse in the judgment of the court. The course of justice must be sought with such objective rationality as we can muster, tempered with mercy, but obedient to the law, which, we do well to remember, is all that empowers a judge to make other people suffer.

Discussion Questions

1. Should any of the following factors have affected Bergman's sentence?

(a) his age

(b) his wealth

(c) the publicity his case attracted

If not, explain why each should be irrelevant to his punishment. If so, should it have increased or decreased his sentence?

2. Which theories of punishment depend upon a belief in "free will"?

Problem

2.12 Part (a) In November 2019, a jury convicted Roger Stone of seven felony counts of making false statements to various government officials, witness tampering, and obstructing a congressional investigation into Russian interference in the 2016 presidential election. Mr. Stone is a long time political consultant and operative described by some as a "dirty trickster."[7] He has also for many years been an associate and informal advisor to President Donald Trump. Prior to August 15, 2015, he was an official on the Trump presidential campaign. Among other things, Mr. Stone told a Congressional Committee that he had never described to anyone involved with the Trump campaign his conversations with a supposed intermediary to Wikileaks, which released emails at various points in the campaign embarrassing to Hillary Clinton, Mr. Trump's opponent in the election. Witnesses who worked for the Trump campaign as well as many emails clearly showed that Mr. Stone's denial was false. He also lied to Congressional investigators about the existence of more than 1,500 email and text messages between Mr. Stone and another witness, whom he attempted to persuade to lie to the Congressional committee conducting the investigation. When persuasion failed, Mr. Stone resorted to threats, telling the witness in a text message to "prepare to die." When this other witness warned Mr. Stone that his lies would catch up with him, he replied "no one cares."[8]

---

7. Sharon LaFraniere and Zach Montague, *Roger Stone Is Convicted of Impeding Investigators in a Bid to Protect President Trump*, THE NEW YORK TIMES (Nov. 15, 2019).

8. *Id.*

Despite an order from the judge presiding over his case not to discuss the case in the media, Mr. Stone posted on Instagram a photo of the judge with an image of a gun site crosshairs next to her head. Mr. Stone faces a maximum possible prison term of 50 years. He is 67 years old and has no prior criminal record. He has expressed no remorse.

At the sentencing hearing, his lawyer spoke about Mr. Stone's advocacy for animal rights, veterans, and NFL players who have suffered brain injuries and recommended the imposition of a sentence involving no prison time. He also argued that Mr. Stone never intended to carry out any of the threats he made. Despite being offered the chance to address the sentencing judge, Mr. Stone remained silent throughout the hearing. As is typical, the federal prosecutors who tried the case against Mr. Stone were trial lawyers, typically referred to as "line" prosecutors, who worked for the United States Attorney's Office for the District of Columbia, where the case was tried. These prosecutors, who were experienced and had worked with the F.B.I. on the investigation of Mr. Stone as well as his trial, submitted a sentencing memorandum recommending that Mr. Stone receive a sentence between seven and nine years.

In a highly unusual if not unprecedented move that caused great controversy, lawyers from the Department of Justice closely associated with Attorney General William Barr submitted a second sentencing memorandum contradicting the memorandum filed by the line prosecutors. The second memorandum stated that a sentence of seven to nine years would be unduly harsh and that a "sentence of incarceration of far less than [five to seven years] would be reasonable." The second memorandum did not recommend a particular sentence or sentencing range. The filing of the second memorandum triggered concern about and numerous accusations of improper political interference by Attorney General Barr in favor of one of President Trump's political allies. Mr. Barr was appointed by and has been strongly supportive of President Trump in ways that have undermined his credibility and independence as the most senior official in federal law enforcement. To protest the filing of the second sentencing memorandum, the line prosecutors withdrew from the case. One resigned from the U.S. Attorney's office.

What punishment should Mr. Stone receive? Why? Should he receive some term of imprisonment?

Part (b) Assume for this part that Mr. Stone receives a sentence that requires him to spend some time incarcerated in a federal prison. After the sentencing, President Trump indicates that he is considering pardoning Mr. Stone. Presidential pardons are typically granted only after careful review by the Office of the Pardon Attorney in the Department of Justice. Mr. Stone's case has received no such review. Should Mr. Stone receive a presidential pardon? If not, why? If so, why?

2. The Purposes of Punishment: A Closer Look

The following pages offer a closer look at the purposes of punishment and some of the challenges and complexities that each presents.

a. Deterrence

Jeremy Bentham, the famous utilitarian philosopher, gave the following classic statement of the deterrence rationale for punishment.

> Pain and pleasure are the great springs of human action. When a man perceives or supposes pain to be the consequence of an act, he is acted upon in such a manner as tends, with a certain force, to withdraw him, as it were, from the commission of that act. If the apparent magnitude, or rather value of that pain be greater than the apparent magnitude or value of the pleasure or good he expects to be the consequence of the act, he will be absolutely prevented from performing it. The mischief which would have ensued from the act, if performed, will also by that means be prevented.[9]

Problem

2.13 If you were a legislator, what range of punishment would you assign to each of the following offenses to assure that, in Bentham's words, "the apparent magnitude" of the pain of punishment is "greater than the apparent magnitude or value of the pleasure or good" a potential offender will gain from committing the offense? How would you determine how much punishment is necessary to deter each offense?

- Attempted residential burglary
- Trading stock on inside information
- Negligent vehicular homicide
- Bribing a mine safety inspector to ignore safety code violations
- Possession of an ounce of cocaine
- Burning a cross on the lawn of black newcomers to a previously all-white neighborhood
- Provoked homicide (i.e. committed in the heat of passion following provocation such as an assault on a family member)

Deterrence is both widely accepted and frequently articulated by legislators, judges, and prosecutors as a purpose of punishment. When a prosecutor, for example, urges

---

9. Jeremy Bentham, *Principles of Penal Law* 396, 402 in Vol. 1, THE WORKS OF JEREMY BENTHAM (John Bouring ed. 1843).

a judge to impose a particular sentence in order to "send a message," she is relying on deterrence reasoning. Reliance on deterrence stems in part from the appeal of its commonsense logic—that people will alter their behavior to avoid unpleasant consequences and thus the threat of punishment, such as time in prison, will discourage people from committing crimes. It is difficult to challenge the claim that the existence of the criminal law and punishment reduces crime to some degree through deterrence. In other words, few would doubt that if we were to repeal and abandon enforcing the criminal law in its entirety, the behavior it currently outlaws and punishes would increase.

But deterrence, like the other purposes of punishment discussed in this chapter, presents complexities and challenges. Deterrence reasoning relies on a number of assumptions the validity of which can be challenged. First, it assumes that potential offenders will know: (1) what the criminal law prohibits and (2) the punishments it imposes for violating those prohibitions. How accurate do you think the first assumption is? It appears valid regarding crimes such as murder, robbery, and assault. But many criminal offenses are more obscure. What about the second assumption? Are the punishments imposed even for well-recognized offenses such as murder, robbery, and assault widely known? Do you, for example, know what the potential and likely punishments are for these offenses in the states where you grew up, where you went to college, or where you are currently going to law school?

As the Bentham quote above makes clear, deterrence also assumes that potential offenders are rational actors who weigh the potential rewards of committing a crime such as robbery or selling illegal drugs against the potential punishments for those crimes. Do you think most potential offenders are such rational calculators? What if the crime is one of passion, such as an assault or homicide that arises from anger or another powerful emotion following an argument, insult, or the discovery of sexual infidelity? What about a potential offender who is intoxicated? Or one who is a drug addict thinking about committing a robbery or burglary to obtain money for drugs?

Some offenders, rather than being the rational calculators Bentham describes, are impulsive and radically present-oriented. Professor John DiIulio describes such criminals in the following excerpt. Is deterrence likely to work with such people?

Help Wanted: Economists, Crime and Public Policy

John J. DiIulio Jr.
10 JOURNAL OF ECONOMIC PERSPECTIVES
3–24 (Winter 1996)

[W]ork by Fleisher and other urban ethnographers suggests that today's crime-prone boys are too radically present-oriented and self-regarding for any type of conventional criminal deterrence to work.

By radically present oriented, I mean that they are almost completely incapable of deferring gratifications for the sake of future rewards. In their lives, there has never been a stable relationship between doing "what's right" and being rewarded and doing "what's wrong" and being punished. Many, in some cases most, of the adults in their lives have been persons who are themselves deviant, delinquent or criminal. Such discipline as they may have received at the hands of parents or other adults has been almost purely arbitrary: the first three times they commit a given prohibited act, nothing happens; the fourth time they get screamed at; the fifth and sixth times nothing happens; the seventh time they get punched in the head; the eighth time nothing happens; and so on. Those crime-prone kids who abuse alcohol or illegal drugs— and many of them do—become even more radically present oriented. Their lived experience, the most powerful teacher of all, counsels that kids who look ahead, stay in school, and "do the right thing" often end up just as jobless, hopeless and miserable as kids who do crime.

Some economists have begun to take such realities into account. For example, in their fine study of work and crime, Witte and Tauchen model the individual as choosing a level of criminal activity rather than the time to allocate to crime "because studies indicate that most criminal acts are unplanned." They also allow for "the possibility of nonmonetary gains from crime." Such work is clearly a step in the right direction. But the extraordinary degree to which today's young street criminals are present oriented, and the extent to which they do crime for fun as well as for profit, has yet to be taken fully into account by economists. "You never think about doing thirty," one young prisoner told me, "when you don't expect to live to thirty."

I suspect that super-impulsive time orientations are analytically tractable. But imagine a radically present-oriented young man who is also unable to feel joy or pain at the joy or pain of others. He is capable of committing the most heinous acts of physical violence for the most trivial reasons (for example, a perception of slight disrespect) without feeling remorse or losing any sleep. He fears neither the stigma of arrest nor the pains of imprisonment. In prison or out, he lives by the code of the streets, a code that reinforces rather than restrains his hair-trigger mentality. If he is part of a gang, then going to prison is very nearly a good "career move." And the things he gets for behaving criminally in a radically present-oriented, totally self-regarding way—money, drugs, status, sex—are their own immediate rewards. So for as long as his youthful energies hold out, he does what comes naturally: murders, assaults, rapes, robs, burglarizes and deals deadly drugs.

I do not have to "imagine" such young men. I have spent years going in and out of county lockups, jails and prisons. These boys are for real, and more are on the way.

If there is a model of criminal deterrence in the literature that mirrors such behavioral propensities, I have yet to come across it. Until economists develop such a model, the suspicion will remain that their notions of deterrence are valuable solely in the seminar room, that their understanding of crime is purely academic. It will not do to make further refinements to conventional deterrence models. Models that assume that young urban street predators are but a highly impulsive breed of middle-aged economics professors are not only intellectually idle, but (should anyone actually be foolish enough to act on them) downright dangerous. The reality simply does not fit the theory; economists need a new theory ...

* * *

If deterrence does not work with young men such as those Professor DiIulio describes, is there another basis on which punishing them can be justified?

Deterrence assumes that potential offenders are strongly motivated to avoid punishments such as a term of imprisonment. While this assumption is certainly well-grounded for most people, as Professor DiIulio suggests, it is not universal. Some repeat offenders become acclimated to prison and the threat of returning thus loses some of its potency. Among certain young men, serving a prison sentence is both a way to gain credibility on the street and also improve their standing in a gang or other criminal organization, especially if they show themselves willing to serve a prison term without cooperating with the government, thus increasing their trustworthiness in the eyes of those higher in the organization.

How much punishment is needed to deter particular offenders and offenses? Legislators passing statutes creating criminal offenses such as those listed in Problem 2.13 must decide what potential punishments should be imposed for those offenses. How do you think they determine what sentencing range will deter potential offenders? How should they?

Judges who rely on deterrence as a purpose of punishment in sentencing a particular defendant also face difficult empirical questions in choosing a particular sentence. If relying on general deterrence, is a five-year prison sentence enough to deter other potential offenders? A 10-year sentence? Or 15 or 20? The group of potential offenders for many crimes is large and many variables will affect the decisions they make about whether or not to commit a particular offense. These variables are likely to differ greatly from one potential offender to another. The judge cannot possibly know all of these variables. How, then, is the judge to calculate how great a sentence is needed to achieve general deterrence?

If the judge is relying on specific deterrence, how is the judge to calculate how large a sentence is necessary to dissuade the offender being sentenced from repeating her offense years down the road when she is released from prison? As with potential offenders who may be generally deterred, many variables, which the judge cannot possibly know about in advance, will likely impact the offender's future decisions about whether or not to reoffend. Again, how can the judge determine what sentence will specifically deter such an offender?

b. Incapacitation

Problem

2.14 Paul, a high school wrestling coach, is facing a potential 17-year prison sentence for molesting nearly two dozen boys. To avoid a lengthy prison sentence and convince the judge to put him on probation, Paul tells the judge that "if it means I have to have a surgical procedure so I have no sexuality, I will do that."[10] If such a surgical procedure were available and Paul willingly underwent the procedure, should that have any impact on the sentence imposed on Paul? To which purpose or purposes of punishment might the surgical procedure be relevant?

Reliance on incapacitation as a purpose of punishment has increased dramatically in recent decades and has been a primary force in expanding the American prison population to record levels. One example of increased reliance on incapacitation has been the enactment by many states of draconian "three strikes" statutes of the sort exemplified in the *Ewing* case, below.

Incapacitation may at first appear simpler and more certain in operation than deterrence because it avoids some of the problems raised by deterrence reasoning, such as whether and when criminals engage in rational calculation. The threat of a mandatory five-year prison term may or may not deter a potential burglar who steals to support a drug habit. But someone who is serving a mandatory five-year prison term is clearly incapacitated from committing a residential burglary while serving that sentence. When thought of in this way, incapacitation can seem a simple and effective, if somewhat crude, way to prevent crime. It also appeals to the natural impulse of society to protect its members from the dangers presented by repeat offenders and high recidivism rates.

Incapacitation reasoning, though, is highly problematic in several ways. Critics argue that reliance on incapacitation as a justification for punishment is basically unfair because it punishes people for crimes they have not committed. It is also inconsistent with retribution, because people cannot be found blameworthy for crimes they might commit in the future but have not actually committed.

Selecting sentences based on incapacitation requires judges and legislators to make predictions about future crimes. In recent years, some states have turned to artificial intelligence to assess future dangerousness. Judges in these states use complicated algorithms developed by private firms to help them make these predictions. Critics argue that predictions about which particular criminals will in fact re-offend are not accurate enough to be the basis for imposing a harsh sentence.

Another objection to using incapacitation to justify punishment is that the criteria used to make predictions about who is most likely to re-offend have a discriminatory impact on the poor and racial minorities. Such criteria are likely to include factors such as a person's level of education, employment history, and family ties. Because poverty increases the chances of inadequate or incomplete education, difficulty finding

---

10. James Ewinger, *Sex Offender's Bid for Freedom Rejected*, CLEVELAND PLAIN DEALER, Sept. 20, 1995, at 1B.

a job, and having a broken family, predictions of future offending that rely on these sorts of criteria are likely to conclude that poorer offenders have a greater likelihood of reoffending than wealthier offenders.

Critics of the use of artificial intelligence algorithms argue that the data used to create them reflect biases that negatively impact offenders with limited resources. Those who support the use of algorithms argue that judges are also likely to reflect common biases and that the algorithms are less likely to be biased than individual judges and can be improved over time. They also point out that algorithms are more likely to produce greater uniformity across many cases.

There has been much criticism in recent decades about the high percentage of the poor and minorities in our prison population, often referred to as "mass incarceration." Increased reliance on incapacitation as a justification for harsh sentencing measures, such as mandatory minimum sentences, has contributed to this problem.

c. Rehabilitation

> ### Problem
>
> 2.15 Johnny is a heroin addict who committed a string of burglaries to support his heroin habit, breaking into houses and apartments to steal electronics equipment and jewelry. Johnny carried no weapons and was careful to make sure no one was in the residences when he committed the burglaries. Eventually, the police caught Johnny in the act of burglarizing a residence when a silent security alarm went off. After he was arrested, the police connected Johnny to approximately 10 burglaries.
>
> Judges in the county in which Johnny was arrested have established a drug court. To be accepted into the drug court, defendants must plead guilty to the offense or offenses with which they are charged and successfully complete a year-long drug treatment program that is closely monitored by a judge. If a defendant completes the drug treatment program, the judge then dismisses all charges to which the defendant earlier pled guilty. Should Johnny, who committed a series of serious theft offenses, be allowed to enter the drug court program and eventually be shielded from any punishment for those offenses? What are the arguments for and against using a drug court program for a defendant such as Johnny?

The aspiration to rehabilitate criminals has influenced American attitudes toward punishment since the colonial era and continues to do so today. Rehabilitation, though, has always competed with other purposes of punishment for the hearts and minds of the public, legislators, and those who work in and study our criminal justice system.

In the colonial era, for example, Calvinists and Quakers held sharply contrasting religious attitudes toward human nature and sin that led to differing views about punishment. Calvinists believed that human beings are inherently evil and need to be deterred by punishment to counter the temptation to sin. Such an attitude supported public and at times gruesome corporal punishment to achieve deterrence. The Quakers, in contrast, believed that human beings are inherently good and that punishment needs to isolate criminals from whatever led them astray and bring them back in touch with their inherent goodness and with God. Rather than public corporal punishments aimed to deter, Quaker attitudes favored punishments aimed to rehabilitate.

The penitentiary, the forerunner of the vast prison system currently found in the United States, was a Quaker innovation. We now tend to see imprisonment as motivated by retribution, deterrence, or incapacitation rather than rehabilitation. Many today view prisons as "criminogenic," creating or reinforcing criminal tendencies rather than reducing or eliminating them. But the penitentiary was originally designed to rehabilitate by instilling repentance rather than fear. Although many now view solitary confinement as unduly harsh and emotionally and psychologically damaging to inmates, isolation was originally aimed at rehabilitation, seen by the Quakers as a way to insulate criminals from the forces that had led them astray and allow them to get back in touch with both God and their own inherent goodness.

In the twentieth and twenty-first centuries, advocates of rehabilitation have come to adopt less of a religious and more of a medical perspective. Rather than seeing a criminal primarily as a sinner, rehabilitation advocates now tend to view a criminal as analogous in many ways to a patient suffering from a physical illness.

Rehabilitation today continues to influence our attitudes toward, and institutions of, punishment. It is a frequently articulated goal of punishment. Many of our current sentencing practices have a rehabilitative foundation. For example, most juvenile offenders are dealt with under systems that are, at least in theory, based primarily on a rehabilitative model. The practice of parole, used today in many states, also reflects a rehabilitative design. Under a parole system those serving prions sentences are released under supervision after serving only a portion of the sentence imposed based on the progress they are assessed to have made toward rehabilitation. In recent years, many cities and counties across the country have created special "problem courts" dealing with specific populations, such as veterans and the mentally ill. Perhaps the most widespread and well-known of these are drug courts. These courts focus primarily on providing a rehabilitative treatment alternative to prison.

Rehabilitation continues to compete with other purposes of punishment, particularly incapacitation. Although some recent developments, such as drug courts, are clearly based on rehabilitation, other developments have been hostile to rehabilitation, such as three strikes laws and high mandatory minimum sentences. Such harsh sentencing measures are motivated primarily by the goal of incapacitating repeat offenders and offer little (if any) possibility for early release. In essence, they reflect the view that certain criminals are beyond the hope of rehabilitation. So today we have somewhat schizoid views about rehabilitation and seem increasingly skeptical of it in relation to certain types of crimes and certain types of offenders.

Rehabilitation may be treated either as a supplement to or as a substitute for punishment. An example of the supplemental approach is making rehabilitative services and treatment available while a person is imprisoned or after they are released. Today's drug courts exemplify the use of rehabilitation as an alternative to punishment. A defendant entering a drug court program typically receives a regimen of treatment to deal with addiction instead of being sent to prison.

Like every other purpose of punishment, the use of rehabilitation as a guide to responding to crime presents a number of theoretical and practical challenges. One is skepticism about whether criminals can be rehabilitated, which is grounded in the very high recidivism rates found in jurisdictions across the United States. Recent research has shown that rehabilitation works, but only under certain conditions. Proponents of rehabilitation argue that state officials in charge of establishing and running rehabilitation programs have often undermined confidence in rehabilitation by failing to base their decisions on valid empirical data.

Rehabilitation programs also face the political challenge of attracting funding from state legislators. It is often politically advantageous for those running for office to appear "tough on crime." Such legislators may fear that supporting rehabilitation programs, even though such programs are likely to reduce future crime, may appear to the public or be labeled by an opponent as being "soft on crime." In response, proponents of rehabilitation have pointed out that current economic realities favor rehabilitation over imprisonment. State prisons are already overcrowded and expensive to run at a time when many state budgets are strained. Rehabilitation programs thus make economic sense because they are cheaper than imprisonment.

d. Retribution

Philosophers and legal academics have long debated whether retribution should serve as a purpose of punishment. But there is little question that retribution as both a justification for and a limitation on punishment continues to influence the thinking of legislators, judges, and the public.

Are you a retributivist? The retributive position has three essential principles: (1) the blameworthy should be punished; (2) punishment must be proportional to the level of blameworthiness; and (3) the blameless (i.e. the innocent) must never be punished. Do you think that any of these principles should play a role in assigning or limiting criminal punishment? Many students resist retribution because they equate it with revenge and view it as necessarily leading to the imposition of harsh punishments. But that is not necessarily so. Retribution can be used to justify punishment under the first and second principles mentioned above. But the second and third principles also serve to limit punishment. For example, the claim that a person who commits a serious crime, such as murder or rape, *should be punished* and that the person's punishment *should be assessed in proportion to the seriousness of the crime* relies on retribution as a *justification* for punishment. In contrast, the position that *only* the blameworthy should be punished and *only* with a punishment *proportional to the seriousness of the crime* relies on retribution as a limitation on punishment. Do you accept retribution as a justification for punishment? How about as a limitation on punishment? Keep this question in mind as you work on Problem 2.16 that appears below and read the *Ewing v. California* case that appears in the next section.

Problem

2.16 You are a legislator in a state in which shoplifting has become a widespread problem. Although the typical shoplifting case in your state involves the theft of items worth between $25 and $50, the aggregate costs imposed on businesses by shoplifting, including the expense of security measures aimed at defeating it, are significant. Many merchant associations and business groups, including the statewide chamber of commerce, are pressing you and other state legislators to address the problem with stiffer sentences. Assume that shoplifters who have been arrested and punished in your state have a high recidivism rate. Many of your fellow legislators decide that neither specific nor general deterrence is likely to work with shoplifters because many shoplifters are drug addicts who steal to buy the drugs to which they are addicted. Due to their addictions, they are typically incapable of the rational calculation and self-control that deterrence requires. Many of your fellow legislators also decide that rehabilitation is too uncertain to deal effectively with the shoplifting problem. Assume that rehabilitation has been shown to have worked with some shoplifting offenders, but has failed with a large number. As a result, some legislators propose a 15-year mandatory sentence for repeat shoplifters in an effort to incapacitate them. How would you, as a legislator, respond to this proposal? Is this mandatory sentencing scheme consistent with deterrence? With incapacitation? With retribution?

The ideas that the criminal law should punish the blameworthy, refrain from punishing the blameless, and impose punishments proportional to blameworthiness appear fairly straightforward. But it is not always clear how one should measure blameworthiness and desert, concepts central to retribution.

Blame can be assessed from a variety of perspectives. It can be viewed as turning on many different factors and there can be significant disagreement on how to weigh particular factors. For example, should assessment of a person's blameworthiness be based on the person's *mental state?* Is someone who kills another purposefully, then, more blameworthy than a person who kills recklessly? Or should blameworthiness depend on the *results* one's conduct brings about? Is someone who attempts to kill but fails just as blameworthy as someone who succeeds in purposefully killing another because both the killer and the would-be killer have the same mental state—purpose to kill? Or is the one who attempts but fails less blameworthy than the one who actually kills because he or she did not actually cause a death?

In assessing blame, should we focus on the criminal? The crime? Both? Imagine two people who each commit residential burglaries. One has no prior record. The other has two prior burglary convictions and has served prison sentences as a consequence of each. Do you think the recidivist is more blameworthy than the first-time offender? If so, why? Or do you think that the recidivist should be treated the same as the first-time offender because both committed the same crime? Because the recidivist has already served two prison sentences for his prior crimes, do you view him as having "paid his debt to society" and thus deserving to be treated the same as the first-time offender?

In addition to requiring that the blameworthy be punished and the blameless not be punished, retribution as a purpose of punishment also requires that punishment be proportional to an offender's level of blame. In other words, more severe punishments should be imposed on more blameworthy offenders and less severe punishments imposed on less blameworthy offenders. As many of the problems in this chapter reveal, assessing an offender's level of blame is not always easy because there are different ways of measuring blame and a wide variety of factors can influence one's assessment of blame.

People often disagree on how to measure blame and on whether and how various factors should influence assessment of an actor's level of blame. They also often disagree on the level of blame that should be assigned to various crimes.

Problem

2.17[11] Rank the following crimes in terms of their moral blameworthiness. If you were a legislator, what range of prison terms would you assign to each of these crimes on the basis of retribution?

- Attempted residential burglary
- Trading stock on inside information
- Negligent vehicular homicide
- Bribing a mine safety inspector to ignore safety code violations
- Possession of an ounce of cocaine
- Burning a cross on the lawn of black newcomers to a previously all-white neighborhood
- Provoked homicide (i.e. committed in the heat of passion following provocation such as an assault on a family member)

---

11. This problem is adapted from David Dolinko, *Three Mistakes of Retributivism*, 39 UCLA L. REV. 1623 (1992).

Even if we could agree on how to rank the relative blameworthiness of various crimes such as those set forth in Problem 2.17, how do we translate those judgments into particular sentences, such as terms of imprisonment?

C. How Much Punishment?

This section focuses on how much punishment should be imposed on an individual defendant. Before turning to that issue, though, it is worth noting the scale of punishment in the United States and how it has grown in recent decades, as reflected in Figure 2.1. The United States in now one of the most punitive countries in the world.

Figure 2.1

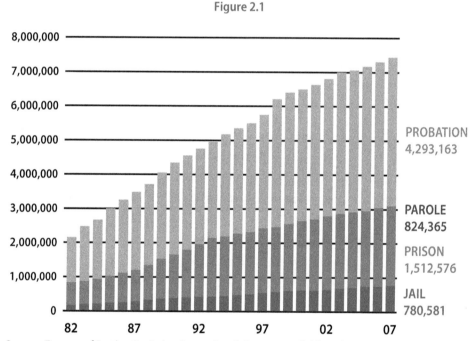

Source: Bureau of Justice Statistics Correctional Surveys available at http://www.ojp.usdoj.gov/bjs/glance/tables/corr2tab.htm
Note: Due to offenders with dual status, the sum of these four correctional categories slightly overstates the total correctional population.

This section focuses on one way in which the criminal law seeks to answer the question of how much punishment should be imposed on a particular defendant, the aspiration of proportionality in sentencing. Proportionality is widely viewed as desirable. Legislatures, for example, often make proportionality one of the goals of sentencing, as the following statutes demonstrate:

Arkansas Code § 16-90-801 Statement of sentencing policy

…

(b) Purpose of Sentencing Standards.

    (1) Though voluntary, the purpose of establishing rational and consistent sentencing standards is to seek to ensure that sanctions imposed following conviction are proportional to the seriousness of the offense of conviction and the extent of the offender's criminal history.

    (2) The standards seek to ensure equitable sanctions which provide that offenders similar with respect to relevant sentencing criteria will receive similar sanctions and offenders substantially different with respect to relevant sentencing criteria will receive different sanctions.

Discussion Questions

1. What is the difference between an *equitable* sentence and a *proportional* sentence?

2. Do you think Ewing's sentence in the case below was equitable? Was it proportional?

New Jersey Code of Criminal Justice § 2C: 1.2 Purposes

The general purposes of the provisions governing the sentencing of offenders are: …

    (4) To safeguard offenders against excessive, disproportionate or arbitrary punishment;

Discussion Questions

1. What is the difference between a sentence being *excessive* and a sentence being *proportional*? Between a sentence being *arbitrary* and a sentence being *proportional*?

2. Do you think Ewing's sentence in the case below was excessive? Was it arbitrary?

Oregon Revised Code § 161.025 Purposes

(1) The general purposes of chapter 743, Oregon Laws 1971 are: …

    (f) To prescribe penalties which are proportionate to the seriousness of offenses and which permit recognition of differences in rehabilitation possibilities among individual offenders.

* * *

Why is proportionality in punishment such a widely shared aspiration? From a retributive perspective, disproportional punishment violates the idea that the punishment should be equivalent to the defendant's blameworthiness. In other words, any punishment imposed beyond what is deserved is essentially punishment without blame and thus violates the retributive principle. Proportional punishment also makes utilitarian sense. Punishment imposed in excess of what is needed to deter, incapacitate, or rehabilitate lacks utility in preventing crime and thus wastes public resources.

Disproportional punishment may also bring about disrespect for the law by the public and by those upon whom it is imposed.

The OXFORD ENGLISH DICTIONARY defines proportion as "[t]he relation existing between things or magnitudes as to size, quantity, number or the like; comparative relation, ratio." Proportionality, then, is a relational concept. Things are not inherently proportional or disproportional. Rather, they have or lack these qualities in relation to something else. In other words, a sentence must be proportional or disproportional to something else. *To what should punishment be proportional? Is it desert? The need for general deterrence? The defendant's future danger?* How do the statutes above answer this question? How do the various opinions that follow in *Ewing* answer it?

California, like many other states, enacted a "three strikes" statute that imposes lengthy mandatory prison terms on repeat offenders. The principal case in this section, *Ewing v. California,* is a United States Supreme Court decision that examines whether a particularly harsh sentence imposed under the California three-strikes statute violates the federal constitution's proportionality requirement. The question of whether a three-strikes statute is good public policy is typically resolved by a legislature. It was the California legislature that enacted the three-strikes statute at issue in the *Ewing* case. But the United States Supreme Court is the final arbiter of whether such a statute violates the United States Constitution. In the following case, the defendant claimed that the sentence imposed on him violated the Eighth Amendment to the United States Constitution, adopted in 1791, which states:

> Excessive bail shall not be required, nor excessive fines imposed, nor cruel and unusual punishments inflicted.

Ewing v. California
538 U.S. 11 (2003)
United States Supreme Court

Justice O'Connor announced the judgment of the Court and delivered an opinion in which The Chief Justice and Justice Kennedy join.

In this case, we decide whether the Eighth Amendment prohibits the State of California from sentencing a repeat felon to a prison term of 25 years to life under the State's "Three Strikes and You're Out" law.

I

California's three strikes law reflects a shift in the State's sentencing policies toward incapacitating and deterring repeat offenders who threaten the public safety. The law was designed "to ensure longer prison sentences and greater punishment for those who commit a felony and have been previously convicted of serious and/or violent felony offenses." On March 3, 1993, California Assemblymen Bill Jones and Jim Costa introduced Assembly Bill 971, the legislative version of what would later become the three strikes law. The Assembly Committee on Public Safety defeated the bill only weeks later. Public outrage over the defeat sparked a voter initiative to add Proposition 184, based loosely on the bill, to the ballot in the November 1994 general election.

On October 1, 1993, while Proposition 184 was circulating, 12-year-old Polly Klaas was kidnapped from her home in Petaluma, California. Her admitted killer, Richard Allen Davis, had a long criminal history that included two prior kidnapping convictions. Davis had served only half of his most recent sentence (16 years for kidnapping, assault, and burglary). Had Davis served his entire sentence, he would still have been in prison on the day that Polly Klaas was kidnapped.

Polly Klaas' murder galvanized support for the three strikes initiative. Within days, Proposition 184 was on its way to becoming the fastest qualifying initiative in California history. On January 3, 1994, the sponsors of Assembly Bill 971 resubmitted an amended version of the bill that conformed to Proposition 184. On January 31, 1994, Assembly Bill 971 passed the Assembly by a 63 to 9 margin. The Senate passed it by a 29 to 7 margin on March 3, 1994. Governor Pete Wilson signed the bill into law on March 7, 1994. California voters approved Proposition 184 by a margin of 72 to 28 percent on November 8, 1994.

California thus became the second State to enact a three strikes law.... Between 1993 and 1995, 24 States and the Federal Government enacted three strikes laws. Though the three strikes laws vary from State to State, they share a common goal of protecting the public safety by providing lengthy prison terms for habitual felons.

California's current three strikes law consists of two virtually identical statutory schemes "designed to increase the prison terms of repeat felons." When a defendant is convicted of a felony, and he has previously been convicted of one or more prior felonies defined as "serious" or "violent" in Cal. Penal Code Ann. §§ 667.5 and 1192.7 sentencing is conducted pursuant to the three strikes law. Prior convictions must be alleged in the charging document, and the defendant has a right to a jury determination that the prosecution has proved the prior convictions beyond a reasonable doubt.

If the defendant has one prior "serious" or "violent" felony conviction, he must be sentenced to "twice the term otherwise provided as punishment for the current felony conviction." If the defendant has two or more prior "serious" or "violent" felony convictions, he must receive "an indeterminate term of life imprisonment." Defendants sentenced to life under the three strikes law become eligible for parole on a date calculated by reference to a "minimum term," which is the greater of (a) three times the term otherwise provided for the current conviction, (b) 25 years, or (c) the term determined by the court pursuant to § 1170 for the underlying conviction, including any enhancements.

Under California law, certain offenses may be classified as either felonies or misdemeanors. These crimes are known as "wobblers." Some crimes that would otherwise be misdemeanors become "wobblers" because of the defendant's prior record. For example, petty theft, a misdemeanor, becomes a "wobbler" when the defendant has previously served a prison term for committing specified theft-related crimes. Other crimes, such as grand theft, are "wobblers" regardless of the defendant's prior record. Both types of "wobblers" are triggering offenses under the three strikes law only when they are treated as felonies. Under California law, a "wobbler" is presumptively a felony and "remains a felony except when the discretion is actually exercised" to make the crime a misdemeanor.

In California, prosecutors may exercise their discretion to charge a "wobbler" as either a felony or a misdemeanor. Likewise, California trial courts have discretion to reduce a "wobbler" charged as a felony to a misdemeanor either before preliminary examination or at sentencing to avoid imposing a three strikes sentence. In exercising this discretion, the court may consider "those factors that direct similar sentencing decisions," such as "the nature and circumstances of the offense, the defendant's appreciation of and attitude toward the offense, ... [and] the general objectives of sentencing."

California trial courts can also vacate allegations of prior "serious" or "violent" felony convictions, either on motion by the prosecution or sua sponte. In ruling whether to vacate allegations of prior felony convictions, courts consider whether, "in light of the nature and circumstances of [the defendant's] present felonies and prior serious and/or violent felony convictions, and the particulars of his background, character, and prospects, the defendant may be deemed outside the [three strikes'] scheme's spirit, in whole or in part." Thus, trial courts may avoid imposing a three strikes sentence in two ways: first, by reducing "wobblers" to misdemeanors (which do not qualify as triggering offenses), and second, by vacating allegations of prior "serious" or "violent" felony convictions.

On parole from a 9-year prison term, petitioner Gary Ewing walked into the pro shop of the El Segundo Golf Course in Los Angeles County on March 12, 2000. He walked out with three golf clubs, priced at $399 apiece, concealed in his pants leg. A shop employee, whose suspicions were aroused when he observed Ewing limp out of the pro shop, telephoned the police. The police apprehended Ewing in the parking lot.

Ewing is no stranger to the criminal justice system. In 1984, at the age of 22, he pleaded guilty to theft. The court sentenced him to six months in jail (suspended), three years' probation, and a $300 fine. In 1988, he was convicted of felony grand theft auto and sentenced to one year in jail and three years' probation. After Ewing completed probation, however, the sentencing court reduced the crime to a misdemeanor, permitted Ewing to withdraw his guilty plea, and dismissed the case. In 1990, he was convicted of petty theft with a prior and sentenced to 60 days in the county jail and three years' probation. In 1992, Ewing was convicted of battery and sentenced to 30 days in the county jail and two years' summary probation. One month later, he was convicted of theft and sentenced to 10 days in the county jail and 12 months' probation. In January 1993, Ewing was convicted of burglary and sentenced to 60 days in the county jail and one year's summary probation. In February 1993, he was convicted of possessing drug paraphernalia and sentenced to six months in the county jail and three years' probation. In July 1993, he was convicted of appropriating lost property and sentenced to 10 days in the county jail and two years' summary probation. In September 1993, he was convicted of unlawfully possessing a firearm and trespassing and sentenced to 30 days in the county jail and one year's probation.

In October and November 1993, Ewing committed three burglaries and one robbery at a Long Beach, California, apartment complex over a 5-week period. He awakened one of his victims, asleep on her living room sofa, as he tried to disconnect her video cassette recorder from the television in that room. When she screamed, Ewing ran out the front door. On another occasion, Ewing accosted a victim in the mailroom of the apartment complex. Ewing claimed to have a gun and ordered the victim to hand over his wallet. When the victim resisted, Ewing produced a knife and forced the victim back to the apartment itself. While Ewing rifled through the bedroom, the victim fled the apartment screaming for help. Ewing absconded with the victim's money and credit cards.

On December 9, 1993, Ewing was arrested on the premises of the apartment complex for trespassing and lying to a police officer. The knife used in the robbery and a glass cocaine pipe were later found in the back seat of the patrol car used to transport Ewing to the police station. A jury convicted Ewing of first-degree robbery and three counts of residential burglary. Sentenced to nine years and eight months in prison, Ewing was paroled in 1999. Only 10 months later, Ewing stole the golf clubs at issue in this case. He was charged with, and ultimately convicted of, one count of felony grand theft of personal property in excess of $400. As required by the three strikes law, the prosecutor formally alleged, and the trial court later found, that Ewing had been convicted previously of four serious or violent felonies for the three burglaries and the robbery in the Long Beach apartment complex.

At the sentencing hearing, Ewing asked the court to reduce the conviction for grand theft, a "wobbler" under California law, to a misdemeanor so as to avoid a three strikes sentence. Ewing also asked the trial court to exercise its discretion to dismiss the allegations of some or all of his prior serious or violent felony convictions, again for purposes of avoiding a three strikes sentence. Before sentencing Ewing, the trial court took note of his entire criminal history, including the fact that he was on parole when he committed his latest offense. The court also heard arguments from defense counsel and a plea from Ewing himself.

In the end, the trial judge determined that the grand theft should remain a felony. The court also ruled that the four prior strikes for the three burglaries and the robbery in Long Beach should stand. As a newly convicted felon with two or more "serious" or "violent" felony convictions in his past, Ewing was sentenced under the three strikes law to 25 years to life.

The California Court of Appeal affirmed in an unpublished opinion. Relying on our decision in *Rummel v. Estelle*, 445 U.S. 263, (1980), the court rejected Ewing's claim that his sentence was grossly disproportionate under the Eighth Amendment. Enhanced sentences under recidivist statutes like the three strikes law, the court reasoned, serve the "legitimate goal" of deterring and incapacitating repeat offenders. The Supreme Court of California denied Ewing's petition for review, and we granted certiorari. We now affirm.

II

The Eighth Amendment, which forbids cruel and unusual punishments, contains a "narrow proportionality principle" that "applies to noncapital sentences." We have most recently addressed the proportionality principle as applied to terms of years in a series of cases beginning with *Rummel v. Estelle.*

In *Rummel*, we held that it did not violate the Eighth Amendment for a State to sentence a three-time offender to life in prison with the possibility of parole. Like Ewing, Rummel was sentenced to a lengthy prison term under a recidivism statute. Rummel's two prior offenses were a 1964 felony for "fraudulent use of a credit card to obtain $ 80 worth of goods or services," and a 1969 felony conviction for "passing a forged check in the amount of $ 28.36." His triggering offense was a conviction for felony theft—"obtaining $120.75 by false pretenses."

This Court ruled that "having twice imprisoned him for felonies, Texas was entitled to place upon *Rummel* the onus of one who is simply unable to bring his conduct within the social norms prescribed by the criminal law of the State." The recidivism statute "is nothing more than a societal decision that when such a person commits yet another felony, he should be subjected to the admittedly serious penalty of incarceration for life, subject only to the State's judgment as to whether to grant him parole." We noted that this Court "has on occasion stated that the Eighth Amendment prohibits imposition of a sentence that is grossly disproportionate to the severity of the crime." But "outside the context of capital punishment, successful challenges to the proportionality of particular sentences have been exceedingly rare." Although we stated that the proportionality principle "would ... come into play in the extreme example ... if a legislature made overtime parking a felony punishable by life imprisonment," we held that "the mandatory life sentence imposed upon this petitioner does not constitute cruel and unusual punishment under the Eighth and Fourteenth Amendments."

In *Hutto v. Davis*, 454 U.S. 370, (1982), the defendant was sentenced to two consecutive terms of 20 years in prison for possession with intent to distribute nine ounces of marijuana and distribution of marijuana. We held that such a sentence was constitutional: "In short, *Rummel* stands for the proposition that federal courts should be reluctant to review legislatively mandated terms of imprisonment, and that successful challenges to the proportionality of particular sentences should be exceedingly rare."

Three years after *Rummel*, in *Solem v. Helm*, 463 U.S. 277, (1983), we held that the Eighth Amendment prohibited "a life sentence without possibility of parole for a seventh nonviolent felony." The triggering offense in *Solem* was "uttering a 'no account' check for $100." We specifically stated that the Eighth Amendment's ban on cruel and unusual punishments "prohibits ... sentences that are disproportionate to the crime committed," and that the "constitutional principle of proportionality has been recognized explicitly in this Court for almost a century." The *Solem* Court then explained that three factors may be relevant to a determination of whether a sentence is so disproportionate that it violates the Eighth Amendment: "(i) the gravity of the offense and the harshness of the penalty; (ii) the sentences imposed on other criminals in the same jurisdiction; and (iii) the sentences imposed for commission of the same crime in other jurisdictions."

Applying these factors in *Solem*, we struck down the defendant's sentence of life without parole. We specifically noted the contrast between that sentence and the sentence in *Rummel*, pursuant to which the defendant was eligible for parole. Indeed, we explicitly declined to overrule *Rummel*: "Our conclusion today is not inconsistent with *Rummel v. Estelle*."

Eight years after *Solem*, we grappled with the proportionality issue again in *Harmelin v. Michigan*. *Harmelin* was not a recidivism case, but rather involved a first-time offender convicted of possessing 672 grams of cocaine. He was sentenced to life in prison without possibility of parole. A majority of the Court rejected *Harmelin's* claim that his sentence was so grossly disproportionate that it violated the Eighth Amendment. The Court, however, could not agree on why his proportionality argument failed. Justice Scalia, joined by The Chief Justice, wrote that the proportionality principle was "an aspect of our death penalty jurisprudence, rather than a generalizable aspect of Eighth Amendment law." He would thus have declined to apply gross disproportionality principles except in reviewing capital sentences.

Justice Kennedy, joined by two other Members of the Court, concurred in part and concurred in the judgment. Justice Kennedy specifically recognized that "the Eighth Amendment proportionality principle also applies to noncapital sentences." He then identified four principles of proportionality review—"the primacy of the legislature, the variety of legitimate penological schemes, the nature of our federal system, and the requirement that proportionality review be guided by objective factors"—that "inform the final one: The Eighth Amendment does not require strict proportionality between crime and sentence. Rather, it forbids only extreme sentences that are 'grossly disproportionate' to the crime." Justice Kennedy's concurrence also stated that *Solem* "did not mandate" comparative analysis "within and between jurisdictions."

The proportionality principles in our cases distilled in Justice Kennedy's concurrence guide our application of the Eighth Amendment in the new context that we are called upon to consider.

For many years, most States have had laws providing for enhanced sentencing of repeat offenders. Yet between 1993 and 1995, three strikes laws effected a sea change in criminal sentencing throughout the Nation. These laws responded to widespread public concerns about crime by targeting the class of offenders who pose the greatest threat to public safety: career criminals.... Though three strikes laws may be relatively new, our tradition of deferring to state legislatures in making and implementing such important policy decisions is longstanding.

Our traditional deference to legislative policy choices finds a corollary in the principle that the Constitution "does not mandate adoption of any one penological theory." A sentence can have a variety of justifications, such as incapacitation, deterrence, retribution, or rehabilitation. Some or all of these justifications may play a role in a

State's sentencing scheme. Selecting the sentencing rationales is generally a policy choice to be made by state legislatures, not federal courts.

When the California Legislature enacted the three strikes law, it made a judgment that protecting the public safety requires incapacitating criminals who have already been convicted of at least one serious or violent crime. Nothing in the Eighth Amendment prohibits California from making that choice. To the contrary, our cases establish that "States have a valid interest in deterring and segregating habitual criminals." Recidivism has long been recognized as a legitimate basis for increased punishment.

California's justification is no pretext. Recidivism is a serious public safety concern in California and throughout the Nation. According to a recent report, approximately 67 percent of former inmates released from state prisons were charged with at least one "serious" new crime within three years of their release. In particular, released property offenders like Ewing had higher recidivism rates than those released after committing violent, drug, or public-order offenses. Approximately 73 percent of the property offenders released in 1994 were arrested again within three years, compared to approximately 61 percent of the violent offenders, 62 percent of the public-order offenders, and 66 percent of the drug offenders.

In 1996, when the *Sacramento Bee* studied 233 three strikes offenders in California, it found that they had an aggregate of 1,165 prior felony convictions, an average of 5 apiece. The prior convictions included 322 robberies and 262 burglaries. About 84 percent of the 233 three strikes offenders had been convicted of at least one violent crime. In all, they were responsible for 17 homicides, 7 attempted slayings, and 91 sexual assaults and child molestations. The *Sacramento Bee* concluded, based on its investigation, that "in the vast majority of the cases, regardless of the third strike, the [three strikes] law is snaring [the] long-term habitual offenders with multiple felony convictions...."

The State's interest in deterring crime also lends some support to the three strikes law. We have long viewed both incapacitation and deterrence as rationales for recidivism statutes: "[A] recidivist statute['s] ... primary goals are to deter repeat offenders and, at some point in the life of one who repeatedly commits criminal offenses serious enough to be punished as felonies, to segregate that person from the rest of society for an extended period of time." Four years after the passage of California's three strikes law, the recidivism rate of parolees returned to prison for the commission of a new crime dropped by nearly 25 percent. Even more dramatically:

> "An unintended but positive consequence of 'Three Strikes' has been the impact on parolees leaving the state. More California parolees are now leaving the state than parolees from other jurisdictions entering California. This striking turnaround started in 1994. It was the first time more parolees left the state than entered since 1976. This trend has continued and in 1997 more than 1,000 net parolees left California."

To be sure, California's three strikes law has sparked controversy. Critics have doubted the law's wisdom, cost-efficiency, and effectiveness in reaching its goals.

This criticism is appropriately directed at the legislature, which has primary responsibility for making the difficult policy choices that underlie any criminal sentencing scheme. We do not sit as a "superlegislature" to second-guess these policy choices. It is enough that the State of California has a reasonable basis for believing that dramatically enhanced sentences for habitual felons "advances the goals of [its] criminal justice system in any substantial way."

III

Against this backdrop, we consider Ewing's claim that his three strikes sentence of 25 years to life is unconstitutionally disproportionate to his offense of "shoplifting three golf clubs." We first address the gravity of the offense compared to the harshness of the penalty. At the threshold, we note that Ewing incorrectly frames the issue. The gravity of his offense was not merely "shoplifting three golf clubs." Rather, Ewing was convicted of felony grand theft for stealing nearly $ 1,200 worth of merchandise after previously having been convicted of at least two "violent" or "serious" felonies. Even standing alone, Ewing's theft should not be taken lightly. His crime was certainly not "one of the most passive felonies a person could commit." To the contrary, the Supreme Court of California has noted the "seriousness" of grand theft in the context of proportionality review. Theft of $1,200 in property is a felony under federal law, 18 U.S.C. § 641, and in the vast majority of States.

That grand theft is a "wobbler" under California law is of no moment. Though California courts have discretion to reduce a felony grand theft charge to a misdemeanor, it remains a felony for all purposes "unless and until the trial court imposes a misdemeanor sentence." "The purpose of the trial judge's sentencing discretion" to downgrade certain felonies is to "impose a misdemeanor sentence in those cases in which the rehabilitation of the convicted defendant either does not require or would be adversely affected by, incarceration in a state prison as a felon." Under California law, the reduction is not based on the notion that a "wobbler" is "conceptually a misdemeanor." Rather, it is "intended to extend misdemeanant treatment to a potential felon." In Ewing's case, however, the trial judge justifiably exercised her discretion not to extend such lenient treatment given Ewing's long criminal history.

In weighing the gravity of Ewing's offense, we must place on the scales not only his current felony, but also his long history of felony recidivism. Any other approach would fail to accord proper deference to the policy judgments that find expression in the legislature's choice of sanctions. In imposing a three strikes sentence, the State's interest is not merely punishing the offense of conviction, or the "triggering" offense: "It is in addition the interest ... in dealing in a harsher manner with those who by repeated criminal acts have shown that they are simply incapable of conforming to the norms of society as established by its criminal law." To give full effect to the State's choice of this legitimate penological goal, our proportionality review of Ewing's sentence must take that goal into account.

Ewing's sentence is justified by the State's public-safety interest in incapacitating and deterring recidivist felons, and amply supported by his own long, serious criminal record.... Ewing's is not "the rare case in which a threshold comparison of the crime committed and the sentence imposed leads to an inference of gross disproportionality."

We hold that Ewing's sentence of 25 years to life in prison, imposed for the offense of felony grand theft under the three strikes law, is not grossly disproportionate and therefore does not violate the Eighth Amendment's prohibition on cruel and unusual punishments. The judgment of the California Court of Appeal is affirmed.

Justice Scalia, concurring in the judgment.

In my concurring opinion in *Harmelin v. Michigan*, I concluded that the Eighth Amendment's prohibition of "cruel and unusual punishments" was aimed at excluding only certain modes of punishment, and was not a "guarantee against disproportionate sentences." Out of respect for the principle of stare decisis, I might nonetheless accept the contrary holding of *Solem v. Helm*—that the Eighth Amendment contains a narrow proportionality principle—if I felt I could intelligently apply it. This case demonstrates why I cannot.

Proportionality—the notion that the punishment should fit the crime—is inherently a concept tied to the penological goal of retribution. "It becomes difficult even to speak intelligently of 'proportionality,' once deterrence and rehabilitation are given significant weight,"—not to mention giving weight to the purpose of California's three strikes law: incapacitation. In the present case, the game is up once the plurality has acknowledged that "the Constitution does not mandate adoption of any one penological theory," and that a "sentence can have a variety of justifications, such as incapacitation, deterrence, retribution, or rehabilitation." That acknowledgment having been made, it no longer suffices merely to assess "the gravity of the offense compared to the harshness of the penalty," that classic description of the proportionality principle (alone and in itself quite resistant to policy-free, legal analysis) now becomes merely the "first" step of the inquiry. Having completed that step (by a discussion which, in all fairness, does not convincingly establish that 25-years-to-life is a "proportionate" punishment for stealing three golf clubs), the plurality must then add an analysis to show that "Ewing's sentence is justified by the State's public-safety interest in incapacitating and deterring recidivist felons."

Which indeed it is—though why that has anything to do with the principle of proportionality is a mystery. Perhaps the plurality should revise its terminology, so that what it reads into the Eighth Amendment is not the unstated proposition that all punishment should be reasonably proportionate to the gravity of the offense, but rather the unstated proposition that all punishment should reasonably pursue the multiple purposes of the criminal law. That formulation would make it clearer than ever, of course, that the plurality is not applying law but evaluating policy.

Because I agree that petitioner's sentence does not violate the Eighth Amendment's prohibition against cruel and unusual punishments, I concur in the judgment....

Justice Breyer, with whom Justice Stevens, Justice Souter, and Justice Ginsburg join, dissenting....

This Court's precedent sets forth a framework for analyzing Ewing's Eighth Amendment claim. The Eighth Amendment forbids, as "cruel and unusual punishments," prison terms (including terms of years) that are "grossly disproportionate." In applying the "gross disproportionality" principle, courts must keep in mind that "legislative policy" will primarily determine the appropriateness of a punishment's "severity," and hence defer to such legislative policy judgments. If courts properly respect those judgments, they will find that the sentence fails the test only in rare instances.... I believe that the case before us is a "rare" case—one in which a court can say with reasonable confidence that the punishment is "grossly disproportionate" to the crime.

Ewing's claim crosses the gross disproportionality "threshold." First, precedent makes clear that Ewing's sentence raises a serious disproportionality question. Ewing is a recidivist. Hence the two cases most directly in point are those in which the Court considered the constitutionality of recidivist sentencing: *Rummel* and *Solem*. Ewing's claim falls between these two cases. It is stronger than the claim presented in *Rummel*, where the Court upheld a recidivist's sentence as constitutional. It is weaker than the claim presented in *Solem*, where the Court struck down a recidivist sentence as unconstitutional....

[T]he comparison [of Ewing's sentence with the sentences imposed in *Solem* and *Rummel*] places Ewing's sentence well within the twilight zone between *Solem* and *Rummel*—a zone where the argument for unconstitutionality is substantial, where the cases themselves cannot determine the constitutional outcome....

[S]ome objective evidence suggests that many experienced judges would consider Ewing's sentence disproportionately harsh. The United States Sentencing Commission (having based the federal Sentencing Guidelines primarily upon its review of how judges had actually sentenced offenders) does not include shoplifting (or similar theft-related offenses) among the crimes that might trigger especially long sentences for recidivists, nor did Congress include such offenses among triggering crimes when it sought sentences "at or near the maximum" for certain recidivists.

... Ewing's "gross disproportionality" argument is a strong one. That being so, his claim must pass the "threshold" test. If it did not, what would be the function of the test? A threshold test must permit arguably unconstitutional sentences, not only actually unconstitutional sentences, to pass the threshold—at least where the arguments for unconstitutionality are unusually strong ones. A threshold test that blocked every ultimately invalid constitutional claim—even strong ones—would not be a threshold test but a determinative test....

Believing Ewing's argument a strong one, sufficient to pass the threshold, I turn to the comparative analysis. A comparison of Ewing's sentence with other sentences requires answers to two questions. First, how would other jurisdictions (or California at other times, i.e., without the three strikes penalty) punish the same offense conduct? Second, upon what other conduct would other jurisdictions (or California) impose the same prison term? Moreover, since hypothetical punishment is beside the point, the relevant prison time, for comparative purposes, is real prison time, i.e., the time that an offender must actually serve....

As to California itself, we know the following: First, between the end of World War II and 1994 (when California enacted the three strikes law), no one like Ewing could have served more than 10 years in prison. We know that for certain because the maximum sentence for Ewing's crime of conviction, grand theft, was for most of that period 10 years....

[W]e know that California has reserved, and still reserves, Ewing-type prison time, i.e., at least 25 real years in prison, for criminals convicted of crimes far worse than was Ewing's. Statistics for the years 1945 to 1981, for example, indicate that typical (nonrecidivist) male first-degree murderers served between 10 and 15 real years in prison, with 90 percent of all such murderers serving less than 20 real years. Moreover, California, which has moved toward a real-time sentencing system (where the statutory punishment approximates the time served), still punishes far less harshly those who have engaged in far more serious conduct. It imposes, for example, upon nonrecidivists guilty of arson causing great bodily injury a maximum sentence of nine years in prison, it imposes upon those guilty of voluntary manslaughter a maximum sentence of 11 years. It reserves the sentence that it here imposes upon (former-burglar-now-golf-club-thief) Ewing, for nonrecidivist, first-degree murderers.

As to other jurisdictions, we know the following: The United States, bound by the federal Sentencing Guidelines, would impose upon a recidivist, such as Ewing, a sentence that, in any ordinary case, would not exceed 18 months in prison. The Guidelines, based in part upon a study of some 40,000 actual federal sentences, reserve a Ewing-type sentence for Ewing-type recidivists who currently commit such crimes as murder, air piracy, robbery (involving the discharge of a firearm, serious bodily injury, and about $1 million), drug offenses involving more than, for example, 20 pounds of heroin, aggravated theft of more than $100 million, and other similar offenses.... Ewing also would not have been subject to the federal "three strikes" law, for which grand theft is not a triggering offense.

With three exceptions, we do not have before us information about actual time served by Ewing-type offenders in other States. We do know, however, that the law would make it legally impossible for a Ewing-type offender to serve more than 10 years in prison in 33 jurisdictions, as well as the federal courts, more than 15 years in 4 other States, and more than 20 years in 4 additional States. In nine other States, the law might make it legally possible to impose a sentence of 25 years or more,— though that fact by itself, of course, does not mean that judges have actually done so. I say "might" because the law in five of the nine last-mentioned States restricts the sentencing judge's ability to impose a term so long that, with parole, it would amount to at least 25 years of actual imprisonment....

The upshot is that comparison of other sentencing practices, both in other jurisdictions and in California at other times (or in respect to other crimes), validates what an initial threshold examination suggested. Given the information available, given the state and federal parties' ability to provide additional contrary data, and given their failure to do so, we can assume for constitutional purposes that the following statement is true: Outside the California three strikes context, Ewing's recidivist sentence is virtually unique in its harshness for his offense of conviction, and by a considerable degree.

… No one argues for Ewing's inclusion within the ambit of the three strikes statute on grounds of "retribution." For reasons previously discussed, in terms of "deterrence," Ewing's 25-year term amounts to overkill. And "rehabilitation" is obviously beside the point. The upshot is that, in my view, the State cannot find in its three strikes law a special criminal justice need sufficient to rescue a sentence that other relevant considerations indicate is unconstitutional.

Justice Scalia and Justice Thomas argue that we should not review for gross disproportionality a sentence to a term of years. Otherwise, we make it too difficult for legislators and sentencing judges to determine just when their sentencing laws and practices pass constitutional muster. I concede that a bright-line rule would give legislators and sentencing judges more guidance. But application of the Eighth Amendment to a sentence of a term of years requires a case-by-case approach. And, in my view, like that of the plurality, meaningful enforcement of the Eighth Amendment demands that application—even if only at sentencing's outer bounds.

A case-by-case approach can nonetheless offer guidance through example. Ewing's sentence is, at a minimum, 2 to 3 times the length of sentences that other jurisdictions would impose in similar circumstances. That sentence itself is sufficiently long to require a typical offender to spend virtually all the remainder of his active life in prison. These and the other factors that I have discussed, along with the questions that I have asked along the way, should help to identify "gross disproportionality" in a fairly objective way—at the outer bounds of sentencing.

Discussion Questions

1. Who decides if a defendant falls within California's three-strikes statute? The prosecutor? The judge? The jury?

2. Justice O'Connor writes: "Recidivism has long been recognized as a legitimate basis for increased punishment." Why is this so? In other words, why should an offender with a prior record receive a harsher sentence than an offender who commits the identical crime but has no prior record?

3. Was Ewing punished for his most recent crime of stealing three golf clubs? Or was he punished for both his most recent offense and his prior offenses? Being punished twice for the same offense is typically viewed as unfair and a violation of the constitutional prohibition on double jeopardy. Are Ewing and other offenders who are sentenced under three-strikes laws being punished twice for crimes?

4. Which purpose of punishment motivated the California legislature to pass the three-strikes statute? Incapacitation? Deterrence? Retribution?

5. Justice Scalia states: "Proportionality—the notion that the punishment should fit the crime—is inherently a concept tied to the penological goal of retribution." Is the idea of proportionality inherently tied to retribution?

6. As Justice O'Connor notes, the crimes committed against Polly Klaas by Richard Allen Davis drove the adoption of the California three-strikes statute. Polly Klaas was a young and vulnerable victim. Richard Allen Davis was a particularly reprehensible and violent criminal who showed no remorse, had a long history of violent crimes, and even taunted Polly Klaas's parents while his case was being resolved. If you do an internet search for images of Polly Klaas and Richard Allen Davis, you will get a sense of the emotional impact the facts and images from this case had on the public and legislators in California. Is a statute such as the California "three strikes" statute, adopted in the shadow of and in reaction to such a terrible crime, likely to be overly harsh?

D. Restorative Justice[12]

In this chapter, we focused on how legislatures, prosecutors, and courts conceive of and implement punishment. What we have not explored in much detail is the role played by victims in this endeavor. A burgeoning victims' rights movement has given victims greater input into the criminal justice process. The rights of victims vary among jurisdictions, but can include the use of victim advocates, allowing victim impact statements at sentencing, and ensuring more transparent communication with prosecutors' offices.

The trend toward implementation of what's known as *restorative justice* also reflects the idea that victims should have a more vibrant role in the criminal justice process. Although restorative justice models vary, the general underlying idea is essentially utilitarian and prospective in orientation. By facilitating a dialogue supervised by a trained facilitator between victim and offender it seeks to achieve an outcome that proves restorative to the victim, to be sure, but also to the community. It also aims to be restorative to the offender, reducing recidivism and the use of prisons. Although a restorative justice dialogue may lead to an apology by the defendant, that is not its central aim. Rather, its goal is to give those who participate an opportunity to be heard and establish a human connection between a victim and a perpetrator.[13]

Restorative justice can be implemented in a number of ways. One model uses what are called Community Courts.[14] The Neighborhood Courts system that started operation in San Francisco in 2012 illustrates this model.

---

12. Our thanks to Lucy Lang and Michelle Mason of the Institute for Innovation in Prosecution at John Jay College of Criminal Justice for their help with our writing of this section.

13. For in depth treatment of restorative justice, see Danielle Sered, *Until We Reckon: Violence, Mass Incarceration, and a Road to Repair* (2019). See also the Common Justice website at common justice.org.

14. Miriam Krinsky and Taylor Phares, *Accountability and Repair: The Prosecutor's Case for Restorative Justice*, 64 N.Y.Law School L. Rev. 31, 40–41 (2020).

The program allows the San Francisco District Attorney's Office the opportunity to divert non-violent cases pre-charge to one of ten Neighborhood Courts, spread over the city's ten police districts. These Neighborhood Courts are facilitated by community-based volunteer "adjudicators" who have been trained in restorative justice principles and facilitate hearings where individuals who caused harm accept responsibility for, and discuss the impact of, their actions. The victim can choose to attend the hearings but also has the option to meet separately with the adjudicator. Adjudicators then create "directives" based on the facts of each case and needs of each party. Sample directives have included cognitive therapy, writing letters of apology, and community service.[15]

Common Justice, based in Brooklyn, New York, operates a restorative justice program that deals with violent felonies in adult courts and works in conjunction with the Brooklyn District Attorney's office.[16] With the consent of both victim and perpetrator, cases are referred to Common Justice.

> ... Common Justice employs a restorative justice "circle" to facilitate conversation between the harmed and responsible parties, aiming to "address the underlying causes of violence and help foster a long-term process of transformation for individuals and communities." ... Trained facilitators extensively prepare with both the harmed parties and those accused of causing the harm before the circles occur. This preparation is centered in a victim-focused approach in order to determine how the circle can best achieve healing for the victim and accountability for the responsible party.
>
> During the circles, participants move toward an agreement on the steps an individual can take to "make things as right as possible," including attending school, paying restitution, and performing community service. Additionally, while Common Justice staff monitor compliance with the circle agreement, responsible parties must also complete an intensive twelve to fifteen-month violence intervention program. Responsible parties who successfully complete both their commitments to those they harmed and the violence intervention program do not serve the jail or prison sentences they would have otherwise faced.[17]

How might restorative justice work in particular cases? Consider, for example, a case in which a teenager with no prior record has been arrested and is charged with illegal possession of a handgun. The restorative dialogue occurs between a group of gun violence victims and the defendant. The process succeeds and the defendant agrees to perform some community service and enroll in an educational program dealing with the impact of gun violence on a community. The prosecutor then agrees to grant the defendant diversion into a program that results in the charge being dis-

---

15. *Id.*
16. Id. at 41–42.
17. *Id.*

missed if the defendant honors the remedial steps that result from the restorative justice dialogue and commits no other offense.

Another example involves a case in which the defendant, while inebriated, damaged the property of a homeowner. Both the victim and the defendant are amenable to a restorative justice dialogue and one takes place under the supervision of a trained facilitator between the defendant and the victim. The dialogue is deemed successful and the vandalism charge is dismissed conditioned on, among other things, the defendant entering and completing an alcohol treatment program and paying restitution to the victim.

Although now typically used when non-violent offenses are at issue, restorative justice may also play a role in a violent offense such as homicide. Take, for example, a homicide that occurred as part of an attempt to rob an elderly man. The victim's adult son, after consulting other family members, tells the prosecutor's office that he is interested in participating in a supervised restorative justice dialogue with the defendant. The defendant is also willing to participate. They enter a dialogue through which the defendant comes to realize the impact of his crime on the victim's family and the son and his family come to understand the circumstances and personal history that contributed to the defendant's crime. The charges are not dropped. But the judge in the case, though not required to do so, takes into account the defendant's having successfully completed the restorative justice process in determining the appropriate sentence and imposes a prison sentence of twenty rather than thirty years.

Advocates for restorative justice make the case that it has been effective where it has been put into use. In addition to achieving its restorative objectives, it has also proved cost effective.

> The success of [the San Francisco Neighborhood Courts] program is evident on many levels. First, the program highlights the importance of involving the community in restorative justice—130 community members have served as voluntary adjudicators in the seven years the program has been operational. Over four thousand cases have been heard since the program began in 2012. Of those cases, 95 percent were successfully resolved, meaning the referred individual completed the assigned directives and was not prosecuted. Compared to the costs of pursuing the cases through the traditional criminal justice system, Neighborhood Courts saved San Francisco taxpayers over $3,500 per case.[18]

The restorative justice movement has gained significant momentum in the last two decades in many countries around the world. The startlingly high magnitude of prison populations in the United States, often referred to simply as "mass incarceration," has made and continues to make the arguments for making use of restorative justice particularly compelling.

---

18. Id. at 40–41.

Despite or perhaps because of its increased popularity and visibility, restorative justice has drawn its share of critics. Some, for instance, argue that it "trivializes" crime and fails to take appropriate account of the blameworthiness of the criminal or the crime. Others are skeptical about how effective some restorative justice programs have been in achieving their stated goals of addressing the needs of victims and reducing crime. Still others argue that more work needs to be done in distinguishing restorative justice programs that work well from those that do not and assessing why those that do work well are successful.

E. Synthesis and Review

As you have seen in this chapter, the purposes of punishment are used in deciding what constitutes punishment, whether someone should be punished, and, if so, what sort of sentence should be imposed on the person. The purposes of punishment are also used in determining what types of punishment a criminal justice system may employ. For example, the purposes of retribution, deterrence, and incapacitation all feature prominently in ongoing debate in the United States about capital punishment. The following two problems and associated materials ask you to use the purposes of punishment to assess the currently controversial issue of solitary confinement and conjugal visitation in prisons.

Problems

2.18 Starting in the 1980s, many states increased their use of solitary confinement, isolating certain prisoners from other inmates and limiting their interaction with prison staff for as much as 23 hours a day, sometimes for decades. Many states built "super-max" prisons in which all inmates are held in isolation. This increased use of solitary confinement was in part a response to problems presented by prison gangs and in part a response to violence resulting from overcrowding that in turn was caused by longer "tough on crime" sentences. As the *Ewing* case illustrates, such harsh sentences became popular with legislatures in the 1980s.

Solitary confinement can have serious negative impacts on the mental health of prisoners, such as heightened psychiatric symptoms and difficulty engaging in normal human interaction. Some studies have shown that solitary confinement increases the likelihood of re-offending and of violence when inmates are released from prison. It is also costly—as much as two to three times as expensive as keeping inmates in the general prison population. Recent years have seen intense criticism of and growing opposition to solitary confinement. Penal authorities are re-examining its use. Should solitary confinement be permitted for adult inmates? For juvenile inmates? What arguments can be made for and against its use? If allowed, what limitations would you place on its use?

2.19 Should prisons encourage and enable inmates to maintain ties with their families? For example, should prison authorities be required to place inmates in prisons near enough to their families to allow frequent visits? Some European countries and a few states, such as New York, Connecticut, California, and Washington, allow prisoners conjugal visits with their spouses. A conjugal visit is one in which an inmate's spouse is allowed to spend an extended period of time with an inmate, usually overnight, in conditions that permit physical contact and sexual intimacy. Should prisons allow conjugal visits for male inmates? For female inmates? What arguments based on the purposes of punishment can be made for and against allowing conjugal visits? What practical problems might conjugal visits present for prison authorities? If such visits are allowed, what limitations, if any, would you place on them?

In this book we focus on American criminal law. But much of what you learn in this course applies to criminal law issues that arise in other countries. In the following two problems, you are asked to apply the purposes of punishment to punishment issues that have arisen in Germany and Israel.

Problems

2.20 Reinhold Hanning, a German citizen, joined the Waffen SS to fight in the German army in World War II. Following Germany's invasion of Russia, he fought against the Russian army on the Eastern Front, where German casualties were particularly high. Hanning was injured in combat and then assigned to a non-combat position as a guard from January 1942 until June 1944 at Auschwitz, a German concentration camp in Poland where nearly one million Jews and tens of thousands of others were executed. At first, he was not aware of the killings, but he admits that eventually he knew what was happening at the camp. Assume the law allows Hanning and dozens of other guards from Auschwitz and similar concentration camps to be prosecuted as accessories to murder. Hanning is now 94 years old and in a wheelchair. Some of the guards are so physically infirm that it is unlikely they will live long enough to stand trial and be sentenced. Should Hanning and other guards like him now be prosecuted and punished? Should it make a difference if they have admitted their crimes and expressed remorse? If convicted, what sentence should be imposed on them?

2.21 Part (a) In an outbreak of violence, roughly 30 Israelis have been killed in attacks by Palestinians. Israeli forces in turn have killed more than 200 Palestinians during attacks, attempted attacks, or suspected attacks on Israeli soldiers or civilians. Nearly half of those involved in actual, attempted, or suspected attacks are Palestinian teenagers. Ten percent are 15 years old or younger.

Dima is a 12-year-old Palestinian girl who lives in the occupied West Bank. Dima became obsessed with reports on television about Israeli military forces killing Palestinians. One day, instead of going to school, Dima hid a kitchen knife under her shirt and walked to a nearby Israeli settlement where she planned to stab and kill an Israeli settler. She later said she wished to become a martyr. Dima stopped at the settlement's entrance in the hope that a guard would search her so she could stab him. But a settler armed with a gun forced Dima to remove the knife from beneath her shirt and drop it. She was then arrested and prosecuted in an Israeli military court for attempted homicide. Dima eventually pled guilty and was sentenced to four and a half months in an Israeli prison. She was released after serving about half of her sentence because of her age.

The Palestinian group Fatah says it has attempted to discourage such attacks by children. The militant Islamist group Hamas has openly encouraged them. Hamas runs the television station on which Dima learned about Israeli forces killing Palestinians. Both Fatah and Hamas celebrated Dima when she was let out of prison with convoys of cars beeping horns and the release of colored balloons, treating Dima as a celebrity. Based on the purposes of punishment, should juveniles such as Dima be criminally prosecuted and sentenced to prison terms? If not, how should Israeli authorities treat them?

Part (b) Assume that a facility aimed at rehabilitating troubled youths was made available to Dima as an alternative to prison, but that Dima's parents rejected that option. Dima's mother was quoted as saying "How could my daughter, who is just 12, go to a place like that? It was a hard decision, but we said 'O.K., put her in jail. At least we know how she will come out.' "[19] Dima has been hyperactive and having trouble in school. When advised by a school counselor that Dima should see a psychiatrist, her parents rejected that advice on the ground that their neighbors would think Dima was "crazy."[20] Should these facts have had any impact on whether or not a prison sentence was appropriate for Dima?

---

19. Diaa Hadid, Rami Nazzai, and Myra Noveck, *As Attacks Surge, Boys and Girls Fill Israeli Jails*, N.Y. Times, April 30, 2016, at A1.

20. *Id.*

Chapter 3

Making Criminal Law

The power to create and define crimes is the power to determine when people will be labeled as criminals, imprisoned, fined, or executed. Who should exercise this power? Who currently exercises it? These questions lie at the center of the materials in this chapter and will recur throughout your study of criminal law.

Federal and state constitutions divide the power of government among three branches—legislative, executive, and judicial. This division is often referred to as the separation of powers and is a cornerstone of the system of government established by the United States constitution. The conventional conception is that the legislature makes the law, the executive branch enforces the law, and the judiciary applies the law. We will see that today the allocation of power among the three branches is considerably more complex and nuanced than this simple description suggests.

Section A in this chapter focuses on legislators and judges, two groups that play the most visible roles in making criminal law. Sections B and C then address how executive branch officials, such as prosecutors and jurors participate in shaping the contours of criminal law.

The starting point for assessing criminal liability today is typically a statute enacted by a legislature. Judges exercise great power in shaping modern criminal law through the interpretation of criminal statutes. How do judges go about this task? How should they go about it? We turn to the topic of statutory interpretation and address these questions in Section D.

Section E deals with the final topic in this chapter, specificity. Here, we turn from the question of who makes criminal law to look at what level of clarity and precision should be required in criminal statutes.

A. Legislators and Judges

The Anglo-American legal system originally relied on judges to formulate criminal law through a body of judicial opinions known as the common law of crimes. As *Khaliq*, the first case in this section, demonstrates, Scotland still recognizes common law crimes. American courts today continue to exercise primary authority as lawmakers in some fields of law, such as torts. But in the United States, the legislature is now widely viewed as having ultimate authority over the creation and definition of criminal offenses, subject only to constitutional constraints. The importance of legislative supremacy in criminal law is stated repeatedly in judicial opinions throughout this book. It is reflected in the following passage from a Florida Supreme Court opinion reversing the controversial conviction of a woman for exposing the fetus she was carrying to cocaine:

> Neither judges nor prosecutors can make criminal laws. This is the purview of the Legislature. If the Legislature wanted to punish the uterine transfer of cocaine from a mother to her fetus, it would be up to the Legislature to consider the attending public policy and constitutional arguments and then pass its Legislation. The Legislature has not done so and the court has no power to make such a law.[1]

The term *legality* is often used to capture this preference for *legislatively defined* crime. It also expresses a preference for *clear* and *advance* definition of crimes, topics we address below. So the notion of legality can thus be seen as having three essential facets. It requires that criminal laws be created and defined (1) by the legislature; (2) with clarity; and (3) in advance of the conduct to which they are applied. The *Keeler* case exemplifies the principle of legality.

What positions do the statutes below take regarding common law crimes?

New Mexico Statutes Annotated

§ 30-1-3 *Construction of Criminal Code*

In criminal cases where no provision of this code is applicable, the common law, as recognized by the United States and the several states of the Union, shall govern.

Florida Statutes

§ 775.01 *Common law of England*

The common law of England in relation to crimes, except so far as the same relates to the modes and degrees of punishment, shall be of full force in this state where there is no existing provision by statute on the subject.

§ 775.02 *Punishment of common-law offenses*

When there exists no such provision by statute, the court shall proceed to punish such offense by fine or imprisonment, but the fine shall not exceed $500, nor the imprisonment 12 months.

Arizona Revised Statute

§ 13-103 *Abolition of common law offenses and affirmative defenses*

A. All common law offenses and affirmative defenses are abolished. No conduct or omission constitutes an offense or an affirmative defense unless it is an offense or an affirmative defense under this title or under another statute or ordinance.

---

1. *Johnson v. Florida*, 602 So. 2d 1288, 1297 (Fla. 1992) (quoting *People v. Bremer*, No. 90-32227-FH (Mich. Cir. Ct. January 31, 1991)).

New Hampshire Revised Statutes

§ 625:6 *All Offenses Defined by Statute*

No conduct or omission constitutes an offense unless it is a crime or violation under this code or under another statute.

Khaliq v. Her Majesty's Advocate

1983 SCCR 483 (3 August, 1983)

[The government alleged that Khaliq and another man had sold to a number of children between the ages of eight and fifteen both glue and paraphernalia for inhaling vapors from the glue, such as tins, tubes, and plastic bags. The defendants challenged the indictment on the ground that what they were charged with doing was not a crime in Scotland. The trial judge ruled on their challenge in the following passages.]

Lord Avonside, ... [The]charge is claimed to be bad on several grounds, the most important of which is that it does not set out a crime known to the law of Scotland. Argument was presented to the effect that if the crime was a "new" crime, it could not be introduced into our criminal law by the decision of a single judge. I accept that. It would be a matter for consideration by a quorum of the High Court....

At the outset I was referred by counsel ... to the fact that while there had been attempts in Parliament to deal—if that be the word—with 'solvent abuse', all that had been achieved was the Solvent Abuse (Scotland) Act 1983. That Act states that a child may be in need of compulsory measures of care within the provisions of the Social Work (Scotland) Act 1968 if 'he has misused a volatile substance by deliberately inhaling, other than for medicinal purposes, that substance's vapour....' I would not brush aside that Act as wholly irrelevant. It does display concern about misuse of volatile substances and shows that there is a defined danger recognised by Parliament.

The initial general approach of counsel for the [defense]was that 'solvents' covered a wide range of substances and that a decision in favour of the Crown in this case could result in many anomalies. There were many types and kinds of 'solvents' legitimately on the public market and open to anyone who wished to buy them. Equally there were many types of drugs which were available without prescription which could be used for wrong and dire purpose and so result in illness or, indeed, death. Cigarettes were dangerous, misused alcohol could lead to death and so on. All that may be so, but I reject argument in terrorem and place no faith in hypotheses of imagination. I am concerned only with the charge before me. Any other case which might arise would depend on the facts and circumstances pertaining to it.

It is not disputed that 'glue' is not listed as a dangerous substance or drug. Nor is it disputed that to possess 'glue' is permissible. Further, in my opinion, it is not a criminal offence for a person who does so to 'misuse glue'.... The real or at least the most important issue in this case lies in the assertion that in respect of the first charge of the indictment no crime has been [charged] "which is known to the law of Scotland." In my opinion that assertion is unfounded…. The great strength of our common law in criminal matters is that it can be invoked to fill a need. It is not static. Over the centuries it has operated unless its jurisdiction is displaced by statute or by decision of the courts. It did not weaken by time or history. It is as alive today in dealing with the present age as it was in dealing with questions raised in the past.

Hume put it thus: "Let us now attend to those offences against the person, which remain on the footing of the common law, and are punishable only with some inferior pain, at the discretion of the Court. These are various in kind and degree; and the law is provided with sundry corresponding terms for them … such as assault, invasion, beating and bruising, blooding and wounding, stabbing, mutilation, demembration, and some others. But although the injury do not come under any of those terms of style, nor be such as can be announced in a single phrase, this circumstance in nowise affects the competency of a prosecution. Let the [charge] … give an intelligible account of it in terms at large; and, if it amount to a real injury, it shall be sustained to infer punishment, less or more … no matter how new or how strange the wrong."

Alison puts the matter thus: "By the common law every new crime, as it successively arises, becomes the object of punishment, provided it be in itself wrong, and hurtful to the persons or property of others."

In my opinion, the claim that the first charge sets out an offence which, it is said, is unknown to 'the law of Scotland' is without substance. The only novelty is that it [charges] the use and abuse of a solvent. It is only comparatively recently that the effect of such abuse has become known to the public. That knowledge is significant, but not decisive in approaching the question of the power of our common law in criminal matters. It would be strange if the common law cannot deal with a known danger and the culpability of those who supply for profit the solvents knowing that abuse and its attendant effects may, in extreme cases, result in the death of the user.

The common law has been overtaken in some instances by Parliament or the decisions of the court, but that apart, it can deal with offences which may have arisen in modern times. The only novelty in the present case is that it involves a supply to the public, and in particular, children and young people, of a substance which lends itself to abuse. If the vapour given off by that substance is inhaled, the user can cause injury to his health and indeed life. This is precisely a situation with which the common law can deal, where the dangers of such a supply are well known.

Put in a positive way, if the [defense] were right in their assertion that these activities did not constitute a crime in the law of Scotland, they can sell or supply solvents well knowing that their young customers have no intention whatsoever of using the substances in an ordinary manner, but, packaged in strange containers as they are, will use the solvents as they might a drug, inhaling the vapours given off by the solvents to the danger of their health or, indeed, to their lives. It might seem that Parliament has found difficulty in dealing with that situation, but, if so, there is all the more reason for applying our common law in criminal matters. I stress what I have said above. This case is not concerned with a "new" crime. It is concerned with the breach of existing common law relating to the use of poisonous, or at least injurious, substances to the danger of health and life. The only novelty is that the abuse of glue, or other solvent, and the danger of such abuses, has only been fully recognised fairly recently.

[The trial judge denied the defendants' challenge to the prosecution. The defendants appealed this ruling to the High Court of Judiciary. The High Court affirmed the trial judge in the following opinion.]

Khaliq v. Her Majesty's Advocate

1984 SCCR 23 (17 November, 1983)

Lord Justice-General Emslie

... In introducing the appellants' primary objection to the relevancy of charge 1, Lord McCluskey reminded us quite correctly that Parliament has not yet subjected solvents to statutory control, fenced by criminal penalties. There are, further, no statutory provisions restricting the supply of solvents to children. Such provisions have, of course, been made in relation to, for example, alcohol and tobacco....

The first and perhaps the only critical question to be answered in this case is whether the Crown's primary submission in support of the relevancy of charge 1 is well founded. The Crown's position is that what is [charged] here is not a new crime but merely a modern example of conduct which our law has for long regarded as criminal. Such conduct is described by Hume in the passage to which reference has already been made and consists in actions of any kind which cause or are a cause of real injury to the person. The Crown case is, in short, that the actions of the appellants, in the particular circumstances [charged], were a cause of real injury to the children referred to resulting from their inhalation of the intoxicating and dangerous fumes emitted by the solvents supplied to them for that specific purpose....

"It would be a mistake," as the Lord Justice-General (Clyde) observed ..."to imagine that the criminal common law of Scotland countenances any precise and exact categorisation of the forms of conduct which amount to crime." It has been pointed out many times in this Court that such is not the nature or quality of the criminal law of Scotland....

It is of course not an objection to the relevancy of a charge alleged to be one of criminal conduct merely to say that it is without precise precedent in previous decisions. The categories of criminal conduct are never to this extent closed. "An old crime may certainly be committed in a new way; and a case, though never occurring before on its facts, may fall within the spirit of a previous decision, or within an established general principle." ... In the case now before us it is to an established general principle that the Lord Advocate resorts in defence of the relevancy and sufficiency of the facts [charged] to constitute an indictable crime, and that general principle is to be found in Hume ... in the passage quoted by the trial judge in his opinion which

I do not find it necessary to repeat. The general principle to be discovered from that passage is that within the category of conduct identified as criminal are acts, whatever their nature may be, which cause real injury to the person. Does this case, though never before occurring on its facts, fall within the general principle as the Lord Advocate contends? In my opinion it does, although the nature of the injury and the act alleged to be a cause of that injury may be new.

Upon the whole matter I am of opinion that the appeals fail and that they should be refused.

Discussion Questions

1. How would the *Khaliq* case be resolved under the New Mexico, Florida, Arizona, and New Hampshire statutes that appear at the beginning of this chapter?

2. Article 7 of the European Convention on Human Rights[2] provides:

> No one shall be held guilty of any criminal offence on account of any act or omission which did not constitute a criminal offence under national or international law at the time when it was committed. Nor shall a heavier penalty be imposed than the one that was applicable at the time the criminal offence was committed.

Which facet of the legality principle does Article 7 reflect? Would Khaliq's conviction be valid under this provision? In other words, was Khaliq convicted of a new crime? Or had he simply found a new way to commit an old crime? If the latter, what is the name of this old crime? How would you define it? Is the crime described by the *Khaliq* judges compatible with all three of the requirements for legality?

3. At his sentencing, Khaliq's lawyer claimed that the police had asked Khaliq to stop selling glue and sniffing paraphernalia to children. When Khaliq asked if what he was doing was a crime, the police told him they "could not say definitely that by doing so [he was] breaking the law." If true, should these facts have any bearing on Khaliq's liability?

4. Khaliq was sentenced by the trial judge to three years of imprisonment. The High Court reduced the sentence to two years, finding that "[a]ll the necessary objectives could have been achieved by a shorter sentence coupled with a clear warning that anyone convicted of a similar crime in future could expect to be punished more severely."[3] Why should Khaliq receive a lesser sentence than someone who commits the same crime in the future?

---

2. The European Convention on Human Rights was made applicable to Scotland in 1998 by the Human Rights Act 1998, ss.1(1); 6(1); (2)(a).

3. *Khaliq v. Her Majesty's Advocate*, 1984 SCCR 212 (14 June 1984).

Keeler v. Superior Court

2 Cal. 3d 619 (1970)
California Supreme Court

Mosk, J.

In this proceeding for writ of prohibition we are called upon to decide whether an unborn but viable fetus is a "human being" within the meaning of the California statute defining murder. We conclude that the Legislature did not intend such a meaning, and that for us to construe the statute to the contrary and apply it to this petitioner would exceed our judicial power and deny petitioner due process of law.

The evidence received at the preliminary examination may be summarized as follows: Petitioner and Teresa Keeler obtained an interlocutory decree of divorce on September 27, 1968. They had been married for 16 years. Unknown to petitioner, Mrs. Keeler was then pregnant by one Ernest Vogt, whom she had met earlier that summer. She subsequently began living with Vogt in Stockton, but concealed the fact from petitioner....

On February 23, 1969, Mrs. Keeler was driving on a narrow mountain road in Amador County ... She met petitioner driving in the opposite direction; he blocked the road with his car, and she pulled over to the side. He walked to her vehicle and began speaking to her. He seemed calm, and she rolled down her window to hear him. He said, "I hear you're pregnant. If you are you had better stay away from the girls and from here." She did not reply, and he opened the car door; as she later testified, "He assisted me out of the car.... [It] wasn't roughly at this time." Petitioner then looked at her abdomen and became "extremely upset." He said, "You sure are. I'm going to stomp it out of you." He pushed her against the car, shoved his knee into her abdomen, and struck her in the face with several blows. She fainted, and when she regained consciousness petitioner had departed.

Mrs. Keeler drove back to Stockton, and the police and medical assistance were summoned. She had suffered substantial facial injuries, as well as extensive bruising of the abdominal wall. A Caesarian section was performed and the fetus was examined *in utero*. Its head was found to be severely fractured, and it was delivered stillborn. The pathologist gave as his opinion that the cause of death was skull fracture with consequent cerebral hemorrhaging, that death would have been immediate, and that the injury could have been the result of force applied to the mother's abdomen. There was no air in the fetus' lungs, and the umbilical cord was intact....

An information was filed charging petitioner, in count I, with committing the crime of murder in that he did "unlawfully kill a human being, to wit Baby Girl Vogt, with malice aforethought." ... His motion to set aside the information for lack of probable cause was denied, and he now seeks a writ of prohibition; ...

I

Penal Code Section 187 provides: "Murder is the unlawful killing of a human being, with malice aforethought." The dispositive question is whether the fetus which petitioner is accused of killing was, on February 23, 1969, a "human being" within the meaning of the statute. If it was not, petitioner cannot be charged with its "murder" and prohibition will lie.

Section 187 was enacted as part of the Penal Code of 1872. Inasmuch as the provision has not been amended since that date, we must determine the intent of the Legislature at the time of its enactment. But section 187 was, in turn, taken verbatim from the first California statute defining murder, part of the Crimes and Punishments Act of 1850. Penal Code Section 5 (also enacted in 1872) declares: "The provisions of this code, so far as they are substantially the same as existing statutes, must be construed as continuations thereof, and not as new enactments." We begin, accordingly, by inquiring into the intent of the Legislature in 1850 when it first defined murder as the unlawful and malicious killing of a "human being."

It will be presumed, of course, that in enacting a statute the Legislature was familiar with the relevant rules of the common law, and, when it couches its enactment in common law language, that its intent was to continue those rules in statutory form. This is particularly appropriate in considering the work of the first session of our Legislature: its precedents were necessarily drawn from the common law, as modified in certain respects by the Constitution and by legislation of our sister states.

We therefore undertake a brief review of the origins and development of the common law of abortional homicide. From that inquiry it appears that by the year 1850 — the date with which we are concerned — an infant could not be the subject of homicide at common law *unless it had been born alive.* Perhaps the most influential statement of the "born alive" rule is that of Coke, in mid-17th century: "If a woman be quick with childe,[5] and by a potion or otherwise killeth it in her wombe, or if a man beat her, whereby the childe dyeth in her body, and she is delivered of a dead childe, this is a great misprision [i.e., misdemeanor], and no murder; but if the childe be born alive and dyeth of the potion, battery, or other cause, this is murder; for in law it is accounted a reasonable creature, *in rerum natura*, when it is born alive." In short, "By Coke's time, the common law regarded abortion as murder only if the foetus is (1) quickened, (2) born alive, (3) lives for a brief interval, and (4) then dies." Whatever intrinsic defects there may have been in Coke's work, the common law accepted his views as authoritative. In the 18th century, for example, Coke's requirement that an infant be born alive in order to be the subject of homicide was reiterated and expanded by both Blackstone and Hale.

...

---

5. "Quickening" is said to occur when movements of the fetus are first sensed or observed, and ordinarily takes place between the 16th and 18th week of pregnancy. Although much of the history of the law of abortion and abortional homicide revolves around this concept, it is of no medical significance and was never adopted into the law of California.

By the year 1850 this rule of the common law had long been accepted in the United States. As early as 1797 it was held that proof the child was born alive is necessary to support an indictment for murder and the same rule was reiterated on the eve of the first session of our Legislature....

We conclude that in declaring murder to be the unlawful and malicious killing of a "human being" the Legislature of 1850 intended that term to have the settled common law meaning of a person who had been born alive, and did not intend the act of feticide—as distinguished from abortion—to be an offense under the laws of California....

It is the policy of this state to construe a penal statute as favorably to the defendant as its language and the circumstances of its application may reasonably permit; just as in the case of a question of fact, the defendant is entitled to the benefit of every reasonable doubt as to the true interpretation of words or the construction of language used in a statute. We hold that in adopting the definition of murder in Penal Code *section 187* the Legislature intended to exclude from its reach the act of killing an unborn fetus.

II

The People urge, however, that the sciences of obstetrics and pediatrics have greatly progressed since 1872, to the point where with proper medical care a normally developed fetus prematurely born at 28 weeks or more has an excellent chance of survival, i.e., is "viable"; that the common law requirement of live birth to prove the fetus had become a "human being" who may be the victim of murder is no longer in accord with scientific fact, since an unborn but viable fetus is now fully capable of independent life; and that one who unlawfully and maliciously terminates such a life should therefore be liable to prosecution for murder under section 187. We may grant the premises of this argument; indeed, we neither deny nor denigrate the vast progress of medicine in the century since the enactment of the Penal Code. But we cannot join in the conclusion sought to be deduced: we cannot hold this petitioner to answer for murder by reason of his alleged act of killing an unborn—even though viable—fetus. To such a charge there are two insuperable obstacles, one "jurisdictional" and the other constitutional.

Penal Code *section 6* declares in relevant part that "No act or omission" accomplished after the code has taken effect "is criminal or punishable, except as prescribed or authorized by this code, or by some of the statutes which it specifies as continuing in force and as not affected by its provisions, or by some ordinance, municipal, county, or township regulation...." This section embodies a fundamental principle of our tripartite form of government, i.e., that subject to the constitutional prohibition against cruel and unusual punishment, the power to define crimes and fix penalties is vested exclusively in the legislative branch. Stated differently there are no common law crimes in California. "In this state the common law is of no effect so far as the specification of what acts or conduct shall constitute a crime is concerned. In order that a public offense be committed, some statute, ordinance or regulation prior in time to the commission of the act, must denounce it."...

Settled rules of construction implement this principle. Although the Penal Code commands us to construe its provisions "according to the fair import of their terms, with a view to effect its objects and to promote justice" (Pen. Code, §4), it is clear the courts cannot go so far as to create an offense by enlarging a statute, by inserting or deleting words, or by giving the terms used false or unusual meanings. Penal statutes will not be made to reach beyond their plain intent; they include only those offenses coming clearly within the import of their language. Indeed, "Constructive crimes— crimes built up by courts with the aid of inference, implication, and strained interpretation—are repugnant to the spirit and letter of English and American criminal law."

Applying these rules to the case at bar, we would undoubtedly act in excess of the judicial power if we were to adopt the People's proposed construction of section 187. As we have shown, the Legislature has defined the crime of murder in California to apply only to the unlawful and malicious killing of one who has been born alive. We recognize that the killing of an unborn but viable fetus may be deemed by some to be an offense of similar nature and gravity; but as Chief Justice Marshall warned long ago, "It would be dangerous, indeed, to carry the principle, that a case which is within the reason or mischief of a statute, is within its provisions, so far as to punish a crime not enumerated in the statute, because it is of equal atrocity, or of kindred character, with those which are enumerated." Whether to thus extend liability for murder in California is a determination solely within the province of the Legislature. For a court to simply declare, by judicial fiat, that the time has now come to prosecute under section 187 one who kills an unborn but viable fetus would indeed be to rewrite the statute under the guise of construing it. Nor does a need to fill an asserted "gap" in the law between abortion and homicide—as will appear, no such gap in fact exists— justify judicial legislation of this nature: to make it "a judicial function 'to explore such new fields of crime as they may appear from time to time' is wholly foreign to the American concept of criminal justice" and "raises very serious questions concerning the principle of separation of powers."

The second obstacle to the proposed judicial enlargement of section 187 is the guarantee of due process of law. Assuming *arguendo* that we have the power to adopt the new construction of this statute as the law of California, such a ruling, by constitutional command, could operate only prospectively, and thus could not in any event reach the conduct of petitioner on February 23, 1969.

The first essential of due process is fair warning of the act which is made punishable as a crime. "That the terms of a penal statute creating a new offense must be sufficiently explicit to inform those who are subject to it what conduct on their part will render them liable to its penalties, is a well-recognized requirement, consonant alike with ordinary notions of fair play and the settled rules of law." "No one may be required at peril of life, liberty or property to speculate as to the meaning of penal statutes. All are entitled to be informed as to what the State commands or forbids." The law of California is in full accord.

This requirement of fair warning is reflected in the constitutional prohibition against the enactment of ex post facto laws. When a new penal statute is applied ret-

rospectively to make punishable an act which was not criminal at the time it was performed, the defendant has been given no advance notice consistent with due process.
And precisely the same effect occurs when such an act is made punishable under a
preexisting statute but by means of an unforeseeable *judicial* enlargement thereof....

"The fundamental principle that 'the required criminal law must have existed when
the conduct in issue occurred,' must apply to bar retroactive criminal prohibitions
emanating from courts as well as from legislatures. If a judicial construction of a
criminal statute is 'unexpected and indefensible by reference to the law which had
been expressed prior to the conduct in issue,' it must not be given retroactive effect." ...

We conclude that the judicial enlargement of section 187 now urged upon us by
the People would not have been forseeable to this petitioner, and hence that its adoption at this time would deny him due process of law.

Let a peremptory writ of prohibition issue restraining respondent court from
taking any further proceedings on Count I of the information, charging petitioner
with the crime of murder.

Burke, Acting C.J., dissenting ... The majority hold that "Baby Girl" Vogt, who, according to medical testimony, had reached the 35th week of development, had a 96
percent chance of survival, and was "definitely" alive and viable at the time of her
death, nevertheless was not a "human being" under California's homicide statutes. In
my view, in so holding, the majority ignore significant common law precedents, frustrate the express intent of the Legislature, and defy reason, logic and common sense.

... The majority pursue the meaning of the term "human being" down the ancient
hallways of the common law, citing Coke, Blackstone and Hale to the effect that the
slaying of a "quickened" (i.e. stirring in the womb) child constituted "a great misprision," but not murder. Although, as discussed below, I strongly disagree with the
premise that the words of our penal statutes must be construed as of 1648 or 1765,
nevertheless, there is much common law precedent which would support the view
that a viable fetus such as Baby Girl Vogt is a human being under [California homicide]
statutes.

The majority cast a passing glance at the common law concept of quickening, but
fail to explain the significance of that concept: At common law, the quickened fetus
was considered to be a human being, a second life separate and apart from its mother.
As stated by Blackstone, in the passage immediately preceding that portion quoted
in the majority opinion, "Life is the immediate gift of God, a right inherent by nature
in every individual; *and it begins in contemplation of law as soon as an infant is able
to stir in the mother's womb.*"

Modern scholars have confirmed this aspect of common law jurisprudence. As
Means observes, "The common law itself prohibited abortion after quickening and
hanging a pregnant felon after quickening, *because the life of a second human being
would thereby be taken,* although it did not call the offense murder or manslaughter."

This reasoning explains why the killing of a quickened child was considered "a
great misprision," although the killing of an unquickened child was no crime at all

at common law. Moreover, although the common law did not apply the labels of "murder" or "manslaughter" to the killing of a quickened fetus, it appears that at common law this "great misprision" was severely punished. As late as 1837, the wilful aborting of a woman quick with child was punishable by *death* in England.

Thus, at common law, the killing of a quickened child was severely punished, since that child was considered to be a human being. The majority would have us assume that the Legislature in 1850 and 1872 simply overlooked this "great misprision" in codifying and classifying criminal offenses in California, or reduced that offense to the lesser offense of illegal abortion with its relatively lenient penalties (Pen. Code, § 274).

In my view, we cannot assume that the Legislature intended a person such as defendant, charged with the malicious slaying of a fully viable child, to suffer only the mild penalties imposed upon common abortionists who, ordinarily, procure only the miscarriage of a nonviable fetus or embryo. To do so would completely ignore the important common law distinction between the quickened and unquickened child.

Of course, I do not suggest that we should interpret the term "human being" in our homicide statutes in terms of the common law concept of quickening. At one time, that concept had a value in differentiating, as accurately as was then scientifically possible, between life and nonlife. The analogous concept of viability is clearly more satisfactory, for it has a well defined and medically determinable meaning denoting the ability of the fetus to live or survive apart from its mother.

The majority opinion suggests that we are confined to common law concepts, and to the common law definition of murder or manslaughter. However, the Legislature, in Penal Code Sections 187 and 192, has defined those offenses for us: homicide is the unlawful killing of a "human being." Those words need not be frozen in place as of any particular time, but must be fairly and reasonably interpreted by this court to promote justice and to carry out the evident purposes of the Legislature in adopting a homicide statute. Thus, Penal Code Section 4, which was enacted in 1872 along with sections 187 and 192, provides: "The rule of the common law, that penal statutes are to be strictly construed, has no application to this code. All its provisions are to be construed according to the fair import of their terms, with a view to effect its objects and to promote justice."

As the majority opinion recognizes, " 'In this state the common law is of no effect so far as the specification of what acts or conduct shall constitute a crime is concerned.' " Instead, we must construe penal statutes in accordance with the "fair import" of their terms, rather than restrict those statutes to common law principles....

Penal Code section 4 ... permits this court fairly to construe the terms of those statutes to serve the ends of justice. Consequently, nothing should prevent this court from holding that Baby Girl Vogt was a human ("belonging or relating to man; characteristic of man")[4] being ("existence, as opp. to nonexistence; specif. life")[5] under California's homicide statutes.

---

4. WEBSTER'S NEW INTERNATIONAL DICTIONARY (2d ed. 1939), page 1211, column 3.

5. *Ibid*, at page 247, column 2.

We commonly conceive of human existence as a spectrum stretching from birth to death. However, if this court properly might expand the definition of "human being" at one end of that spectrum, we may do so at the other end. Consider the following example: All would agree that "Shooting or otherwise damaging a corpse is not homicide...." In other words, a corpse is not considered to be a "human being" and thus cannot be the subject of a "killing" as those terms are used in homicide statutes. However, it is readily apparent that our concepts of what constitutes a "corpse" have been and are being continually modified by advances in the field of medicine, including new techniques for life revival, restoration and resuscitation such as artificial respiration, open heart massage, transfusions, transplants and a variety of life-restoring stimulants, drugs and new surgical methods. Would this court ignore these developments and exonerate the killer of an apparently "drowned" child merely because that child would have been pronounced dead in 1648 or 1850? Obviously not. Whether a homicide occurred in that case would be determined by medical testimony regarding the capability of the child to have survived prior to the defendant's act. And that is precisely the test which this court should adopt in the instant case.

The common law reluctance to characterize the killing of a quickened fetus as a homicide was based solely upon a presumption that the fetus would have been born dead. This presumption seems to have persisted in this country at least as late as 1876. Based upon the state of the medical art in the 17th, 18th and 19th centuries, that presumption may have been well-founded. However, as we approach the 21st century, it has become apparent that "This presumption is not only contrary to common experience and the ordinary course of nature, but it is contrary to the usual rule with respect to presumptions followed in this state."

There are no accurate statistics disclosing fetal death rates in "common law England," although the foregoing presumption of death indicates a significantly high death experience. On the other hand, in California the fetal death rate in 1968 is estimated to be 12 deaths in 1,000, a ratio which would have given Baby Girl Vogt a 98.8 percent chance of survival. If, as I have contended, the term "human being" in our homicide statutes is a fluid concept to be defined in accordance with present conditions, then there can be no question that the term should include the fully viable fetus.

The majority suggest that to do so would improperly create some new offense. However, the offense of murder is no new offense. Contrary to the majority opinion, the Legislature has not "defined the crime of murder in California to apply only to the unlawful and malicious killing of one who has been born alive." Instead, the Legislature simply used the broad term "human being" and directed the courts to construe that term according to its "fair import" with a view to effect the objects of the homicide statutes and promote justice. What justice will be promoted, what objects effectuated, by construing "human being" as excluding Baby Girl Vogt and her unfortunate successors? Was defendant's brutal act of stomping her to death any less an act of homicide than the murder of a newly born baby? No one doubts that the term "human being" would include the elderly or dying persons whose potential for life has nearly lapsed;

their proximity to death is deemed immaterial. There is no sound reason for denying the viable fetus, with its unbounded potential for life, the same status.

The majority also suggest that such an interpretation of our homicide statutes would deny defendant "fair warning" that his act was punishable as a crime. Aside from the absurdity of the underlying premise that defendant consulted Coke, Blackstone or Hale before kicking Baby Girl Vogt to death, it is clear that defendant had adequate notice that his act could constitute homicide. Due process only precludes prosecution under a new statute insufficiently explicit regarding the specific conduct proscribed, or under a preexisting statute "by means of an unforeseeable *judicial* enlargement thereof."

Our homicide statutes have been in effect in this state since 1850. The fact that the California courts have not been called upon to determine the precise question before us does not render "unforeseeable" a decision which determines that a viable fetus is a "human being" under those statutes. Can defendant really claim surprise that a 5-pound, 18-inch, 34-week-old, living, viable child is considered to be a human being? ...

In summary, I have shown that at common law, the slaying of a quickened fetus was a "great misprision" and was severely punished, since that fetus was considered to be a human being. We should not presume that the Legislature ignored these common law developments and intended to punish the malicious killing of a viable fetus as the lesser offense of illegal abortion. Moreover, apart from the common law approach, our Legislature has expressly directed us to construe the homicide statutes in accordance with the fair import of their terms. There is no good reason why a fully viable fetus should not be considered a "human being" under those statutes. To so construe them would not create any new offense, and would not deny defendant fair warning or due process ...

The trial court's denial of defendant's motion to set aside the information was proper, and the peremptory writ of prohibition should be denied.

* * *

The California Legislature responded to the *Keeler* decision by modifying California Penal Code Section 187 to include a fetus as a category of murder victim.

Discussion Questions

1. Who do you find more persuasive? Justice Mosk writing for the majority or Justice Burke writing in dissent? In what ways do the two opinions differ in their reasoning?

2. How would the *Keeler* case be resolved under the New Mexico, Florida, Arizona, and New Hampshire statutes that appear at the beginning of this chapter?

3. How would Khaliq have fared if he had been prosecuted in California? How would Keeler have fared in Scotland?

4. Was the prosecution in *Keeler* trying to convict Keeler of a new crime? Or was it prosecuting him for committing an old crime in a new way?

5. Should what Keeler did be treated as a type of homicide? Should feticide be made criminal? Does Justice Mosk directly answer or even address either of these questions? On what question does he focus? Why?

Problem

3.1 *Drafting a Feticide Statute.* You are a legislative assistant to a member of the California legislature who, after reading the *Keeler* case, wants to enact legislation making feticide a crime. She asks you to draft a criminal statute. In writing that statute, how will you address the following?

    (a) a medical doctor performing an abortion.

    (b) a driver who recklessly causes an auto accident that results in the death of a fetus being carried by a pregnant passenger in the driver's car. Assume the driver knew the passenger was pregnant.

    (c) a pregnant woman whose fetus dies because she abused cocaine during the pregnancy.

---

1. The Rule of Lenity

Justice Mosk in *Keeler* writes that "it is the policy of this state to construe a penal statute as favorably to the defendant as its language and the circumstances of its application may reasonably permit; just as in the case of a question of fact, the defendant is entitled to the benefit of every reasonable doubt as to the true interpretation of words or the construction of language used in a statute." This policy regarding the interpretation of criminal statutes is sometimes referred to as the rule of strict construction of criminal statutes or simply the rule of lenity.

United States v. Wiltberger

18 U.S. 76, 95 (1820) United States Supreme Court

Marshall, C.J.

… The rule that penal laws are to be construed strictly, is perhaps not much less old than construction itself. It is founded on the tenderness of the law for the rights of individuals; and on the plain principle that the power of punishment is vested in the legislative, not in the judicial department. It is the legislature, not the Court, which is to define a crime, and ordain its punishment.

* * *

Legislatures and courts vary in their attitudes toward the rule of lenity, as the following provisions and cases reveal.

Florida Statutes

§ 775.021 *Rules of Construction*

(1) The provisions of [the Florida Criminal Code] and offenses defined by other statutes shall be strictly construed; when the language is susceptible of differing constructions, it shall be construed most favorably to the accused.

Arizona Revised Statute

§ 13-104

The general rule that a penal statute is to be strictly construed does not apply to [the Arizona Criminal Code], but the provisions herein must be construed according to the fair meaning of their terms to promote justice and effect the objects of the law....

Kentucky Revised Statutes

§ 446.080

(1) All statutes of this state shall be liberally construed with a view to promote their objects and carry out the intent of the legislature....

(2) There shall be no difference in the construction of civil, penal and criminal statutes.

State v. Maggio

432 So. 2d 854, 856 (1983)
Louisiana Supreme Court

Dennis, J.

... [N]umerous state legislatures, frustrated in the field of criminal law, have abrogated or modified the rule [of strict construction of criminal statutes]. Some states expressly repudiated the common law rule of construction and substituted a rule calling for a construction of criminal laws according to the "fair import of their terms." Other states have gone even further and have opted for a "liberal" construction of their criminal laws.

Louisiana took what might be termed a "middle ground" approach somewhere between the old common law rule and the "liberal" rule adopted by other states. At the time of the drafting of the comprehensive criminal code, the members of the Louisiana State Law Institute refused to embrace a rule of either strict or liberal construction. Instead the Law Institute recommended, and the legislature subsequently enacted, a rule of construction which provides:

> The articles of this Code cannot be extended by analogy so as to create crimes not provided for herein; however, in order to promote justice and to effect the objects of the law, all of its provisions shall be given a genuine construction, according to the fair import of their words, taken in their usual sense, in connection with the context, and with reference to the purpose of the provision. Louisiana Revised Statutes 14:3.

* * *

Courts at times place restrictions on the operation of the rule of lenity, as the following passage reveals.

Muscarello v. United States
524 U.S. 125, 138 (1998)
United States Supreme Court

Breyer, J.

... The simple existence of some statutory ambiguity ... is not sufficient to warrant application of [the] rule of lenity, for most statutes are ambiguous to some degree. "The rule of lenity applies only if, after seizing everything from which aid can be derived, ... we can make no more than a guess as to what Congress intended." To invoke the rule, we must conclude that there is a "'grievous ambiguity or uncertainty' in the statute."

Discussion Questions

1. Justice Dennis in *State v. Maggio,* quoted above, identifies three different approaches courts may use in interpreting vague statutes: "strict" interpretation (the rule of lenity); "liberal" interpretation; and "fair" interpretation, a middle position between strict and liberal interpretation. What are the arguments for and against each approach?

2. If you were a *legislator*, would you favor adopting or rejecting the rule of lenity? Would your view change if you were a *judge* responsible for interpreting and applying criminal statutes?

3. Both the majority and dissent in *Keeler* acknowledge the existence of California Penal Code Section 4, which rejects the rule of lenity. Nonetheless, the majority relies on the rule of lenity. Courts often ignore legislative efforts to jettison or modify the rule of lenity. Why do you think they might do so? Is this practice valid?

2. Analogy

What if the prosecution had argued in *Keeler* that although feticide was not covered by California's homicide statutes at the time Keeler assaulted his wife and killed the fetus she was carrying, the purposeful killing of an unborn fetus is both wrongful and similar in nature and gravity to homicide and therefore should be punished in the same way as homicide. In other words, one might argue that what Keeler did was *analogous* to homicide. He was just as blameworthy and just as dangerous as one who commits murder by purposefully killing a person who has been born, and thus Keeler should receive the same punishment as a murderer. Do you find this reasoning persuasive in regard to Keeler's conduct? Such reasoning relies on the idea of extending a criminal statute by *analogy*. If an act is wrongful and harmful to society but has not been made criminal by a statute, the principle of analogy allows the act to be punished in the same way as an analogous offense.

Criminal codes in Germany and Russia at times explicitly adopted the idea of punishment by analogy. For example, the 1925 Russian Criminal Code provided:

> Where a socially dangerous act has not been expressly dealt with in the present code, the basis of responsibility in respect thereof shall be determined in conformity with those articles of the code which deal with the crimes most closely resembling it.[4]

No American jurisdiction currently accepts punishment by analogy. The Louisiana statute quoted in the *Maggio* case above, for example, explicitly rejects it: "The articles of this Code cannot be extended *by analogy* so as to create crimes not provided for herein" (emphasis added). Though he does not use the word *analogy*, Justice Mosk's majority opinion in *Keeler* also clearly rejects the idea of punishment by analogy in the following passage in which he quotes Chief Justice Marshall:

> We recognize that the killing of an unborn but viable fetus may be deemed by some to be an offense of *similar nature and gravity*; but as Chief Justice Marshall warned long ago, "It would be dangerous, indeed, to carry the principle, that a case which is within the reason or mischief of a statute, is within its provisions, so far as to punish a crime not enumerated in the statute, because it is *of equal atrocity, or of kindred character, with those which are enumerated*." Whether to thus extend liability for murder in California is a determination solely within the province of the Legislature. (emphasis added)

What arguments can be made for and against punishment by analogy? Do you agree with Chief Justice Marshall that "[i]t would be dangerous" to make use of punishment by analogy? If so, why?

* * *

Almost all American jurisdictions now recognize only statutory crimes. As the statutes set forth at the beginning of this section reflect, in a few states common law crimes continue in theory to supplement statutory crimes. But in these states, courts rarely, if ever, use the power such statutes give them to create or recognize nonstatutory crimes.

Courts still play a crucial role in the development of criminal law through interpreting and filling gaps in statutes. Although common law crimes are virtually defunct in the United States, you will see throughout this course that the common law remains an important resource and reference point for legislatures drafting and courts interpreting criminal statutes. The *Keeler* court, for example, begins its analysis of the

---

4. The Penal Code of the Russian Socialist Federal Soviet Republic, Article 16 (H.M. Stationery Office 1934) cited in Note, *The Use of Analogy in Criminal Law*, 47 Columbia L. Rev. 613, 619 (1947).

meaning of California Penal Code Section 187 by examining the common law of abortional homicide. Similarly, Justice Burke begins his dissent in *Keeler* with a discussion of common law. As the *Keeler* majority notes, California has rejected common law crimes. Why, then, do both the majority and dissent in *Keeler* rely so extensively on common law? Both opinions assume that Keeler is being prosecuted for a statutory and not a common law offense. But both opinions use common law to help figure out what the California legislature intended when it enacted California Penal Code Section 187. You will see many judges making similar use of common law in virtually every chapter of this book to help them interpret statutes creating criminal offenses.

Statutory criminal law in some jurisdictions is an accumulation of statutes enacted in piecemeal fashion over many years. Federal criminal law, for example, includes a piracy statute enacted in 1790 along with modern statutes dealing with terrorism, computer crime, and white-collar fraud. The piecemeal enactment of such legislation may result in inconsistency, redundancy, and failure to address general questions of criminal law that cut across many statutes, such as issues of interpretation and mental state. Accordingly, many state legislatures have replaced an accumulation of criminal provisions with a comprehensive set of simultaneously enacted statutes, often referred to as a code. Jeremy Bentham, an influential proponent of statutory law and critic of common law, coined the term "codification" for this process. When a jurisdiction enacts a criminal code in this fashion, it tends to reduce inconsistency and redundancy and often prompts the legislature to address broad questions that can arise under many statutes. Codification also gives the legislature an opportunity to prune dead wood—outdated statutes no longer enforced—from its criminal laws.

3. Common Law versus Statutes

What explains the modern preference for legislative supremacy in criminal law? The question of whether judges or legislators should create and define crimes necessarily implicates two other questions. One is the *form* that criminal law should take. Legislatures create law in the form of statutes, while judges do so through judicial opinions, sometimes referred to as case law. The second is the *process* by which criminal law should be created. A legislature acts through an overtly political process the sole aim of which is to create statutes. It does not apply the statutes it creates to any particular person or set of facts. Judges, on the other hand, are primarily concerned with adjudicating particular cases and produce law only as necessary to resolve those cases.

One can use a variety of criteria to answer the questions of who should create and define crimes and whether criminal law should take the form of statutes or case law. Below we address a few possibilities. Can you think of others?

a. Legitimacy

Criminal law authorizes imposition of more severe sanctions than civil law. Violation of tort or contract law typically results in an award of money damages. Though a criminal violation can trigger monetary fines and restitution similar in form and function to money damages, it may and often does result in imprisonment and in some cases execution. A criminal conviction also stigmatizes more severely than a civil judgment and can make it difficult and in some cases virtually impossible to find a job or even a place to live. A criminal conviction can also result in loss of the right to vote, inability to live in public housing, disqualification from receiving welfare, ineligibility for student loans, and other serious consequences. The consequences of a conviction have an especially harsh impact on those who are poor or otherwise disadvantaged. Accordingly, it is particularly important that criminal laws be democratically legitimate and viewed as such by those subject to them and by society in general.

Concern that the judicial branch is undemocratic is a common theme in American law and politics. American colonists, for example, were suspicious of judges and the common law they created because of the judges' allegiance to the English crown. American judges have referred to themselves as "oligarchic"[5] and "a small and unrepresentative segment of our society."[6]

Legislatures are typically viewed as more representative of the electorate than judges. Voters directly elect legislators, who stand for reelection regularly. Some judges are appointed rather than elected and, in the case of federal judges, are appointed for life and may not be removed from office except for serious misdeeds. Other judges stand for election, but typically serve longer terms than legislators and thus are not as often subject to popular control.

Parts of the legislative process are more open to public scrutiny and input than the judicial process, a fact that may enhance its apparent democratic legitimacy. Candidates for legislative office openly debate the virtues and vices of legislation. After elections, public debate by legislators often continues during the drafting and voting process. Legislative committees regularly hold hearings that are open to the public and press and may even be televised. Citizens can and often do contact their representatives and ask them to vote for or against particular legislation.

In comparison, court processes are less open to public scrutiny and input. Appellate courts are the source of most judge-made law. Though not easy to obtain, the public

---

5. *American Federation of Labor v. American Sash & Door Co.*, 335 U.S. 538, 555–556 (1949) (Frankfurter, J., dissenting) ("Because the powers exercised by this Court are inherently oligarchic, Jefferson all of his life thought of the Court as 'an irresponsible body' and 'independent of the nation itself.' The Court is not saved from being oligarchic because it professes to act in the service of humane ends. As history amply proves, [t]he judiciary is prone to misconceive the public good by confounding private notions with constitutional requirements, and such misconceptions are not subject to legitimate displacement by the will of the people except at too slow a pace.").

6. *Atkins v. Virginia*, 536 U.S. 304, 349 (2002) (Scalia, J., dissenting).

does have access to briefs written by lawyers representing the parties in a case. Hearings are public and sometimes covered by the press. How judges vote and their supporting reasoning regularly appear in published opinions. But the judges' decision-making process and any debate among judges who disagree are usually shielded from public scrutiny until an opinion is filed. Although courts have discretion to allow those who are not parties to express their views to the court through amicus briefs, judges view as inappropriate the receipt of public comment on a case pending before the court or the legal issues it may resolve.

The idealized image of legislatures as representative of and responsive to the majority of the electorate has suffered in recent decades. Considerable attention has been given to the role of special interest groups in funding campaigns and influencing legislation. And despite the open nature of some aspects of the legislative process, such as debate and voting on the final versions of legislation, much of the legislative process is hidden from public view and subject to complex procedural rules that are not easily understood. The fate of much legislation is often resolved out of public view and in ways that are far from transparent and subject to accountability.

Electoral accountability and openness suggest that legislators should be more responsive to the majority will than judges. But accountability to the majority raises concern about the protection of individual rights and the interests of groups such as racial, ethnic, and religious minorities, those suffering social and economic disadvantages, and those holding unconventional views. Criminal sanctions in the United States are imposed disproportionately on minority groups. Who is more likely to protect minority interests from oppression at the hands of the majority — legislators or judges?

In recent decades, legislators have been subject to enormous pressure to be seen as "tough on crime." While many groups lobby legislators either to enact new crimes or to increase the punishment for existing crimes, few if any lobby on behalf of those who have been or will be subject to criminal statutes either to repeal outdated criminal laws or to reduce punishments. Often great pressure is exerted on legislators to increase the scope and severity of the criminal law in the aftermath of particularly notorious and highly publicized crimes, as the kidnapping and murder of Polly Klass led to California's adoption of its three strikes law as described in the *Ewing* case in Chapter 2. These political dynamics have been a major factor in increasing the severity of the American criminal justice system in recent decades and the rise in mass incarceration.

b. Accessibility and Comprehensibility

Criminal law ideally should be both accessible and comprehensible. In other words, the criminal law should be easy to find and to understand. Accessibility and comprehensibility of criminal law are important for several reasons. "The criminal law is a particularly public and visible part of the law. It is important that its authority and legitimacy should not be undermined by perceptions that it is intelligible only to experts."[7] Accessible and comprehensible criminal law makes it possible for potential offenders to have advance notice of what is and is not criminal. The clearer the threat of punishment, one would presume, the greater the deterrent effect of the criminal law. And blame is easier to assign if the offender acted when he knew or could easily have learned that his conduct violated the law. Increased accessibility and clarity also make it possible for lawyers to advise their clients more accurately and efficiently.

Accessibility and comprehensibility are also important for increasing accuracy and the efficiency of those administering the criminal law—police, judges, law clerks, prosecutors, defense counsel, and jurors—particularly when dealing with the high volume of cases typical of many modern criminal courts. Obscurity and ambiguity in the definition of offenses, for example, increases the rate of appeals and reversals based on erroneous interpretations of the charged offense.

A standard argument on behalf of statutory law is that it is more accessible than case law. One can locate with relative ease the criminal statutes of a particular jurisdiction. Legal publishers often offer compact, single-volume paperback versions of a jurisdiction's criminal statutes that prosecutors, defense lawyers, and judges keep at their desks and can carry with them to court.

Judges, by contrast, typically developed the common law definitions of offenses through a gradual, incremental process in a series of opinions over many years. Charting the definition of an offense often required reading numerous cases. Finding these opinions could be a time-consuming and tedious task even for lawyers and required sophistication in the use of secondary sources and legal research tools. Treatise writers such as Blackstone summarized the common law to help lawyers find and understand it. Today, although the Internet and search engines provide greater accessibility to case law, tracking down case law treating a particular issue often remains challenging.

With legislative definition of crime, a statute provides a useful starting point for determining the definition of an offense. But how easy it is to find the full definition of an offense depends on how the legislature drafts the statute. Some criminal statutes are models of clarity. Others simply adopt the common law definition of a crime or do little more than announce the existence of an offense, leaving to the prosecutors, juries, and courts the difficult task of defining its elements. At other times, a statute can be a dense and intimidating text filled with ambiguity and complex, ill-defined terms. Even when the elements are spelled out, the meaning of statutory language must be determined by the judges called on to apply those statutes. Often, then, the task of learning what a statutory offense requires involves researching case law through a process similar to what the common law required. One clear advantage of statutorily defined crimes is that annotated versions of a jurisdiction's criminal statutes typically collect key cases developing and refining the definition of an offense and place them immediately after the text of the statute.

---

7. The Law Commission, A Criminal Code for England and Wales 6 (1989).

Are statutes easier to understand than common law? The fact that a legislature is free to use simple, modern language in stating the law while the common law tends to cling tenaciously to outdated terminology suggests so. At times, the common law camouflaged evolving criminal law by attaching multiple meanings to well-worn terminology, meanings often at odds with common usage. In addition, a statute's only function is to state the law, while a judicial opinion's primary function is to resolve a particular case. In resolving that case, the judge may state the law leading to that resolution clearly, or she may do so ambiguously, leaving the reader to extrapolate the law from the resolution of the case, a skill referred to in law school as learning how to "read" a case. The meaning of a case is often subject to dispute, such as when judges disagree on the application of prior cases, known as precedent, to a new situation.

These factors suggest that statutes should be more comprehensible than case law. But, as pointed out above, statutes as well as judicial opinions may be poorly drafted. At times, legislatures purposefully leave a certain element vague because of failure to achieve agreement among the legislators regarding that element.

You can make your own judgments on the relative comprehensibility of statutes and cases as you encounter each type of law in this and other courses.

c. Prospective versus Retrospective Operation

Statutes in theory operate only prospectively. Indeed, retrospective operation of a criminal statute is barred by the federal constitution's prohibition of *ex post facto* laws. The common law, by contrast, is typically viewed as being able to create a new crime or expand the definition of an existing crime to meet a new situation and apply it retrospectively. Indeed, the ability of the common law to adapt to new situations is often praised as one of its primary virtues.

Critics have complained about the retroactivity of the common law. Bentham caustically described the common law as "dog law" because of its retrospective operation:

> When your dog does anything you want to break him of you wait til he does it, and then beat him for it. This is the way you make laws for your dog; and this is the way judges made law for you and me.[8]

Critics of common law also point out that as the body of statutory law has grown, society has less need for the common law's ability to create new crimes. An English report recommending the codification of English criminal law argues that:

> [t]he common law method of resolving uncertainty by "retrospective" declaration of the law is objectionable in principle. It may lead to the conviction of a defendant on the basis of criminal liability not known to exist in that form before he acted.... On the other hand, the effect of an appeal may be to narrow the law retrospectively, either by acknowledging the existence of a defence to criminal liability which was not previously recognised or by al-

---

8. III THE WORKS OF JEREMY BENTHAM 235 (Bowring ed. 1838–1843).

tering the definition of a criminal offence.... Such a change may give rise to a suggestion not only that the conviction in the earlier case was unsafe but also cast doubt on the validity of the convictions in other cases during the intervening ... period which had been based on the terms of the direction approved in the earlier case. Such suggestions, which are inherent in the development of the law on a case by case basis, must undermine confidence in this important branch of the law. Statutory changes, on the other hand, do not have retrospective effect. They come into force only after full [legislative] debate with the commencement of the provisions of the statute. Earlier cases are unaffected.[9]

Though statutes in theory do not operate retrospectively, they may do so in practice. If a statute contains ambiguities that are resolved by court interpretation only after the defendant has acted or been convicted, although the statute existed prior to the defendant's act, its meaning was not established until after the fact. A court might remedy this problem by refusing to apply a new interpretation of a statute to a particular case, choosing to apply it only to future cases.

d. Balancing the Particular and the General

Justice Holmes wrote:

> Great cases like hard cases make bad law. For great cases are called great, not by reason of their real importance ... but because of some accident of immediate overwhelming interest which appeals to the feelings and distorts the judgement. These immediate interests exercise a kind of hydraulic pressure which makes what previously was clear seem doubtful, and before which even well settled principles of law will bend.[10]

Because common law is created in the process of resolving cases, the judges who shape it at times encounter a tension between doing justice to the litigants in the cases before them and doing justice to litigants in future cases. Common law courts, then, must simultaneously use two focal points, one narrow and present-oriented, the other broad and future-oriented. Does this responsibility to do justice to the particular litigants before it distort the judgment of common law courts, resulting in the creation of rules unjust to the parties in future cases? Or does the experience of applying rules to actual cases give judges insight and wisdom to help them craft better rules?

Because it does not resolve controversies involving particular parties, a legislature is not subject to a tension between adjudicating a particular case and creating a general rule. Its exclusive role is to create rules to be generally applied in the future. Its focus is solely broad and future-oriented.

---

9. THE LAW COMMISSION, A CRIMINAL CODE FOR ENGLAND AND WALES 7–8 (1989).

10. *Northern Securities Co. v. United States*, 193 U.S. 197, 400–401 (1904).

Particular cases, though, as noted previously may have a powerful and at times pernicious impact on a legislature. High-profile cases at times generate great pressure for legislators to enact or revise criminal statutes to respond to public concern about a particular case. In doing so, they may fail to give adequate consideration to a law's long-term impact. John Hinckley's shooting of President Reagan, for example, triggered a wave of legislative activity across the United States restricting access to the insanity defense. And, as Justice O'Connor pointed out in the *Ewing* case in Chapter 2, the well-publicized kidnapping and murder of Polly Klaas in California spurred enactment of California's draconian three-strikes law.

e. Keeping Criminal Law Current

Are judges or legislators better able to keep the criminal law in touch with current social needs and attitudes? Judges must typically wait for litigants to present a case giving them the opportunity to change the law. If no such case comes before them, they are unable to reform the law no matter how much it needs to be changed.

Common law gives great weight to the principle of *stare decisis*—the idea that in determining the law applicable to a particular situation a court is bound by the decisions of earlier courts that have spoken on the issue. Judges today vary in their fidelity to *stare decisis*. At times, judges openly announce that a judicially created rule needs to be changed and then change it. But the principle of *stare decisis* may nonetheless prove a stumbling block to judicial law reform.

Legislators are not bound by *stare decisis*. Nor do they have to wait for a party to a lawsuit to bring a case before them to change the law. They are free to revisit and revise a statute at any time. Also, because of their electoral accountability they are often thought to be more in touch with the needs and attitudes of the electorate than judges and so know what laws need to be changed.

In practice, though, there are many practical and political roadblocks to legislative reform. Lack of time due to crowded legislative agendas, lack of consensus within a political party or between political parties about what shape reform should take, or the fact that different parties control the executive and legislative branches are all potential barriers to legislative reform. Fear of being viewed by voters or labeled by an opponent as being "soft on crime" discourages legislators from voting to repeal or modify criminal statutes to create greater leniency. For example, despite increased public support across the United States, the decriminalization of medical and recreational marijuana that has occurred in many states in recent years has not come from the action of state legislatures. Instead, referenda that enable voters to bypass state legislatures has driven decriminalization.

f. Institutional Competence

There are a number of additional reasons one might expect a legislature to do a better job of creating law than courts, including criminal law. One is that the legislative process involves deliberation by, and input from, many more people than the resolution of a court case. This fact, one might argue, should make it less likely that a bad criminal law will be created by a legislature than by a court.

In addition, the legislature can hold hearings through which it gathers facts relevant to proposed legislation. It can also summon experts and those with firsthand experience with the problem the legislation addresses to hear their views. Its committees often have professional staff who can collect data and study an issue. A court may also utilize data about a particular problem that has already been published or otherwise made available. It can also learn the views of experts and others with firsthand experience through the filings of the parties or amici. But courts typically have no ability to generate and an ability inferior to the legislature to gather this sort of information.

But legislatures often fail in actual practice to give careful consideration to the laws they pass. Congressman Dan Rostenkowski, for example, voted for the Federal Sentencing Guidelines both in committee and on the floor of the House. Later convicted of mail fraud and sentenced to serve a work term in a federal prison, he had the chance firsthand to learn how the Guidelines work. He later admitted in a radio interview that he had been completely unaware of what the Guidelines were about when he voted for them.[11]

B. The Executive Branch

The executive branch does not make criminal law. It enforces criminal laws enacted by the legislature. That, at least, is the conventional view of the executive branch's role in the criminal justice system. Closer examination, however, reveals that executive branch officials shape the criminal law in a number of ways.

Executive officials are important players in the political process of creating criminal legislation. Criminal issues sometimes feature prominently in presidential and gubernatorial campaigns and on the legislative agendas of newly elected officials. Appointed and career officials in the federal Department of Justice and elected state attorneys general and the lawyers in their offices can and often do draft and submit proposed criminal statutes to the legislature. They also lobby for or against and provide testimony, empirical data, and advice on criminal statutes the legislature is considering.

Executive clemency—the power to pardon offenders exercised by the president for federal offenses and governors in some states for state offenses—also gives the executive branch power to nullify the application of the criminal law in particular cases.

The executive branch can also influence criminal law in less obvious ways. The positions taken by government lawyers and the arguments they advance play a role in influencing both trial and appellate court interpretation of criminal statutes. Pros-

---

11. National Public Radio, *This American Life*, Episode 143, "Sentencing" (10/22/1999).

ecutorial charging policy provides another example. Our criminal justice system gives prosecutors a large measure of discretion over whether to prosecute a case. A prosecutorial policy not to prosecute a particular crime can effectively nullify an act of the legislature. Fornication and adultery laws still exist in some jurisdictions, for example, but prosecutors largely ignore them. A prosecutorial policy to prosecute offenses recognized by the legislature only under specified conditions effectively "rewrites" a statute. Statutory rape laws, for example, once routinely prohibited sexual intercourse with a female under a certain age even if the female consented and the male was close in age to the victim. Prosecutors, though, often declined to file criminal charges when the intercourse was consensual and occurred between teenagers close in age, in effect creating an age span exemption not found in the language of the statute. Modern legislators have followed the lead set by such prosecutorial policies and now typically incorporate an explicit age span exemption in statutory rape laws.

Executive branch officials also play a role in defining offenses when the legislature explicitly delegates to them the power to create and define crimes. The following case provides an example of explicit, also referred to as express, delegation of the power to define what is criminal by the legislature to an executive branch official, here the state fire marshal.

Connecticut v. White

204 Conn. 410 (1987)
Connecticut Supreme Court

Santaniello, J.

The defendant, Gordon L. White, was charged ... with three counts of failing to provide a smoke detector in violation of Connecticut state fire safety code §§ 11-1.8.1 and 11-3.3.3.1, and General Statutes §§ 29-292 and 29-295. After a jury trial, the defendant was found guilty.... On appeal, the defendant ... claims ... that the state fire safety code provisions exceed the scope of authority conferred by the code's enabling statute.... We find error.

The jury could reasonably have found the following facts: The defendant owned a three family residential building located at 1387 Corbin Avenue in New Britain. On December 25, 1982, at approximately 5:30 a.m., Edward Ross, an occupant of the first floor apartment, awoke to find smoke filtering into his apartment. After waking up his wife, their child, and his brother-in-law, and escorting them outside, Ross summoned the New Britain fire department. The fire department arrived at the scene almost immediately and began battling a fire which had broken out on the second floor. Several firefighters entered the second floor apartment, which was full of smoke, and discovered the bodies of Maryann Jones and her two young children, Lindsay and Brandy, the occupants of that apartment, lying dead on the floor. The medical examiner concluded that all three had died from asphyxia caused by smoke inhalation.

It was estimated that the fire, apparently caused by an electrical overload from a wall outlet into which a quartz heater had been plugged, began smoldering at approximately 2:30 a.m., but did not break out in the apartment until about 5:30 a.m. As a result of the slow burning nature of the fire, the apartment was covered with soot and was filled with thick smoke. There were no smoke detectors in the building.

At trial, the state introduced evidence regarding how a smoke detector works, the cost of a smoke detector, how it is installed, and its effectiveness. Additionally, testimony was introduced that had smoke detectors been installed in the defendant's building, the occupants would have been alerted to the fire in sufficient time to enable them to escape.

Evidence was also introduced that the defendant owned another multifamily apartment building located in East Hartford. In May, 1982, the defendant received notice from the East Hartford fire marshal informing him that he was required to furnish smoke detectors in his East Hartford building. The defendant installed smoke detectors in the East Hartford building, but he did not install smoke detectors in his New Britain building. Additionally, prior to December, 1982, the defendant undertook renovations on the New Britain property but did not obtain building permits for the work he performed.

At the conclusion of the state's case, the defendant moved for a judgment of acquittal claiming that: ... the state had failed to prove that the defendant had violated Connecticut fire safety code §§ 11-1.8.1 and 11-3.3.3.1 and General Statutes §§ 29-292 and 29-295 because the state did not establish that a building permit had been issued on or after October 1, 1976, for the building in question. The defendant also argued that the fire safety code was inconsistent with its enabling statute in contravention of General Statutes § 29-293. The court denied the defendant's motion....

II

The defendant ... complains that the fire safety code regulations exceed the scope of authority conferred by § 29-292,[4] the code's enabling legislation. We agree.

---

4. "[General Statutes (Rev. to 1983)] Sec. 29-292. (Formerly Sec. 29-40). Fire safety code. Smoke detection and warning equipment. Certificate of occupancy. Review of plans and specifications; fees.

(a) The state fire marshal and the codes and standards committee shall adopt, promulgate and administer a fire safety code and at any time may amend the same. The regulations in said code shall provide for reasonable safety from fire, smoke and panic therefrom, in all buildings and areas adjacent thereto except in private dwellings occupied by one or two families and upon all premises except those used for manufacturing, and shall include provision for smoke detection and warning equipment in residential buildings designed to be occupied by two or more families for which a building permit is issued on or after October 1, 1976, and in new residential buildings designed to be occupied by one or more families for which a building permit for new occupancy is issued on or after October 1, 1978, to provide Level Four Protection, as defined in the 1974 edition of Number Seventy-four of the National Fire Protection Association. Said regulations shall provide the requirements for markings and literature which shall accompany such equipment sufficient to inform the occupants and owners of such buildings of the purpose, protective limitations and correct installation, operating, testing,

It is well established that although the power to make law is vested exclusively in the legislature, the legislature may create a law designed to accomplish a particular purpose and may expressly authorize an administrative agency to "fill up the details" by prescribing rules and regulations for the operation and enforcement of that law. It is necessary, however, that the enabling statute declare legislative policy, establish primary standards or lay down an intelligible principle to which the administrative officer or body must conform. If the legislature fails to prescribe the limits of the power delegated with reasonable clarity, or the power is too broad, its attempt to delegate is a nullity. While the modern trend of the legislature is liberal in approving delegation under broad regulatory standards so as to facilitate the operational functions of administrative agencies, agencies must, nonetheless, act according to the strict statutory authority.

To address the defendant's claim that the fire safety code exceeds the authority conferred by its enabling statute, a review of the original act, its relevant amendment and the relevant code provision is necessary. In 1947, the legislature passed Public Acts 1947, No. 419, which provided that "[t]he state fire marshal shall establish a fire safety code and at any time may amend the same. The regulations in said code shall provide for reasonable safety from fire, smoke, and panic therefrom, in all buildings except in private dwellings occupied by one or two families, and upon all premises except those used for manufacturing." General Statutes (1949 Rev.) § 3665. The purpose of the statute was to give the fire marshal the ability to enact reasonable minimum requirements for safety in new and existing buildings.

---

maintenance and replacement procedures and servicing instructions for such equipment and shall require that smoke detection and warning equipment which is installed in such residential buildings shall be capable of sensing visible or invisible smoke particles, that the manner and location of installing smoke detectors shall be approved by the local fire marshal or building official, that such installation shall not exceed the standards under which such equipment was tested and approved and that such equipment, when activated, shall provide an alarm suitable to warn the occupants.

"(b) No certificate of occupancy shall be issued for any residential building designed to be occupied by two or more families for which a building permit is issued on or after October 1, 1976, or any new residential building designed to be occupied by one or more families for which a building permit for new occupancy is issued on or after October 1, 1978, unless the local fire marshal or building official has certified that said building is equipped with smoke detection and warning equipment complying with the fire safety code.

"(c) Detailed plans and specifications of structures subject to the state fire safety code may be submitted to the state fire marshal for review and a determination concerning compliance with the state fire safety code. The state fire marshal shall develop a schedule of fees for reviewing such plans and specifications, which schedule shall provide for fees payable to the state treasurer in amounts of not less than ten dollars nor more than one hundred dollars, depending upon the complexity of the review."

For almost thirty years, this act remained substantially unchanged.[5] In 1976, however, the legislature passed No. 76-78 of the 1976 Public Acts (Public Act No. 76-78) which amended § 20-40, the predecessor of § 29-292, mandating, in relevant part, that the regulations "shall include provision for smoke detection systems in residential buildings designed to be occupied by two or more families for which a building permit is issued on or after [October 1, 1976]."

The fire safety code, passed pursuant to § 29-292, requires that smoke detectors be installed in "each guest room, suite or sleeping area of hotels, motels, lodging or rooming houses, and dormitories, and in each dwelling unit within apartment houses and one- and two-family dwellings...." Connecticut State Fire Safety Code (1981) § 11-1.8.1.[6]

The defendant contends that the enabling statute, as amended by Public Act No. 76-78, limits the fire marshal's ability to promulgate regulations concerning smoke detectors in buildings designed to be occupied by two or more families to those buildings for which a building permit has been issued on or after October 1, 1976. Because the fire safety code does not require that smoke detectors be installed only in those buildings, the defendant argues that the code exceeds its express statutory authority.

There is no question that the legislature, in originally enacting § 29-292, conferred upon the fire marshal broad authority to pass rules and regulations to "provide for reasonable safety from fire, smoke and panic therefrom," and that such a conferral was a valid delegation of authority. Had the original statute been in effect during this case, there would be little doubt that the challenged fire safety code regulations would be valid. The legislature, however, amended the enabling statute in 1976. The question thus becomes whether the legislature, in passing Public Act No. 76-78, intended to limit the fire marshal's authority to pass regulations with respect to smoke detectors for residential buildings designed to be occupied by two or more families.

In determining whether the legislature was limiting the authority of the fire marshal to promulgate regulations, we are guided by the well established principles of statutory construction which require us to ascertain and give effect to the apparent intent of the legislature. When the language of the statute is plain and unambiguous, we need look no further than the words themselves because we assume that the language expresses the legislature's intent. If, however, the language is unclear, we must ascertain the intent of the legislature by examining the language of the statute, its legislative history and the purpose the statute is to serve.

An examination of the statute fails to reveal whether the legislature, in enacting Public Act No. 76-78, intended to authorize the fire marshal in promulgating the fire

5. In 1958, General Statutes § 3665 was transferred and set out as § 29-40 and in 1983 the statute was transferred and set out as § 29-292.

6. On March 10, 1987, the Code for Safety to Life from Fire in Buildings and Structures of the National Fire Protection Association, Inc., Standard 101, 1985 edition, was adopted by reference as the Connecticut fire safety code. See Connecticut State Fire Safety Code § 29-292-1. For the purpose of this appeal, however, the code provisions as they existed at the time relevant to this action govern our disposition of the case.

safety code to require smoke detectors only in multifamily buildings for which a building permit was issued after October 1, 1976, as the defendant claims, or, as the state argues, intended to set a minimum standard for the installation of smoke detectors and allow the fire marshal to set additional standards regarding smoke detectors.

The state contends that the plain language of the amendment demonstrates that the legislature did not intend to limit the authority of the fire marshal, but rather intended the amendment to direct that "the Code include at least that class of buildings." (Emphasis added.) The state argues that the amendment's language that the regulations "shall *include* provision for smoke detection systems" (emphasis added) mandated that the fire marshal *at least include* such a regulation in the code, but did not proscribe him from further regulating in that area. The state claims that the word "include" is a word of enlargement, not one of limitation, and cites to Webster's Third New International Dictionary, which defines "include" as "to place, list or rate as part or component of a whole or larger group, class or aggregate ... to take in, enfold, or comprise as a discrete or subordinate part or item of a larger aggregate...."

We have recognized in the past, however, that the word "include" may be considered a word of limitation as well as a word of enlargement. In *Hartford Electric Light Co. v. Sullivan*, we recognized that the most likely common use of the term "shall include" is one of limitation. In that case, however, we could not conclude with certainty that it was so employed. Similarly, in the present case we cannot conclude that the word "include" is used as a word of limitation or a word of enlargement.

Because we find the legislative intent unclear from the language of the statute itself, we must turn to other tools of statutory interpretation. Unfortunately the legislative history of Public Act No. 76-78 is of little help. While debate on the amendment indicates that it was enacted to require smoke detectors in all new buildings occupied by two or more families for which a building permit was issued after the enumerated date, it does not indicate whether the legislature intended to preclude the fire marshal from further promulgating regulations for the installation of smoke detectors in other multifamily buildings.

We find it significant, however, that the legislature chose to delineate carefully the types of buildings in which it required the installation of smoke detectors, rather than to mandate generally the installation of smoke detectors and to defer to the fire marshal's authority the promulgation of such regulations. When a statute provides that a thing shall be done in a certain way, it carries with it an implied prohibition against doing that thing a different way. "An enumeration of powers in a statute is uniformly held to forbid things not enumerated." Had the General Assembly intended that the fire marshal be allowed to promulgate more comprehensive regulations, it could easily have broadened the requirements for smoke detector regulations. Instead it specifically set forth that smoke detectors were required in buildings for which building permits were issued on or after October 1, 1976.

Moreover, we agree with the defendant that, because § 29-292 is penal in nature, the statute and the code provision should be construed strictly and we should resolve any ambiguity in the defendant's favor. The fact that this statute has a penal component cannot be seriously doubted, as demonstrated by the defendant's conviction. Thus, because the legislative intent behind Public Act No. 76-78 is not entirely clear, we construe §29-292 to limit the fire marshal's authority in passing regulations with regard to the installation of smoke detectors. To the extent that fire safety code §11-1.8.1 regulates beyond that legislative mandate, it exceeds the scope of its statutory authority. The defendant cannot be convicted of violating §11-1.8.1 unless it is shown that a building permit had been issued for his building on or after the enumerated date. At trial no such evidence was introduced. Accordingly, the defendant's convictions for such violations must be set aside.

Discussion Questions

1. Why do legislatures sometimes expressly authorize administrative agencies to create and define criminal offenses? What are the advantages and disadvantages of such a practice?

2. What is the statutory language at issue in the *White* case? What were the competing positions of the prosecution and defense regarding the meaning of that language? Is the word *include* one of enlargement or limitation? What do you think the legislature intended *include* to mean in this context? Which should control the outcome of the case—what a word means or what the legislature intended it to mean?

* * *

In addition to explicit, or express, delegation exemplified in *White*, the legislature may also implicitly delegate power to prosecutors by passing a criminal statute that is silent or ambiguous, creating space the executive can fill through the policies it adopts regarding the selection of cases to prosecute. Implicit delegation is also referred to as *implied delegation*. The United States Congress has passed a number of laws that allow federal prosecutors to exercise a large measure of power and effectively transfer to them the task of defining the elements of the offense. Professor Dan Kahan describes this interaction between the legislature and prosecutors in the following excerpt.

Three Conceptions of Federal Criminal-Lawmaking

Dan M. Kahan

1 BUFF. CRIM. L.R. 5, 15–16 (1997)

Congress predictably and systematically delegates lawmaking power by drafting criminal statutes in exceedingly general or open-textured terms.... The beneficiaries of this lawmaking abdication are individual prosecutors, who as a result of it face little constraint in advancing broad and innovative readings of incompletely specified statutes. If courts disavow the normative discretion to specify what broadly worded statutes do and don't cover, the only sensible limiting principles that will exist are the ones that individual U.S. Attorneys elect to recognize based on their own sense of institutional self-restraint.

And they display precious little of that. Individual U.S. Attorneys are extraordinarily ambitious and routinely enter electoral politics after leaving office. Consequently, while in office, they face significant incentives to advance imaginative readings of vague criminal offenses in order to please influential local interests. Consider Rudolph Giuliani, whose innovative insider-trading prosecutions, it has been alleged, were calculated to win the approval of the established Wall Street firms that were then being routed by Michael Milken and other financial innovators. When Giuliani later ran for Mayor of New York, these firms were among his key supporters.

C. The Jury

Problem

3.2 *Cameras in the Jury Room?* You are the judge in a capital murder trial. A public television station files a motion seeking to film the trial, including the jury's deliberation and rendering of its verdict, for later broadcast as part of an award-winning documentary series the station has created on the criminal justice system. The documentary's purpose is to educate the public on how criminal justice is administered in the courtroom. The state in which you sit has allowed filming of trials for a number of years, but to date cameras have never gone into a jury room in your state. A few other states have allowed filming of jury deliberations in criminal cases for educational purposes. The station proposes to place unattended cameras and microphones in the jury room so that no person other than the jurors would be physically present in the jury room. They also suggest that early in the jury selection process any potential juror who objects to being filmed be removed from the potential pool for that case. The defendant, after consulting with his lawyer, consents to having the jury deliberations filmed and agrees to waive any claim of error based on the filming. How would you rule on the television station's motion? What are the potential advantages and disadvantages of allowing cameras into the jury room? Would your ruling depend on whether or not the prosecuting attorney objects? Would your resolution be different if the case did not involve capital punishment?

The Sixth Amendment to the United States Constitution provides:

> In all criminal prosecutions, the accused shall enjoy the right to a speedy and public trial, by an impartial jury of the State and district wherein the crime shall have been committed ...

Roughly 90 to 95 percent of criminal cases in both federal and state courts are resolved without any sort of trial through a guilty plea that is often the result of negotiation between the prosecution and defense. But because of the Sixth Amendment, most criminal trials are jury trials. The following excerpt captures the rationale for trial by jury.

Duncan v. Louisiana
391 U.S. 145, 156 (1968)
United States Supreme Court

Providing an accused with the right to be tried by a jury of his peers gave him an inestimable safeguard against the corrupt or overzealous prosecutor and against the compliant, biased, or eccentric judge. If the defendant preferred the common-sense judgment of a jury to the more tutored but perhaps less sympathetic reaction of the single judge, he was to have it. Beyond this, the jury trial provisions in the Federal and State Constitutions reflect a fundamental decision about the exercise of official power—a reluctance to entrust plenary powers over the life and liberty of the citizen to one judge or to a group of judges. Fear of unchecked power, so typical of our State and Federal Governments in other respects, found expression in the criminal law in this insistence upon community participation in the determination of guilt or innocence.

* * *

The materials in this section address the role of the jury in criminal cases. The conventional modern view, expressed in the following jury instruction, is that jurors play no role in making criminal law.

Model Jury Instruction 3.02[12]

It is your duty to find from the evidence what the facts are. You will then apply the law, as I give it to you, to those facts. You must follow my instructions on the law, even if you thought the law was different or should be different.

Do not allow sympathy or prejudice to influence you. The law demands of you a just verdict, unaffected by anything except the evidence, your common sense, and the law as I give it to you.

* * *

Despite what this instruction states, jurors may play a role in shaping criminal law in two primary ways. First, they may do so when required to apply a vague or am-

---

12. Manual of Model Criminal Jury Instructions for the District Courts of the Eighth Circuit (2000).

biguous statute. In the previous section, we saw how a statute that is silent or ambiguous on a particular point effectively delegates lawmaking power to executive branch officials through their discretionary power to choose cases for prosecution. Silence or ambiguity in a criminal statute may similarly delegate power to jurors to shape the criminal law through their power to interpret vague statutes.

Second, even if a statute is clear, jurors may exercise power over the substantive criminal law through what is called jury nullification. *United States v. Dougherty*, below, addresses whether jurors should be told they have the power to nullify. This power is similar to the nullification power prosecutors may exercise by refusing to prosecute cases under certain statutes.

In the selection below, Professor Matthew Harrington describes the historical evolution of the view that jurors are to determine only the facts and not the law in criminal cases.

The Law-Finding Function of the American Jury
Matthew P. Harrington
1999 WIS. L. REV. 377, 377–380 (1999)

It has become something of an article of faith in the legal community that it is "the duty of the court to expound the law and that of the jury to apply the law as thus declared." In practice, this is often interpreted to mean that the judge alone has the power to determine the law and the jury is limited to applying the law to the facts. The standard allocation of power between judge and jury is thought to be as old as the common law itself.

In truth, however, this division of labor is of relatively recent origin. Until the early years of this century, many American lawyers and judges believed that juries had the power to declare both the law and the facts. The jury thus had the ability to take upon itself the right to determine the entire controversy. As late as 1895, Supreme Court Justice Shiras asserted:

> The jury ... are intrusted with the decision of both the law and the facts involved in [the] issue. To assist them in the decision of the facts, they hear the testimony of witnesses; but they are not bound to believe the testimony. To assist them in the decision of the law, they receive the instructions of the judge; but they are not obliged to follow his instructions.

This ability to determine the law was something more than the power to bring in a general verdict, however. American judges actually asserted an almost plenary power in the jury to decide the law as it saw fit. Most recognized that juries might ignore their instructions, and bring in a verdict contrary to the law stated in the charge. For many years, therefore, courts were reluctant to order new trials on the grounds that the verdict was against the law. "It doth not vitiate a verdict," the Connecticut Supreme Court once declared, "that the jury have mistaken the law or the evidence; for ... they are judges of both."

The jury's power over law has its origins in the struggle against the royal prerogative. In seventeenth-century England, the jury's ability to bring in a general verdict of acquittal was celebrated as a bulwark of liberty. In several notable cases, juries stood up for individual rights against oppressive or unjust prosecutions. This characteristic of jury practice became especially valuable in the colonists' own struggle against the Crown. Colonial juries often refused to convict in cases brought under the navigation acts and sedition laws. Royal officials saw the coercive power of parliamentary legislation hampered by the inability to obtain convictions. The jury's power to nullify unpopular laws made it an important vehicle for the expression of the popular will.

Judges were not alone in their adherence to the jury's law-finding function. Lawyers, too, recognized the jury's power over law, and relied on it in presenting their case. Eighteenth-century lawyers did not hesitate to argue the law to juries, often citing cases and pointing to eminent legal authorities, such as Blackstone, to convince the jury to adopt their own view of the law. This privilege was so jealously guarded that it became the source of a great deal of controversy when judges later attempted to restrict the practice.

The jury's power over law was aided by the fact that few judges in the colonial period had formal legal training; many were simply administrative or legislative officers whose position gave them the right to adjudicate disputes, or prominent members of the community. Knowledge of the law was not a prerequisite to being a judge. As a result, the judge who presided at the trial did not look all that much different from the jury. "In background, experiences, and outlook [juries] were much like the litigants whose disputes they determined, and not very different from the judges who oversaw them." They were neighbors from nearby towns, who shared the same common beliefs and assumptions as the parties before them. Their lack of formal training meant that colonial judges did not usually instruct the jury on the law. Even when they did, judges were quick to advise the jury that they were not bound by the judge's view of the law as stated in the charge.

The relationship between judge and jury did not change much in the years immediately following the Revolution. Although the business of judging was becoming more professionalized, many judges still refused to instruct the jury that it was bound by the charge. This was certainly true in criminal cases, mainly because judges still revered the jury's role as a check on oppressive prosecutions. Nonetheless, many judges refused to instruct the jury on the law in civil suits as well. The jury's power over law in the first decade of the Republic did not, therefore, look very much different than in the colonial era.

In time, however, members of the bench and bar gradually came to the conclusion that the jury's power over law must be restrained. In civil cases, judges and lawyers joined with merchant interests to limit the jury's law-finding function as a means of promoting a stable commercial environment. Such stability was thought necessary to the Republic as a means of putting the new nation on a firm economic footing, allowing it to provide for the welfare of its citizens and assume a place of prominence in the family of nations. This instrumentalist view of the law made judges increasingly willing to devise some means to force juries to adhere to the law as stated in the court's charge. It was not long before American judges resorted to the English doctrine of new trials to reverse verdicts where juries had brought in a verdict contrary to their instructions. This program was so successful that by 1820, the jury's power over law had all but disappeared.

The jury's law-finding function in criminal cases was to survive much longer, however. Adherence to the view of the jury as a bulwark of liberty meant that many judges were more reluctant to intrude upon the jury's power to bring in a general verdict in criminal trials. Constitutional prohibitions on double jeopardy also meant that the power to grant new trials in criminal cases was severely limited. The inability to order a new trial in cases where the jury brought in a verdict of acquittal made it difficult to enforce complete compliance with the court's instructions. The jury's power to acquit "in the teeth of both law and facts" meant that it would always retain some variant of its earlier law-finding function. Nonetheless, by the end of the nineteenth century, judges shed their earlier hesitance and took upon themselves the power to grant new trials in cases of conviction. More importantly, judges also began to instruct juries that they were bound by the law as stated in the charge. They increasingly sought to prevent counsel from advising the jury of its right to nullify and prohibit lawyers from making any sort of legal argument to the jury. In so doing, judges eventually succeeded in burying the jury's law-finding function in the dusts of time. The judges were so successful that few lawyers, and almost no juror, ever has but the faintest inkling of the enormous prerogative that once belonged to the jury.

What is especially striking about the decline of the jury's power over law is the way in which it was carried out. The drive to limit the law-finding function was entirely a judge-led exercise, carried out without legislative warrant and sometimes in the face of legislative enactments to the contrary. Three factors played a role in this effort: Foremost among these was the growing desire for stability in the law. Both judges and lawyers were concerned about the need to provide a stable legal regime. This was so not only to ensure stability in the commercial law, but also to ensure that the criminal law might be fixed and uniform. The increasing diversity of juries was also a factor. The "men of the neighborhood" who adjudicated disputes in the town and county courts were no more. As the nation became diverse and jury service was opened to a wider segment of the population, juries could no longer be counted on to speak from a common set of beliefs and experiences. The way was cleared for inconsistent and contradictory verdicts. Perhaps worse, from the judges' point of view, was the increasing tendency of juries to bring in verdicts at odds with the judges' own views and experiences. Finally, the movement was also fueled by the increasing professionalization of the bench and bar. As legal education became more sophisticated, judges became more convinced that the bench was the proper place in which to lodge the law-finding function.

In the end, the American judiciary succeeded in delegitimizing the jury's power over law by means of a careful and creative reinterpretation of the common law governing the allocation of power between judge and jury. The transformation was long and arduous, marked by a great deal of hesitancy and many missteps; but, the results have been long lasting.

Discussion Questions

1. What are the advantages and disadvantages of having jurors rather than judges or legislators define what is criminal?

2. How would Khaliq and Keeler have fared if a jury had been entrusted with the task of defining the criminal law in their cases?

* * *

United States v. Dougherty
473 F.2d 1113 (D.C. Cir. 1972)
United States Court of Appeals for the D.C. Circuit

Leventhal, Circuit Judge.

Seven of the so-called "D.C. Nine" bring this joint appeal from convictions arising out of their unconsented entry into the Washington offices of the Dow Chemical Company, and their destruction of certain property therein.... The undisputed evidence showed that on Saturday, March 22, 1969, appellants broke into the locked fourth floor Dow offices at 1030 15th Street, N.W., Washington, D.C., threw papers and documents about the office and into the street below, vandalized office furniture and equipment, and defaced the premises by spilling about a bloodlike substance. The prosecution proved its case through Dow employees who testified as to the lack of permission and extent of damage, members of the news media who had been summoned to the scene by the appellants and who witnessed the destruction while recording it photographically, and police officers who arrested appellants on the scene....

[The jury acquitted the defendants of burglary but convicted on unlawful entry and malicious destruction of property.]

The Issue of Jury Nullification

[Appellants] say that the jury has a well-recognized prerogative to disregard the instructions of the court even as to matters of law, and that they accordingly have the legal right that the jury be informed of its power.... There has evolved in the Anglo-American system an undoubted jury prerogative-in-fact, derived from its power to bring in a general verdict of not guilty in a criminal case, that is not reversible by the court....

The pages of history shine on instances of the jury's exercise of its prerogative to disregard uncontradicted evidence and instructions of the judge. Most often commended are the 18th century acquittal of Peter Zenger of seditious libel, on the plea of Andrew Hamilton, and the 19th century acquittals in prosecutions under the fugitive slave law. The values involved drop a notch when the liberty vindicated by the verdict relates to the defendant's shooting of his wife's paramour, or purchase during Prohibition of alcoholic beverages....

Since the jury's prerogative of lenity, again in Learned Hand's words, introduces a "slack into the enforcement of law, tempering its rigor by the mollifying influence of current ethical conventions," it is only just, say appellants, that the jurors be so told. It is unjust to withhold information on the jury power of "nullification," since conscientious jurors may come, ironically, to abide by their oath as jurors to render verdicts offensive to their individual conscience, to defer to an assumption of necessity that is contrary to reality.

This so-called right of jury nullification is put forward in the name of liberty and democracy, but its explicit avowal risks the ultimate logic of anarchy. This is the concern voiced by Judge Sobeloff in *United States v. Moylan*:

> To encourage individuals to make their own determinations as to which laws they will obey and which they will permit themselves as a matter of conscience to disobey is to invite chaos. No legal system could long survive if it gave every individual the option of disregarding with impunity any law which by his personal standard was judged morally untenable. Toleration of such conduct would not be democratic, as appellants claim, but inevitably anarchic.

The statement that avowal of the jury's prerogative runs the risk of anarchy, represents, in all likelihood, the habit of thought of philosophy and logic, rather than the prediction of the social scientist. But if the statement contains an element of hyperbole, the existence of risk and danger, of significant magnitude, cannot be gainsaid. In contrast, the advocates of jury "nullification" apparently assume that the articulation of the jury's power will not extend its use or extent, or will not do so significantly or obnoxiously. Can this assumption fairly be made? We know that a posted limit of 60 m.p.h. produces factual speeds 10 or even 15 miles greater, with an understanding all around that some "tolerance" is acceptable to the authorities, assuming conditions warrant. But can it be supposed that the speeds would stay substantially the same if the speed limit were put: Drive as fast as you think appropriate, without the posted limit as an anchor, a point of departure?

Our jury system is a resultant of many vectors, some explicit, and some rooted in tradition, continuity and general understanding without express formulation. A constitution may be meaningful though it is unwritten, as the British have proved for 900 years.

The jury system has worked out reasonably well overall, providing "play in the joints" that imparts flexibility and avoids undue rigidity. An equilibrium has evolved — an often marvelous balance — with the jury acting as a "safety valve" for exceptional cases, without being a wildcat or runaway institution. There is reason to believe that the simultaneous achievement of modest jury equity and avoidance of intolerable caprice depends on formal instructions that do not expressly delineate a jury charter to carve out its own rules of law. We have taken due and wry note that those whose writings acclaim and invoke Roscoe Pound's 1910 recognition of the value of the jury as safety valve, omit mention of the fact that in the same article he referred to "the extreme decentralization that allows a local jury or even a local prosecutor to hold up instead of uphold the law of the state" as one of the conditions that "too often result in a legal paralysis of legal administration," that his writings of that period are expressly concerned with the evils of the "extravagant powers" of juries, and that in 1931 he joined the other distinguished members of the Wickersham Commission in this comment:

> In a number of jurisdictions juries are made judges of the law in criminal cases, thus inviting them to dispense with the rules of law instead of finding the facts. The juror is made judge of the law not to ascertain what it is, but to judge of its conformity to his personal ideals and ascertain its validity on that basis.... It is significant that there is most satisfaction with criminal juries in those jurisdictions which have interfered least with the conception of a trial of the facts unburdened with further responsibility and instructed as to the law and advised as to the facts by the judge.

The way the jury operates may be radically altered if there is alteration in the way it is told to operate. The jury knows well enough that its prerogative is not limited to the choices articulated in the formal instructions of the court. The jury gets its understanding as to the arrangements in the legal system from more than one voice. There is the formal communication from the judge. There is the informal communication from the total culture—literature (novel, drama, film, and television); current comment (newspapers, magazines and television); conversation; and, of course, history and tradition. The totality of input generally conveys adequately enough the idea of prerogative, of freedom in an occasional case to depart from what the judge says. Even indicators that would on their face seem too weak to notice—like the fact that the judge tells the jury it must acquit (in case of reasonable doubt) but never tells the jury in so many words that it must convict—are a meaningful part of the jury's total input. Law is a system, and it is also a language, with secondary meanings that may be unrecorded yet are part of its life.

When the legal system relegates the information of the jury's prerogative to an essentially informal input, it is not being duplicitous, chargeable with chicane and intent to deceive. The limitation to informal input is, rather a governor to avoid excess: the prerogative is reserved for the exceptional case, and the judge's instruction is retained as a generally effective constraint. We "recognize a constraint as obligatory upon us when we require not merely reason to defend our rule departures, but damn good reason." The practicalities of men, machinery and rules point up the danger of articulating discretion to depart from a rule, that the breach will be more often and casually invoked. We cannot gainsay that occasionally jurors uninstructed as to the prerogative may feel themselves compelled to the point of rigidity. The danger of the excess rigidity that may now occasionally exist is not as great as the danger of removing the boundaries of constraint provided by the announced rules.

We should also note the inter-relation of the unanimity requirement for petit juries, which was applicable to this trial, and is still the general rule though no longer constitutionally required for state courts. This is an additional reason—a material consideration, though neither a necessary nor sufficient condition—to brake the wheels of those who would tell the petit jurors they are to determine the rules of law, either directly or by telling them they are free to disregard the judge's statement of the rules. The democratic principle would not be furthered, as proponents of jury nullification claim, it would be disserved by investing in a jury that must be unanimous the function not merely of determining facts, hard enough for like-minded resolution, but of determining the rules of law.

Rules of law or justice involve choice of values and ordering of objectives for which unanimity is unlikely in any society, or group representing the society, especially a society as diverse in cultures and interests as ours. To seek unity out of diversity, under the national motto, there must be a procedure for decision by vote of a majority or prescribed plurality—in accordance with democratic philosophy. To assign the role of mini-legislature to the various petit juries, who must hang if not unanimous, exposes criminal law and administration to paralysis, and to a deadlock that betrays rather than furthers the assumptions of viable democracy.

Moreover, to compel a juror involuntarily assigned to jury duty to assume the burdens of mini-legislator or judge, as is implicit in the doctrine of nullification, is to put untoward strains on the jury system. It is one thing for a juror to know that the law condemns, but he has a factual power of lenity. To tell him expressly of a nullification prerogative, however, is to inform him, in effect, that it is he who fashions the rule that condemns. That is an overwhelming responsibility, an extreme burden for the jurors' psyche. And it is not inappropriate to add that a juror called upon for an involuntary public service is entitled to the protection, when he takes action that he knows is right, but also knows is unpopular, either in the community at large or in his own particular grouping, that he can fairly put it to friends and neighbors that he was merely following the instructions of the court.

In the last analysis, our rejection of the request for jury nullification doctrine is a recognition that there are times when logic is not the only or even best guide to sound conduct of government. For machines, one can indulge the person who likes to tinker in pursuit of fine tuning. When men and judicial machinery are involved, one must attend to the many and complex mechanisms and reasons that lead men to change their conduct—when they know they are being studied; when they are told of the consequences of their conduct; and when conduct exercised with restraint as an unwritten exception is expressly presented as a legitimate option.

What makes for health as an occasional medicine would be disastrous as a daily diet. The fact that there is widespread existence of the jury's prerogative, and approval of its existence as a "necessary counter to casehardened judges and arbitrary prosecutors," does not establish as an imperative that the jury must be informed by the judge of that power. On the contrary, it is pragmatically useful to structure instructions in such wise that the jury must feel strongly about the values involved in the case, so strongly that it must itself identify the case as establishing a call of high conscience, and must independently initiate and undertake an act in contravention of the established instructions. This requirement of independent jury conception confines the happening of the lawless jury to the occasional instance that does not violate, and viewed as an exception may even enhance, the over-all normative effect of the rule of law. An explicit instruction to a jury conveys an implied approval that runs the risk of degrading the legal structure requisite for true freedom, for an ordered liberty that protects against anarchy as well as tyranny.

Finally, we are aware that the denial of defendants' request for a nullification instruction will be considered by them to negative some, or perhaps most, of the value of the right of *pro se* representation which we have recognized. This point could be answered in terms of logic: The right of self-representation is given for reasons recognized by the law, and cannot be a springboard to establish the validity of other advantages or conditions that lie in its tactical wake. Thus, a defendant's ability to present his demeanor and often even a kind of testimony, without exposure to impeachment or cross-examination, may be a tactical consequence of *pro se* representation, and even a moving cause of its invocation, but this is not to say it is an objective of the law. But defendants' position merits a more spacious answer, that lies outside the domain of formal logic. It is this. The jury system provides flexibility for the consideration of interests of justice outside the formal rules of law. This embraces whatever extra the defendant conveys by personal representation, whether through demeanor or sincerity of justification. But it is subject to the overriding consideration that what is tolerable or even desirable as an informal, self-initiated exception, harbors grave dangers to the system if it is opened to expansion and intensification through incorporation in the judge's instruction.

[The judgment was reversed on other grounds.]

Discussion Question

Can a judge make sure that jurors are following the law as the judge instructs them? If so, how?

Problems

3.3 Does the jury play a role in defining what is criminal under the following statutes? If so, what facets of each statute invite the jury to define the law?

(a) It is a third degree felony to kill another negligently. A person acts negligently if she should have been aware of a substantial and unjustifiable risk of death and in so failing grossly deviates from what a reasonable person would have done.

(b) Manslaughter is the intentional killing of another under the influence of actual and reasonable provocation. Reasonable provocation is any provocation which would cause a reasonable person to lose self-control.

3.4 Should jurors have the power to nullify the application of criminal statutes in particular cases? Is jury nullification always prompted by a disposition toward leniency and mercy? How do you think a jury would use that power in the following cases?

(a) a battered wife is charged with the murder of her abusive husband;

(b) in a state in which euthanasia is illegal, a husband is charged with the murder by drug overdose of his wife who suffered from a painful, terminal illness and wished to end her life;

(c) in a county in which discrimination against a certain minority group is widespread, a young man is charged with assaulting a member of that minority group.

3.5 Write a jury instruction informing the jury of their obligations regarding enforcement of the criminal law.

D. Statutory Interpretation

Judges exercise significant power to shape criminal law through the interpretation of statutes written and enacted by the legislature. Considerable controversy and debate surround the question of how judges should go about this task, whether they should wield the power to interpret sparingly or expansively and what resources they should use when interpreting a statute. In this section, we examine three approaches to statutory interpretation. *Church of the Holy Trinity v. United States* exemplifies the *intentionalist* approach to statutory interpretation. As many of the cases you will read in this course and some of the cases you have already read demonstrate, intentionalism is currently the dominant mode of interpretation used by both state and federal judges in the United States. In the reading selection following *Holy Trinity*, Justice Antonin Scalia criticizes *Holy Trinity* and the intentionalist approach it exemplifies and defends a different approach to statutory interpretation known as *textualism*. The final excerpt in this section, by Professor William Eskridge, describes a third view of how judges should interpret statutes, known as *dynamic* statutory interpretation. In the problems below as well as in much of the rest of the material in this book, you will have opportunities to apply these various approaches.

Problems

3.6 A pandemic driven by a new form of coronavirus is spreading across the world causing many deaths. The virus can result in, among other things, a headache, sore throat, and serious chest cough. If an infected person's immune system and medical intervention are not equal to the task of fighting off the viral infection, the person develops pneumonia in both lungs, filling them with fluid and making it impossible for the person breathe, resulting in death.

Infected patients have inundated hospitals in many cities in the United States. Hospital supplies such as ventilators and protective gear, including gloves and face masks, are in short supply and daily death totals are increasing. Public health officials have warned the public frequently through television, radio, and newspapers that the coronavirus is very serious and is spread by fluids from an infected person entering the mouth, nose, or eyes of an uninfected person. The governor of the state in which the prosecutions described below take place has ordered all residents to sequester at home and emphasized in numerous appearances the importance of social distancing: keeping at least six feet between people and avoiding public gatherings to fight spread of the virus. Trips to a market to buy food and to a pharmacy to obtain medication are not prohibited.

The defendants described in Parts (a), (b), and (c) below have each been charged under the following statute:

Terroristic Threats

(a) A person commits a crime under this statute if the person communicates, either directly or indirectly, a threat of serious physical harm to another person. To violate this statute, the person must have either:

   (1) purpose to terrorize another or to cause evacuation of a building, place of assembly, or public transportation facility, or otherwise cause serious public inconvenience; or

   (2) reckless disregard of the risk of terrorizing another or causing inconvenience as described in Part (a)(1), above.

Violation of this statute is a misdemeanor punishable by up to one year of imprisonment and a $25,000 fine.

(b) Violation of this statute constitutes a felony punishable by up to two years of imprisonment and a $50,000 fine if:

   (1) the threat causes the occupants of the building, place of assembly, or public transportation facility to be diverted from their normal or customary operations; or

   (2) the threat involves the use of a biological agent.

(a) George enters a grocery store and walks within a few feet of a store employee who is stocking shelves to ask her a question. The employee asks George not to stand so close to her. George responds by stepping even closer to the employee, coughing, and then laughingly telling her he has the coronavirus. Has George violated the statute? If so, is the violation a misdemeanor or a felony?

(b) Margaret enters a grocery store intending to shoplift a twelve-pack of her favorite beer. When she nears the fresh fruit and produce section, she deliberately begins to cough and spit onto the fruit and produce on display. While doing so, she shouts out that she has the coronavirus. Panic in the store ensues, with many customers and some employees fleeing from the market. Amid the chaos, Margaret picks up the twelve-pack and walks out of the store. A store employee follows her and writes down her license plate number as she drives away. Margaret is soon under arrest. It turns out she is not infected by the coronavirus. However, because they did not know at the time of the incident whether Margaret did or did not in fact have the virus, the store's owners had to dispose of $35,000 worth of food. Has Margaret violated the statute? If so, is the violation a misdemeanor or a felony?

(c) Cody enters a pharmacy, walks up to the shelves where deodorants are on display, and begins slowly and methodically to lick the deodorant containers. While doing so, he records a cellphone video of himself licking the containers, at the end of which he asks "Who's scared of coronavirus?" He then posts the video on the internet using various social media sites. The local police receive complaints from local residents, as well as from people in other parts of the United States, the Netherlands, Ireland, and the United Kingdom. Has Cody violated the statute? If so, is the violation a misdemeanor or a felony?

3.7 Ryan is 16 years old and a sophomore in high school. His girlfriend, Theresa, is a 15-year-old high school freshman. Ryan and Theresa have been physically intimate for several months and recently began having sexual intercourse. With her cell phone, Theresa takes a sexually suggestive nude picture of herself and sends it via text messaging to Ryan. Ryan then reciprocates by using his cell phone to take a similarly sexually suggestive nude photo of himself and then text messaging it to Theresa. Ryan and Theresa each tell a few close friends about their exchange of photos, but neither one shows or sends the photographs to anyone else. A teacher overhears one of these conversations and the school principal confiscates both Ryan's and Theresa's cell phones and turns them over to the local police, who find the photos on both phones. Both Ryan and Theresa are now charged with distribution of child pornography under the following statute:

It is a felony to distribute a pornographic photo image of a child. A "child" under this statute is any person 16 years of age or younger. A pornographic image is one that reveals the private body parts of a child in a sexually suggestive manner.

Both Ryan's lawyer and Theresa's lawyer make a joint motion before trial to dismiss the charges against them on the ground that their conduct does not fall within the statute. The trial judge holds a hearing on whether or not to grant the motion. What arguments can be made for and against dismissal? Assume that the photos of Ryan and Theresa qualify as pornographic photo images of a child under the statute. Assume also that this statute was enacted in 1975, decades before modern cell phones were created and widely used by consumers and decades before text messaging was offered in connection with cell phones.

3.8 You are a judge in a city near Mountain View Park, a state park containing several tracts designated as "wilderness areas." In 1964, when the state legislature created wilderness areas, it passed the following statute:

> Use of any motorized vehicle or mechanical transport within any part of a State Park designated as a wilderness area is hereby prohibited. Any person violating this provision is subject to a $1,000 fine and/or 3 months imprisonment.

When the legislature enacted this statute, mountain bikes—bicycles built to climb mountain trails using fat tires with chunky treads—had not been invented. In the past few years, though, mountain bikes have become popular in the park, including its wilderness areas. In response to complaints from hikers and environmental groups, the State Department of Parks and Recreation recently banned mountain bikes from wilderness areas on the ground that a mountain bike is "mechanical transport" under the above statute.

Keith is an avid mountain biker and owner of a mountain bike shop located near the Park. To protest the State's mountain bike ban, Keith and a group of fellow mountain bikers rode their mountain bikes into a wilderness area where they were cited by a Park Ranger for violation of the statute. You are assigned as the trial judge in Keith's case. In a pretrial motion, Keith's attorney argues that the statute under which Keith has been charged does not apply to mountain bikes. How would you rule?

In making your ruling, consider the following:

(a) Prior to being designated as wilderness areas, hiking, horseback riding, cross country skiing, as well as the canoeing were common in these park lands. The legislative history indicates that the legislature was aware of these uses at the time it passed the statute and indicates no purpose to ban these uses.

(b) Mountain bikers claim that they do less damage to wilderness areas than hikers or horses. Hikers typically drive to a trailhead, requiring the establishment of parking areas and restrooms. Horses are heavier than mountain bikes and therefore have greater impact on trails. Both hikers and horseback riders regularly camp overnight in wilderness areas, requiring the establishment of camping areas and resulting in greater impact from fire rings, trash, and human waste. Mountain bikers rarely camp in a wilderness area.

(c) Participation nationally in mountain biking has increased in the past five years to a figure of 7.1 million people.

(d) The Park Service has also banned hang gliders and backcountry skateboards from wilderness areas under the statute.

3.9 Consider the following statute:

It is unlawful for any person to sell or transfer to a minor any firearm, pistol, Springfield rifle or other repeating rifle, bowie knife or dirk, brass knuckles, slingshot, or electric weapon or device. A person who violates this section commits a felony of the second degree.

(a) Lonnie is arrested and charged with selling aluminum knuckles to a minor. Is he liable under the statute? Would your answer differ if the legislature had added the words "or other" just before the word "knuckles"? Would it be significant if the legislative history revealed that the legislature considered substituting "metal" for "brass" but chose not to do so?

(b) Theresa runs a small fashion boutique selling trendy women's clothes and accessories. One item she brought back from a recent trip to an out-of-state fashion show is called the "brass knuckles" handbag. It is made of snakeskin with a handle of brass knuckles and described as "a hard-rock mix of sophistication and street style." Theresa sells one such handbag to a minor. Is she liable under the statute?

3.10 Sean was recently arrested for engaging in what has come to be known as "upskirting." Sean surreptitiously approached two different women who were working at a shopping mall. While standing behind each woman and holding his cell phone's camera below his waist level, he reached his camera beneath each woman's skirt, pointed it upward and snapped a photograph. After he was arrested, police retrieved photos on Sean's cell phone camera that revealed the undergarments of each woman. Although of relatively recent origin, upskirting has become a growing problem across the United States, with websites devoted to posting and disseminating photos and videos of unsuspecting women on the

Internet. Some states have adopted statutes specifically addressing and criminalizing upskirting. But the legislature in the state in which Sean is being prosecuted has not adopted such a statute. Sean is charged under the following statute:

> A person commits the crime of voyeurism if, for the purpose of arousing or gratifying the sexual desire of any person, he or she knowingly views, photographs, or films another person, without that person's knowledge and consent, in a place where he or she would have a reasonable expectation of privacy.

The statute defines "place where he or she would have a reasonable expectation of privacy" as:

> (i) A place where a reasonable person would believe that he or she could disrobe in privacy, without being concerned that his or her undressing was being photographed or filmed by another; or

> (ii) A place where one may reasonably expect to be safe from casual or hostile intrusion or surveillance

Sean's lawyer files a motion to dismiss on the ground that his conduct does not fall within this statute. What arguments can be made on Sean's behalf? What arguments can be made by the prosecution? If you were the judge, which way would you rule?

1. Intentionalism

As you will see in the court opinions you read in this course and other courses, intentionalism, the subject of this subsection, is by far the predominant method of interpretation used by state and federal judges in the United States.

Church of the Holy Trinity v. United States

143 U.S. 457 (1892)
United States Supreme Court

Brewer, J.

Plaintiff in error is a corporation duly organized and incorporated as a religious society under the laws of the state of New York. E. Walpole Warren was, prior to September, 1887, an alien residing in England. In that month the plaintiff in error made a contract with him, by which he was to remove to the city of New York, and enter into its service as rector and pastor; and, in pursuance of such contract, Warren did so remove and enter upon such service. It is claimed by the United States that this contract on the part of the plaintiff in error was forbidden by [the statute below]; and an action was commenced to recover the penalty prescribed by that act. The circuit court held that the contract was within the prohibition of the statute, and rendered judgment accordingly, and the single question presented for our determination is whether it erred in that conclusion.

The first section describes the act forbidden, and is in these words:

> Be it enacted by the senate and house of representatives of the United States of America, in congress assembled, that from and after the passage of this act it shall be unlawful for any person, company, partnership, or corporation, in any manner whatsoever, to prepay the transportation, or in any way assist or encourage the importation or migration, of any alien or aliens, any foreigner or foreigners, into the United States, its territories, or the District of Columbia, under contract or agreement, parole or special, express or implied, made previous to the importation or migration of such alien or aliens, foreigner or foreigners, to perform labor or service of any kind in the United States, its territories, or the District of Columbia.

It must be conceded that the act of the corporation is within the letter of this section, for the relation of rector to his church is one of service, and implies labor on the one side with compensation on the other. Not only are the general words 'labor' and 'service' both used, but also, as it were to guard against any narrow interpretation and emphasize a breadth of meaning, to them is added 'of any kind;' and, further, as noticed by the circuit judge in his opinion, the fifth section, which makes specific exceptions, among them professional actors, artists, lecturers, singers, and domestic servants, strengthens the idea that every other kind of labor and service was intended to be reached by the first section. While there is great force to this reasoning, we cannot think congress intended to denounce with penalties a transaction like that in the present case. It is a familiar rule that a thing may be within the letter of the statute and yet not within the statute, because not within its spirit nor within the intention of its makers. This has been often asserted, and the Reports are full of cases illustrating its application. This is not the substitution of the will of the judge for that of the legislator; for frequently words of general meaning are used in a statute, words broad enough to include an act in question, and yet a consideration of the whole legislation, or of the circumstances surrounding its enactment, or of the absurd results which follow from giving such broad meaning to the words, makes it unreasonable to believe that the legislator intended to include the particular act....

In *U.S. v. Kirby* ... the defendants were indicted for the violation of an act of congress providing 'that if any person shall knowingly and willfully obstruct or retard the passage of the mail, or of any driver or carrier, or of any horse or carriage carrying the same, he shall, upon conviction, for every such offense, pay a fine not exceeding one hundred dollars.' The specific charge was that the defendants knowingly and willfully retarded the passage of one Farris, a carrier of the mail, while engaged in the performance of his duty, and also in like manner retarded the steamboat Gen. Buell, at that time engaged in carrying the mail. To this indictment the defendants pleaded specially that Farris had been indicted for murder by a court of competent authority in Kentucky; that a bench-warrant had been issued and placed in the hands of the defendant Kirby, the sheriff of the county, commanding him to arrest Farris, and bring him before the court to answer to the indictment; and that, in obedience to this warrant, he and the other defendants, as his posse, entered upon the steamboat Gen. Buell and arrested Farris, and used only such force as was necessary to accomplish that arrest. The question as to the sufficiency of this plea was certified to this court, and it was held that the arrest of Farris upon the warrant from the state court was not an obstruction of the mail, or the retarding of the passage of a carrier of the mail, within the meaning of the act. In its opinion the court says: 'All laws should receive a sensible construction. General terms should be so limited in their application as not to lead to injustice, oppression, or an absurd consequence. It will always, therefore, be presumed that the legislature intended exceptions to its language which would avoid results of this character. The reason of the law in such cases should prevail over its letter.

The common sense of man approves the judgment mentioned by Puffendorf, that the Bolognian law which enacted 'that whoever drew blood in the streets should be punished with the utmost severity,' did not extend to the surgeon who opened the vein of a person that fell down in the street in a fit. The same common sense accepts the ruling, cited by Plowden, that the statute … which enacts that a prisoner who breaks prison shall be guilty of felony, does not extend to a prisoner who breaks out when the prison is on fire, 'for he is not to be hanged because he would not stay to be burnt.' …

Among other things which may be considered in determining the intent of the legislature is the title of the act. We do not mean that it may be used to add to or take from the body of the statute, but it may help to interpret its meaning…."Where the intent is plain, nothing is left to construction. Where the mind labors to discover the design of the legislature, it seizes everything from which aid can be derived; and in such case the title claims a degree of notice, and will have its due share of consideration." …

Now, the title of this act is, "An act to prohibit the importation and migration of foreigners and aliens under contract or agreement to perform labor in the United States, its territories, and the District of Columbia." Obviously the thought expressed in this reaches only to the work of the manual laborer, as distinguished from that of the professional man. No one reading such a title would suppose that congress had in its mind any purpose of staying the coming into this country of ministers of the gospel, or, indeed, of any class whose toil is that of the brain. The common understanding of the terms 'labor' and 'laborers' does not include preaching and preachers, and it is to be assumed that words and phrases are used in their ordinary meaning. So whatever of light is thrown upon the statute by the language of the title indicates an exclusion from its penal provisions of all contracts for the employment of ministers, rectors, and pastors.

Again, another guide to the meaning of a statute is found in the evil which it is designed to remedy; and for this the court properly looks at contemporaneous events, the situation as it existed, and as it was pressed upon the attention of the legislative body….

The situation which called for this statute was briefly but fully stated by Mr. Justice Brown when, as district judge, he decided the case of *U.S. v. Craig*: 'The motives and history of the act are matters of common knowledge. It had become the practice for large capitalists in this country to contract with their agents abroad for the shipment of great numbers of an ignorant and servile class of foreign laborers, under contracts by which the employer agreed, upon the one hand, to prepay their passage, while, upon the other hand, the laborers agreed to work after their arrival for a certain time at a low rate of wages. The effect of this was to break down the labor market, and to reduce other laborers engaged in like occupations to the level of the assisted immigrant. The evil finally became so flagrant that an appeal was made to congress for relief by the passage of the act in question, the design of which was to raise the standard of foreign immigrants, and to discountenance the migration of those who had not sufficient means in their own hands, or those of their friends, to pay their passage.'

It appears, also, from the petitions, and in the testimony presented before the committees of congress, that it was this cheap, unskilled labor which was making the trouble, and the influx of which congress sought to prevent. It was never suggested that we had in this country a surplus of brain toilers, and, least of all, that the market for the services of Christian ministers was depressed by foreign competition. Those were matters to which the attention of congress, or of the people, was not directed. So far, then, as the evil which was sought to be remedied interprets the statute, it also guides to an exclusion of this contract from the penalties of the act.

A singular circumstance, throwing light upon the intent of congress, is found in this extract from the report of the senate committee on education and labor, recommending the passage of the bill: "The general facts and considerations which induce the committee to recommend the passage of this bill are set forth in the report of the committee of the house. The committee report the bill back without amendment, although there are certain features thereof which might well be changed or modified, in the hope that the bill may not fail of passage during the present session. Especially would the committee have otherwise recommended amendments, substituting for the expression, 'labor and service,' whenever it occurs in the body of the bill, the words 'manual labor' or 'manual service,' as sufficiently broad to accomplish the purposes of the bill, and that such amendments would remove objections which a sharp and perhaps unfriendly criticism may urge to the proposed legislation. The committee, however, believing that the bill in its present form will be construed as including only those whose labor or service is manual in character, and being very desirous that the bill become a law before the adjournment, have reported the bill without change." And, referring back to the report of the committee of the house, there appears this language: "It seeks to restrain and prohibit the immigration or importation of laborers who would have never seen our shores but for the inducements and allurements of men whose only object is to obtain labor at the lowest possible rate, regardless of the social and material well-being of our own citizens, and regardless of the evil consequences which result to American laborers from such immigration." ...

We find, therefore, that the title of the act, the evil which was intended to be remedied, the circumstances surrounding the appeal to congress, the reports of the committee of each house, all concur in affirming that the intent of congress was simply to stay the influx of this cheap, unskilled labor.

But, beyond all these matters, no purpose of action against religion can be imputed to any legislation, state or national, because this is a religious people. This is historically true. From the discovery of this continent to the present hour, there is a single voice making this affirmation....

Suppose, in the congress that passed this act, some member had offered a bill which in terms declared that, if any Roman Catholic church in this country should contract with Cardinal Manning to come to this country, and enter into its service as pastor and priest, or any Episcopal church should enter into a like contract with Canon Farrar, or any Baptist church should make similar arrangements with Rev. Mr. Spurgeon, or any Jewish synagogue with some eminent rabbi, such contract should be adjudged unlawful and void, and the church making it be subject to prosecution and punishment. Can it be believed that it would have received a minute of approving thought or a single vote? Yet it is contended that such was, in effect, the meaning of this statute. The construction invoked cannot be accepted as correct. It is a case where there was presented a definite evil, in view of which the legislature used general terms with the purpose of reaching all phases of that evil; and thereafter, unexpectedly, it is developed that the general language thus employed is broad enough to reach cases and acts which the whole history and life of the country affirm could not have been intentionally legislated against. It is the duty of the courts, under those circumstances, to say that, however broad the language of the statute may be, the act, although within the letter, is not within the intention of the legislature, and therefore cannot be within the statute.

The judgment will be reversed, and the case remanded for further proceedings in accordance with this opinion.

2. Textualism

Textualism, as explained and defended by Justice Scalia below, is an approach to statutory interpretation that, at least in theory, relies *solely* on the text of the statute, i.e., the words the legislature used. As you will see in the court opinions you read in this and other courses, very few judges adopt a textualist approach. As you saw in the *Holy Trinity* case, above, judges who adopt an intentionalist stance when interpreting a statute also take into account the language of the statute at issue. A key difference between textualism and intentionalism is that textualism makes use of *only statutory language* while intentionalism uses statutory language *in addition to other interpretive resources such as legislative history.*

A Matter of Interpretation 16–37 (1997)

Antonin Scalia

"INTENT OF THE LEGISLATURE"

... You will find it frequently said in judicial opinions of my court and others that the judge's objective in interpreting a statute is to give effect to "the intent of the legislature." This principle, in one form or another, goes back at least as far as Blackstone.... I think, that it is simply incompatible with democratic government, or indeed, even with fair government, to have the meaning of a law determined by what the lawgiver meant, rather than by what the lawgiver promulgated.... It is the *law* that governs, not the intent of the lawgiver. That seems to me the essence of the famous American ideal set forth in the Massachusetts constitution: A government of laws, not of men. Men may intend what they will; but it is only the laws that they enact which bind us.

In reality, however, if one accepts the principle that the object of judicial interpretation is to determine the intent of the legislature, being bound by genuine but unexpressed legislative intent rather than the law is only the *theoretical* threat. The *practical* threat is that, under the guise or even the self-delusion of pursuing unexpressed legislative intents, common-law judges will in fact pursue their own objectives and desires, extending their lawmaking proclivities from the common law to the statutory field. When you are told to decide, not on the basis of what the legislature said, but on the basis of what it *meant,* and are assured that there is no necessary connection between the two, your best shot at figuring out what the legislature meant is to ask yourself what a wise and intelligent person *should* have meant; and that will surely bring you to the conclusion that the law means what you think it *ought* to mean—which is precisely how judges decide things under the common law. As Dean Landis of Harvard Law School (a believer in the search for legislative intent) put it in a 1930 article:

> [T]he gravest sins are perpetrated in the name of the intent of the legislature. Judges are rarely willing to admit their role as actual lawgivers, and such admissions as are wrung from their unwilling lips lie in the field of common and not statute law....

CHURCH OF THE HOLY TRINITY

To give some concrete form to the danger I warn against, let me describe what I consider to be the prototypical case involving the triumph of supposed "legislative intent" (a handy cover for judicial intent) over the text of the law. It is called *Church of the Holy Trinity v. United States* and was decided by the Supreme Court of the United States in 1892. The Church of the Holy Trinity, located in New York City, contracted with an Englishman to come over to be its rector and pastor. The United States claimed that this agreement violated a federal statute that made it unlawful for any person to "in any way assist or encourage the importation or migration of any alien ... into the United States ... under contract or agreement ... made previous to the importation or migration of such alien ... to perform labor or service of any kind in the United States...."

... The Court proceeds to conclude from various extratextual indications, including even a snippet of legislative history (highly unusual in those days), that the statute was intended to apply only to manual labor—which renders the exceptions for actors, artists, lecturers, and singers utterly inexplicable.... That being so, it says, "[t]he construction invoked [by the prosecution] cannot be accepted as correct." It concludes:

> It is a case where there was presented a definite evil, in view of which the legislature used general terms with the purpose of reaching all phases of that evil, and thereafter, unexpectedly, it is developed that the general language thus employed is broad enough to reach cases and acts which the whole history and life of the country affirm could not have been intentionally legislated against. It is the duty of the courts, under those circumstances, to say that, however broad the language of the statute may be, the act, although within the letter, is not within the intention of the legislature, and therefore cannot be within the statute.

Well of course I think that the act was within the letter of the statute, and was therefore within the statute: end of case. Congress can enact foolish statutes as well as wise ones, and it is not for the courts to decide which is which and rewrite the former. I acknowledge an interpretative doctrine of what the old writers call lapsus linguae (slip of the tongue), and what our modern cases call "scrivener's error," where on the very face of the statute it is clear to the reader that a mistake of expression (rather than of legislative wisdom) has been made. For example, a statute may say "defendant" when only "criminal defendant" (i.e., not "civil defendant") makes sense. The objective import of such a statute is clear enough, and I think it not contrary to sound principles of interpretation, in such extreme cases, to give the totality of context precedence over a single word. But to say that the legislature obviously misspoke is worlds away from saying that the legislature obviously overlegislated. *Church of the Holy Trinity* is cited to us whenever counsel wants us to ignore the narrow, deadening text of the statute, and pay attention to the life-giving legislative intent. It is nothing but an invitation to judicial lawmaking.

There are more sophisticated routes to judicial lawmaking than reliance upon unexpressed legislative intent, but they will not often be found in judicial opinions because they are too obvious a usurpation. Calling the court's desires "unexpressed legislative intent" makes everything seem all right....

[A] modern and forthright approach to according courts the power to revise statutes is set forth in Professor Eskridge's recent book, *Dynamic Statutory Interpretation*. The essence of it is acceptance of the proposition that it is proper for the judge who applies a statute to consider "not only what the statute means abstractly, or even on the basis of legislative history, but also what it ought to mean in terms of the needs and goals of our present day society." The law means what it ought to mean.

I agree ... that many decisions can be cited which, by subterfuge, accomplish precisely what ... Eskridge and other honest nontextualists propose. As I have said, "legislative intent" divorced from text is one of those subterfuges; and as I have described,

Church of the Holy Trinity is one of those cases. What I think is needed, however, is not rationalization of this process but abandonment of it. It is simply not compatible with democratic theory that laws mean whatever they ought to mean, and that un-elected judges decide what that is.

It may well be that the statutory interpretation adopted by the Court in *Church of the Holy Trinity* produced a desirable result; and it may even be (though I doubt it) that it produced the unexpressed result actually intended by Congress, rather than merely the one desired by the Court. Regardless, the decision was wrong because it failed to follow the text. The text is the law, and it is the text that must be observed....

TEXTUALISM

The philosophy of interpretation I have described above is known as textualism. In some sophisticated circles, it is considered simpleminded—"wooden," "unimag-inative," "pedestrian." It is none of that. To be a textualist in good standing, one need not be too dull to perceive the broader social purposes that a statute is designed, or could be designed, to serve; or too hidebound to realize that new times require new laws. One need only hold the belief that judges have no authority to pursue those broader purposes or write those new laws.

Textualism should not be confused with so-called strict constructionism, a degraded form of textualism that brings the whole philosophy into disrepute. I am not a strict constructionist, and no one ought to be—though better that, I suppose, than a non-textualist. A text should not be construed strictly, and it should not be construed le-niently; it should be construed reasonably, to contain all that it fairly means....

LEGISLATIVE HISTORY

Let me turn now ... to an interpretive device whose widespread use is relatively new: legislative history, by which I mean the statements made in the floor debates, committee reports, and even committee testimony, leading up to the enactment of the legislation. My view that the objective indication of the words, rather than the intent of the legislature, is what constitutes the law leads me, of course, to the con-clusion that legislative history should not be used as an authoritative indication of a statute's meaning. This was the traditional English, and the traditional American, practice. Chief Justice Taney wrote:

> In expounding this law, the judgment of the court cannot, in any degree, be influenced by the construction placed upon it by individual members of Congress in the debate which took place on its passage, nor by the motives or reasons assigned by them for supporting or opposing amendments that were offered. The law as it passed is the will of the majority of both houses, *and the only mode in which that will is spoken is in the act itself;* and we must gather their intention from the language there used, comparing it, when any ambiguity exists, with the laws upon the same subject, and looking, if nec-essary, to the public history of the times in which it was passed.[40]

---

40. Aldridge v. Williams, 44 U.S. (3 How.) 9, 24 (1985) (emphasis added).

That uncompromising view generally prevailed in this country until the present century. The movement to change it gained momentum in the late 1920s and 1930s, driven, believe it or not, by frustration with common-law judges' use of "legislative intent" and phonied-up canons to impose their own views—in those days views opposed to progressive social legislation. I quoted earlier an article by Dean Landis inveighing against such judicial usurpation. The solution he proposed was not the banishment of legislative intent as an interpretive criterion, but rather the use of legislative history to place that intent beyond manipulation....

In the past few decades, however, we have developed a legal culture in which lawyers routinely—and I do mean routinely—make no distinction between words in the text of a statute and words in its legislative history. My Court is frequently told, in briefs and in oral argument, that "Congress said thus-and-so" when in fact what is being quoted is not the law promulgated by Congress, nor even any text endorsed by a single house of Congress, but rather the statement of a single committee of a single house, set forth in a committee report. Resort to legislative history has become so common that lawyerly wags have popularized a humorous quip inverting the oft-recited (and oft-ignored) rule as to when its use is appropriate: "One should consult the text of the statute," the joke goes, "only when the legislative history is ambiguous." Alas, that is no longer funny. Reality has overtaken parody. A few terms ago, I read a brief that *began* the legal argument with a discussion of legislative history and then continued (I am quoting it verbatim): "Unfortunately, the legislative debates are not helpful. Thus, we turn to the other guidepost in this difficult area, statutory language."

As I have said, I object to the use of legislative history on principle, since I reject intent of the legislature as the proper criterion of the law. What is most exasperating about the use of legislative history, however, is that it does not even make sense for those who *accept* legislative intent as the criterion. It is much more likely to produce a false or contrived legislative intent than a genuine one. The first and most obvious reason for this is that, with respect to 99.99 percent of the issues of construction reaching the courts, there is no legislative intent, so that any clues provided by the legislative history are bound to be false. Those issues almost invariably involve points of relative detail, compared with the major sweep of the statute in question. That a majority of both houses of Congress (never mind the President, if he signed rather than vetoed the bill) entertained *any* view with regard to such issues is utterly beyond belief. For a virtual certainty, the majority was blissfully unaware of the *existence* of the issue, much less had any preference as to how it should be resolved.

But assuming, contrary to all reality, that the search for "legislative intent" is a search for something that exists, that something is not likely to be found in the archives of legislative history. In earlier days, when Congress had a smaller staff and enacted less legislation, it might have been possible to believe that a significant number of senators or representatives were present for the floor debate, or read the committee reports, and actually voted on the basis of what they heard or read. Those days, if they ever existed, are long gone. The floor is rarely crowded for a debate, the members generally being occupied with committee business and reporting to the floor only when a quorum call is demanded or a vote is to be taken. And as for committee reports, it is not even certain that the members of the issuing *committees* have found time to read them....

Ironically, but quite understandably, the more courts have relied upon legislative history, the less worthy of reliance it has become. In earlier days, it was at least genuine and not contrived—a real part of the legislation's *history*, in the sense that it was part of the *development* of the bill, part of the attempt to inform and persuade those who voted. Nowadays, however, when it is universally known and expected that judges will resort to floor debates and (especially) committee reports as authoritative expressions of "legislative intent," affecting the courts rather than informing the Congress has become the primary purpose of the exercise. It is less that the courts refer to legislative history because it exists than that legislative history exists because the courts refer to it. One of the routine tasks of the Washington lawyer-lobbyist is to draft language that sympathetic legislators can recite in a prewritten "floor debate"—or, even better, insert into a committee report....

Since there are no rules as to how much weight an element of legislative history is entitled to, it can usually be either relied upon or dismissed with equal plausibility. If the willful judge does not like the committee report, he will not follow it; he will call the statute not ambiguous enough, the committee report too ambiguous, or the legislative history (this is a favorite phrase) "as a whole, inconclusive." It is ordinarily very hard to demonstrate that this is false so convincingly as to produce embarrassment.... Legislative history provides, moreover, a uniquely broad playing field. In any major piece of legislation, the legislative history is extensive, and there is something for everybody....

I think it is time to call an end to a brief and failed experiment, if not for reasons of principle then for reasons of practicality.... The most immediate and tangible change the abandonment of legislative history would effect is this: Judges, lawyers, and clients will be saved an enormous amount of time and expense. When I was head of the Office of Legal Counsel in the Justice Department, I estimated that 60 percent of the time of the lawyers on my staff was expended finding, and poring over, the incunabula of legislative history. What a waste. We did not use to do it, and we should do it no more.

Discussion Questions

1. Justice Scalia argues that the text of a statute is the only legitimate source for determining what the law is. What if the text is ambiguous? Justice William A. Bablitch of the Wisconsin Supreme Court has written:

> ... *"That depends on what the meaning of the word 'is' is."* William Jefferson Clinton.... Language is inherently ambiguous—perhaps not as ambiguous as the quotation above would have us believe, but the quote makes a point: plain meaning is frequently in the eye of the beholder. What is plain to one may be ambiguous to another.[13]

---

13. *State v. Peters*, 263 Wis. 2d 475, 494–95 (2003) (Bablitch, J., concurring).

Do you agree that language is inherently ambiguous? If so, how does reliance on the text of a statute alone, as textualism dictates, provide adequate guidance to judges interpreting statutes?

2. How would a textualist interpret "human being" in the California murder statute in the context of the *Keeler* case? Justice Burke in his *Keeler* dissent argues that the words "human being ... need not be frozen in place as of any particular time." Would Justice Scalia agree? In other words, if the meaning of words in a statute, such as "human being," changes over time, should courts restrict the statute to the original meaning at the time the statute was enacted? Or should courts use the new meanings the words in the statute acquire over time?

3. What if application of the literal text of a statute to a particular situation would produce an absurd result? How might Justice Scalia respond to this question?

4. Which theory of interpretation puts fewer constraints on judges: intentionalism or textualism? Justice Aharon Barak has written that a judge "who holds that the purpose of the statute may be learned only from its language" has more discretion than a judge "who will seek guidance from every reliable source."[14] How might Justice Scalia respond to this claim?

On the Uses of Legislative History in Interpreting Statutes

Stephen Breyer
65 S. CAL. L. REV. 845 (1992)

INTRODUCTION

Until recently an appellate court trying to interpret unclear statutory language would have thought it natural, and often helpful, to refer to the statute's "legislative history." The judges might have examined congressional floor debates, committee reports, hearing testimony, and presidential messages in an effort to determine what Congress really "meant" by particular statutory language. Should courts refer to legislative history as they try to apply statutes correctly? Is this practice wise, helpful, or proper? Lawyers and judges, teachers and legislators, have begun to reexamine this venerable practice, often with a highly critical eye. Some have urged drastically curtailing, or even totally abandoning, its use. Some argue that courts use legislative history almost arbitrarily. Using legislative history, Judge Leventhal once said, is like "looking over a crowd and picking out your friends." Others maintain that it is constitutionally improper to look beyond a statute's language, or that searching for "congressional intent" is a semi-mystical exercise like hunting the snark....

I should like to defend the classical practice and convince you that those who attack it ought to claim victory once they have made judges more sensitive to problems of the abuse of legislative history; they ought not to condemn its use altogether. They should confine their attack to the outskirts and leave the citadel at peace....

---

14. AHARON BARAK, JUDICIAL DISCRETION 62 (1989).

I concede at the outset that my arguments are more pragmatic than theoretical. They rest upon two important assumptions. First, I assume that appellate courts are in part administrative institutions that aim to help resolve disputes and, while doing so, interpret, and thereby clarify, the law. Second, I assume that law itself is a human institution, serving basic human or societal needs. It is therefore properly subject to praise, or to criticism, in terms of certain pragmatic values, including both formal values, such as coherence and workability, and widely shared substantive values, such as helping to achieve justice by interpreting the law in accordance with the "reasonable expectations" of those to whom it applies. If you do not accept these assumptions, then I am unlikely to convince you of the legitimate role of legislative history in the judicial process. If you do accept them and if, through example, I can suggest to you that legislative history helps appellate courts reach interpretations that tend to make the law itself more coherent, workable, or fair, then I may convince you that courts should not abandon the practice.

THE CRITICISMS OF THE USE OF LEGISLATIVE HISTORY

... Although many of [the criticisms of the use of legislative history] have considerable logical and practical force, the question you should ask is whether they are strong enough to force us to abandon, or significantly to curtail, the often useful practice of looking to legislative history.... Why, of all the many tools judges use to help interpret unclear statutory language (context, tradition, custom, precedent, dictionary meanings, administrability, and so on), should they not use this one?

A. LACK OF UTILITY

The argument most frequently heard against the use of legislative history is that it does not help. Critics quote Justice Jackson's remark that "legislative history here, as usual, is more vague than the statute we are called upon to interpret." Again they will point to Judge Leventhal's comment that searching congressional documents for a statute's legislative history is like "looking over a crowd and picking out your friends." One can easily find examples of vague or conflicting legislative history. The critics do so, and they cite them.

This kind of argument is strongest when aimed at "misuse" of history. But, how strong a case can it make for abandonment? Logically, the argument is open to the response, "If the history is vague, or seriously conflicting, do not use it." No one claims that history is *always* useful; only that it *sometimes* helps.

Moreover, those who oppose the use of legislative history often illustrate their arguments with Supreme Court cases, for unlike lower courts, the Supreme Court frequently interprets statutory provisions arising out of serious political disagreement. The warring legislative parties, in such cases, often leave no legislative history stone unturned in their efforts to influence subsequent judicial interpretations.

Federal courts of appeals, however, consider many more cases each year, and many more less important cases, than does the Supreme Court. Indeed, they decide about nine thousand cases by written opinion, compared to about 150 in the Supreme Court. Their workload includes many unclear statutory provisions where lack of clarity does *not* reflect major political controversy. Such cases usually do not involve conflicting legislative history; in fact, the history itself often is clear enough to clarify the statute....

B. CONSTITUTIONAL ARGUMENTS

Two types of constitutional arguments are made against the use of legislative history. The first concerns the Constitution's requirements for enacting a law. A bill must pass both houses of Congress and obtain the President's signature or a veto override. The result, says the Constitution, is a statute; and that statute, not a floor speech or committee report or testimony or presidential message or congressional "intent," is the law. The use of legislative history, according to this argument, tends to make these other matters—report language and floor speeches—the "law" even though they had received neither a majority vote nor a presidential signature.

Second, the Constitution vests "legislative" power in a Congress made up of elected members. It does not vest legislative power in congressional staff or in lobbyists. Yet these unelected individuals write the floor statements, testimony, reports, and messages that make up legislative history. Indeed, the elected members may not even read these materials. Thus, to use legislative history not only makes "law" out of that which is not law, but also permits the exercise of legislative power by those who do not constitutionally possess it.

These arguments overstate their case. The "statute-is-the-only-law" argument misses the point. No one claims that legislative history is a statute, or even that, in any strong sense, it is "law." Rather, legislative history is helpful in trying to understand the meaning of the words that do make up the statute or the "law." A judge cannot interpret the words of an ambiguous statute without looking beyond its words for the words have simply ceased to provide univocal guidance to decide the case at hand. Can the judge, for example, ignore a dictionary or the historical interpretive practice of the agency that customarily applies some words? Is a dictionary or an historic agency interpretive practice "law?" It is "law" only in a weak sense that does not claim the status of a statute, and in a sense that violates neither the letter nor the spirit of the Constitution.

The delegation argument ("the Senator did not write, or even read, the report") is susceptible to the same type of criticism. After all, no one elected lexicographers or agency civil servants to Congress. The Constitution nowhere grants them legislative power. Yet, judges universally seek their help in resolving interpretive problems.

More importantly, this argument misunderstands how Congress works as an institution. The relevant point here is that nothing in the Constitution seems to prohibit Congress from using staff and relying upon groups and institutions in the way I have described. And, for purposes of establishing the legislator's personal responsibility, that description does not distinguish between different kinds of documents—between committee reports, floor statements, or statutory text. Rather, it holds the legislator personally responsible for the work of staff, and it correlates the legislator's direct personal involvement, not according to the kind of document, but according to the significance of the decision at issue. That is to say, the personal involvement of the individual legislator in the statute's text itself may or may not be greater than the legislator's involvement with report language or a floor statement. Involvement is a function of the importance of the substantive, procedural, or political *issue* facing the legislator, not of the "category" of the text that happens to embody that particular issue. It is not obvious that in the late twentieth century there is some better way to organize Congress's work. But regardless of the merits of this process, nothing about it makes a court's reference to legislative history seem *constitutionally* suspect....

The complex legislative process I have described relies heavily upon interactions of legislators, staff, and interest groups to create, review, criticize, and amend legislative language, reports, and floor statements. The process is reasonably open and fair so long as those whom the legislation will likely affect have roughly equal access to the legislative process. However, critics of the congressional process challenge this assumption strongly and often. Most critics concede that trade associations, labor unions, executive departments, and certain public interest groups, all under the watchful eye of the press, participate fully in the process on behalf of those they represent. But they ask several familiar questions. For example, are there not many disadvantaged groups who are excluded from the legislative process? Indeed, is the ordinary citizen adequately represented as a "typical citizen" rather than as a member of some organized interest group? Moreover, does ideology drive congressional staff more than the desire to reflect the will of the voter? Perhaps because we are all familiar with such criticism, my description of the legislative process did not fully dispel doubts about the legitimacy of the use of legislative history.

If these questions disturb you, then you might ask yourself whether judicial abandonment of the use of legislative history would make matters better or worse. Certainly abandonment would eliminate one factor that favors public hearings, public reports vetted by staff, and fairly detailed floor debates. It would also make it easier for legislators to justify amending legislation after it leaves committee, while it is on the floor of the House or Senate, or even while both Houses of Congress confer upon the bill after it passed each in different versions. To the extent that a change weakens the publicly accessible committee system and diminishes the need for public justification, it increases the power of the "special interests" (and here I use that term pejoratively) to secure legislation that is not in the "public interest." Thus, if judges abandon the use of legislative history, Congress will not necessarily produce better laws....

I did not dwell upon the problems of the legislative process, however, because my focus was the judiciary. I have simply argued that, viewed in light of the judiciary's important objective of helping to maintain coherent, workable statutory law, the case for abandoning the use of legislative history has not yet been made. Present practice has proved useful; the alternatives are not promising; radical change is too problematic. The "problem" of legislative history is its "abuse," not its "use." Care, not drastic change, is all that is warranted.

Discussion Questions

1. Justice Breyer does not contest that legislative history can be abused and at times has been abused by courts interpreting statutes. If so, why doesn't he recommend abandoning the use of legislative history?

2. Justice Breyer suggests that "judicial abandonment of the use of legislative history" might make the legislative process less open and fair. How so?

3. What do you think Justice Breyer means when he says that "[t]he warring legislative parties, in [cases involving serious political disagreement] often leave no legislative history stone unturned in their efforts to influence subsequent judicial interpretations"?

Problem

3.11 Look back at Problem 3.2, dealing with cameras in the jury room. Assume the jurisdiction in which that Problem occurs has the following statute:

No person shall be permitted to be with a jury while it is deliberating.

Assume also that the case has drawn notoriety and that a member of the state senate has introduced a bill currently being considered by the senate judiciary committee to amend this statute by adding the following language: "Nor shall any camera, microphone, or other recording device be permitted in a jury room while a jury is deliberating." How do you think Justice Brewer would interpret this statute to resolve Problem 3.2? How do you think Justice Scalia would interpret it? How would you interpret the statute?

---

3. Dynamic Statutory Interpretation

Dynamic statutory interpretation, the subject of this subsection, is an alternative to both textualism and intentionalism. Its primary advocate is Professor William Eskridge, the author of the following excerpt. Few, if any, judges openly adopt a dynamic approach to interpretation. But as you read judicial opinions in this and other courses, ask yourself whether some judges are in fact using a dynamic approach despite the fact that they say that they are adopting an intentionalist approach.

Dynamic Statutory Interpretation

William N. Eskridge, Jr.
135 U. Pa. L. Rev. 1479 (1987)

Federal judges interpreting the Constitution typically consider not only the constitutional text and its historical background, but also its subsequent interpretational history, related constitutional developments, and current societal facts. Similarly, judges interpreting common law precedents normally consider not only the text of the precedents and their historical context, but also their subsequent history, related legal developments, and current societal context. In light of this, it is odd that many judges and commentators believe judges should consider only the text and historical context when interpreting statutes, the third main source of law. Statutes, however, should—like the Constitution and the common law—be interpreted "dynamically," that is, in light of their present societal, political, and legal context.

Traditional doctrine teaches that statutes should not be interpreted dynamically. Prevailing approaches to statutory interpretation treat statutes as static texts. Thus, the leading treatise states that "[f]or the interpretation of statutes, 'intent of the legislature' is the criterion that is most often cited." This "intentionalist" approach asks how the legislature originally intended the interpretive question to be answered, or would have intended the question to be answered had it thought about the issue when it passed the statute. A "modified intentionalist" approach uses the original purpose of the statute as a surrogate for original intent, especially when the latter is uncertain; the proper interpretation is the one that best furthers the purpose the legislature had in mind when it enacted the statute.

Theoretically, these "originalist" approaches to statutory interpretation assume that the legislature fixes the meaning of a statute on the date the statute is enacted. The implicit claim is that a legislator interpreting the statute at the time of enactment would render the same interpretation as a judge interpreting the same statute fifty years later. This implication seems counterintuitive. Indeed, the legal realists argued this point earlier in the century. For example, gaps and ambiguities exist in all statutes, typically concerning matters as to which there was little legislative deliberation and, hence, no clear intent. As society changes, adapts to the statute, and generates new variations of the problem which gave rise to the statute, the unanticipated gaps and ambiguities proliferate. In such circumstances, it seems sensible that "the quest is not properly for the sense originally intended by the statute, [or] for the sense sought originally to be put into it, but rather for the sense which can be quarried out of it in the light of the new situation." Moreover, as time passes, the legal and constitutional context of the statute may change. Should not an interpreter "ask [her]self not only what the legislation means abstractly, or even on the basis of legislative history, but also what it ought to mean in terms of the needs and goals of our present day society[?]" …

The static vision of statutory interpretation prescribed by traditional doctrine is strikingly outdated. In practice, it imposes unrealistic burdens on judges, asking them to extract textual meaning that makes sense in the present from historical materials whose sense is often impossible to recreate faithfully. As doctrine, it is intellectually antediluvian, in light of recent developments in the philosophy of interpretation. Interpretation is not static, but dynamic. Interpretation is not an archeological discovery,[1] but a dialectical creation. Interpretation is not mere exegesis

---

1. Professor T. Alexander Aleinikoff suggested to me the idea that traditional statutory interpretation is like an archeological expedition. He compares the "archeological metaphor" with a "nautical metaphor," in which Congress turns the statute out to sea and leaves it to drift unpredictably.

to pinpoint historical meaning, but hermeneutics to apply that meaning to current problems and circumstances.

The dialectic of statutory interpretation is the process of understanding a text created in the past and applying it to a present problem. This process cannot be described simply as the recreation of past events and past expectations, for the "best" interpretation of a statute is typically the one that is most consonant with our current "web of beliefs" and policies surrounding the statute. That is, statutory interpretation involves the present-day interpreter's understanding and reconciliation of three different perspectives, no one of which will always control. These three perspectives relate to (1) the statutory text, which is the formal focus of interpretation and a constraint on the range of interpretive options available (textual perspective); (2) the original legislative expectations surrounding the statute's creation, including compromises reached (historical perspective); and (3) the subsequent evolution of the statute and its present context, especially the ways in which the societal and legal environment of the statute has materially changed over time (evolutive perspective).

Under dynamic statutory interpretation, the textual perspective is critical in many cases. The traditional understanding of the "rule of law" requires that statutes enacted by the majoritarian legislature be given effect, and that citizens have reasonable notice of the legal rules that govern their behavior. When the statutory text clearly answers the interpretive question, therefore, it normally will be the most important consideration. Exceptions, however, do exist because an apparently clear text can be rendered ambiguous by a demonstration of contrary legislative expectations or highly unreasonable consequences. The historical perspective is the next most important interpretive consideration; given the traditional assumptions that the legislature is the supreme lawmaking body in a democracy, the historical expectations of the enacting legislature are entitled to deference. Hence, when a clear text and supportive legislative history suggest the same answer, they typically will control.

The dynamic model, however, views the evolutive perspective as most important when the statutory text is not clear and the original legislative expectations have been overtaken by subsequent changes in society and law. In such cases, the pull of text and history will be slight, and the interpreter will find current policies and societal conditions most important. The hardest cases, obviously, are those in which a clear text or strong historical evidence or both, are inconsistent with compelling current values and policies....

The three perspectives implicated in dynamic interpretation ... suggest a continuum. In many cases, the text of the statute will provide determinate answers, though we should trust our reading of the text primarily when the statute is recent and the context of enactment represents considered legislative deliberation and decision on the interpretive issue. This is one end of the continuum: the text controls. At the opposite end of the continuum are those cases where neither the text nor the historical context of the statute clearly resolves the interpretive question, and the societal and legal context of the statute has changed materially. In those cases, the evolutive context controls. In general, the more detailed the text is, the greater weight the interpreter will give to textual considerations; the more recent the statute and the clearer the legislative expectations, the greater weight the interpreter will give to historical considerations; the more striking the changes in circumstances (changes in public values count more than factual changes in society), the greater weight the interpreter will give to evolutive considerations. The [dynamic] model very roughly reflects this continuum....

Historical scholarship suggests that our constitutional system of government was not meant to be one of rigid separation of powers or pure majoritarianism. Instead, the polity created by the Constitution requires a government that is deliberative and promotes the common good, at least on important matters. Judicial lawmaking from statutes has a constructive role to play in such a polity, especially in light of the tendency of the legislature to produce too little up-to-date public-seeking policy and not to produce well-integrated policies. The vision of a tripartite government and the legitimacy of the system are not served by a straitjacketed theory of statutory interpretation but are better served by a flexible approach that is sensitive to current policy concerns....

To a substantial extent, the metaphor of judge as cipher has been replaced with the vision of a creative lawmaker whose judgment in "hard" statutory cases, where the statutory text does not answer the question determinately, rests in large part on the judge's subjective views of the statute and the justice of the particular case. In 1920, Judge Benjamin Cardozo confessed that the nature of the judicial process is "uncertainty" rather than objective answers, and that "the process in its highest reaches is not discovery, but creation." Although Cardozo and his contemporaries usually spoke of judicial creativity in connection with the judge's common law powers, they clearly saw the judge's creative role extending to statutory interpretation as well.

Discussion Questions

1. What meaning would a judge using dynamic statutory interpretation give the words "human being" in the California murder statute in the context of the *Keeler* case? Would the dynamic view be receptive to Justice Burke's argument in his *Keeler* dissent that the words "human being ... need not be frozen in place as of any particular time"?

2. Which approaches to statutory interpretation do the majority and dissenting opinions in *Keeler* reflect?

Problem

3.12 In the following statutes, legislatures provide guidance to courts on how to interpret statutes. Do these statutes endorse an intentionalist, textualist, or dynamic approach? Or some combination of these? Do they agree or disagree with the *Holy Trinity* case?

Minnesota Statutes

§ 645.16 *Legislative intent controls*

The object of all interpretation and construction of laws is to ascertain and effectuate the intention of the legislature. Every law shall be construed, if possible, to give effect to all its provisions.

When the words of a law in their application to an existing situation are clear and free from all ambiguity, the letter of the law shall not be disregarded under the pretext of pursuing the spirit.

When the words of a law are not explicit, the intention of the legislature may be ascertained by considering, among other matters:

(1) The occasion and necessity for the law;

(2) The circumstances under which it was enacted;

(3) The mischief to be remedied;

(4) The object to be attained;

(5) The former law, if any, including other laws upon the same or similar subjects;

(6) The consequences of a particular interpretation;

(7) The contemporaneous legislative history; and

(8) Legislative and administrative interpretations of the statute.

§ 645.17 *Presumptions in ascertaining legislative intent*

In ascertaining the intention of the legislature the courts may be guided by the following presumptions:

(1) the legislature does not intend a result that is absurd, impossible of execution, or unreasonable;

(2) the legislature intends the entire statute to be effective and certain;

(3) the legislature does not intend to violate the constitution of the United States or of this state;

(4) when a court of last resort has construed the language of a law, the legislature in subsequent laws on the same subject matter intends the same construction to be placed upon such language; and

(5) the legislature intends to favor the public interest as against any private interest.

Iowa Code

§ 4.6 *Ambiguous statutes — interpretation*

If a statute is ambiguous, the court, in determining the intention of the legislature, may consider among other matters:

1. The object sought to be attained.

2. The circumstances under which the statute was enacted.

3. The legislative history.

4. The common law or former statutory provisions, including laws upon the same or similar subjects.

5. The consequences of a particular construction.

6. The administrative construction of the statute.

7. The preamble or statement of policy.

Texas Government Code

§ 311.023 *Statute Construction Aids*

In construing a statute, whether or not the statute is considered ambiguous on its face, a court may consider among other matters the:

(1) object sought to be attained;

(2) circumstances under which the statute was enacted;

(3) legislative history;

(4) common law or former statutory provisions, including laws on the same or similar subjects;

(5) consequences of a particular construction;

(6) administrative construction of the statute; and

(7) title (caption), preamble, and emergency provision.

E. Specificity

A System of Penal Law for the United States of America 2 (1828)

Edward Livingston

Penal laws should be written in plain language, clearly and unequivocally expressed, that they may neither be misunderstood nor perverted; they should be so concise, as to be remembered with ease; and all technical phrases, or words they contain, should be clearly defined. They should be promulgated in such a manner as to force a knowledge of their provisions upon the people; to this end, they should not only be published, but taught in the schools; and publicly read on stated occasions.

Discussion Questions

1. Livingston wants criminal statutes to be written in language that is plain, clear, and concise. This certainly seems like a good idea for a number of reasons examined in this Section. As you read the various statutes you encounter in this course, ask yourself if it is possible for a modern criminal code, covering topics as diverse as computer crime, child pornography, sexual offenses, and homicide, to be made plain, clear, and concise.

2. Livingston, writing in 1828, also suggests that criminal laws be taught in school and publicly read. Today these ideas may well strike you as quaint. But isn't public awareness of our criminal laws important for deterrence to work? Are there ways we could increase public awareness of those laws?

* * *

Gang violence and shootings have plagued Chicago for decades. In 1992, to combat gang violence and intimidation in some of its neighborhoods, Chicago enacted the following ordinance:

> (a) Whenever a police officer observes a person whom he reasonably believes to be a criminal street gang member loitering in any public place with one or more other persons, he shall order all such persons to disperse and remove themselves from the area. Any person who does not promptly obey such an order is in violation of this section.
>
> (b) It shall be an affirmative defense to an alleged violation of this section that no person who was observed loitering was in fact a member of a criminal street gang.
>
> (c) As used in this section:
>
>> (1) 'Loiter' means to remain in any one place with no apparent purpose.
>>
>> (2) 'Criminal street gang' means any ongoing organization, association in fact or group of three or more persons, whether formal or informal, having as one of its substantial activities the commission of one or more of the criminal acts enumerated in paragraph (3), and whose members individually or collectively engage in or have engaged in a pattern of criminal gang activity.
>>
>> ...
>>
>> (5) 'Public place' means the public way and any other location open to the public, whether publicly or privately owned.
>
> (e) Any person who violates this Section is subject to a fine of not less than $100 and not more than $500 for each offense, or imprisonment for not more than six months, or both.

Discussion Questions

If you were a Chicago city council member, would you have voted for or against this ordinance? What if you represented a poor neighborhood suffering from gang violence? What if you represented one of the more affluent neighborhoods in Chicago?

* * *

Jesus Morales, convicted under the ordinance, challenged his conviction on appeal and sought review in the United States Supreme Court.

City of Chicago v. Morales

527 U.S. 41 (1999)
United States Supreme Court

Justice Stevens announced the judgment of the Court and delivered the opinion of the Court with respect to Parts I, II, and V, and an opinion with respect to Parts III, IV, and VI, in which Justice Souter and Justice Ginsburg join.

I

Before the ordinance was adopted, the city council's Committee on Police and Fire conducted hearings to explore the problems created by the city's street gangs, and more particularly, the consequences of public loitering by gang members. Witnesses included residents of the neighborhoods where gang members are most active, as well as some of the aldermen who represent those areas. Based on that evidence, the council made a series of findings that are included in the text of the ordinance and explain the reasons for its enactment.

The council found that a continuing increase in criminal street gang activity was largely responsible for the city's rising murder rate, as well as an escalation of violent and drug related crimes. It noted that in many neighborhoods throughout the city, "the burgeoning presence of street gang members in public places has intimidated many law abiding citizens." Furthermore, the council stated that gang members "establish control over identifiable areas ... by loitering in those areas and intimidating others from entering those areas; and ... members of criminal street gangs avoid arrest by committing no offense punishable under existing laws when they know the police are present...." It further found that "loitering in public places by criminal street gang members creates a justifiable fear for the safety of persons and property in the area" and that "aggressive action is necessary to preserve the city's streets and other public places so that the public may use such places without fear." Moreover, the council concluded that the city "has an interest in discouraging all persons from loitering in public places with criminal gang members."

The ordinance creates a criminal offense punishable by a fine of up to $500, imprisonment for not more than six months, and a requirement to perform up to 120 hours of community service. Commission of the offense involves four predicates. First, the police officer must reasonably believe that at least one of the two or more persons present in a "public place" is a "criminal street gang member." Second, the persons must be "loitering," which the ordinance defines as "remaining in any one place with no apparent purpose." Third, the officer must then order "all" of the persons to disperse and remove themselves "from the area." Fourth, a person must disobey the officer's order. If any person, whether a gang member or not, disobeys the officer's order, that person is guilty of violating the ordinance.

Two months after the ordinance was adopted, the Chicago Police Department promulgated General Order 92-4 to provide guidelines to govern its enforcement. That order purported to establish limitations on the enforcement discretion of police officers "to ensure that the anti-gang loitering ordinance is not enforced in an arbitrary or discriminatory way." The limitations confine the authority to arrest gang members who violate the ordinance to sworn "members of the Gang Crime Section" and certain other designated officers, and establish detailed criteria for defining street gangs and membership in such gangs. In addition, the order directs district commanders to "designate areas in which the presence of gang members has a demonstrable effect on the activities of law abiding persons in the surrounding community," and provides that the ordinance "will be enforced only within the designated areas." The city, however, does not release the locations of these "designated areas" to the public.

II

During the three years of its enforcement, the police issued over 89,000 dispersal orders and arrested over 42,000 people for violating the ordinance....

The Illinois Supreme Court ... held "that the gang loitering ordinance violates due process of law in that it is impermissibly vague on its face and an arbitrary restriction on personal liberties." ...

III

The basic factual predicate for the city's ordinance is not in dispute. As the city argues in its brief, "the very presence of a large collection of obviously brazen, insistent, and lawless gang members and hangers-on on the public ways intimidates residents, who become afraid even to leave their homes and go about their business. That, in turn, imperils community residents' sense of safety and security, detracts from property values, and can ultimately destabilize entire neighborhoods." The findings in the ordinance explain that it was motivated by these concerns. We have no doubt that a law that directly prohibited such intimidating conduct would be constitutional, but this ordinance broadly covers a significant amount of additional activity. Uncertainty about the scope of that additional coverage provides the basis for respondents' claim that the ordinance is too vague.

We are confronted at the outset with the city's claim that it was improper for the state courts to conclude that the ordinance is invalid on its face. The city correctly points out that imprecise laws can be attacked on their face under two different doctrines. First, the overbreadth doctrine permits the facial invalidation of laws that inhibit the exercise of First Amendment rights if the impermissible applications of the law are substantial when "judged in relation to the statute's plainly legitimate sweep." Second, even if an enactment does not reach a substantial amount of constitutionally protected conduct, it may be impermissibly vague because it fails to establish standards for the police and public that are sufficient to guard against the arbitrary deprivation of liberty interests.

While we, like the Illinois courts, conclude that the ordinance is invalid on its face, we do not rely on the overbreadth doctrine. We agree with the city's submission that the law does not have a sufficiently substantial impact on conduct protected by the First Amendment to render it unconstitutional. The ordinance does not prohibit speech. Because the term "loiter" is defined as remaining in one place "with no apparent purpose," it is also clear that it does not prohibit any form of conduct that is apparently intended to convey a message. By its terms, the ordinance is inapplicable to assemblies that are designed to demonstrate a group's support of, or opposition to, a particular point of view. Its impact on the social contact between gang members and others does not impair the First Amendment "right of association" that our cases have recognized.

On the other hand, as the United States recognizes, the freedom to loiter for innocent purposes is part of the "liberty" protected by the Due Process Clause of the Fourteenth Amendment. We have expressly identified this "right to remove from one place to another according to inclination" as "an attribute of personal liberty" protected by the Constitution. Indeed, it is apparent that an individual's decision to remain in a public place of his choice is as much a part of his liberty as the freedom of movement inside frontiers that is "a part of our heritage" or the right to move "to whatsoever place one's own inclination may direct" identified in Blackstone's Commentaries. 1 W. Blackstone, Commentaries on the Laws of England 130 (1765).

There is no need, however, to decide whether the impact of the Chicago ordinance on constitutionally protected liberty alone would suffice to support a facial challenge under the overbreadth doctrine. For it is clear that the vagueness of this enactment makes a facial challenge appropriate. This is not an ordinance that "simply regulates business behavior and contains a scienter requirement." It is a criminal law that contains no *mens rea* requirement, and infringes on constitutionally protected rights. When vagueness permeates the text of such a law, it is subject to facial attack.

Vagueness may invalidate a criminal law for either of two independent reasons. First, it may fail to provide the kind of notice that will enable ordinary people to understand what conduct it prohibits; second, it may authorize and even encourage arbitrary and discriminatory enforcement. Accordingly, we first consider whether the ordinance provides fair notice to the citizen and then discuss its potential for arbitrary enforcement.

IV

"It is established that a law fails to meet the requirements of the Due Process Clause if it is so vague and standardless that it leaves the public uncertain as to the conduct it prohibits...." The Illinois Supreme Court recognized that the term "loiter" may have a common and accepted meaning, but the definition of that term in this ordinance—"to remain in any one place with no apparent purpose"—does not. It is difficult to imagine how any citizen of the city of Chicago standing in a public place with a group of people would know if he or she had an "apparent purpose." If she were talking to another person, would she have an apparent purpose? If she were frequently checking her watch and looking expectantly down the street, would she have an apparent purpose?

Since the city cannot conceivably have meant to criminalize each instance a citizen stands in public with a gang member, the vagueness that dooms this ordinance is not the product of uncertainty about the normal meaning of "loitering," but rather about what loitering is covered by the ordinance and what is not. The Illinois Supreme Court emphasized the law's failure to distinguish between innocent conduct and conduct threatening harm.[24] Its decision followed the precedent set by a number of state courts that have upheld ordinances that criminalize loitering combined with some other overt act or evidence of criminal intent. However, state courts have uniformly invalidated laws that do not join the term "loitering" with a second specific element of the crime.

The city's principal response to this concern about adequate notice is that loiterers are not subject to sanction until after they have failed to comply with an officer's order to disperse. "Whatever problem is created by a law that criminalizes conduct people normally believe to be innocent is solved when persons receive actual notice from a police order of what they are expected to do." We find this response unpersuasive for at least two reasons.

First, the purpose of the fair notice requirement is to enable the ordinary citizen to conform his or her conduct to the law. "No one may be required at peril of life, liberty or property to speculate as to the meaning of penal statutes." Although it is true that a loiterer is not subject to criminal sanctions unless he or she disobeys a dispersal order, the loitering is the conduct that the ordinance is designed to prohibit. If the loitering is in fact harmless and innocent, the dispersal order itself is an unjustified impairment of liberty. If the police are able to decide arbitrarily which members of the public they will order to disperse, then the Chicago ordinance becomes indistinguishable from the law we held invalid in *Shuttlesworth v. Birmingham*, 382 U.S. 87, 90, 15 L. Ed. 2d 176, 86 S. Ct. 211 (1965).[29] Because an officer may issue an order only after prohibited conduct has already occurred, it cannot provide the kind of advance notice that will protect the putative loiterer from being ordered to disperse. Such an order cannot retroactively give adequate warning of the boundary between the permissible and the impermissible applications of the law.

Second, the terms of the dispersal order compound the inadequacy of the notice afforded by the ordinance. It provides that the officer "shall order all such persons to disperse and remove themselves from the area." This vague phrasing raises a host of questions. After such an order issues, how long must the loiterers remain apart? How far must they move? If each loiterer walks around the block and they meet again

---

24. 177 Ill. 2d at 452, 687 N.E.2d at 61. One of the trial courts that invalidated the ordinance gave the following illustration: "Suppose a group of gang members were playing basketball in the park, while waiting for a drug delivery. Their apparent purpose is that they are in the park to play ball. The actual purpose is that they are waiting for drugs. Under this definition of loitering, a group of people innocently sitting in a park discussing their futures would be arrested, while the 'basketball players' awaiting a drug delivery would be left alone." Chicago v. Youkhana, Nos. 93 MCI 293363 et al. (Ill. Cir. Ct., Cook Cty., Sept. 29, 1993), reprinted in App. to Pet. for Cert. 45a.

29. "Literally read ... this ordinance says that a person may stand on a public sidewalk in Birmingham only at the whim of any police officer of that city. The constitutional vice of so broad a provision needs no demonstration." 382 U.S. 87 at 90.

at the same location, are they subject to arrest or merely to being ordered to disperse again? As we do here, we have found vagueness in a criminal statute exacerbated by the use of the standards of "neighborhood" and "locality." We remarked in *Connally* that "both terms are elastic and, dependent upon circumstances, may be equally satisfied by areas measured by rods or by miles."

Lack of clarity in the description of the loiterer's duty to obey a dispersal order might not render the ordinance unconstitutionally vague if the definition of the forbidden conduct were clear, but it does buttress our conclusion that the entire ordinance fails to give the ordinary citizen adequate notice of what is forbidden and what is permitted. The Constitution does not permit a legislature to "set a net large enough to catch all possible offenders, and leave it to the courts to step inside and say who could be rightfully detained, and who should be set at large." This ordinance is therefore vague "not in the sense that it requires a person to conform his conduct to an imprecise but comprehensible normative standard, but rather in the sense that no standard of conduct is specified at all."

V

The broad sweep of the ordinance also violates "'the requirement that a legislature establish minimal guidelines to govern law enforcement.'" There are no such guidelines in the ordinance. In any public place in the city of Chicago, persons who stand or sit in the company of a gang member may be ordered to disperse unless their purpose is apparent. The mandatory language in the enactment directs the police to issue an order without first making any inquiry about their possible purposes. It matters not whether the reason that a gang member and his father, for example, might loiter near Wrigley Field is to rob an unsuspecting fan or just to get a glimpse of Sammy Sosa leaving the ballpark; in either event, if their purpose is not apparent to a nearby police officer, she may—indeed, she "shall"—order them to disperse.

Recognizing that the ordinance does reach a substantial amount of innocent conduct, we turn, then, to its language to determine if it "necessarily entrusts lawmaking to the moment-to-moment judgment of the policeman on his beat." As we discussed in the context of fair notice, the principal source of the vast discretion conferred on the police in this case is the definition of loitering as "to remain in any one place with no apparent purpose."

As the Illinois Supreme Court interprets that definition, it "provides absolute discretion to police officers to determine what activities constitute loitering." We have no authority to construe the language of a state statute more narrowly than the construction given by that State's highest court. "The power to determine the meaning of a statute carries with it the power to prescribe its extent and limitations as well as the method by which they shall be determined."

Nevertheless, the city disputes the Illinois Supreme Court's interpretation, arguing that the text of the ordinance limits the officer's discretion in three ways. First, it does not permit the officer to issue a dispersal order to anyone who is moving along or who has an apparent purpose. Second, it does not permit an arrest if individuals obey a dispersal order. Third, no order can issue unless the officer reasonably believes that one of the loiterers is a member of a criminal street gang.

Even putting to one side our duty to defer to a state court's construction of the scope of a local enactment, we find each of these limitations insufficient. That the ordinance does not apply to people who are moving—that is, to activity that would not constitute loitering under any possible definition of the term—does not even address the question of how much discretion the police enjoy in deciding which stationary persons to disperse under the ordinance.[32] Similarly, that the ordinance does not permit an arrest until after a dispersal order has been disobeyed does not provide any guidance to the officer deciding whether such an order should issue. The "no apparent purpose" standard for making that decision is inherently subjective because its application depends on whether some purpose is "apparent" to the officer on the scene.

Presumably an officer would have discretion to treat some purposes—perhaps a purpose to engage in idle conversation or simply to enjoy a cool breeze on a warm evening—as too frivolous to be apparent if he suspected a different ulterior motive. Moreover, an officer conscious of the city council's reasons for enacting the ordinance might well ignore its text and issue a dispersal order, even though an illicit purpose is actually apparent.

It is true, as the city argues, that the requirement that the officer reasonably believe that a group of loiterers contains a gang member does place a limit on the authority to order dispersal. That limitation would no doubt be sufficient if the ordinance only applied to loitering that had an apparently harmful purpose or effect, or possibly if it only applied to loitering by persons reasonably believed to be criminal gang members. But this ordinance, for reasons that are not explained in the findings of the city council, requires no harmful purpose and applies to non-gang members as well as suspected gang members.[34] It applies to everyone in the city who may remain in one place with one suspected gang member as long as their purpose is not apparent to an officer observing them. Friends, relatives, teachers, counselors, or even total strangers might unwittingly engage in forbidden loitering if they happen to engage in idle conversation with a gang member.

---

32. It is possible to read the mandatory language of the ordinance and conclude that it affords the police no discretion, since it speaks with the mandatory "shall." However, not even the city makes this argument, which flies in the face of common sense that all police officers must use some discretion in deciding when and where to enforce city ordinances.

34. Not all of the respondents in this case, for example, are gang members. The city admits that it was unable to prove that Morales is a gang member but justifies his arrest and conviction by the fact that Morales admitted "that he knew he was with criminal street gang members." Reply Brief for Petitioner 23, n. 14. In fact, 34 of the 66 respondents in this case were charged in a document that only accused them of being in the presence of a gang member. Tr. of Oral Arg. 34, 58.

Ironically, the definition of loitering in the Chicago ordinance not only extends its scope to encompass harmless conduct, but also has the perverse consequence of excluding from its coverage much of the intimidating conduct that motivated its enactment. As the city council's findings demonstrate, the most harmful gang loitering is motivated either by an apparent purpose to publicize the gang's dominance of certain territory, thereby intimidating nonmembers, or by an equally apparent purpose to conceal ongoing commerce in illegal drugs. As the Illinois Supreme Court has not placed any limiting construction on the language in the ordinance, we must assume that the ordinance means what it says and that it has no application to loiterers whose purpose is apparent. The relative importance of its application to harmless loitering is magnified by its inapplicability to loitering that has an obviously threatening or illicit purpose.

Finally, in its opinion striking down the ordinance, the Illinois Supreme Court refused to accept the general order issued by the police department as a sufficient limitation on the "vast amount of discretion" granted to the police in its enforcement. We agree. That the police have adopted internal rules limiting their enforcement to certain designated areas in the city would not provide a defense to a loiterer who might be arrested elsewhere. Nor could a person who knowingly loitered with a well-known gang member anywhere in the city safely assume that they would not be ordered to disperse no matter how innocent and harmless their loitering might be.

VI

In our judgment, the Illinois Supreme Court correctly concluded that the ordinance does not provide sufficiently specific limits on the enforcement discretion of the police "to meet constitutional standards for definiteness and clarity." We recognize the serious and difficult problems testified to by the citizens of Chicago that led to the enactment of this ordinance. "We are mindful that the preservation of liberty depends in part on the maintenance of social order." However, in this instance the city has enacted an ordinance that affords too much discretion to the police and too little notice to citizens who wish to use the public streets.

Accordingly, the judgment of the Supreme Court of Illinois is affirmed.

Problem

3.13 You are the attorney for a city considering enacting the following as an ordinance. The city council asks you to: (1) provide an opinion about whether the proposed ordinance would be constitutionally valid; (2) review the constitutional strengths and weaknesses of the statute; (3) make suggestions for redrafting the ordinance to cure any constitutional weaknesses.

A person commits a violation if he loiters or prowls in a place, at a time, or in a manner not usual for law-abiding individuals under circumstances that warrant alarm for the safety of persons or property in the vicinity. Among the circumstances which may be considered in determining whether such alarm is warranted is the fact that the actor takes flight upon appearance of a peace officer, refuses to identify himself, or manifestly endeavors to conceal himself or any object. Unless flight by the actor or other circumstances makes it impracticable, a peace officer shall, prior to any arrest for an offense under this section, afford the actor an opportunity to dispel any alarm which would otherwise be warranted, by requesting him to identify himself and explain his presence and conduct. No person shall be convicted of an offense under this Section if the peace officer did not comply with the preceding sentence, or if it appears at trial that the explanation given by the actor was true and, if believed by the peace officer at the time, would have dispelled the alarm.

State v. Pomianek

221 N.J. 66 (2015)
Supreme Court of New Jersey

Justice Albin delivered the opinion of the Court.

Defendant David Pomianek, Jr., and co-defendant Michael Dorazo, Jr., were charged in a sixteen-count indictment with two counts of second-degree official misconduct; twelve counts of fourth-degree bias intimidation; and two counts of third-degree hindering apprehension or prosecution. The court denied defendant's pretrial motion to dismiss the bias-intimidation counts based on a constitutional challenge to the bias-intimidation statute....

The events relevant to this appeal occurred on April 4, 2007, in an old garage used for storage by the Gloucester Township Department of Public Works. A number of Public Works employees were assigned to the building that day, including defendant, Dorazo, and Steven Brodie, Jr. The three men worked in the Parks and Recreations Division. Defendant and Dorazo, who are Caucasian, worked as truck drivers. Brodie, who is African-American, worked as a laborer. The hierarchy in the Parks Division is supervisor, truck driver, and laborer.

Brodie testified that a number of the employees were horsing around in the building—throwing footballs and acting "out of control." In the building was a sixteen-foot long and eight-foot wide steel storage cage on a landing, thirteen steps above ground level. The cage was enclosed by a heavy chain-link fence on three sides and a cinder block wall on the fourth side and was secured by a sliding chain-link door with a padlock. According to Brodie, defendant was wrestling with a coworker in the storage cage. The coworker attempted to close the cage door on defendant, but defendant managed to slip through it.

Shortly afterwards, in a ruse, Dorazo approached Brodie and told him that their supervisor needed an item from the cage. Brodie dutifully walked up the steps into the cage and asked Dorazo, "Where is it?" Then, Dorazo shut the cage door, locking Brodie inside.

A number of Public Works Department employees began laughing, but Brodie found no humor in his predicament. At the time, defendant was sitting on a lawn-mower on the ground level of the garage. Brodie recalled defendant saying, "Oh, you see, you throw a banana in the cage and he goes right in," which triggered more laughter among the men, including defendant and Dorazo. Brodie considered the remark to be "racial" in nature. To Brodie, this was not a harmless caper; instead, he "was locked in a cage like an animal." From his perspective, the line about "throwing the banana in there" was like "being called a monkey in a cage." Brodie admitted, however, that he never heard defendant call him a monkey.

Brodie remained in the cage for three to five minutes until an employee unlocked the sliding door. Brodie felt humiliated and embarrassed. After his release, Brodie walked into the new Public Works building, followed by Dorazo, who said, "You all right, buddy? We were just joking around." Brodie replied, "Yeah, yeah, I'm fine."

Two Parks Division employees generally corroborated Brodie's account. One testified that defendant said, "You can throw a banana in a cage and lock a monkey in there," and the other remembered defendant calling out, "He looks like a monkey in a cage, let's throw him some bananas." The two witnesses maintained that defendant's voice could be heard from a distance but, as noted, Brodie did not hear the reference to "monkey."

Brodie also testified to another incident involving defendant and Dorazo that he believed had racial overtones. Several months earlier, an African-American laborer, Rashaan McDaniel, was vacuuming leaves on the street with a hose attached to a truck that Dorazo was driving. Brodie observed Dorazo give two bungee cords to defendant, who from behind began lightly "tapping" McDaniel on the shoulders with the cords. Brodie did not consider defendant's hijinks a joking matter. In Brodie's view, defendant was making a statement about "slavery because [there was] a black man working and he's getting whipped as he's working." No criminal charges arose from that incident.

At the conclusion of the trial, the jury acquitted defendant of all counts alleging that he falsely imprisoned or harassed Brodie either *with the purpose* to intimidate him or *knowing* that his conduct would cause Brodie to be intimidated because of his race, color, national origin, or ethnicity. In addition, defendant was acquitted of the lesser-included offense of false imprisonment.

Defendant, however, was found guilty of two fourth-degree bias-intimidation crimes, one for harassment by alarming conduct and the other for harassment by communication. N.J.S.A. 2C:16-1(a)(3). The jury reached its verdict based on two discrete findings: (1) the offenses were committed "under circumstances that caused Steven Brodie to be intimidated" and (2) considering the manner in which those offenses were committed, Brodie "*reasonably believed*" either that the offenses were "committed with a purpose to intimidate him" or that "he was selected to be the target because of his race, color, national origin, or ethnicity." The jury also convicted defendant of official misconduct, based in part on the finding that he committed the crime of bias intimidation. The jury was charged that it could not find defendant guilty of misconduct in office unless it first determined that he had committed a crime. The bias-intimidation convictions, therefore, were a necessary predicate to the misconduct-in-office verdict. Last, the jury convicted defendant of the petty disorderly persons' offenses of harassment by alarming conduct and harassment by communication.

The trial court sentenced defendant on the charge of second-degree official misconduct to a four-year probationary term, conditioned on defendant serving 270 days on weekends in the county jail. The court imposed the identical sentence on each of the bias-intimidation counts and imposed a thirty-day term on the harassment count. All of the sentences were made to run concurrent to one another. In addition, the court imposed statutorily required fines and penalties.

Defendant appealed.... The State rejects the notion that subsection (a)(3) is unconstitutionally vague "because it upgrades the predicate crime based on the victim's perception of the defendant's conduct." The State insists that the victim's objectively reasonable perception of the defendant's intent to intimidate on the basis of bias satisfies the mens rea requirement and gives fair notice for due process purposes. According to the State, the First and Fourteenth Amendments do not protect a defendant from his "subjective ignorance or indifference as a defense to bias intimidation."

Moreover, to the extent that subsection (a)(3) can be characterized as a "strict liability" statute, the State submits that it is no different than other statutes that criminalize activity based on attendant circumstances without regard to the defendant's mental state. One such strict-liability statute, according to the State, is N.J.S.A. 2C:35-7(a), which penalizes drug distribution within 1000 feet of a school zone, even when the defendant is unaware of his location....

... [D]efendant argues that N.J.S.A. 2C:16-1(a)(3), by focusing on what a "reasonable" victim believes is the defendant's motivation rather than on what the defendant actually intends, fails to give a person of reasonable intelligence fair notice of the conduct that is forbidden. Defendant maintains that the statute offends the Due Process Clause of the Fourteenth Amendment on vagueness grounds because "[a] defendant should not be obliged to guess whether his conduct is criminal." Defendant also contends that unlike such strict-liability statutes as the one enhancing criminal penalties for drug distribution within 1000 feet of a school-zone, where the boundary of a school zone is an objective fact, *N.J.S.A.* 2C:35-7(a), subsection (a)(3) criminalizes a defendant's conduct based on the victim's perception.

Amici, the Rutherford Institute, ACLU, and ACDL ... echo defendant's due process argument that N.J.S.A. 2C:16-1(a)(3) does not give fair notice of where the line is drawn for conduct that is proscribed because the victim's "belief will depend wholly upon the thoughts, memories or experiences of which [the defendant] almost certainly cannot know." Amici note that one of the purposes of the traditional scienter requirement is to give clear notice of acts that are criminal in nature. That notice is absent when criminality depends on whether the victim reasonably believes he was targeted on the basis of bias rather than on the defendant's subjective intent. Amici emphasize that a defendant "cannot control and may not even be aware of" the victim's beliefs and that "there is a real risk that bias will be reasonably perceived by a victim even where it does not exist."

The primary issue before us is one of constitutional interpretation — whether subsection (a)(3) of the bias-intimidation statute, N.J.S.A. 2C:16-1, violates the ... Due Process Clause of the Fourteenth Amendment of the United States Constitution. Because the issue is purely legal in nature, we owe no deference to either the trial court's or Appellate Division's conclusions of law. Our review therefore is de novo.

We begin with a discussion of the text and history of the bias-intimidation statute and then examine whether subsection (a)(3) satisfies the due process demands of the Fourteenth Amendment. We must answer whether the line separating lawful from criminal conduct in subsection (a)(3) is so vague that a reasonable person would not have fair notice when that line is crossed....

N.J.S.A. 2C:16-1 provides:

a. A person is guilty of the crime of bias intimidation if he commits, attempts to commit, conspires with another to commit, or threatens the immediate commission of an offense specified in chapters 11 through 18 of Title 2C of the New Jersey Statutes ...

(1) with a purpose to intimidate an individual or group of individuals because of race, color, religion, gender, disability, sexual orientation, gender identity or expression, national origin, or ethnicity; or

(2) knowing that the conduct constituting the offense would cause an individual or group of individuals to be intimidated because of race, color, religion, gender, disability, sexual orientation, gender identity or expression, national origin, or ethnicity; or

(3) under circumstances that caused any victim of the underlying offense to be intimidated and the victim, considering the manner in which the offense was committed, reasonably believed either that (a) the offense was committed with a purpose to intimidate the victim or any person or entity in whose welfare the victim is interested because of race, color, religion, gender, disability, sexual orientation, gender identity or expression, national origin, or ethnicity, or (b) the victim or the victim's property was selected to be the target of the offense because of the victim's race, color,

religion, gender, disability, sexual orientation, gender identity or expression, national origin, or ethnicity.

Generally, bias intimidation is punishable by a sentence one degree higher than the underlying crime that forms the basis for the bias-intimidation charge. In this case, the underlying charges were the petty disorderly persons' offenses of harassment by communication and alarming conduct. Harassment is punishable by a sentence not to exceed thirty days' imprisonment. However, when the victim of the harassment is subjected to bias intimidation, a fourth-degree crime has been committed and the crime is punishable by a sentence not to exceed eighteen months' imprisonment.

Under subsections (a)(1) and (a)(2), a defendant commits bias intimidation when he acts "with a purpose to intimidate" or with "knowledge" that his conduct will intimidate a person based on an immutable characteristic, such as a person's race or color. Those state-of-mind requirements are the traditional means of determining criminal liability. Unlike subsections (a)(1) and (a)(2), subsection (a)(3) focuses not on the state of mind of the accused, but rather on the victim's perception of the accused's motivation for committing the offense. Thus, if the victim *reasonably believed* that the defendant committed the offense of harassment with the purpose to intimidate or target him based on his race or color, the defendant is guilty of bias intimidation. Under subsection (a)(3), a defendant may be found guilty of bias intimidation even if he had no purpose to intimidate or knowledge that his conduct would intimidate a person because of his race or color. In other words, an innocent state of mind is not a defense to a subsection (a)(3) prosecution; the defendant is culpable for his words or conduct that led to the victim's reasonable perception even if that perception is mistaken.

Subsection (a)(3) was not part of New Jersey's original "hate crime" law. The original version provided for an extended term of imprisonment if, at sentencing, the trial judge found by a preponderance of evidence that "[t]he defendant in committing the crime acted *with a purpose to intimidate* an individual or group of individuals because of race, color, gender, handicap, religion, sexual orientation or ethnicity." The United States Supreme Court struck down that statute because it allowed the trial court to impose a sentence greater than the one authorized by the jury verdict in contravention of the Sixth Amendment right to trial by jury. [The] *Apprendi* [case] made clear that bias motivation in the sentence-enhancement provision was an element of the offense, disguised as a sentencing factor. Notably, N.J.S.A. 2C:44-3(e) hinged a sentence enhancement on a defendant's intent to intimidate, not on the victim's perception of defendant's motivation.

In response to *Apprendi*, the Legislature enacted N.J.S.A. 2C:16-1, the current bias-intimidation statute. The original bill sponsored in the Senate corrected the constitutional defect in N.J.S.A. 2C:44-3(e) and provided that the purpose to intimidate on the basis of bias would be treated as an element of the offense and tried to the jury. Later, a substitute bill was introduced that included the present version of section (a)(3), which unlike sections (a)(1) and (a)(2), contains no scienter requirement. The legislative history gives no insight into the Legislature's reason for including subsection (a)(3). The Senate Judiciary Committee and Assembly Judiciary Committee Statements ... explained that a "person would be guilty of bias intimidation *if the person commits any crime listed in the bill with a purpose to intimidate* an individual or group of individuals because of race, color, religion, gender, handicap, sexual orientation or ethnicity." In those Statements, no mention is made of the provision that allows for a bias-crime conviction based on a victim's reasonable belief that a defendant possessed a purpose to commit bias intimidation, even if the defendant had no such purpose.

Subsection (a)(3) is unique among bias-crime statutes in this nation. It is the only statute that authorizes a bias-crime conviction based on the victim's perception that the defendant committed the offense with the purpose to intimidate, regardless of whether the defendant actually had the purpose to intimidate. For a defendant to be found guilty of bias intimidation in other jurisdictions, a finding of the defendant's bias-motivated state of mind, such as malice and specific intent, is required. *See, e.g.*, Colo. Rev. Stat. § 18-9-121(2) (2014) ("A person commits a bias-motivated crime if, with the intent to intimidate or harass another person because of that person's actual or perceived race, color, religion, ancestry, national origin, physical or mental disability, or sexual orientation...."); Idaho Code Ann. § 18-7902 (2014) ("It shall be unlawful for any person, maliciously and with the specific intent to intimidate or harass another person because of that person's race, color, religion, ancestry, or national origin...."); Okla. Stat. tit. 21, § 850 (2013) ("No person shall maliciously and with the specific intent to intimidate or harass another person because of that person's race, color, religion, ancestry, national origin or disability...."). Those out-of-state statutes are comparable to subsections (a)(1) and (a)(2) of N.J.S.A. 2C:16-1.

With this backdrop, we next address whether subsection (a)(3) of N.J.S.A. 2C:16-1 passes muster under the Due Process Clause of the Fourteenth Amendment.

The Due Process Clause of the Fourteenth Amendment of the United States Constitution guarantees that "[n]o State shall ... deprive any person of life, liberty, or property, without due process of law...." A fundamental element of due process is that a law "must give fair notice of conduct that is forbidden or required." "A conviction fails to comport with due process if the statute under which it is obtained fails to provide a person of ordinary intelligence fair notice of what is prohibited...." A person should be on notice that he is engaged in wrongdoing before he "is brought to the bar of justice for condemnation in a criminal case."

A statute that criminalizes conduct "in terms so vague that [persons] of common intelligence must necessarily guess at its meaning ... violates the first essential of due process of law." The inherent vice in vague laws is that they do not draw clear lines separating criminal from lawful conduct. A penal statute should not be "a trap" for the unwary.

In *Mortimer*, we ultimately rejected a due process vagueness challenge to the entirety of N.J.S.A. 2C:33-4(d) (repealed by *L.* 2001, *c.* 443, § (3), which classified as a fourth-degree crime harassment that is motivated by bias. 2C:33-4(d) criminalized the defendant's conduct if the defendant "acted, at least in part, with ill will, hatred or bias toward, and with a purpose to intimidate, an individual or group of individuals because of race, color, religion, sexual orientation or ethnicity." We struck from the statute the language—"at least in part with ill will, hatred or bias toward"—on vagueness grounds because those words failed to give sufficient notice of "what that part of the statute proscribe[d]." The reconstructed statute read as follows: "A person commits a crime of the fourth degree if in committing an offense under this section, he acted ... with a purpose to intimidate an individual or group of individuals because of race, color, religion, sexual orientation or ethnicity." The reconstructed statute survived due process scrutiny because the statute's mens rea—"with purpose to intimidate"—penalizes a defendant who "*selects* a victim because of the victim's group identification or inherent characteristics." Although we upheld "subsection d, thereby *permitting an inquiry into a person's motive to commit one of the predicate offenses*, we caution[ed] that our decision [was] not an invitation to inquire into an actor's beliefs, expressions, and associations generally."

The United States Supreme Court in *Mitchell* likewise rejected a constitutional challenge to a statute that provided for a penalty enhancement when the defendant "intentionally" committed certain crimes because of an immutable characteristic, such as race, religion, or color. The statute passed muster under the First and Fourteenth Amendments because a defendant is not punished because of his "bigoted beliefs" but because of his "discriminatory motive." The Court recognized that "bias-motivated crimes are more likely to provoke retaliatory crimes, inflict distinct emotional harms on their victims, and incite community unrest."

What distinguishes the statutes upheld in *Mortimer* and *Mitchell* from subsection (a)(3) of N.J.S.A. 2C:16-1 is that in those statutes the defendant is penalized for intentionally targeting the victim based on an immutable characteristic, such as race or color, whereas subsection (a)(3) penalizes the defendant even if he has no motive to discriminate, so long as the victim reasonably believed he acted with a discriminatory motive.

While the State is correct that our upholding of the constitutionality of the bias-harassment statute in *Mortimer* does not ineluctably lead to the conclusion that subsection (a)(3) is unconstitutional, the reasoning in *Mortimer* lends no support to the State's argument. Indeed, the concern we expressed in *Mortimer*—the need to avoid "inquiry into an actor's beliefs, expressions, and associations generally"—may be realized when the focus is on the victim's reasonable perceptions as opposed to the defendant's actual motivation. A bigot who harasses a neighbor for no reason other than that the neighbor is playing music too loudly in the evening may be convicted of bias intimidation under subsection (a)(3) if the neighbor reasonably believes, under the circumstances, that the bigot acted based on his racial, religious, or nativist sentiments. That is because subsection (a)(3) does not require that a defendant have a bias motive to be convicted of bias intimidation. Significantly, we found that the statute in *Mortimer* was "rationally related to [a] legitimate State interest" because criminalizing "bias-motivated harassment" advanced the goal of deterrence. The goal of deterrence surely is diminished when a person has no motive to commit a bias crime and is unaware that his conduct or speech has crossed over into the realm of criminal misconduct.

The State compares subsection (a)(3) to other strict-liability statutes, but statutes without scienter requirements have due process limitations. A strict-liability statute will violate due process if it "offend[s] fundamental notions of justice." The due process bar to a strict-liability statute applies "when the underlying conduct is so passive, so unworthy of blame, that the persons violating the proscription would have no notice that they were breaking the law." As with vague statutes, notice is a key component to a due process review of strict-liability statutes. Strict-liability statutes that have withstood constitutional scrutiny typically involve an element of an offense that involves an ascertainable fact of which a defendant can make himself aware to avoid criminal liability.

For example, N.J.S.A. 2C:35-7(a), a statute criminalizing the distribution of drugs within 1000 feet of a school, is constitutional without requiring proof that the defendant knew that he was within the prohibited zone. Significantly, a defendant has the ability to determine his location in relationship to a school. In *State v. Fearick*, we rejected the constitutional challenge to a statute that imposed a mandatory jail sentence on a defendant who was involved in an accident while driving with a suspended license. The statute did not accord defendant a defense based on his lack of fault in causing the accident. Notably, a defendant is on statutory notice that if he drives while suspended, the happenstance of an accident, even if not his fault, would subject him to a harsh penalty. In *Maldonado,* we upheld the constitutionality of a statute that imposed strict liability on a drug distributor whose drugs proximately caused death. The defendant was on notice of the inherent dangers of drugs and their potential to cause death.

Unlike the defendants in those cases involving strict-liability statutes, defendant here could not readily inform himself of a fact and, armed with that knowledge, take measures to avoid criminal liability. Defendant was guilty of a crime under N.J.S.A. 2C:16-1(a)(3) even if he had no intent to commit bias intimidation, so long as the victim reasonably believed that defendant targeted him on account of his race or color. Of course, a victim's reasonable belief about whether he has been subjected to bias may well depend on the victim's personal experiences, cultural or religious upbringing and heritage, and reaction to language that is a flashpoint to persons of his race, religion, or nationality. A tone-deaf defendant may intend no bias in the use of crude or insensitive language, and yet a victim may reasonably perceive animus. The defendant may be wholly unaware of the victim's perspective, due to a lack of understanding of the emotional triggers to which a reasonable person of that race, religion, or nationality would react. Nothing in the history of the bias-intimidation statute suggests that the Legislature intended to criminalize conduct through the imposition of an amorphous code of civility or criminalize speech that was not intended to intimidate on the basis of bias. It bears repeating that no other bias-intimidation statute in the nation imposes criminal liability based on the victim's reasonable perceptions....

N.J.S.A. 2C:16-1(a)(3) fails to set a standard that places a reasonably intelligent person on notice when he is crossing a proscribed line. That is so because guilt may depend on facts beyond the knowledge of the defendant or not readily ascertainable by him.

Indeed, the facts of this case illustrate how subsection (a)(3) exceeds its constitutional bounds. After Dorazo lured Brodie into the storage cage in the Public Works garage and locked the cage door, defendant remarked—according to Brodie—"Oh, you see, you throw a banana in the cage and he goes right in." Although the jury concluded that defendant acted with the purpose to harass Brodie, it rejected the State's theory that defendant acted with the purpose to intimidate or target Brodie on account of his race or color. However, because Brodie, an African-American victim, reasonably believed under the circumstances that defendant's words were racially motivated—even though the jury concluded they were not—defendant was convicted of bias intimidation.

Subsection (a)(3) required defendant to predict that the reasonable African-American would consider defendant's words as constituting the motive for a crime, even though he had no such motive. Persons who belong to specific ethnic, religious, or racial groups that have been historically exposed to bigotry will be particularly sensitive to language that is deemed offensive, based on their communal and individual experiences. But defendant did not possess the communal and individual experiences of the reasonable victim in this case. Subsection (a)(3) criminalizes defendant's failure to apprehend the reaction that his words would have on another. Here, subsection (a)(3) penalizes, as a bias crime, coarse and insensitive language that may have been uttered as part of a terrible prank.

In summary, we conclude that because N.J.S.A. 2C:16-1(a)(3) fails to give adequate notice of conduct that it proscribes, the statute is unconstitutionally vague and violates notions of due process protected by the Fourteenth Amendment. Defendant was convicted not based on what he was thinking but rather on his failure to appreciate what the victim was thinking....

It bears emphasizing that the twin pillars of the bias-intimidation statute—subsections (a)(1) and (a)(2) of N.J.S.A. 2C:16-1—still stand. A defendant is prohibited from acting with the purpose to commit bias intimidation or with knowledge that his conduct constitutes bias intimidation. With the striking of subsection (a)(3), New Jersey's bias-intimidation law now conforms to its original form, the statute's explanatory statement contained in the legislative history, the laws of the rest of the nation, and the United States Constitution....

We remand to the trial court for entry of judgment consistent with this opinion.

Discussion Questions

1. Do you agree with the Court that "[t]he goal of deterrence surely is diminished when a person has no motive to commit a bias crime and is unaware that his conduct or speech has crossed over into the realm of criminal misconduct"? Do you think Section (a)(3) of the New Jersey statute would have any deterrent effect?

2. The Court states that the jury concluded that the defendant's words were not racially motivated. Did the jury reach such a conclusion?

3. If you were a New Jersey legislator, how could you amend the New Jersey statute to cure the constitutional problems raised in the *Pomianek* case?

F. Synthesis and Review

Problem

3.14 Laverne recently gave birth to a baby boy, Earl. Laverne has given birth to two previous babies born with cocaine addictions. Laverne admitted to her pediatrician that she regularly used cocaine while pregnant with Earl and that she used cocaine while in labor just a few hours prior to Earl's delivery. Urine tests demonstrate that Earl has cocaine in his bloodstream and medical expert testimony will establish that if Laverne took cocaine while in labor it would have remained in her bloodstream until well after Earl was delivered. Laverne is charged with violating the following statute:

> It is a felony punishable by up to 15 years imprisonment for anyone to deliver cocaine to a person under the age of 18 years.

The prosecution's theory is that Laverne delivered cocaine to Earl, who was clearly under 18 years of age, through her umbilical cord during the roughly two minutes that passed between his emergence from the birth canal and the severance of the umbilical cord by the obstetrician.

Is Laverne liable for violating the statute? What problems would the prosecution encounter in prosecuting Laverne?

Three Conceptions of Federal Criminal-Lawmaking

Dan M. Kahan

1 Buff. Crim. L.R. 5, 16–18 (1997)

What's needed ideally ... is a third conception of federal criminal lawmaking — one that conserves the efficiency of delegated criminal lawmaking but that avoids the coordination and the legitimacy problems associated with overt federal common-lawmaking.

A Realizable Ideal: An Administrative Law of Crimes

That third conception is what I [refer] to ... as the administrative-law conception of federal criminal-lawmaking. On this view, filling in incompletely specified criminal statutes is the responsibility not of courts or individual U.S. Attorneys but of an executive agency; that agency could be one newly minted for this purpose, but I'll assume here that it would be the Department of Justice. The Department would exercise its delegated-lawmaking power by issuing formal interpretations of ambiguous or generally worded criminal statutes. For its interpretations to be binding on courts, the Department would have to comply with standard administrative-law requirements, including those obliging the agency to justify its position through notice-and-comment rulemaking or its equivalent, and to do so prior to defending its position in litigation.

This administrative-law approach would conserve essentially all of the efficiency benefits associated with implied delegation. Congress enjoys the institutional economies of incomplete specification regardless of whether it's the Judiciary or an administrative agency that finishes the task. In addition, agencies, like courts, can update the law more quickly than Congress, and can use its contact with actual cases to tailor the law to unforeseen circumstances. Indeed, because the Justice Department has more experience with criminal law enforcement than does any court, and because it is more unified than the Judiciary, an administrative regime would likely enhance both the quality and the consistency of federal criminal-lawmaking relative to the existing common-lawmaking baseline.

In addition, an administrative law of crimes would avoid the asserted tensions between common-lawmaking and the values of democracy and fair notice. Because the Justice Department is accountable to the President, its judgments on contentious issues are likely to be closer to those of the national electorate than are those of courts. What's more, under the so-called rule against "post hoc rationalizations," the Justice Department would be obliged to issue its interpretations of ambiguous statutes before defending them in court, thus avoiding the unfair surprise sometimes associated with common-lawmaking.

Discussion Questions

1. Under the approach Professor Kahan describes, the Department of Justice would be required to issue formal interpretations of ambiguous statutes. Would such formal interpretations ameliorate the problems the *Morales* court identifies?

2. Should we explicitly and openly require the executive branch to define crimes and give them the power to do so as suggested by Professor Kahan? What limits would exist on that power? Would an open grant of such power be better or worse than the current system of implicit delegation?

Chapter 4

Conduct

A. The Elements of an Offense

One objective of a law school course is to teach the fundamental skill of legal analysis, which in criminal law often focuses on statutes. In analyzing statutes, lawyers generally break them down into parts and refer to those parts as the elements of the offense. Distinguishing among the various elements of an offense is critical to clear legal analysis. This chapter focuses on the conduct element.

Consider the following criminal statute:

Cal. Penal Code Ann. § 459

Every person who enters any house, room, … shop, … store, … or other building … with intent to commit … larceny or any felony is guilty of burglary.

Enters is the conduct element of this statute.

Although this chapter focuses on conduct, it will help you develop your skill in analyzing criminal statutes to begin practicing identifying all of the elements of offenses you encounter in the reading. Start in this chapter by identifying each of the non-mental elements of an offense. In the next chapter you will identify the mental elements of offenses. The Model Penal Code divides the non-mental elements into three categories: (1) conduct elements; (2) result elements; and (3) circumstance elements. Although every offense has at least one conduct element, not all offenses have result or circumstance elements. Problem 3.1 in Chapter 3 required you to draft a feticide statute. The non-mental elements of feticide include: (1) some sort of conduct; (2) death—a result element; and (3) that the death be of a fetus—a circumstance element. These non-mental elements can be diagrammed as follows:

Conduct
Death
Of Fetus

The California burglary statute that appears above has two non-mental elements: (1) enters—a conduct element; and (2) that the place entered be a house, room, shop, store or other building—a circumstance element. These non-mental elements can be diagrammed as follows:

Enters
House, room, shop, store or other building

Problems

4.1 Identify the conduct elements in the following statutes.

Wash. Rev. Code

Part (a) § 9A.52.120

A person is guilty of computer trespass in the first degree if the person, without authorization, intentionally gains access to a computer system or electronic data base of another; and (a) The access is made with the intent to commit another crime; or (b) The violation involves a computer data base maintained by a government agency.

United States Code

Part (b) 18 § 2339B

Whoever knowingly provides material support or resources to a foreign terrorist organization, or attempts or conspires to do so, shall be fined under this title or imprisoned not more than 20 years, or both, and, if the death of any person results, shall be imprisoned for any term of years or for life. To violate this paragraph, a person must have knowledge that the organization is a designated terrorist organization ... that the organization has engaged or engages in terrorist activity ... or that the organization has engaged or engages in terrorism....

Tex. Penal Code Ann.

Part (c) § 49.03

A person commits an offense if the person consumes an alcoholic beverage while operating a motor vehicle in a public place and is observed doing so by a peace officer.

* * *

4.2 Diagram all the non-mental elements in each of the statutes in Problem 4.1.

As the statutes above demonstrate, legislatures typically require some sort of conduct for criminal liability. Lawyers often refer to the conduct element in a criminal statute using the Latin phrase *actus reus*, which literally means "guilty act." You should be aware, though, that lawyers and judges vary in the meanings they attach to the phrase *actus reus*. Some employ *actus reus* in a narrow sense consistent with its Latin meaning to refer only to the conduct element of a crime. Unfortunately, others use *actus reus* in a broader sense to refer not only to the conduct element but collectively to all non-mental elements of an offense, including results and circumstances. To avoid this confusing ambiguity and to emphasize the importance of distinguishing conduct from other non-mental elements, we use the words "conduct" or "act" rather than *actus reus* in referring to the subject matter of this chapter.

Section B of this chapter examines why conduct is typically viewed as a necessary ingredient in defining crimes. Section C focuses on what constitutes conduct. Section D deals with status and the difficulties that may arise in distinguishing status, which generally may not be penalized, from conduct.

Section E treats both the requirement that conduct be voluntary in order to be penalized as well as what voluntariness entails. A defendant may take many steps in a course of conduct leading to a criminal charge. From among those many acts, how should one choose the conduct on which to base criminal liability? This choice in focal point is the subject of Section F on timeframing.

It is sometimes said that there can be no crime without an act. The final three sections of this chapter allow you to assess the validity of this generalization. Each provides examples in which the criminal law is sometimes viewed as dispensing with any conduct requirement. Section G deals with crimes based on omission, the failure to act. Section H focuses on possession, a common basis for criminal liability and one that has been described as neither an act nor an omission. This chapter ends with Section I's exploration of the topic of vicarious liability, the controversial practice of imposing criminal punishment on one person based on the actions of another person. Jurisdictions vary in their acceptance of vicarious criminal liability.

Problems

4.3 One summer night, Rickford walks several times by the open window of a ground-level apartment in the city where he lives. As he walks by, he repeatedly looks into the open window, trying to see the woman who lives in the apartment. The woman sees Rickford reach his hand inside the window and open the curtain so it does not obstruct his view into the apartment. She calls the police and a nearby patrolman arrests Rickford, who is charged with first degree burglary under the following statute:

> Whoever enters a building without consent and with intent to commit
> a crime, or enters a building without consent and commits a crime
> while in the building, either directly or as an accomplice, commits bur-
> glary in the first degree ... if:

> (a) the building is a dwelling and another person, not an accomplice, is present in it when the burglar enters or at any time while the burglar is in the building; …

The crime the prosecution alleges Rickford intended to commit in reaching through the window and moving the curtain is interference with privacy, defined in the following statute:

> A person is guilty of a gross misdemeanor who:
>
> (1) enters upon another's property;
>
> (2) surreptitiously gazes, stares, or peeps in the window or any other aperture of a house or place of dwelling of another; and
>
> (3) does so with intent to intrude upon or interfere with the privacy of a member of the household.

Did Rickford violate the first-degree burglary statute? Did he enter the apartment building? What arguments can you make for Rickford? For the prosecution?

4.4 A police officer responds to a report of an assault in the parking lot of a gas station. James has a laceration on his face and tells the officer he was assaulted. The officer asks James about a plastic bag that is sticking out of his pocket. James removes the bag, which contains a small amount of marijuana, from his pocket and hands it to the officer. James then says he wants to use the bathroom and buy a pack of cigarettes at the gas station's store. James goes into the store with the officer following him. As he rounds a corner in the store on his way to the bathroom, James reaches into the right pocket of his cargo pants and removes another, larger bag of marijuana, which had not been visible before. James throws the bag into a large cardboard bin of snack foods. It lands on top of the items in the bin and James makes no attempt to conceal the bag in the bin. The officer immediately retrieves the bag and arrests James, who is charged with one count of possession of marijuana and one count of tampering with physical evidence. The tampering statute reads:

> A person commits the offense of tampering with physical evidence if, believing that an official proceeding is pending or about to be instituted, he destroys, mutilates, conceals, removes, or alters physical evidence with the intent to impair its verity or availability in the pending or prospective official proceeding.

Is James liable under this statute? Did he fulfill any of the conduct elements listed in the statute?

B. Why Require Conduct?

Why do legislatures routinely include a conduct element in defining crimes? In answering this question, it is helpful to refer to the purposes of punishment.

From a retributive perspective, criminal punishment requires blameworthiness. Though some religions treat bad thoughts alone as sinful,[1] the criminal law views thoughts alone as insufficiently blameworthy to justify state-imposed criminal punishment. Blame sufficient to warrant criminal sanction attaches only when the person entertaining bad thoughts chooses to act on them.

From a deterrent perspective, the threat of punishment aims to reduce crime by influencing the potential offender in the period between thought and action. Requiring conduct gives that threat the opportunity to dissuade the potential offender from turning bad thoughts into action.

To what extent can we control our thoughts? Without such control, it is difficult to find bad thoughts blameworthy. And the threat of punishment, no matter how severe, cannot deter thoughts if they are outside one's control.

From an incapacitation perspective, a conduct requirement may or may not make sense. The person who thinks about crime but poses no risk of actually acting on her thoughts presents no future danger and accordingly is not in need of incapacitation. A conduct requirement thus protects the idle daydreamer. But what about those who do act on their thoughts?

Consider the case of Buford O. Furrow Jr. According to newspaper accounts,[2] he was a heavily armed white supremacist who revealed to psychiatric workers that he was fantasizing about committing a mass killing. A few months later, he shot six people, killing one, at a Jewish community center in Los Angeles.[3] Waiting until someone with bad thoughts does act means losing the opportunity to intervene preemptively and prevent harm.

Consider also the notorious case of Gilberto Valle, a New York City police officer whose prosecution was the subject of a 2015 HBO documentary titled *Thought Crimes: The Case of the Cannibal Cop*. Valle was accused of conspiring online with other men to kidnap, kill, cook, and eat a number of women he knew. Valle's wife turned him in to police when she found detailed and gruesome "chats" on his computer setting forth how he planned to carry out these crimes and the names of planned victims. Valle was charged with conspiracy but claimed that these chats, all of which took place on a bizarre fetishist web site, were merely fantasies he never intended to carry

---

1. *See, e.g.,* Exodus 20:17 ("You shall not covet your neighbor's house; you shall not covet your neighbor's wife or his male servant or his female servant or his ox or his donkey or anything that belongs to your neighbor.") (New Amer. Stand.).

2. Barry Meier, *A Violent Creed Is No Bar to Gun Ownership*, N.Y. Times, Aug. 16, 1999, at A16.

3. *Id.*

out. His lawyer argued that he should not be punished for simply entertaining evil thoughts. A federal jury convicted Valle. But the trial judge overturned the conviction on the ground that fantasizing about crimes is not itself a crime. The Second Circuit affirmed the trial judge's action. Both the Furrow and Valle cases raise the difficult question of balancing freedom of thought with protecting society from future crime.

Defenders of the conduct requirement also frequently rely on practical grounds. If the state were to punish bad thoughts, how would it determine which people were actually thinking bad thoughts? Conduct provides circumstantial evidence to help prove what the offender was thinking.

One way to grasp both the theoretical and practical reasons why criminal law regularly insists on an act is to imagine a criminal justice system without such a requirement. Under such a system, "thinking about killing another human being" or "thinking about stealing the property of another" could be crimes. Under such provisions, who among us would not qualify as a criminal? What means would the police need to adopt to detect such crime? How would the government prove guilt? How could someone charged with such a crime demonstrate her innocence? If thoughts were already criminalized, what incentive would there be to stop someone from converting thoughts into actions? Imagine also the size and scope of the criminal justice apparatus that would be necessary to enforce such a system.

C. What Is an Act?

Problems

4.5 Consider the following legislative definitions:

New York Penal Law

§ 15.00

"Act" means a bodily movement.

Utah Code Ann.

§ 76-1-601(1)

"Act" means a voluntary bodily movement and includes speech.

Evil Emil tells his blind companion that the medicine his companion needs is in the bottle to his companion's left. In fact, the bottle to the left contains poison. Emil's companion picks up and swallows the contents of the bottle on the left and dies. Has Emil acted under the New York statute? The Utah statute?

4.6 Ross and Joey are both in love with Rachel. When Joey finds out that Rachel has become involved romantically with Ross, Joey violently assaults Ross in a jealous rage when he encounters them together at a local bar. As a result of Joey's assault, Ross is completely paralyzed. Brain surgeons implant a small sensor in Ross's brain that allows his brain to control a computer, a television, and a robot using only his thoughts. One day Joey comes to Ross's apartment to express his remorse and beg forgiveness. While Joey is on his knees weeping, Ross by his thoughts directs the robot he controls to grab Joey by his throat and strangle him to death. Is Ross criminally liable for the death of Joey? Did Ross act?

4.7 You are a justice of a state supreme court. You and the other justices have agreed to review a series of cases raising questions about the scope of the following criminal statute:

Driving while under the influence of alcohol or drugs

No person shall operate any vehicle, streetcar, or trackless trolley within this state if the person is under the influence of alcohol, a drug of abuse, or alcohol and a drug of abuse.

The facts in these cases are as follows. Assume the prosecutor can prove that the defendant in each was under the influence of alcohol at the time he entered his car.

Case 1. At 1:30 a.m. in the middle of a cold and snowy January night, the sound of a car motor running in his driveway awoke Timothy. When he investigated, he found that a stranger, Allen, had parked his car in Timothy's driveway with the motor running. Allen was asleep in the driver's seat and did not wake or stir when Timothy shone a flashlight through the car window into his face. Timothy called the police. The arresting officer concluded that Allen had been in Timothy's driveway a considerable time since no tire tracks were visible behind Allen's car in the freshly fallen snow.

Case 2. After ending a 15-hour work shift at 10 p.m., Michael drove to McDuffie's Bar, parked his car and went inside where he stayed until the bar closed at 2:30 a.m. Police found Michael at 4 a.m. passed out and slumped over the steering wheel of his car, which was still in the same space in McDuffie's lot where he had parked it at 10 p.m. The motor was running at idle speed, the transmission was in neutral, and the emergency brake was engaged. It was 15 degrees outside and the heater in the car was on. Michael admitted to the arresting police officers that he was intoxicated and told them he had decided to follow his lawyer's advice not to drive if he "had more than two beers."

Case 3. Police found Bradley asleep in the driver's seat of his car. The car was parked in a lot belonging to a county park. Its motor was not running, but its radio was on. The key was in the ignition, but turned to the left or "ACC" position. The key needs to be turned in the opposite direction, to the right, to start the engine.

Allen, Michael, and Bradley were each charged with violating the statute above. The lower courts have disagreed on whether or not the conduct of Allen, Michael, and Bradley fall within the statute. How would you rule in each case?

D. Status

Legislatures typically require that a person do something in order to incur criminal liability. But is it ever permissible to punish a person for *being* rather than *doing* something? This question, which the criminal law frames as whether a person may be punished for his or her *status*, was the focus of two landmark U.S. Supreme Court cases that appear below.

Robinson v. California

370 U.S. 660 (1962)
United States Supreme Court

Stewart, J. A California statute makes it a criminal offense for a person to "be addicted to the use of narcotics."[1] This appeal draws into question the constitutionality of that provision of the state law, as construed by the California courts in the present case.

The appellant was convicted after a jury trial in the Municipal Court of Los Angeles. The evidence against him was given by two Los Angeles police officers. Officer Brown testified that he had had occasion to examine the appellant's arms one evening on a street in Los Angeles some four months before the trial. The officer testified that at that time he had observed "scar tissue and discoloration on the inside" of the appellant's right arm, and "what appeared to be numerous needle marks and a scab which was approximately three inches below the crook of the elbow" on the appellant's left arm. The officer also testified that the appellant under questioning had admitted to the occasional use of narcotics.

Officer Lindquist testified that he had examined the appellant the following morning in the Central Jail in Los Angeles. The officer stated that at that time he had observed discolorations and scabs on the appellant's arms, and he identified photographs which had been taken of the appellant's arms shortly after his arrest the night before. Based upon more than ten years of experience as a member of the Narcotic Division of the Los Angeles Police Department, the witness gave his opinion that "these marks and the discoloration were the result of the injection of hypodermic needles into the

---

1. The statute is § 11721 of the California Health and Safety Code. It provides:
   "No person shall use, or be under the influence of, or be addicted to the use of narcotics, excepting when administered by or under the direction of a person licensed by the State to prescribe and administer narcotics. It shall be the burden of the defense to show that it comes within the exception. Any person convicted of violating any provision of this section is guilty of a misdemeanor and shall be sentenced to serve a term of not less than 90 days nor more than one year in the county jail. The court may place a person convicted hereunder on probation for a period not to exceed five years and shall in all cases in which probation is granted require as a condition thereof that such person be confined in the county jail for at least 90 days. In no event does the court have the power to absolve a person who violates this section from the obligation of spending at least 90 days in confinement in the county jail."

tissue into the vein that was not sterile." He stated that the scabs were several days old at the time of his examination, and that the appellant was neither under the influence of narcotics nor suffering withdrawal symptoms at the time he saw him. This witness also testified that the appellant had admitted using narcotics in the past.

The appellant testified in his own behalf, denying the alleged conversations with the police officers and denying that he had ever used narcotics or been addicted to their use. He explained the marks on his arms as resulting from an allergic condition contracted during his military service. His testimony was corroborated by two witnesses.

The trial judge instructed the jury that the statute made it a misdemeanor for a person "either to use narcotics, or to be addicted to the use of narcotics.... That portion of the statute referring to the 'use' of narcotics is based upon the 'act' of using. That portion of the statute referring to 'addicted to the use' of narcotics is based upon a condition or status. They are not identical.... To be addicted to the use of narcotics is said to be a status or condition and not an act. It is a continuing offense and differs from most other offenses in the fact that [it] is chronic rather than acute; that it continues after it is complete and subjects the offender to arrest at any time before he reforms. The existence of such a chronic condition may be ascertained from a single examination, if the characteristic reactions of that condition be found present."

The judge further instructed the jury that the appellant could be convicted under a general verdict if the jury agreed *either* that he was of the "status" *or* had committed the "act" denounced by the statute. "All that the People must show is either that the defendant did use a narcotic in Los Angeles County, or while in the City of Los Angeles he was addicted to the use of narcotics".... Under these instructions the jury returned a verdict finding the appellant "guilty of the offense charged." ...

The broad power of a State to regulate the narcotic drugs traffic within its borders is not here in issue. More than forty years ago ... this Court explicitly recognized the validity of that power: "There can be no question of the authority of the State in the exercise of its police power to regulate the administration, sale, prescription and use of dangerous and habit-forming drugs.... The right to exercise this power is so manifest in the interest of the public health and welfare, that it is unnecessary to enter upon a discussion of it beyond saying that it is too firmly established to be successfully called in question."

Such regulation, it can be assumed, could take a variety of valid forms. A State might impose criminal sanctions, for example, against the unauthorized manufacture, prescription, sale, purchase, or possession of narcotics within its borders. In the interest of discouraging the violation of such laws, or in the interest of the general health or welfare of its inhabitants, a State might establish a program of compulsory treatment for those addicted to narcotics. Such a program of treatment might require periods of involuntary confinement. And penal sanctions might be imposed for failure to comply with established compulsory treatment procedures. Or a State might choose to attack the evils of narcotics traffic on broader fronts also—through public health education, for example, or by efforts to ameliorate the economic and social conditions under which those evils might be thought to flourish. In short, the range of valid choice which a State might make in this area is undoubtedly a wide one, and the wisdom of any particular choice within the allowable spectrum is not for us to decide. Upon that premise we turn to the California law in issue here.

It would be possible to construe the statute under which the appellant was convicted as one which is operative only upon proof of the actual use of narcotics within the State's jurisdiction. But the California courts have not so construed this law. Although there was evidence in the present case that the appellant had used narcotics in Los Angeles, the jury were instructed that they could convict him even if they disbelieved that evidence. The appellant could be convicted, they were told, if they found simply that the appellant's "status" or "chronic condition" was that of being "addicted to the use of narcotics." And it is impossible to know from the jury's verdict that the defendant was not convicted upon precisely such a finding.

The instructions of the trial court ... amounted to "a ruling on a question of state law that is as binding on us as though the precise words had been written" into the statute. Indeed, in their brief in this Court counsel for the State have emphasized that it is "the proof of addiction by circumstantial evidence ... by the tell-tale track of needle marks and scabs over the veins of his arms, that remains the gist of the section."

This statute, therefore, is not one which punishes a person for the use of narcotics, for their purchase, sale or possession, or for antisocial or disorderly behavior resulting from their administration. It is not a law which even purports to provide or require medical treatment. Rather, we deal with a statute which makes the "status" of narcotic addiction a criminal offense, for which the offender may be prosecuted "at any time before he reforms." California has said that a person can be continuously guilty of this offense, whether or not he has ever used or possessed any narcotics within the State, and whether or not he has been guilty of any antisocial behavior there.

It is unlikely that any State at this moment in history would attempt to make it a criminal offense for a person to be mentally ill, or a leper, or to be afflicted with a venereal disease. A State might determine that the general health and welfare require that the victims of these and other human afflictions be dealt with by compulsory treatment, involving quarantine, confinement, or sequestration. But, in the light of contemporary human knowledge, a law which made a criminal offense of such a disease would doubtless be universally thought to be an infliction of cruel and unusual punishment in violation of the Eighth and Fourteenth Amendments.

We cannot but consider the statute before us as of the same category. In this Court counsel for the State recognized that narcotic addiction is an illness. Indeed, it is apparently an illness which may be contracted innocently or involuntarily. We hold that a state law which imprisons a person thus afflicted as a criminal, even though he has never touched any narcotic drug within the State or been guilty of any irregular behavior there, inflicts a cruel and unusual punishment in violation of the Fourteenth Amendment. To be sure, imprisonment for ninety days is not, in the abstract, a punishment which is either cruel or unusual. But the question cannot be considered in the abstract. Even one day in prison would be a cruel and unusual punishment for the "crime" of having a common cold.

We are not unmindful that the vicious evils of the narcotics traffic have occasioned the grave concern of government. There are, as we have said, countless fronts on which those evils may be legitimately attacked. We deal in this case only with an individual provision of a particularized local law as it has so far been interpreted by the California courts.

Reversed.

Five years later, the Supreme Court addressed the constitutionality of a conviction under the following statute in light of *Robinson*:

> Whoever shall get drunk or be found in a state of intoxication in any public place, or at any private house except his own, shall be fined not exceeding one hundred dollars.

Powell v. Texas

392 U.S. 514 (1968)
United States Supreme Court

Marshall, J. In late December 1966, appellant was arrested and charged with being found in a state of intoxication in a public place, in violation of Texas Penal Code, Art. 477 (1952), which reads as follows:

> "Whoever shall get drunk or be found in a state of intoxication in any public place, or at any private house except his own, shall be fined not exceeding one hundred dollars."

Appellant was tried, ... found guilty, and fined $ 20. He appealed [and] a trial *de novo* was held. His counsel urged that appellant was "afflicted with the disease of chronic alcoholism," that "his appearance in public [while drunk was] ... not of his own volition," and therefore that to punish him criminally for that conduct would be cruel and unusual, in violation of the Eighth and Fourteenth Amendments to the United States Constitution. The trial judge in the county court, sitting without a jury, made certain findings of fact, but ruled as a matter of law that chronic alcoholism was not a defense to the charge....

The principal testimony was that of Dr. David Wade, a Fellow of the American Medical Association, duly certificated in psychiatry.... Dr. Wade sketched the outlines of the "disease" concept of alcoholism; noted that there is no generally accepted definition of "alcoholism"; alluded to the ongoing debate within the medical profession over whether alcohol is actually physically "addicting" or merely psychologically "habituating"; and concluded that in either case a "chronic alcoholic" is an "involuntary drinker," who is "powerless not to drink," and who "loses his self-control over his drinking." He testified that he had examined appellant, and that appellant is a "chronic alcoholic," who "by the time he has reached [the state of intoxication] ... is not able to control his behavior, and [who] ... has reached this point because he has an uncontrollable compulsion to drink." Dr. Wade also responded in the negative to the question whether appellant has "the willpower to resist the constant excessive consumption of alcohol." He added that in his opinion jailing appellant without medical attention would operate neither to rehabilitate him nor to lessen his desire for alcohol.

On cross-examination, Dr. Wade admitted that when appellant was sober he knew the difference between right and wrong, and he responded affirmatively to the question whether appellant's act of taking the first drink in any given instance when he was sober was a "voluntary exercise of his will." Qualifying his answer, Dr. Wade stated that "these individuals have a compulsion, and this compulsion, while not completely overpowering, is a very strong influence, an exceedingly strong influence, and this compulsion coupled with the firm belief in their mind that they are going to be able to handle it from now on causes their judgment to be somewhat clouded."

Appellant testified concerning the history of his drinking problem. He reviewed his many arrests for drunkenness; testified that he was unable to stop drinking; stated that when he was intoxicated he had no control over his actions and could not remember them later, but that he did not become violent; and admitted that he did not remember his arrest on the occasion for which he was being tried. On cross-examination, appellant admitted that he had had one drink on the morning of the trial and had been able to discontinue drinking. In relevant part, the cross-examination went as follows:

"Q. You took that one at eight o'clock because you wanted to drink?

"A. Yes, sir.

"Q. And you knew that if you drank it, you could keep on drinking and get drunk?

"A. Well, I was supposed to be here on trial, and I didn't take but that one drink.

"Q. You knew you had to be here this afternoon, but this morning you took one drink and then you knew that you couldn't afford to drink any more and come to court; is that right?

"A. Yes, sir, that's right.

"Q. So you exercised your will power and kept from drinking anything today except that one drink?

"A. Yes, sir, that's right.

"Q. Because you knew what you would do if you kept drinking, that you would finally pass out or be picked up?

"A. Yes, sir.

"Q. And you didn't want that to happen to you today?

"A. No, sir.

"Q. Not today?

"A. No, sir.

"Q. So you only had one drink today?

"A. Yes, sir."

On redirect examination, appellant's lawyer elicited the following:

"Q. Leroy, isn't the real reason why you just had one drink today because you just had enough money to buy one drink?

"A. Well, that was just give to me.

"Q. In other words, you didn't have any money with which you could buy any drinks yourself?

"A. No, sir, that was give to me.

"Q. And that's really what controlled the amount you drank this morning, isn't it?

"A. Yes, sir.

"Q. Leroy, when you start drinking, do you have any control over how many drinks you can take?

"A. No, sir."

Evidence in the case then closed. The State made no effort to obtain expert psychiatric testimony of its own, or even to explore with appellant's witness the question of appellant's power to control the frequency, timing, and location of his drinking bouts, or the substantial disagreement within the medical profession concerning the nature of the disease, the efficacy of treatment and the prerequisites for effective treatment. It did nothing to examine or illuminate what Dr. Wade might have meant by his reference to a "compulsion" which was "not completely overpowering," but which was "an exceedingly strong influence," or to inquire into the question of the proper role of such a "compulsion" in constitutional adjudication. Instead, the State contented itself with a brief argument that appellant had no defense to the charge because he "is legally sane and knows the difference between right and wrong." Following this abbreviated exposition of the problem before it, the trial court indicated its intention to disallow appellant's claimed defense of "chronic alcoholism." ...

[T]he inescapable fact is that there is no agreement among members of the medical profession about what it means to say that "alcoholism" is a "disease." One of the principal works in this field states that the major difficulty in articulating a "disease concept of alcoholism" is that "alcoholism has too many definitions and disease has practically none." This same author concludes that *a disease is what the medical profession recognizes as such.* In other words, there is widespread agreement today that "alcoholism" is a "disease," for the simple reason that the medical profession has concluded that it should attempt to treat those who have drinking problems. There the agreement stops. Debate rages within the medical profession as to whether "alcoholism" is a separate "disease" in any meaningful biochemical, physiological or psychological sense, or whether it represents one peculiar manifestation in some individuals of underlying psychiatric disorders.

Nor is there any substantial consensus as to the "manifestations of alcoholism." E. M. Jellinek, one of the outstanding authorities on the subject, identifies five different types of alcoholics which predominate in the United States, and these types display a broad range of different and occasionally inconsistent symptoms. Moreover, wholly distinct types, relatively rare in this country, predominate in nations with different cultural attitudes regarding the consumption of alcohol. Even if we limit our consideration to the range of alcoholic symptoms more typically found in this country, there is substantial disagreement as to the manifestations of the "disease" called "alcoholism." Jellinek, for example, considers that only two of his five alcoholic types can truly be said to be suffering from "alcoholism" as a "disease," because only these two types attain what he believes to be the requisite degree of physiological dependence on alcohol. He applies the label "gamma alcoholism" to "that species of alcoholism in which (1) acquired increased tissue tolerance to alcohol, (2) adaptive cell metabolism..., (3) withdrawal symptoms and 'craving,' i.e., physical dependence, and (4) loss of control are involved." A "delta" alcoholic, on the other hand, "shows the first three characteristics of gamma alcoholism as well as a less marked form of the fourth characteristic—that is, instead of loss of there is inability to abstain." Other authorities approach the problems of classification in an entirely different manner and, taking account of the large role which psycho-social factors seem to play in "problem drinking," define the "disease" in terms of the earliest identifiable manifestations of any sort of abnormality in drinking patterns.

Dr. Wade appears to have testified about appellant's "chronic alcoholism" in terms similar to Jellinek's "gamma" and "delta" types, for these types are largely defined, in their later stages, in terms of a strong compulsion to drink, physiological dependence and an inability to abstain from drinking. No attempt was made in the court below, of course, to determine whether Leroy Powell could in fact properly be diagnosed as a "gamma" or "delta" alcoholic in Jellinek's terms. The focus at the trial, and in the dissent here, has been exclusively upon the factors of loss of control and inability to abstain. Assuming that it makes sense to compartmentalize in this manner the diagnosis of such a formless "disease," tremendous gaps in our knowledge remain, which the record in this case does nothing to fill.

The trial court's "finding" that Powell "is afflicted with the disease of chronic alcoholism," which "destroys the afflicted person's will power to resist the constant, excessive consumption of alcohol" covers a multitude of sins. Dr. Wade's testimony that appellant suffered from a compulsion which was an "exceedingly strong influence," but which was "not completely overpowering" is at least more carefully stated, if no less mystifying. Jellinek insists that conceptual clarity can only be achieved by distinguishing carefully between "loss of control" once an individual has commenced to drink and "inability to abstain" from drinking in the first place. Presumably a person would have to display both characteristics in order to make out a constitutional defense, should one be recognized. Yet the "findings" of the trial court utterly fail to make this crucial distinction, and there is serious question whether the record can be read to support a finding of either loss of control or inability to abstain.

Dr. Wade did testify that once appellant began drinking he appeared to have no control over the amount of alcohol he finally ingested. Appellant's own testimony concerning his drinking on the day of the trial would certainly appear, however, to cast doubt upon the conclusion that he was without control over his consumption of alcohol when he had sufficiently important reasons to exercise such control. However that may be, there are more serious factual and conceptual difficulties with reading this record to show that appellant was unable to abstain from drinking. Dr. Wade testified that when appellant was sober, the act of taking the first drink was a "voluntary exercise of his will," but that this exercise of will was undertaken under the "exceedingly strong influence" of a "compulsion" which was "not completely overpowering." Such concepts, when juxtaposed in this fashion, have little meaning.

Moreover, Jellinek asserts that it cannot accurately be said that a person is truly unable to abstain from drinking unless he is suffering the physical symptoms of withdrawal. There is no testimony in this record that Leroy Powell underwent withdrawal symptoms either before he began the drinking spree which resulted in the conviction under review here, or at any other time. In attempting to deal with the alcoholic's desire for drink in the absence of withdrawal symptoms, Jellinek is reduced to unintelligible distinctions between a "compulsion" (a "psychopathological phenomenon" which can apparently serve in some instances as the functional equivalent of a "craving" or symptom of withdrawal) and an "impulse" (something which differs from a loss of control, a craving or a compulsion, and to which Jellinek attributes the start of a new drinking bout for a "gamma" alcoholic). Other scholars are equally unhelpful in articulating the nature of a "compulsion." It is one thing to say that if a man is deprived of alcohol his hands will begin to shake, he will suffer agonizing pains and ultimately he will have hallucinations; it is quite another to say that a man has a "compulsion" to take a drink, but that he also retains a certain amount of "free will" with which to resist. It is simply impossible, in the present state of our knowledge, to ascribe a useful meaning to the latter statement. This definitional confusion reflects, of course, not merely the undeveloped state of the psychiatric art but also the conceptual difficulties inevitably attendant upon the importation of scientific and medical models into a legal system generally predicated upon a different set of assumptions.

II.

Despite the comparatively primitive state of our knowledge on the subject, it cannot be denied that the destructive use of alcoholic beverages is one of our principal social and public health problems. The lowest current informed estimate places the number of "alcoholics" in America (definitional problems aside) at 4,000,000, and most authorities are inclined to put the figure considerably higher. The problem is compounded by the fact that a very large percentage of the alcoholics in this country are "invisible"—they possess the means to keep their drinking problems secret, and the traditionally uncharitable attitude of our society toward alcoholics causes many of them to refrain from seeking treatment from any source. Nor can it be gainsaid that the legislative response to this enormous problem has in general been inadequate.

There is as yet no known generally effective method for treating the vast number of alcoholics in our society. Some individual alcoholics have responded to particular forms of therapy with remissions of their symptomatic dependence upon the drug.

But just as there is no agreement among doctors and social workers with respect to the causes of alcoholism, there is no consensus as to why particular treatments have been effective in particular cases and there is no generally agreed-upon approach to the problem of treatment on a large scale. Most psychiatrists are apparently of the opinion that alcoholism is far more difficult to treat than other forms of behavioral disorders, and some believe it is impossible to cure by means of psychotherapy; indeed, the medical profession as a whole, and psychiatrists in particular, have been severely criticized for the prevailing reluctance to undertake the treatment of drinking problems. Thus it is entirely possible that, even were the manpower and facilities available for a full-scale attack upon chronic alcoholism, we would find ourselves unable to help the vast bulk of our "visible"—let alone our "invisible"—alcoholic population.

However, facilities for the attempted treatment of indigent alcoholics are woefully lacking throughout the country. It would be tragic to return large numbers of helpless, sometimes dangerous and frequently unsanitary inebriates to the streets of our cities without even the opportunity to sober up adequately which a brief jail term provides. Presumably no State or city will tolerate such a state of affairs. Yet the medical profession cannot, and does not, tell us with any assurance that, even if the buildings, equipment and trained personnel were made available, it could provide anything more than slightly higher-class jails for our indigent habitual inebriates. Thus we run the grave risk that nothing will be accomplished beyond the hanging of a new sign— reading "hospital"—over one wing of the jailhouse.

One virtue of the criminal process is, at least, that the duration of penal incarceration typically has some outside statutory limit; this is universally true in the case of petty offenses, such as public drunkenness, where jail terms are quite short on the whole. "Therapeutic civil commitment" lacks this feature; one is typically committed until one is "cured." Thus, to do otherwise than affirm might subject indigent alcoholics to the risk that they may be locked up for an indefinite period of time under the same conditions as before, with no more hope than before of receiving effective treatment and no prospect of periodic "freedom."

Faced with this unpleasant reality, we are unable to assert that the use of the criminal process as a means of dealing with the public aspects of problem drinking can never be defended as rational. The picture of the penniless drunk propelled aimlessly and endlessly through the law's "revolving door" of arrest, incarceration, release and re-arrest is not a pretty one. But before we condemn the present practice across-the-board, perhaps we ought to be able to point to some clear promise of a better world for these unfortunate people. Unfortunately, no such promise has yet been forthcoming. If, in addition to the absence of a coherent approach to the problem of treatment, we consider the almost complete absence of facilities and manpower for the implementation of a rehabilitation program, it is difficult to say in the present context that the criminal process is utterly lacking in social value. This Court has never held that anything in the Constitution requires that penal sanctions be designed solely to achieve therapeutic or rehabilitative effects, and it can hardly be said with assurance that incarceration serves such purposes any better for the general run of criminals than it does for public drunks.

Ignorance likewise impedes our assessment of the deterrent effect of criminal sanctions for public drunkenness. The fact that a high percentage of American alcoholics conceal their drinking problems, not merely by avoiding public displays of intoxication but also by shunning all forms of treatment, is indicative that some powerful deterrent operates to inhibit the public revelation of the existence of alcoholism. Quite probably this deterrent effect can be largely attributed to the harsh moral attitude which our society has traditionally taken toward intoxication and the shame which we have associated with alcoholism. Criminal conviction represents the degrading public revelation of what Anglo-American society has long condemned as a moral defect, and the existence of criminal sanctions may serve to reinforce this cultural taboo, just as we presume it serves to reinforce other, stronger feelings against murder, rape, theft, and other forms of antisocial conduct.

Obviously, chronic alcoholics have not been deterred from drinking to excess by the existence of criminal sanctions against public drunkenness. But all those who violate penal laws of any kind are by definition undeterred. The long-standing and still raging debate over the validity of the deterrence justification for penal sanctions has not reached any sufficiently clear conclusions to permit it to be said that such sanctions are ineffective in any particular context or for any particular group of people who are able to appreciate the consequences of their acts. Certainly no effort was made at the trial of this case, beyond a monosyllabic answer to a perfunctory one-line question, to determine the effectiveness of penal sanctions in deterring Leroy Powell in particular or chronic alcoholics in general from drinking at all or from getting drunk in particular places or at particular times.

III.

Appellant claims that his conviction on the facts of this case would violate the Cruel and Unusual Punishment Clause of the Eighth Amendment as applied to the States through the Fourteenth Amendment. The primary purpose of that clause has always been considered, and properly so, to be directed at the method or kind of punishment imposed for the violation of criminal statutes; the nature of the conduct made criminal is ordinarily relevant only to the fitness of the punishment imposed.

Appellant, however, seeks to come within the application of the Cruel and Unusual Punishment Clause announced in *Robinson* v. *California*, 370 U.S. 660 (1962), which involved a state statute making it a crime to "be addicted to the use of narcotics." This Court held there that "a state law which imprisons a person thus afflicted [with narcotic addiction] as a criminal, even though he has never touched any narcotic drug within the State or been guilty of any irregular behavior there, inflicts a cruel and unusual punishment...."

On its face the present case does not fall within that holding, since appellant was convicted, not for being a chronic alcoholic, but for being in public while drunk on a particular occasion. The State of Texas thus has not sought to punish a mere status, as California did in *Robinson;* nor has it attempted to regulate appellant's behavior in the privacy of his own home. Rather, it has imposed upon appellant a criminal sanction for public behavior which may create substantial health and safety hazards, both for appellant and for members of the general public, and which offends the moral and esthetic sensibilities of a large segment of the community. This seems a far cry from convicting one for being an addict, being a chronic alcoholic, being "mentally ill, or a leper...."

Robinson so viewed brings this Court but a very small way into the substantive criminal law. And unless *Robinson* is so viewed it is difficult to see any limiting principle that would serve to prevent this Court from becoming, under the aegis of the Cruel and Unusual Punishment Clause, the ultimate arbiter of the standards of criminal responsibility, in diverse areas of the criminal law, throughout the country.

It is suggested in dissent that *Robinson* stands for the "simple" but "subtle" principle that "[criminal] penalties may not be inflicted upon a person for being in a condition he is powerless to change." *Post,* at 567. In that view, appellant's "condition" of public intoxication was "occasioned by a compulsion symptomatic of the disease" of chronic alcoholism, and thus, apparently, his behavior lacked the critical element of *mens rea.* Whatever may be the merits of such a doctrine of criminal responsibility, it surely cannot be said to follow from *Robinson.* The entire thrust of *Robinson's* interpretation of the Cruel and Unusual Punishment Clause is that criminal penalties may be inflicted only if the accused has committed some act, has engaged in some behavior, which society has an interest in preventing, or perhaps in historical common law terms, has committed some *actus reus.* It thus does not deal with the question of whether certain conduct cannot constitutionally be punished because it is, in some sense, "involuntary" or "occasioned by a compulsion."

Likewise, as the dissent acknowledges, there is a substantial definitional distinction between a "status," as in *Robinson,* and a "condition," which is said to be involved in this case. Whatever may be the merits of an attempt to distinguish between behavior and a condition, it is perfectly clear that the crucial element in this case, so far as the dissent is concerned, is whether or not appellant can legally be held responsible for his appearance in public in a state of intoxication. The only relevance of *Robinson* to this issue is that because the Court interpreted the statute there involved as making a "status" criminal, it was able to suggest that the statute would cover even a situation in which addiction had been acquired involuntarily. That this factor was not determinative in the case is shown by the fact that there was no indication of how Robinson himself had become an addict.

Ultimately, then, the most troubling aspects of this case, were *Robinson* to be extended to meet it, would be the scope and content of what could only be a constitutional doctrine of criminal responsibility. In dissent it is urged that the decision could be limited to conduct which is "a characteristic and involuntary part of the pattern of the disease as it afflicts" the particular individual, and that "[it] is not foreseeable" that it would be applied "in the case of offenses such as driving a car while intoxicated, assault, theft, or robbery." That is limitation by fiat. In the first place, nothing in the logic of the dissent would limit its application to chronic alcoholics. If Leroy Powell cannot be convicted of public intoxication, it is difficult to see how a State can convict an individual for murder, if that individual, while exhibiting normal behavior in all other respects, suffers from a "compulsion" to kill, which is an "exceedingly strong influence," but "not completely overpowering." Even if we limit our consideration to chronic alcoholics, it would seem impossible to confine the principle within the arbitrary bounds which the dissent seems to envision.

It is not difficult to imagine a case involving psychiatric testimony to the effect that an individual suffers from some aggressive neurosis which he is able to control when sober; that very little alcohol suffices to remove the inhibitions which normally contain these aggressions, with the result that the individual engages in assaultive behavior without becoming actually intoxicated; and that the individual suffers from a very strong desire to drink, which is an "exceedingly strong influence" but "not completely overpowering." Without being untrue to the rationale of this case ... the Court could not avoid holding such an individual constitutionally unaccountable for his assaultive behavior.

Traditional common-law concepts of personal accountability and essential considerations of federalism lead us to disagree with appellant. We are unable to conclude, on the state of this record or on the current state of medical knowledge, that chronic alcoholics in general, and Leroy Powell in particular, suffer from such an irresistible compulsion to drink and to get drunk in public that they are utterly unable to control their performance of either or both of these acts and thus cannot be deterred at all from public intoxication. And in any event this Court has never articulated a general constitutional doctrine of *mens rea*. We cannot cast aside the centuries-long evolution of the collection of interlocking and overlapping concepts which the common law has utilized to assess the moral accountability of an individual for his antisocial deeds. The doctrines of *actus reus, mens rea,* insanity, mistake, justification, and duress have historically provided the tools for a constantly shifting adjustment of the tension between the evolving aims of the criminal law and changing religious, moral, philosophical, and medical views of the nature of man. This process of adjustment has always been thought to be the province of the States.

...

Affirmed.

* * *

What, then, is the significance of the status of addiction to drugs or alcohol? Despite the fact that a drug addict cannot be prosecuted for being an addict, an addict can be prosecuted for acts that violate the law, such as using or selling drugs or, as we saw in the *Ewing* case, stealing property to obtain money to buy drugs.

How do you think the criminal justice system should treat addiction? This question is currently the subject of considerable debate. Critics of our current criminal justice system argue that adopting what is sometimes called a "medical model" to the problem of addiction focused on rehabilitation is more humane, less costly, and more productive than punishment in reducing recidivism. These critics also argue that use of a "criminal model" focused on punishment has contributed to the harshness of our criminal justice system and the problem of what is called "mass incarceration." Do you agree with this critique? Should rehabilitation be offered as a substitute for (i.e., instead of) imprisonment? For example, instead of imposing a prison sentence, a judge could grant probation and make participation in a rehabilitation program a condition. Should rehabilitation be offered as a supplement (i.e., in addition to) prison? For example, rehabilitation services could be made much more widely available to people serving prison sentences in anticipation of their release? What are the arguments for and against each position?

Judges in cities across the United States have created drug courts, described in Problem 2.15 in Chapter 2. Defendants are offered the opportunity to participate in drug court, but not required to do so. To enter drug court, defendants typically must plead guilty to the charged offense. They are then placed in a treatment program and their progress is closely monitored by the judge. Those in treatment usually must appear regularly in court to discuss with the judge and an assigned social worker their progress as well as any problems or setbacks they encounter. Upon successful completion of the treatment program, the charge against them is dropped. If they fail to complete the treatment program, judgment is entered on the basis of their earlier guilty plea and they receive a criminal sentence. Is the drug court a sound compromise between punishment and treatment? Would it be preferable to make those who suffer addictions exempt from criminal punishment?

E. Voluntariness

Problems

4.8 As he prepared to leave a wedding reception, Dwight realized he was too inebriated to drive safely and asked a friend for a ride home. In the parking lot, Dwight's friend was drawn into a fistfight with his brother. Police arrived and ordered everyone to disperse. Due to his drunken condition, Dwight hesitated. When Dwight failed to respond, a police officer told him that if he failed to get into his truck and drive away, the officer would arrest him. Dwight entered his truck, started the motor and promptly backed his truck into a police car. Dwight was then arrested and charged with driving under the influence. Was Dwight's driving a voluntary act?

4.9 Dick and Jane, a newly married couple, take a vacation together. During the vacation, they decide to visit an establishment called "Burgers and Bullets" that allows visitors to fire various high-powered weapons, such as machine guns. Dick is an experienced gun owner but Jane has no experience with guns.

At Dick's suggestion, Jane takes a lesson in firing an Uzi submachine gun. Her instructor, Charles, stands next to Jane and demonstrates firing an Uzi both in single-shot mode and in full automatic mode. He explains what he is doing to Jane. Charles asks Jane "Are you ready to try it?" and Jane nervously answers "Yes. I think so." Charles then puts the gun on full automatic and hands it to Jane. Jane aims the gun down the range at the target and pulls the trigger. Because of the Uzi's powerful recoil, Jane stumbles backward, falling, and almost immediately loses control of the Uzi, which begins to fire upward and then backward. Several bullets strike Charles in the head, killing him. Can Jane be held liable for homicide based on the death of Charles? Could anyone else be held liable for homicide based on his death?

4.10 Larry was convicted of a sexual offense and subsequently served a prison sentence. After his release, state law requires him to register his address with state officials. In large part because of both his criminal record and his status as a sex offender, Larry has been both unemployed and homeless since his release from prison. Larry has already been prosecuted and convicted once for failing to register his address and now is facing a second such prosecution. The penalty for a second conviction of failure to register by a sex offender is an automatic life sentence. Larry's explanation for failing to register an address is that he is homeless and thus has no address to register. His lawyer argues that the state's sex offender restrictions leave sex offenders with virtually no place they can live. One of the lawyers representing Larry reported that she "had scoured the state for homeless shelters that would accept male sex offenders and could find only one, which was full."[4] Larry has been largely transient since his release from prison, frequently spending the night sleeping under various freeway overpasses. Is Larry's conviction for failing to register an address consistent with the principles you have studied in this and prior chapters? What arguments could you make for him if you were his lawyer?

4.11 The deadly coronavirus has hit some major cities in the United States severely. The mayor of one city issues an order that everyone who lives in the city must shelter in place at their residence. The order exempts certain categories of "essential" workers, such as medical personnel and police officers. Some residents defy the order by doing things such as gathering to socialize in parks and places of worship. The number of people in the city infected with the virus continues to rise as does the number of deaths attributed to the virus. The mayor and city council then pass a temporary ordinance that makes it a misdemeanor for anyone to violate the ordinance. John has been living for the past year in a shelter for homeless men run by a non-profit organization. There are

---

4. Shaila Dewan, *Homelessness Could Mean Life in Prison for Offender*, N.Y. Times, August 3, 2007, at A13.

many homeless men in the city and conditions in the shelter are crowded. One of the men who lives at the shelter was recently tested and diagnosed as having been infected with the virus. However, his symptoms were not serious enough for the man to be admitted to one of the city hospitals, which are struggling to deal with virus victims who are seriously ill. The citywide policy for hospitals has been to instruct those who test positive for the virus but have no serious symptoms to return to their residences and contact the hospital if their symptoms worsen. Consequently, the infected man returned to the shelter. Fearful that he will contract the virus, John decides to leave the shelter, live on the street, and sleep in a city park. Has John violated the ordinance?

Martin v. State

31 Ala. App. 334 (1944)Court of Appeals of Alabama

Simpson, J.

Appellant was convicted of being drunk on a public highway, and appeals. Officers of the law arrested him at his home and took him onto the highway, where he allegedly committed the proscribed acts, viz., manifested a drunken condition by using loud and profane language.

The pertinent provisions of our statute are: "Any person who, while intoxicated or drunk, appears in any public place where one or more persons are present, * * * and manifests a drunken condition by boisterous or indecent conduct, or loud and profane discourse, shall on conviction, be fined", etc....

Under the plain terms of this statute, a voluntary appearance is presupposed. The rule has been declared, and we think it sound, that an accusation of drunkenness in a designated public place cannot be established by proof that the accused, while in an intoxicated condition, was involuntarily and forcibly carried to that place by the arresting officer.

Conviction of appellant was contrary to this announced principle and, in our view, erroneous. It appears that no legal conviction can be sustained under the evidence, so, consonant with the prevailing rule, the judgment of the trial court is reversed and one here rendered discharging appellant.

Discussion Questions

1. Did the language of the statute save Martin? Or a general principle not found in the statute?

2. Would Martin have been liable if the statute had penalized only "appearing in any public place in a drunken condition"? What if the statute had penalized only "manifesting a drunken condition by boisterous or indecent conduct"?

Model Penal Code

§ 2.01

(1) A person is not guilty of an offense unless his liability is based on conduct that includes a voluntary act or the omission to perform an act of which he is physically capable.

(2) The following are not voluntary acts within the meaning of this Section:

    (a) a reflex or convulsion;

    (b) a bodily movement during unconsciousness or sleep;

    (c) conduct during hypnosis or resulting from hypnotic suggestion;

    (d) a bodily movement that otherwise is not a product of the effort or determination of the actor, either conscious or habitual.

Discussion Question

How would Martin have fared under the Model Penal Code provisions above?

* * *

Martin and the Model Penal Code require that conduct be voluntary to qualify for criminal liability. What, though, does it mean for conduct to be voluntary? Students, lawyers, and judges are often led astray when the law gives a familiar word a legal meaning that differs from the word's meaning in everyday usage. Such a word is sometimes called a legal "term of art." To avoid being misled, it is important to be aware of the special meanings criminal law gives certain words. The word *voluntary* is a good example. In common usage, *voluntary* typically means free from coercion or interference. Was Dwight's conduct in Problem 4.8 voluntary under this common meaning? In the context of the criminal law's voluntary act requirement, the word voluntary has a narrower meaning. Conduct is generally voluntary if the actor made a conscious choice to act, even if coercion influenced the choice. Was Dwight's conduct in Problem 4.8 voluntary under this narrower legal meaning of voluntary? Is it desirable for the criminal law to give words legal meanings that differ from their common meanings?

Problem

4.12 Part (a). Jeff was arrested for robbery. At the time of the arrest, one of the arresting officers conducted a pat-down search of Jeff. Another officer conducted a pat-down search of Jeff before placing him in the back of a police car for transport to a detention facility. Neither officer found any weapons or contraband on Jeff during these searches. The arresting officers then transported Jeff in the back of their police cruiser to the detention facility where he would be held prior to his trial. When they arrived at the detention facility, the arresting officers warned Jeff that he should tell them if he had any weapons or contraband on him because bringing such items into a detention facility is a felony. Jeff stated that he did not possess anything the officers needed to be concerned about. Once inside the detention facility, another officer searched Jeff before placing him in his cell. Suspicious of Jeff's evasive leg movements during this search, the officer focused his search on Jeff's legs and found marijuana hidden inside one of Jeff's pants cuffs. Jeff was indicted under the following statute:

> It is a felony for anyone to knowingly convey or attempt to convey any drug of abuse onto the grounds of a detention facility.

Assume that marijuana is illegal in the jurisdiction and qualifies as a drug of abuse. Is Jeff liable under the statute?

Part (b). Assume that Jeff swallowed several balloons of heroin just prior to his arrest to prevent the officers from finding them. The balloons were in Jeff's digestive system when he was transported to and entered the detention facility. When the balloons later emerged from Jeff's digestive tract, he attempted to flush the heroin down a toilet, but was caught by officers at the detention facility before he could do so. Assume that heroin qualifies as a drug of abuse. Is Jeff liable under the statute for conveying heroin onto the grounds of the detention facility?

F. Timeframing[5]

Statutes vary in how they describe the conduct element. The language chosen can give prosecutors and juries more or less leeway in selecting the culpable act. Consider the *Decina* case and the problems that follow.

People v. Decina

138 N.E. 2d 799 (1956)
Court of Appeals of New York

Froessel, J.

At about 3:30 p.m. on March 14, 1955, a bright, sunny day, defendant was driving, alone in his car.... At a point south of an overhead viaduct of the Erie Railroad, defendant's car swerved to the left, across the center line in the street, so that it was completely in the south lane, traveling 35 to 40 miles per hour. It then veered sharply to the right ... and continued thereafter at a speed estimated to have been about 50 or 60 miles per hour or more....

---

5. For perhaps the classic exposition of the time frame issue, *see* Mark Kelman, *Interpretive Construction in the Substantive Criminal Law*, 33 Stan. L. Rev. 591 (1981).

A group of six schoolgirls were walking north on the easterly sidewalk ... when defendant's car struck them from behind.... Three of the children, 6 to 12 years old, were found dead on arrival by the medical examiner, and a fourth child, 7 years old, died in a hospital two days later as a result of injuries sustained in the accident.

After striking the children, defendant's car continued on.... With its horn blowing steadily—apparently because defendant was "stooped over" the steering wheel—the car proceeded on the sidewalk until it finally crashed through a 7¼-inch brick wall of a grocery store, injuring at least one customer and causing considerable property damage. An injured customer in the store, after receiving first aid, pressed defendant for an explanation of the accident and he told her: "I blacked out from the bridge." ...

Defendant ... at the age of 7 ... was struck by an auto and suffered a marked loss of hearing. In 1946 he was treated in this same hospital for an illness during which he had some convulsions. Several burr holes were made in his skull and a brain abscess was drained. Following this operation defendant had no convulsions from 1946 through 1950. In 1950 he had four convulsions, caused by scar tissue on the brain. From 1950 to 1954 he experienced about 10 or 20 seizures a year, in which his right hand would jump although he remained fully conscious. In 1954, he had 4 or 5 generalized seizures with loss of consciousness, the last being in September, 1954, a few months before the accident. Thereafter he had more hospitalization, a spinal tap, consultation with a neurologist, and took medication daily to help prevent seizures.

On the basis of this medical history, Dr. Wechter made a diagnosis of Jacksonian epilepsy, and was of the opinion that defendant had a seizure at the time of the accident....

We turn first to the [defendant's claim] that his demurrer should have been sustained, since the *indictment* here does not charge a crime. The *indictment* states essentially that defendant, *knowing* "that he was subject to epileptic attacks or other disorder rendering him likely to lose consciousness for a considerable period of time", was culpably negligent "in that he *consciously* undertook to and *did operate* his Buick sedan on a public highway" (emphasis supplied) and "while so doing" suffered such an attack which caused said automobile "to travel at a fast and reckless rate of speed, jumping the curb and driving over the sidewalk" causing the death of 4 persons. In our opinion, this clearly states a violation of section 1053-a of the Penal Law. The statute does not require that a defendant must deliberately intend to kill a human being, for that would be murder. Nor does the statute require that he knowingly and consciously follow the precise path that leads to death and destruction. It is sufficient, we have said, when his conduct manifests a "disregard of the consequences which may ensue from the act, and indifference to the rights of others. No clearer definition, applicable to the hundreds of varying circumstances that may arise, can be given. Under a given state of facts, whether negligence is culpable is a question of judgment." ...

Assuming the truth of the indictment, as we must on a demurrer, this defendant knew he was subject to epileptic attacks and seizures that might strike *at any time*. He also knew that a moving motor vehicle uncontrolled on a public highway is a highly dangerous instrumentality capable of unrestrained destruction. With this *knowledge*, and without anyone accompanying him, he deliberately took a chance by making a conscious choice of a course of action, in disregard of the consequences which he knew might follow from his conscious act, and which in this case did ensue. How can we say as a matter of law that this did not amount to culpable negligence within the meaning of section 1053-a?

To hold otherwise would be to say that a man may freely indulge himself in liquor in the same hope that it will not affect his driving, and if it later develops that ensuing intoxication causes dangerous and reckless driving resulting in death, his unconsciousness or involuntariness at that time would relieve him from prosecution under the statute. His awareness of a condition which he knows may produce such consequences as here, and his disregard of the consequences, renders him liable for culpable negligence, as the courts below have properly held.... To have a sudden sleeping spell, an unexpected heart or other disabling attack, without any prior knowledge or warning thereof, is an altogether different situation ... and there is simply no basis for comparing such cases with the flagrant disregard manifested here....

Desmond, J. (Concurring in part and dissenting in part). I think the indictment should be dismissed because it alleges no crime. Defendant's demurrer should have been sustained.

The indictment charges that defendant knowing that "he was subject to epileptic attacks or other disorder rendering him likely to lose consciousness" suffered "an attack and loss of consciousness which caused the said automobile operated by the said defendant to travel at a fast and reckless rate of speed" and to jump a curb and run onto the sidewalk "thereby striking and causing the death" of 4 children. Horrible as this occurrence was and whatever necessity it may show for new licensing and driving laws, nevertheless this indictment charges no crime known to the New York statutes. Our duty is to dismiss it....

Now let us test by its consequences this new construction of section 1053-a. Numerous are the diseases and other conditions of a human being which make it possible or even likely that the afflicted person will lose control of his automobile. Epilepsy, coronary involvements, circulatory diseases, nephritis, uremic poisoning, diabetes, Meniere's Syndrome, a tendency to fits of sneezing, locking of the knee, muscular contractions — any of these common conditions may cause loss of control of a vehicle for a period long enough to cause a fatal accident. An automobile traveling at only 30 miles an hour goes 44 feet in a second. Just what is the court holding here? No less than this: that a driver whose brief blackout lets his car run amuck and kill another has killed that other by reckless driving. But any such "recklessness" consists necessarily not of the erratic behavior of the automobile while its driver is unconscious, but of his driving at all when he knew he was subject to such attacks. Thus, it must be that such a blackout-prone driver is guilty of reckless driving, Vehicle and Traffic Law,

§ 58, whenever and as soon as he steps into the driver's seat of a vehicle. Every time he drives, accident or no accident, he is subject to criminal prosecution for reckless driving or to revocation of his operator's license. And how many of this State's 5,000,000 licensed operators are subject to such penalties for merely driving the cars they are licensed to drive? No one knows how many citizens or how many or what kind of physical conditions will be gathered in under this practically limitless coverage of section 1053-a of the Penal Law and section 58 and subdivision 3 of section 71 of the Vehicle and Traffic Law. It is no answer that prosecutors and juries will be reasonable or compassionate. A criminal statute whose reach is so unpredictable violates constitutional rights....

Problems

4.13 Daniel is severely allergic to bee stings. His doctor told him a bee sting could kill him by causing a reaction severe enough to close down his airways and suffocate him in minutes, unless he gives himself an injection of epinephrine. The doctor gives Daniel an epinephrine injection kit and advises Daniel to keep it with him at all times. One day Daniel is driving in his car with the windows open on a busy street in the middle of the day when a bee flies in the window and starts buzzing around his head. Upon hearing the bee, Daniel realizes he left his injection kit at home. Daniel panics and starts wildly waving his arms around his head to shoo the bee away. In doing so, he lets go of the steering wheel of his car, which crashes into and demolishes a new police car worth $40,000. Luckily no one is hurt. But Daniel is charged under the following statute:

> Anyone who damages government property in excess of $1,000 is guilty of a misdemeanor punishable by 6 months in jail or a $5,000 fine.

Is Daniel liable for violating the statute?

4.14 Reconsider the following problem in light of what you have learned in this chapter.

Laverne recently gave birth to a baby boy, Earl. Laverne has previously given birth to two cocaine-addicted babies. Laverne admitted to her pediatrician that she regularly used cocaine while pregnant with Earl and that she used cocaine while in labor just a few hours prior to Earl's delivery. Urine tests demonstrate that Earl has cocaine in his bloodstream and medical expert testimony will establish that if Laverne took cocaine while in labor it would have remained in her bloodstream until well after Earl was delivered. Laverne is charged with violating the following statute:

> It is a felony punishable by up to 15 years imprisonment for anyone to deliver cocaine to a person under the age of 18 years.

The prosecution's theory is that Laverne delivered cocaine to Earl, who was clearly under 18 years of age, through her umbilical cord during the roughly two minutes that passed between his emergence from the birth canal and the severance of the umbilical cord by the obstetrician. What conduct on the part of Laverne is the prosecutor likely to focus on? What conduct is Laverne's lawyer likely to focus on?

4.15 Demy is a successful recording artist with a large entourage. Many of these folks hang out at Demy's large house, swim in her pool, borrow her designer clothes, and use Demy's fame and connections to promote their own musical careers. Demy begins to suspect that one member of her entourage, Tricia, is stealing money from her. When Demy and Tricia attend the birthday party of a mutual friend at a club, Demy asks Tricia to hold her purse while they are at the party. At the end of the evening, when Tricia returns the purse, Demy finds that $3,000 is missing from it. As Demy is leaving the party, she retrieves a handgun from the glove box of her SUV, gets into the passenger seat of Tricia's car and demands that Tricia return the money. Tricia states that she did not take and does not have the missing $3,000. With the gun in her right hand, Demy grabs hold of Tricia's purse with her left hand and a tug-of-war ensues. Tricia uses both hands to retain control of her purse. As she starts to lose the tug-of-war, Demy reaches for the purse with her right hand. As she does so, the gun in her hand discharges and a bullet strikes Tricia in the abdomen. Demy is charged with felony assault. At trial, Demy testifies that she did not intend to pull the trigger or to shoot Tricia and that she simply wanted to scare Tricia with the gun so she would return her money. Demy's lawyer calls a firearms expert who testifies that Demy had pulled the trigger reflexively during the struggle for the purse. What arguments could you make for Demy? What arguments could you make for the prosecution? If you were on the jury, would you convict or acquit Demy? Why?

G. Omission

Orthodox theory holds that criminal liability may not be imposed without a voluntary act. In the materials that follow, though, you will see that criminal liability may be imposed for an omission. Can the imposition of liability for *failure to act* be squared with the principle that criminal liability requires an act?

Criminal laws penalize omissions in two different ways. Some statutes expressly make failure to act an element of a crime, such as the Deadbeat Parents Act, 18 U.S.C. § 228:

> Any person who ... willfully fails to pay a support obligation with respect
> to a child who resides in another State, if such obligation has remained

unpaid for a period longer than 1 year, or is greater than $5,000 ... shall
be punished ... [by] a fine ... imprisonment for not more than 6 months,
or both.

An omission may also be penalized when the language of the relevant statute
speaks in terms of an act, such as killing. As the following case reveals, criminal law
here treats an omission coupled with a duty as the equivalent of an act. How does
the use of omission in the *Jones* case differ from the use of omission in the Deadbeat
Parents Act?

Jones v. United States

308 F.2d 307 (1962)
United States Court of Appeals for the D.C. Circuit

Wright, Circuit Judge.

[Jones was convicted at trial of] involuntary manslaughter through failure to perform
[her] legal duty of care for Anthony Lee Green, which failure resulted in his death....
In late 1957, Shirley Green became pregnant, out of wedlock, with a child, Robert
Lee, subsequently born August 17, 1958. Apparently to avoid the embarrassment of
the presence of the child in the Green home, it was arranged that appellant, a family
friend, would take the child to her home after birth. Appellant did so, and the child
remained there continuously until removed by the police on August 5, 1960. Initially
appellant made some motions toward the adoption of Robert Lee, but these came to
nought, and shortly thereafter it was agreed that Shirley Green was to pay appellant
$72 a month for his care. According to appellant, these payments were made for only
five months. According to Shirley Green, they were made up to July, 1960.

Early in 1959 Shirley Green again became pregnant, this time with the child Anthony Lee, whose death is the basis of appellant's conviction. This child was born
October 21, 1959. Soon after birth, Anthony Lee developed a mild jaundice condition,
attributed to a blood incompatibility with his mother. The jaundice resulted in his
retention in the hospital for three days beyond the usual time, or until October 26,
1959, when, on authorization signed by Shirley Green, Anthony Lee was released by
the hospital to appellant's custody. Shirley Green, after a two or three day stay in the
hospital, also lived with appellant for three weeks, after which she returned to her
parents' home, leaving the children with appellant. She testified she did not see them
again, except for one visit in March, until August 5, 1960. Consequently, though
there does not seem to have been any specific monetary agreement with Shirley Green
covering Anthony Lee's support,[5] appellant had complete custody of both children
until they were rescued by the police.

With regard to medical care, the evidence is undisputed. In March, 1960, appellant
called a Dr. Turner to her home to treat Anthony Lee for a bronchial condition. Ap-

---

5. It was uncontested that during the entire period the children were in appellant's home, appellant
had ample means to provide food and medical care.

pellant also telephoned the doctor at various times to consult with him concerning Anthony Lee's diet and health. In early July, 1960, appellant took Anthony Lee to Dr. Turner's office where he was treated for 'simple diarrhea.' At this time the doctor noted the 'wizened' appearance of the child and told appellant to tell the mother of the child that he should be taken to a hospital. This was not done.

On August 2, 1960, two collectors for the local gas company had occasion to go to the basement of appellant's home, and there saw the two children. Robert Lee and Anthony Lee at this time were age two years and ten months respectively. Robert Lee was in a 'crib' consisting of a framework of wood, covered with a fine wire screening, including the top which was hinged. The 'crib' was lined with newspaper, which was stained, apparently with feces, and crawling with roaches. Anthony Lee was lying in a bassinet and was described as having the appearance of a 'small baby monkey.' One collector testified to seeing roaches on Anthony Lee.

On August 5, 1960, the collectors returned to appellant's home in the company of several police officers and personnel of the Women's Bureau.... The officers removed the children to the D.C. General Hospital where Anthony Lee was diagnosed as suffering from severe malnutrition and lesions over large portions of his body, apparently caused by severe diaper rash. Following admission, he was fed repeatedly, apparently with no difficulty, and was described as being very hungry. His death, 34 hours after admission, was attributed without dispute to malnutrition. At birth, Anthony Lee weighed six pounds, fifteen ounces—at death at age ten months, he weighed seven pounds, thirteen ounces. Normal weight at this age would have been approximately 14 pounds....

Appellant ... takes exception to the failure of the trial court to charge that the jury must find beyond a reasonable doubt, as an element of the crime, that appellant was under a legal duty to supply food and necessities to Anthony Lee....

> "The law recognizes that under some circumstances the omission of a duty owed by one individual to another, where such omission results in the death of the one to whom the duty is owing, will make the other chargeable with manslaughter. * * * This rule of law is always based upon the proposition that the duty neglected must be a legal duty, and not a mere moral obligation. It must be duty imposed by law or by contract, and the omission to perform the duty must be the immediate and direct cause of death."

There are at least four situations in which the failure to act may constitute breach of a legal duty. One can be held criminally liable: first, where a statute imposes a duty to care for another; second, where one stands in a certain status relationship to another; third, where one has assumed a contractual duty to care for another; and fourth, where one has voluntarily assumed the care of another and so secluded the helpless person as to prevent others from rendering aid.

It is the contention of the Government that either the third or the fourth ground is applicable here. However, it is obvious that in any of the four situations, there are critical issues of fact which must be passed on by the jury—specifically in this case, whether appellant had entered into a contract with the mother for the care of Anthony

Lee or, alternatively, whether she assumed the care of the child and secluded him from the care of his mother, his natural protector. On both of these issues, the evidence is in direct conflict, appellant insisting that the mother was actually living with appellant and Anthony Lee, and hence should have been taking care of the child herself, while Shirley Green testified she was living with her parents and was paying appellant to care for both children.

In spite of this conflict, the instructions given in the case failed even to suggest the necessity for finding a legal duty of care. The only reference to duty in the instructions was the reading of the indictment which charged, inter alia, that the defendants 'failed to perform their legal duty.' A finding of legal duty is the critical element of the crime charged and failure to instruct the jury concerning it was plain error.

Reversed and remanded.

Problem

4.16 Will and Johnny manufacture and distribute methamphetamine. Will is an experienced chemist who "cooks" the methamphetamine. Johnny, who is considerably younger than Will, assists in the cooking and distributes the methamphetamine through his friends in the drug world. Recently, Johnny has become romantically involved with his neighbor, Joanne. Both Johnny and Joanne are recovering heroin addicts. Joanne relapses into heroin use and, as she does so, starts to re-involve Johnny in heroin use. Johnny's heroin use makes Will nervous and he urges Johnny to break off his relationship with Joanne. But Johnny refuses. One day, Johnny fails to show up for a meeting with Will and to answer his cell phone. Concerned, Will goes to Johnny's apartment. There he finds Johnny and Joanne in bed surrounded by heroin paraphernalia. Both are obviously under the influence of heroin. While Will is there, he sees Joanne convulse, vomit, and begin to suffocate due to the vomit in her throat. Will could easily save Joanne by clearing her throat or turning her onto her side. Instead, while Johnny remains asleep, Will simply watches Joanne die. Is Will criminally liable for Joanne's death?

Model Penal Code

§ 2.01 (3)

Liability for the commission of an offense may not be based on an omission unaccompanied by action unless:

    (a) the omission is expressly made sufficient by the law defining the offense; or

    (b) a duty to perform the omitted act is otherwise imposed by law.

* * *

Subsection (a) here refers to statutes such as the Deadbeat Parents Act discussed above. In accord with *Jones*, Subsection (b) adopts the conventional view that omission plus duty can fulfill the conduct requirement of a statute whose language does not mention omission.

Often it is easy to distinguish an act from a failure to act—an omission. But the line between act and omission is not easily drawn in some cases, and the prosecution and defense may disagree about how to classify a particular case. Characterizing the facts of a case as showing an *act* by a defendant usually favors the prosecution because that characterization eliminates the need to show the existence of a duty. Showing the existence of a duty may present the prosecutor with both legal and evidentiary challenges.

As *Jones* points out, a "status relationship" such as husband-wife or parent-child typically gives rise to a duty. Cases may arise that test the boundaries of such legal categories. Consider, for example, a Connecticut case, *State v. Miranda*, 715 A.2d 680 (1998), in which the defendant, a man, was living with a woman for several years along with her children from a prior relationship. The man and woman had lived together long enough to establish a "common law marriage," a situation in which the law treats a couple as if they were married despite never having gone through any marriage ceremony. The defendant had not adopted the woman's children. Did a common law marital relationship give rise to a duty on the man's part, based on what the *Jones* court termed "status" relationship, to rescue or report the woman's severe abuse of her children? This was an issue of first impression in Connecticut and the prosecutor had to brief and argue for an extension of the duty to rescue in the trial, appellate, and supreme courts before prevailing. The prosecutor also had the burden of obtaining and presenting sufficient evidence at trial to show that a common law marriage existed between the defendant and the woman. None of this would have been necessary if the case had involved action rather than omission on the part of the defendant. In other words, there is simply less for the prosecution to prove in cases involving action rather than omission.

The *Jones* court stated that there were "at least four situations" that give rise to a duty to act. Another potential source of a duty to act not mentioned in *Jones* is based on "creation of the peril." Actor A, a man hunting alone, recklessly shoots at something moving in some brush thinking it might be a deer. What was moving in the brush, though, was another man hunting alone, Actor B. A's shot hits and seriously wounds B in the leg. A does not know B. A sees that B is seriously wounded, bleeding badly, and unable to walk. All this takes place in a remote wooded area. If A fails to help B and B dies as a result, A might be prosecuted on the basis of his *act* of shooting B. Or A could be prosecuted on the basis of his failure to aid B, an *omission*, because A put B "in peril" by his prior reckless act.

The following Problem illustrates the malleability that may arise in characterizing a set of facts as showing act or omission.

Problem

4.17 Katy and Julia are roommates. Both are also law students. Late in the semester, Julia is working on a research paper and checks out a large number of books from the library. Because her room is not large, Julia stacks these books in multiple piles in the hallway outside her room. Katy must walk down this hallway to get to the living room, kitchen, and the one bathroom in the apartment. Late one night when the hallway is dark and the stacks of books have become quite large, Katy trips over the books on her way to the bathroom, falls, and breaks her leg. She cannot move or reach the phone to summon help. Julia hears Katy fall, opens the door to her room and sees Katy on the hallway floor in great pain and unable to move. Does Julia have a duty to rescue Katy? If so, on what basis? In other words, if Julia fails to help Katy and Katy dies as a result, could Julia be criminally liable for homicide? And under what theory? Act? Omission? Both?

H. Possession

Legislators frequently create criminal statutes that use possession as the conduct element. Possession of illegal drugs, chemicals used to make illegal drugs, machine guns, burglar's tools, certain types of explosives, and any firearm if the actor is a felon are just a few examples. Why do you think legislators make such extensive use of possession? After all, isn't the real concern with such items their actual use? Isn't the ultimate concern with possession of a machine gun not someone *having* it, but someone *using* it to cause great harm? Is the same true for the other items listed above? Why then do you think legislators so often choose to focus on possession rather than actual use?

Criminal law's use of possession is subject to a number of criticisms. One is that it is too broad in scope, especially the concepts of joint and constructive possession. Another critique is that the boundaries of possession are so vague they fail to provide clear notice and are malleable by police and prosecutors, concerns expressed by the U.S. Supreme Court in *City of Chicago v. Morales*, in Chapter 3, Section E, above, on specificity. Is possession an act? A mental state? A relationship? Some combination of each of these?

As you read the materials below, see if you agree or disagree with these criticisms. Would it be practical for criminal law to do away with crimes of possession? Could the concept of possession be clarified and narrowed? If so, how?

Oklahoma Uniform Jury Instructions
(2nd Edition)

Possession — Actual physical custody, or knowledge of the substance's presence, as well as power and intent to control its use or disposition.

Ninth Circuit Pattern Jury Instructions (Criminal Cases) Chapter 3. § 3.16
Possession — Defined

A person has possession of something if the person knows of its presence and has physical control of it, or knows of its presence and has the power and intention to control it.

More than one person can be in possession of something if each knows of its presence and has the power and intention to control it.

The concept of possession is often broken down into categories. One of these is *"actual"* possession. A person carrying a machine gun in his hands is said to have actual possession of it. Another category is called *"constructive"* possession. The leader of a drug cartel, for example, rarely takes "actual" possession of the drugs because doing so can be very risky. Instead, she relies on subordinates to take actual possession of the drugs to transport and sell them. Such a leader, though, maintains constructive possession because she knows where they are, who has them, and she has the "power and intention" to control them. Possession can also be *"sole"* or *"joint."* A person carrying a machine gun, who owns it and has exclusive control over it is said to have sole possession. Illegal drugs being transported by car for sale between two cities at the direction of those at the top of a drug gang's hierarchy are jointly possessed by the driver of the car and those for whom he is acting. Do the Oklahoma and Ninth Circuit instructions, above, include all four of these categories?

Problem

4.18 Dwayne is a drug dealer and a felon, having served time for possession of a controlled substance with intent to distribute. Dwayne is arrested one day trying to sell drugs to an undercover police officer. A criminal statute forbids a felon from possessing a firearm. Would Dwayne be liable under any of the following circumstances?

(a) Dwayne is arrested with a 9mm pistol in his hand, which he was using to threaten the undercover police officer.

(b) Police find the gun in Dwayne's pocket when they search him at the time of arrest.

(c) Dwayne is arrested in his truck and police find the gun under the driver's seat.

(d) Same as (c), except police find the gun in the truck's unlocked glove box. What if the glove box was locked?

(e) Police find the gun in a closed zippered bag along with money and drug scales under a tarp in the bed of the truck.

(f) Police obtain a warrant and search the apartment Dwayne shares with his girlfriend, Rose. During the search, the police find the gun under some clothes on a shelf in a closet shared by Dwayne and Rose. Rose tells the police that the gun is hers and that she keeps it for protection when Dwayne is not at home. Police find one of Dwayne's fingerprints on the gun.

Model Penal Code

§ 2.01

(1) Possession is an act, within the meaning of this Section, if the possessor knowingly procured or received the thing possessed or was aware of his control thereof for a sufficient period to have been able to terminate his possession.

* * *

How to define possession in the context of child pornography and the use of computers has raised challenges in recent years as the following problems, statutes, and case illustrate.

Problems

4.19 Albert owns a house in a downtown area of a major city and rents out several bedrooms to help with his mortgage payments. Paul is one of Albert's tenants. One day the mailman delivers, along with mail for Albert and some of the other tenants, a large manila envelope addressed to Paul. Albert fails to notice that the envelope is addressed to Paul and opens it. In the envelope is a magazine. Puzzled, Albert flips through the magazine and finds that it contains multiple pictures of child pornography. Paul apparently purchased the magazine from an illicit website. Concerned that the magazine itself may be illegal, Albert places it in a locked drawer in a desk in the basement of his house where he maintains an office and calls the police. Has Albert violated any of the statutes below? If so, which one(s)?

4.20 Michael searches online and finds an Internet chat room for people interested in child pornography. On a bulletin board related to the chat room, someone has posted information about a gathering at a private home in the city where Michael lives. At the gathering, videos containing child pornography will be shown and offered for sale. Michael attends the gathering, spends about a half-hour watching various videos, then leaves without buying anything. Has Michael violated any of the statutes below? If so, which one(s)?

4.21 Lonnie uses a publicly accessible computer at an Internet café to search for websites that post images of child pornography. He finds several websites and spends about half an hour browsing through various images. The computer does not allow Lonnie to download any images to its hard drive. Nor does the computer allow Lonnie either to print any images or download them to a portable storage device. All it allows Lonnie to do is view the images. Carol, another patron of the café, sees the images that Lonnie is watching and complains to the café's owner, John, who shuts down the computer that Lonnie has been using and asks Lonnie to leave. Has Lonnie violated any of the statutes below? Has Carol? How about John, the owner of the café and the computer? If so, which one(s)?

4.22 Bart uses his home computer to search for and access various websites that post images of child pornography. He spends about an hour browsing through various images. But he does not download any of the images to his computer's hard drive or any portable storage device. Nor does he print any of the images. However, Bart's computer automatically downloads the images he was watching to a "temporary Internet file cache" on his computer. Bart did not intend to have these images downloaded to his cache file. Nor was he aware that his computer would automatically download the images. Has Bart violated any of the statutes below? If so, which one(s)?

4.23 Part (a) Dennis and his wife, Margaret, own and share a home computer. Dennis uses it to search for and access various websites that post images of child pornography. On a number of separate occasions, Dennis spends several hours viewing these images and saves about 100 of them to the hard drive of the computer so he can access them later. Has Dennis violated any of the statutes below? If so, which one(s)?

Part (b) Dennis's wife, Margaret, notices the files Dennis has placed on the hard drive and opens them. Horrified, she closes the files and calls the police. Has Margaret violated any of the statutes below? If so, which one(s)?

Virginia Code

§ 18.2-374.1:1

A. Any person who knowingly possesses child pornography is guilty of a Class 6 felony.

18 U.S.C.

§ 2252A

Any person who ...

(a)(5)(B) knowingly possesses, or knowingly accesses with intent to view, any book, magazine, periodical, film, videotape, computer disk, or any other material that contains an image of child pornography ... [is guilty of a felony];

Ohio Revised Code

§ 2907.323

No person shall do any of the following:

...

(3) Possess or view any material or performance that shows a minor who is not the person's child or ward in a state of nudity, unless one of the following applies:

(a) The material or performance is sold, disseminated, displayed, possessed, controlled, brought or caused to be brought into this state, or presented for a bona fide artistic, medical, scientific, educational, religious, governmental, judicial, or other proper purpose, by or to a physician, psychologist, sociologist, scientist, teacher, person pursuing bona fide studies or research, librarian, member of the clergy, prosecutor, judge, or other person having a proper interest in the material or performance.

(b) The person knows that the parents, guardian, or custodian has consented in writing to the photographing or use of the minor in a state of nudity and to the manner in which the material or performance is used or transferred.

New Jersey Statutes

§ 2C:24-4.

...

(b) A person commits a crime ... if he knowingly possesses, knowingly views, or knowingly has under his control, through any means, including the Internet, an item depicting the sexual exploitation or abuse of a child.

The following statute is applied and interpreted in the *Barger* case, below:

Oregon Revised Statutes

§ 163.686

(1) A person commits the crime of encouraging child sexual abuse in the second degree if the person:

> (a)(A)(i) Knowingly possesses or controls any photograph, motion picture, videotape or other visual recording of sexually explicit conduct involving a child for the purpose of arousing or satisfying the sexual desires of the person or another person; [and] ...

> (B) Knows or is aware of and consciously disregards the fact that creation of the visual recording of sexually explicit conduct involved child abuse[.]

State v. Barger

247 P.3d 309 (2011)
Supreme Court of Oregon

Gillette J.

This criminal case involves the following question: Can a person be found guilty of "possess[ing] or control[ling]" digital images of sexually explicit conduct involving a child, as that phrase in used in ORS 163.686(1)(a), based on evidence showing only that the person searched for and found such images through the Internet on his or her computer? Although the trial court in the present case acknowledged that "the world of the Internet presses * * * the boundaries of what we normally understand to be possession and control," it ultimately concluded that a jury *could* find defendant guilty under ORS 163.686(1)(a) based solely on such evidence. As we explain below, we disagree with that conclusion: The statute requires something more than simply accessing and looking at incorporeal material of the kind involved here to "possess" or "control" that material. Accordingly, we reverse both the circuit court judgment and the Court of Appeals decision affirming that judgment.

In the course of investigating a report that defendant had sexually abused a child, a City of Eugene Police Officer, Sullivan, talked to defendant's wife, who told him that there was some "weird" material on the couple's home computer. Defendant's wife showed the computer to Sullivan, who looked at the computer's web-address history and saw three addresses that, based on their titles, seemed suspicious.

A few weeks later, the Eugene police asked defendant's wife if she would allow them to take the computer and examine it. She consented. Thereafter, Eugene police detective Williams, who was certified in computer forensics, took possession of the computer, made a copy of the hard drive, and used certain forensic software to examine that hard drive. Based on Williams's findings, defendant was charged with eight counts of Encouraging Child Sexual Abuse in the Second Degree, ORS 163.686, by possessing or controlling a visual recording of sexually explicit conduct involving a child. Each charge was based on a separate digital image that Williams found in the computer's "temporary internet file cache."

As Williams later explained at defendant's jury trial, temporary Internet files found in a computer are the product of an automatic function of a computer's web browser. Whenever a computer user visits a web page, the browser creates a copy of the web page and stores it in a temporary Internet file "cache," where it remains until the space is used up and written over, or it is erased. If a user calls up the same web page at some later date, the browser simply accesses the copy from the temporary files, rather than going through the slower process of downloading the same information from the web page. Computer users with ordinary skills would not necessarily be aware of that function or know how to go about accessing information stored in the temporary Internet file cache.

Williams testified that, when he received the computer, only one of the three addresses that had triggered Sullivan's suspicions remained in the web-address registry but that, by examining other Internet activity files, he was able to identify two other suspicious web addresses that someone had accessed in the recent past. Williams stated that he checked all three web sites and that all appeared to contain pornographic images of prepubescent girls and girls in their early teens.

Williams testified that he then searched for similar images that might be stored on the computer's hard drive, using certain words and phrases commonly used in child pornography. He acknowledged that he did not find any images of that kind that had been purposefully copied and saved in any user's personal files. He did, however, discover sexually explicit images of prepubescent girls in the computer's temporary Internet file cache.

The prosecution then presented the specific evidence that it asserts established defendant's guilt of the eight charges of Encouraging Child Sexual Abuse. The evidence included the eight digital images, all of which Williams had discovered in the temporary Internet file cache of defendant's computer, and which were the bases of the charges. Williams acknowledged that there was nothing about the images that identified what web site they had come from and that there was no way to know with absolute certainty whether the images had been accessed intentionally by a user or "were the result of pop-up windows or browser redirects." Williams further explained, however, that pornographic pop-ups and redirects occur almost exclusively when a computer user visits another pornographic web site.

After presenting Williams's testimony, the state rested. Defendant then moved for a judgment of acquittal, arguing that there was no evidence that the eight images at issue had made their way onto the hard drive through any intentional or knowing action by him and that, even if it was possible to infer that defendant had *accessed* the images through web browsing, that inference was insufficient to establish defendant's knowing *possession* or *control* of those images. The trial judge denied defendant's motion, and the jury ultimately returned guilty verdicts on all eight charges. On defendant's appeal, the Court of Appeals affirmed without opinion. We allowed defendant's petition for review.

Before this court, defendant argues that, although the state's evidence might support an inference that he had accessed and viewed the images at issue, the evidence would not support an inference that he ever knowingly "possess[ed] or control[led]" them within the meaning of ORS 163.686(1)(a).

Because there is no evidence in the record suggesting that defendant knew about the computer's automatic caching function or how to access material in the cache, the state does not now argue, and never has argued, that defendant "knowingly possess[ed] or control[led]" the images at issue insofar as they existed in his computer's temporary Internet file cache. Instead, the state's position is a more simple one. It argues that, because defendant's computer gave him the capability to print, save, e-mail, and otherwise manipulate the images in question, his actions of intentionally accessing one or more web sites that contained the proscribed images, thus causing those images to be displayed on his computer screen, constituted "possess[ion] and control[]" in the required sense. The question for this court thus is a narrow one: Can a computer user be found to have knowingly "possess[ed] or control[led]" digital images of child sexual abuse, within the meaning of ORS 163.686(1)(a)(A)(i), based solely on evidence showing that, at some time in the past, he intentionally accessed those digital images using his computer's Internet browser and—by reasonable inference—looked at them?

The answer to that question depends on what the legislature that enacted ORS 163.686(1)(a) intended by the phrase "possesses or controls" and on whether an activity that is commonplace now but was far less common at the time of the statute's enactment comes within the meaning that the legislature intended for that statute. To determine the legislature's intent, we employ the methodology set out in ORS 174.020 and *State v. Gaines.* Specifically, we first consider the text and context of the statute and then, if we so choose, consider any legislative history that the parties might proffer.

... [T]he operative words in the present inquiry are the verbs "possesses" and "controls." The verb "control" is not statutorily defined, but its common meaning, as set out in *Webster's Third New Int'l Dictionary* 496 (unabridged ed. 2002), is "to exercise restraining or directing influence over: REGULATE, CURB." The word "possess," on the other hand, *is* statutorily defined: For purposes of most Oregon criminal statutes, including ORS 163.686, it means "to have physical possession or otherwise to exercise dominion or control over property." ORS 161.015(9). As this court explained in *State v. Fries,* that definition of the word "possess" encompasses two alternative ways of possessing property that this court traditionally has recognized: (1) *physically* controlling the property ("actual" possession) and (2) exercising some *other* kind of dominion or control over the property ("constructive" possession). Put differently, to "possess" a thing traditionally means to control it, and "actual possession" and "constructive possession" are simply different types of control.

Because the idea of control is inherent in the statutory term "possess," it is odd that the legislature chose to define the crime of encouraging child sexual abuse in terms both of "possessing" and of "controlling" certain kinds of images. The state explains that choice as a considered decision to recognize that "control" *itself* may be both actual and constructive, and to define the crime set out in ORS 163.686(1)(a) in terms of (1) actual possession, *i.e.*, physical control of an object; (2) constructive possession, *i.e.*, "dominion or power" over the object that is not necessarily exercised; and (3) actual control, *i.e.*, active restraint or direction of the object.

That explanation is creative, but it is not persuasive. We think it highly unlikely that the legislature engaged in that kind of parsing of terms or that it even recognized that, in light of the statutory definition of the term "possess," the inclusion of the term "control" was duplicative. Instead, we believe it is more logical to conclude that the legislature's choice of words reflects its desire to ensure that the crime not be limited to a narrow, solely physical, concept of possession. In other words, it would appear that the legislature used *two* words to convey the same broad meaning that ORS 161.015(9) actually conveys in the single word "possess" and that, at least in the criminal law context, this court traditionally has ascribed to that word; *viz.*, to *physically or bodily* possess or control something *or* to exercise dominion or control (*i.e.*, a restraining or directing influence) over it *in some other way*.

At this stage of our interpretive process, we also consider the statutory context in which the wording under consideration appears. Defendant points to a contextual clue—a related section of the provision under consideration—that we agree is relevant. The "possesses or controls" wording at issue in this case appears in a subparagraph of ORS 163.686—subparagraph (1)(a)(A)(i)—that describes one way of committing the crime of Encouraging Child Sexual Abuse in the Second Degree. However, the next subparagraph of the statute describes an *alternative* way to commit the same crime. It states that a person commits the crime by

> "Knowingly pay[ing], exchang[ing] or giv[ing] anything of value to *obtain or view* a photograph, motion picture, videotape or other visual recording of sexually explicit conduct involving a child for the purpose of arousing or satisfying the sexual desires of the person or another person."

ORS 163.686(1)(a)(A)(ii) (emphasis added).

There are two significant things about subparagraph (ii). The first is that it is an alternative definition of the same crime—Encouraging Child Sexual Abuse in the Second Degree—that is defined in subparagraph (i), discussed at length above. The second is that it criminalizes the actions of paying to obtain and view visual recordings of child sexual abuse. Although other state legislatures have chosen to criminalize the act of viewing child pornography in and of itself, the wording of ORS 163.686(1)(a)(A)(ii) demonstrates to us that the Oregon legislature made a different choice: It chose *not* to criminalize the act of *viewing* child pornography, unless that act is accompanied by paying, exchanging, or giving "anything" *of value*. (That same requirement is true of the act of "obtaining" child pornography.)

That legislative choice is relevant to our reading of ORS 163.686. Whatever "knowingly possess[ing] or control[ling]" recordings of child sexual abuse might mean in subparagraph (1)(a)(A)(i), it involves something different than simply "obtain[ing]" or "view[ing]" digital images: The legislature clearly has chosen to criminalize the act of "view[ing]" or "obtain[ling]" visual recordings of sexually explicit conduct involving children under ORS 163.686(1)(a)(A)(ii) *only if that act is accompanied by the payment, exchange, or giving of something "of value*," an element that is not required under ORS 163.686(1)(a)(A)(i).

A final source of contextual evidence is the body of cases that interpret or discuss the definition of "possess" provided by ORS 161.015(9)—the statute that, as discussed, applies to ORS 163.686(1)(a)(A)(i) and therefore expresses the meaning that the legislature intended to convey by the phrase "possesses and controls" in ORS 163.686(1)(a)(A)(i). In general, those cases deal with possession of tangible objects—firearms, drugs, forged checks, and the like—and thus are not perfect analogies for determining how the concepts of actual and constructive possession apply to a digital image that once appeared on a computer screen and now is retained in some form on the computer's hard drive. Certain of the cases *are* relevant, however, to the extent that they show that even *constructive* possession of a thing, *i.e.*, dominion or control over it, cannot be established merely by showing that the thing was in close proximity or physically available to a potential possessor. *See, e.g., State v. Casey,* 346 Ore 54, 203 P3d 202 (2009) (fact that visitor's gun, which had been left on counter in defendant's home, was in close proximity to defendant when he went into home to retrieve items for police officers waiting outside would not support defendant's conviction on charge of felon in possession of firearm); *see also State v. Daniels,* 348 Ore 513, 234 P3d 976 (2010) (rejecting state's claim that methamphetamine found in defendant's home, in a purse that belonged to defendant's girlfriend, was constructively in defendant's possession because it was *available* for his use).

With the foregoing background concerning the meaning of the phrase "possesses or controls" in ORS 163.686(1)(a)(A)(i) in mind, we turn to the specific question that this case presents: Does a computer user's act of accessing an Internet web page and intentionally calling digital images of child sexual abuse onto a computer screen constitute "possess[ion] or control[]" of those images within the meaning of that statute? The state asserts that it does, and offers three different explanations for its answer.

First, the state contends that, insofar as a computer user has physical control over a computer screen, he or she has physical control ("actual" possession) of any images that appear on it. The state points to the fact that a computer user can move his or her monitor from one place to another and thereby display the image appearing on the screen wherever he or she chooses. We think, however, that that argument misses the point: The intangible nature of a web image is analogous to seeing something that a visitor has temporarily placed in one's own home. One may be *aware* of it, may even have asked the visitor to bring it for viewing, but one does not thereby *possess* the item.

The state argues, next, that a computer user "controls" a digital image of child pornography by actively navigating to the web site where it resides, thereby bringing the image to his computer screen. We think, however, that this argument suffers from some of the same defects as the preceding one: Looking for something on the Internet is like walking into a museum to look at pictures—the pictures are where the person expected them to be, and he can look at them, but that does not in any sense give him possession of them.

Finally, the state argues that, to establish that defendant "controlled" the images at issue at the time that they appeared on his computer screen, the state need only show that, at that time, defendant had the *ability* to direct or influence the images (by, for example, showing that he had the ability to save, copy, print, or e-mail them), and that it need not show that defendant actually *exercised* any such influence or control. In support of that theory, the state points to certain of this court's cases that describe constructive possession in terms of a "right" to control the object in question.

The state's position is problematic in a number of respects. First, it assumes that, when this court in [earlier cases] described constructive possession in terms of the "right" to control a thing, it meant nothing more than a bare and practical "ability" to exercise a directing or restraining influence. We do not read the cases that way. *Oare* and *Weller* both involved property that was physically present in places to which the defendants had access, so that the defendants physically could have taken up and moved or otherwise used the items. In both cases, this court found that physical ability to be insufficient by itself to support a charge of constructive possession. And, although this court in *Barnes* held that a jury *could* infer that the defendant claimed a right to control (and therefore possessed) the moonshine whiskey at issue in that case, its conclusion in that regard was based on the existence of evidence that the defendant was not only at the site where the whiskey was concealed, but had tools and containers designed to remove the whiskey from its hiding place. We conclude from the foregoing, then, that when the court in *Oare* and other cases referred to a "right" to control a thing, it was referring to something akin to a *legal* right to do so—a concept that is useful in discussing the distinction between "ownership," "possession," and mere "custody" of property, but one that is not helpful here.

What is more, there is no support in this court's cases for the idea that a mere unexercised *ability* to manipulate a thing can constitute constructive possession of it. Indeed, *State v. Casey*, discussed earlier, is to the contrary. In that case, this court considered and rejected the state's contention that a visitor's gun, which had been left on a counter in the defendant's trailer, was under the defendant's "dominion and control" (and, thus, in his constructive possession) when he went into the trailer to retrieve certain items for police officers who were waiting outside. It is clear from that decision that the mere fact that an object is within a person's reach, and that the person thus has a physical *ability* to exercise some directing or restraining influence over it, is insufficient to establish constructive possession of the object. And, to the extent that, in *Daniels, Oare* and *Weller*, this court also declined to infer possession or control from the mere fact of proximity or availability, those cases convey a similar message.

A final problem with the state's theory about the meaning of "control" is that it would sweep in more factual scenarios than we believe the legislature could possibly have intended. If the mere *ability* to cause an item to appear on a computer screen is sufficient to constitute "control" or constructive "possession" of the item for purposes of ORS 163.686(1)(a)(A)(i), then *any* person who uses the Internet (and, indeed, any person who is within physical reach of some tangible item of child pornography) can be deemed to be guilty of violating that statute, at least insofar as the element of possession or control is involved. Of course, the state contends that a person who already has accessed an image of child sexual abuse on his computer has a more direct and immediate ability to save, print, or otherwise control that image than does a computer user who has not accessed the image, and that that directness and immediacy makes the difference. But that argument still is nothing more than the assertion, rejected by this court most recently in *Casey*, that the *ability* to possess or control a thing means that one actually *is* possessing or controlling it.

In a final version of that argument, the state insists that a person who uses a computer to look at images of child pornography does more than just *view* the images that he brings to the screen. It contends that, because computers have the *capacity* to save, print, post, and transmit those images "with only a few mouse clicks," web browsing for child pornography is qualitatively different from other methods of "viewing" child pornography, and falls within the intended meaning of the phrase "possesses or controls" in ORS 163.686(1)(a)(A)(i). But we think that our recent holdings in *Casey* and *Daniels* fully answer that argument, particularly where the state fails to explain why existence of those capacities in the viewing device would transform viewing into possession. Neither do we see anything in the statutory wording that would support that idea.

For the foregoing reasons, we are not persuaded by the state's theories as to how and why, in the absence of some additional action by a computer user beyond that proved here, the user could be deemed to "possess" or "control," in any sense that this court heretofore has recognized, a digital image that he or she has called up on a computer screen. Instead, we are satisfied that the statute before us, ORS 163.686(1)(a)(A)(i), when read in the light of its context (particularly *ORS 163.686(1)(a)(A)(ii)*), embodies a considered legislative choice not to criminalize the mere "obtaining" or "viewing" of child pornography without consideration. Thus, we conclude that the acts at issue here—navigating to a website and bringing the images that the site contains to a computer screen—are not acts that the legislature intended to criminalize.

Applying our conclusions to the record in this case, we hold that defendant's motion for a judgment of acquittal should have been granted. There is no evidence in the record that, at any time, defendant "possess[ed] or control[led]" any of the eight images that are the subject of the charges against him under ORS 163.686(1)(a)(A)(i).

The decision of the Court of Appeals is reversed. The judgment of the circuit court is reversed, and the case is remanded to the circuit court with instructions to enter a judgment of acquittal.

Discussion Questions

1. State courts have divided on whether accessing child pornography on the Internet constitutes possession or control of such materials. Courts in Alaska and Georgia have ruled, like the *Barger* court, that it does not. Courts in Illinois and Pennsylvania, as well as a federal court of appeals, have ruled that it does. Which, in your opinion, is the better view?

2. Should viewing child pornography be enough to trigger criminal liability?

3. The *Barger* opinion tells us that Detective Williams "checked all three websites and that all appeared to contain pornographic images of prepubescent girls and girls in their early teens." Did Detective Williams violate any of the above statutes?

* * *

Subsequent to the *Barger* opinion, the Oregon legislature amended the statute at issue in that case as follows:

Oregon Revised Statutes

§ 163.686

(1) A person commits the crime of encouraging child sexual abuse in the second degree if the person:

(a) (A)(i) Knowingly possesses or controls, or knowingly accesses with the intent to view, a visual recording of sexually explicit conduct involving a child for the purpose of arousing or satisfying the sexual desires of the person or another person; or

(ii) Knowingly pays, exchanges or gives anything of value to obtain or view a visual recording of sexually explicit conduct involving a child for the purpose of arousing or satisfying the sexual desires of the person or another person; and

(B) Knows or is aware of and consciously disregards the fact that creation of the visual recording of sexually explicit conduct involved child abuse; or

(b) (A) Knowingly pays, exchanges or gives anything of value to observe sexually explicit conduct by a child or knowingly observes, for the purpose of arousing or gratifying the sexual desire of the person, sexually explicit conduct by a child; and

(B) Knows or is aware of and consciously disregards the fact that the conduct constitutes child abuse.

How did the Oregon legislature change the statute? How would the *Barger* case come out under the amended statute?

I. Vicarious Liability

The word *vicarious* is derived from a Latin word, *vicar*, meaning the representative of another person. Webster's defines vicarious as meaning "endured, suffered, or performed by one person in place of another." Vicarious authority, for example, is authority exercised by one person on behalf of another. Is vicarious liability consistent with the act requirement?

States are divided, some accepting and some rejecting vicarious criminal liability. Should the criminal law recognize vicarious liability, punishing one person based on the conduct of another? What are the arguments in favor of vicarious liability? Are they retributive? Utilitarian? Both? What are the arguments against vicarious liability? Again, are they retributive? Utilitarian? Both? It is useful in considering these questions to look back at an example of vicarious punishment you encountered in Problem 2.9 in Chapter 2 on punishment. This problem involved imprisonment on a "correctional planet" of a family member of a drug offender.

State v. Guminga

395 N.W.2d 344 (1986)
Minnesota Supreme Court

Yetka, J.

On May 29, 1985, the state filed a criminal complaint in Hennepin County Municipal Court against George Joseph Guminga, defendant....

On March 29, 1985, in the course of an undercover operation, two investigators for the City of Hopkins entered Lindee's Restaurant, Hopkins, Minnesota, with a 17-year-old woman. All three ordered alcoholic beverages. The minor had never been in Lindee's before, and the waitress did not ask the minor her age or request identification. When the waitress returned with their orders, the minor paid for all the drinks. After confirming that the drink contained alcohol, the officers arrested the waitress for serving intoxicating liquor to a minor in violation of Minn.Stat. § 340.73 (1984). The owner of Lindee's, defendant George Joseph Guminga, was subsequently charged with violation of section 340.73 pursuant to Minn.Stat. § 340.941 (1984), which imposes vicarious criminal liability on an employer whose employee serves intoxicating liquor to a minor. The state does not contend that Guminga was aware of or ratified the waitress's actions....

The certified question of law before this court is as follows:

Whether Minn. Stat. § 340.941, on its face, violates the defendant's right to due process of law under the Fourteenth Amendment to the United States Constitution and analogous provisions of the Constitution of the State of Minnesota.

We find that the statute in question does violate the due process clauses of the Minnesota and the United States Constitutions and thus answer the question in the affirmative....

Minn. Stat. § 340.73 (1984) provides:

> It is unlawful for any person, except a licensed pharmacist to sell, give, barter, furnish, deliver, or dispose of, in any manner, either directly or indirectly, any intoxicating liquors or nonintoxicating malt liquors in any quantity, for any purpose, to any person under the age of 19 years.

* * *

> Whoever in any way procures intoxicating liquor or nonintoxicating malt liquor for the use of any person named in this section shall be deemed to have sold it to that person. Any person violating any of the provisions of this section is guilty of a gross misdemeanor.

Minn. Stat. § 340.941 (1984) imposes vicarious criminal liability on the employer for an employee's violation of section 340.73:

> Any sale of liquor in or from any public drinking place by any clerk, barkeep, or other employee authorized to sell liquor in such place is the act of the employer as well as that of the person actually making the sale; and every such employer is liable to all the penalties provided by law for such sale, equally with the person actually making the same.

Under Minn. Stat. § 609.03 (1984), a defendant who commits a gross misdemeanor may be sentenced to "imprisonment for not more than one year or to payment of a fine of not more than $3,000 or both." In addition, a defendant convicted under section 340.941 may, at the discretion of the licensing authority, have its license suspended, revoked or be unable to obtain a new license.... As a gross misdemeanor, a conviction under section 340.941 would also affect a defendant's criminal history score were he or she to be convicted of a felony in the future....

Since this is not an appeal from a conviction, we do not yet know whether, if found guilty, Guminga would be subjected to imprisonment, a suspended sentence, or a fine....

We find that criminal penalties based on vicarious liability under Minn. Stat. § 340.941 are a violation of substantive due process and that only civil penalties would be constitutional. A due process analysis of a statute involves a balancing of the public interests protected against the intrusion on personal liberty while taking into account any alternative means by which to achieve the same end.... The private interests affected, however, include liberty, damage to reputation and other future disabilities arising from criminal prosecution for an act which Guminga did not commit or ratify. Not only could Guminga be given a prison sentence or a suspended sentence, but, in the more likely event that he receives only a fine, his liberty could be affected by a longer presumptive sentence in a possible future felony conviction. Such an intrusion on personal liberty is not justified by the public interest protected, especially when there are alternative means by which to achieve the same end, such as civil fines or license suspension, which do not entail the legal and social ramifications of a criminal conviction....

The dissent's citation to an article by Sayre, *Criminal Responsibility for the Acts of Another*, 43 Harv. L. Rev. 689 (1930), is ... inapposite. After finding numerous opinions on *both* sides of the question of whether to impose vicarious criminal liability, Professor Sayre states: "The liquor cases embody numerous diverging and conflicting views, and cannot be reconciled." Professor Sayre noted:

> The danger is that criminal courts may forget the fundamental distinctions between criminal and civil liability for another's acts, and begin to use as precedents for true-crime cases those liquor cases which virtually adopt the doctrine of *respondeat superior*.

Professor Sayre went on to summarize the appropriate legal principle in these terms:

> As the decisions indicate, a sharp line must be drawn between true crimes involving serious punishments and petty misdemeanors involving only light monetary fines. Where the offense is in the nature of a true crime, that is, where it involves moral delinquency or is punishable by imprisonment or a serious penalty, it seems clear that the doctrine of *respondeat superior* must be repudiated as a foundation for criminal liability.

Finally, far from endorsing criminal sanctions for violation of vicarious liability statutes, commentators LaFave and Scott believe that such sanctions are a mistake.

> To the extent that vicarious liability can be justified in the criminal law, it should not be utilized to bring about the type of moral condemnation which is implicit when a sentence of imprisonment is imposed. On the other hand, imposition of a fine is consistent with the rationale behind vicarious criminal liability. Vicarious liability is imposed because of the nature and inherent danger of certain business activities and the difficulties of establishing actual fault in the operation of such businesses. A fine, unlike imprisonment, is less personal and is more properly viewed as a penalty on the business enterprise.

> Yet, it must be recognized that the imposition of criminal liability for faultless conduct is contrary to the basic Anglo-American premise of criminal justice that crime requires personal fault on the part of the accused. Perhaps the answer should be the same as the answer proposed in the case of strict-liability crimes: it is proper for the legislature to single out some special areas of human activity and impose vicarious liability on employers who are without personal fault, but the matter should not be called a "crime" and the punishment should not include more than a fine or forfeiture or other civil penalty; that is, it should not include imprisonment. As the law now stands, however, in almost all jurisdictions imprisonment and the word "criminal" may be visited upon perfectly innocent employers for the sins of their employees.

LaFave & Scott, Handbook on Criminal Law § 32 at 227–28 (1972)....

The dissent argues that vicarious liability is necessary as a deterrent so that an owner will impress upon employees that they should not sell to minors. However, it does not distinguish between an employer who vigorously lectures his employees and one who does not. According to the dissent, each would be equally guilty. We believe it is a deterrent enough that the employee who sells to the minor can be charged under the statute and that the business is subject to fines or suspension or revocation of license.

In this last quarter of the twentieth century, there is doubt whether the United States Supreme Court would uphold a conviction under the provisions of the United States Constitution. Even if it were to do so, the statute we hold violates Minn. Const. art. I, §7, which states:

> [No] person shall be held to answer for a criminal offense without due process of law ... nor be deprived of life, liberty or property without due process of law.

We specifically and exclusively decide the question under the provisions of the Minnesota Constitution herein cited. We find that, in Minnesota, no one can be convicted of a crime punishable by imprisonment for an act he did not commit, did not have knowledge of, or give expressed or implied consent to the commission thereof.

Discussion Questions

1. Did Guminga "sell, give, barter, furnish, deliver or dispose of" liquor to a minor? If not, on what basis was he charged with violating Minnesota §340.73?

2. The Minnesota legislature in §340.941 chose to create vicarious criminal liability for employers who own and operate businesses that sell liquor. How can the Minnesota Supreme Court override this legislative choice? Is such an override consistent with the notion of legislative supremacy in making criminal law? Could the state prosecutor have sought review in the United States Supreme Court of the Minnesota Supreme Court's decision in *Guminga*?

3. How might the Minnesota legislature rewrite the statutes at issue to remedy the constitutional defect found by the *Guminga* court and still create an incentive for employers to prevent their employees from selling liquor to minors?

Problem

4.24 "Collective punishment" refers to the deplorable practice of government actors, often in times of war, imposing punishment on innocent people in retaliation for acts by others. Many instances have involved occupying armies retaliating against civilians for attacks by resistance movements. In World War

II, the commander of the German army occupying Yugoslavia ordered that "for every German soldier harmed" one hundred civilians from all segments of society be killed, leading to the deaths of thousands of civilians.[6] In response to such atrocities, the Fourth Geneva Convention was enacted in 1949. Article 33 states:

> No protected person may be punished for any offense he or she has not personally committed. *Collective penalties ... are prohibited* (emphasis added).

Nonetheless, the use of collective punishment continues. North Korea, for example, employs a "three generations of punishment" policy.[7] People viewed as hostile to the government in act or attitude are deemed criminals and sentenced to life imprisonment along with their families. In addition, the next two generations of such families remain imprisoned for life. Human rights organizations and others complain that the Syrian government and some of its opponents during the ongoing civil war in Syria have employed and continue to employ collective punishment measures, such as using planes to bomb civilian targets[8] and bulldozers to raze neighborhoods or entire villages.[9]

Does collective punishment resemble vicarious liability of the sort used by the Minnesota legislature in the statute at issue in *Guminga*? If so, what do you see as the similarity? Does collective punishment differ from vicarious liability? If so, what do you see as the difference?

---

6. Marie-Janine Calic, *A History of Yugoslavia* 125 (2019).

7. U.S. Department of State, *Prisons of North Korea* (www.state.gov/j/drl/).

8. *See, e.g.,* Richard Spencer, *Syria: Assad used chemical attacks to drive wedge between civilians and rebels*, The Times (April 13, 2020) ("The reports demonstrate how the regime managed to reverse the "asymmetrical warfare" of rebel forces operating among civilians, by using its air power to prosecute a ruthless policy of "collective punishment" that split the people from the insurgents.)

9. *See, e.g.,* Amnesty International, *Syria: US ally's razing of villages amounts to war crimes.* (October 13, 2015) (www.amnesty.org/en/latest/news/2015/syria-us-allys-razing-of-villages-amounts-to-war-crimes/).

J. Synthesis and Challenges

Problem

4.25 Julie is a 40-year-old substitute English teacher in an elementary school. She is a complete novice in regard to computer use. In her own words, she "has no clue" about computers. She does not own one and has rarely used one. She has never used the computers in the classrooms where she substitute teaches.

One day when she is substituting for the regular English teacher, Julie leaves the classroom for a few minutes just prior to class. When she returns, several students are gathered around the classroom computer watching a hair styling website. When Julie tries to shut down the website, a barrage of pop-up ads for Internet pornography websites start to appear on the computer's screen. Julie tries for several minutes to stop the pop-up ads, but she is unable to do so. She also does not know how to turn the computer off. Eventually she turns the computer's screen away from the students and toward the white board at the front of the classroom. After about an hour, during which the ads continue to appear on the computer screen, there is a break in the class. Julie then goes to the teachers' lounge and finds another teacher who helps her shut down the computer.

The computer at issue had filters on it to prevent access to pornography and to protect it from spyware and malware. Due to an oversight by the school's information services manager, the filters had not been properly updated for several weeks. The children in the class tell their parents about the episode and several of the parents complain to the school district. Following the parents' complaints, the district attorney is considering charging Julie under the following statute:

Injury or risk of injury to, or impairing morals of, children.

Any person who willfully or unlawfully causes or permits any child under the age of sixteen years to be placed in such a situation that the life or limb of such child is endangered, the health of such child is likely to be injured or the morals of such child are likely to be impaired, or does any act likely to impair the health or morals of any such child, … shall be guilty of … a … felony….

Has Julie violated the statute? Based on what you have learned in this chapter, what arguments could you make on Julie's behalf to convince the district attorney not to charge her?

Rethinking the Conduct Requirement

Scholars have focused on rethinking the conduct element of crimes. Consider the proposals of Professors Douglas Husak and Deborah Denno.

It is often stated that criminal liability requires an act and many scholars adhere to this view. Professor Douglas Husak, though, takes the position that criminal liability does not depend on the principle of an act, but on a different principle, which he calls the "control requirement."[10] He explains the notion of control as follows:

> The core idea behind the control requirement is that a person lacks responsibility for those states of affairs he or she is unable to prevent from taking place or obtaining.... I propose to explicate control in terms of what it is reasonable to expect of persons. A person lacks control over a state of affairs and neither is nor ought to be criminally liable for it if it is unreasonable to expect him or her to have prevented that state of affairs from obtaining....[11]

> Defenders of the act requirement must strain to explain liability for omissions. *Some* explanation is required, if the act requirement is to be preserved.... I believe that this normative basis is easily described. Criminal liability should sometimes be imposed for omissions because persons are able to exercise control over a state of affairs by not acting, and persons may be subject for moral and criminal condemnation for some of those untoward states of affairs over which they exercise sufficient control. This basis can be extended far beyond the category of omissions, thus opening the door to further kinds of exceptions to the act requirement.[12]

As indicated at the beginning of this chapter, it is typically thought to be improper to punish thoughts. What implications does Professor Husak's control requirement have for punishing thoughts? He maintains that the control requirement exempts most thoughts from punishment:

> [T]he best reason to resist criminal liability for the vast majority of thoughts is that persons lack the requisite degree of control over most of their mental processes to be responsible for them. Consider beliefs. A person cannot control whether or not he or she believes the Earth to be round, for example. A person simply evaluates the evidence and forms a judgment about the shape of the Earth, without exercising much if any control over the outcome. For this reason, liability for beliefs would be unjustifiable.[13]

---

10. Douglas Husak, *Does Criminal Liability Require an Act?* In Philosophy and the Criminal Law: Principle and Critique 60 (Antony Duff, ed., Cambridge U. Press, 1998).
11. *Id.* at 77–78.
12. *Id.* at 82.
13. *Id.* at 87.

But Professor Husak contends that the control requirement supports punishment for thoughts a person controls:

> I will call those thoughts that are sufficiently under the control of persons "mental acts." Clearly, some mental acts exist. For example, whether a person decides to rob a bank, deliberates over time, anticipates every contingency, and carefully plans an escape seems no less under individual control than whether he or she commits any number of acts that unquestionably are the proper objects of criminal liability.[14]

Discussion Questions

1. Look back over the criminal law's treatment of the issues you studied in this chapter, such as status, omission, and possession. Does Professor Husak's control principle provide a more convincing explanation of the criminal law's treatment of these issues than an act requirement? Does a control requirement better serve the purposes of the criminal law than an act requirement?

2. Do you agree with Professor Husak's argument that a person lacks control over her beliefs?

3. What implications would Professor Husak's control principle have for criminal law's use of vicarious liability? Is vicarious liability consistent with an "act" requirement? With a "control" requirement?

Crime and Consciousness: Science and Involuntary Acts

Deborah W. Denno
87 Minn. L. Rev. 269 (2002)

In 1906 Edouard Claparede experimented with the mind. He pricked the hand of a memory-impaired patient while greeting her with a pin concealed between his fingers. As always, the patient failed to recognize Claparede when the two met again; yet, she refused to shake his hand, explaining that it might be unpleasant but she did not know why. With this test, Claparede revealed the dynamics of "covert awareness"—the inconsistency between individuals' conscious acts and their unconscious memories, perceptions, and judgments.

Claparede's research was unusual for its time. For most of the twentieth century, the topic of consciousness, apart from Freudian theory, was not considered fit for serious scientific study. Consciousness was the "ghost in the machine," an unobservable, immeasurable, phenomenon rendered irrelevant to objective science. Starting in the 1970s, however, interest in the topic surged to the current point of "explosion." The scientific "race" to understand consciousness is on and the potential for discovery seems boundless.

---

14. *Id.*

The race within science has far-reaching legal implications. Criminal law, in particular, presumes that most human behavior is voluntary and that individuals are consciously aware of their acts. On the other hand, it also presumes that individuals who act unconsciously, such as sleepwalkers, are not "acting" at all. Under the criminal law's voluntary act requirement, unconscious individuals can be totally acquitted even if their behavior causes serious harm.

In contrast to these legal "dichotomies" (voluntary/involuntary, conscious/unconscious), modern neuroscientific research has revealed a far more fluid and dynamic relationship between conscious and unconscious processes. If such fluidity exists, human behavior is not always conscious or voluntary in the "either/or" way that the voluntary act requirement presumes. Rather, consciousness manifests itself in degrees that represent varying levels of awareness. [My writing] ... confronts this clash between legal and scientific perspectives on consciousness by proposing new ways to structure the voluntary act requirement so that it incorporates the insights of modern science on the human mind....

Despite the differences and debates among cognitive scientists on the topic, one idea becomes clear: No consensus of scientific support exists for the concept of a conscious/unconscious dichotomy. [In my writing, I propose] ... that the voluntary act requirement should be simplified and consist of three parts: (1) voluntary acts, (2) involuntary acts, and 3) semi-voluntary acts. Semi-voluntary acts would incorporate cases that have previously been shoehorned into the first two categories.... Semi-voluntary acts would include ... those who acted involuntarily or semi-voluntarily but demonstrate the potential to be dangerous again [for example, a violent sleepwalker].... Classifying [a violent sleepwalker's, like Kenneth] Parks's behavior as semi-voluntary would preclude an unqualified acquittal for him, but, at the same time, avoid the injustice or putting someone like Parks in an institution for the criminally insane.... The result of integrating increasing knowledge about the unconscious into the criminal law will mean that individuals will be held both more and less responsible than the conventional understanding....

If the criminal law can confront and modify the chimera of "either/or" embedded in the voluntary act requirement, it can join science with a more nuanced, and more just, view of the human mind.

Discussion Questions

1. Upon whom would jurors or judges rely in determining that an act was semi-voluntary?

2. How should punishment for semi-voluntary acts be graded?

Professor Denno criticizes use of the "legal dichotomies" of voluntary/involuntary and conscious/unconscious. She argues that modern research reveals that consciousness is not in fact dichotomous, but rather is fluid and "manifests itself in degrees that represent varying levels of awareness." In other words, she rejects approaching consciousness and voluntariness as if they present a binary choice with only two irreconcilable possibilities. Instead, she urges us to recognize consciousness and voluntariness as existing in degrees. The word *dichotomous* is used to describe issues and questions that present only two possible choices. In contrast, the word *continuous* describes something that exists in gradations. As you continue with your study of criminal law, you will encounter and it will be useful to recognize and to distinguish between subjects and questions that are dichotomous in nature and ones that are continuous in nature. Keep an eye out for some of each in the next chapter, Mental States.

Chapter 5

Mental States

A. Introduction

Legislatures regularly include one or more mental state requirements in defining crimes. The mental element is often referred to by the Latin phrase *mens rea*, meaning "guilty mind." Consider, for example, the following hypothetical criminal statute:

Aggravated Burglary

A person is guilty of aggravated burglary if the person intentionally enters a building that is a residential dwelling with intent to commit a felony therein. To be liable under this statute the prosecution must prove that the person knew at the time of entry that the building entered was a residential dwelling. The prosecution need not prove that any resident of the building was present in the building at the time of entry.

The mental elements of this offense are: (1) intent to enter; (2) knowledge that the building is a dwelling; and (3) intent to commit a felony inside the building. The mental and non-mental elements of this offense may be diagrammed as follows:

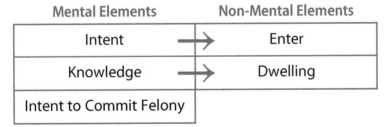

Mental Elements		Non-Mental Elements
Intent	→	Enter
Knowledge	→	Dwelling
Intent to Commit Felony		

Problems

5.1 Identify the mental state or states the following statutes require for conviction.

Vehicular Assault

A person is liable for the crime of vehicular assault if the person while driving (1) causes serious injury to another person and (2) is either reckless or negligent regarding such serious injury to another.

Sale of Controlled Substance Near a School

It is a felony to sell a controlled substance within 1,000 feet of any school. To be liable under this statute the prosecution must prove that the person knew at the time of the sale that the substance sold was a controlled substance. The prosecution need not prove any culpable mental state on the part of the person regarding the fact that the sale took place within 1,000 feet of a school.

Criminally Negligent Homicide

A person commits the crime of criminally negligent homicide if he causes the death of another person by criminal negligence.

* * *

5.2 Diagram all of the non-mental and mental elements of the above offenses.

This chapter focuses on the mental element in crimes. The first section describes how legislatures use mental states to define and grade crimes. It identifies common problems and sources of confusion regarding mental states. Section A also introduces basic concepts and vocabulary, comparing the Model Penal Code's use of the words *purpose, knowledge, recklessness* and *negligence,* with the more traditional term *intent.* At times, legislatures create crimes that dispense in whole or in part with mental state. We examine this controversial practice, known as *strict* or *absolute* liability, in Section B.

Legislatures often enact statutes that are silent or otherwise ambiguous regarding mental state, leaving it to courts to decide what mental states should apply or if strict liability should be imposed. Such statutes are a perennial source of uncertainty and confusion in criminal law and create challenging issues of statutory interpretation for judges, a topic we examine in Section C.

Sections D and E address how the criminal law responds to a defendant's claim that she was ignorant or mistaken about a matter of fact or law. Questions of ignorance and mistake can often be resolved easily if the legislature clearly defined the mental states required for conviction. But, as mentioned in the previous paragraph, legislatures often write statutes that are ambiguous on mental states, causing considerable confusion in the treatment of ignorance and mistake.

Sections F and G deal with two mental states encountered less often than those covered in Section A. Section F treats *willful blindness,* a term used to describe the mental state of a person who goes out of his or her way to avoid knowledge. In the *Jewell* case in Section F, for example, the defendant consciously avoided knowledge that a car he was paid to drive from Mexico into the United States contained marijuana. Section G deals with conditional purpose, the idea that one may have purpose to do an act or cause a result only if some condition is fulfilled. For example, a robber may intend to use force only if the victim of the crime resists. Jurisdictions vary on whether they find conditional purpose sufficient for liability under a statute that requires purpose.

What impact should intoxication with alcohol or drugs have on criminal liability? Should the fact that a defendant was drunk when she killed someone, for example, aggravate punishment? Should it mitigate punishment? Or should it be treated as irrelevant? Section H on intoxication looks at these and related questions.

Describe the mental states of the people in the following problems using your own words. Then, once you have read and studied the Model Penal Code's mental state terms later in this Chapter, come back to these problems and decide which Model Penal Code terms best fit each person.

Problems

5.3 In July 2016, the U.S. Director of National Intelligence released a brief report containing the government's estimate of how many "non-combatants" have been killed by U.S. drone strikes outside war zones. The report provides the following summary:

- Total Number of Strikes Against Terrorist Targets Outside Areas of Active Hostilities: 473
- Combatant Deaths: [Between] 2372–2581
- Non-Combatant Deaths: [Between] 64–116

What mental state or states do you think the drone operators had about the combatant deaths? What mental state or states do you think the drone operators had about the non-combatant deaths?

5.4 Delores was charged with running a prostitution business by telephone from her home. Over a period of 12 years, she employed more than 100 women whom she refers to as "subcontractors." When confronted with the charges, Delores responded that she ran a completely legal high-end escort service that was not intended to involve the exchange of sex for money. In fact, she claims that she explicitly directed her female subcontractors not to engage in the illegal exchange of sex for money and her contracts with the women expressly prohibited such conduct. Rather, the male customers were to pay $300 for 90 minutes of "fantasy" conversation and companionship. It turns out that many of Delores's subcontractors were in fact engaging in prostitution with her escort service's customers. What mental state or states do you think Delores had about the fact that some of her subcontractors were engaging in illegal prostitution?

5.5 Rod and Sandra are the parents of twin girls, Daria and Lilly, who are born fused together at both the chest and abdomen. Daria, referred to by doctors as the "cardiac twin," is born with a heart. Lilly, referred to by doctors as the "acardiac twin," is born without a heart. Lilly survives after birth because Daria's heart pumps blood not only through Daria's circulatory system but also through Lilly's circulatory system by way of a shared umbilical cord. Unless the girls are separated soon after birth, both will die. The only hope for saving Daria is to separate her from Lilly. But that means that Lilly will certainly die. The operation also poses a substantial risk to Daria's life. In other words, either: (1) both girls will die or (2) Lilly will die and Daria might survive if the operation is successful. Rod and Sandra consent to the operation in the hope of saving Daria's life and the surgeons perform the operation. When performing the operation, what mental state or states do the surgeons have regarding Daria's death? When performing the operation, what mental state or states do the surgeons have regarding Lilly's death?

5.6 During a late-season professional baseball game between teams that are both vying for a spot in the postseason playoffs, a relief pitcher is brought in with his team ahead by several runs and a few innings left to play. The opposing team then loads the bases and the relief pitcher gives up a home run and the opposing team takes the lead. The player who hit the home run exuberantly celebrates as he runs around the bases. On the very next pitch, the relief pitcher hits the next batter from the opposing team with a fastball. The batter then charges the pitcher and throws his batting helmet at the pitcher, hitting him. What was the mental state of the pitcher about hitting the batter? What was the mental state of the batter who charged the pitching mound about hitting the pitcher with his helmet?

5.7 Kristen, a hospital surgical technician who is also a drug addict, stole pain medication from dozens of hospital patients who were recovering from surgery, causing them to experience very serious pain. Kristen also swapped needles she used to inject herself with those used to inject the recovering surgical patients, thus infecting many of the patients with the hepatitis C virus that Kristen herself carried. Assume Kristen knew that she was infected with the hepatitis C virus at the time she swapped the needles. What was Kristen's mental state about stealing the pain medication? What was her mental state about the pain she caused the patients? What was her mental state about the hepatitis C infection she gave to some of the patients?

1. The Functions of Mental States

Mental states serve two important functions in criminal law. One is in distinguishing criminal conduct from conduct that is either wholly innocent or that should be subject only to civil sanctions. In many jurisdictions, for example, one who kills another person with simple negligence regarding the death is not subject to criminal liability, but only to civil tort liability in a suit brought by a private plaintiff for wrongful death seeking monetary damages. In contrast, one who kills another person with gross negligence regarding the death is subject to a criminal action brought by the state seeking criminal punishment in addition to being subject to civil tort liability.

The second function mental states serve is the grading of criminal offenses, distinguishing between and among more and less serious offenses. For example, one who kills another person with purpose regarding the death qualifies for a higher level of offense and punishment than one who kills another person with either gross negligence or recklessness regarding the death.

a. Distinguishing Criminal from Non-Criminal Conduct

Why do legislatures use mental state as an ingredient in defining crimes? Supreme Court Justice Robert Jackson, who served as a prosecutor at the Nuremberg war crime trials following World War II, offered the following explanation:

> The contention that an injury can amount to a crime only when inflicted by intention is no provincial or transient notion. It is as universal and persistent in mature systems of law as belief in freedom of the human will and a consequent ability and duty of the normal individual to choose between good and evil. A relation between some mental element and punishment for a harmful act is almost as instinctive as the child's familiar exculpatory "But I didn't mean to" ...[1]

As this passage suggests, a defendant's mental state is closely tied to our intuitive sense of blameworthiness. Therefore, from a retributive perspective, it makes sense to rely on mental state to determine which actors are blameworthy and should be criminally sanctioned.

Compare, for example, a political extremist who sends a letter containing anthrax to a government office and a mail carrier who delivers the letter. The extremist's purpose is to infect and kill a legislator whom the extremist has targeted because of the legislator's support of abortion rights. The mail carrier, by contrast, does not know the letter is contaminated. His only purpose is to deliver mail, not hurt anyone. The legislator opens the letter, is infected, and dies. The extremist and the mail carrier both played a role — "acted" — in bringing about the legislator's death. But we think of the extremist as a blameworthy criminal because she had purpose to kill and the mail carrier as innocent because he had no blameworthy mental state concerning the legislator's death.

b. Grading Offenses

Mental states are useful in establishing degrees of blameworthiness. The architecture of the law of homicide, for example, is built on gradations of mental state regarding

---

1. *Morissette v. United States*, 342 U.S. 246, 250 (1952).

the victim's death. The Model Penal Code's homicide hierarchy places those who kill with purpose or knowledge regarding the death, such as the extremist who mailed anthrax in the previous hypothetical, in its highest homicide category, murder. Those who kill recklessly—by consciously engaging in highly risky conduct, such as drag racing—typically fall in a homicide category just below murder called manslaughter and are exposed to less punishment than those convicted of murder. The Model Penal Code creates a third homicide category of negligent homicide for those who kill by engaging in highly risky conduct when they should be, but are not, aware of the risk of death. Under the Model Penal Code, negligent homicide entails less punishment than both murder and manslaughter.

2. Sources of Difficulty

Despite the obvious and intuitive appeal of mental states in marking the boundaries of the criminal law and grading offenses, the treatment of mental states is often the source of considerable confusion and difficulty in criminal law. Three aspects of mental states regularly cause trouble. Each is examined below. Time invested in understanding these sources of difficulty will pay large dividends throughout the course. It is worthwhile reading the following sections several times and raising questions you have about this material in class to make sure you have a good grasp of it.

a. Mental State Is a Question of Degree

Early criminal law took a crude, simplistic approach to mental state. It treated mental state inquiries as posing binary (i.e. either/or) propositions. A person either had a guilty mental state or did not. Virtually any sort of morally blameworthy mental state sufficed as a guilty mental state.

This attitude, which continues to impede the clear analysis and drafting of mental elements, deems a mental state inquiry as analogous, in modern terms, to the power switch on a cell phone or a guitar amplifier that has only on/off positions with no gradations in between.

In contrast, modern criminal law uses a more sophisticated, nuanced approach in assessing mental states. It treats mental state inquiries as posing questions of degree. As the Model Penal Code's homicide hierarchy, described above, illustrates, a variety of mental states that differ in blameworthiness may qualify a defendant for criminal sanctions. This modern approach views mental state as analogous to the volume control on a cell phone or guitar amplifier, rather than its power switch. As one moves up the hierarchy of mental states from negligence to purpose, for example, blame increases just as the sound coming from a cell phone or amplifier increases as one presses a certain button or turns a knob to increase the volume.

Failure by legislators and judges to recognize the fact that mental states take a variety of forms with varying degrees of blameworthiness and failure to distinguish clearly among those various mental states has been and continues to be a common problem in the criminal law's treatment of mental state.

b. Multiple Mental States

The common law originally took the simplistic view that each criminal offense had only one of two possible mental states, either what it termed "specific intent" or "general intent."

The modern view recognizes that criminal statutes may and often do require more than one mental state for conviction. The burglary statute at the outset of this chapter is an example. It requires *intent* about entering, *knowledge* that the building entered is a dwelling, and *intent* to commit a felony inside the dwelling.

As such statutes implicitly recognize, a person is capable of simultaneously having more than one mental state. Take, for example, someone transporting stolen archaeological artifacts into the United States. One mental state the person may possess is *purpose* to transport the objects at issue—the conscious objective of moving them from one place to another. At the same time, the person may have a second mental state, *knowledge,* that the objects are archaeological artifacts. The person may at the same time have a third mental state, *recklessness,* regarding the fact that the artifacts are stolen. A person might have all three of these mental states at the same time or lack one or more of them.

Failure to distinguish clearly among multiple mental states required by a statute for conviction and among multiple mental states possessed by a particular defendant has been and continues to be a common problem in the criminal law's treatment of mental state.

c. Mental State Is Relational

A third critical aspect of mental state is that it is relational, an idea we encountered in studying proportionality. Suppose someone asked you "Do you belong?" You would be unable to respond unless the questioner provided a reference point by answering a second question, "To what?" Your answers to the question would vary with the reference point—e.g., your family, the Hell's Angels Motorcycle Club, the Sierra Club, your law school class, or a Colombian drug cartel.

The same is true with mental state. If we were to ask "What is the mental state of the person in our stolen artifacts hypothetical?" it would be impossible to answer the question clearly without specifying the reference point for the mental state—the act of transporting the artifacts, their status as artifacts, or their status as stolen. The defendant may have purpose to transport the objects, but not realize that they are artifacts or that they are stolen. Or the person might know they are artifacts, but not know they are stolen. That a crime may require, and an offender may possess, more than one mental state makes it critical *to specify to what the mental state pertains* in order to avoid confusion. The common law often failed to do so and, unfortunately, many legislators, judges, and criminal lawyers today often fail to do so.

Criminal law's treatment of mental state has evolved from crude to relatively sophisticated by recognizing: (1) that mental state is a question of degree, (2) that crimes and criminal defendants can have more than one mental state, and (3) that mental state is relational. Your mastery of mental state, which is central to all subsequent chapters of this book and to virtually every type of crime, will turn in large part on being familiar with these sources of difficulty. However, you will see that the level of sophistication and clarity in dealing with these three topics still varies greatly from one legislature, judge, and lawyer to the next.

3. The Vocabulary of Mental States

The criminal law's traditional treatment of mental state was abysmal, resulting in widespread confusion and discontent. Consider the following passage from a Senate report proposing reform of the federal criminal law's handling of mental state:

> Present Federal criminal law is composed of a bewildering array of terms used to describe the mental element of an offense. The National Commission's consultant on this subject identified 78 different terms used in present law. These range from the traditional "knowingly," "willfully," and "maliciously," to the redundant "willful, deliberate, malicious, and premeditated," to the conclusory "unlawfully," "improperly," and "feloniously," to the self-contradictory "wilfully neglects." No Federal statute attempts a comprehensive and precise definition of the terms used to describe the requisite state of mind. Nor are the terms defined in the statutes in which they are used. Instead the task of giving substance to the "mental element" used in a particular statute has been left to the courts.[2]

This report was written in 1977. Today, more than four decades later, Congress has yet to remedy this sorry situation.

This report identifies two problems in the treatment of *mens rea*. One is the sheer number and variety of mental state terms. The second is the fact that these terms are either poorly defined or not defined at all. This lack of clarity in the language of mental states reflects an underlying conceptual failure to divide mental states into separate categories. In other words, lack of clarity in *speaking* about mental states often reflects a more basic problem of lack of precision in *thinking* about mental states.

a. Model Penal Code Terminology

The Model Penal Code exemplifies a more recent stage in the evolution of the criminal law's treatment of mental states. The Model Penal Code seeks to remedy the vocabulary problems described in the report quoted above by using four primary mental states—purpose, knowledge, recklessness, and negligence—and attempting to define each with precision. It recognizes that a person may simultaneously entertain more than one mental state and that the definition of a crime often entails use of multiple mental states. It also insists on specifying what the mental state pertains to and analyzing mental state separately for each non-mental element of an offense.

---

2. Criminal Code Reform Act of 1977, Senate Report No. 605, 95th Cong.,1st Sess. 55 (1977).

The Model Penal Code defines these four mental states in Section 2.02. The following Comment to that section explains the drafters' goals.

Comment to Model Penal Code

§ 2.02 General Requirements of Culpability

[This] section ... attempts the extremely difficult task of articulating the kinds of culpability that may be required for the establishment of liability. It delineates four levels of culpability: purpose, knowledge, recklessness and negligence. It requires that one of these levels of culpability must be proved with respect to each "material element" of the offense, which may involve (1) the nature of the forbidden conduct, (2) the attendant circumstances, or (3) the result of conduct. *The question of which level of culpability suffices to establish liability must be addressed separately with respect to each material element,* and will be resolved either by the particular definition of the offense or the general provisions of this section. (emphasis added)

The purpose of articulating these distinctions in detail is to advance the clarity of draftsmanship in the delineation of the definitions of specific crimes, to provide a distinct framework against which those definitions may be tested, and to dispel the obscurity with which the culpability requirement is often treated when such concepts as "general criminal intent," "mens rea," "presumed intent," "malice," "wilfulness," "scienter" and the like have been employed. What Justice Jackson called "the variety, disparity and confusion" of judicial definitions of "the requisite but elusive mental element" in crime should, insofar as possible, be rationalized by a criminal code.

The Model Code's approach is based upon the view that *clear analysis requires that the question of the kind of culpability required to establish the commission of an offense be faced separately with respect to each material element of the crime.* (emphasis added)

Under the Code, therefore, the problem of the kind of culpability that is required for conviction must be faced separately with respect to each material element of the offense, although the answer may in many cases be the same with respect to each element.

* * *

Examine the following MPC provisions carefully to see how they define *purpose, knowledge, recklessness,* and *negligence.* It is worth spending time to make sure you understand each of these because they will recur throughout the course, with every crime that we study.

Model Penal Code

§ 2.02 General Requirements of Culpability.

(2) Kinds of Culpability Defined.

(a) Purposely.

A person acts purposely with respect to a material element of an offense when:

(i) if the element involves the nature of his conduct or a result thereof, it is his conscious object to engage in conduct of that nature, or to cause such result; and

(ii) if the element involves the attendant circumstances, he is aware of the existence of such circumstances or he believes or hopes that they exist.

(b) Knowingly.

A person acts knowingly with respect to a material element of an offense when:

(i) if the element involves the nature of his conduct or the attendant circumstances, he is aware that his conduct is of that nature or that such circumstances exist; and

(ii) if the element involves a result of his conduct, he is aware that it is practically certain that his conduct will cause such a result.

Comment

Purpose and Knowledge. In defining the kinds of culpability, the Code draws a narrow distinction between acting purposely and knowingly, one of the elements of ambiguity in legal usage of the term "intent." Knowledge that the requisite external circumstances exist is a common element in both conceptions. But action is not purposive with respect to the nature or result of the actor's conduct unless it was his conscious object to perform an action of that nature or to cause such a result. It is meaningful to think of the actor's attitude as different if he is simply aware that his conduct is of the required nature or that the prohibited result is practically certain to follow from his conduct....

Most recent legislative revisions and proposals have adopted, though with varying terminology, the Model Code's distinction between purpose and knowledge. They, like the Code, have made these levels of culpability depend on the actual state of mind of the actor rather than on what a reasonable man in the circumstances would have contemplated.

Model Penal Code

§ 2.02 General Requirements of Culpability.

(c) Recklessly.

A person acts recklessly with respect to a material element of an offense when he consciously disregards a substantial and unjustifiable risk that the material element exists or will result from his conduct. The risk must be of such a nature and degree that, considering the nature and purpose of the actors conduct and the circumstances known to him, its disregard involves a gross deviation from the standard of conduct that a law-abiding person would observe in the actor's situation.

Comment

Recklessness. An important discrimination is drawn between acting either purposely or knowingly and acting recklessly. As the Code uses the term, recklessness involves conscious risk creation. It resembles acting knowingly in that a state of awareness is involved, but the awareness is of risk, that is of a probability less than substantial certainty; the matter is contingent from the actor's point of view. Whether the risk relates to the nature of the actor's conduct, or to the existence of the requisite attendant circumstances, or to the result that may ensue, is immaterial; the concept is the same, and is thus defined to apply to any material element.

The risk of which the actor is aware must of course be substantial in order for the recklessness judgment to be made. The risk must also be unjustifiable. Even substantial risks, it is clear, may be created without recklessness when the actor is seeking to serve a proper purpose, as when a surgeon performs an operation that he knows is very likely to be fatal but reasonably thinks to be necessary because the patient has no other, safer chance. Some principle must, therefore, be articulated to indicate the nature of the final judgment to be made after everything has been weighed. Describing the risk as "substantial" and "unjustifiable" is useful but not sufficient, for these are terms of degree, and the acceptability of a risk in a given case depends on a great many variables. Some standard is needed for determining *how* substantial and *how* unjustifiable the risk must be in order to warrant a finding of culpability. There is no way to state this value judgment that does not beg the question in the last analysis; the point is that the jury must evaluate the actor's conduct and determine whether it should be condemned. The Code proposes, therefore, that this difficulty be accepted frankly, and that the jury be asked to measure the substantiality and unjustifiability of the risk by asking whether its disregard, given the actor's perceptions, involved a gross deviation from the standard of conduct that a law-abiding person in the actor's situation would observe.

Ultimately, then, the jury is asked to perform two distinct functions. First, it is to examine the risk and the factors that are relevant to how substantial it was and to the justifications for taking it. In each instance, the question is asked from the point of view of the actor's perceptions, i.e., to what extent he was aware of risk, of factors relating to its substantiality and of factors relating to its unjustifiability. Second, the jury is to make the culpability judgment in terms of whether the defendant's conscious disregard of the risk justifies condemnation. Considering the nature and purpose of his conduct and the circumstances known to him, the question is whether the defendant's disregard of the risk involved a gross deviation from the standards of conduct that a law-abiding person would have observed in the actor's situation....

Most recent undertakings to revise criminal codes have substantially accepted the Model Code's formulation of recklessness.

Model Penal Code

§ 2.02 General Requirements of Culpability.

(d) Negligently.

A person acts negligently with respect to a material element of an offense when he should be aware of a substantial and unjustifiable risk that the material element exists or will result from this conduct. The risk must be of such a nature and degree that the actors failure to perceive it, considering the nature and purpose of his conduct and the circumstances known to him, involves a gross deviation from the standard of care that a reasonable person would observe in the actor's situation.

Comment

Negligence. The fourth kind of culpability is negligence. It is distinguished from purposeful, knowing or reckless action in that it does not involve a state of awareness. A person acts negligently under this subsection when he inadvertently creates a substantial and unjustifiable risk of which he ought to be aware.... As in the case of recklessness, both the substantiality of the risk and the elements of justification in the situation form the relevant standards of judgment. And again it is quite impossible to avoid tautological articulation of the final question. The tribunal must evaluate the actor's failure of perception and determine whether, under all the circumstances, it was serious enough to be condemned. The jury must find fault, and must find that it was substantial and unjustified; that is the heart of what can be said in legislative terms.

As with recklessness, the jury is asked to perform two distinct functions. First, it is to examine the risk and the factors that are relevant to its substantiality and justifiability. In the case of negligence, these questions are asked not in terms of what the actor's perceptions actually were, but in terms of an objective view of the situation as it actually existed. Second, the jury is to make the culpability judgment, this time in terms of whether the failure of the defendant to perceive the risk justifies condemnation. Considering the nature and purpose of his conduct and the circumstances known to him, the question is whether the defendant's failure to perceive a risk involves a gross deviation from the standard of care that a reasonable person would observe in the actor's situation.

Formulation of the standard in these terms is believed to be a substantial improvement over the traditional approach to defining negligence for purposes of criminal liability. Much of this confusion is dispelled by a clear-cut distinction between recklessness and negligence in terms of the actor's awareness of the risk involved. Clarity is also promoted by formulating the inquiry in terms of the specific factors to which attention is directed in the Model Code.

A further point in the Code's concept of negligence merits attention. The standard for ultimate judgment invites consideration of the "care that a reasonable person would observe in the actor's situation." There is an inevitable ambiguity in "situation." If the actor were blind or if he had just suffered a blow or experienced a heart attack, these would certainly be facts to be considered in a judgment involving criminal liability, as they would be under traditional law. But the heredity, intelligence or temperament of the actor would not be held material in judging negligence, and could not be without depriving the criterion of all its objectivity. The Code is not intended to displace discriminations of this kind, but rather to leave the issue to the courts.

No one has doubted that purpose, knowledge, and recklessness are properly the basis for criminal liability, but some critics have opposed any penal consequences for negligent behavior. Since the actor is inadvertent by hypothesis, it has been argued that the "threat of punishment for negligence must pass him by, because he does not realise that it is addressed to him." So too, it has been urged that education or corrective treatment, not punishment, is the proper social method for dealing with persons with inadequate awareness, since what is implied is not a moral defect. This analysis, however, oversimplifies the issue. When people have knowledge that conviction and sentence, not to speak of punishment, may follow conduct that inadvertently creates improper risk, they are supplied with an additional motive to take care before acting, to use their faculties and draw on their experience in gauging the potentialities of contemplated conduct. To some extent, at least, this motive may promote awareness and thus be effective as a measure of control. Moreover, moral defect can properly be imputed to instances where the defendant acts out of insensitivity to the interests of other people, and not merely out of an intellectual failure to grasp them. In any event legislators act on these assumptions in a host of situations, and it would be dogmatic to assert that they are wholly wrong. Accordingly, negligence, as here defined, should not be wholly rejected as a ground of culpability that may suffice for purposes of penal law, though it should properly not generally be deemed sufficient in the definition of specific crimes and it should often be differentiated from conduct involving higher culpability for the purposes of sentence....

Most recent legislative revisions and proposals have adopted definitions of negligence similar to that of the Model Code.

Model Penal Code

§ 2.02 General Requirements of Culpability.

(5) Substitutes for Negligence, Recklessness and Knowledge.

When the law provides that negligence suffices to establish an element of an offense, such element also is established if a person acts purposely or knowingly, or recklessly. When recklessness suffices to establish an element, such element also is established if a person acts purposefully or knowingly. When acting knowingly suffices to establish an element, such element also is established if a person acts purposely.

Discussion Questions

1. What distinguishes each Model Penal Code mental state from the others?

2. Jerome Hall referred to the phrase "wilful, wanton negligence" as "the apex of [judicial] infelicity" in defining mental state and described it as suggesting "a triple contradiction."[3] What is the triple contradiction?

3. Does the Model Penal Code satisfactorily define each mental state? Do these definitions delegate any lawmaking to judges? To jurors? If so, how are they consistent with the idea of legislative supremacy in criminal lawmaking we studied in Chapter 3?

4. The Model Penal Code Comment on Negligence states:

If the actor were blind or if he had just suffered a blow or experienced a heart attack, these would certainly be facts to be considered in a judgment involving criminal liability, as they would be under traditional law. But the heredity, intelligence or temperament of the actor would not be held material in judging negligence, and could not be without depriving the criterion of all its objectivity.

---

3. Jerome Hall, General Principles of the Criminal Law 124 (2d ed.1960).

Why are the facts listed in the first sentence of this quote relevant to criminal liability? Why are the facts listed in the second sentence irrelevant? How are they relevant to negligence under the Model Penal Code?

5. Should criminal liability be imposed based on negligence? What are the arguments for and against such liability? How do those arguments relate to the purposes of punishment we studied in Chapter 2?

MPC Breakdown

MPC recklessness has five key components:

MPC negligence shares many, but not all, of the components of MPC recklessness. In what ways are they the same? How do they differ? Construct a diagram similar to the one above for MPC negligence.

The "Other Minds" Question

"The sphygmograph records with graphic certainty the fluctuations of the pulse. There is no instrument yet invented that records with equal certainty the fluctuations of the mind." *People v. Zackowitz*, 254 N.Y. 192, 195 (1930) (Cardozo, J.).

Can we discover the mental state of another person? Can we determine whether someone acts with *purpose* to kill? Whether someone crossing a border *knows* that a package she is carrying contains an illegal narcotic? Whether a gun dealer *knows* that the person he sells a firearm to is a minor? Whether a parent is *aware* of the risk that striking a small child with a fist might kill the child? How does a prosecutor at a trial months or even years after the event in question prove such mental states beyond a reasonable doubt? How can we expect juries to resolve such issues? Philosophers refer to this as the "other minds" problem—the difficulty in determining what is going on inside the mind of another.[4]

---

4. *See* Rebecca Dresser, *Culpability and Other Minds*, 2 S. CAL. INTERDISC. L.J. 41 (1993).

The law of evidence recognizes two types of evidence—direct and circumstantial. Direct evidence is evidence that, if believed, establishes the point it is offered to prove without the necessity of drawing any inferences. Circumstantial evidence, by contrast, requires the use of one or more inferences to prove the point. Imagine you wish to prove to a jury that it snowed between midnight and sunrise on a particular night. First, you call a witness who was awake and outside at 2 a.m. on the date in question and she testifies that she saw and felt the snow coming down. Second, you call a witness who testifies that the ground and streets around his house were completely dry and without a trace of snow when he went to bed at midnight. This witness also testifies that he saw and drove through a foot of snow at sunrise the next day as he went to work. The first witness provides direct evidence of the fact that it snowed during the night. If believed, her testimony establishes your point without the jury having to draw any inferences. The second witness provides circumstantial evidence that it snowed during the night. In order to conclude that it snowed between midnight and sunrise, the jury must draw an inference: if there was no snow on the ground at midnight and a foot of snow on the ground at sunrise, then it must have snowed between midnight and sunrise.

Circumstantial evidence is often referred to as if it is necessarily weaker than direct evidence. News reporters sometimes state that "the prosecution has only a circumstantial case" to convey the view that the prosecution's evidence in the case is weak. But circumstantial evidence is not inherently weaker than direct evidence. Direct evidence may be weak or strong depending on the particular witness. Qualities such as a witness's sincerity and capacity to accurately perceive, remember, and recount events about which the witness testifies vary from witness to witness. And circumstantial evidence may be weak or strong depending on the strength of the inferences it supports.

Prosecutors and defense lawyers use both sorts of evidence in criminal cases in general and to prove or disprove subjective mental states in particular. At times, the prosecutor will have access to direct evidence. The defendant may have made a statement of his mental state to another person, such as a friend or even the victim. The statement may have been recorded by an undercover informant or a court authorized telephone wiretap or heard by an accomplice who agrees to cooperate and testify for the government. The defendant may have made a confession after the crime, including a statement of her mental state at the time of the offense. The defense may also rely on direct evidence, such as the defendant taking the stand and testifying that he did not have the requisite mental state—for example "I didn't intend to kill [the victim]. It was an accident."

Both sides also typically rely heavily on circumstantial evidence to help prove or disprove a required mental state. In a homicide case, for example, the use of a deadly weapon pointed at a vital part of the victim's body such as the head, neck, or heart, the firing of multiple shots, or the presence of a motive, such as revenge or financial gain, are examples of circumstantial evidence that would help a prosecutor prove purpose to kill.

Prosecutors often use evidence that a reasonable person *would have known* something or *would have been aware* of a risk in a particular situation as circumstantial evidence that a defendant *actually knew* something or *actually realized* a risk. Use of such evidence is often the source of confusion between the objective standard of negligence and mental states, such as knowledge. For example, if the minor who purchased a gun from a gun dealer was so small in stature and young in appearance that a reasonable person would have concluded he was underage, then the jury may infer that the defendant actually was aware that the purchaser was underage. If all that was required regarding the purchaser's age was simple negligence, the jury would not need to draw any inference. But if knowledge regarding age is required to convict, the jury must take an additional inferential step from what *a reasonable person would have known* to what *the defendant actually did know* about the purchaser being underage. If the jury refuses to take that step, perhaps concluding that the defendant is not very perceptive or intelligent or the jury simply believes the defendant's testimony that he did not know, they should acquit.

Problems

5.8 Look back at *State v. Pomianek,* which you read in Chapter 3 in connection with the topic of specificity.

(a) What mental states did the New Jersey legislature use in the hate crime statute at issue in *Pomianek*?

(b) The New Jersey Supreme Court found the statute at issue in *Pomianek* unconstitutionally vague. Assume you are a New Jersey legislator. Following the *Pomianek* case, how might you rewrite the statute so that it would be constitutional?

5.9 Late one evening, from the window of his apartment several stories above the street, Dino observes two men beating a third man on the sidewalk. One of the assailants is kicking the victim and the other is beating him about the head with a pipe. The victim screams for help and pleads with the men not to hurt or kill him. Dino fetches his 25-caliber automatic handgun, but by the time he returns to the window the beating has stopped. The victim is standing on the sidewalk and the former assailants are walking away. Dino yells at the men to halt. When they begin to run, despite seeing other people on the street near the men, Dino fires several "warning shots" to frighten the men as they flee. One of Dino's bullets nearly strikes an innocent passerby. What is Dino's mental state regarding injury to the passerby?

5.10 Lorna is having an affair with Jerome. Together they plan to kill Lorna's husband to remove him as an obstacle to their relationship and to collect on a

$1 million insurance policy. One evening shortly thereafter, Lorna and her husband are returning by car to their house. Lorna is behind the wheel and when they arrive home, her husband gets out and walks in front of the car to open the garage door. When he does so, Lorna hits the gas, running over him and killing him. What is Lorna's mental state regarding the death of her husband?

5.11 Rich is a member of a radical animal rights group. Karen, another member of the group, is incarcerated in the county jail awaiting trial on charges of having broken into a research lab at a local university and freed a number of research animals. Rich decides to spring Karen from jail. To do so, he plans to use a powerful explosive to dismantle the main door to the jail. Rich is experienced in the use of explosives from his days working in the mining industry. He calculates that the explosive will do great damage to anything within 50 feet of the door, but he knows that Karen's cell is several hundred feet away from the door, far enough so that the explosive will not injure her. Rich plants the explosive charge and as he does so he observes that a deputy sheriff is sitting just inside the door. Although Rich would prefer not to hurt the deputy, he nonetheless sets off the charge, killing the deputy, and then frees Karen. What is Rich's mental state regarding the death of the deputy?

5.12 Kathleen is a research doctor conducting a cancer study on human volunteer subjects. The information obtained from the study could save thousands of lives, but Kathleen is informed that there is a 10 percent chance that one or more of the subjects could die. Kathleen conducts the study, during which one of the subjects does in fact die. What is Kathleen's mental state regarding the subject's death?

5.13 In the early stages of the Covid-19 pandemic, government health officials warn the public that any large gathering of people poses an unacceptable risk of spreading the virus, a novel coronavirus that can be fatal. They also warn the public that asymptomatic people infected with the virus can spread it to others. The governor accordingly bans any such gatherings, including musical concerts, business conventions, and large church services.

Part (a). Having heard the warnings about the virus and knowing of the governor's ban, Reverend Dave nonetheless holds his regular Sunday service and roughly 150 people attend. What is Reverend Dave's mental state regarding the possibility of one or more of the attendees at the service becoming infected with the virus? What is his mental state about the possibility of one or more of the attendees dying from Covid-19?

Part (b). Ron is a well-known conservative radio personality with a nationwide daily broadcast. He has heard the warnings from public health officials and read the news reports about the Covid-19 deaths in countries such as China and Italy. He also knows that the company that employs him has taken a number of precautionary measures to avoid spreading the disease within the company, including measures to protect Ron. Nonetheless, Ron tells his listeners that the coronavirus is a "hoax" invented by political opponents of the country's current president. What is Ron's mental state regarding the possibility of one or more of his listeners becoming infected with the virus? What is his mental state about the possibility of one or more of his listeners dying from Covid-19?

5.14 Terry is an electrician and owner of an electrical supply company. He is certified as an electrical inspector by the state and works in that capacity for several towns near the town in which he lives. One day Terry installs some electric heaters in the basement of an elderly neighbor's house in return for $1,200. Shortly afterward, a fire breaks out in the basement of the neighbor's house and one of the neighbor's grandchildren dies in the fire. The local fire marshal testifies that the heaters Terry installed caused the fire. He also testifies that Terry's installation of the heaters resulted in numerous violations of the electrical code. One heater was installed directly beneath an outlet in violation of the manufacturer's instructions. The heater was also stamped as being a 120-volt unit but was wired to a 220-volt circuit. The heater was not properly grounded and the heater's internal thermostat did not function properly. The fire marshal also testified that these violations were uncommon and that he had never witnessed so many violations at one site. Terry admits his electrical work for his neighbor violated the electrical code. But he testifies that these violations were to save his neighbor money and that he believed his work on the house was safe. What was Terry's mental state regarding the death of his neighbor's grandchild?

5.15 Christine decides to end a troubled relationship with Randall, her boyfriend of several months. The day after informing Randall of her decision, Christine heads to work in her car. While driving to work, she notices Randall following her in his car. Christine tries to lose him by making several detours from her usual route. Randall runs several stop signs to keep up with Christine and drives his car within a few feet of the rear of her car while going more than 40 mph. Christine eventually loses sight of Randall, arrives at work and starts to walk across the parking lot outside the building in which she works. As she does so, she sees Randall's car speeding toward her across the parking lot and she freezes. Randall continues toward her, honking his horn, and swerves at the last minute to avoid her by about two feet. What is Randall's mental state regarding injury to Christine?

b. Traditional Terminology: Intent

Of all the words used to describe the mental component in crime, the one most frequently used is probably *intent*. At times, intent is used to mean "purpose," a use that conforms to the meaning of intent in common usage. Some criminal codes explicitly define intent in this way:

Maine Criminal Code

Ch.15, § 352

Intent to deprive "means to have the conscious object … [t]o withhold property permanently or for so extended a period or to use under such circumstances that a substantial portion of its economic value, or the use and benefit thereof, would be lost; …"

Alabama Criminal Code

§ 13A-2-2

(1) Intentionally. A person acts intentionally with respect to a result or to conduct described by a statute defining an offense, when his purpose is to cause that result or to engage in that conduct.

Problem

5.16 Judges often stretched and distorted the boundaries of the word *intent* and gave it meanings at odds with its meaning in common usage. In the passages below, how is intent defined? Which Model Penal Code mental state is closest to the definition of intent given in each of the cases below?

State v. Roufa

241 La. 474 (1961)
Louisiana Supreme Court

Hamlin, J.

Roufa was charged by bill of information with a violation of LSA-R.S. 14:106(2), the Louisiana Obscenity Statute. Paragraph Two of the Louisiana Obscenity Statute recites:

Obscenity is the intentional … [p]roduction, sale, exhibition, possession with intention to display, exhibit, or sell, or the advertisement of, any obscene, lewd, lascivious, filthy, or sexually indecent print, picture, motion picture, written composition, model, instrument, contrivance or thing of whatsoever description.

... We conclude that the word "Intentional" and the phrase "With Intention" in the Louisiana Obscenity Statute mean that knowledge is implied where one has criminal intent. It leaps to the mind that knowledge is necessary to intention and that one cannot have intention without knowledge.... The actual obscenity of the publications allegedly intentionally possessed by the defendant will be a question of fact for the trial court's determination. The criminal intent or guilty knowledge of the defendant will also be a question of fact for the trial court's determination.

Regina v. Faulknor
13 Cox Crim Cases 550 (1877)

[T]o constitute an offense under the Malicious Injuries to Property Act, the act done must be in fact intentional and wilful, although the intention and will may (perhaps) be held to exist in, or be proved by, the fact that the accused knew that the injury would be the probable result of his unlawful act, and yet did the act reckless of such consequences.

Woodward v. State
144 So. 895 (1932)
Supreme Court of Mississippi

Intent is a necessary element of assault and battery ... "An assault and battery is the unlawful touching of another by the aggressor himself or by any other substance put in motion by him." An assault and battery may be committed with a motor vehicle by striking a person, or a vehicle in which he is riding, either intentionally or by driving so negligently as to constitute a reckless disregard of human life and safety. Of course, mere negligence would not impute an intent. If negligence be relied on, then it must amount to reckless, willful, and wanton disregard of the rights of others, in which case the intent is imputed to the accused.

State v. Clardy
73 S.C. 340 (1905)
South Carolina Supreme Court

The Court charged that "a criminal intent is attributed to a person who even does a grossly careless act," which in light of the undisputed facts, meant, that "a criminal intent is attributed to a person who kills another with a deadly weapon from gross carelessness," but the jury were left to determine whether such act was done with gross carelessness. So the language of the charge, "the law presumes that he intended to do what he actually did do," in the light of the facts, simply means, "the law, in the case of a homicide with a deadly weapon under circumstances showing gross carelessness, presumes that he intended to do what he actually did do." ... The Circuit Judge, recognizing the rule that there must be a criminal intent for every common law crime, and having previously clearly stated the law concerning murder and voluntary manslaughter, was submitting to the jury the law as to voluntary manslaughter, in which gross negligence supplies the place of criminal intent.

* * *

Compare the treatment of intent in the cases above with the Model Penal Code approach described in the following comment:

Comment to Model Penal Code

§ 2.02 General Requirements of Culpability

The Model Code's approach to purpose and knowledge is in fundamental disagreement with the position of the House of Lords in *Director of Public Prosecutions v. Smith*. That case effectively equated "intent to inflict grievous bodily harm" with what the defendant as a reasonable man must be taken to have contemplated, thus erecting an objective instead of a subjective inquiry to determine what the defendant "intended." In the Code's formulation, both "purposely" and "knowingly," as well as "recklessly," are meant to ask what, in fact, the defendant's mental attitude was. It was believed to be unjust to measure liability for serious criminal offenses on the basis of what the defendant should have believed or what most people would have intended.

* * *

Legislators have also given the word *intent* many meanings, as in the following Kansas statute.

Kansas Statutes Annotated

§ 21-3201. Criminal intent

(a) Except as otherwise provided, a criminal intent is an essential element of every crime defined by this code. Criminal intent may be established by proof that the conduct of the accused person was intentional or reckless. Proof of intentional conduct shall be required to establish criminal intent, unless the statute defining the crime expressly provides that the prohibited act is criminal if done in a reckless manner.

(b) Intentional conduct is conduct that is purposeful and willful and not accidental. As used in this code, the terms "knowing," "willful," "purposeful," and "on purpose" are included within the term "intentional."

(c) Reckless conduct is conduct done under circumstances that show a realization of the imminence of danger to the person of another and a conscious and unjustifiable disregard of that danger. The terms "gross negligence," "culpable negligence," "wanton negligence" and "wantonness" are included within the term "recklessness" as used in this code.

Discussion Questions

1. As you saw above, the Model Penal Code does not use intent as one of its mental states. Why do you think those who drafted the Model Penal Code chose not to use intent?

2. The *Roufa* case states that "one cannot have intention without knowledge." Is this true? Consider the following hypothetical: Two organized crime groups are fighting with one another to control and profit from various criminal activities, such as drug distribution, illegal gambling, and extorting "protection money" from legitimate business owners by threatening them with violence. One group hires a professional "hit man" to assassinate the boss of the rival group. An informant tells the hit man that the rival boss's office has a large glass window and tells the hit man where it is. The hit man takes up a position on a rooftop several hundred yards from the building the rival gang uses as its headquarters. He has a high-powered rifle with a scope. But there is a high wind and it is difficult to see through the glass window. Although his goal is to kill the rival boss, he realizes that under these conditions — the distance, the wind, and the window — he has at best about a 50% chance of hitting and killing him. Nonetheless, he takes several shots in an attempt to kill the rival boss and then flees the scene. At the time he fired the shots, what was the mental state of the hit man? Using traditional terminology, did he have *intent* to kill his target? Did he *know* that his target would die? What MPC mental states did he fulfill?

3. What does it mean in *Woodward* and *Clardy* to impute, attribute, or presume intent?

B. Strict Liability

According to Justice Jackson, crime is "a compound concept, *generally* constituted only from concurrence of an evil-meaning mind with an evil-doing hand" (emphasis added). But there exists a category of crimes that require no evil-meaning mind, no mental state, as the following statute reveals:

Colorado Revised Statutes

§ 18-1-502 Requirements for criminal liability in general and for offenses of strict liability and of mental culpability

The minimum requirement for criminal liability is the performance by a person of conduct which includes a voluntary act or the omission to perform an act which he is physically capable of performing. If that conduct is all that is required for commission of a particular offense, or if an offense or some material element thereof does not require a culpable mental state on the part of the actor, the offense is one of "strict liability." If a culpable mental state on the part of the actor is required with respect to any material element of an offense, the offense is one of "mental culpability."

* * *

Strict liability is sometimes referred to as absolute liability. The statutory definitions of strict liability crimes often read like their civil counterparts in torts and lack any mental state terminology. If one does an act and other non-mental elements are fulfilled, one is liable. This Section starts with the *Balint* case, one of the earliest Supreme Court analyses of strict liability crimes.

United States v. Balint

258 U.S. 250 (1922)
United States Supreme Court

Taft. C.J.

Defendants were indicted for a violation of the Narcotic Act of December 17, 1914. The indictment charged them with unlawfully selling to another a certain amount of a derivative of opium and a certain amount of a derivative of coca leaves, not in pursuance of any written order on a form issued in blank for that purpose by the Commissioner of Internal Revenue, contrary to provisions of § 2 of the act. The defendants demurred to the indictment on the ground that it failed to charge that they had sold the inhibited drugs knowing them to be such. The statute does not make such knowledge an element of the offense. The District Court sustained the demurrer and quashed the indictment. The correctness of this ruling is the question before us.

While the general rule at common law was that the scienter was a necessary element in the indictment and proof of every crime, and this was followed in regard to statutory crimes even where the statutory definition did not in terms include it there has been a modification of this view in respect to prosecutions under statutes the purpose of which would be obstructed by such a requirement. It is a question of legislative intent to be construed by the court. It has been objected that punishment of a person for an act in violation of law when ignorant of the facts making it so, is an absence of due process of law. But that objection was considered and overruled in *Shevlin-Carpenter*, in which it was held that in the prohibition or punishment of particular acts, the State may in the maintenance of a public policy provide "that he who shall do them shall do them at his peril and will not be heard to plead in defense good faith or ignorance." Many instances of this are to be found in regulatory measures in the exercise of what is called the police power where the emphasis of the statute is evidently upon achievement of some social betterment rather than the punishment of the crimes as in cases of mala in se. So, too, in the collection of taxes, the importance to the public of their collection leads the legislature to impose on the taxpayer the burden of finding out the facts upon which his liability to pay depends and meeting it at the peril of punishment. Again where one deals with others and his mere negligence may be dangerous to them, as in selling diseased food or poison, the policy of the law may, in order to stimulate proper care, require the punishment of the negligent person though he be ignorant of the noxious character of what he sells.

The question before us, therefore, is one of the construction of the statute and of inference of the intent of Congress. The Narcotic Act has been held by this court to be a taxing act with the incidental purpose of minimizing the spread of addiction to the use of poisonous and demoralizing drugs.

Section 2 of the Narcotic Act [reads:]

> Part of § 2 of an act entitled An Act To Provide for the registration of, with collectors of internal revenue, and to impose a special tax upon all persons who produce, import, manufacture, compound, deal in, dispense, sell, distribute, or give away opium or coca leaves, their salts, derivatives, or preparations, and for other purposes.

> Sec. 2. That it shall be unlawful for any person to sell, barter, exchange, or give away any of the aforesaid drugs except in pursuance of a written order of the person to whom such article is sold, bartered or exchanged, or given, on a form to be issued in blank for that purpose by the Commissioner of Internal Revenue.

It is very evident from a reading of it that the emphasis of the section is in securing a close supervision of the business of dealing in these dangerous drugs by the taxing officers of the Government and that it merely uses a criminal penalty to secure recorded evidence of the disposition of such drugs as a means of taxing and restraining the traffic. Its manifest purpose is to require every person dealing in drugs to ascertain at his peril whether that which he sells comes within the inhibition of the statute, and if he sells the inhibited drug in ignorance of its character, to penalize him. Congress weighed the possible injustice of subjecting an innocent seller to a penalty against the evil of exposing innocent purchasers to danger from the drug, and concluded that the latter was the result preferably to be avoided. Doubtless considerations as to the opportunity of the seller to find out the fact and the difficulty of proof of knowledge contributed to this conclusion. We think the demurrer to the indictment should have been overruled.

Discussion Questions

1. What are the non-mental elements required for violation of Section 2 of the Narcotic Act? Balint's mental state about which of these non-mental elements was at issue?

2. Chief Justice Taft uses the word *scienter* in his opinion. Like the noun *science* ("knowledge attained through study or practice"), scienter derives from a Latin verb meaning to know. Scienter literally means "knowingly." What meaning does the context suggest Chief Justice Taft gives to scienter? You may remember that Justice Thomas also used the word scienter in his opinion in *Hendricks,* where he took the lack of a scienter requirement in the Kansas Sexually Violent Predator Act as indicating a lack of intent on the part of the Kansas legislature to punish those falling under that act. What does the context suggest Justice Thomas meant by scienter in *Hendricks*?

3. The phrase "at his peril" is often used especially by courts to describe strict liability. What does the phrase mean? Try writing a sentence that clearly and completely expresses the thinking behind this phrase.

4. The *Balint* opinion indicates that strict liability is sometimes objected to as "an absence of due process of law." What connection is there between the presence or absence of a mental state and due process? Remember that the Minnesota Supreme Court in *Guminga* found vicarious liability a violation of due process. What similarities are there between strict liability and vicarious liability?

5. Was the purpose of Congress to impose strict liability in Section 2 of the Narcotic Act "manifest"—that is, easily understood or recognized? If so, what is it about the statute that makes this legislative purpose easy to understand?

6. How do the rationales for strict liability examined in *Balint* relate to the purposes of punishment? Are they retributive? Utilitarian?

In contrast to *Balint*, the Model Penal Code rejects the use of strict liability in crimes, as reflected in the following provisions.

Model Penal Code

§ 2.02 (1) Minimum Requirements of Culpability.

Except as provided in Section 2.05, a person is not guilty of an offense unless he acted purposely, knowingly, recklessly or negligently, as the law may require, with respect to each material element of the offense. . . .

Comment

Objective. This section expresses the Code's basic requirement that unless some element of mental culpability is proved with respect to each material element of the offense, no valid criminal conviction may be obtained. This requirement is subordinated only to the provision of Section 2.05 for a narrow class of strict liability offenses that are limited to those for which no severer sentence than a fine may be imposed.

1. The Strict Liability Debate

Should mental state be eliminated in certain criminal offenses, either entirely or in relation to one particular non-mental element? This question is the source of considerable debate. The arguments in favor of strict liability are primarily utilitarian. Proponents claim that strict liability makes enforcement easier, cheaper and more effective, protects society by increasing deterrence, and addresses special needs in the area of regulatory or public welfare crimes. Critics advance both retributive and utilitarian arguments to attack strict liability.

Eliminating mental state does make enforcement easier and cheaper. Requiring the prosecution to prove fewer elements means the government needs to invest fewer resources investigating, preparing, and trying cases. Echoing the "other minds" problem, the argument can be made that mental state is difficult to investigate and prove, particularly in regulatory crimes. Such proof problems give defendants opportunities to falsely claim lack of a culpable mental state.

Those in favor of strict liability argue that it increases the deterrent effect of a criminal prohibition compared with a similar prohibition requiring proof of mental state. The thinking here is that jettisoning mental state increases certainty of conviction, in turn increasing deterrence. As deterrence increases, harm to society from the criminal behavior should correspondingly decrease.

Special need in the area of regulatory crimes is also frequently invoked in defense of strict liability. As the Supreme Court stated in *United States v. Morissette*:

> The industrial revolution multiplied the number of workmen exposed to injury from increasingly powerful and complex mechanisms, driven by freshly discovered sources of energy, requiring higher precautions by employers. Traffic of velocities, volumes and varieties unheard of came to subject the wayfarer to intolerable casualty risks if owners and drivers were not to observe new cares and uniformities of conduct. Congestion of cities and crowding of quarters called for health and welfare regulations undreamed of in simpler times. Wide distribution of goods became an instrument of wide distribution of harm when those who dispersed food, drink, drugs, and even securities, did not comply with reasonable standards of quality and integrity, disclosure and care. Such dangers have engendered increasingly numerous and detailed regulations which heighten the duties of those in control of particular industries, trades, properties or activities that affect public health, safety or welfare.

Strict liability can be criticized by drawing on the retributive limiting principle we encountered at the outset of the course—that there should be no criminal punishment without blame and that there is no blame without a culpable mental state. Critics of strict liability also counter the utilitarian argument for increased deterrence by pointing out the lack of empirical support for the claimed increase in deterrence. Disconnecting criminal punishment from blame may also breed disrespect for and cynicism toward the criminal law among the group one seeks to deter and among the public in general. Such disrespect and cynicism might well decrease deterrence. They also might increase jury nullification, resulting in less certainty of conviction, undermining deterrence.

The assumption underlying the deterrence argument is that those subject to regulation under a strict liability statute will respond to the imposition of strict liability by expending extra effort to adhere to the law. But a utilitarian argument against strict liability challenges this assumption. It asserts that strict liability deters more than we want it to by discouraging not only criminal conduct but also socially desirable conduct.[5] Imposing strict liability on food distributors, for example, for selling contaminated food in addition to deterring sale of contaminated food may also drive people out of the food distribution business. Such over-deterrence may also produce

---

5. Phillip Johnson, *Strict Liability: The Prevalent View*, ENCYCLOPEDIA OF CRIME AND JUSTICE 1518, 1520–1521 (1983).

the unintended consequence of increasing the very harm it seeks to prevent. If strict liability does in fact drive some people to abandon entirely the regulated activity on which strict liability is imposed, who will choose to leave? One possibility is that careful businesspeople will decide to abandon the activity because they are exposed to liability even if they act without culpability. Who, then, is likely to remain? The careless—those who are poor risk calculators and those who are non-calculators— may disproportionately choose to stay in the field. If the careful leave and the careless remain, the harm the strict liability measure seeks to avoid may well increase.[6]

In response to the retributive argument against strict liability as imposing punishment without blame, a strict liability proponent might argue that the punishments imposed in strict liability offenses are typically small, usually limited to fines, so lack of blame is not critical. A critic might counter that if the punishments are limited to monetary fines, then civil enforcement is a more appropriate route to imposition of a monetary penalty. Imposition of a civil penalty is also more certain than imposition of a criminal sanction since the civil system has a lower burden of proof than the criminal system and poses fewer barriers to enforcement. Civil liability, for example, unlike criminal liability, gives rise to no constitutional privilege against self-incrimination. Thus, the threat of a civil monetary penalty may be a more certain and thus a more effective deterrent than a criminal fine.

The strict liability advocate may also argue that just because mental state and blame are not required to be proven as an element of the offense, convicted defendants are not necessarily blameless. Police and prosecutors may exercise their discretion to prosecute only cases in which they are convinced there is blame, even if they are not required to prove it. The police officers' and prosecutors' sense of retributive justice might lead them to do this. But self-interest may also dictate prosecuting only people with culpable mental states because police and prosecutors may fear jury nullification unless the evidence strongly suggests some level of blame. Juries may nullify and judges may impose only monetary punishment unless blame is shown.

The notion that insuring culpability should be entrusted to police and prosecutors raises serious questions of whether we can trust police and prosecutors to perform this task. It also raises the possibility of discriminatory enforcement. Jury nullification may not be reliable for protecting blameless defendants because the judge may choose not to admit defense evidence showing lack of mental state on the ground that such evidence is irrelevant because mental state is not an element of the crime and therefore not an issue in the case. The existence of mandatory sentencing guidelines may severely curtail the judge's ability to make sure that strict liability crimes are never punished with imprisonment.

---

6. Stephen J. Schulhofer, *Harm and Punishment: A Critique of Emphasis on the Results of Conduct in the Criminal Law*, 122 U. Pa. L. Rev. 1497, 1586–1587 (1974).

2. A Compromise Position

A compromise position between requiring the government to prove a subjective mental state and abandoning mental state entirely through strict liability is the idea of lowering the culpability requirement to simple negligence and shifting the burden of proof to the defendant. If the defendant can prove by a preponderance of the evidence that she acted with reasonable care, then no liability is imposed. This approach remedies the difficulties of proving subjective mental state on the part of the government by changing from a subjective standard to an objective standard and putting the burden of proving reasonableness on the defendant.

Problems

5.17 You are counsel to a committee of a state legislature that is considering modifying the treatment of mental state in its drug possession statute. The statute in your state currently makes it a felony to possess with intent to distribute any amount of a controlled substance. Felony possession carries prison terms that can be as high as 10 to 15 years for first offenders and life imprisonment for repeat offenders. The same statute makes simple possession of a controlled substance a misdemeanor with a maximum sentence of one year's imprisonment. Simple possession is possession without intent to distribute of less than a specified quantity of a controlled substance.

Currently the drug statute in your state, like the federal drug laws and the drug laws of 47 other states, requires that the prosecution prove beyond a reasonable doubt that the actor knew that the substance the actor possessed was a controlled substance.

The Florida legislature became the first in the nation to deviate from this pattern by: (1) eliminating knowledge of the illicit nature of the controlled substance as an offense element; and (2) creating an affirmative defense in which a defendant can avoid conviction if she proves her lack of knowledge of the substance's illicit nature. In other words, the Florida legislature shifted the burden of proof regarding knowledge of the illicit nature of a substance possessed from the prosecution to the defendant. Recall from Chapter 3 that the definition of possession requires that a defendant know of the presence of a substance in order to possess it. The Florida legislature clarified that under its new approach the prosecution must still prove that the defendant knew of the *presence* of the substance. Thus the legislature distinguished between knowledge of the *presence* of the substance and knowledge of its *illicit nature*. Its new approach applies only to the second of these types of knowledge.

The legislature in your state wants your advice. Should the legislature adopt the Florida approach?

5.18 The previous problem describes how the Florida legislature shifted the burden of proof regarding knowledge of the illicit nature of a controlled substance in a drug possession statute. Instead of this "burden shifting" approach, would it be preferable for a legislature simply to apply strict liability regarding the illicit nature of a substance possessed by someone? Under such an approach, the legislature would eliminate entirely such knowledge as an offense element and not create any sort of affirmative defense allowing a defendant to defeat liability by proving he lacked such knowledge.

Part (a). Should the legislature use strict liability in regard to the illicit nature of the substance possessed when the drug possession charged is a felony? What are the arguments for and against this approach?

Part (b). Should the legislature use strict liability in regard to the illicit nature of the substance possessed when the drug possession charged is misdemeanor simple possession without intent to distribute? What are the arguments for and against this approach?

C. Resolving Statutory Ambiguity

As pointed out in the introduction to this chapter, legislatures often draft statutes that are silent or otherwise ambiguous regarding mental state. Prosecutors, defense lawyers, and judges are then left to decide what mental state should be applied or if strict liability should be imposed. Statutes silent or ambiguous regarding mental state are a regular source of uncertainty and confusion in criminal law and create challenging issues of statutory interpretation for lawyers to argue and for judges to decide. We examine such statutes and how judges interpret them in this section.

Problem

5.19 Amanda is a private security guard at a military base that provides housing for United States Coast Guard personnel and their families. In a parking area Amanda regularly patrols, there is an old camper-trailer of the sort that is towed behind a car or truck and can be opened into a large canvas tent upon reaching a camping area. The camper trailer has not been moved in more than two years. It has a flat tire and no license plate. One day Amanda decides to take the camper trailer and use it for her family. She takes it home, cleans it, repairs the tire, and begins using it with her family. A few months later, she is arrested and charged under the statute below. Amanda claims that she thought the camper trailer had been abandoned. It turns out that the camper-trailer belongs to a Coast Guard enlisted man. Because he has been on several long tours of duty, he has had no opportunity to use the camper-trailer in recent years.

Assume that the military base where Amanda was employed is within the special maritime and territorial jurisdiction of the United States and that the trailer's value is $1,200. Is Amanda liable under the following statute? If you represented Amanda, what arguments would you make on her behalf? If you were the prosecutor, what evidence would help you to convict?

18 United States Code

§ 661

Whoever, within the special maritime and territorial jurisdiction of the United States, takes and carries away, with intent to steal or purloin, any personal property of another shall be punished as follows:

If the property taken is of a value exceeding $1,000, or is taken from the person of another, by a fine under this title, or imprisonment for not more than five years, or both; in all other cases, by a fine under this title or by imprisonment not more than one year, or both.

Would the following facts make a difference in determining Amanda's liability? If so, why?

(1) Amanda took the camper-trailer off the base in the middle of the day.

(2) Amanda took the camper-trailer off the base in the middle of the night.

(3) Amanda made several attempts to identify and locate the owner.

(4) Amanda made no attempt to identify or locate the owner.

The defendant in the following case was charged with violating the following statute:

18 United States Code

§ 641

Whoever embezzles, steals, purloins, or knowingly converts to his use or the use of another, or without authority, sells, conveys, or disposes of any record, voucher, money, or thing of value of the United States [s]hall be fined not more than $10,000 or imprisoned not more than ten years, or both; but if the value of such property does not exceed the sum of $100, he shall be fined not more than $1,000 or imprisoned not more than one year, or both.

Morissette v. United States

342 U.S. 246 (1952)
United States Supreme Court

Jackson, J.

On a large tract of uninhabited and untilled land in a wooded and sparsely populated area of Michigan, the Government established a practice bombing range over which the Air Force dropped simulated bombs at ground targets. These bombs consisted of a metal cylinder about forty inches long and eight inches across, filled with sand and enough black powder to cause a smoke puff by which the strike could be located. At various places about the range signs read "Danger—Keep Out—Bombing Range." Nevertheless, the range was known as good deer country and was extensively hunted.

Spent bomb casings were cleared from the targets and thrown into piles "so that they will be out of the way." They were not stacked or piled in any order but were dumped in heaps, some of which had been accumulating for four years or upwards, and were exposed to the weather and rusting away.

Morissette, in December of 1948, went hunting in this area but did not get a deer. He thought to meet expenses of the trip by salvaging some of these casings. He unloaded three tons of them on his truck and took them to a nearby farm, where they were flattened by driving a tractor over them. After expending this labor and trucking them to market in Flint, he realized $84.

The loading, crushing and transporting of these casings were all in broad daylight, in full view of passersby, without the slightest effort at concealment. When an investigation was started, Morissette voluntarily, promptly and candidly told the whole story to the authorities, saying that he had no intention of stealing but thought the property was abandoned, unwanted and considered of no value to the government. He was indicted, however, on the charge that he "did unlawfully, wilfully and knowingly steal and convert" property of the United States of a value of $84, in violation of 18 U.S.C. §641, which provides that "whoever embezzles, steals, purloins, or knowingly converts" government property is punishable by fine and imprisonment. Morissette was convicted and sentenced to imprisonment for two months or to pay a fine of $200.

On his trial, Morissette, as he had at all times told investigating officers, testified that from appearances he believed the casings were cast-off and abandoned, that he did not intend to steal the property, and took it with no wrongful or criminal intent. The trial court, however, was unimpressed, and ruled: "He took it because he thought it was abandoned and he knew he was on government property.... That is no defense.... I don't think anybody can have the defense they thought the property was abandoned on another man's piece of property." The court stated: "I will not permit you to show this man thought it was abandoned.... I hold in this case that there is no question of abandoned property." The court refused to submit or to allow counsel to argue to the jury whether Morissette acted with innocent intention.

I.

The contention that an injury can amount to a crime only when inflicted by intention is no provincial or transient notion. It is as universal and persistent in mature systems of law as belief in freedom of the human will and a consequent ability and duty of the normal individual to choose between good and evil. A relation between some mental element and punishment for a harmful act is almost as instinctive as the child's familiar exculpatory "But I didn't mean to," and has afforded a rational basis for a tardy and unfinished substitution of deterrence and reformation in place of retaliation and vengeance as the motivation for public prosecution. Unqualified acceptance of this doctrine by English common law in the Eighteenth Century was indicated by Blackstone's sweeping statement that to constitute any crime there must first be a "vicious will." Common-law commentators of the Nineteenth Century early pronounced the same principle, although a few exceptions not relevant to our present problem came to be recognized.

Crime, as a compound concept, generally constituted only from concurrence of an evil-meaning mind with an evil-doing hand, was congenial to an intense individualism and took deep and early root in American soil. As the states codified the common law of crimes, even if their enactments were silent on the subject, their courts assumed that the omission did not signify disapproval of the principle but merely recognized that intent was so inherent in the idea of the offense that it required no statutory affirmation. Courts, with little hesitation or division, found an implication of the requirement as to offenses that were taken over from the common law. The unanimity with which they have adhered to the central thought that wrongdoing must be conscious to be criminal is emphasized by the variety, disparity and confusion of their definitions of the requisite but elusive mental element. However, courts of various jurisdictions, and for the purposes of different offenses, have devised working formulae, if not scientific ones, for the instruction of juries around such terms as "felonious intent," "criminal intent," "malice aforethought," "guilty knowledge," "fraudulent intent," "wilfulness," "scienter," to denote guilty knowledge, or "mens rea," to signify an evil purpose or mental culpability. By use or combination of these various tokens, they have sought to protect those who were not blameworthy in mind from conviction of infamous common-law crimes.

However, the *Balint* ... [offense] ... belong[s] to a category of another character, with very different antecedents and origins. The [crime] ... there involved depend[s] on no mental element but consist[s] only of forbidden acts or omissions. This, while not expressed by the Court, is made clear from examination of a century-old but accelerating tendency, discernible both here and in England, to call into existence new duties and crimes which disregard any ingredient of intent.

While many of these duties are sanctioned by a more strict civil liability, lawmakers, whether wisely or not, have sought to make such regulations more effective by invoking criminal sanctions to be applied by the familiar technique of criminal prosecutions and convictions. This has confronted the courts with a multitude of prosecutions, based on statutes or administrative regulations, for what have been aptly called "public welfare offenses." These cases do not fit neatly into any of such accepted classifications of common-law offenses, such as those against the state, the person, property, or public morals. Many of these offenses are not in the nature of positive aggressions or invasions, with which the common law so often dealt, but are in the nature of neglect where the law requires care, or inaction where it imposes a duty. Many violations of such regulations result in no direct or immediate injury to person or property but merely create the danger or probability of it which the law seeks to minimize. While such offenses do not threaten the security of the state in the manner of treason, they may be regarded as offenses against its authority, for their occurrence impairs the efficiency of controls deemed essential to the social order as presently constituted. In this respect, whatever the intent of the violator, the injury is the same, and the consequences are injurious or not according to fortuity. Hence, legislation applicable to such offenses, as a matter of policy, does not specify intent as a necessary element. The accused, if he does not will the violation, usually is in a position to prevent it with no more care than society might reasonably expect and no more exertion than it might reasonably exact from one who assumed his responsibilities. Also, penalties commonly are relatively small, and conviction does no grave damage to an offender's reputation. Under such considerations, courts have turned to construing statutes and regulations which make no mention of intent as dispensing with it and holding that the guilty act alone makes out the crime. This has not, however, been without expressions of misgiving....

After the turn of the Century, a new use for crimes without intent appeared when New York enacted numerous and novel regulations of tenement houses, sanctioned by money penalties. Landlords contended that a guilty intent was essential to establish a violation. Judge Cardozo wrote the answer:

> "The defendant asks us to test the meaning of this statute by standards applicable to statutes that govern infamous crimes. The analogy, however, is deceptive. The element of conscious wrongdoing, the guilty mind accompanying the guilty act, is associated with the concept of crimes that are punished as infamous.... Even there it is not an invariable element.... But in the prosecution of minor offenses, there is a wider range of practice and of power. Prosecutions for petty penalties have always constituted in our law a class by themselves.... That is true though the prosecution is criminal in form."

Tenement House Department v. McDevitt, 215 N.Y. 160, 168 (1915).

Soon, employers advanced the same contention as to violations of regulations prescribed by a new labor law. Judge Cardozo, again for the court, pointed out, as a basis for penalizing violations whether intentional or not, that they were punishable only by fine "moderate in amount," but cautiously added that in sustaining the power so to fine unintended violations "we are not to be understood as sustaining to a like length the power to imprison. We leave that question open." ...

Neither this Court nor, so far as we are aware, any other has undertaken to delineate a precise line or set forth comprehensive criteria for distinguishing between crimes that require a mental element and crimes that do not. We attempt no closed definition, for the law on the subject is neither settled nor static. The conclusion reached in the *Balint* case ... has our approval and adherence for the circumstances to which it was there applied. A quite different question here is whether we will expand the doctrine of crimes without intent to include those charged here.

Stealing, larceny, and its variants and equivalents, were among the earliest offenses known to the law that existed before legislation; they are invasions of rights of property which stir a sense of insecurity in the whole community and arouse public demand for retribution, the penalty is high and, when a sufficient amount is involved, the infamy is that of a felony, which, says Maitland, is "... as bad a word as you can give to man or thing." State courts of last resort, on whom fall the heaviest burden of interpreting criminal law in this country have consistently retained the requirement of intent in larceny-type offenses. If any state has deviated, the exception has neither been called to our attention nor disclosed by our research.

Congress, therefore, omitted any express prescription of criminal intent from the enactment before us in the light of an unbroken course of judicial decision in all constituent states of the Union holding intent inherent in this class of offense, even when not expressed in a statute. Congressional silence as to mental elements in an Act merely adopting into federal statutory law a concept of crime already so well defined in common law and statutory interpretation by the states may warrant quite contrary inferences than the same silence in creating an offense new to general law, for whose definition the courts have no guidance except the Act. Because the [offense] ... before this Court in the *Balint* ... case ... [was] of this latter class, we cannot accept ... [it] as authority for eliminating intent from offenses incorporated from the common law....

[W]hen congress borrows terms of art in which are accumulated the legal tradition and meaning of centuries of practice, it presumably knows and adopts the cluster of ideas that were attached to each borrowed word in the body of learning from which it was taken and the meaning its use will convey to the judicial mind unless otherwise instructed. In such case, absence of contrary direction may be taken as satisfaction with widely accepted definitions, not as a departure from them.

We hold that mere omission from § 641 of any mention of intent will not be construed as eliminating that element from the crimes denounced.

Knowledge, of course, is not identical with intent and may not have been the most apt words of limitation. But knowing conversion requires more than knowledge that defendant was taking the property into his possession. He must have had knowledge of the facts, though not necessarily the law, that made the taking a conversion. In the case before us, whether the mental element that Congress required be spoken of as knowledge or as intent, would not seem to alter its bearing on guilt. For it is not apparent how Morissette could have knowingly or intentionally converted property that he did not know could be converted, as would be the case if it was in fact abandoned or if he truly believed it to be abandoned and unwanted property.

Of course, the jury, considering Morissette's awareness that these casings were on government property, his failure to seek any permission for their removal and his self-interest as a witness, might have disbelieved his profession of innocent intent and concluded that his assertion of a belief that the casings were abandoned was an afterthought. Had the jury convicted on proper instructions it would be the end of the matter. But juries are not bound by what seems inescapable logic to judges. They might have concluded that the heaps of spent casings left in the hinterland to rust away presented an appearance of unwanted and abandoned junk, and that lack of any conscious deprivation of property or intentional injury was indicated by Morissette's good character, the openness of the taking, crushing and transporting of the casings, and the candor with which it was all admitted. They might have refused to brand Morissette as a thief. Had they done so, that too would have been the end of the matter.

Reversed.

Discussion Questions

1. Was Morissette's case more difficult to resolve than Amanda's case in Problem 5.19? How does the text of 18 U.S.C. §641 used in *Morissette* differ from the text of 18 U.S.C. §661 used in Amanda's case?

2. The *Morissette* court distinguishes between traditional common law crimes and new public welfare or regulatory crimes. What significance does the court attach to this distinction?

3. Rewrite 18 U.S.C. §641 to reflect the *Morissette* court's interpretation of that statute. What changes would you make to the language of §641?

* * *

Ambiguity about mental state is a common problem in criminal statutes. Two common problems are: (1) the statute is silent about mental state; or (2) the statute mentions a mental state, but it is not clear to which non-mental elements that mental state applies. As you will see below, because these two problems occur so often the Model Penal Code created specific rules for dealing with each.

1. Statutes Silent on Mental State

Problem

5.20 John was arrested after police saw him leave a clandestine laboratory set up in a garage to extract pseudoephedrine from cold pills, a step in the process of manufacturing methamphetamine. John received $500 for "washing" cold pills to extract the pseudoephedrine, but claims he was unaware that it was to be used to make methamphetamine. He had seen ephedrine advertised as a weight loss and body-building agent. The man who hired John to "wash" the pseudoephedrine told him it was to be used to make ephedrine. When John asked some of his co-workers and was told the pseudoephedrine was to be used to make methamphetamine, he became scared, stopped work, and left the garage where the pills were being washed. John is charged under the following statute:

> Every person who manufactures or assists in the manufacturing
> of methamphetamine shall be punished in the state prison by
> a term of up to ten years.

At trial, John's wife testifies that John does not use or have any involvement with methamphetamine or any other illegal drug. A former work supervisor testifies that John is an honest and conscientious worker, does not drink or use illegal drugs, and is somewhat naïve about worldly matters.

Possession or sale of methamphetamine is a crime. The statute penalizing possession and sale makes no mention of mental state, but the courts have required knowledge that the substance possessed or sold is methamphetamine in order to sustain a criminal conviction. The manufacturing of methamphetamine at one time was covered by the same statute that penalizes possession and sale. But the legislature made manufacturing a separate offense in order to impose a higher penalty on manufacturing. Assume that a person who extracts pseudoephedrine is engaged in the process of manufacturing methamphetamine. Is John liable?

If a statute is silent about mental state, what inference should a judge or prosecutor draw about what the legislature intended? That the legislature intended to do away with mental state entirely and create a strict liability offense? How do the Model Penal Code and the *Elonis* case in this section deal with such silence?

Model Penal Code

§ 2.02 General Requirements of Culpability

(1) Minimum Requirements of Culpability. Except as provided in Section 2.05, a person is not guilty of an offense unless he acted purposely, knowingly, recklessly or negligently, as the law may require, with respect to each material element of the offense....

Comment

Objective. This section expresses the Code's basic requirement that unless some element of mental culpability is proved with respect to each material element of the offense, no valid criminal conviction may be obtained. This requirement is subordinated only to the provision of Section 2.05 for a narrow class of strict liability offenses that are limited to those for which no severer sentence than a fine may be imposed.

(3) Culpability Required Unless Otherwise Provided. When the culpability sufficient to establish a material element of an offense is not prescribed by law, such element is established if a person acts purposely, knowingly or recklessly with respect thereto.

Comment

Offense Silent as to Culpability. Subsection (3) provides that unless the kind of culpability sufficient to establish a material element of an offense has been prescribed by law, it is established if a person acted purposely, knowingly or recklessly with respect thereto. This accepts as the basic norm what usually is regarded as the common law position. More importantly, it represents the most convenient norm for drafting purposes. When purpose or knowledge is required, it is conventional to be explicit. And since negligence is an exceptional basis of liability, it should be excluded as a basis unless explicitly prescribed.

* * *

The defendant in the following case was prosecuted under this federal statute:

18 U.S.C.

§ 875 (c)

Whoever transmits in interstate or foreign commerce any communication containing any threat to kidnap any person or any threat to injure the person of another, shall be fined under this title or imprisoned not more than five years, or both.

Elonis v. United States

135 S. Ct. 2001 (2015)
Supreme Court of the United States

Chief Justice Roberts delivered the opinion of the Court.

Federal law makes it a crime to transmit in interstate commerce "any communication containing any threat ... to injure the person of another." Petitioner was convicted of violating this provision under instructions that required the jury to find that he communicated what a reasonable person would regard as a threat. The question is whether the statute also requires that the defendant be aware of the threatening nature of the communication....

I

Anthony Douglas Elonis was an active user of the social networking Web site Facebook. Users of that Web site may post items on their Facebook page that are accessible to other users, including Facebook "friends" who are notified when new content is posted. In May 2010, Elonis's wife of nearly seven years left him, taking with her their two young children. Elonis began "listening to more violent music" and posting self-styled "rap" lyrics inspired by the music. Eventually, Elonis changed the user name on his Facebook page from his actual name to a rap-style nom de plume, "Tone Dougie," to distinguish himself from his "on-line persona." The lyrics Elonis posted as "Tone Dougie" included graphically violent language and imagery. This material was often interspersed with disclaimers that the lyrics were "fictitious," with no intentional "resemblance to real persons." Elonis posted an explanation to another Facebook user that "I'm doing this for me. My writing is therapeutic."

Elonis's co-workers and friends viewed the posts in a different light. Around Halloween of 2010, Elonis posted a photograph of himself and a co-worker at a "Halloween Haunt" event at the amusement park where they worked. In the photograph, Elonis was holding a toy knife against his co-worker's neck, and in the caption Elonis wrote, "I wish." Elonis was not Facebook friends with the co-worker and did not "tag" her, a Facebook feature that would have alerted her to the posting. But the chief of park security was a Facebook "friend" of Elonis, saw the photograph, and fired him.

In response, Elonis posted a new entry on his Facebook page:

> "Moles! Didn't I tell y'all I had several? Y'all sayin' I had access to keys for all the f***in' gates. That I have sinister plans for all my friends and must have taken home a couple. Y'all think it's too dark and foggy to secure your facility from a man as mad as me? You see, even without a paycheck, I'm still the main attraction. Whoever thought the Halloween Haunt could be so f***in' scary?"

This post became the basis for Count One of Elonis's subsequent indictment, threatening park patrons and employees.

Elonis's posts frequently included crude, degrading, and violent material about his soon-to-be ex-wife. Shortly after he was fired, Elonis posted an adaptation of a satirical sketch that he and his wife had watched together. In the actual sketch, called "It's Illegal to Say...," a comedian explains that it is illegal for a person to say he wishes to kill the President, but not illegal to explain that it is illegal for him to say that. When Elonis posted the script of the sketch, however, he substituted his wife for the President. The posting was part of the basis for Count Two of the indictment, threatening his wife:

> "Hi, I'm Tone Elonis.
>
> Did you know that it's illegal for me to say I want to kill my wife? ...
>
> It's one of the only sentences that I'm not allowed to say....
>
> Now it was okay for me to say it right then because I was just telling you that it's illegal for me to say I want to kill my wife....
>
> Um, but what's interesting is that it's very illegal to say I really, really think someone out there should kill my wife....
>
> But not illegal to say with a mortar launcher.
>
> Because that's its own sentence....
>
> I also found out that it's incredibly illegal, extremely illegal to go on Facebook and say something like the best place to fire a mortar launcher at her house would be from the cornfield behind it because of easy access to a getaway road and you'd have a clear line of sight through the sun room....
>
> Yet even more illegal to show an illustrated diagram.
>
> [diagram of the house]...."

The details about the home were accurate. At the bottom of the post, Elonis included a link to the video of the original skit, and wrote, "Art is about pushing limits. I'm willing to go to jail for my Constitutional rights. Are you?"

After viewing some of Elonis's posts, his wife felt "extremely afraid for [her] life." A state court granted her a three-year protection-from-abuse order against Elonis (essentially, a restraining order). Elonis referred to the order in another post on his "Tone Dougie" page, also included in Count Two of the indictment:

"Fold up your [protection-from-abuse order] and put it in your pocket

Is it thick enough to stop a bullet?

Try to enforce an Order

that was improperly granted in the first place

Me thinks the Judge needs an education

on true threat jurisprudence

And prison time'll add zeros to my settlement …

And if worse comes to worse

I've got enough explosives

to take care of the State Police and the Sheriff's Department."

At the bottom of this post was a link to the Wikipedia article on "Freedom of speech." Elonis's reference to the police was the basis for Count Three of his indictment, threatening law enforcement officers.

That same month, interspersed with posts about a movie Elonis liked and observations on a comedian's social commentary, Elonis posted an entry that gave rise to Count Four of his indictment:

"That's it, I've had about enough

I'm checking out and making a name for myself

Enough elementary schools in a ten mile radius

to initiate the most heinous school shooting ever imagined

And hell hath no fury like a crazy man in a Kindergarten class

The only question is … which one?"

Meanwhile, park security had informed both local police and the Federal Bureau of Investigation about Elonis's posts, and FBI Agent Denise Stevens had created a Facebook account to monitor his online activity. After the post about a school shooting, Agent Stevens and her partner visited Elonis at his house. Following their visit, during which Elonis was polite but uncooperative, Elonis posted another entry on his Facebook page, called "Little Agent Lady," which led to Count Five:

"You know your s***'s ridiculous

when you have the FBI knockin' at yo' door

Little Agent lady stood so close

Took all the strength I had not to turn the b**** ghost

Pull my knife, flick my wrist, and slit her throat

Leave her bleedin' from her jugular in the arms of her partner

[laughter]

So the next time you knock, you best be serving a warrant
And bring yo' SWAT and an explosives expert while you're at it

Cause little did y'all know, I was strapped wit' a bomb

Why do you think it took me so long to get dressed with no shoes on?

I was jus' waitin' for y'all to handcuff me and pat me down

Touch the detonator in my pocket and we're all goin'

[BOOM!]

Are all the pieces comin' together?

S***, I'm just a crazy sociopath

that gets off playin' you stupid f***s like a fiddle

And if y'all didn't hear, I'm gonna be famous

Cause I'm just an aspiring rapper who likes the attention

who happens to be under investigation for terrorism

cause y'all think I'm ready to turn the Valley into Fallujah

But I ain't gonna tell you which bridge is gonna fall

into which river or road

And if you really believe this s***

I'll have some bridge rubble to sell you tomorrow

[BOOM!] [BOOM!] [BOOM!]"

A grand jury indicted Elonis for making threats to injure patrons and employees of the park, his estranged wife, police officers, a kindergarten class, and an FBI agent, all in violation of 18 U.S.C. § 875(c). In the District Court, Elonis moved to dismiss the indictment for failing to allege that he had intended to threaten anyone. The District Court denied the motion, holding that Third Circuit precedent required only that Elonis "intentionally made the communication, not that he intended to make a threat." At trial, Elonis testified that his posts emulated the rap lyrics of the well-known performer Eminem, some of which involve fantasies about killing his ex-wife. In Elonis's view, he had posted "nothing ... that hasn't been said already." The Government presented as witnesses Elonis's wife and co-workers, all of whom said they felt afraid and viewed Elonis's posts as serious threats.

Elonis requested a jury instruction that "the government must prove that he intended to communicate a true threat." The District Court denied that request. The jury instructions instead informed the jury that

"A statement is a true threat when a defendant intentionally makes a statement in a context or under such circumstances wherein a reasonable person would foresee that the statement would be interpreted by those to whom the maker communicates the statement as a serious expression of an intention to inflict bodily injury or take the life of an individual."

The Government's closing argument emphasized that it was irrelevant whether Elonis intended the postings to be threats — "it doesn't matter what he thinks." A jury convicted Elonis on four of the five counts against him, acquitting only on the charge of threatening park patrons and employees. Elonis was sentenced to three years, eight months' imprisonment and three years' supervised release.

Elonis renewed his challenge to the jury instructions in the Court of Appeals, contending that the jury should have been required to find that he intended his posts to be threats. The Court of Appeals disagreed, holding that the intent required by Section 875(c) is only the intent to communicate words that the defendant understands, and that a reasonable person would view as a threat. We granted certiorari.

II

A

An individual who "transmits in interstate or foreign commerce any communication containing any threat to kidnap any person or any threat to injure the person of another" is guilty of a felony and faces up to five years' imprisonment. 18 U.S.C. §875(c). This statute requires that a communication be transmitted and that the communication contain a threat. It does not specify that the defendant must have any mental state with respect to these elements. In particular, it does not indicate whether the defendant must intend that his communication contain a threat.

Elonis argues that the word "threat" itself in Section 875(c) imposes such a requirement. According to Elonis, every definition of "threat" or "threaten" conveys the notion of an intent to inflict harm. See *E.g.*, 11 Oxford English Dictionary 353 (1933) ("to declare (usually conditionally) one's intention of inflicting injury upon"); Webster's New International Dictionary 2633 (2d ed. 1954) ("*Law*, specif., an expression of an intention to inflict loss or harm on another by illegal means"); Black's Law Dictionary 1519 (8th ed. 2004) ("A communicated intent to inflict harm or loss on another").

These definitions, however, speak to what the statement conveys — not to the mental state of the author. For example, an anonymous letter that says "I'm going to kill you" is "an expression of an intention to inflict loss or harm" regardless of the author's intent. A victim who receives that letter in the mail has received a threat, even if the author believes (wrongly) that his message will be taken as a joke.

For its part, the Government argues that Section 875(c) should be read in light of its neighboring provisions, Sections 875(b) and 875(d). Those provisions also prohibit certain types of threats, but expressly include a mental state requirement of an "intent to extort." See 18 U.S.C. §875(b) (proscribing threats to injure or kidnap made "with intent to extort"); § 875(d) (proscribing threats to property or reputation made "with intent to extort"). According to the Government, the express "intent to extort" requirements in Sections 875(b) and (d) should preclude courts from implying an unexpressed "intent to threaten" requirement in Section 875(c). *See Russello v. United States*, 464 U.S. 16, 23, 104 S. Ct. 296, 78 L. Ed. 2d 17 (1983) ("[W]here Congress includes particular language in one section of a statute but omits it in another section of the same Act, it is generally presumed that Congress acts intentionally and purposely] in the disparate inclusion or exclusion.").

The Government takes this *expressio unius est exclusio alterius* canon too far. The fact that Congress excluded the requirement of an "intent to extort" from Section 875(c) is strong evidence that Congress did not mean to confine Section 875(c) to crimes of extortion. But that does not suggest that Congress, at the same time, also meant to exclude a requirement that a defendant act with a certain mental state in communicating a threat. The most we can conclude from the language of Section 875(c) and its neighboring provisions is that Congress meant to proscribe a broad class of threats in Section 875(c), but did not identify what mental state, if any, a defendant must have to be convicted.

In sum, neither Elonis nor the Government has identified any indication of a particular mental state requirement in the text of Section 875(c).

B

The fact that the statute does not specify any required mental state, however, does not mean that none exists. We have repeatedly held that "mere omission from a criminal enactment of any mention of criminal intent" should not be read "as dispensing with it." *Morissette v. United States*, 342 U.S. 246, 250 (1952). This rule of construction reflects the basic principle that "wrongdoing must be conscious to be criminal." As Justice Jackson explained, this principle is "as universal and persistent in mature systems of law as belief in freedom of the human will and a consequent ability and duty of the normal individual to choose between good and evil." The "central thought" is that a defendant must be "blameworthy in mind" before he can be found guilty, a concept courts have expressed over time through various terms such as *mens rea*, scienter, malice aforethought, guilty knowledge, and the like. Although there are exceptions, the "general rule" is that a guilty mind is "a necessary element in the indictment and proof of every crime." We therefore generally "interpret criminal statutes to include broadly applicable scienter requirements, even where the statute by its terms does not contain them."

This is not to say that a defendant must know that his conduct is illegal before he may be found guilty. The familiar maxim "ignorance of the law is no excuse" typically holds true. Instead, our cases have explained that a defendant generally must "know the facts that make his conduct fit the definition of the offense," even if he does not know that those facts give rise to a crime....

To take another example, in *Posters 'N' Things, Ltd. v. United States*, this Court interpreted a federal statute prohibiting the sale of drug paraphernalia. Whether the items in question qualified as drug paraphernalia was an objective question that did not depend on the defendant's state of mind. But, we held, an individual could not be convicted of selling such paraphernalia unless he "knew that the items at issue [were] likely to be used with illegal drugs." Such a showing was necessary to establish the defendant's culpable state of mind....

Section 875(c), as noted, requires proof that a communication was transmitted and that it contained a threat. The "presumption in favor of a scienter requirement should apply to *each* of the statutory elements that criminalize otherwise innocent conduct." The parties agree that a defendant under Section 875(c) must know that he is transmitting a communication. But communicating *something* is not what makes the conduct "wrongful." Here "the crucial element separating legal innocence from wrongful conduct" is the threatening nature of the communication. The mental state requirement must therefore apply to the fact that the communication contains a threat.

Elonis's conviction, however, was premised solely on how his posts would be understood by a reasonable person. Such a "reasonable person" standard is a familiar feature of civil liability in tort law, but is inconsistent with "the conventional requirement for criminal conduct—*awareness* of some wrongdoing." Having liability turn on whether a "reasonable person" regards the communication as a threat—regardless of what the defendant thinks—"reduces culpability on the all-important element of the crime to negligence," and we "have long been reluctant to infer that a negligence standard was intended in criminal statutes." Under these principles, "what [Elonis] thinks" does matter.

The Government is at pains to characterize its position as something other than a negligence standard, emphasizing that its approach would require proof that a defendant "comprehended [the] contents and context" of the communication. The Government gives two examples of individuals who, in its view, would lack this necessary mental state—a "foreigner, ignorant of the English language," who would not know the meaning of the words at issue, or an individual mailing a sealed envelope without knowing its contents. But the fact that the Government would require a defendant to actually know the words of and circumstances surrounding a communication does not amount to a rejection of negligence. Criminal negligence standards often incorporate "the circumstances known" to a defendant. Courts then ask, however, whether a reasonable person equipped with that knowledge, not the actual defendant, would have recognized the harmfulness of his conduct. That is precisely the Government's position here: Elonis can be convicted, the Government contends, if he himself knew the contents and context of his posts, and a reasonable person would have recognized that the posts would be read as genuine threats. That is a negligence standard....

There is no dispute that the mental state requirement in Section 875(c) is satisfied if the defendant transmits a communication for the purpose of issuing a threat, or with knowledge that the communication will be viewed as a threat. In response to a question at oral argument, Elonis stated that a finding of recklessness would not be sufficient. Neither Elonis nor the Government has briefed or argued that point, and we accordingly decline to address it. See *Department of Treasury, IRS v. FLRA*, 494 U.S. 922, 933 (1990) (this Court is "poorly situated" to address an argument the Court of Appeals did not consider, the parties did not brief, and counsel addressed in "only the most cursory fashion at oral argument").

Both Justice Alito and Justice Thomas complain about our not deciding whether recklessness suffices for liability under Section 875(c). Justice Alito contends that each party "argued" this issue, but they did not address it at all until oral argument, and even then only briefly....

Justice Alito also suggests that we have not clarified confusion in the lower courts. That is wrong. Our holding makes clear that negligence is not sufficient to support a conviction under Section 875(c), contrary to the view of nine Courts of Appeals. There was and is no circuit conflict over the question Justice Alito and Justice Thomas would have us decide — whether recklessness suffices for liability under Section 875(c). No Court of Appeals has even addressed that question. We think that is more than sufficient "justification" for us to decline to be the first appellate tribunal to do so.

We may be "capable of deciding the recklessness issue," but following our usual practice of awaiting a decision below and hearing from the parties would help ensure that we decide it correctly.

The judgment of the United States Court of Appeals for the Third Circuit is reversed, and the case is remanded for further proceedings consistent with this opinion.

It is so ordered.

Discussion Questions

1. Did the trial court in its instructions to the jury require any culpable mental state on the part of Elonis about whether his posts would be viewed as threats by those reading them? If so, what mental state?

2. How would the *Elonis* case have been resolved under the Model Penal Code?

3. Justice Roberts states that "the conventional requirement for criminal conduct" is "*awareness* of some wrongdoing." Is this consistent with the Model Penal Code? With the Model Penal Code's rules of interpretation regarding vague statutes?

2. Statutes that Include a Mental State

If a statute that has multiple non-mental elements includes a mental state, what inference should a judge or prosecutor draw about which non-mental elements that mental state applies to? Only the non-mental element the mental state appears closest to in the statute? All the statute's non-mental elements? Or something in between? How do the Model Penal Code and the *Flores-Figuero* case in this section deal with such ambiguity?

Problem

5.21 You are a public defender appointed to represent a client charged with second degree burglary under the statute that appears below. Your client admits entering the building in question, a warehouse, intending to steal some property inside the building.

Burglary in the second degree.

A person is guilty of burglary in the second degree when he knowingly enters or remains unlawfully in a building with intent to commit a crime therein, and when:

1. In effecting entry or while in the building or in the immediate flight therefrom, he or another participant in the crime:

   a. Is armed with explosives or a deadly weapon;

   b. Causes physical injury to any person who is not a participant in the crime; or

2. The building is a dwelling.

Part (a) Your client did not know that the warehouse in question was a dwelling. He carefully surveyed the warehouse for several weeks prior to his entry and accurately determined that the warehouse closes each day at 5 p.m. and that all employees appear to leave at that time. Your client checked with the city and found that no residential occupancy permit had been issued for the warehouse. Your client even went so far as to ask some of the employees at the warehouse, whom he met at local bar, and they informed him that the building was not used as a dwelling. Unfortunately for your client, it turns out that a small section of an upper floor in the rear of the building serves as an apartment for a watchman who lives in the building and uses a rear entrance to enter and to exit. Is your client liable under the burglary statute?

Part (b) Assume for this part that the warehouse was not a dwelling. Your client agreed with a friend together to steal some laptop computers and cash from a shipping office inside the warehouse and split the proceeds of the theft. Your client did not know that the friend was carrying a loaded handgun in a jacket pocket at the time they entered the warehouse. Your client discovered that his friend was carrying the handgun when they were arrested leaving the warehouse and the police searched both your client and his friend incident to their arrests. Is your client liable under the burglary statute?

Part (c) Assume for this part that the warehouse was not a dwelling and that your client acted *alone* and was *unarmed*. Your client thought that there was no one in the warehouse at the time he entered it. As he was rummaging around the warehouse looking for property to steal, a watchman appeared, turned on the lights and demanded to know who was in the building. Your client hid behind some crates until the watchman passed his hiding place, then ran for the door to make his escape. The watchman heard your client fleeing and gave chase. In so doing, the watchman slipped and fell, breaking an arm and spraining his knee. Is your client liable under the burglary statute?

Part (d) You have been hired as counsel for the committee of the state legislature responsible for drafting and amending the state's criminal laws. You are directed by the committee chair to propose amendments to its burglary statute to clarify its application to situations such as those presented in Parts (a), (b), and (c) of this Problem. What amendments do you suggest?

Model Penal Code

§ 2.02 General Requirements of Culpability

…

(4) Prescribed Culpability Requirement Applies to All Material Elements. When the law defining an offense prescribes the kind of culpability that is sufficient for the commission of an offense, without distinguishing among the material elements thereof, such provision shall apply to all the material elements of the offense, unless a contrary purpose plainly appears.…

Comment

Ambiguous Culpability Requirements. Subsection (4) seeks to assist in the resolution of a common ambiguity in penal legislation, the statement of a particular culpability requirement in the definition of an offense in such a way that it is unclear whether the requirement applies to all the elements of the offense or only to the element that it immediately introduces.…

The Code proceeds in the view that if a particular kind of culpability has been articulated at all by the legislature as sufficient with respect to any element of the offense, the assumption is that it was meant to apply to all material elements. Hence this construction is required, unless a "contrary purpose plainly appears." When a distinction is intended, as it often is, proper drafting ought to make it clear.

[An example] may help to clarify the intended scope of the provision and to illustrate its relationship with Subsection 3. False imprisonment is defined by Section 212.3 of the Model Code to include one who "knowingly restrains another unlawfully so as to interfere substantially with his liberty." Plainly, the word "knowingly" is intended to modify the restraint, so that the actor must, in order to be convicted under this section, know that he is restraining his victim. The question whether "knowingly" also qualifies the unlawful character of the restraint is not clearly answered by the definition of the offense, but is answered in the affirmative by the subsection under discussion.…

Flores-Figueroa v. United States

556 U.S. 646 (2009)
Supreme Court of the United States

Justice Breyer delivered the opinion of the Court.

A federal criminal statute forbidding "[a]ggravated identity theft" imposes a mandatory consecutive 2-year prison term upon individuals convicted of certain other crimes *if*, during (or in relation to) the commission of those other crimes, the offender "*knowingly* transfers, possesses, or uses, without lawful authority, *a means of identification of another person.*" 18 U.S.C. § 1028A(a)(1) (emphasis added). The question is whether the statute requires the Government to show that the defendant *knew* that the "means of identification" he or she unlawfully transferred, possessed, or used, in fact, belonged to "another person." We conclude that it does.

The statutory provision in question references a set of predicate crimes, including, for example, theft of government property, fraud, or engaging in various unlawful activities related to passports, visas, and immigration. It then provides that if any person who commits any of those other crimes (in doing so) "knowingly transfers, possesses, or uses, without lawful authority, a means of identification of another person," the judge must add two years' imprisonment to the offender's underlying sentence. All parties agree that the provision applies only where the offender knows that he is transferring, possessing, or using *something.* And the Government reluctantly concedes that the offender likely must know that he is transferring, possessing, or using that *something* without lawful authority. But they do not agree whether the provision requires that a defendant also know that the *something* he has unlawfully transferred is, for example, a real ID belonging to another person rather than, say, a fake ID (*i.e.,* a group of numbers that does not correspond to any real Social Security number).

Petitioner Ignacio Flores-Figueroa argues that the statute requires that the Government prove that he *knew* that the "means of identification" belonged to someone else, *i.e.,* was "a means of identification *of another person.*" The Government argues that the statute does not impose this particular knowledge requirement. The Government concedes that the statute uses the word "knowingly," but that word, the Government claims, does not modify the statute's last phrase ("a means of identification of another person") or, at the least, it does not modify the last three words of that phrase ("of another person").

The facts of this case illustrate the legal problem. Ignacio Flores-Figueroa is a citizen of Mexico. In 2000, to secure employment, Flores gave his employer a false name, birth date, and Social Security number, along with a counterfeit alien registration card. The Social Security number and the number on the alien registration card were not those of a real person. In 2006, Flores presented his employer with new counterfeit Social Security and alien registration cards; these cards (unlike Flores' old alien registration card) used his real name. But this time the numbers on both cards were in fact numbers assigned to other people.

Flores' employer reported his request to U.S. Immigration and Customs Enforcement. Customs discovered that the numbers on Flores' new documents belonged to other people. The United States then charged Flores with two predicate crimes, namely, entering the United States without inspection, 8 U.S.C. § 1325(a), and misusing immigration documents, 18 U.S.C. § 1546(a). And it charged him with aggravated identity theft, 18 U.S.C. § 1028A(a)(1), the crime at issue here.

Flores moved for a judgment of acquittal on the "aggravated identity theft" counts. He claimed that the Government could not prove that he *knew* that the numbers on the counterfeit documents were numbers assigned to other people. The Government replied that it need not prove that knowledge, and the District Court accepted the Government's argument. After a bench trial, the court found Flores guilty of the predicate crimes and aggravated identity theft. The Court of Appeals upheld the District Court's determination. And we granted certiorari to consider the "knowledge" issue—a matter about which the Circuits have disagreed. Compare *United States v. Godin*, 534 F.3d 51 (CA1 2008) (knowledge requirement applies to "of another person"); *United States v. Miranda-Lopez*, 532 F.3d 1034 (CA9 2008) (same); *United States v. Villanueva-Sotelo*, 380 U.S. App. D.C. 11, 515 F.3d 1234 (CADC 2008) (same), with *United States v. Mendoza-Gonzalez*, 520 F.3d 912 (CA8 2008) (knowledge requirement does not apply to "of another person"); *United States v. Hurtado*, 508 F.3d 603 (CA11 2007) (per curiam) (same); *United States v. Montejo*, 442 F.3d 213 (CA4 2006) (same).

There are strong textual reasons for rejecting the Government's position. As a matter of ordinary English grammar, it seems natural to read the statute's word "knowingly" as applying to all the subsequently listed elements of the crime. The Government cannot easily claim that the word "knowingly" applies only to the statute's first four words, or even its first seven. It makes little sense to read the provision's language as heavily penalizing a person who "transfers, possesses, or uses, without lawful authority" a *something*, but does not know, at the very least, that the "something" (perhaps inside a box) is a "means of identification." Would we apply a statute that makes it unlawful "*knowingly* to possess drugs" to a person who steals a passenger's bag without knowing that the bag has drugs inside?

The Government claims more forcefully that the word "knowingly" applies to all but the statute's last three words, *i.e.*, "of another person." The statute, the Government says, does not require a prosecutor to show that the defendant *knows* that the means of identification the defendant has unlawfully used in fact belongs to another person. But how are we to square this reading with the statute's language?

In ordinary English, where a transitive verb has an object, listeners in most contexts assume that an adverb (such as knowingly) that modifies the transitive verb tells the listener how the subject performed the entire action, including the object as set forth in the sentence. Thus, if a bank official says, "Smith knowingly transferred the funds to his brother's account," we would normally understand the bank official's statement as telling us that Smith knew the account was his brother's. Nor would it matter if the bank official said "Smith knowingly transferred the funds to the account of his brother." In either instance, if the bank official later told us that Smith did not know the account belonged to Smith's brother, we should be surprised.

Of course, a statement that does *not* use the word "knowingly" may be unclear about just what Smith knows. Suppose Smith mails his bank draft to Tegucigalpa, which (perhaps unbeknownst to Smith) is the capital of Honduras. If the bank official says, "Smith sent a bank draft to the capital of Honduras," he has expressed next to nothing about Smith's knowledge of that geographic identity. But if the official were to say, "Smith *knowingly* sent a bank draft to the capital of Honduras," then the official has suggested that Smith knows his geography.

Similar examples abound. If a child knowingly takes a toy that belongs to his sibling, we assume that the child not only knows that he is taking something, but that he also knows that what he is taking is a toy *and* that the toy belongs to his sibling. If we say that someone knowingly ate a sandwich with cheese, we normally assume that the person knew both that he was eating a sandwich and that it contained cheese. Or consider the Government's own example, "'John knowingly discarded the homework of his sister.'" The Government rightly points out that this sentence "does not *necessarily*" imply that John knew whom the homework belonged to. But that is what the sentence, as *ordinarily* used, does imply.

At the same time, dissimilar examples are not easy to find. The Government says that "knowingly" modifies only the verbs in the statute, while remaining indifferent to the subject's knowledge of at least part of the transitive verb's object. In certain contexts, a listener might understand the word "knowingly" to be used in that way. But the Government has not provided us with a single example of a sentence that, when used in typical fashion, would lead the hearer to believe that the word "knowingly" modifies only a transitive verb without the full object, *i.e.*, that it leaves the hearer gravely uncertain about the subject's state of mind in respect to the full object of the transitive verb in the sentence. The likely reason is that such sentences typically involve special contexts or themselves provide a more detailed explanation of background circumstances that call for such a reading. As Justice Alito notes, the inquiry into a sentence's meaning is a contextual one. No special context is present here.

The manner in which the courts ordinarily interpret criminal statutes is fully consistent with this ordinary English usage. That is to say courts ordinarily read a phrase in a criminal statute that introduces the elements of a crime with the word "knowingly" as applying that word to each element. For example, in *Liparota v. United States*, this Court interpreted a federal food stamp statute that said, "'[w]hoever knowingly uses, transfers, acquires, alters, or possesses coupons or authorization cards *in any manner not authorized by [law]'*" is subject to imprisonment. The question was whether the word "knowingly" applied to the phrase "in any manner not authorized by [law]." The Court held that it did, despite the legal cliche "ignorance of the law is no excuse."

More recently, [in *United States v. X-Citement Video*] we had to interpret a statute that penalizes "[a]ny person who—(1) knowingly transports or ships [using any means or facility of] interstate or foreign commerce by any means including by computer or mails, any visual depiction, if—(A) the producing of such visual depiction involves the use of a minor engaging in sexually explicit conduct." In issue was whether the term "knowingly" in paragraph (1) modified the phrase "the use of a minor" in sub-paragraph (A). The language in issue in *X-Citement Video* (like the language in *Liparota*) was more ambiguous than the language here not only because the phrase "the use of a minor" was not the direct object of the verbs modified by "knowingly," but also because it appeared in a different subsection. Moreover, the fact that many sex crimes involving minors do not ordinarily require that a perpetrator know that his victim is a minor supported the Government's position. Nonetheless, we again found that the intent element applied to "the use of a minor." Again the Government, while pointing to what it believes are special features of each of these cases, provides us with no convincing counterexample, although there may be such statutory instances....

The Government also considers the statute's purpose to be a circumstance showing that the linguistic context here is special. It describes that purpose as "provid[ing] enhanced protection for individuals whose identifying information is used to facilitate the commission of crimes." And it points out that without the knowledge requirement, potential offenders will take great care to avoid wrongly using IDs that belong to others, thereby enhancing the protection that the statute offers.

The question, however, is whether Congress intended to achieve this enhanced protection by permitting conviction of those who do not *know* the ID they unlawfully use refers to a real person, *i.e.*, those who do not *intend* to cause this further harm. And, in respect to this latter point, the statute's history (outside of the statute's language) is inconclusive.

On the one hand, some statements in the legislative history offer the Government a degree of support. The relevant House Report refers, for example, both to "identity theft" (use of an ID belonging to someone else) and to "identity fraud" (use of a false ID), often without distinguishing between the two. And, in equating fraud and theft, Congress might have meant the statute to cover both—at least where the fraud takes the form of using an ID that (without the offender's knowledge) belongs to someone else.

On the other hand, Congress separated the fraud crime from the theft crime in the statute itself. The title of one provision (not here at issue) is "Fraud and related activity in connection with identification documents, authentication features, and information." 18 U.S.C. § 1028. The title of another provision (the provision here at issue) uses the words "identity *theft*." § 1028A (emphasis added). Moreover, the examples of theft that Congress gives in the legislative history all involve instances where the offender would know that what he has taken identifies a different real person. H. R. Rep. No. 108-528, at 4–5 (identifying as examples of "identity theft" "'dumpster diving,'" "accessing information that was originally collected for an authorized purpose," "hack[ing] into computers," and "steal[ing] paperwork likely to contain personal information").

Finally, and perhaps of greatest practical importance, there is the difficulty in many circumstances of proving beyond a reasonable doubt that a defendant has the necessary knowledge. Take an instance in which an alien who unlawfully entered the United States gives an employer identification documents that *in fact* belong to others. How is the Government to prove that the defendant *knew* that this was so? The Government may be able to show that such a defendant knew the papers were not his. But perhaps the defendant did not care whether the papers (1) were real papers belonging to another person or (2) were simply counterfeit papers. The difficulties of proof along with the defendant's necessary guilt of a predicate crime and the defendant's necessary knowledge that he has acted "without lawful authority," make it reasonable, in the Government's view, to read the statute's language as dispensing with the knowledge requirement.

We do not find this argument sufficient, however, to turn the tide in the Government's favor. For one thing, in the classic case of identity theft, intent is generally not difficult to prove. For example, where a defendant has used another person's identification information to get access to that person's bank account, the Government can prove knowledge with little difficulty. The same is true when the defendant has gone through someone else's trash to find discarded credit card and bank statements, or pretends to be from the victim's bank and requests personal identifying information. Indeed, the examples of identity theft in the legislative history (dumpster diving, computer hacking, and the like) are all examples of the types of classic identity theft where intent should be relatively easy to prove, and there will be no practical enforcement problem. For another thing, to the extent that Congress may have been concerned about criminalizing the conduct of a broader class of individuals, the concerns about practical enforceability are insufficient to outweigh the clarity of the text. Similar interpretations that we have given other similarly phrased statutes also created practical enforcement problems. But had Congress placed conclusive weight upon practical enforcement, the statute would likely not read the way it now reads. Instead, Congress used the word "knowingly" followed by a list of offense elements. And we cannot find indications in statements of its purpose or in the practical problems of enforcement sufficient to overcome the ordinary meaning, in English or through ordinary interpretive practice, of the words that it wrote.

We conclude that § 1028A(a)(1) requires the Government to show that the defendant knew that the means of identification at issue belonged to another person. The judgment of the Court of Appeals is reversed, and the case is remanded for further proceedings consistent with this opinion.

Justice Scalia, with whom Justice Thomas joins, concurring in part and concurring in the judgment.

I agree with the Court that to convict petitioner for "knowingly transfer[ring], possess[ing], or us[ing], without lawful authority, a means of identification of another person," the Government must prove that he "*knew* that the 'means of identification' he ... unlawfully transferred, possessed, or used, in fact, belonged to 'another person.'" "Knowingly" is not limited to the statute's verbs.... [O]nce the statute's knowledge requirement is understood to modify the object of those verbs, there is no reason to believe it does not extend to the phrase which limits that object ("of another person"). Ordinary English usage supports this reading, as the Court's numerous sample sentences amply demonstrate.

But the Court is not content to stop at the statute's text, and I do not join that further portion of the Court's opinion. First, the Court relies in part on the principle that "courts ordinarily read a phrase in a criminal statute that introduces the elements of a crime with the word 'knowingly' as applying that word to each element." If that is meant purely as a description of what most cases do, it is perhaps true, and perhaps not. I have not canvassed all the cases and am hence agnostic. If it is meant, however, as a normative description of what courts *should* ordinarily do when interpreting such statutes … then I surely do not agree. The structure of the text in *X-Citement Video* plainly separated the "use of a minor" element from the "knowingly" requirement, wherefore I thought (and think) that case was wrongly decided. It is one thing to infer the common-law tradition of a *mens rea* requirement where Congress has not addressed the mental element of a crime. It is something else to expand a *mens rea* requirement that the statutory text has carefully limited.

I likewise cannot join the Court's discussion of the (as usual, inconclusive) legislative history. Relying on the statement of a single Member of Congress or an unvoted-upon (and for all we know unread) Committee Report to expand a statute beyond the limits its text suggests is always a dubious enterprise. And consulting those incunabula with an eye to making criminal what the text would otherwise permit is even more suspect. Indeed, it is not unlike the practice of Caligula, who reportedly "wrote his laws in a very small character, and hung them up upon high pillars, the more effectually to ensnare the people." The statute's text is clear, and I would reverse the judgment of the Court of Appeals on that ground alone.

Justice Alito, concurring in part and concurring in the judgment.

While I am in general agreement with the opinion of the Court, I write separately because I am concerned that the Court's opinion may be read by some as adopting an overly rigid rule of statutory construction. The Court says that "[i]n ordinary English, where a transitive verb has an object, listeners in most contexts assume that an adverb (such as knowingly) that modifies the transitive verb tells the listener how the subject performed the entire action, including the object as set forth in the sentence." The Court adds that counterexamples are "not easy to find," and I suspect that the Court's opinion will be cited for the proposition that the *mens rea* of a federal criminal statute nearly always applies to every element of the offense.

I think that the Court's point about ordinary English usage is overstated. Examples of sentences that do not conform to the Court's rule are not hard to imagine. For example: "The mugger knowingly assaulted two people in the park—an employee of company X and a jogger from town Y." A person hearing this sentence would not likely assume that the mugger knew about the first victim's employer or the second victim's hometown. What matters in this example, and the Court's, is context.

More to the point, ordinary writers do not often construct the particular kind of sentence at issue here, *i.e.*, a complex sentence in which it is important to determine from the sentence itself whether the adverb denoting the actor's intent applies to every characteristic of the sentence's direct object. Such sentences are a staple of criminal codes, but in ordinary speech, a different formulation is almost always used when the speaker wants to be clear on the point. For example, a speaker might say: "Flores-Figueroa used a Social Security number that he knew belonged to someone else" or "Flores-Figueroa used a Social Security number that just happened to belong to a real person." But it is difficult to say with the confidence the Court conveys that there is an "ordinary" understanding of the usage of the phrase at issue in this case.

In interpreting a criminal statute such as the one before us, I think it is fair to begin with a general presumption that the specified *mens rea* applies to all the elements of an offense, but it must be recognized that there are instances in which context may well rebut that presumption. For example, 18 U.S.C. §2423(a) makes it unlawful to "knowingly transpor[t] an individual who has not attained the age of 18 years in interstate or foreign commerce ... with intent that the individual engage in prostitution, or in any sexual activity for which any person can be charged with a criminal offense." The Courts of Appeals have uniformly held that a defendant need not know the victim's age to be guilty under this statute. ...

In the present case, however, the Government has not pointed to contextual features that warrant interpreting 18 U.S.C. §1028A(a)(1) in a similar way. Indeed, the Government's interpretation leads to exceedingly odd results. Under that interpretation, if a defendant uses a made-up Social Security number without having any reason to know whether it belongs to a real person, the defendant's liability under §1028A(a)(1) depends on chance: If it turns out that the number belongs to a real person, two years will be added to the defendant's sentence, but if the defendant is lucky and the number does not belong to another person, the statute is not violated.

I therefore concur in the judgment and join the opinion of the Court except insofar as it may be read to adopt an inflexible rule of construction that can rarely be overcome by contextual features pointing to a contrary reading.

Discussion Questions

1. Justice Breyer states that applying the word "knowingly" to the circumstance element "of another person" is the most natural reading of the language in the statute. He also concludes that the practical enforcement problems raised by the government are insufficient "to outweigh the clarity of the text." But he also notes that federal appellate courts had divided relatively equally on how to interpret this statute. If the interpretation Justice Breyer adopts is the most natural reading of the statute and the statute's text is as clear as Justice Breyer says, why did roughly half of the appellate courts reject this interpretation?

2. How would the statute at issue in *Flores-Figueroa* be interpreted under the Model Penal Code?

3. Whose interpretive approach is more similar to the Model Penal Code's? Justice Breyer's? Or Justice Alito's?

4. Where have you previously encountered the sort of practical enforcement problems raised by the government in *Flores-Figueroa*?

5. In Chapter 3 you read an excerpt from an article by Justice Breyer on the use of legislative history in statutory interpretation. Is Justice Breyer's treatment of legislative history in *Flores-Figueroa* consistent with the views he expresses in his article?

D. Mistake of Fact

Problem

5.22 Jane was convicted after a jury trial under a statute that states: "It is a felony punishable by 10 years imprisonment knowingly to sell crack cocaine within 1,000 feet of any school." The school in question was a preschool serving children of families with working parents and located in a light industrial building in a primarily commercial area. Jane was arrested by an undercover police officer in front of the building in which the preschool was located. Jane testified at trial and admitted that she did in fact sell a small amount of crack cocaine within 1000 feet of the preschool, but claimed that she was mistaken about whether the building in question contained a school. She believed the building and the surrounding area were strictly commercial.

At Jane's trial, the judge gave the following instruction on mistake of fact:

"Ladies and gentlemen of the jury, Jane the defendant has admitted in her testimony selling the crack cocaine in question within a prohibited distance from a school. But she claims to have been mistaken about whether the building in question contained a school. Now the statute in question punishes only knowingly selling crack cocaine within 1000 feet of a school, and the defendant has admitted that she knew she was selling the crack cocaine in question. If you find that the defendant's mistake negates the knowledge required by the statute, then you should acquit her. However, you should acquit her on the basis of her mistake only if you find her mistake is one for which you think there is a reasonable explanation or excuse."

Assume the preschool qualifies as a "school," the amount of crack cocaine qualifies for prosecution under the statute, and that Jane is prosecuted in a Model Penal Code jurisdiction. You are an appellate judge reviewing Jane's conviction. Should you reverse Jane's conviction? Why? What, if anything, did the trial judge do wrong in instructing the jury? Write the instruction the trial judge should give to the jury if you reverse and grant Jane a new trial.

What does a defendant mean when she makes a claim of ignorance, mistake, or accident regarding a factual matter relevant to a crime? Is she saying that she did not commit the crime in question because some element of the crime has not been proven? Or is she saying that she did commit the crime—that is she admits all the elements have been proven—but she should nonetheless be relieved of liability because of ignorance, mistake, or accident? In answering these questions, consider the following definitions of ignorance, mistake, and knowledge from two dictionaries and a federal jury instruction.

The Oxford English Dictionary

ignorance: the fact or condition of being ignorant; want of knowledge ...

Webster's New Collegiate Dictionary

mistake: a misunderstanding of the meaning or implication of something; a wrong action or statement proceeding from faulty judgment, inadequate knowledge, or inattention.

accident: an event occurring by chance ...; lack of intention ...; an unfortunate event resulting from carelessness, unawareness, ignorance or a combination of causes

Ninth Circuit Manual of Model Jury Instructions—Criminal (2000)
5.6 Knowingly Defined

An act is done knowingly if the defendant is aware of the act and does not act through ignorance, mistake, or accident.... You may consider evidence of the defendant's words, acts, or omissions, along with all the other evidence, in deciding whether the defendant acted knowingly.

Problems

Assume the following problems arise in a Model Penal Code jurisdiction. Diagram the elements of the crime involved in each problem, then decide which box is relevant to resolving the defendant's claims in each.

5.22 Knowing possession of cocaine is a crime. Janet is a cocaine dealer. Janet has regular runners she uses to deliver cocaine around town. One day, though, Janet gets a call from a customer who wants some cocaine in a hurry but none of her regular runners is available. Janet decides to use a legitimate local delivery service to get the cocaine to her customer. Ivan, an employee of the delivery company, responds to Janet's call in his delivery truck. Janet gives him a box of groceries, tells him she wants them delivered to a friend, and provides the address. Included in the box is a clear jar of white powder, which is marked "sugar" but actually contains cocaine. It turns out that police have had Janet under surveillance for some time. They follow Ivan and arrest him just after he delivers the box, including the cocaine, to Janet's customer. Is Ivan liable for knowing possession of cocaine?

Should it make any difference how Ivan describes his mental state? Consider the following variations:

    (a) "I didn't know the white stuff in the jar was cocaine."

    (b) "I thought the white stuff in the jar was sugar. The label said sugar."

    (c) "I was mistaken about what the white powder was."

    (d) "I was ignorant of the true nature of the white powder."

5.23 Assume possession of a sword cane is a crime and that strict liability applies to whether the cane contains a sword. When her father dies, Shelly inherits his entire estate. She cleans out his attic and discards many items, but retains a number of things, including a cane she thinks would look great hanging on the wall of her library. Shelly is unaware that the cane from her father's attic is a sword cane. Before hanging it on the wall, she takes it, along with some other items, to an antique dealer for an appraisal. The antique dealer discovers the true nature of the cane when he inspects it and calls the police, who charge Shelly. Is Shelly liable for possession of the sword cane?

Should it make any difference how Shelly describes her mental state? Consider the following variations:

    (a) "I didn't know it was a sword cane."

    (b) "I thought it was simply a cane."

    (c) "I was mistaken about the nature of the cane."

    (d) "I was ignorant of the nature of the cane."

5.24 Assume that killing another person with purpose to cause that death is murder. Silvia and her friend Vince often play practical jokes on one another. One night Silvia decides to frighten Vince by pointing her revolver, which she thinks is unloaded, at Vince's head and pulling the trigger. Silvia usually keeps the revolver empty. But just to be sure, she opens the gun and quickly checks the chambers. In doing so, she fails to notice a single bullet in the chamber just to the left of the firing pin. Silvia puts the gun to Vince's head, pulls the trigger, and the gun fires. Vince drops dead and Silvia collapses in shock and remorse. Is Silvia liable for murder on the basis of purposefully causing Vince's death?

Should it make any difference how Silvia describes her mental state? Consider the following variations:

    (a) "It wasn't my purpose to kill Vince. I just wanted to scare him."

    (b) "I thought the gun was unloaded."

(c) "I was mistaken about whether the gun was loaded."

(d) "I was ignorant of the fact that a bullet was in the gun."

5.25 Assume that killing another human being with negligence regarding the death is negligent homicide. Perry and Ann are the parents of Jack, a three-year-old boy. One day, Jack comes home from school with a sore throat, fever, and runny nose. Perry and Ann treat Jack with cold medicine and decide to keep him home from school the next day. The next morning, Ann wakes up, goes into Jack's room, and finds him dead in his bed. An autopsy reveals that Jack had a rare allergy and that his symptoms were the result of his having eaten some unusual food at school. Inflammation in his throat had become so severe that Jack was unable to breathe. The medical examiner determines that if Perry and Ann had brought Jack to a hospital emergency room as soon as he came home from school, Jack could have been saved through the administration of medicine to counter his allergic reaction. Are Perry and Ann liable for negligent homicide for their failure to take Jack to an emergency room?

Should it make any difference how Perry and Ann describe their mental states? Consider the following variations:

(a) "We didn't know he had an allergy or was suffering an allergic reaction."

(b) "We thought he just had a cold."

(c) "We were mistaken about what he was suffering from and how much danger it posed."

(d) "We were ignorant of how serious Jack's condition was."

1. Mistake as Evidence of Mental State

The preferable way to approach claims of mistake, ignorance, or accident is to treat such claims simply as offering evidence regarding mental state, or, more precisely, evidence that the defendant lacked a particular mental state. In other words, in making a claim of mistake or ignorance, a defendant is simply addressing an element of the charged offense. As with all offense elements, the burden of proof is on the government to prove a required mental state and the standard of proof is beyond reasonable doubt.

When a defendant claims to lack a mental state required for conviction of a crime, it raises a factual issue for the jury to resolve. Both the prosecution and defense can present direct and circumstantial evidence on such a question. The defendant may testify, for example, that he lacked a mental state; that is, that he was ignorant or mistaken or caused some result by accident. Such testimony qualifies as direct evidence. The defendant may also offer circumstantial evidence to prove the same point. In Problem 5.24, for example, the fact that the victim was a friend of the defendant, Silvia, makes it less likely that Silvia would purposefully have killed him. If Janet in Problem 5.22 paid Ivan only his normal fee to deliver the box containing the jar of white powder, it makes it less likely that Ivan knew the jar contained cocaine. The prosecution may also offer direct evidence of a defendant's mental state, such as a confession or a tape-recorded phone call in which the defendant admitted having the required mental state. Often the prosecution relies on circumstantial evidence of mental state. In Problem 5.24, if a quarrel had recently taken place between Silvia and her victim, it would be a piece of circumstantial evidence tending to show that Silvia did have purpose to kill. In Problem 5.22, if Janet had paid Ivan a very large sum above his normal fee to deliver the box, it would tend to show that Ivan knew or was aware of a substantial risk that the box contained something illegal. A useful exercise is to review each of the problems from 5.22 through 5.25, identify the various pieces of evidence, and see what, if any, bearing each has on the mental state issue presented in that problem.

After evaluating and weighing the evidence presented by both sides, direct and circumstantial, the jury finally determines whether the government has met its burden of proving beyond a reasonable doubt that the defendant did have the required mental state. Thus, a defendant should win if the jury concludes that there exists reasonable doubt about whether he or she had a required mental state.

Problem

5.26 Would the defendants in Problems 5.22 through 5.25 above be held liable under the following statutes?

Iowa Criminal Code

§ 701.6. Ignorance or mistake

… Evidence of an accused person's ignorance or mistake as to a matter of … fact … shall be admissible in any case where it shall tend to prove the existence or nonexistence of some element of the crime with which the person is charged.

Model Penal Code

§ 2.04 Ignorance or Mistake

(1) Ignorance or mistake as to a matter of fact or law is a defense if:

    (a) the ignorance or mistake negatives the purpose, knowledge, belief, recklessness or negligence required to establish a material element of the offense; or

(b) the law provides that the state of mind established by such ignorance or mistake constitutes a defense.

Comment

Relation of Ignorance or Mistake to Culpability Requirements. Subsection (1) states the conventional position under which the significance of ignorance by the defendant of a matter of fact or law, or a mistake as to such matters, is determined by the mental state required for the commission of the offense involved. Thus ignorance or mistake is a defense when it negatives the existence of a state of mind that is essential to the commission of an offense, or when it establishes a state of mind that constitutes a defense under a rule of law relating to defenses. In other words, ignorance or mistake has only evidential import; it is significant whenever it is logically relevant, and it may be logically relevant to negate the required mode of culpability or to establish a special defense.

5.27 The following jury instructions are pattern instructions for use in cases of mistake of fact. The bracketed words and blank spaces in each mark the language the trial judge tailors to the charge in the particular case. If you were the trial judge in Problems 5.22 through 5.25 above, in which cases would it be appropriate to give either instruction? How would you tailor the language of each instruction to the charge in each problem? Would the defendants in those problems be held liable under either instruction?

Ohio Jury Instructions 409.03 Mistake of fact

1. Unless the defendant had the required _____ [mental state] he is not guilty of the crime of _____.

2. In determining whether the defendant had the required _____ [mental state], you will consider whether he acted under a mistake of fact regarding _____.

3. If the defendant had an honest belief arrived at in good faith in the existence of such facts and acted in accordance with the facts as he believed them to be, he is not guilty of _____ as _____ [mental state] is an essential element of that offense.

Pattern Jury Instructions (Criminal Cases) Prepared by the Committee on Pattern Criminal Jury Instructions, First Circuit.

5.02 Mental State That Is Inconsistent with the Requisite Culpable State of Mind

Evidence has been presented of defendant's mistake. Such mistake may be inconsistent with _____ [the requisite culpable state of mind for the charged offense]. If after considering the evidence of mistake, together with all the other evidence, you have a reasonable doubt that defendant acted with _____ [the requisite culpable state of mind], then you must find defendant not guilty.

Below is the New York statute under which the defendant in the following case was convicted:

New York Penal Code

§ 120.05 Assault in the second degree

A person is guilty of assault in the second degree when: …

4. He recklessly causes serious physical injury to another person by means of a deadly weapon or a dangerous instrument; …

People v. Rypinski

57 A.D.2d 260 (1990)
Appellate Division of the Supreme Court of New York

Pine, J.

Defendant was convicted, after a jury trial, of reckless assault in the second degree (Penal Law § 120.05 [4]), as a purported lesser included offense of reckless assault in the first degree (Penal Law § 120.10 [3]). He was acquitted of two companion counts of intentional assault and one count of criminal possession of a weapon. He contends on appeal that the court erroneously refused to charge that a mistake of fact is a defense to reckless assault. No issue is raised with respect to the propriety of charging assault in the second degree as a lesser included offense.

The evidence established that defendant, who had been drinking all evening, shot Gordon Ulrich above the left knee in the early morning hours of January 1, 1985 after an argument concerning defendant's girlfriend.

Prosecution witnesses testified that, before defendant got a rifle from his car, he threatened to blow the victim's brains out. They also testified that, after the gun discharged, defendant said "I'm sorry, it was an accident. I didn't mean to hurt anybody."

Defendant testified that he was a member of a conservation society and used its rifle range. He said that he intended to go there on January 1st, that he had cleaned the rifle the day before, that he always kept three rounds of ammunition in the rifle (one in the chamber and two in the clip), and that he had removed and replaced the three rounds while cleaning the gun. He said he had thrown it in the back seat of his car because he was having trouble opening his trunk.

He testified that he was drunk and that, when he knew there would be trouble, he pulled the rifle from the back seat of his car. He further testified that: "as I stood by the door, I ejected it three times. And the gun was unloaded as far as I knew because I always had the three rounds in it. And I turned away from my car. I had the rifle in my right hand, and I was hanging on to the car with my left as I was walking. I didn't even reach to the end of the car and the rifle discharged. I don't know how it went off. It was unloaded as far as I knew. And I was surprised as everybody else. I was in shock that it went off. I looked around. I heard people screaming, and

I looked and I seen somebody on the ground. I walked over to the person and I seen him bleeding. I put my hand on him and I says, I'm sorry, it was an accident."

Defendant conceded that he did not look in the chamber to see whether the gun was unloaded. He testified that the only way the gun could have been loaded was that he had not put one bullet in the chamber and two "in the ready" as he thought, but had mistakenly put three "in the ready". If he had done that, there would still have been a bullet in the chamber after he cocked the rifle three times.

Defendant requested the court to charge that the jury could consider whether a mistake of fact negated the culpable mental state required for each of the three assault counts charged in the indictment. His request was granted with respect to the intentional counts only. Although there was no specific request for a mistake of fact charge on the purported lesser included reckless assault crime of which defendant was convicted, we find that the issue whether a mistake of fact defense applies to reckless conduct is preserved on this record.

The mistake of fact defense is found in Penal Law § 15.20 (1) (a), which provides:

"A person is not relieved of criminal liability for conduct because he engages in such conduct under a mistaken belief of fact, unless:

"(a) Such factual mistake negatives the culpable mental state required for the commission of an offense."

Recklessness is a culpable mental state defined in Penal Law § 15.05 (3). It requires that the actor be aware of and consciously disregard a substantial and unjustifiable risk that a result will occur or that a circumstance exists.

In *People v Marrero*, the Court of Appeals ... held: "Although the drafters of the New York statute did not adopt the precise language of the Model Penal Code provision ... it is evident and has long been believed that the Legislature intended the New York statute to be similarly construed. In fact, the legislative history of section 15.20 is replete with references to the influence of the Model Penal Code provision."

Section 2.04 (1) (a) of the Model Penal Code provides:

"(1) Ignorance or mistake as to a matter of fact or law is a defense if:

"(a) the ignorance or mistake negatives the purpose, knowledge, belief, recklessness or negligence required to establish a material element of the offense" (emphasis added).

The commentary notes that the mistake of fact need not be reasonable in order to exculpate a defendant of a crime requiring intentional or knowing action. The commentary also notes that New York is in accord with the Model Penal Code in not requiring that the mistake be reasonable.

It is clear that Penal Law § 15.20 (1) (a), in referring to a culpable mental state required for the commission of an offense, included recklessness as a culpable mental state because that mental state is defined as such in Penal Law § 15.05 (3) and recklessness is specifically mentioned in Model Penal Code § 2.04. Therefore, the court erred in refusing to so charge the jury. Defendant's conviction must be reversed, the sentence thereon vacated, and the indictment dismissed. The People may re-present appropriate charges to another Grand Jury if so advised.

Discussion Questions

1. Assume Rypinski is retried on a charge of reckless assault. Draft the instruction on mistake of fact the trial judge should give the jury at the retrial.

2. Rypinski claimed to have been mistaken about the gun being loaded. What evidence supports his claim? What evidence tends to disprove his claim? If you were a juror at a retrial, would you convict or acquit?

3. Should the trial judge have given an instruction on mistake? The appellate court in *Rypinski* said yes. But why is an instruction on mistake required if the judge instructed the jury on the mental elements of the offense?

4. Why did the appellate court in *Rypinski* not simply remand the case for a new trial? Why did the court dismiss the indictment and require the prosecutor to re-present the case to another grand jury?

2. Reasonableness

> Uncertainty as to the precise significance of the defendant's mistake or ignorance of the surrounding facts is attributable in part to assertions, usually unexplained, in some decisions that the error must be a reasonable one....
>
> Wayne R. LaFave, Criminal Law 282 (4th ed. 2003)

Comment to Model Penal Code § 2.04 Ignorance or Mistake

The critical legislative decisions [about ignorance and mistake] ... relate to the establishment of the culpability for specific offenses as they are defined in the criminal code.... To put the matter as this subsection does is not to say anything that would not otherwise be true, even if no provision on the subject were made. As Glanville Williams has summarized the matter, the rule relating to mistake "is not a new rule; and the law could be stated equally well without reference to mistake ... it is impossible to assert that a crime requiring intention or recklessness can be committed although the accused laboured under a mistake negativing the requisite intention or recklessness. Such an assertion carries its own refutation." This obvious point has, however, sometimes been overlooked in general formulations purporting to require that mistake be reasonable if it is to exculpate, without regard to the mode of culpability required to commit the crime. This is unexceptionable in the case of mistake regarding an element of an offense as to which negligence is the culpability level. There is no justification ... for requiring that ignorance or mistake be reasonable if the crime or the element of the crime involved requires acting purposely or knowingly for its commission.

It is true, of course, that whether recklessness or negligence suffices as a mode of culpability with respect to a given element of an offense is often raised for the first time in dealing with a question of mistake. That this may happen emphasizes the importance of perceiving that the question relates to the underlying rule as to the kind of culpability required with respect to the particular element of the offense involved. Generalizations about mistake of fact and mistake of law, or about honest and reasonable mistakes as relevant to general and specific intent crimes, tend to obscure rather than clarify that simple point.

Problems

5.28 What effect does the inclusion of a reasonableness requirement have on the operation of the following Texas and New Jersey mistake statutes?

Texas Penal Code

§ 8.02. Mistake of Fact

(a) It is a defense to prosecution that the actor through mistake formed a reasonable belief about a matter of fact if his mistaken belief negated the kind of culpability required for commission of the offense.

New Jersey Code of Criminal Justice

§ 2C:2-4 Ignorance or mistake

a. Ignorance or mistake as to a matter of fact ... is a defense if the defendant reasonably arrived at the conclusion underlying the mistake and:

   (1) It negatives the culpable mental state required to establish the offense; or

   (2) The law provides that the state of mind established by such ignorance or mistake constitutes a defense.

5.29 If the defendants in Problems 5.22 through 5.25 were required to prove that their mistakes were reasonable in order to be acquitted, what impact would such a requirement have on the definition of the offense in each statute? How would it affect the liability of the defendants in those Problems?

What explains the tendency of legislators and judges to add a reasonableness requirement for mistake to exculpate even if the statute in question requires knowledge for conviction? One possible explanation is the intuitive allure of reasonableness. It may just seem reasonable to require a defendant's mistake to be reasonable. Or, phrased differently, it may seem intuitively objectionable to allow an unreasonable defendant to escape liability.

Another possible explanation is semantic, the failure to appreciate that claims of mistake or ignorance are ways of talking about mental state. Because the vocabulary is different — using terms such as *ignorance* and *mistake* rather than *knowledge, purpose,* or *intent* — some legislators and judges seem not to realize that requiring the government to prove knowledge and simultaneously insisting that the defendant be reasonable are inconsistent. When legislators and judges use two different "languages" regarding mental state they may fail to see inconsistencies that would be more apparent if only one language were used. Imagine if a contractor building a house was forced simultaneously to use both imperial units of measurement (e.g. yards, feet, inches) and metric units of measurement (e.g. meters, centimeters, millimeters). Using two different standards requiring conversion increases the risk of error. The same is true when legislators and judges address mental state using two different languages—the standard vocabulary of mental state and the vocabulary of mistake and ignorance.

The way lawyers tend to frame issues of mistake and ignorance may also contribute to the confusion. Typically, the topic of ignorance and mistake is introduced by asking whether either "is a defense." Due to imprecision in use of the term "defense," as described in the next paragraph, this way of posing the question may mask the connection between mental state and mistake and can prompt lawyers, judges, and legislators to view them as unrelated.

The term "defense" is used by lawyers, legislators, and judges to refer to two different ways of defeating liability. At times they use "defense" to refer to strategies in which the defendant contests one of the elements of the offense. Examples are alibi and mistaken identity. Each essentially attempts to establish that the defendant did not engage in the prohibited conduct. In an alibi defense, the defendant tries to show that he could not have committed the act because he was elsewhere at the time of the offense. A mistaken identity defense tries to show that one or more witnesses has wrongly identified the defendant as the person who committed the act. Mistake and ignorance properly fall within this broad use of "defense." Just as alibi and mistaken identity contest the conduct element, an assertion of ignorance or mistake contests mental state.

But "defense" is also used to refer to strategies such as self-defense and necessity in which the defendant *admits fulfillment of the elements* of the offense, but nonetheless seeks to avoid liability by asserting a principle that justifies or excuses the defendant despite admission that she committed the acts and had the requisite mental states. This second meaning of "defense" is sometimes referred to as "confession and avoidance"—confessing fulfillment of the elements but avoiding liability through assertion of an overriding principle. If a defendant uses self-defense to try to defeat liability for an aggravated assault, the defendant admits the elements of the crime—conduct, injury to the victim, causation and purpose to injure—but argues that she should nonetheless be exonerated because she had a good reason for doing so, to prevent the victim from injuring her or another. Necessity provides another example of a defense in which the defendant confesses fulfillment of the offense elements. In the famous case of *Regina v. Dudley and Stephens,* after having been shipwrecked and stranded in a lifeboat for many days without food and water, Dudley killed, and he and other crew members cannibalized, a member of his crew. Dudley admitted the elements of murder—conduct, death, causation, and purpose to kill—but nonetheless sought to avoid liability by arguing that the intentional killing of the victim was necessary and justifiable in order to save others.

As discussed above, when a defendant makes a claim of mistake in a case in which the government is required to prove the defendant's knowledge, the defendant is contesting fulfillment of an element of the crime rather than using confession and avoidance. Nonetheless, judges and legislators who are not careful in their use of the term defense may equate a "defense" of mistake or ignorance with confession and avoidance, prompting them to fail to see the relation between mistake or ignorance claims and the mental elements of the offense.

E. Mistake of Law

The often-repeated statement that ignorance or mistake of law is never a defense is the source of much confusion. Many times, as in the *Baker* case below, a mistake about or ignorance of a criminal statute does not prevent a person from being convicted. But at other times, as in the *Ratzlaf* and *Smith* (*David*) cases, below, a mistake or ignorance about the law does in fact insulate a person from conviction. As you read these cases, think about how you might rewrite the above statement about ignorance or mistake of law so that it accurately describes the results in all the cases in this section.

1. The Law Defining the Charged Offense

Problems

5.30 Jane is the leader of a community organization for girls in a western state. The group is trying to raise money for a trip to Disney World. As a fund-raising venture, Jane and some of the other mothers silk-screen t-shirts to sell to summer visitors to a nearby national park. On the t-shirts, Jane uses the image of Smokey the Bear, a figure popular with tourists because of the many forest fires that have plagued the western United States in recent years. Jane and the other mothers are arrested and charged under the following statute:

> Whoever reproduces for monetary gain the image of Smokey the Bear without the prior written permission of the United States Forest Service is punishable by a fine of up to $1,000 and/or six months imprisonment.

Jane and the other mothers did not obtain permission from the Forest Service and were unaware of the existence of this statute. Are they liable?

5.31 Leonard moves to the United States from a foreign country to be near his children and grandchildren. He is 70 years old and speaks little English. He spends most of his time at a community center with other elderly men from his native country. They pass much of their time playing card games in which substantial sums change hands. This type of gambling is a common and completely acceptable pastime for elderly gentlemen in Leonard's native country. One day, the community center is raided and Leonard and his fellow card players are charged under the following statute.

> It is a misdemeanor to participate in gambling, including playing card games for money, betting on horses, or other forms of lottery or chance without a state license.

Leonard and his colleagues had no idea that gambling is illegal without a license in the state where he now lives. Moreover, Leonard reads no English. Is Leonard liable under the statute?

a. The Conventional Position

United States v. Baker

807 F.2d 427 (5th Cir. 1986)
United States Court of Appeals for the Fifth Circuit

Reavley, J.

Paul Baker appeals his conviction for trafficking in counterfeit goods, claiming that an element of the offense is knowledge of the criminality of the conduct and that the jury should have been so charged. We reject his contention and affirm his conviction.

[T]he Trademark Counterfeiting Act subjects to criminal penalties anyone who intentionally traffics or attempts to traffic in goods or services and knowingly uses a counterfeit mark on or in connection with such goods or services. (Codified at 18 U.S.C. § 2320).

Paul Baker was convicted under this new statute for dealing in counterfeit watches. He does not dispute that he intentionally dealt in the watches. He also admits that he knew the "Rolex" watches he sold were counterfeit. His contention is that the statute requires that he act with knowledge that his conduct is criminal and that he would not have done so had he known he was committing a crime.

Although this is a case of first impression as to this statute, the underlying legal principles are well established. "The definition of the elements of a criminal offense is entrusted to the legislature, particularly in the case of federal crimes, which are solely creatures of statute." Thus our job on this appeal is to determine what Congress intended when it enacted the statute. Both the language of the statute and the legislative history lead to the inescapable conclusion that Baker need not have known that his conduct was a crime.

The statute clearly sets out the elements of the crime and the mental state required for each element. The defendant must intentionally deal in goods and he must knowingly use a counterfeit mark in connection with those goods. There is no ambiguity in this language and nothing in the statute suggests that any other mental state is required for conviction.

Our reading of the statute is confirmed by resort to the legislative history. The committee reports on the bill contain detailed descriptions of the mental states required for conviction, yet nowhere do they state that knowledge of illegality is an element of the crime.

It is not surprising that Congress would allow conviction of one who knows that he is selling bogus "Rolex" watches even though he does not know his conduct is punishable as a crime. While it is true that the "general principle that ignorance or mistake of law is no excuse is usually greatly overstated," the principle continues to be valid to the extent that ordinarily "the criminal law does not require knowledge that an act is illegal, wrong, or blameworthy." Baker's claim is merely that, even though he had the mental states required by the face of the statute, he should not be convicted because he did not know that Congress had passed a statute criminalizing his conduct. This clearly is not the law. A defendant cannot "avoid prosecution by simply claiming that he had not brushed up on the law."

Discussion Questions

1. The *Baker* court states that "[b]oth the language of the statute and the legislative history" lead the court to reject Baker's argument. How does the language of the statute help the court resolve the case? To what language is the court referring? How does the statute's legislative history help the court?

2. The Model Penal Code Comment that follows refers to "the conventional position" on mistake of law. What is this conventional position according to the *Baker* court? To what law does this conventional position refer?

Problem

5.32 How would the *Baker* case be resolved under the following Model Penal Code provisions?

Model Penal Code

§ 2.02(9) Culpability as to Illegality of Conduct

Neither knowledge nor recklessness or negligence as to whether conduct constitutes an offense or as to the existence, meaning or application of the law determining the elements of an offense is an element of such offense, unless the definition of the offense or the Code so provides.

Comment

Culpability as to Illegality of Conduct. Subsection (9) states the conventional position that knowledge of the existence, meaning or application of the law determining the elements of an offense is not an element of that offense, except in the unusual situations where the law defining the offense or the Code so provides....

The proper arena for the principle that ignorance or mistake of law does not afford an excuse is thus with respect to the particular law that sets forth the definition of the crime in question. It is knowledge of *that* law that is normally not a part of the crime, and it is ignorance or mistake as to *that* law that is denied defensive significance by this subsection of the Code and by the traditional common law approach to the issue.

Model Penal Code

§ 2.04 Ignorance or Mistake

(1) Ignorance or mistake as to a matter of fact or law is a defense if:

(a) the ignorance or mistake negatives the purpose, knowledge, belief, recklessness or negligence required to establish a material element of the offense; or

(b) the law provides that the state of mind established by such ignorance or mistake constitutes a defense.

5.33 How would the *Baker* case be resolved under the following Iowa Criminal Code provision?

Iowa Criminal Code

§ 701.6. *Ignorance or mistake*

All persons are presumed to know the law. Evidence of an accused person's ignorance or mistake as to a matter of fact or law shall be admissible in any case where it shall tend to prove the existence or nonexistence of some element of the crime with which the person is charged.

Do the MPC and Iowa provisions on mistake of law differ? If so, how?

b. Special Cases

i. Statutes Requiring Culpability Regarding Illegality

Comment to Model Penal Code
§ 2.02 (9) Culpability as to Illegality of Conduct.

It needs to be recognized, however, that there may be *special cases* where *knowledge of the law defining the offense should be part of the culpability requirement for its commission*, i.e., where a belief that one's conduct is not a violation of the law or, at least, such a belief based on reasonable grounds, ought to engender a defense. Such a result might be brought about directly by the definition of the crime, e.g., by explicitly requiring awareness of a regulation, violation of which is denominated as an offense. It also may be brought about by a general provision in the Code indicating circumstances in which mistakes about the law defining an offense will constitute a defense. In either case, the result is exceptional and arises only when the governing law "so provides." (emphasis added)

Problem

5.34 Tara is charged with violating a misdemeanor criminal statute dealing with political campaign contributions. The statute reads:

> All campaign contributions must be made by check. Anyone who makes a campaign contribution in cash of over $20 with the purpose of influencing an election is guilty of a misdemeanor. In order to secure a conviction under this statute, the prosecution must prove that the person making the campaign contribution in cash knew of the existence of this statute.

Tara is critical of her city's current mayor. Tara heard the woman challenging the mayor in an upcoming election give a speech and was impressed. Unaware of the above statute, Tara made a $50 cash contribution to the challenger's campaign, hoping to help the challenger unseat the current mayor. Tara admits making a campaign contribution in cash of over $20 with the purpose of influencing the mayoral election. But Tara argues that her lack of knowledge of the existence of the charged offense means she didn't violate it. Phrased differently, she says that her ignorance of the law under which she is charged shields her from liability for violating that law.

Part (a) Is evidence of Tara's lack of knowledge (e.g., her own testimony) relevant to her liability under the statute?

Part (b) Is she relying here on a challenge to proof or confession and avoidance strategy?

Part (c) Assume at trial that the prosecution offers no evidence that Tara knew of the statute. At the end of the prosecution's case, Tara's lawyer asks the judge to dismiss the case. You are the judge. How should you rule on the motion?

Ratzlaf v. United States

510 U.S. 135 (1994)
United States Supreme Court

Ginsburg, J.

Federal law requires banks and other financial institutions to file reports with the Secretary of the Treasury whenever they are involved in a cash transaction that exceeds $10,000 ... It is illegal to "structure" transactions—i.e., to break up a single transaction above the reporting threshold into two or more separate transactions — for the purpose of evading a financial institution's reporting requirement ... "A person willfully violating" this antistructuring provision is subject to criminal penalties.... This case presents a question on which the Courts of Appeals have divided: Does a defendant's purpose to circumvent a bank's reporting obligation suffice to sustain a conviction for "willfully violating" the antistructuring provision? We hold that the "willfulness" requirement mandates something more. To establish that a defendant "willfully violated" the antistructuring law, the Government must prove that the defendant acted with knowledge that his conduct was unlawful.

I

On the evening of October 20, 1988, defendant ... Waldemar Ratzlaf ran up a debt of $160,000 playing blackjack at the High Sierra Casino in Reno, Nevada. The casino gave him one week to pay. On the due date, Ratzlaf returned to the casino with cash of $100,000 in hand. A casino official informed Ratzlaf that all transactions involving more than $10,000 in cash had to be reported to state and federal authorities. The official added that the casino could accept a cashier's check for the full amount without triggering any reporting requirement. The casino helpfully placed a limousine at Ratzlaf's disposal, and assigned an employee to accompany him to banks in the vicinity. Informed that banks too, are required to report cash transactions in excess of $10,000, Ratzlaf purchased cashier's checks, each for less than $10,000 and each from a different bank. He delivered these checks to the High Sierra Casino.

Based on this endeavor, Ratzlaf was charged with "structuring transactions" to evade the banks' obligation to report cash transactions exceeding $10,000.... The trial judge instructed the jury that the Government had to prove defendant's knowledge of the banks' reporting obligation and his attempt to evade that obligation, but did not have to prove that the defendant knew the structuring was unlawful. Ratzlaf was convicted, fined, and sentenced to prison.

Ratzlaf maintained on appeal that he could not be convicted of "willfully violating" the antistructuring law solely on the basis of his knowledge that a financial institution must report currency transactions in excess of $10,000 and his intention to avoid such reporting. To gain a conviction for "willful" conduct, he asserted, the Government must prove he was aware of the illegality of the "structuring" in which he engaged. The Ninth Circuit upheld the trial court's construction of the legislation and affirmed Ratzlaf's conviction.... We granted certiorari ... and now conclude that, to give effect to the statutory "willfulness" specification, the Government had to prove Ratzlaf knew the structuring he undertook was unlawful. We therefore reverse the judgment of the Court of Appeals....

"No person shall for the purpose of evading the reporting requirements of section 5313(a) with respect to such transaction—

...

(3) structure or assist in structuring, or attempt to structure or assist in structuring, any transaction with one or more domestic financial institutions."

The criminal enforcement provision at issue, 31 U.S.C. § 5322(a), sets out penalties for "a person willfully violating," inter alia, the anti-structuring provision. Section 5322(a) reads:

> "A person willfully violating this subchapter ... or a regulation prescribed under this subchapter ... shall be fined not more than $250,000, or imprisoned for not more than five years, or both."

Section 5324 forbids structuring transactions with a "purpose of evading the reporting requirements of section 5313(a)." Ratzlaf admits that he structured cash transactions, and that he did so with knowledge of, and a purpose to avoid, the banks' duty to report currency transactions in excess of $10,000. The statutory formulation (§ 5322) under which Ratzlaf was prosecuted, however, calls for proof of "willfulness" on the actor's part. The trial judge in Ratzlaf's case, with the Ninth Circuit's approbation, treated § 5322(a)'s "willfulness" requirement essentially as surplusage — as words of no consequence. Judges should hesitate so to treat statutory terms in any setting, and resistance should be heightened when the words describe an element of a criminal offense....

Willful, this Court has recognized, is a "word of many meanings," and "its construction is often ... influenced by its context." ... Accordingly, we view §§ 5322(a) and 5324(3) mindful of the complex of provisions in which they are embedded. In this light, we count it significant that § 5322(a)'s omnibus "willfulness" requirement, when applied to other provisions in the same subchapter, consistently has been read by the Courts of Appeals to require both "knowledge of the reporting requirement" and a "specific intent to commit the crime," i.e., "a purpose to disobey the law." ...

Undoubtedly there are bad men who attempt to elude official reporting requirements in order to hide from Government inspectors such criminal activity as laundering drug money or tax evasion. But currency structuring is not inevitably nefarious. Consider, for example, the small business operator who knows that reports filed under [the relevant section] are available to the Internal Revenue Service. To reduce the risk of an IRS audit, she brings $9,500 in cash to the bank twice each week, in lieu of reporting over $10,000 once each week. That person, if the United States is right, has committed a criminal offense, because she structured cash transactions "for the specific purpose of depriving the Government of the information that [the relevant section] is designed to obtain." ... Nor is a person who structures a currency transaction invariably motivated by a desire to keep the Government in the dark....

But under the Government's construction an individual would commit a felony against the United States by making cash deposits in small doses, fearful that the bank's reports would increase the likelihood of burglary, or in an endeavor to keep a former spouse unaware of his wealth....

In § 5322, Congress subjected to criminal penalties only those "willfully violating" § 5324, signaling its intent to require for conviction proof that the defendant knew not only of the bank's duty to report cash transactions in excess of $10,000, but also of his duty not to avoid triggering such a report. There are, we recognize, contrary indications in the statute's legislative history. But we do not resort to legislative history to cloud a statutory text that is clear. Moreover, were we to find [the relevant section's] "willfulness" requirement ambiguous as applied..., we would resolve any doubt in favor of the defendant....

We do not dishonor the venerable principle that ignorance of the law generally is no defense to a criminal charge.... In particular contexts, however, Congress may decree otherwise. That, we hold, is what Congress has done with respect to [this statute] and the provisions it controls. To convict Ratzlaf of the crime with which he was charged, ... the jury had to find he knew the structuring in which he engaged was unlawful. Because the jury was not properly instructed in this regard, we reverse the judgment of the Ninth Circuit and remand this case for further proceedings consistent with this opinion.

Dissent, Blackmun, J.

On October 27, 1988, ... Waldemar Ratzlaf arrived at a Nevada casino with a shopping bag full of cash to pay off a $160,000 gambling debt. He told casino personnel he did not want any written report of the payment to be made. The casino vice president informed Ratzlaf that he could not accept a cash payment of more than $10,000 without filing a report.

Ratzlaf, along with his wife and a casino employee, then proceeded to visit several banks in and around Stateline, Nevada and South Lake Tahoe, California, purchasing separate cashier's checks, each in the amount of $9,500. At some banks the Ratzlafs attempted to buy two checks — one for each of them — and were told that a report would have to be filed; on those occasions they canceled the transactions. Ratzlaf then returned to the casino and paid off $76,000 of his debt in cashier's checks. A few weeks later, Ratzlaf gave three persons cash to purchase cashier's checks in amounts less than $10,000. The Ratzlafs themselves also bought five more such checks in the course of a week.

A jury found beyond a reasonable doubt that Ratzlaf knew of the financial institutions' duty to report cash transactions in excess of $10,000 and that he structured transactions for the specific purpose of evading the reporting requirements.

The Court today, however, concludes that these findings are insufficient ... because a defendant also must have known that the structuring in which he engaged was illegal. Because this conclusion lacks support in the text of the statute, conflicts in my view with the basic principles governing the interpretation of criminal statutes, and is squarely undermined by the evidence of congressional intent, I dissent.

"The general rule that ignorance of the law or a mistake of law is no defense to criminal prosecution is deeply rooted in the American legal system." ... Thus, the term "willfully" in criminal law generally refers to consciousness of the act but not to consciousness that the act is unlawful.... Unlike other provisions of the subchapter, the antistructuring provision identifies the purpose that is required for a ... violation: "evading the reporting requirements." The offense of structuring, therefore, requires

(1) knowledge of a financial institution's reporting requirements, and (2) the structuring of a transaction for the purpose of evading those requirements. These elements define a violation that is "willful" as that term is commonly interpreted. The majority's additional requirement that an actor have actual knowledge that structuring is prohibited strays from the statutory text, as well as from our precedents interpreting criminal statutes generally and "willfulness" in particular.

In interpreting federal criminal tax statutes, this Court has defined the term "willfully" as requiring the "voluntary, intentional violation of a known legal duty." ... Our rule in the tax area, however, is an "exception to the traditional rule," applied "largely due to the complexity of the tax laws." ... The rule is inapplicable here, where, far from being complex, the provisions involved are perhaps among the simplest in the United States Code.

Although I believe the statutory language is clear in light of our precedents, the legislative history confirms that Congress intended to require knowledge of (and purpose to evade) the reporting requirements but not specific knowledge of the illegality of structuring.

Discussion Questions

1. Didn't Ratzlaf make the same argument as Baker? If so, why did Ratzlaf win and Baker lose? How do you think Justice Ginsburg would rule on Baker's argument? Has Justice Ginsburg in *Ratzlaf* turned the conventional position on mistake of law on its head? Or can the *Ratzlaf* case be squared with the conventional position?

2. Do you believe that the Court's interpretation of "willfully" effectuated congressional intent? Consider the following:

> In direct response to the *Ratzlaf* decision, Congress amended § 5324 effective September 23, 1994, by deleting the statutory "willfulness" requirement for *all* criminal prosecutions brought under 31 U.S.C. 5324.... The effect of this legislative "fix" was to *eliminate entirely* the statutory willfulness requirement in all criminal prosecutions for violation of the "structuring" provisions of Section 5324(a)(3). Under the "*Ratzlaf fix*"—applicable to offenses *completed* after the statute's effective date—it is only necessary to prove that criminal defendants prosecuted under 31 U.S.C. § 5324 acted for the purpose of evading the CTR reporting requirements.[7]

3. Justice Blackmun in his dissent indicates that he differs with Justice Ginsburg in his approach to: (a) the text of the statute, (b) statutory interpretation, and (c) use of legislative intent. What approach does each justice take to each of these topics?

4. The lower courts in *Ratzlaf* apparently treated "willfulness" as surplusage. Surplusage is extraneous or unnecessary matter. Why would judges at both the trial and appellate levels treat a word placed in a statute by a legislature as being of "no consequence"?

---

7. U.S. Dep't of Justice, Criminal Resource Manual, § 2033 Structuring, http://www.usdoj.gov/usao/eousa/foia_reading_room/usam/title9/crm02033.htm (accessed 9/13/2017).

5. Note that Ratzlaf—or actually Ratzlaf's lawyers—admitted in the Supreme Court that Ratzlaf met all the statutory elements except "willfulness." Why would a lawyer do such a thing? If Ratzlaf is retried after the Supreme Court's reversal of his conviction, does the prosecutor still have to prove the elements Ratzlaf admitted? If so, can she use Ratzlaf's admission to prove them?

6. How would the *Ratzlaf* case be resolved under the Model Penal Code?

ii. Reliance on Official Interpretation

The conventional view, exemplified by *Baker*, is that no mental state is required regarding the existence or meaning of the criminal law a defendant is charged with violating. However, some statutes are written or interpreted as adopting the unconventional position of requiring the prosecution to prove some mental state regarding illegality. The federal statute at issue in *Ratzlaf* is an example of such an unconventional statute.

What happens, though, if a government agent, such as a police officer, misleads an actor about the illegality of the actor's conduct? If the statute under which the actor is charged adopts the unconventional position requiring knowledge of illegality and the actor lacks the required knowledge due to the actor's reliance on a statement by a government agent, the question of liability is easy to resolve. The actor would lack a required mental state and would not be liable.

But what if such a defendant is charged under a statute adopting the conventional position? Should the fact that the defendant was misled by a government agent be treated as irrelevant? Or should the defendant be relieved of liability? The materials in this section address this problem.

Model Penal Code

§ 2.04. Ignorance or Mistake.

(3) A belief that conduct does not legally constitute an offense is a defense to prosecution for that offense based upon such conduct when:

(a) the statute or other enactment defining the offense is not known to the actor and has not been published or otherwise made reasonably available prior to the conduct alleged; or

(b) he acts in reasonable reliance upon an official statement of the law, afterward determined to be invalid or erroneous, contained in:

   (i) a statute or other enactment;

   (ii) a judicial decision, opinion or judgment;

   (iii) an administrative order or grant of permission; or

   (iv) an official interpretation of the public officer or body charged by law with responsibility for the interpretation, administration or enforcement of the law defining the offense.

Texas Penal Code

§ 8.03 Mistake of Law

(a) It is no defense to prosecution that the actor was ignorant of the provisions of any law after the law has taken effect.

(b) It is an affirmative defense to prosecution that the actor reasonably believed the conduct charged did not constitute a crime and that he acted in reasonable reliance upon:

  (1) an official statement of the law contained in a written order or grant of permission by an administrative agency charged by law with responsibility for interpreting the law in question; or

  (2) a written interpretation of the law contained in an opinion of a court of record or made by a public official charged by law with responsibility for interpreting the law in question.

Discussion Question

Does the Texas statute differ from the Model Penal Code? If so, how?

Problem

5.35 Reverend Bill Hopkins is a minister in a state that has liberal marriage laws that allow couples to marry quickly. Nearby states have more stringent marriage laws and so many couples travel to the state where Reverend Bill lives to get married. In order to stem the increase in out-of-state couples coming to the state to get married, the state enacts the following statute:

> Anyone who places or maintains in a public space any billboard,
> sign, poster or display of any kind intended to aid in the solicitation
> or performance of marriages is guilty of a misdemeanor.

Reverend Bill wants to put up four signs on public roads near his church that say "Reverend William Hopkins, Information" with arrows pointing toward his church. One of the signs is illuminated so it is visible at night. Prior to putting the signs up, Reverend Bill asks an Assistant District Attorney, who is a member of his church, whether his signs violate the statute above. The Assistant District Attorney advises him that the signs do not violate the statute. Reverend Bill then puts up the four signs. A few months later, Rev. Bill is charged with four counts of violating the statute above. Is he liable under the Model Penal Code provision that appears above? What about under the Texas Penal Code section on mistake of law?

5.36 Andrew is charged under a state statute that prohibits a felon from possessing a firearm. Andrew has always been an avid hunter. He is now on probation after being convicted of a state felony. Following the instructions of his probation officer, Andrew sold several hunting rifles he had owned. He continued hunting deer with a bow and arrow. When his bow was damaged, his fellow hunters suggested that he could hunt with a muzzle-loading rifle.[8] They believed that a felon is allowed to possess a muzzle loader.

Andrew tried to learn if what he had been told is true. A local gun dealer accurately informed him that the state does not require a criminal background check for the sale of a muzzle-loading rifle. Andrew also contacted the Federal Bureau of Alcohol, Tobacco and Firearms ("ATF") and the state Department of Game and Fisheries. Officials at both agencies told him that a felon is allowed to possess a muzzle loader. Finally, Andrew asked his probation officer, who advised him that under the state's felon firearm possession statute a muzzle loader does not qualify as a firearm and that a felon such as Andrew can legally possess a muzzle loader. Relying on what he had been told, Andrew bought a muzzle loader and obtained the appropriate state license to hunt with it. He was subsequently arrested for violating the felon firearm possession statute and informed that what his probation officer and others had told him is inaccurate.

Andrew admits at trial that all elements of the offense were fulfilled. He also admits that he knew of the existence of the felon firearm statute. But he seeks to avoid conviction on the ground that he was mistaken about the meaning of the word "firearm" (i.e., that "firearm" in the felon firearm statute includes a muzzle loader) because he relied on and was misled by what others had told him about the charged offense.

Part (a) Is Andrew's testimony about his conversations with any of the following people relevant to his liability for the charged offense? If so, which ones and why are they relevant?

1. his fellow hunters

2. the local gun dealer

3. the ATF

4. the state Department of Game and Fisheries

5. his probation officer

Part (b) Is his strategy here one of challenge to proof or confession and avoidance?

Part (c) Is Andrew liable under the Model Penal Code?

Part (d) Is Andrew liable in Texas?

---

8. A muzzle-loading rifle is one in which the projectile and the propellant charge are loaded from the muzzle, the forward, open end of the gun's barre. *Muzzleloader*, WIKIPEDIA, https://en.wikipedia.org/wiki/Muzzleloader [https://perma.cc/Z4ZA-XWN4] (last updated Jan. 28, 2019).

As we have seen, a defendant being misled by a government agent will relieve the defendant of liability if the jurisdiction has adopted a statute such as the Model Penal Code's "reasonable reliance on official statement" provision and that provision's elements are fulfilled. Apart from such statutory relief, a defendant who is misled by a government agent may also be relieved of liability under the due process clause of the federal constitution, as in the following case. The due process clause obviously applies in federal court and in every state jurisdiction, regardless of whether the jurisdiction has adopted a reliance statute such as Model Penal Code Section 2.04.

Cox v. Louisiana
379 U.S. 559 (1965)
United States Supreme Court

Goldberg, J.

[Defendant] was convicted of violating a Louisiana statue which provides:

"Whoever, with the intent of interfering with, obstructing, or impeding the administration of justice, or with the intent of influencing any judge, juror, witness, or court officer, in the discharge of his duty pickets or parades in or near a building housing a court of the State of Louisiana ... shall be fined not more than five thousand dollars or imprisoned not more than one year, or both."

[Defendant] was ... sentenced to the maximum penalty under the statute of one year in jail and a $5,000 fine.... The record here clearly shows that the officials present gave permission for the demonstration to take place across the street from the courthouse. Cox testified that they gave him permission to conduct the demonstration on the far side of the street. This testimony is not only uncontradicted but is corroborated by the State's witnesses who were present. Police Chief White testified that he told Cox "he must confine" the demonstration "to the west side of the street." James Erwin, news director of radio station WIBR, agreed that Cox was given permission for the assembly as long as it remained within a designated time. When Sheriff Clemmons sought to break up the demonstration, he first announced, "now, you have been allowed to demonstrate." The Sheriff testified that he had "no objection" to the students "being assembled on that side of the street." ...

[Defendant] was ... sentenced to the maximum penalty under the statute of one year in jail and a $5,000 fine.... [Defendant] was convicted for demonstrating not "in", but "near" the courthouse. It is undisputed that the demonstration took place on the west sidewalk, the far side of the street, exactly 101 feet from the courthouse steps and, judging from the pictures in the record, approximately 125 feet from the courthouse itself. The question is raised as to whether the failure of the statute to define the word "near" renders it unconstitutionally vague.... It is clear that there is some lack of specificity in a word such as "near." While this lack of specificity may not render the statute unconstitutionally vague, at least as applied to a demonstration within the sight and hearing of those in the courthouse, it is clear that the statute, with respect to the determination of how near the courthouse a particular demonstration can be, foresees a degree of on-the-spot administrative interpretation by officials charged with responsibility for administering and enforcing it. It is apparent that demonstrators, such as those involved here, would justifiably tend to rely on this administrative interpretation of how "near" the courthouse a particular demonstration might take place. Louisiana's statutory policy of preserving order around the courthouse would counsel encouragement of just such reliance. This administrative discretion to construe the term "near" concerns a limited control of the streets and other areas in the immediate vicinity of the courthouse and is the type of narrow discretion which this Court has recognized as the proper role of responsible officials in making determinations concerning the time, place, duration, and manner of demonstrations.... Obviously, telling demonstrators how far from the courthouse steps is "near" the courthouse for purposes of a permissible peaceful demonstration is a far cry from allowing one to commit, for example, murder, or robbery.

Thus, the highest police officials of the city, in the presence of the Sheriff and Mayor, in effect told the demonstrators that they could meet where they did, 101 feet from the courthouse steps, but could not meet closer to the courthouse. In effect, [defendant] was advised that a demonstration at the place it was held would not be one "near" the courthouse within the terms of the statute.... The Due Process Clause does not permit convictions to be obtained under such circumstances....

Reversed.

Discussion Questions

1. Was Cox mistaken about the law? Was he misled about the law? About what law was he mistaken and misled?

2. Did the error raise an issue about the defendant's mental state with respect to the *existence* of the statute in question? His mental state with respect to the *meaning* of the statute? His mental state with respect to a *non-mental element* in the statute? Did the court's decision turn on any of these questions?

3. How would Cox have fared under the Model Penal Code Section 2.04?

4. How would Cox have fared under Texas Penal Code § 8.03 Mistake of Law, set forth above?

2. Mistake Regarding Circumstances That Include a Legal Element

Problem

5.37 Part (a) Vince, a Vermont resident, wants to divorce his wife, Maggie, who is not willing to consent to a divorce. Vince goes on the internet to a legal advice website and reads that U.S. residents can obtain quick divorces in Mexico. Assume that under Mexican law a married person can obtain a divorce without the other spouse either consenting or being present. Vince travels to Mexico and complies with the legal requirements for a Mexican divorce. He returns to Vermont with his Mexican decree of divorce, completely convinced that he is validly divorced from Maggie and now legally free to marry someone other than Maggie. Several months later, Vince marries a woman named Emmy Lou in a civil ceremony conducted in the state of Vermont by a Vermont justice of the peace. Shortly thereafter, on the basis of a complaint from Maggie, Vince is charged with bigamy under the following statute:

> Any person who marries in Vermont without having a valid divorce
> or annulment of a prior marriage is guilty of bigamy, a felony.

To his dismay, Vince learns that Vermont does not recognize Mexican divorces as valid in the state of Vermont. Therefore, under Vermont law, Vince, at the time he married Emmy Lou, was (and still is) legally married to Maggie. Is Vince criminally liable for violation of the Vermont bigamy statute? What if Vermont has adopted the Model Penal Code's provisions on statutory interpretation and mistake?

Part (b) What if Vince, instead of going to the internet for legal advice, consults a reputable divorce lawyer who unfortunately misadvises Vince that a Mexican divorce is valid in the state of Vermont?

Comment to Model Penal Code § 2.02 General Requirements of Culpability

It should be noted that the general principle that ignorance or mistake of law is no excuse is greatly overstated; it has no application, for example, *when the circumstances made material by the definition of the offense include a legal element.* Thus it is immaterial in theft, when claim of right is adduced in defense, that the claim involves a legal judgment as to the right of property. Claim of right is a defense because the property must belong to someone else for the theft to occur and the defendant must have culpable awareness of that fact. Insofar as this point is involved, there is no need to state a special principle; the legal element involved is simply an aspect of the attendant circumstances, with respect to which knowledge, recklessness or negligence, as the case may be, is required for culpability by Subsections (1) and (3). The law involved is not the law defining the offense; it is some other legal rule that characterizes the attendant circumstances that are material to the offense. (emphasis added)

Regina v. Smith (David)
Q.B. 354 1973 (1974)

On June 26, 1973, ... the appellant, David Raymond Smith, pleaded not guilty to an indictment charging him ... with contravening section 1(1) of the Criminal Damage Act 1971. On June 28, 1973, the jury ... convicted the appellant and he was discharged conditionally for 12 months and was ordered to pay £ 40 compensation. He appealed against conviction....

In 1970 the appellant became the tenant of a ground-floor flat.... The letting included a conservatory. In the conservatory the appellant and his brother, who lived with him, installed some electric wiring for use with stereo equipment. Also, with the landlord's permission, they put up roofing material and asbestos wall panels and laid floor boards. There is no dispute that the roofing, wall panels and floor boards became part of the house and, in law, the property of the landlord. Then in 1972 the appellant gave notice to quit and asked the landlord to allow the appellant's brother to remain as tenant of the flat. On September 18, 1972, the landlord informed the appellant that his brother could not remain. On the next day the appellant damaged the roofing, wall panels and floorboards he had installed in order—according to the appellant and his brother—to gain access to and remove the wiring. The extent of the damage was £ 130. When interviewed by the police, the appellant said: "Look, how can I be done for smashing my own property. I put the flooring and that in, so if I want to pull it down it's a matter for me."...

The appellant's defence was that he honestly believed that the damage he did was to his own property, that he believed that he was entitled to damage his own property and therefore he had a lawful excuse for his actions causing the damage. In the course of his summing up the deputy judge directed the jury in these terms:

"Now, in order to make the offence complete, the person who is charged with it must destroy or damage that property belonging to another, 'without lawful excuse,' and that is something that one has got to look at a little more, members of the jury, because you have heard here that, so far as each defendant was concerned, it never occurred to them, and, you may think, quite naturally never occurred to either of them, that these various additions to the house were anything but their own property.... But members of the jury, the Act is quite specific, and so far as the defendant David Smith is concerned lawful excuse is the only defence which has been raised. It is said that he had a lawful excuse by reason of his belief, his honest and genuinely held belief that he was destroying property which he had a right to destroy if he wanted to. But, members of the jury, I must direct you as a matter of law, and you must, therefore, accept it from me, that belief by the defendant David Smith that he had the right to do what he did is not lawful excuse within the meaning of the Act. Members of the jury, it is an excuse, it may even be a reasonable excuse, but it is not, members of the jury, a lawful excuse, because, in law, he had no right to do what he did. Members of the jury, as a matter of law, the evidence, in fact, discloses, so far as David Smith is concerned, no lawful excuse at all, because, as I say, the only defence which he has raised is the defence that he thought he had the right to do what he did. I have directed you that that is not a lawful excuse, and, members of the jury, it follows from that that so far as David Smith is concerned, I am bound to direct you as a matter of law that you must find him guilty of this offence with which he is charged."

It is contended for the appellant that that is a misdirection in law, and that, as a result of the misdirection, the entire defence of the appellant was wrongly withdrawn from the jury.

Section 1 of the Criminal Damage Act 1971 reads:

"(1) A person who without lawful excuse destroys or damages any property belonging to another intending to destroy or damage any such property or being reckless as to whether any such property would be destroyed or damaged, shall be guilty of an offence." ...

It is argued for the appellant that an honest, albeit erroneous, belief that the act causing damage or destruction was done to his own property provides a defence to a charge brought under section 1(1). The argument is ... that the offence charged includes the act causing the damage or destruction and the element of mens rea. The element of mens rea relates to all the circumstances of the criminal act. The criminal act in the offence is causing damage to or destruction of "property belonging to another" and the element of mens rea, therefore, must relate to "property belonging to another." Honest belief, whether justifiable or not, that the property is the defendant's own negatives the element of mens rea....

It is conceded by Mr. Gerber that there is force in the argument that the element of mens rea extends to "property belonging to another." But, it is argued, the section creates a new statutory offence and that it is open to the construction that the mental element in the offence relates only to causing damage to or destroying property. That if in fact the property damaged or destroyed is shown to be another's property the offence is committed although the defendant did not intend or foresee damage to another person's property....

If the direction given by the deputy judge in the present case is correct, then the offence created by section 1(1) of the Act of 1971 involves a considerable extension of the law in a surprising direction. Whether or not this is so depends upon the construction of the section. Construing the language of section 1(1) we have no doubt that the actus reus is "destroying or damaging any property belonging to another." It is not possible to exclude the words "belonging to another" which describes the "property." Applying the ordinary principles of mens rea, the intention and recklessness and the absence of lawful excuse required to constitute the offence have reference to property belonging to another. It follows that in our judgment no offence is committed under this section if a person destroys or causes damage to property belonging to another if he does so in the honest though mistaken belief that the property is his own, and provided that the belief is honestly held it is irrelevant to consider whether or not it is a justifiable belief.

In our judgment, the direction given to the jury was a fundamental misdirection in law. The consequence was that the jury were precluded from considering facts capable of being a defence to the charge and were directed to convict.

For these reasons ... we allowed the appeal and ordered that the conviction be quashed.

Discussion Questions

1. How does the *Smith(David)* case differ from the *Baker* and *Ratzlaf* cases?
2. How would Smith have fared under the Model Penal Code?

F. Willful Blindness

The "willful blindness" doctrine examined in this section is widely adopted in state and federal criminal law. A willful blindness instruction is sometimes referred to as an "ostrich instruction." Why is that? But willful blindness is not often defined clearly or consistently. As you will see below, authorities don't even agree on whether to use "willful" or "wilful" in addressing this doctrine. Pay close attention to the way willful blindness is defined by Model Penal Code § 2.02(7), the First Circuit Pattern Instruction that follows it, and the *Jewell* case. How do they differ? Which approach is preferable?

Problem

5.38 Gwen is a bank trust officer. One day she approaches her friend Richard, a stockbroker and sometime art dealer, to ask for his help. Gwen tells Richard that the beneficiary of one of the trusts she administers is an older man, Bob, who has become quite fond of her. Bob's older brother died and left stock in a trust for Bob, which has increased enormously in value. Bob is a man of simple tastes who withdraws only a few hundred dollars a month from the thousands of dollars in interest available to him. The rest of the trust's income keeps accumulating. Gwen tells Richard that Bob wants to make a gift to her because she has been so kind to him over the years, but bank regulations will not let her take the money directly from Bob. Gwen proposes to write Richard a series of 10 checks for $3,000 each from Bob's trust account. All Richard has to do is deposit the checks in his account and then write a check to Gwen. For his help, Gwen offers to allow Richard to keep half the money. Gwen will wind up with $15,000 and Richard will wind up with $15,000. Gwen offers to further explain the bank regulations and to have Richard meet Bob, but Richard tells Gwen that he doesn't want to know any more than she has told him. Gwen and Richard go ahead with the transaction. Six months later, an FBI agent calls on Richard. It turns out that Gwen was embezzling the money from Bob's trust account without Bob's knowledge or consent. Richard is charged with a felony under a statute that reads:

> Anyone who receives money in excess of $1,000 knowing that it is
> either stolen or embezzled is guilty of a felony punishable by up to
> five years in prison.

Is Richard criminally liable under the statute?

The MPC Approach to Willful Blindness

The willful blindness problem proved important enough to merit special attention in the Model Penal Code provisions on culpability.

§ 2.02 (7) Requirement of Knowledge Satisfied by Knowledge of High Probability.

When knowledge of the existence of a particular fact is an element of an offense, such knowledge is established if a person is aware of a high probability of its existence, unless he actually believes it does not exist.

The following commentary to the MPC explains the MPC position.

Comment

Knowledge Satisfied by High Probability. Subsection (7) deals with the situation that British commentators have denominated "wilful blindness" or "connivance," the case of the actor who is aware of the probable existence of a material fact but does not determine whether it exists or does not exist. Whether such cases should be viewed as instances of acting recklessly or knowingly presents a subtle but important question.

The Code proposes that the case be viewed as one of acting knowingly when what is involved is a matter of existing fact, but not when what is involved is the result of the defendant's conduct, necessarily a matter of the future at the time of acting. The position reflects what was believed to be the normal policy of criminal enactments that rest liability on acting "knowingly." The inference of "knowledge" of an existing fact is usually drawn from proof of notice of high probability of its existence, unless the defendant establishes an honest, contrary belief. Subsection (7) solidifies this usual result and clarifies the terms in which the issue is submitted to the jury.

Some recently revised and proposed codes have included similar language....

Pattern Jury Instructions (Criminal Cases) Prepared by the Committee on Pattern Criminal Jury Instructions, First Circuit (1998)

2.14 "Willful Blindness" As A Way of Satisfying Knowingly

In deciding whether the defendant acted knowingly, you may infer that the defendant had knowledge of a fact if you find that he/she deliberately closed his/her eyes to a fact that otherwise would have been obvious to him/her. In order to infer knowledge, you must find that two things have been established. First, that the defendant was aware of a high probability of the fact in question. Second, that the defendant consciously and deliberately avoided learning of that fact. That is to say, the defendant willfully made himself blind to that fact. It is entirely up to you to determine whether he deliberately closed his eyes to the fact and, if so, what inference, if any, should be drawn. However, it is important to bear in mind that mere negligence or mistake in failing to learn the fact is not sufficient. There must be a deliberate effort to remain ignorant of the fact.

Comment

… "The danger of an improper willful blindness instruction is 'the possibility that the jury will be led to employ a negligence standard and convict a defendant on the impermissible ground that he should have known [an illegal act] was taking place.'" *United States v. Brandon*, 17 F.3d 409, 453 (1st Cir. 1994).

Discussion Questions

1. How does the MPC's treatment of willful blindness compare with the First Circuit's? Which is preferable?

2. Why is it impermissible to convict someone on the ground that he *should have known* some fact, such as, in the following case, whether a car he was driving contained marijuana?

United States v. Jewell

532 F.2d 697 (1976)
United States Court of Appeals for the Ninth Circuit

Browning, J.

… It is undisputed that [Jewell] entered the United States driving an automobile in which 110 pounds of marihuana worth $6,250 had been concealed in a secret compartment between the trunk and rear seat. [Jewell] testified that he did not know the marihuana was present. There was circumstantial evidence from which the jury could infer that appellant had positive knowledge of the presence of the marihuana, and that his contrary testimony was false.

[Jewell] testified that a week before the incident in question he sold his car for $100 to obtain funds "to have a good time." He then rented a car for about $100, and he and a friend drove the rented car to Mexico. [Jewell] and his friend were unable to explain their whereabouts during the period of about 11 hours between the time they left Los Angeles and the time they admitted arriving in Mexico.

Their testimony regarding acquisition of the load car follows a pattern common in these cases: they were approached in a Tijuana bar by a stranger who identified himself only by his first name "Ray." He asked them if they wanted to buy marihuana, and offered to pay them $100 for driving a car north across the border. [Jewell] accepted the offer and drove the load back, alone. [Jewell's] friend drove the ... rented car back to Los Angeles.

[Jewell] testified that the stranger instructed him to leave the load car at the address on the car registration slip with the keys in the ashtray. The person living at that address testified that he had sold the car a year earlier and had not seen it since. When the Customs agent asked [Jewell] about the secret compartment in the car, [Jewell] did not deny knowledge of its existence, but stated that it was in the car when he got it....

On the other hand there was evidence from which the jury could conclude that appellant spoke the truth — that although appellant knew of the presence of the secret compartment and had knowledge of facts indicating that it contained marihuana, he deliberately avoided positive knowledge of the presence of the contraband to avoid responsibility in the event of discovery.... The Drug Enforcement Administration agent testified that [Jewell] stated "he thought there was probably something wrong and something illegal in the vehicle, but that he checked it over. He looked in the glove box and under the front seat and in the trunk, prior to driving it. *He didn't find anything and therefore he assumed that the people at the border wouldn't find anything either*" (emphasis added). [Jewell] was asked at trial whether he had seen the special compartment when he opened the trunk. He responded, "Well, you know, I saw a void there, but I didn't know what it was." He testified that he did not investigate further.... The jury would have been justified in accepting all of the testimony as true and concluding that although [defendant] was aware of facts making it virtually certain that the secret compartment concealed marihuana, he deliberately refrained from acquiring positive knowledge of the fact. If the jury concluded the latter was indeed the situation, and if positive knowledge is required to convict, the jury would have no choice consistent with its oath but to find appellant not guilty even though he deliberately contrived his lack of positive knowledge.

[The jury convicted Jewell under the following statutes: (1) knowingly or intentionally importing a controlled substance, 21 U.S.C. § 952(a), 960(a)(1); (2) knowingly or intentionally possessing, with intent to distribute, a controlled substance 21 U.S.C. § 841 (a)(1).]

[Jewell] tendered an instruction that to return a guilty verdict the jury must find that the defendant knew he was in possession of marihuana. The trial judge rejected the instruction....

The court instructed the jury that "knowingly" meant voluntarily and intentionally and not by accident or mistake.... The court continued: The Government can complete their burden of proof by proving, beyond a reasonable doubt, that if the defendant was not actually aware that there was marijuana in the vehicle he was driving when he entered the United States his ignorance in that regard was solely and entirely a result of his having made a conscious purpose to disregard the nature of that which was in the vehicle, with a conscious purpose to avoid learning the truth.

The legal premise of these instructions is firmly supported by leading commentators here and in England. Professor Rollin M. Perkins writes, "One with a deliberate antisocial purpose in mind ... may deliberately 'shut his eyes' to avoid knowing what would otherwise be obvious to view. In such cases, so far as criminal law is concerned, the person acts at his peril in this regard, and is treated as having 'knowledge' of the facts as they are ultimately discovered to be." ... Professor Glanville Williams states, on the basis of both English and American authorities, "To the requirement of actual knowledge there is one strictly limited exception.... [The] rule is that if a party has his suspicion aroused but then deliberately omits to make further enquiries, because he wishes to remain in ignorance, he is deemed to have knowledge." Professor Williams concludes, "The rule that wilful blindness is equivalent to knowledge is essential, and is found throughout the criminal law.... It is, at the same time, an unstable rule, because judges are apt to forget its very limited scope. A court can properly find wilful blindness only where it can almost be said that the defendant actually knew.... It requires in effect a finding that the defendant intended to cheat the administration of justice. Any wider definition would make the doctrine of wilful blindness indistinguishable from the civil doctrine of negligence in not obtaining knowledge.

The substantive justification for the rule is that deliberate ignorance and positive knowledge are equally culpable. The textual justification is that in common understanding one "knows" facts of which he is less than absolutely certain. To act "knowingly," therefore, is not necessarily to act only with positive knowledge, but also to act with an awareness of the high probability of the existence of the fact in question. When such awareness is present, "positive" knowledge is not required.

This is the analysis adopted in the Model Penal Code. Section 2.02(7) states: "When knowledge of the existence of a particular fact is an element of an offense, such knowledge is established if a person is aware of a high probability of its existence, unless he actually believes that it does not exist." ...

"Deliberate ignorance" instructions have been approved in prosecutions under criminal statutes prohibiting "knowing" conduct by the Courts of Appeals of the Second, Sixth, Seventh, and Tenth Circuits. In many other cases, Courts of Appeals reviewing the sufficiency of evidence have approved the premise that "knowingly" in criminal statutes is not limited to positive knowledge, but includes the state of mind of one who does not possess positive knowledge only because he consciously avoided it. These lines of authority appear unbroken. Neither the dissent nor the briefs of either party has cited a case holding that such an instruction is error or that such evidence is not sufficient to establish "knowledge."

There is no reason to reach a different result under the statute involved in this case. Doing so would put this court in direct conflict with Courts of Appeals in two other circuits that have approved "deliberate ignorance" instructions in prosecutions under 21 U.S.C. §841(a), or its predecessor, 21 U.S.C. §174. Nothing is cited from the legislative history of the Drug Control Act indicating that Congress used the term "knowingly" in a sense at odds with prior authority. Rather, Congress is presumed to have known and adopted the "cluster of ideas" attached to such a familiar term of art. *Morissette v. United States*, 342 U.S. 246 (1952)....

Appellant's narrow interpretation of "knowingly" is inconsistent with the Drug Control Act's general purpose to deal more effectively "with the growing menace of drug abuse in the United States." Holding that this term introduces a requirement of positive knowledge would make deliberate ignorance a defense. It cannot be doubted that those who traffic in drugs would make the most of it. This is evident from the number of appellate decisions reflecting conscious avoidance of positive knowledge of the presence of contraband—in the car driven by the defendant or in which he is a passenger, in the suitcase or package he carries, in the parcel concealed in his clothing....

It is worth emphasizing that the required state of mind differs from positive knowledge only so far as necessary to encompass a calculated effort to avoid the sanctions of the statute while violating its substance. "A court can properly find wilful blindness only where it can almost be said that the defendant actually knew." ...

No legitimate interest of an accused is prejudiced by such a standard, and society's interest in a system of criminal law that is enforceable and that imposes sanctions upon all who are equally culpable requires it.

The conviction is affirmed.

Kennedy, J., dissenting.

[One] problem [with the wilful blindness doctrine] is that the English authorities seem to consider wilful blindness a state of mind distinct from, but equally culpable as, "actual" knowledge. When a statute specifically requires knowledge as an element of a crime, however, the substitution of some other state of mind cannot be justified even if the court deems that both are equally blameworthy....

Finally, the wilful blindness doctrine is uncertain in scope. There is disagreement as to whether reckless disregard for the existence of a fact constitutes wilful blindness or some lesser degree of culpability. Some cases have held that a statute's scienter requirement is satisfied by the constructive knowledge imputed to one who simply fails to discharge a duty to inform himself. There is also the question of whether to use an "objective" test based on the reasonable man, or to consider the defendant's subjective belief as dispositive.

The approach adopted in section 2.02(7) of the Model Penal Code clarifies, and, in important ways restricts the English doctrine.... This provision requires an awareness of a high probability that a fact exists, not merely a reckless disregard, or a suspicion followed by a failure to make further inquiry. It also establishes knowledge as a matter of subjective belief, an important safeguard against diluting the guilty state of mind required for conviction. It is important to note that section 2.02(7) is a definition of knowledge, not a substitute for it....

In light of the Model Penal Code's definition, the "conscious purpose" jury instruction is defective in three respects. First, it fails to mention the requirement that Jewell have been aware of a high probability that a controlled substance was in the car. It is not culpable to form "a conscious purpose to avoid learning the truth" unless one is aware of facts indicating a high probability of that truth. To illustrate, a child given a gift-wrapped package by his mother while on vacation in Mexico may form a conscious purpose to take it home without learning what is inside; yet his state of mind is totally innocent unless he is aware of a high probability that the package contains a controlled substance. Thus, a conscious purpose instruction is only proper when coupled with a requirement that one be aware of a high probability of the truth.

The second defect in the instruction as given is that it did not alert the jury that Jewell could not be convicted if he "actually believed" there was no controlled substance in the car. The failure to emphasize, as does the Model Penal Code, that subjective belief is the determinative factor, may allow a jury to convict on an objective theory of knowledge—that a reasonable man should have inspected the car and would have discovered what was hidden inside. One recent decision reversed a jury instruction for this very deficiency—failure to balance a conscious purpose instruction with a warning that the defendant could not be convicted if he actually believed to the contrary.

Third, the jury instruction clearly states that Jewell could have been convicted even if found ignorant or "not actually aware" that the car contained a controlled substance. This is unacceptable because true ignorance, no matter how unreasonable, cannot provide a basis for criminal liability when the statute requires knowledge. A proper jury instruction based on the Model Penal Code would be presented as a way of defining knowledge, and not as an alternative to it.

Discussion Questions

1. What is willful blindness? Is it a substitute for or a type of knowledge? Should courts use willful blindness when a statute calls for knowledge? Why does Judge (former Justice) Kennedy in his dissent emphasize that willful blindness is "a way of defining knowledge, and not ... an alternative to it"?

2. What are the difficulties in treating willful blindness as a proxy for knowledge? Is there another mental state or combination of mental states that better captures the culpability reflected in willful blindness?

3. In *Keeler*, the court interpreted the word "human being" not to include a fetus. In *Martin*, the court interpreted the word "appear" to include a voluntariness requirement. Is the *Jewell* court's interpretation of the word "knowingly" to include willful blindness akin to either the interpretation in *Keeler* or the interpretation in *Martin*?

4. Judge Browning cites the *Morissette* case in support of his interpretation of the statutes under which Jewell was charged. How does *Morissette* support Judge Browning's interpretation?

5. Is the instruction given by the trial court in *Jewell* consistent with the MPC standard in 2.02(7)?

6. Which defines willful blindness most clearly? Judge Browning's opinion in *Jewell*? Judge Kennedy's dissent in *Jewell*? The Model Penal Code? Or the First Circuit Pattern jury instruction that appears at the outset of this Section?

G. Conditional Purpose/Intent

Problem

5.39 Part (a) A large percentage of the men who frequent a homeless shelter are heroin addicts. The re-use of hypodermic needles by multiple addicts is increasing the incidence of HIV infection among these men. The shelter's medical director tries to get each addict to stop using heroin and enter the shelter's drug rehabilitation program. To the addicts who refuse to enter the rehab program, however, she provides clean hypodermic needles, telling them: "I want you and urge you to stop using heroin and enter our rehab program. But if you are going to use heroin, please use this clean needle so you won't get infected with HIV." Under the *Holloway* case, is it the medical director's purpose to have these addicts use the needles she gives them to inject themselves with heroin? How about under the Model Penal Code?

Part (b) Keith approached 15-year-old Anna, falsely told her he lost his cell phone, and asked her to dial his phone to help him find it. Later that day, Keith began to send Anna text messages proposing a sexual relationship. At one point, Keith offered to send Anna a nude picture of himself, but only if she first sent him a nude picture of herself. No exchange of photos took place. Instead, Anna reported Keith to the police and Keith was arrested and his cell phone seized and searched pursuant to a warrant. On Keith's cell phone were a variety of nude photos of Keith. Keith has been charged with the crime of "possession of matter harmful to a minor with intent to disseminate that matter." At the end of the prosecution's case at trial, Keith's lawyer asks the judge to dismiss the charge arguing that Keith's refusal to send Anna a nude photo of himself until she sent him a photo of herself means that the prosecution failed to prove that Keith had the intent to disseminate required by the statute. How should the judge rule under *Holloway*? Under the Model Penal Code?

> ## The MPC Approach to Conditional Purpose
>
> **2.02(6) Requirement of purpose satisfied if purpose is conditional**
>
> When a particular purpose is an element of an offense, the element is established although such purpose is conditional, unless the condition negatives the harm or evil sought to be prevented by the law defining the offense.

In the following case, the defendant was charged and convicted under this statute:

Whoever, with the intent to cause death or serious bodily harm takes a motor vehicle that has been transported, shipped, or received in interstate or foreign commerce from the person or presence of another by force and violence or by intimidation, or attempts to do so, shall —

(1) be fined under this title or imprisoned not more than 15 years, or both....

Holloway v. United States

526 U.S. 1 (1999)
United States Supreme Court

Stevens. J.

Carjacking "with the intent to cause death or serious bodily harm" is a federal crime. The question presented in this case is whether that phrase requires the Government to prove that the defendant had an unconditional intent to kill or harm in all events, or whether it merely requires proof of an intent to kill or harm if necessary to effect a carjacking. Most of the judges who have considered the question have concluded, as do we, that Congress intended to criminalize the more typical carjacking carried out by means of a deliberate threat of violence, rather than just the rare case in which the defendant has an unconditional intent to use violence regardless of how the driver responds to his threat.

I

A jury found petitioner guilty on three counts of carjacking, as well as several other offenses related to stealing cars. In each of the carjackings, petitioner and an armed accomplice identified a car that they wanted and followed it until it was parked. The accomplice then approached the driver, produced a gun, and threatened to shoot unless the driver handed over the car keys. The accomplice testified that the plan was to steal the cars without harming the victims, but that he would have used his gun if any of the drivers had given him a "hard time." When one victim hesitated, petitioner punched him in the face but there was no other actual violence.

The District Judge instructed the jury that the Government was required to prove beyond a reasonable doubt that the taking of a motor vehicle was committed with the intent "to cause death or serious bodily harm to the person from whom the car was taken." After explaining that merely using a gun to frighten a victim was not sufficient to prove such intent, he added the following statement over the defendant's objection:

"In some cases, intent is conditional. That is, a defendant may intend to engage in certain conduct only if a certain event occurs.

"In this case, the government contends that the defendant intended to cause death or serious bodily harm if the alleged victims had refused to turn over their cars. If you find beyond a reasonable doubt that the defendant had such an intent, the government has satisfied this element of the offense...."

In his postverdict motion for a new trial, petitioner contended that this instruction was inconsistent with the text of the statute. The District Judge denied the motion, stating that there "is no question that the conduct at issue in this case is precisely what Congress and the general public would describe as carjacking, and that Congress intended to prohibit it in § 2119." He noted that the statute as originally enacted in 1992 contained no intent element but covered all carjackings committed by a person "possessing a firearm." A 1994 amendment had omitted the firearm limitation, thus broadening the coverage of the statute to encompass the use of other weapons, and also had inserted the intent requirement at issue in this case. The judge thought that an "odd result" would flow from a construction of the amendment that "would no longer prohibit the very crime it was enacted to address except in those unusual circumstances when carjackers also intended to commit another crime—murder or a serious assault." Moreover, the judge determined that even though the issue of conditional intent has not been discussed very often, at least in the federal courts, it was a concept that scholars and state courts had long recognized.

Over a dissent that accused the majority of "a clear judicial usurpation of congressional authority," the Court of Appeals affirmed. The majority was satisfied that "the inclusion of a conditional intent to harm within the definition of specific intent to harm" was not only "a well-established principle of common law," but also, and "most importantly," comported "with a reasonable interpretation of the legislative purpose of the statute." The alternative interpretation, which would cover "only those carjackings in which the carjacker's sole and unconditional purpose at the time he committed the carjacking was to kill or maim the victim," the court concluded, was clearly at odds with the intent of the statute's drafters.

To resolve an apparent conflict with a decision of the Ninth Circuit, we granted certiorari.

II

Writing for the Court in *United States v. Turkette*, Justice White reminded us that the language of the statutes that Congress enacts provides "the most reliable evidence of its intent." For that reason, we typically begin the task of statutory construction by focusing on the words that the drafters have chosen. In interpreting the statute at issue, "we consider not only the bare meaning" of the critical word or phrase "but also its placement and purpose in the statutory scheme."

The specific issue in this case is what sort of evil motive Congress intended to describe when it used the words "with the intent to cause death or serious bodily harm" in the 1994 amendment to the carjacking statute. More precisely, the question is whether a person who points a gun at a driver, having decided to pull the trigger if the driver does not comply with a demand for the car keys, possesses the intent, at that moment, to seriously harm the driver. In our view, the answer to that question does not depend on whether the driver immediately hands over the keys or what the offender decides to do after he gains control over the car. At the relevant moment, the offender plainly does have the forbidden intent.

The opinions that have addressed this issue accurately point out that a carjacker's intent to harm his victim may be either "conditional" or "unconditional." The statutory phrase at issue theoretically might describe (1) the former, (2) the latter, or (3) both species of intent. Petitioner argues that the "plain text" of the statute "unequivocally" describes only the latter: that the defendant must possess a specific and unconditional intent to kill or harm in order to complete the proscribed offense. To that end, he insists that Congress would have had to insert the words "if necessary" into the disputed text in order to include the conditional species of intent within the scope of the statute. Because Congress did not include those words, petitioner contends that we must assume that Congress meant to provide a federal penalty for only those carjackings in which the offender actually attempted to harm or kill the driver (or at least intended to do so whether or not the driver resisted).

We believe, however, that a commonsense reading of the carjacking statute counsels that Congress intended to criminalize a broader scope of conduct than attempts to assault or kill in the course of automobile robberies. As we have repeatedly stated, "the meaning of statutory language, plain or not, depends on context." When petitioner's argument is considered in the context of the statute, it becomes apparent that his proffered construction of the intent element overlooks the significance of the placement of that element in the statute. The carjacking statute essentially is aimed at providing a federal penalty for a particular type of robbery. The statute's mens rea component thus modifies the act of "taking" the motor vehicle. It directs the factfinder's attention to the defendant's state of mind at the precise moment he demanded or took control over the car "by force and violence or by intimidation." If the defendant has the proscribed state of mind at that moment, the statute's scienter element is satisfied.

Petitioner's reading of the intent element, in contrast, would improperly transform the mens rea element from a modifier into an additional actus reus component of the carjacking statute; it would alter the statute into one that focuses on attempting to harm or kill a person in the course of the robbery of a motor vehicle. Indeed, if we accepted petitioner's view of the statute's intent element, even Congress' insertion of the qualifying words "if necessary," by themselves, would not have solved the deficiency that he believes exists in the statute. The inclusion of those words after the intent phrase would have excluded the unconditional species of intent—the intent to harm or kill even if not necessary to complete a carjacking. Accordingly, if Congress had used words such as "if necessary" to describe the conditional species of intent, it would also have needed to add something like "or even if not necessary" in order to cover both species of intent to harm. Given the fact that the actual text does not mention either species separately—and thus does not expressly exclude either—that text is most naturally read to encompass the mens rea of both conditional and unconditional intent, and not to limit the statute's reach to crimes involving the additional actus reus of an attempt to kill or harm.

Two considerations strongly support the conclusion that a natural reading of the text is fully consistent with a congressional decision to cover both species of intent. First, the statute as a whole reflects an intent to authorize federal prosecutions as a significant deterrent to a type of criminal activity that was a matter of national concern.[9] Because that purpose is better served by construing the statute to cover both the conditional and the unconditional species of wrongful intent, the entire statute is consistent with a normal interpretation of the specific language that Congress chose. Indeed, petitioner's interpretation would exclude from the coverage of the statute most of the conduct that Congress obviously intended to prohibit.

Second, it is reasonable to presume that Congress was familiar with the cases and the scholarly writing that have recognized that the "specific intent" to commit a wrongful act may be conditional. The facts of the leading case on the point are strikingly similar to the facts of this case. In *People v. Connors*, the Illinois Supreme Court affirmed the conviction of a union organizer who had pointed a gun at a worker and threatened to kill him forthwith if he did not take off his overalls and quit work. The Court held that the jury had been properly instructed that the "specific intent to kill" could be found even though that intent was "coupled with a condition" that the defendant would not fire if the victim complied with his demand. That holding has been repeatedly cited with approval by other courts and by scholars. Moreover, it reflects the views endorsed by the authors of the Model Criminal Code. The core principle that emerges from these sources is that a defendant may not negate a proscribed intent by requiring the victim to comply with a condition the defendant has no right to impose; "an intent to kill, in the alternative, is nevertheless an intent to kill."

This interpretation of the statute's specific intent element does not, as petitioner suggests, render superfluous the statute's "by force and violence or by intimidation" element. While an empty threat, or intimidating bluff, would be sufficient to satisfy the latter element, such conduct, standing on its own, is not enough to satisfy § 2119's specific intent element. In a carjacking case in which the driver surrendered or otherwise lost control over his car without the defendant attempting to inflict, or actually inflicting, serious bodily harm, Congress' inclusion of the intent element requires

---

9. Although the legislative history relating to the carjacking amendment is sparse, those members of Congress who recorded comments made statements reflecting the statute's broad deterrent purpose. See 139 Cong. Rec. 27867 (1993) (statement of Sen. Lieberman) ("Th[e 1994] amendment will broaden and strengthen the [carjacking] law so our U.S. attorneys will have every possible tool available

the Government to prove beyond a reasonable doubt that the defendant would have
at least attempted to seriously harm or kill the driver if that action had been necessary
to complete the taking of the car.

In short, we disagree with petitioner's reading of the text of the Act and think it
unreasonable to assume that Congress intended to enact such a truncated version of
an important criminal statute. The intent requirement of §2119 is satisfied when the
Government proves that at the moment the defendant demanded or took control
over the driver's automobile the defendant possessed the intent to seriously harm or
kill the driver if necessary to steal the car (or, alternatively, if unnecessary to steal the
car). Accordingly, we affirm the judgment of the Court of Appeals.

It is so ordered.

Scalia, J. dissenting.

The issue in this case is the meaning of the phrase, in 18 U.S.C. §2119, "with the
intent to cause death or serious bodily harm." (For convenience' sake, I shall refer to
it in this opinion as simply intent to kill.) As recounted by the Court, petitioner's accomplice, Vernon Lennon, "testified that the plan was to steal the cars without harming
the victims, but that he would have used his gun if any of the drivers had given him
a 'hard time.'" The District Court instructed the jury that the intent element would
be satisfied if petitioner possessed this "conditional" intent. Today's judgment holds
that instruction to have been correct.

I dissent from that holding because I disagree with the following, utterly central,
passage of the opinion:

"[A] carjacker's intent to harm his victim may be either 'conditional' or 'unconditional.' The statutory phrase at issue theoretically might describe (1) the former,
(2) the latter, or (3) both species of intent."

I think, to the contrary, that in customary English usage the unqualified word "intent" does not usually connote a purpose that is subject to any conditions precedent
except those so remote in the speaker's estimation as to be effectively nonexistent—
and it never connotes a purpose that is subject to a condition which the speaker hopes
will not occur. (It is this last sort of "conditional intent" that is at issue in this case,
and that I refer to in my subsequent use of the term.) "Intent" is "[a] state of mind
in which a person seeks to accomplish a given result through a course of action."
Black's Law Dictionary 810 (6th ed. 1990). One can hardly "seek to accomplish" a
result he hopes will not ensue.

_____

to them to attack the problem"); 140 Cong. Rec. E858 (May 5, 1994) (extension of remarks by Rep.
Franks) ("We must send a message to [carjackers] that committing a violent crime will carry a severe
penalty."). There is nothing in the 1994 amendment's legislative history to suggest that Congress
meant to create a federal crime for only the unique and unusual subset of carjackings in which the
offender intends to harm or kill the driver regardless of whether the driver accedes to the offender's
threat of violence.

The Court's division of intent into two categories, conditional and unconditional, makes the unreasonable seem logical. But Aristotelian classification says nothing about linguistic usage. Instead of identifying two categories, the Court might just as readily have identified three: unconditional intent, conditional intent, and feigned intent. But the second category, like the third, is simply not conveyed by the word "intent" alone. There is intent, conditional intent, and feigned intent, just as there is agreement, conditional agreement, and feigned agreement—but to say that in either case the noun alone, without qualification, "theoretically might describe" all three phenomena is simply false. Conditional intent is no more embraced by the unmodified word "intent" than a sea lion is embraced by the unmodified word "lion."

If I have made a categorical determination to go to Louisiana for the Christmas holidays, it is accurate for me to say that I "intend" to go to Louisiana. And that is so even though I realize that there are some remote and unlikely contingencies—"acts of God," for example—that might prevent me. (The fact that these remote contingencies are always implicit in the expression of intent accounts for the humorousness of spelling them out in such expressions as "if I should live so long," or "the Good Lord willing and the creek don't rise.") It is less precise, though tolerable usage, to say that I "intend" to go if my purpose is conditional upon an event which, though not virtually certain to happen (such as my continuing to live), is reasonably likely to happen, and which I hope will happen. I might, for example, say that I "intend" to go even if my plans depend upon receipt of my usual and hoped-for end-of-year bonus.

But it is not common usage—indeed, it is an unheard-of usage—to speak of my having an "intent" to do something, when my plans are contingent upon an event that is not virtually certain, and that I hope will not occur. When a friend is seriously ill, for example, I would not say that "I intend to go to his funeral next week." I would have to make it clear that the intent is a conditional one: "I intend to go to his funeral next week if he dies." The carjacker who intends to kill if he is met with resistance is in the same position: he has an "intent to kill if resisted"; he does not have an "intent to kill." No amount of rationalization can change the reality of this normal (and as far as I know exclusive) English usage. The word in the statute simply will not bear the meaning that the Court assigns.

The Government makes two contextual arguments to which I should respond. First, it points out that the statute criminalizes not only carjackings accomplished by "force and violence" but also those accomplished by mere "intimidation." Requiring an unconditional intent, it asserts, would make the number of covered carjackings accomplished by intimidation "implausibly small." That seems to me not so. It is surely not an unusual carjacking in which the criminal jumps into the passenger seat and forces the person behind the wheel to drive off at gunpoint. A carjacker who intends to kill may well use this modus operandi, planning to kill the driver in a more secluded location. Second, the Government asserts that it would be hard to imagine an unconditional-intent-to-kill case in which the first penalty provision of §2119 would apply, i.e., the provision governing cases in which no death or bodily harm has occurred. That is rather like saying that the crime of attempted murder should not exist, because someone who intends to kill always succeeds.

Notwithstanding the clear ordinary meaning of the word "intent," it would be possible, though of course quite unusual, for the word to have acquired a different meaning in the criminal law. The Court does not claim — and falls far short of establishing — such "term-of-art" status. It cites five state cases (representing the majority view among the minority of jurisdictions that have addressed the question) saying that conditional intent satisfies an intent requirement; but it acknowledges that there are cases in other jurisdictions to the contrary. As I understand the Court's position, it is not that the former cases are right and the latter wrong, so that "intent" in criminal statutes, a term of art in that context, includes conditional intent; but rather that "intent" in criminal statutes may include conditional intent, depending upon the statute in question. That seems to me not an available option. It is so utterly clear in normal usage that "intent" does not include conditional intent, that only an accepted convention in the criminal law could give the word a different meaning. And an accepted convention is not established by the fact that some courts have thought so some times. One must decide, I think, which line of cases is correct, and in my judgment it is that which rejects the conditional-intent rule....

Ultimately, the Court rests its decision upon the fact that the purpose of the statute — which it says is deterring carjacking — "is better served by construing the statute to cover both the conditional and the unconditional species of wrongful intent." It supports this statement, both premise and conclusion, by two unusually uninformative statements from the legislative history (to stand out in that respect in that realm is quite an accomplishment) that speak generally about strengthening and broadening the carjacking statute and punishing carjackers severely. But every statute intends not only to achieve certain policy objectives, but to achieve them by the means specified. Limitations upon the means employed to achieve the policy goal are no less a "purpose" of the statute than the policy goal itself. Under the Court's analysis, any interpretation of the statute that would broaden its reach would further the purpose the Court has found. Such reasoning is limitless and illogical.

The Court confidently asserts that "petitioner's interpretation would exclude from the coverage of the statute most of the conduct that Congress obviously intended to prohibit." It seems to me that one can best judge what Congress "obviously intended" not by intuition, but by the words that Congress enacted, which in this case require intent (not conditional intent) to kill. Is it implausible that Congress intended to define such a narrow federal crime? Not at all. The era when this statute was passed contained well publicized instances of not only carjackings, and not only carjackings involving violence or the threat of violence (as of course most of them do); but also of carjackings in which the perpetrators senselessly harmed the car owners when that was entirely unnecessary to the crime. I have a friend whose father was killed, and whose mother was nearly killed, in just such an incident — after the car had already been handed over. It is not at all implausible that Congress should direct its attention to this particularly savage sort of carjacking — where killing the driver is part of the intended crime.

Indeed, it seems to me much more implausible that Congress would have focused upon the ineffable "conditional intent" that the Court reads into the statute, sending courts and juries off to wander through "would-a, could-a, should-a" land. It is difficult enough to determine a defendant's actual intent; it is infinitely more difficult to determine what the defendant planned to do upon the happening of an event that the defendant hoped would not happen, and that he himself may not have come to focus upon. There will not often be the accomplice's convenient confirmation of conditional intent that exists in the present case. Presumably it will be up to each jury whether to take the carjacker ("Your car or your life") at his word. Such a system of justice seems to me so arbitrary that it is difficult to believe Congress intended it. Had Congress meant to cast its carjacking net so broadly, it could have achieved that result—and eliminated the arbitrariness—by defining the crime as "carjacking under threat of death or serious bodily injury." Given the language here, I find it much more plausible that Congress meant to reach—as it said—the carjacker who intended to kill....

This seems to me not a difficult case. The issue before us is not whether the "intent" element of some common-law crime developed by the courts themselves—or even the "intent" element of a statute that replicates the common-law definition—includes, or should include, conditional intent. Rather, it is whether the English term "intent" used in a statute defining a brand new crime bears a meaning that contradicts normal usage. Since it is quite impossible to say that longstanding, agreed-upon legal usage has converted this word into a term of art, the answer has to be no. And it would be no even if the question were doubtful. I think it particularly inadvisable to introduce the new possibility of "conditional-intent" prosecutions into a modern federal criminal-law system characterized by plea bargaining, where they will predictably be used for in terrorem effect. I respectfully dissent.

H. Intoxication

Should the fact that someone was intoxicated with alcohol or another drug play a role in determining criminal liability or punishment? If so, should it mitigate or aggravate?

The criminal law's answers to these questions have changed over time and vary significantly today from jurisdiction to jurisdiction. *Montana v. Egelhoff*, below, traces the evolution of the common law's position and describes recent legislative developments on intoxication. As described in *Egelhoff*, the common law moved to a compromise position on intoxication, allowing mitigation in one category of offenses the common law labeled specific intent crimes, but disallowing it in another category the common law labeled general intent crimes. *Egelhoff* also describes a recent legislative trend of returning toward an earlier common law position of severely restricting the use of intoxication. Legislatures in most states have dealt with the subject of intoxication by statute. The selection of statutes that appears after *Egelhoff* represents a range of approaches found in current statutory provisions.

The criminal law's vacillation and variation in dealing with intoxication is partly a product of our society's ambivalence about alcohol. Though intoxication statutes do not distinguish among intoxicants, alcohol is by far the most popular drug in the United States and the most frequent source of intoxication problems in criminal law. Accordingly, our views about alcohol have played a dominant role in shaping our attitudes about the impact of intoxication on criminal liability.

While most people who drink do so safely, those who heavily consume alcohol produce an impact that ripples outward to encompass their families, friends, and communities. Consider the following data about alcohol and its costs in the United States.

- In 2010, alcohol misuse problems cost the United States $249 billion.

- A 2012 study indicated that more than 10 percent of U.S. children live with a parent with alcohol problems.

Researchers estimate that each year:

- 696,000 students between the ages of 18 and 24 are assaulted by another student who has been drinking.

- 97,000 students between the ages of 18 and 24 report experiencing alcohol-related sexual assault or date rape.

- Roughly 20 percent of college students meet the criteria for an Alcohol Use Disorder.

In 2014:

- 37.9 percent of college students ages 18–22 engaged in binge drinking (five or more drinks on an occasion) in the past month compared with 33.5 percent of other persons of the same age.

- 24.7 percent of people ages 18 or older reported that they engaged in binge drinking in the past month.

- 16.3 million adults ages 18 and older (6.8 percent of this age group) had an Alcohol Use Disorder.

- Nearly 88,000 people die from alcohol-related causes annually, making alcohol the fourth leading preventable cause of death in the United States.

- Alcohol-impaired driving fatalities accounted for 9,967 deaths (31 percent of overall driving fatalities).

* * *

Alcohol is legal, widely accepted, and typically used without negative consequences. At the same time, alcohol has a high correlation with crime and imposes significant human and economic costs. So, is drinking blameworthy? Is it something the criminal law should seek to deter? Our culture's schizophrenic views about alcohol are captured in the following statement from a congressman asked to explain his attitude toward whiskey:

> If you mean the demon drink that poisons the mind, pollutes the body, desecrates family life and inflames sinners, then I'm against it. But if you mean the elixir of Christmas cheer, the shield against winter chill, the taxable potion that puts needed funds into public coffers to comfort little crippled children, then I'm for it. This is my position, and I will not compromise.[10]

What view, then, should the criminal law take toward alcohol? As you read *Egelhoff* and the statutes on intoxication below, try to articulate the policies underlying various legal rules about intoxication. Do you think the differences result from disagreement about the relevance of intoxication in proving or disproving the elements of a charged offense? Or do policies unrelated to relevance explain the divergence in approaches to intoxication? The following passage, written by Chief Justice Traynor, is a useful starting point in answering these questions.

People v. Hood

1 Cal. 3d 444 (1969)
California Supreme Court

A significant effect of alcohol is to distort judgment and relax the controls on aggressive and anti-social impulses. Alcohol apparently has less effect on the ability to engage in simple goal-directed behavior, although it may impair the efficiency of that behavior. In other words, a drunk man is capable of forming an intent to do something simple, such as strike another, unless he is so drunk that he has reached the stage of unconsciousness. What he is not as capable as a sober man of doing is exercising judgment about the social consequences of his acts or controlling his impulses toward anti-social acts. He is more likely to act rashly and impulsively and to be susceptible to passion and anger.

Montana v. Egelhoff

518 U.S. 37 (1996)
United States Supreme Court

Scalia, J. We consider in this case whether the Due Process Clause is violated by Montana Code Annotated § 45-2-203, which provides, in relevant part, that voluntary intoxication "may not be taken into consideration in determining the existence of a mental state which is an element of [a criminal] offense."

I

In July 1992, while camping out in the Yaak region of northwestern Montana to pick mushrooms, respondent made friends with Roberta Pavola and John Christenson,

---

10. M. Lender and J. Martin, Drinking in America: A History 169 (1982).

who were doing the same. On Sunday, July 12, the three sold the mushrooms they had collected and spent the rest of the day and evening drinking, in bars and at a private party in Troy, Montana. Some time after 9 p.m., they left the party in Christenson's 1974 Ford Galaxy station wagon. The drinking binge apparently continued, as respondent was seen buying beer at 9:20 p.m. and recalled "sitting on a hill or a bank passing a bottle of Black Velvet back and forth" with Christenson.

At about midnight that night, officers of the Lincoln County, Montana, sheriff's department, responding to reports of a possible drunk driver, discovered Christenson's station wagon stuck in a ditch along U.S. Highway 2. In the front seat were Pavola and Christenson, each dead from a single gunshot to the head. In the rear of the car lay respondent, alive and yelling obscenities. His blood-alcohol content measured .36 percent over one hour later. On the floor of the car, near the brake pedal, lay respondent's .38 caliber handgun, with four loaded rounds and two empty casings; respondent had gunshot residue on his hands.

Respondent was charged with two counts of deliberate homicide, a crime defined by Montana law as "purposely" or "knowingly" causing the death of another human being. Mont. Code Ann. § 45-5-102 (1995). A portion of the jury charge, uncontested here, instructed that "[a] person acts purposely when it is his conscious object to engage in conduct of that nature or to cause such a result," and that "[a] person acts knowingly when he is aware of his conduct or when he is aware under the circumstances his conduct constitutes a crime; or, when he is aware there exists the high probability that his conduct will cause a specific result." Respondent's defense at trial was that an unidentified fourth person must have committed the murders; his own extreme intoxication, he claimed, had rendered him physically incapable of committing the murders, and accounted for his inability to recall the events of the night of July 12. Although respondent was allowed to make this use of the evidence that he was intoxicated, the jury was instructed, pursuant to Mont. Code Ann. § 45-2-203 (1995), that it could not consider respondent's "intoxicated condition ... in determining the existence of a mental state which is an element of the offense." The jury found respondent guilty on both counts, and the court sentenced him to 84 years' imprisonment.

The Supreme Court of Montana reversed. It reasoned (1) that respondent "had a due process right to present and have considered by the jury all relevant evidence to rebut the State's evidence on all elements of the offense charged," and (2) that evidence of respondent's voluntary intoxication was "clearly ... relevant to the issue of whether [respondent] acted knowingly and purposely." Because § 45-2-203 prevented the jury from considering that evidence with regard to that issue, the court concluded that the State had been "relieved of part of its burden to prove beyond a reasonable doubt every fact necessary to constitute the crime charged," and that respondent had therefore been denied due process. We granted certiorari.

II

The cornerstone of the Montana Supreme Court's judgment was the proposition that the Due Process Clause guarantees a defendant the right to present and have considered by the jury "all relevant evidence to rebut the State's evidence on all elements of the offense charged." Respondent does not defend this categorical rule; he acknowledges that the right to present relevant evidence "has not been viewed as absolute." That is a wise concession, since the proposition that the Due Process Clause guarantees the right to introduce all relevant evidence is simply indefensible. As we have said: "The accused does not have an unfettered right to offer [evidence] that is incompetent, privileged, or otherwise inadmissible under standard rules of evidence." Relevant evidence may, for example, be excluded on account of a defendant's failure to comply with procedural requirements. And any number of familiar and unquestionably constitutional evidentiary rules also authorize the exclusion of relevant evidence. For example, Federal (and Montana) Rule of Evidence 403 provides: "Although relevant, evidence may be excluded if its probative value is substantially outweighed by the danger of unfair prejudice, confusion of the issues, or misleading the jury, or by considerations of undue delay, waste of time, or needless presentation of cumulative evidence" (emphasis added). Hearsay rules similarly prohibit the introduction of testimony which, though unquestionably relevant, is deemed insufficiently reliable. Of course, to say that the right to introduce relevant evidence is not absolute is not to say that the Due Process Clause places no limits upon restriction of that right. But it is to say that the defendant asserting such a limit must sustain the usual heavy burden that a due process claim entails:

> "Preventing and dealing with crime is much more the business of the States than it is of the Federal Government, and ... we should not lightly construe the Constitution so as to intrude upon the administration of justice by the individual States. Among other things, it is normally 'within the power of the State to regulate procedures under which its laws are carried out,' ... and its decision in this regard is not subject to proscription under the Due Process Clause unless 'it offends some principle of justice so rooted in the traditions and conscience of our people as to be ranked as fundamental.'"

Respondent's task, then, is to establish that a defendant's right to have a jury consider evidence of his voluntary intoxication in determining whether he possesses the requisite mental state is a "fundamental principle of justice."

Our primary guide in determining whether the principle in question is fundamental is, of course, historical practice. Here that gives respondent little support. By the laws of England, wrote Hale, the intoxicated defendant "shall have no privilege by this voluntary contracted madness, but shall have the same judgment as if he were in his right senses." According to Blackstone and Coke, the law's condemnation of those suffering from dementia affectata was harsher still: Blackstone, citing Coke, explained that the law viewed intoxication "as an aggravation of the offence, rather than as an excuse for any criminal misbehaviour." This stern rejection of inebriation as a defense became a fixture of early American law as well. The American editors of the 1847 edition of Hale wrote:

> "Drunkenness, it was said in an early case, can never be received as a ground to excuse or palliate an offence: this is not merely the opinion of a speculative philosopher, the argument of counsel, or the obiter dictum of a single judge, but it is a sound and long established maxim of judicial policy, from which perhaps a single dissenting voice cannot be found. But if no other authority could be adduced, the uniform decisions of our own Courts from the first establishment of the government, would constitute it now a part of the common law of the land."

The historical record does not leave room for the view that the common law's rejection of intoxication as an "excuse" or "justification" for crime would nonetheless permit the defendant to show that intoxication prevented the requisite mens rea. Hale, Coke, and Blackstone were familiar, to say the least, with the concept of mens rea, and acknowledged that drunkenness "deprive[s] men of the use of reason." It is inconceivable that they did not realize that an offender's drunkenness might impair his ability to form the requisite intent; and inconceivable that their failure to note this massive exception from the general rule of disregard of intoxication was an oversight. Hale's statement that a drunken offender shall have the same judgment "as if he were in his right senses" must be understood as precluding a defendant from arguing that, because of his intoxication, he could not have possessed the mens rea required to commit the crime. And the same must be said of the exemplar of the common-law rule cited by both Hale and Blackstone....

Against this extensive evidence of a lengthy common-law tradition decidedly against him, the best argument available to respondent is the one made by his amicus and conceded by the State: Over the course of the 19th century, courts carved out an exception to the common law's traditional across-the-board condemnation of the drunken offender, allowing a jury to consider a defendant's intoxication when assessing whether he possessed the mental state needed to commit the crime charged, where the crime was one requiring a "specific intent." The emergence of this new rule is often traced to an 1819 English case, in which Justice Holroyd is reported to have held that "though voluntary drunkenness cannot excuse from the commission of crime, yet where, as on a charge of murder, the material question is, whether an act was premeditated or done only with sudden heat and impulse, the fact of the party being intoxicated [is] a circumstance proper to be taken into consideration." 1 W. Russell, Crimes and Misdemeanors 8 (citing *King v. Grindley*, Worcester Sum Assizes 1819, MS). This exception was "slow to take root," however, even in England. Indeed, in the 1835 case of *King v. Carroll*, Justice Park claimed that Holroyd had "retracted his opinion" in *Grindley*, and said "there is no doubt that that case is not law." In this country, as late as 1858 the Missouri Supreme Court could speak as categorically as this:

"To look for deliberation and forethought in a man maddened by intoxication is vain, for drunkenness has deprived him of the deliberating faculties to a greater or less extent; and if this deprivation is to relieve him of all responsibility or to diminish it, the great majority of crimes committed will go unpunished. This however is not the doctrine of the common law; and to its maxims, based as they obviously are upon true wisdom and sound policy, we must adhere."

And as late as 1878, the Vermont Supreme Court upheld the giving of the following instruction at a murder trial:

" 'The voluntary intoxication of one who without provocation commits a homicide, although amounting to a frenzy, that is, although the intoxication amounts to a frenzy, does not excuse him from the same construction of his conduct, and the same legal inferences upon the question of premeditation and intent, as affecting the grade of his crime, which are applicable to a person entirely sober.' "

Eventually, however, the new view won out, and by the end of the 19th century, in most American jurisdictions, intoxication could be considered in determining whether a defendant was capable of forming the specific intent necessary to commit the crime charged.

On the basis of this historical record, respondent's amicus argues that "the old common-law rule ... was no longer deeply rooted at the time the Fourteenth Amendment was ratified." That conclusion is questionable, but we need not pursue the point, since the argument of amicus mistakes the nature of our inquiry. It is not the State which bears the burden of demonstrating that its rule is "deeply rooted," but rather respondent who must show that the principle of procedure violated by the rule (and allegedly required by due process) is " 'so rooted in the traditions and conscience of our people as to be ranked as fundamental.' " Thus, even assuming that when the Fourteenth Amendment was adopted the rule Montana now defends was no longer generally applied, this only cuts off what might be called an a fortiori argument in favor of the State. The burden remains upon respondent to show that the "new common-law" rule — that intoxication may be considered on the question of intent — was so deeply rooted at the time of the Fourteenth Amendment (or perhaps has become so deeply rooted since) as to be a fundamental principle which that Amendment enshrined.

That showing has not been made. Instead of the uniform and continuing acceptance we would expect for a rule that enjoys "fundamental principle" status, we find that fully one-fifth of the States either never adopted the "new common-law" rule at issue here or have recently abandoned it.

It is not surprising that many States have held fast to or resurrected the common-law rule prohibiting consideration of voluntary intoxication in the determination of mens rea, because that rule has considerable justification — which alone casts doubt upon the proposition that the opposite rule is a "fundamental principle." A large number of crimes, especially violent crimes, are committed by intoxicated offenders; modern studies put the numbers as high as half of all homicides, for example. Disallowing consideration of voluntary intoxication has the effect of increasing the punishment for all unlawful acts committed in that state, and thereby deters drunkenness or irresponsible behavior while drunk. The rule also serves as a specific deterrent, ensuring that those who prove incapable of controlling violent impulses while voluntarily intoxicated go to prison. And finally, the rule comports with and implements society's moral perception that one who has voluntarily impaired his own faculties should be responsible for the consequences.

There is, in modern times, even more justification for laws such as §45-2-203 than there used to be. Some recent studies suggest that the connection between drunkenness and crime is as much cultural as pharmacological—that is, that drunks are violent not simply because alcohol makes them that way, but because they are behaving in accord with their learned belief that drunks are violent. This not only adds additional support to the traditional view that an intoxicated criminal is not deserving of exoneration, but it suggests that juries—who possess the same learned belief as the intoxicated offender—will be too quick to accept the claim that the defendant was biologically incapable of forming the requisite mens rea. Treating the matter as one of excluding misleading evidence therefore makes some sense.

In sum, not every widespread experiment with a procedural rule favorable to criminal defendants establishes a fundamental principle of justice. Although the rule allowing a jury to consider evidence of a defendant's voluntary intoxication where relevant to mens rea has gained considerable acceptance, it is of too recent vintage, and has not received sufficiently uniform and permanent allegiance, to qualify as fundamental, especially since it displaces a lengthy common law tradition which remains supported by valid justifications today....

"The doctrines of actus reus, mens rea, insanity, mistake, justification, and duress have historically provided the tools for a constantly shifting adjustment of the tension between the evolving aims of the criminal law and changing religious, moral, philosophical, and medical views of the nature of man. This process of adjustment has always been thought to be the province of the States." The people of Montana have decided to resurrect the rule of an earlier era, disallowing consideration of voluntary intoxication when a defendant's state of mind is at issue. Nothing in the Due Process Clause prevents them from doing so, and the judgment of the Supreme Court of Montana to the contrary must be reversed.

Discussion Questions

1. Which theories of punishment support the Montana intoxication statute?

2. Which theories of punishment support the modified common law position of allowing the defendant to introduce intoxication evidence in cases involving specific intent crimes?

* * *

As *Egelhoff* illustrates, criminal defendants frequently seek to use intoxication as evidence that they lacked a mental state required for liability, such as purpose to kill. Resolving such a claim is not an easy task. Alcohol produces its physiological effects on both body and mind in degrees that range from barely perceptible to coma with many gradations in between. The extent of both intoxication and impairment of mental function can often be difficult to determine with precision. Common experience and research have shown that alcohol affects perception, memory, and cognition. Evidence of alcohol use by a witness is routinely admitted at trial for jurors to use in assessing the ability of the witness to perceive and remember what she recounts in her testimony. But precisely how and to what degree alcohol affects mental function is not entirely clear and still the subject of research. Alcohol's effects are subject to significant variation depending on a multitude of factors such as body weight, gender, food consumption, rate of drinking, and drinking experience. The same amount of alcohol, for example, can intoxicate a novice drinker but have much less effect on a person with a history of heavy drinking.

For these reasons, claims about how much a defendant drank and how it affected his or her mental processes may be easy to make but difficult for the government to refute. If a defendant is arrested at the time of the crime, blood-alcohol level evidence may be obtained. But if no such timely arrest is made, it may be even harder to disprove false claims about drinking and its effect on the mind. These practical problems in accurately assessing intoxication claims provide one set of reasons a legislature might resist allowing defendants to use intoxication evidence to disprove a mental state.

The effects of alcohol are also subject to much public misunderstanding. A leading pharmacology treatise, for example, reports that "[t]he public often views alcoholic drinks as stimulating, but [alcohol] is primarily a central nervous system depressant."[11] Justice Scalia stated in *Egelhoff* that recent studies suggest that the correlation of crime with intoxication "is as much cultural as pharmacological." One of the articles he cited explains this cultural phenomenon:

> Although popular thought may hold that alcohol makes people behave in out-of-character ways, recent research suggests that it does not. MacAndrew and Edgerton, in their cross-cultural review of drunken comportment and its consequences, concluded that the pharmacological action of ethanol cannot account for the transformations in social behavior that occur when people drink, as those transformations vary widely from culture to culture and in the same culture across time periods. Their contention that the effects of alcohol are instead culturally learned spurred research showing that certain of these effects are exhibited by people who only think that they have imbibed.[12]

---

11. GOODMAN & GILMAN, THE PHARMACOLOGICAL BASIS OF THERAPEUTICS 430 (10th ed. 2001).

12. Barbara Critchlow, *The Powers of John Barleycorn: Beliefs About the Effects of Alcohol on Social Behavior*, Vol. 41 No. 7 AM. PSYCHOLOGIST 751, 751 (1986).

The MacAndrew and Edgerton study referred to in this passage concludes by describing the authors' thesis that "the way people comport themselves when they are drunk is determined not by alcohol's toxic assault upon the seat of moral judgment, conscience, or the like, but by what their society makes of and imparts to them concerning the state of drunkenness.... The moral, then, is this. Since societies, like individuals, get the sorts of drunken comportment they allow, they deserve what they get."[13]

Discussion Questions

1. Justice Scalia argues in *Egelhoff* that public misperceptions provide support for restricting evidence of intoxication because jurors, based on their learned beliefs that drunks are violent, "will be too quick to accept the claim that the defendant was biologically incapable of forming the requisite *mens rea*." Does the Montana rule protect against this danger?

2. Does the existence of "learned beliefs" about alcohol provide a rationale for restricting evidence of intoxication aside from the possibility of jurors being misled by the evidence? Are there steps the criminal law should take to address such beliefs in addition to restricting the uses that can be made of intoxication in criminal cases?

3. If violent behavior is the result of "learned beliefs" about alcohol rather than a pharmacological "assault" on the brain, does that fact change the blameworthiness of drinking? Does it make drinking more or less dangerous?

Problems

Should evidence that the defendant was intoxicated be admitted in the following cases? In answering each, apply the statutes that follow the problems.

5.40 Alan goes to a party at the apartment of Chris, an acquaintance of one of Alan's friends. Alan wears his 10-year-old black leather jacket to the party. When Alan arrives at the party, Chris hangs Alan's jacket, along with those of his other guests, in a hall closet outside his bedroom. At the party, Alan consumes a large quantity of alcohol. Just before midnight, Alan decides to leave the party. Alan walks to the closet where Chris hung his jacket. When Alan opens the closet door, instead of taking his own jacket, he takes a similar, brand-new black leather jacket belonging to Chris and leaves the party. Someone observes Alan's conduct and calls the police, who arrest Alan a few hours later and charge him with theft. Assume Alan is charged under the following statute:

---

13. Craig MacAndrew and Robert B. Edgerton, Drunken Comportment: A Social Explanation 165, 173 (1969).

Theft

Anyone who knowingly takes the property of another with intent to permanently deprive the owner of it is guilty of theft.

Alan admits that he took Chris's jacket, but argues that because of the alcohol he had consumed he thought the jacket he took was in fact his.

5.41 After several hours of drinking, James begins bragging to Michael about his lack of fear of firearms. Michael decides to test James's claims with a revolver he recently purchased. While showing the gun to James, Michael puts the gun to James's head. To Michael's amazement, the gun goes off, killing James.

Part (a) Michael claims he was simply trying to frighten James and believed that when he pulled the trigger the gun was unloaded. He argues that because of the alcohol he consumed, he failed to remember that he had placed bullets in the gun a few days earlier. Does it make any difference if:

(1) Michael is charged with reckless homicide?

(2) Michael is charged with negligent homicide?

Part (b) Michael claims that he did not intend to pull the trigger of the gun but merely meant to place it against James's head to frighten him. He argues that because of the alcohol he consumed, his motor skills were impaired and he did not have adequate control of his trigger finger.

5.42 Joel is on a business trip to a large city. One night after he has had quite a few drinks in the bar of the hotel where he is staying, a young woman approaches him and engages him in conversation. Joel buys her several drinks. About an hour later, Joel offers the young woman $100 to go to his room with him and have sex. She agrees. As they leave the bar together, both are arrested by an undercover police officer who overheard their conversation. Joel is charged under the following statute:

A person is guilty of patronizing a prostitute in the third degree when, being over twenty-one years of age, he patronizes a prostitute and the person patronized is less than seventeen years of age.

Joel is 30 years old. The young woman turns out to be 16 years old. Joel wants to introduce evidence of his drinking to show he lacked the required mental state regarding the prostitute being less than 17. May Joel introduce evidence of his drinking?

Part (a) Assume the statute requires *knowledge* regarding the prostitute's being less than 17.

Part (b) Assume the statute requires *recklessness* regarding the prostitute's being less than 17.

Part (c) Assume the statute requires *negligence* regarding the prostitute's being less than 17.

Part (d) Assume that the statute assigns *strict liability* regarding the prostitute's being less than 17.

Montana Code Annotated

§ 45-2-203 Responsibility — intoxicated condition

A person who is in an intoxicated condition is criminally responsible for his conduct and an intoxicated condition is not a defense to any offense and may not be taken into consideration in determining the existence of a mental state which is an element of the offense unless the defendant proves that he did not know that it was an intoxicating substance when he consumed, smoked, sniffed, injected, or otherwise ingested the substance causing the condition.

Ohio Revised Code

§ 2901.21 Requirements for criminal liability

Voluntary intoxication may not be taken into consideration in determining the existence of a mental state that is an element of a criminal offense. Voluntary intoxication does not relieve a person of a duty to act if failure to act constitutes a criminal offense. Evidence that a person was voluntarily intoxicated may be admissible to show whether or not the person was physically capable of performing the act with which the person is charged.

Minnesota Statutes

§ 609.075 Intoxication as defense

An act committed while in a state of voluntary intoxication is not less criminal by reason thereof, but when a particular intent or other state of mind is a necessary element to constitute a particular crime, the fact of intoxication may be taken into consideration in determining such intent or state of mind.

Iowa Code

§ 701.5 Intoxicants or drugs

The fact that a person is under the influence of intoxicants or drugs neither excuses the person's act nor aggravates the person's guilt, but may be shown where it is relevant in proving the person's specific intent or recklessness at the time of the person's alleged criminal act or in proving any element of the public offense with which the person is charged.

Model Penal Code

§ 2.08.

(1) … intoxication of the actor is not a defense unless it negatives an element of the offense.

(2) When recklessness establishes an element of the offense, if the actor, due to self-induced intoxication, is unaware of a risk of which he would have been aware had he been sober, such unawareness is immaterial.

Discussion Questions

1. How does each of these statutes differ from the original common law position on intoxication described in *Egelhoff*?

2. Why does the Model Penal Code's intoxication provision devote a separate section to recklessness? What is the effect of that section? Why does the Model Penal Code's intoxication provision not specifically address negligence?

3. You learned in studying the subject of mistake that the term "defense" is used to encompass two different ways of defeating liability. One is by contesting an element of the offense. The other is when the defendant admits the elements but seeks to avoid liability by asserting some other principle. The word "defense" is often used in referring to intoxication. Use of the word "defense" in the context of intoxication is associated with which of these ways of defeating liability?

4. A number of jurisdictions have left the law on intoxication to judges to develop through a common law process. Should legislators or judges be making the law in this area? Or should the significance of intoxication be left to the jury to handle in its role as the finder of fact?

I. Synthesis and Challenges

Problems

5.43 South African criminal law recognizes the concept of "conscious negligence" which is described as follows:

> Conscious negligence exists where the accused foresees only a remote possibility of a consequence resulting and fails to take the steps that a reasonable man would have taken to guard against this possibility.
>
> For instance, in *R v Hedley* the accused was found guilty of culpable homicide where he fired a rifle shot at a cormorant near the edge of a dam. The bullet ricocheted off the surface of the water, near some huts which the accused admitted seeing before he fired, and killed a woman. Broome JP said: 'He knew that the bullet he was firing would strike the

water and might ricochet, and that if it did ricochet it might pass near the huts and so might hit someone. It is true that the likelihood of harm was small, but on the other hand the harm, if it resulted, would be very serious.'

In other words, Hedley foresaw the remote possibility that he might kill someone when he fired the shot. Since a reasonable person would not have fired the shot in these circumstances, he was consciously negligent in doing so.[14]

What similarities does conscious negligence have to the mental states recognized by the Model Penal Code? How does it differ from those mental states? Should conscious negligence be a basis for criminal liability?

5.44 The Restatement Second of Torts gives the following definitions:

§ 8 A Intent

The word "intent" is used throughout the Restatement of this Subject to denote that the actor desires to cause consequences of his act, or that he believes that the consequences are substantially certain to result from it.

§ 500 Reckless Disregard of Safety Defined

The actor's conduct is in reckless disregard of the safety of another if he does an act or intentionally fails to do an act which it is his duty to the other to do, knowing or having reason to know of facts which would lead a reasonable man to realize, not only that his conduct creates an unreasonable risk of physical harm to another, but also that such risk is substantially greater than that which is necessary to make his conduct negligent.

§ 282 Negligence Defined

In the Restatement of this Subject, negligence is conduct which falls below the standard established by law for the protection of others against unreasonable risk of harm. It does not include conduct recklessly disregardful of an interest of others.

How do these tort law definitions of each of these terms compare with criminal law definitions of each? Is it desirable for mental state terminology to be consistent across different areas of substantive law?

5.45 It is sometimes said to be a "maxim" of criminal law that "ignorance or mistake of law is never a defense." As the cases and problems in this Chapter demonstrate, though, ignorance or mistake of law at times does insulate a defendant from liability. Rewrite the ignorance of the law maxim so that it accurately reflects the nuances of the law you learned in this Chapter.

---

14. Jonathan Burchell & John Milton, Principles of Criminal Law 321–322 (2d ed.1997).

Chapter 6

Homicide

A. Introduction

Homicides represent a relatively small percentage of overall crime. But the topic of homicide draws a level of popular and academic attention disproportionate to that percentage. Portrayals of crime on television and in the movies commonly focus on homicide. Homicides draw extensive news coverage. Academics also give a great deal of attention to the law of homicide. A number of factors may explain this level of attention. The crimes of murder and manslaughter were among the first recognized by the common law. The criminal justice system's most severe sanctions are imposed in homicide cases, including the death penalty. Homicide can also have a devastating impact on family members and other surviving victims. Perhaps because of the attention given homicides in both the news and popular media, homicides also seriously undermine society's sense of security.

The architecture of the law of homicide throughout American jurisdictions has many common features. All homicides require the same three non-mental elements — (1) some form of conduct, (2) a resulting death, and (3) a causative link between the conduct and the death. The law of homicide revolves in large measure around the actor's mental state regarding the death. So, another common feature across jurisdictions is the role played by the mental element pertaining to the death. Someone who causes death with purpose in regard to that death will initially qualify for murder in virtually every jurisdiction. A killing done with recklessness regarding the death initially qualifies for manslaughter. Someone who causes a death with simple negligence as to the death may escape criminal liability for homicide entirely.

The following diagram shows the key mental state in the architecture of homicide law:

Mental Elements		Non-Mental Elements
Purpose	→	Conduct
Key Mental State	→	Death

Because of the role played by mental state in the hierarchy of homicide, the organization of this chapter is keyed to the actor's mental state regarding death. We start with premeditation and deliberation, a standard that is widely considered the most demanding and blameworthy. In many jurisdictions, proof of premeditation and deliberation raises an "ordinary" murder that was committed with purpose from second degree to first degree murder. Next we turn to provocation, a doctrine that can reduce an actor's liability from murder to manslaughter, even though the actor killed with purpose regarding the death. The section following provocation deals with reckless murder, cases in which the degree of recklessness regarding death is so extreme that a killing that normally would be treated as manslaughter is raised to murder. We then continue down the mental state continuum and treat reckless and negligent killings. The chapter's final category of homicide incorporates a strict liability component regarding the death. This is felony murder.

As noted previously, the law of homicide has a number of features that are fairly uniform from jurisdiction to jurisdiction, such as a purposeful killing initially qualifying for murder, recognition of some sort of extreme reckless murder, and provocation reducing murder to manslaughter. But there are some aspects of the law of homicide that vary dramatically from jurisdiction to jurisdiction. Jurisdictions disagree, for example, on whether to divide murder into separate degrees. And those that do divide murder into degrees differ on the criteria they use in drawing that distinction. States also vary on what qualifies as provocation and whether to subsume negligent and reckless killing under a single category called manslaughter or create separate crimes, with negligent homicide warranting a lesser penalty.

Our federal system of government is responsible for jurisdictional variation in the criminal law. States are allowed and encouraged to shape their criminal law as they see fit within the bounds of the Constitution. You will encounter jurisdictional variations not just in homicide but in many other areas throughout this book. Try to spot such variations and decipher what policy or political issues may cause states to differ on these points. At the same time, note jurisdictional uniformity when you find it. Don't let jurisdictional variations mask the fact that there are many points on which jurisdictions are quite uniform. You will need to recognize both jurisdictional uniformity as well as variation to master criminal law.

B. Purposeful Killings

This section deals with homicides in which the actor has purpose regarding the resulting death. Such homicides may be diagrammed as follows:

Mental Elements		Non-Mental Elements
Purpose	→	Conduct
Purpose	→	Death

1. Degrees of Murder

Problems

6.1 Will and Andy manufactured and distributed methamphetamine successfully for a number of years. During that time they aligned themselves with a number of people in the drug world. These included a gang headed by a man named Matt, whose members assisted in cooking (i.e. creating) and distributing the methamphetamine, and a woman named Catie, who helped them both to procure chemical components and distribute the methamphetamine overseas. When Will and Andy attempt to end their association with Matt's gang, Matt kidnaps Andy, holds him hostage, and forces him to cook methamphetamine. With Andy under their control, Matt and Catie decide they can do without Will and attempt to kill him. Will goes underground and carefully plans a counter-attack on Matt and Catie.

(a) Catie is an avid coffee drinker and always stops at a particular Starbucks location for her morning coffee. Will manages to sneak ricin, a powerful poison, into Catie's coffee. This poison causes flu-like symptoms. In a phone call to Catie after she has taken the ricin, Will gloats and admits to Catie that he put the poison in her coffee. Shortly after the phone call ends, Catie dies. What level of homicide does Will qualify for based on Catie's death under the statutes and cases in this section?

(b) Will buys a .50 caliber machine gun and an old car with an enormous trunk. He mounts the machine gun inside the trunk so that it will pop up and automatically begin to fire in a sweeping pattern when he opens the trunk using a remote control. Will drives the car to confront Matt and parks the car in front of a building where he knows Matt and his gang are. Will walks into the building and sees that Andy is also in the room. After a brief and unproductive conversation with Matt, Will hits the remote and dives to the floor, taking Andy down with him as the machine gun begins to fire. The machine gun kills Matt and all but one of his gang members. What level of homicide does Will qualify for based on the deaths of Matt and his fellow gang members under the statutes and cases in this section?

(c) Will survives but is fatally wounded. Andy survives with no wounds as does Ted, Matt's nephew and a member of his gang. Ted was in charge of keeping Andy hostage and forcing him to cook methamphetamine for the gang. Ted was brutal toward Andy. To intimidate Andy after an attempt to escape, Ted went to the house of a woman Andy loved and shot and killed her in front of Andy. Ted then threatened Andy that if he didn't cooperate, he would also kill the woman's son, whom Andy also loves. Andy is on the floor in chains when the machine gun stops firing. When he sees that Ted is alive, Andy attacks him in a fit of anger. During the struggle, Andy manages to get his wrist chains around Ted's neck and chokes him to death. What level of homicide does Andy qualify for based on Ted's death under the statutes and cases in this section?

6.2 Bill and Robert are sheriff's deputies who have worked together for years. They are and for many years have been close personal friends. One day when they are on duty together, Bill and Robert respond in their patrol car to a report of gun shots having been fired at a house. Living in the house at the time the shots are fired are Earl and his pregnant girlfriend, Deborah. The shots neighbors heard and reported were fired by Earl when, after a quarrel, he shot and killed Deborah. Earl backs his car into the driveway and is trying to load Deborah's body into the car's trunk when Bill and Robert arrive at the house. When he sees the officers, Earl runs into the house. Robert goes to the rear of the house while Bill calls for back-up and covers the front of the house. When Robert approaches the rear of the house, Earl surprises and kills him with a single shot to his head. Earl then goes to the front door and tries to get to his car. While trying to reach the car, Earl fires his gun at Bill and Bill fires back. Earl misses Bill, but Bill hits Earl with three shots. None of Bill's shots that hit Earl are fatal, but they disable him, allowing Bill to handcuff Earl and take away his gun. After picking up Earl's gun, Bill calls out to Robert: "Bob? ... Bob? ... Bob?" Hearing no reply, Bill walks to the back of the house and finds Robert's dead body. About 30 seconds after finding Robert's body, Bill walks back to the front of the house and at close range fires a single shot into Earl's chest, killing him instantly. Later evidence reveals that Earl was a convicted felon and a member of a white supremacist prison gang called the Aryan Brotherhood. Bill is a well-respected member of his community with a spotless record as a police officer. Residents of the community rally to his support and raise thousands of dollars in donations for his defense. What level of homicide does Bill qualify for under the statutes and cases in this section based on Earl's death?

6.3 Martha and Jim have been a devoted married couple for 42 years. They have three children and five grandchildren. Four years ago, Jim was diagnosed with terminal bone cancer. Martha has been a loving caregiver, attending to Jim's every need and wish. Despite radiation, chemotherapy, and various experimental medical procedures, the cancer continues to progress, causing Jim enormous pain. Jim has been bed-bound for three months. He is in almost constant pain and paralyzed from the neck down. Martha administers morphine in liquid form to Jim several times a day to try to manage the pain. Because some of Jim's bones are very fragile, when Martha moves Jim to change the linens or wash him, it can cause Jim's bones to fracture, producing excruciating pain. Jim's doctor tells Martha that, although one cannot predict with certainty, because Jim is still able to eat and none of his vital organs has failed, Jim is likely to live anywhere from three months to a year more. When Jim learns of the doctor's prognosis, he begs Martha to end his suffering. Martha believes that if she steadily increases the amount of morphine she gives Jim, he will die a painless death while asleep or in a coma. On a calm day, when Jim's pain seems under better control, she discusses her plan with Jim. Jim readily agrees. The next morning, Martha begins increasing the morphine dosage. Wanting to eliminate Jim's pain and provide him peace, she continues to increase the morphine dosage, adjusting it five times over the following 24 hours. She sits with Jim, holding his hand, and singing their favorite songs. Finally, Jim drifts into a coma and dies 12 hours later. The coroner determines that the cause of death was morphine overdose. What was Martha's mental state with respect to Jim's death? Should Martha's conduct be treated as a crime? If so, of what crime should Martha be convicted?

Consider the following statutes. Do they recognize degrees of murder? If so, on what bases do they distinguish between first and second degree murder?

California Penal Code Annotated

§ 189 Murder; degrees

All murder which is perpetrated by means of a destructive device or explosive, a weapon of mass destruction, knowing use of ammunition designed primarily to penetrate metal or armor, poison, lying in wait, torture, or by any other kind of willful, deliberate, and premeditated killing, or which is committed in the perpetration of, or attempt to perpetrate arson, rape, carjacking, robbery, burglary, mayhem, kidnapping, train wrecking, or any act punishable under [enumerated sexual offenses], or any murder which is perpetrated by means of discharging a firearm from a motor vehicle intentionally at another person outside of the vehicle with the intent to inflict death is murder of the first degree. All other kinds of murders are of the second degree.

To prove the killing was "deliberate and premeditated," it shall not be necessary to prove the defendant maturely and meaningfully reflected upon the gravity of his or her act.

Kansas Statutes Annotated

§ 21-3401 Murder in the first degree.

Murder in the first degree is the killing of a human being committed:

(a) intentionally and with premeditation; or

(b) in the commission of, attempt to commit, or flight from an inherently dangerous felony as defined in K.S.A. 21-3436 and amendments thereto.

Kansas Statutes Annotated

§ 21-3402 Murder in the second degree.

Murder in the second degree is the killing of a human being committed:

  (a) intentionally; or

  (b) unintentionally but recklessly under circumstances manifesting extreme indifference to the value of human life.

Hawaii Revised Statutes

§ 707-701. Murder in the first degree

(1) A person commits the offense of murder in the first degree if the person intentionally or knowingly causes the death of:

  (a) More than one person in the same or separate incident;

  (b) A law enforcement officer, judge, or prosecutor arising out of the performance of official duties;

  (c) A person known by the defendant to be a witness in a criminal prosecution and the killing is related to the person's status as a witness;

  (d) A person by a hired killer, in which event both the person hired and the person responsible for hiring the killer shall be punished under this section;

  (e) A person while the defendant was imprisoned;

  (f) A person from whom the defendant has been restrained, by order of any court, including an ex parte order, from contacting, threatening, or physically abusing …;

  (g) A person who is being protected by a police officer ordering the defendant to leave the premises of that protected person … during the effective period of that order;

  (h) A person known by the defendant to be a witness in a family court proceeding and the killing is related to the person's status as a witness; or

  (i) A person whom the defendant restrained with intent to:

    (i)   Hold the person for ransom or reward; or

    (ii) Use the person as a shield or hostage.

Model Penal Code

§ 210.2 Murder

(1) Except as provided in Section 210.3(1)(b), criminal homicide constitutes murder when:

  (a) it is committed purposely or knowingly; or

  (b) it is committed recklessly under circumstances manifesting extreme indifference to the value of human life. Such recklessness and indifference are presumed if the actor is engaged or is an accomplice in the commission of, or an attempt to commit, or flight after committing or attempting to commit robbery, rape or deviate sexual intercourse by force or threat of force, arson, burglary, kidnapping or felonious escape.

2. Premeditation and Deliberation

Murder historically required "malice aforethought." The meaning of this phrase has varied over time and still engenders debate. Courts usually interpret this phrase to encompass intent to kill, which sometimes is referred to as "express malice." Malice aforethought also encompasses three other categories that the law treats as legally equivalent to intent to kill. These are sometimes referred to as "implied malice." The first is intent to do serious bodily injury. The second is extreme recklessness that reveals an indifference to the value of human life. The third category is felony murder.

Each of the four categories that comprise malice aforethought — intent to kill, intent to do serious bodily injury, extreme recklessness, and felony murder — can support a charge of murder. Jurisdictions that divide murder into degrees elevate murder to first degree murder if additional circumstances or mental states are present. Perhaps the most common of these is premeditation and deliberation, the subject of this section.

Compare the various definitions of premeditation and deliberation in the following cases. Which is preferable? If you were a legislator, which approach would you favor?

State v. Bingham

40 Wash. App. 553 (1985)
Court of Appeals of Washington

Worswick, C. J.

We are asked to decide whether the time to effect death by manual strangulation is alone sufficient to support a finding of premeditation in the absence of any other evidence supporting such a finding. We hold it is not. Accordingly, we reverse the conviction of Charles Dean Bingham for aggravated first degree murder....

Leslie Cook, a retarded adult living at the Laurisden Home in Port Angeles, was raped and strangled on February 15, 1982. Bingham was the last person with whom she was seen. The two of them got off the Port Angeles-Sequim bus together at Sequim about 6 p.m. on February 15. They visited a grocery store and two residences. The last of these was Enid Pratt's where Bingham asked for a ride back to Port Angeles. When he was refused, he said they would hitchhike. They took the infrequently traveled Old Olympic Highway. Three days later, Cook's body was discovered in a field approximately ¼ mile from the Pratt residence.

At trial, the State's expert testified that, in order to cause death by strangulation, Cook's assailant would have had to maintain substantial and continuous pressure on her windpipe for 3 to 5 minutes. The State contended that this alone was enough to raise an inference that the murder was premeditated.... Therefore, it allowed the issue of premeditation to go to the jury. The jury convicted Bingham of aggravated first degree murder, rape being the aggravating circumstance. On appeal, counsel for Bingham concedes that a finding of guilty of murder was justified; he challenges only the finding of premeditation, contending that the evidence was insufficient to support it. We agree.

Premeditation is a separate and distinct element of first degree murder. It involves the mental process of thinking over beforehand, deliberation, reflection, weighing or reasoning for a period of time, however short, after which the intent to kill is formed. The time required for manual strangulation is sufficient to permit deliberation. However, time alone is not enough. The evidence must be sufficient to support the inference that the defendant not only had the time to deliberate, but that he actually did so. To require anything less would permit a jury to focus on the method of killing to the exclusion of the mental process involved in the separate element of premeditation.

The concept of premeditation had a slow but sure beginning in Anglo-American legal history. More than 500 years ago, English jurists arrived at the not surprising conclusion that the worst criminals—and those most deserving of the ultimate punishment—were those who planned to kill and then did so. Thus began the movement toward classification of homicides that resulted in restriction of the death penalty to those involving "malice prepensed" or "malice aforethought." When Washington's first criminal code was enacted in 1854, the Territorial Legislature abandoned this archaic language and used the phrase "deliberate and premeditated malice" in defining first degree murder. It thereby made a clear separation between a malicious intent and the process of deliberating before arriving at that intent.

Our Supreme Court recognized the need for evidence of both time for and fact of deliberation in *State v. Arata*, 56 Wash. 185, 189 (1909). Although it reversed a first degree murder conviction because a portion of an instruction was erroneous, it approved the remainder of the instruction, saying:

> ... [I]n substance, the law knows no specific time; if the man reflects upon the act a moment antecedent to the act, it is sufficient; the time of deliberation and premeditation need not be long; if it furnishes room for reflection *and the facts show that such reflection existed*, then it is sufficient deliberation ...

* * *

The subject of premeditation appears frequently in Washington cases. However, it is seldom discussed in a way that affords clear, objective guidance to trial judges in determining the sufficiency of the evidence to support it. Nevertheless, review of these cases reveals that in each one where the evidence has been found sufficient, there has been some evidence beyond time from which a jury could infer the fact of deliberation. This evidence has included, *inter alia*, motive, acquisition of a weapon, and planning directly related to the killing.

Unless evidence of both time for and fact of deliberation is required, premeditation could be inferred in any case where the means of effecting death requires more than a moment in time. For all practical purposes, it would merge with intent; proof of intent would become proof of premeditation. However, the two elements are separate. Premeditation cannot be inferred from intent.

Premeditation can be proved by direct evidence, or it can be proved by circumstantial evidence where the inferences drawn by the jury are reasonable and the evidence supporting the jury's findings is substantial. There was no such evidence here, either direct or circumstantial.

There was no evidence that Bingham had known Cook before February 15 or that he had a motive to kill her. By chance, they took the same bus. When Cook's companion on the bus refused to go to Sequim with her, Bingham offered to see that Cook got back to the Laurisden Home later. That was apparently still his intention when he asked for a ride at the Pratt residence. It could be inferred that between there and the field ¼ mile away, he decided to rape her. A reasonable jury could not infer from this beyond a reasonable doubt that he also planned to kill her. There is no other evidence to support a finding of premeditation. The fact of strangulation, without more, leads us to conclude that the jury only speculated as to the mental process involved in premeditation. This is not enough. The premeditation finding cannot stand....

Reversed. Remanded for entry of judgment and sentence for second degree murder.

People v. Morrin
187 N.W.2d 434 (1971)
Court of Appeals of Michigan

First-degree and second-degree murder are separate offenses, carrying vastly different penalties, distinguished only by the requirement that a homicide punishable as first-degree murder be committed with premeditation and deliberation. If premeditation and deliberation are ill-defined, the jury is left with no objective standards upon which to base its verdict. Convictions of the two offenses will be distributed not on the basis of ascertainable criteria, but entirely as products of the subjective, wholly individualist determinations of different juries.

The United States Supreme Court has frequently ruled that juries cannot be permitted to determine criminal liability without a reasonably ascertainable standard of guilt. Absent such standards, the jury has the sort of naked and arbitrary power which is inconsistent with due process.

Accordingly, it underscores the difference between the statutory degrees of murder to emphasize that premeditation and deliberation must be given independent meaning in a prosecution for first-degree murder. The ordinary meaning of the terms will suffice. To premeditate is to think about beforehand; to deliberate is to measure and evaluate the major facets of a choice or problem. As a number of courts have pointed out, premeditation and deliberation characterize a thought process undisturbed by hot blood. While the minimum time necessary to exercise this process is incapable of exact determination, the interval between initial thought and ultimate action should be long enough to afford a reasonable man time to subject the nature of his response to a "second look."

Discussion Questions

1. Should courts or the legislature specify a minimum amount of time required to establish premeditation and deliberation?

2. What criteria beyond time should courts consider in determining whether the killer premeditated and deliberated?

Byford v. Nevada

116 Nev. 215 (2000)
Supreme Court of Nevada

Shearing, J.

In 1992, the State charged appellant Robert Royce Byford and two codefendants, Christopher Garth Williams and Todd Smith, with the murder of Monica Wilkins. Smith later pleaded guilty to one count of accessory to murder and agreed to testify against Byford and Williams.... Byford and Williams were ... convicted. Byford received a death sentence, and Williams a term of life in prison without the possibility of parole.

Byford, Williams, and two teenage girls were visiting Smith at his parents' residence in Las Vegas on March 8, 1991. Byford was twenty years old, Williams seventeen, and Smith nineteen. Monica Wilkins, who was eighteen, called and told Smith she would pay him for a ride home from a local casino. Smith drove his jeep to pick Wilkins up, accompanied by Williams and one of the girls. After Smith picked up Wilkins and her friend, Jennifer Green, he asked Wilkins for gas money. Wilkins had Smith stop at a Burger King so that she could get some money. Williams went inside the store to see what was taking her so long, and Wilkins told him that she had gotten another ride. Smith and Williams were upset with Wilkins, and after they drove away, Williams fired a handgun out the window of the jeep.

Smith testified that Wilkins had angered him, Williams, and Byford before because she had invited them to her apartment to party but then left with other men. Byford and Williams had talked about "getting rid of her" because she was always "playing games with our heads." Smith participated in the talk but took the threats as jokes.

Later that night, Smith, Williams, and Byford were together at Smith's house when Wilkins called again for a ride home. Accompanied by Byford and Williams, Smith drove to pick her up. Smith then drove all four of them to the desert outside of town to find a party that Byford heard was taking place. Wilkins told the other three that she had taken LSD earlier and was hallucinating. Smith drove to the usual area for parties, but they found no party. They then stopped so that everyone could urinate. Wilkins walked up a ravine to do so.

Smith testified to the following. As Wilkins finished, Byford handed Williams a handgun and said he "couldn't do it." Smith asked Byford what he was doing with the gun, and Byford told Smith to "stay out of it." Williams then shot Wilkins in the back three to five times. She screamed and fell to the ground. Wilkins got up, walked to Williams, and asked him why he had shot her. He told her that he had only shot around her. Wilkins walked up out of the ravine but then felt the back of her neck, saw that she was bleeding, and again confronted Williams. Williams told her that he shot her because she was "a bitch." He then walked behind her and shot her again repeatedly. Wilkins screamed and fell to the ground again. Byford then took the gun from Williams, said that he would "make sure the bitch is dead," and fired two shots into her head. Byford then got a can of gasoline from the jeep and poured it on Wilkins. Byford tried to hand a lighter to Smith and get him to light the gasoline, but Smith refused. Byford called him a "wussie" and lit the body. As it burned, the three drove off. As they returned to Las Vegas, Byford pointed the handgun at Smith and threatened to kill him if he ever told anyone....

The instructions defining the mens rea required for first-degree murder.

The jury in this case was instructed:

> Premeditation is a design, a determination to kill, distinctly formed in the mind at any moment before or at the time of the killing.

> Premeditation need not be for a day, an hour or even a minute. It may be as instantaneous as successive thoughts of the mind. For if the jury believes from the evidence that the act constituting the killing has been preceded by and has been the result of premeditation, no matter how rapidly the premeditation is followed by the act constituting the killing, it is willful, deliberate and premeditated murder.

We will refer to this as the *Kazalyn* instruction because it first appears in this court's case law in *Kazalyn v. State*, 108 Nev. 67, 75 (1992).

Byford argues that this instruction is improper because it mandates a finding of willful, deliberate, and premeditated murder based only on the existence of premeditation. Although we reject this argument as a basis for any relief for Byford, we recognize that it raises a legitimate concern which this court should address.

We conclude that the evidence in this case is clearly sufficient to establish deliberation and premeditation on Byford's part. Byford and Williams had talked of "getting rid" of the victim on prior occasions. On the night of the murder, Byford handed the gun to Williams, saying that he (Byford) "couldn't do it," and told Smith to "stay out of it." Thus, it is evident that Byford and Williams discussed shooting the victim before doing so. Williams and Byford then calmly and dispassionately shot the victim in the absence of any provocation, confrontation, or stressful circumstances of any kind. Williams first shot her several times and then, after a passage of some time, shot her several more times. Byford watched this transpire, and when the victim was helpless on the ground, he took the gun from Williams, said that he would make sure she was dead, and shot her in the head twice. This evidence was sufficient for the jurors to reasonably find that before acting to kill the victim Byford weighed the reasons for and against his action, considered its consequences, distinctly formed a design to kill, and did not act simply from a rash, unconsidered impulse.

The *Kazalyn* instruction, however, does raise a concern which we will now consider.

[The Nevada murder statute] provides in relevant part that murder perpetrated by "willful, deliberate and premeditated killing" is first-degree murder. In this regard, willful means intentional. Therefore, willful first-degree murder requires that the killer actually intend to kill. Not every murder requires an intent to kill. For example, murder can also exist when a killer acts with a reckless disregard for human life amounting to "an abandoned and malignant heart." However, such a murder would not constitute willful first-degree murder.

In addition to willfulness, the statutory provision in question requires deliberation and premeditation. These are the truly distinguishing elements of first-degree murder under this provision. But the jurisprudence of Nevada, like that of other states, has shown a "trend toward a confusion of premeditation and deliberation." We therefore take this opportunity to "adhere to long-established rules of law and … abandon the modern tendency to muddle the line between first- and second-degree murder."

The *Kazalyn* instruction and some of this court's prior opinions have underemphasized the element of deliberation. The neglect of "deliberate" as an independent element of the *mens rea* for first-degree murder seems to be a rather recent phenomenon. Before *Kazalyn*, it appears that "deliberate" and "premeditated" were both included in jury instructions without being individually defined but also without "deliberate" being reduced to a synonym of "premeditated." We did not address this issue in our *Kazalyn* decision, but later the same year, this court expressly approved the *Kazalyn* instruction, concluding that "deliberate" is simply redundant to "premeditated" and therefore requires no discrete definition. *See Powell v. State,* 108 Nev. 700, 708–10, (1992). Citing *Powell*, this court went so far as to state that "the terms premeditated, deliberate and willful are a single phrase, meaning simply that the actor intended to commit the act and intended death as the result of the act." *Greene v. State,* 113 Nev. 157, 168, (1997).

We conclude that this line of authority should be abandoned. By defining only premeditation and failing to provide deliberation with any independent definition, the *Kazalyn* instruction blurs the distinction between first- and second-degree murder. *Greene's* further reduction of premeditation and deliberation to simply "intent" unacceptably carries this blurring to a complete erasure.

We acknowledge that the jurisprudence of this court on this issue has not been consistent, but in *Powell* we overlooked earlier pronouncements of this court which recognized that "deliberate" and "premeditated" define distinct elements. In *Hern v. State,* this court stated: "It is clear from the statute that *all three elements*, willfulness, deliberation, and premeditation, must be proven beyond a reasonable doubt before an accused can be convicted of first degree murder." (Emphasis added.)

In sum, the *Kazalyn* instruction and *Powell* and its progeny do not do full justice to the phrase "willful, deliberate, and premeditated." Deliberation remains a critical element of the *mens rea* necessary for first-degree murder, connoting a dispassionate weighing process and consideration of consequences before acting. "In order to establish first-degree murder, the premeditated killing must also have been done deliberately, that is, with coolness and reflection."

Because deliberation is a distinct element of *mens rea* for first-degree murder, we direct the district courts to cease instructing juries that a killing resulting from premeditation is "willful, deliberate, and premeditated murder." Further, if a jury is instructed separately on the meaning of premeditation, it should also be instructed on the meaning of deliberation.

Accordingly, we set forth the following instructions for use by the district courts in cases where defendants are charged with first-degree murder based on willful, deliberate, and premeditated killing.

> Murder of the first degree is murder which is perpetrated by means of any kind of willful, deliberate, and premeditated killing. All three elements — willfulness, deliberation, and premeditation — must be proven beyond a reasonable doubt before an accused can be convicted of first-degree murder.

> Willfulness is the intent to kill. There need be no appreciable space of time between formation of the intent to kill and the act of killing.

> Deliberation is the process of determining upon a course of action to kill as a result of thought, including weighing the reasons for and against the action and considering the consequences of the action.

> A deliberate determination may be arrived at in a short period of time. But in all cases the determination must not be formed in passion, or if formed in passion, it must be carried out after there has been time for the passion to subside and deliberation to occur. A mere unconsidered and rash impulse is not deliberate, even though it includes the intent to kill.

> Premeditation is a design, a determination to kill, distinctly formed in the mind by the time of the killing.

> Premeditation need not be for a day, an hour, or even a minute. It may be as instantaneous as successive thoughts of the mind. For if the jury believes from the evidence that the act constituting the killing has been preceded by and has been the result of premeditation, no matter how rapidly the act follows the premeditation, it is premeditated.

> The law does not undertake to measure in units of time the length of the period during which the thought must be pondered before it can ripen into an intent to kill which is truly deliberate and premeditated. The time will vary with different individuals and under varying circumstances.

> The true test is not the duration of time, but rather the extent of the reflection. A cold, calculated judgment and decision may be arrived at in a short period of time, but a mere unconsidered and rash impulse, even though it includes an intent to kill, is not deliberation and premeditation as will fix an unlawful killing as murder of the first degree....

We affirm Byford's conviction and sentence of death.

* * *

Courts take different approaches to the definition and application of the phrase "premeditation and deliberation." Compare the approaches in *Bingham*, *Morrin*, and *Byford* above with those in *Carroll*, *Young*, and *Carmichael* below.

Commonwealth v. Carroll

412 Pa. 525 (1963)
Supreme Court of Pennsylvania

Bell, C.J.

The defendant, Carroll, pleaded guilty generally to an indictment charging him with the murder of his wife, and was tried by a Judge without a jury in the Court of Oyer and Terminer of Allegheny County. That Court found him guilty of first-degree murder and sentenced him to life imprisonment. Following argument and denial of motions in arrest of judgment and for a new trial, defendant took this appeal. The only questions involved are thus stated by the appellant:

(1) "Does not the evidence sustain a conviction no higher than murder in the second degree?"

(2) "Does not the evidence of defendant's good character, together with the testimony of medical experts, including the psychiatrist for the Behavior Clinic of Allegheny County, that the homicide was not premeditated or intentional, *require* the Court below to fix the degree of guilt of defendant no higher than murder in the second degree?

The defendant married the deceased in 1955, when he was serving in the Army in California. Subsequently he was stationed in Alabama, and later in Greenland. During the latter tour of duty, defendant's wife and two children lived with his parents in New Jersey. Because this arrangement proved incompatible, defendant returned to the United States on emergency leave in order to move his family to their own quarters. On his wife's insistence, defendant was forced to secure a "compassionate transfer" back to the States, and subsequently to resign from the Army in July of 1960, by which time he had attained the rank of Chief Warrant Officer. Defendant was a hard worker, earned a substantial salary and bore a very good reputation among his neighbors.

In 1958, decedent-wife suffered a fractured skull while attempting to leave defendant's car in the course of an argument. Allegedly this contributed to her mental disorder, which was later diagnosed as a schizoid personality type. In 1959 she underwent psychiatric treatment at the mental hygiene clinic in Aberdeen, Maryland. She complained of nervousness and told the examining doctor "I feel like hurting my children." This sentiment sometimes took the form of sadistic "discipline" toward their very young children. Nevertheless, upon her discharge from the clinic, the doctors considered her much improved. With this background we come to the immediate events of the crime.

In January, 1962, defendant was selected to attend an electronics school in Winston-Salem, North Carolina, for nine days. His wife greeted this news with violent argument. Immediately prior to his departure for Winston-Salem, at the suggestion and request of his wife, he put a *loaded* .22 caliber pistol on the windowsill at the head of their common bed, so that she would feel safe. On the evening of January 16, 1962, defendant returned home and told his wife that he had been temporarily assigned to teach at a school in Chambersburg, which would necessitate his absence from home four nights out of seven for a ten week period. A violent and protracted argument ensued at the dinner table and continued until four o'clock in the morning.

Defendant's own statement after his arrest details the final moments before the crime: "We went into the bedroom a little before 3 o'clock on Wednesday morning where we continued to argue in short bursts. Generally she laid with her back to me facing the wall in bed and would just talk over her shoulder to me. I became angry and more angry especially what she was saying about my kids and myself, and sometime between 3 and 4 o'clock in the morning I remembered the gun on the window sill over my head. I think she had dozed off. *I reached up and grabbed the pistol and brought it down and shot her twice in the back of the head.*"[1]

Defendant's testimony at the trial elaborated this theme. He started to think about the children, "seeing my older son's feet what happened to them. I could see the bruises on him and Michael's chin was split open, four stitches. I didn't know what to do. I wanted to help my boys. Sometime in there she said something in there, she called me some kind of name. I kept thinking of this. *During this time I either thought or felt—I thought of the gun, just thought of the gun.* I am not sure whether I felt my hand move toward the gun—I saw my hand move, the next thing—the only thing I can recollect after that is right after the shots or right during the shots I saw the gun in my hand just pointed at my wife's head. She was still lying on her back—I mean her side. I could smell the gunpowder and I could hear something—it sounded like running water. I didn't know what it was at first, didn't realize what I'd done at first. Then I smelled it. I smelled blood before....'" "Q. At the time you shot her, Donald, were you fully aware and intend to do what you did? A. I don't know positively. All I remember hearing was two shots and feeling myself go cold all of a sudden."

Shortly thereafter defendant wrapped his wife's body in a blanket, spread and sheets, tied them on with a piece of plastic clothesline and took her down to the cellar. He tried to clean up as well as he could. That night he took his wife's body, wrapped in a blanket with a rug over it to a desolate place near a trash dump. He then took the children to his parents' home in Magnolia, New Jersey. He was arrested the next Monday in Chambersburg where he had gone to his teaching assignment.

Although defendant's brief is voluminous, the narrow and only questions which he raises on this appeal are as hereinbefore quoted. Both are embodied in his con-

---

1. When pressed on cross-examination defendant approximated that five minutes elapsed between his wife's last remark and the shooting.

tention that the crime amounted only to second degree murder and that his conviction should therefore be reduced to second degree or that a new trial should be granted....

The specific intent to kill which is necessary to constitute in a nonfelony murder, murder in the first degree, may be found from a defendant's words or conduct or from the attendant circumstances together with all reasonable inferences therefrom, and may be inferred from the intentional use of a deadly weapon on a vital part of the body of another human being.

It is well settled that a jury or a trial Court can believe all or a part of or none of a defendant's statements, confessions or testimony, or the testimony of any witness.

If we consider only the evidence which is favorable to the Commonwealth, it is without the slightest doubt sufficient in law to prove first degree. However, even if we believe all of defendant's statements and testimony, there is no doubt that this killing constituted murder in the first degree. Defendant first urges that there was insufficient time for premeditation in the light of his good reputation. This is based on an isolated and oft repeated statement in *Commonwealth v. Drum*, that "'no time is too short for a wicked man to frame in his mind his scheme of murder.'" Defendant argues that, conversely, a long time is necessary to find premeditation in a "good man." We find no merit in defendant's analogy or contention. As Chief Justice Maxey appropriately and correctly said in *Commonwealth v. Earnest*: "Whether the intention to kill and the killing, that is, the premeditation and the fatal act, were within a brief space of time or a long space of time is immaterial if the killing was in fact intentional, willful, deliberate and premeditated.... As Justice Agnew said in *Com. v. Drum*: 'The law fixes upon no length of time as necessary to form the intention to kill, but leaves the existence of a fully formed intent as a fact to be determined by the jury, from all the facts and circumstances in the evidence.'"

Defendant further contends that the time and place of the crime, the enormous difficulty of removing and concealing the body, and the obvious lack of an escape plan, militate against and make a finding of premeditation legally impossible. This is a "jury argument"; it is clear as crystal that such circumstances do not negate premeditation. This contention of defendant is likewise clearly devoid of merit.

Defendant's most earnestly pressed contention is that the *psychiatrist's opinion* of what *defendant's state of mind must have been and was at the time of the crime*, clearly establishes not only the lack but also the legal impossibility of premeditation. Dr. Davis, a psychiatrist of the Allegheny County Behavior Clinic, testified that defendant was "for a number of years ... passively going along with a situation which he ... [was] not controlling and he ... [was] not making any decisions, and finally a decision ... [was] forced on him.... He had left the military to take this assignment, and he was averaging about nine thousand a year; he had a good job. He knew that if he didn't accept this teaching assignment in all probability he would be dismissed from the Government service, and at his age and his special training he didn't know whether he would be able to find employment. More critical to that was the fact that at this point, as we understand it, his wife issued an ultimatum that if he went and gave this training course she would leave him.... He was so dependent upon her he didn't want her to leave. He couldn't make up his mind what to do. He was trapped...."

The doctor then gave *his opinion* that "rage," "desperation," and "panic" produced "an impulsive automatic reflex type of homicide ... as opposed to an intentional premeditated type of homicide.... Our feeling was that if this gun had fallen to the floor he wouldn't have been able to pick it up and consummate that homicide. And I think if he had to load the gun he wouldn't have done it. This is a matter of opinion, but this is our opinion about it."

There are three answers to this contention. First, as we have hereinbefore stated, neither a Judge nor a jury has to believe all or any part of the testimony of the defendant or of any witness. Secondly, the opinion of the psychiatrists was based to a large extent upon statements made to them by the defendant, which need not be believed and which are in some instances opposed by the facts themselves. Thirdly, a psychiatrist's opinion of a defendant's impulse or lack of intent or state of mind is, in this class of case, entitled to very little weight, and this is especially so when defendant's own actions, or his testimony or confession, or the facts themselves, belie the opinion....

Defendant's *own statement* after his arrest, upon which his counsel so strongly relies, *as well as his testimony at his trial,* clearly convict him of first degree murder and justify the finding and sentence of the Court below. Defendant himself described his actions at the time he killed his wife. From his own statements and from his own testimony, it is clear that, terribly provoked by his allegedly nagging, belligerent and sadistic wife,[2] defendant remembered the gun, deliberately took it down, and deliberately fired two shots into the head of his sleeping wife. There is no doubt that this was a wilful, deliberate and premeditated murder.

Young v. State
428 So. 2d 155 (1982)
Alabama Court of Criminal Appeals

Premeditation and deliberation in the law of homicide are synonymous terms meaning simply that the accused, before he committed the fatal act, intended that he would commit the act at the time that he did and that death would result. It does not mean that the accused "must have sat down and reflected over it or thought over it for any appreciable length of time."

Premeditation and deliberation may be formed while the killer is "pressing the trigger that fired the fatal shot." There need be no "appreciable space of time between the formation of the intention to kill and the act of killing." Such space of time is

---

2. While this picture of his wife is different from that depicted by her neighbors, if defendant's version is true, the remedy lies in a commutation by the Board of Pardons and not by a disregard of the law by the Courts.

"immaterial." "It was possible for the defendant to have framed a premeditated as well as a malicious design to kill after taking up the gun and before it was fired."

Carmichael v. State
340 Ark. 598, 602 (2000)
Supreme Court of Arkansas

Premeditated and deliberated murder occurs when it is the killer's conscious object to cause death and he forms that intention before he acts and as a result of a weighing of the consequences of his course of conduct. Premeditation is not required to exist for a particular length of time. It may be formed in an instant and is rarely capable of proof by direct evidence but must usually be inferred from the circumstances of the crime. Similarly, premeditation and deliberation may be inferred from the type and character of the weapon, the manner in which the weapon was used, the nature, extent, and location of the wounds, and the accused's conduct. One can infer premeditation from the method of death itself where the cause of death is strangulation.

Discussion Question

How do the "premeditation and deliberation" standards in *Carroll, Young,* and *Carmichael* differ from those in *Bingham, Morrin,* and *Byford*? Which is preferable?

3. The Provocation Doctrine

The first thing to know about the provocation doctrine is its function. If successfully invoked, it reduces a homicide from a more serious level to a less serious level, typically murder to manslaughter, and thus reduces the potential punishment that can be imposed on a defendant. Another important thing to know about provocation is that all American jurisdictions recognize some form of this defense.

Some, but not all, jurisdictions label manslaughter that results from application of the provocation doctrine "voluntary manslaughter." What do you think the word *voluntary* means here? How does it differ from the meaning of voluntary (1) in common usage; and (2) in the context of the voluntary act requirement you studied in Chapter 4 on conduct?

Discussion Questions

1. What significance, if any, do you think the criminal law should attach to the fact that a defendant was provoked? Should it mitigate or aggravate liability? Or should it be treated as irrelevant?

2. From a retributive point of view, does it make sense to reduce the punishment of an actor who was provoked at the time of killing?

3. From a deterrence point of view, does it make sense to reduce the punishment of an actor who was provoked at the time of killing? Is a provoked killer likely to be *less* dangerous than an unprovoked killer? Or *more* dangerous?

a. Actual Provocation

Certain features of the provocation doctrine are consistent from state to state. For example, its function of reducing murder to manslaughter is uniform from state to state. The subjective requirement that the defendant be "actually provoked" is also uniform from state to state. Many students struggle with understanding the actual provocation requirement, thinking that because it incorporates the word *provocation* it refers to things done or said by the victim or someone else to the person who does the killing. The actual provocation requirement instead refers to the internal mental and emotional *reaction of the killer* to the provoking event. It requires, simply, that the provoking act caused the killer himself or herself to actually experience an intense emotional reaction — *e.g.*, anger, rage — at the time of the killing.

Another way of thinking about the actual provocation requirement is to contrast it with the requirement of deliberation you encountered in the previous section on degrees of murder. Using traditional terminology, an actor who is actually provoked is described as acting in "hot blood" while an actor who deliberates is described as acting in "cold blood." The *Byford* court stated that a deliberate decision to kill "must not be formed in passion." In contrast, a provoked decision to kill *must* be formed in passion.

Problem

6.5 Daren and Annette have been married for 10 years. In the last few years, there has been considerable discord in their marriage. Annette on a number of occasions has expressed her unhappiness and that she is thinking of ending the marriage and divorcing Daren. Daren starts to suspect that Annette may be having an affair. Annette works as an accountant at a software company and her work hours typically are from around 8:30 a.m. until about 5:30 p.m. But recently, Annette has been coming home very late at night and Daren can tell she has been drinking. One night when Annette is asleep, Daren takes her cellphone, which is not password protected, and looks at her call history. He sees a large number of phone calls almost every day for the past few months to and from the same number that he does not immediately recognize. In the voicemail folder on the phone, there is a recent message that Annette failed to delete that is from the same number that appears so frequently in her call history. Daren listens to the message, recognizes the voice, and realizes that is from Jeremy, one of Annette's co-workers at the software company. In the message, Jeremy tells Annette that he will meet her the following evening at a high-end hotel.

The next evening, Daren waits outside Annette's workplace and follows her to the hotel, where she and Jeremy have a romantic dinner and then go up to a hotel room for several hours. Daren is furious, but manages to contain his anger and not reveal what he has learned to Annette. Daren hires a private investigator who follows Annette and Jeremy for months. The private investigator records and reports to Daren the details of their many meetings and also secretly photographs them on many occasions having dinner at various restaurants and entering and leaving the hotel they regularly use for their trysts.

One evening while Daren is brooding over Annette's affair with Jeremy, he watches an episode of the television show *How to Get Away with Murder* that deals with the provocation doctrine. The next day, he goes to the law library and reads up on his state's homicide laws, including the provocation doctrine. Under his state's version of the provocation doctrine, a husband witnessing his wife engaged in the act adultery qualifies as "legally adequate provocation." Daren buys a handgun and goes to a firing range to practice using it.

One evening almost a year after he first saw Annette and Jeremy together, Daren follows them, watches them eat dinner, and then follows them back to the hotel. Earlier that day, Daren had booked a room in the same hotel right next door to the one Annette and Jeremy regularly use and left a suitcase containing his loaded handgun in that room. After Annette and Jeremy go into their room, Daren enters his room and listens carefully through the adjoining wall with audio enhancement gear he obtained from his private investigator. When Daren hears sounds that indicate that Annette and Jeremy are *in flagrante delicto*, he calmly takes the gun out of his suitcase and checks to make sure it is loaded and that the safety is off. He takes a deep breath and says to himself "This is the moment I've been waiting for." Daren then kicks open the door to Annette and Jeremy's room, walks into the room, sees Annette and Jeremy engaged in sexual intercourse, and coolly says "Gotcha. I'm going to kill you both and I'm only going to be convicted of manslaughter because of the provocation doctrine." He then shoots and kills both Annette and Jeremy. Is Daren right? Does he qualify for the provocation doctrine?

b. Limitations on Provocation

Jurisdictions consistently impose objective limitations on use of the provocation doctrine. One such limitation is a reasonableness requirement, that the provoking event would have agitated a reasonable person. Other examples include categorical limitations on the sorts of events that can trigger a provocation defense, the amount of time that may elapse between the provoking event and the killing (sometimes referred to as "cooling time") and whether the defense is available if the defendant, either purposefully or accidentally, killed someone other than the person responsible for the provocation. Jurisdictions can also differ on whether and how much they "tailor" the objective reasonableness standard to characteristics of the defendant such as age, ethnicity, race, and gender. In sum, there is a great deal of variation from jurisdiction to jurisdiction regarding these objective limitations.

As you read through the statutes and cases that follow, compare and contrast the approaches adopted by various states. Some are more generous and some more restrictive in allowing defendants access to the provocation defense. In part, that may reflect the positions of different state legislatures in the debate about whether recognizing a provocation defense is a good idea.

Problems

6.6 David and his girlfriend Kelly are at a dance club one night celebrating a friend's birthday. Out on the dance floor, a man whom his friends call "Rowdy Roddy" is dancing wildly and accidentally knocks into Kelly and spills his drink on her dress. Rather than apologize, Roddy curses Kelly for having gotten in his way. David intervenes and a heated argument ensues. The club's bouncers separate the men and David and Kelly decide to leave. Several of Roddy's friends follow David and Kelly out into the club's poorly lit parking lot, where they assault and seriously injure David. Afterward, David drives back to his house, retrieves a handgun he legally owns, and returns to the club's parking lot. There he shoots and kills a man he believes is one of the men who assaulted him. The parking lot is dark, and David's vision is impaired because of the injuries he sustained to his head in the assault. It turns out that the man he shot is not one of the men who assaulted him. About 10 minutes elapsed between the time David was assaulted and his shooting the man. A police officer describes David's face as being so swollen that one eye was completely closed. Kelly described the swelling of David's head from the assault as making his eyes appear "like they were sitting on the side of his head." Does David qualify for a provocation defense under the statutes and cases below?

6.7 Reconsider Problem 6.2. Bill and Robert are sheriff's deputies who have worked together for years. They have been close personal friends for many years. Robert is the godfather of Bill's oldest son. One day when they are on duty together, Bill and Robert respond in their patrol car to a report of gun shots having been fired at a house. Living in the house at the time the shots were fired are Earl and his pregnant girlfriend, Deborah. The shots neighbors heard and reported had been fired by Earl when, after a quarrel, he had shot and killed Deborah. Earl backs his car into the driveway and is trying to load Deborah's body into the car's trunk when Bill and Robert arrive at the house. When he sees the officers, Earl runs into the house. Robert goes to the rear of the house while Bill calls for back-up and covers the front of the house. When Robert approaches the rear of the house, Earl surprises and kills him with a single shot to his head. Earl then goes to the front door and tries to get to his car. While trying to reach the car to escape, Earl fires his gun at Bill and Bill fires back. Earl misses Bill but Bill hits Earl with three shots. None of the shots that hit Earl are fatal, but they disable him, allowing Bill to take away his gun and handcuff Earl. After picking up Earl's gun, Bill calls out to Robert: "Bob? ... Bob? ... Bob?" Hearing no reply, Bill walks to the back of the house and finds Robert's dead body. About 30 seconds after finding Robert's body, Bill walks back to the front of the house and at close range fires a single shot into Earl's chest, killing him instantly. Later evidence reveals that Earl was a convicted felon and a member of a white supremacist prison gang called the Aryan Brotherhood. Bill is a well-respected member of his community with a spotless record as a police officer. Residents of the community rally to his support and raise thousands of dollars in donations for his defense. Does Bill qualify for a provocation defense under the statutes and cases below?

6.8 Reconsider Problem 6.1(c). Andy survives with no wounds as does Ted, Matt's nephew and a member of his gang. Ted was in charge of keeping Andy hostage and forcing him to cook methamphetamine for the gang. Ted was brutal toward Andy. To intimidate Andy after an attempt to escape, Ted went to the house of a woman Andy loved and shot and killed her in front of Andy. Ted then threatened Andy that if he didn't cooperate, he would also kill the woman's son, whom Andy also loves. Andy is on the floor in chains when the machine gun stops firing. When he sees that Ted is alive, Andy attacks him in a fit of anger. During the struggle, Andy manages to get his wrist chain around Ted's neck and chokes him to death. Does Andy qualify for a provocation defense in his killing of Ted under the cases and statutes below?

i. Categorical Limitations

In England the provocation doctrine was traditionally limited to—and in some U.S. jurisdictions is still limited to—certain categories of provoking acts often referred to as "legally adequate" provocation. In such jurisdictions, as you will see in the *Dennis* case, only provoking acts that fall within these categories qualify for mitigation. One example of such a category is battery. If a defendant killed a victim in response to the victim battering the defendant or a member of the defendant's family, the defendant could make use of the provocation doctrine. The Maryland case below involves another common category of legally adequate provocation, adultery.

Dennis v. State
105 Md. App. 687 (1995)
Court of Special Appeals of Maryland

Wilner, C.J.

On the evening of August 21, 1993, appellant, armed with a handgun, went to the home of Mark Bantz, apparently kicked in the door, entered the house, and shot

Mr. Bantz nine times—in the chest, in the head, and in the back. At least three of the wounds were fatal.

As a consequence of this conduct, a jury in the Circuit Court for Baltimore County convicted appellant of premeditated first degree murder, burglary, and unlawful use of a handgun, for which substantial sentences were imposed. Appellant complains in this appeal that the court refused to instruct the jury properly on the crime of manslaughter.... We find no merit in these complaints and shall therefore affirm the judgments entered by the circuit court.

Although appellant claimed to have no memory of the actual killing, his defense was that it must have occurred in the heat of passion, as the result of a dual, or mixed, provocation ... [a] two-month adulterous relationship [between defendant's wife, Robin, and Bantz], culminating in the sight of seeing them in an amorous embrace; and knowledge gained earlier in the day that, on the previous evening, Bantz had smoked cocaine in the presence of appellant's 12-year-old son.

Appellant and Robin met while they were teenagers; they began to live together and married when Robin became pregnant. Appellant worked hard to support his family, and all, apparently, went well until late 1990 or early 1991, when they began to suffer financial difficulties due, according to appellant, to Robin's spending habits....

[O]n June 26, 1993, Robin left the marital home, telling appellant that she was going to live with a female friend. About a week later, Robin confessed that she was, in fact, living with Mr. Bantz. Appellant became "emotionally upset" at this news, at least in part because he knew that Bantz was "involved with drugs." This concern heightened when he learned, in mid-July, that Robin too had begun smoking cocaine. She rejected his pleas to come home, "because of the drugs and the sex." Appellant then made two threats against Bantz—one in a conversation with Bantz's parents and one in a letter he wrote to Robin.

By late July or early August, appellant began to accept the situation. Although still professing strong feelings for Robin, he said that he "was starting to learn to accept the fact that she wasn't going to come home" and to focus his attention on raising his son. By August, he continued, "I was doing fairly good with all of this. I was pretty much coming back to earth." On Tuesday, August 17, however, Robin told appellant that she wanted to return. The next day, appellant picked her up from work, took her to Bantz's house to get some of her belongings, and had dinner and spent the night with her.

Notwithstanding this romantic interlude and the representation that her affair with Bantz was over, Robin asked for a little more time to make up her mind. She said that Bantz had moved back with his parents and allowed her to remain in the home they had shared until she could decide what she wanted to do. It is not clear whether appellant and Robin had contact the next day, but on Thursday, August 19, they again spent the evening together. On Friday evening, at Robin's request, appellant allowed his son to stay with Robin. When appellant took his son to the house, Bantz was not there.

On Saturday, appellant learned from his son that Bantz had come to the house on Friday evening, and that, as they were watching television, Bantz smoked cocaine. Appellant decided to investigate. He tried to reach Robin by telephone, but, when there was no answer, he drove to Bantz's house. He had with him in the car a .22 caliber handgun, allegedly because of a hunting trip planned for the next day.[1] Appellant stopped on the way and called Robin again, this time getting through to her; stating that she was going out with a girlfriend, she asked him to stay away, but he told her he was coming.

When he arrived at the home, appellant saw Bantz's father's truck, thereby indicating Bantz's presence. He approached the house, opened the screen door, and looked through the window. He described in his testimony what he saw:

> "I seen [Bantz] standing there, and he had his hands around my wife, and they were kind of, like embraced in, I don't know, some kind of mood, I guess.
>
> He had her dress all hiked up around her. I could see her, you know. It was kind of hard to take.
>
> * * *
>
> She was—it was, like, her back and [Bantz's] belly. He had her kind of around in front of him, and the best way I can say it, he had her all hooked up.
>
> * * *
>
> He had her dress kind of hiked up around her and it just looked like he was maybe feeling her private parts or so.
>
> * * *
>
> It looked like they were getting ready to engage in some kind of sex act."

Appellant claimed to have no memory of what next occurred, and, because he and Robin reconciled, she refused to testify. Testimony from two police officers who responded to the scene in response to emergency calls from Robin indicate that the front door had been kicked in and that the nine bullets fired into Bantz's head and body had been fired from at least 18 inches away; they were not contact wounds.

When counsel and the court first conferred on jury instructions, the court indicated that it proposed to give the Pattern Jury Instruction on voluntary manslaughter drafted by the Maryland State Bar Association Committee on Criminal Pattern Jury Instructions (MPJI-Cr 4:17.4C). In pertinent part, that instruction states that a killing in hot blooded response to "legally adequate provocation" is a mitigating circumstance, that in order for such a mitigating circumstance to exist in the particular case, five factors must be present: (1) the defendant reacted to something in "a hot blooded rage"; (2) the rage was caused by something "the law recognizes as legally adequate provocation" and that the only act the jury could find to be adequate provocation under the evidence

---

1. In fact, a hunting trip, as such, was not planned. Hunting was not allowed in August. Testimony by appellant's friend, who was to accompany him, indicated that they were intending to "scout out" areas for a future hunting trip, and that appellant was bringing his pistol for "snakes or wild dogs."

in this case is "the sudden discovery of the defendant's spouse in an act of sexual intercourse"; (3) the defendant was still enraged when he killed the victim; (4) there was not enough time between the provocation and the killing for a reasonable person's rage to cool; and (5) the victim was the person who provoked the rage.

Appellant raised no objection then, and raises no complaint now, about any aspect of that proposed instruction other than the language in element (2) declaring that the only adequate provocation under the facts of this case would be if appellant suddenly discovered Robin "in an act of sexual intercourse." ... [T]he court ... agreed to modify the instruction ... to read "sudden discovery by the Defendant of the Defendant's spouse in the act of sexual intercourse or his having strong reason to believe that it recently took place." It gave the instruction in that form....

After some period of deliberation, the jury sent a note asking the court to "clarify the term recent in the description of legal provocation in terms of recently had sexual intercourse, and must it be intercourse?" That provoked another discussion between counsel and the court ... [after which, the Court] instructed the jury that "recent is a term which is imprecise, and its meaning is within your sound discretion" and "intercourse is to be interpreted as having its usual and generally accepted meaning."

In this appeal, appellant complains that the court erred in limiting the provocation to the discovery of actual sexual intercourse, i.e., coition. He urges that (1) the conduct observed by him "was sufficient to constitute an 'act of sexual intercourse' necessary to form legally adequate provocation for the killing," (2) even if it was not, the law should recognize "significant sexual contact" or "sexual intimacy" as sufficient provocation, and (3) in any event, the jury should have been instructed to consider "the victim's illicit drug use in the presence of appellant's child" as sufficient provocation.

To constitute a mitigating factor sufficient to negate the element of malice, and thereby reduce murder to manslaughter, the provocation must be "adequate." In *Girouard*, the Court explained that, for a provocation to be "adequate," it must be "calculated to inflame the passion of a *reasonable* [person] and tend to cause [that person] to act for the moment from passion rather than reason." (Emphasis added.) That describes one aspect of "adequacy." There is another, which flows from the requirement that the passion be that of a reasonable person; the provocation must be one the law is prepared to recognize as minimally sufficient, in proper circumstances, to overcome the restraint normally expected from reasonable persons. There are many "slings and arrows of outrageous fortune" that people either must tolerate or find an alternative way, other than homicide, to redress.

Judge Moylan commented on this in *Tripp v. State*:

> We begin with the proposition that there must be not simply provocation in psychological fact, but one of certain fairly-well defined classes of provocation recognized as being adequate as a matter of law....

We are not dealing here with the entire universe of situations that might have the required effect. One type of conduct that the common law has long and consistently recognized as legally adequate is observing one's spouse in an act of adultery. The *Girouard* Court confirmed that "discovering one's spouse in the act of sexual intercourse with another" constitutes sufficient provocation.[3] In *Tripp*, we allowed a modest expansion. We there observed:

> "The law anciently required a spouse unexpectedly to discover the erring spouse *in flagrante delicto*. In its more modern and liberalized manifestations, it has been extended to situations where the spouse has suddenly been told of the other spouse's infidelity or has strong reason to believe that there has been such infidelity. *Even in the liberalized forms, however, the indispensable predicate is sexual intercourse.*" (Emphasis added.)

We need not determine here whether the term "sexual intercourse" might properly include any conduct other than coition. It is enough for us to reject the proposition that mere "sexual intimacy" or "significant sexual contact"—the standard urged by appellant—suffices. Those terms are much too general and cover far too great a range of conduct to be legally acceptable. It is clear that the kind of conduct allegedly observed by appellant as he peered through the window does not fall within any reasonable definition of "sexual intercourse."

Appellant's alternative assertion is that legally adequate provocation can be fashioned from the combination of Robin's earlier adultery, Bantz's corruption of her and appellant's son with drugs, and the suggestive embrace that he actually witnessed. That argument, though couched in terms of expanding the concept of adequate provocation, more significantly implicates, and fails to satisfy, the required causation between the provocation, the passion, and the killing.

By his own testimony, any passion generated by the knowledge that Robin had been engaged in an adulterous affair had cooled long before appellant appeared at Bantz's house. He had, in effect, forgiven Robin for her past infidelity and agreed to resume the marital relationship. Nor can provocation be found from the revelation of Bantz's drug use on Friday evening.... [A]lthough appellant testified that he "didn't like it," he offered no evidence that he was, in any way, enraged by that revelation....

What appellant seeks to do is to combine three separate grievances, arising or occurring at different times, none of which individually can constitute legally adequate provocation as of the time appellant actually shot Bantz, and make the combination suffice as provocation. A few States, notably California and Pennsylvania, have ap-

---

3. At a more ancient time, it appears that the killing of a man caught in the act of adultery with the defendant's wife was regarded as entirely justifiable. Blackstone notes in his discussion of the crime of manslaughter that

> "if a man takes another in the act of adultery with his wife and kills him directly on the spot, though this was allowed by the laws of Solon, as likewise by the Roman civil law, (if the adulterer was found in the husband's own house,) and also among the ancient Goths, yet in England it is not absolutely ranked in the class of justifiable homicide ... but it is manslaughter. It is, however, the lowest degree of it; and therefore in such a case the court directed the burning in the hand to be gently inflicted, because there could not be a greater provocation."

W. Blackstone, *Commentaries on the Laws of England*, Book IV* 191–92 (Lewis ed., 1922) (footnotes omitted). As Judge Moylan noted in *Tripp*, we have advanced somewhat in the past 200 years.

parently found sufficient provocation from what appears to be "the last straw" theory — a smoldering resentment or pent-up rage resulting from earlier insults or humiliating events culminating in a triggering event that, by itself, might be insufficient. Maryland has not adopted that view; nor, apparently, have most other States. In *Tripp*, we rejected the "long smoldering grudge" or "slow burn" as adequate. In *Girouard*, the Court of Appeals rejected taunts and verbal assaults as adequate provocation, even when taking on their humiliating and enraging character from antecedent events.

Antecedent events may be relevant in determining whether the triggering event in fact produced the hot blood necessary to rebut malice — they may support or detract from that nexus — but they do not suffice to give the triggering event a legal quality it does not otherwise have. Discovering one's spouse in an embrace with a paramour will not constitute adequate provocation because at some earlier time he or she committed adultery with that paramour. That is a matter for the divorce court; it does not reduce murder to some lesser offense.... We find no error in the court's instructions....

Discussion Questions

1. Should the law allow the discovery of adultery to reduce murder to manslaughter? Do reasonable people respond to adultery with lethal force? If so, why doesn't the doctrine provide for complete acquittal? If reasonable people don't respond with lethal force, why reduce the charge from murder to manslaughter?

2. If the discovery of adultery is legally adequate provocation, should sexual infidelity in *non-marital* relationships also qualify as legally adequate provocation?

* * *

In 1994, a Maryland judge sentenced a man who, after hours of drinking and arguing with his wife, shot and killed her with a hunting rifle. The defendant, a truck driver, found his wife in bed with another man. The sentence was 18 months in jail with possibility of work release and 50 hours of community service. At the time of sentencing, the judge made the following comments:

> "I seriously wonder how many married men — married five, four years — would have the strength to walk away without inflicting some corporal punishment.... I'm forced to impose a sentence ... only because I think I must do it to make the system honest...."[1]

The judge's comments sparked controversy and, three years later, in 1997, the Maryland legislature enacted the following statute:

Maryland Crim. Law Code Ann.

§ 2-207(b)

(b) Spousal adultery not a mitigating factor. — The discovery of one's spouse engaged in sexual intercourse with another person does not constitute legally adequate provo-

---

1. Megan Rosenfeld, *Is Adultery Cause to Kill Your Wife?*, San Jose Mercury News, Oct. 19, 1994 at 1 & back page.

cation for the purpose of mitigating a killing from the crime of murder to voluntary manslaughter even though the killing was provoked by that discovery.

* * *

Just as England did over time, a number of courts and legislatures in the United States moved away from the rigidity of the traditional provocation test. The case below provides an early example of a more modern and expansive approach to provocation.

Maher v. People

10 Mich. 212 (1862)
Supreme Court of Michigan

Christiancy, J.

... To the question, what shall be considered in law a reasonable or adequate provocation for such state of mind, so as to give to a homicide, committed under its influence, the character of manslaughter? On principle, the answer, as a general rule, must be, anything the natural tendency of which would be to produce such a state of mind in ordinary men, and which the jury are satisfied did produce it in the case before them—not such a provocation as must, by the laws of the human mind, produce such an effect with the *certainty that physical effects follow from physical causes*; for then the individual could hardly be held morally accountable. Nor, on the other hand, must the provocation, in every case, be held sufficient or reasonable, because such a state of excitement has followed from it; for then, by habitual and long continued indulgence of evil passions, a bad man might acquire a claim to mitigation which would not be available to better men, and on account of that very wickedness of heart which, in itself, constitutes an aggravation both in morals and in law.

In determining whether the provocation is sufficient or reasonable, *ordinary human nature*, or the average of men recognized as men of fair average mind and disposition, should be taken as the standard—unless, indeed, the person whose guilt is in question be shown to have some peculiar weakness of mind or infirmity of temper, not arising from wickedness of heart or cruelty of disposition.

It is, doubtless, in one sense, the province of the court to define what, in law, will constitute a reasonable or adequate provocation, but not, I think, in ordinary cases, to determine whether the provocation proved in the particular case is sufficient or reasonable....

The judge, it is true, must, to some extent, assume to decide upon the sufficiency of the alleged provocation, when the question arises upon the admission of testimony; and when it is so clear as to admit of no reasonable doubt upon any theory, that the alleged provocation could not have had any tendency to produce such state of mind, in ordinary men, he may properly exclude the evidence; but, if the alleged provocation be such as to admit of any reasonable doubt, whether it might not have had such tendency, it is much safer, I think, and more in accordance with principle, to let the evidence go to the jury under the proper instructions.... The law can not with justice assume, by the light of past decisions, to catalogue all the various facts and combinations of facts which shall be held to constitute reasonable or adequate provocation. Scarcely two past cases can be found which are identical in all their circumstances; and there is no reason to hope for greater uniformity in future. Provocations will be given without reference to any previous model, and the passions they excite will not consult the precedents.

The same principles which govern, as to the extent to which the passions must be excited and reason disturbed, apply with equal force to the time during which its continuance may be recognized as a ground for mitigating the homicide to the degree of manslaughter, or, in other words, to the question of cooling time. This, like the provocation itself, must depend upon the nature of man and the laws of the human mind, as well as upon the nature and circumstances of the provocation, the extent to which the passions have been aroused, and the fact, whether the injury inflicted by the provocation is more or less permanent or irreparable.... No precise time, therefore, *in hours or minutes,* can be laid down by the court, as a rule of law, within which the passions *must be held* to have subsided and reason to have resumed its control, without setting at defiance the laws of man's nature, and ignoring the very principle on which provocation and passion are allowed to be shown, at all, in mitigation of the offense. The question is one of reasonable time, depending upon all the circumstances of the particular case; and where the law has not defined, and can not without gross injustice define the precise time which shall be deemed reasonable.

Discussion Questions

1. How does the *Maher* Court's approach to provocation differ from the traditional approach exemplified in the *Dennis* case?

2. Is the *Maher* approach preferable? How might this last question be answered from the point of view of a defendant? From the point of view of a victim? From society's point of view?

3. Which theories of punishment do you think support the modern, expansive approach to provocation?

ii. Words

Can a provocateur's language alone give rise to a provocation defense? Should homicide law ever allow what a victim says to give rise to a provocation defense? Consider the following variations:

- What if the words themselves alone enraged a defendant, as in the case of an insult or racial slur made by the victim toward the defendant or a member of the defendant's family?
- What if the words *informed* the defendant of an act by the victim, such as the battery or rape of a family member? What if the victim admits sexual infidelity

to a spouse? Should the criminal law require that a defendant actually witness—
that is, observe firsthand—a provoking act in order to claim provocation?

· What if words are mixed with acts?

How do the following Georgia provocation statute and Georgia Supreme Court case
deal with the issue of words as provocation?

Georgia Code Annotated

§ 16-5-2 Voluntary Manslaughter

(a) A person commits the offense of voluntary manslaughter when he causes the death
of another human being under circumstances which would otherwise be murder and
if he acts solely as the result of a sudden, violent, and irresistible passion resulting from
serious provocation sufficient to excite such passion in a reasonable person; however,
if there should have been an interval between the provocation and the killing sufficient
for the voice of reason and humanity to be heard, of which the jury in all cases shall be
the judge, the killing shall be attributed to deliberate revenge and be punished as murder.

Scott v. State

291 Ga. 156 (2012)
Supreme Court of Georgia

Thompson, J.

Appellant Steven Scott was convicted of felony murder, aggravated assault and
possession of a firearm during the commission of a crime in connection with the
shooting death of Dan Smith, the boyfriend of Scott's sister. He appeals from the
denial of his motion for new trial, contending the trial court erred by excluding from
trial evidence that the victim had been molesting appellant's niece and refusing to
charge the jury on the lesser included offense of voluntary manslaughter. For the reasons that follow, we reverse.

Viewed in the light most favorable to the verdict, the evidence authorized the jury
to conclude that on the day of the crimes appellant's 16-year-old niece told him she
had been molested by the victim. Appellant walked to a convenience store to get a
beer, which he stated calmed him down, then returned home to continue talking to
his niece. When the child's mother and the victim arrived to pick her up, the child,
her mother, and appellant went inside the house to talk privately. Minutes later, appellant exited the house, asked the victim why he did it, and fatally shot the victim
as he sat in his car....

Appellant contends the trial court erred by refusing to charge the jury on the lesser
included offense of voluntary manslaughter. Voluntary manslaughter occurs when
one kills another human being under circumstances which would otherwise be
murder, if the killer "acts solely as the result of a sudden, violent, and irresistible passion resulting from serious provocation sufficient to excite such passion in a reasonable
person." "On the trial of a murder case, if there be any evidence, however slight, as

to whether the offense is murder or voluntary manslaughter, instruction as to the law of both offenses should be given the jury."

In this case, appellant proffered evidence supporting an inference that he shot the victim in the heat of passion during a confrontation about the victim's molestation of appellant's niece. Appellant testified he learned of the molestation one or two hours before the shooting. Immediately prior to the shooting, appellant's sister, when informed about the molestation, stated she did not believe her daughter. Appellant stated he then retrieved his gun for his own protection and went outside to talk to the victim. Appellant asked the victim why he did it, and the victim taunted him by saying "she's my b____, I can do whatever I want." At that point, appellant stated he "lost it," "blacked out," and started shooting. In light of this testimony, we conclude the slight evidence necessary to show provocation to support a charge on voluntary manslaughter was present.[2] See *Glidewell v. State* (evidence supported voluntary manslaughter charge where husband discovered spouse's intent to take child with her to meet paramour at hotel); *Banks v. State*, (evidence that defendant shot victim after learning victim was beating his daughter sufficient to warrant voluntary manslaughter charge). While we adhere to the view that "words alone, regardless of the degree of their insulting nature, will not in any case justify the excitement of passion so as to reduce the crime from murder to manslaughter," in this case there is slight evidence from which a jury could conclude the victim's words in connection with his conduct served as the "serious provocation sufficient to excite ... a sudden, violent and irresistible passion." Accordingly, it was error not to instruct the jury on the lesser included charge of voluntary manslaughter and under the circumstances of this case, we cannot say the error was harmless.

It follows that the trial court's ruling that appellant could not introduce evidence relevant to prove provocation was harmful error.

Judgment reversed.

iii. Time Limitations

What impact, if any, should the passage of time have on the availability of a provocation defense? Should provocation doctrine place a limit on the amount of time that can pass between a provoking event and a defendant's lethal response? If so, should it be measured in minutes? Hours? Days? Traditional doctrine put fairly strict time limits on how long anger and loss of control can qualify for mitigation under

---

2. The State contends the only provocation was the niece's disclosure of the molestation, and thus, there was a sufficient cooling period. See OCGA § 16-5-2 (a) ("if there should have been an interval between the provocation and the killing sufficient for the voice of reason and humanity to be heard ... the killing shall be attributed to deliberate revenge and be punished as murder"). This argument, however, ignores the cumulative effect of the victim's alleged conduct, appellant's discovery of the molestation, his sister's refusal to believe her daughter, and the victim's taunt that the child was his "b____ [and he could] do whatever [he] want[ed]."

the provocation doctrine. The materials below reveal that legislators and courts have taken a number of different approaches to the question of time limitation, some quite strict and others much more generous. How does the Georgia Supreme Court handle the issue of time in the *Scott* case, above? How does the Michigan Supreme Court handle it in the *Maher* case, above?

Louisiana Statutes Annotated

§ 14:31 Manslaughter

A. Manslaughter is:

  (1) A homicide which would be murder under either Article 30 (first degree murder) or Article 30.1 (second degree murder), but the offense is committed in sudden passion or heat of blood immediately caused by provocation sufficient to deprive an average person of his self-control and cool reflection. Provocation shall not reduce a homicide to manslaughter if the jury finds that the offender's blood had actually cooled, or that an average person's blood would have cooled, at the time the offense was committed.

State v. Pierce

64 Ohio St. 2d 281 (1980)
Supreme Court of Ohio

This appeal arises from the conviction of Homer C. Pierce, Jr. (hereinafter "defendant-appellant"), for the December 23, 1976, aggravated murder of Jeffrey LaPorte in Massillon, Ohio.

The relevant facts are not in dispute. As early as November 11, 1976, defendant, by his own admission, threatened LaPorte with serious bodily harm because LaPorte was spending time with defendant's wife. Also, as of that same date, defendant and his wife were contemplating legal separation. Several days later, defendant agreed to a divorce on the condition that his wife would not see LaPorte or any other man for two months. Shortly thereafter, defendant agreed to permit his wife to see LaPorte in public. Upon seeing them together in public, however, defendant became upset and decided to leave Massillon for a while.

On the night of December 16, 1976, contemporaneous with his return to Massillon, defendant admitted telephoning his wife at her home. Upon determining that LaPorte was then in her company, defendant further admitted threatening LaPorte with serious bodily harm. After defendant hung up, his wife telephoned the police who thereupon arrived at her home. A December 16, 1976, police report includes (1) defendant's wife's statement that defendant was holding a gun to the telephone and clicking it during his conversation with her; and (2) LaPorte's statement that defendant had threatened to kill him. While the police were still on the scene, defendant telephoned a second time. Defendant admitted that he conversed with the police during this second call and that he informed them that he owned a .22 caliber weapon.

At least four witnesses, in addition to defendant's wife, testified that defendant had threatened LaPorte sometime during the months of November and December, 1976. In a handwritten last will and testament dated December 18, 1976, defendant left his property to his sisters and his life insurance to his stepdaughter. A Firearms Transaction Record of December 19, 1976, indicates that defendant purchased a Winchester 30-30 rifle from a local store.... On the evening of December 22, 1976, defendant spoke to his wife, LaPorte and some of his wife's relatives and friends on the telephone. During these calls, a fight between defendant and LaPorte, which never materialized, was discussed.

At approximately 6:00 a.m. on the next morning, December 23, defendant visited a restaurant where both LaPorte and his brother were employed. There, defendant learned from LaPorte's brother that LaPorte was still at home where he was preparing to depart for the restaurant. Defendant left the restaurant and drove to LaPorte's home. When defendant arrived at LaPorte's home (approximately 6:30 a.m.), LaPorte had just entered his vehicle which was parked in front of his home. Defendant thereupon repeatedly fired a long-barreled automatic weapon containing 30-30 ammunition at LaPorte, killing him. The killing was witnessed by LaPorte's mother....

The grand jury indicted defendant for aggravated murder, R.C. 2903.01, to which defendant pleaded not guilty and not guilty by reason of insanity. Subsequent to trial, the jury was instructed on aggravated murder; on the lesser-included offenses of murder, R. C. 2903.02; on voluntary manslaughter, R. C. 2903.03; and on the defense of insanity. On August 1, 1979, the jury found defendant guilty of aggravated murder, and conviction and sentence were entered accordingly. On appeal, the Court of Appeals affirmed this conviction.

The cause is now before this court pursuant to an allowance of a motion for leave to appeal.... [D]efendant-appellant argues that the trial court's instruction on voluntary manslaughter was prejudicial because it included inadequate definitions of both extreme emotional distress and serious provocation.

The Court of Appeals found it unnecessary to consider this argument, ruling that defendant was not entitled to an instruction on voluntary manslaughter. We agree....

State v. Muscatello provides that in a prosecution for aggravated murder, an instruction on the lesser-included offense of voluntary manslaughter must be submitted to the jury if "the defendant produces or elicits some evidence on the mitigating circumstance of extreme emotional stress ..." *State v. Muscatello*, however, defines an act committed under extreme emotional stress as "one performed under the influence of sudden passion or in the heat of blood without time and opportunity for reflection or for passions to cool."

Further, under Ohio law, the lesser-included offense of voluntary manslaughter does not embrace "a deliberate, calculated homicide [merely] *** because extreme emotional stress brought on by the requisite provocation caused the laying of plans for the killing, as well as the killing itself * * *." "It is upon just such fact-patterns that defendants enjoy the opportunity of obtaining relief by means other than a resort to deadly force."

Defendant introduced evidence of his emotional stress which he alleged was caused by the breakdown of his marriage; his contact with his wife, LaPorte and others during the six weeks preceding the killing; and a number of idiosyncratic personality traits. Further, defendant introduced evidence of his telephone conversations on the night before the killing, December 22, 1976, with his wife, some of his wife's relatives and friends, and LaPorte, in which a fight between defendant and LaPorte, which never materialized, was discussed.

Even assuming that these telephone conversations on the night before the killing could constitute requisite provocation, defendant was not entitled to an instruction on voluntary manslaughter. Given the period of time which elapsed between these telephone conversations and the killing on the next morning (during which there is no evidence of provocation), such killing was not, as a matter of law, committed under extreme emotional stress, since no finder of fact could possibly conclude that the killing was "performed under the influence of sudden passion or in the heat of blood, *without time and opportunity for reflection or for passions to cool.*" Therefore, we conclude that defendant was not entitled to an instruction on voluntary manslaughter.

Discussion Questions

1. What time limit does the *Pierce* Court place on provocation? What rationale supports this limit?

2. What if Pierce had encountered LaPorte two hours after the telephone conversations? Would he have been able to claim provocation in Ohio?

* * *

The following case reveals that California takes a very different approach to time limits than Ohio.

People v. Wharton
53 Cal. 3d 522 (1991)
Supreme Court of California

Lucas, J.

... Defendant requested the following special jury instruction: "A defendant may act in the heat of passion at the time of the killing as a result of a series of events which occur over a considerable period of time. When the provocation extends for a long time, you must take such period of time into account in determining whether there was a sufficient cooling period for the passion to subside. The burden is on the prosecution to establish beyond a reasonable doubt that the defendant did not act in the heat of passion." The trial court rejected the proposed instruction on the dual grounds that it was an incorrect statement of the law and that the correct legal points raised were adequately covered in other instructions.

Defendant challenges both reasons for the trial court's refusal to give his requested instruction. We agree with defendant's initial point that provocation sufficient to reduce murder to manslaughter need not occur instantaneously, but may occur over a period of time. *People v. Berry* is illustrative. In *Berry*, the defendant's wife Rachel traveled alone to Israel three days after their wedding. When she returned, she announced that she loved another man, they had been sexually intimate, and she now wanted a divorce. For a period of 13 days, "Rachel continually provoked defendant with sexual taunts and incitements, alternating acceptance and rejection of him." The defendant killed Rachel.

... [W]e concluded that the "two-week period of provocatory conduct" by the defendant's wife was sufficient to justify an instruction on voluntary manslaughter based on heat of passion. The key element is not the duration of the source of provocation but "'whether or not defendant's reason was, at the time of his act, so disturbed or obscured by some passion ... to such an extent as would render ordinary men of average disposition liable to act rashly or without due deliberation and reflection, and from this passion rather than from judgment.'" ...

Defendant's second point—that his proposed instruction was not duplicative of other instructions—also has merit as to some portions of the instruction. The jury was given comprehensive instructions on heat of passion and provocation, including one stating that "the killing must have occurred while the slayer was acting under the direct and immediate influence of ... heat of passion," and that "the question as to whether the cooling period has elapsed and reason has returned is not measured by the standard of the accused, but the duration of the cooling period is the time it would take an average or ordinarily reasonable person to have cooled his heat of passion and for his reason to have returned." In addition, the jury was told that the prosecution bore the burden of proving defendant did not act while under the heat of passion.

Despite these instructions, defendant's proposed instruction raised two points not covered by the standard CALJIC instructions delivered by the court. First, the jury was not informed that provocation could occur over a "considerable period of time." Second, it was not told that if provocation occurred over such a period, the jury "must" take that period of time into account in determining the effect of the cooling-off period....

A criminal defendant is entitled, on request, to an instruction "pinpointing" the theory of his defense. As we recently explained, however, instructions that attempt to relate particular facts to a legal issue are generally objectionable as argumentative and the effect of certain facts on identified theories "is best left to argument by counsel, cross-examination of the witnesses, and expert testimony where appropriate."

Whether the period of provocation was long or short, the jury should consider all the facts to determine whether "sufficient time ha[d] elapsed between the provocation and the fatal blow for passion to subside and reason to return." By directing that the jury "must" take into account the long period of provocation in determining the effect of a cooling-off period, defendant's proposed instruction improperly singled out one factor, favorable to defendant, and improperly elevated it over other factors that the jury should also consider. This portion of the instruction was thus objectionable as argumentative and properly refused, albeit for the wrong reason, by the trial court.

By contrast, the court erred in refusing to instruct the jury, at defendant's request, that legally adequate provocation could occur over a considerable period of time. It was defendant's theory at trial that no single action on the part of the victim provoked the fatal blow but that the book-throwing incident was merely the culmination of his pent-up frustration and anger emanating from his ongoing dysfunctional relationship with the victim. In other words, his defense theory at trial was that he killed after enduring provocatory conduct by the victim over a period of weeks.

The People argue there was insufficient evidence of this theory to justify the instruction. We disagree; defendant proffered evidence from which reasonable persons could have concluded there was sufficient provocation to reduce murder to manslaughter.

Problem

6.9 Consider the excerpted facts below from *People v. Nesler*, 16 Cal. 4th 561, 941 P.2d 87 (1997). Of what level of homicide should Nesler be convicted? Does she qualify for a provocation defense under California law? Would she qualify under Ohio law?

Daniel Driver allegedly raped defendant's son, W., at a Christian camp where Driver worked. Driver told W., who was then seven years of age, that Driver would kill him, his sister, and defendant if W. told anyone what had happened. Several months later, W. disclosed to defendant what Driver had done. In May 1989, a complaint was filed against Driver, alleging seven counts of child molestation involving four boys, including W. Driver, however, had fled and was not apprehended until late 1992 or early 1993.

During this period, W. became hypervigilant and expected Driver to kidnap and kill him. He also began asking defendant questions about suicide, and once defendant found him with a gun. Fearing that W. would kill himself, she obtained counseling for him. Defendant told her sister, Jannette Martinez, that when defendant was a child she had been raped in the same manner as W., and that there was a time when she, too, wanted to die.

Before Driver's preliminary hearing took place in April 1993, defendant protested when she learned that W. would have to face Driver at the hearing. She suggested videotaping W.'s testimony, but that alternative was unavailable; defendant then asked that the hearing at least be closed to the public. On the morning of the hearing, W. began vomiting and continued to do so after he arrived at the courthouse. Defendant appeared nervous, upset, and extremely anxious about W. She told an investigator that W. might not be able to testify, and she attempted to reassure and encourage the boy. When Driver arrived at the courthouse for the hearing, he looked at W. and grinned with a mean, disgusted, and haughty look. Defendant lunged for Driver, but Martinez grabbed her arm. Defendant again asked someone from the district attorney's office whether the courtroom could be closed, but an open hearing was held.

After W. entered the waiting room for witnesses, he continued to vomit. The mother of one of the other boys said that she did not believe her testimony had gone well, and that Driver had smirked at her and her son when they testified. This woman also said that she was convinced Driver was "going to walk," and that she wanted to get a gun and kill him. She told defendant to try to do better than she and her son had done. After this exchange, defendant became nervous and started pacing.

Defendant and W. were to be the last witnesses to testify at the preliminary hearing. Just before they were called, defendant asked the investigator whether he and other employees in the district attorney's office would get in trouble if "something happened" to Driver. Believing that defendant was referring to a previous assault upon Driver by another inmate in the jail, the investigator gave a negative response. Defendant and Martinez entered the courtroom, and the prosecutor told them to take a seat. The judge was not present, and a shackled Driver was sitting in a chair approximately one foot from defense counsel. Defendant stood behind the defense attorney, drew a gun she had taken from Martinez's purse, and shot Driver five times in the left side of the head and neck; a sixth bullet missed Driver and was found in the wall. The gun's muzzle was within two to three feet of Driver's head, and the shots were fired in rapid succession. Driver was killed almost instantly.

iv. Victim Identity

Typically, the person killed in a case raising a potential provocation defense is the person who provided the provocation. In other words, the victim and the provocateur are usually the same person. In an adultery situation, for example, the spouse who engages in the adultery and his or her lover are often both the provocateurs and the victims. In most of the problems set forth at the outset of this section the provocateur and the victim are the same person.

But that is not always the case. Sometimes the provocateur does not wind up being the victim. For example, in Problem 6.6 above, David was provoked by a group of men who assaulted him. When David returned to the scene of the assault with his gun, he wound up shooting and killing a man he thought was one of the men who assaulted him, but in fact he shot an innocent man he mistook for one of the men who beat him. Should this disqualify David from using a provocation defense? What should happen under the provocation doctrine when one person provides the provocation but the person provoked winds up killing *a different* person?

How do the following statute and jury instruction handle this "victim identity" question? How would David in Problem 6.6 fare under each?

18 Pennsylvania Consolidated Statutes Annotated

§ 2503 Voluntary Manslaughter

(a) A person who kills an individual without lawful justification commits voluntary manslaughter if at the time of the killing he is acting under a sudden and intense passion resulting from serious provocation by:

(1) the individual killed; or

(2) another whom the actor endeavors to kill, but he negligently or accidentally causes the death of the individual killed.

Maryland State Bar Association Committee on Criminal Pattern Jury Instructions, Maryland Pattern Jury Instruction Criminal 4:17.4C VOLUNTARY MANSLAUGHTER

Killing in hot blooded response to legally adequate provocation is a mitigating circumstance. In order for this mitigating circumstance to exist in this case, the following five factors must be present: (1) the defendant reacted to something in a hot blooded rage, that is, the defendant actually became enraged; (2) the rage was caused by something the law recognizes as legally adequate provocation, that is, something that would cause a reasonable person to become enraged enough to kill or inflict serious bodily harm.... ; (3) the defendant was still enraged when [he] [she] killed the victim, that is, the defendant's rage had not cooled by the time of the killing; (4) there was not enough time between the provocation and the killing for a reasonable person's rage to cool; and (5) the victim was the person who provoked the rage.

Discussion Question

Which is preferable, Pennsylvania's approach or Maryland's?

v. "Tailoring" the Reasonableness Standard

The defendant in the following case, Camplin, was a 15-year-old boy. After being raped and then ridiculed by a man, Camplin grabbed a heavy metal pan and struck the man in the head, killing him. A primary issue at trial was whether the reasonableness of Camplin's emotional response to the rape and ridicule should be judged from the point of view of a reasonable adult or from the point of view of a reasonable 15-year-old. The trial judge instructed the jury that they were required to use the adult standard.

Director of Public Prosecutions v. Camplin

(1978) English House of Lords

Opinion of Lord Diplock.

... As I have already pointed out, for the purposes of the law of provocation the "reasonable man" has never been confined to the adult male. It means an ordinary person of either sex, not exceptionally excitable or pugnacious, but possessed of such powers of self-control as everyone is entitled to expect that his fellow citizens will exercise in society as it is today. A crucial factor in the defense of provocation from earliest times has been the relationship between the gravity of provocation and the way in which the accused retaliated, both being judged by the social standards of the day.

When Hale was writing in the seventeenth century, pulling a man's nose was thought to justify retaliation with a sword; when *Mancini v. Director of Public Prosecutions* [1942] A.C.I. was decided by this House, a blow with a fist would not justify retaliation with a deadly weapon. But so long as words unaccompanied by violence could not in law amount to provocation the relevant proportionality between provocation and retaliation was primarily one of degrees of violence. Words spoken to the accused before the violence started were not normally to be included in the proportion sum. But now that the law has been changed so as to permit of words being treated as provocation even though unaccompanied by any other acts, the gravity of verbal provocation may well depend upon the particular characteristics or circumstances of the person to whom a taunt or insult is addressed. To taunt a person because of his race, his physical infirmities or some shameful incident in his past may well be considered by the jury to be more offensive to the person addressed, however equable his temperament, if the facts on which the taunt is founded are true than it would be if they were not. It would stultify much of the mitigation of the previous harshness of the common law in ruling out verbal provocation as capable of reducing murder to manslaughter if the jury could not take into consideration all those factors which in their opinion would affect the gravity of taunts or insults when applied to the person whom they are addressed....

That he was only 15 years of age at the time of the killing is the relevant characteristic of the accused in the instant case. It is a characteristic which may have its effects on temperament as well as physique. If the jury think that the same power of self-control is not to be expected in an ordinary, average or normal boy of 15 as in an older person, are they to treat the lesser powers of self-control possessed by an ordinary, average or normal boy of 15 as the standard of self-control with which the conduct of the accused is to be compared?

It may be conceded that in strict logic there is a transition between treating age as a characteristic that may be taken into account in assessing the gravity of the provocation addressed to the accused and treating it as a characteristic to be taken into account in determining what is the degree of self-control to be expected of the ordinary person with whom the accused's conduct is to be compared. But to require old heads upon young shoulders is inconsistent with the law's compassion to human infirmity to which Sir Michael Foster ascribed the doctrine of provocation more than two centuries ago. The distinction as to the purposes for which it is legitimate to take the age of the accused into account involves considerations of too great nicety to warrant a place in deciding a matter of opinion, which is no longer one to be decided by a judge trained in logical reasoning but by a jury drawing on their experience of how ordinary human beings behave in real life....

In my opinion a proper direction to a jury on the question left to their exclusive determination by section 3 of the Act of 1957 would be on the following lines. The judge should state what the question is using the very terms of the section. He should then explain to them that the reasonable man referred to in the question is a person having the power of self-control to be expected of an ordinary person of the sex and age of the accused, but in other respects sharing such of the accused's characteristics as they think would affect the gravity of the provocation to him; and that the question is not merely whether such a person would in like circumstances be provoked to lose his self-control but also whether he would react to the provocation as the accused did.

I accordingly agree with the Court of Appeal that the judge ought not to have instructed the jury to pay no account to the age of the accused even though they themselves might be of opinion that the degree of self-control to be expected in a boy of that age was less than in an adult. So to direct them was to impose a fetter on the right and duty of the jury which the Act accords to them to act upon their own opinion on the matter.

Discussion Question

To which of the following characteristics, if any, should the reasonableness standard be tailored?

- Gender
- Sexual orientation
- Race
- Ethnicity

- Religion
- Physical handicap
- Mental handicap

Problems

6.10 Stanley lost both legs at his hip joints five years ago following a terrible auto accident. After the accident, Stanley became bitter. He lost his job. His relationship with his wife, June, and his son, James, became distant and tense. Several years ago, Stanley learned from a friend that June was having an affair with another man. One day Stanley finds a letter written by June to her paramour. That evening, when June returns from work, Stanley confronts her with the letter. June admits the adultery and angrily begins taunting Stanley, calling him "only half a man." Furious, Stanley pulls out a loaded handgun and fires away at June, screaming "you're a dead woman, June." June, however, manages to dive for cover without being hit by any bullets. Unfortunately, though, James walks through the door at this very moment, is hit in the head by one of Stanley's bullets, and is killed instantly. What is the homicide liability of Stanley for the death of James?

6.11 Consider the following excerpted facts from the Michigan case of *People v. Schmitz*, 231 Mich. App. 521 (1998):

> This case arises from defendant's killing of Scott Amedure with a shotgun on March 9, 1995. Three days before the shooting, defendant appeared with Amedure and Donna Riley in Chicago for a taping of an episode of the Jenny Jones talk show, during which defendant was surprised by Amedure's revelation that he had a secret crush on [the defendant]. After the taping, defendant told many friends and acquaintances that he was quite embarrassed and humiliated by the experience and began a drinking binge. On the morning of the shooting, defendant found a sexually suggestive note from Amedure on his front door. Defendant then drove to a local bank, withdrew money from his savings account, and purchased a 12-gauge pump-action shotgun and some ammunition. Defendant then drove to Amedure's trailer, where he confronted Amedure about the note. When Amedure just smiled at him, defendant walked out of the trailer, stating that he had to shut off his car. Instead, defendant retrieved the shotgun and returned to the trailer. Standing at the front door, defendant fired two shots into Amedure's chest, leaving him with no chance for survival. Defendant left the scene and telephoned 911 to confess to the shooting.

Should the trial judge instruct the jury on the provocation defense? If so, how should the reasonableness requirement be stated to the jury?

vi. The Model Penal Code's Approach: Extreme Mental or Emotional Disturbance

Model Penal Code

§ 210.3 Manslaughter

(1) Criminal homicide constitutes manslaughter when: …

(b) a homicide which would otherwise be murder is committed under the influence of extreme mental or emotional disturbance for which there is reasonable explanation or excuse. The reasonableness of such explanation or excuse shall be determined from the viewpoint of a person in the actor's situation under the circumstances as he believes them to be.

* * *

What positions does the MPC provision above take on the various limitations examined previously in this section?

- Categorical limits?
- Words as provocation?
- Time limits?
- Victim identity?
- Tailoring?

Comments to Model Penal Code § 210.3:

The critical element in the Model Penal Code formulation is the clause requiring that reasonableness be assessed "from the viewpoint of a person in the actor's situation." The word "situation" is designedly ambiguous. On the one hand, it is clear that personal handicaps and some external circumstances must be taken into account. Thus, blindness, shock from traumatic injury, and extreme grief are all easily read into the term "situation." This result is sound, for it would be morally obtuse to appraise a crime for mitigation of punishment without reference to these factors. On the other hand, it is equally plain that idiosyncratic moral values are not part of the actor's situation. An assassin who kills a political leader because he believes it is right to do so cannot ask that he be judged by the standard of a reasonable extremist. Any other result would undermine the normative message of the criminal law. In between these two extremes, however, there are matters neither as clearly distinct from individual blameworthiness as blindness or handicap nor as integral a part of moral depravity as a belief in the rightness of killing. Perhaps the classic illustration is the unusual sensitivity to the epithet "bastard" of a person born illegitimate. An exceptionally punctilious sense of personal honor or an abnormally fearful temperament may also serve to differentiate an individual actor from the hypothetical reasonable man, yet none of these factors is wholly irrelevant to the ultimate issue of culpability. The proper role of such factors cannot be resolved satisfactorily by abstract definition of what may constitute adequate provocation. The Model Code endorses a formulation that affords sufficient flexibility to differentiate in particular cases between those special aspects of the actor's situation that should be deemed material for purpose of grading and those that should be ignored. There thus will be room for interpretations of the word "situation," and that is precisely the flexibility desired. There will be opportunity for argument about the reasonableness of explanation or excuse, and that too is a ground on which argument is required. In the end the question is whether the actor's loss of self-control can be understood in terms that arouse sympathy in the ordinary citizen. Section 210.3 faces this issue squarely and leaves the ultimate judgment to the ordinary citizen in the function of a juror assigned to resolve the specific case.

c. Battered Spouses

What problems would a battered spouse or child encounter in trying to use the provocation defense if the battered spouse or child killed the battering spouse or parent? Should legislatures modify the provocation defense to allow battered spouses and children to make use of the provocation defense?

State v. Goff

2013 Ohio App. LEXIS 27; 2013 WL 139545 (2013)
Court of Appeals of Ohio

When Megan [Goff] was 15 years old, she and her family moved next door to William. At the time, William was 40 years old, and he lived alone. Eventually, Megan and William developed a sexual relationship. Megan married William when she was 19 years old. When Megan was 21 years old, she gave birth to a daughter. A few years later, Megan gave birth to a son. Megan claimed that William was often emotionally abusive during the marriage. Additionally, Megan claimed that William had threatened to become violent on several occasions.

Megan and William's marital difficulties escalated in late 2005 and early 2006. Megan claimed that, during that time period, William told her that he was going to kill her and the children. According to Megan, William kicked the couple's son in the stomach on January 18, 2006. Later that same day, Megan left the marital residence with her children. They went to a domestic violence shelter in Kentucky. Megan also filed domestic violence charges against William. (As a result of the domestic violence charges, law enforcement removed 63 guns from the home.) In addition to filing the domestic violence charges, Megan initiated divorce proceedings.

Megan claimed that William attempted to track her and the children down after they left the residence. While Megan and the children were staying at the domestic violence shelter in Kentucky, an employee of the shelter spotted a man resembling William near the shelter. This caused the shelter to go on lock down. Shortly after that incident, Megan and the children left the shelter. Eventually, they moved into an apartment in West Virginia.

In early March 2006, Megan recorded a phone conversation that she had with William. (The recording was played at trial.) At the beginning of the conversation, Megan informed William that she was recording the call. During the conversation,

William admitted that he previously said he was going to kill Megan and the children. He claimed the statement was for "shock value" based on statements Megan had made about suicide. (Megan responded by telling William that he was taking her comments out of context and that she had been referring to what she would do if she was ever terminally ill.)

Apparently, Megan and William had at least one unrecorded phone conversation on March 17, 2006. According to Megan, William again told her that he would kill her and the children. She testified that, after speaking with William on March 17, she became convinced that he was going to carry out his threat.

Megan drove to William's house on Saturday, March 18, 2006. She stated that she intended to persuade William to kill her but not the children. Megan claimed that she believed that if William killed her, it would somehow prevent him from killing the children.

Megan arrived at the house armed with two handguns. (Megan claimed that she carried two guns because, earlier in their marriage, William had advised her to always carry two guns in case one of the guns jammed.) Megan testified that, after she knocked on the door, William answered and said, "I didn't think you had the guts." She also claimed that William told her to "get in here." Next, Megan stated that, after she entered the house, she did not feel that she could get out of the house because William blocked the door. Megan testified that William told her that her mother "was going to have a birthday present and it was going to be two dead grand kids and a dead daughter." (Megan's mother's birthday was on the following Monday, i.e., March 20.)

Shortly thereafter, Megan shot William multiple times, and he died as a result of the gunshot wounds. Megan called 911 to report that she had shot William. The recording of the 911-call was played at trial. During the 911-call, the dispatcher struggled to convince Megan to calm down. Megan claimed she feared that William would still be able to harm her despite his multiple gunshot wounds. Megan told Det. Bollinger that she killed William because she feared that he would kill her and the children. Megan claimed that she shot William in self-defense and that she suffered from battered woman's syndrome. A psychiatrist testified that, in his opinion, Megan believed that she and her children were in imminent danger of death or serious bodily injury when she shot William....

Discussion Question

1. Ms. Goff's lawyer requests that the judge instruct the jury on provocation. Should the judge give such an instruction, telling the jurors they should convict Ms. Goff of manslaughter if they find the elements of a provocation defense are satisfied?

2. Ms. Goff's lawyer also asks the judge to instruct the jurors that the emotion of fear (rather than anger) can be the basis of a provocation defense? Should the judge give such an instruction?

Fear vs. Anger

As you have seen, the emotional state that can trigger a provocation defense is described in a variety of ways. Some states use language, such as "hot blooded rage" or "irresistible passion," that strongly suggests that an emotional state of *anger* is required. Does an emotional state of *fear* also support a provocation defense? Should it? Jurisdictions vary in answering this question. In the following excerpt, Professor Michal Buchandler-Raphael argues that fear should be so recognized.

Fear-Based Provocation

Michal Buchandler-Raphael

67 Am. U. L. Rev. 1719 (2018)

A. The Psychology of Fear

… [P]sychologists now agree that emotions serve "an adaptive coordination role" that trigger a set of behavioral responses, one important implication of these research findings concerns individuals' resulting behavioral responses to fear. Psychological researcher Joseph Cesario notes that the behavioral outcomes of fear may consist of five distinct responses, including flee, freeze, hide, attack, and assess risk. While lay societal perceptions often assume that fear is more likely to result in a flee or freeze response rather than in aggression, Cesario found that the more common responses to fear are either flight or fight.…

Another research finding pertains to the duration of experiencing fear. In general, researchers agree that full-blown emotions are commonly short-lived, and that fear, specifically, is often an acute, sudden, and short-lived reaction to an immediate threat. While "[e]motions are initially elicited rapidly and can trigger swift action," psychological research also recognizes that once activated, "some emotions … can trigger more systemic thoughts." Consequently, researchers now "distinguish[] between the cognitive consequences of an emotion-elicitation phase and an emotion-persistence phase." Furthermore, researchers note that fear sometimes carries ongoing consequences—particularly that fear and anticipatory anxiety about a future dangerous event may linger longer in circumstances where a person has been subjected to continuous abuse for an extended period of time. In such cases, the longevity of the psychological repercussions of past physical abuse continues to have an impact on some individuals' future perception of risk. A growing body of research suggests that victims of long-term physical and emotional abuse experience a variety of symptoms long after the actual abuse has ended, including fear, anxiety, stress, and anger. For example, severe past trauma and abuse that results in intense fear may cause long-term stress, negatively affecting all areas of functioning. Research further shows that domestic violence victims suffer from a host of serious long-term mental health problems even after separating from abusive partners, including depression, anxiety, and PTSD. Moreover, the traumatic effects of physical abuse are especially exacerbated in the case of spousal abuse due to the fact that the abused person is emotionally involved with the abuser, therefore further explaining why fear may linger on, even when the threat of harm has been completely removed.…

B. Psychological Research's Implications for Fear-Based Provocation

Psychological research findings offer important insights on the scope of the provocation defense, and particularly on recognizing fear-based provocation. Understanding how fear affects a person's judgment and decision making processes explains why the prevalent perception of provocation as an anger-based defense proves unfit for accommodating the experiences of fearful killers. Since provocation's elements are incompatible with the way fear operates, even in jurisdictions that do not view provocation and self-defense as mutually exclusive, fearful killers trying to rely on provocation are often unsuccessful.

The subsections below elaborate on the three main features that defendants who kill out of fear experience: (1) fear results in interference with defendants' reasoning and judgment processes; (2) fear is often cumulative, simmering slowly over a prolonged time period; and (3) fear might linger for long periods, resulting in a failure to cool off, even with lapse of time. While these three factors are critical for recognizing fear-based provocation, they are currently not embedded in existing understanding of anger-based provocation.

1. Fear-based provocation's rationale: impaired judgment

Psychological research reveals that intense fear may result in significantly impaired thought processes, leading defendants to act out of distorted reasoning and judgment. Acknowledging that fear undermines rational judgment explains why fearful people might kill. Yet, as previously noted, the main rationale upon which anger-based provocation is predicated is the notion of loss of control. This model, however, is unsuitable to capture the distinct features characterizing the typical responses of fearful killers.

One implication of the psychological finding that fear may impair rational judgment is that fear does not necessarily result in a visible response that may be characterized as loss of control. In fact, fearful killers may outwardly appear calm, cool, composed, and in control of their actions. Defendants who externally exhibit visible signs of control of their emotions may lead decision makers to conclude mistakenly that these defendants killed in acts of calculated and deliberate revenge, seeking personal vendetta against the deceased individuals who wronged them. But in fact, these fearful killers might have killed as a result of significant distortion in their judgment and rational thinking. Predicating the provocation defense on the loss of control rationale therefore raises a concern regarding disparate treatment of angry and fearful killers. Angry defendants whose behavior is *externally* manifested as an impulsive act of loss of control might be treated more favorably than fearful killers whose typical response might be perceived by decision makers as the exact opposite of loss of control that is as deliberate and calculated.

Shifting provocation's focal point from loss of control towards the destruction of reasoning and judgment provides a coherent rationale for recognizing fear-based provocation. Conceding that a fearful killer's thought process has been significantly distorted as a result of the deceased's threatening behavior offers normative grounds for mitigation. When defendants kill in response to such threats, their moral culpability is diminished compared to defendants who kill in other circumstances. Put differently, when distortion in a defendant's judgment is powerful enough, it is sufficient to make the act of killing far less morally culpable than it would have been absent such distortion. Since a defendant's ability to rationally assess the situation is significantly undermined by the impact of fear, mitigating charges from murder to manslaughter is warranted.

Emphasizing the impact of fear on defendants' decision making processes is also consistent with a basic tenet of criminal law, under which the degree of criminal liability ought to be derivative and proportional to the degree of defendants' moral culpability. Recognizing fear-based provocation would allow the law to reflect proper gradations of criminal culpability based on varying levels of moral blameworthiness. Reducing murder to voluntary manslaughter, rather than completely acquitting of any crime, reflects prevailing societal perceptions that killing in circumstances falling short of self-defense still warrants criminal penalty. But at the same time, it acknowledges that a defendant whose cognitive and volitional capabilities were significantly impaired is not as morally culpable as one whose capabilities remained intact.

Additionally, conceding that both anger and fear may distort rational judgments should also take into consideration the fact that the psychological reality is that these emotions sometimes overlap, operating jointly. Grounding a defense on decision makers' determination of whether the killer was primarily angry or primarily fearful is inherently problematic because it lacks support in psychological research. Since in some cases the same deceased's behavior that angers a defendant also establishes the defendant's fear of physical violence, legal doctrine ought to acknowledge that provocation may often be triggered by an indistinguishable combination of fear and anger. If both anger and fear may destruct defendants' rational judgment, even if such destruction is differently manifested, there is no principled basis for the law's privileging one emotion over the other. Anger and fear ought to be similarly treated, with both providing grounds for mitigation of murder charges to manslaughter.

2. The cumulative impact of fear

The provocation defense was traditionally not available to defendants who were subjected to multiple provoking acts over an extended period of time. Existing provocation doctrine still envisions a raging defendant who has undertaken a spontaneous act of aggression, triggered by a single and sudden provoking event. Only a minority of jurisdictions recognize the notion of cumulative provocation, namely the additive effect of previous multiple physical abuses as adequate provocation culminating in the killing. A key impediment to incorporating a fear-based trigger into existing provocation defense lies with many jurisdictions' refusal to recognize the cumulative effect of a series of triggering incidents, increasingly building up over a long period of time. Since many jurisdictions define provocation as requiring a sudden and serious incident, a series of past provoking incidents in the course of prolonged abuse would not satisfy this requirement. This is especially apparent when defendants kill following the deceased's threat to kill in the future, but given previous threats of a similar nature, the specific threat preceding the killing is not deemed in itself sudden and sufficiently serious. Psychological research demonstrates that particularly in cases of domestic abuse, a killing may result from a "slow burn" reaction to fear of an abuser, accumulating over a prolonged time period of abuse. Case law further illustrates that domestically battered people who were subjected to physical abuse for a long time may kill their abusers in response to many past abusive incidents. In these circumstances, the killing is the culmination of slow simmering of multiple incidents, which are often part of a repetitive pattern of abuse that gradually builds up over time. Provocation law's emphasis on the suddenness of the triggering incident proves inapt in cases where defendants did not react in response to one serious sudden incident but rather in response to the cumulative effect of a series of actual or threatened violence.

3. The lingering effect of fear

The cooling off requirement presents an additional obstacle for fearful killers trying to establish the elements of the provocation defense. Since provocation doctrine requires a sudden act, the presence of a cooling off period typically negates any mitigating effect which the provocation might have had. Most courts require that a relatively short interval — often only a few minutes — occur between the provocation and the killing. While many jurisdictions have relaxed the cooling off requirement, leaving the issue to the jury, the impact of this element persists as juries might reject the defense in cases where they believe that there was sufficient time for the defendant's passions to cool off. Despite many jurisdictions' shifting from a stringent cooling off requirement towards evaluating the lapse of time factor under reasonableness standards, provocation's temporal requirement still presents a significant hurdle for fearful killers attempting to raise the provocation defense. This enduring limitation fails to take into account the psychological research findings that fear may carry lingering effects.

Commentators observe that even if the temporal requirement is modified, existing emphasis on the jury's evaluation of the reasonableness of the defendant's reaction to the provoking incident remains problematic, especially for killers who are women. Additionally, the cooling off requirement has proven especially problematic for people who suffered domestic abuse, often women, who endured long term terror by their abusers. These abused people may first exhibit symptoms of depression and desperation and react violently only after a lapse of time between the last battering incident and the killing. The problem is especially apparent when these defendants kill their abusers in non-confrontational circumstances, such as when the abusers were sleeping since the defendants had ample time to cool off after the most recent battering incident. The current view of the provocation defense, with its deeply embedded assumption that passage of time provides defendants with sufficient time to cool off and regain back control, is inconsistent with the actual experiences of these fearful killers.

The judicial reluctance to acknowledge the lingering effects of fear is incompatible with the psychological research. This research buttresses abused defendants' claims that their continuous abuse placed them in a perpetual state of terror that never dissipated, and that their reactive aggression was a response to extreme fear of future violence by the abuser. This research further rebuts the myth that time heals all wounds, supporting battered defendants' perceptions of long-lasting fear. In sum, the elements of existing provocation defense demonstrate that current law is not informed by the psychological research on how fear operates and its lingering impact.

Discussion Question

1. Should the criminal law recognize fear-based provocation as Professor Buchandler-Raphael argues? If so, how would you draft the elements of such a defense?

2. If a fear-based provocation instruction were given in Ms. Goff's case, how do you think the jury would respond?

3. What implications does recognition of fear-based provocation have for battered spouses?

d. Provocation Outside the Homicide Context

The provocation defense is something of an anomaly because although it can reduce murder to manslaughter, outside the homicide context it generally does not mitigate a criminal offense. Should provocation mitigate non-homicide offenses? Should a defendant have his or her offense level reduced because a provocateur's conduct prompted the defendant to seriously injure rather than kill the provocateur? Or prompted the defendant to damage the victim's property rather than kill the victim? Does it make sense based on the purposes of punishment that defendants who kill provocateurs receive mitigation while those who simply injure provocateurs or their property do not receive mitigation? In relation to these questions, consider the following problem based on the infamous beating of Rodney King by Los Angeles police officers.

Problem

6.14 After spending the night watching a basketball game at a friend's house, Rodney was driving in the early morning hours on a freeway with two other men in his car. Two police officers saw that Rodney was speeding and attempted to pull him over. Rodney had been drinking and his blood-alcohol level was twice the legal limit. Rodney was on parole for a previous robbery conviction and attempted to outrun the officers because a drunk-driving charge would have violated his parole and possibly sent him back to prison. Rodney led the officers on a high-speed chase for five hours. Several police cars and a police helicopter chased Rodney as he left the freeway and drove onto residential streets at speeds between 55 and 80 mph. Eventually several police cars cornered and trapped Rodney's car. When Rodney got out of his car, one witness said that he giggled and waved at the police helicopter overhead. Four officers swarmed Rodney to subdue and handcuff him. Rodney resisted and one of the police officers twice shocked him with a Taser device. Rodney rose from the ground and rushed toward one of the officers and collided with him. Another officer struck Rodney with a baton and several officers surrounded Rodney and continued to strike him with their batons even after he had been restrained. Assume a jury convicts the police officers of a criminal civil rights violation based on their use of excessive force after Rodney had been restrained. Did Rodney provoke the police officers' use of excessive force? If so, should that mitigate their criminal punishment? Does it mitigate their punishment under the following Federal Sentencing Guideline?

United States Sentencing Guidelines
§ 5k2.10. Victim's Conduct (Policy Statement).

If the victim's wrongful conduct contributed significantly to provoking the offense behavior, the court may reduce the sentence below the guideline range to reflect the nature and circumstances of the offense. In deciding ... the extent of a sentence reduction, the court should consider:

1. The size and strength of the victim, or other relevant physical characteristics, in comparison with those of the defendant.

2. The persistence of the victim's conduct and any efforts by the defendant to prevent confrontation.

3. The danger reasonably perceived by the defendant, including the victim's reputation for violence.

4. The danger actually presented to the defendant by the victim.

5. Any other relevant conduct by the victim that substantially contributed to the danger presented.

6. The proportionality and reasonableness of the defendant's response to the victim's provocation.

Victim misconduct ordinarily would be insufficient to warrant application of this provision in the context of offenses under Chapter Two, Part A, Subpart 3 (Criminal Sexual Abuse). In addition, this provision usually would not be relevant in the context of non-violent offenses. There may, however, be unusual circumstances in which substantial victim misconduct would warrant a reduced penalty in the case of a non-violent offense. For example, an extended course of provocation and harassment might lead a defendant to steal or destroy property in retaliation.

C. Extreme Reckless Murder

In this section, we focus on murder based on extreme recklessness. This category of homicide can be diagrammed as follows:

Mental Elements		Non-Mental Elements
Purpose	→	Conduct
Extreme Recklessness	→	Death

Several issues recur throughout the materials on extreme reckless murder. One is the normative question of whether some people who kill recklessly—that is, without either purpose or knowledge about the resulting death—should be treated and labeled as murderers. Are some who kill with recklessness as blameworthy as those who kill with purpose or knowledge? Are some as dangerous? The common law said "yes" to these questions by treating extreme recklessness as a type of "implied malice" thereby including some reckless killings as murder. Following that lead, murder statutes across the United States currently include some type of reckless murder. As the *Fleming* case, below, reveals, the federal murder statute includes certain reckless killings as does the Model Penal Code. So, it is clear that across the United States some reckless killings do qualify as murders.

But *which* reckless killings qualify as murder? This question, as you will see in the materials below, does not have a clear answer. The common law used colorful verbiage, such as an actor having an "abandoned and malignant heart" to describe what brought certain killers within this category of murder. Current statutes and cases often use similarly colorful but not terribly enlightening language in dealing with reckless murder.

Reckless killings typically qualify for manslaughter, a category of homicide we will examine in the next section of this Chapter. What distinguishes reckless killings that qualify for *murder* from those that qualify for *manslaughter*? Although virtually every American jurisdiction recognizes extreme reckless murder, none does a good job of distinguishing the criteria for extreme reckless murder from the criteria for reckless manslaughter. Here are some possibilities to consider:

- the magnitude of the risk taken
- the unjustifiability of the risk taken
- the degree of deviation from reasonableness
- whether the killer was *aware* of the risk

- whether the killer was violating some law other than homicide law
- whether the killer had an antisocial motive
- whether the killer had *purpose* regarding the risk taken (as opposed to purpose regarding the death itself)
- whether the killer was truly *indifferent* to whether someone died

As you read the materials that follow, compare the various criteria that are used in formulating what is required for extreme reckless murder. What combination of factors do the courts and legislators rely on in assessing whether the defendant possessed extreme recklessness? Which of these factors do the *Fleming* and *Berry* opinions rely on? Which does the Model Penal Code rely on?

Problems

6.15 Both Christopher and Beth are recovering heroin addicts participating in a government-supervised drug treatment program. They regularly take methadone, a synthetic narcotic used to wean addicts off heroin, which is legally provided to them as part of their treatment program. For the past two years, Christopher and Beth have been raising their three-year-old nephew, Jordi. Jordi is the son of Beth's sister, who had been raising Jordi as a single parent. She died of cancer when Jordi was six months old. Since that time Christopher and Beth have been raising Jordi. Friends and relatives state unequivocally that Christopher and Beth cared deeply for Jordi.

A few days ago, Beth asked Christopher to store some extra methadone in their refrigerator. Christopher did so, but he placed the methadone, which had been mixed with cranberry juice to make it more palatable, in a plastic cup that Jordi regularly used. After playing outside, Jordi came in looking for something to drink. He drank the methadone and cranberry juice mixture, then fell asleep. Both Christopher and Beth had forgotten that the methadone was in the refrigerator. Beth was away from the house when Jordi drank the methadone. She came home in the early evening and found Jordi asleep. When she could not rouse him, she called 911. Jordi died shortly thereafter from drinking the methadone. Friends and relatives say that Christopher and Beth have been devastated by Jordi's death. Are Christopher and Beth liable for homicide? For murder?

6.16 Craig and Andy are friends. One night at Craig's house, Craig suggests a game of "Russian Roulette." Andy agrees. Craig fetches his handgun, places it against Andy's head, and pulls the trigger. The gun fires and Andy is instantly killed. Is Craig liable for homicide? For murder? Would the following factual variations make a difference in his liability?

(a) Craig thinks the gun is empty when he pulls the trigger and he fails to check it before pulling the trigger.

(b) Craig thinks the gun is empty when he fetches it and fails to check all the chambers of the gun's barrel. The gun has a six-chambered revolver that rotates clockwise. Craig places a single bullet in the chamber immediately to the right of the firing pin. He then closes the barrel, puts the gun to Andy's head, and pulls the trigger. The bullet that kills Andy is not the one Craig placed in the chamber to the right of the firing pin. It turns out that Craig's brother earlier that day had placed several other bullets in the gun. It is one of these that kills Andy.

(c) There is only one bullet in the gun, which Craig places there before firing. Craig spins the barrel once, then fires three times with the gun placed against Andy's head. The third shot kills Andy.

(d) There is only one bullet in the gun, which Craig places there before firing. Craig places the gun against Andy's head. Craig fires three times, spinning the barrel prior to each shot. The third shot kills Andy.

(e) Craig and Andy take turns putting the gun to their own heads and firing, spinning the barrel before each pull of the trigger. Andy goes first and Craig second. Nothing happens on either of these pulls of the trigger. Andy then takes another turn placing the gun against his own head and firing. On this third turn, the gun goes off, killing Andy.

Before reading the *Fleming* case, read the following federal statute under which Fleming was tried and convicted. Does it set forth a category of reckless murder? If so, what language does it use to do so? Is reckless murder first or second degree murder under this statute?

18 United States Code

§ 1111 -Murder

(a) Murder is the unlawful killing of a human being with malice aforethought. Every murder perpetrated by poison, lying in wait, or any other kind of willful, deliberate, malicious, and premeditated killing; or committed in the perpetration of, or attempt to perpetrate, any arson, escape, murder, kidnaping, treason, espionage, sabotage, aggravated sexual abuse or sexual abuse, burglary, or robbery; or perpetrated from a premeditated design unlawfully and maliciously to effect the death of any human being other than him who is killed, is murder in the first degree.
Any other murder is murder in the second degree.

United States v. Fleming

739 F.2d 945 (4th Cir. 1984)
United States Court of Appeals for the Fourth Circuit

Winter, C.J.

This case requires us to decide whether a non-purposeful vehicular homicide can ever amount to murder. We conclude that it can.

Defendant David Earl Fleming was convicted of second-degree murder, in violation of 18 U.S.C. § 1111, in the death of Margaret Jacobsen Haley. Mrs. Haley was the driver of an automobile with which an automobile operated by the defendant collided when defendant lost control while traveling at a high rate of speed.

Fleming's car was observed at about 3:00 p.m. on June 15, 1983, traveling southbound on the George Washington Memorial Parkway in northern Virginia at speeds variously estimated by witnesses as between 70 and 100 miles per hour. The speed limit on the Parkway is, at most points, 45 miles per hour. Fleming several times directed his southbound car into the northbound lanes of the Parkway in order to avoid traffic congestion in the southbound lanes. Northbound traffic had to move out of his way in order to avoid a head-on collision. At one point, a pursuing police officer observed Fleming steer his car into the northbound lanes, which were separated from the southbound lanes at that point and for a distance of three-tenths of a mile by a raised concrete median, and drive in the northbound lanes, still at a high rate of speed, for the entire length of the median. At two other points, Fleming traveled in northbound lanes that were separated from the southbound lanes by medians.

Approximately six miles from where his car was first observed traveling at excessive speed, Fleming lost control of it on a sharp curve. The car slid across the northbound lanes, striking the curb on the opposite side of the highway. After striking the curb, Fleming's car straightened out and at that moment struck the car driven by Mrs. Haley that was coming in the opposite direction. Fleming's car at the moment of impact was estimated by witnesses to have been traveling 70 to 80 miles per hour; the speed limit at that point on the Parkway was 30 miles per hour. Mrs. Haley received multiple severe injuries and died before she could be extricated from her car.

Fleming was pulled from the wreckage of his car and transported to a Washington hospital for treatment. His blood alcohol level was there tested at .315 percent.

Fleming was indicted by a grand jury on a charge of second-degree murder and a number of other charges which are not relevant to this appeal. He was tried before a jury on the murder charge and convicted.

Defendant maintains that the facts of the case cannot support a verdict of murder. Particularly, defendant contends that the facts are inadequate to establish the existence of malice aforethought, and thus that he should have been convicted of manslaughter at most.

Malice aforethought, as provided in 18 U.S.C. § 1111(a), is the distinguishing characteristic which, when present, makes a homicide murder rather than manslaughter.[2] Whether malice is present or absent must be inferred by the jury from the whole facts and circumstances surrounding the killing.

Proof of the existence of malice does not require a showing that the accused harbored hatred or ill will against the victim or others. Neither does it require proof of an intent to kill or injure. Malice may be established by evidence of conduct which is "reckless and wanton and a gross deviation from a reasonable standard of care, of such a nature that a jury is warranted in inferring that defendant was aware of a serious risk of death or serious bodily harm." To support a conviction for murder, the government need only have proved that defendant intended to operate his car in the manner in which he did with a heart that was without regard for the life and safety of others.[3]

We conclude that the evidence regarding defendant's conduct was adequate to sustain a finding by the jury that defendant acted with malice aforethought. It is urged upon us, however, that a verdict of murder in this case should be precluded by the existence of a statute defining and proscribing involuntary manslaughter, 18 U.S.C. § 1112(a).[4] Defendant maintains that vehicular homicide where no purpose on the part of the accused to have caused death or injury has been shown should result only in conviction of involuntary manslaughter. Otherwise, defendant argues, all drunk driving homicides and many reckless driving ones will be prosecutable as murder. We are not persuaded by the argument.

The difference between malice, which will support conviction for murder, and gross negligence, which will permit of conviction only for manslaughter, is one of degree rather than kind. In the vast majority of vehicular homicides, the accused has not exhibited such wanton and reckless disregard for human life as to indicate the

---

2. Malice aforethought is a concept that originated with the common law and is used in 18 U.S.C. § 1111(a) in its common law sense. The statute's terms, since known to and derived from the common law, are referable to it for interpretation. Accordingly, we do not confine our consideration of the precedents to decisions of federal courts interpreting the federal statute, but rather consider other sources which may shed light on the issues of this case.

3. We note that, even assuming that subjective awareness of the risk is required to establish murder where the killing resulted from reckless conduct, an exception to the requirement of subjective awareness of risk is made where lack of such awareness is attributable solely to voluntary drunkenness.... Defendant's state of voluntary intoxication thus would not have been relevant to whether the jury could have inferred from the circumstances of the crime that he was aware of the risk created by his conduct.

4. 18 U.S.C. § 1112(a) provides:
   Manslaughter is the unlawful killing of a human being without malice. It is of two kinds:
   Voluntary—Upon a sudden quarrel or heat of passion.
   Involuntary—In the commission of an unlawful act not amounting to a felony, or in the commission in an unlawful manner, or without due caution and circumspection, of a lawful act which might produce death.

presence of malice on his part. In the present case, however, the facts show a deviation from established standards of regard for life and the safety of others that is markedly different in degree from that found in most vehicular homicides. In the average drunk driving homicide, there is no proof that the driver has acted while intoxicated with the purpose of wantonly and intentionally putting the lives of others in danger. Rather, his driving abilities were so impaired that he recklessly put others in danger simply by being on the road and attempting to do the things that any driver would do. In the present case, however, danger did not arise only by defendant's determining to drive while drunk. Rather, in addition to being intoxicated while driving, defendant drove in a manner that could be taken to indicate depraved disregard of human life, particularly in light of the fact that because he was drunk his reckless behavior was all the more dangerous....

Defendant also contends that the district court erred in admitting into evidence defendant's driving record which showed previous convictions for driving while intoxicated. The driving record would not have been admissible to show that defendant had a propensity to drive while drunk. However, the driving record was relevant to establish that defendant had grounds to be aware of the risk his drinking and driving while intoxicated presented to others. It thus was properly admitted.

Affirmed.

Discussion Questions

1. Under the *Fleming* opinion, what distinguishes reckless murder from manslaughter? Are the criteria for reckless murder objective or subjective?

2. Does Judge Winter clarify whether or not awareness of risk is required for Fleming to be convicted of murder?

3. Judge Winter notes that "In the average drunk driving homicide, there is no proof that the driver has acted while intoxicated with the purpose of wantonly and intentionally putting the lives of others in danger." Is there a difference between having purpose regarding a resulting death and purpose regarding creating a risk of death? Are they equally blameworthy? Equally dangerous?

4. In your view, should there be a category of reckless murder? If so, what would you use to distinguish reckless murder from manslaughter?

* * *

In a California case affirming the conviction of a drunk driver for murder, *People v. Watson*, 30 Cal. 3d 290 (1981), the California Supreme Court described the standard that the prosecution has to prove in order for a court to uphold a murder charge:

> [w]hen a person does "an act, the natural consequences of which are dangerous to life, which act was deliberately performed by a person who knows that his conduct endangers the life of another and who acts with conscious disregard for life".... Phrased a different way, malice may be implied when defendant does an act with a high probability that it will result in death and does it with a base antisocial motive and with a wanton disregard for human life.

In the passage that follows, then Chief Justice Rose Bird dissented in the *Watson* case:

> The fact that [defendant] was under the influence of alcohol made his driving more dangerous. A high percentage of accidents are caused by such drivers. No one holds a brief for this type of activity. However, a rule should not be promulgated by this court that driving while under the influence of alcohol is sufficient to establish an act "likely to kill." Death or injury is not the probable result of driving while under the influence of alcohol. "Thousands, perhaps hundreds of thousands, of Californians each week reach home without accident despite their driving intoxicated." The majority also fail to demonstrate that it is reasonable to infer that [defendant] had a conscious disregard for life. Can a conscious disregard for life be established by the fact that several hours *before* the accident [defendant] drove his car to a bar? The majority hold as a matter of law that he "must have known" he would have to drive his car later and that he wilfully drank alcohol until he was under its influence....
>
> The majority's reasoning also perpetuates the fiction that when a person drinks socially, he wilfully drinks to come under the influence of alcohol and with this knowledge drives home at a later time. This unfounded conclusion ignores social reality. "[T]ypically [a person] sets out to drink without becoming intoxicated, and because alcohol distorts judgment, he overrates his capacity, and misjudges his driving ability after drinking too much."

Discussion Questions

1. Under the passage from the majority opinion in *Watson*, what distinguishes reckless murder from manslaughter? Are these criteria for reckless murder objective or subjective?

2. Would Fleming have been convicted under the *Watson* standard?

3. Upon which criterion or criteria does Chief Justice Bird focus in her dissent? Who is more convincing? The *Watson* majority? Or Chief Justice Bird?

Berry v. Superior Court

208 Cal. App. 3d 783 (1989)
The California Court of Appeals

Agliano, P.J.

The People have charged Michael Patrick Berry, defendant, with the murder of two and one-half-year-old James Soto who was killed by Berry's pit bull dog. Defendant also stands accused of negligent keeping of a mischievous animal which kills a human being (Pen. Code, § 399); marijuana cultivation; and misdemeanor keeping of a fighting dog. By this statutorily authorized petition for a writ of prohibition, defendant seeks dismissal of the charges of murder.... He claims the evidence taken at the preliminary hearing falls legally short of establishing implied malice sufficient to bind over for murder; the factual findings of the magistrate rule out malice; and there is no evidence that the animal was mischievous or was kept without ordinary care.

A reviewing court may not substitute its judgment as to the weight of the evidence for that of the magistrate, and, if there is some evidence to support the information, the court will not inquire into its sufficiency.... Every legitimate inference that may be drawn from the evidence must be drawn in favor of the information." Our task is to decide whether "a person of ordinary caution or prudence would be led to believe and conscientiously entertain a strong suspicion that defendant committed the crime charged."

We have concluded, for reasons we shall state, that judged by this standard of review the record here will support a prosecution for murder. The other charges may also go forward....

The record shows that on June 13, 1987, James Soto, then aged two years and eight months, was killed by a pit bull dog named "Willy" owned by defendant. The animal was tethered near defendant's house but no obstacle prevented access to the dog's area. The victim and his family lived in a house which stood on the same lot, sharing a common driveway. The Soto family had four young children, then aged ten, four and one-half, two and one-half, and one year.

On the day of the child's death, his mother, Yvonne Nunez, left the child playing on the patio of their home for a minute or so while she went into the house, and when she came out the child was gone. She was looking for him when within some three to five minutes her brother-in-law, Richard Soto, called her and said defendant's dog had attacked James. Meanwhile the father, Arthur Soto, had come upon the dog Willy mauling his son. He screamed for defendant to come get the dog off the child; defendant did so. The child was bleeding profusely. Although an on-call volunteer fireman with paramedical training who lived nearby arrived within minutes and attempted to resuscitate the child, James died before an emergency crew arrived at the scene.

There was no evidence that Willy had ever before attacked a human being, but there was considerable evidence that he was bred and trained to be a fighting dog and that he posed a known threat to people. Defendant bought Willy from a breeder of fighting dogs, who informed defendant of the dog's fighting abilities, his gameness, wind, and exceptionally hard bite. The breeder told defendant that in a dog fight "a dog won't go an hour with Willy and live."

The police searched defendant's house after the death of James and found many underground publications about dog fighting; a pamphlet entitled "42 day keep" which set out the 6-week conditioning procedures used to prepare a dog for a match; a treadmill used to condition a dog and increase its endurance; correspondence with Willy's breeder, Gene Smith; photographs of dog fights; and a "break stick," used to pry fighting dogs apart since they will not release on command. One of Smith's letters dated December 7, 1984, described Willy as having an exceptionally hard bite. Two women who knew defendant testified he told them he had raised dogs for fighting purposes and had fought pit bulls.

Richard Soto testified defendant told him he used the treadmill to increase the strength and endurance of his dogs. Defendant also told both Arthur and Richard Soto that he would not fight his dogs for less than $500 and he told Richard Willy had had matches as far away as South Carolina. The victim's mother testified defendant had several dogs. He told her not to be concerned about the dogs, that they would not bother her children, except for "one that he had on the side of the house" which was behind a six-foot fence. Defendant further said this dangerous dog was Willy but that she need not be concerned since he was behind a fence. There was a fence where the dog was tethered on the west side of defendant's house, but the fence was not an enclosure and did not prevent access to the area the dog could reach.

The police found some 243 marijuana plants growing behind defendant's house. Willy was tethered in such location that anyone wanting to approach the plants would have to cross the area the dog could reach. That area was readily accessible to anyone.

An animal control officer qualified as an expert on fighting dogs testified. He said pit bull dogs are selectively bred to be aggressive towards other animals. They give no warning of their attack, attack swiftly, silently and tenaciously. Although many recently bred pit bulls have good dispositions near human beings and are bred and raised to be pets, there are no uniform breeding standards for temperament and the animal control officers consider a pit bull dangerous unless proved otherwise.

Defendant's counsel placed great emphasis on certain testimony of the animal control officer, Miller. Counsel claimed that Miller testified Willy's attack on James was completely unpredictable, and that the People are bound by this testimony and therefore cannot argue that defendant ought to have foreseen what would happen. The testimony occurred during cross-examination, as follows: defendant's counsel asked Miller whether he knew of any prior attacks by Willy, and he said no. Then counsel quoted from an article written by Miller saying that even pit bulls with no prior history of aggression have been known to become highly aggressive "when at large, when in a pack, when confronted by any aggressive dog or under other unpredictable situations." Miller affirmed he believed this. Then counsel ruled out such factors as the dog being at large, in a pack, and so forth, and then said the dog being confronted by the little boy "would come under this unpredictable situation then, wouldn't he?" and Miller said yes. Counsel then asked, "So then what you are saying is is [sic] that without any prior knowledge of unpredictability, Willy could cause an attack such as this, isn't that true?" and Miller said yes.

When testifying, Arthur Soto denied having told any investigator that defendant had warned him about Willy. Counsel interrogating him insinuated that he was afraid to testify about prior warnings because he might jeopardize his civil lawsuit against defendant. Later an officer who had investigated the death and had interviewed Arthur testified pursuant to Evidence Code section 1237 that Arthur had told the officer defendant had warned Arthur to "keep the kids away from the killer dog," meaning Willy.

First, defendant claims that as a matter of law the record does not show implied malice sufficient to require him to stand trial for a charge of second degree murder. As stated above, the issue at this stage of the proceedings is not whether the evidence establishes guilt beyond a reasonable doubt, but rather whether the evidence is sufficient to lead a man of ordinary caution or prudence to believe and conscientiously entertain a strong suspicion of his guilt of this offense, or whether there is some rational ground for assuming the possibility of his guilt.

The case of *People v. Watson,* a case involving reckless driving under the influence, states that the test of implied malice in an unintentional killing is actual appreciation of a high degree of risk that is objectively present. There must be a high probability that the act done will result in death and it must be done with a base antisocial motive and with wanton disregard for life. The conduct in Watson, held sufficient to ground a finding of malice, was reckless speeding while intoxicated. Defendant had prior knowledge of the hazards of drunk driving.

The recent decision in *People v. Protopappas* further elaborates the definition of implied malice. That case found sufficient evidence of implied malice to support the defendant dentist's convictions of the murders of three of his patients, who died because of his recklessness. He clearly did not intend to kill them; as the decision pointed out, it was in his interests to keep them alive so that he could continue to collect fees from them. Further, his failure to provide proper treatment for them could be characterized as an act of omission or neglect rather than an affirmative act of homicide. But the appellate court found sufficient evidence of malice because the jury could infer from his conduct that he actually appreciated the risk to his patients and exhibited extreme indifference to their welfare in failing to provide the proper treatment and care and in administering anesthesia to them in grossly negligent fashion. The court found substantial evidence Protopappas's treatment of his patients was "aggravated, culpable, gross, or reckless" neglect ... [which] involved such a high degree of probability that it would result in death that it constituted "a wanton disregard for human life" making it second degree murder. The *Protopappas* court further elaborated the requirements of implied malice thus: "wantonness, an extreme indifference to [the victim's] life, and subjective awareness of the very high probability of her death."

Interestingly, the court in *Protopappas* referred to the dentist's conduct as "the health care equivalent of shooting into a crowd or setting a lethal mantrap in a dark alley." Similarly here, the People seek to analogize defendant's manner of keeping Willy as the equivalent of setting a lethal mantrap, since anyone could have approached the dog and been at risk of attack.

Another decision which thoughtfully explores the nature of implied malice is *People v. Love....* Love observes that the "continuum of death-causing behavior for which society imposes sanctions is practically limitless with the gradations of more culpable conduct imperceptibly shading into conduct for the less culpable. Our high court has drawn this line placing in the more culpable category not only those deliberate life-endangering acts which are done with a subjective awareness of the risk involved, but also life-endangering conduct which is 'only' done with the awareness the conduct is contrary to the laws of society...."

The decision in *Love* sets forth two prerequisites for affixing second degree murder liability upon an unintentional killing. One requirement is the defendant's extreme indifference to the value of human life, a condition which must be demonstrated by showing the probability that the conduct involved will cause death. Another requirement is awareness either (1) of the risks of the conduct, *or* (2) that the conduct is contrary to law. Here, evidence of the latter requirement is first, that the very possession of Willy may have constituted illegal keeping of a fighting dog. Second, there is evidence that defendant kept Willy to guard marijuana plants, also conduct with elements of illegality and antisocial purpose. Thus the second element which *Love* required could be satisfied here in a number of ways.

Defendant argues that the elements posited in *Love*—awareness of high risk of antisocial or illegal conduct—are insufficient. He says a further requirement is that the defendant have actively killed the victim, rather than being guilty of passive omissions which result in the death....

However, despite defendant's argument that all second degree murders involve acts of commission rather than omission, at least two cases of second degree murder, *Protopappas* and *Burden* arguably rest on reckless failure to provide proper care or treatment. The *Protopappas* court described the defendant's conduct there in precisely those terms. *Burden* rests on a father's neglect in caring for his son, namely, allowing him to starve to death. The *Burden* court said that "the common law does not distinguish between homicide by act and homicide by omission." "Willful failure of a person to perform a legal duty, whereby the death of another is caused, is murder...."

Almost any behavior can alternately be stated as a sin of omission or of commission. Therefore the distinction of active and passive behavior is not a reliable means of distinguishing intentional and unintentional homicide. For example defendant seeks to distinguish the spring gun case (*People v. Ceballos*) as one involving an active act of setting the trap; but his conduct could equally be described as stationing the dog in a dangerous location. Rather, as the cases hold, attention is best focused on the difference in mental state, in the defendant's intent. Death by agency of an "abandoned and malignant heart," more precisely defined in *Watson, supra,* as a subjective appreciation of a high risk of death, is murder; by gross negligence alone is manslaughter.

Have we here evidence of the elements of second degree murder as described in these decisions, namely, the high probability the conduct will result in the death of a human being, a subjective appreciation of the risk, and a base antisocial purpose or motive? The People point to these facts: The homes of defendant and the victim's family shared a lot and were in close proximity, the Soto family had four very young children and defendant knew this; defendant knew the dog Willy was dangerous to the children, as evidenced by the mother's testimony that he told her that the dog could be dangerous but was behind a fence; defendant in fact lulled Yvonne into a false sense of security by assuring her the dangerous dog was behind a fence when he was in fact accessible; defendant bred fighting dogs and had knowledge of the nature and characteristics of fighting pit bulls; defendant had referred to Willy as a "killer dog"; pit bulls in fact are sometimes dangerous and will attack unpredictably and without warning; and Willy was a proven savage fighting dog.

From this mass of evidence it is possible to isolate facts which standing alone would not suffice as the basis of a murder charge. For example, we do not believe that a showing that Willy was dangerous to other dogs, without more, would be sufficient to bind over his owner on a murder charge; there is no evidence in this record that dogs who are dangerous to their own kind are ipso facto dangerous to human beings and therefore there is no support for an inference that the owner of such a dog should be aware of any such danger. But the evidence amassed here goes beyond demonstrating that Willy was aggressive towards his own kind. We believe this record shows first, that Willy's owner may have been actually aware of the dog's potential danger to human beings. This mental state may be proved by showing he kept the dog chained, he warned the child's parents that the dog was dangerous to children, and he spoke of the dog as dangerous. Second, the testimony of the animal control officer could support an inference that fighting pit bull dogs are dangerous to human beings, and the record of defendant's extensive knowledge of the breed could support an inference that he knew such dogs are dangerous.

Defendant argues that the testimony of the animal control officer, Miller, regarding the dangerousness of pit bulls, conclusively establishes that Willy's attack was "unpredictable" in the sense that it could not reasonably have been anticipated. This interpretation is not compelled. Some of that testimony consists of responses to ungrammatical questions and as such does not establish any proposition with certainty.[1] But a possible fair reading of Miller's testimony is that he used "unpredictable" not in the sense that no one could predict whether the dog would ever attack, but rather, in the sense that the dog could be expected to attack without advance warning or apparent cause. Thus Miller's testimony could support an inference that pit bulls are known to be liable to attack human beings. There is also evidence, consisting mainly of physical evidence seized from defendant's home, showing that defendant is a connoisseur of fighting pit bull dogs and had sought out a vicious dog in order to have him fight successfully.

Thus there is a basis from which the trier of fact could derive the two required elements of implied malice, namely existence of an objective risk and subjective awareness of that risk. Additionally, there is arguably some base and antisocial purpose involved in keeping the dog (1) because harboring a fighting dog is illegal and (2) because there is some evidence the dog was kept to guard an illegal stand of marijuana. Illegality of the underlying conduct is not an element of the charge, but may be relevant on the issue of subjective intent.

We do not know the actual probability that a death could result from defendant's conduct in keeping the dog. Presumably that is a question of fact to be submitted to

---

1. The question counsel asked Miller was "So then what you are saying is is [sic] that without any prior knowledge of unpredictability, Willy could cause an attack such as this, isn't that true?" to which he said yes. As a matter of English grammar there is no reliable inference that can be based on this interrogation.

the court or jury upon appropriate instructions requiring that it find a high probability that death would result from the circumstances before it can convict of murder.

Defendant emphasizes the facts that Willy had never before attacked a human being and that he was kept chained on the premises. First, the fact that the dog was kept chained lessened little the risk which he posed, in view of the close proximity of very young children, the obvious risk of a child's wandering near, and indeed being attracted to a seemingly harmless pet, and the easy accessibility to his vicinity. The mere fact he was chained clearly cannot, under the circumstances of record, absolve the owner of blame. Also, the fact that defendant took the precaution of restraining the dog is a fact which might show he knew the dog was dangerous.... A similar inference may rest on the facts the dog was a pit bull, bought for his fighting ability, bred and conditioned as a fighting dog, kept chained, and described by defendant as a killer.... These circumstances clearly support an inference defendant knew his dog was dangerous to humans....

We conclude that it is for the jury to resolve the factual issues of probability of death and subjective mental state. There is sufficient evidence to justify trial for murder on an implied malice theory....

The petition for writ of prohibition is denied.

Discussion Questions

1. Does the *Berry* opinion do a better job than the *Fleming* opinion of clarifying what distinguishes reckless murder from manslaughter? Are the criteria for reckless murder under *Berry* objective or subjective?

2. Does the *Berry* opinion clarify whether or not awareness of risk is required for Berry to be convicted of murder?

3. Should animal owners ever be liable for homicide based on the actions of their animals? For murder? Should it matter what type of animal it is?

4. Is the owner's presence or absence at the time of the attack relevant? Imagine that Mr. Berry saw his pit bull attack his neighbor's child and ran outside screaming "release" to the dog, but the dog failed to release the child. Should that affect the defendant's liability?

5. The *Berry* court refers to the "high probability of death" standard for implied malice as described by *Watson*. Is the magnitude of the risk of death an appropriate standard? What does "high probability" mean? 10 percent? 20 percent? 90 percent?

6. The jury ultimately acquitted Berry of murder but convicted him of manslaughter. What factors do you think might have influenced the jury to convict Berry of manslaughter rather than murder?

The Model Penal Code Approach to Reckless Murder

As noted at the outset of this Section, the Model Penal Code has a category of reckless murder, reflected in the following language.

Model Penal Code § 210.2 Murder

(1) Except as provided in Section 210.3(1) (b), criminal homicide constitutes murder when: ...

(b) it is committed recklessly under circumstances manifesting extreme indifference to the value of human life....

Discussion Questions

1. What criteria does the Model Penal Code use to distinguish reckless murder from manslaughter? Does the MPC formulation for reckless murder differ from the formulation in the *Fleming* opinion? In the *Berry* opinion? Does it improve on the formulations found in *Fleming* and *Berry*? Is it clearer?

2. What do you think it means for "circumstances" to manifest "extreme indifference to the value of human life"? Does this convey a subjective or objective criterion?

3. Apply the MPC approach to reckless murder to the problems set forth at the outset of this Section. Would the defendants in those problems qualify for murder under the MPC standard?

* * *

Problem

6.17 You are a legislator in a jurisdiction that is redrafting its murder statute. Would you recognize reckless murder? If so, how would you draft the criteria for reckless murder?

Final Thoughts on Extreme Reckless Murder

The category of murder that we have referred to as extreme reckless murder and that the common law called "malignant heart" murder has been around for a long time. Despite this fact, legislatures and courts still struggle to define it clearly.

- What lessons should we draw from the persistence of this ambiguity? Should we abandon this category of murder if we can't define it well?

- Do the definitions in this section satisfy the due process specificity requirement we studied in Chapter 2? In other words, do the various verbal formulas, such as "abandoned and malignant heart" and "extreme indifference," provide adequate notice to defendants about the line between murder and manslaughter? Do they provide adequate guidance to prosecutors, judges, and jurors?

- When statutory and judicial definitions of this category of murder are vague, who winds up exercising increased power in setting the boundaries of what constitutes murder?

D. Manslaughter

In this section, we shift our attention from murder to manslaughter. Unlike manslaughter that results from application of the provocation doctrine, the focus here, as it was when we examined extreme reckless murder, is on issues of risk and awareness of risk. What was the probability that the harm would occur? What type of harm was risked? Was there any good reason for taking the risk? While some jurisdictions often require a subjective awareness of risk, as the statutes below reveal, other jurisdictions permit a finding of manslaughter without subjective awareness, relying instead on negligence.

Model Penal Code

§ 210.3 Manslaughter.

(1) Criminal homicide constitutes manslaughter when:

    (a) it is committed recklessly; ...

* * *

The elements of Model Penal Code manslaughter under § 210.3 can be diagrammed as follows:

Mental Elements		Non-Mental Elements
Purpose	→	Conduct
Recklessness	→	Death

18 Pennsylvania Consolidated Statutes Annotated

§ 2504 Involuntary Manslaughter

(a) General Rule — A person is guilty of involuntary manslaughter when as a direct result of the doing of an unlawful act in a reckless or grossly negligent manner, or the doing of a lawful act in a reckless or grossly negligent manner, he causes the death of another person.

New York Penal Law

§ 125.15 Manslaughter in the Second Degree

A person is guilty of manslaughter in the second degree when:

1. He recklessly causes the death of another person; ...

Problem

6.18 Diagram the elements of manslaughter under the Pennsylvania and New York statutes above.

Note the various labels different states attach to the type of manslaughter covered in this section. Some use just the word "manslaughter." Others use the terms "involuntary manslaughter" or "second degree manslaughter." The important thing to pay attention to here is how the crime is defined rather than the label attached to it.

Discussion Questions

1. Should a negligent killing in which the actor was unaware of the risk of death be given the same homicide classification—manslaughter—and receive the same potential penalties as a reckless killing in which the actor was aware of the risk of death? Are those who kill negligently and those who kill recklessly equally blameworthy? Equally dangerous?

2. Based on the statutes above, how does manslaughter differ from reckless murder?

Problems

6.19 Chris is an avid cyclist living in a city with a large cycling community. Chris's favorite route is a 40-mile loop that runs from a city park near his house to another park in a rural area outside the city, then back to the city park. Chris subscribes to an Internet website that allows cyclists to record and post their times for various cycling routes using the GPS built into their cell phones. Chris held the record for the best time on the loop route until a few weeks ago, when another cyclist beat Chris's record by several minutes.

One morning Chris sets out to reclaim the record. On the way out, he rides faster than he ever has. He heads back into the city on pace to set a new record. Once back in the city, Chris runs through red lights and stop signs at several intersections. He comes over a hill and as he descends toward an intersection near the park that marks the end of his route, he is going about 35 mph in a 25-mph zone. When he is about 100 yards from the intersection, the light turns red. Several people, including an elderly man, are in the crosswalk. Chris does not brake when he reaches the crosswalk, but tries to weave his way through the pedestrians without slowing down. He collides with the elderly man, knocking him to the ground. Chris is thrown from his bike onto the ground. A few days later, the elderly man, who was hospitalized following the collision, dies from head injuries he suffered when Chris knocked him to the ground. Is Chris liable for manslaughter? Assume that there is no precedent in the jurisdiction for a cyclist being prosecuted for manslaughter.

6.20 Mary Walker is the mother of four-year-old Laura. One day while attending pre-school, Laura began to cry and complain of pain in her neck. The pain appeared so severe that her teacher and the school nurse took Laura to the emergency room of the local hospital after notifying her mother. The doctor at the emergency room admitted Laura and immediately ordered a battery of tests which showed that Laura was suffering from acute purulent meningitis. Mary arrived at the hospital while the tests were being performed. After the test results were examined, the doctors treating Laura told Mary that Laura was suffering from acute purulent meningitis and that Laura's only chance of survival depended on her receiving immediate medical treatment.

The doctors asked Mary to consent to the recommended medical treatment of Laura. Mary, however, is a member of a religious group whose members believe that disease is a "physical manifestation of errors of the mind." The use of medicine is believed to perpetuate such error and is therefore prohibited within their faith. Accordingly, Mary refused to consent to the suggested medical treatment for Laura. Instead, she contacted a "prayer practitioner" of her faith who prayed for Laura and visited her on several occasions. During the three weeks following the initial diagnosis, Laura lost weight and grew increasingly disoriented and irritable. On the twentieth day following the initial diagnosis, Laura died of acute purulent meningitis having received no medical treatment. The prosecution will present at trial expert medical testimony that with treatment Laura had a very good chance of surviving the illness. Mary will testify at trial that at the time she refused treatment, she believed that the use of prayer rather than medical treatment was in her daughter's best interest and would in fact cure Laura.

The prosecution charges Mary with manslaughter based on Laura's death. Is she liable for manslaughter? Assume that homicide liability in this case would infringe neither the free exercise of religion clause nor the establishment of religion clause of the federal or applicable state constitution.

Commonwealth v. Welansky

316 Mass. 383 (1944)
Supreme Court of Massachusetts

Lummus, J.

On November 28, 1942, and for about nine years before that day, a corporation named New Cocoanut Grove, Inc., maintained and operated a "night club" in Boston, having an entrance at 17 Piedmont Street, for the furnishing to the public for compensation of food, drink, and entertainment consisting of orchestra and band music, singing and dancing. It employed about eighty persons. The corporation, its officers and employees, and its business, were completely dominated by the defendant Barnett Welansky, who is called in this opinion simply the defendant, since his codefendants were acquitted by the jury. He owned, and held in his own name or in the names of others, all the capital stock. He leased some of the land on which the corporate business was carried on, and owned the rest, although title was held for him by his sister. He was entitled to, and took, all the profits. Internally, the corporation was operated without regard to corporate forms, as though the business were that of the defendant as an individual. It was not shown that responsibility for the number or condition of safety exits had been delegated by the defendant to any employee or other person.

The defendant was accustomed to spend his evenings at the night club, inspecting the premises and superintending the business. On November 16, 1942, he became suddenly ill, and was carried to a hospital, where he was in bed for three weeks and remained until discharged on December 11, 1942. During his stay at the hospital, although employees visited him there, he did not concern himself with the night club, because, as he testified, he "knew it would be all right" and that "the same system ... [he] had would continue" during his absence. There is no evidence of any act, omission or condition at the night club on November 28, 1942 (apart from the lighting of a match hereinafter described), that was not within the usual and regular practice during the time before the defendant was taken ill when he was at the night club nearly every evening....

[There were only two entrances and exits intended for the normal use of the night club's patrons. There were also five emergency exits, described as follows.]

(1) A door, opening outward to Piedmont Street, two and one half feet wide, at the head of the stairway leading to and from the basement Melody Lounge. That door apparently was not visible from the greater part of the foyer, for it was in a passageway that ran from one end of the foyer past the office to the stairway. That door was marked "Exit" by an electric sign. It was equipped with a "panic" or "crash" bar, intended to unbolt and open the door upon pressure from within the building. But on the evidence it could have been found that the device just mentioned was regularly made ineffective by having the door locked by a separate lock operated by a key that was kept in a desk in the office. Late in the evening of November 28, 1942, firemen found that door locked and had to force it open with an axe. The jury were entitled to disbelieve the testimony of the defendant that he had instructed the head waiter, who died in the occurrence of that evening, always to keep that door unlocked. It

may be observed that if that door should be left so that it could be opened by means of the panic bar, a patron might leave through that door without paying his bill. It does not appear that anyone watched that door to prevent patrons from so doing.

(2) A door two and one third feet wide leading from the foyer, near the revolving door, into the small vestibule adjoining the office, already described. From that vestibule another similar door, swinging inward, gave egress to Piedmont Street, near the revolving door. The door to Piedmont Street could not be opened fully, because of a wall shelf. And that door was commonly barred in the evening, as it was on November 28, 1942, by a removable board with clothing hooks on it, and by clothing, for in the evening the office and vestibule were used for checking clothing.

(3) A door, opening outward, from the middle of the wall of the main dining room to Shawmut Street, and marked "Exit" by an electric sign. The opening was about three and two thirds feet wide. The defendant testified that this was the principal exit provided for emergencies. From the sides of the opening hung double doors, equipped with "panic" bars intended to unbolt and open the doors upon pressure from within. But on the evening of November 28, 1942, one of the two doors did not open upon pressure, and had to be hammered with a table before it would open. Besides, the "panic" doors were hidden from the view of diners by a pair of "Venetian" wooden doors, swinging inward, and fastened by a hook, which had to be opened before one could operate the "panic" doors. In addition, dining tables were regularly placed near the Venetian doors, one of them within two feet, and these had to be moved away in order to get access to the doors. That condition prevailed on the evening of November 28, 1942.

(4) The service door, two and one half feet wide, swinging inward, leading to Shawmut Street at 8 Shawmut Street. This door was ... in a part of the premises to which patrons were not admitted and which they could not see. This door was known to employees, but doubtless not to patrons. It was kept locked by direction of the defendant, and the key was kept in a desk in the office.

(5) The door, two and three fourths feet wide, swinging inward, leading from a corridor into which patrons had no occasion to go, to Shawmut Street at 6 Shawmut Street. No patron was likely to know of this door. It was kept locked by direction of the defendant, but he ordered the key placed in the lock at seven every evening.

We now come to the story of the fire. A little after ten o'clock on the evening of Saturday, November 28, 1942, the night club was well filled with a crowd of patrons. It was during the busiest season of the year. An important football game in the afternoon had attracted many visitors to Boston. Witnesses were rightly permitted to testify that the dance floor had from eighty to one hundred persons on it, and that it was "very crowded." Witnesses were rightly permitted to give their estimates, derived from their observations, of the number of patrons in various parts of the night club. Upon the evidence it could have been found that at that time there were from two hundred fifty to four hundred persons in the Melody Lounge, from four hundred to five hundred in the main dining room and the Caricature Bar, and two hundred fifty in the Cocktail Lounge. Yet it could have been found that the crowd was no larger than it had been on other Saturday evenings before the defendant was taken ill, and that there had been larger crowds at earlier times. . . .

A bartender in the Melody Lounge noticed that an electric light bulb which was in or near the cocoanut husks of an artificial palm tree in the corner had been turned off and that the corner was dark. He directed a sixteen year old bar boy who was waiting on customers at the tables to cause the bulb to be lighted. A soldier sitting with other persons near the light told the bar boy to leave it unlighted. But the bar boy got a stool, lighted a match in order to see the bulb, turned the bulb in its socket, and thus lighted it. The bar boy blew the match out, and started to walk away. Apparently the flame of the match had ignited the palm tree and that had speedily ignited the low cloth ceiling near it, for both flamed up almost instantly. The fire spread with great rapidity across the upper part of the room, causing much heat. The crowd in the Melody Lounge rushed up the stairs, but the fire preceded them. People got on fire while on the stairway. The fire spread with great speed across the foyer and into the Caricature Bar and the main dining room, and thence into the Cocktail Lounge. Soon after the fire started the lights in the night club went out. The smoke had a peculiar odor. The crowd was panic stricken, and rushed and pushed in every direction through the night club, screaming, and overturning tables and chairs in their attempts to escape.

The door at the head of the Melody Lounge stairway was not opened until firemen broke it down from outside with an axe and found it locked by a key lock, so that the panic bar could not operate. Two dead bodies were found close to it, and a pile of bodies about seven feet from it. The door in the vestibule of the office did not become open, and was barred by the clothing rack. The revolving door soon jammed, but was burst out by the pressure of the crowd. The head waiter and another waiter tried to get open the panic doors from the main dining room to Shawmut street, and succeeded after some difficulty. The other two doors to Shawmut Street were locked, and were opened by force from outside by firemen and others. Some patrons escaped through them, but many dead bodies were piled up inside them. A considerable number of patrons escaped through the Broadway door, but many died just inside that door. Some employees, and a great number of patrons, died in the fire. Others were taken out of the building with fatal burns and injuries from smoke, and died within a few days.

The defendant [was] indicted for manslaughter. . . . [The Commonwealth specified] among other things that the alleged misconduct of the defendant consisted in causing or permitting or failing reasonably to prevent defective wiring, the installation of inflammable decorations, the absence of fire doors, the absence of "proper means of egress properly maintained" and "sufficient proper" exits, and overcrowding. . . .

The defendant was found guilty . . . [and] sentenced to imprisonment in the State prison upon each count for a term of not less than twelve years and not more than fifteen years, the first day of said term to be in solitary confinement and the residue at hard labor.

The Commonwealth disclaimed any contention that the defendant intentionally killed or injured the persons named in the indictments as victims. It based its case on involuntary manslaughter through wanton or reckless conduct. The judge instructed the jury correctly with respect to the nature of such conduct.

Usually wanton or reckless conduct consists of an affirmative act, like driving an automobile or discharging a firearm, in disregard of probable harmful consequences to another. But where, as in the present case, there is a duty of care for the safety of business visitors invited to premises which the defendant controls, wanton or reckless conduct may consist of intentional failure to take such care in disregard of the probable harmful consequences to them or of their right to care.

To define wanton or reckless conduct so as to distinguish it clearly from negligence and gross negligence is not easy. Sometimes the word "wilful" is prefaced to the words "wanton" and "reckless" in expressing the concept. That only blurs it. Wilful means intentional. In the phrase "wilful, wanton or reckless conduct," if "wilful" modifies "conduct" it introduces something different from wanton or reckless conduct, even though the legal result is the same. Wilfully causing harm is a wrong, but a different wrong from wantonly or recklessly causing harm. If "wilful" modifies "wanton or reckless conduct" its use is accurate. What must be intended is the conduct, not the resulting harm. The words "wanton" and "reckless" are practically synonymous in this connection, although the word "wanton" may contain a suggestion of arrogance or insolence or heartlessness that is lacking in the word "reckless." But intentional conduct to which either word applies is followed by the same legal consequences as though both words applied.

The standard of wanton or reckless conduct is at once subjective and objective.... Knowing facts that would cause a reasonable man to know the danger is equivalent to knowing the danger. The judge charged the jury correctly when he said, "To constitute wanton or reckless conduct, as distinguished from mere negligence, grave danger to others must have been apparent, and the defendant must have chosen to run the risk rather than alter his conduct so as to avoid the act or omission which caused the harm. If the grave danger was in fact realized by the defendant, his subsequent voluntary act or omission which caused the harm amounts to wanton or reckless conduct, no matter whether the ordinary man would have realized the gravity of the danger or not. But even if a particular defendant is so stupid [or] so heedless ... that in fact he did not realize the grave danger, he cannot escape the imputation of wanton or reckless conduct in his dangerous act or omission, if an ordinary normal man under the same circumstances would have realized the gravity of the danger. A man may be reckless within the meaning of the law although he himself thought he was careful."

The essence of wanton or reckless conduct is intentional conduct, by way either of commission or of omission where there is a duty to act, which conduct involves a high degree of likelihood that substantial harm will result to another....

The words "wanton" and "reckless" are thus not merely rhetorical or vituperative expressions used instead of negligent or grossly negligent. They express a difference in the degree of risk and in the voluntary taking of risk so marked, as compared with negligence, as to amount substantially and in the eyes of the law to a difference in kind....

For many years this court has been careful to preserve the distinction between negligence and gross negligence, on the one hand, and wanton or reckless conduct on the other. In pleadings as well as in statutes the rule is that "negligence and wilful and wanton conduct are so different in kind that words properly descriptive of the one commonly exclude the other."

Notwithstanding language used commonly in earlier cases, and occasionally in later ones, it is now clear in this Commonwealth that at common law conduct does not become criminal until it passes the borders of negligence and gross negligence and enters into the domain of wanton or reckless conduct. There is in Massachusetts at common law no such thing as "criminal negligence."

Judgments affirmed.

Discussion Questions

1. How does the Massachusetts definition of manslaughter in *Welansky* compare with the Pennsylvania, MPC, and New York definitions in the statutes that preceded the *Welansky* case?

2. Does Massachusetts allow a manslaughter conviction to be based on negligence?

Problem

6.21 After graduating from law school, you are working as counsel to the Judiciary Committee of the Senate of the State of Massachusetts. Assume that *Commonwealth v. Welansky* is currently the controlling case on the definition of manslaughter in Massachusetts. The Senator who chairs the Judiciary Committee is troubled by the *Welansky* case's imprecision in defining manslaughter. She wants you to draft a statute to rectify *Welansky's* ambiguities and clarify how manslaughter is defined in Massachusetts. She asks you to write her a short memo on *Welansky* in two parts: (1) identify the analytical and logical weaknesses in the opinion by Justice Lummus in *Welansky* and (2) draft a statute that remedies these weaknesses.

As you read the *Hall* case that follows, think about how the court's analysis of manslaughter in *Hall* differs from that in *Welansky*. If you were a legislator, which approach to manslaughter would you adopt?

People v. Hall

999 P.2d 207 (2000)
Colorado Supreme Court

Bender, J.

We hold that Nathan Hall must stand trial for the crime of reckless manslaughter. While skiing on Vail mountain, Hall flew off of a knoll and collided with Allen Cobb, who was traversing the slope below Hall. Cobb sustained traumatic brain injuries and died as a result of the collision. The People charged Hall with felony reckless manslaughter.

At a preliminary hearing to determine whether there was probable cause for the felony count, the county court found that Hall's conduct "did not rise to the level of dangerousness" required under Colorado law to uphold a conviction for manslaughter, and the court dismissed the charges. On appeal, the district court affirmed the county court's decision. The district court determined that in order for Hall's conduct to have been reckless, it must have been "at least more likely than not" that death would result. Because the court found that "skiing too fast for the conditions" is not "likely" to cause a another person's death, the court concluded that Hall's conduct did not constitute a "substantial and unjustifiable" risk of death. Thus, the district court affirmed the finding of no probable cause.

The charge of reckless manslaughter requires that a person "recklessly cause the death of another person." For his conduct to be reckless, the actor must have consciously disregarded a substantial and unjustifiable risk that death could result from his actions. We hold that, for the purpose of determining whether a person acted recklessly, a particular result does not have to be more likely than not to occur for the risk to be substantial and unjustifiable. A risk must be assessed by reviewing the particular facts of the individual case and weighing the likelihood of harm and the degree of harm that would result if it occurs. Whether an actor consciously disregarded such a risk may be inferred from circumstances such as the actor's knowledge and experience, or from what a similarly situated reasonable person would have understood about the risk under the particular circumstances.

We hold that under the particular circumstances of this case, whether Hall committed the crime of reckless manslaughter must be determined by the trier of fact. Viewed in the light most favorable to the prosecution, Hall's conduct—skiing straight down a steep and bumpy slope, back on his skis, arms out to his sides, off-balance, being thrown from mogul to mogul, out of control for a considerable distance and period of time, and at such a high speed that the force of the impact between his ski and the victim's head fractured the thickest part of the victim's skull—created a substantial and unjustifiable risk of death to another person. A reasonable person could infer that the defendant, a former ski racer trained in skier safety, consciously disregarded that risk. For the limited purposes of a preliminary hearing, the prosecution provided sufficient evidence to show probable cause that the defendant recklessly caused the victim's death. Thus, we reverse the district court's finding of no probable cause and we remand the case to that court for trial.

On April 20, 1997, the last day of the ski season, Hall worked as a ski lift operator on Vail mountain. When he finished his shift and after the lifts closed, Hall skied down toward the base of the mountain. The slopes were not crowded.

On the lower part of a run called "Riva Ridge," just below where the trail intersects with another called "North Face Catwalk," Hall was skiing very fast, ski tips in the air, his weight back on his skis, with his arms out to his sides to maintain balance. He flew off of a knoll and saw people below him, but he was unable to stop or gain control because of the moguls.

Hall then collided with Cobb, who had been traversing the slope below Hall. The collision caused major head and brain injuries to Cobb, killing him. Cobb was taken to Vail Valley Medical Center, where efforts to resuscitate him failed. Hall's blood alcohol level was .009, which is less than the limit for driving while ability impaired. A test of Hall's blood for illegal drugs was negative.

The People charged Hall with manslaughter and misdemeanor charges that are not relevant to this appeal. At the close of the prosecution's case at the preliminary hearing, the People requested that, with respect to the manslaughter count, the court consider the lesser-included charge of criminally negligent homicide.

The county court held a preliminary hearing to determine whether there was probable cause to support the felony charges against Hall. At the preliminary hearing, the People presented testimony from an eyewitness, the coroner who conducted the autopsy on Cobb's body, an investigator from the District Attorney's office, and the detective who investigated the accident for the Eagle County Sheriff's department.

Judge Buck Allen, who serves as a judge for several mountain towns and lives in Vail, testified that he is an expert skier and familiar with Vail's slopes. He was making a final run for the day when he first noticed Hall on the slope. Allen was on part of the run called "Lower Riva," which is just below the "North Face Catwalk." From that part of the slope, Allen had a direct line of sight to the bottom of the run. Allen said that he could see other skiers traversing the slope below him at least from their waists up and that there were no blind spots on that part of the run.

Hall passed Allen skiing "at a fairly high rate of speed." Allen estimated that Hall was skiing about three times as fast as he was. Allen stated that Hall was "sitting back" on his skis, tips in the air, with his arms out to his sides in an effort to maintain his balance. Hall was skiing straight down the fall line; that is, he was skiing straight down the slope of the mountain without turning from side-to-side or traversing the slope. Hall "bounded off the bumps as he went," and "the terrain was controlling [Hall]" rather than the other way around. In Allen's opinion, Hall was skiing too fast for the skill level he demonstrated, and Hall was out of control "if you define 'out of control' as [not] being able to stop or avoid someone." Although he watched Hall long enough to note Hall's unsafe skiing—approximately two or three seconds—Allen did not see the collision.

Detective McWilliam investigated the collision for the Eagle County Sheriff's office. McWilliam testified that Deputy Mossness said that while Hall could not remember the collision, Hall admitted that as he flew off a knoll and looked down, he saw people below him but could not stop because of the bumps:

> Mr. Hall told [the deputy] that he had been skiing that day, he was an employee of Vail Associates. That he was coming down the mountain and that he—he said he flew off of a knoll, looked down and saw some people below him down the slope, tried to slow down, and that because of the bumps, he wasn't able to stop. And he doesn't remember beyond that point. But he was told that somebody—that he had collided with someone.

McWilliam testified that he interviewed Jonathan Cherin, an eyewitness to the collision between Hall and Cobb. Cherin stated that he saw Hall skiing straight down the slope at a high speed and out of control. He said that Cobb, who appeared to be an inexperienced skier, traversed the slope below Hall when Hall hit some bumps, became airborne, and struck Cobb.

McWilliam testified that Deputy Bishop, an officer on the scene, told McWilliam about the observations of other witnesses to the collision. Bruce Yim said that Hall was skiing too fast, that he was out of control, and that Hall collided with Cobb as Cobb traversed the slope. Loic Lemaner, who was skiing below Cobb at the time of the collision, saw Hall after the collision. Lemaner said that after the collision, Hall struck Lemaner's skis and poles, breaking one of Lemaner's poles in half.

McWilliam said that the trail was 156 feet across at the point of the collision. Cobb's body came to rest slightly to the right of the center of the slope. Hall came to rest in the center of the trail, approximately eighty-three feet below Cobb's body.

Upon cross-examination, McWilliam testified that in eleven years' experience in Eagle County, he was aware of two other collisions between skiers on Vail mountain that resulted in the death of a skier. McWilliam said that deaths on Vail mountain from such collisions are rare.

Sandberg, an investigator for the District Attorney's office, testified that he spoke with Mark Haynes, who had been Hall's high school ski coach. Haynes told Sandberg that in the years he coached Hall, Hall was one of the top two or three skiers on the team and that Hall was "talented and aggressive." Haynes said that Hall participated in slalom and giant slalom races when he was in high school. Haynes taught his skiers to ski safely and under control.

Dr. Ben Galloway, the coroner who performed the autopsy on Cobb's body, testified that Cobb died from a single and traumatic blow to his head that fractured his skull and caused severe brain injuries. The coroner said that the injury was consistent with the impact from an object, such as a ski, striking Cobb's head on a perpendicular plane. In addition to the skull fractures and brain injuries, Cobb had a contusion or bruise around his right eye and had an abrasion across his nose. Although he noted the effects of the failed resuscitation efforts, Galloway saw no signs of trauma to any other parts of Cobb's body, indicating that Cobb's head was the sole area of contact.

Galloway testified that Hall struck Cobb just below his right ear, in an area of the skull where the bones are thickest and "it takes more force to fracture those areas" than other areas of the skull. Galloway described the injury as an "extensive basal skull fracture" with "components" or smaller fractures that extended from the major fracture. The damage to Cobb's skull resulted in "contusions or bruises" on Cobb's brain, a subdural hemorrhage near the brain stem, and "marked swelling of the brain due to cerebral edema." This trauma to Cobb's brain led to cardiorespiratory failure, the cause of Cobb's death. Galloway noted that as a result of the bleeding from Cobb's brain, Cobb aspirated blood into his lungs, "which certainly compromised his ability to breathe." Galloway found that the severe head injury was the sole cause of Cobb's death.

Galloway testified that "it would take considerable force" to cause such an injury: ...

> In my experience in my practice spanning some 25 years, you most commonly
> see this type of fracturing when someone is thrown out of an automobile or
> a moving vehicle and sustains a basal skull fracture.

Following the presentation of these witnesses, the county court considered whether there was sufficient evidence to find probable cause that Hall recklessly caused Cobb's death. The county court reviewed other Colorado manslaughter cases where courts found substantial and unjustified risks of death resulting from conduct such as firing a gun at a person or kicking an unconscious person in the head. The court found that Hall's conduct—which the court characterized as skiing "too fast for the conditions"—did not involve a substantial and unjustifiable risk of death and "does not rise to the level of dangerousness required under the current case law" to sustain a count of manslaughter. Because Hall's conduct did not, in the court's view, involve a substantial and unjustifiable risk of death, the court found that the prosecution failed to provide sufficient proof that Hall acted recklessly. The county court therefore dismissed the manslaughter count.

The prosecution appealed the county court's decision to the district court.... The district court agreed with the county court that the prosecution failed to establish probable cause. The court held that Hall's conduct did not involve a substantial risk of death because any risk created by Hall had a less than fifty percent chance of causing another's death....

The People petitioned this court ... and we granted certiorari to consider the following:

> (1) Whether the district court erred by establishing "more likely than not" as
> the level of substantial risk of death that a defendant must disregard for a
> finding of probable cause that he caused the death of another recklessly; and

> (2) Whether the district court reviewed the wrong criteria and neglected the
> evidence relating specifically to this case in affirming the county court's dis-
> missal of a manslaughter charge at preliminary hearing.

... To demonstrate that Hall committed the crime of manslaughter, the prosecution must provide sufficient evidence to show that the defendant's conduct was reckless. Thus, we focus on describing the mental state of recklessness and determining whether Hall's conduct meets that definition.

As Colorado's criminal code defines recklessness, "A person acts recklessly when he consciously disregards a substantial and unjustifiable risk that a result will occur or that a circumstance exists." Thus, in the case of manslaughter, the prosecution must show that the defendant's conduct caused the death of another and that the defendant:

1) consciously disregarded

2) a substantial and

3) unjustifiable risk that he would

4) cause the death of another.

We examine these elements in detail.

Substantial and Unjustifiable Risk

To show that a person acted recklessly, the prosecution must establish that the person's conduct created a "substantial and unjustifiable" risk. The district court construed some of our earlier cases as requiring that the risk of death be "at least more likely than not" to constitute a substantial and unjustifiable risk of death. In interpreting our cases, the court relied on an erroneous definition of a "substantial and unjustifiable" risk. Whether a risk is substantial must be determined by assessing both the likelihood that harm will occur and the magnitude of the harm should it occur. We hold that whether a risk is unjustifiable must be determined by assessing the nature and purpose of the actor's conduct relative to how substantial the risk is. Finally, in order for conduct to be reckless, the risk must be of such a nature that its disregard constitutes a gross deviation from the standard of care that a reasonable person would exercise.

A risk does not have to be "more likely than not to occur" or "probable" in order to be substantial. A risk may be substantial even if the chance that the harm will occur is well below fifty percent. Some risks may be substantial even if they carry a low degree of probability because the magnitude of the harm is potentially great. For example, if a person holds a revolver with a single bullet in one of the chambers, points the gun at another's head and pulls the trigger, then the risk of death is substantial even though the odds that death will result are no better than one in six. As one court remarked,

> If the potential of a risk is death, that risk is always serious. Therefore, only some likelihood that death will occur might create for most people a "substantial and unjustifiable" risk....

Conversely, a relatively high probability that a very minor harm will occur probably does not involve a "substantial" risk. Thus, in order to determine whether a risk is substantial, the court must consider both the likelihood that harm will occur and the magnitude of potential harm, mindful that a risk may be "substantial" even if the odds of the harm occurring are lower than fifty percent.

Whether a risk is substantial is a matter of fact that will depend on the specific circumstances of each case. Some conduct almost always carries a substantial risk of death, such as engaging another person in a fight with a deadly weapon or firing a gun at another. In such instances, the substantiality of the risk may be evident from the nature of the defendant's conduct and the court will not have to examine the specific facts in detail.

Other conduct requires a greater inquiry into the facts of the case to determine whether it creates a substantial risk of death....

As well as being substantial, a risk must be unjustifiable in order for a person's conduct to be reckless. Whether a risk is justifiable is determined by weighing the nature and purpose of the actor's conduct against the risk created by that conduct. If a person consciously disregards a substantial risk of death but does so in order to advance an interest that justifies such a risk, the conduct is not reckless. For example, if a surgeon performs an operation on a patient that has a seventy-five percent chance of killing the patient, but the patient will certainly die without the operation, then the conduct is justified and thus not reckless even though the risk is substantial.

In addition to the separate analyses that are applied to determine whether a risk is both "substantial" and "unjustified," the concept of a "substantial and unjustifiable risk" implies a risk that constitutes a gross deviation from the standard of care that a reasonable law-abiding person would exercise under the circumstances.... A substantial and unjustifiable risk must constitute a "gross deviation" from the reasonable standard of care in order to justify the criminal sanctions imposed for criminal negligence or reckless conduct, as opposed to the kind of deviation from the reasonable standard of care that results in civil liability for ordinary negligence.

Whether a risk is substantial and unjustified is a question of fact. Hence, at trial, the trier of fact must determine whether the facts presented prove beyond a reasonable doubt that the risk was substantial and unjustified. In the limited context of a preliminary hearing, the court must determine whether a risk was substantial and unjustified by considering the evidence presented in the light most favorable to the prosecution, and the court must ask whether a reasonable person could "entertain" the belief—though not necessarily conclude beyond a reasonable doubt—that the defendant's conduct was reckless based on that evidence.

Conscious Disregard

In addition to showing that a person created a substantial and unjustifiable risk, the prosecution must demonstrate that the actor "consciously disregarded" the risk in order to prove that she acted recklessly. A person acts with a conscious disregard of the risk created by her conduct when she is aware of the risk and chooses to act despite that risk. In contrast to acting "intentionally" or "knowingly," the actor does not have to intend the result or be "practically certain" that the result will occur, he only needs to be "aware" that the risk exists.

Although recklessness is a less culpable mental state than intentionally or knowingly, it involves a higher level of culpability than criminal negligence. Criminal negligence requires that, "through a gross deviation from the standard of care that a reasonable person would exercise," the actor fails to perceive a substantial and unjustifiable risk that a result will occur or a circumstance exists. An actor is criminally negligent when he should have been aware of the risk but was not, while recklessness requires that the defendant actually be aware of the risk but disregard it. Thus, even if she should be, a person who is not actually aware that her conduct creates a substantial and unjustifiable risk is not acting recklessly.

A court or trier of fact may infer a person's subjective awareness of a risk from the particular facts of a case, including the person's particular knowledge or expertise....

In addition to the actor's knowledge and experience, a court may infer the actor's subjective awareness of a risk from what a reasonable person would have understood under the circumstances. When a court infers the defendant's subjective awareness of a risk from what a reasonable person in the circumstances would have known, the court may consider the perspective of a reasonable person in the situation and with the knowledge and training of the actor. Although a court can infer what the defendant actually knew based on what a reasonable person would have known in the circumstances, a court must not confuse what a reasonable person would have known in the circumstances with what the defendant actually knew. Thus, if a defendant engaged in conduct that a reasonable person would have understood as creating a substantial and unjustifiable risk of death, the court may infer that the defendant was subjectively aware of that risk, but the court cannot hold the defendant responsible if she were actually unaware of a risk that a reasonable person would have perceived.

Hence, in a reckless manslaughter case, the prosecution must prove that the defendant acted despite his subjective awareness of a substantial and unjustifiable risk of death from his conduct. Because absent an admission by the defendant such awareness cannot be proven directly, the court or trier of fact may infer the defendant's awareness of the risk from circumstances such as the defendant's training, knowledge, and prior experiences, or from what a reasonable person would have understood under the circumstances.

Risk of Death

The final element of recklessness requires that the actor consciously disregard a substantial and unjustifiable risk of a particular result, and in the case of manslaughter the actor must risk causing death to another person. The risk can be a risk of death to another generally; the actor does not have to risk death to a specific individual. Because the element of a "substantial and unjustifiable risk" measures the likelihood and magnitude of the risk disregarded by the actor, any risk of death will meet the requirement that the actor, by his conduct, risks death to another. That is, only a slight risk of death to another person is necessary to meet this element....

The district court's conclusion that Hall's conduct did not represent a substantial and unjustifiable risk of death rested on an erroneous construction of recklessness. Relying on two of our earlier cases, the court found that for a risk to be "substantial" it must "be at least more likely than not that death would result." As discussed, a risk of death that has less than a fifty percent chance of occurring may nonetheless be a substantial risk depending on the circumstances of the particular case. Because the district court applied a flawed interpretation of the law, we hold that the district court's assessment of probable cause was in error....

We first ask whether the prosecution presented sufficient evidence to show that Hall's conduct created a substantial and unjustifiable risk of death. Like other activities that generally do not involve a substantial risk of death, such as driving a car or installing a heater, "skiing too fast for the conditions" is not widely considered behavior that constitutes a high degree of risk. However, we hold that the specific facts in this case support a reasonable inference that Hall created a substantial and unjustifiable risk that he would cause another's death.

Several witnesses stated that Hall was skiing very fast. Allen and the other eyewitnesses all said that Hall was travelling too fast for the conditions, at an excessive rate of speed, and that he was out of control. Allen said that Hall passed him on the slope travelling three times faster than Allen, himself an expert skier. Sandberg presented testimony that Hall was a ski racer, indicating that Hall was trained to attain and ski at much faster speeds than even skilled and experienced recreational skiers. The witnesses said that Hall was travelling straight down the slope at such high speeds that, because of his lack of control, he would not have been able to stop or avoid another person.

In addition to statements of witnesses, the nature of Cobb's injuries and other facts of the collision support the inference that Hall was skiing at an inordinately high speed when he struck Cobb.... Thus, based on the testimony of the witnesses and the coroner's examination of Cobb's body, a reasonable person could conclude that Hall was skiing at very high speeds, thereby creating a risk of serious injury or death in the event of a skier-to-skier collision.

In addition to Hall's excessive speed, Hall was out of control and unable to avoid a collision with another person.... [A] reasonably prudent person could have concluded that Hall was unable to anticipate or avoid a potential collision with a skier on the trail below him.

While skiing ordinarily carries a very low risk of death to other skiers, a reasonable person could have concluded that Hall's excessive speed, lack of control, and improper technique for skiing bumps significantly increased both the likelihood that a collision would occur and the extent of the injuries that might result from such a collision, including the possibility of death, in the event that a person like Cobb unwittingly crossed Hall's downhill path. McWilliam testified that he was aware of only two other deaths from skier collisions on Vail mountain in the past eleven years, but a reasonable person could have determined that Hall's conduct was precisely the type of skiing that risked this rare result.

We next ask whether a reasonable person could have concluded that Hall's creation of a substantial risk of death was unjustified. To the extent that Hall's extremely fast and unsafe skiing created a risk of death, Hall was serving no direct interest other than his own enjoyment....

In addition to our conclusion that a reasonable person could have entertained the belief that Hall's conduct created a substantial and unjustifiable risk, we must ask whether Hall's conduct constituted a "gross deviation" from the standard of care that a reasonable law-abiding person (in this case, a reasonable, law-abiding, trained ski racer and resort employee) would have observed in the circumstances.

As we noted, the nature of the sport involves moments of high speeds and temporary losses of control. However, the General Assembly imposed upon a skier the duty to avoid collisions with any person or object below him. See § 33-44-109(2).[14] Although this statute may not form the basis of criminal liability, it establishes the minimum standard of care for uphill skiers and, for the purposes of civil negligence suits, creates a rebuttable presumption that the skier is at fault whenever he collides with skiers on the slope below him. A violation of a skier's duty in an extreme fashion, such as here, may be evidence of conduct that constitutes a "gross deviation" from the standard of care imposed by statute for civil negligence. Hall admitted to Deputy Mossness that as he flew off a knoll, he saw people below him but was unable to stop; Hall was travelling so fast and with so little control that he could not possibly have respected his obligation to avoid skiers below him on the slope. Additionally, Hall skied in this manner for some time over a considerable distance, demonstrating that his high speeds and lack of control were not the type of momentary lapse of control or inherent danger associated with skiing. Based on the evidence, a reasonable person could conclude that Hall's conduct was a gross deviation from the standard of care that a reasonable, experienced ski racer would have exercised knowing that other people were on the slope in front of him and that he could not see the area below the knolls and bumps over which he was jumping.

Having determined that Hall's conduct created a substantial and unjustified risk of death that is a gross deviation from the reasonable standard of care under the circumstances, we next ask whether a reasonably prudent person could have entertained the belief that Hall consciously disregarded that risk. Hall is a trained ski racer who had been coached about skiing in control and skiing safely. Further, he was an employee of a ski area and had a great deal of skiing experience. Hall's knowledge and training could give rise to the reasonable inference that he was aware of the possibility that by skiing so fast and out of control he might collide with and kill another skier unless he regained control and slowed down....

Although the risk that he would cause the death of another was probably slight, Hall's conduct created a risk of death. Hall's collision with Cobb involved enough force to kill Cobb and to simulate the type of head injury associated with victims in car accidents. Even though it is a rare occurrence, the court heard testimony that two skiers in the past eleven years died on Vail mountain alone from skier-to-skier collisions. Based on the evidence presented at the preliminary hearing, a reasonable person could conclude that Hall's conduct involved a risk of death.

---

14. Section 33-44-109(2) states:
   Each skier has the duty to maintain control of his speed and course at all times when skiing and to maintain a proper lookout so as to be able to avoid other skiers and objects. However, the primary duty shall be on the person skiing downhill to avoid collision with any person or objects below him.

Thus, interpreting the facts presented in the light most favorable to the prosecution, we hold that a reasonably prudent and cautious person could have entertained the belief that Hall consciously disregarded a substantial and unjustifiable risk that by skiing exceptionally fast and out of control he might collide with and kill another person on the slope.

Obviously, this opinion does not address whether Hall is ultimately guilty of any crime. Rather, we hold only that the People presented sufficient evidence to establish probable cause that Hall committed reckless manslaughter, and the court should have bound Hall's case over for trial.

Discussion Questions

1. How does the mental state standard in *Hall* differ from that in *Welansky*? Which is preferable? Why?

2. How might Hall's conviction affect the behavior of skiers in Colorado? Of resort operators?

E. Negligent Killing

The focus of this section is negligent killing. Some jurisdictions, as you saw in the previous section, treat both reckless and negligent killing as manslaughter. But the Model Penal Code and some states treat negligent killing as a separate and lesser crime called negligent homicide.

Model Penal Code

§ 210.4 Negligent Homicide.

    (1) Criminal homicide constitutes negligent homicide when it is committed negligently.

* * *

The elements of Model Penal Code negligent homicide under § 210.4 can be diagrammed as follows:

Mental Elements		Non-Mental Elements
Purpose	$\longrightarrow$	Conduct
Negligence	$\longrightarrow$	Death

Problems

6.22 Joshua is the father of three-year-old Lucas. Joshua has a .45 caliber handgun that he keeps in a closet. One morning he takes the handgun out of the closet, intending to take it to a local firing range. But before Joshua can leave for the range, his wife asks him to help her put together a swing set she bought for Lucas. Joshua slips the handgun beneath the cushions of a couch in the living room to hide it and goes out into the back yard to help his wife. Shortly thereafter, Joshua and his wife hear a shot. Immediately they run inside and find Lucas dead on the living room floor. Lucas found Joshua's handgun and accidentally shot himself in the head. Investigation reveals that Joshua recently gave Lucas a .22 caliber rifle for Christmas and had been instructing Lucas on how to use it. The police also find a photograph, taken by Joshua's wife, that shows Joshua crouching in the snow and showing Lucas how to shoot the rifle. They find another photograph, taken by Joshua, that shows Lucas holding an AR 15 assault rifle. Is Joshua liable for homicide based on the death of Lucas? If so, for which level of homicide?

6.23 Patricia is the 26-year-old mother of four-year-old Malcolm. Patricia's boyfriend, Robert, is a private security guard. One day when the battery in Patricia's car dies, Robert lends Patricia his car to make a trip to the grocery store. Patricia sets out for the grocery store with her mother in the front passenger seat and Malcolm in the back seat. Malcolm is not in a car seat, nor is he restrained by a seat belt. Robert's bulletproof security vest and his gun belt are on the floor of the back seat where Malcolm is sitting. Patricia stops for a red light and as she accelerates the car after the stop, Robert's .40 caliber handgun, which Robert had placed under the driver's seat, slides out from under the driver's seat onto the floor in front of the rear seat where Malcolm is sitting. Malcolm picks up the gun and while he is playing with it, the gun goes off.

Part (a) Assume that the bullet from the gun passes through the *driver's* seat from behind and kills Patricia. Is Robert liable for homicide? If so, for which level of homicide?

Part (b) Assume that the bullet from the gun passes through the front *passenger's* seat and kills Patricia's mother. Is Robert liable for homicide? Is Patricia? If so, for which level of homicide?

6.24 Jeffrey, who is 12 years old, is riding in the back of a pickup truck in the rural area where he and his family live. In the back of the truck with him are his sister, Cassie, who is 11 years old, and two other children. Jeffrey starts playing with a pistol his father had lent him to scare coyotes. Believing he removed all the bullets from the pistol, Jeffrey points the pistol at Cassie's head and pulls the trigger. The pistol fires and Cassie is instantly killed. Is Jeffrey liable for homicide? Is Jeffrey's father liable for homicide? If so, for which level of homicide?

6.25 Andrew is 16 years old and enrolled in a gun safety class. His father, Don, keeps an unloaded 20-gauge shotgun in a family gun cabinet that is locked. One day, excited about going to his gun safety class that evening, Andrew unlocks the cabinet and removes the shotgun. He places a single shell in the shotgun and pulls the hammer back. At this point Andrew becomes frightened and decides to put the gun back in the case. But as he attempts to do so, his finger slips and the shotgun fires, killing his 12-year-old sister. Andrew immediately calls 911, but by the time paramedics arrive, his sister is dead. Is Andrew liable for homicide? Is Don? If so, for which level of homicide?

6.26 A construction crew is working at night on a seldom-used road. They have dug a trench to access electrical connections underground. Before their break at 2:00 a.m., they place reflective orange cones around the trench and hang reflective tape from cone to cone so that it encircles the trench at a height of 12 inches. Car headlights would clearly reveal and highlight the reflective tape, warning drivers to beware. A bicyclist cycles by in the dark. When his tire hits the reflective tape, he is thrown into the trench and dies. Is the supervisor of the construction crew liable for homicide? If so, for which level of homicide?

Reconsider at this point **Problem 6.20**:

Mary Walker is the mother of four-year-old girl Laura. One day while attending pre-school, Laura began to cry and complain of pain in her neck. The pain appeared so severe that her teacher and the school nurse took Laura to the emergency room of the local hospital after notifying her mother. The doctor at the emergency room admitted Laura and immediately ordered a battery of tests which showed that Laura was suffering from acute purulent meningitis. Mary arrived at the hospital while the tests were being performed. After the test results were examined, the doctors treating Laura told Mary that Laura was suffering from acute purulent meningitis and that Laura's only chance of survival depended on her receiving immediate medical treatment.

The doctors asked Mary to consent to the recommended medical treatment of Laura. Mary, however, is a member of a religious group whose members believe that disease is a "physical manifestation of errors of the mind." The use of medicine is believed to perpetuate such error and is therefore discouraged within their faith. Accordingly, Mary refused to consent to the suggested medical treatment for Laura. Instead, she contacted a "prayer practitioner" of her faith who prayed for Laura and visited her on several occasions. During the three weeks following the initial diagnosis, Laura lost weight and grew increasingly disoriented and irritable. On the twentieth day following the initial diagnosis, Laura died of acute purulent meningitis having received no medical treatment. The prosecution will present at trial expert medical testimony that with medical treatment Laura had a very good chance of surviving the illness. Mary will testify at trial that at the time she refused treatment, she believed that the use of prayer rather than medical treatment was in her daughter's best interest and would in fact cure Laura.

Would Mary be liable for homicide based on negligence if she was prosecuted under the manslaughter statute used in *State v. Williams*, below? Would she be liable for negligent homicide under the Model Penal Code?

Criminal law typically requires a level of negligence that exceeds the simple or ordinary negligence that may give rise to tort liability in a civil lawsuit. Such negligence is often termed *gross negligence*. Some jurisdictions do, however, impose homicide liability based on simple or ordinary negligence. Should negligent killing ever be a criminal offense? Or should liability for negligent killing be limited to civil money damages? What are the comparative advantages and disadvantages of criminal and civil liability as a deterrent to negligent killing?

The *Williams* case and the Problem that follows it below raise a number of troubling issues about the intersection of criminal law with poverty, race, and being viewed by some as an "outsider" to their community.

State v. Williams

4 Wash. App. 908 (1971)
Court of Appeals of Washington

Horowitz, C.J.

Defendants, husband and wife, were charged by information filed October 3, 1968, with the crime of manslaughter for negligently failing to supply their 17-month child with necessary medical attention, as a result of which he died on September 12, 1968. Upon entry of findings, conclusions and judgment of guilty, sentences were imposed on April 22, 1969. Defendants appeal.

The defendant husband, Walter Williams, is a 24-year-old full-blooded Sheshone Indian with a sixth-grade education. His sole occupation is that of laborer. The defendant wife, Bernice Williams, is a 20-year-old part Indian with an 11th grade education. At the time of the marriage, the wife had two children, the younger of whom was a 14-month old son. Both parents worked and the children were cared for by the 85-year-old mother of the defendant husband. The defendant husband assumed parental responsibility with the defendant wife to provide clothing, care and medical attention for the child. Both defendants possessed a great deal of love and affection for the defendant wife's young son.

The court expressly found:

That both defendants were aware that William Joseph Tabafunda was ill during the period September 1, 1968 to September 12, 1968. The defendants were ignorant. They did not realize how sick the baby was. They thought that the baby had a toothache and no layman regards a toothache as dangerous to life. They loved the baby and gave it aspirin in hopes of improving its condition. They did not take the baby to a doctor because of fear that the Welfare Department would take the baby away from them. They knew that medical help was available because of previous experience. They had no excuse that the law will recognize for not taking the baby to a doctor....

The defendants Walter L. Williams and Bernice J. Williams were negligent in not seeking medical attention for William Joseph Tabafunda.

That as a proximate result of this negligence, William Joseph Tabafunda died....

From these and other findings, the court concluded that the defendants were each guilty of the crime of manslaughter as charged.... Defendants take no exception to the findings but contend that the findings do not support the conclusions that the defendants are guilty of manslaughter as charged....

Parental duty to provide medical care for a dependent minor child was recognized at common law and characterized as a natural duty. In Washington, the existence of the duty is commonly assumed and is stated at times without reference to any particular statute. The existence of the duty also is assumed, but not always defined, in statutes that provide special criminal and civil sanctions for the performance of that duty.... [A]t common law, in the case of involuntary manslaughter, the breach [of the duty to provide medical care] had to amount to more than mere ordinary or simple negligence — gross negligence was essential. In Washington, however, RCW 9.48.060[2] (since amended by Laws of 1970, ch. 49, § 2) and RCW 9.48.150[3] supersede both voluntary and involuntary manslaughter as those crimes were defined at common law. Under these statutes the crime is deemed committed even though the death of the victim is the proximate result of only simple or ordinary negligence.

The concept of simple or ordinary negligence describes a failure to exercise the "ordinary caution" necessary to make out the defense of excusable homicide. RCW 9.48.150. Ordinary caution is the kind of caution that a man of reasonable prudence would exercise under the same or similar conditions. If, therefore, the conduct of a defendant, regardless of his ignorance, good intentions and good faith, fails to measure up to the conduct required of a man of reasonable prudence, he is guilty of ordinary negligence because of his failure to use "ordinary caution." If such negligence proximately causes the death of the victim, the defendant, as pointed out above, is guilty of statutory manslaughter....

In the instant case ... the defendant husband is not the father of the minor child, nor has he adopted that child. Nevertheless, the evidence shows that he had assumed responsibility with his wife for the care and maintenance of the child, whom he greatly loved. Such assumption of responsibility, characterized in the information as that required of a "guardian and custodian," is sufficient to impose upon him the duty to furnish necessary medical care.

The remaining issue of proximate cause requires consideration of the question of when the duty to furnish medical care became activated. If the duty to furnish such care was not activated until after it was too late to save the life of the child, failure to furnish medical care could not be said to have proximately caused the child's death. Timeliness in the furnishing of medical care also must be considered in terms of "ordinary caution." The law does not mandatorily require that a doctor be called for a

---

2. RCW 9.48.060 provided in part: "In any case other than those specified in RCW 9.48.030, 9.48.040 and 9.48.050, homicide, not being excusable or justifiable, is manslaughter."

3. RCW 9.48.150 provides: "Homicide is excusable when committed by accident or misfortune in doing any lawful act by lawful means, with ordinary caution and without any unlawful intent."

child at the first sign of any indisposition or illness. The indisposition or illness may appear to be of a minor or very temporary kind, such as a toothache or cold. If one in the exercise of ordinary caution fails to recognize that his child's symptoms require medical attention, it cannot be said that the failure to obtain such medical attention is a breach of the duty owed. In our opinion, the duty as formulated in *People v. Pierson*, 176 N.Y. 201, (1903) ... properly defines the duty contemplated by our manslaughter statutes RCW 9.48.060 and RCW 9.48.150. The court there said:

> We quite agree that the Code does not contemplate the necessity of calling a physician for every trifling complaint with which the child may be afflicted which in most instances may be overcome by the ordinary household nursing by members of the family; that a reasonable amount of discretion is vested in parents, charged with the duty of maintaining and bringing up infant children; and that the standard is at what time would an ordinarily prudent person, solicitous for the welfare of his child and anxious to promote its recovery, deem it necessary to call in the services of a physician.

It remains to apply the law discussed to the facts of the instant case....

Dr. Gale Wilson, the autopsy surgeon and chief pathologist for the King County Coroner, testified that the child died because an abscessed tooth had been allowed to develop into an infection of the mouth and cheeks, eventually becoming gangrenous. This condition, accompanied by the child's inability to eat, brought about malnutrition, lowering the child's resistance and eventually producing pneumonia, causing the death. Dr. Wilson testified that in his opinion the infection had lasted for approximately 2 weeks, and that the odor generally associated with gangrene would have been present for approximately 10 days before death. He also expressed the opinion that had medical care been first obtained in the last week before the baby's death, such care would have been obtained too late to have saved the baby's life. Accordingly, the baby's apparent condition between September 1 and September 5, 1968 became the critical period for the purpose of determining whether in the exercise of ordinary caution defendants should have provided medical care for the minor child.

The testimony concerning the child's apparent condition during the critical period is not crystal clear, but is sufficient to warrant the following statement of the matter. The defendant husband testified that he noticed the baby was sick about 2 weeks before the baby died. The defendant wife testified that she noticed the baby was ill about a week and a half or 2 weeks before the baby died. The evidence showed that in the critical period the baby was fussy; that he could not keep his food down; and that a cheek started swelling up. The swelling went up and down, but did not disappear. In that same period, the cheek turned "a bluish color like." The defendants, not realizing that the baby was as ill as it was or that the baby was in danger of dying, attempted to provide some relief to the baby by giving the baby aspirin during the critical period and continued to do so until the night before the baby died. The defendants thought the swelling would go down and were waiting for it to do so; and defendant husband testified, that from what he had heard, neither doctors nor dentists pull out a tooth "when it's all swollen up like that." There was an additional explanation for not calling a doctor given by each defendant. Defendant husband testified that "the way the cheek looked, * * * and that stuff on his hair, they would think we were neglecting him and take him away from us and not give him back." Defendant wife testified that the defendants were "waiting for the swelling to go down," and also that they were afraid to take the child to a doctor for fear that the doctor would report them to the welfare department, who, in turn, would take the child away. "It's just that I was so scared of losing him." They testified that they had heard that the defendant husband's cousin lost a child that way. The evidence showed that the defendants did not understand the significance or seriousness of the baby's symptoms. However, there is no evidence that the defendants were physically or financially unable to obtain a doctor, or that they did not know an available doctor, or that the symptoms did not continue to be a matter of concern during the critical period. Indeed, the evidence shows that in April 1968 defendant husband had taken the child to a doctor for medical attention.

In our opinion, there is sufficient evidence from which the court could find, as it necessarily did, that applying the standard of ordinary caution, *i.e.*, the caution exercisable by a man of reasonable prudence under the same or similar conditions, defendants were sufficiently put on notice concerning the symptoms of the baby's illness and lack of improvement in the baby's apparent condition in the period from September 1 to September 5, 1968 to have required them to have obtained medical care for the child. The failure so to do in this case is ordinary or simple negligence, and such negligence is sufficient to support a conviction of statutory manslaughter.

The judgment is affirmed.

Discussion Questions

1. Were Walter and Bernice Williams blameworthy? If so, was their blameworthiness based on their mental state about the baby's death? Would your view of their blameworthiness change if their failure to recognize the baby's condition was the result of lack of medical sophistication? Or lack of education?

2. Were Walter and Bernice Williams blameworthy because they objectively deviated from what a reasonable parent would have done?

3. Were Walter and Bernice dangerous? In other words, did society need to deter them? To incapacitate them?

4. Would Walter and Bernice Williams have had a better chance of acquittal under the Model Penal Code's definition of negligence? Why?

Consider the following information in evaluating whether the parents in the *Williams* case were negligent:

Removing Children: The Destruction of American Indian Families

William Byler
9 Civil Rights 19 (Summer 1977)

Surveys of States with large Indian populations conducted by the Association on American Indian Affairs (AAIA) in 1969 and again in 1974 indicate that approximately 25–35 percent of all Indian children are separated from their families and placed in foster homes, adoptive homes, or institutions....

The disparity in placement rates for Indian[s] and non-Indians is shocking.... In the state of Washington, the Indian adoption rate is 19 times greater and the foster care rate ten times greater [than for non-Indians]....

How are we to account for this disastrous situation? The reasons appear very complex.... [They] include a lack of rational federal and state standards governing child welfare matters, a breakdown in due process, economic incentives, and the harsh social conditions in so many Indian communities....

Very few Indian children are removed from their families on the grounds of physical abuse.... In judging the fitness of a particular family, many social workers, ignorant of Indian cultural values and social norms, ... frequently discover neglect or abandonment where none exists.

* * *

Congress recognized the concerns raised in William Byler's work and enacted the Indian Child Welfare Act of 1978, 25 U.S.C. §§ 1901–1963, to address and remedy unwarranted removal of children from Indian homes and the failure to place children with families that share the values of Indian culture.

In particular, the Act acknowledged "that an alarmingly high percentage of Indian families are broken up by the removal, often unwarranted, of their children from them by nontribal public and private agencies and that an alarmingly high percentage of such children are placed in non-Indian foster and adoptive homes and institutions; and ... that the States ... have often failed to recognize the essential tribal relations of Indian people and the cultural and social standards prevailing in Indian communities and families." 25 U.S.C. § 1901 (4), (5) (1990). The Act aimed to establish "minimum Federal standards for the removal of Indian children from their families and the placement of such children in foster or adoptive homes which will reflect the unique values of Indian culture...." 25 U.S.C. § 1902 (1990).

Problem

6.27 Born in France, Haya grew up in Gambia and entered the United States legally when she was twenty-three. She stayed illegally, taking up residence in New York and finding part-time work in hair salons. She is a practicing Muslim who worships at a mosque in her neighborhood. She married a man who drives a taxi and has had two children with him, one three years old, the other eighteen months.

Haya and her family temporarily shared an apartment with a friend in a public housing project. On the afternoon in question, Haya's husband was working and Haya took the girls with her to a nearby laundromat and placed several loads in to wash. They then returned to the apartment. Later that afternoon, one of the girls heard the jingle of an ice cream truck outside and said "Mommy, ice cream!" Haya ran down to the street to buy the girls ice cream but missed the truck. Since she was already outside, she decided to return to the laundromat to dry the clothes. For approximately forty minutes, she waited in the laundromat for the clothes to dry. During this time, Haya mistakenly thought her roommate was in the apartment. When Haya left the apartment earlier to buy ice cream, she left incense burning on a table. It eventually dropped onto a couch that started a fire that engulfed the entire apartment. As Haya was returning to the apartment, she saw the fire trucks responding to the fire and became hysterical. Both her daughters died in the ensuing blaze. Haya has been devastated by the deaths. A few months after the fire, she told investigators "It's something I will deal with for the rest of my life."

The district attorney is considering charging Haya with two counts of negligent homicide, each of which carries a potential sentence of four years in prison. She has no criminal record. There have been no earlier reports of neglect or other complaints about her care of the children. Because of the publicity the case has attracted, Haya's illegal status is known to immigration authorities. If she is not criminally charged, she will be deported almost immediately. If she is criminally charged, she will be deported at the conclusion of her case, including any prison term she may receive.

Part (a) If you were the prosecutor, would you present Haya's case to a grand jury for indictment? How do the purposes of punishment we studied at the start of the course bear on your decision? Do you think a jury would be likely to find her guilty of negligent homicide if her case were to go to trial? Would you make her a guilty plea offer? If so, on what terms?

Part (b) If you were Haya's lawyer, what arguments would you make to try to convince the prosecutor not to charge Haya? Which purposes of punishment might you invoke? Would you advise her to accept a guilty plea offer? If so, on what terms?

F. Felony Murder

The felony murder doctrine in its purest form holds any felon and accomplices liable for murder when a death is caused by "the perpetration or attempt to perpetrate a felony." The original common law doctrine was extremely broad. Liability attached even if the killing was accidental or the fatal blow was struck by the intended victim or by a police officer responding to the felony. England, the country that created the felony murder rule, abandoned it decades ago. Similarly, the Model Penal Code rejects the felony murder rule, a stance consistent with the Model Penal Code's rejection of strict liability.

The felony murder rule may be diagrammed as follows:

Mental Elements		Non-Mental Elements
Purpose	→	Conduct
None (Strict Liability)	→	Death

As described in the *Aaron* case below, some states have done away with the felony murder rule. But it has proved popular with state legislators and accordingly most states retain it in some form. As you will see below, many states have placed limitations on the felony murder rule. This section is organized according to those limitations.

After an introductory problem, this Section begins with the basic felony murder rule. This first section contrasts West Virginia's relatively broad felony murder rule, applied by the West Virginia Supreme Court in the *Sims* case, with the Michigan Supreme Court's rejection of the felony murder rule in *Aaron*. The felony murder rule makes use of strict liability regarding the death element in homicide. So the arguments for and against the felony murder rule echo the arguments for and against strict liability that you studied in Chapter 5 on Mental States. It is a good idea to briefly review those arguments as you start your study of the felony murder rule.

After the *Aaron* case, you will study the Model Penal Code's alternative to the felony murder rule. Because we examine this Model Penal Code provision in the Section of this book devoted to felony murder, some students erroneously conclude that the Model Penal Code's provision is a form of felony murder. It is not. Felony murder relies on strict liability regarding the death element. The Model Penal Code's provision relies on extreme recklessness regarding the death and not strict liability. So, the Model Penal Code's provision is not a type of felony murder, but an alternative to felony murder.

We then study five common limitations jurisdictions place on the felony murder rule: (1) enumeration; (2) the inherent dangerousness requirement; (3) the merger doctrine; (4) the agency rule, also known as the "in furtherance" requirement; and (5) the res gestae requirement.

HOMICIDE

Problem

6.28 As a result of a downturn in the local economy, Henry recently lost his job. To make some much-needed cash, Henry has been earning money gardening in yards around town. One day, in order to ask a question, Henry goes to the back door of the home of the Juarez family for whom he gardens. Henry notices an envelope with a large sum of money on the kitchen table. His rent is due and he feels desperate. Henry tries the kitchen door and finds it unlocked. He walks quietly into the kitchen, intending to take $400, just enough to pay his rent. Just as he steps towards the table and puts his hand on the envelope, he slips and falls on the freshly waxed kitchen floor. Mrs. Juarez hears the noise and comes running into the kitchen. She too slips on the waxed floor. Unfortunately, Mrs. Juarez hits her head on the granite counter as she slides to the floor. As a result of the fall, Mrs. Juarez suffers a severe head injury from which she dies a week later. Is Henry liable for felony murder under the following statute?

> Murder by poison, lying in wait, imprisonment, starving, or by any willful, deliberate and premeditated killing, or in the commission of, or attempt to commit, arson, kidnapping, sexual assault, robbery, burglary, breaking and entering, escape from lawful custody, or a felony offense of manufacturing or delivering a controlled substance … is murder of the first degree. All other murder is murder of the second degree.

Assume that burglary is defined as: Entry into a structure with the intent to commit theft.

1. The Basic Rule

State v. Sims

162 W. Va. 212 (1978)
Supreme Court of Appeals of West Virginia

Miller, J.

Paul Sims, after pleading guilty to first degree murder, contends that he was coerced into the plea as a result of the trial court's ruling in connection with the felony-murder rule.

The claimed coercion occurred when the trial court ruled preliminarily to the trial that as a matter of law Sims' defense of an accidental discharge of his shotgun during the commission of a burglary would not permit the jury to reduce the crime below first degree murder. We refuse to overturn the guilty plea.

The operative facts are these: Around 2:00 a.m. on January 16, 1976, the defendant Paul Sims, Clay Grimmer and Arthur Burns went to the home of Mr. and Mrs. Oscar Schmidt located in Brooke County, West Virginia. After cutting the telephone wires on the outside of the house, Sims and Burns proceeded onto the front porch of the home. Both men were armed. Sims carried a 20-gauge sawed-off shotgun and Burns had a pistol.

The Schmidts' bedroom adjoined the porch. While Sims remained on the porch adjacent to the windows, his companion Burns broke the windows and stepped through them into the bedroom. Sims pointed his shotgun and a flashlight into the bedroom. Shortly after Burns had entered the bedroom, Walter Schmidt, the son of Oscar Schmidt, entered the bedroom from another portion of the house.

Apparently as a result of this distraction, Oscar Schmidt was able to seize his pistol and fire it at Sims. The bullet struck Sims' right arm, and he claimed this caused an involuntary muscle spasm in his trigger finger which resulted in the discharge of the shotgun, killing Walter Schmidt.

In support of the defendant's theory that the bullet wound caused an involuntary muscle reaction, his attorneys took a deposition from the neurologist who treated him for the injury. Since the doctor was not available for testimony at the trial, the prosecuting and defense attorneys stipulated that his deposition would be read at trial.

Based upon his examination and treatment of the defendant's wound, together with his expert knowledge of the involved nerves and muscles, the doctor concluded it was possible that the bullet wound caused an involuntary muscle reflex resulting in the discharge of the shotgun.

It is to be noted that the State did not agree with the involuntary reflex theory and vigorously cross-examined the doctor, who conceded that the same type of wound might instead have caused the defendant to drop the gun.

The trial court proceeded to rule *in limine* that even assuming the defendant's theory to be true, it would not present a factual defense to mitigate the first degree murder verdict required under this State's felony-murder rule.

The issue before us on this direct appeal relates to the voluntariness of the guilty plea based on the theory that the plea was coerced as a result of the court's preliminary ruling that deprived the defendant of a key factual defense. However, the focus is not upon the court's ruling, but the competency of defendant's counsel in advising the guilty plea in light of the court's ruling.

[T]he guilty plea in this case can only be invalidated if it can be found that Sims' counsel was not acting with reasonable competency when he advised that an involuntary homicide would not mitigate the crime of felony-murder. There is no dispute that the killing occurred during the course of an attempted burglary. There is also no dispute that the guilty plea was prompted by defendant's belief that he had no defense to the felony-murder crime.

Our inquiry is narrowed to a consideration of whether our felony-murder rule, which by statute makes the crime first degree murder, admits any amelioration from first degree by virtue of the fact that the homicide was accidental.

Our felony-murder statute alters the scope of the common law rule by confining its application to the crimes of arson, rape, robbery and burglary or the attempt to commit such crimes. W.Va. Code, 61-2-1.[5] Traditionally at common law, the commission of, or the attempt to commit, any felony which resulted in a homicide was deemed murder....

Our statute enumerates three broad categories of homicide constituting first degree murder: (1) murder by poison, lying in wait, imprisonment, starving; (2) by any wilful, deliberate and premeditated killing; (3) in the commission of, or attempt to commit, arson, rape, robbery or burglary....

It is defendant's contention that this State's felony-murder statute warrants the conclusion that malice is an element of the crime and that an accidental homicide committed during one of the designated felonies will not invoke the felony-murder rule. The third syllabus of *State ex rel. Peacher v. Sencindiver,* ___ W.Va. ___, 233 S.E.2d 425 (1977), is cited as supporting this point....

[But i]n each of [the] ... cases cited by *Peacher* the courts found that the felony-murder crime historically did not require malice, premeditation or deliberate intent to kill as an element of proof....

[From a review of the law of other jurisdictions, t]wo salient facts emerge.... First, in those jurisdictions having felony-murder statutes similar to ours, the courts recognize that their statutes embody the common law concept of the crime of felony-murder. Second, the common law created this substantive crime so as not to include the element that the homicide has to be committed with malice or an intent to kill.

The defendant argues, however, that a literal reading of our statute would suggest that by the use of the term "murder" as the initial subject of the sentence setting out the categories of first degree murder, it was intended that the State must initially prove what amounts to a common law murder before it can invoke the felony-murder rule. Stripping the statute of its other categories of first degree murder, the defendant presents the statute as follows:

> "Murder * * * in the commission of, or attempt to commit, arson, rape, robbery or burglary, is murder of the first degree."

He submits that this is a fair reading of the third syllabus of *Peacher.* From a purely grammatical standpoint, it would have been better usage to begin the independent

---

5. "Murder by poison, lying in wait, imprisonment, starving, or by any wilful, deliberate and premeditated killing, or in the commission of, or attempt to commit, arson, rape, robbery or burglary, is murder of the first degree. All other murder is murder of the second degree."

clause defining the crime of felony-murder with the term "homicide." However this may be, we do not approach the question of what the statute means as if we were on a maiden voyage and were forced upon uncharted seas without compass or sextant.

The felony-murder rule was a part of our substantive criminal law long before this State was formed. No case, either from this Court or from the Virginia court, has ever broken from the historical common law precedent to suggest that proof of an intentional killing is an element of the felony-murder crime. This principle is not only settled in the Virginias, but exists uniformly in all other states which have similar statutes.

In the few cases where such argument, as here advanced, has been considered, it has been flatly rejected as violating the historical common law concepts of the crime of felony-murder....

The use of the term "murder" in the statute, W.Va. Code, 61-2-1, and in the third syllabus of *Peacher* as it relates to the crime of felony-murder, means nothing more than it did at common law—a homicide.

The defendant's trial counsel competently advised him as to the guilty plea, as there could be no reasonable expectation under the settled principles of our law that an unintended homicide committed in the course of an attempted burglary would constitute a defense to first degree murder arising out of the felony-murder rule.

For these reasons, we affirm the judgment of the Circuit Court of Brooke County.

Discussion Questions

1. Would Sims have been liable under any category of homicide other than felony murder? If so, what category? In other words, did the prosecutors need the felony murder rule in order to convict Sims of homicide? To convict Sims of murder?

2. Was the firing of the gun a voluntary act by Sims? If not, would that negate his liability? On what conduct by Sims is his homicide liability based?

3. The court says that Sims argues for "a literal reading" of the statute at issue. What method of statutory interpretation is Sims relying on? What method of interpretation does the court end up using? What language in the opinion supports your answer?

4. The court says that "[f]rom a purely grammatical standpoint, it would have been better usage to begin the independent clause defining the crime of felony-murder with the term 'homicide.'" Is that true? How would you rewrite that clause to reflect the court's decision in *Sims*?

People v. Stamp

2 Cal. App. 3d 203, 208–209 (1969)
California Court of Appeal

Defendant Koory and Stamp, armed with a gun and a blackjack, entered the rear of a building housing the offices of General Amusement Company, ordered the employees they found there to go to the front of the premises, where the two secretaries were working. Stamp, the one with the gun, then went into the office of Carl Honeyman, the owner and manager. Thereupon, Honeyman, looking very frightened and pale, emerged from the office in a "kind of hurry." He was apparently propelled by Stamp who had hold of him by an elbow.

The robbery victims were required to lie down on the floor while the robbers took the money and fled out the back door. As the robbers, who had been on the premises 10 to 15 minutes, were leaving, they told the victims to remain on the floor for five minutes so that no one would "get hurt."

Honeyman, who had been lying next to the counter, had to use it to steady himself in getting up off the floor. Still pale, he was short of breath, sucking air, and pounding and rubbing his chest. As he walked down the hall, in an unsteady manner, still breathing hard and rubbing his chest, he said he was having trouble "keeping the pounding down inside" and that his heart was "pumping too fast for him" ... 15 or 20 minutes after the robbery had occurred, he collapsed on the floor.... [H]e was pronounced dead on arrival at the hospital. The coroner's report listed the immediate cause of death as heart attack....

The victim was an obese, 60 year-old man, with a history of heart disease, who was under a great deal of pressure due to the intensely competitive nature of his business. Additionally, he did not take good care of his heart.

Three doctors ... testified that although Honeyman had an advanced case of atherosclerosis, a progressive and ultimately fatal disease, there must have been some immediate upset to his system which precipitated the attack. It was their conclusion in response to a hypothetical question that but for the robbery there would have been no fatal seizure at that time.... There was opposing testimony to the effect that it could not be said with reasonable medical certainty that fright could ever be fatal.

Under the felony-murder rule of section 189 of the Penal Code, a killing committed in either the perpetration of or an attempt to perpetrate robbery is murder of the first degree. This is true whether the killing is wilfull, deliberate and premeditated, or merely accidental or unintentional, and whether or not the killing is planned as part of the commission of the robbery....

The doctrine presumes malice aforethought on the basis of the commission of a felony inherently dangerous to human life.... This is a rule of substantive law in California and not merely an evidentiary shortcut to finding malice as it withdraws from the jury the requirement that they find either express malice or the implied malice which is manifested in an intent to kill.... Under this rule no intentional act is necessary other than the attempt to or the actual commission of the robbery itself....

There is no requirement that the killing occur, "while committing" or "while engaged in" the felony, or that the killing be "a part of" the felony, other than that the few acts be a part of one continuous transaction....

The doctrine is not limited to those deaths which are foreseeable.... As long as the homicide is the direct causal result of the robbery the felony-murder rule applies whether or not the death was a natural or probable consequence of the robbery.... So long as life is shortened as a result of the felonious act, it does not matter that the victim might have died soon anyway.

* * *

In contrast to the *Sims* and *Stamp* courts, which both approved the felony murder rule, the Michigan Supreme Court rejected it in the *Aaron* case below. The *Aaron* opinion provides a detailed review of the arguments for and against the felony murder rule.

People v. Aaron

409 Mich. 672 (1980)
Supreme Court of Michigan

Fitzgerald, J.

The existence and scope of the felony-murder doctrine have perplexed generations of law students, commentators and jurists in the United States and England, and have split our own Court of Appeals. In these cases, we must decide whether Michigan has a felony-murder rule which allows the element of malice required for murder to be satisfied by the intent to commit the underlying felony or whether malice must be otherwise found by the trier of fact. We must also determine what is the *mens rea* required to support a conviction under Michigan's first-degree murder statute.

Defendant Aaron was convicted of first-degree felony murder as a result of a homicide committed during the perpetration of an armed robbery. The jury was instructed that they could convict defendant of first-degree murder if they found that defendant killed the victim during the commission or attempted commission of an armed robbery....

History of the Felony-Murder Doctrine

Felony murder has never been a static, well-defined rule at common law, but throughout its history has been characterized by judicial reinterpretation to limit the harshness of the application of the rule. Historians and commentators have concluded that the rule is of questionable origin and that the reasons for the rule no longer exist, making it an anachronistic remnant, "a historic survivor for which there is no logical or practical basis for existence in modern law." ...

At early common law, the felony-murder rule went unchallenged because at that time practically all felonies were punishable by death. It was, therefore, "of no particular moment whether the condemned was hanged for the initial felony or for the death accidentally resulting from the felony." Thus, as Stephen and Perkins point out, no injustice was caused directly by application of the rule at that time....

Case law of Nineteenth-Century England reflects the efforts of the English courts to limit the application of the felony-murder doctrine....

In this century, the felony-murder doctrine was comparatively rarely invoked in England and in 1957 England abolished the felony-murder rule. Section 1 of England's Homicide Act provides that a killing occurring in a felony-murder situation will not amount to murder unless done with the same malice aforethought as is required for all other murder....

Limitation of the Felony-Murder Doctrine in the United States

While only a few states have followed the lead of Great Britain in abolishing felony murder, various legislative and judicial limitations on the doctrine have effectively narrowed the scope of the rule in the United States. Perkins states that the rule is "somewhat in disfavor at the present time" and that "courts apply it where the law requires, but they do so grudgingly and tend to restrict its application where circumstances permit".

The draftsmen of the Model Penal Code have summarized the limitations imposed by American courts as follows:

(1) "The felonious act must be dangerous to life."

(2) and (3) "The homicide must be a natural and probable consequence of the felonious act." "Death must be 'proximately' caused." Courts have also required that the killing be the result of an act done in the furtherance of the felonious purpose and not merely coincidental to the perpetration of a felony. These cases often make distinctions based on the identity of the victim (*i.e.*, whether the decedent was the victim of the felony or whether he was someone else, *e.g.*, a policeman or one of the felons) and the identity of the person causing the death.

(4) "The felony must be *malum in se*."

(5) "The act must be a common-law felony."

(6) "The period during which the felony is in the process of commission must be narrowly construed."

(7) "The underlying felony must be 'independent' of the homicide."

Some courts, recognizing the questionable wisdom of the rule, have refused to extend it beyond what is required.... Other courts have required a finding of a separate *mens rea* connected with the killing in addition to the intent associated with the felony.... Kentucky and Hawaii have specifically abolished the felony-murder doctrine. Ohio has effectively abolished the felony-murder rule. Seven states have downgraded the offense and consequently reduced the punishment.

Three states require a demonstration of *mens rea* beyond the intent to cause the felony....

Other restrictions of the common-law rule include the enumeration of felonies which are to be included within the felony-murder category, and the reduction to manslaughter of killings in the course of non-enumerated felonies....

Finally, a limitation of relatively recent origin is the availability of affirmative defenses where a defendant is not the only participant in the commission of the underlying felony. The New York statute provides, as do similar statutes of nine other states, an affirmative defense to the defendant when he:

> "(a) Did not commit the homicidal act or in any way solicit, request, command, importune, cause or aid the commission thereof; and

> "(b) Was not armed with a deadly weapon, or any instrument, article or substance readily capable of causing death or serious physical injury and of a sort not ordinarily carried in public places by law-abiding persons; and

> "(c) Had no reasonable ground to believe that any other participant was armed with such a weapon, instrument, article or substance; and

> "(d) Had no reasonable ground to believe that any other participant intended to engage in conduct likely to result in death or serious physical injury."

... The numerous modifications and restrictions placed upon the common-law felony-murder doctrine by courts and legislatures reflect dissatisfaction with the harshness and injustice of the rule. Even though the felony-murder doctrine survives in this country, it bears increasingly less resemblance to the traditional felony-murder concept. To the extent that these modifications reduce the scope and significance of the common-law doctrine, they also call into question the continued existence of the doctrine itself.

The Requirement of Individual Culpability for Criminal Responsibility

"If one had to choose the most basic principle of the criminal law in general ... it would be that criminal liability for causing a particular result is not justified in the absence of some culpable mental state in respect to that result...."

The most fundamental characteristic of the felony-murder rule violates this basic principle in that it punishes all homicides, committed in the perpetration or attempted perpetration of proscribed felonies whether intentional, unintentional or accidental, without the necessity of proving the relation between the homicide and the perpetrator's state of mind. This is most evident when a killing is done by one of a group of co-felons....

The felony-murder rule's most egregious violation of basic rules of culpability occurs where felony murder is categorized as first-degree murder. All other murders carrying equal punishment require a showing of premeditation, deliberation and willfulness while felony murder only requires a showing of intent to do the underlying felony. Although the purpose of our degree statutes is to punish more severely the more culpable forms of murder, an accidental killing occurring during the perpetration of a felony would be punished more severely than a second-degree murder requiring intent to kill, intent to cause great bodily harm, or wantonness and willfulness. Furthermore, a defendant charged with felony murder is permitted to raise defenses only to the mental element of the felony, thus precluding certain defenses available to a defendant charged with premeditated murder who may raise defenses to the mental element of murder (*e.g.*, self-defense, accident). Certainly, felony murder is no more reprehensible than premeditated murder.

LaFave & Scott explain the felony-murder doctrine's failure to account for a defendant's moral culpability as follows:

> "The rationale of the doctrine is that one who commits a felony is a bad person with a bad state of mind, and he has caused a bad result, so that we should not worry too much about the fact that the fatal result he accomplished was quite different and a good deal worse than the bad result he intended. Yet it is a general principle of criminal law that one is not ordinarily criminally liable for bad results which differ greatly from intended results."

The failure of the felony-murder rule to consider the defendant's moral culpability is explained by examining the state of the law at the time of the rule's inception. The concept of culpability was not an element of homicide at early common law. The early definition of malice aforethought was vague. The concept meant little more than intentional wrongdoing with no other emphasis on intention except to exclude homicides that were committed by misadventure or in some otherwise pardonable manner. Thus, under this early definition of malice aforethought, an intent to commit the felony would in itself constitute malice. Furthermore, as all felonies were punished alike, it made little difference whether the felon was hanged for the felony or for the death....

Today, however, malice is a term of art. It does not include the nebulous definition of intentional wrongdoing. Thus, although the felony-murder rule did not broaden the definition of murder at early common law, it does so today. We find this enlargement of the scope of murder unacceptable, because it is based on a concept of culpability which is "totally incongruous with the general principles of our jurisprudence" today.

The Felony-Murder Doctrine in Michigan
A. Murder and Malice Defined

In order to understand the operation of any state's felony-murder doctrine, initially it is essential to understand how that state defines murder and malice.

In Michigan, murder is not statutorily defined. This Court early defined the term as follows:

> "Murder is where a person of sound memory and discretion unlawfully kills any reasonable creature in being, in the peace of the state, with malice prepense or aforethought, either express or implied." *People v Potter*, 5 Mich 1 (1858)....

We agree with the following analysis of murder and malice aforethought presented by LaFave & Scott:

> "Though murder is frequently defined as the unlawful killing of another 'living human being' with 'malice aforethought', in modern times the latter phrase does not even approximate its literal meaning. Hence it is preferable not to rely upon that misleading expression for an understanding of murder but rather to consider the various types of murder (typed according to the mental element) which the common law came to recognize and which exist today in most jurisdictions:

"(1) intent-to-kill murder;

"(2) intent-to-do-serious-bodily-injury murder;

"(3) depraved-heart murder [wanton and willful disregard that the natural tendency of the defendant's behavior is to cause death or great bodily harm]; and

"(4) felony murder."

. . .

Our focus in this opinion is upon the last category of murder, *i.e.*, felony murder. We do not believe the felony-murder doctrine, as some courts and commentators would suggest, abolishes the requirement of malice, nor do we believe that it equates the *mens rea* of the felony with the *mens rea* required for a non-felony murder. We construe the felony-murder doctrine as providing a separate definition of malice, thereby establishing a fourth category of murder. The effect of the doctrine is to recognize the intent to commit the underlying felony, in itself, as a sufficient *mens rea* for murder. This analysis of the felony-murder doctrine is consistent with the historical development of the doctrine.

The question we address today is whether Michigan recognizes the felony-murder doctrine and, accordingly, the category of malice arising from the underlying felony. The relevant inquiry is first whether Michigan has a statutory felony-murder doctrine. If it does not, it must then be determined whether Michigan has or should have a common-law felony-murder doctrine.

B. Statutory Felony Murder

Michigan does not have a statutory felony-murder doctrine which designates as murder any death occurring in the course of a felony without regard to whether it was the result of accident, negligence, recklessness or willfulness. Rather, Michigan has a statute which makes a *murder* occurring in the course of one of the enumerated felonies a first-degree murder:

"Murder which is perpetrated by means of poison, lying in wait, or other wilful, deliberate, and premeditated killing, or which is committed in the perpetration, or attempt to perpetrate arson, criminal sexual conduct in the first or third degree, robbery, breaking and entering of a dwelling, larceny of any kind, extortion, or kidnapping, is murder of the first degree, and shall be punished by imprisonment for life." MCL 750.316; MSA 28.548....

Thus, we conclude that Michigan has not codified the common-law felony-murder rule. The use of the term "murder" in the first-degree statute requires that a murder must first be established before the statute is applied to elevate the degree.

C. Common-Law Felony Murder in Michigan

The prosecution argues that even if Michigan does not have a statutory codification of the felony-murder rule, the common-law definition of murder included a homicide in the course of a felony. Thus, the argument continues, once a homicide in the course of a felony is proven, under the common-law felony-murder rule a murder has been established and the first-degree murder statute then becomes applicable....

Our research has uncovered no Michigan cases, nor do the parties refer us to any, which have expressly considered whether Michigan has or should continue to have a common-law felony-murder doctrine....

However, our finding that Michigan has never specifically adopted the doctrine which defines malice to include the intent to commit the underlying felony is not the end of our inquiry. In Michigan, the general rule is that the common law prevails except as abrogated by the Constitution, the Legislature or this Court. Const 1963, art 3, § 7....

The cases before us today squarely present us with the opportunity to review the doctrine and to consider its continued existence in Michigan. Although there are no Michigan cases which specifically abrogate the felony-murder rule, there exist a number of decisions of this Court which have significantly restricted the doctrine in Michigan and which lead us to conclude that the rule should be abolished....

Accordingly, we hold today that malice is the intention to kill, the intention to do great bodily harm, or the wanton and willful disregard of the likelihood that the natural tendency of defendant's behavior is to cause death or great bodily harm. We further hold that malice is an essential element of any murder, as that term is judicially defined, whether the murder occurs in the course of a felony or otherwise. The facts and circumstances involved in the perpetration of a felony may evidence an intent to kill, an intent to cause great bodily harm, or a wanton and willful disregard of the likelihood that the natural tendency of defendant's behavior is to cause death or great bodily harm; however, the conclusion must be left to the jury to infer from all the evidence....

Practical Effect of Abrogation of the Common-Law Felony-Murder Doctrine

From a practical standpoint, the abolition of the category of malice arising from the intent to commit the underlying felony should have little effect on the result of the majority of cases. In many cases where felony murder has been applied, the use of the doctrine was unnecessary because the other types of malice could have been inferred from the evidence.

Abrogation of this rule does not make irrelevant the fact that a death occurred in the course of a felony. A jury can properly infer malice from evidence that a defendant intentionally set in motion a force likely to cause death or great bodily harm.... If the jury concludes that malice existed, they can find murder and, if they determine that the murder occurred in the perpetration or attempted perpetration of one of the enumerated felonies, by statute the murder would become first-degree murder.

The difference is that the jury may not find malice from the intent to commit the underlying felony alone. The defendant will be permitted to assert any of the applicable defenses relating to *mens rea* which he would be allowed to assert if charged with premeditated murder....

In the past, the felony-murder rule has been employed where unforeseen or accidental deaths occur and where the state seeks to prove vicarious liability of co-felons. In situations involving the vicarious liability of co-felons, the individual liability of each felon must be shown. It is fundamentally unfair and in violation of basic principles of individual criminal culpability to hold one felon liable for the unforeseen and unagreed-to results of another felon. In cases where the felons are acting intentionally or recklessly in pursuit of a common plan, the felony-murder rule is unnecessary because liability may be established on agency principles.

Finally, in cases where the death was purely accidental, application of the felony-murder doctrine is unjust and should be precluded. The underlying felony, of course, will still be subject to punishment....

Discussion Questions

1. Do you support retention of the felony murder rule? Or abolition? Is your reasoning retributive? Or utilitarian?

2. Despite extensive criticism, many jurisdictions retain the felony murder rule. What do you think explains its continued vitality?

The Model Penal Code's Alternative to Felony Murder
Model Penal Code § 210.2

Murder

(1) Except as provided in Section 210.3(1) (b), criminal homicide constitutes murder when: ...

    (b) it is committed recklessly under circumstances manifesting extreme indifference to the value of human life. *Such recklessness and indifference are presumed if the actor is engaged or is an accomplice in the commission of, or an attempt to commit, or flight after committing or attempting to commit robbery, rape or deviate sexual intercourse by force or threat of force, arson, burglary, kidnapping or felonious escape* (emphasis added).

Note that the Model Penal Code's alternative to felony murder incorporates a presumption that someone committing or attempting to commit the listed felonies has extreme indifference to life and thus qualifies for murder. This presumption is a rebuttable one, which means that the defendant may introduce evidence to try to persuade the jury that he or she did *not* have extreme indifference to life. After hearing any such evidence from the defense, in order to convict, the jurors must ultimately conclude that the prosecution has proven the defendant's extreme indifference to life beyond reasonable doubt.

In contrast to the Model Penal Code provision, a defendant charged solely with felony murder is not allowed to introduce evidence that he or she lacked any of the mental states that qualify for murder, such as purpose, knowledge, or extreme indifference to life, because none of those mental states is required for conviction of felony murder. For the same reason, jurors, in order to convict on a felony murder charge, need not conclude that the prosecution has proven any mental state regarding the death beyond a reasonable doubt.

Problem

6.29 Imagine a burglary scenario in which you, as defense counsel, could introduce evidence to try to rebut the presumption of extreme indifference under the MPC and argue that your client did not harbor extreme indifference. What evidence relating to the burglary would suggest the absence of extreme indifference?

Discussion Questions

1. What are the advantages and disadvantages of the MPC provision compared with the felony murder rule?

2. Does the MPC provision make use of strict liability?

3. How would the defendants in the felony murder cases described earlier in this chapter have fared under the MPC approach?

Consider the following excerpt in which Professors David Crump and Susan Waite Crump defend the felony murder rule.

In Defense of the Felony Murder Doctrine

David Crump and Susan Waite Crump
8 Harv. J.L. Law & Pub. Pol'y 359 (1985)

Differences in result must be taken into account as part of actus reus if classification and grading are to be rational. For example, murder and attempted murder may require similar mental states (indeed, attempted murder generally requires proof of a higher mental element), but no common law jurisdiction treats the two offenses as one, and certainly none treats attempted murder more severely. The only difference justifying this classification is that death results in one offense but not in the other. Similarly, it is a misdemeanor for a person to operate a motor vehicle while impaired by drugs or alcohol, but if this conduct causes the death of a human being, the offense in some jurisdictions is elevated to the status of homicide. Most jurisdictions treat vehicular homicide more severely than the misdemeanor of alcohol-impaired driving, even though the actions and mental states of the defendant may be equivalent or identical....

The classification and grading of offenses so that the entire scheme of defined crimes squares with societal perceptions of proportionality—of "just deserts"—is a fundamental goal of the law of crimes.

The felony murder doctrine serves this goal, just as do the distinctions inherent in the separate offenses of attempted murder and murder, or impaired driving and vehicular homicide. Felony murder reflects a societal judgment that an intentionally committed robbery that causes the death of a human being is qualitatively more serious than an identical robbery that does not. Perhaps this judgment could have been embodied in a newly defined offense called "robbery-resulting-in-death"; but while a similar approach has been adopted in some areas of the criminal law, such a proliferation of offense definitions is undesirable. Thus the felony murder doctrine reflects the conclusions that a robbery that causes death is more closely akin to murder than to robbery. If this conclusion accurately reflects societal attitudes, and if classification of crimes is to be influenced by such attitudes in order to avoid depreciation of the seriousness of the offense and to encourage respect for the law, then the felony murder doctrine is an appropriate classificatory device....

Juries provide another index of the public's attitude toward felony murder. Kalven and Zeisel [researchers on jury issues] were surprised to find that jurors faced with actual felony murder cases agreed with the doctrine. The jury research revealed in public attitudes a resistance to the criminalization of many kinds of socially disapproved events (including some homicides), but *not* felony murder....

Scholarly criticisms of felony murder have tended to neglect its relationship to proportionality and grading. The criticisms erroneously tend to regard mens rea as the only legitimate determinant of the grade of a homicide resulting from a felony. This reasoning sometimes leads modern writers into the same rigid formalism, divorced from policy, that they rightly reject in historical justifications of the rule. Mens rea is not a "unified field theory" of homicide, and while such a theory might make the subject artificially "logical" or "consistent," it does not reflect our society's more complex understanding of the nature, function, and purpose of criminal law. The fallacy of this approach is its denigration of actus reus and its failure to include the result of defendant's conduct as a determinant of just disposition. The importance of this factor is demonstrated by the attempted murder and alcohol-impaired driving examples given above. Simply put, if one must categorize a robbery causing death as either a robbery or a murder, it is the latter category that is the "better fit"; calling such a crime robbery, and robbery only, would distort its significance in the scheme of crime grading....

A purpose of sentencing closely related to proportionality is that of condemnation....

Condemnation itself is a multifaceted idea. It embodies the notion of reinforcement of societal norms and values as a guide to the conduct of upright persons, as opposed to less upright ones who presumably require the separate prod of "deterrence." The felony murder rule serves this purpose by distinguishing crimes that cause human deaths, thus reinforcing the reverence for human life. To put the argument differently, characterizing a robbery-homicide solely as robbery would have the undesirable effect of communicating to the citizenry that the law does not consider a crime that takes a human life to be different from one that does not—a message that would be indistinguishable, in the minds of many, from a devaluation of human life.

Another aspect of condemnation is the expression of solidarity with the victims of crime. If we as a society label a violent offense in a manner that depreciates its significance, we communicate to the victim by implication that we do not understand his suffering. He may be left with the impression that he is unprotected—or even that he is disoriented, having himself failed to understand the rules of the game. Felony murder is a useful doctrine because it reaffirms to the surviving family of a felony-homicide victim the kinship the society as a whole feels with him by denouncing in the strongest language of the law the intentional crime that produced the death....

Deterrence is the policy most often recognized in the cases. Scholars, however, tend to dismiss this rationale, using such arguments as the improbability that felons will know the law, the unlikelihood that a criminal who has formed the intent to commit a felony will refrain from acts likely to cause death, or the assertedly small number of felony-homicides.

The trouble with these criticisms is that they underestimate the complexity of deterrence. There may be more than a grain of truth in the proposition that felons, if considered as a class, evaluate risks and benefits differently than members of other classes in society. The conclusion does not follow, however, that felons cannot be deterred, or that criminals are so different from other citizens that they are impervious to inducements or deterrents that would affect people in general. There is mounting evidence that serious crime is subject to deterrence if consequences are adequately communicated. The felony murder rule is just the sort of simple, commonsense, readily enforceable, and widely known principle that is likely to result in deterrence....

The argument against deterrence often proceeds on the additional assumption that felony murder is addressed only to accidental killings and cannot result in their deterrence. By facilitating proof and simplifying the concept of liability, however, felony murder may deter intentional killings as well. The robber who kills intentionally, but who might claim under oath to have acted accidentally, is thus told that he will be deprived of the benefit of this claim. By institutionalizing this effect and consistently condemning robbery-homicides as qualitatively more blameworthy than robberies, the law leads the robber who kills intentionally to expect this treatment for himself. Furthermore, the contrary argument proves too much even as to robbery-killings that are factually accidental. The proposition that accidental killings cannot be deterred is inconsistent with the widespread belief that the penalizing of negligence, and even the imposition of strict liability, may have deterrent consequences....

Another advantage of the felony murder rule ... is that it may aid in the optimal allocation of criminal justice resources. A small minority of cases is tried before juries. The efforts of judges, courtroom time, lawyering on both sides, and support services are all scarce resources. Although we resist thinking of criminal justice in these terms, and few would be willing to put a specific dollar price upon its proper function, the quality of our justice is limited by the scarcity of these resources and by the efficiency with which we allocate them....

One of our choices might be to improve the allocation of criminal justice resources by adopting some version of the felony murder rule. The rule has beneficial allocative consequences because it clearly defines the offense, simplifies the task of the judge and jury with respect to questions of law and fact, and thereby promotes efficient administration of justice....

Obviously, reliance upon this policy should be limited carefully. The failure to recognize the effects of our decisions upon the use of scarce resources, however, would be equally dangerous, threatening to lower the quality of criminal justice generally.

* * *

Before we turn to limitations on the felony murder rule, consider the constitutional criticisms of the felony murder rule in the following excerpt from an article by Professors Scott Sundby and Nelson Roth:

The Felony-Murder Rule: A Doctrine at Constitutional Crossroads
Nelson E. Roth and Scott E. Sundby
70 CORNELL L. REV. 446, 491–92 (1985)

The felony-murder rule has been criticized almost from its inception as a harsh legal doctrine with insufficient policy justifications. Two basic conceptualizations of felony murder have emerged: the rule is viewed either as providing a conclusive presumption of the culpability required for murder, or as a distinct crime for which the killing does not have a separate mens rea element apart from the felony.

The Supreme Court's holding in *Sandstrom v. Montana* constitutionally prohibits conclusive presumptions because they violate a defendant's presumption of innocence and because they intrude upon the jury's duty to affirmatively find each element of the offense. The felony-murder rule violates both rationales of [a]defendant's culpability for murder....

Those courts that have attempted to avoid the due process problems of mandatory presumptions have characterized the felony-murder rule as a distinct crime without a separate mens rea element for the homicide. The Supreme Court has recently indicated, however, that eighth amendment and due process restrictions limit the ability of legislatures and courts to create and sanction nonregulatory crimes that do not contain a requirement of culpability. In *Enmund v. Florida* and *United States v. United States Gypsum Co.*, the Court has noted that a relationship between culpability and punishment is intrinsic to our criminal system. The felony-murder rule violates this basic principle of our legal system when justified as a strict liability crime.

The felony-murder rule arose from obscure historical origins and has developed haphazardly into a harsh and unjust legal doctrine. It is perhaps fitting, therefore, that two separate lines of constitutional doctrines, developing independently, have come together in such a way that it is impossible to conceptualize felony murder in a manner that does not run afoul of constitutional guarantees.

2. Limitations on the Felony Murder Rule

Problem

6.30 A gang controls distribution of heroin in certain neighborhoods of a major city and in doing so makes use of what are called "stash houses." In a "stash house" the gang keeps a large amount of heroin from which it replenishes its street dealers as their supplies run low. In recent months, the gang's stash houses have been robbed and large amounts of the gang's heroin supply have been stolen by a man named Otis. Otis makes his living, as he puts it, "ripping and running." In other words, he and his associates rob drug dealers of both drugs and money. One day Otis and three of his associates—Keisha, Tammy, and Darnell—decide to rob a particular stash house used by the gang. Otis and his crew see that the stash house is well-guarded, so they come up with a clever ruse to distract and get the jump on the armed guards. Tammy, dressed in a jogging outfit, runs up to the stash house carrying a handful of paper flyers, crying hysterically, and pretending that she is a mother looking for her missing daughter. Tammy's act distracts the guards long enough for Otis and Keisha to get the jump on the them and force them to lower their guns. Once inside the stash house, Otis threatens to shoot and kill the guards if they don't immediately turn over the drug stash. Unbeknownst to Otis, the gang has more armed men on the roof at the back of the house who prepare to attack Otis and his crew. At the last moment, Otis figures out that he has walked into a trap and tells his three compatriots to retreat. As Otis's crew runs down the street toward their getaway car, the gang's armed guards open fire. Otis's crew shoots back and, in doing so, Darnell, firing over his shoulder, accidentally hits and kills Tammy. When Keisha sees Tammy dead in the street, she starts walking toward the guards and fires and kills one of them. Otis then grabs Keisha and she and Darnell and Otis make their escape. Assume that Otis, Darnell, and Keisha are all caught and prosecuted. Are any or all of them liable for homicide based on the death of Tammy? Are any or all of them liable for felony murder based on the death of Tammy? Are any or all of them liable for homicide based on the death of the guard Keisha shot and killed?

The history of the felony murder rule, particularly in this century, has seen the felony murder rule restricted in many ways. The sections that follow address four of the most common limitations.

a. Enumeration

Legislatures can limit the scope of the felony murder rule by enumerating—that is, specifically naming—the felonies that can support a felony murder conviction.

The absence of a felony from such a statutory list excludes it as a possible basis for a felony murder charge. The following Wisconsin statute exemplifies this approach.

Wisconsin Statutes

§ 940.03 Felony murder

Whoever causes the death of another human being while committing or attempting to commit [various forms of battery, threatening a witness, prosecutor, judge, or law enforcement officer, false imprisonment, kidnapping, first degree sexual assault, arson, armed burglary, or armed robbery] may be imprisoned for not more than 15 years in excess of the maximum term of imprisonment provided by law for that crime or attempt.

* * *

Under this statute, a prosecutor could not base a felony murder charge on the felonies of unarmed robbery, unarmed burglary, grand theft, or dozens of other felonies.

In states that divide murder into degrees, sometimes the legislature enumerates felonies for only one of the jurisdiction's degrees of murder. Enumeration is commonly used when legislatures seek to limit liability for first degree murder. The West Virginia statute at issue in the *Sims* case, above, for example, limits first-degree felony murder convictions to the commission of or attempt to commit arson, rape, robbery, or burglary.

What role should drug cases play in any felony murder scheme? In states that use the enumeration limitation, should felony drug offenses be included in the list of felonies that trigger felony murder liability? Or should there be a separate statute creating felony murder for deaths arising from drug offenses? If so, which drug offenses? The next Problem raises these issues.

Problem

6.31 Lewis and Daniel are friends who play together in a band. Each is twenty-four years old. Lewis is a heroin addict and Daniel an occasional heroin user. Late one night after band practice they decide to buy and share some heroin. They pool their money, Lewis contributing $10 and Daniel $30. With Lewis at the wheel of his car, they drive together to a neighborhood known for heroin dealing. Lewis spots a man standing on a corner and honks his horn. In apparent response, the man whistles. Lewis gets out of the car and walks over to the man. He gives the man the pooled $40 and the man give him four glassine packets of heroin. On the way home, Lewis hands Daniel two of the packets and Daniel puts them into his pocket. They then drive to the apartment they share. Once there, they go to their separate bedrooms where each separately prepares and injects himself with the contents of one heroin packet. Early the following morning, while still in separate bedrooms, each injects himself with the contents of the second packet of heroin. The following afternoon, Lewis wakes up and finds Daniel on a couch in the apartment's living room dead. The medical examiner later determines that Daniel died from a heroin overdose and had no other drugs in his system.

Lewis is charged under the following statutes:

Distribution of a Controlled Substance

It shall be unlawful to manufacture, distribute, or dispense a controlled substance. Any person who violates this provision with an amount of heroin less than a pound is punishable with a maximum potential sentence of five years' imprisonment.

Drug-Induced Murder

Any person who manufactures, distributes, or dispenses any controlled substance is strictly liable for any death which results from the injection, inhalation, or ingestion of that substance and is guilty of murder with a maximum potential sentence of 20 years' imprisonment.

The legislature passed the Drug-Induced Murder statute in response to a dramatic increase in deaths resulting from heroin use. When it did so, the legislature made the following statement: "It is the policy of this state to distinguish between drug offenders based on the seriousness of the offense, considering principally the nature, quantity, and purity of the controlled substance involved, and the role of the actor in the overall distribution network. It is important to identify the most serious offenders and offenses to guard against sentencing disparity."

Part (a) Lewis's lawyer files a motion to dismiss both charges on the ground that Lewis's conduct does not fall within either statute. What arguments can Lewis's lawyer make? What arguments can be made by the prosecution? If you were the judge, how would you rule?

Part (b) The Drug-Induced Murder statute under which Lewis is charged explicitly uses strict liability regarding death as the basis for murder liability. If you were a legislator, would you vote for or against this statute? What are the arguments for adopting it? What are the arguments against adopting it?

b. *Inherently Dangerous Felony*

The inherently dangerous felony limitation restricts the types of felonies upon which the prosecution can base a charge of felony murder. What felonies do you consider inherently dangerous? How do you assess the inherent dangerousness of a felony? Should it matter if the felon is very careful during the felony?

People v. Sanchez

86 Cal. App. 4th 970 (2001)
Court of Appeal of California

Scotland, J.

One passenger was killed and two were seriously injured when defendant Refugio Anthony Sanchez crashed his car while trying to elude pursuing police officers. Criminal charges were filed, and defendant was convicted of a number of offenses, including second degree murder. (Pen. Code, § 187, subd. (a).) Sentenced to state prison, he appeals.

In the published portion of this opinion, we agree with defendant that his murder conviction must be reversed because the trial court erred in instructing the jury, pursuant to the felony-murder doctrine, that a person who kills a human being while violating Vehicle Code section 2800.3 is guilty of second degree murder.... As we shall explain, in determining whether the felonious violation of section 2800.3 is inherently dangerous to human life as required for application of the second degree felony-murder doctrine, we must look to the elements of the statute in the abstract, rather than to defendant's specific conduct. In doing so, we conclude that, because dispositive elements of section 2800.3 can be satisfied by conduct that does not necessarily pose a high probability of death, it is not a felony inherently dangerous to human life. Thus, section 2800.3 cannot serve as the predicate crime for application of the second degree felony-murder doctrine.

Around 2:00 a.m. on March 1, 1998, Officer John Morris saw defendant's car run a stop sign and two red lights at speeds between 35 to 55 miles per hour. Morris turned on the red lights and siren of his marked patrol vehicle and pursued the car, which barely missed colliding with another vehicle while speeding through an intersection. Goldie McCowan, one of three passengers in defendant's car, told defendant to pull over because police were behind them. Defendant refused to do so, claiming he could get away. Eventually, all the passengers pleaded for defendant to pull over. But "[h]e just turned up the music" and drove faster.

Defendant accelerated to speeds between 85 to 100 miles per hour. As he drove down a residential street at high speed, defendant came to a 90-degree turn in the road. Unable to make the turn, defendant lost control of the car, the right rear of which "swung out" and "clipped the guardrail." After hitting the guardrail, the car flipped upside down and crashed into a house. Skid marks indicated that defendant's car was traveling at approximately 84 miles per hour when he lost control at the turn in the road.

Officer Morris stopped to render aid and arrest the driver. Flames were coming out of the front of the car, and smoke and gasoline pouring out of the back. A car door was open, and one of the passengers was facedown on the ground, with the vehicle partially on top of her. Morris heard a woman in the back of the car screaming for help.

As others who had joined the pursuit attended to the passengers, Officer Bobby Daniels and another officer pulled defendant from the car. Defendant, who did not appear to be injured, was belligerent and continually screamed at the officers. Noticing that defendant had a strong odor of alcohol on his breath and was unable to stand on his own, Officer Daniels concluded that defendant was under the influence of alcohol. Subsequent testing revealed that defendant had a blood-alcohol level of .18 percent.

One of the passengers, Lakisha Davis, died as a result of the crash. Goldie McCowan suffered a broken right arm, a fractured collarbone, and injuries to her hip. Shanise Shaver was cut and bruised on her hand, head, and stomach.

Prior to the fatal crash, defendant had been convicted of driving under the influence of alcohol and his driver's license had been suspended....

The jury was presented with two alternative theories to support defendant's conviction of second degree murder: (1) he acted with implied malice in unlawfully killing Lakisha Davis, or (2) he caused her death while committing a felony that is inherently dangerous to human life but is not enumerated in Penal Code section 189 (the second degree felony-murder rule).[3] ...

The second degree felony-murder theory applies when a defendant commits a homicide during the perpetration of a felony that is inherently dangerous to human life but is not enumerated in Penal Code section 189. "'The felony-murder doctrine, whose ostensible purpose is to deter those engaged in felonies from killing negligently or accidentally, operates to posit the existence of that crucial mental state—and thereby to render irrelevant evidence of actual malice or the lack thereof—when the killer is engaged in a felony whose inherent danger to human life renders logical an imputation of malice on the part of all who commit it.'" In other words, a defendant who kills a human being during the commission of a felony that is inherently dangerous to human life is deemed to have acted with malice aforethought, i.e., committed murder. A felony is inherently dangerous to human life when it "carr[ies] 'a high probability' that death will result." (*People v. Patterson* (1989) 49 Cal. 3d 615, 627 italics omitted.)....

[T]he difference between implied malice and felony murder is that, under the implied malice theory, when the defendant kills a person while committing an act which, by its nature, poses a high probability that the act will result in death, the trier of fact *may infer* the defendant killed with malice aforethought; whereas, under the

---

3. A person who kills a human being during the commission of a felony enumerated in Penal Code section 189 is guilty of first degree felony murder.

felony-murder theory, if the inherently dangerous act is a felony, the defendant is *deemed* to have killed with malice aforethought as a matter of law.

In this case, defendant's appeal addresses only the second theory tendered by the prosecutor, that defendant was guilty of felony murder based upon his violation of section 2800.3, which was charged as a felony.[4]

Over defendant's objection, the trial court agreed with the prosecutor that the felonious violation of section 2800.3 is an inherently dangerous felony that can support a murder conviction via the second degree felony-murder doctrine. Consequently, the court instructed the jury as follows: "Every person who unlawfully kills a human being with malice aforethought *or during the commission or attempted commission of evading a peace officer, a felony inherently dangerous to human life,* is guilty of the crime of murder in violation of Section 187 of the Penal Code. In order to prove this crime, each of the following elements must be proved: One, a human being was killed; and two, the killing was unlawful; and three, the killing was done with malice aforethought *or occurred during the commission or attempted commission of evading a peace officer, a felony inherently dangerous to human life. Evading a peace officer is a felony inherently dangerous to human life.*" (Italics added.) The court further instructed that "[t]he unlawful killing of a human being whether intentional, unintentional, or accidental, *which occurs during the commission or attempted commission of a crime of evading a peace officer is murder of the second degree when the perpetrator had the specific intent to commit that crime.*" (Italics added.)

Defendant contends "it was error for the court to predicate a felony[-]murder instruction upon a violation of section 2800.3." We agree for reasons that follow.

Under specified conditions satisfied by the evidence in this case, "[a]ny person who, while operating a motor vehicle and with the intent to evade, willfully flees or otherwise attempts to elude a pursuing peace officer's motor vehicle, is guilty of a misdemeanor...." (§ 2800.1.) Section 2800.3 provides that "[w]henever willful flight or attempt to elude a pursuing peace officer in violation of Section 2800.1 proximately causes death or serious bodily injury to any person, the person driving the pursued vehicle, upon conviction, shall be punished by [confinement in state prison or county jail]...." [and is guilty of a felony.]

[T]o serve as the basis for the second degree felony-murder rule, the predicate crime must be a felony inherently dangerous to human life, i.e., there must be a high probability that death will result from its commission. "In determining whether a felony is inherently dangerous [to human life], the court looks to the elements of the felony *in the abstract,* 'not the "particular" facts of the case,' i.e., not to the defendant's specific conduct."[6]

---

4. Section 2800.3 is not a felony enumerated in Penal Code section 189.

6. "This form of analysis is compelled because there is a killing in every case where the [felony-murder] rule might potentially be applied. If in such circumstances a court were to examine the particular facts of the case prior to establishing whether the underlying felony is inherently dangerous [to human life], ... the existence of the dead victim might appear to lead inexorably to the conclusion that the underlying felony is exceptionally hazardous. [But such an analysis would be] unjustifiable bootstrapping" (*People v. Burroughs, supra,* 35 Cal. 3d at p. 830).

In *People v. Burroughs*, the Supreme Court laid out the analytical model for determining whether, in the abstract, the elements of a felony make the crime inherently dangerous to human life. Courts "look first to the primary element of the offense at issue, then to the 'factors elevating the offense to a felony,' ... In this examination we are required to view the statutory definition of the offense as a whole, taking into account even nonhazardous ways of violating the provisions of the law which do not necessarily pose a threat to human life." Thus, if dispositive elements of the statute may be established by conduct that does not endanger human life, it is not a felony inherently dangerous to human life.

As can be seen from the statutory language quoted above, the primary element of section 2800.3 is that, while operating a motor vehicle and with the intent to evade, a person willfully flees or otherwise attempts to elude a pursuing peace officer's motor vehicle. Common sense and common experience indicate that attempts by drivers to flee or otherwise elude pursuing peace officers often involve conduct that is inherently dangerous to human life. This case is a prime example of such reprehensible misconduct. But, as the Supreme Court has instructed, we must examine the crime in the abstract. And, as can be attested to by those who watched the ludicrous pursuit of Orenthal James Simpson in his white Bronco, a driver can flee or otherwise attempt to elude pursuing officers in a manner that does not pose a high probability of death to anyone. Hence, the primary element of section 2800.3 fails to support a determination that the offense is an inherently dangerous felony.

Therefore, we turn to the factor that elevates the misconduct from a misdemeanor to a felony, i.e., when the person driving the pursued vehicle proximately causes death "or" serious bodily injury to any person while fleeing or otherwise attempting to elude a pursuing peace officer. " 'Serious bodily injury' means a serious impairment of physical condition, including, but not limited to, the following: loss of consciousness; concussion; bone fracture; protracted loss or impairment of function of any bodily member or organ; a wound requiring extensive suturing; and serious disfigurement."

That "death" and "serious bodily injury" are identified in the disjunctive as separate risks in section 2800.3 indicates the Legislature intended that a person may violate the section without necessarily endangering human life....

Because dispositive elements of the statute can be satisfied by conduct that does not necessarily pose a high probability of death, the violation of section 2800.3, in the abstract, is not a felony inherently dangerous to human life. Consequently, it cannot serve as the predicate crime for application of the second degree felony-murder rule.

Discussion Questions

1. How does the *Sanchez* court determine if a felony is inherently dangerous? What probability is required for the danger of death to be inherent?

2. What does it mean for a felony to be inherently dangerous in the abstract?

3. Unlike California courts, some courts base their assessment of inherent danger on the facts of the case. What is the significance of assessing the inherent danger of a felony in the context of the facts of the particular case rather than in the abstract?

4. Should shooting into an inhabited dwelling qualify as an inherently dangerous felony?

5. Should the felony described below qualify?

> Except as otherwise authorized by law, any person who willfully discharges a firearm in a grossly negligent manner which could result in injury or death to a person is guilty of a public offense.... Cal. Penal Code Ann. § 246.3 (West 1999).

c. The Merger Doctrine

Like the inherent danger limitation, courts use the merger doctrine to limit the types of felonies upon which the prosecution can base a felony murder charge. If a felony "merges" with a homicide, that means it cannot support a felony murder charge. This doctrine is sometimes referred to as the "independent" felony rule. A felony must be independent of the homicide in order to support a felony murder charge. In other words, a felony that "merges" is not "independent."

Barnett v. State

783 So. 2d 927 (2000)
Court of Criminal Appeals of Alabama

Cobb, Judge.

The appellant, Andrae Barnett, was indicted and convicted of felony murder, a violation of § 13A-6-2(a)(3), Ala. Code 1975. Barnett was sentenced to 50 years in the state penitentiary....

On the afternoon of October 17, 1998, Morris Givens and his brother Andrae Barnett went to Daphne Golson's house to pick up Givens's three-year old daughter Jamari and take her to the fair. Daphne Golson is Jamari's mother and Givens's former girlfriend. Golson, her mother, her daughter Jamari, and her boyfriend Kevon Moses were at the home when Givens and Barnett arrived....

Golson stepped off the porch.... She then began to argue with Givens. While Golson and Givens were arguing, a separate altercation began between Moses and Barnett. Golson heard a noise behind her and turned; Barnett was holding a garden hoe. According to Golson, Barnett had the hoe in his hands and Moses was backing away from Barnett. As he backed away, Moses tripped over Givens's feet, fell on his stomach, and was hit in the back of the head with the hoe by Barnett. Moses died as a result of the blow to the head. Subsequently, Barnett was arrested and indicted on the charge of felony murder.

On appeal, Barnett asserts that the trial court erred by allowing him to be charged with felony murder when the underlying felony was assault, because he argues, assault was an essential part of the homicide itself....

Barnett's felony-murder conviction was premised on the underlying felony of assault in the first degree. Whether felony murder can be premised on a murder resulting from a first degree assault is a question of first impression in Alabama. The indictment stated that Barnett

> "did commit or attempt to commit the crime of Assault First Degree, a felony clearly dangerous to human life and, in the furtherence [sic] of committing or attempting to commit Assault in the First Degree on KEVON MOSES did cause the death of KEVON MOSES by striking him with a garden hoe, in violation of Section 13A-6-2, Code of Alabama, 1975."

Under Alabama law, a person commits the crime of felony murder when

> "he commits or attempts to commit arson in the first degree, burglary in the first or second degree, escape in the first degree, kidnapping in the first degree, rape in the first degree, robbery in any degree, sodomy in the first degree, or any other felony clearly dangerous to human life and, in the course of and in furtherance of the crime that he is committing or attempting to commit, or in immediate flight therefrom, he, or another participant if there be any, causes the death of any person."

Assault in the first degree is defined at § 13A-6-20(a)(1), Ala.Code 1975:

> "(a) A person commits the crime of assault in the first degree if:
>
> (1) With intent to cause serious physical injury to another person, he causes serious physical injury to any person by means of a deadly weapon or a dangerous instrument."

In *People v. Ireland*, the Supreme Court of California addressed whether assault with a deadly weapon could constitute the predicate felony for a felony-murder charge. The appellant in *Ireland* shot and killed his wife. During the trial, the trial court instructed the jury that it could convict Ireland of felony murder if it determined that he committed the underlying felony of assault with a deadly weapon. In discussing this issue, the Supreme Court of California stated:

> "We have concluded that the utilization of the felony-murder rule in circumstances such as those before us extends the operation of that rule 'beyond any rational function it is designed to serve.' To allow such use of the felony-murder rule would effectively preclude the jury from considering the issue of malice aforethought in all cases wherein homicide has been committed as a result of a felonious assault—a category which includes the great majority of all homicides. This kind of bootstrapping finds support neither in logic nor in law. We therefore hold that a second degree felony-murder instruction may not properly be given when it is based upon a felony which is an integral part of the homicide and which the evidence produced by the prosecution shows to be an offense included in fact within the offense charged."

Other jurisdictions have construed their felony-murder laws in a similar manner, and have held that felonious assault merges into the homicide....

Conceived in the nineteenth century, the merger doctrine bars the use of the felony-murder rule when the underlying felony directly results in, or is an integral part of, the homicide.... Thus, under the merger doctrine, the elements of the underlying felony must be independent of the homicide. We believe that the California Supreme Court's rationale in *Ireland* is sound and that the "merger doctrine" should be applied in felony-murder cases in which the underlying felony is the assault that results in the victim's death.

To read the "clearly dangerous to human life" language in the felony murder rule as allowing an assault on the homicide victim to be the predicate felony for felony murder would offend the statutory construction of Alabama's homicide laws. The Legislature has defined those acts that constitute murder as well as those acts that constitute manslaughter. *See* §§ 13A-6-2 and 13A-6-3, Ala.Code 1975. If prosecutors could prove murder by proving the intent element of assault as opposed to the requisite mens rea for murder or manslaughter, §§ 13A-6-2(a)(1) and (2), 13A-6-2(b), and 13A-6-3, Ala Code 1975 would effectively be eliminated. Clearly, such a result would be contrary to legislative intent....

Reversed and remanded.

* * *

Not every jurisdiction abides by the merger or "independent" felony limitation. Notably, in June 2020, Minnesota Attorney General Keith Ellison filed second-degree murder charges against Minneapolis Police Officer Derek Chauvin for killing an unarmed black man, George Floyd, by kneeling on his neck for more than eight minutes, even as Floyd insisted "I can't breathe." Ellison indicated that the precise theory underlying this charge was felony murder: That Chauvin committed assault, a felony, and that led to Floyd's death. Under Minnesota law, "any felony, not otherwise proscribed, which, as committed, involved special danger to human life, could serve as a predicate felony." *State v. Branson*, 487 N.W.2d 880 (Minn. 1992). Minnesota courts have subsequently affirmed several felony murder convictions in which assault served as the underlying felony.[2] If the killing of Floyd had occurred in Alabama, would prosecutors be able to file felony murder charges? How might the murder of Floyd be distinguished from the facts of the *Barnett* case? Or would the merger doctrine provide an insurmountable barrier to prosecution in Alabama?

* * *

Legislatures commonly designate particular felonies as ones that can support a first-degree murder conviction. These enumerated felonies are not generally subject to the inherent danger or merger limitations. Rather, courts often treat such enumerated felonies as having a legislative exemption from the inherent danger and

---

2. Amy Swearer, *A More Fitting Criminal Charge in George Floyd's Death*, The Heritage Foundation, June 2, 2020, available at https://www.heritage.org/crime-and-justice/commentary/more-fitting-criminal-charge-george-floyds-death.

merger requirements. In contrast, even enumerated felonies may be subject to other limitations, like the agency and res gestae limitations discussed below.

d. "Agency" and "In Furtherance"

Unlike the inherent danger and merger limitations, the agency and "in furtherance" limitations do not focus on the type of felony. Although these two limitations are often lumped together and often lead to the same results, they are not identical. Three different variations tend to be collapsed under these headings. Since these cases frequently involve shooting deaths, we'll use hypothetical "shooters" to explain these variations.

A "shooter ID" rule. The agency limitation narrows felony murder by looking to the identity of the shooter, in particular, whether the shooter was a co-felon of the person charged with felony murder. Each felon acts as an agent for the other robbers. Assume, for example, that during a bank robbery committed by a team of several robbers, a police officer responding to a silent alarm accidentally shot and killed an innocent bank customer. Since the police officer clearly was not acting as an *agent* of the bank robbers when he shot the customer, the agency limitation or "shooter ID" rule would eliminate felony murder here. In other words, the *shooter* has to be a *felon* to support felony murder.

A "victim ID" rule. What if during the robbery one felon accidentally shot and killed another felon? Since the shooter was a felon, the agency requirement addressed above under the "shooter ID" rule is met. Nonetheless, some jurisdictions do *not* impose felony murder in this situation, requiring that the *victim not* be a felon, *i.e.*, not an agent of the person charged with felony murder. In other words, the victim must be a *non-felon*, such as a police officer, customer, or other bystander. Reasoning offered to support this "victim ID" rule typically is that the felony murder rule was not created to protect felons from being shot.

A "motivation" rule. A distinct but analogous way of limiting felony murder is to look to the *motivation* rather than the *identity* of the shooter. If the shooter's motive was to further the felony (*i.e.*, to help it succeed), the shooting meets the "in furtherance" requirement and triggers felony murder. But if the shooter was acting to resist the felony, the shooting death would not trigger felony murder.

In most cases, one who shoots and kills "in furtherance" of a felony is a felon and one who shoots in resistance to the felony is not a felon. Instead one who shoots in resistance typically is a policeman, bank guard, or bystander. Therefore, the "motivation" or "in furtherance" rule typically achieves the same results as the "shooter ID" version of the agency rule.

As you read the materials in this section, ask yourself whether and why these issues are important. Is the identity of the shooter or the victim significant from the perspective of the purposes of punishment?

Consider the Delaware statute that follows:

Delaware Code Annotated

§ 635 Murder in the second degree

A person is guilty of murder in the second degree when:

(2) In the course of and in furtherance of the commission or attempted commission of any felony not specifically enumerated in § 636 of this title or immediate flight therefrom, the person, with criminal negligence, causes the death of another person.

Note here that Delaware has modified its felony murder rule, rejecting strict liability and requiring at least negligence regarding the death.

Discussion Question

What does the statutory language "in furtherance of the commission" mean?

Weick v. State

420 A.2d 159 (1980)
Supreme Court of Delaware

Herrmann, C.J.

On appeal, the defendants petition this court to reverse their convictions for Murder in the Second Degree under 11 Del.C. § 635(2); and Conspiracy in the Second Degree under 11 Del.C. § 512(1)....

The facts giving rise to the indictments were stipulated for the purposes of trial as follows:

In November, 1977, the defendants agreed with each other and with a fifth person, Eugene Edgar Weick, to seize by force a quantity of marijuana held illegally by Robert and Kathy Fitzgerald. To this end, the defendants Frank Weick, Eugene Weick and Messick armed themselves with loaded sawed-off shotguns. Then they and the defendants Jerry and Gary Connelly proceeded to the Fitzgerald residence.

Messick, his shotgun hidden under his coat, was admitted to the house by Robert Fitzgerald. Once inside, Messick produced the shotgun and forced Fitzgerald into a rear room of the house. At that point, Frank Weick trained his shotgun on Fitzgerald through a window in that room.

Simultaneously, Kathy Fitzgerald came out of a bedroom and observed what was occurring in the rear of the house. She returned to the bedroom and obtained a 30-30 caliber rifle. On re-exiting from the bedroom she observed Eugene Weick breaking through the kitchen door. She fired the rifle at Eugene and the bullet struck him in the face. Messick and Frank Weick retreated from the house, taking Eugene with them, and met the Connellys, who had been awaiting them in the getaway car. They placed their injured cohort in the car and fled the scene, failing to consummate the intended drug theft. Eugene subsequently died of the bullet wound he received at the hands of Mrs. Fitzgerald. The criminal charges brought against the defendants were based upon that homicide.

The defendants contend: (1) that §635(2) was applied to them improperly in that it was used as the basis for convictions and sentences for the killing of a co-felon by the intended victim of the felony....

Under §635(2), the Statute upon which the Murder convictions were based, a person is guilty of Murder in the Second Degree when:

> "(i)n the course of and in furtherance of the commission or attempted commission of any felony not specifically enumerated in §636 of this title or immediate flight therefrom, he, with criminal negligence, causes the death of another person."

The defendants contend that this section was improperly applied to them because, manifestly, §635(2) was not intended to punish one who commits a felony for a homicide that occurs during the perpetration of that felony but is not committed by him, his agent, or some one under his control. We agree.

Section 635(2) is the statutory substitute for the common-law felony-murder rule.

"[W]ith the general trend toward mitigation in the severity of punishment for many felonies, and with the addition of many statutory felonies of a character less dangerous than was typical of most common law felonies, the irrationality and unfairness of an unlimited felony-murder rule become increasingly apparent." Consequently, limitations were placed on the scope of the rule. One such restriction was the requirement of a causal connection between the felony and the murder. Another restraint placed on the rule by some courts was the requirement that the killing be performed by the felon, his accomplices, or one associated with the felon in his unlawful enterprise.

In the development of the felony-murder rule through the common law and by statute, the latter limitation has become the majority rule.... The parameters of this rule are probably best defined by *Commonwealth v. Redline,* Pa.Supr., 391 Pa. 486 (1958) in which it was stated:

> "In adjudging a felony-murder, it is to be remembered at all times that the thing which is imputed to a felon for a killing incidental to his felony is *malice* and *not the act of killing.* The mere coincidence of homicide and felony is not enough to satisfy the requirements of the felony murder doctrine. It is necessary ... to show that the conduct causing death was done in furtherance of the design to commit the felony. Death must be a consequence of the felony ... and not merely coincidence."

We think that this rule clearly applies to §635(2). That section requires that the homicide be committed "in the course of and in furtherance" of the commission or attempted commission of any felony not enumerated in §636. Certainly the killing of a co-felon by the victim or a police officer, or the accidental killing of an innocent bystander by the victim or a police officer, can hardly be considered to be "in furtherance" of the commission or attempted commission of a felony. Indeed, the homicide in the instant case was an attempt to prevent the felony....

The case is remanded to the Superior Court for further proceedings in accordance herewith.

* * *

Compare the position taken in the above decision with that taken below in *Oimen*. What explains the difference?

State v. Oimen

184 Wis. 2d 423 (1994)
Supreme Court of Wisconsin

Heffernan, C.J.

... We accepted review limited to the following two issues: whether the felony murder statute, sec. 940.03, applies to a defendant whose co-felon is killed by the intended felony victim; and whether the circuit court erred in instructing the jury on the elements of felony murder.

We conclude that under sec. 940.03, a defendant can be charged with felony murder for the death of a co-felon when the killing was committed by the victim of the underlying felony. Sec. 940.03 limits liability to those deaths caused by a defendant committing or attempting to commit a limited number of inherently dangerous felonies, but it contains no other limitations on liability. The state need only prove that the defendant caused the death, and that the defendant caused the death while committing or attempting to commit one of the five listed felonies. The defendant's acts need not be the sole cause of death. Thus, Oimen was appropriately charged with felony murder for the death of a co-felon, Shawn Murphy McGinnis, who was killed by Tom Stoker, the victim of the underlying felony....

[Evidence suggested that Oimen helped plan the robbery and provided information about the victim and the sums of money the victim kept at his home as well as a diagram of the intended victim's house. Oimen waited up the street in the getaway vehicle until the shooting of McGinnis by the intended victim, at which time, Oimen apparently drove away.]

The jury found Oimen guilty on all counts....

The first issue we address on review is whether a defendant may be charged with felony murder under sec. 940.03, when that defendant's co-felon is killed by the intended victim of the underlying felony. Statutory construction is a question of law that this court determines de novo. The principal objective of statutory construction is to ascertain and give effect to the legislature's intent. In determining that intent, we first resort to the language of the statute

Section 940.03, states:

> Whoever causes the death of another human being while committing or attempting to commit a crime specified in s. 940.225(1) or (2)(a) [first degree sexual assault and second degree sexual assault with use or threat of force or violence], 943.02 [arson], 943.10(2) [armed burglary] or 943.32(2) [armed

452   6 · HOMICIDE

robbery] may be imprisoned for not more than 20 years in excess of the maximum period of imprisonment provided by law for that crime or attempt.

We conclude that the plain meaning of sec. 940.03, allows a defendant to be charged with felony murder when a co-felon is killed by the intended felony victim. Section 940.03, contains two elements, which were set forth in the jury instructions: the defendant must cause a death and the defendant must cause the death while committing or attempting to commit one of the five listed felonies. "Causes" has a consistent, well-established meaning in Wisconsin criminal law. An actor causes death if his or her conduct is a "substantial factor" in bringing about that result. As long as an actor's conduct is a "substantial factor" in bringing about a death, the plain language of sec. 940.03 places no limits on whose death it is that results. Under sec. 940.03, it is irrelevant that McGinnis, the person who was killed, was a co-felon. It is also irrelevant for purposes of sec. 940.03 that the rifle shot fired by Stoker was the immediate cause of McGinnis's death. A "substantial factor" need not be the sole cause of death....

The conclusion we reach regarding the elements of felony murder liability, based on the plain language of sec. 940.03, is supported by the legislative history. Sec. 940.03 became law when the legislature revised the law of homicide. These revisions were drafted by the Wisconsin Judicial Council's Special Committee on Homicide and Lesser Included Offenses ["Homicide Law Committee"].... The Homicide Law Committee discussions indicate that the Judicial Council decided to recommend only one limitation on liability—the major limitation of restricting felony murder liability to killings that occur during the course of five listed felonies.

The Homicide Law Committee discussed and rejected other limitations on felony murder liability....

A brief discussion by members of the Homicide Law Committee indicates that sec. 940.03 was not meant to be restricted to situations in which the person killed was the victim of the underlying felony. A member of the committee raised the possibility of having a longer list of underlying felonies and limiting the statute's coverage to killings of the victim of those crimes. However, another committee member stated the victim limitation could present problems and asked whether patrons at a retail store would be "victims" if killed in an armed robbery when only cash register proceeds had been taken. The other committee member agreed that limiting the statute's coverage to death of victims of the underlying felony could prove to be complicated. We could find no further discussion suggesting that sec. 940.03 was to apply only to murders of certain individuals such as bystanders or victims of the underlying felony. No such limiting language was proposed....

[T]he committee [also] made no effort to ... limit liability to the "trigger person" when it developed the fall back provision that became sec. 940.03.

Oimen points out that the vast majority of state courts that have addressed this issue have concluded that the applicable statute does not make a felon liable for murder when the killing was done by a victim of the felony. These states take what has been termed the "agency approach" to felony murder liability, under which a felon can only be liable for death when the killing was committed by an individual acting in concert with him, i.e. acting in furtherance of the underlying felony. We believe that sec. 940.03 and the accompanying legislative history indicate that the legislature did not intend to impose liability only when there is an "agency" relationship ... [W]e note that the cases adopting the agency approach appear to be grounded in policy concerns—dissatisfaction with the strict liability aspect of felony murder, or a concern that liability in such cases "erodes the relation between criminal liability and moral culpability." While that concern is not unreasonable, that policy determination is one for the legislature to make and the Wisconsin legislature's determination is to the contrary.

Realizing that application of the felony murder statute could lead to harsh results in some cases, the Homicide Law Committee explained that any potential harshness can be mitigated at sentencing.... Decision affirmed.

Discussion Questions

1. Could a killing during an enumerated felony fail to create felony murder liability? If so, how?

2. How do the agency and in furtherance limitations differ from the inherent danger limitation?

e. Res Gestae

When does liability for felony murder end? What if someone is killed while the felony is being committed? What if the killing happens two hours after the felony is completed? What if police identify the felons months or even years after the felony was committed and someone is killed when the police try to capture them? Felony murder statutes are not precise in setting a temporal restriction on felony murder, often using language such as "in the commission of" or "during" the felony. These questions are addressed under a fourth limitation on the felony murder rule we consider in this section, the *res gestae* limitation. It focuses on how closely tied the killing is to the felony.

Courts here often focus on time, whether the felony was still in progress at the time of the killing or, if the felony had been completed, how much time transpired between completion of the felony and the death. Courts applying the res gestae limitation also consider the distance between the place of the felony and the place of the death as well as the strength of the causal connection between the felony and the death. Again, as you read the materials that follow, ask yourself if and why issues of time, space, and causal connection should be important in establishing the bounds of felony murder liability.

State v. Adams

339 Mo. 926 (1936)
Supreme Court of Missouri

Ellison, J.

The appellant was convicted of murder in the first degree, the jury inflicting the death penalty, for the fatal shooting of Clarence Green, night marshal of the town of Campbell in Dunklin County, in March, 1934. It was not controverted at the trial that just preceding the homicide the appellant and two accomplices were engaged in burglarizing a filling station at Campbell. But he contended the burglarious enterprise had been abandoned, that he was in flight, and that Green was shot by another of the burglars for which he is not responsible....

Summarizing the evidence as briefly as possible, it was conceded by appellant's counsel in open court at the trial, and the undisputed evidence showed it, that he and two accomplices had broken into a White Eagle gasoline filling station at Campbell about eleven o'clock at night and had carried out and deposited on the ground certain articles of property which they were stealing, and had gone back presumably for more loot when the deceased Clarence Green, together with Rodney Brown, city marshal, and two other men, drove up to the filling station. The three burglars fled across lots into a wooded section behind the station. Green and Brown followed in pursuit, being guided mainly by sound since it was too dark to see the fugitives in the woods, though the moon was shining. How far from the filling station the chase continued the record does not clearly show — perhaps several hundred feet — but at any rate, Brown testified that Green was about twenty feet ahead of him and some fifty feet from what the witnesses called "the fourth fence" when suddenly one gunshot was fired by someone straight ahead of Green who sagged down and then started to straighten up. Several more shots came from an oblique direction. From their rapid succession it appeared they had been fired from an automatic shotgun. Green reeled in a semicircle for about fifteen feet, fell, and died without uttering a word....

[W]e must ... pass on the assignments in [the] motion for new trial charging the homicide was not committed in the perpetration or attempted perpetration of the burglary — this because the court gave instructions authorizing a conviction on that theory, and the appellant complains there was no evidence to support them. The seventh instruction declared any homicide committed in the perpetration or attempted perpetration of a burglary is murder in the first degree, and the eighth instruction told the jury the perpetration or attempted perpetration of a burglary consists not only in burglariously breaking and entering a building and seizing property therein with intent to steal and carry it away, but includes also the act of asportation, and continues until the property has been reduced to the unmolested dominion of the burglars. This instruction then went on to advise the jury that if they found the killing of Green was done by the appellant, or others with whom he knowingly acted in joint concert, while the appellant and such others were engaged in the perpetration or attempted perpetration of a burglary as above defined, the law would presume and supply the several mental ingredients necessary to make the homicide murder in the first degree.

The appellant's motion points to the undisputed evidence showing that when the officers approached the filling station the three accomplices abandoned the burglary and all dominion over the property they had seized, and fled from the premises, the fatal shooting occurring thereafter. He maintains that under these facts the homicide was not committed in the perpetration or attempted perpetration of the burglary within the meaning of the statute; and that he cannot be held guilty of murder in the first degree on that theory, either as the actual killer, or as a co-conspirator in the antecedent burglary if the fatal shot was fired by another of the trio....

It is held in many jurisdictions, including Missouri, that when the homicide is within the *res gestae* of the initial crime and is an emanation thereof, it is committed in the *perpetration* of that crime in the statutory sense. Thus it has been often ruled that the statute applies where the initial crime and the homicide were parts of one continuous transaction, and were closely connected in point of time, place and causal relation, as where the killing was done in flight from the scene of the crime to prevent detection, or promote escape. The same rule has been followed in cases of *attempted* robbery where there was no asportation, the robbers being compelled to flee without obtaining any property. [T]his is the prevailing doctrine in this country....

The undisputed evidence in this case shows the killing of Green was of the *res gestae* of the burglary. Instruction No. 8, if it was erroneous in the respect above pointed out, was error in favor of the appellant, rather than against him, because it allowed a conviction on the theory that the homicide was committed in the perpetration or attempted perpetration of the burglary, only if the jury found the killing was done during the actual burglary or the asportation of the property sought to be taken....

But the instruction could have done no harm in this case, because, as we have shown, the undisputed evidence shows the homicide was committed within the *res gestae* of the burglary, and the question of asportation and possession was immaterial....

Date of execution set for December 18, 1936.

* * *

How far does the res gestae of a felony extend? Consider the following standard from *State v. Williams*, 776 So. 2d 1066 (2001):

> The crux of this case is the breadth of the phrase "engaged in the perpetration of ... any felony" in the felony murder statute....
>
> In deciding whether a killing falls under the felony murder statute, the more recent supreme court case of *Parker v. State*, 641 So. 2d 369, 376 (Fla.1994), looked for a "break in the chain of circumstances" between the killing and the underlying felony....
>
> To find what the supreme court calls "a break in the chain of circumstances" between the killing and the underlying felony, courts focus on the time, dis-

tance, and causal relationship between the underlying felony and the killing. "Neither the passage of time nor separation in space from the felonious act to the killing precludes a felony murder conviction when it can be said ... that the killing is a predictable result of the felonious transaction." ...

[O]ne of the most important factors to consider in deciding if there has been a "break in the chain of circumstances" is whether the "fleeing felon has reached a place of temporary safety." *Parker*, 570 So. 2d at 1051 (quoting Lafave, Substantive Criminal Law, §7.5 (1986)). If the felon has gained a place of temporary safety after commission of the felony and before the death of the victim, the felony murder rule generally does not apply.

G. Synthesis and Review

Problem

6.32 Sarah is a member of a radical white supremacist group dedicated to ridding the United States of the pernicious influences of "alien" racial and religious groups. In order to help fund her group's activities, she decides to kidnap for ransom Stephen, the son of a prominent newspaper owner. The family's newspaper is liberal in its political point of view and has been highly critical of the white supremacist movement. Sarah and a group of confederates abduct Stephen early one morning while he is on his way to work and take him to a remote wooded area in the countryside. In order to keep Stephen out of sight and out of trouble while negotiating the group's $1 million ransom demand, Sarah and her confederates bury Stephen alive in a wooden box, the dimensions of which are roughly 6 ft., by 4 ft., by 4 ft. The box is buried by Sarah approximately three feet underground in a sandy, wooded area. In the box, Sarah leaves a small electric light bulb connected to several car batteries. In order to provide Stephen with air, Sarah buries next to the box an air tank with a day's supply of air in it. A mouthpiece is connected from the tank to the box for Stephen to breathe through. One of her confederates asks Sarah, "Don't you think he might suffocate? He's not worth anything to us dead." Sarah replies, "It's a risk worth taking. Their newspaper has tried to suffocate our movement."

The next day, Sarah makes several telephone calls to Stephen's family demanding $1 million in ransom. Acting on the advice of the FBI and local police, Stephen's family initially stalls for several hours and resists Sarah's ransom demands. During the delay, the FBI traces the calls to the telephone booth Sarah has been using to make the ransom calls. While Sarah is making her final ransom call on the day after Stephen was buried, the FBI arrests her. At the time of her arrest, she is alone. Her confederates hear of the arrest and, afraid that Sarah may talk, head for Canada, leaving Stephen buried in the box. At the border her confederates are all killed in a shootout with Canadian and United States police.

During intense interrogation in the days following her arrest, Sarah refuses to reveal the whereabouts of Stephen. The police inform Sarah that Stephen has not been found and that her confederates have all been killed. A week after Sarah's arrest, while Sarah is still in custody and refusing to talk, police dogs locate the site at which Stephen had been buried alive. When the box is uncovered, Stephen is found dead. A medical examiner later determines: (1) that Stephen died from suffocation two days before the police discovered the location of the box and (2) that Stephen would have lived if his location had been discovered two days earlier.

Is Sarah liable for homicide? If so, what type of homicide? Assessing Sarah's homicide liability requires you to draw on some of the materials you learned earlier in the course, such as those dealing with conduct.

6.33 Carlton makes his living selling heroin. He buys "uncut" (*i.e.*, pure) heroin from his supplier. Uncut heroin is lethal to inject, so Carlton, like other dealers, "cuts" (*i.e.*, dilutes) the heroin he sells with other substances such as baking powder, starch, sucrose, and powdered milk before putting it into small plastic bags, each of which is meant for a single injection. Carlton usually does this by putting the heroin and the cutting agents into a common food blender and mixing them.

Recently the heroin Carlton has been receiving from his supplier has been of low quality and Carlton's customers have complained that the heroin he is selling is "weak." To remedy this problem, Carlton decides to add to his heroin fentanyl, a powerful but potentially dangerous synthetic opioid. Carlton asks his supplier to provide him with fentanyl and the supplier agrees to do so. The supplier warns Carlton that the fentanyl is very dangerous and that Carlton must be careful not to mix too much fentanyl into the heroin or it will kill those who use it. Carlton is aware that in the city where he lives an increasing number of heroin users in recent years have died from using heroin laced with too much fentanyl. These deaths and the dangers of heroin mixed with fentanyl have received great publicity.

Carlton cuts a new batch of heroin he is preparing to sell. As usual, he does it in a food blender. But this time he adds some fentanyl. Unfortunately, a blender is too crude a device to distribute the fentanyl evenly throughout the batch of heroin. As a result, some of the individual bags of heroin Carlton prepares wind up not having much fentanyl, if any, and others have too much fentanyl and are deadly.

Maria, one of Carlton's customers, is a young executive. After suffering a serious back injury in an auto accident, she became addicted to the oxycodone she was prescribed for pain. When her treatment for the back injury ended about a year after the accident, she started using heroin because her doctors would no longer prescribe oxycodone for her. One day Carlton comes to Maria's condominium to deliver heroin. Maria complains that the heroin Carlton has been supplying her recently is too weak to satisfy her needs. When she tells him she plans to look for another dealer, Carlton tells her that the heroin he has with him is much better and offers to let her try it. Maria takes a bag, prepares it, and injects it while Carlton waits.

Shortly after she injects the heroin, Maria falls to the floor and starts convulsing. Carlton then realizes he put too much fentanyl in the bag he gave Maria. Rather than calling 911, Carlton flees the apartment. Maria dies from a fentanyl overdose. Carlton's image as well as that of his car and its license plate are captured on a security camera at Maria's condominium complex and Carlton is arrested. A medical examiner determines that if Maria had received medical assistance, in particular the drug naloxone, within a half hour of her collapse, she would have survived. The prosecution also proves that if Carlton had called 911 when Maria collapsed, a medical team equipped with naloxone from a nearby fire station would have arrived within 15 minutes. Is Carlton liable for homicide in regard to Maria's death? If so, what level of homicide?

Chapter 7

Causation

A. Introduction

Legislatures often include a result element when defining crimes. All homicide of-fenses, for example, require a *death*. Other examples of result elements found in criminal statutes are *serious bodily injury* and *damage to property*. When a crime re-quires a result, the prosecution must prove not only that the result occurred but also that the defendant's conduct *caused* that result. By contrast, crimes without a result element do not require proof of causation. Theft, reckless driving, and attempt are examples of crimes that lack result elements and accordingly do not require proof of causation. Our previous homicide diagrams should then be modified to include the requirement of causation:

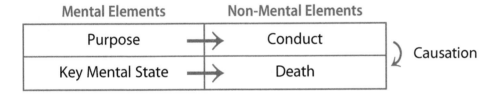

An assault statute that makes it a crime to engage in conduct that results in serious bodily injury to another person with purpose regarding such injury would be dia-grammed as follows:

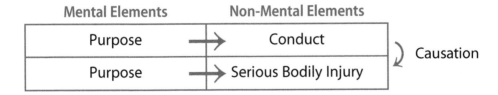

A statute that makes it a crime to damage the property of another with recklessness regarding the resulting damage and knowledge that the property belonged to someone else would be diagrammed as follows:

Mental Elements		Non-Mental Elements	
Purpose	⟶	Conduct	⎫
Recklessness	⟶	Damage to Property	⎬ Causation
Knowledge	⟶	Of Another	⎭

This chapter addresses two central questions. First, why is causation ever a prerequisite for criminal liability? Second, what is required to satisfy causation? In answering the first, think about the following scenario. Defendant Uno, intending to kill victim Quatro, sprinkles a fatal dose of cyanide poison on the brownies that Uno knows Quatro will eat at lunch. Meanwhile, en route home from the gym early that same morning, Quatro's car is struck by a drunk driver, killing both Quatro and the drunk driver. Should Uno be liable for Quatro's death? Intuition may suggest that Uno should not be held liable for a death he played no role in bringing about and the criminal law accords with your intuition. Uno would not be held liable for Quatro's death because of a lack of causation between Uno's conduct and Quatro's death. What underlies this intuition? In answering this question, look back to the purposes of punishment. Does a retributive concern about blame explain causation requirements? Does it make any difference if one measures blame by reference to mental state or by reference to any harm that actually occurs? Or do utilitarian concerns about danger drive causation?

Consider a second scenario. A and B leave a bar one minute apart. Both are severely intoxicated and drive at 75 mph to their respective homes, which are just a few houses apart. A and B run the same multiple stop signs and red lights along the way. A arrives home without causing any harm. B, just one minute behind A, hits a school bus carrying a soccer team returning from a game. B survives but several young people on the bus are killed. Who should be punished? A, who caused no harm? B, who caused several deaths? If both should be punished, should B be punished more severely than A? If so, why? If not, why not?

If one uses harm to assess blame, it makes sense to punish B more severely than A from a retributive perspective because B's driving brought about several deaths. But what if one uses mental state rather than harm to assess blame? Is A's mental state any less blameworthy than B's? If one relies on the utilitarian purposes of punishment to determine whether and how severely A and B should be punished, it is difficult to distinguish between A and B. A's conduct was just as dangerous as B's. Both seem equally in need of deterrence and incapacitation. Which theories of punishment, then, support treating A and B differently? Should homicide liability and severity of punishment hinge on B's "bad luck" in striking or A's "good luck" in missing the bus? What does this hypothetical scenario suggest about the use of causation as an ingredient in formulating criminal liability?

To answer the second inquiry and determine what is required to satisfy causation, we begin with a typical criminal jury instruction succinctly stating the basic law of causation and a problem asking you to apply the instruction to the facts of a number of cases you have already studied. The jury instruction reveals that the test for causation has two components, which may seem familiar to you if you have already taken a course in tort law. The prosecution must prove both. The first is often referred to as *cause in fact* or *but for cause* and the second as *proximate cause*. The materials that follow the introductory problem examine both cause in fact and proximate cause in detail.

The law of causation is often criticized as murky and indeterminate. See if you agree with this assessment as you decide whether causation is fulfilled in each of the cases in Problem 7.1.

Although legislatures have primary authority in criminal law, they have shown little interest in the law of criminal causation. Most states do not have a statute addressing causation. Rather, judges largely control the development of the law of causation through a common law process. The law you will encounter in this chapter, unlike most of the other chapters in this book, is almost exclusively in the form of judicial opinions.

Problem

7.1 *Jury Instruction on Causation*.[1] The state alleges that the defendant's act caused the death at issue in this case. Cause is an essential element in a homicide offense. An act causes death if: (1) without the act the death would not have occurred and (2) the act produces the death in a natural and continuous sequence. The defendant's responsibility is not limited to the immediate or most obvious result of the defendant's act. The defendant is also responsible for the natural and foreseeable consequences that follow, in the ordinary course of events, from the act.

> (a) Put yourself in the role of a juror and apply the above instruction to the following cases.
>
> > (1) *Keeler v. Superior Court* (Ch. 3) (in utero fetus dies after defendant, with the goal of killing the fetus, assaults pregnant ex-wife). Did Keeler's conduct cause the death of the fetus his former wife was carrying?

---

1. This instruction is based on *Ohio Jury Instructions—Criminal*, 409.55.

(2) *Jones v. United States* (Ch. 4) (10-month-old infant, Anthony Lee, who had been in the defendant's care, dies of malnutrition). Did Jones' failure to act cause the death of Anthony Lee?

(3) *Commonwealth v. Carroll* (Ch. 6) (defendant shoots wife after argument about defendant taking teaching position that would require his absence from the home several nights a week). Did Carroll's conduct cause his wife's death?

(4) *United States v. Fleming* (Ch. 6) (victim dies after intoxicated defendant collides with victims' car on wrong side of highway). Did Fleming's conduct cause the deaths of those who died in the collision?

(5) *Berry v. Superior Court* (Ch. 6) (child dies after being mauled by defendant's pit bull, Willy). Did Berry's conduct cause the death of his neighbor's child?

(6) *Commonwealth v. Welansky* (Ch. 6) (many victims, unable to escape, die in the fire at the Cocoanut Grove). Did Welansky's conduct cause the deaths of those who died in the Cocoanut Grove fire?

(7) *People v. Hall* (Ch. 6) (victim skier dies after being struck in the head by defendant skier). Did Hall's conduct cause the death of the skier he struck?

(8) *State v. Williams* (Ch. 6) (17-month-old child dies after parents fail to provide medical attention). Did his parents' failure to provide medical attention cause the child's death?

(b) What is required under this instruction for a jury to find that someone caused a death?

(c) Who is making the law of criminal causation under an instruction such as the one that appears above? The legislature? The judge? The jury?

B. Cause in Fact

Cause in fact is sometimes referred to as factual or "but for" cause. The jury instruction in Problem 7.1 above uses the standard test for cause in fact, whether "without the [defendant's] act, the death would not have occurred." This same test is often expressed using the phrase "but for." That is, if the result would not have occurred "but for" the defendant's act, then cause in fact is fulfilled. Recall the *Stamp* felony-murder case from Chapter 6 in which the victim of a robbery died from a heart attack less than one hour after the robbery. The medical expert's testimony that "but for the robbery there would have been no fatal seizure at that time" provided the evidentiary basis for the jury to find that the robbery was a cause in fact of the victim's death, fulfilling the first component of causation.

The cause in fact inquiry is a factual one, whether the defendant's conduct in some way contributed to the result. This component of causation has been described as adopting a "scientific notion of causation. Whether cigarette smoking causes cancer, whether the presence of hydrogen or helium caused an explosion, are factual questions to be resolved by the best science the courts can muster."[2]

You should keep in mind that cause in fact is a necessary but not sufficient condition for criminal liability. Many acts fulfill the test for cause in fact even though they do not warrant criminal punishment. A, for example, hires B to work as a sales clerk in A's store. During a robbery of the store, B is shot and killed. If A had not hired B, B would not have been killed in the robbery. A's act of hiring B thus meets the test for cause in fact of B's homicide though it obviously does not merit criminal punishment. The second component of causation — proximate cause — serves an important limiting function by sifting, from the many acts that fulfill cause in fact, those upon which criminal liability may be imposed.

Problems

7.2 Was cause in fact fulfilled in each of the cases in Problem 7.1?

7.3 Mary and Jim recently refinanced their mortgage with a new bank. Mary takes care of the couple's banking chores and did most of the work on the refinancing. One evening, because Mary knows she has a busy schedule the following day, she asks Jim to stop by the bank during his lunch hour to pick up a form to have their monthly mortgage payment automatically deducted from their joint checking account. Jim's typical routine is to exercise during his lunch hour by running or lifting weights at a gym. The next day, Jim goes to the bank during his lunch hour and happens to arrive in the middle of a bank robbery. Police surround the bank and the robbers take Jim hostage. Jim is shot and killed in an exchange of gunfire between the robbers and pursuing police. Is Mary's act of asking Jim to visit the bank during his lunch hour a cause in fact of Jim's death?

7.4 Stephen, a former nursing home administrator, was recently fired. His employers discovered that in order to increase profits, Stephen had drastically cut the nursing home staff while simultaneously increasing the number of residents. After Stephen made the staff cuts, Geraldine, an elderly resident of the nursing home, wandered outside during the night, where she died of exposure. You are the local prosecutor. Public attention is focused on Geraldine's death and her relatives demand that you charge Stephen with manslaughter based on Geraldine's death. Could you prove beyond a reasonable doubt that Stephen's conduct was a cause in fact of Geraldine's death?

---

2. Michael S. Moore, *Causation*, in 1 ENCYCLOPEDIA OF CRIME AND JUSTICE 152 (2d ed. 2002).

7.5 A police officer sitting in his patrol car one evening at around 10:30 observes Timothy, who is driving a 1979 Chevy Malibu, engaged in what the officer believes is a drug transaction in a downtown city neighborhood. The officer follows Timothy and after Timothy makes a left turn without using his turn signal, the officer signals Timothy to pull over. As the officer approaches Timothy's car on foot, Timothy accelerates and drives away. Shortly thereafter, Timothy's speeding Malibu passes a parked police patrol car. As it does, Timothy's car backfires. The officers misinterpret the backfire and conclude that someone in Timothy's car fired a shot at them. The officers then radio a report giving a description of Timothy's car and stating that someone in the car fired a shot at them.

The police officers commence a high-speed chase of Timothy's car that lasts 22 minutes. During the chase, Timothy drives erratically and dangerously at speeds up to 100 mph, going in and out of parking lots and swerving to avoid police cars attempting to stop him. Sixty-two police cars and more than 100 officers join the chase, which eventually ends when Timothy drives his car into a parking lot that has only one exit and his car is cornered by several police cars. Even after being blocked, Timothy continues to try to escape, driving his car toward several police cars and officers who had gotten out of their cars. Michael is a police officer in one of those cars. Once Timothy is cornered, refuses to surrender, and drives his car toward the police, the officers surrounding him open fire. Over a 12-second period, 13 police officers, including Michael, fire more than 100 shots at Timothy's car. Michael fires his gun 49 times. When the other officers stop shooting, Michael continues to fire, eventually climbing up onto the hood of Timothy's car where he fires a total of 15 shots at Timothy and Melissa through the windshield.

No gun is found in Timothy's car and none is found along the route of the chase. Investigators also examine videos of the chase from traffic cameras and "dash cams" located in police patrol cars and find no evidence of either Timothy or Melissa having a gun. The prosecutor's office concludes that both Timothy and Melissa were unarmed. But many of the officers involved in the chase believed that Melissa was firing from Timothy's car in part because of backfires from Timothy's car and the many erroneous police radio reports warning that the passenger in Timothy's car had a gun and was firing at the police. In addition, the police cars and officers that surrounded Timothy's car created a dangerous "cross-fire" situation. Many officers mistook bullets that came in their direction and hit their cars as having been fired by Timothy or Melissa when in fact those bullets were fired by other officers aiming at Timothy's car.

Later toxicology reports reveal that Timothy's blood-alcohol level was very high and that he was also under the influence of crack cocaine at the time of his death. Those reports showed the presence of both crack cocaine and marijuana in Melissa's blood. Melissa had apparently been "binge smoking" crack cocaine, taking repeated hits to try to regain a "high." A medical expert determines that Timothy was hit by 23 bullets and that four of those shots were "fatal"—i.e. that each of the four shots was independently capable of killing Timothy. Melissa was hit by 24 bullets and six of the shots that struck Melissa were "fatal."

The prosecutor is considering filing homicide charges against Michael. What causation problems might the prosecutor face in pursuing homicide charges against Michael?

7.6 Jeffrey and Jennifer are charged with manslaughter based on the death of Jeffrey's six-year-old son, Billy. Jennifer is Jeffrey's girlfriend and lived with Jeffrey and Billy. On the evening prior to Billy's death, Jennifer beat Billy and left him severely bruised. During this beating, she struck Billy several times forcefully in the head. The following morning, Billy was slow to get out of bed. Jeffrey then beat Billy again, delivering a number of blows to Billy's head. Later that afternoon, Billy lost consciousness and was taken to the emergency room of a local hospital where he died. The prosecution calls the coroner as an expert witness. She testifies that one particularly severe blow to the head appears to have caused Billy's death, but she is unable to determine whether the blow was one struck by Jennifer the evening prior to Billy's death or by Jeffrey on the morning of Billy's death. Both Jeffrey and Jennifer ask the trial judge to grant a motion for acquittal for failure to prove causation. How should the judge rule?

Burrage v. United States

134 S. Ct. 881 (2014)
Supreme Court of the United States

Scalia, J.

[The] Controlled Substances Act imposes a 20-year mandatory minimum sentence on a defendant who unlawfully distributes a Schedule I or II drug, when "death or serious bodily injury results from the use of such substance." We consider whether the mandatory-minimum provision applies when use of a covered drug supplied by the defendant contributes to, but is not a but-for cause of, the victim's death or injury.

Joshua Banka, a long-time drug user, died on April 15, 2010, following an extended drug binge. The episode began on the morning of April 14, when Banka smoked marijuana at a former roommate's home. Banka stole oxycodone pills from the roommate before departing and later crushed, cooked, and injected the oxycodone. Banka and his wife, Tammy Noragon Banka (Noragon), then met with petitioner Marcus

Burrage and purchased one gram of heroin from him. Banka immediately cooked and injected some of the heroin and, after returning home, injected more heroin between midnight and 1 a.m. on April 15. Noragon went to sleep at around 5 a.m., shortly after witnessing Banka prepare another batch of heroin. When Noragon woke up a few hours later, she found Banka dead in the bathroom and called 911. A search of the couple's home and car turned up syringes, 0.59 grams of heroin, alprazolam and clonazepam tablets, oxycodone pills, a bottle of hydrocodone, and other drugs.

Burrage pleaded not guilty to a superseding indictment alleging two counts of distributing heroin in violation of § 841(a)(1). Only one of those offenses, count 2, is at issue here.... Count 2 alleged that Burrage unlawfully distributed heroin on April 14, 2010, and that "death ... resulted from the use of th[at] substance"—thus subjecting Burrage to the 20-year mandatory minimum of § 841(b)(1)(C).

Two medical experts testified at trial regarding the cause of Banka's death. Dr. Eugene Schwilke, a forensic toxicologist, determined that multiple drugs were present in Banka's system at the time of his death, including heroin metabolites, codeine, alprazolam, clonazepam metabolites, and oxycodone. (A metabolite is a "product of metabolism," Webster's New International Dictionary 1544 (2d ed. 1950), or, as the Court of Appeals put it, "what a drug breaks down into in the body.") Although morphine, a heroin metabolite, was the only drug present at a level above the therapeutic range—*i.e.*, the concentration normally present when a person takes a drug as prescribed—Dr. Schwilke could not say whether Banka would have lived had he not taken the heroin. Dr. Schwilke nonetheless concluded that heroin "was a contributing factor" in Banka's death, since it interacted with the other drugs to cause "respiratory and/or central nervous system depression." The heroin, in other words, contributed to an overall effect that caused Banka to stop breathing. Dr. Jerri McLemore, an Iowa state medical examiner, came to similar conclusions. She described the cause of death as "mixed drug intoxication" with heroin, oxycodone, alprazolam, and clonazepam all playing a "contributing" role. Dr. McLemore could not say whether Banka would have lived had he not taken the heroin, but observed that Banka's death would have been "[v]ery less likely."

The District Court denied Burrage's motion for a judgment of acquittal, which argued that Banka's death did not "result from" heroin use because there was no evidence that heroin was a but-for cause of death. The court also declined to give Burrage's proposed jury instructions regarding causation. One of those instructions would have required the Government to prove that heroin use "was the proximate cause of [Banka's] death." Another would have defined proximate cause as "a cause of death that played a substantial part in bringing about the death," meaning that "[t]he death must have been either a direct result of or a reasonably probable consequence of the cause and except for the cause the death would not have occurred." The court instead gave an instruction requiring the Government to prove "that the heroin distributed by the Defendant was a contributing cause of Joshua Banka's death." The jury convicted Burrage on both counts, and the court sentenced him to 20 years' imprisonment, consistent with § 841(b)(1)(C)'s prescribed minimum.

The Court of Appeals for the Eighth Circuit affirmed Burrage's convictions. As to the causation-in-fact element of count 2, the court held that the District Court's contributing-cause instruction was consistent with its earlier decision in *United States v. Monnier*, 412 F. 3d 859, 862 (CA8 2005). As to proximate cause, the court held that Burrage's proposed instructions "d[id] not correctly state the law" because "a showing of 'proximate cause' is not required."

We granted certiorari on two questions: Whether the defendant may be convicted under the "death results" provision (1) when the use of the controlled substance was a "contributing cause" of the death, and (2) without separately instructing the jury that it must decide whether the victim's death by drug overdose was a foreseeable result of the defendant's drug-trafficking offense.

As originally enacted, the Controlled Substances Act "tied the penalties for drug offenses to both the type of drug and the quantity involved, with no provision for mandatory minimum sentences." That changed in 1986 when Congress enacted the Anti-Drug Abuse Act, which redefined the offense categories, increased the maximum penalties and set minimum penalties for many offenders, including the "death results" enhancement at issue here. With respect to violations involving distribution of a Schedule I or II substance (the types of drugs defined as the most dangerous and addictive) the Act imposes sentences ranging from 10 years to life imprisonment for large-scale distributions, from 5 to 40 years for medium-scale distributions, and not more than 20 years for smaller distributions, the type of offense at issue here. These default sentencing rules do not apply, however, when "death or serious bodily injury results from the use of [the distributed] substance." In those instances, the defendant "shall be sentenced to a term of imprisonment which ... shall be not less than twenty years or more than life," a substantial fine, "or both."[3]

Because the "death results" enhancement increased the minimum and maximum sentences to which Burrage was exposed, it is an element that must be submitted to the jury and found beyond a reasonable doubt. Thus, the crime charged in count 2 of Burrage's superseding indictment has two principal elements: (i) knowing or intentional distribution of heroin and (ii) death caused by ("resulting from") the use of that drug....

The law has long considered causation a hybrid concept, consisting of two constituent parts: actual cause and legal cause. When a crime requires "not merely conduct but also a specified result of conduct," a defendant generally may not be convicted unless his conduct is "both (1) the actual cause, and (2) the 'legal' cause (often called

---

3. Although this language, read literally, suggests that courts may impose a fine or a prison term, it is undisputed here that the "death results" provision mandates a prison sentence. Courts of Appeals have concluded, in effect, that the "or" is a scrivener's error. The best evidence of that is the concluding sentence of §841(b)(1)(C), which states that a court "shall not place on probation or suspend the sentence of any person sentenced under the provisions of this subparagraph *which provide for a mandatory term of imprisonment if death or serious bodily injury results*." (Emphasis added.)

the 'proximate cause') of the result." Those two categories roughly coincide with the two questions on which we granted certiorari. We find it necessary to decide only the first: whether the use of heroin was the actual cause of Banka's death in the sense that § 841(b)(1)(C) requires.

The Controlled Substances Act does not define the phrase "results from," so we give it its ordinary meaning. A thing "results" when it "[a]rise[s] as an effect, issue, or outcome *from* some action, process or design." 2 The New Shorter Oxford English Dictionary 2570 (1993). "Results from" imposes, in other words, a requirement of actual causality. "In the usual course," this requires proof "'that the harm would not have occurred' in the absence of—that is, but for—the defendant's conduct." *University of Tex. Southwestern Medical Center v. Nassar*, 570 U.S. ___, at ___, 133 S. Ct. 2517 (2013) (quoting Restatement of Torts § 431, Comment *a* (1934)). The Model Penal Code reflects this traditional understanding; it states that "[c]onduct is the cause of a result" if "it is an antecedent but for which the result in question would not have occurred." That formulation represents "*the minimum* requirement for a finding of causation when a crime is defined in terms of conduct causing a particular result."

Thus, "where A shoots B, who is hit and dies, we can say that A [actually] caused B's death, since but for A's conduct B would not have died." The same conclusion follows if the predicate act combines with other factors to produce the result, so long as the other factors alone would not have done so—if, so to speak, it was the straw that broke the camel's back. Thus, if poison is administered to a man debilitated by multiple diseases, it is a but-for cause of his death even if those diseases played a part in his demise, so long as, without the incremental effect of the poison, he would have lived.

This but-for requirement is part of the common understanding of cause. Consider a baseball game in which the visiting team's leadoff batter hits a home run in the top of the first inning. If the visiting team goes on to win by a score of 1 to 0, every person competent in the English language and familiar with the American pastime would agree that the victory resulted from the home run. This is so because it is natural to say that one event is the outcome or consequence of another when the former would not have occurred but for the latter. It is beside the point that the victory also resulted from a host of *other* necessary causes, such as skillful pitching, the coach's decision to put the leadoff batter in the lineup, and the league's decision to schedule the game. By contrast, it makes little sense to say that an event resulted from or was the outcome of some earlier action if the action merely played a nonessential contributing role in producing the event. If the visiting team wound up winning 5 to 2 rather than 1 to 0, one would be surprised to read in the sports page that the victory resulted from the leadoff batter's early, non-dispositive home run.

Where there is no textual or contextual indication to the contrary, courts regularly read phrases like "results from" to require but-for causality. Our interpretation of statutes that prohibit adverse employment action "because of" an employee's age or complaints about unlawful workplace discrimination is instructive. Last Term, we addressed Title VII's antiretaliation provision, which states in part:

"It shall be an unlawful employment practice for an employer ... to discriminate against any individual ... *because* he has opposed any practice made an unlawful employment practice by this subchapter, or *because* he has made a charge, testified, assisted, or participated in any manner in an investigation, proceeding, or hearing under this subchapter." (emphasis added).

Given the ordinary meaning of the word "because," we held that [this section] "require[s] proof that the desire to retaliate was [a] but-for cause of the challenged employment action." The same result obtained in an earlier case interpreting a provision in the Age Discrimination in Employment Act that makes it "unlawful for an employer ... to discharge any individual or otherwise discriminate against any individual with respect to his compensation, terms, conditions, or privileges of employment, *because of* such individual's age." Relying on dictionary definitions of "[t]he words 'because of'"—which resemble the definition of "results from" recited above—we held that "[t]o establish a disparate-treatment claim under the plain language of [§623(a)(1)] ... a plaintiff must prove that age was [a] 'but for' cause of the employer's adverse decision."

Our insistence on but-for causality has not been restricted to statutes using the term "because of." We have, for instance, observed that "[i]n common talk, the phrase 'based on' indicates a but-for causal relationship," and that "the phrase, 'by reason of,' requires at least a showing of 'but for' causation." State courts, which hear and decide the bulk of the Nation's criminal matters, usually interpret similarly worded criminal statutes in the same manner.

In sum, it is one of the traditional background principles "against which Congress legislate[s]," that a phrase such as "results from" imposes a requirement of but-for causation. The Government argues, however, that distinctive problems associated with drug overdoses counsel in favor of dispensing with the usual but-for causation requirement. Addicts often take drugs in combination, as Banka did in this case, and according to the National Center for Injury Prevention and Control, at least 46 percent of overdose deaths in 2010 involved more than one drug. This consideration leads the Government to urge an interpretation of "results from" under which use of a drug distributed by the defendant need not be a but-for cause of death, nor even independently sufficient to cause death, so long as it contributes to an aggregate force (such as mixed-drug intoxication) that is itself a but-for cause of death.

In support of its argument, the Government can point to the undoubted reality that courts have not *always* required strict but-for causality, even where criminal liability is at issue. The most common (though still rare) instance of this occurs when multiple sufficient causes independently, but concurrently, produce a result. To illustrate, if "A stabs B, inflicting a fatal wound; while at the same moment X, acting independently, shoots B in the head ... also inflicting [a fatal] wound; and B dies from the combined effects of the two wounds," A will generally be liable for homicide even though his conduct was not a but-for cause of B's death (since B would have died from X's actions in any event). We need not accept or reject the special rule developed for these cases, since there was no evidence here that Banka's heroin use was an independently sufficient cause of his death. No expert was prepared to say that Banka would have died from the heroin use alone.

Thus, the Government must appeal to a second, less demanding (but also less well established) line of authority, under which an act or omission is considered a cause-in-fact if it was a "substantial" or "contributing" factor in producing a given result. Several state courts have adopted such a rule, but the American Law Institute declined to do so in its Model Penal Code. One prominent authority on tort law asserts that "a broader rule ... has found general acceptance: The defendant's conduct is a cause of the event if it was a material element and a substantial factor in bringing it about." W. Keeton, D. Dobbs, R. Keeton, & D. Owen, Prosser and Keeton on Law of Torts §41, p. 267 (5th ed. 1984) (footnote omitted). But the authors of that treatise acknowledge that, even in the tort context, "[e]xcept in the classes of cases indicated" (an apparent reference to the situation where each of two causes is independently effective) "no case has been found where the defendant's act could be called a substantial factor when the event would have occurred without it." The authors go on to offer an alternative rule—functionally identical to the one the Government argues here—that "[w]hen the conduct of two or more actors is so related to an event that their combined conduct, viewed as a whole, is a but-for cause of the event, and application of the but-for rule to them individually would absolve all of them, the conduct of each is a cause in fact of the event." Yet, as of 1984, "no judicial opinion ha[d] approved th[at] formulation." The "death results" enhancement became law just two years later.

We decline to adopt the Government's permissive interpretation of §841(b)(1). The language Congress enacted requires death to "result from" use of the unlawfully distributed drug, not from a combination of factors to which drug use merely contributed. Congress could have written §841(b)(1)(C) to impose a mandatory minimum when the underlying crime "contributes to" death or serious bodily injury, or adopted a modified causation test tailored to cases involving concurrent causes, as five States have done, see Ala. Code §13A-2-5(a) (2005); Ark. Code Ann. §5-2-205 (2006); Me. Rev. Stat. Ann., Tit. 17-A, §33 (2006); N. D. Cent. Code Ann. §12.1-02-05 (Lexis 2012); Tex. Penal Code Ann. §6.04 (West 2011). It chose instead to use language that imports but-for causality. Especially in the interpretation of a criminal statute subject to the rule of lenity, we cannot give the text a meaning that is different from its ordinary, accepted meaning, and that disfavors the defendant.

The Government objects that the ordinary meaning of "results from" will "unduly limi[t] criminal responsibility" and "cannot be reconciled with sound policy." We doubt that the requirement of but-for causation for this incremental punishment will prove a policy disaster. A cursory search of the Federal Reporter reveals that but-for causation is not nearly the insuperable barrier the Government makes it out to be. *See, e.g., United States v. Krieger*, 628 F. 3d 857, 870–871 (CA7 2010) (affirming "death results" conviction based on expert testimony that, although the victim had several drugs in her system, the drug distributed by the defendant was a but-for cause of death); *United States v. Webb*, 655 F. 3d 1238, 1254–1255 (CA11 2011) (per curiam) (same). Moreover, even when the prosecution is unable to prove but-for causation, the defendant will still be liable for violating § 841(a)(1) and subject to a substantial default sentence under § 841(b)(1).

Indeed, it is more likely the Government's proposal "cannot be reconciled with sound policy," given the need for clarity and certainty in the criminal law. The judicial authorities invoking a "substantial" or "contributing" factor test in criminal cases differ widely in their application of it. Compare *Wilson v. State*, 24 S. W. 409, 410 (Tex. Crim. App. 1893) (an act is an actual cause if it "contributed materially" to a result, even if other concurrent acts would have produced that result on their own), with *Cox v. State*, 305 Ark. 244, 248, 808 S. W. 2d 306, 309 (1991) (causation cannot be found where other concurrent causes were clearly sufficient to produce the result and the defendant's act was clearly insufficient to produce it (applying Ark. Code Ann. § 5-2-205 (1987)).

Here the Government is uncertain about the precise application of the test that it proposes. Taken literally, its "contributing-cause" test would treat as a cause-in-fact every act or omission that makes a positive incremental contribution, however small, to a particular result. But at oral argument the Government insisted that its test excludes causes that are "not important enough" or "too insubstantial." Unsurprisingly, it could not specify how important or how substantial a cause must be to qualify. Presumably the lower courts would be left to guess. That task would be particularly vexing since the evidence in § 841(b)(1) cases is often expressed in terms of probabilities and percentages. One of the experts in this case, for example, testified that Banka's death would have been "[v]ery less likely" had he not used the heroin that Burrage provided. Is it sufficient that use of a drug made the victim's death 50 percent more likely? Fifteen percent? Five? Who knows. Uncertainty of that kind cannot be squared with the beyond-a-reasonable-doubt standard applicable in criminal trials or with the need to express criminal laws in terms ordinary persons can comprehend.

But in the last analysis, these always-fascinating policy discussions are beside the point. The role of this Court is to apply the statute as it is written—even if we think some other approach might "'accor[d] with good policy.'" As we have discussed, it is written to require but-for cause.

We hold that, at least where use of the drug distributed by the defendant is not an independently sufficient cause of the victim's death or serious bodily injury, a defendant cannot be liable under the penalty enhancement provision of 21 U.S.C. § 841(b)(1)(C) unless such use is a but-for cause of the death or injury. The Eighth Circuit affirmed Burrage's conviction based on a markedly different understanding of the statute, and the Government concedes that there is no "evidence that Banka would have lived but for his heroin use." Burrage's conviction with respect to count 2 of the superseding indictment is therefore reversed, and the case is remanded for further proceedings consistent with this opinion.

* * *

Note the trial court's failure to distinguish clearly between cause-in-fact and proximate cause. Note also that Justice Scalia uses *civil* cases involving areas of law such as age discrimination as authority in determining the requirements of causation in

Burrage, a criminal case. He also makes use of the Restatement of Torts in his analysis. The fact that he makes use of these civil sources in a criminal case indicates that he views the principles of causation in civil and criminal cases as the same, basically interchangeable. Keep this in mind when you read later cases in this chapter. Some of these take the position that criminal causation and tort causation are the same. Others take the position that civil and criminal causation differ.

Discussion Questions

1. Should the fact that a death results from the distribution of heroin trigger a 20-year mandatory minimum sentence? Isn't such a death a serious risk with all heroin distribution? Do the purposes of punishment support treating a person whose heroin distribution results in a death more severely than other heroin distributors?

2. When a court is trying to figure out the meaning of words such as "results from" or "because" used by a legislature in a statute, should the court look to the "common meaning" of those words (i.e., the meaning given the words in everyday usage) or the technical, legal meaning that lawyers give such words? Which does Justice Scalia use in *Burrage*?

3. Justice Scalia approves making use of "the traditional background principles 'against which Congress legislates'" in interpreting a statute. Is use of such principles consistent with textualist interpretation? With intentionalist interpretation?

C. Proximate Cause

Proximate cause is sometimes referred to as legal cause or cause in law. As the jury instruction in Problem 7.1 illustrates, the test for proximate cause is vague. That instruction uses several phrases to guide the jury in resolving the proximate cause question. The result must occur "in a natural and continuous sequence" though causation is "not limited to the immediate or most obvious result." The defendant is "responsible for the natural and foreseeable consequences that follow, in the ordinary course of events, from the act." Does the vagueness inherent in words such as "natural," "foreseeable," "ordinary," and "continuous" delegate the job of determining causation standards to jurors?

Use of the words "natural" and "foreseeable" and the phrase "in the ordinary course of events" indicate that probability plays an important role in determining proximate cause. Generally, the higher the probability that a result will follow from the defendant's act, the greater the likelihood that the defendant's act will be found to have proximately caused that result. The probability issue in causation is often addressed in terms of foreseeability, perhaps the most frequently invoked test in determining proximate cause. A defendant is usually held to have proximately caused a foreseeable result and not to have proximately caused an unforeseeable result. What, though, must be foreseeable? The result? The manner in which the result occurred? Both? And how foreseeable must the result and/or the manner of its occurrence be? In other words, what level of probability is required for a finding of proximate cause? The law on proximate cause typically is not clear in answering these questions, giving judges and juries considerable latitude in determining the boundaries of proximate cause.

If a second person is involved in bringing about a result required for criminal liability, the causation analysis often becomes more complex and issues other than foreseeability may play a role. A subsequent actor sometimes insulates a prior actor from criminal liability. In the jargon of causation, the second actor is often referred to as an "intervening cause" who may "break the causal chain" between the first actor and the result. Saying that a second actor breaks the causal chain between a prior actor's conduct and a result means that the first actor will not be found to have proximately caused the result.

The precise conditions under which a subsequent actor's conduct breaks the causal chain are the source of considerable confusion in the law of causation. Courts are often neither clear nor consistent in their treatment of intervening cause cases. The mental state and blameworthiness of the second actor play major roles in determining whether a second actor will relieve a first actor of causal responsibility. Take, for example, a case in which A wishes to kill C. A disguises a bomb as a toy, wraps it in a package, and sends it to C using B, a courier. B is paid by A to deliver the package and is unaware of A's plan and the content of the package. B delivers the package to C, who opens it and is killed. In this hypothetical, B's conduct does play a role in bringing about C's death and thus B's conduct is a cause in fact of C's death. But because B has an innocent mental state and no blame in relation to C's death, B's act will not relieve A of liability. In other words, B's conduct does not break the causal chain between A's conduct and C's death.

But what if the intervening actor is blameworthy? Will the actor then break the causal chain? The higher the intervenor's mental state and blame, the greater the chance that the intervenor will break the causal chain. In the cases that follow, what level of blame is required on the part of an intervenor in order for her to break the causal chain? Is negligence sufficient? How about recklessness? Knowledge? Purpose?

In contrast to the inquiry underlying cause in fact, which is factual in nature, the proximate cause inquiry requires the jury to assess blame and responsibility. In other words, while cause in fact is concerned with finding out what happened, proximate cause is concerned with allocating responsibility, determining who should be held responsible for what happened.

Keep in mind that a finding of causation alone is not equivalent to a finding of criminal liability. The other elements of an offense, such as mental state and a voluntary act, must also be satisfied.

Problem

7.7 Was proximate cause fulfilled in each of the cases in Problem 7.1?

1. Intervening Actors Other Than the Victim

Problems

7.8 Look back at Problems 6.22, 6.23, and 6.24 in Chapter 6, Homicide. They describe a variety of situations in which a gun owner allowed a minor access to a gun and the minor shot and killed another person. Are the minors in any of these cases intervenors who break the chain of causation between the gun owner's conduct and the death of the victim? If so, in which cases?

7.9 Steve and Orville live on a small farm with a group of roughly 20 other people in a post-apocalyptic world in which most of the population are zombies who eat human flesh. The countryside around the farm is infested with zombies. The group is running low on medical supplies. Steve and Orville volunteer for a dangerous mission in which they will go to an abandoned school in a nearby town to obtain a stash of much-needed medical supplies. Steve and Orville manage to get into the school and obtain the supplies without alerting the zombies to their presence. But as they are leaving the school, zombies spot and start chasing them. Steve and Orville start to run, but the zombies gain on them. Orville sustained a leg injury inside the school and is limping. Steve turns to Orville, says "I'm sorry," and shoots Orville in the leg. Orville collapses on the pavement and the zombies attack and kill (i.e., eat) Orville. The fact that the zombies cease their pursuit of Steve to focus on consuming Orville allows Steve to escape and return to the farm with the needed medical supplies. Assume that Steve's shot alone would not have killed Orville. Is Steve's act of shooting Orville the proximate cause of Orville's death? Do the zombies who kill and consume Orville break the causal chain between Steve's act of shooting Orville and Orville's death?

7.10 D was convicted at trial for armed robbery. A testified as an expert witness for the prosecution at trial that D's fingerprint matched a fingerprint found on a gun used in the robbery. In reality, the results of A's comparison between D's fingerprints and fingerprints found on the gun were inconclusive. But A believed that D had committed the robbery and wanted to help strengthen the prosecution's case. A subsequent audit of the police forensic science laboratory determines that A committed perjury at D's trial when he testified. Without this evidence, it is unlikely the jury would have convicted D. D later dies. Could A be held liable for homicide under any of the following scenarios?

Part (a) D was killed when a state owned and operated bus transporting him to prison crashed. Assume the driver of the bus was negligent.

Part (b) D was purposefully killed by another prisoner once he arrived at prison.

Part (c) Assume D's case involved a capital homicide rather than an armed robbery. D was executed by the state following his conviction.

7.11 Otto, an officer in the army, is happily married to Debra. Ian, another army officer and friend of Otto's, is romantically interested in Debra. When Otto is deployed overseas, Ian approaches Debra several times and tries to convince her to have an affair with him. Debra spurns each of Ian's advances. Angered at Debra's rejections, Ian hatches a plan for revenge. When Otto's deployment ends, Ian invites him to a bar for a drink "to celebrate his safe return." After Otto has had quite a few drinks, Ian expresses concern for Otto and tells him that Debra has been unfaithful while he was away on deployment. Ian also offers Otto "evidence" of the supposed affair. He falsely tells Otto that he followed Debra on several occasions when she spent the night with the fictional officer and hands him a forged love letter from the officer to Debra. Angry and intoxicated, Otto, drives home, confronts Debra, and accuses her of having an affair. An argument ensues in which Debra truthfully protests her innocence. But Otto does not believe her. Enraged, Otto kills Debra by shooting her several times with a handgun. Has Ian caused Debra's death? Could Ian be held liable for homicide?

People v. Flenon

202 N.W.2d 471 (1972)
Court of Appeals of Michigan

V.J. Brennan, P. J., and McGregor and Bronson, JJ. All concurred.

Defendant was convicted by jury verdict of murder in the first degree and sentenced to life imprisonment. He appeals this conviction as a matter of right....

In the early morning hours of March 21, 1970, defendant left a house in Detroit carrying a shotgun for the avowed purpose of "getting back" at an unidentified person. He proceeded down the street until he encountered a group of persons including Carl Johnson, the deceased. Upon realizing the defendant had a gun, the group dispersed. Defendant chased the deceased, cornered him behind a parked car and shot him in the upper part of his leg.

Carl Johnson was rushed to a hospital where his right leg was amputated high above the knee because of the severity of the wound. Five weeks later, Carl Johnson was released and returned home. Within a short period of time he substantially weakened and was readmitted to the hospital where he died. The cause of death was found by the doctor performing the autopsy to be serum hepatitis and pneumonia.

Defendant's first allegation of error is that there was an insufficient causal connection between the gunshot wound and death by serum hepatitis to sustain his conviction....

The causation problem in the instant case is compounded by defendant's allegation that serum hepatitis constituted an independent intervening cause suspending his liability. The concept of medical mistreatment becoming an intervening cause was considered in *People v Cook*, 39 Mich 236 (1878). There the victim received medical treatment including the administration of morphine after being shot by defendant. Since the victim's death was attributed to the morphine, defendant claimed that this medicine produced death independent of the wound and suspended his liability. The *Cook* Court found that morphine was a proper and appropriate medicine given by competent and skillful physicians. The legal principles applied by the *Cook* Court depended upon whether the wound was considered mortal and were summarized by its statement that:

"In a case where the *wound is not mortal*, the injured person may recover, and thus no homicide has been committed. If, however, death does result, the accused will be held responsible, unless it was occasioned, not by the wound, but by *grossly erroneous medical treatment*. But where the *wound is a mortal one*, there is no chance for the injured person to recover, and therefore the reason which permits the showing of death from medical treatment does not exist." (Emphasis added.)

Although the *Cook* Court did not clearly indicate the nature of the wound at issue, it concluded that the victim's death could not be attributed to the independent act of a third person. Failing to find the wound inflicted in the present case from which the deceased initially recovered to be mortal, the type of medical treatment rendered requires further inquiry.

The Court in *People v Cook, supra,* terminated the defendant's responsibility only if the medical treatment was *grossly erroneous*. This principle was affirmed by the Court's statement in *People v Townsend*, 214 Mich 267, 278–279 (1921), that:

" 'He who inflicted the injury is liable even though the medical or surgical treatment which was the direct cause of the death was *erroneous* or *unskilful*, or although the death was due to the negligence or failure by the deceased to procure treatment or take proper care of the wound.' " (Emphasis added.)

This standard which requires something more than ordinary negligence before exculpating a defendant is sound. The concept of an intervening cause is predicated upon foreseeability. Since humans are not infallible, a doctor's negligence is foreseeable and cannot be used by a defendant to exonerate himself from criminal liability.

An application of these standards to the instant case requires an understanding of the alleged intervening cause. The only expert witness testifying at trial was offered by the people. This witness discussed the disease of serum hepatitis and opined that the deceased contracted this disease from the blood transfusion received during the operation to amputate his leg. After indicating that the deceased received a total of 11 pints of blood during medical treatment, he testified that there was a 100% possibility of *exposure* to the disease after receipt of six pints of blood. The incidence of death after such exposure is .01% to 3%.[10] This testimony leads us to the conclusion that the victim's exposure to serum hepatitis upon receiving a blood transfusion necessitated by the injury inflicted by the defendant is clearly foreseeable. Whether the victim contracts the disease and dies depends upon his susceptibility to it. Defendant must take his victim as he finds him and may not escape liability because a majority of the people are able to withstand contraction of the disease or death following such contraction. This disease injected through medical intervention is similar to the injection of morphine causing death in the *Cook* case and cannot itself constitute an intervening cause.

The medical evidence concerning this disease similarly precludes a finding that the medical profession's inability to prevent or cure such a prevailing disease constitutes gross mistreatment or an intervening cause. This disease cannot be cultured, precluding experimental testing except by human volunteers, is impossible to detect or screen out from blood, and its cause is currently unknown. The justifiable conclusion based upon this data is that serum hepatitis is an unavoidable risk indigenous to blood transfusions....

Affirmed.

Discussion Questions

1. Should causation analysis in cases such as *Flenon* depend on whether the initial wound was mortal? Do any theories of punishment justify distinguishing between mortal and nonmortal wounds?

2. Should causation analysis turn on the distinction between negligence and gross negligence? Or should the chain of causation be severed only when a subsequent actor displays a higher level of culpability, such as recklessness, knowledge, or purpose?

People v. Kibbe

35 N.Y.2d 407 (1974)
Court of Appeals of New York

Gabrielli, J.

Subdivision 2 of section 125.25 of the Penal Law provides, in pertinent part, that "[a] person is guilty of murder" when "[under] circumstances evincing a depraved indifference to human life, he recklessly engages in conduct which creates a grave risk of death to another person, and thereby causes the death of another person".

The factual setting of the bizarre events of a cold winter night of December 30, 1970, as developed by the testimony ... reveal the following: During the early evening the defendants were drinking in a Rochester tavern along with the victim, George Stafford. The bartender testified that Stafford was displaying and "flashing" one hun-

---

10. The mortality rate increases with age and may go as high as 20% or 30%. 2 Gray, Attorneys' Textbook of Medicine (3d ed), §38.36, p. 38–53.

dred dollar bills, was thoroughly intoxicated and was finally "shut off" because of his inebriated condition. At some time between 8:15 and 8:30 p.m., Stafford inquired if someone would give him a ride to Canandaigua, New York, and the defendants, who, according to their statements, had already decided to steal Stafford's money, agreed to drive him there in Kibbe's automobile. The three men left the bar and proceeded to another bar where Stafford was denied service due to his condition. The defendants and Stafford then walked across the street to a third bar where they were served, and each had another drink or two.

After they left the third bar, the three men entered Kibbe's automobile and began the trip toward Canandaigua. Krall drove the car while Kibbe demanded that Stafford turn over any money he had. In the course of an exchange, Kibbe slapped Stafford several times, took his money, then compelled him to lower his trousers and to take off his shoes to be certain that Stafford had given up all his money; and when they were satisfied that Stafford had no more money on his person, the defendants forced Stafford to exit the Kibbe vehicle.

As he was thrust from the car, Stafford fell onto the shoulder of the rural two-lane highway on which they had been traveling. His trousers were still down around his ankles, his shirt was rolled up towards his chest, he was shoeless and he had also been stripped of any outer clothing. Before the defendants pulled away, Kibbe placed Stafford's shoes and jacket on the shoulder of the highway. Although Stafford's eyeglasses were in the Kibbe vehicle, the defendants, either through inadvertence or perhaps by specific design, did not give them to Stafford before they drove away. It was sometime between 9:30 and 9:40 p.m. when Kibbe and Krall abandoned Stafford on the side of the road. The temperature was near zero, and, although it was not snowing at the time, visibility was occasionally obscured by heavy winds which intermittently blew previously fallen snow into the air and across the highway; and there was snow on both sides of the road as a result of previous plowing operations. The structure nearest the point where Stafford was forced from the defendants' car was a gasoline service station situated nearly one half of a mile away on the other side of the highway. There was no artificial illumination on this segment of the rural highway.

At approximately 10:00 p.m. Michael W. Blake, a college student, was operating his pickup truck in the northbound lane of the highway in question. Two cars, which were approaching from the opposite direction, flashed their headlights at Blake's vehicle. Immediately after he had passed the second car, Blake saw Stafford sitting in the road in the middle of the northbound lane with his hands up in the air. Blake stated that he was operating his truck at a speed of approximately 50 miles per hour, and that he "didn't have time to react" before his vehicle struck Stafford. After he brought his truck to a stop and returned to try to be of assistance to Stafford, Blake observed that the man's trousers were down around his ankles and his shirt was pulled up around his chest. A Deputy Sheriff called to the accident scene also confirmed the fact that the victim's trousers were around his ankles, and that Stafford was wearing no shoes or jacket.

At the trial, the Medical Examiner of Monroe County testified that death had occurred fairly rapidly from massive head injuries. In addition, he found proof of a high degree of intoxication with a .25%, by weight, of alcohol concentration in the blood.

For their acts, the defendants were convicted of murder, robbery in the second degree and grand larceny in the third degree. However, the defendants basically challenge only their convictions of murder, claiming that the People failed to establish beyond a reasonable doubt that their acts "caused the death of another".... [W]e are required to determine whether the defendants may be convicted of murder for the occurrences which have been described. They contend that the actions of Blake, the driver of the pickup truck, constituted both an intervening and superseding cause which relieves them of criminal responsibility for Stafford's death. There is, of course, no statutory provision regarding the effect of an intervening cause of injury as it relates to the criminal responsibility of one who sets in motion the machinery which ultimately results in the victim's death; and there is surprisingly little case law dealing with the subject. Moreover, analogies to causation in civil cases are neither controlling nor dispositive, since, as this court has previously stated: "A distance separates the negligence which renders one criminally liable from that which establishes civil liability"; and this is due in large measure to the fact that the standard or measure of persuasion by which the prosecution must convince the trier of all the essential elements of the crime charged, is beyond a reasonable doubt. However, to be a sufficiently direct cause of death so as to warrant the imposition of a criminal penalty therefor, it is not necessary that the ultimate harm be intended by the actor. It will suffice if it can be said beyond a reasonable doubt, as indeed it can be here said, that the ultimate harm is something which should have been foreseen as being reasonably related to the acts of the accused.

In *People v. Kane,* the defendant inflicted two serious pistol shot wounds on the body of a pregnant woman. The wounds caused a miscarriage; the miscarriage caused septic peritonitis, and the septic peritonitis, thus induced, caused the woman's death on the third day after she was shot. Over the defendant's insistence that there was no causal connection between the wounds and the death and, in fact, that the death was due to the intervention of an outside agency, namely, the negligent and improper medical treatment at the hospital, this court affirmed the conviction "even though the medical treatment may also have had some causative influence."

We subscribe to the requirement that the defendants' actions must be a *sufficiently direct cause* of the ensuing death before there can be any imposition of criminal liability, and recognize, of course, that this standard is greater than that required to serve as a basis for tort liability. Applying these criteria to the defendants' actions, we conclude that their activities on the evening of December 30, 1970 were a sufficiently direct cause of the death of George Stafford so as to warrant the imposition of criminal sanctions. In engaging in what may properly be described as a despicable course of action, Kibbe and Krall left a helplessly intoxicated man without his eyeglasses in a position from which, because of these attending circumstances, he could not extricate himself and whose condition was such that he could not even protect himself from the elements. The defendants do not dispute the fact that their conduct evinced a depraved indifference to human life which created a grave risk of death, but rather they argue that it was just as likely that Stafford would be miraculously rescued by a good samaritan. We cannot accept such an argument. There can be little doubt but that Stafford would have frozen to death in his state of undress had he remained on the shoulder of the road. The only alternative left to him was the highway, which in his condition, for one reason or another, clearly foreboded the probability of his resulting death.

Under the conditions surrounding Blake's operation of his truck (i.e., the fact that he had his low beams on as the two cars approached; that there was no artificial lighting on the highway; and that there was insufficient time in which to react to Stafford's presence in his lane), we do not think it may be said that any supervening wrongful act occurred to relieve the defendants from the directly foreseeable consequences of their actions. In short, we will not disturb the jury's determination that the prosecution proved beyond a reasonable doubt that their actions came clearly within the statute and "[caused] the death of another person"....

Orders affirmed.

Discussion Questions

1. Who was a potential intervenor in *Kibbe*? Stafford, the victim? Blake, the driver of the truck that hit the victim?

2. Was Stafford's conduct responsive to the defendants' initial conduct or coincidental? What about Blake's conduct?

3. Was the result in *Kibbe* (i.e., Stafford's death) foreseeable? Was the manner in which it occurred foreseeable? How likely does the result and/or manner have to be in order to be foreseeable?

4. How much deference should courts give jurors on questions of proximate causation?

2. The Victim as Intervenor

Problems

7.12 Robert is a freshman in college. One afternoon after classes he goes to the college gym and plays in a pick-up basketball game. During the game, Robert gets into a shoving match with Steve, another player. After the game, Steve continues to verbally spar with Robert and the two wind up in a fistfight. Robert prevails in the altercation and walks away when Steve is on the ground and unable to fight any more. That evening, Steve and several of his friends go to

Robert's dorm to retaliate. They plan to gang up on Robert and allow Steve to assault Robert. Robert hears a knock on his door and when he looks through the peephole he sees Steve and his friends, who begin to pound on the door shouting that they are going to beat Robert and challenging him to come outside. They also attempt to force the door open. Meanwhile, Robert goes to the window of his dorm room and attempts to leap to the ground to escape. In doing so, he falls badly and breaks his neck. An ambulance is called, but Robert is dead by the time help arrives. Is the conduct of Steve and his friends a proximate cause of Robert's death? Consider the following variables. Would any make a difference in your determination of proximate causation?

   (a) Robert's room is on the second floor of the dorm

   (b) Robert's room is on the fourth floor of the dorm

   (c) Robert's room is on the eighth floor of the dorm

   (d) Steve was accompanied by two friends

   (e) Steve was accompanied by four friends

   (f) Steve was accompanied by eight friends

   (g) Steve and his friends were brandishing baseball bats

   (h) Steve and his friends were carrying knives hidden in their pockets

7.13 Read the following excerpt setting forth the facts in *Commonwealth v. Carter*, a recent Massachusetts manslaughter case that received considerable publicity. Did Michelle Carter cause Conrad Roy's death? Or did Roy's own acts break any potential chain of causation between Carter's conduct and his death? What arguments could Carter's lawyer make? What arguments could the prosecution make? If you were the judge, how would you rule? (Note that Massachusetts, unlike most states, does not make it a crime to coerce someone to commit suicide.)

Commonwealth v. Carter

481 Mass. 352 (2019)
Supreme Judicial Court of Massachusetts

At age seventeen, Michelle Carter was charged with involuntary manslaughter as a youthful offender for the suicide death of Conrad Roy, age eighteen. On July 13, 2014, the victim's body was found in his truck.... He had committed suicide by inhaling carbon monoxide that was produced by a gasoline-powered water pump located in the truck.

[The defendant and the victim] first met in 2012.... Thereafter, they rarely saw each other in person, but they maintained a long-distance relationship by electronic text messaging and cell phone conversations. A frequent subject of their communications was the victim's fragile mental health, including his suicidal thoughts. Between October 2012 and July 2014, the victim attempted suicide several times by various means, including overdosing on over-the-counter medication, drowning, water poisoning, and suffocation. None of these attempts succeeded, as the victim abandoned each attempt or sought rescue.

At first, the defendant urged the victim to seek professional help for his mental illness. Indeed, in early June 2014, the defendant, who was planning to go to McLean Hospital for treatment of an eating disorder, asked the victim to join her, saying that the professionals there could help him with his depression and that they could mutually support each other. The victim rebuffed these efforts, and the tenor of their communications changed. As the victim continued researching suicide methods and sharing his findings with the defendant, the defendant helped plan how, where, and when he would do so, and downplayed his fears about how his suicide would affect his family. She also repeatedly chastised him for his indecision and delay, texting, for example, that he "better not be bull shiting me and saying you're gonna do this and then purposely get caught" and made him "promise" to kill himself....

In the days leading to July 12, 2014, the victim continued planning his suicide, including by securing a water pump that he would use to generate carbon monoxide in his closed truck. On July 12, the victim drove his truck to a local store's parking lot and started the pump. While the pump was operating, filling the truck with carbon monoxide, the defendant and victim were in contact by cell phone. Cell phone records showed that one call of over forty minutes had been placed by the victim to the defendant, and a second call of similar length by the defendant to the victim, during the time when police believe the victim was in his truck committing suicide. There is no contemporaneous record of what the defendant and victim said to each other during those calls.

The defendant, however, sent a text to a friend at 8:02 P.M., shortly after the second call: "he just called me and there was a loud noise like a motor and I heard moaning like someone was in pain, and he wouldn't answer when I said his name. I stayed on the phone for like 20 minutes and that's all I heard." And at 8:25 P.M., she again texted that friend: "I think he just killed himself." She sent a similar text to another friend at 9:24 P.M.: "He called me, and I heard like muffled sounds and some type of motor running, and it was like that for 20 minutes, and he wouldn't answer. I think he killed himself." Weeks later, on September 15, 2014, she texted the first friend again, saying in part:

> "I failed [the victim] I wasn't supposed to let that happen and now I'm realizing I failed him. [H]is death is my fault like honestly I could have stopped him I was on the phone with him and he got out of the car because it was working and he got scared and I fucking told him to get back in ... because

I knew he would do it all over again the next day and I couldn't have him live the way he was living anymore I couldn't do it I wouldn't let him."

The judge found that the victim got out of the truck, seeking fresh air, in a way similar to how he had abandoned his prior suicide attempts.... The judge found that when the defendant realized he had gotten out of the truck, she instructed him to get back in, knowing that it had become a toxic environment and knowing the victim's fears, doubts, and fragile mental state. The victim followed that instruction. Thereafter, the defendant, knowing the victim was inside the truck and that the water pump was operating—the judge noted that she could hear the sound of the pump and the victim's coughing—took no steps to save him. She did not call emergency personnel, contact the victim's family, or instruct him to get out of the truck. The victim remained in the truck and succumbed to the carbon monoxide.

State v. Echols

919 S.W.2d 634 (1995)
Court of Criminal Appeals of Tennessee

Summers, J.

The defendant Robert L. Echols was convicted by a jury of aggravated robbery, and the trial court entered judgment. On appeal, he claims that the evidence is insufficient to support his conviction because his conduct was not the cause of the victim's injury. We affirm the judgment of the trial court.

Shortly after 6:00 a.m. on June 17, 1993, the victim unlocked her door and an outer wrought iron security door to take out the garbage. Meanwhile, the defendant who had "been up all night smoking drugs" was walking home. As he walked past the victim's house he saw her purse. While the victim was gathering the garbage, the defendant opened the door and grabbed the victim's purse. When the victim went outside to scream for help and look for the defendant, she fell. She was later admitted to the hospital where she was diagnosed with a fractured bone in her hip. The victim remained in the hospital for four days and later underwent three weeks of rehabilitation. She testified that she was in a "lot of pain."

One element of aggravated robbery is that the alleged victim suffer serious bodily injury. This offense requires a defendant to cause a certain result—serious bodily injury. The necessary causal relationship between the conduct and the result is that the defendant's conduct be both 1) the "but for" cause or "cause in fact" and 2) the "proximate" or "legal cause" of the result.

The defendant essentially contends that the evidence fails to establish that his conduct was the proximate cause of the victim's serious bodily injury. Rather, he appears to assert that the victim's own conduct was the cause of her injury. A defendant's conduct is the proximate cause of the natural and probable consequences of his conduct.

Where sufficiency of the evidence is challenged, the relevant question for an appellate court is whether, after viewing the evidence in the light most favorable to the prosecution, any rational trier of fact could have found the essential elements of the crime or crimes beyond a reasonable doubt. This standard applies to evidence of causation. The evidence amply supports a finding that the defendant's conduct was the proximate cause of the victim's injury. The victim's act of quickly exiting the house to scream for help and look for the defendant is a natural and probable response to the defendant's conduct. Her actions were normal and instinctive under the circumstances. That the victim's own conduct may also be a proximate cause of her injury is of no consequence to the defendant's situation. "One whose wrongdoing is a concurrent proximate cause of an injury may be criminally liable the same as if his wrongdoing were the sole proximate cause of the injury."

Affirmed.

Discussion Questions

1. Can the victim of a crime be an intervenor who breaks the causal chain between a defendant's conduct and the victim's injury or death?

2. The court emphasizes that the victim's conduct was a *response* to the defendant's conduct. Why is this significant?

3. The court also emphasizes that the victim's conduct was "normal and instinctive." Why is this significant?

Several famous causation cases, including the following case, deal with fearful or otherwise distraught victims bringing about their own deaths in response to clearly blameworthy conduct by the defendants in the case. One of the reasons this case attracted great attention is that the defendant was the Grand Dragon of the Indiana Ku Klux Klan, an infamous and violent white supremacist group that came into being in the years following the Civil War and has been responsible for numerous acts of violence against black people, including lynchings.

Stephenson v. State

205 Ind. 141 (1932)
Supreme Court of Indiana

[The defendant was charged with murder.] The victim of this homicide is Miss Madge Oberholtzer, who was a resident of the City of Indianapolis and lived with her father and mother.... She was twenty-eight years of age ... and had always been in good health.... [S]he was employed by the State Superintendent of Public Instruction as manager of the Young Peoples' Reading Circle.

[Defendant Stephenson became infatuated with Miss Oberholtzer after meeting her at a public social gathering. She at first did not respond to his many phone calls but eventually agreed to have dinner with the him. Weeks later, the defendant invited her to his house. When she arrived, the defendant and his associates immediately forced her to drink a sedative that made her feel ill and dazed. They prevented her from leaving or calling anyone. In response to her protests, defendant Stephenson said "No, you cannot go home. Oh yes! you are going with me to

Chicago. I love you more than any woman I have ever known." After arming themselves with pistols, the men took her by car against her will to a reserved compartment on a train.]

[In the train compartment,] Stephenson ... took hold of the bottom of her dress and pulled it over her head, against her wishes, and she tried to fight him away, but was weak and unsteady. [Then Stephenson sexually assaulted Ms. Oberholtzer. The next morning the men took her from the train to a hotel in Hammond, Indiana, where she was forced to share a room with the defendant.] Before they left the train, Stephenson was flourishing his revolver and the victim asked him to shoot her. He held the revolver against her side and she said to him again to kill her, but he put the gun away in his grip.... [At the hotel] she asked Stephenson to give her some money, for she had none, so that she might purchase herself a hat. Stephenson told [one of the other men] to give her money and he gave her $15.00 and took her out in the automobile. [The man] waited for her while she went into a store and purchased a hat, for which she paid $ 12.50. When she returned to the car, she asked [him] to drive her to a drug store so that she might purchase some rouge. He then drove the car to a drug store, where she purchased a box of bichloride of mercury tablets, put them in her coat pocket and returned with [the driver] in the automobile to the hotel.... [At the hotel] Miss Oberholtzer laid out eighteen of the bichloride of mercury tablets and at once took six of them.... She only took six of the tablets because they burnt her so. Earlier in the morning she had taken Stephenson's revolver and thought to kill herself in Stephenson's presence while he was asleep. It was then she decided to try and get poison and take it in order to save her mother from disgrace. She knew it would take longer for the mercury tablets to kill her. After she had taken the tablets, she lay down on the bed and became very ill....

On the journey back to Indianapolis she screamed for a doctor, and said she wanted a hypodermic to relieve the pain, but the men refused to stop. She begged Stephenson to leave her along the road some place, that someone would stop and take care of her, and said to Stephenson, that he was even then more cruel to her than he had been the night before. He promised to stop at the next town, but did not.... She vomited in the car all over the back seat and the luggage. Stephenson did nothing to make her comfortable on the trip. He said to [one of the other men], "This takes guts to do this ... she is dying".

[Once back in Indianapolis, the defendant allowed Miss Oberholtzer to return to her home. She was very ill and attended to by several doctors. The expert testimony at the trial established that several of the wounds she received from the defendant had resulted in serious infections. Because of the presence of the bichloride of mercury in her system, her body was unable to overcome these infections and she died.]

It was stated that taking into consideration the facts given in evidence of the taking of possession of Miss Oberholtzer by appellant; her trip to Hammond; the taking of the poison; the return home and the time intervening from then until her death, a delay of twenty-four to twenty-six hours in administering remedies for mercuric chloride poisoning, materially reduced her chances of recovery.

Appellant very earnestly argues that the evidence does not show appellant guilty of murder. He points out in his brief that after they reached the hotel, Madge Oberholtzer left the hotel and purchased a hat and the poison, and voluntarily returned to his room, and at the time she took the poison she was in an adjoining room to him, and that she swallowed the poison without his knowledge, and at a time when he was not present. From these facts he contends that she took her life by committing suicide; that her own act in taking the poison was an intervening responsible agent which broke the causal connection between his acts and the death; that his acts were not the proximate cause of her death, but the taking of the poison was the proximate cause of death....

In the case of *Rex* v. *Beech*, the prosecutrix was the village nurse and lived alone. At 11:45 P. M. on an evening in November the appellant came to her house when she was in bed. He entered the house by breaking a window and went upstairs to the bedroom occupied by the prosecutrix. The door was locked and the appellant threatened to break it open if the prosecutrix would not let him in. She refused and the appellant then tried to burst open the door. The prosecutrix called out, that if he got in he would not find her in the room, and as the appellant continued his attack upon the door the prosecutrix jumped out of the window sustaining injuries. The prosecutrix also testified that the appellant had attempted to interfere with her on a previous occasion when she had threatened to take poison if he touched her. The court approved the proposition as stated by the lower court as follows: "Whether the conduct of the prisoner amounted to a threat of causing injury to the young woman; was the act of jumping the natural consequence of the conduct of the prisoner and was the grievous bodily harm the result of the conduct of the prisoner." The court held that if these questions were answered in the affirmative he would be guilty. In *Rex* v. *Valade*, where the accused induced a young girl under the age of consent to go along with him to a secluded apartment, and there had criminal sexual intercourse with her, following which she jumped from a window to the street to get away from him and was killed by the fall. The accused was held guilty of murder. Bishop, in his work on Criminal Law, says, "When suicide follows a wound inflicted by the defendant his act is homicidal, if deceased was rendered irresponsible by the wound and as a natural result of it." We do not understand that the rule laid down by Bishop, that the wound which renders the deceased mentally irresponsible is necessarily limited to a physical wound. We should think the same rule would apply if a defendant engaged in the commission of a felony such as rape or attempted rape and inflicts upon his victim both physical and mental injuries, the natural and probable result of which would render the deceased mentally irresponsible and suicide followed, we think he would be guilty of murder. In the case at bar appellant is charged with having caused the death of Madge Oberholtzer while engaged in the crime of attempted rape.

Appellant argues that the deceased was a free agent on this trip to purchase a hat and, etc., and that she voluntarily returned to the room in the hotel. This was a question for the jury and the evidence would justify them in reaching a contrary conclusion. Appellant's chauffeur accompanied her on this trip, and the deceased had, before she left appellant's home in Indianapolis, attempted to get away and also made two unsuccessful attempts to use the telephone to call help. She was justified in concluding that any attempt she might make, while purchasing a hat or while in the drug store, to escape or secure assistance would be no more successful in Hammond than it was in Indianapolis. We think the evidence shows that the deceased was at all times from the time she was entrapped by the appellant at his home on the evening of March 15th till she was returned to her home two days later, in the custody and absolute control of appellant. Neither do we think the fact that the deceased took the poison some four hours after they left the drawing-room on the train or after the crime of attempted rape had been committed necessarily prevents it from being part of the attempted rape. Suppose they had not left the drawing-room on the train, and instead of the deceased taking poison she had secured possession of appellant's revolver and shot herself or thrown herself out of the window of the car and died from the fall. We can see no vital difference. At the very moment Madge Oberholtzer swallowed the poison she was subject to the passion, desire and will of appellant. She knew not what moment she would be subjected to the same demands that she was while in the drawing-room on the train. What would have prevented appellant from compelling her to submit to him at any moment? The same forces, the same impulses, that would impel her to shoot herself during the actual attack or throw herself out of the car window after the attack had ceased, was pressing and overwhelming her at the time she swallowed the poison. The evidence shows that she was so weak that she staggered as she left the elevator to go to the room in the hotel, and was assisted, by appellant and Gentry. That she was very ill so much so that she could not eat, all of which was the direct and proximate result of the treatment accorded her by appellant.

We think the situation no different here than we find in the *Beech* case or the *Valade* case, *supra*. To say that there is no causal connection between the acts of appellant and the death of Madge Oberholtzer, and that the treatment accorded her by appellant had no causal connection with the death of Madge Oberholtzer would be a travesty on justice. The whole criminal program was so closely connected that we think it should be treated as one transaction, and should be governed by the same principles of law as was applied in the case of *Rex* v. *Beech* and *Rex* v. *Valade, supra*. We therefore conclude that the evidence was sufficient and justified the jury in finding that appellant by his acts and conduct rendered the deceased distracted and mentally irresponsible, and that such was the natural and probable consequence of such unlawful and criminal treatment, and that the appellant was guilty of murder in the second degree as charged in the first count of the indictment.

Discussion Questions

1. Was Madge Oberholtzer's conduct forseeable? Would it have made a difference to the causation analysis if she had killed herself with Stephenson's gun in one of the hotel rooms?

2. Was the victim's conduct a *response* to the defendant's conduct.

3. Was the victim's conduct here "normal and instinctive," as the court discussed in *Echols*?

Commonwealth v. Root

403 Pa. 571, 170 A.2d 310 (1961)
Pennsylvania Supreme Court

Jones, C.J.

The appellant was found guilty of involuntary manslaughter for the death of his competitor in the course of an automobile race between them on a highway. The trial court overruled the defendant's demurrer to the Commonwealth's evidence and, after verdict, denied his motion in arrest of judgment. On appeal from the judgment of sentence entered on the jury's verdict, the Superior Court affirmed. We granted allocatur because of the important question present as to whether the defendant's unlawful and reckless conduct was a sufficiently direct cause of the death to warrant his being charged with criminal homicide.

The testimony, which is uncontradicted in material part, discloses that, on the night of the fatal accident, the defendant accepted the deceased's challenge to engage in an automobile race; that the racing took place on a rural 3-lane highway; that the night was clear and dry, and traffic light; that the speed limit on the highway was 50 miles per hour; that, immediately prior to the accident, the two automobiles were being operated at varying speeds of from 70 to 90 miles per hour; that the accident occurred in a no-passing zone on the approach to a bridge where the highway narrowed to two directionally-opposite lanes; that, at the time of the accident, the defendant was in the lead and was proceeding in his right-hand lane of travel; that the deceased, in an attempt to pass the defendant's automobile, when a truck was closely approaching from the opposite direction, swerved his car to the left, crossed the highway's white dividing line and drove his automobile on the wrong side of the highway head-on into the oncoming truck with resultant fatal effect to himself.

This evidence would of course amply support a conviction of the defendant for speeding, reckless driving and, perhaps, other violations of The Vehicle Code.... In any event, unlawful or reckless conduct is only one ingredient of the crime of involuntary manslaughter. Another essential and distinctly separate element of the crime is that the unlawful or reckless conduct charged to the defendant was the direct cause of the death in issue. The first ingredient is obviously present in this case but, just as plainly, the second is not.

While precedent is to be found for application of the tort law concept of "proximate cause" in fixing responsibility for criminal homicide, the want of any rational basis for its use in determining criminal liability can no longer be properly disregarded. When proximate cause was first borrowed from the field of tort law and applied to homicide prosecutions in Pennsylvania, the concept connoted a much more direct casual relation in producing the alleged culpable result than it does today. Proximate cause, as an essential element of a tort founded in negligence, has undergone in recent times, and is still undergoing, a marked extension. More specifically, this area of civil law has been progressively liberalized in favor of claims for damages for personal injuries to which careless conduct of others can in some way be associated. To persist in applying the tort liability concept of proximate cause to prosecutions for criminal homicide after the marked expansion of *civil* liability of defendants in tort actions for negligence would be to extend possible *criminal* liability to persons chargeable with unlawful or reckless conduct in circumstances not generally considered to present the likelihood of a resultant death.

In this very case the Superior Court mistakenly opined that "The concept of proximate cause as applied in tort cases is applicable to similar problems of causation in criminal cases. *Commonwealth v. Almeida.*" It is indeed strange that the *Almeida* case should have been cited as authority for the above quoted statement; the rationale of the Almeida case was flatly rejected by this Court in *Commonwealth v. Redline*, where we held that the tort liability concept of proximate cause is not a proper criterion of causation in a criminal homicide case. True enough, *Commonwealth v. Redline* was a murder case, but the distinction between murder and involuntary manslaughter does not rest upon a differentiation in causation; it lies in the state of mind of the offender. If one kills with malice aforethought, he is chargeable with murder; and if death, though unintentional, results directly from his unlawful or reckless conduct, he is chargeable with involuntary manslaughter. In either event, the accused is not guilty unless his conduct was a cause of death sufficiently direct as to meet the requirements of the *criminal*, and not the *tort*, law.

The instant case is one of first impression in this State; and our research has not disclosed a single instance where a district attorney has ever before attempted to prosecute for involuntary manslaughter on facts similar to those established by the record now before us. The closest case, factually, would seem to be *Commonwealth v. Levin*, which affirmed the defendant's conviction of involuntary manslaughter. In the *Levin* case two cars were racing on the streets of Philadelphia at speeds estimated at from 85 to 95 miles per hour. The defendant's car, in the left-hand lane, was racing alongside of the car in which the deceased was a passenger when the defendant turned his automobile sharply to the right in front of the other car, thereby causing the driver of the latter car to lose control and smash into a tree, the passenger being thrown to the road and killed as a result of the impact. It is readily apparent that the elements of causation in the *Levin* case were fundamentally different from those in the present case. Levin's act of cutting his automobile sharply in front of the car in which the deceased was riding directly forced that car off of the road and into the tree. The defendant's reckless and unlawful maneuver was the direct cause of the crucial fatality. In the instant case, the defendant's conduct was not even remotely comparable. Here, the action of the deceased driver in recklessly and suicidally swerving his car to the left lane of a 2-lane highway into the path of an oncoming truck was not forced upon him by any act of the defendant; it was done by the deceased and by him alone, who thus directly brought about his own demise. The *Levin* case was properly decided but it cannot, by any ratiocination, be utilized to justify a conviction in the present case.

Legal theory which makes guilt or innocence of criminal homicide depend upon such accidental and fortuitous circumstances as are now embraced by modern tort law's encompassing concept of proximate cause is too harsh to be just....

Even if the tort liability concept of proximate cause were to be deemed applicable, the defendant's conviction of involuntary manslaughter in the instant case could not be sustained under the evidence. The operative effect of a supervening cause would have to be taken into consideration. *Commonwealth v. Redline.* But, the trial judge refused the defendant's point for charge to such effect and erroneously instructed the jury that "negligence or want of care on the part of ... [the deceased] is no defense to the criminal responsibility of the defendant...."

The Superior Court, in affirming the defendant's conviction in this case, approved the charge above mentioned, despite a number of decisions in involuntary manslaughter cases holding that the conduct of the deceased victim must be considered in order to determine whether the defendant's reckless acts were the proximate (i.e., sufficiently direct) cause of his death. The Superior Court dispensed with th[e] decisional authority by expressly overruling [past decisions] ... on the ground that there can be more than one proximate cause of death. The point is wholly irrelevant. Of course there can be more than one proximate cause of death just as there can also be more than one direct cause of death. For example, in the so-called "shield" cases where a felon interposes the person of an innocent victim between himself and a pursuing officer, if the officer should fire his gun at the felon to prevent his escape and fatally wound the person used as a shield, the different acts of the policeman and the felon would each be a direct cause of the victim's death.

If the tort liability concept of proximate cause were to be applied in a criminal homicide prosecution, then the conduct of the person whose death is the basis of the indictment would have to be considered, not to prove that it was merely an *additional* proximate cause of the death, but to determine, under fundamental and long recognized law applicable to proximate cause, whether the subsequent wrongful act *superseded* the original conduct chargeable to the defendant. If it did in fact supervene, then the original act is so insulated from the ensuing death as not to be its proximate cause.

Under the uncontradicted evidence in this case, the conduct of the defendant was not the proximate cause of the decedent's death as a matter of law. In *Kline v. Moyer and Albert,* the rule is stated as follows: "Where a second actor has become aware of the existence of a potential danger created by the negligence of an original tortfeasor, and thereafter, by an independent act of negligence, brings about an accident, the first tort-feasor is relieved of liability, because the condition created by him was merely a circumstance of the accident and not its proximate cause."

In *Johnson v. Angretti,* while Angretti was driving his truck eastward along a highway, a bus, traveling in the same direction in front of him, stopped to take on a passenger. Angretti swerved his truck to the left into the lane of oncoming traffic in an attempt to pass the bus but collided with a tractor-trailer driven by the plaintiff's decedent, who was killed as a result of the collision. In affirming the entry of judgment n.o.v. in favor of the defendant bus company, we held that any negligence on the part of the bus driver, in suddenly bringing his bus to a halt in order to pick up a passenger, was not a proximate cause of the death of the plaintiff's decedent since the accident "was due entirely to the intervening and superseding negligence of Angretti in allowing his truck to pass over into the pathway of the westbound tractor-trailer...."

In the case now before us, the deceased was aware of the dangerous condition created by the defendant's reckless conduct in driving his automobile at an excessive rate of speed along the highway but, despite such knowledge, he recklessly chose to swerve his car to the left and into the path of an oncoming truck, thereby bringing about the head-on collision which caused his own death.

To summarize, the tort liability concept of proximate cause has no proper place in prosecutions for criminal homicide and more direct casual connection is required for conviction. In the instant case, the defendant's reckless conduct was not a sufficiently direct cause of the competing driver's death to make him criminally liable therefor.

The judgment of sentence is reversed and the defendant's motion in arrest of judgment granted.

Eagen, J., dissenting

The opinion of the learned Chief Justice admits, under the uncontradicted facts, that the defendant, at the time of the fatal accident involved, was engaged in an unlawful and reckless course of conduct. Racing an automobile at 90 miles per hour, trying to prevent another automobile going in the same direction from passing him, in a no-passing zone on a two-lane public highway, is certainly all of that. Admittedly also, there can be more than one direct cause of an unlawful death. To me, this is self-evident. But, says the majority opinion, the defendant's recklessness was not a direct cause of the death. With this, I cannot agree.

If the defendant did not engage in the unlawful race and so operate his automobile in such a reckless manner, this accident would never have occurred. He helped create the dangerous event. He was a vital part of it. The victim's acts were a natural reaction to the stimulus of the situation. The race, the attempt to pass the other car and forge ahead, the reckless speed, all of these factors the defendant himself helped create. He was part and parcel of them. That the victim's response was normal under the circumstances, that his reaction should have been expected and was clearly foreseeable, is to me beyond argument. That the defendant's recklessness was a substantial factor is obvious. All of this, in my opinion, makes his unlawful conduct a direct cause of the resulting collision.

The cases cited in support of the majority opinion are not in point. For instance, in *Johnson v. Angretti,* this Court, in affirming the trial court, found that the bus driver *was not guilty of any negligence or violation of The Vehicle Code* in bringing the bus to a stop. The Court, as dicta, then went on to say, "Moreover it is clear that such alleged violation bore no casual relation whatever to the happening of the accident which was due entirely to the intervening and superseding negligence of Angretti in allowing his truck to pass over into the pathway of the westbound tractor-trailer instead of bringing his vehicle to a stop as Osterling [the driver of the truck directly behind the bus and in front of Angretti] had done and *as he admitted he could readily have done without colliding with the truck ahead of him.* The situation created by the stopping of the bus was merely a circumstance of the accident and not its proximate cause (citing cases)." It is readily apparent that the instant case and the *Angretti* case are distinguishable in all the important factors. In the present case there was (1) recklessness and a violation of The Vehicle Code; (2) a joint venture or common enterprise of racing; (3) no proof that Hall could have guided his car back into the right-hand lane behind Root after he became aware of the danger of the oncoming truck....

In the present case, there wasn't any evidence that Hall saw the oncoming truck when he pulled out to pass Root. This would have been suicide, against which there is a presumption. The act of passing was not an "extraordinary negligent" act, but rather a "normal response" to the act of "racing." Furthermore, as Hall pulled out to pass, Root "dropped off" his speed to 90 miles an hour. Such a move probably prevented Hall from getting back into the right-hand lane since he was alongside of Root at the time and to brake the car at that speed would have been fatal to both himself and Root. Moreover, the dangerous condition of which the deceased had to become aware of before the defendant was relieved of his direct casual connection with the ensuing accident, was not the fact that the defendant was driving at an excessive rate of speed along the highway. He knew that when the race began many miles and minutes earlier. *The dangerous condition necessary was an awareness of the oncoming truck and the fact that at the rate of speed Root was traveling he couldn't safely pass him.* This important fact was not shown and, therefore, was a question for the fact-finders and not a question that could be decided as a matter of law.

The majority opinion states, "Legal theory which makes guilt or innocence of criminal homicide depend upon such *accidental and fortuitous circumstances* as are now embraced by modern tort law's encompassing concept is ... too harsh to be just." If the resulting death had been dependent upon "accidental and fortuitous circumstances" or, as the majority also say, "in circumstances not generally considered to present the likelihood of a resultant death," we would agree that the defendant is not criminally responsible. However, acts should be judged by their tendency under the known circumstances, not by the actual intent which accompanies their performance. Every day of the year, we read that some teen-agers, or young adults, somewhere in this country, have been killed or have killed others, while racing their automobiles. Hair-raising, death-defying, lawbreaking rides, which encompass "racing" are the rule rather than the exception, and endanger not only the participants, but also every motorist and passenger on the road. To call such resulting accidents "accidental and fortuitous," or unlikely to result in death, is to ignore the cold and harsh reality of everyday occurrences. Root's actions were as direct a cause of Hall's death as those in the "shield" cases. Root's shield was his high speed and any approaching traffic in his quest to prevent Hall from passing, which he knew Hall would undertake to do, the first time he thought he had the least opportunity....

But, says the majority opinion, these are principles of tort law and should not in these days be applied to the criminal law. But such has been the case since the time of Blackstone. These same principles have always been germane to both crimes and tort. They have been repeatedly so applied throughout the years and were employed in a criminal case in Pennsylvania as long as one hundred and seventeen years ago....

While the victim's foolhardiness in this case contributed to his own death, he was not the only one responsible and it is not he alone with whom we are concerned. It is the people of the Commonwealth who are harmed by the kind of conduct the defendant pursued. Their interests must be kept in mind.

Discussion Questions

1. The conduct of the defendants in *Kibbe* was found to have proximately caused the victim's death. The conduct of the defendant in *Root*, however, was determined not to have proximately caused the victim's death. What explains the different outcomes in the two cases in terms of proximate cause?

2. Was the result in *Root* foreseeable? What about the manner in which it occurred? Were the victim driver's actions foreseeable? Were they a response to Root's actions? What was the blameworthiness of Root? Of the victim driver?

3. Does timeframing (discussed in Chapter 4, Section F) play a role in the outcome of *Root*? Which opinion uses narrow timeframing and which uses broad timeframing? How does the choice about timeframing affect causation analysis?

Commonwealth v. Carlson

447 Mass. 79 (2006)
Supreme Judicial Court of Massachusetts

Reaney, J.

We transferred this case here on our own motion to consider the scope of criminal liability for the negligent operation of a motor vehicle that results, in the circumstances described below, in death. A jury in the East Brookfield Division of the District Court Department convicted the defendant on a complaint charging motor vehicle homicide by negligent operation. The evidence at trial demonstrated that Carol Suprenant (victim) was hospitalized with chest and lung injuries suffered as a result of an accident caused by the defendant's negligent operation of an automobile and died of respiratory failure four days later after her doctors, at her request, removed her from a ventilator that allowed her to breathe and might have ensured her survival. The defendant appeals from her conviction, challenging (as she did at trial) the sufficiency of the evidence proving causation and claiming (for the first time on appeal) that the trial judge's instructions to the jury on the concept of superseding causes were inadequate. We affirm the conviction.

The jury could have found the following facts. On July 4, 2002, the victim and her husband, Robert Suprenant, left their home in Spencer to attend a cookout at their daughter's home. At about noon, the Suprenants were traveling south on Mechanic Street and had just entered the intersection of Mechanic and Chestnut Streets, when their automobile was struck on the passenger side by an automobile traveling east on Chestnut Street operated by the defendant. The force of impact pushed the Suprenants' automobile a distance of approximately fifteen to twenty feet, across the road, over a sidewalk, and into a chain link fence. Traffic entering the intersection from the defendant's direction was controlled by both a stop sign and blinking red light. A jury could infer that the defendant had failed to stop (or yield the right of way) at the intersection and, thus, was negligent. The victim was transferred from the accident scene by emergency medical personnel to St. Vincent's Hospital at Worcester Medical Center.

As a result of the accident, the victim suffered multiple chest wall fractures, including fractures of the ribs and sternum and a lung contusion. The victim had suffered for several years prior to the accident from chronic obstructive pulmonary disease (COPD), a condition which makes it difficult to breathe and thus, to supply oxygen to the bloodstream, and had required the use of an oxygen tank in her home to assist in her breathing.[2] The trauma to her chest compromised her ability to breathe as she had before the accident, to the point where she could no longer oxygenate her blood by normal breathing. That night in the intensive care unit, the victim was intubated and placed on a ventilator.[3] The next morning, the doctors removed the victim from the ventilator, and she was transferred from the intensive care unit to a medical floor in the hospital.

Over the next few days, the victim's breathing difficulties increased. Three doctors separately advised the victim of the need to reintubate her and place her again on a ventilator in order to assist her breathing. At first the victim, who had in the past repeatedly told her daughter-in-law (and health proxy) that she never wanted to be kept alive by a ventilator, refused permission for the doctors to do so. After speaking with family members and her doctors, however, the victim acquiesced and allowed herself to be reintubated, at least temporarily, in order to determine if her health would improve.

The next morning the victim's kidneys began to fail, and doctors advised the victim that her worsening condition would require dialysis. At this point, the victim stated

2. The victim's primary care physician testified at trial that the victim's condition would have gradually deteriorated over time and that the disease would have shortened her life. He opined that, based on the severity of her disease, the victim could have expected to enjoy only three to six more years of "good quality" life.

3. Intubation is a procedure where a hollow tube, one-half to three-quarters of an inch in circumference, is inserted into the mouth and approximately six to eight inches into the windpipe. The tube enables oxygen to be delivered directly into the lungs by means of a ventilator. A ventilator was described at trial as a "mechanical breathing machine" that pushes air into and out of the lungs by way of a pressure piston.

that she no longer wished to be attached to a ventilator. Two doctors on the medical staff of the hospital met separately with the victim to discuss the nature of the circumstances facing her and the probable consequences of forgoing mechanical ventilation. The victim's personal physician also spoke with her at great length about her decision and encouraged her to remain on the breathing tube and ventilator to allow her situation time to improve. The victim understood (a jury could infer) that her death was probable if she did not allow intubation and that, conversely, her injuries were potentially survivable if she remained on the ventilator. The victim was adamant that she did not want to be intubated. On July 8, she was taken off the ventilator and the intubation tube was removed. She died a few hours later from respiratory failure.

At trial one doctor testified that, if the accident had not happened, the victim probably would not have needed a ventilator and could have continued being on home oxygen in her usual fragile state of health, but that the chest injuries suffered in the accident "tipped the scales against her." He also opined that the victim's decision not to be intubated "likely played a role in her death." Another doctor stated his opinion "to a reasonable degree of medical certainty" that the victim would have survived her injuries if she had agreed to mechanical ventilatory support, and might even have returned to the state she was in before the accident, but conceded as well that the victim might have required "chronic and continuous ventilatory support." The victim's daughter-in-law assessed the situation as follows: "We all knew that it was a possibility that she might not make it, but [the doctors] couldn't give us a guarantee that she would make it without ... hav[ing] to be on a [ventilator] for the rest of her life, and she didn't want to live like that, and we couldn't force her to do that." The victim's primary care physician testified, "I do think her mind was made up."

The judge denied the defendant's motions for the entry of a required finding of not guilty presented at the close of the Commonwealth's case and at the close of all the evidence. The defendant argues that the Commonwealth's proof was insufficient to sustain the conviction because no rational jury could have determined, beyond a reasonable doubt, that the victim's death from respiratory failure was proximately caused by the defendant's negligence. The defendant asserts that the victim's death was a direct result of her independent decision not to undertake medical procedures that could be considered appropriate for a person in her condition and that would, in all probability, have allowed her to survive the accident. The defendant concedes that the victim had the right to make an informed decision to forgo life support, but argues that the victim's choice broke the chain of causation and relieved the defendant of criminal responsibility for the victim's death. We disagree.

The defendant was not entitled to a required finding of not guilty. The standard of causation under G. L. c. 90, §24G, is the same as that employed in tort law. Conduct is a proximate cause of death if the conduct, "by the natural and continuous sequence of events, causes the death and without which the death would not have occurred." There is no question that the defendant's negligent failure to stop, or yield the right of way, at the intersection (for which the defendant accepts responsibility in this appeal) set in motion a chain of events that resulted in the victim's death. The victim's injuries from the accident exacerbated serious preexisting health problems and required her to be intubated and placed on the ventilator. Her ultimate decision to be removed from life support was not an independent occurrence but the final step in the continuous sequence of events that began with the defendant's negligent operation of her automobile. "But for" the negligence, the accident would not have occurred, and the victim would not have been forced into the position of having to make what was, in retrospect, a true life-or-death decision.

The general rule is that intervening conduct of a third party will relieve a defendant of culpability for antecedent negligence only if such an intervening response was not reasonably foreseeable. "This is just another way of saying that an intervening act of a third party that was not reasonably foreseeable in the circumstances would prevent the victim's death from following naturally and continuously from the defendant's conduct." Whether an intervening act was reasonably foreseeable and, thus, followed naturally from the defendant's conduct, or unforeseeable and, thus, broke the chain of causation as a matter of law, is a question of fact for the jury to decide based on an assessment of the circumstances.

Here, the victim's choice was between invasive life support that might have assured her survival, but could also have led to a life of ventilator dependence (and, we may assume, continued pain and suffering), or acceptance of "comfort measures" only. The record shows that the victim was intelligent and coherent at all times. She had an absolute right to make the decision that she did. Modern medicine can sometimes prolong or sustain life by way of invasive procedures, but it is common knowledge that some patients will refuse to consent to such procedures. The jury were warranted in determining, in the circumstances of this case, that the victim's decision to forgo invasive life support was reasonably foreseeable.[4]

The defendant poses the question: "In the realm of crimes of negligence, should the tort concept of 'you take your victim as you find him' apply ... even though, by pure chance and coincidence, it has the effect of turning an act of simple negligence into a serious crime?" The answer to this question is "yes." ...

The defendant's suggestion that she should not be held accountable for the victim's death, because the same injuries would have been minor if inflicted on a healthy young person, has no merit. Our long-standing rule in Massachusetts, in criminal law as well as in tort, is that "the wrongdoer takes the victim as he or she finds him."

---

4. The defendant's attempt to assign blame to the victim for her own death, because she "made the deliberate choice to ... engage in irrational and self-destructive behavior" is not persuasive. There is no contributory negligence in the law of motor vehicle homicide. We also reject the defendant's attempt to apply the tort doctrine of "avoidable consequences" to this criminal matter.

We now consider the defendant's argument that the judge's instructions to the jury on causation were so inadequate and confusing as to require a new trial. The defendant asserted no challenge to the judge's instructions at trial. She is entitled to relief only if she demonstrates error in the instructions that created a substantial risk of a miscarriage of justice, namely, "a substantial danger that the jury was misled by [an] erroneous instruction, and that the instruction may have materially influenced their appraisal of the [evidence]." There was no error.

The judge properly charged the jury on the elements of negligent motor vehicle homicide. He advised the jury that there may be more than one cause of a person's death, but that the Commonwealth is required to prove beyond a reasonable doubt that the defendant "directly and substantially set in motion a chain of events that produced the death in a natural and continuous sequence," and that the death would not have occurred without the defendant's actions. This is a correct statement of the law.

The judge instructed the jury on the law of intervening events and superseding causes, as set forth in the margin,[5] in accordance with what has been said in this opinion.[6] The judge emphasized that the jury must acquit the defendant "if the death would not have occurred without the intervention of another person or event, and a reasonable person in the same circumstances would not have foreseen the likely possibility of such a result."[7] There was no possibility that the jury did not understand that they must find beyond a reasonable doubt that the defendant's negligence directly set in motion a continuous chain of events that produced the death, and that they must acquit the defendant if the death would not have occurred without the intervention of some other person or event that was not reasonably foreseeable. The judge's instructions focused the jury's attention on the issue of causation and correctly left the issue of foreseeability to the jury.

The order staying the defendant's sentence on her conviction of homicide by negligent operation of a motor vehicle is vacated. The judgment of conviction is affirmed.

---

5. "If the defendant's actions would not have brought about the death all by themselves without the intervention of some other person or event, the defendant is still held responsible as the cause of death if two conditions are met. First, the defendant's actions directly and substantially set in motion a natural, continuous sequence of events to cause the death. And second, a reasonable person in the defendant's position would have foreseen that her actions could easily result in serious injury or death to someone like the victim."

6. The instructions tracked, substantially, Instruction 5.27 of the Model Jury Instructions for Use in the District Court (1995). The judge's use of the word "result" instead of the word "event" was immaterial and did not change the essential meaning of the instruction.

7. The jury returned during deliberations seeking a copy of the law of negligent motor vehicle homicide. The judge responded by repeating the substance of his earlier instructions. The jury later requested clarification on the issue of causation and asked for specific examples that would help to distinguish between what is, and what is not, a "major factor in the cause of death." The judge declined to give examples but repeated, for the third time, his instructions on the elements of negligent motor vehicle homicide and on intervening events and superseding causes.

Discussion Questions

1. Who is a potential intervening actor in this case? The victim? The doctors who took her off the ventilator? Why does the court find that neither the victim nor the doctors broke the causal chain between the defendant's acts and the victim's death?

2. Under Massachusetts law, who decides whether an actor breaks a chain of causation? The judge? The jury?

3. The "Eggshell Victim" Rule

State v. Jenkins

276 S.C. 209 (1981)
South Carolina Supreme Court

Robert Hamilton Jenkins was convicted of murder and sentenced to life imprisonment. His grounds for this appeal include the assertion that the trial judge erred in failing to submit to the jury as possible verdicts assault and battery with intent to kill and assault and battery of a high and aggravated nature. We find no reversible error and affirm.

Appellant's indictment for murder followed the death of a stabbing victim. The evidence reflects that the victim identified the appellant as the assailant before being rushed to a hospital for treatment of serious wounds to the neck and arms. The victim lost substantial amounts of blood and was in a state of shock before reaching the hospital.

In order to determine the extent of the victim's injuries to the major blood vessels, an arteriogram was performed. Although the arteriogram is a common procedure, the victim suffered a rare, fatal reaction to the dye used in the arteriogram procedure. The evidence includes medical testimony that the victim's immediate cause of death was the reaction to the dye, that she probably would have survived absent the reaction, but that she probably would not have survived without medical treatment.

The trial judge submitted to the jury three possible verdicts—murder, manslaughter, and not guilty. He properly instructed the jury that there must be a causal relationship between the defendant's act and the death of the deceased before criminal liability may be imposed. The jury's verdict of guilty of murder necessarily included a finding adverse to appellant on the causation issue, which finding excluded a verdict for an offense not involving the victim's death.

Additionally, appellant does not in this Court challenge the sufficiency of the evidence to sustain the conviction of murder. Under such circumstances, we conclude there was no prejudicial error in refusing to submit to the jury the two degrees of assault and battery. The verdict in this case is consistent with those cases holding that one who inflicts an injury on another is deemed by law to be guilty of homicide where the injury contributes mediately or immediately to the death of the other.

... Accordingly, we affirm the lower court's determination of those issues under Rule 23 of the Rules of Practice of this Court.

Discussion Questions

1. How likely was it that the victim would die? How likely was it that the victim would die *from a fatal reaction to the arteriogram dye*? Which is the relevant inquiry for determining proximate cause?

2. *Jenkins* provides an example of what is often called the "eggshell victim" rule. Is this rule consistent with the requirement of foreseeability?

D. The Model Penal Code and Causation

Model Penal Code

§ 2.03 Causal Relationship between Conduct and Result; Divergence between Result Designed or Contemplated and Actual Result or between Probable and Actual Result

(1) Conduct is the cause of a result when:

    (a) it is an antecedent but for which the result in question would not have occurred; and

    (b) the relationship between the conduct and result satisfies any additional causal requirements imposed by the Code or by the law defining the offense.

(2) When purposely or knowingly causing a particular result is an element of an offense, the element is not established if the actual result is not within the purpose or the contemplation of the actor unless:

    (a) the actual result differs from that designed or contemplated, as the case may be, only in the respect that a different person or different property is injured or affected or that the injury or harm designed or contemplated would have been more serious or more extensive than that caused; or

    (b) the actual result involves the same kind of injury or harm as that designed or contemplated and is not too remote or accidental in its occurrence to have a [just] bearing on the actor's liability or on the gravity of his offense.

(3) When recklessly or negligently causing a particular result is an element of an offense, the element is not established if the actual result is not within the risk of which the actor is aware or, in the case of negligence, of which he should be aware unless:

    (a) the actual result differs from the probable result only in the respect that a different person or different property is injured or affected or that the probable injury or harm would have been more serious or more extensive than that caused; or

    (b) the actual result involves the same kind of injury or harm as the probable result and is not too remote or accidental in its occurrence to have a [just] bearing on the actor's liability or on the gravity of the offense.

(4) When causing a particular result is a material element of an offense for which absolute liability is imposed by law, the element is not established unless the actual result is a probable consequence of the actor's conduct.

Discussion Questions

1. Does the MPC simply state the law of criminal causation reflected in the other materials in this chapter? Or does the MPC change the law of criminal causation? If so, what does it change? Are these changes an improvement? Apply the MPC to each of the cases and problems in this chapter. Would any come out differently?

2. Does causation determine what is "just"? Or does what is "just" determine causation?

Problem

7.14 Draft a jury instruction on causation for use in a jurisdiction that has adopted the MPC provision on causation. Does your MPC instruction differ from the jury instruction on causation that appears in Section 7.1 at the outset of this chapter? If so, how?

E. Synthesis and Review

1. In most cases requiring proof of causation, proximate cause is resolved quite easily. But in a small number of cases, proximate cause proves to be highly problematic. Why is it that proximate cause is usually very easy to resolve but on occasion is very difficult? What distinguishes easy causation cases from difficult ones?

2. The Court in *Kibbe* and the majority in *Root* say that the law of causation in criminal law is *different from* and *more demanding* than the law of causation in torts. The Court in *Carlson,* though, says that the causation standard used in criminal law is "the *same* as that employed in tort law."(emphasis added) The dissenting justice in *Root* also states that the law of causation is the same in tort and criminal cases. Note also that Justice Scalia in the *Burrage* case treated criminal and civil causation standards as interchangeable. If you have already studied causation in torts, which of these views do you think is more accurate? Are tort causation standards different from criminal causation standards? Or are they the same? If they are different, on what points do you think they differ? Cause in fact? Proximate cause? Intervening cause? The eggshell victim rule?

3. Should criminal causation standards differ from tort causation standards? If so, should criminal causation standards be narrower or broader in terms of the scope of causal responsibility? Why? Should criminal standards be narrower on the ground

that the consequences of criminal liability, such as being labeled a criminal, potential imprisonment, and various collateral consequences (e.g., loss of voting rights and disqualification from public benefits) are more severe than the consequences of a civil judgment, typically money damages? Or should they be broader on the ground that criminal defendants usually have a more blameworthy mental state than civil defendants. In other words, shouldn't the scope of causal responsibility be greater for someone who kills with purpose regarding the death at issue, as in many murder cases, than for someone who kills with simple negligence, as in a tort action based on wrongful death?

4. Would it be preferable for judges in criminal cases, rather than using the proximate cause terminology you learned about in this Chapter, to instruct the jury simply to find that the defendant caused the result in question if the jurors conclude that in their judgment it is "fair and just" to impose causal responsibility on the defendant? Do you think such an instruction would cause jurors to act differently than they do under jury instructions currently in use?

5. Are the problems that exist in the law of causation due to the fact that judges have developed causation doctrine through a common-law process? If legislatures addressed causation through statutes, is it likely the law of causation would be in better shape? How might such a statute read?

6. As stated at the outset of this chapter, the conventional view is that only crimes requiring a result also require causation. Professor Michael Moore has written that this "dogma ... is manifestly false."[3] He argues that "a causal judgment is involved in all actions prohibited or required by the criminal law." Theft, for example, is typically viewed as a crime that does not require a result, and thus does not require causation. But Professor Moore argues that "a theft occurs ... only when an actor's voluntary act *causes* movement ('asportation') of the goods stolen." Do you agree with Professor Moore? How could a crime such as burglary be analyzed as involving a causal element?

---

3. Michael S. Moore, *Causation* in 1 ENCYCLOPEDIA OF CRIME AND JUSTICE 151 (2d ed.2002).

Chapter 8

Justifications and Excuses

A. Introduction

Justifications and excuses are ways of defeating criminal liability. "A justification renders a nominal violation of the criminal law lawful and therefore exempt from criminal sanctions.... Those who act [with a legal justification] exercise a privilege and act in conformity with the law."[1] In contrast, an excuse "concedes that the violation is unjustified, but seeks to exempt the particular actor from responsibility for the unjustified act. A claim of justification maintains that the act is right; a claim of excuse concedes that the act in the abstract is wrong, but argues that the actor is not personally responsible for having committed the act. Injuring an innocent person is wrong, but if the actor is insane, his condition precludes his being held responsible for the wrongful act."[2]

The distinction between a justification and an excuse can be important. For example, someone who aids a criminal act for which a justification exists will also usually have the benefit of that justification. Excuse, however, typically is personal to the actor. A sane person who aids an insane person to kill cannot make use of the insanity excuse.

Both justifications and excuses are defenses. The term "defense" can encompass two different ways of defeating liability. Sometimes it is used to refer to defense strategies, such as alibi, mistaken identity, mistake of fact, and intoxication, in which a defendant is essentially contesting the prosecution's proof of one of the elements of the offense. Alibi and mistaken identity, for example, are ways of arguing that the defendant did not engage in the prohibited conduct — someone else did. Mistake of fact and intoxication are typically used to show that the defendant lacked a required mental state.

But "defense" is also used to refer to strategies such as self-defense and necessity, in which the defendant admits fulfillment of the elements but nonetheless seeks to avoid liability by asserting some other principle. This second meaning is sometimes referred to as "confession and avoidance" — confessing to fulfilling the elements but avoiding liability through assertion of an overriding principle.[3] Under this latter

---

1. George P. Fletcher, Justification, Theory, Encyclopedia of Crime and Justice, Vol. 3, 941 (Sanford H. Kadish ed., The Free Press 1983).

2. *Id.* at 942.

3. A Dictionary of Law 96 (Elizabeth A. Martin ed., Oxford University Press 1997) ("**confession and avoidance** A pleading in the defence that, while admitting or assuming the truth of the material facts alleged in the statement of the claim (the **confession**), seeks to avoid or destroy the legal con-

meaning of defense, even if the prosecution proves every element of the crime, the jury should acquit the defendant if it finds the defense applicable. This is often called a "true" or "affirmative" defense. This type of affirmative defense usually places some burden on the defendant to demonstrate the existence of the circumstances that trigger the defense. This burden may require only the production of some evidence or require the defense to prove the existence of the defense by a standard such as a preponderance of the evidence.

This chapter focuses on four affirmative defenses. It begins with a combined treatment of self-defense and its twin, defense of others, and then turns to the defense of necessity. These defenses are regularly accorded the status of justifications. The chapter concludes with duress and insanity, defenses that represent excuses.

B. Self-Defense and Defense of Others

1. Introduction

A legal system is possible only if the state enjoys a monopoly of force. When private individuals appeal to force and decide who shall enjoy the right to "life, liberty and the pursuit of happiness," there can be no pretense of the rule of law. Yet the state's monopoly also entails an obligation to secure its citizens against violence. When individuals are threatened with immediate aggression, when the police cannot protect them, the monopoly of the state gives way. The individual right of survival reasserts itself.[4]

What do jurisdictions require for a successful assertion of self-defense and defense of others? As you read the statutes and cases in this Section, look for similarities and differences in what they require for a successful self-defense claim.

After exploring how self-defense may arise in the context of police-civilian encounters, we consider the perspective from which self-defense must be assessed, that of a hypothetical reasonable person. Recall the importance of the question of "reasonableness" and "tailoring" in our earlier study of mental state and homicide law. Next, we look at reasonableness in the context of domestic violence in *State v. Norman*. We then turn to the rules on retreat and the potential right of self-defense for an initial aggressor. Finally, we examine the Model Penal Code approach on defensive force.

---

sequences of those facts by alleging further facts constituting some defence to the claim (the **avoidance**). An example is a plea of self-defence to an action for assault."); Black's Law Dictionary 293 (Bryan A. Garner ed., West 1997) ("**confession and avoidance.** A plea in which a defendant admits allegations but pleads additional facts that deprive the admitted facts of an adverse legal effect.").

4. George P. Fletcher, A Crime of Self-Defense 18 (U. of Chi. Press 1988).

Problems

8.1 One Halloween, when Fred was a child, he knocked on the door of a house while trick-or-treating. A man with red hair in an elaborate vampire costume opened the door. Fred was terrified. Since that time, Fred has been frightened of red-haired men. Fred works as a repossession agent, a job in which he is often threatened by those whose cars he has been hired to repossess. Earlier today, Fred was repossessing a car when a red-haired man confronted Fred and demanded that Fred cease his repossession. The man was much larger than Fred and yelled and cursed at Fred in an angry tone of voice. The man displayed no weapon nor did he threaten Fred with physical harm. Nonetheless, Fred flashed back to his childhood terror and pulled out his .22 semi-automatic. As the man came within arm's length of Fred, Fred became convinced he was in mortal danger and fired three shots, killing the man. Does Fred have a viable self-defense claim?

8.2 Sheila and her neighbor Yolanda have been feuding for years. Their dispute has grown quite acrimonious. Because they are both fencing and archery enthusiasts, Yolanda challenges Sheila to a fencing match. Sheila accepts. As part of the match, Yolanda stabs Sheila in the leg. Does Yolanda have a viable self-defense claim?

8.3 Consider the following news account of a California trial:

> The defendant, from the Eritrea region of Ethiopia, claimed that he suffered headaches and stomachaches because an Ethiopian woman he had dated was a *bouda* controlled by the Evil Spirit and inflicting pain on him. After begging her several times to stop, he said, he went to her apartment with a gun, intending only to frighten her, but shot her twice.... [The defense attorney] presented testimony from UC Berkeley anthropology professor, William Shack, who said Ethiopians from the Etritea area do indeed believe that the Evil Spirit inflicts pain through a woman selected as a *bouda*.... A psychologist also testified that because of the defendant's war-torn background he was unusually likely to interpret physical pain according to the culture of his upbringing.[5]

Does the defendant have a viable self-defense claim?

Arkansas Code Annotated

§ 5-2-607. Justification.

  (a) A person is justified in using deadly physical force upon another person if he reasonably believes that the other person is:

    (1) Committing or about to commit a felony involving force or violence;

---

5. Myrna Oliver, *Immigrant Crimes, Cultural Defense — A Legal Tactic*, L.A. TIMES, July 15, 1988, at 1.

(2) Using or about to use unlawful deadly physical force; or

(3) Imminently endangering his or her life or imminently about to victimize [any family or household members] from the continuation of a pattern of domestic abuse.

Illinois Compiled Statutes

§ 7-1. Use of Force in Defense of Person.

A person is justified in the use of force against another when and to the extent that he reasonably believes that such conduct is necessary to defend himself or another against such other's imminent use of unlawful force. However, he is justified in the use of force which is intended or likely to cause death or great bodily harm only if he reasonably believes that such force is necessary to prevent imminent death or great bodily harm to himself or another, or the commission of a forcible felony.

Colorado Revised Statutes

§ 18-1-704. Use of Physical Force in Defense of a Person

(1) Except as provided … a person is justified in using physical force upon another person in order to defend himself or a third person from what he reasonably believes to be the use or imminent use of unlawful physical force by that other person, and he may use a degree of force which he reasonably believes to be necessary for that purpose.

(2) Deadly physical force may be used only if a person reasonably believes that a lesser degree of force is inadequate and:

(a) The actor has reasonable grounds to believe, and does believe, that he or another person is in imminent danger of being killed or of receiving great bodily injury; …

(4) Notwithstanding the provisions of subsection (1) of this section, a person is not justified in using physical force if: …

(c) The physical force involved is the product of a combat by agreement not specifically authorized by law.

Discussion Questions

1. How do the Arkansas, Illinois, and Colorado statutes differ? How are they alike?

2. How do these statutes distinguish between deadly and nondeadly force? Are the differences significant?

3. Why does the Colorado statute prevent a defendant from prevailing on a self-defense claim if he or she engaged in combat by agreement? Why don't the other statutes have a similar provision?

4. Are the terms "about to" and "imminent" synonymous?

2. Police-Civilian Encounters and the Black Lives Matter Movement

In recent years, police shootings of black men have resulted in protests and stirred an impassioned national debate about race across the United States. The Black Lives Matter movement has awakened much of the nation to the indignities suffered by people of color, including death at the hands of police officers.

Police advocates point out that the wide proliferation of handguns in the United States makes police work here much more dangerous than in other countries in which access to guns is severely curtailed and that this reality must be taken into account in explaining police use of deadly force. In an effort to reduce the frequency of such shootings, some police departments have sought to change the way their officers use deadly force. The Camden, New Jersey, police department, for example, has begun training its police officers to use alternatives to deadly force whenever possible in interacting with a potentially dangerous person.[6]

Prosecutors and grand juries have often been reluctant to criminally charge police officers involved in such shootings and petit juries have often been reluctant to convict them, so criminal convictions in these cases are rare, though they do happen. Families of the victims have been more successful in civil suits seeking monetary damages brought against the municipality employing the police officer, often resulting in large settlements.

In many of these cases, the police officer claims that self-defense justified the killing. Some people are understandably skeptical of these claims, viewing these incidents as predicated on implicit—and occasionally explicit—biases against African Americans. Under the statutes and cases in this section, should such claims be successful if the victim turns out to have been unarmed? Which elements of self-defense do you think would likely be contested in such cases? Which elements of self-defense do you think would be contested in the following problem?

Problems

8.4 Part (a) David, who is 16 years old, gives his friend, Tom, who is 12 years old, a replica air gun that shoots plastic pellets. David and Tom are both black. The air gun is a replica of a real Colt handgun. Unless examined carefully and at close range, the replica air gun appears identical to a real Colt handgun. To

---

6. Joseph Goldstein, *Changes in Policing Take Hold in One of the Nation's Most Dangerous Cities*, N.Y. TIMES, April 2, 2017, https://www.nytimes.com/2017/04/02/nyregion/camden-nj-police-shootings.html?mcubz=0.

avoid having replica air guns mistaken for real guns, manufacturers place a bright orange ring at the end of a replica gun's barrel. Because the air gun no longer worked, David had removed the orange ring from the end of its barrel before he gave it to Tom. Tom takes the air gun with him to Douglas Park, a public park next to a city recreation center in a low income, predominantly black neighborhood. In the park, Tom begins playing with the gun, pointing it at several people. A man who sees Tom calls 911 and tells the operator "There's a kid in Douglas Park with a pistol. You know it's probably a fake, but he's pointing it at everybody." The 911 operator asks the caller to describe the person with the gun and the man says "He's a kid, male, about 5 feet 6 inches tall, and black." The 911 operator then sends out a radio report to officers in the vicinity of Douglas Park: "A black male in Douglas Park is pointing a gun at people." Two police officers, Frank and Christopher, are on duty in a patrol car near Douglas Park when they hear the 911 report. They drive to the park with Frank behind the wheel and Christopher in the front passenger seat. As they approach the park, Christopher takes out his handgun. They see Tom sitting on a bench and Frank drives the patrol car to within 20 feet of Tom. Later that day, Frank gives the following account of the shooting to fellow officers. Christopher tells them he agrees with Frank's statement.

> *It was a valid shooting. Through my cruiser's loudspeaker, I told him to raise his hands. When we were within 20 feet, Chris jumped out of the car with his weapon drawn. Instead of raising his hands, he pulled the gun out of his waist band. Chris told him to drop it, but he didn't. Chris fired several times, hitting and killing him. After Chris told him to drop the gun, Chris gave him about 20 seconds before he fired his weapon.*

Under these facts, does Christopher have a valid claim of self-defense?

Part (b) Assume for this part that a surveillance camera at the park captured the shooting on video. It contradicts Frank and Christopher's account in Part (a) on some important points. The recording shows that rather than waiting for 20 seconds, Christopher fired the fatal shots at Tom *as Christopher was getting out of the cruiser.* Although there is no audio recording, the video shows Christopher firing so quickly that there would not have been time for any warning or command by Christopher to Tom. The video is unclear on whether Tom had pulled the air gun from his waistband. Considering what the video reveals and that it contradicts Frank and Christopher's earlier account, does Christopher have a valid claim of self-defense?

Part (c) Assume the 911 operator included in the radio report the witness's statement that the gun was "probably a fake" and that the person with the gun was "a kid." Does Christopher have a valid claim of self-defense?

Part (d) You are the attorney representing the city that employs Frank and Christopher in a civil action brought by Tom's family against the city. Assume the city is vicariously liable for the actions of its employees, Christopher and

Frank, and that the same principles of self-defense found in this chapter apply to a wrongful death action. Would you advise the city to settle the case or go to trial? If you advise settlement, how much would you advise the city to offer in settlement?

8.5 Michael is a tall, twenty-one-year-old African American in a city with a history of fraught relations between the nearly all-white police force and the black community. This history includes at least two recent incidents in which police officers shot and killed unarmed black men. Late one night, Michael is walking down the street when two police officers, responding to reports of gunfire in the neighborhood, suddenly approach him with their weapons raised. The police do not notify Michael about the reason for their presence or, for that matter, say anything. Michael shoots the officer closest to him in the shoulder, causing him to drop his gun. Would Michael succeed with a self-defense claim?

3. A Matter of Perspective: The "Reasonable Person"

In weighing a self-defense claim, should courts use a subjective test and ask whether the defendant genuinely believed he was in harm's way? Or should the test be objective and assess whether a reasonable person would have felt threatened under the circumstances? Neither approach is perfect. A purely subjective test might allow people with idiosyncratic and unusually-elevated fears of violence to escape conviction, whereas taking a wholly objective stance might deny relief to people with legitimate fears that stem from tragic personal experience. Although jurisdictions vary in how they answer these questions, many states blend the two approaches by adopting an objective test with a subjective twist. Consider the approach in New York:

New York Penal Law § 35.15 Justification;
use of physical force in defense of a person.

1. A person may, subject to the provisions of subdivision two, use physical force upon another person when and to the extent he or she reasonably believes such to be necessary to defend himself, herself or a third person from what he or she reasonably believes to be the use or imminent use of unlawful physical force by such other person ...

2. A person may not use deadly physical force upon another person under circumstance specified in subdivision one unless: (a) The actor reasonably believes that such other person is using or about to use deadly physical force.

People v. Umali

10 N.Y.3d 417 (2008)
New York Court of Appeals

JUDGE GRAFFEO.

As relevant to this appeal, justification is comprised of both subjective and objective elements. The subjective element is concerned with whether the defendant believed that the use of deadly force was necessary; while under the objective prong, the jury must consider whether a reasonable person in the defendant's circumstances would have believed that deadly force was required. When a defense of justification is raised, "the People must prove beyond a reasonable doubt that [the] defendant's conduct was not justified" (*People v. Craig*, 78 N.Y.2d 616, 619 n. 1, 578 N.Y.S.2d 471, 585 N.E.2d 783 [1991]). In other words, the People must demonstrate beyond a reasonable doubt that the defendant did not believe deadly force was necessary or that a reasonable person in the same situation would not have perceived that deadly force was necessary (*see e.g. People v. Goetz*, 68 N.Y.2d 96, 115, 506 N.Y.S.2d 18, 497 N.E.2d 41 [1986]).

The *Goetz* case cited in *Umali* attained great notoriety and provoked a powerful response throughout the nation, particularly among New Yorkers. It involved a white subway rider, Bernie Goetz, who opened fire on four African-American teenagers "after one or two of the youths approached him and asked for $5." The Court of Appeals considered Goetz's personal experiences, which including being the victim of past muggings, in evaluating how a "reasonable person" in the actor's situation would have perceived the threat and found the evidence sufficient to submit a self-defense instruction to the jury.

Ultimately, the jury in the criminal trial acquitted Goetz of all the charges except criminal possession of a weapon in the third degree. One of the victims of the shooting, Darrell Cabey, who remained paralyzed, sued Goetz. The jury in this civil case found in favor of Mr. Cabey and awarded him the sum of $43,000,000.[7] What might explain the profoundly disparate results in the criminal and civil cases?

The *Goetz* case arguably also represented a key chapter in the story of the burgeoning "gun rights" movement. Consider these reflections from a former National Rifle Association leader thirty years after that fatal day on a New York City subway:

> Looking back, it was a defining moment for the emerging gun rights movement led by the National Rifle Association — and I know because I was that young NRA spokesman. The era prior had been about eliminating the right to even own a handgun; now the debate would be transformed into the lawful

---

7. Associated Press, *Jury Hands Down $43M Verdict in Lawsuit against Goetz*, ARIZ. DAILY WILDCAT, Aug. 2, 2004, http://wildcat.arizona.edu//papers/89/144/11_1_m.html.

ability to carry one. The following year Florida passed the first modern "**shall issue**" statute mandating the issuance of a carry license if the applicant met certain basic standards. No longer could Palm Beach, Broward and Dade Counties Florida prevent their citizens from having the same self-defense rights as other Floridians.[8]

Discussion Questions

What are the advantages and disadvantages of an objective standard? What are the advantages and disadvantages of a subjective standard?

4. Defense of Others

As the statutes earlier in the chapter and the New York statute in the *Goetz* case illustrate, the doctrine of defense of others largely parallels that of self-defense. Commonly, a defendant must meet the same requirements for each.

But sometimes courts have distinguished a self-defense claim from one for defense of others. For example, under a traditional self-defense claim, if the defendant made an honest but reasonable error about the need to use deadly defensive force, the defendant generally still benefited from a defensive force defense. If the defendant used deadly force against a gun-wielding assailant, but the assailant turned out to be a police officer engaged in a legitimate arrest and a person in the defendant's situation could have reasonably mistaken the officer for someone intending unlawful deadly harm, the defendant could still usually invoke a perfect self-defense claim. In contrast, some courts have not upheld such a claim when the defendant misperceived the situation and was acting in defense of a third party.[9] Historically, some courts have also limited the right to use deadly force to defend third parties to those with whom the defendant has a specific relationship, like a spousal or parental relationship.[10]

5. Self-Defense and Domestic Violence

The issue of self-defense arises in many factual contexts. Much debate over the past several decades has focused on its use in the domestic violence context. A substantial portion of this debate revolves around the effects of domestic violence on the person battered and the requirements of reasonableness and imminence. Contrast the majority and dissent approaches to these issues in the *Norman* case below.

---

8. Richard Feldman, *Bernie Goetz "The Subway Gunman" Thirty Years Later,* Huffington Post, Dec. 23, 2014.

9. Wayne R. LaFave, Criminal Law 550–52 (4th ed. 2000).

10. *Id.* at 553.

State v. Norman

324 N.C. 253 (1989)
Supreme Court of North Carolina

Mitchell, J.

The defendant was tried ... upon a proper indictment charging her with the first degree murder of her husband. The jury found the defendant guilty of voluntary manslaughter. The defendant appealed from the trial court's judgment sentencing her to six years imprisonment.

The Court of Appeals granted a new trial, citing as error the trial court's refusal to submit a possible verdict of acquittal by reason of perfect self-defense. Notwithstanding the uncontroverted evidence that the defendant shot her husband three times in the back of the head as he lay sleeping in his bed, the Court of Appeals held that the defendant's evidence that she exhibited what has come to be called "the battered wife syndrome" entitled her to have the jury consider whether the homicide was an act of perfect self-defense and, thus, not a legal wrong.

We conclude that the evidence introduced in this case would not support a finding that the defendant killed her husband due to a reasonable fear of imminent death or great bodily harm, as is required before a defendant is entitled to jury instructions concerning either perfect or imperfect self-defense. Therefore, the trial court properly declined to instruct the jury on the law relating to self-defense. Accordingly, we reverse the Court of Appeals.

At trial, the State presented the testimony of Deputy Sheriff R. H. Epley of the Rutherford County Sheriff's Department, who was called to the Norman residence on the night of 12 June 1985. Inside the home, Epley found the defendant's husband, John Thomas Norman, lying on a bed in a rear bedroom with his face toward the wall and his back toward the middle of the room. He was dead, but blood was still coming from wounds to the back of his head. A later autopsy revealed three gunshot wounds to the head, two of which caused fatal brain injury. The autopsy also revealed a .12 percent blood alcohol level in the victim's body.

Later that night, the defendant related an account of the events leading to the killing, after Epley had advised her of her constitutional rights and she had waived her right to remain silent. The defendant told Epley that her husband had been beating her all day and had made her lie down on the floor while he slept on the bed. After her husband fell asleep, the defendant carried her grandchild to the defendant's mother's house. The defendant took a pistol from her mother's purse and walked the short distance back to her home. She pointed the pistol at the back of her sleeping husband's head, but it jammed the first time she tried to shoot him. She fixed the gun and then shot her husband in the back of the head as he lay sleeping. After one shot, she felt her husband's chest and determined that he was still breathing and making sounds. She then shot him twice more in the back of the head. The defendant told Epley that she killed her husband because "she took all she was going to take from him so she shot him."

The defendant presented evidence tending to show a long history of physical and mental abuse by her husband due to his alcoholism. At the time of the killing, the thirty-nine-year-old defendant and her husband had been married almost twenty-five years and had several children. The defendant testified that her husband had started drinking and abusing her about five years after they were married. His physical abuse of her consisted of frequent assaults that included slapping, punching and kicking her, striking her with various objects, and throwing glasses, beer bottles and other objects at her. The defendant described other specific incidents of abuse, such as her husband putting her cigarettes out on her, throwing hot coffee on her, breaking glass against her face and crushing food on her face. Although the defendant did not present evidence of ever having received medical treatment for any physical injuries inflicted by her husband, she displayed several scars about her face which she attributed to her husband's assaults.

The defendant's evidence also tended to show other indignities inflicted upon her by her husband. Her evidence tended to show that her husband did not work and forced her to make money by prostitution, and that he made humor of that fact to family and friends. He would beat her if she resisted going out to prostitute herself or if he was unsatisfied with the amounts of money she made. He routinely called the defendant "dog," "bitch" and "whore," and on a few occasions made her eat pet food out of the pets' bowls and bark like a dog. He often made her sleep on the floor. At times, he deprived her of food and refused to let her get food for the family. During those years of abuse, the defendant's husband threatened numerous times to kill her and to maim her in various ways.

The defendant said her husband's abuse occurred only when he was intoxicated, but that he would not give up drinking. She said she and her husband "got along very well when he was sober," and that he was "a good guy" when he was not drunk. She had accompanied her husband to the local mental health center for sporadic counseling sessions for his problem, but he continued to drink.

In the early morning hours on the day before his death, the defendant's husband, who was intoxicated, went to a rest area off I-85 near Kings Mountain where the defendant was engaging in prostitution and assaulted her. While driving home, he was stopped by a patrolman and jailed on a charge of driving while impaired. After the defendant's mother got him out of jail at the defendant's request later that morning, he resumed his drinking and abuse of the defendant.

The defendant's evidence also tended to show that her husband seemed angrier than ever after he was released from jail and that his abuse of the defendant was more frequent. That evening, sheriff's deputies were called to the Norman residence, and the defendant complained that her husband had been beating her all day and she could not take it anymore. The defendant was advised to file a complaint, but she said she was afraid her husband would kill her if she had him arrested. The deputies told her they needed a warrant before they could arrest her husband, and they left the scene.

The deputies were called back less than an hour later after the defendant had taken a bottle of pills. The defendant's husband cursed her and called her names as she was attended by paramedics, and he told them to let her die. A sheriff's deputy finally chased him back into his house as the defendant was put into an ambulance. The defendant's stomach was pumped at the local hospital, and she was sent home with her mother.

While in the hospital, the defendant was visited by a therapist with whom she discussed filing charges against her husband and having him committed for treatment. Before the therapist left, the defendant agreed to go to the mental health center the next day to discuss those possibilities. The therapist testified at trial that the defendant seemed depressed in the hospital, and that she expressed considerable anger toward her husband. He testified that the defendant threatened a number of times that night to kill her husband and that she said she should kill him "because of the things he had done to her."

The next day, the day she shot her husband, the defendant went to the mental health center to talk about charges and possible commitment, and she confronted her husband with that possibility. She testified that she told her husband later that day: "J. T., straighten up. Quit drinking. I'm going to have you committed to help you." She said her husband then told her he would "see them coming" and would cut her throat before they got to him.

The defendant also went to the social services office that day to seek welfare benefits, but her husband followed her there, interrupted her interview and made her go home with him. He continued his abuse of her, threatening to kill and to maim her, slapping her, kicking her, and throwing objects at her. At one point, he took her cigarette and put it out on her, causing a small burn on her upper torso. He would not let her eat or bring food into the house for their children.

That evening, the defendant and her husband went into their bedroom to lie down, and he called her a "dog" and made her lie on the floor when he lay down on the bed. Their daughter brought in her baby to leave with the defendant, and the defendant's husband agreed to let her baby-sit. After the defendant's husband fell asleep, the baby started crying and the defendant took it to her mother's house so it would not wake up her husband. She returned shortly with the pistol and killed her husband.

The defendant testified at trial that she was too afraid of her husband to press charges against him or to leave him. She said that she had temporarily left their home on several previous occasions, but he had always found her, brought her home and beaten her. Asked why she killed her husband, the defendant replied: "Because I was scared of him and I knowed when he woke up, it was going to be the same thing, and I was scared when he took me to the truck stop that night it was going to be worse than he had ever been. I just couldn't take it no more. There ain't no way, even if it means going to prison. It's better than living in that. That's worse hell than anything."

The defendant and other witnesses testified that for years her husband had frequently threatened to kill her and to maim her. When asked if she believed those threats, the defendant replied: "Yes. I believed him; he would, he would kill me if he got a chance. If he thought he wouldn't a had to went to jail, he would a done it."

Two expert witnesses in forensic psychology and psychiatry who examined the defendant after the shooting, Dr. William Tyson and Dr. Robert Rollins, testified that the defendant fit the profile of battered wife syndrome. This condition, they testified, is characterized by such abuse and degradation that the battered wife comes to believe she is unable to help herself and cannot expect help from anyone else. She believes that she cannot escape the complete control of her husband and that he is invulnerable to law enforcement and other sources of help.

Dr. Tyson, a psychologist, was asked his opinion as to whether, on 12 June 1985, "it appeared reasonably necessary for Judy Norman to shoot J. T. Norman?" He replied: "I believe that ... Mrs. Norman believed herself to be doomed ... to a life of the worst kind of torture and abuse, degradation that she had experienced over the years in a progressive way; that it would only get worse, and that death was inevitable...." Dr. Tyson later added: "I think Judy Norman felt that she had no choice, both in the protection of herself and her family, but to engage, exhibit deadly force against Mr. Norman, and that in so doing, she was sacrificing herself, both for herself and for her family."

Dr. Rollins, who was the defendant's attending physician at Dorothea Dix Hospital when she was sent there for evaluation, testified that in his opinion the defendant was a typical abused spouse and that "[s]he saw herself as powerless to deal with the situation, that there was no alternative, no way she could escape it." Dr. Rollins was asked his opinion as to whether "on June 12th, 1985, it appeared reasonably necessary that Judy Norman would take the life of J. T. Norman?" Dr. Rollins replied that in his opinion, "that course of action did appear necessary to Mrs. Norman."

Based on the evidence that the defendant exhibited battered wife syndrome, that she believed she could not escape her husband nor expect help from others, that her husband had threatened her, and that her husband's abuse of her had worsened in the two days preceding his death, the Court of Appeals concluded that a jury reasonably could have found that her killing of her husband was justified as an act of perfect self-defense. The Court of Appeals reasoned that the nature of battered wife syndrome is such that a jury could not be precluded from finding the defendant killed her husband lawfully in perfect self-defense, even though he was asleep when she killed him. We disagree.

The right to kill in self-defense is based on the necessity, real or reasonably apparent, of killing an unlawful aggressor to save oneself from *imminent* death or great bodily harm at his hands. Our law has recognized that self-preservation under such circumstances springs from a primal impulse and is an inherent right of natural law.

In North Carolina, a defendant is entitled to have the jury consider acquittal by reason of *perfect* self-defense when the evidence, viewed in the light most favorable to the defendant, tends to show that at the time of the killing it appeared to the defendant and she believed it to be necessary to kill the decedent to save herself from imminent death or great bodily harm. That belief must be reasonable, however, in that the circumstances as they appeared to the defendant would create such a belief in the mind of a person of ordinary firmness. Further, the defendant must not have been the initial aggressor provoking the fatal confrontation. A killing in the proper exercise of the right of *perfect* self-defense is always completely justified in law and constitutes no legal wrong.

Our law also recognizes an *imperfect* right of self-defense in certain circumstances, including, for example, when the defendant is the initial aggressor, but without intent to kill or to seriously injure the decedent, and the decedent escalates the confrontation to a point where it reasonably appears to the defendant to be necessary to kill the decedent to save herself from imminent death or great bodily harm. Although the culpability of a defendant who kills in the exercise of *imperfect* self-defense is reduced, such a defendant is *not justified* in the killing so as to be entitled to acquittal, but is guilty at least of voluntary manslaughter.

The defendant in the present case was not entitled to a jury instruction on either perfect or imperfect self-defense. The trial court was not required to instruct on *either* form of self-defense unless evidence was introduced tending to show that at the time of the killing the defendant reasonably believed herself to be confronted by circumstances which necessitated her killing her husband to save herself from *imminent* death or great bodily harm. No such evidence was introduced in this case, and it would have been error for the trial court to instruct the jury on *either* perfect or imperfect self-defense....

The killing of another human being is the most extreme recourse to our inherent right of self-preservation and can be justified in law only by the utmost real or apparent necessity brought about by the decedent. For that reason, our law of self-defense has required that a defendant claiming that a homicide was justified and, as a result, inherently lawful by reason of perfect self-defense must establish that she reasonably believed at the time of the killing she otherwise would have immediately suffered death or great bodily harm. Only if defendants are required to show that they killed due to a reasonable belief that death or great bodily harm was imminent can the justification for homicide remain clearly and firmly rooted in necessity....

The term "imminent," as used to describe such perceived threats of death or great bodily harm as will justify a homicide by reason of perfect self-defense, has been defined as "immediate danger, such as must be instantly met, such as cannot be guarded against by calling for the assistance of others or the protection of the law." Black's Law Dictionary 676 (5th ed. 1979). Our cases have sometimes used the phrase "about to suffer" interchangeably with "imminent" to describe the immediacy of threat that is required to justify killing in self-defense.

The evidence in this case did not tend to show that the defendant reasonably believed that she was confronted by a threat of imminent death or great bodily harm.

The evidence tended to show that no harm was "imminent" or about to happen to the defendant when she shot her husband. The uncontroverted evidence was that her husband had been asleep for some time when she walked to her mother's house, returned with the pistol, fixed the pistol after it jammed and then shot her husband three times in the back of the head. The defendant was not faced with an instantaneous choice between killing her husband or being killed or seriously injured. Instead, *all* of the evidence tended to show that the defendant had ample time and opportunity to resort to other means of preventing further abuse by her husband. There was no action underway by the decedent from which the jury could have found that the defendant had reasonable grounds to believe either that a felonious assault was imminent or that it might result in her death or great bodily injury. Additionally, no such action by the decedent had been underway immediately prior to his falling asleep....

The reasoning of our Court of Appeals in this case proposes to change the established law of self-defense by giving the term "imminent" a meaning substantially more indefinite and all-encompassing than its present meaning. This would result in a substantial relaxation of the requirement of real or apparent necessity to justify homicide. Such reasoning proposes justifying the taking of human life not upon the reasonable belief it is necessary to prevent death or great bodily harm — which the imminence requirement ensures — but upon purely subjective speculation that the decedent probably would present a threat to life at a future time and that the defendant would not be able to avoid the predicted threat.

The Court of Appeals suggests that such speculation would have been particularly reliable in the present case because the jury, based on the evidence of the decedent's intensified abuse during the thirty-six hours preceding his death, could have found that the decedent's passive state at the time of his death was "but a momentary hiatus in a continuous reign of terror by the decedent [and] the defendant merely took advantage of her first opportunity to protect herself." Requiring jury instructions on perfect self-defense in such situations, however, would still tend to make opportune homicide lawful as a result of mere subjective predictions of indefinite future assaults and circumstances. Such predictions of future assaults to justify the defendant's use of deadly force in this case would be entirely speculative, because there was no evidence that her husband had ever inflicted any harm upon her that approached life-threatening injury, even during the "reign of terror." It is far from clear in the defendant's poignant evidence that any abuse by the decedent had ever involved the degree of physical threat required to justify the defendant in using deadly force, even when those threats were imminent. The use of deadly force in self-defense to prevent harm other than death or great bodily harm is excessive as a matter of law.

As we have stated, stretching the law of self-defense to fit the facts of this case would require changing the "imminent death or great bodily harm" requirement to something substantially more indefinite than previously required and would weaken our assurances that justification for the taking of human life remains firmly rooted in real or apparent necessity. That result in principle could not be limited to a few cases decided on evidence as poignant as this. The relaxed requirements for perfect self-defense proposed by our Court of Appeals would tend to categorically legalize the opportune killing of abusive husbands by their wives solely on the basis of the wives' testimony concerning their subjective speculation as to the probability of future felonious assaults by their husbands. Homicidal self-help would then become a lawful solution, and perhaps the easiest and most effective solution, to this problem. . . .

For the foregoing reasons, we conclude that the defendant's conviction for voluntary manslaughter and the trial court's judgment sentencing her to a six-year term of imprisonment were without error. Therefore, we must reverse the decision of the Court of Appeals which awarded the defendant a new trial.

Reversed.

Justice Martin, dissenting.

At the outset it is to be noted that the peril of fabricated evidence is not unique to the trials of battered wives who kill. The possibility of invented evidence arises in all cases in which a party is seeking the benefit of self-defense. Moreover, in this case there were a number of witnesses other than defendant who testified as to the actual presence of circumstances supporting a claim of self-defense. This record contains no reasonable basis to attack the credibility of evidence for the defendant. . . .

At the heart of the majority's reasoning is its unsubstantiated concern that to find that the evidence presented by defendant would support an instruction on self-defense would "expand our law of self-defense beyond the limits of immediacy and necessity." Defendant does not seek to expand or relax the requirements of self-defense and thereby "legalize the opportune killing of allegedly abusive husbands by their wives," as the majority overstates. Rather, defendant contends that the evidence as gauged by the existing laws of self-defense is sufficient to require the submission of a self-defense instruction to the jury. The proper issue for this Court is to determine whether the evidence, viewed in the light most favorable to the defendant, was sufficient to require the trial court to instruct on the law of self-defense. I conclude that it was. . . .

A defendant is entitled to an instruction on self-defense when there is evidence, viewed in the light most favorable to the defendant, that these four elements existed at the time of the killing:

(1) it appeared to defendant and he believed it to be necessary to kill the deceased in order to save himself from death or great bodily harm; and

(2) defendant's belief was reasonable in that the circumstances as they appeared to him at the time were sufficient to create such a belief in the mind of a person of ordinary firmness; and

(3) defendant was not the aggressor in bringing on the affray, i.e., he did not aggressively and willingly enter into the fight without legal excuse or provocation; and

(4) defendant did not use excessive force, i.e., did not use more force than was necessary or reasonably appeared to him to be necessary under the circumstances to protect himself from death or great bodily harm. . . .

Evidence presented by defendant described a twenty-year history of beatings and other dehumanizing and degrading treatment by her husband. In his expert testimony a clinical psychologist concluded that defendant fit "and exceed[ed]" the profile of an abused or battered spouse, analogizing this treatment to the dehumanization process suffered by prisoners of war under the Nazis during the Second World War and the brainwashing techniques of the Korean War. The psychologist described the defendant as a woman incarcerated by abuse, by fear, and by her conviction that her husband was invincible and inescapable:

> Mrs. Norman didn't leave because she believed, fully believed that escape was totally impossible. There was no place to go. [S]he had left before; he had come and gotten her. She had gone to the Department of Social Services. He had come and gotten her. The law, she believed the law could not protect her; no one could protect her, and I must admit, looking over the records, that there was nothing done that would contradict that belief. She fully believed that he was invulnerable to the law and to all social agencies that were available; that nobody could withstand his power. As a result, there was no such thing as escape.

When asked if he had an opinion whether it appeared reasonably necessary for Judy Norman to shoot her husband, this witness responded:

> Yes.... I believe that in examining the facts of this case and examining the psychological data, that Mrs. Norman believed herself to be doomed ... to a life of the worst kind of torture and abuse, degradation that she had experienced over the years in a progressive way; that it would only get worse, and that death was inevitable; death of herself, which was not such, I don't think was such an issue for her, as she had attempted to commit suicide, and in her continuing conviction of J. T. Norman's power over her, and even failed at that form of escape. I believe she also came to the point of beginning to fear for family members and her children, that were she to commit suicide that the abuse and the treatment that was heaped on her would be transferred onto them.

This testimony describes defendant's perception of circumstances in which she was held hostage to her husband's abuse for two decades and which ultimately compelled her to kill him. This testimony alone is evidence amply indicating the first two elements required for entitlement to an instruction on self-defense.

In addition to the testimony of the clinical psychologist, defendant presented the testimony of witnesses who had actually seen defendant's husband abuse her. These witnesses described circumstances that caused not only defendant to believe escape was impossible, but that also convinced *them* of its impossibility. Defendant's isolation and helplessness were evident in testimony that her family was intimidated by her husband into acquiescing in his torture of her. Witnesses also described defendant's experience with social service agencies and the law, which had contributed to her sense of futility and abandonment through the inefficacy of their protection and the strength of her husband's wrath when they failed. Where torture appears interminable and escape impossible, the belief that only the death of the oppressor can provide relief is reasonable in the mind of a person of ordinary firmness, let alone in the mind of the defendant, who, like a prisoner of war of some years, has been deprived of her humanity and is held hostage by fear....

Evidence presented in the case sub judice revealed no letup of tension or fear, no moment in which the defendant felt released from impending serious harm, even while the decedent slept.... Psychologists have observed and commentators have described a "constant state of fear" brought on by the cyclical nature of battering as well as the battered spouse's perception that her abuser is both "omnipotent and unstoppable." *See* Comment, *The Admissibility of Expert Testimony on the Battered Woman Syndrome in Support of a Claim of Self-Defense,* 15 Conn. L. Rev. 121, 131 (1982). Constant fear means a perpetual anticipation of the next blow, a perpetual expectation that the next blow will kill. "[T]he battered wife is constantly in a heightened state of terror because she is certain that one day her husband will kill her during the course of a beating.... Thus from the perspective of the battered wife, the danger is constantly 'immediate.'" Eber, *The Battered Wife's Dilemma: To Kill or To Be Killed,* 32 Hastings L.J. 895, 928–29 (1981). For the battered wife, if there is no escape, if there is no window of relief or momentary sense of safety, then the next attack, which could be the fatal one, is imminent. In the context of the doctrine of self-defense, "imminent" is a term the meaning of which must be grasped from the defendant's point of view. Properly stated, the second prong of the question is not whether the threat was *in fact* imminent, but whether defendant's belief in the impending nature of the threat, given the circumstances as she saw them, was reasonable in the mind of a person of ordinary firmness.[1]

Defendant's intense fear, based on her belief that her husband intended not only to maim or deface her, as he had in the past, but to kill her, was evident in the testimony of witnesses who recounted events of the last three days of the decedent's life. This testimony could have led a juror to conclude that defendant reasonably perceived a threat to her life as "imminent," even while her husband slept. Over these three days, her husband's anger was exhibited in an unprecedented crescendo of violence. The evidence showed defendant's fear and sense of hopelessness similarly intensifying, leading to an unsuccessful attempt to escape through suicide and culminating in her belief that escape would be possible only through her husband's death.

Defendant testified that on 10 June, two days before her husband's death, he had again forced her to go to a rest stop near Kings Mountain to make money by prostitution. Her daughter Phyllis and Phyllis's boyfriend Mark Navarra accompanied her on this occasion because, defendant said, whenever her husband took her there, he would beat her. Phyllis corroborated this account. She testified that her father had

---

1. This interpretation of the meaning of "imminent" is reflected in the Comments to the Model Penal Code: "The actor must believe that his defensive action is immediately necessary and the unlawful force against which he defends must be force that he apprehends will be used on the present occasion, but he need not apprehend that it will be immediately used." Model Penal Code § 3.04 comment (ALI 1985).

arrived some time later and had begun beating her mother, asking how much money she had. Defendant said they all then drove off. Shortly afterwards an officer arrested defendant's husband for driving under the influence. He spent the night in jail and was released the next morning on bond paid by defendant's mother.

Defendant testified that her husband was argumentative and abusive all through the next day, 11 June. Mark Navarra testified that at one point defendant's husband threw a sandwich that defendant had made for him on the floor. She made another; he threw it on the floor, as well, then insisted she prepare one without touching it. Defendant's husband had then taken the third sandwich, which defendant had wrapped in paper towels, and smeared it on her face. Both Navarra and Phyllis testified that they had later watched defendant's husband seize defendant's cigarette and put it out on her neck, the scars from which defendant displayed to the jury.

A police officer testified that he arrived at defendant's home at 8:00 that evening in response to a call reporting a domestic quarrel. Defendant, whose face was bruised, was crying, and she told the officer that her husband had beaten her all day long and that she could not take it any longer. The officer told her that he could do nothing for her unless she took out a warrant on her husband. She responded that if she did, her husband would kill her. The officer left but was soon radioed to return because defendant had taken an overdose of pills. The officer testified that defendant's husband was interfering with ambulance attendants, saying "Let the bitch die." When he refused to respond to the officer's warning that if he continued to hinder the attendants, he would be arrested, the officer was compelled to chase him into the house.

Defendant's mother testified that her son-in-law had reacted to the discovery that her daughter had taken the pills with cursing and obscenities and threats such as, "Now, you're going to pay for taking those pills," and "I'll kill you, your mother and your grandmother." His rage was such that defendant's mother feared he might kill the whole family, and knowing defendant's sister had a gun in her purse, she took the gun and placed it in her own.

Defendant was taken to the hospital, treated, and released at 2:30 a.m. She spent the remainder of the night at her grandmother's house. Defendant testified that the next day, 12 June, she felt dazed all day long. She went in the morning to the county mental health center for guidance on domestic abuse. When she returned home, she tried to talk to her husband, telling him to "straighten up. Quit drinking.... I'm going to have you committed to help you." Her husband responded, "If you do, I'll see them coming and before they get here, I'll cut your throat."

Later, her husband made her drive him and his friend to Spartanburg to pick up the friend's paycheck. On the way, the friend testified, defendant's husband "started slapping on her" when she was following a truck too closely, and he periodically poured his beer into a glass, then reached over and poured it on defendant's head. At one point defendant's husband lay down on the front seat with his head on the arm rest, "like he was going to go to sleep," and kicked defendant, who was still driving, in the side of the head.

Mark Navarra testified that in the year and a half he had lived with the Normans, he had never seen defendant's husband madder than he was on 12 June, opining that it was the DUI arrest two days before that had ignited J.T.'s fury. Phyllis testified that her father had beaten her mother "all day long." She testified that this was the third day defendant's husband had forbidden her to eat any food. Phyllis said defendant's family tried to get her to eat, but defendant, fearing a beating, would not. Although Phyllis's grandmother had sent over a bag of groceries that day, defendant's husband had made defendant put them back in the bag and would not let anyone eat them.

Early in the evening of 12 June, defendant's husband told defendant, "Let's go to bed." Phyllis testified that although there were two beds in the room, her father had forbidden defendant from sleeping on either. Instead, he had made her lie down on the concrete floor between the two beds, saying, "Dogs don't lay in the bed. They lay in the floor." Shortly afterward, defendant testified, Phyllis came in and asked her father if defendant could take care of her baby while she went to the store. He assented and eventually went to sleep. Defendant was still on the floor, the baby on the small bed. The baby started to cry and defendant "snuck up and took him out there to [her] mother's [house]." She asked her mother to watch the baby, then asked if her mother had anything for headache, as her head was "busting." Her mother responded that she had some pain pills in her purse. Defendant went in to get the pills, "and the gun was in there, and I don't know, I just seen the gun, and I took it out, and I went back there and shot him."

From this evidence of the exacerbated nature of the last three days of twenty years of provocation, a juror could conclude that defendant believed that her husband's threats to her life were viable, that serious bodily harm was imminent, and that it was necessary to kill her husband to escape that harm. And from this evidence a juror could find defendant's belief in the necessity to kill her husband not merely reasonable but compelling.

The third element for entitlement to an instruction on self-defense requires that there be evidence that the defendant was not the aggressor in bringing on the affray. If the defendant was the aggressor and killed with murderous intent, that is, the intent to kill or inflict serious bodily harm, then she is not entitled to an instruction on self-defense. A hiatus between provocation by the decedent and the killing can mark the initiation of a new confrontation between the defendant and the decedent, such that the defendant's earlier perception of imminent danger no longer appears reasonable and the defendant becomes the aggressor....

Where the defendant is a battered wife, there is no analogue to the victim-turned-aggressor.... Where the defendant is a battered wife, the affray out of which the killing arises can be a continuing assault. There was evidence before the jury that it had not been defendant but her husband who had initiated "the affray," which the jury could have regarded as lasting twenty years, three days, or any number of hours preceding his death. And there was evidence from which the jury could infer that in defendant's mind the affray reached beyond the moment at which her husband fell asleep. Like the ongoing threats of death or great bodily harm, which she might reasonably have perceived as imminent, her husband continued to be the aggressor and she the victim.

Finally, the fourth element of self-defense poses the question of whether there was any evidence tending to show that the force used by defendant to repel her husband was not excessive, that is, more than reasonably appeared to be necessary under the circumstances. This question is answered in part by abundant testimony describing defendant's immobilization by fear caused by abuse by her husband. Three witnesses, including the decedent's best friend, all recounted incidents in which defendant passively accepted beating, kicks, commands, or humiliating affronts without striking back. From such evidence that she was paralyzed by her husband's presence, a jury could infer that it reasonably appeared to defendant to be necessary to kill her husband in order ultimately to protect herself from the death he had threatened and from severe bodily injury, a foretaste of which she had already experienced....

It is to be remembered that defendant does not have the burden of persuasion as to self-defense; the burden remains with the state to prove beyond a reasonable doubt that defendant intentionally killed decedent without excuse or justification. If the evidence in support of self-defense is sufficient to create a reasonable doubt in the mind of a rational juror whether the state has proved an intentional killing without justification or excuse, self-defense must be submitted to the jury. This is such a case.

Discussion Questions

1. What is the rule regarding self-defense in North Carolina as expressed in the *Norman* case?

2. Why do the majority and dissent come to different conclusions? How does each define the word *imminent*?

3. To which requirements of self-defense is battered woman syndrome testimony relevant?

* * *

Consider the Utah statute and the expression of legislative intent behind the 1994 revision to Utah's self-defense statute below. How might a court using this statute have resolved the issues in *Norman*?

Utah Code Annotated

§ 76-2-402. Force in Defense of a Person — Forcible Felony Defined.

(1) A person is justified in threatening or using force against another when and to the extent that he or she reasonably believes that force is necessary to defend himself or a third person against such other's imminent use of unlawful force. However, that person is justified in using force intended or likely to cause death or serious bodily injury only if he or she reasonably believes that force is necessary to prevent death or serious bodily injury to himself or a third person as a result of the other's imminent use of unlawful force, or to prevent the commission of a forcible felony....

(5) In determining imminence or reasonableness under Subsection (1), the trier of fact may consider, but is not limited to, any of the following factors:

　　(a) the nature of the danger;

　　(b) the immediacy of the danger;

　　(c) the probability that the unlawful force would result in death or serious bodily injury;

　　(d) the other's prior violent acts or violent propensities; and

　　(e) any patterns of abuse or violence in the parties' relationship.

* * *

The legislative history of the above Utah Code Section contains the following statement of legislative intent:

> Amendments made by this act to Section 76-2-402, regarding self-defense, are intended to clarify that justification of the use of force in defense of a person applies equally to all persons including victims of abuse in ongoing relationships. It is intended that otherwise competent evidence regarding a victim's response to patterns of domestic abuse or violence be considered by the trier of fact in determining imminence or reasonableness in accordance with that section, and that the evidence be considered when useful in understanding the perceptions or conduct of a witness.

6. Retreat

Traditionally, a nonaggressor was not required to retreat before employing force, even deadly force, if the requirements of self-defense were otherwise met. More recently, however, and particularly following promulgation of the Model Penal Code, a number of jurisdictions adopted retreat requirements.[11] Under a retreat requirement, if an actor threatened by the use of unlawful force can avoid the use of defensive force by safely retreating, the actor must do so. Such a requirement can be seen as consistent with the generally accepted view that defensive force should be used only when it is necessary. What rationales support a no-retreat approach? Which support a retreat requirement? If safe retreat is available, is deadly defensive force ever necessary?

---

11. *See* Model Penal Code § 3.04 (Commentaries at 55) (ALI 1985).

Problem

8.6 Bob and Judy, a married couple, argue about the division of property in anticipation of their legal separation. Bob insists on keeping the antique rifle that Judy inherited from her father before she and Bob married. The argument gets so heated that Judy pulls a knife and threatens Bob with serious injury if he does not give her the rifle. Bob responds by pointing the rifle at Judy and firing, causing her serious injury. Does Bob have a viable self-defense claim under the excerpted statutes below?

Arkansas Code Annotated

§ 5-2-607. Use of Deadly Physical Force in Defense of a Person.

(a) A person is justified in using deadly physical force upon another person if he reasonably believes that the other person is:

(2) Using or about to use unlawful deadly physical force....

   (b) A person may not use deadly physical force in self-defense if he knows that he can avoid the necessity of using that force with complete safety:

(1) By retreating, except that a person is not required to retreat if he is in his dwelling and was not the original aggressor, or ...

(2) By surrendering possession of property to a person claiming a lawful right thereto.

Nebraska Revised Statutes

§ 28-1409. Use of Force in Self-Protection

(4) The use of force shall not be justifiable under this section ... if: ...

   (b) The actor knows that he can avoid the necessity of using such force with complete safety by retreating or by surrendering possession of a thing to a person asserting a claim of right thereto or by complying with a demand that he abstain from any action which he has no duty to take, except that:

   (i) The actor shall not be obliged to retreat from his dwelling or place of work, unless he was the initial aggressor or is assailed in his place of work by another person whose place of work the actor knows it to be....

Montana Code Annotated

§ 45-3-102. Use of Force in Defense of Person

A person is justified in the use of force or threat to use force against another when and to the extent that he reasonably believes that such conduct is necessary to defend himself or another against such other's imminent use of unlawful force. However, he is justified in the use of force likely to cause death or serious bodily harm only if he reasonably believes that such force is necessary to prevent imminent death or serious bodily harm to himself or another or to prevent the commission of a forcible felony.

Discussion Questions

1. What rules about retreat does each statute adopt?

2. How do the concepts of necessity of using force and retreat relate to one another?

3. How would the retreat rules apply to the *Norman* case?

* * *

Even when jurisdictions require retreat, it is not typically required within one's residence. This exception to the retreat requirement is known as the "castle exception." As the Nebraska Code above illustrates, some jurisdictions, following the Model Penal Code approach, extend the castle exception beyond the home to the non-aggressor's place of work.

Discussion Questions

1. What purposes does the castle exception serve?

2. What risks might it present?

Since 2005, a number of states have passed so-called "Stand Your Ground" or "Make My Day" laws that, in general, reject the duty to retreat and return to the traditional view that a nonaggressor may defend herself in the face of a threat, even if safe retreat is possible and regardless of the location of the incident. This modification of self-defense doctrine has made headlines, most notably, after the tragic 2012 shooting of an African-American teenager, Trayvon Martin, in which the white perpetrator George Zimmerman successfully relied on Florida's version of the law at trial to obtain an acquittal.[12] Indeed, there is some data indicating that Stand Your Ground defenses have disproportionately benefitted white men. A study of Stand Your Ground cases in Florida, for instance, examined 237 cases between 2005 and 2013 and found roughly a 40% probability of conviction for a male defendant in a "domestic" case (where the incident took place on the defendant's property), whereas for women it soared to 80%. That same study determined that, accounting for both domestic and non-domestic cases, the probability of conviction was approximately 10% lower for white defendants with white victims as compared with black defendants.[13]

In states that have adopted stand your ground laws, the requirements of imminence, proportionality, and necessity still apply.

---

12. Lizette Alvarez & Cara Buckley, *Zimmerman Is Acquitted in Trayvon Martin Killing*, N.Y. TIMES, July 13, 2013.

13. Justin Murphy, *Are "Stand Your Ground" Laws Racist and Sexist? A Statistical Analysis of Cases in Florida, 2005 to 2013*, 99 SOCIAL SCIENCE QUARTERLY, Issue 1, pp. 439–452 (March 2018).

Florida Statutes Annotated

§ 776.013 Home protection; use or threatened use of deadly force; presumption of fear of death or great bodily harm. —

(1) A person who is in a dwelling or residence in which the person has a right to be has no duty to retreat and has the right to stand his or her ground and use or threaten to use

   (a) Nondeadly force against another when and to the extent that the person reasonably believes that such conduct is necessary to defend himself or herself or another against the other's imminent use of unlawful force; or

   (b) Deadly force if he or she reasonably believes that using or threatening to use such force is necessary to prevent imminent death or great bodily harm to himself or herself or another or to prevent the imminent commission of a forcible felony.

(2) A person is presumed to have held a reasonable fear of imminent peril of death or great bodily harm to himself or herself or another when using or threatening to use defensive force that is intended or likely to cause death or great bodily harm to another if:

   (a) The person against whom the defensive force was used or threatened was in the process of unlawfully and forcefully entering, or had unlawfully and forcibly entered, a dwelling, residence, or occupied vehicle, or if that person had removed or was attempting to remove another against that person's will from the dwelling, residence, or occupied vehicle; and

   (b) The person who uses or threatens to use defensive force knew or had reason to believe that an unlawful and forcible entry or unlawful and forcible act was occurring or had occurred.

Discussion Questions

1. What is your view on the merits of "Stand Your Ground" laws?

2. In some states, Stand Your Ground laws grant immunity from prosecution,[14] while in other jurisdictions it is treated as an affirmative defense, like self-defense more generally. The immunity approach requires that a defendant asserting self-defense be given a pretrial hearing at which a judge determines whether the defendant has a viable self-defense claim. If the judge rules in the defendant's favor at the conclusion of the hearing, the case is dismissed and no jury trial takes place. Immunity arguably represents a "far greater right" than a classic affirmative defense because it prevents a case from going to trial.[15] What are the advantages and disadvantages of allowing someone who establishes that they fall under the Florida provision above to be immune from prosecution and evade trial?

---

14. *See, e.g., Jefferson v. State*, 264 So.3d 1019 (Fla. 2d D.C.A. 2018).

15. *State v. Collins*, 425 P.3d 630 (Kan. Ct. App. 2018).

3. If your state were to pass a Stand Your Ground law, what features, if any, would you recommend including in the statute to safeguard against potential gender and racial bias in its application?

7. Initial Aggressor Rules

Defensive force implies a response needed to protect against aggression by another. Initial aggressors generally lack the right to resort to defensive force. Nonetheless, under certain circumstances, an initial aggressor can gain the right to use defensive force. According to the two statutes that follow, under what circumstances may an initial aggressor make use of defensive force?

Problem

8.7 Candace discovers that Sammie was intimate with Candace's boyfriend earlier in the week. Candace encounters Sammie at a party and begins an argument with her. Candace hurls nasty racial and gender-based epithets at her. Sammie pokes Candace on her arm with the thin metal pick used for removing clam hors d'oeuvres from their shells. Candace responds by grabbing her clam pick and stabbing Sammie in her leg. Candace continues her assault on Sammie. Sammie, still holding the metal pick in a threatening manner toward Candace, says: "Wait, I'm bleeding." Can Sammie or Candace prevail on a self-defense claim under the statutes that follow?

Texas Penal Code Annotated

§ 9.31. Self-Defense.

(a) Except as provided in Subsection (b), a person is justified in using force against another when and to the degree he reasonably believes the force is immediately necessary to protect himself against the other's use or attempted use of unlawful force.

(b) The use of force against another is not justified:

  (1) in response to verbal provocation alone;

* * *

  (3) if the actor consented to the exact force used or attempted by the other.
  (4) if the actor provoked the other's use or attempted use of unlawful force, unless:

   (i) the actor abandons the encounter, or clearly communicates to the other his intent to do so reasonably believing he cannot safely abandon the encounter; and

   (ii) the other nevertheless continues or attempts to use unlawful force against the actor....

Colorado Revised Statutes

§ 18-1-704. Use of Physical Force in Defense of a Person.

(1) Except as provided in subsections (2) and (3) of this section, a person is justified in using physical force upon another person in order to defend himself or a third person from what he reasonably believes to be the use or imminent use of unlawful physical force by that other person, and he may use a degree of force which he reasonably believes to be necessary for that purpose.

(2) Deadly physical force may be used only if a person reasonably believes a lesser degree of force is inadequate and:

(a) The actor has reasonable ground to believe, and does believe, that he or another person is in imminent danger of being killed or of receiving great bodily injury; or

(b) The other person is using or reasonably appears about to use physical force against the occupant of a dwelling or business establishment while committing or attempting to commit burglary....

(c) The other person is committing or reasonably appears about to commit kidnapping, ... robbery, ... sexual assault ... or assault....

(3) Notwithstanding the provisions of subsection (1) of this section, a person is not justified in using physical force if:

(a) With intent to cause bodily injury or death to another person, he provokes the use of unlawful force by that other person; or

(b) He is the initial aggressor; except that his use of physical force upon another person under the circumstances is justifiable if he withdraws from the encounter and effectively communicates to the other person his intent to do so, but the latter nevertheless continues or threatens the use of unlawful physical force; or

(c) The physical force involved is the product of a combat by agreement not specifically authorized by law.

Discussion Questions

1. What does the Texas statute require for an initial aggressor to regain the right to self-defense?

2. How does the Colorado statute differ from the Texas statute on the requirements for regaining the right to self-defense by an initial aggressor?

3. How would Norman fare under the Texas and Colorado statutes?

8. Model Penal Code Treatment of Self-Defense

Model Penal Code

§ 3.04 Use of Force in Self-Protection.

(1) **Use of Force Justifiable for Protection of the Person.** Subject to the provisions of this Section and of Section 3.09, the use of force upon or toward another person is justifiable

when the actor believes that such force is immediately necessary for the purpose of protecting himself against the use of unlawful force by such other person on the present occasion.

(2) **Limitations on Justifying Necessity for Use of Force....**

(b) The use of deadly force is not justifiable under this Section unless the actor believes that such force is necessary to protect himself against death, serious bodily injury, kidnapping or sexual intercourse compelled by force or threat; nor is it justifiable if:

(i) the actor, with the purpose of causing death or serious bodily injury provoked the use of force against himself in the same encounter; or

(ii) the actor knows that he can avoid the necessity of using such force with complete safety by retreating or by surrendering possession of a thing to a person asserting a claim of right thereto or by complying with a demand that he abstain from any action that he has no duty to take, except that:

(A) the actor is not obliged to retreat from his dwelling or place of work, unless he was the initial aggressor or is assailed in his place of work by another person whose place of work the actor knows it to be....

(c) Except as required by paragraph ... (b) of this Subsection, a person employing protective force may estimate the necessity thereof under the circumstances as he believes them to be when the force is used, without retreating, surrendering possession, or doing any other act that he has no legal duty to do or abstaining from any lawful action.

Model Penal Code

§ 3.09 Reckless or Negligent Use of Otherwise Justifiable Force

(2) When the actor believes that the use of force upon or toward the person of another is necessary for any of the purposes for which such belief would establish a justification under Sections 3.03 to 3.08 but the actor is reckless or negligent in having such belief or in acquiring or failing to acquire any knowledge or belief that is material to the justifiability of his use of force, the justification afforded by those Sections is unavailable in a prosecution for an offense for which recklessness or negligence, as the case may be, suffices to establish culpability.

Discussion Question

What happens under the Model Penal Code when the defendant genuinely but erroneously believes in the need for self-defense?

C. Necessity

1. Introduction

A necessity defense may be triggered when an actor engages in what would otherwise be a crime in order to avoid a greater harm. Trespassing onto someone's land to avoid being struck by a speeding automobile is a classic example. Trespass is a crime. But avoiding the greater harm of serious bodily injury justifies the trespass and exonerates the actor.

Necessity is a justification. Someone acting under the pressure of necessity engages in conduct that society approves of and encourages. Someone aiding in the criminal activity of an individual with a valid necessity defense usually may also avail herself of the defense.

Commentators and courts commonly view necessity as a "true affirmative" defense. As the introductory materials to this chapter indicate, asserting a true affirmative defense means that the actor admits the elements that constitute the offense (confession), but then offers a rationale justifying his conduct and asks the fact-finder to acquit him (avoidance).

We begin our study of necessity by analyzing statutory approaches to the defense and applying them to a series of problems. We then turn to the common law approach to necessity and perhaps the most famous case in Anglo-American criminal law, *The Queen v. Dudley & Stephens*. Next, we examine application of the necessity defense to civil disobedience. Finally, we explore the Model Penal Code approach to necessity, known as the choice of evils.

Problems

8.8 Mr. and Mrs. Smith become convinced that their daughter is being brainwashed by a satanic cult. The cult forbids family visitors. The Smiths hire a private detective who, by spying through an open window, videotapes some of the cult's practices. The video reveals worship services in which Adolf Hitler is revered as a deity and initiation ceremonies that involve forced fasting for periods of up to 21 days. The video shows the Smith's daughter looking very gaunt and dazed. The Smiths estimate that their daughter has lost 20 pounds in the two weeks that she has lived at the complex. They fear for her physical and mental well-being. They hire a deprogramming service to kidnap their daughter and work with her to unlearn the cult's message. During the kidnapping, the Smiths' daughter resists violently. Neighbors call the police because of the commotion. The Smiths and the deprogrammers are arrested and charged with kidnapping and trespass. Would the statutes below provide Mr. and Mrs. Smith or the deprogrammers with a necessity defense?

8.9 Part (a) "On July 22, 1992, [Arlin] Budoo was a passenger in a car whose other occupants were Monte Glen, Sean Branch, Isaiah Taylor, and Michael Douglas. When Glen became aware that Branch, Taylor and Douglas planned to kill him, he fled the car. However, Taylor followed and shot him 10 times. Budoo witnessed the murder. Budoo initially refused to provide any information about the murder because he was afraid for himself and his family. Eventually he gave a statement to [the police]..., but declined any police protection." The prosecution granted him immunity, but he refused to testify before the grand jury. The government offered to protect Budoo and discuss "witness security with him. [He] declined to even discuss what his options would be under the Witness Protection Program."

"Despite his refusal to testify before the grand jury, Budoo was subpoenaed to appear as a witness at the trial of Taylor on July 24, 1993. However, upon learning that a witness who testified the previous day had been murdered, Budoo once again refused to testify.... Budoo was charged with contempt ... in that he willfully and knowingly disobeyed an order of the Court to testify, thereby causing an obstruction of the orderly administration of justice."[16]

Would the statutes below afford Mr. Budoo a necessity defense?

Part (b) Same as **Part (a)**, except that the defendant belonged to a gang in which killings of gang members were common to enforce order and loyalty within the gang. Would the Arizona statute below afford the defendant a defense under these circumstances?

8.10 Anti-abortion protestors block the entrance to a clinic that offers medical services to women. Of the services offered, five percent involve abortion procedures. Police arrest the protestors for trespassing and blocking a public sidewalk. At trial, the protestors prove that their efforts on the day in question prevented three women from obtaining abortions. The government proves that 50 other women were denied non-abortion related medical services. Would the statutes below provide a necessity defense for the protestors?

8.11 Richard is a heroin addict. Prison officers at the Racine facility find him injecting himself in his cell. "He specifically asserts that his illegal drug use was made necessary by the Department of Corrections (DOC) depriving him of the methadone it promised to provide...."[17] "Unfortunately, as a result of what the State acknowledges was a 'mistake' by DOC personnel, [Richard] was not provided with methadone when he entered Racine. Although he tried, through counsel, to get the DOC to live up to the transfer agreement, the

---

16. *Budoo v. United States*, 677 A.2d 51, 52–54 (1996).
17. *Wisconsin v. Anthuber*, 201 Wis. 2d 512, 515 (1996).

health officers at Racine could not cooperate because the facility was not certified to administer methadone ... On August 7, a prison guard caught [Richard] injecting heroin into his foot."[18] Would the statutes below provide a necessity defense for Richard?

8.12 A wildfire is roaring up a hillside toward seven houses at the top of the hillside and a small enclave of 10 houses on the far side of the hill. George burns down the seven houses at the top of the hillside to create a fire break and prevent the fire from reaching the enclave of 10 houses. Would the statutes below provide George a necessity defense?

8.13 A married couple, Jennifer and Jason, were at their family cabin in a rural area that lacked cellphone coverage. After an evening of drinking, they got into an argument, which escalated and resulted in Jason pushing Jennifer. Jennifer sought refuge in her car parked outside the cabin. Jason jumped on the vehicle and pounded on the windshield to the point that it cracked. Jennifer drove to a tavern a mile up the road to seek help, and at the tavern she was promptly arrested for suspected drunk driving. A urine test later revealed that Jennifer had a blood alcohol content of .16, twice the legal limit. Would the statutes below provide Jennifer a necessity defense?[19]

Arizona Revised Statutes

§ 13-417. Necessity Defense.

A. Conduct that would otherwise constitute an offense is justified if a reasonable person was compelled to engage in the proscribed conduct and the person had no reasonable alternative to avoid imminent public or private injury greater than the injury that might reasonably result from the person's own conduct.

B. An accused person may not assert the defense under subsection A if the person intentionally, knowingly or recklessly placed himself in the situation in which it was probable that the person would have to engage in the proscribed conduct.

C. An accused person may not assert the defense under subsection A for offenses involving homicide or serious physical injury.

---

18. *Id.* at 516.
19. *Axelberg v. Commissioner of Public Safety*, 848 N.W.2d 206 (Minn. 2014).

New York Penal Law

§ 35.05. Justification; generally.

[C]onduct which would otherwise constitute an offense is justifiable and not criminal when....

2. Such conduct is necessary as an emergency measure to avoid an imminent public or private injury which is about to occur by reason of a situation occasioned or developed through no fault of the actor, and which is of such gravity that, according to ordinary standards of intelligence and morality, the desirability and urgency of avoiding such injury clearly outweigh the desirability of avoiding the injury sought to be prevented by the statute defining the offense in issue. The necessity and justifiability of such conduct may not rest upon considerations pertaining only to the morality and advisability of the statute, either in its general application or with respect to an application to a particular class of cases arising thereunder.

18 Pennsylvania Consolidated Statutes Annotated

§ 503. Justification generally.

(a) **general rule.** — Conduct which the actor believes to be necessary to avoid a harm or evil to himself or another is justifiable if:

   (1) the harm or evil sought to be avoided by such conduct is greater than that sought to be prevented by the law defining the offense charged;

   (2) neither this title nor other law defining the offense provides exceptions or defenses dealing with the specific situation involved; and

   (3) a legislative purpose to exclude the justification claimed does not otherwise plainly appear.

(b) **choice of evils.** — When the actor was reckless or negligent in bringing about the situation requiring a choice of harms or evils or in appraising the necessity for his conduct, the justification afforded by this section is unavailable in a prosecution for any offense for which recklessness or negligence, as the case may be, suffices to establish culpability.

Wisconsin Statutes

§ 939.47. Necessity.

Pressure of natural physical forces which causes the actor reasonably to believe that his or her act is the only means of preventing imminent public disaster, or imminent death or great bodily harm to the actor or another and which causes him or her so to act, is a defense to a prosecution for any crime based on that act, except that if the prosecution is for first-degree intentional homicide, the degree of the crime is reduced to 2nd-degree intentional homicide.

Discussion Questions

   1. Are there any features common to all of the statutes above?

   2. Are there any features unique to only one of the statutes?

Problem

8.14 You are a state legislator. A committee on which you serve has been assigned the task of writing a necessity statute. Draft the statute. What elements would your statute have? Why?

2. Necessity and the Common Law

"Leading cases are the very stuff of which the common law is made, and [according to one of its historians] no leading case in the common law is better known than that of *Regina v. Dudley and Stephens.*"[20]

The Queen v. Dudley and Stephens

14 Law Reports 273 (1884)
December 9

At the trial before Huddleston, B., at the Devon and Cornwall Winter Assizes, November 7, 1884, the jury, at the suggestion of the learned judge, found the facts of the case in a special verdict which stated "that, on July 5,1884, the prisoners, Thomas Dudley and Edward Stephens, with one Brooks, all able-bodied English seamen, and the deceased also an English boy, between seventeen and eighteen years of age, ... were cast away in a storm on the high seas 1600 miles from the Cape of Good Hope, and were compelled to put into an open boat belonging to the said yacht. That in this boat they had no supply of water and no supply of food, except two 1 lb. tins of turnips, and for three days they had nothing else to subsist upon. That on the fourth day they caught a small turtle, upon which they subsisted for a few days, and this was the only food they had up to the twentieth day when the act now in question was committed. That on the twelfth day the remains of the turtle were entirely consumed, and for the next eight days they had nothing to eat. That they had no fresh water, except such rain as they from time to time caught in their oilskin capes. That the boat was drifting on the ocean, and was probably more than 1000 miles away from land. That on the eighteenth day, when they had been seven days without food and five without water, the prisoners spoke to Brooks as to what should be done if no succour came, and suggested that some one should be sacrificed to save the rest, but Brooks dissented, and the boy, to whom they were understood to refer, was not consulted. That on the 24th of July, the day before the act now in question, the prisoner Dudley proposed to Stephens and Brooks that lots should be cast who should be put to death to save the rest, but Brooks refused to consent, and it was not put to the boy, and in point of fact there was no drawing of lots. That on that day the pris-

---

20. A.W. BRIAN SIMPSON, CANNIBALISM AND THE COMMON LAW: THE STORY OF THE TRAGIC LAST VOYAGE OF THE MIGNONETTE AND THE STRANGE LEGAL PROCEEDINGS TO WHICH IT GAVE RISE, *ix* (U. of Chicago Press 1984).

oners spoke of their having families, and suggested it would be better to kill the boy that their lives should be saved, and Dudley proposed that if there was no vessel in sight by the morrow morning, the boy should be killed. That next day, the 25th of July, no vessel appearing, Dudley told Brooks that he had better go and have a sleep, and made signs to Stephens and Brooks that the boy had better be killed. The prisoner Stephens agreed to the act, but Brooks dissented from it. That the boy was then lying at the bottom of the boat quite helpless, and extremely weakened by famine and by drinking sea water, and unable to make any resistance, nor did he ever assent to his being killed. The prisoner Dudley offered a prayer asking forgiveness for them all if either of them should be tempted to commit a rash act, and that their souls might be saved. That Dudley, with the assent of Stephens, went to the boy, and telling him that his time was come, put a knife into his throat and killed him then and there; that the three men fed upon the body and blood of the boy for four days; that on the fourth day after the act had been committed the boat was picked up by a passing vessel, and the prisoners were rescued, still alive, but in the lowest state of prostration. That they were carried to the port of Falmouth, and committed for trial at Exeter. That if the men had not fed upon the body of the boy they would probably not have survived to be so picked up and rescued, but would within the four days have died of famine. That the boy, being in a much weaker condition, was likely to have died before them. That at the time of the act in question there was no sail in sight, nor any reasonable prospect of relief. That under these circumstances there appeared to the prisoners every probability that unless they then fed or very soon fed upon the boy or one of themselves they would die of starvation. That there was no appreciable chance of saving life except by killing some one for the others to eat. That assuming any necessity to kill anybody, there was no greater necessity for killing the boy than any of the other three men." But whether upon the whole matter by the jurors found the killing of Richard Parker by Dudley and Stephens be felony and murder the jurors are ignorant, and pray the advice of the Court thereupon, and if upon the whole matter the Court shall be of opinion that the killing of Richard Parker be felony and murder, then the jurors say that Dudley and Stephens were each guilty of felony and murder as alleged in the indictment...."

Lord Coleridge, C.J. The two prisoners, Thomas Dudley and Edwin Stephens, were indicted for the murder of Richard Parker on the high seas.... They were tried before my Brother Huddleston ... and, under the direction of my learned Brother, the jury returned a special verdict, the legal effect of which has been argued before us, and on which we are now to pronounce judgment.

The special verdict as, after certain objections by Mr. Collins to which the Attorney General yielded, it is finally settled before us is as follows. [His Lordship read the special verdict as above set out.] From these facts, stated with the cold precision of a special verdict, it appears sufficiently that the prisoners were subject to terrible temptation, to sufferings which might break down the bodily power of the strongest man, and try the conscience of the best. Other details yet more harrowing, facts still more loathsome and appalling, were presented to the jury, and are to be found recorded in my learned Brother's notes. But nevertheless this is clear, that the prisoners put to death a weak and unoffending boy upon the chance of preserving their own lives by feeding upon his flesh and blood after he was killed, and with the certainty of depriving *him*, of any possible chance of survival. The verdict finds in terms that "if the men had not fed upon the body of the boy they would *probably* not have survived," and that "the boy being in a much weaker condition was *likely* to have died before them." They might possibly have been picked up next day by a passing ship; they might possibly not have been picked up at all; in either case it is obvious that the killing of the boy would have been an unnecessary and profitless act. It is found by the verdict that the boy was incapable of resistance, and, in fact, made none; and it is not even suggested that his death was due to any violence on his part attempted against, or even so much as feared by, those who killed him. Under these circumstances the jury say that they are ignorant whether those who killed him were guilty of murder, and have referred it to this Court to determine what is the legal consequence which follows from the facts which they have found....

There remains to be considered the real question in the case—whether killing under the circumstances set forth in the verdict be or be not murder. The contention that it could be anything else was, to the minds of us all, both new and strange, and we stopped the Attorney General in his negative argument in order that we might hear what could be said in support of a proposition which appeared to us to be at once dangerous, immoral, and opposed to all legal principle and analogy.... First it is said that it follows from various definitions of murder in books of authority, which definitions imply, if they do not state, the doctrine, that in order to save your own life you may lawfully take away the life of another, when that other is neither attempting nor threatening yours, nor is guilty of any illegal act whatever towards you or any one else. But if these definitions be looked at they will not be found to sustain this contention....

[T]he doctrine contended for receives no support from the great authority of Lord Hale.... [H]e says that "the necessity which justifies homicide is of two kinds: (1) the necessity which is of a private nature; (2) the necessity which relates to the public justice and safety. The former is that necessity which obligeth a man to his own defence and safeguard...." As touching the first of these—viz., homicide in defence of, a man's own life, which is usually styled se defendendo. It is not possible to use words more clear to shew that Lord Hale regarded the private necessity which justified, and alone justified, the taking the life of another for the safeguard of one's own to be what is commonly called "self-defence." (Hale's Pleas of, the Crown, i. 478.)

But if this could be even doubtful upon Lord Hale's words, Lord Hale himself has made it clear. For in the chapter in which he deals with the exemption created by compulsion or necessity he thus expresses himself:—"If a man be desperately assaulted and in peril of death, and cannot otherwise escape unless, to satisfy his assailant's fury, he will kill an innocent person then present, the fear and actual force will not acquit him of the crime and punishment of murder, if he commit the fact, for he ought rather to die himself than kill an innocent; but if he cannot otherwise save his own life the law permits him in his own defence to kill the assailant, for by the violence of the assault, and the offence committed upon him by the assailant himself, the law of nature, and necessity, hath made him his own protector...." (Hale's Pleas of the Crown, vol. i. 51.).

* * *

Now, except for the purpose of testing how far the conservation of a man's own life is in all cases and under all circumstances, an absolute, unqualified, and paramount duty, we exclude from our consideration all the incidents of war. We are dealing with a case of private homicide, not one imposed upon men in the service of their Sovereign and in the defence of their country. Now it is admitted that the deliberate killing of this unoffending and unresisting boy was clearly murder, unless the killing can be justified by some well-recognised excuse admitted by the law. It is further admitted that there was in this case no such excuse, unless the killing was justified by what has been called "necessity." But the temptation to the act which existed here was not what the law has ever called necessity. Nor is this to be regretted. Though law and morality are not the same, and many things may be immoral which are not necessarily illegal, yet the absolute divorce of law from morality would be of fatal consequence; and such divorce would follow if the temptation to murder in this case were to be held by law an absolute defence of it. It is not so. To preserve one's life is generally speaking a duty, but it may be the plainest and the highest duty to sacrifice it. War is full of instances in which it is a man's duty not to live, but to die. The duty, in case of ship-wreck, of a captain to his crew, of the crew to the passengers, of soldiers to women and children ... ; these duties impose on men the moral necessity, not of the preser-vation, but of the sacrifice of their lives for others from which in no country, least of all, it is to be hoped, in England, will men ever shrink, as indeed, they have not shrunk. It is not correct, therefore, to say that there is any absolute or unqualified necessity to preserve one's life.... Who is to be the judge of this sort of necessity? By what measure is the comparative value of lives to be measured? Is it to be strength, or intellect, or 'what? It is plain that the principle leaves to him who is to profit by it to determine the necessity which will justify him in deliberately taking another's life to save his own. In this case the weakest, the youngest, the most unresisting, was chosen. Was it more necessary to kill him than one of the grown men? The answer must be "No."

* * *

... There is no safe path for judges to tread but to ascertain the law to the best of their ability and to declare it according to their judgment; and if in any case the law appears to be too severe on individuals, to leave it to the Sovereign to exercise that prerogative of mercy which the Constitution has intrusted to the hands fittest to dis-pense it.

It must not be supposed that in refusing to admit temptation to be an excuse for crime it is forgotten how terrible the temptation was; how awful the suffering; how hard in such trials to keep the judgment straight and the conduct pure. We are often compelled to set up standards we cannot reach ourselves, and to lay down rules which we could not ourselves satisfy. But a man has no right to declare temptation to be an excuse, though he might himself have yielded to it, nor allow compassion for the criminal to change or weaken in any manner the legal definition of the crime. It is therefore our duty to declare that the prisoners' act in this case was wilful murder, that the facts as stated in the verdict are no legal justification of the homicide; and to say that in our unanimous opinion the prisoners are upon this special verdict guilty of murder.[1] The Court then proceeded to pass sentence of death upon the prisoners.[2]

Discussion Questions

1. What does the *Dudley and Stephens* case illustrate about the traditional common law approach to the defense of necessity?

2. Is the situation of being without food and water for an extended period unique to shipwrecks of the 1800s? Are you aware of any modern examples of this situation?

3. Is the result in *Dudley and Stephens* too harsh? Is the approach the case takes to necessity too limited?

4. What does the fact that the sentence of death was later commuted to six months' imprisonment suggest about the purposes behind the sentences in the case?

5. Why do you think Brooks escaped prosecution?

Consider the following comments from historian A.W. Brian Simpson:

In effect, all the witnesses to the killing of Richard Parker were defendants. In the contemporary state of the law, it was quite out of the question for them to be required to give their account of what happened or give sworn evidence in court and thereby expose themselves to cross-examination to elicit the facts.... It was plain, too, that the defense of necessity would be raised; the legal status of this defense was problematical, and its application might well depend on the precise conditions in the *Mignonette's* dinghy. Only a witness who had actually been there could speak convincingly about them.

[The prosecutor,] Mr. Danckwerts therefore needed such a witness, and the only candidates were Dudley, Stephens, and Brooks. One of them must appear for the crown, and the obvious choice was Brooks, who was of subordinate status and had taken no active part in the killing.[21]

---

1. My brother Grove has furnished me with the following suggestion, too late to be embodied in the judgment but well worth preserving: "If the two accused men were justified in killing Parker, then if not rescued in time, two of the three survivors would be justified in killing the third, and of the two who remained the stronger would be justified in killing the weaker, so that three men might be justifiably killed to give the fourth a chance of survival." — C.

2. This sentence was afterwards commuted by the Crown to six months' imprisonment.

21. *Supra* n. 15 at 90.

According to historian Simpson, records indicate that public opinion strongly supported Dudley and Stephens during much of the pre-trial and trial phase of the case.[22] In explaining the context of the times regarding cannibalism by stranded seafarers, Mr. Simpson explains: "[M]aritime survival cannibalism, preceded by the drawing of lots and killing, was a socially accepted practice among seamen until the end of the days of sail...."[23] "In spite of the frequent occurrence of survival cannibalism, often preceded by deliberate killing, and the abundant evidence of a nautical custom legitimating the practice of killing under necessity, the survivors of the *Mignonette* have always been regarded as the first and indeed only individuals who have ever faced trial for murder for a killing committed in such circumstances."[24] Mr. Simpson suggests that British authorities had been seeking a case "to bring the custom of the sea before a court of law for condemnation"[25] for some time.

6. Would any of the statutes at the beginning of the chapter have provided Dudley and Stephens with a necessity defense?

Problem

8.15 The elements of a necessity defense vary. Compare the elements as enumerated below from the Ohio case of Columbus v. Spingola[26] with the statutes at the beginning of this section.

> (1) [T]he harm must be committed under the pressure of physical or natural force, rather than human force; (2) the harm sought to be avoided is greater than, or at least equal to that sought to be prevented by the law defining the offense charged; (3) the actor reasonably believes at that moment that his act is necessary and is designed to avoid the greater harm; (4) the actor must be without fault in bringing about the situation; and (5) the harm threatened must be imminent, leaving no alternative by which to avoid the greater harm.

---

22. *Id.* at 87.
23. *Id.* at 145.
24. *Id.* at 161.
25. *Id.* at 195.
26. *Columbus v. Spingola*, 144 Ohio App. 3d 76, 83 (2001).

3. Civil Disobedience

Defendants have raised the necessity defense in a host of contexts. A common one is civil disobedience, the subject of the *Schoon* case that follows.

United States v. Schoon

971 F.2d 193 (9th Cir. 1992)
United States Court of Appeals for the Ninth Circuit

Boochever, Circuit Judge.

Gregory Schoon, Raymond Kennon, Jr., and Patricia Manning appeal their convictions for obstructing activities of the Internal Revenue Service Office in Tucson, Arizona, and failing to comply with an order of a federal police officer. Both charges stem from their activities in protest of United States involvement in El Salvador. They claim the district court improperly denied them a necessity defense. Because we hold the necessity defense inapplicable in cases like this, we affirm.

On December 4, 1989, thirty people, including appellants, gained admittance to the IRS office in Tucson, where they chanted "keep America's tax dollars out of El Salvador," splashed simulated blood on the counters, walls, and carpeting, and generally obstructed the office's operation. After a federal police officer ordered the group, on several occasions, to disperse or face arrest, appellants were arrested.

At a bench trial, appellants proffered testimony about conditions in El Salvador as the motivation for their conduct. They attempted to assert a necessity defense, essentially contending that their acts in protest of American involvement in El Salvador were necessary to avoid further bloodshed in that country. While finding appellants motivated solely by humanitarian concerns, the court nonetheless precluded the defense as a matter of law, relying on Ninth Circuit precedent. The sole issue on appeal is the propriety of the court's exclusion of a necessity defense as a matter of law.

A district court may preclude a necessity defense where "the evidence, as described in the defendant's offer of proof, is insufficient as a matter of law to support the proffered defense." To invoke the necessity defense, therefore, the defendants colorably must have shown that: (1) they were faced with a choice of evils and chose the lesser evil; (2) they acted to prevent imminent harm; (3) they reasonably anticipated a direct causal relationship between their conduct and the harm to be averted; and (4) they had no legal alternatives to violating the law. We review *de novo* the district court's decision to bar a necessity defense.

The district court denied the necessity defense on the grounds that (1) the requisite immediacy was lacking; (2) the actions taken would not abate the evil; and (3) other legal alternatives existed. Because the threshold test for admissibility of a necessity defense is a conjunctive one, a court may preclude invocation of the defense if "proof is deficient with regard to any of the four elements."

While we could affirm substantially on those grounds relied upon by the district court, we find a deeper, systemic reason for the complete absence of federal case law recognizing a necessity defense in an indirect civil disobedience case. As used in this opinion, "civil disobedience" is the wilful violation of a law, undertaken for the purpose of social or political protest.... Indirect civil disobedience involves violating a law or interfering with a government policy that is not, itself, the object of protest. Direct civil disobedience, on the other hand, involves protesting the existence of a law by breaking that law or by preventing the execution of that law in a specific instance in which a particularized harm would otherwise follow. This case involves indirect civil disobedience because these protestors were not challenging the laws under which they were charged. In contrast, the civil rights lunch counter sit-ins, for example, constituted direct civil disobedience because the protestors were challenging the rule that prevented them from sitting at lunch counters. Similarly, if a city council passed an ordinance requiring immediate infusion of a suspected carcinogen into the drinking water, physically blocking the delivery of the substance would constitute direct civil disobedience: protestors would be preventing the execution of a law in a specific instance in which a particularized harm — contamination of the water supply — would otherwise follow.

While our prior cases consistently have found the elements of the necessity defense lacking in cases involving indirect civil disobedience, we have never addressed specifically whether the defense is available in cases of indirect civil disobedience. Indeed, some other courts have appeared doubtful. Today, we conclude, for the reasons stated below, that the necessity defense is inapplicable to cases involving indirect civil disobedience.

Necessity is, essentially, a utilitarian defense. It therefore justifies criminal acts taken to avert a greater harm, maximizing social welfare by allowing a crime to be committed where the social benefits of the crime outweigh the social costs of failing to commit the crime. Pursuant to the defense, prisoners could escape a burning prison, a person lost in the woods could steal food from a cabin to survive; an embargo could be violated because adverse weather conditions necessitated sale of the cargo at a foreign port; a crew could mutiny where their ship was thought to be unseaworthy; and property could be destroyed to prevent the spread of fire.

What all the traditional necessity cases have in common is that the commission of the "crime" averted the occurrence of an even greater "harm." In some sense, the necessity defense allows us to act as individual legislatures, amending a particular criminal provision or crafting a one-time exception to it, subject to court review, when a real legislature would formally do the same under those circumstances. For example, by allowing prisoners who escape a burning jail to claim the justification of necessity, we assume the lawmaker, confronting this problem, would have allowed for an exception to the law proscribing prison escapes.

Because the necessity doctrine is utilitarian, however, strict requirements contain its exercise so as to prevent nonbeneficial criminal conduct. For example, "'if the criminal act cannot abate the threatened harm, society receives no benefit from the criminal conduct.'" Similarly, to forgive a crime taken to avert a lesser harm would fail to maximize social utility. The cost of the crime would outweigh the harm averted by its commission. Likewise, criminal acts cannot be condoned to thwart threats, yet to be imminent, or those for which there are legal alternatives to abate the harm.

Analysis of three of the necessity defense's four elements leads us to the conclusion that necessity can never be proved in a case of indirect civil disobedience. We do not rely upon the imminent harm prong of the defense because we believe there can be indirect civil disobedience cases in which the protested harm is imminent.

1. Balance of Harms

It is axiomatic that, if the thing to be averted is not a harm at all, the balance of harms necessarily would disfavor any criminal action. Indirect civil disobedience seeks first and foremost to bring about the repeal of a law or a change of governmental policy, attempting to mobilize public opinion through typically symbolic action. These protestors violate a law, not because it is unconstitutional or otherwise improper, but because doing so calls public attention to their objectives. Thus, the most immediate "harm" this form of protest targets is the *existence* of the law or policy. However, the mere existence of a constitutional law or governmental policy cannot constitute a legally cognizable harm. *See* Comment, *Political Protest and the Illinois Defense of Necessity,* 54 U. Chi. L. Rev. 1070, 1083 (1987) ("In a society based on democratic decision making, this is how values are ranked—a protester cannot simply assert that her view of what is best should trump the decision of the majority of elected representatives.")....

The protest in this case was in the form of indirect civil disobedience, aimed at reversal of the government's El Salvador policy. That policy does not violate the Constitution, and appellants have never suggested as much. There is no evidence that the procedure by which the policy was adopted was in any way improper; nor is there any evidence that appellants were prevented systematically from participating in the democratic processes through which the policy was chosen. The most immediate harm the appellants sought to avert was the existence of the government's El Salvador policy, which is not in itself a legally cognizable harm. Moreover, any harms resulting from the operation of this policy are insufficiently concrete to be legally cognizable as harms for purposes of the necessity defense.

Thus, as a matter of law, the mere existence of a policy or law validly enacted by Congress cannot constitute a cognizable harm. If there is no cognizable harm to prevent, the harm resulting from criminal action taken for the purpose of securing the repeal of the law or policy necessarily outweighs any benefit of the action.

2. Causal Relationship between Criminal Conduct and Harm to be Averted

This inquiry requires a court to judge the likelihood that an alleged harm will be abated by the taking of illegal action. In the sense that the likelihood of abatement is required in the traditional necessity cases, there will never be such likelihood in cases of indirect political protest. In the traditional cases, a prisoner flees a burning cell and averts death, or someone demolishes a home to create a firebreak and prevents the conflagration of an entire community. The nexus between the act undertaken and the result sought is a close one. Ordinarily it is the volitional illegal act alone which, once taken, abates the evil.

In political necessity cases involving indirect civil disobedience against congressional acts, however, the act alone is unlikely to abate the evil precisely because the action is indirect. Here, the IRS obstruction, or the refusal to comply with a federal officer's order, are unlikely to abate the killings in El Salvador, or immediately change Congress's policy; instead, it takes another *volitional* actor not controlled by the protestor to take a further step; Congress must change its mind.

3. Legal Alternatives

A final reason the necessity defense does not apply to these indirect civil disobedience cases is that legal alternatives will never be deemed exhausted when the harm can be mitigated by congressional action. As noted above, the harm indirect civil disobedience aims to prevent is the continued existence of a law or policy. Because congressional action can *always* mitigate this "harm," lawful political activity to spur such action will always be a legal alternative. On the other hand, we cannot say that this legal alternative will always exist in cases of direct civil disobedience, where protestors act to avert a concrete harm flowing from the operation of the targeted law or policy.

The necessity defense requires the absence of any legal alternative to the contemplated illegal conduct which could reasonably be expected to abate an imminent evil. A prisoner fleeing a burning jail, for example, would not be asked to wait in his cell because someone might conceivably save him; such a legal alternative is ill-suited to avoiding death in a fire. In other words, the law implies a reasonableness requirement in judging whether legal alternatives exist.

Where the targeted harm is the existence of a law or policy, our precedents counsel that this reasonableness requirement is met simply by the possibility of congressional action. For example, in *Dorrell*, an indirect civil disobedience case involving a trespass on Vandenburg Air Force Base to protest the MX missile program, we rejected Dorrell's claims that legal alternatives, like lobbying Congress, were unavailable because they were futile.... Without expressly saying so, *Dorrell* decided that petitioning Congress to change a policy is *always* a legal alternative in such cases, regardless of the likelihood of the plea's success. Thus, indirect civil disobedience can never meet the necessity defense requirement that there be a lack of legal alternatives.

As have courts before us, we could assume, as a threshold matter, that the necessity defense is conceivably available in these cases, but find the elements never satisfied. Such a decision, however, does not come without significant costs. First, the failure of the federal courts to hold explicitly that the necessity defense is unavailable in these cases results in district courts expending unnecessary time and energy trying to square defendants' claims with the strict requirements of the doctrine. Second, such an inquiry oftentimes requires the courts to tread into areas constitutionally committed to other branches of government. For example, in *May*, which involved trespass on a naval base to protest American nuclear weapons policy, we noted that, "[t]o consider defendants' argument [that trespassing was justified by the nefariousness of the Trident missile] would put us in the position of usurping the functions that the Constitution has given to the Congress and to the President." Third, holding out the possibility of the defense's applicability sets a trap for the unwary civil disobedient, rather than permitting the individual to undertake a more realistic cost-benefit analysis before deciding whether to break the law in political protest. Fourth, assuming the applicability of the defense in this context may risk its distortion in traditional cases. Finally, some commentators have suggested that the courts have sabotaged the usually low threshold for getting a defense theory before the jury as a means of keeping the necessity defense from the jury.

The real problem here is that litigants are trying to distort to their purposes an age-old common law doctrine meant for a very different set of circumstances. What these cases are really about is gaining notoriety for a cause—the defense allows protestors to get their political grievances discussed in a courtroom. It is precisely this political motive that has left some courts, like the district court in this case, uneasy. Because these attempts to invoke the necessity defense "force the courts to choose among causes they should make legitimate by extending the defense of necessity" and because the criminal acts, themselves, do not maximize social good, they should be subject to a *per se* rule of exclusion.

Thus, we see the failure of any federal court to recognize a defense of necessity in a case like ours not as coincidental, but rather as the natural consequence of the historic limitation of the doctrine. Indirect protests of congressional policies can never meet all the requirements of the necessity doctrine. Therefore, we hold that the necessity defense is not available in such cases.

Affirmed.

Discussion Questions

1. Reconsider the problem at the beginning of this section involving the abortion protestors blocking access to the clinic. Should a court characterize their actions as direct or indirect civil disobedience? Which prong(s) of the necessity defense might bar use of the necessity defense in abortion protestor cases?

2. What if animal rights protestors free all the animals used for experimentation in a college laboratory, arguing that they were saving the animals from pain and suffering in lab cages and undergoing experimentation? Would these protestors have a necessity defense?

4. Model Penal Code Treatment of Necessity

Model Penal Code

§ 3.02. Justification Generally: Choice of Evils.

(1) Conduct which the actor believes to be necessary to avoid a harm or evil to himself or another is justifiable, provided that:

(a) the harm or evil sought to be avoided by such conduct is greater than that sought to be prevented by the law defining the offense charged; and

(b) neither the Code nor other law defining the offense provides exceptions or defenses dealing with the specific situation involved; and

(c) a legislative purpose to exclude the justification claimed does not otherwise plainly appear.

(2) When the actor was reckless or negligent in bringing about the situation requiring a choice of harms or evils or in appraising the necessity for his conduct, the justification afforded by this Section is unavailable in a prosecution for any offense for which recklessness or negligence, as the case may be, suffices to establish culpability.

Discussion Questions

1. What do you see as the advantages of the MPC approach to necessity? What are its limitations?

2. Which statute, at the start of the Necessity section, reflects the MPC treatment of necessity?

Review Problems

8.16 Doctors are able to recover a viable liver from a recently deceased individual. The liver is needed for a patient on the transplant list in a hospital in a nearby city. As soon as the recipient hospital hears that a liver is available, they begin preparing the recipient patient for surgery. An ambulance from the donor hospital begins the journey of 50 miles, with the liver packed for transportation. The ambulance turns on its lights and travels at 100 mph in a posted 70-mph zone. Just before it reaches the recipient hospital, the local police pull the ambulance over and charge the driver with a speeding violation.[27]

---

27. This problem is adapted from news accounts which reported a case in England in 2003, in which an ambulance driver was cited for speeding while carrying a liver from a hospital in Leeds to one in Cambridge for a transplant operation.

Associated Press, *Ambulance Driver Charged with Speeding While Delivering Liver*, STAR TRIBUNE, http://www.startribune.com/viewers/story.php?template=print_a&story=3930823 (accessed June 16, 2003); itv.com news, *Speeding charge for ambulance*, http://www.itv.com/news/38417.html (accessed June 16, 2003).

Assume that the speeding statute reads as follows:

> It is unlawful to exceed the posted speed limit. This section does not apply to law enforcement vehicles. Nor does it apply to fire trucks when they are proceeding to the scene of an emergency. Nor does this section apply to ambulances that are proceeding to the scene of an accident or carrying a patient to the hospital.

You represent the ambulance driver. What arguments would you make on the driver's behalf? How would your argument change, if, unlike the situation in the real case upon which the problem above is based, the ambulance driver had caused an accident in which someone was injured en route to deliver the liver? What if the accident caused someone's death?

8.17 A pizza deliveryman delivered pizza to a remote location. Shortly thereafter, he entered a bank with a bulge under his t-shirt and presented a note demanding cash. The teller gave him the cash. Shortly thereafter, the police arrested him. The bulge turned out to be a bomb that the delivery man begged police to remove. In the real case, the bomb detonated and killed the deliveryman. Imagine instead that the deliveryman had survived and that shortly before the bank robbery, he had delivered pizza to would-be bank robbers who had attached the bomb to his chest and told him to rob the bank or they would detonate the bomb. As directed, he completed the robbery and brought the proceeds to the would-be bank robbers who removed the bomb. Subsequently, the government prosecuted the pizza deliveryman. As his attorney, what arguments would you raise in his defense?[28]

8.18 Necessity defenses often arise in prison escape cases where inmates claim that they essentially had no choice but to flee given the danger of life behind bars. Note that the crime of "prison escape" is treated as a felony in many jurisdictions. Consider whether a necessity defense is viable in the following circumstances:

(a) Jay, an inmate, is a member of an ethnic group that is vastly underrepresented in the prison population, making him susceptible to harm. Although he has never actually been attacked, he is worried that an assault from other inmates is imminent. He escapes from the facility. Could Jay successfully draw upon a necessity defense if he were later charged with prison escape? Assume further that the facility allows for "protective custody"—an administrative procedure that puts vulnerable inmates in solitary confinement for their own safety—but he is fearful of the psychological trauma caused by long-term isolation.

---

28. CBS Evening News, *Forced to Become Human Bomb?*, (accessed Sept. 2, 2003) http://www.cbsnews.com/stories/2003/09/01/eveningnews/main57 (accessed July 20, 2004).

(b) Leslie, an inmate who identifies as LGBTQ+ and gender-nonconforming, is placed in a facility for male inmates. They has experienced sexual assault twice at the hands of other prisoners while incarcerated. They also spent several weeks in protective custody, during which a corrections officer made unwanted sexual advances. They escape the prison. Could Leslie successfully utilize a defense of necessity to justify the crime of prison escape?

(c) Carl, an inmate, is housed in an overcrowded state prison. A fire breaks out and the inmates begin to suffer from the effects of smoke inhalation. Corrections officers have abandoned the facility and there does not appear to be any coordinated, state-sanctioned effort to transfer the prisoners to safety. Is Carl justified on the grounds of necessity if he commits the crime of prison escape?

(d) Similar to (c) above: Carl, an inmate, is housed in an overcrowded state prison. The facility is decrepit and full of mold. Carl has a respiratory condition that makes mold especially hazardous to his health. He has notified the warden about the situation and even spent time in the infirmary, but no prison official has acted to remove the mold. His condition is worsening; Carl escapes. Would he succeed in raising a necessity defense?

D. Duress

"The defense of duress ... serves to excuse behavior where extrinsic circumstances compel a person to perform unlawful acts which he did not otherwise wish to do."[29] In a classic example of duress, a stranger holds a gun to the actor's temple and threatens the actor with instant death if the actor does not commit a crime, for example, a battery by hitting an innocent third party. The actor must choose between the risk that the stranger will carry out the threat and committing the crime of battery. If the actor chooses to strike the innocent third party, all the elements of the crime of battery will be fulfilled. The actor here makes a reluctant but conscious decision and corresponding physical movement to strike another. She therefore has done a voluntary act. In addition, battery often requires no more mental state than a purpose to do the act with knowledge that the act is likely to cause the offensive physical contact with the third party. Consequently, with both the conduct and mental state elements satisfied, absent the duress defense, the actor would be guilty of battery.[30]

---

29. *Working Papers of the National Commission on Reform of Federal Criminal Laws*, Vol. 1, IX, 273 (U.S. Gov't Printing Office 1970).

30. *Id.*

The argument in favor of this excuse defense is that "[t]here is no just reason to impose criminal sanctions, or try to reform a man, because he committed unlawful acts which anyone else, given the circumstances, would also have committed."[31] The theories of punishment we have studied fail to justify punishment here. Retribution fails, as there is little to suggest moral blameworthiness in the actor's response to the threat. Similarly, when the actor's plight meets the requirements of the defense, she has, in society's cost-benefit calculus, chosen an acceptable response, one we would not wish to deter her or someone else from choosing. Nor do incapacitation or rehabilitation seem appropriate responses. We would be removing the actor from society, trying to alter her response, or publicly denouncing her to prevent her from engaging in conduct that society finds acceptable and no different from what we would lawfully expect from others similarly situated.

Because courts and legislators have usually treated duress as an excuse rather than a justification, they often place a burden on the defense to produce evidence or to prove duress by a preponderance of evidence. Given that duress and necessity share a number of characteristics, some jurisdictions treat them as overlapping defenses. Others consider them distinct.

Oregon Revised Statutes Annotated

§ 161.270. Duress.

(1) The commission of acts which would otherwise constitute an offense, other than murder, is not criminal if the actor engaged in the proscribed conduct because the actor was coerced to do so by the use or threatened use of unlawful physical force upon the actor or a third person, which force or threatened force was of such nature or degree to overcome earnest resistance.

(2) Duress is not a defense for one who intentionally or recklessly places oneself in a situation in which it is probable that one will be subjected to duress.

Arizona Revised Statutes

§ 13-412. Duress.

A. Conduct which would otherwise constitute an offense is justified if a reasonable person would believe that he was compelled to engage in the proscribed conduct by the threat or use of immediate physical force against his person or the person of another which resulted or could result in serious physical injury which a reasonable person in the situation would not have resisted.

B. The defense provided by subsection A is unavailable if the person intentionally, knowingly or recklessly placed himself in a situation in which it was probable that he would be subjected to duress.

---

31. *Id.*

C. The defense provided by subsection A is unavailable for offenses involving homicide or serious physical injury.

Washington Revised Code

§ 9A.16.060. Duress.

(1) In any prosecution for a crime, it is a defense that:

- (a) The actor participated in the crime under compulsion by another who by threat or use of force created an apprehension in the mind of the actor that in case of refusal he or she or another would be liable to immediate death or immediate grievous bodily injury; and
- (b) That such apprehension was reasonable upon the part of the actor; and
- (c) That the actor would not have participated in the crime except for the duress involved.

(2) The defense of duress is not available if the crime charged is murder, manslaughter, or homicide by abuse.

(3) The defense of duress is not available if the actor intentionally or recklessly places himself or herself in a situation in which it is probable that he or she will be subject to duress.

(4) The defense of duress is not established solely by showing that a married person acted on the command of his or her spouse.

Model Penal Code

§ 2.09. Duress.

(1) It is an affirmative defense that the actor engaged in the conduct charged to constitute an offense because he was coerced to do so by the use of, or a threat to use, unlawful force against his person or the person of another, that a person of reasonable firmness in his situation would have been unable to resist.

(2) The defense provided by this Section is unavailable if the actor recklessly placed himself in a situation in which it was probable that he would be subjected to duress. The defense is also unavailable if he was negligent in placing himself in such a situation, whenever negligence suffices to establish culpability for the offense charged.

Problem

8.19 The 18-year-old defendant had worked at Floyd Culver's garage and become acquainted with both Mr. and Mrs. Culver. One night, according to the defendant, Mrs. Culver, a 45-year-old woman, "came in an automobile [to the park where the defendant was located] and asked him to go down town with her. While driving along she told him that she wanted him to break into the filling station. She also drew a pistol and told him that if he did not do so she would kill him. She held the pistol on him until the automobile stopped across the street from the station. She then got out of the car and followed him to the station and kept the pistol pointed at him until he broke into the station. He did not want to break in, but was afraid of [Mrs.] Culver.... The mother of the [defendant] testified that after her son was arrested [Mrs.] Culver came to her home and told her that it was all her fault, that she had told her son that if he did not break into the building she would blow his brains out, and showed [the] witness the gun she had used. [The defendant's mother] was corroborated by her daughter, who claims to have been present when the conversation occurred."[32] Should the defendant be excused on the basis of duress?

United States v. Contento-Pachon

723 F.2d 691 (9th Cir. 1984)
United States Court of Appeals for the Ninth Circuit

Boochever, Circuit Judge.

This case presents an appeal from a conviction for unlawful possession with intent to distribute a narcotic controlled substance in violation of 21 U.S.C. §841(a)(1) (1976). At trial, the defendant attempted to offer evidence of duress and necessity defenses. The district court excluded this evidence on the ground that it was insufficient to support the defenses. We reverse because there was sufficient evidence of duress to present a triable issue of fact.

The defendant-appellant, Juan Manuel Contento-Pachon, is a native of Bogota, Colombia and was employed there as a taxicab driver. He asserts that one of his passengers, Jorge, offered him a job as the driver of a privately-owned car. Contento-Pachon expressed an interest in the job and agreed to meet Jorge and the owner of the car the next day.

Instead of a driving job, Jorge proposed that Contento-Pachon swallow cocaine-filled balloons and transport them to the United States. Contento-Pachon agreed to consider the proposition. He was told not to mention the proposition to anyone, otherwise he would "get into serious trouble." Contento-Pachon testified that he did not contact the police because he believes that the Bogota police are corrupt and that they are paid off by drug traffickers.

Approximately one week later, Contento-Pachon told Jorge that he would not carry the cocaine. In response, Jorge mentioned facts about Contento-Pachon's personal life, including private details which Contento-Pachon had never mentioned to Jorge. Jorge told Contento-Pachon that his failure to cooperate would result in the death of his wife and three year-old child.

---

32. *Nall v. Commonwealth*, 208 Ky. 700, 701–02 (1925).

The following day the pair met again. Contento-Pachon's life and the lives of his family were again threatened. At this point, Contento-Pachon agreed to take the cocaine into the United States.

The pair met two more times. At the last meeting, Contento-Pachon swallowed 129 balloons of cocaine. He was informed that he would be watched at all times during the trip, and that if he failed to follow Jorge's instruction he and his family would be killed.

After leaving Bogota, Contento-Pachon's plane landed in Panama. Contento-Pachon asserts that he did not notify the authorities there because he felt that the Panamanian police were as corrupt as those in Bogota. Also, he felt that any such action on his part would place his family in jeopardy.

When he arrived at the customs inspection point in Los Angeles, Contento-Pachon consented to have his stomach x-rayed. The x-rays revealed a foreign substance which was later determined to be cocaine.

At Contento-Pachon's trial, the government moved to exclude the defenses of duress and necessity. The motion was granted. We reverse.

A. DURESS

There are three elements of the duress defense: (1) an immediate threat of death or serious bodily injury, (2) a well-grounded fear that the threat will be carried out, and (3) no reasonable opportunity to escape the threatened harm. Sometimes a fourth element is required: the defendant must submit to proper authorities after attaining a position of safety.

Factfinding is usually a function of the jury, and the trial court rarely rules on a defense as a matter of law. If the evidence is insufficient as a matter of law to support a duress defense, however, the trial court should exclude that evidence.

The trial court found Contento-Pachon's offer of proof insufficient to support a duress defense because he failed to offer proof of two elements: immediacy and inescapability. We examine the elements of duress.

Immediacy: The element of immediacy requires that there be some evidence that the threat of injury was present, immediate, or impending. "[A] veiled threat of future unspecified harm" will not satisfy this requirement. The district court found that the initial threats were not immediate because "they were conditioned on defendant's failure to cooperate in the future and did not place defendant and his family in immediate danger."

Evidence presented on this issue indicated that the defendant was dealing with a man who was deeply involved in the exportation of illegal substances. Large sums of money were at stake and, consequently, Contento-Pachon had reason to believe that Jorge would carry out his threats. Jorge had gone to the trouble to discover that Contento-Pachon was married, that he had a child, the names of his wife and child, and the location of his residence. These were not vague threats of possible future harm.

According to the defendant, if he had refused to cooperate, the consequences would have been immediate and harsh.

Contento-Pachon contends that he was being watched by one of Jorge's accomplices at all times during the airplane trip. As a consequence, the force of the threats continued to restrain him. Contento-Pachon's contention that he was operating under the threat of immediate harm was supported by sufficient evidence to present a triable issue of fact.

Escapability: The defendant must show that he had no reasonable opportunity to escape. The district court found that because Contento-Pachon was not physically restrained prior to the time he swallowed the balloons, he could have sought help from the police or fled. Contento-Pachon explained that he did not report the threats because he feared that the police were corrupt. The trier of fact should decide whether one in Contento-Pachon's position might believe that some of the Bogota police were paid informants for drug traffickers and that reporting the matter to the police did not represent a reasonable opportunity of escape.

If he chose not to go to the police, Contento-Pachon's alternative was to flee. We reiterate that the opportunity to escape must be reasonable. To flee, Contento-Pachon, along with his wife and three year-old child, would have been forced to pack his possessions, leave his job, and travel to a place beyond the reaches of the drug traffickers. A juror might find that this was not a reasonable avenue of escape. Thus, Contento-Pachon presented a triable issue on the element of escapability.

Surrender to Authorities: As noted above, the duress defense is composed of at least three elements. The government argues that the defense also requires that a defendant offer evidence that he intended to turn himself in to the authorities upon reaching a position of safety. Although it has not been expressly limited, this fourth element seems to be required only in prison escape cases. Under other circumstances, the defense has been defined to include only three elements.

The Supreme Court in *United States v. Bailey*, 444 U.S. 394, 413 (1980), noted that "escape from federal custody ... is a continuing offense and ... an escapee can be held liable for failure to return to custody as well as for his initial departure." This factor would not be present in most crimes other than escape.

In cases not involving escape from prison there seems little difference between the third basic requirement that there be no reasonable opportunity to escape the threatened harm and the obligation to turn oneself in to authorities on reaching a point of safety. Once a defendant has reached a position where he can safely turn himself in to the authorities he will likewise have a reasonable opportunity to escape the threatened harm.

That is true in this case. Contento-Pachon claims that he was being watched at all times. According to him, at the first opportunity to cooperate with authorities without alerting the observer, he consented to the x-ray. We hold that a defendant who has acted under a well-grounded fear of immediate harm with no opportunity to escape may assert the duress defense, if there is a triable issue of fact whether he took the opportunity to escape the threatened harm by submitting to authorities at the first reasonable opportunity.

B. NECESSITY

The defense of necessity is available when a person is faced with a choice of two evils and must then decide whether to commit a crime or an alternative act that constitutes a greater evil. Contento-Pachon has attempted to justify his violation of 21 U.S.C. §841(a)(1) by showing that the alternative, the death of his family, was a greater evil.

Traditionally, in order for the necessity defense to apply, the coercion must have had its source in the physical forces of nature. The duress defense was applicable when the defendant's acts were coerced by a human force. W. LaFave & A. Scott, *Handbook on Criminal Law* §50 at 383 (1972). This distinction served to separate the two similar defenses. But modern courts have tended to blur the distinction between duress and necessity....

The defense of necessity is usually invoked when the defendant acted in the interest of the general welfare. For example, defendants have asserted the defense as a justification for (1) bringing laetrile into the United States for the treatment of cancer patients, (2) unlawfully entering a naval base to protest the Trident missile system, (3) burning Selective Service System records to protest United States military action.

Contento-Pachon's acts were allegedly coerced by human, not physical forces. In addition, he did not act to promote the general welfare. Therefore, the necessity defense was not available to him. Contento-Pachon mischaracterized evidence of duress as evidence of necessity. The district court correctly disallowed his use of the necessity defense.

Contento-Pachon presented credible evidence that he acted under an immediate and well-grounded threat of serious bodily injury, with no opportunity to escape. Because the trier of fact should have been allowed to consider the credibility of the proffered evidence, we reverse. The district court correctly excluded Contento-Pachon's necessity defense.

Reversed and remanded.

Coyle, District Judge (dissenting in part and concurring in part):

[I]n its Order the district court stated:

> The first threat made to defendant and his family about three weeks before the flight was not immediate; the threat was conditioned upon defendant's failure to cooperate in the future and did not place the defendant and his family in immediate danger or harm. Moreover, after the initial threat and until he went to the house where he ingested the balloons containing cocaine, defendant and his family were not physically restrained and could have sought help from the police or fled. No such efforts were attempted by defendant.

Thus, defendant's own offer of proof negates two necessary elements of the defense of duress.

In cases where the defendant's duress has been raised, the courts have indicated that the element of immediacy is of crucial importance. The trial court found that the threats made against the defendant and his family lacked the requisite element of immediacy. This finding is adequately supported by the record. The defendant was outside the presence of the drug dealers on numerous occasions for varying lengths of time. There is no evidence that his family was ever directly threatened or even had knowledge of the threats allegedly directed against the defendant.

Moreover, the trial court found that the defendant and his family enjoyed an adequate and reasonable opportunity to avoid or escape the threats of the drug dealers in the weeks before his flight. Until he went to the house where he ingested the balloons containing cocaine, defendant and his family were not physically restrained or prevented from seeking help. The record supports the trial court's findings that the defendant and his family could have sought assistance from the authorities or have fled. Cases considering the defense of duress have established that where there was a reasonable legal alternative to violating the law, a chance to refuse to do the criminal act and also to avoid the threatened danger, the defense will fail. Duress is permitted as a defense only when a criminal act was committed because there was no other opportunity to avoid the threatened danger.

Discussion Questions

1. How should "immediacy" be defined in the context of duress?

2. Would the *Contento-Pachon* case have come out differently if those threatening Contento-Pachon had urged him to commit robbery? How about kidnapping a child?

3. If no one had been on the airplane watching Contento-Pachon, would the immediacy criterion have been satisfied?

E. Insanity and Mental Illness

1. Introduction

Mental illness is an important issue in the criminal justice system. Some observers believe that defendants in a substantial portion of criminal cases suffer from mental illness.[33]

Although mental illness may be part of the subtext in many cases, formal recognition of mental illness in criminal cases generally falls under three rubrics: (1) insanity, (2) effect on required mental state (diminished capacity), and (3) incompetence. Insanity and diminished capacity, as used here, relate to the defendant's

---

33. One scholar describes the situation and some of the studies as follows:

The prevalence of mental disorders among persons with criminal justice involvement is

mental state *at the time of the offense*. For competence, we look instead at the defendant's mental condition and ability to understand the criminal proceedings *at the time of prosecution*. Before turning to the focal point of this section, insanity, we briefly describe and contrast insanity, diminished capacity, and incompetence.

Of the three, insanity is perhaps the most widely known. In a criminal case, the presumption is that the defendant was sane at the time of the commission of the acts. As a result, the law commonly treats insanity as an affirmative defense. Even if the defendant succeeds and the fact-finder declares the defendant not guilty by reason of insanity, this insanity acquittal, unlike other acquittals, does not necessarily result in release. Instead, courts regularly commit the defendant for evaluation and treatment of the underlying mental illness. The court may ultimately commit the defendant to a mental institution for longer than the defendant would have served had the defendant been convicted and sentenced.

The insanity defense has provoked substantial controversy over the course of its existence. It appears to be raised, however, in only a small percentage of cases. According to one multijurisdictional study, "the insanity defense was raised in approximately one percent of all felony cases."[34] Of these, the study indicates that only 26 percent were successful.[35]

The criminal justice system also sometimes recognizes the impact of mental illness on the defendant's capacity to entertain the required mental state for the crime.[36] For

---

staggering. Each year about 700,000 adults with serious mental illness come into contact with the criminal justice system. Justice Department statistics indicate that sixteen percent of jail and prison inmates have a serious mental illness but these estimates rise to 35% when they include less serious disorders.... Indeed, a recent study in Michigan found that 31% of its prison population required psychiatric care. The largest study to date, sampling 3,332 inmates in New York prisons, found that 80% had severe disorders requiring treatment and another 16% had mental disorders requiring periodic mental health services.

Richard E. Redding, Why It Is Essential to Teach About Mental Health Issues in Criminal Law (And a Primer on How To Do It), 14 WASH. U. J. L. & POL'Y 407, 408–09 (2004).

34. Lisa A. Callahan et al., *The Volume and Characteristics of Insanity Defense Pleas: An Eight-State Study*, 19 BULL. AM. ACAD. PSYCH. & LAW, 331, 334 (1991).

35. *Id.*

36. Some jurisdictions distinguish between the defendant's capacity to entertain the required mental state ("diminished capacity") and her actually having possessed the required mental state at the time of the offense ("diminished actuality"). In jurisdictions that do not recognize diminished capacity, but do recognize diminished actuality, instead of asking whether the defendant had the capacity to entertain the mental state, the question becomes whether, as a result of the mental illness, the circumstances demonstrate that the defendant in fact lacked the mental state at the time of the offense. California Penal Code § 28 provides a statutory example of how a jurisdiction may draw the distinction:

Cal. Penal Code § 28 (2003). Mental Disease.

(a) Evidence of mental disease, mental defect, or mental disorder shall not be admitted to show or negate the capacity to form any mental state, including, but not limited to, purpose, intent, knowledge, premeditation, deliberation, or malice aforethought, with which the accused committed the act. Evidence of mental disease ... is admissible solely on the issue of whether or not the accused actually formed a required specific intent, premeditated, deliberated, or harbored malice aforethought, when a specific intent crime is charged.

example, theft requires that the defendant believe that the property taken belongs to another. If a defendant's mental illness makes him incapable of understanding that the property belongs to someone else, the defendant would lack the mental state required for the crime. Courts and commentators sometimes refer to this as "diminished capacity."[37] Instead of serving as a true affirmative defense, the mental illness affects evaluation of whether the prosecution has proven the requisite mental state for one or more of the charges. Both insanity and diminished capacity involve an evaluation of the defendant's state of mind at the time of the offense.

Competence relates to the defendant's ability to understand the proceedings and assist in the defense. It focuses on a different period of time than insanity. Competence deals with the defendant's ability to understand the legal proceedings at the time they occur. Unlike insanity, lack of competence is not a defense. While insanity can extinguish liability, lack of competence bars prosecution while the defendant is incompetent. A court may delay or suspend criminal proceedings while the defendant is incompetent. If a court has suspended proceedings due to the defendant's incompetence, proceedings can resume if the defendant (re)gains competence and is able to understand the criminal proceedings. Tests for determining competence vary, depending on the stage of the proceedings. Competency litigation has raised the issue of whether the state should be allowed to medicate defendants against their will in order to return them to competence and continue legal proceedings against them, including execution.

The next section reviews one state's struggle to select a definition of insanity. A series of opinions reflect the evolution of the state's insanity law. Following those, we focus on a quandary of the law of insanity. To qualify as insane, must the individual lack knowledge that her conduct is *morally* wrong? Or must she lack knowledge that her conduct is *legally* wrong? The section then proceeds to canvass several of the most common legal definitions of insanity. Then, we focus on the rationales for and critiques of the insanity defense.

2. Case Study: One State's Struggle to Choose an Insanity Test

Over the centuries, English and American courts and commentators developed several definitions of insanity. Perhaps the most famous and widely used is the M'Naghten test. The Model Penal Code standard, developed by experts under the auspices of the American Law Institute (ALI), represents another highly influential test. Both of these tests are discussed in the following opinion.

---

37. For a discussion of the related doctrine of "partial responsibility," *see* WAYNE LaFAVE, CRIMINAL LAW 451–460 (4th ed 2003).

People v. Drew

22 Cal.3d 333 (1978)
Supreme Court of California

Tobriner, J.

For over a century California has followed the M'Naghten[1] test to define the defenses of insanity and idiocy. The deficiencies of that test have long been apparent, and judicial attempts to reinterpret or evade the limitations of M'Naghten have proven inadequate. We shall explain why we have concluded that we should discard the M'Naghten language, and update the California test of mental incapacity as a criminal defense by adopting the test proposed by the American Law Institute....

The purpose of a legal test for insanity is to identify those persons who, owing to mental incapacity, should not be held criminally responsible for their conduct. The criminal law rests on a postulate of free will—that all persons of sound mind are presumed capable of conforming their behavior to legal requirements and that when any such person freely chooses to violate the law, he may justly be held responsible. From the earliest days of the common law, however, the courts have recognized that a few [categories of] persons lack the mental capacity to conform to the strictures of the law.... The principle that mental incapacity constitutes a defense to crime is today accepted in all American jurisdictions.

The California Penal Code codifies the defense of mental incapacity.... [S]ection 26 specifies that "All persons are capable of committing crimes except those belonging to the following classes" and includes among those classes "Idiots" and "Lunatics"* and insane persons.

Although the Legislature has thus provided that "insanity" is a defense to a criminal charge, it has never attempted to define that term. The task of describing the circumstances under which mental incapacity will relieve a defendant of criminal responsibility has become the duty of the judiciary.

Since *People v. Coffman* (1864) 24 Cal. 230, 235, the California courts have followed the M'Naghten rule to define the defense of insanity. The curious origin of the M'-Naghten rule has been frequently recounted. In 1843 Daniel M'Naghten, afflicted with paranoia, attempted to assassinate the Prime Minister of England, and succeeded in killing the Prime Minister's secretary. M'Naghten's acquittal on grounds of insanity so disturbed Queen Victoria that she summoned the House of Lords to obtain the opinion of the judges on the law of insanity. The 15 judges of the common law courts were called in an extraordinary session, "under a not subtle atmosphere of pressure" to answer five hypothetical questions on the law of criminal responsibility.

---

1. Daniel M'Naghten was inconsistent in the spelling of his name, and courts and commentators ever since have shared in that inconsistency. We follow the spelling in the Clark and Finnelly report of the M'Naghten case.

* The term "lunatics" ... probably referred to persons who had lucid intervals; "insane persons" to those who lacked lucid intervals. The cases do not distinguish between the two terms.

In response to two of the questions propounded the judges stated that "to establish a defence on the ground of insanity, it must be clearly proved that, at the time of the committing the act, the party accused was labouring under such a defect of reason, from disease of the mind, as not to know the nature and quality of the act he was doing; or, if he did know it, that he did not know he was doing what was wrong." Although an advisory opinion, and thus most questionable authority, this language became the basis for the test of insanity in all American states except New Hampshire.

Despite its widespread acceptance, the deficiencies of M'Naghten have long been apparent. Principal among these is the test's exclusive focus upon the cognitive capacity of the defendant, an outgrowth of the then current psychological theory under which the mind was divided into separate independent compartments, one of which could be diseased without affecting the others. As explained by Judge Ely of the Ninth Circuit: "The M'Naghten rules fruitlessly attempt to relieve from punishment only those mentally diseased persons who have no cognitive capacity...." This formulation does not comport with modern medical knowledge that an individual is a mentally complex being with varying degrees of awareness. It also fails to attack the problem presented in a case wherein an accused may have understood his actions but was incapable of controlling his behavior. Such a person has been allowed to remain a danger to himself and to society whenever, under *M'Naghten*, he is imprisoned without being afforded such treatment as may produce rehabilitation and is later, potentially recidivistic, released."[7]

M'Naghten's exclusive emphasis on cognition would be of little consequence if all serious mental illness impaired the capacity of the affected person to know the nature and wrongfulness of his action.... Current psychiatric opinion, however, holds that mental illness often leaves the individual's intellectual understanding relatively unimpaired, but so affects his emotions or reason that he is unable to prevent himself from committing the act. "[I]nsanity does not only, or primarily, affect the cognitive or intellectual faculties, but affects the whole personality of the patient, including both the will and the emotions. An insane person may therefore often know the nature and quality of his act and that it is wrong and forbidden by law, and yet commit it as a result of the mental disease." (Rep. Royal Com. on Capital Punishment, 1949–1953, p. 80.)

The annals of this court are filled with illustrations of the above statement: the deluded defendant in *People v. Gorshen* who believed he would be possessed by devilish visions unless he killed his foreman; the schizophrenic boy in *People v. Wolff*, who knew that killing his mother was murder but was unable emotionally to control his conduct despite that knowledge; the defendant in *People v. Robles* (1970), suffering from organic brain damage, who mutilated himself and killed others in sudden rages. To ask whether such a person knows or understands that his act is "wrong" is to ask

---

7. Numerous other cases and writers have cited M'Naghten's failure to include a volitional element in its test of insanity.

a question irrelevant to the nature of his mental illness or to the degree of his criminal responsibility.

Secondly, "M'Naghten's single track emphasis on the cognitive aspect of the personality recognizes no degrees of incapacity. Either the defendant knows right from wrong or he does not.... But such a test is grossly unrealistic.... As the commentary to the American Law Institute's Model Penal Code observes, 'The law must recognize that when there is no black and white it must content itself with different shades of gray.'"

In short, M'Naghten purports to channel psychiatric testimony into the narrow issue of cognitive capacity, an issue often unrelated to the defendant's illness or crime. The psychiatrist called as a witness faces a dilemma: either he can restrict his testimony to the confines of M'Naghten, depriving the trier of fact of a full presentation of the defendant's mental state, or he can testify that the defendant cannot tell "right" from "wrong" when that is not really his opinion because by so testifying he acquires the opportunity to put before the trier of fact the reality of defendant's mental condition....

Even if the psychiatrist is able to place before the trier of fact a complete picture of the defendant's mental incapacity, that testimony reaches the trier of fact weakened by cross-examination designed to show that defendant knew right from wrong. As a result, conscientious juries have often returned verdicts of sanity despite plain evidence of serious mental illness and unanimous expert testimony that the defendant was insane.

[Over the years, innovative modifications to the M'Naghten rule set forth by California courts have failed] to cure its basic defects....

In our opinion the continuing inadequacy of M'Naghten as a test of criminal responsibility cannot be cured by further attempts to interpret language dating from a different era of psychological thought, nor by the creation of additional concepts designed to evade the limitations of M'Naghten. It is time to recast M'Naghten in modern language, taking account of advances in psychological knowledge and changes in legal thought.

The definition of mental incapacity appearing in section 4.01 of the American Law Institute's Model Penal Code represents the distillation of nine years of research, exploration, and debate by the leading legal and medical minds of the country. It specifies that "A person is not responsible for criminal conduct if at the time of such conduct as a result of mental disease or defect he lacks substantial capacity either to appreciate the criminality [wrongfulness] of his conduct or to conform his conduct to the requirements of law."[8]

---

8. The American Law Institute takes no position as to whether the term "criminality" or the term "wrongfulness"' best expresses the test of criminal responsibility; we prefer the term "criminality."

Subdivision 2 of the American Law Institute test provides that "the terms 'mental disease or defect' do not include an abnormality manifested only by repeated criminal or otherwise anti-social conduct." The language, designed to deny an insanity defense to psychopaths and sociopaths, is not relevant to the present case. The question whether to adopt subdivision 2 of the ALI test is one which we defer to a later occasion.

Adhering to the fundamental concepts of free will and criminal responsibility, the American Law Institute test restates M'Naghten in language consonant with current legal and psychological thought....

The advantages [of the ALI test] may be briefly summarized. First, the ALI test adds a volitional element, the ability to conform to legal requirements, which is missing from the M'Naghten test. Second, it avoids the all-or-nothing language of M'-Naghten and permits a verdict based on lack of substantial capacity. Third, the ALI test is broad enough to permit a psychiatrist to set before the trier of fact a full picture of the defendant's mental impairments and flexible enough to adapt to future changes in psychiatric theory and diagnosis. Fourth, by referring to the defendant's capacity to "appreciate" the wrongfulness of his conduct the test confirms our holding in *People v. Wolff*, that mere verbal knowledge of right and wrong does not prove sanity....

In light of the manifest superiority of the ALI test, the only barrier to the adoption of that test we perceive lies in the repeated judicial declarations that any change in the M'Naghten rule requires legislative action. This pronouncement rests on two bases: the lengthy history of the M'Naghten rule in California and the failure of the 1927 Legislature, when it revised the procedures for pleading and trying the defense of insanity, to overturn the M'Naghten test.

The concept that an extended line of judicial decisions, accompanied by legislative inaction, can freeze the evolution of judicial principles, divesting the courts of authority to overturn their prior decisions, is not in good repute.... [T]he judiciary has the responsibility for legal doctrine which it has created.[11] The power of the court to reshape judicial doctrine does not authorize us to overturn constitutionally valid statutes. But as Justice Mosk explained in his concurring opinion in *People v. Kelly*, the M'Naghten rule is not an integral part of the statutory structure of California criminal law. The Legislature has never enacted the M'Naghten rule as a test of insanity, and its provisions relating to criminal responsibility do not incorporate the M'Naghten formula. Thus replacement of the M'Naghten rule with the ALI test will not contradict or nullify any legislative enactment.

Discussion Questions

1. Why does the California Supreme Court, rather than the California legislature, undertake the task of changing the insanity standard from M'Naghten to the ALI test?

2. What advantages does change by the Court have? What disadvantages?

---

11. When the law governing a subject has been shaped and guided by judicial decision, legislative inaction does not necessarily constitute a tacit endorsement of the precise stage in the evolution of the law extant at the time when the Legislature did nothing; it may signify that the Legislature is willing to entrust the further evolution of legal doctrine to judicial development.

3. Should there be a different standard for insanity for medical diagnosis than for legal attribution of responsibility? Or should the standards be the same?

4. What does Justice Tobriner imply about the dilemma of a psychiatrist testifying under the M'Naghten standard?

5. What, according to the Court, does the ALI test purport to do in relation to the M'Naghten standard?

6. How is mental disease determined under M'Naghten? Under the ALI test? Who should determine whether the defendant's mental condition qualifies as a mental disease or defect?

People v. Fields

35 Cal. 3d 329 (1983)
Supreme Court of California

Broussard, J.

… Defendant, after presenting no defense of significance at the guilt phase of the trial, offered a defense of insanity. He presented evidence that he had an "antisocial personality" which, he claimed, constituted a form of insanity under the American Law Institute (ALI) test we endorsed in *People v. Drew* (1978)….[19]

[In *Drew*, we deferred the question of whether to adopt subdivision 2 of the American Law Institute test because it was not relevant to that case. Subdivision 2] provides that "the terms 'mental disease or defect' do not include an abnormality manifested only by repeated criminal or otherwise antisocial conduct.' This language [was] designed to deny an insanity defense to psychopaths and sociopaths…." Forecasting that the California Supreme Court would adopt subdivision 2 of the ALI test, the trial judge in the present case instructed the jury in accord with that provision. The present case thus presents the issue we deferred deciding in *Drew*.

Defense counsel called as his only expert witness Dr. Ronald Markman, who testified that defendant suffered from an "antisocial personality" (the current psychiatric term for psychopaths and sociopaths),[20] that this condition is a "mental disease," and that because of this disease defendant was unable to conform his behavior to legal requirements. He described defendant as a person who lacks the interest, concern, or ability to conform to social roles, and was unable to benefit from experience. On cross-examination, however, he was asked whether his views would change if the

---

19. An initiative measure effective June 8, 1982, enacted a statutory definition of insanity (see Pen. Code, § 25, subd. (b)) which resembles the M'Naghten test rejected by this court in *People v. Drew*. The considerations of policy barring extension of the insanity defense to psychopaths discussed in this opinion apply with equal force to cases arising under the new statutory definition.

20. The terms "psychopath" and "sociopath" are used interchangeably in the psychiatric literature; the newer term "antisocial personality" is roughly equivalent although, as we will explain later in this opinion, the profession has attempted to establish specific criteria for use of this term which may make it narrower than the earlier designations.

term "mental disease" did not include an abnormality "manifested only by repeated or otherwise antisocial conduct." Markman replied that under this definition defendant would not be insane.

When the trial judge, over defendant's objection, instructed the jury on subdivision 2 of the ALI test, the defense case was destroyed. As the prosecutor pointed out to the jury, under subdivision 2's definition of mental disease, Dr. Markman agreed with the prosecution experts that defendant was sane, and no testimony whatever supported the insanity defense.

Before explaining our reasons for approving the court's instruction based on subdivision 2, it is important to note what that subdivision does and does not do. Although it was designed to deny an insanity defense to psychopaths and sociopaths, it does not have that precise effect. What it does is prevent consideration of a mental illness if that illness is manifested only by a series of criminal or antisocial acts. If that illness manifests itself in some other way as well, then it can be considered as a "mental disease" under the ALI test, and instances of criminal or antisocial conduct can be ascribed to that disease or cited as evidence of its severity. (Thus Dr. Markham may have been mistaken when, in response to a question excluding consideration of "an abnormality manifested only by repeated or otherwise antisocial conduct," he stated that "by definition, you are excluding the antisocial personality.")

In effect, subdivision 2 operates to define a prima facie case for an insanity defense: if the defense expert can point to no symptom, no manifestation, of defendant's condition except repeated criminal or antisocial acts, that condition cannot be considered grounds for finding defendant insane. Whether this requirement denies the insanity defense to a person with an "antisocial personality" will depend upon the individual case, and on the ability of the psychiatrist to base a diagnosis upon facts additional to a list of defendant's criminal or antisocial acts.

We advance three reasons for approving subdivision 2 of the ALI test. First, that provision has been endorsed by the overwhelming weight of authority. [S]even federal circuits have considered the issue, with five adopting subdivision 2 and two rejecting that provision; fourteen states have adopted subdivision 2 either through legislation or judicial decision. No state has rejected it.

Second, subdivision 2 is consistent with the majority view of psychiatrists and psychologists that proof of a series of criminal or antisocial acts is insufficient to demonstrate mental disease. The standard authority for classification and diagnosis of mental illness is the American Psychiatric Association's Diagnostic and Statistical Manual. The term "antisocial personality" first appeared in the second edition of this manual (DSM-II) in 1968. In defining that term, the manual stated explicitly that "[a] mere history of repeated legal or social offenses is not sufficient to justify this diagnosis."[24]

---

24. The description of antisocial personality in DSM-II states that persons with this illness are those "who are basically unsocialized and whose behavior pattern brings them repeatedly into conflict with society. They are incapable of significant loyalty to individuals, groups, or social values. They

... [W]e foresee harmful legal and social consequences if an expert's diagnosis of mental illness and opinion of insanity could be based solely on recidivist behavior. If a pattern of antisocial behavior is sufficient basis for an insanity defense, then a substantial proportion of serious criminal offenders would be able to assert this defense. It may be that few would succeed in persuading a jury. But the assertion of the insanity defense by recidivists with no apparent sign of mental illness except their penchant for criminal behavior would burden the legal system, bring the insanity defense itself into disrepute, and imperil the ability of persons with definite mental illness to assert that defense.

We have considered carefully the views of the Ninth Circuit in *Wade v. United States* (9th Cir. 1970), the leading decision rejecting subdivision 2 of the ALI test. The *Wade* court reasoned that it was preferable for dangerous psychopaths to be found insane, because a defendant convicted of crime must be released when he has served his sentence but one found insane could be confined indefinitely....

Against this asserted advantage of an insanity finding—an advantage which is nonexistent when the underlying crime carries a sentence of life imprisonment—we must balance a substantial disadvantage. To classify persons with "antisocial personality" as insane would put in the mental institutions persons for whom there is currently no suitable treatment and who would be a constant danger to the staff and other inmates. Mental hospitals are not designed for this type of person; prisons are.

Indeed, the "antisocial personality" is the classic criminal; our prisons are largely populated by such persons. To classify such persons as insane would radically revise the criminal law—insanity, instead of a rare exception to the rule of criminal accountability, would become the ordinary defense in a felony trial. Absent a better understanding of the disorder of "antisocial personality" and some effective treatment for this condition, such an expansive role for the insanity defense would work more harm than good.

Discussion Questions

1. Should the insanity defense include "psychopaths"?
2. Which theories of punishment support the result reached by the Court?

---

are grossly selfish, callous, irresponsible, impulsive, and unable to feel guilt or to learn from experience and punishment. Frustration tolerance is low. They tend to blame others or offer plausible rationalizations for their behavior. A mere history of repeated legal or social offenses is not sufficient to justify this diagnosis."

People v. Skinner

39 Cal. 3d 765 (1985)
Supreme Court of California

Grodin, J.

For over a century prior to the decision in *People v. Drew* (1978), California courts framed this state's definition of insanity, as a defense in criminal cases, upon the two-pronged test adopted by the House of Lords in *M'Naghten's* Case (1843).... Over the years the M'Naghten test became subject to considerable criticism and was abandoned in a number of jurisdictions. In *Drew* this court followed suit, adopting the test for mental incapacity proposed by the American Law Institute....

In June 1982 the California electorate adopted an initiative measure, popularly known as Proposition 8, which (among other things) for the first time in this state established a statutory definition of insanity: "In any criminal proceeding ... in which a plea of not guilty by reason of insanity is entered, this defense shall be found by the trier of fact only when the accused person proves by a preponderance of the evidence that he or she was incapable of knowing or understanding the nature and quality of his or her act *and* of distinguishing right from wrong at the time of the commission of the offense." (Penal Code, § [25 (b)])

It is apparent from the language of section 25(b) that it was designed to eliminate the *Drew* test and to reinstate the prongs of the M'Naghten test. However, the section uses the conjunctive "and" instead of the disjunctive "or" to connect the two prongs. Read literally, therefore, section 25(b) would do more than reinstate the M'Naghten test. It would strip the insanity defense from an accused who, by reason of mental disease, is incapable of knowing that the act he was doing was wrong. That is, in fact, the interpretation adopted by the trial court in this case.

Defendant claims that the purpose of the electorate in adopting section 25(b) was to restore the M'Naghten test as it existed in California prior to this court's decision in *People v. Drew*. If read literally, he argues, section 25(b) would violate both the state and federal Constitutions by imposing criminal responsibility and sanctions on persons who lack the mens rea essential to criminal culpability.

The People do not dispute the proposition that the intent of the electorate was to reinstate the pre-*Drew* test of legal insanity. They argue, however, that section 25(b), "amplifies" and "clarifies" the M'Naghten test. Amicus curiae, the Criminal Justice Legal Foundation, agrees that the intent was not to adopt a stricter test than that applicable prior to *Drew*, but suggest that in fact there is no difference between the two prongs of the M'Naghten test—ability to distinguish between right and wrong, and knowledge of the nature and quality of the particular criminal act.

Mindful of the serious constitutional questions that might arise were we to accept a literal construction of the statutory language, and of our obligation wherever possible both to carry out the intent of the electorate and to construe statutes so as to preserve their constitutionality, we shall conclude that section 25(b) was intended to, and does, restore the M'Naghten test as it existed in this state before *Drew*. We shall also conclude that under that test there exist two distinct and independent bases upon which a verdict of not guilty by reason of insanity might be returned.

Defendant appeals from a judgment of conviction of second degree murder entered upon his pleas of nolo contendere and not guilty by reason of insanity, and a finding by the court, after a jury was waived, that he was sane at the time of the offense. In finding the defendant sane, the judge acknowledged that it was more likely than not that defendant suffered from a mental disease, paranoid schizophrenia, which played a significant part in the killing. The judge stated that under the *Drew* test of legal insanity defendant would qualify as insane, and also found that "under the right-wrong prong of section 25(b), the defendant would qualify as legally insane; but under the other prong, he clearly does not." Concluding that by the use of the conjunctive "and" in section 25(b), the electorate demonstrated an intent to establish a stricter test of legal insanity than the M'Naghten test, and to "virtually eliminate" insanity as a defense, the judge found that defendant had not established that he was legally insane.

Probation was denied and defendant was sentenced to a term of 15 years to life in the state prison.

Defendant strangled his wife while he was on a day pass from the Camarillo State Hospital at which he was a patient. Evidence offered at the trial on his plea of not guilty by reason of insanity included the opinion of a clinical and forensic psychologist that defendant suffered from either classical paranoiac schizophrenia, or schizoaffective illness with significant paranoid features. A delusional product of this illness was a belief held by defendant that the marriage vow "till death do us part" bestows on a marital partner a God-given right to kill the other partner who has violated or was inclined to violate the marital vows, and that because the vows reflect the direct wishes of God, the killing is with complete moral and criminal impunity. The act is not wrongful because it is sanctified by the will and desire of God.

Although there was also evidence that would have supported a finding that defendant was sane, it was apparently the evidence summarized above upon which the trial judge based his finding that defendant met one, but not both, prongs of the M'-Naghten test. Defendant knew the nature and quality of his act. He knew that his act was homicidal. He was unable to distinguish right and wrong, however, in that he did not know that this particular killing was wrongful or criminal....

We conclude, as did the Court of Appeal in *Horn* that section 25(b) reinstated the M'Naghten test as it was applied in California prior to *Drew* as the test of legal insanity in criminal prosecutions in this state.

Although the People agree that the purpose of section 25(b) was to return the test of legal insanity in California to the pre-ALI-*Drew* version of the M'Naghten test, they argue that reversal of this judgment is not required because both prongs of that test are actually the same. The findings of the trial judge in this case illustrate the fallacy inherent in this argument. It is true that a person who is unaware of the nature and quality of his act by definition cannot know that the act is wrong. In this circumstance the "nature and quality" prong subsumes the "right and wrong" prong.

The reverse does not necessarily follow, however. The expert testimony in this case supported the findings of the trial court that this defendant was aware of the nature and quality of his homicidal act. He knew that he was committing an act of strangulation that would, and was intended to, kill a human being. He was not able to comprehend that the act was wrong because his mental illness caused him to believe that the act was not only morally justified but was expected of him. He believed that the homicide was "right." ...

Courts in a number of jurisdictions which have considered the question have come to the conclusion as we do, that a defendant who is incapable of understanding that his act is morally wrong is not criminally liable merely because he knows the act is unlawful. Justice Cardozo, in an opinion for the New York Court of Appeal, eloquently expressed the underlying philosophy: "In the light of all these precedents, it is impossible, we think, to say that there is any decisive adjudication which limits the word 'wrong' in the statutory definition to legal as opposed to moral wrong.... The interpretation placed upon the statute by the trial judge may be tested by its consequences. A mother kills her infant child to whom she has been devotedly attached. She knows the nature and quality of the act; she knows that the law condemns it; but she is inspired by an insane delusion that God has appeared to her and ordained the sacrifice. *It seems a mockery to say that, within the meaning of the statute, she knows that the act is wrong.* If the definition propounded by the trial judge is right, it would be the duty of a jury to hold her responsible for the crime. We find nothing either in the history of the rule, or in its reason or purpose, or in judicial exposition of its meaning, to justify a conclusion so abhorrent.... Knowledge that an act is forbidden by law will in most cases permit the inference of knowledge that, according to the accepted standards of mankind, it is also condemned as an offense against good morals. Obedience to the law is itself a moral duty. If, however, there is an insane delusion that God has appeared to the defendant and ordained the commission of a crime, we think it cannot be said of the offender that he knows the act to be wrong." ...

Kaus, J., Broussard, J., Reynoso, J., and Lucas, J., concurred....

Bird, C.J. Dissenting.

In June of 1982, the voters adopted a ballot measure which radically altered the test for criminal insanity in this state. (Pen. Code, § [25 (b)] ... popularly known as Prop. 8.) I cannot ignore the fact that they adopted language which unambiguously requires the accused to demonstrate that "he or she was incapable of knowing or understanding the nature and quality of his or her act *and* of distinguishing right from wrong at the time of the commission of the offense." There is nothing in the statute, in Proposition 8 as a whole, or in the ballot arguments that implies that the electorate intended "and" to be "or." However unwise that choice, it is not within this court's power to ignore the expression of popular will and rewrite the statute.

Since appellant failed to establish his insanity under the test enunciated in Penal Code section [25 (b),] I cannot join the decision of my brethren.

Discussion Questions

1. Why, in 1982, might the electorate have reinstated a more restrictive definition of insanity than the Court's then-applicable *Drew* definition?

2. Should the Court have followed the literal language of the statute? What theories of interpretation, if any, support the Court's decision?

3. Moral Wrong versus Legal Wrong

One of the most controversial issues in the M'Naghten definition involves the distinction between moral and legal wrong, discussed briefly in the *Skinner* case. The Washington Supreme Court addresses this issue in the *Crenshaw* case.

State v. Crenshaw

98 Wash. 2d 78 (1983)
Supreme Court of Washington

Brachtenbach, J.

Petitioner Rodney Crenshaw pleaded not guilty and not guilty by reason of insanity to the charge of first degree murder of his wife, Karen Crenshaw. A jury found him guilty....

[Here, we consider] the propriety of the insanity defense instruction which explained the right-wrong standard in the *M'Naghten* test in terms of "legal" right and wrong....

Before turning to the legal issues, the facts of the case must be recounted. While defendant and his wife were on their honeymoon in Canada, petitioner was deported as a result of his participation in a brawl. He secured a motel room in Blaine, Washington, and waited for his wife to join him. When she arrived 2 days later, he immediately thought she had been unfaithful—he sensed "it wasn't the same Karen ... she'd been with someone else."

Petitioner did not mention his suspicions to his wife; instead he took her to the motel room and beat her unconscious. He then went to a nearby store, stole a knife, and returned to stab his wife 24 times, inflicting a fatal wound. He left again, drove to a nearby farm where he had been employed and borrowed an ax. Upon returning to the motel room, he decapitated his wife with such force that the ax marks cut into the concrete floor under the carpet and splattered blood throughout the room.

Petitioner then proceeded to conceal his actions. He placed the body in a blanket, the head in a pillowcase, and put both in his wife's car. Next, he went to a service station, borrowed a bucket and sponge, and cleaned the room of blood and finger-prints. Before leaving, petitioner also spoke with the motel manager about a phone bill, then chatted with him for awhile over a beer.

When Crenshaw left the motel he drove to a remote area 25 miles away where he hid the two parts of the body in thick brush. He then fled, driving to the Hoquiam area, about 200 miles from the scene of the crime. There he picked up two hitchhikers, told them of his crime, and enlisted their aid in disposing of his wife's car in a river. The hitchhikers contacted the police and Crenshaw was apprehended shortly thereafter. He voluntarily confessed to the crime.

The defense of not guilty by reason of insanity was a major issue at trial. Crenshaw testified that he followed the Moscovite religious faith, and that it would be improper for a Moscovite not to kill his wife if she committed adultery. Crenshaw also has a history of mental problems, for which he has been hospitalized in the past. The jury, however, rejected petitioner's insanity defense, and found him guilty of murder in the first degree.

Insanity is an affirmative defense the defendant must establish by a preponderance of the evidence. Sanity is presumed, even with a history of prior institutional com-mitments from which the individual was released upon sufficient recovery.

The insanity defense is not available to all who are mentally deficient or deranged; legal insanity has a different meaning and a different purpose than the concept of medical insanity. A verdict of not guilty by reason of insanity completely absolves a defendant of any criminal responsibility. Therefore, "the defense is available only to those persons who have lost contact with reality so completely that they are beyond any of the influences of the criminal law."

Petitioner assigned error to insanity defense instruction 10 which reads:

> In addition to the plea of not guilty, the defendant has entered a plea of in-sanity existing at the time of the act charged.
>
> Insanity existing at the time of the commission of the act charged is a de-fense.
>
> For a defendant to be found not guilty by reason of insanity you must find that, as a result of mental disease or defect, the defendant's mind was affected to such an extent that the defendant was unable to perceive the nature and quality of the acts with which the defendant is charged or was unable to tell right from wrong with reference to the particular acts with which defendant is charged.
>
> What is meant by the terms "right and wrong" refers to knowledge of a person at the time of committing an act that he was acting contrary to the law.

But for the last paragraph, this instruction tracks the language of WPIC 20.01, which is the *M'Naghten* test as codified in RCW 9A.12.010. Petitioner contends, however, that the trial court erred in defining "right and wrong" as legal right and wrong rather than in the moral sense.

We find this instruction was not reversible error on ... alternative grounds: (1) The *M'Naghten* opinion amply supports the "legal" wrong definition as used in this case, (2) under these facts, "moral" wrong and "legal" wrong are synonymous, therefore the "legal" wrong definition did not alter the meaning of the test....

The definition of the term "wrong" in the *M'Naghten* test has been considered and disputed by many legal scholars. In Washington, we have not addressed this issue previously.

The confusion arises from apparent inconsistencies in the original *M'Naghten* case. In response to the House of Lords first question, the justices replied that if an accused knew he was acting contrary to law but acted under a partial insane delusion that he was redressing or revenging some supposed grievance or injury, or producing some supposed public benefit, "he is nevertheless punishable ... if he knew at the time of committing such crime that he was acting *contrary to law; ... the law of the land*." (Italics ours.) *M'Naghten's Case,* 8 Eng. Rep. 718, 722 (1843). In this answer, the justices appear to approve the legal standard of wrong when there is evidence that the accused knew he was acting contrary to the law.

This has been characterized as inconsistent with the justices' response to the second and third questions, regarding how a jury should be instructed on the insanity defense:

> If the question were to be put [to a jury] as to the knowledge of the accused solely and exclusively with reference to the law of the land, it might tend to confound the jury, by inducing them to believe that an actual knowledge of the law of the land was essential in order to lead to a conviction; whereas the law is administered upon the principle that every one must be taken conclusively to know it, without proof that he does know it. If the accused was conscious that the act was one which he ought not to do, and if that act was at the same time contrary to the law of the land, he is punishable; and the usual course therefore has been to leave the question to the jury, whether the party accused had a sufficient degree of reason to know that he was doing an act that was wrong: and this course we think is correct, accompanied with such observations and explanations as the circumstances of each particular case may require.

M'Naghten, at 723. This response appears to require both that the accused be "conscious that the act was one which he ought not to do" and that the act be "contrary to the law."

A close examination of these answers, however, shows they are reconcilable in the context of this case. First, the similarities between the hypothetical in the first question and Crenshaw's situation should afford that answer great weight. If, arguendo, Crenshaw was delusional, his delusion was only partial, for it related only to his perceptions of his wife's infidelity. His behavior towards others, *i.e.*, the motel manager and the woman who loaned him the ax, at the time of the killing was normal. Crenshaw also "knew he was acting contrary to law" (*M'Naghten*, at 720), as evidenced by his sophisticated attempts to hide his crime and by the expert, psychiatric testimony. Furthermore, he acted with a view "of redressing or revenging [the] supposed grievance" (*M'Naghten*, at 720) of his wife's infidelity. Thus, the Crenshaw situation fits perfectly into the first hypothetical, and the trial court understandably relied on this passage in approving the challenged instruction....

Alternatively, the statement in instruction 10 may be approved because, in this case, legal wrong is synonymous with moral wrong. This conclusion is premised on two grounds.

First, in discussing the term "moral" wrong, it is important to note that it is society's morals, and not the individual's morals, that are the standard for judging moral wrong under *M'Naghten*. If wrong meant moral wrong judged by the individual's own conscience, this would seriously undermine the criminal law, for it would allow one who violated the law to be excused from criminal responsibility solely because, in his own conscience, his act was not morally wrong. This principle was emphasized by Justice Cardozo:

> The anarchist is not at liberty to break the law because he reasons that all government is wrong. The devotee of a religious cult that enjoins polygamy or human sacrifice as a duty is not thereby relieved from responsibility before the law ...

(Citations omitted.) *People v. Schmidt*, 216 N.Y. 324, 340, 110 N.E. 945, 950 (1915)....

There is evidence on the record that Crenshaw knew his actions were wrong according to society's standards, as well as legally wrong. Dr. Belden testified:

> I think Mr. Crenshaw is quite aware on one level that he is in conflict with the law *and with people*. However, this is not something that he personally invests his emotions in.

(Italics ours.) We conclude that Crenshaw knew his acts were morally wrong from society's viewpoint and also knew his acts were illegal. His personal belief that it was his duty to kill his wife for her alleged infidelity cannot serve to exculpate him from legal responsibility for his acts.

A narrow exception to the societal standard of moral wrong has been drawn for instances wherein a party performs a criminal act, knowing it is morally and legally wrong, but believing, because of a mental defect, that the act is ordained by God: such would be the situation with a mother who kills her infant child to whom she is devotedly attached, believing that God has spoken to her and decreed the act. Although the woman knows that the law and society condemn the act, it would be unrealistic to hold her responsible for the crime, since her free will has been subsumed by her belief in the deific decree.

This exception is not available to Crenshaw, however. Crenshaw argued only that he followed the Moscovite faith and that Moscovites believe it is their duty to kill an unfaithful wife. This is not the same as acting under a deific command. Instead, it is akin to "[t]he devotee of a religious cult that enjoins ... human sacrifice as a duty

[and] is *not* thereby relieved from responsibility before the law". (Italics ours.) Crenshaw's personal "Moscovite" beliefs are not equivalent to a deific decree and do not relieve him from responsibility for his acts.

Once moral wrong is equated with society's morals, the next step, equating moral and legal wrong, follows logically. The law is, for the most part, an expression of collective morality.

Most cases involving the insanity defense involve serious crimes for which society's moral judgment is identical with the legal standard. Therefore, a number of scholars have concluded that, as a practical matter, the way in which a court interprets the word "wrong" will have little effect on the eventual outcome of a case.

4. Insanity Definitions

Problems

M'Naghten and four other influential insanity definitions appear following the problems below. Apply each to the problems. Consider their similarities and their differences. Which one is preferable?

8.20 Andrea Yates, the mother of five young children between the ages of six months and seven years, drowned each of her children, one after the other, in the bathtub of their family home. In response to questioning about the acts, Mrs. Yates indicated that the children had not done anything to make her angry and that she had been considering drowning them for some time. She explained that her thoughts about drowning her children were part of her realization that she had "not been a good mother to them." She explained this by noting that "[t]hey weren't developing correctly." They had, in her view, behavioral and learning problems. She stated that she "realized it was time to be punished ... for not being a good mother."[38] She explained: "After I kill them, they would go up to heaven and be with God and be safe."[39] Two years earlier, she had attempted suicide and been treated for depression. Assuming that Mrs. Yates suffered from postpartum psychosis, a severe mental disease, should the jury have found her insane under Texas law? What about any of the other definitions provided after Problem 8.21 below?

---

38. This problem is based upon the Transcript of Andrea Yates's statement to the police by the Associated Press, HOUSTON CHRON., *Transcript of Andrea Yates' Confession*, wysiwg://41/http://www.chron.com/ ... tory.mpl/special/drownings/1266294 (accessed July 28, 2004), and the Glenn article cited in the next footnote.

39. Mike Glenn et al., *June 20: Mom Held in Killing 5 Kids*, HOUSTON CHRON., Dec. 24, 2001, *available at* wysiwyg://33/http://www.chron.com/cs/CDA/story.hts/topstory2/949223 (accessed on July 28, 2004).

Texas Penal Code Annotated

§ 8.01. Insanity.

(a) It is an affirmative defense to prosecution that, at the time of the conduct charged, the actor, as a result of severe mental disease or defect, did not know that his conduct was wrong.

(b) The term "mental disease or defect" does not include an abnormality manifested only by repeated criminal or otherwise antisocial conduct.

Problem

8.21 The defendant, John Hinckley, shot then-President Ronald Reagan. Evidence presented at trial suggested that Hinckley was obsessed with the actress Jodi Foster and that he believed that killing President Reagan would impress her. Assume that Hinckley suffered from psychosis, a severe mental illness, and genuinely believed that President Reagan's death would produce this desired result. Under the tests below, should the factfinder acquit Hinckley?

---

1. *Federal Test:* "It is an affirmative defense to a prosecution under any Federal statute that, at the time of the commission of the acts constituting the offense, the defendant, as a result of a severe mental disease or defect, was unable to appreciate the nature and quality or the wrongfulness of his acts. Mental disease or defect does not otherwise constitute a defense." 18 U.S.C.S. § 17 (2003).

2. *M'Naghten Test:* "[T]o establish a defence on the ground of insanity, it must be clearly proved that, at the time of the committing of the act, the party accused was labouring under such a defect of reason, from disease of the mind, as not to know the nature and quality of the act he was doing; or, if he did know it, that he did not know he was doing what was wrong." *M'Naghten's Case*, 8 Eng. Rep. 718, 722 (1843).

3. *Model Penal Code Test:* "A person is not responsible for criminal conduct if at the time of such conduct as a result of mental disease or defect he lacks substantial capacity either to appreciate the criminality [wrongfulness] of his conduct or to conform his conduct to the requirements of law.[40]

[A]s used in this Article, the terms 'mental disease or defect' do not include an abnormality manifested only by repeated criminal or otherwise antisocial conduct." Model Penal Code § 4.01 (ALI 1985).

---

40. The Model Penal Code drafters explain the inclusion of the alternatives of "criminality" and "wrongfulness" as follows: "Wrongfulness is suggested as a possible alternative to criminality, though it is recognized that few cases are likely to arise in which the variation will be determinative." Model Penal Code, Commentaries, Complete Statutory Text, Art. 4, p. 62.

4. *Irresistible Impulse Test:* "[T]he degree of insanity which will relieve the accused of the consequences of a criminal act must be such as to create in his mind an uncontrollable impulse to commit the offense charged. This impulse must be such as to override the reason and judgment and obliterate the sense of right and wrong to the extent that the accused is deprived of the power to choose between right and wrong. The mere ability to distinguish right from wrong is no longer the correct test either in civil or criminal cases, where the defense of insanity is interposed.... [T]he accused must be capable, not only of distinguishing between right and wrong, but that he was not impelled to do the act by an irresistible impulse, which means before it will justify a verdict of acquittal that his reasoning powers were so far dethroned by his diseased mental condition as to deprive him of the will power to resist the insane impulse to perpetrate the deed, though knowing it to be wrong." *Smith v. United States*, 36 F.2d 548, 549 (1929).

5. *Durham Test:* "[A]n accused is not criminally responsible if his unlawful act was the product of mental disease or mental defect." *Durham v. United States*, 214 F.2d 862, 874–75 (1954).

5. Rationales for and against an Insanity Defense

Despite overwhelming acceptance under federal and state law of some version of an insanity defense, its utility, desirability, and scope remain controversial. Particular cases often spark renewed debate about the existence, nature, and language of the defense. For instance, the jury's acquittal of John Hinckley by reason of insanity on the charge of the attempted assassination of President Reagan had a profound effect on the treatment of legal insanity in this country. "During the three-year period following the *Hinckley* acquittal, Congress and half the states enacted changes in the insanity defense, all designed to limit it in some respect. Congress and nine states narrowed the substantive test of insanity; Congress and seven states shifted the burden of proof to the defendant; eight states supplemented the insanity verdict with a separate verdict of guilty but mentally ill; and one state (Utah) abolished the defense altogether."[41]

In 1966, Congress established a Commission to "undertake a complete review and recommend revision of the federal criminal laws."[42] As part of its task, the Commission reviewed a host of arguments about potential abolition of the insanity defense. In reading what follows from the Commission's report, which argument do you find most persuasive?

---

41. PETER W. LOW ET AL., THE TRIAL OF JOHN W. HINCKLEY, JR.: A CASE STUDY IN THE INSANITY DEFENSE 126–27 (Foundation Press, Inc. 1986). The Model Penal Code test applied in the federal courts at the time of Hinckley's trial.
42. *Supra* n. 28 at 248–53 (1970).

Working Papers of The National Commission on Reform of Federal Criminal Law

Vol. 1, IX (U.S. Gov't Printing Office 1970)

In Support of Abolishing the Insanity Defense:

* There is a shortage of "[t]rained mental health personnel." Their time should be devoted to serving "in disposition and treatment of persons who have engaged in criminal conduct" rather than "in courthouses so that they will be available to engage in retrospective reconstructions of criminal responsibility."

* "Insanity is frequently and properly called a 'rich man's defense,' for the wealthy can sift the pool of potential expert witnesses for those who will produce favorable testimony in a convincing manner." (noting the "fairly extreme example [of] *Wright v. United States*, in which eleven psychiatrists examined the defendant and testified before the jury.").

* "Key terms in the conventionally utilized insanity tests (particularly when one goes beyond *M'Naghten*) such as 'mental disease,' and 'capacity to conform,' are vague at best, and perhaps meaningless. The insanity defense invites semantic jousting, metaphysical speculation, and intuitive moral judgments in the guise of factual determinations."

* "The literature reveals great uncertainty as to the function of insanity defenses. Currently, it perhaps is most commonly stated as designed to remove from the criminal process those who are deemed to be not blameworthy. Left unclear is the establishment of criteria for determining blameworthiness and the identification of persons meeting such criteria."

* "The crucial decisions with respect to persons, including mentally abnormal persons, who commit criminal acts involve disposition. An insanity defense is a poor device for determination of whether persons ought to be institutionalized and, if so, to what facility they are to be directed. It is far more rational to face this question frankly and directly. Large numbers of defendants who could present effective insanity defenses under present standards do not do so either because the possibility is not recognized or because it is avoided, commonly out of fear of more lengthy detention and/or more painful stigmatization."

* "The criminal process has the advantages of determinate maximum periods of detention, and proportionality between the seriousness of the offense and the penalty. Persons channeled out of the criminal system by the insanity defense are subject to incarceration, possibly for life. The criteria for release, such as 'recovered sanity,' and no longer 'dangerous,' are subject to such wide variations of meaning as to afford little protection to the 'patient.'"

* "A number of informed observers believe that it is therapeutically desirable to treat behavioral deviants as responsible for their conduct rather than as involuntary victims playing a sick role."

In Support of Retaining the Insanity Defense:

* "There is a powerful root feeling in our culture tha[t] an 'insane' person is not appropriately subject to the condemnation implicit in criminal conviction and sentencing. We sense a lack of culpability.... In part these feelings may be attributable to a subjective sense of freedom to avoid criminal conduct ourselves and our lack of identification with grossly abnormal offenders, whom we feel to be different from ourselves in the sense of being less free."

* "To abolish the insanity defense would be to seem to recognize that criminal sanction may be imposed irrespective of whether the defendant freely chose his course of conduct, thus weakening what is at least a useful myth."

* "Criminal convictions carry added sanctions of loss of reputation, self-deprecation, and (frequently) civil legal liabilities."

* "If a special insanity defense is eliminated, there will be greater need to provide means for channeling mentally abnormal persons away from correctional institutions and into mental hospitals."

6. "Guilty but Mentally Ill"

As noted above, in the aftermath of the Hinckley case, a number of states passed laws allowing for a verdict of "guilty but mentally ill" (GBMI). These laws generally represent an alternative, rather than a replacement, for the insanity defense in situations where a defendant's illness is insufficient to excuse him from criminal responsibility, but still worrisome enough to justify mandatory treatment. After a GBMI verdict, a defendant typically is sentenced as if he were found guilty but the court then decides the extent to which he needs mental health treatment. If and when the defendant is considered "cured" of the underlying mental health problem, he then usually must serve out the remainder of his prison sentence—unlike a person deemed not guilty by reason of insanity who would be freed from mental health commitment upon a finding that he is no longer suffering from the illness. At bottom, "the guilty but mentally ill verdict is intended to provide an 'in-between' classification whereby a defendant bears the legal responsibility for criminal conduct, but is provided treatment while incarcerated for mental illness."[43] What are the pros and cons of this option?

---

43. *Star v. Commonwealth*, 313 S.W.3d 30, 35–36 (Ky. 2010).

Problem

8.22 Consider the following statute:

It shall be a defense to a prosecution under any statute that the defendant, as a result of mental disease or defect, lacked a culpable mental state required as an element of the crime charged. Mental disease or defect is not otherwise a defense.

(A) What is the effect of this statute? Does it abolish the insanity defense? Does it re-define it?

(B) Is what the defense is allowed to do under this statute a challenge to proof? Or an example of confession and avoidance?

Chapter 9

Rape

A. Introduction

In his 1760s Commentaries, William Blackstone defined common law rape as the "carnal knowledge of a woman forcibly and against her will."[1] In recent decades, many state legislatures redefined rape, making it, according to Professor Susan Estrich, the "subject of substantive criminal law in great[est] ferment."[2] Widespread criticism of the traditional approach to defining the crime of rape and the criminal justice system's treatment of rape victims fueled this ferment. Much of the criticism centered on the deep distrust of rape complainants that permeates the history of rape law.

For example, until reforms in recent decades, unlike other crime victims, judges routinely instructed jurors to be wary of the testimony of rape complainants. A limited number of jurisdictions still authorize the use of such a cautionary instruction. Similarly, courts treated rape complainants like accomplices to the crime, by requiring corroboration of their testimony. This meant that, for most every other crime, a victim's testimony by itself could support a conviction. But for rape, victim testimony alone was insufficient as a matter of law.

In addition, rape complainants had to report the offense promptly, a rule that became known as the "prompt complaint" rule. Although longer statutes of limitations existed for rape, under common law, failure to report promptly created "a strong but not conclusive presumption against a woman,"[3] even if the report fell

---

1. WILLIAM BLACKSTONE, COMMENTARIES ON THE LAWS OF ENGLAND, Book IV Ch. 15 p. 208 (Thomas M. Cooley ed., Callaghan and Company 1879).

2. Susan Estrich, *Teaching Rape Law*, 102 YALE L.J. 509, 516 (1992).

3. Model Penal Code Commentaries, 420–421, citing 4 W. BLACKSTONE COMMENTARIES * 211; 1 W. HAWKINS, PLEAS OF THE CROWN 170 (3d ed 1788). The Model Penal Code's provision on Prompt Complaint reads: "No prosecution may be instituted or maintained under this Article unless the alleged offense was brought to the notice of public authority within [3] months of its occurrence or, where the alleged victim was less than [16] years old or otherwise incompetent to make complaint, within [3] months after a parent, guardian or other competent person specially interested in the victim learns of the offense." Contrast the MPC position above with the language of the Montana statute, which declares: "(4) Evidence of failure to make a timely complaint or immediate outcry does not raise any presumption as to the credibility of the victim." Mont. Code Ann. §45-5-511 (4).

well within the statute of limitations. Some jurisdictions, following the lead of the Model Penal Code in the 1950s, went further and enacted a complete bar to rape prosecutions when the victim did not report promptly. In the wake of rape law reform, many jurisdictions eliminated the formal doctrinal requirement of prompt complaint.

Another troubling aspect of the law of rape that has drawn heated criticism is what is known as the "marital exemption." This exemption meant that conduct that would qualify as rape outside of a marriage did not qualify as rape if the people involved were married. In other words, a husband could force his wife to engage in sexual acts without her consent and not violate the law of rape. Blackstone's definition of rape included such an exemption. As the MPC provisions you will read in this Chapter reveal, the original version of the MPC's rape statute retains this exemption. The marital exemption is now largely an artifact of the law of rape, having been abandoned in virtually every American jurisdiction. Currently pending revisions to the MPC do away with it as well.

The cautionary instruction, the corroboration requirement, and the prompt complaint rule are three obvious manifestations of the criminal law's distrust of rape victims. Such distrust continues to influence today's legal discourse on rape law and reform efforts.

The tendency of some victims not to reveal or report sexual offenses against them along with inadequate and otherwise problematic responses by police and prosecutors have long posed barriers to the effective enforcement of criminal law penalizing rape and other sexual offenses. Victims are often reluctant, even fearful, of reporting sex offenses for a variety of reasons, such as self-blaming, fear of embarrassment, social stigmatization, possible retaliation from the perpetrator, and wariness of participating in the criminal process. Police have too often been unsupportive of victims of sexual offenses and dismissive or openly skeptical of their allegations. Both police and prosecutors have at times been highly pessimistic about their ability to succeed in obtaining convictions in rape cases. In recent decades, some police departments and prosecutor offices have consciously sought to change these attitudes.

The MeToo movement has brought an international spotlight to these issues. Activist Tarana Burke coined the term MeToo in 2006 for use on social media to provide support to victims of sexual abuse. In 2017, highly publicized allegations by many women of repeated sexual offenses and sexual harassment by movie producer Harvey Weinstein sparked an exponential expansion of the movement through a social media campaign. After a trial in early 2020 that drew significant media attention, Weinstein was convicted by a jury of rape and sexual assault in New York state court, then sentenced to twenty-three years in prison. Public disclosure of the complaints against Weinstein, along with his high profile prosecution following a controversial initial decision by the prosecutor not to file charges, resulted in many people in the United States and around the world coming forth publicly to reveal that they were victims of sex crimes and sexual harassment, especially in the workplace.

Use of the slogan "Believe Women" arose from the MeToo movement. It is aimed at achieving something long overdue, dispelling the distrust of women that, as described above, has long permeated the law of rape. A proponent has written that the slogan means "don't assume women as a gender are especially deceptive or vindictive, and recognize that false allegations are less common than real ones."[4] It gained momentum after the controversial confirmation of Brett Kavanaugh as a Supreme Court Justice in 2018, despite Professor Christine Blassey Ford's compelling congressional testimony chronicling how Kavanaugh had sexually assaulted her.

The MeToo movement and the Believe Women slogan have drawn negative responses from some quarters. Critics complain that those against whom public complaints of sexual misconduct are made have inadequate opportunity to defend themselves before suffering serious damage to their careers, reputations, and families. They contend that, regardless of whether a criminal prosecution results, those who are the subjects of such complaints end up being unfairly condemned in the court of public opinion without being afforded a presumption of innocence or a chance to be heard. Other critics are skeptical of the veracity of some of the allegations the MeToo movement has brought to light. They argue that the Believe Women slogan demands or at least prompts categorical acceptance of any complaint of sexual misconduct without consideration of the evidence and without concern for the possibility that some complaints may be false.

What lasting impact the MeToo movement, the Believe Women slogan, and the ideas and concerns that drive them may have on the substantive criminal law, criminal procedure, and police practices dealing with sex crimes and victims remains to be seen. As you read the materials in this Chapter, consider what impact they may already have had on your thinking and feelings about how the law deals with sexual misconduct. What impact do you think this movement, this slogan, and the ideas behind them may have on actors in the criminal justice system, such as prosecutors, defense lawyers, judges, and jurors? What impact do you think they *should* have?

This section begins with background information about rape. We consider statistics, studies, and demographics. Following this background information, we turn to the elements of rape. Starting with Blackstone's formulation, we look at what has changed and what has remained unchanged about rape law since Blackstone's time.

Our inquiry begins with the conduct element — how legislatures have altered Blackstone's "carnal knowledge of a woman" as the starting point in defining rape. We then turn to two other elements of Blackstone's definition, "forcibly and against her will." The crime of rape historically required, and in many jurisdictions continues to require, proof of both force and lack of consent. In defining and applying force and lack of consent, courts have focused on whether and to what extent the victim resisted. Accordingly, we study force, lack of consent, and resistance together. In the last section, we focus on the crime of statutory rape, in which, rather than consent or

---

4. Sady Doyle, *Despite What You May Have Heard, "Believe Women" Has Never Meant "Ignore Facts,"* ELLE (November, 2017).

force, the ages of the involved parties generally control whether the sexual conduct qualifies as criminal.

B. Context: Statistics, Studies, and Demographics

The National Intimate Partner and Sexual Violence Survey (NISVS): 2010 Summary Report, **National Center for Injury Prevention and Control**
Michelle Black et al.
Centers for Disease Control and Prevention
(Atlanta: CDC, Nov. 2011)

From January 22, 2010 through December 31, 2010 NISVS used a dual-frame sampling strategy to interview a total of 18,049 individuals via cellular phone and land line about their experiences with rape and other forms of sexual violence. Of the total interviews conducted 9,970 were women and 8,079 were men. The survey defined rape to include "any completed or attempted vaginal (for women), oral, or anal penetration through the use of physical force (such as being pinned or held down, or by the use of violence) or threats to physically harm and includes times when the victim was drunk, high, drugged, or passed out and unable to consent." The survey found that:

> Nearly 1 in 5 women in the United States has been raped in her lifetime (18.3%). This is translated to almost 22 million women in the United States. The most common form of rape victimization experienced by women was completed forced penetration, experienced by 12.3% of women.... Approximately 1 in 71 men in the United States (1.4%) reported having been raped in his lifetime, which translates to almost 1.6 million men in the United States.

* * *

The National Intimate Partner and Sexual Violence Survey (NISVS): An Overview of 2010 Findings on Victimization by Sexual Orientation, **National Center for Injury Prevention and Control**

• Approximately 1 in 8 lesbian women (13%), [and] nearly half of bisexual women (46%) ... have been raped in their lifetime....

• Four in 10 gay men (40%), [and] nearly half of bisexual men (47%) ... have experienced [sexual violence] other than rape in their lifetime.

* * *

James, S. E., Herman, J. L., Rankin, S.,
Keisling, M., Mottet, L., & Anafi, M. (2016).
The Report of the 2015 U.S. Transgender Survey. Washington, DC:
National Center for Transgender Equality.

Nearly half (47%) of respondents have been sexually assaulted at some point in their lifetime.... Respondents who have participated in sex work (72%), those who have experienced homelessness (65%), and people with disabilities (61%) were more likely to have been sexually assaulted in their lifetime.

* * *

National Institute of Justice, *Victims and Perpetrators,* https://www.nij.gov/topics/crime/rape-sexual-violence/Pages/ victims-perpetrators.aspx (Oct. 2010).

Research on sexual violence indicates that—[s]exual violence may occur in any type of relationship, but most perpetrators of sexual assault are known to their victims. Among victims ages 18 to 29, two-thirds had a prior relationship with the offender. The Bureau of Justice Statistics (BJS) reports that 6 in 10 rape or sexual assault victims said that they were assaulted by an intimate partner, relative, friend or acquaintance.

* * *

Criminal Victimization 2018, Rachel E. Morgan, Ph.D., and Barbara A. Oudekerk, Ph.D., *BJS Statisticians,* (Sept. 2019), is the most recent national crime victimization report from the U.S. Bureau of Justice Statistics. It provides the following data on the number of reported rapes and sexual assaults as well as victimization rates from 2014 through 2018:

	Number	Rate
2014:	284,350	1.1 per thousand
2015:	431,840	1.6 per thousand
2016:	298,410	1.1 per thousand
2017:	393,980	1.4 per thousand
2018:	734,630	2.7 per thousand

* * *

Cognitive Processing Therapy for Rape Victims: A Treatment Manual 4
Patricia A. Resick & Monica K. Schnicke (Sage 1996)

Sexual assault ... is a traumatic event from which many victims never fully recover. Many victims develop problems with depression, poor self-esteem, interpersonal difficulties, and sexual dysfunctions.... However, the most frequently observed disorder that develops as a result of sexual assault is post-traumatic stress disorder (PTSD).

Problem

9.1 After graduating from law school, you are working as legal counsel for the Criminal Justice Committee of the senate in the state where you live and practice. The Committee wants to replace your state's current rape statute. The Committee has asked you to draft a new statute for the committee to consider. The Committee is concerned because studies have shown that rape is both underreported by victims and under-prosecuted by police and district attorneys in your state. Another problem the Committee seeks to address is jury nullification. Studies have shown that jurors are often reluctant to convict defendants of rape if they learn of conduct on the part of the alleged victim that they view as "contributory fault." The Committee chair asks that you keep these problems in mind as you draft your proposed statute. Here are the key questions you will need to consider in drafting your statute:

(1) *What should the crime be called?* The common law used, and your state's current statute uses, the term "rape" to label a crime involving nonconsensual sexual intercourse. But many states have abandoned the term rape and substituted terms such as "sexual assault," "sexual battery," or "sexual abuse."

(2) *How should the conduct element of the offense be defined?* The common law used the phrase "carnal knowledge"—an awkward circumlocution for sexual intercourse. Your state's current rape statute defines the conduct element as "sexual intercourse." What are the downsides of the current definition? What alternatives are there?

(3) *Should your statute include "lack of consent" as an element of the offense?* The common law definition of rape required that the sexual intercourse be accomplished "against the will" of the victim, the equivalent of lack of consent. In an effort to avoid putting the victim "on trial," the Model Penal Code eliminated a lack of consent element and defined the required conduct on the part of the perpetrator as forcible compulsion.

(4) *Should your statute include a "force" element?* The common law definition of rape included a force element and so do many modern statutes. If you include a force element, should you provide a definition of the word "force" in your statute? If so, how should you define it?

(5) *Should your statute include a resistance requirement?* In other words, should conviction require that the prosecution prove that the victim resisted? If so, under what circumstances? If so, should physical resistance be required? What about verbal resistance? What purpose would physical or verbal resistance likely serve?

(6) *How should your statute define the mental state(s) required for conviction?* The common law did not clearly address this question. Many modern statutes also fail to address it.

(7) *Should your statute create grades or degrees of sexual offenses with graduated penalties?* If so, on what basis should the grades or degrees be based? As we saw in Chapter 6, homicide offenses are graded according to the actor's mental state about the resulting death. Under the Model Penal Code, for example, purpose, knowledge, or extreme recklessness regarding death qualify for murder, recklessness for manslaughter, and negligence for negligent homicide. In similar fashion, should the actor's mental state about, for example, the victim's lack of

consent be used to grade your statute? Or you could grade the statute based on harm that resulted or was risked? For example, serious bodily injury resulting to the victim could serve to distinguish grades of offenses. A third possibility would be to rely on the actor's conduct, such as the use of a weapon, to grade offenses.

C. Conduct

Blackstone defined rape as the "carnal knowledge of a woman forcibly and against her will." Carnal knowledge meant sexual intercourse involving at least slight penile penetration of the vaginal area. This definition of rape required a male perpetrator and a female victim. Reform efforts led many legislatures to define the primary conduct more broadly. Modern legislatures have also attached a variety of labels to current versions of the common law crime of rape. These include, for example, sexual assault, sexual abuse, and criminal sexual assault, as well as rape.

Problem

9.2 Consider the four factual scenarios described below and the statutes that follow. Apply each statute to each of the scenarios. Assume that all other elements are fulfilled. Which of the statutes covers the conduct described?

Part (a) John has sexual intercourse with Karen.

Part (b) Arthur anally penetrates Fred.

Part (c) Karen engages in oral sex with Jessica.

Part (d) Jill masturbates Tom.

Idaho Code

§ 18-6101. Rape defined

Rape is defined as the penetration, however slight, of the oral, anal or vaginal opening with a penis accomplished under any one (1) of the following circumstances: ...

(4) Where the victim resists but her resistance is overcome by force or violence....

New York Penal Code

§ 130.30. Rape in the first degree

A person is guilty of rape in the first degree when he or she engages in sexual intercourse with another person:

(1) By forcible compulsion....

Illinois Compiled Statutes

§ 5/11-1.20. Criminal Sexual Assault

(a) A person commits criminal sexual assault if that person commits an act of penetration and:

(1) uses force or threat of force....

§ 5/11-0.1 Definitions

"Sexual penetration" means any contact, however slight, between the sex organ or anus of one person and an object or the sex organ, mouth, or anus of another person, or any intrusion, however slight, of any part of the body of one person or of any animal or object into the sex organ or anus of another person, including, but not limited to, cunnilingus, fellatio, or anal penetration. Evidence of emission of semen is not required to prove sexual penetration.

Iowa Code

§ 709.1. Sexual abuse defined

Any sex act between persons is sexual abuse by either of the persons when the act is performed with the other person in any of the following circumstances:

1. The act is done by force or against the will of the other....

Massachusetts General Laws

Ch. 265 § 22. Rape

(b) Whoever has sexual intercourse or unnatural sexual intercourse with a person, and compels such person to submit by force and against his will....

Discussion Questions

1. Which statute provides the broadest coverage of conduct?

2. Assume that the Massachusetts Criminal Code fails to define "unnatural sexual intercourse." What concerns would that failure raise?

3. Which statutory language regarding conduct would you choose as a state legislator? Why?

1. Force, Resistance, and/or Lack of Consent

In addition to the conduct element of carnal knowledge, Blackstone's definition of rape required that the act be committed "forcibly and against her will." In defining and applying these elements, courts looked to the resistance of rape victims. Courts gauged the existence and extent of force by analyzing how much resistance the defendant had overcome. Resistance communicated that the contact was against the victim's will, that she had not consented. Consent was presumed absent a physical manifestation of lack of consent and resistance disproved the presumption. Over time, courts accepted threat or fear of serious injury as a proxy for force. In this section, we study the interaction among these components.

The MeToo movement has prompted a reexamination of the entire concept of consent and sexual activity. As you read the treatment of consent and lack of consent in the cases and statutes in this section, ask yourself the following questions. When, if ever, should a court find lack of consent when a man in a position of power, such as Harvey Weinstein in the movie industry, directly or indirectly pressures a woman in a less powerful position to engage in sexual activity? Should imbalance of power between two parties to a sexual act be a factor in evaluating consent? If so, in every case? And, if not in every case, which ones?

People v. Warren

113 Ill. App. 3d 1(1983)
Illinois Court of Appeals

Karns, Justice.

Defendant, Joel F. Warren, was charged by information with two counts of deviate sexual assault. Following a bench trial, defendant was convicted on both counts and was sentenced to a term of six years in prison.

On appeal, defendant contends that the State did not prove him guilty of deviate sexual assault beyond a reasonable doubt. Specifically, defendant argues that the State failed to prove that the acts complained of were committed by force or threat of force or against the will of the complainant. Defendant further contends that he was denied due process of law when the court convicted him on the basis of an improper standard of guilt.

At the time of the incident, defendant, Joel Warren, was 30 years of age and was a student at Southern Illinois University. Complainant was 32 years of age and worked as a volunteer at Synergy, an organization located in Carbondale, Illinois.

Complainant testified that on the afternoon of July 1, 1980, she rode her bicycle to Horstman's Point, which overlooks the Carbondale City Reservoir in Carbondale. While complainant was standing alone at Horstman's Point, defendant approached her and initiated and engaged in a conversation with her. Although complainant did not know defendant, she responded to his conversation which was general in nature.

Complainant started to walk away from the lake in the direction of her bicycle which was at the top of the hill. While she walked up the hill, defendant continued talking as he walked alongside of her. Complainant testified that when she got on her bicycle defendant placed his hand on her shoulder. At this time, complainant stated, "No, I have to go now," to which defendant responded, "This will only take a minute. My girlfriend doesn't meet my needs." Defendant also told her that "I don't want to hurt you."

According to complainant, defendant then lifted her off the ground and carried her into a wooded area adjacent to the reservoir. Upon entering the woods, defendant placed complainant on the ground and told her to put her head on his backpack. Defendant then told her to take her pants down which she did part way. Defendant pulled her pants completely off and placed them underneath her. He then proceeded to pull up complainant's tank top shirt and began kissing her breasts and vaginal area. After he finished kissing complainant, defendant sat up and unzipped his pants and complainant performed an act of fellatio upon him.

At the completion of this second act, defendant gave complainant an article of clothing to wipe her mouth. Complainant then dressed and defendant picked her up again and carried her back to her bicycle. Defendant testified that complainant asked him, "Is that all?" to which he answered, "Yes."

Complainant got on her bicycle and rode to Synergy, where she spoke to a volunteer worker who referred her to the Women's Center in Carbondale. At the Women's Center, she spoke with Mary Kay Bachman, with whom she went to the Carbondale Police Department. Complainant related the incident to Officer William Kilquist, who testified that complainant appeared to be very upset. Officer Kilquist further testified that no formal report was prepared at the request of complainant.

On February 15, 1981, complainant saw defendant while she was jogging and reported him to the police as the man with whom she had sexual relations. Defendant was arrested at his home later that day by Officers Hunziker and Hawk of the Southern Illinois Police Department and charged with deviate sexual assault.

At the outset, we note that there are no significant inconsistencies in the testimony of the two parties. Instead, we are faced with facts which are susceptible of more than one reading. Defendant admits that he performed the acts upon which the deviate sex charges are based. He contends, however, that the acts complained of were performed without force or threat of force.

Reviewing courts are especially charged with the duty of carefully examining the evidence in rape or deviate sexual assault cases and it is the duty of the reviewing court to reverse the judgment unless the evidence is sufficient to remove all reasonable doubt of defendant's guilt and create an abiding conviction that he is guilty of the crime charged. The ultimate issue presented for review in the instant case is whether the State satisfactorily proved that the acts complained of were committed by force or threat of force as required to constitute deviate sexual assault.

To sustain a conviction for deviate sexual assault, there must be evidence that defendant, by force or threat, compelled another to perform or submit to any act of deviate sexual conduct. There is, however, no definite standard which fixes the amount of force which is required to sustain the charge of rape or deviate sexual assault. Each case must be examined on the basis of its own particular facts.

In the present case, the State contends that defendant coerced complainant into engaging in deviate sexual acts by threatening to use physical force. The State maintains that this threat was conveyed by defendant's statement that "I don't want to hurt you," the implication being that he would hurt her if she did not comply. Although this interpretation has some merit, we do not believe that it is the most reasonable conclusion drawn from the facts. Defendant did not make the above statement while brandishing a weapon or applying physical force, a circumstance which would support the State's construction. Instead, we find that the record is devoid of any attendant circumstances which suggest that complainant was compelled to submit to defendant.

In addition, the State argues that the threat of force was conveyed by the disparity of size and strength between the parties. The record shows that at the time of the incident complainant was 5'2" tall weighing 100 to 105 pounds, whereas defendant was 6'3" and 185 pounds. The State further maintains that the seclusion of the woods contributed to this threat of force. Although it is proper to consider such factors in weighing the evidence, we do not believe that the evidence taken as a whole supports the State's conclusion. Aside from picking up complainant and carrying her into and out of the woods, defendant did not employ his superior size and strength. Furthermore, complainant did not attempt to flee or in any meaningful way resist the sexual advances of defendant.

Much of the State's case rests upon its contention that complainant's absence of effort in thwarting defendant's advances was motivated by her overwhelming fear. In support of this position, the State offers complainant's statement that she did not attempt to flee because, "it was in the middle of the woods and I didn't feel like I could get away from him and I thought he'd kill me." Moreover, complainant stated that she did not yell or scream because the people she had seen in the area were too far away and that under the circumstances she felt that screaming "would be bad for me."

Despite professing fear for her safety, complainant concedes that defendant did not strike her or threaten to strike her or use a weapon. When defendant picked up complainant and carried her into the wooded area, she did not protest but merely stated, "I can walk." Although she maintained that she stiffened up to make it harder for him to carry her, defendant did not recall any resistance. At no time did complainant tell defendant to leave her alone or put her down. Furthermore, complainant did not object when defendant instructed her to take off her pants, but instead she complied with his request by pulling down her pants part way....

In the case before us, defendant maintains that once complainant became aware that defendant intended to engage in sexual relations it was incumbent upon her to resist. This resistance would have the effect of giving defendant notice that his acts were being performed without her consent. It is well settled that if complainant had the use of her faculties and physical powers, the evidence must show such resistance as will demonstrate that the act was against her will. If the circumstances show resistance to be futile or life endangering or if the complainant is overcome by superior strength or paralyzed by fear, useless or foolhardy acts of resistance are not required. We cannot say that any of the above factors are present here. Complainant's failure to resist when it was within her power to do so conveys the impression of consent regardless of her mental state, amounts to consent and removes from the act performed an essential element of the crime. We do not mean to suggest, however, that the complainant did in fact consent; however, she must communicate in some objective manner her lack of consent.

Defendant's second contention is that the trial court violated his due process by applying an erroneous standard of guilt. Defendant maintains that the trial court created a new standard of guilt in determining that defendant used "psychological force" to overcome the will of complainant....

Although the trial court employed a new term in entering its judgment, we believe it is clear that the court applied the statutory standard of guilt. We believe, however, that the State has not proved that defendant committed deviate sexual acts by force or threat of force as required by statute. Consequently, the judgment of conviction for deviate sexual assault is reversed.

Harrison, Presiding Justice:

I respectfully dissent.

It is well settled that a victim need not resist when to do so would be futile or life endangering, or where she is overcome by superior strength or paralyzed by fear. Such was the case here. The victim testified that she did not scream because there was no one in the vicinity to hear her screams. She considered escaping but decided that an attempt would be futile because she could not outrun the defendant in the woods. She testified that she resisted when he carried her into the woods, although she did not strike or otherwise physically assault him because of the likelihood that such behavior would anger him. She was overpowered by him physically (compare 5 ft. 2 in., 100 lbs. to 6 ft. 3 in., 185 lbs.) and felt extremely vulnerable in such an isolated area where no one was around to help her. Under these circumstances, where violent resistance might only have provoked the defendant, her acquiescence was reasonable and did not constitute consent.

In addition, the victim made an immediate complaint to a counseling center and to the police. A prompt complaint to authorities has been held sufficient corroboration. And even if uncorroborated, the testimony of the witness alone can be sufficient to justify the conviction if that testimony is clear and convincing. In my view, her account of the episode and the reasons explaining her behavior were clear and convincing. Therefore, I would affirm the defendant's conviction for deviate sexual assault.

Discussion Questions

1. Why is the majority not persuaded that physically lifting a stranger off her feet and carrying her some distance to an isolated wooded area constitutes the use of force? Should the relative sizes of the defendant and the complainant play a role in determining whether force was used?

2. How is force defined here? How is it related to a threat? Why does the Court conclude that a threat was not present?

3. What role does the fact that the woman complained promptly play in the dissent's analysis?

4. From the dissent's discussion, what appears to be the role of corroboration in sexual offenses in Illinois in 1983?

Problem

9.3 Consider the following facts from a Pennsylvania case:

> The complainant, a female college student, left her class, went to her dormitory room where she drank a martini, and then went to a lounge to await her boyfriend. When her boyfriend failed to appear, she went to another dormitory to find a friend, Earl Hassel. She knocked on the door, but received no answer. She tried the doorknob and, finding it unlocked, entered the room and discovered a man sleeping on the bed. The complainant originally believed the man to be Hassel, but it turned out to be Hassel's roommate, [the Defendant]. [He] asked her to stay for a while and she agreed. He requested a back-rub and she declined. He suggested that she sit on the bed, but she declined and sat on the floor
>
> [Defendant] then moved to the floor beside her, lifted up her shirt and bra and massaged her breasts. He then unfastened his pants and unsuccessfully attempted to put his penis in her mouth. They both stood up, and he locked the door. He returned to push her onto the bed, and removed her undergarments from one leg. He then penetrated her vagina with his penis. After withdrawing and ejaculating on her stomach, he stated, "Wow, I guess we just got carried away," to which she responded, "No, we didn't get carried away, you got carried away."
>
> The complainant repeatedly said "no" throughout the encounter, but took no physical action to discourage or impede the defendant. She states that the defendant "put me down on the bed. He didn't throw me on the bed. It was kind of like a push." She also states that the defendant's hands were not restraining her in any manner, though the weight of his body was on top of her. The evidence also shows that the door could have been easily unlocked and that the complainant was aware of this but did not attempt to unlock the door or leave the room.[4]

Has the defendant violated the following statutes?

---

4. Based upon and quotations from *Commonwealth v. Berkowitz*, 415 Pa. Super. 505 (1992).

Pennsylvania Consolidated Statutes

§ 3121. Rape

A person commits a felony of the first degree when he or she engages in sexual intercourse with a complainant:

(1) By forcible compulsion....

Pennsylvania Consolidated Statutes

§ 3124.1 Sexual Assault

Except as provided in section 3121 (relating to rape) or 3123 (relating to involuntary deviate sexual intercourse), a person commits a felony of the second degree when that person engages in sexual intercourse or deviate sexual intercourse with a complainant without the complainant's consent.

Idaho Code

§ 18-6101. Rape defined

Rape is defined as the penetration, however slight, of the oral, anal or vaginal opening with the perpetrator's penis accomplished with a female ...

(4) Where the victim resists but her resistance is overcome by force or violence....

Discussion Questions

1. What are the elements of each statute? What are the differences among the statutes?

2. How should "forcible compulsion" be interpreted? Is "forcible compulsion" something distinct from lack of consent? Does it incorporate lack of consent?

3. Do you favor having *both* force and a lack of consent elements? A force element without a lack of consent element? A lack of consent element without a force element? What do you see as the possible advantages and disadvantages of each of these approaches?

4. Reconsider the *Warren* case. Would Warren be liable under either Pennsylvania or Idaho law?

State in Interest of M.T.S.

129 N.J. 422 (1992)
Supreme Court of New Jersey

Handler, J.

Under New Jersey law a person who commits an act of sexual penetration using physical force or coercion is guilty of second-degree sexual assault. The sexual assault statute does not define the words "physical force." The question posed by this appeal is whether the element of "physical force" is met simply by an act of non-consensual penetration involving no more force than necessary to accomplish that result.

That issue is presented in the context of what is often referred to as "acquaintance rape." The record in the case discloses that the juvenile, a seventeen-year-old boy, engaged in consensual kissing and heavy petting with a fifteen-year-old girl and thereafter engaged in actual sexual penetration of the girl to which she had not consented. There was no evidence or suggestion that the juvenile used any unusual or extra force or threats to accomplish the act of penetration.

The trial court determined that the juvenile was delinquent for committing a sexual assault. The Appellate Division reversed the disposition of delinquency, concluding that non-consensual penetration does not constitute sexual assault unless it is accompanied by some level of force more than that necessary to accomplish the penetration. We granted the State's petition for certification....

The New Jersey Code of Criminal Justice, N.J.S.A. 2C:14-2c(1), defines "sexual assault" as the commission "of sexual penetration" "with another person" with the use of "physical force or coercion."[1] An unconstrained reading of the statutory language indicates that both the act of "sexual penetration" and the use of "physical force or coercion" are separate and distinct elements of the offense. Neither the definitions section of *N.J.S.A.* 2C:14-1 to -8, nor the remainder of the Code of Criminal Justice provides assistance in interpreting the words "physical force." The initial inquiry is, therefore, whether the statutory words are unambiguous on their face and can be understood and applied in accordance with their plain meaning....

The parties offer two alternative understandings of the concept of "physical force" as it is used in the statute. The State would read "physical force" to entail any amount of sexual touching brought about involuntarily. A showing of sexual penetration coupled with a lack of consent would satisfy the elements of the statute. The Public Defender urges an interpretation of "physical force" to mean force "used to overcome lack of consent." That definition equates force with violence and leads to the conclusion that sexual assault requires the application of some amount of force in addition to the act of penetration.

Current judicial practice suggests an understanding of "physical force" to mean "any degree of physical power or strength used against the victim, even though it entails no injury and leaves no mark." *Model Jury Charges, Criminal* 3 (revised Mar. 27, 1989).... The dictionary provides several definitions of "force," among which are the following: (1) "power, violence, compulsion, or constraint exerted upon or against a person or thing," (2) "a general term for exercise of strength or power, esp. physical, to overcome resistance," or (3) "strength or power of any degree that is exercised with-

---

1. The sexual assault statute, N.J.S.A.: 2C:14-2c(1), reads as follows:
   c. An actor is guilty of sexual assault if he commits an act of sexual penetration with another person under any one of the following circumstances:
   (1) The actor uses physical force or coercion, but the victim does not sustain severe personal injury; ...
Sexual assault is a crime of the second degree.

out justification or contrary to law upon a person or thing." *Webster's Third New International Dictionary* 887 (1961).

Thus, as evidenced by the disagreements among the lower courts and the parties, and the variety of possible usages, the statutory words "physical force" do not evoke a single meaning that is obvious and plain. Hence, we must pursue avenues of construction in order to ascertain the meaning of that statutory language. Those avenues are well charted. When a statute is open to conflicting interpretations, the court seeks the underlying intent of the legislature, relying on legislative history and the contemporary context of the statute. With respect to a law, like the sexual assault statute, that "alters or amends the previous law or creates or abolishes types of actions, it is important, in discovering the legislative intent, to ascertain the old law, the mischief and the proposed remedy." We also remain mindful of the basic tenet of statutory construction that penal statutes are to be strictly construed in favor of the accused. Nevertheless, the construction must conform to the intent of the Legislature. . . .

Under traditional rape law, in order to prove that a rape had occurred, the state had to show both that force had been used and that the penetration had been against the woman's will. Force was identified and determined not as an independent factor but in relation to the response of the victim, which in turn implicated the victim's own state of mind. "Thus, the perpetrator's use of force became criminal only if the victim's state of mind met the statutory requirement. The perpetrator could use all the force imaginable and no crime would be committed if the state could not prove additionally that the victim did not consent." Although the terms "non-consent" and "against her will" were often treated as equivalent, under the traditional definition of rape, both formulations squarely placed on the victim the burden of proof and of action. Effectively, a woman who was above the age of consent had actively and affirmatively to withdraw that consent for the intercourse to be against her will. As a Delaware court stated, "[i]f sexual intercourse is obtained by milder means, or with the consent or silent submission of the female, it cannot constitute the crime of rape."

The presence or absence of consent often turned on credibility. To demonstrate that the victim had not consented to the intercourse, and also that sufficient force had been used to accomplish the rape, the state had to prove that the victim had resisted. According to the oft-quoted Lord Hale, to be deemed a credible witness, a woman had to be of good fame, disclose the injury immediately, suffer signs of injury, and cry out for help. Courts and commentators historically distrusted the testimony of victims, "assuming that women lie about their lack of consent for various reasons: to blackmail men, to explain the discovery of a consensual affair, or because of psychological illness." Evidence of resistance was viewed as a solution to the credibility problem; it was the "outward manifestation of nonconsent, [a] device for determining whether a woman actually gave consent."

The resistance requirement had a profound effect on the kind of conduct that could be deemed criminal and on the type of evidence needed to establish the crime. . . . In many jurisdictions the requirement was that the woman have resisted

to the utmost…."[A] mere tactical surrender in the face of an assumed superior physical force is not enough. Where the penalty for the defendant may be supreme, so
must resistance be unto the uttermost." Other states followed a "reasonableness" standard, while some required only sufficient resistance to make non-consent reasonably
manifest….

That the law put the rape victim on trial was clear. The resistance requirement
had another untoward influence on traditional rape law. Resistance was necessary
not only to prove non-consent but also to demonstrate that the force used by the defendant had been sufficient to overcome the victim's will. The amount of force used
by the defendant was assessed in relation to the resistance of the victim. In New
Jersey, the amount of force necessary to establish rape was characterized as "'the
degree of force sufficient to overcome any resistance that had been put up by the female.'" Resistance, often demonstrated by torn clothing and blood, was a sign that
the defendant had used significant force to accomplish the sexual intercourse. Thus,
if the defendant forced himself on a woman, it was her responsibility to fight back,
because force was measured in relation to the resistance she put forward. Only if she
resisted, causing him to use more force than was necessary to achieve penetration,
would his conduct be criminalized. Indeed, the significance of resistance as the proxy
for force is illustrated by cases in which victims were unable to resist; in such cases
the force incident to penetration was deemed sufficient to establish the "force" element
of the offense.

The importance of resistance as an evidentiary requirement set the law of rape
apart from other common-law crimes, particularly in the eyes of those who advocated
reform of rape law in the 1970s….

They emphasized that rape had its legal origins in laws designed to protect the
property rights of men to their wives and daughters. Although the crime had evolved
into an offense against women, reformers argued that vestiges of the old law remained,
particularly in the understanding of rape as a crime against the purity or chastity of
a woman. The burden of protecting that chastity fell on the woman, with the state
offering its protection only after the woman demonstrated that she had resisted sufficiently….

Critics of rape law agreed that the focus of the crime should be shifted from the
victim's behavior to the defendant's conduct, and particularly to its forceful and assaultive, rather than sexual, character. Reformers also shared the goals of facilitating
rape prosecutions and of sparing victims much of the degradation involved in bringing
and trying a charge of rape…. [A]ll proponents of reform shared a central premise:
that the burden of showing non-consent should not fall on the victim of the crime.
In dealing with the problem of consent the reform goal was not so much to purge
the entire concept of consent from the law as to eliminate the burden that had been
placed on victims to prove they had not consented.

Similarly, with regard to force, rape law reform sought to give independent significance to the forceful or assaultive conduct of the defendant and to avoid a defi-

nition of force that depended on the reaction of the victim. Traditional interpretations of force were strongly criticized for failing to acknowledge that force may be understood simply as the invasion of "bodily integrity." In urging that the "resistance" requirement be abandoned, reformers sought to break the connection between force and resistance.

The history of traditional rape law sheds clearer light on the factors that became most influential in the enactment of current law dealing with sexual offenses....

Since the 1978 reform, the Code has referred to the crime that was once known as "rape" as "sexual assault." The crime now requires "penetration," not "sexual intercourse." It requires "force" or "coercion," not "submission" or "resistance." It makes no reference to the victim's state of mind or attitude, or conduct in response to the assault.... It emphasizes the assaultive character of the offense by defining sexual penetration to encompass a wide range of sexual contacts, going well beyond traditional "carnal knowledge."[2] Consistent with the assaultive character, as opposed to the traditional sexual character, of the offense, the statute also renders the crime gender-neutral: both males and females can be actors or victims....

The Legislature's concept of sexual assault and the role of force was significantly colored by its understanding of the law of assault and battery. As a general matter, criminal battery is defined as "the unlawful application of force to the person of another." The application of force is criminal when it results in either (a) a physical injury or (b) an offensive touching. Any "unauthorized touching of another [is] a battery. Thus, by eliminating all references to the victim's state of mind and conduct, and by broadening the definition of penetration to cover not only sexual intercourse between a man and a woman but a range of acts that invade another's body or compel intimate contact, the Legislature emphasized the affinity between sexual assault and other forms of assault and battery....

The understanding of sexual assault as a criminal battery, albeit one with especially serious consequences, follows necessarily from the Legislature's decision to eliminate nonconsent and resistance from the substantive definition of the offense. Under the new law, the victim no longer is required to resist and therefore need not have said or done anything in order for the sexual penetration to be unlawful. The alleged victim is not put on trial, and his or her responsive or defensive behavior is rendered immaterial. We are thus satisfied that an interpretation of the statutory crime of sexual assault to require physical force in addition to that entailed in an act of involuntary or unwanted sexual penetration would be fundamentally inconsistent with

---

2. The reform replaced the concept of carnal abuse, which was limited to vaginal intercourse, with specific kinds of sexual acts contained in a broad definition of penetration: Sexual penetration means vaginal intercourse, cunnilingus, fellatio or anal intercourse between persons or insertion of the hand, finger or object into the anus or vagina either by the actor or upon the actor's instruction. [N.J.S.A. 2C:14-1.]

the legislative purpose to eliminate any consideration of whether the victim resisted or expressed non-consent....

We conclude, therefore, that any act of sexual penetration engaged in by the defendant without the affirmative and freely-given permission of the victim to the specific act of penetration constitutes the offense of sexual assault. Therefore, physical force in excess of that inherent in the act of sexual penetration is not required for such penetration to be unlawful. The definition of "physical force" is satisfied under N.J.S.A. 2C:14-2c(1) if the defendant applies any amount of force against another person in the absence of what a reasonable person would believe to be affirmative and freely-given permission to the act of sexual penetration.

Under the reformed statute, permission to engage in sexual penetration must be affirmative and it must be given freely, but that permission may be inferred either from acts or statements reasonably viewed in light of the surrounding circumstances....

Our understanding of the meaning and application of "physical force" under the sexual assault statute indicates that the term's inclusion was neither inadvertent nor redundant. The term "physical force," like its companion term "coercion," acts to qualify the nature and character of the "sexual penetration." Sexual penetration accomplished through the use of force is unauthorized sexual penetration. That functional understanding of "physical force" encompasses the notion of "unpermitted touching" derived from the Legislature's decision to redefine rape as a sexual assault. As already noted, under assault and battery doctrine, any amount of force that results in either physical injury or offensive touching is sufficient to establish a battery. Hence, as a description of the method of achieving "sexual penetration," the term "physical force" serves to define and explain the acts that are offensive, unauthorized, and unlawful.

That understanding of the crime of sexual assault fully comports with the public policy sought to be effectuated by the Legislature. In redefining rape law as sexual assault, the Legislature adopted the concept of sexual assault as a crime against the bodily integrity of the victim. Although it is possible to imagine a set of rules in which persons must demonstrate affirmatively that sexual contact is unwanted or not permitted, such a regime would be inconsistent with modern principles of personal autonomy. The Legislature recast the law of rape as sexual assault to bring that area of law in line with the expectation of privacy and bodily control that long has characterized most of our private and public law. In interpreting "physical force" to include any touching that occurs without permission we seek to respect that goal....

Each person has the right not only to decide whether to engage in sexual contact with another, but also to control the circumstances and character of that contact. No one, neither a spouse, nor a friend, nor an acquaintance, nor a stranger, has the right or the privilege to force sexual contact.

We emphasize as well that what is now referred to as "acquaintance rape" is not a new phenomenon. Nor was it a "futuristic" concept in 1978 when the sexual assault law was enacted. Current concern over the prevalence of forced sexual intercourse between persons who know one another reflects both greater awareness of the extent of such behavior and a growing appreciation of its gravity. Notwithstanding the stereotype of rape as a violent attack by a stranger, the vast majority of sexual assaults are perpetrated by someone known to the victim. One respected study indicates that more than half of all rapes are committed by male relatives, current or former husbands, boyfriends or lovers. Similarly, contrary to common myths, perpetrators generally do not use guns or knives and victims generally do not suffer external bruises or cuts. Although this more realistic and accurate view of rape only recently has achieved widespread public circulation, it was a central concern of the proponents of reform in the 1970s.

The insight into rape as an assaultive crime is consistent with our evolving understanding of the wrong inherent in forced sexual intimacy....

In a case such as this one, in which the State does not allege violence or force extrinsic to the act of penetration, the factfinder must decide whether the defendant's act of penetration was undertaken in circumstances that led the defendant reasonably to believe that the alleged victim had freely given affirmative permission to the specific act of sexual penetration....

In these cases neither the alleged victim's subjective state of mind nor the reasonableness of the alleged victim's actions can be deemed relevant to the offense. The alleged victim may be questioned about what he or she did or said only to determine whether the defendant was reasonable in believing that affirmative permission had been freely given....

If there is evidence to suggest that the defendant reasonably believed that such permission had been given, the State must demonstrate either that defendant did not actually believe that affirmative permission had been freely-given or that such a belief was unreasonable under all of the circumstances. Thus, the State bears the burden of proof throughout the case....

Because "physical force" as an element of sexual assault in this context requires the *absence* of affirmative and freely-given permission, the "consent" necessary to negate such "physical force" under a defense based on consent would require the *presence* of such affirmative and freely-given permission. Any lesser form of consent would render the sexual penetration unlawful and cannot constitute a defense....

We acknowledge that cases such as this are inherently fact sensitive and depend on the reasoned judgment and common sense of judges and juries. The trial court concluded that the victim had not expressed consent to the act of intercourse, either through her words or actions. We conclude that the record provides reasonable support for the trial court's disposition.

Accordingly, we reverse the judgment of the Appellate Division and reinstate the disposition of juvenile delinquency for the commission of second-degree sexual assault.

Discussion Questions

1. What method of statutory interpretation is Justice Handler using in the M.T.S. case? Textualist? Intentionalist? Dynamic?

2. Is the offensive touching element in criminal battery as described in M.T.S. subjective or objective? Is a lack of consent element in a rape statute subjective or objective? What about an affirmative permission requirement?

3. Under the M.T.S. case, what are the elements of second degree sexual assault in New Jersey?

4. Are force and penetration redundant in New Jersey in sexual assault cases involving intercourse after *M.T.S.*? What about force and lack of consent?

* * *

2. Other Types of Coercion

"The law of rape has generally refused to recognize coercion, apart from physical violence or threats of it."[5] As an example, consider Professor Schulhofer's discussion of *Commonwealth v. Biggs*, 320 Pa. Super. 265 (1983):

> In Pennsylvania, John Biggs repeatedly had sex with his seventeen-year-old daughter. He told her that if she told anyone, he would show people nude pictures of her. If he had forced her to pay him in cash for not showing the pictures, he would be guilty of blackmail, a serious felony in nearly all states. But Biggs could not be convicted of blackmail because he obtained sex, not money. At the same time he could not be convicted of rape, because, as the appellate court put it, he obtained his daughter's compliance "by threats, not of force, but of humiliation."[6]

The statutes of some jurisdictions now permit convictions for sexual offenses when coercion involves a threat other than a threat of physical force.

3. Fraud

The traditional law of rape permitted convictions based upon fraud only in limited circumstances. The first generally involved medical examinations if the doctor deceived a woman into believing that he was using an appropriate medical instrument to examine her, and instead penetrated her with his penis. In these cases, courts have treated women as deceived about the essential fact of intercourse, i.e., the patient consented to a medical exam, not intercourse. The second type of case that courts recognized as rape based on fraud was when the perpetrator deceived a woman into

---

5. Stephen Schulhofer, Unwanted Sex: The Culture of Intimidation and the Failure of Law, 114 (Harv. U. Press 1998).

6. *Id.*

believing that he was her husband. Although the law found this harder to classify as deception regarding the essential fact of intercourse, courts have, although not consistently, convicted defendants of rape in this situation.[7] Some state statutes address these situations:

Colorado Revised Statutes

§ 18-3-402. Sexual assault

(1) Any actor who knowingly inflicts sexual intrusion or sexual penetration on a victim commits sexual assault if: ...

  c) The actor knows that the victim submits erroneously, believing the actor to be the victim's spouse; or ...

  g) The actor, while purporting to offer a medical service, engages in treatment or examination of a victim for other than a bona fide medical purpose or in a manner substantially inconsistent with reasonable medical practices.

* * *

Outside the contexts considered above, the law historically refused to recognize as rape some types of deception used to persuade the complainant to consent to intercourse.[8] According to Professor Patricia Falk, "[t]he legislative prohibition of sexual penetration or contact accomplished by fraud that occurs outside of professional treatment contexts continues to be a difficult problem. No doubt wary of casting their nets too wide, state legislatures have been quite conservative, tending to enact very specific provisions to cover a few factual scenarios rather than passing more global fraud statutes."[9] But there are exceptions. Consider the following statute.

Tennessee Code Annotated

§ 39-13-503. Rape

(a) Rape is unlawful sexual penetration of a victim by the defendant or of the defendant by a victim accompanied by any of the following circumstances: ...

  (4) The sexual penetration is accomplished by fraud.

* * *

In 1999, a man convicted of rape and attempted rape under the Tennessee statute challenged the validity of its rape by fraud provision.[10] The appellant, who "came to be known as the 'Fantasy Man,' would call young women late at night, impersonating their fiancé or lover." He would tell the woman that "he had a special fantasy from

7. WAYNE LAFAVE, CRIMINAL LAW 767 (3d ed. 2000). The law often labeled these types of fraud, "fraud in the factum."

8. *Id.* This type of fraud generally fell under the rubric, "fraud in the inducement."

9. Patricia J. Falk, *Rape by Fraud and Rape by Coercion*, 64 BROOK. L. REV. 39, 118–119 (1998).

10. *Tennessee v. Mitchell*, 1999 Tenn. Crim. App. LEXIS 772 (1999).

the movie, *Nine and ½ Weeks*, and that he wanted her to act out a scene from the movie with him." The fantasy involved the women blindfolding themselves and waiting unclothed for the appellant with the understanding that they would then "act out the fantasy and have sexual intercourse...."

Was appellant's conduct covered by the Tennessee statute?

Defining fraud has challenged legislators and scholars. Should fraud encompass a defendant who falsely promises to marry the complainant if the complainant agrees to intercourse? What about one who falsely claims he is not married?

4. Lack of Consent

Although the materials already presented in this chapter raise issues related to consent, we examine the issue in greater depth in the materials that follow. Recall that the common law definition of rape required that the act be committed both "forcibly," the subject covered in-depth earlier in the chapter, and "against her will," the subject of this section. This section begins with the traditional view of consent and its relationship to resistance and progresses to more modern treatments of consent.

a. *The Traditional View*

Brown v. State
127 Wis. 193 (1906)
Supreme Court of Wisconsin

Dodge, J.

... As the statement of facts discloses, the only mooted question was that of prosecutrix's physical resistance to the act of intercourse, and, as to this, counsel for plaintiff in error urges, with great force, that there was not evidence sufficient to satisfy any reasonable mind, beyond reasonable doubt, of such resistance as the law makes sine qua non to the crime of rape. We need not reiterate those considerations of the ease of assertion of the forcible accomplishment of the sexual act, with impossibility of defense save by direct denial, or of the proneness of the woman, when she finds the fact of her disgrace discovered or likely of discovery, to minimize her fault by asserting vis major, which have led courts, and none more strenuously than this, to hold to a very strict rule of proof in such cases. Not only must there be entire absence of mental consent or assent, but there must be the most vehement exercise of every physical means or faculty within the woman's power to resist the penetration of her person, and this must be shown to persist until the offense is consummated. We need not mention the exception where the power of resistance is overcome by unconsciousness, threats, or exhaustion, for, in this case, there is no proof of any of those things. Further, it is settled in this state that no mere general statements of the prosecutrix, involving her conclusions, that she did her utmost and the like, will suffice to establish this essential fact, but she must relate the very acts done, in order that the jury and the court may judge whether any were omitted. Turning to the testimony of prosecutrix, we find it limited to the general statement, often repeated, that she tried as hard as she could to get away. Except for one demand, when first seized, to "let me go," and inarticulate screams, she mentions no verbal protests. While we would reasonably recognize the limitations resting on many people in attempting expression and description, we cannot conceive it possible that one whose mind and exertions had, during an encounter of this sort, been set on resistance, could or would in narrative mention nothing but escape or withdrawal. A woman's means of protection are not limited to that, but she is equipped to interpose most effective obstacles by means of hands and limbs and pelvic muscles. Indeed, medical writers insist that these obstacles are practically insuperable in absence of more than the usual relative disproportion of age and strength between man and woman, though no such impossibility is recognized as a rule of law. In addition to the interposition of such obstacles is the ability and tendency of reprisal, of counter physical attack. It is hardly within the range of reason that a man should come out of so desperate an encounter as the determined normal woman would make necessary, without signs thereof upon his face, hands, or clothing. Yet this prosecutrix, of at least fair intelligence, education, and ability of expression, in her narrative mentions no single act of resistance or reprisal. It is inconceivable that such efforts should have been forgotten if they were made, or should fail of prominence in her narrative. The distinction between escape and resistance is admirably discussed by Ryan, C. J., in *State v. Welch*, 37 Wis. 201. Resistance is opposing force to force (Bouvier), not retreating from force. These illustrations but serve to point the radical difference between the mental conception of resistance and escape and emphasize the improbability that if the former existed only the latter would have been mentioned. This court does not hold, with some, that, as matter of law, rape cannot be established by the uncorroborated testimony of the sufferer, but, in common with all courts, recognizes that, without such corroboration, her testimony must be most clear and convincing. Among the corroborating circumstances almost universally present in cases of actual rape are the signs and marks of the struggle upon the clothing and persons of the participants, and the complaint by the sufferer at the earliest opportunity. In the present case the former is absolutely wanting, for the one-inch rip in prosecutrix's underwear was not shown to be of a character or location significant of force or violence. Not a bruise or scratch on either was proved, and none existed on prosecutrix, for she was carefully examined by physicians. Her outer clothing not only presented no tearing, but no disarray, so far as the testimony goes. When one pauses to reflect upon the terrific resistance which the determined woman should make, such a situation is wellnigh incredible. The significance of the other corroborative circumstance, that of immediate disclosure, is much weakened in this case by the fact that prosecutrix turned from her way to friends and succor to arrange her underclothing and there discovered a condition making silence impossible. Such facts cannot but suggest a doubt whether her encounter would ever have been disclosed had not the discovery of blood aroused her fear that she was injured and must seek medical aid, or at least that she could not conceal from her family what had taken place. Nor is this thoughtfulness of the disarrangement of her clothing consistent with the outraged woman's terror-stricken flight to friends to give the alarm and seek aid which is to be expected. We are convinced that there was no evidence of the resistance which is essential to the crime of rape, and that the motion for new trial should have been granted on that ground.

Judgment and sentence reversed, and cause remanded for a new trial.

Discussion Questions

1. What purposes would a resistance requirement serve?

2. Do you think the judge's assumptions about female behavior in response to sexual aggression were realistic in 1906? Do you they are realistic today?

b. Consent in Transition

People v. Barnes

42 Cal. 3d 284 (1986)
Supreme Court of California

Bird, C. J.

At common law, the crime of rape was defined as "the carnal knowledge of a woman forcibly and against her will." Historically, it was considered inconceivable that a woman who truly did not consent to sexual intercourse would not meet force with force. The law originally demanded "utmost resistance" from the woman to ensure she had submitted rather than consented.

California long ago rejected this "primitive rule" of utmost resistance. "A woman who is assaulted need not resist to the point of risking being beaten into insensibility. If she resists to the point where further resistance would be useless or, ... until her resistance is overcome by force or violence, submission thereafter is not consent." In our state, it had long been the rule that the resistance required by former section 261, subdivision 2, was only that which would reasonably manifest refusal to consent to the act of sexual intercourse.

Nevertheless, courts refused to uphold a conviction of rape by force where the complainant had exhibited little or no resistance. The law demanded some measure of resistance, for it remained a tenet that a virtuous woman would by nature resist a sexual attack.

The requirement that a woman resist her attacker appears to have been grounded in the basic distrust with which courts and commentators traditionally viewed a woman's testimony regarding sexual assault....

Such wariness of the complainant's credibility created "an exaggerated insistence on evidence of resistance." As an objective indicator of nonconsent, the requirement of resistance insured against wrongful conviction based solely on testimony the law considered to be inherently suspect. In our state, it supplied a type of intrinsic corroboration of the prosecuting witness's testimony, a collateral demanded even when extrinsic corroboration was not required. Thus did the resistance requirement continue even in its modified form, to nurture and reflect the perspective, still held by some modern commentators, that "human nature will impel an unwilling woman to resist unlawful sexual intercourse with great effort."

Recently, however, the entire concept of resistance to sexual assault has been called into question.... It has been suggested that while the presence of resistance may well be probative on the issue of force or nonconsent, its absence may not.

For example, some studies have demonstrated that while some women respond to sexual assault with active resistance, others "freeze." One researcher found that many women demonstrate "psychological infantilism"—a frozen fright response—in the face of sexual assault. The "frozen fright" response resembles cooperative behavior. Indeed, as Symonds notes, the "victim may smile, even initiate acts, and may appear relaxed and calm." Subjectively, however, she may be in a state of terror. Symonds also reports that the victim may make submissive signs to her assailant and engage in propitiating behavior in an effort to inhibit further aggression. These findings belie the traditional notion that a woman who does not resist has consented. They suggest that lack of physical resistance may reflect a "profound primal terror" rather than consent.

Additionally, a growing body of authority holds that to resist in the face of sexual assault is to risk further injury. In a 1976 study of rape victims and offenders, the Queen's Bench Foundation found that over half of the sexual assault offenders studied reported becoming more violent in response to victim resistance. Injury as reported by victims correlated with some form of resistance, including verbal stalling, struggling and slapping. Those victims who resisted during coitus suffered increased violence as the assailant forced compliance. Victim resistance, whether passive or active, tended to precede an increase or intensification of the assailant's violence.

On the other hand, other findings indicate that resistance has a direct correlation with *deterring* sexual assault. Of the 75 convicted rapists the Queen's Bench Foundation questioned, half believed that their sexual assaults could have been deterred by active victim resistance. [Susan] Brownmiller argues that submissive behavior is *not* necessarily helpful to a rape victim and suggests that strong resistance on the part of women can thwart rape. She suggests it would be well for women to undergo systematic training in self-defense in order to fight back against their attackers.

Reflecting the foregoing uncertainties about the advisability of resistance, the Queen's Bench Foundation concluded: "Overall, the research findings suggest that rape prevention is more possible through vigorous resistance[;] however, resistance incurs greater risk of injury. When confronted with attack, each woman must make a choice which is highly personal and may be affected by situational factors beyond her control." These conclusions are also contained in a pamphlet for distribution to the general public in which the reader is advised that physical resistance may increase the danger or may thwart the attack; the woman must therefore evaluate the threat she faces and decide how to react based on the kind of person she is.

In sum, it is not altogether clear what the absence of resistance indicates in relation to the issue of consent. Nor is it *necessarily* advisable for one who is assaulted to resist the attack. It is at least arguable that if it fails to deter, resistance may well increase the risk of bodily injury to the victim. This possibility, as well as the evolution in societal expectations as to the level of danger a woman should risk when faced with sexual assault, are reflected in the Legislature's elimination of the resistance requirement. In so amending section 261, subdivision (2), the Legislature has demonstrated its unwillingness to dictate a prescribed response to sexual assault. For the first time, the Legislature has assigned the decision as to whether a sexual assault should be resisted to the realm of personal choice.

The elimination of the resistance requirement is also consistent with the modern trend of removing evidentiary obstacles unique to the prosecution of sexual assault cases. For example, in enacting section 1112 in 1980, the Legislature barred psychiatric examinations of rape complainants which had been authorized.... In recent years, the Legislature has also prohibited the instructional admonition that an "unchaste woman" is more likely to consent than her chaste counterpart ... and has largely precluded the use of evidence of a complaining witness's sexual conduct to prove consent.

This court has made similar strides. Over a decade ago, the use of CALJIC No. 10.22, embodying the deprecatory "Hale instruction,"[18] was disapproved. That holding laid to juridical rest the notion that "those who claim to be victims of sexual offenses are presumptively entitled to less credence than those who testify as the alleged victims of other crimes." ...

By removing resistance as a prerequisite to a rape conviction, the Legislature has brought the law of rape into conformity with other crimes such as robbery, kidnapping and assault, which require force, fear, and nonconsent to convict. In these crimes, the law does not expect falsity from the complainant who alleges their commission and thus demand resistance as a corroboration and predicate to conviction. Nor does the law expect that in defending oneself or one's property from these crimes, a person must risk injury or death by displaying resistance in the face of attack. The amendment of section 261, subdivision (2), acknowledges that previous expectational disparities, which singled out the credibility of rape complainants as suspect, have no place in a modern system of jurisprudence.

This court therefore concludes that the Legislature's purposes in amending section 261 were (1) to relieve the state of the need to establish resistance as a prerequisite to

---

18. Former CALJIC No. 10.22 read: "'A charge such as that made against the defendant in this case is one which is easily made and, once made, difficult to defend against, even if the person accused is innocent. [¶.] Therefore, the law requires that you examine the testimony of the female person named in the information with caution.'" (*People v. Rincon-Pineda, supra,* 14 Cal.3d at p. 871.) The instruction was based on Sir Matthew Hale's well-worn 17th century admonition that the testimony of "sometimes ... malicious and false" rape complainants must be cautiously scrutinized since rape "'is an accusation easily to be made and hard to be proved, and harder to be defended by the party accused, tho never so innocent.' [Citation.]" (*Id.,* at pp. 873, 874, 875.)

a rape conviction, and (2) to release rape complainants from the potentially dangerous burden of resisting an assailant in order to substantiate allegations of forcible rape.

As noted, it is no longer proper to instruct the jury that it must find the complainant resisted before it may return a verdict of guilt. Nor may lack of resistance be employed by courts—like the Court of Appeal here—to support a finding of insufficient evidence of rape under section 261, subdivision (2).[19]

* * *

Consider the following definitions of consent. The first three are found in statutes. The fourth is from the Antioch College Sexual Offense Policy. Upon whom does the burden regarding consent fall in each?

Wisconsin Statutes

§ 940.225. Sexual assault

(4) "Consent", as used in this section, means words or overt actions by a person who is competent to give informed consent indicating a freely given agreement to have sexual intercourse or sexual contact.

Florida Statutes

§ 794.011. Sexual battery

(a) "Consent" means intelligent, knowing, and voluntary consent and does not include coerced submission. "Consent" shall not be deemed or construed to mean the failure by the alleged victim to offer physical resistance to the offender.

Illinois Compiled Statutes

§ 11-1.70. Defenses

(a) It shall be a defense to any offense under [the sexual offense section of this Code] … where force or threat of force is an element of the offense that the victim consented. "Consent" means a freely given agreement to the act of sexual penetration or sexual conduct in question. Lack of verbal or physical resistance or submission by the victim resulting from the use of force or threat of force by the accused shall not constitute consent. The manner of dress of the victim at the time of the offense shall not constitute consent.

---

19. The statutory change does not mean that when resistance does exist, it is irrelevant to nonconsent. Absence of resistance may also continue to be probative of whether the accused honestly and reasonably believed he was engaging in consensual sex. (See *People v. Mayberry*, (1975) 15 Cal.3d 143, 155 [125 Cal.Rptr. 745, 542 P.2d 1337].)

The Antioch College Sexual Offense Policy (Consent)

1. For the purpose of this policy, "consent" shall be defined as follows: the act of willingly and verbally agreeing to engage in specific sexual contact or conduct.

2. If sexual contact and/or conduct is not mutually and simultaneously initiated, then the person who initiates sexual contact/conduct is responsible for getting the verbal consent of the other individual(s) involved.

* * *

5. The Model Penal Code

a. Original Provisions

Unlike traditional approaches to rape, the Model Penal Code's original provisions on rape and other sexual offenses do not formally include a lack of consent provision. Instead, they focus on force or compulsion. These provisions on rape and related offenses follow:

Model Penal Code

§ 213.1. Rape and Related Offenses

(1) <u>Rape</u>. A male who has sexual intercourse with a female not his wife is guilty of rape if:

a) he compels her to submit by force or by threat of imminent death, serious bodily injury, extreme pain or kidnapping, to be inflicted on anyone; or

b) he has substantially impaired her power to appraise or control her conduct by administering or employing without her knowledge drugs, intoxicants or other means for the purpose of preventing resistance; or

c) the female is unconscious; or

d) the female is less than 10 years old.

Rape is a felony of the second degree unless i) in the course thereof the actor inflicts serious bodily injury upon anyone, or ii) the victim was not a voluntary social companion of the actor upon the occasion of the crime and had not previously permitted him sexual liberties, in which cases the offense is a felony of the first degree.

(2) Gross Sexual Imposition. A male who has sexual intercourse with a female not his wife commits a felony of the third degree if:

a) he compels her to submit by any threat that would prevent resistance by a woman of ordinary resolution; or

b) he knows she suffers from a mental disease or defect which renders her incapable of appraising the nature of her conduct; or

c) he knows that she is unaware that a sexual act is being committed upon her or that she submits because she mistakenly supposes that he is her husband.

Discussion Questions

1. How do the elements in the MPC provision on rape differ from the elements in Blackstone's definition?

2. What are the consequences of eliminating consent as an element? Do the MPC provisions focus more on the defendant or on the complainant?

3. Under the MPC provisions, would it matter if the complainant had been out drinking at a bar or had worn revealing clothing?

4. Under the MPC, would it matter if the defendant and the complainant had a prior relationship but had not had sexual contact?

b. Proposed MPC Revisions[11]

When the MPC's original sexual offense provisions were written and adopted six decades ago, in the late 1950s and early 1960s, they were progressive in several respects for their time. They reflected the social attitudes and values of the era in which they were written. In the intervening decades, these attitudes and values changed, driven in large part by the feminist movement. During those years, these sections of the MPC have become the focal point of substantial criticism.[12] In response, the American Law Institute has drafted proposed revisions, including those that appear below. Some aspects of these revisions have sparked continuing controversy.[13]

§ 213.1. Forcible Rape

(1) An actor is guilty of Forcible Rape if he or she causes another person to engage in an act of sexual penetration or oral sex by knowingly or recklessly:

   (a) using physical force or restraint, or making an express or implied threat of bodily injury or physical force or restraint; or

   (b) making an express or implied threat to inflict bodily injury on someone else.

Forcible Rape is a felony of the second degree and a registrable offense.

(2) *Aggravated Forcible Rape.* An actor is guilty of Aggravated Forcible Rape if he or she violates subsection (1) of this Section and in doing so:

   (a) knowingly uses a deadly weapon to cause the other person to engage in the act of sexual penetration or oral sex; or

   (b) knowingly acts with one or more persons who participate in the sexual penetration or oral sex, or who assist in the use of force, threat, or restraint when it occurs; or

---

11. At the time of this writing, the ALI's revisions are under consideration but have not yet been adopted. The revisions that appear here are from Tentative Draft No. 3 (2017).

12. Deborah W. Denno, *Why the Model Penal Code's Sexual Offense Provisions Should Be Pulled and Replaced*, 1 Ohio St. J. Crim. L. 207 (2003).

13. Robert Weisberg, *Sexual Offenses*, Reforming Criminal Justice: A Report by the Academy of Justice Vol. 1, 139 (2017).

(c) knowingly or recklessly causes serious bodily injury to the other person or to someone else.

Aggravated Forcible Rape is a felony of the first degree and a registrable offense.

§ 213.4 *Sexual Penetration or Oral Sex without Consent*

(1) An actor is guilty of Sexual Penetration or Oral Sex Without Consent if he or she knowingly or recklessly engages in an act of sexual penetration or oral sex without the consent of the other person.

(2) Sexual Penetration or Oral Sex Without Consent is a felony of the fifth degree, except that it is a felony of the fourth degree when the act occurs in disregard of the other person's expressed unwillingness, or is so sudden or unexpected that the other person has no adequate opportunity to express unwillingness before the act occurs.

Discussion Questions

1. How do the offense elements in the MPC revisions differ from the original MPC provisions?

2. What positions do the MPC revisions adopt in regard to the issues we addressed earlier in this chapter?

3. Which aspects of the MPC revisions do you think sparked controversy and debate?

D. Mental States

1. Regarding Force or Fear

Statutes dealing with sexual offenses are frequently silent on the issue of mental state concerning force. Should any mental state be required? If so, what mental state? What inference should be drawn from legislative silence on this issue? How would such silence be treated under the Model Penal Code?

The question of the accused's mental state regarding force rarely arises in cases involving guns, knives, other weapons, or explicit threats of violence. In those circumstances, it is highly likely that the accused had purpose or knowledge with respect to the use of force. In other circumstances, the issue of mental state proves more difficult. For example, when the case involves the accused acting aggressively sexually and using a threatening tone of voice in pursuing sexual contact and the accused is substantially larger than the victim, should prosecutors in rape cases have to prove a particular mental state regarding force?

Sometimes courts focus on the actor's mental state regarding a victim's fear rather than the actor's mental state regarding force, though these are closely related issues. For example, in Maryland, courts look to whether "the acts and threats of the defendant were reasonably calculated to create in the mind of the victim ... a real apprehension, due to fear, of imminent bodily harm...."[14] What does "reasonably calculated" mean here? What mental state should the law require with respect to a victim's fear?

Professor Kit Kinports explains that "[v]ery little attention has been paid to the mens rea applicable to the element of force, that is, the defendant's state of mind with respect to the presence of force."[15] She concludes that:

> the elements of force and nonconsent are duplicative of one another. A woman who did not consent to intercourse was, by definition, forced, and one who was forced did not consent. By the same token, a defendant who knew (or should have known) that the victim did not consent also knew (or should have known) that he was forcing her to submit. Therefore, proof of either lack of consent on the part of the victim or the use of force on the part of the defendant — plus the accompanying mens rea — ought to suffice to support a rape conviction. And the fact that courts routinely ignore questions of mens rea and force, in contravention of the general criminal law presumption that a mens rea requirement attaches to every material element of the crime, demonstrates that they too recognize, at least implicitly, that the traditional "conjunction of force and nonconsent" is ... "redundant."[16]

2. Regarding Lack of Consent

What mental state, if any, on the part of an actor is the prosecution required to prove regarding lack of consent? What mental state, if any, in your view should be required regarding lack of consent? Knowledge? Recklessness? Negligence?

Texas Code Annotated

§ 39-13-503. Rape

a) Rape is unlawful sexual penetration of a victim by the defendant or of the defendant by a victim accompanied by any of the following circumstances:

  (1) Force or coercion is used to accomplish the act;

  (2) The sexual penetration is accomplished without the consent of the victim and the defendant knows or has reason to know at the time of the penetration that the victim did not consent;

---

14. *State v. Rusk*, 289 Md. 230, 242 (1981) (quoting *Hazel v. State*, 221 Md. 464 (1960).
15. Kit Kinports, *Rape and Force: The Forgotten Mens Rea*, 4 Buff. Crim. L. Rev. 755, 759 (2001).
16. *Id.* at 798–799.

Sexual Offences Act 1956 [England]

Section: 1 Rape of woman or man

It is an offence for a man to rape a woman. [A] man commits rape if

(1) he has sexual intercourse with a woman [whether vaginal or anal] who at the time of the intercourse does not consent to it; and

(2) at the time he knows that she does not consent to the intercourse or is reckless as to whether she consents to it.

Commonwealth v. Lopez

433 Mass. 722 (2001)
Supreme Judicial Court of Massachusetts

Spina, J.

The defendant, Kenny Lopez, was convicted on two indictments charging rape and one indictment charging indecent assault and battery on a person over the age of fourteen years. We granted his application for direct appellate review. The defendant claims error in the judge's refusal to give a mistake of fact instruction to the jury. He asks us to recognize a defendant's honest and reasonable belief as to a complainant's consent as a defense to the crime of rape, and to reverse his convictions and grant him a new trial. Based on the record presented, we decline to do so, and affirm the convictions.

1. *Background.* We summarize facts that the jury could have found. On May 8, 1998, the victim, a seventeen year-old girl, was living in a foster home in Springfield. At approximately 3 P.M., she started walking to a restaurant where she had planned to meet her biological mother. On the way, she encountered the defendant. He introduced himself, asked where she was going, and offered to walk with her. The victim met her mother and introduced the defendant as her friend. The defendant said that he lived in the same foster home as the victim and that "they knew each other from school." Sometime later, the defendant left to make a telephone call. When the victim left the restaurant, the defendant was waiting outside and offered to walk her home. She agreed.

The two walked to a park across the street from the victim's foster home and talked for approximately twenty to thirty minutes. The victim's foster sisters were within earshot, and the victim feared that she would be caught violating her foster mother's rules against bringing "a guy near the house." The defendant suggested that they take a walk in the woods nearby. At one point, deep in the woods, the victim said that she wanted to go home. The defendant said, "trust me," and assured her that nothing would happen and that he would not hurt her. The defendant led the victim down a path to a secluded area.

The defendant asked the victim why she was so distant and said that he wanted to start a relationship with her. She said that she did not want to "get into any relationship." The defendant began making sexual innuendos to which the victim did not respond. He grabbed her by her wrist and began kissing her on the lips. She pulled away and said, "No, I don't want to do this." The defendant then told the victim that if she "had sex with him, [she] would love him more." She repeated, "No, I don't want to. I don't want to do this." He raised her shirt and touched her breasts. She immediately pulled her shirt down and pushed him away.

The defendant then pushed the victim against a slate slab, unbuttoned her pants, and pulled them down. Using his legs to pin down her legs, he produced a condom and asked her to put it on him. The victim said, "No." The defendant put the condom on and told the victim that he wanted her to put his penis inside her. She said, "No." He then raped her, and she began to cry. A few minutes later, the victim made a "jerking move" to her left. The defendant became angry, turned her around, pushed her face into the slate, and raped her again. The treating physician described the bruising to the victim's knees as "significant." The physician opined that there had been "excessive force and trauma to the [vaginal] area" based on his observation that there was "a lot of swelling" in her external vaginal area and her hymen had been torn and was "still oozing." The doctor noted that in his experience it was "fairly rare" to see that much swelling and trauma.

The defendant told the victim that she "would get in a lot of trouble" if she said anything. He then grabbed her by the arm, kissed her, and said, "I'll see you later." The victim went home and showered. She told her foster mother, who immediately dialed 911. The victim cried hysterically as she spoke to the 911 operator.

The defendant's version of the encounter was diametrically opposed to that of the victim. He testified that the victim had been a willing and active partner in consensual sexual intercourse. Specifically, the defendant claimed that the victim initiated intimate activity, and never once told him to stop. Additionally, the defendant testified that the victim invited him to a party that evening so that he could meet her friends. The defendant further claimed that when he told her that he would be unable to attend, the victim appeared "mildly upset."

Before the jury retired, defense counsel requested a mistake of fact instruction as to consent.[1] The judge declined to give the instruction, saying that, based "both on the law, as well as on the facts, that instruction is not warranted." Because the defendant's theory at trial was that the victim actually consented and not that the defendant was "confused, misled, or mistaken" as to the victim's willingness to engage in sexual intercourse, the judge concluded that the ultimate question for the jury was simply whether they believed the victim's or the defendant's version of the encounter. The decision not to give the instruction provides the basis for this appeal.

---

1. The defendant proposed the following instruction: "If the Commonwealth has not proved beyond a reasonable doubt that the defendant was not motivated by a reasonable and honest belief that the complaining witness consented to sexual intercourse, you must find the defendant not guilty."

2. *Mistake of fact instruction....* In *Commonwealth v. Ascolillo*, 405 Mass. 456, 541 N.E.2d 570 (1989), we held that the defendant was not entitled to a mistake of fact instruction, and declined to adopt a rule that "in order to establish the crime of rape the Commonwealth must prove *in every case* not only that the defendant intended intercourse but also that he did not act pursuant to an honest and reasonable belief that the victim consented" (emphasis added). Neither the plain language of our rape statute nor this court's decisions prior to the *Ascolillo* decision warrant a different result.

A fundamental tenet of criminal law is that culpability requires a showing that the prohibited conduct (actus reus) was committed with the concomitant mental state (mens rea) prescribed for the offense. The mistake of fact "defense" is available where the mistake negates the existence of a mental state essential to a material element of the offense.[3] In determining whether the defendant's honest and reasonable belief as to the victim's consent would relieve him of culpability, it is necessary to review the required elements of the crime of rape....

The current rape statute, G. L. c. 265, § 22 (b), provides in pertinent part:

"Whoever has sexual intercourse or unnatural sexual intercourse with a person and compels such person to submit by force and against his will, or compels such person to submit by threat of bodily injury, shall be punished by imprisonment in the state prison for not more than twenty years."

This statute follows the common-law definition of rape, and requires the Commonwealth to prove beyond a reasonable doubt that the defendant committed (1) sexual intercourse (2) by force or threat of force and against the will of the victim.

As to the first element, there has been very little disagreement. Sexual intercourse is defined as penetration of the victim, regardless of degree. The second element has proven to be more complicated. We have construed the element, "by force and against his will," as truly encompassing two separate elements each of which must independently be satisfied. Therefore, the Commonwealth must demonstrate beyond a reasonable doubt that the defendant committed sexual intercourse (1) by means of physical force; nonphysical, constructive force; or threats of bodily harm, either explicit or implicit; and (2) at the time of penetration, there was no consent.

Although the Commonwealth must prove lack of consent, the "elements necessary for rape do not require that the defendant intend the intercourse be without consent." Historically, the relevant inquiry has been limited to consent in fact, and no mens rea or knowledge as to the lack of consent has ever been required.

A mistake of fact as to consent, therefore, has very little application to our rape statute. Because G. L. c. 265, § 22, does not require proof of a defendant's knowledge

---

3. Thus understood, a mistake of fact is not truly a defense, but rather a means of demonstrating that the prosecution has failed to prove beyond a reasonable doubt the essential elements of the crime....

of the victim's lack of consent or intent to engage in nonconsensual intercourse as a material element of the offense, a mistake as to that consent cannot, therefore, negate a mental state required for commission of the prohibited conduct. Any perception (reasonable, honest, or otherwise) of the defendant as to the victim's consent is consequently not relevant to a rape prosecution.

This is not to say, contrary to the defendant's suggestion, that the absence of any mens rea as to the consent element transforms rape into a strict liability crime. It does not. Rape, at common law and pursuant to G. L. c. 265, § 22, is a general intent crime, and proof that a defendant intended sexual intercourse by force coupled with proof that the victim did not in fact consent is sufficient to maintain a conviction.

Other jurisdictions have held that a mistake of fact instruction is necessary to prevent injustice. New Jersey, for instance, does not require the force necessary for rape to be anything more than what is needed to accomplish penetration. Thus, an instruction as to a defendant's honest and reasonable belief as to consent is available in New Jersey to mitigate the undesirable and unforeseen consequences that may flow from this construction. By contrast, in this Commonwealth, unless the putative victim has been rendered incapable of consent, the prosecution must prove that the defendant compelled the victim's submission by use of physical force; nonphysical, constructive force; or threat of force. Proof of the element of force, therefore, should negate any possible mistake as to consent.

We also have concerns that the mistake of fact defense would tend to eviscerate the long-standing rule in this Commonwealth that victims need not use any force to resist an attack. A shift in focus from the victim's to the defendant's state of mind might require victims to use physical force in order to communicate an unqualified lack of consent to defeat any honest and reasonable belief as to consent. The mistake of fact defense is incompatible with the evolution of our jurisprudence with respect to the crime of rape.

We are cognizant that our interpretation is not shared by the majority of other jurisdictions. States that recognize a mistake of fact as to consent generally have done so by legislation....

The mistake of fact "defense" has been recognized by judicial decision in some States. In 1975, the Supreme Court of California became the first State court to recognize a mistake of fact defense in rape cases....

Other State courts have employed a variety of different constructions in adopting the mistake of fact defense....

However, the minority of States sharing our view is significant. Whether such a defense might, in some circumstances, be appropriate is a difficult question that we may consider on a future case where a defendant's claim of reasonable mistake of fact is at least arguably supported by the evidence. This is not such a case.

Judgments affirmed.

Discussion Questions

1. Who has the burden of proof on mental state regarding lack of consent under the Texas and English statutes? Who has the burden of proof on mistake regarding lack of consent under *Lopez*?

2. Is the treatment of mistake in *Lopez* consistent with the treatment of mistake of fact you studied in Chapter 5, *Mental States*, earlier in the course?

3. If a statute requires force beyond the act of penetration itself, what are the risks of eliminating a mental state requirement regarding consent?

E. Incapacity to Consent

Modern rape statutes commonly prohibit intercourse when there is a proxy for force and/or lack of consent, such as the administration of certain intoxicants, unconsciousness of the victim, and lack of legal capacity to consent. The Kansas statute below provides an example.

Kansas Statutes Annotated

§ 21-5503. Rape.

a) Rape is:

(1) Knowingly engaging in sexual intercourse with a victim who does not consent to the sexual intercourse under any of the following circumstances:

  (A) When the victim is overcome by force or fear; or

  (B) when the victim is unconscious or physically powerless;

(2) Knowingly engaging in sexual intercourse with a victim when the victim is incapable of giving consent because of mental deficiency or disease, or when the victim is incapable of giving consent because of the effect of any alcoholic liquor, narcotic, drug or other substance, which condition was known by the offender or was reasonably apparent to the offender;

F. Rape Shield Statutes

At one time, a defendant in a rape case could admit into evidence the sexual history of the complainant under two different theories. First, it was admissible on the issue of consent. The assumption was that if a woman had consented to sexual intercourse on prior occasions, the earlier consent made it more likely that she consented to sexual intercourse on the occasion at issue in the rape charge. Second, courts admitted it on the issue of credibility. The assumption was that a woman who had engaged in past consensual intercourse was less credible than a woman who had not.

The admission of sexual history in rape cases effectively "put the victim on trial," resulting in humiliation and embarrassment of the complainant and effectively discouraging survivors of sexual violence from reporting or agreeing to cooperate in the prosecution of rapes. Sexual history evidence also tended to trigger in juries the passing of harsh judgments on the complainant and the acquittal of defendants who had in fact committed rape if the jury found moral fault with the complainant's sexual history. In addition, the inferences underlying the traditional theories of admissibility on consent as well as credibility came to be viewed as based on gender stereotypes rather than reality. There typically is no correlation between sexual history and either consent or credibility. Accordingly, legislatures altered the rules on admissibility of sexual history in rape cases by enacting what are commonly called "rape shield" statutes.

Federal Rule of Evidence 412. Sex-Offense Cases: The Victim's Sexual Behavior or Predisposition

(a) Prohibited Uses. The following evidence is not admissible in a … criminal proceeding involving alleged sexual misconduct:

(1) evidence offered to prove that a victim engaged in other sexual behavior; or

(2) evidence offered to prove a victim's sexual predisposition.

(b) Exceptions.

(1) *Criminal Cases.* The court may admit the following evidence in a criminal case:

(A) evidence of specific instances of a victim's sexual behavior, if offered to prove that someone other than the defendant was the source of semen, injury, or other physical evidence;

(B) evidence of specific instances of a victim's sexual behavior with respect to the person accused of the sexual misconduct, if offered by the defendant to prove consent or if offered by the prosecutor; and

(C) evidence whose exclusion would violate the defendant's constitutional rights.

Problem

9.4 Harold is the defendant in a rape case. He and the complainant, Susan, were classmates in college. Several years after graduation, each returned to the college campus for the weekend to attend a football game and class reunion. During the weekend, Harold and Susan attended the same reunion party. When the party was over, Susan gave Harold a ride to his hotel, where the act of sexual intercourse on which the rape charge is based took place. Harold admits that he had sexual intercourse with Susan on the evening in question, but asserts that she consented. Susan states that she did not consent, that Harold forced her to have sexual intercourse. Harold wishes to introduce the following items of evidence on the issue of consent.

(a) The testimony of Thomas that two weeks prior to the evening of the incident giving rise to the charges against Harold, Thomas met Susan in a bar on campus and later the same evening had consensual sexual intercourse with her in his hotel room.

(b) The testimony of Jane, a friend of Harold's, that, at the reunion party on the evening in question, Susan was "snuggling up to Harold, you know, kind of hanging all over him."

(c) The testimony of Jorge that Susan is, in his view, "very sexually active."

(d) The testimony of Maria that Susan is "widely known as promiscuous."

(e) The testimony of Harold that he and Susan had consensual sexual intercourse several times in the weeks prior to the reunion weekend.

G. Rape Trauma Syndrome

Rape Trauma Syndrome (RTS) describes a collection of common reactions that a sexual assault survivor may manifest.[17] It can serve to explain the conduct of a survivor that might be perceived by laypersons as inconsistent with how they expect a sexual assault survivor to act. In this way, it might be used to explain unanticipated conduct, like delay in reporting a rape or the calm demeanor of a survivor after a rape. The *Taylor* case that follows offers an overview and application of RTS.

People v. Taylor
75 N.Y.2d 277 (1990)
Court of Appeals of New York

... In these two cases, we consider whether expert testimony that a complaining witness has exhibited behavior consistent with "rape trauma syndrome" is admissible at the criminal trial of the person accused of the rape. Both trial courts admitted the testimony and the Appellate Division affirmed in both cases. We now affirm in *People v Taylor* and reverse in *People v Banks*....

---

17. David Faigman et al., Science in the Law, Social and Behavioral Science Issues 270 (West 2002).

I. *People v. Taylor*

On July 29, 1984, the complainant, a 19-year-old Long Island resident, reported to the town police that she had been raped and sodomized at gunpoint on a deserted beach near her home. The complainant testified that at about nine that evening she had received a phone call from a friend, telling her that he was in trouble and asking her to meet him at a nearby market in half an hour. Twenty minutes later, the same person called back and changed the meeting place. The complainant arrived at the agreed-upon place, shut off the car engine and waited. She saw a man approach her car and she unlocked the door to let him in. Only then did she realize that the person who had approached and entered the car was not the friend she had come to meet. According to the complainant, he pointed a gun at her, directed her to nearby Clarke's Beach, and once they were there, raped and sodomized her.

The complainant arrived home around 11:00 p.m., woke her mother and told her about the attack. Her mother then called the police. Sometime between 11:30 p.m. and midnight, the police arrived at the complainant's house. At that time, the complainant told the police she did not know who her attacker was. She was taken to the police station where she described the events leading up to the attack and again repeated that she did not know who her attacker was. At the conclusion of the interview, the complainant was asked to step into a private room to remove the clothes that she had been wearing at the time of the attack so that they could be examined for forensic evidence. While she was alone with her mother, the complainant told her that the defendant, John Taylor, had been her attacker. The time was approximately 1:15 a.m. The complainant had known the defendant for years, and she later testified that she happened to see him the night before the attack at a local convenience store.

Her mother summoned one of the detectives and the complainant repeated that the defendant had been the person who attacked her. The complainant said that she was sure that it had been the defendant because she had had ample opportunity to see his face during the incident. The complainant subsequently identified the defendant as her attacker in two separate lineups. He was arrested on July 31, 1984, and was indicted by the Grand Jury on one count of rape in the first degree, two counts of sodomy in the first degree and one count of sexual abuse in the first degree.

The defendant's first trial ended without the jury being able to reach a verdict. At his second trial, the Judge permitted Eileen Treacy, an instructor at the City University of New York, Herbert Lehman College, with experience in counseling sexual assault victims, to testify about rape trauma syndrome. The prosecutor introduced this testimony for two separate purposes. First, Treacy's testimony on the specifics of rape trauma syndrome explained why the complainant might have been unwilling during the first few hours after the attack to name the defendant as her attacker where she had known the defendant prior to the incident. Second, Treacy's testimony that it was common for a rape victim to appear quiet and controlled following an attack, responded to evidence that the complainant had appeared calm after the attack and tended to rebut the inference that because she was not excited and upset after the attack, it had not been a rape. At the close of the second trial, the defendant was convicted of two counts of sodomy in the first degree and one count of attempted rape in the first degree and was sentenced to an indeterminate term of 7 to 21 years on the two sodomy convictions and 5 to 15 years on the attempted rape conviction.

II. *People v. Banks*

On July 7, 1986, the defendant Ronnie Banks approached the 11-year-old complainant, who was playing with her friends in the City of Rochester. The complainant testified that the defendant told her to come to him and when she did not, he grabbed her by the arm and pulled her down the street. According to the complainant, the defendant took her into a neighborhood garage where he sexually assaulted her. The complainant returned to her grandmother's house, where she was living at the time. The next morning, she told her grandmother about the incident and the police were contacted. The defendant was arrested and charged with three counts involving forcible compulsion—rape in the first degree, sodomy in the first degree and sexual abuse in the first degree—and four counts that were based solely on the age of the victim—rape in the second degree, sodomy in the second degree, sexual abuse in the second degree and endangering the welfare of a child.

At trial, the complainant testified that the defendant had raped and sodomized her. In addition, she and her grandmother both testified about the complainant's behavior following the attack. Their testimony revealed that the complainant had been suffering from nightmares, had been waking up in the middle of the night in a cold sweat, had been afraid to return to school in the fall, had become generally more fearful and had been running and staying away from home. Following the introduction of this evidence, the prosecution sought to introduce expert testimony about the symptoms associated with rape trauma syndrome.

Clearly, the prosecution, in an effort to establish that forcible sexual contact had in fact occurred, wanted to introduce this evidence to show that the complainant was demonstrating behavior that was consistent with patterns of response exhibited by rape victims. The prosecutor does not appear to have introduced this evidence to counter the inference that the complainant consented to the incident, since the 11-year-old complainant is legally incapable of consent (Penal Law § 130.05 [3] [a]). Unlike *Taylor*, the evidence was not offered to explain behavior exhibited by the victim that the jury might not understand; instead, it was offered to show that the behavior that the complainant had exhibited after the incident was consistent with a set of symptoms commonly associated with women who had been forcibly attacked. The clear implication of such testimony would be that because the complainant exhibited these symptoms, it was more likely than not that she had been forcibly raped.

The Judge permitted David Gandell, an obstetrician-gynecologist on the faculty of the University of Rochester, Strong Memorial Hospital, with special training in treating victims of sexual assault, to testify as to the symptoms commonly associated with rape trauma syndrome. After Gandell had described rape trauma syndrome he testified hypothetically that the kind of symptoms demonstrated by the complainant were consistent with a diagnosis of rape trauma syndrome. At the close of the trial, the defendant was acquitted of all forcible counts and was convicted on the four statutory counts. He was sentenced to indeterminate terms of 3½ to 7 years on the rape and sodomy convictions and to definite one-year terms on the convictions of sexual abuse in the second degree and endangering the welfare of a child.

III. Rape Trauma Syndrome

In a 1974 study rape trauma syndrome was described as "the acute phase and long-term reorganization process that occurs as a result of forcible rape or attempted forcible rape. This syndrome of behavioral, somatic, and psychological reactions is an acute stress reaction to a life-threatening situation" (Burgess & Holmstrom, *Rape Trauma Syndrome, 131 Am J Psychiatry* 981, 982 [1974]). Although others had studied the reactions of rape victims prior to this publication, the Burgess and Holmstrom identification of two separate phases in a rape victim's recovery has proven enormously influential.

According to Burgess and Holmstrom, the rape victim will go through an acute phase immediately following the incident. The behavior exhibited by a rape victim after the attack can vary. While some women will express their fear, anger and anxiety openly, an equal number of women will appear controlled, calm, and subdued. Women in the acute phase will also experience a number of physical reactions. These reactions include the actual physical trauma that resulted from the attack, muscle tension that could manifest itself in tension headaches, fatigue, or disturbed sleep patterns, gastrointestinal irritability and genitourinary disturbance. Emotional reactions in the acute phase generally take the form of fear, humiliation, embarrassment, fear of violence and death, and self-blame.

As part of the long-term reorganizational phase, the victim will often decide to make a change in her life, such as a change of residence. At this point, the woman will often turn to her family for support. Other symptoms that are seen in this phase are the occurrence of nightmares and the development of phobias that relate to the circumstances of the rape. For instance, women attacked in their beds will often develop a fear of being indoors, while women attacked on the street will develop a fear of being outdoors.

While some researchers have criticized the methodology of the early studies of rape trauma syndrome, Burgess and Holmstrom's model has nonetheless generated considerable interest in the response and recovery of rape victims and has contributed to the emergence of a substantial body of scholarship in this area ...

We realize that rape trauma syndrome encompasses a broad range of symptoms and varied patterns of recovery.... We are satisfied, however, that the relevant scientific community has generally accepted that rape is a highly traumatic event that will in many women trigger the onset of certain identifiable symptoms.

We note that the American Psychiatric Association has listed rape as one of the stressors that can lead to posttraumatic stress disorder (American Psychiatric Association, Diagnostic & Statistical Manual of Mental Disorders 247, 248 [3d ed rev 1987] [DSM III-R]). According to DSM III-R, there is an identifiable pattern of responses that can follow an intensely stressful event. The victim who suffers from posttraumatic stress disorder will persistently reexperience the traumatic event in a number of ways, as through dreams, flashbacks, hallucinations, or intense distress at exposure to events that resemble or symbolize the traumatic event. The victim will also avoid stimuli that he or she associates with the trauma. Finally, the victim will experience "persistent symptoms of increased arousal," which could include difficulty in falling or staying asleep, sudden outbursts of anger, or difficulty concentrating. While the diagnostic criteria for posttraumatic stress disorder that are contained in DSM III-R have convinced us that the scientific community has accepted that rape as a stressor can have marked, identifiable effects on a victim's behavior, we would further note that although rape trauma syndrome can be conceptualized as a posttraumatic stress disorder, victims of rape will often exhibit peculiar symptoms — like a fear of men — that are not commonly exhibited by victims of other sorts of trauma....

IV. The Law

Having concluded that evidence of rape trauma syndrome is generally accepted within the relevant scientific community, we must now decide whether expert testimony in this area would aid a lay jury in reaching a verdict. "[Expert] opinion is proper when it would help to clarify an issue calling for professional or technical knowledge, possessed by the expert and beyond the ken of the typical juror" (*De Long v County of Erie*, 60 NY2d 296, 307)....

[R]ape is a crime that is permeated by misconceptions. Society and law are finally realizing that it is an act of violence and not a sexual act.... Studies have shown that one of the most popular misconceptions about rape is that the victim by behaving in a certain way brought it on herself. For that reason, studies have demonstrated that jurors will under certain circumstances blame the victim for the attack and will refuse to convict the man accused. Studies have also shown that jurors will infer consent where the victim has engaged in certain types of behavior prior to the incident....

Because cultural myths still affect common understanding of rape and rape victims and because experts have been studying the effects of rape upon its victims only since the 1970's, we believe that patterns of response among rape victims are not within the ordinary understanding of the lay juror. For that reason, we conclude that introduction of expert testimony describing rape trauma syndrome may under certain circumstances assist a lay jury in deciding issues in a rape trial....

Among those States that have allowed such testimony to be admitted, the purpose for which the testimony was offered has proven crucial. A number of States have allowed testimony of rape trauma syndrome to be admitted where the defendant concedes that sexual intercourse occurred, but contends that it was consensual....

Other States have permitted the admission of this testimony where it was offered to explain behavior exhibited by the complainant that might be viewed as inconsistent with a claim of rape. In *People v Hampton* (746 P2d 947), the Colorado Supreme Court held that in a case where the complainant waited 89 days to report an attack, expert testimony that a rape victim who is assaulted by someone she knows is more reluctant to report an attack was admissible to explain the delay in reporting.... Other States that have permitted the admission of expert testimony of this type to explain inconsistencies in the behavior of the complainant, especially where a child is involved....

Having concluded that evidence of rape trauma syndrome can assist jurors in reaching a verdict by dispelling common misperceptions about rape, and having reviewed the different approaches taken by the other jurisdictions that have considered the question, we too agree that the reason why the testimony is offered will determine its helpfulness, its relevance and its potential for prejudice. In the two cases now before us, testimony regarding rape trauma syndrome was offered for entirely different purposes. We conclude that its admission at the trial of John Taylor was proper, but that its admission at the trial of Ronnie Banks was not.

As noted above, the complaining witness in *Taylor* had initially told the police that she could not identify her assailant. Approximately two hours after she first told her mother that she had been raped and sodomized, she told her mother that she knew the defendant had done it. The complainant had known the defendant for years and had seen him the night before the assault. We hold that under the circumstances present in this case, expert testimony explaining that a rape victim who knows her assailant is more fearful of disclosing his name to the police and is in fact less likely to report the rape at all was relevant to explain why the complainant may have been initially unwilling to report that the defendant had been the man who attacked her. Behavior of this type is not within the ordinary understanding of the jury and testimony explaining this behavior assists the jury in determining what effect to give to the complainant's initial failure to identify the defendant. This evidence provides a possible explanation for the complainant's behavior that is consistent with her claim that she was raped. As such, it is relevant.

Rape trauma syndrome evidence was also introduced in *Taylor* in response to evidence that revealed the complainant had not seemed upset following the attack. We note again in this context that the reaction of a rape victim in the hours following her attack is not something within the common understanding of the average lay juror. Indeed, the defense would clearly want the jury to infer that because the victim was not upset following the attack, she must not have been raped. This inference runs contrary to the studies cited earlier, which suggest that half of all women who have been forcibly raped are controlled and subdued following the attack. Thus, we conclude that evidence of this type is relevant to dispel misconceptions that jurors might possess regarding the ordinary responses of rape victims in the first hours after their attack. We do not believe that evidence of rape trauma syndrome, when admitted for that express purpose, is unduly prejudicial.

The admission of expert testimony describing rape trauma syndrome in *Banks*, however, was clearly error. As we noted earlier, this evidence was not offered to explain behavior that might appear unusual to a lay juror not ordinarily familiar with the patterns of response exhibited by rape victims. We conclude that evidence of rape trauma syndrome is inadmissible when it inescapably bears solely on proving that a rape occurred, as was the case here.

Discussion Questions

1. Should courts prohibit or allow introduction of RTS evidence to prove that a rape occurred? Why?

2. Is there really a distinction between proving that a rape occurred and that a victim did not act inconsistently with having been raped?

H. Statutory Rape

1. Historical and Contemporary Justifications

The common law did not penalize consensual sexual intercourse with a minor as a form of rape.[18] But the English Parliament enacted a statute creating the crime of "statutory rape."[19] While lack of consent was a critical element of common law rape, the minor's consent or lack thereof was and is irrelevant to an offense of statutory rape. Statutory rape laws have been in use for centuries during which both the laws and their purposes have evolved. Examination of those purposes reveals a range of rationales, many of which continue to cause controversy.

Whose interests do these statutes protect? The interests of minors? Their parents? Or society? Preventing the loss of chastity in young women provided an early motivation for laws criminalizing sexual intercourse with minors. Indeed, for many years, young women who lost their chastity also lost the protection afforded by the law of statutory rape. Chastity was viewed as precious in part because its loss adversely affected a father's financial interests.

> Under customary dowry practices, a non-virgin was considered less desirable for marriage, and therefore less likely to bring financial reward to her father upon marriage. Indeed, if she failed to marry, a daughter represented a life-long financial burden to her father. From this perspective, statutory rape laws were an outgrowth of biblical precepts, by which virginity was so highly prized that a man who took a girl's virginity without her father's permission was considered to have committed a theft against the father. The father could demand compensation either in the form of payment, or by forcing the rapist to marry the victim.[20]

Loss of chastity also raised fears about the immoral influence of an unchaste young woman on other members of society. The Missouri Supreme Court in a 1923 statutory rape case expressed this view:

---

18. Wayne R. LaFave, Criminal Law 777 (3d ed. 2000).

19. *Id.*

20. Michelle Oberman, *Girls in the Master's House: Of Protection, Patriarchy and the Potential for Using the Master's Tools to Reconfigure Statutory Rape Law*, 50 DePaul L. Rev. 799, 802 (2001).

The purpose of the lawmakers ... is manifest. Experience has shown that girls under the age of 16, as the statute now reads, are not always able to resist temptation. They lack the discretion and firmness that comes with maturer years. Fathers and mothers know that this is true of boys as well.... A lecherous woman is a social menace; she is more dangerous than T.N.T.

This wretched girl was young in years but old in sin and shame. A number of callow youths, of otherwise blameless lives so far as this record shows, fell under her seductive influence. They flocked about her, if her story is to be believed, like moths about the flame of a lighted candle and probably with the same result. The girl was a common prostitute as the record shows. The boys were immature and doubtless more sinned against than sinning.[21]

Chastity was important, then, to fathers and society, and the Missouri Supreme Court thought young women could not be trusted to guard it on their own. Young women were thus seen simultaneously as both innocent and a potential menace. Over time, the view of women's chastity as a commodity, of value to the patriarch of the family, and the view of young women as corrupting influences triggered substantial criticism. In more recent decades, this criticism along with changing social attitudes have discredited these views as legitimate motivations for statutory rape laws.

More recent discussions shift the focus from the goals of preserving chastity and virtue to pragmatic concerns with illegitimate pregnancy. In *Michael M. v. Superior Court*, 450 U.S. 464 (1981), a 17-year-old male challenged a California statutory rape law as a violation of equal protection because it protected only females and penalized only males. The California Supreme Court upheld the statute. The United States Supreme Court affirmed the California Supreme Court. Justice Rehnquist explained that:

[T]eenage pregnancies, which have increased dramatically over the last two decades, have significant social, medical, and economic consequences for both the mother and her child, and the State. Of particular concern to the State is that approximately half of all teenage pregnancies end in abortion. And of those children who are born, their illegitimacy makes them likely candidates to become wards of the State. We need not be medical doctors to discern that young men and young women are not similarly situated with respect to the problems and the risks of sexual intercourse. Only women may become pregnant, and they suffer disproportionately the profound physical, emotional, and psychological consequences of sexual activity. The statute at issue here protects women from sexual intercourse at an age when those consequences are particularly severe.

---

21. *State v. Snow*, 252 S.W.629, 632 (1923).

Because virtually all of the significant harmful and inescapably identifiable consequences of teenage pregnancy fall on the young female, a legislature acts well within its authority when it elects to punish only the participant who, by nature, suffers few of the consequences of his conduct. It is hardly unreasonable for a legislature acting to protect minor females to exclude them from punishment. Moreover, the risk of pregnancy itself constitutes a substantial deterrence to young females. No similar natural sanctions deter males. A criminal sanction imposed solely on males thus serves to roughly "equalize" the deterrents on the sexes.[22]

In addition to the costs imposed on society, sexual activity can result in emotional, psychological, and physical harm to minors, such as transmission of HIV and other diseases. The following case study description gives a vivid sense of some of these potential harms.

Case 6

When this subject was 11, a 16-year-old baby-sitter pulled off his pajamas and sat on him putting his penis in her vagina. He did not understand what was happening but remembers feeling terrified, confused, and ashamed. He had no previous sexual experience, had never ejaculated, and did not ejaculate during the intercourse. Subsequently, he did not masturbate and avoided any direct sexual contact. At 19, he met his wife. There was no premarital genital petting or any attempt at intercourse. On their wedding night he was impotent and did not allow her to touch him. He was seen with his wife for sex therapy, the complaint being his aversion to sexual activity and an unconsummated marriage due to primary impotence. It is worth noting that he had been in psychotherapy for 2 years prior to his marriage but had shared his sexual history with neither his therapist nor his wife.[23]

Are the dangers of sexual activity the same for teenagers as they are for preadolescent children? Some commentators argue that consensual adolescent sexuality is not necessarily harmful and that current statutory rape provisions are too restrictive as applied to adolescents. They argue that sexual activity offers benefits as well as problems for adolescents.

---

22. *Michael M. v. Superior Court*, 450 U. S. 464 (1981).
23. Philip M. Sarrel & William H. Masters, *Sexual Molestation of Men by Women*, 11 Archives of Sexual Behavior 117 (1982).

Meaningful Consent:
Toward a New Generation of Statutory Rape Laws

Heidi Kitrosser

4 Va. J. Soc. Policy & L. 287, 322–326 (1997)

Positive Aspects of Adolescent Sexuality

Sexual activity in adolescence is extremely common. In the United States, about sixty percent of unmarried eighteen-year-olds are sexually active, a figure consistent across many Western nations, although there is variation within groups. Aside from the frequency of adolescent sex, the literature on adolescent sexuality suggests that adolescent sex can play a positive role in young people's lives, both through the nature of the sexual experience itself, and through the potential for the experience to serve as a growth tool, preparing an adolescent to deal with future relationships....

Researchers also note that sexual experimentation "is one way in today's society for young people to gain a sense of independence from parents, to begin the process of growing up and taking on adult roles."

Indeed, even though many teenagers, particularly girls, find their first coital experience unrewarding, "many teenagers find subsequent sexual intercourse to be a positive experience...."

Problems in Adolescent Sexuality

While [confronting sexual feelings in adolescence] can contribute to successful sexual development, their unsuccessful resolution can affect and be affected by experiences in the sexual domain. Adolescents can use sex indiscriminately in an attempt to bolster popularity and self-esteem, a strategy that is not always successful.... Sex can be used to gain power over others, or can become the inappropriate focus of identity formation, for example the person who feels they are defined by their level of sexual attractiveness. Selverstone suggests that sexual involvement is one of the ways we learn to feel lovable, but that inappropriate involvement and sexual risk-taking can be counterproductive in the quest toward self-definition and personal integration.

Within this framework of enhanced vulnerability, it is notable that many of the destructive aspects of adolescent sexuality, particular those related to coercive sexual norms, reflect the same framework of male aggressiveness and female passivity that permeates notions of heterosexual sex generally. For example, girls are less likely to envision sex as something for their own pleasure, and more likely to think of sex as something that they are supposed to "give" to boys. Boys, in turn, often feel that it is their role to pressure girls into having sex.

As to the latter, one study found, for example, that:

> Many boys who might not consider rape or physical force were not averse to strong persuasion in order to get their own way sexually. A variety of techniques such as shaming, teasing, trickery, and perseverance were considered

appropriate.... In all, over two-thirds of the teenage boys interviewed said they would try to convince a reluctant female partner to have sex. They appeared to regard their partner's reticence as a weak barrier to intercourse, one which it was part of the male role to overcome.

Research further indicates that the psychology of teenage girls in our society is such that they are often particularly vulnerable to such pressures due to limited self-esteem and the correlative assumption that their opinions and feelings are not worth expressing....

Aside from diminished self-esteem and a desire to be perceived as "feminine," the reaction to the physical process of becoming a woman also contributes to girls' insecurity. Most girls view the physical changes of adolescence—the complete alteration of the body's shape—not as an empowering experience, but as a loss of control. As they reach puberty, girls become objects of male desire, and the experience of seeing and valuing (or devaluing) themselves through the eyes of others is a traumatic one.

Thus, one of the most insidious aspects of girls' psycho-social development is that they become less certain of their physical boundaries and less able to declare their own limits, at precisely the time at which they begin to explore their own sexuality. The implications of this convergence of bodily maturity and moral dispossession are particularly disturbing because male sexual initiative remains a societal norm.

Hence, while sexuality in adolescence is an extremely common phenomenon, and is not necessarily unhealthy or coercive, it is underscored by the same sexist norms of male aggressiveness and female passivity that makes heterosexual sex problematic in general. Furthermore, these norms occur within a framework of particular vulnerability due to the difficult period of adolescence. While this framework of vulnerability makes both boys and girls vulnerable sexually, a sexist social context clearly heightens this vulnerability in the case of females, again reflective of broader social norms.

* * *

An additional problem is the incidence of violence in adolescent dating relationships. Studies have revealed that roughly 10 percent of high school students report the occurrence of violence in dating relationships.

Statutory rape laws also give prosecutors an alternative means for prosecuting a forcible rape against a minor. In *Michael M.*, which was prosecuted as a statutory rape case, for example,

> The evidence adduced at a preliminary hearing showed that at approximately midnight on June 3, 1978, petitioner [a 17½-year-old male] and two friends approached Sharon, a 16½-year-old female, and her sister as they waited at a bus stop. Petitioner and Sharon, who had already been drinking, moved away from the others and began to kiss. After being struck in the face for rebuffing petitioner's initial advances, Sharon submitted to sexual intercourse with petitioner.

Some have estimated that half of all rapes are committed against adolescents. Earlier in this chapter we discussed the problems prosecutors encounter obtaining convictions in forcible rape cases. Think back on those materials and assess why the prosecutor may have chosen to prosecute in *Michael M.* for statutory rape rather than forcible rape.

Discussion Questions

1. If you were a state legislator, would you favor or oppose penalizing consensual sexual intercourse involving minors? Should sexual activity other than intercourse be penalized? Are such laws sexist attempts to secure male control over female sexuality? Do they treat females as incapable of making choices about sex? Or are they simply a logical response to existing "sexist" patterns of male and female behavior?

2. If you favor such laws, on which rationale(s) would you rely? How does the choice of rationale affect your answers to the following questions:

(a) What age limits should the statute set?

(b) Should sex between adolescents close in age be exempted? If so, what age span should the exemption use?

(c) Should the statute recognize both males and females as potential perpetrators? As potential victims? Should it include homosexual as well as heterosexual activity?

3. Can the legislative purpose behind a statute change over time? In interpreting a statute, should a court focus on the intent of the legislature that enacted the statute? Or the reasons the current legislature would give for enacting the statute if it came before them today? What significance should attach to the fact that a statute was originally enacted for a sexist reason?

4. Should the criminal law penalize video depictions of sexual activity by those who appear to be minors but are in fact of legal age? What are the arguments for and against such a criminal prohibition?

2. Non-Mental Elements

Problems

Apply the statutes that appear below to the following factual scenarios. Assume in each problem that both parties are willing participants in sexual intercourse.

9.5 (a) Roy is a 30-year-old high school math teacher who recently went through a difficult divorce. He has been tutoring Doris, a 15-year-old female student in one of his classes. Doris develops a crush on Roy and begins buying him gifts and sending him flowers. One evening, Roy invites Doris to his house and the two have sexual intercourse.

(b) What if Doris is 16?

(c) What if the teacher in Part (a) is female and the student male?

(d) What if the teacher and student in Part (a) are both male? Both female?

(e) Assume Doris engaged in sexual intercourse on prior occasions with males other than Roy. Would this affect Roy's liability?

(f) What if, rather than being her teacher, Roy is Doris's stepfather?

9.6 (a) Arthur is an 18-year-old high school senior. Julie, his girlfriend, is 15 and a high school freshman. Arthur invites Julie to his senior prom and Julie accepts. Without informing Julie, Arthur reserves a hotel room for the night of the dance. After the dance, Arthur and Julie go to the hotel room and have intercourse.

(b) What if Arthur is 17 and Julie 15?

(c) What if Arthur is 16 and Julie 15?

Idaho Code

§ 16101 Rape Defined

Rape is defined as the penetration, however slight, of the oral, anal, or vaginal opening with the perpetrator's penis accomplished with a female under the following circumstances:

1. Where the female is under the age of eighteen (18) years.

Alabama Code

§ 13A-6-62 Rape; second degree

(a) A person commits the crime of rape in the second degree if:

(1) Being 16 years old or older, he or she engages in sexual intercourse with a member of the opposite sex less than 16 and more than 12 years old; provided, however, the actor is at least two years older than the member of the opposite sex

Georgia Code Annotated

§ 16-6-3 Statutory rape

(a) A person commits the offense of statutory rape when he or she engages in sexual intercourse with any person under the age of 16 years and not his or her spouse, provided that no conviction shall be had for this offense on the unsupported testimony of the victim.

(b) A person convicted of the offense of statutory rape shall be punished by imprisonment for not less than one nor more than 20 years; provided, however, that if the person so convicted is 21 years of age or older, such person shall be punished by imprisonment for not less than 10 nor more than 20 years; provided, further, that if the victim is 14 or 15 years of age and the person so convicted is no more than three years older than the victim, such person shall be guilty of a misdemeanor.

Louisiana Statutes Annotated

§ 80

A. Felony carnal knowledge of a juvenile is committed when:

(1) A person who is nineteen years of age or older has sexual intercourse, with consent, with a person who is twelve years of age or older but less than seventeen years of age, when the victim is not the spouse of the offender; or

(2) A person who is seventeen years of age or older has sexual intercourse, with consent, with a person who is twelve years of age or older but less than fifteen years of age, when the victim is not the spouse of the offender; or ...

B. As used in this Section, "sexual intercourse" means anal, oral, or vaginal sexual intercourse

C. Lack of knowledge of the juvenile's age shall not be a defense. Emission is not necessary, and penetration, however slight, is sufficient to complete the crime.

D. Whoever commits the crime of felony carnal knowledge of a juvenile shall be fined not more than five thousand dollars, or imprisoned, with or without hard labor, for not more than ten years, or both....

Arizona Revised Statutes

§ 13-1405 Sexual conduct with a minor; classification

A. A person commits sexual conduct with a minor by intentionally or knowingly engaging in sexual intercourse or oral sexual contact with any person who is under eighteen years of age.

B. Sexual conduct with a minor who is under fifteen years of age is a class 2 felony.... Sexual conduct with a minor who is at least fifteen years of age is a class 6 felony. Sexual conduct with a minor who is at least fifteen years of age is a class 2 felony if the person is the minor's parent, stepparent, adoptive parent, legal guardian or foster parent and the convicted person is not eligible for suspension of sentence, probation, pardon or release from confinement ... until the sentence imposed has been served or commuted.

* * *

Note that the Idaho statute is gender-specific, recognizing only male perpetrators and female victims. Such statutes were once common. But a new generation of gender-neutral laws has largely replaced gender-specific statutes. Modern statutes controlling sexual activity with minors often give names other than "statutory rape" to the crimes they create and vary in the scope of conduct they prohibit. Some seem to contemplate only traditional intercourse, while others reach a broader range of sexual activity. These laws often use age span provisions excluding from criminal sanction or lessening punishment for sexual activity between people fairly close in age. What underlying purpose do these age span exemptions reflect? Another common feature is the recognition of certain status categories, such as parent or teacher, as an aggravating element.

3. Mental States

Problem

9.7 Apply the statutes and cases that appear below to the following factual scenarios. Assume that both parties are willing participants in sexual intercourse.

(a) Raymond is a 20-year-old man. A friend introduced Raymond to Erica, who was 13 at the time. The two subsequently talked occasionally by telephone. One evening, Raymond, apparently wishing to call for a ride home, approached Erica's house at about nine o'clock. Erica opened her bedroom window, through which Raymond entered. Raymond later stated that "she just told me to get a ladder and climb up to her window." The two talked and later engaged in sexual intercourse. Raymond left at about 4:30 the following morning. Nine months later, Erica gave birth to a baby, of which Raymond is the biological father. Raymond wishes to introduce into evidence testimony that Erica and her friends told him that she was 16 years old and that he believed them. Should the trial judge admit this testimony?

(b) Same facts as (a) above, except assume that Raymond is mentally disabled. His I.Q. is 52 and his school guidance counselor describes him as a mildly retarded person who reads on the third-grade level, does arithmetic on the fifth-grade level, and interacts with others socially at school at the level of someone 11 or 12 years of age. Should the trial judge admit the testimony about Erica and her friends telling Raymond that Erica was 16 years old and his belief in their representations?

Ohio Revised Code Annotated

§ 2907.04 Unlawful sexual conduct with minor

(A) No person who is eighteen years of age or older shall engage in sexual conduct with another, who is not the spouse of the offender, when the offender knows the other person is thirteen years of age or older but less than sixteen years of age, or the offender is reckless in that regard.

(B) Whoever violates this section is guilty of unlawful sexual conduct with a minor.

   (1) Except as otherwise provided in divisions (B)(2), (3), and (4) of this section, unlawful sexual conduct with a minor is a felony of the fourth degree.

(2) Except as otherwise provided in division (B)(4) of this section, if the offender is less than four years older than the other person, unlawful sexual conduct with a minor is a misdemeanor of the first degree.

Model Penal Code

§ 213.6 Mistake as to Age

Whenever in this Article the criminality of conduct depends on a child's being below the age of 10, it is no defense that the actor did not know the child's age, or reasonably believed the child to be older than 10. When criminality depends on the child's being below a critical age other than 10, it is a defense for the actor to prove by a preponderance of the evidence that he reasonably believed the child to be above the critical age.

Florida Statutes

§ 794.021 Ignorance or belief as to victim's age no defense

When, in this chapter, the criminality of conduct depends upon the victim's being below a certain specified age, ignorance of the age is no defense. Neither shall misrepresentation of age by such person nor a bona fide belief that such person is over the specified age be a defense.

Louisiana Statutes Annotated

§ 80

. . .

C. Lack of knowledge of the juvenile's age shall not be a defense. Emission is not necessary, and penetration, however slight, is sufficient to complete the crime....

Arizona Revised Statutes

§ 13-1405 Sexual conduct with a minor

A. A person commits sexual conduct with a minor by intentionally or knowingly engaging in sexual intercourse or oral sexual contact with any person who is under eighteen years of age.

Discussion Questions

1. Jurisdictions vary in their treatment of mental state regarding age in statutory rape. What approach is reflected in each of the above statutes?

2. In what context earlier in the course have you encountered the position exemplified in Model Penal Code § 213.6?

* * *

Though some criminal codes explicitly address mental state concerning age, many are silent on the issue, leaving courts to grapple with the issue, as in the following opinions.

State v. Elton

657 P.2d 1261 (1982)
Supreme Court of Utah

Per Curiam.

The defendant, 19, had sexual intercourse with a 14-year-old female, not his wife, and was found guilty by a jury of violating U.C.A., 1953, 76-5-401.[1] The offense is a third-degree felony, punishable by up to five years in prison. The trial court spared defendant the prison term, conditioned on a probationary completion of a half-way house program.

Defendant urges three points on appeal to the effect that (1) the offense charged requires a specific criminal intent, (2) his mistake in appraising the girl's age constitutes a defense to the charge, and (3) failure to allow evidence as to defendant's "belief" or "mistake" as to the girl's age, together with failure to instruct thereon, was error.

Defendant concedes that Utah courts, as elsewhere, traditionally have considered and approved sanctions for offenses like that charged here, connoting a "strict liability" that is implicit in the offense itself, whether those words are included in the legislation defining the offense or not. Such offenses have been considered to be punishable without the necessity of pleading or proving specific intent. Since they are malum prohibitum *crimes, criminal responsibility attaches whenever the prohibited act is fully accomplished.*

The defendant's whole thesis is to the effect that it would be ludicrous if the legislature intended that one be guilty of a felony if the sex act occurred shortly before a girl's sixteenth birthday, but guilty only of a misdemeanor if it happened a few minutes after that magic date. Irrespective of such hypothetics, defendant contends that he should be excused from criminal liability if he "believed" or was "mistaken" as to the girl's age.

Courts generally have not gone along with any of defendant's concepts as to what the law *should be,* leaving that determination to the legislature. Courts have taken the position that a statute calling for the protection of young women below a specific age is necessary and contributive to the common welfare. In rare instances, where one may not have intended to do violence because of belief or mistake, the law wisely has provided a mitigating process. This mitigating and ameliorating process has been employed in this very case in the sentencing phase, where the trial court placed the defendant on probation rather than impose a prison term.

The defendant cites but one case supporting his contention that his own subjective belief that the girl was 16 or over, should constitute a defense to the statutory charge.[2] This case has been rejected in numerous other jurisdictions. We agree in such rejection and quote with approval language found in the following two well-reasoned opinions apropos to the questions raised here:

---

1. "A person commits unlawful sexual intercourse if that person has sexual intercourse with a person, not that person's spouse, who is under sixteen years of age."

2. *People v. Hernandez,* 61 Cal. 2d 529 (1964).

The arbitrary age of consent in these cases has been established by our legislature as a matter of public policy for the obvious protection of young and
immature females. We cannot properly make exceptions. Therefore, in a
prosecution for alleged statutory rape a defendant's knowledge of the age of
the girl involved is immaterial and his reasonable belief that she is over the
age of eighteen years is no defense.[3]

Petitioner claims that his honest belief that the prosecutrix of the statutory rape
charge was over 16 years of age should constitute a defense, of constitutional dimen-
sions, to statutory rape. The effect of *mens rea* and mistake on state criminal law has
generally been left to the discretion of the states. The Supreme Court has never held
that an honest mistake as to the age of the prosecutrix is a constitutional defense to
statutory rape, and nothing in the Court's recent decisions clarifying the scope of
procreative privacy suggests that a state may no longer place the risk of mistake as
to the prosecutrix's age on the person engaging in sexual intercourse with a partner
who may be young enough to fall within the protection of the statute. Petitioner's
argument is without merit.

Affirmed.

State v. Elton

680 P.2d 727 (1984)
Supreme Court of Utah

Stewart, Justice.

We have previously issued a *per curiam* opinion in this case, now published at 657
P.2d 1261.... We later withdrew that opinion for the purpose of rehearing the case
and addressing more fully an issue of first impression. Upon reconsideration, we
vacate our previous opinion and set aside the trial court's judgment of conviction
and remand.

Defendant was convicted of the crime of unlawful sexual intercourse, a third degree
felony, under U.C.A., 1953, § 76-5-401, which provided:[1]

(1) A person commits unlawful sexual intercourse if that person has sexual
intercourse with a person, not that person's spouse, who is under sixteen
years of age.

(2) Unlawful sexual intercourse is a felony of the third degree except when
at the time of intercourse the actor is no more than three years older than
the victim, in which case it is a class B misdemeanor. Evidence that the actor
was not more than three years older than the victim at the time of the intercourse shall be raised by the defendant.

---

3. *State v. Fulks*, 83 S.D. 433, 436 (1968).
1. The section has since been amended. 1983 Utah Laws ch. 88, § 16.

On September 16, 1981, defendant engaged in sexual intercourse with a girl, not his wife, who was fourteen years of age. Defendant was nineteen years of age at the time and therefore more than three years older than the girl. Defendant testified that the girl told him she was eighteen years of age and that he believed her representation. The girl testified that she participated in the act voluntarily, but that she told the defendant that she was fifteen years old. Although the trial court allowed testimony showing that the defendant knew the girl's age, the trial court excluded any further testimony by the defendant concerning the reasonableness of his belief as to the girl's age and instructed the jury that mistake as to the girl's age was no defense to the charge.

On this appeal, defendant argues that the trial court erred in (1) excluding the proffered evidence substantiating the basis of the defendant's alleged belief that the girl was over the age of sixteen years and (2) rejecting the defendant's requested jury instruction that a reasonable mistake as to the girl's age constituted a defense to the crime as charged. We note that even if the requested instruction had been given and the jury had found in accordance therewith, the defendant still would have been guilty of fornication under Utah law. U.C.A., 1953, § 76-7-104.

I.

The Utah Criminal Code follows the common law in establishing the basic proposition that a person cannot be found guilty of a criminal offense unless he harbors a requisite criminal state of mind or unless the prohibited act is based on strict liability. At the time in question, § 76-2-101 stated:

No person is guilty of an offense unless his conduct is prohibited by law and:

(1) He acts intentionally, knowingly, recklessly or with criminal negligence with respect to each element of the offense as the definition of the offense requires; or

(2) His acts constitute an offense involving strict liability.[2]

Thus, for an act to constitute a crime, the act must be prohibited and the defendant must be shown to have possessed a culpable or criminal state of mind, a *mens rea*, "with respect to each element of the offense," unless the offense involves a strict liability offense. An established first principle of the criminal law, with few exceptions, is that the doing of a wrongful act without the requisite culpable mental state does not constitute a crime. Nor does the harboring of a criminal mental state, not translated into a prohibited act, constitute a crime.

---

2. The section has since been amended. 1983 Utah Laws ch. 90, § 1; ch. 98, § 1.

Under the Utah Criminal Code, a crime may be a strict liability crime only if the statute specifically states it to be such.[3] At the time in dispute, § 76-2-102 stated:

Every offense not involving strict liability shall require a culpable mental state, and when the definition of the offense does not specify a culpable mental state, intent, knowledge, or recklessness shall suffice to establish criminal responsibility. *An offense shall involve strict liability only when a statute defining the offense clearly indicates a legislative purpose to impose strict liability for the conduct by use of the phrase "strict liability" or other terms of similar import.* [Emphasis added.][4]

The unlawful sexual intercourse statute, § 76-5-401, *supra*, does not clearly indicate "a legislative purpose to impose strict liability" as required by § 76-2-102 to establish a strict liability offense. It does not even impliedly indicate a legislative purpose to impose strict liability. Thus, a crime of unlawful sexual intercourse, a crime different from the crime of fornication, cannot be proved unless the state proves the requisite criminal state of mind as to each element of the offense. § 76-2-101(1).

The elements of the degree of unlawful sexual intercourse charged here are:

(1) an act of sexual intercourse, (2) with a person, not the defendant's spouse, (3) who is under sixteen years of age. The punishment is enhanced if the defendant is more than three years older than the other person. § 76-5-401(2). In proving unlawful sexual intercourse, therefore, the state must prove a culpable mental state by showing that the defendant "act[ed] intentionally, knowingly, recklessly or with criminal negligence," § 76-2-101(1), as those terms are defined in § 76-2-103.

Clearly, the requisite culpable mental state as to the first and second elements of the offense is established by showing that defendant intentionally engaged in sexual intercourse with a female not his wife. However, since the crime of unlawful sexual intercourse is not a strict liability offense, the critical issue is what mental state must exist as to the victim's age.[5] On its face, the unlawful sexual intercourse statute does not require intent as to all elements of the crime. The *mens rea* necessary for the third element of the crime requires a consideration of the purposes of the statute. No doubt

---

3. Strict criminal liability is clearly an exception to long-established principles of criminal liability. Under Utah law, strict liability exists only when the statute defining the offense expressly so states. Generally, strict criminal liability is employed only in certain business or economic regulations. The United States Supreme Court discussed the subject of strict liability in *Morissette v. United States*, 342 U.S. 246, 96 L. Ed. 288, 72 S. Ct. 240 (1952), in which a defendant's conviction was overturned because no *mens rea* was shown and the crime was not a regulatory offense.

4. This section has since been amended. 1983 Utah Laws, ch. 90, § 2.

5. We shall refer to the girl in this case as the "victim" where helpful and for ease of reference, although arguably this is a so-called "victimless" crime. Indeed, both the girl and the defendant could have been charged with violating § 76-5-401. The act prohibited is not rape but a consensual act on the part of both parties. However that may be, the policy of law is to prevent persons from engaging in intercourse outside of marriage.

one purpose of the statute is to deter persons from engaging in intercourse with young, immature persons and to avoid the consequent risk of pregnancies because those subject to the prohibitions of the statute, both males and females, are not likely to be fully knowledgeable in any realistic way about the personal and social consequences of an out-of-wedlock pregnancy. The statute seeks to establish barriers around, and provide a measure of protection to, younger, more impressionable, and perhaps more persuadable persons in order to prevent them from engaging in sexual intercourse out of wedlock.

To accomplish those purposes and still remain true to long-established fundamental principles of the criminal law, which have been incorporated in the Utah Criminal Code, we hold that as to the third element of the crime, there must be proof of a culpable mental state which establishes that the defendant was at least criminally negligent as to the age of the partner. That is, the prosecution must prove that the defendant either was aware of the fact that the partner was underage or that the defendant ought to have been aware of a substantial and unjustifiable risk that his partner was underage. § 76-2-103(4). The test as to the latter part of the standard is an objective, reasonable person test.

Furthermore, § 76-2-304 provides that unless otherwise provided, ignorance or mistake of fact which disproves the culpable mental state is a defense to the crime charged but does not relieve a person from being prosecuted for a lesser included offense. There is no inconsistency in requiring a *mens rea* of criminal negligence as to age and an affirmative defense of mistake of fact as to age. The *mens rea* requirement may be based on objective criteria, while the ignorance or mistake of fact defense bears upon the subjective state of mind of the defendant.[6]

II.

We recognize that a number of courts have held that a defendant is strictly liable with respect to the age of a victim and that mistake of age is not a defense to the crime charged here. Many courts have argued that the crime is a strict liability offense because the age of the girl is not an element of the offense; therefore, no *mens rea* is required as to that.... In such jurisdictions, the state would not have to prove that a defendant had knowledge of the partner's age or was criminally negligent in failing to ascertain it, and a defendant's reasonable mistake as to the victim's age would be irrelevant.

Other jurisdictions strive to satisfy the *mens rea* requirement and still disallow the defense of mistake of age by hypothesizing the necessary *mens rea* in the intention to have intercourse with a nonspouse, without requiring any *mens rea* as to the partner's age. That is, the defendant's intent to do one unlawful act is deemed to suffice for the commission of another, unintended act. R. Perkins, *Criminal Law* 819 (2d

---

6. In a similar case, the California court held that a defendant is entitled to introduce evidence of mistake of age. *People v. Hernandez*, 61 Cal. 2d 529 (1964).

ed. 1969). Thus, where the law makes intercourse with any nonspouse illegal, irrespective of age (as under the Utah fornication statute, § 76-7-104), the theory is that since the defendant intended to commit *an* illegal act that constitutes fornication at least, the unlawful intention or *mens rea* necessary for that crime is transferable to the charge of unlawful sexual intercourse.

Under that theory, the prosecution is not required to prove the *mens rea* as to the element of age, and the defendant's evidence of mistake is not recognized on the ground that because the defendant had a criminal intent to commit a crime, even though the intended crime is not the one with which he is charged. That is, the act of intercourse would be criminal under the unlawful sexual intercourse statute even if the defendant acted reasonably in attempting to ascertain the age of the victim and even if the victim actively misled the defendant. Thus, the *mens rea* of a lesser crime (fornication) is held to satisfy the *mens rea* required for a more serious crime (unlawful sexual intercourse or statutory rape). Other courts impose strict liability by not requiring a *mens rea* as to the age of the victim.

However unrealistic the position may be in a particular case, the criminal law presumes that one knows the criminal law. Paradoxically, if one does know the elements of the unlawful intercourse law and takes every possible precaution to avoid violation of that law, he may still be guilty of violating that law on the doctrine of transferred intent, i.e., that the criminal intent to commit one wrong may be used to convict one of another criminal act, or on the doctrine of strict liability. That is at odds with the belief that in a free society one should be held responsible for criminal activity only if he is culpable by virtue of a criminal or wrongful intent to do the wrongful act.

Both theories flout the constitutional principle that one should be responsible to ascertain and understand the criminal law and should be held accountable only for those acts of criminal conduct for which he or she is mentally culpable in the criminal sense. It is not consonant with our principles of criminal liability when dealing with *malum in se* crimes to hold a person responsible for a crime he did not intend to commit and indeed may even have taken every precaution to avoid committing, even though he intended to commit a lesser crime. To hold one liable for a greater crime which he actually sought to avoid committing on the ground that he committed a lesser crime turns the doctrine of lesser included offenses on its head and raises fundamental questions which may have constitutional implications.

In addition, it is fundamentally unfair to allow the victim in such a crime—who necessarily has also violated the law—to mislead the defendant as to an element of the crime and then place the blame for the mistake on the defendant rather than the person who created the deceit and entrapped the defendant into committing a crime he or she attempted to avoid. Finally, the theory that the age of the victim is not an element of the offense is plainly wrong. Surely no one would contend that if a prosecutor failed to prove the age of the girl, a conviction for unlawful intercourse could stand.

III.

The prosecution argued at trial and the trial court held that defendant's mental state with respect to the girl's age was irrelevant. That is, the trial court held that no *mens rea* was required for the third element of the crime. In denying the defendant the opportunity to present evidence as to mistake of age, the trial court stated, "I think ... just intentionally knowing that you are having intercourse with a given individual, who it turns out is within the age restrictions that would cause this matter to be a felony." Thus, the intent to engage in sexual intercourse, with knowledge that the girl was not his spouse, was held sufficient to satisfy the *mens rea* requirement for all elements. In other words, the prosecution was only required to prove the elements of the crime of fornication, *see* § 76-7-104, of the more serious crime of unlawful sexual intercourse, a third degree felony. Thus, although the prosecution presented evidence that the defendant knew the girl was under sixteen, the defendant was not allowed to rebut that evidence.

Because defendant's mental state with respect to the age of the girl was considered irrelevant, his proffered defense based on a reasonable mistake as to her age was disallowed. The exclusion of the defendant's evidence does not comport with the provisions of the Utah Criminal Code.

The defense of mistake of fact is established by § 76-2-304:

> (1) Unless otherwise provided, ignorance or mistake of fact which disproves the culpable mental state is a defense to any prosecution for that crime....
> (3) Although an actor's ignorance or mistake of fact or law may constitute a defense to the offense charged, he may nevertheless be convicted of a lesser included offense of which he would be guilty if the fact or law were as he believed.

Under subsection (1), if a defendant acts under a reasonable mistake of fact as to the victim's age, that mistake is a defense to the crime of unlawful sexual intercourse. Under subsection (3), such a defendant is still guilty of a lesser included offense of fornication. In other words, a defendant may rebut the prosecution's evidence that the defendant had knowledge or should have had knowledge of the victim's age by proving that he or she was misled by the partner's affirmatively misrepresenting his or her age. Of course, a misrepresentation is not an absolute defense. If the trier of fact were to conclude that the defendant had not relied on the misrepresentation, the defendant could still be convicted of the crime charged. Clearly the physical appearance of the victim may be persuasive against a defendant. The physical appearance of a very young girl would, at least in some cases, negate any affirmative misrepresentation she might make. But a defendant's showing that he acted reasonably under all the circumstances to avoid transgressing the statute in question may rebut the prosecution's charge that defendant acted with criminal negligence.

IV.

This construction of the statutes does not subvert the objectives of the law.[8] We certainly do not question the proposition that young people should be protected from sexual exploitation by older, more experienced persons until they reach the legal age of consent and can more maturely comprehend and appreciate the consequences of their sexual acts. However, where a younger participant intentionally misrepresents his or her age, so that the older participant reasonably relies on the misrepresentations as to the partner's age, the "victim" and society's interests generally are still protected by the statute prohibiting fornication. Not to require the prosecution to prove a *mens rea* as to the element of age and to deny the defense of mistake of fact would subject an honestly misled party, whether adult or fellow teenager, to criminal liability brought about by a sophisticated youth who seeks to abuse the criminal law for his or her own sensual indulgences or for even more insidious purposes, such as blackmail or an attempt to avoid community or familial condemnation by denying that he or she enticed another to participate in the sexual act. The unlawful sexual intercourse statute was not aimed at defendants such as these, nor should it place such weapons in the hands of those who would deny their own responsibilities. The denial of evidence of mistake of fact in such cases would subject the defendant to a liability out of proportion with his or her culpability.

Reversed and remanded for proceedings consistent with this opinion.

* * *

As Justice Stewart mentions in the second *Elton* opinion, the Utah legislature enacted the following statute in 1983:

Utah Code Annotated

§ 76-3-304.5 Mistake as to victim's age not a defense

(2) It is not a defense to the crime of unlawful sexual activity with a minor,.... that the actor mistakenly believed the victim to be 16 years of age or older at the time of the alleged offense or was unaware of the victim's true age.

* * *

This statute was enacted after the first but prior to the second *Elton* opinion. With which opinion is the statute consistent? Why do you think the legislature passed this statute? In *State v. Martinez*, 14 P.3d 114 (2000), the Utah Court of Appeals held that an amended version of this Utah provision imposes strict liability for sex offenses involving victims under the age of 16, but that "no such provision precludes a mistake of fact defense when the alleged victim is a minor of sixteen or seventeen."

---

8. We recognize that our decision in this case may have only limited significance, as the Legislature has amended the Utah Criminal Code in 1983 to disallow mistake of fact as to age as a defense to the crime of unlawful sexual intercourse: "It is not a defense to the crime of unlawful sexual intercourse, ... that the actor mistakenly believed the victim to be sixteen years of age or older at the time of the alleged offense or was unaware of the victim's true age." U.C.A., 1953, § 76-2-304.5(2). That provision, however, is not applied retroactively to the facts of this case....

4. Constitutional Issues

In the next case, the defendant was charged under the following Ohio statute:

> No person shall engage in sexual conduct with another who is not the spouse of the offender or who is the spouse of the offender but is living separate and apart from the offender, when any of the following applies: ...

> (b) The other person is less than 13 years of age, whether or not the offender knows the age of the other person.

In re D.B.

129 Ohio St. 3d 104 (2011)
Supreme Court of Ohio

[The defendant, D.B., a 12-year-old boy, was charged in juvenile court with multiple counts of statutory rape and forcible rape of M.G., an 11-year-old boy. D.B. was also charged with one count of statutory rape of A.W., a 12-year-old boy. Prior to trial, the prosecution dropped the count charging D.B. with the statutory rape of A.W., who testified against D.B. at trial. At the close of the trial, the judge decided the prosecution had not proven that D.B. used force against M.G. and acquitted D.B. of all charges of forcible rape. But he found D.B. guilty of five counts of statutory rape of M.G.]

Lanziger, J.

... A.W. testified that he had observed D.B. and M.G. engage in anal sex. A.W. testified that D.B. "bribed" M.G. with video games to engage in sexual conduct. Both A.W. and M.G. stated that the sexual conduct was always initiated by D.B. and that D.B. would either bargain with, or use physical force on, M.G. to convince M.G. to engage in sexual conduct.

According to A.W., D.B. and M.G. did not engage in sexual conduct until M.G. himself agreed to the activity. D.B.'s father testified that while D.B. was significantly bigger than other children his age, he was not an aggressive child and he never used his size to bully or intimidate other children.

Defense counsel moved for acquittal at the conclusion of the state's case. The court dismissed the counts [alleging forcible rape] after finding that no specific evidence existed to support them. Determining that there was no basis for finding that D.B. had engaged in forcible sexual conduct, the court also dismissed those portions of [other] counts ... that alleged forcible rape. D.B.'s motion to dismiss the counts alleging a violation of R.C. 2907.02(A)(1)(b) was denied.

The hearing resumed on March 4, 2008.... Following the presentation of the defense's case, the court stated that while there was "no question whatsoever" that the sexual acts detailed in the remaining counts took place, it could not find that D.B used force during any of the acts. The court therefore adjudicated D.B. delinquent based on the violation of R.C. 2907.02(A)(1)(b) alleged in [five] counts [in the complaint].

At the dispositional hearing, the court committed D.B. to the Department of Youth Services for a minimum of five years to the maximum period of his 21st birthday, suspended the commitment, and placed D.B. on probation for an indefinite period of time. The court further ordered D.B. to attend counseling and group therapy.

On appeal to the Fifth District Court of Appeals, D.B. argued that application of R.C. 2907.02(A)(1)(b) violated his federal rights to due process and equal protection, that the juvenile court abused its discretion in adjudicating him delinquent for rape.... The court of appeals upheld the constitutionality of R.C. 2907.02(A)(1)(b) as applied and held that the trial court did not abuse its discretion in adjudicating D.B. delinquent for rape for engaging in sexual conduct with an 11-year-old child. We accepted jurisdiction over appellant's proposition of law, which states that application of R.C. 2907.02(A)(1)(b) to a child under the age of 13 violates the Due Process and Equal Protection Clauses of the United States and Ohio Constitutions.[2]

Analysis

D.B. does not assert that R.C. 2907.02(A)(1)(b) is unconstitutional on its face, meaning that it can never be applied without violating constitutional rights, but asserts that it is unconstitutional as applied to him. "A statute may be challenged as unconstitutional on the basis that it is invalid on its face or as applied to a particular set of facts. In an as-applied challenge, the challenger 'contends that application of the statute in the particular context in which he has acted, or in which he proposes to act, [is] unconstitutional.'" Thus, we focus on the statute and its particular application in an as-applied challenge.

R.C. 2907.02(A)(1)(b) criminalizes what is commonly known as "statutory rape." The statute holds offenders strictly liable for engaging in sexual conduct with children under the age of 13—force is not an element of the offense because a child under the age of 13 is legally presumed to be incapable of consenting to sexual conduct.

R.C. 2907.02(A)(1) provides:

> "No person shall engage in sexual conduct with another who is not the spouse of the offender or who is the spouse of the offender but is living separate and apart from the offender, when any of the following applies: ...
>
> "(b) The other person is less than 13 years of age, whether or not the offender knows the age of the other person."

The statute furthers the state's interest in protecting young children. Indeed, the Legislature Service Commission stated that R.C. 2907.02(A)(1)(b) was created to protect a prepubescent child from the sexual advances of another because "engaging in sexual conduct with such a person indicates vicious behavior on the part of the offender."

D.B. argues that R.C. 2907.02(A)(1)(b) is unconstitutional in two ways. First, he argues that the statute is vague as applied to children under the age of 13 and thus violates his right to due process. Second, he argues that the statute was applied in an arbitrary manner in this case in contravention of his constitutional right to equal protection. This case thus asks whether a child's federal constitutional rights are violated when, as a member of the class protected under R.C. 2907.02(A)(1)(b), he or she is adjudicated delinquent based upon a violation of this statute.

A. Due Process

D.B. argues that R.C. 2907.02(A)(1)(b) is unconstitutional as applied to him because it fails to provide guidelines that designate which actor is the victim and which is the offender, resulting in arbitrary and discriminatory enforcement. "It is fundamental that a court must 'presume the constitutionality of lawfully enacted legislation.'" Accordingly, "the legislation in question 'will not be invalidated unless the challenger establishes that it is unconstitutional beyond a reasonable doubt.'"

Juvenile delinquency hearings "must measure up to the essentials of due process and fair treatment." Due process is not satisfied if a statute is unconstitutionally vague. "A statute can be impermissibly vague for either of two independent reasons. First, if it fails to provide people of ordinary intelligence a reasonable opportunity to understand what conduct it prohibits. Second, if it authorizes or even encourages arbitrary and discriminatory enforcement."

The United States Supreme Court has identified the second reason as the primary concern of the vagueness doctrine: "[T]he more important aspect of vagueness doctrine 'is not actual notice, but the other principal element of the doctrine—the requirement that a legislature establish minimal guidelines to govern law enforcement.' Where the legislature fails to provide such minimal guidelines, a criminal statute may permit 'a standardless sweep [that] allows policemen, prosecutors, and juries to pursue their personal predilections.'" This prong of the vagueness doctrine not only upholds due process, but also serves to protect the separation of powers: "It would certainly be dangerous if the legislature could set a net large enough to catch all possible offenders, and leave it to the courts to step inside and say who could be rightfully detained, and who should be set at large. This would, to some extent, substitute the judicial for the legislative department of the government."

As applied to children under the age of 13 who engage in sexual conduct with other children under the age of 13, R.C. 2907.02(A)(1)(b) is unconstitutionally vague because the statute authorizes and encourages arbitrary and discriminatory enforcement. When an adult engages in sexual conduct with a child under the age of 13, it is clear which party is the offender and which is the victim. But when two children under the age of 13 engage in sexual conduct with each other, each child is both an offender and a victim, and the distinction between those two terms breaks down.

---

2. Because appellant argued only a violation of his federal constitutional rights of due process and equal protection during his appeal to the Fifth District, we will not address his allegations regarding the state constitution in this opinion.

The facts of this case provide an example of the temptation for prosecutors to label one child as the offender and the other child as the victim. Based apparently upon the theory that D.B. forced M.G. to engage in sexual conduct, the state alleged that D.B., but not M.G., had engaged in conduct that constituted statutory rape. However, while the theory of D.B. as the aggressor was consistent with the counts alleging a violation of RC. 2907.02(A)(2), which proscribes rape by force, this theory is incompatible with the counts alleging a violation of statutory rape because anyone who engages in sexual conduct with a minor under the age of 13 commits statutory rape regardless of whether force was used. Thus, if the facts alleged in the complaint were true, D.B. and M.G. would both be in violation of RC. 2907.02(A)(1)(b).

The prosecutor's choice to charge D.B. but not M.G. is the very definition of discriminatory enforcement. D.B. and M.G. engaged in sexual conduct with each other, yet only D.B. was charged.[3] The facts of this case demonstrate that R.C. 2907.02(A)(1)(b) authorizes and encourages arbitrary and discriminatory enforcement when applied to offenders under the age of 13. The statute is thus unconstitutionally vague as applied to this situation.

It must be emphasized that the concept of consent plays no role in whether a person violates R.C. 2907.02(A)(1)(b): children under the age of 13 are legally incapable of consenting to sexual conduct. Furthermore, whether D.B. used force to engage in sexual conduct does not play a role in our consideration of R.C. 2907.02(A)(1)(b). The trial court found that D.B. did not use force. Whether an offender used force is irrelevant to the determination whether the offender committed rape under R.C. 2907.02(A)(1)(b).

We note that while we hold that R.C. 2907.02(A)(1)(b) is unconstitutional as applied to a child under the age of 13 who engages in sexual conduct with another child under the age of 13, a child under the age of 13 may be found guilty of rape if additional elements are shown: the offender substantially impairs the other person's judgment or control, R.C. 2907.02(A)(1)(a); the other person's ability to resist or consent is substantially impaired because of a mental or physical condition, R.C. 2907.02(A)(1)(c); or the offender compels the other person to submit by force or threat of force, R.C. 2907.02(A)(2). None of those additional elements was present here.

B. Equal Protection

Application of R.C. 2907.02(A)(1)(b) in this case also violates D.B.'s federal right to equal protection. "The Equal Protection Clause directs that 'all persons similarly circumstanced shall be treated alike.'"

The plain language of the statute makes it clear that every person who engages in sexual conduct with a child under the age of 13 is strictly liable for statutory rape, and

---

3. Furthermore, the initial complaint detailed sexual conduct between D.B. and A.W., yet charged only D.B. with rape in violation of R.C. 2907.02(A)(1)(b).

the statute must be enforced equally and without regard to the particular circumstances of an individual's situation. R.C. 2907.02(A)(1)(b) offers no prosecutorial exception to charging an offense when every party involved in the sexual conduct is under the age of 13; conceivably, the principle of equal protection suggests that both parties could be prosecuted as identically situated. Because D.B. and M.G. were both under the age of 13 at the time the events in this case occurred, they were both members of the class protected by the statute, and both could have been charged under the offense. Application of the statute in this case to a single party violates the Equal Protection Clause's mandate that persons similarly circumstanced shall be treated alike.

All three boys allegedly engaged in sexual conduct with a person under the age of 13; however, only D.B. was charged with a violation of R.C. 2907.02(A)(1)(b). This arbitrary enforcement of the statute violates D.B.'s right to equal protection. We accordingly hold that application of the statute in this case violated D.B.'s federal equal-protection rights. The statute is unconstitutional as applied to him.

Judgment reversed and cause remanded.

Discussion Questions

1. How could the Ohio legislature clarify the statute at issue in *In re: D.B.* to cure the vagueness and equal protection problems identified by the court? How should the statute be clarified?

2. Would the prosecution have satisfied equal protection if D.B. and both the other boys had been charged? If all had been charged, who would have testified against D.B.? Are there any reasons that would justify the prosecution in treating two boys such as D.B. and M.G. differently? What if the charges against one of the other boys had been dropped in exchange for his agreeing to testify against D.B.? Would that have been a satisfactory reason for treating one of them differently? What if D.B. had a prior history of engaging in sexual conduct with other juveniles and the others did not? What if M.G. had been 9 rather than 11? What if he had been 6 rather than 11?

3. The court states that "consent plays no role in whether a person violates" the statutory rape statute. If M.G. did not consent to D.B.'s conduct, would it be fair to say that M.G. *engaged in sexual conduct* as required by the statute? The court also states that "whether D.B. used force to engage in sexual conduct does not play a role in our consideration of" the statutory rape statute. If D.B. did use force against M.G., would it still be fair to say that M.G. *engaged in sexual conduct* as required by the statute?

4. The court states that "[t]he plain language of the statute makes it clear that every person who engages in sexual conduct with a child under the age of 13 is strictly liable for statutory rape...." Does the plain language of the Ohio statute clearly impose strict liability? If so, what language in the statute imposes strict liability? Or is the statute ambiguous about mental state? What statutory language addresses mental state? How could it be clarified?

Synthesis and Review

In recent years, sexual violence and other coercive sexual behavior on college and university campuses has been the focus of considerable concern and attention. The incidence of such violence and behavior is and has been shockingly high. A 2015 survey by the Association of American Universities, for example, found that more than one-fourth of undergraduate women at a large number of major universities reported having experienced unwanted sexual contact, ranging from touching to rape.[24] A follow-up 2019 survey revealed even higher rates of sexual misconduct.[25] The reluctance of student victims to report misconduct by another student and the failure of many colleges and universities to adopt adequate preventive measures, encourage reporting, or impose disciplinary sanctions are and have been problems. During the Obama administration, the Department of Education demanded that colleges and universities address these issues and provided guidelines that schools must follow in order for them to receive federal funding. Some of these guidelines were widely seen as appropriate and long overdue. Others, though, generated significant criticism and controversy. Debate about how colleges and universities should deal with sexual misconduct on campus is ongoing.

Problem

9.8 What in your view is the appropriate approach for a college or university to adopt for dealing with sexual misconduct? Consider the possibilities described below. What do you see as the potential arguments for and against each? Is there an approach to sexual misconduct that you think would be more appropriate and effective than the options described below? Which approach or combination of approaches do you think is preferable? Are there measures you think should be adopted in addition to the measures listed below?

(a) Alert the local police and prosecutor about a complaint, then wait until any criminal action is resolved before commencing a disciplinary proceeding. If the case results in a criminal conviction, expel the student who is the subject of the complaint. If the case does not result in prosecution or ends with a verdict of not guilty, take no disciplinary action.

(b) Have the school immediately conduct its own investigation and, if warranted, begin a disciplinary action regardless of whether a criminal case is pending or under investigation.

---

24. Richard Perez-Pena, *1 in 4 Women Experience Sexual Assault on Campus*, NEW YORK TIMES (Sept. 21, 2015); AAU Climate Survey on Sexual Assault and Sexual Misconduct (2015).
25. AAU Campus Climate Survey (2019).

(c) In the disciplinary proceeding, require that the misconduct be proven *beyond reasonable doubt* before any disciplinary action is taken.

(d) In the disciplinary proceeding, require that the misconduct be proven by a *preponderance of the evidence* before any disciplinary action is taken.

(e) While a disciplinary proceeding is pending, place restrictions on the subject of the complaint, such as having no contact with the complainant, banning the subject from student housing, banning the subject from campus except to attend classes, or banning the subject from the campus entirely.

Chapter 10

Attempt

A. Introduction

Modern criminal law regularly treats an attempt to commit a crime as a separate offense. Attempt is an example of a category of crimes known as *anticipatory* offenses, as are solicitation and conspiracy. Each is anticipatory in the sense of looking forward to the commission of some other crime in the future, often referred to as the target offense. An attempt to commit a murder, for example, anticipates the target offense of murder. Conspiracy to commit bank robbery anticipates the crime of bank robbery. The adjective *inchoate*—meaning something in an initial or early stage, only partially developed—is also used to describe such offenses.

This chapter begins by examining the conduct required for attempt. Legislatures as well as courts vary greatly in regard to the conduct required for attempt. Some allow early steps in a course of conduct aimed at committing an offense to trigger attempt liability. Others rely on much later steps to trigger attempt liability. Some, for example, require that a person be dangerously close to accomplishing the target offense. Still others take positions between these two extremes.

We then turn to mental states. As you have seen in prior chapters, crimes can and often do include more than one mental state. The same is true for attempt. Legislatures typically designate intent as one of these mental states. The Model Penal Code and jurisdictions that have adopted its mental state terms use the word purpose rather than intent in relation to attempt. We saw in the chapter on mental states that the word *intent* has been given a variety of meanings by courts and legislatures. In the context of attempt, intent is generally given the same meaning it has in common usage, the same meaning as *purpose* under the Model Penal Code.

To what must this intent or purpose pertain? The conduct element required for attempt? The conduct required for commission of the target offense? Any result elements in the target offense? Any circumstance elements in the target offense? As these questions suggest, clear analysis of attempt liability requires one to distinguish among and assess separately multiple mental states. Many statutes and cases, unfortunately, fail to resolve these questions.

Following mental state, we address the question of whether a person can cancel liability for attempt by abandoning a course of conduct prior to committing the target offense. Then we deal with the problem of impossibility—whether a person will be held legally responsible for trying to commit a crime that it is not possible for the person to commit.

In Chapter 4, in relation to the conduct requirement, we addressed the tension that may arise between incapacitation on the one hand and retribution and deterrence on the other. A person typically must act on evil intentions in order to be sufficiently blameworthy to deserve criminal punishment. Conduct serves the practical function of providing concrete circumstantial evidence of an actor's culpable mental state. The conduct requirement also gives deterrence a chance to work. It is between formation of a purpose to commit a crime and action based on that purpose when the threats underlying deterrence in theory do their work. The Latin phrase for this period in which a potential offender may have a change of heart is "locus poenitentiae"—literally a place for repentance.

But waiting until someone acts on evil intentions reduces and may even eliminate the opportunity for police to intervene and incapacitate a dangerous person. Anticipatory offenses such as attempt and conspiracy respond to the desire to incapacitate an actor before she has committed the target offense. But can we be sure an anticipatory offender really is harboring an evil purpose if she has not yet acted on it? And how do we know she would not have been deterred by the threat of punishment for the target offense if she is arrested and not allowed to choose whether to commit the target offense? This tension pitting incapacitation against retribution and deterrence underlies all anticipatory offenses. As you read the statutes and cases in this chapter, see how legislatures and courts have weighed and balanced concerns about blame, deterrence and incapacitation.

B. Punishment

How should attempts be punished? Consider the facts described in the following Problem:

Problem

10.1 In October, 2018, Robert D. Bowers attacked a synagogue in Pennsylvania and killed multiple victims using a gun. In October, 2019, Richard Holzer planned to attack a synagogue in Colorado using explosives, but was arrested before he could do so. He met with undercover FBI agents posing as fellow white supremacists and was arrested when he accepted fake explosives from the agents. In earlier conversations, Holzer expressed his hatred of Jewish people and his plan to destroy the synagogue. Assume that Holzer intended to kill multiple people in the attack and that he is guilty of attempted murder. Both Bowers and Holzer hold white supremacist and virulently antisemitic beliefs and were motivated by these beliefs in planning their crimes. Assuming both men have similar criminal records, should Holzer, who *attempted* to murder multiple victims but did not succeed get the *same punishment* as Bowers, who *succeeded* in murdering multiple victims? Or should Holzer get a *lesser punishment* than Bowers? What are the competing arguments for each position? In answering these questions, consider the purposes of punishment you have studied throughout this course.

As the statutes below reflect, jurisdictions vary in how they answer the question of whether people who attempt a crime, such as Holzer, should get the same punishment as those who succeed in committing that target crime, such as Bowers. What position does each statute take on this question? How do they differ? Which statute do you think reflects the preferable view?

Montana Code Annotated

§ 45-4-103 Attempt

(3) A person convicted of the offense of attempt shall be punished not to exceed the maximum provided for the offense attempted.

Minnesota Statutes

§ 609.17 Attempts

4. Whoever attempts to commit a crime may be sentenced as follows:

   (1) If the maximum sentence provided for the crime is life imprisonment, to not more than 20 years; or

   (2) For any other attempt, to not more than one-half of the maximum imprisonment or fine or both provided for the crime attempted, but such maximum in any case shall not be less than imprisonment for 90 days or a fine of $100.

Model Penal Code

§ 5.05

(1) <u>Grading.</u> Except as otherwise provided in this Section, attempt, solicitation and conspiracy are crimes of the same grade and degree as the most serious offense that is attempted or solicited or is an object of the conspiracy. An attempt, solicitation or

conspiracy to commit a [capital crime or a] felony of the first degree is a felony of the
second degree.

C. Conduct

In Chapter 4 you encountered the general proposition that criminal law does not
punish evil intentions alone. Rather, some form of conduct is typically required.
Based on the materials in this section, do you think the crime of attempt is consistent
with this proposition?

Problems

10.2 Gwen is a radical environmentalist who decides to assassinate Albert, the
president of Oilco, an oil and gas exploration company. Oilco has obtained permission to drill for oil and gas in an area recognized until recently as wilderness
protected from such drilling. To enact her plan, Gwen first hacks into Oilco's
computer and learns Albert's home address. She then follows Albert for several
days to determine when and on what route he drives to and from work each
day. Gwen scouts the route for a good place for an ambush. Albert lives in a
rural area about an hour outside the city in which Oilco has its headquarters.
Gwen chooses a wooded spot about a mile from Albert's house for the assassination and constructs a shelter of tree limbs so she cannot be seen from the
road. She buys a high-powered deer hunting rifle and ammunition from a local
gun dealer using a false name and identification papers. On the day she has
chosen for the shooting, Gwen dons camouflage hunting clothes and takes up
her position in the woods with the hunting rifle. About half an hour later, Albert
drives by Gwen's location. Gwen takes aim and fires, but she misses and Albert
escapes unharmed. Assume that the police had legally wiretapped Gwen's telephone, recorded statements by Gwen to other radical environmentalists about
her plan to kill Albert, and placed her under surveillance. Under the statutes
and cases below, at what point could the police have arrested Gwen for attempted
murder? Would it make a difference if Gwen's shot had taken place during deer
hunting season?

10.3 In April 2007, a Virginia Tech student armed with two handguns shot and
killed 32 students and faculty on that university's campus before killing himself.
Throughout the United States the Virginia Tech shootings received enormous
publicity.

Three months after the Virginia Tech shootings, in July 2007, a licensed gun
dealer in a midwestern university town becomes concerned when he learns that
Kenneth, a student at the local university, has purchased online and is awaiting
delivery of four semi-automatic firearms: three Hi-Point .380 caliber semiau-

tomatic handguns and a Vulcan Mac 10 .45 caliber semiautomatic handgun. After Kenneth repeatedly calls the dealer, seeming anxious about delivery of the guns, the dealer notifies the university's campus police about the pending delivery of the guns to Kenneth. The police find parked on campus a car registered to Kenneth. They legally search the car and in a compartment inside it they find a piece of paper on which is written:

> SEND 2 to … paypal account if this account doesn't reach $50,000 in the next 7 days then a murderous rampage similar to the VT shooting will occur at another highly populated university. THIS IS NOT A JOKE!

In the car, the police also find a knit watch cap and ski mask.

The police then arrest Kenneth at his on-campus apartment. During a search of the apartment the police find a loaded .25 caliber handgun in Kenneth's dresser. Under state law, a student must obtain written permission from university police to bring a firearm onto a university campus. Kenneth did not seek or obtain such permission for the handgun found in his dresser.

Kenneth is charged with attempt to commit a terrorist threat. The target offense Kenneth is charged with attempting to commit is defined as follows:

> A person is guilty of making a terrorist threat when, with the intent to intimidate or coerce a significant portion of a civilian population, he or she in any manner knowingly threatens to commit or threatens to cause the commission of a terrorist act and thereby causes a reasonable expectation or fear of the imminent commission of a terrorist act.

At trial, Kenneth's defense lawyer calls some of Kenneth's friends who testify to their good opinion of his character, that he is president of his fraternity, and that he and his friends share a hobby of shooting firearms. Is Kenneth liable for attempt to make a terrorist threat?

Montana Code Annotated

§ 45-4-103 Attempt

(1) A person commits the offense of attempt when, with the purpose to commit a specific offense, he does any act toward the commission of such offense.

Wisconsin Statutes

§ 939.32

(3) An attempt to commit a crime requires that the actor have an intent to perform acts and attain a result which, if accomplished, would constitute such crime and that the actor does acts toward the commission of the crime which demonstrate unequivocally,

under all the circumstances, that the actor formed that intent and would commit the crime except for the intervention of another person or some other extraneous factor.

Model Penal Code

§ 5.01. Criminal Attempt

(1) **Definition of Attempt.** A person is guilty of an attempt to commit a crime if ... he:

    (a) purposely engages in conduct that would constitute the crime if the attendant circumstances were as he believes them to be; or

    (b) when causing a particular result is an element of the crime, does or omits to do anything with the purpose of causing or with the belief that it will cause such result without further conduct on his part; or

    (c) purposely does or omits to do anything that, under the circumstances as he believes them to be, is an act or omission constituting a substantial step in a course of conduct planned to culminate in his commission of the crime.

(2) **Conduct Which May Be Held Substantial Step Under Subsection (1)(c).** Conduct shall not be held to constitute a substantial step under Subsection (1)(c) of this Section unless it is strongly corroborative of the actor's criminal purpose. Without negativing the sufficiency of other conduct, the following, if strongly corroborative of the actor's criminal purpose, shall not be held insufficient as a matter of law:

    (a) lying in wait, searching for or following the contemplated victim of the crime;

    (b) enticing or seeking to entice the contemplated victim of the crime to go to the place contemplated for its commission;

    (c) reconnoitering the place contemplated for the commission of the crime;

    (d) unlawful entry of a structure, vehicle or enclosure in which it is contemplated that the crime will be committed;

    (e) possession of materials to be employed in the commission of the crime, that are specially designed for such unlawful use or that can serve no lawful purpose of the actor under the circumstances;

    (f) possession, collection or fabrication of materials to be employed in the commission of the crime, at or near the place contemplated for its commission, if such possession, collection or fabrication serves no lawful purpose of the actor under the circumstances;

    (g) soliciting an innocent agent to engage in conduct constituting an element of the crime.

Discussion Questions

1. What is the key language in each subsection of MPC Section 5.01(1) — (a), (b), and (c) — for determining conduct sufficient to constitute an attempt? Note that the language in each section differs.

2. What is the significance and function of the list of examples set forth in Model Penal Code Section 5.01(2), such as lying in wait and soliciting an innocent agent?

* * *

In relation to Question 2, above, many students misinterpret the list in MPC Section 5.01(2) as providing examples of acts that automatically fulfill the substantial step requirement. But the MPC explains that the significance of these examples is that they "shall not be held insufficient as a matter of law." What this means is that if a defendant has engaged in any of these acts, the trial judge may not grant a motion for acquittal on behalf of the defendant but must let the jury resolve the question of whether the defendant's conduct constituted a substantial step strongly corroborative of the actor's purpose. Similarly, this list prevents an appellate court from reversing a defendant's attempt conviction on the grounds of insufficiency regarding the conduct element if the prosecution has proven beyond reasonable doubt that the defendant engaged in one of the acts on this list. So, the function of this list is to entrust to the jury the question of whether the defendant went far enough for attempt liability in the factual settings described in MPC Section 5.01 (2). In other words, a judge cannot find any act on the list legally insufficient. But jurors are not *required* to find any of the acts on the list sufficient, although they may do so.

"Complete" and "Incomplete" Attempts

The words "complete" and "incomplete" are sometimes used to classify attempts. A complete attempt is one in which an actor intending to commit a target offense does everything on the actor's part necessary to bring about the offense but nonetheless fails. In Problem 10.2, for example, once Gwen fires her rifle at Albert, her intended victim, her attempt to murder him is "complete." Be careful about this terminology. The fact that an attempt is "incomplete" does *not* mean that the actor's conduct failed to go far enough for the actor to be liable for attempt. This is because many jurisdictions and the Model Penal Code use conduct tests for attempt liability that trigger liability well before the actor has taken his or her final step, as your analysis of Problem 10.2 demonstrated.

The Model Penal Code does not use the word "complete" in its treatment of attempt. But the Model Penal Code and jurisdictions that have patterned their attempt statutes based on the Model Penal Code do have a section that deals specifically with factual situations that would fall in that category. Model Penal Code Section 5.01(1)(b) states that a person is guilty of an attempt if "when causing a particular result is an element of the crime, [he] does or omits to do anything with the purpose of causing or with the belief that it will cause such result *without further conduct on his part.* (emphasis added).

Problem

10.3 Glenn is the pastor of a rural Christian church that practices speaking in tongues and the laying on of hands, and whose members are often swept up in spiritual ecstasy during services. Inspired by a Bible verse in which Jesus tells his disciples that those who believe in him "shall take up serpents, and if they drink any deadly thing, it shall not hurt them,"[1] the church's members also practice snake handling and, at times, drink the poison strychnine. Darlene is Glenn's wife and a member of his congregation. Cages located behind Glenn's and Darlene's house contain numerous poisonous canebrake rattlesnakes used in the church's services.

Part (a) Glenn has suspected for some time that Darlene has been sexually involved with another member of his congregation. One night after he has consumed several drinks, Glenn points a loaded gun at Darlene and accuses her of being unfaithful. He then forces her at gunpoint to walk outside and place her arm inside a snake cage. A snake bites Darlene. Glenn then holds Darlene at gunpoint inside the house while her hand swells and blackens due to the snake venom. He also compels her to write a false suicide note that he dictates. Does Glenn's conduct toward Darlene at this point qualify as a "complete" attempt?

Part (b) Glenn for a second time forces Darlene to place her arm inside a snake cage and she is bitten again. Back inside the house, Glenn continues to drink, eventually passing out and dropping the gun. Darlene makes her way into the kitchen where she calls her sister, who calls 911. Police and an ambulance respond. Darlene is taken to a hospital where she is treated and survives.[2] Does Glenn's conduct at this point qualify as "complete" for the purposes of attempt.

Part (c) Taking into account the facts in both Part (a) and Part (b), should Glenn be liable for just one attempt? Or for two attempts?

Part (d) Under the statutes and cases that follow, at what point would Glenn have become liable for the attempted murder of Darlene?

In the materials below, you will learn about and compare different tests used by various jurisdictions to define the conduct required for an attempt. You will notice that modern legislative definitions of attempt do not use the term "complete." But as you review the conduct tests used in these states, ask yourself whether an actor whose conduct would qualify as a "complete" attempt would satisfy each of these tests.

---

1. Mark 16:18.

2. This fact pattern is based on the prosecution of Glenn Summerford, *Summerford v. State*, 621 Ala. Crim. App LEXIS 194 (1993), described in detail by investigative journalist Dennis Covington in his book, SALVATION ON SAND MOUNTAIN (1995).

Kansas v. Gobin

216 Kan. 278 (1975)
Kansas Supreme Court

Fromme. J.

... The Kansas Criminal Code defines an attempt as follows:

"An attempt is any overt act toward the perpetration of a crime done by a person who intends to commit such crime but fails in the perpetration thereof or is prevented or intercepted in executing such crime." ...

Next let us consider the type of an overt act necessary to support an attempt to commit any crime. The essential elements to establish an attempt have been repeatedly set forth in our cases ... where it is said:

"[the Kansas attempt statute] contains three essential elements (1) the intent to commit the crime, (2) an overt act toward the perpetration of the crime, and (3) a failure to consummate it...."

The comment of the committee on pattern jury instructions covering attempts is:

"A problem inherent in the law of attempts concerns the point when criminal liability attaches for the overt act. On the one hand mere acts of preparation are insufficient while, on the other, if the accused has performed the final act necessary for the completion of the crime, he could be prosecuted for the crime intended and not for an attempt. The overt act lies somewhere between these two extremes and each case must depend upon its own particular facts...."

It becomes apparent from reading the ... cases that no definite rule as to what constitutes an overt act for the purposes of an attempt can or should be laid down. Each case must depend largely on its particular facts and the inferences which the jury may reasonably draw therefrom. The problem should be approached with a desire to accomplish substantial justice.

Discussion Questions

1. The *Gobin* court states that "no definite rule as to what constitutes an overt act for the purposes of an attempt can or should be laid down." Is the court's position consistent with the language of the Kansas Criminal Code?

2. If neither the legislature nor the courts define the conduct required for an attempt, who will wind up determining what conduct warrants an attempt conviction?

3. What do you think the adjective "overt" means in the Kansas attempt statute? What, if anything, does it add to the statute's requirements for an attempt conviction?

4. If a defendant *succeeds* in completing the target offense, won't she have satisfied any conduct requirement for attempt? Should completion of the target offense eliminate attempt liability? Does completion of the target offense eliminate attempt liability under the Kansas attempt statute?

People v. Rizzo

246 N.Y. 334 (1927)
New York Court of Appeals

Crane, J.

The police of the city of New York did excellent work in this case by preventing the commission of a serious crime. It is a great satisfaction to realize that we have such wide-awake guardians of our peace. Whether or not the steps which the defendant had taken up to the time of his arrest amounted to the commission of a crime, as defined by our law, is, however, another matter. He has been convicted of an attempt to commit the crime of robbery in the first degree and sentenced to State's prison. There is no doubt that he had the intention to commit robbery if he got the chance. An examination, however, of the facts is necessary to determine whether his acts were in preparation to commit the crime if the opportunity offered, or constituted a crime in itself, known to our law as an attempt to commit robbery in the first degree.

Charles Rizzo, the defendant, appellant, with three others, Anthony J. Dorio, Thomas Milo and John Thomasello, on January 14th planned to rob one Charles Rao of a payroll valued at about $1,200 which he was to carry from the bank for the United Lathing Company. These defendants, two of whom had firearms, started out in an automobile, looking for Rao or the man who had the payroll on that day. Rizzo claimed to be able to identify the man and was to point him out to the others who were to do the actual holding up. The four rode about in their car looking for Rao. They went to the bank from which he was supposed to get the money and to various buildings being constructed by the United Lathing Company. At last they came to One Hundred and Eightieth street and Morris Park avenue. By this time they were watched and followed by two police officers. As Rizzo jumped out of the car and ran into the building all four were arrested. The defendant was taken out from the building in which he was hiding. Neither Rao nor a man named Previti, who was also supposed to carry a payroll, were at the place at the time of the arrest. The defendants had not found or seen the man they intended to rob; no person with a payroll was at any of the places where they had stopped and no one had been pointed out or identified by Rizzo. The four men intended to rob the payroll man, whoever he was; they were looking for him, but they had not seen or discovered him up to the time they were arrested.

Does this constitute the crime of an attempt to commit robbery in the first degree? The Penal Law, section 2, prescribes, "An act, done with intent to commit a crime, and tending but failing to effect its commission, is 'an attempt to commit that crime.'" The word "tending" is very indefinite. It is perfectly evident that there will arise differences of opinion as to whether an act in a given case is one tending to commit a crime. "Tending" means to exert activity in a particular direction. Any act in preparation to commit a crime may be said to have a tendency towards its accomplishment. The procuring of the automobile, searching the streets looking for the desired victim, were in reality acts tending toward the commission of the proposed crime.

The law, however, has recognized that many acts in the way of preparation are too remote to constitute the crime of attempt. The line has been drawn between those acts which are remote and those which are proximate and near to the consummation. The law must be practical, and, therefore, considers those acts only as tending to the commission of the crime which are so near to its accomplishment that in all reasonable probability the crime itself would have been committed but for timely interference. The cases which have been before the courts express this idea in different language, but the idea remains the same. The act or acts must come or advance very near to the accomplishment of the intended crime. In *People v. Mills* it was said: "Felonious intent alone is not enough, but there must be an overt act shown in order to establish even an attempt. An overt act is one done to carry out the intention, and it must be such as would naturally effect that result, unless prevented by some extraneous cause." In *Hyde v. United States* it was stated that the act amounts to an attempt when it is so near to the result that the danger of success is very great. "There must be dangerous proximity to success." Halsbury in his "Laws of England" says: "An act, in order to be a criminal attempt, must be immediately, and not remotely, connected with and directly tending to the commission of an offence." *Commonwealth v. Peaslee* refers to the acts constituting an attempt as coming very near to the accomplishment of the crime.

The method of committing or attempting crime varies in each case so that the difficulty, if any, is not with this rule of law regarding an attempt, which is well understood, but with its application to the facts. As I have said before, minds differ over proximity and the nearness of the approach.

How shall we apply this rule of immediate nearness to this case? The defendants were looking for the payroll man to rob him of his money. This is the charge in the indictment. Robbery is defined in section 2120 of the Penal Law as "the unlawful taking of personal property, from the person or in the presence of another, against his will, by means of force, or violence, or fear of injury, immediate or future, to his person;" and it is made robbery in the first degree by section 2124 when committed by a person aided by accomplices actually present. To constitute the crime of robbery the money must have been taken from Rao by means of force or violence, or through fear. The crime of attempt to commit robbery was committed if these defendants did an act tending to the commission of this robbery. Did the acts above described come dangerously near to the taking of Rao's property? Did the acts come so near the commission of robbery that there was reasonable likelihood of its accomplishment but for the interference? Rao was not found; the defendants were still looking for him; no attempt to rob him could be made, at least until he came in sight; he was not in the building at One Hundred and Eightieth street and Morris Park avenue. There was no man there with the payroll for the United Lathing Company whom these defendants could rob. Apparently no money had been drawn from the bank for the payroll by anybody at the time of the arrest. In a word, these defendants had planned to commit a crime and were looking around the city for an opportunity to commit it, but the opportunity fortunately never came. Men would not be guilty of an attempt at burglary if they had planned to break into a building and were arrested while they were hunting about the streets for the building not knowing where it was. Neither would a man be guilty of an attempt to commit murder if he armed himself and started out to find the person whom he had planned to kill but could not find him. So here these defendants were not guilty of an attempt to commit robbery in the first degree when they had not found or reached the presence of the person they intended to rob.

For these reasons, the judgment of conviction of this defendant, appellant, must be reversed and a new trial granted.

A very strange situation has arisen in this case. I called attention to the four defendants who were convicted of this crime of an attempt to commit robbery in the first degree. They were all tried together upon the same evidence, and jointly convicted, and all sentenced to State's prison for varying terms. Rizzo was the only one of the four to appeal to the Appellate Division and to this court. His conviction was affirmed by the Appellate Division by a divided court, two of the justices dissenting, and we have now held that he was not guilty of the crime charged. If he were not guilty, neither were the other three. As the others, however, did not appeal, there is no remedy for them through the court; their judgments stand, and they must serve their sentences. This of course is a situation which must in all fairness be met in some way. Two of these men were guilty of the crime of carrying weapons, pistols, contrary to law, for which they could be convicted. Two of them, John Thomasello and Thomas Milo, had also been previously convicted, which may have had something to do with their neglect to appeal. However, the law would fail in its function and its purpose if it permitted these three men whoever or whatever they are to serve a sentence for a crime which the courts subsequently found and declared had not been committed. We, therefore, suggest to the district attorney of Bronx county that he bring the cases of these three men to the attention of the Governor to be dealt with as to him seems proper in the light of this opinion.

The judgment of the Appellate Division and that of the County Court should be reversed and a new trial ordered.

Discussion Questions

1. In *Rizzo*, which branch of New York's state government winds up defining the conduct required for attempt in New York? The legislature? The courts?

2. What role did statutory text and legislative intent play in Justice Crane's analysis? What statutory arguments might the prosecutor have made in support of the government's position that Rizzo's conduct was sufficient for attempt liability? Is Justice Crane's analysis consistent with the language of the New York attempt statute?

3. What test does *Rizzo* use for the conduct element of an attempt? What are the advantages and disadvantages of this test?

4. If not guilty of attempt, can you think of another anticipatory crime Rizzo and his partners appear to have committed?

5. Justice Crane states that Rizzo's three co-defendants were not guilty of attempt despite their convictions. Why, then, does he conclude that "they must serve their sentences"? Should the court have taken steps to free them? To have them retried? Or resentenced? Should the prosecutor have taken such steps?

United States v. Jackson

560 F.2d 112 (2d Cir. 1977)
United States Court of Appeals for the Second Circuit

Bryan, Senior District Judge.

Robert Jackson, William Scott, and Martin Allen appeal from judgments of conviction entered on November 23, 1976 in the United States District Court for the Eastern District of New York after a trial before Chief Judge Jacob Mishler without a jury.

Count one of the indictment alleged that between June 11 and June 21, 1976 the appellants conspired to commit an armed robbery of the Manufacturers Hanover Trust branch located at 210 Flushing Avenue, Brooklyn, New York, in violation of 18 U.S.C. §371. Counts two and three each charged appellants with an attempted robbery of the branch on June 14 and on June 21, 1976, respectively, in violation of 18 U.S.C. §§2113(a) and 2. Count four charged them with possession of two unregistered sawed-off shotguns on June 21, 1976, in violation of 26 U.S.C. §5861(d) and 18 U.S.C. §2.

After a suppression hearing on July 23, 1976 and a one-day trial on August 30, 1976, Chief Judge Mishler filed a memorandum of decision finding each defendant guilty on all four counts.

Appellants' principal contention is that the court below erred in finding them guilty on counts two and three. While they concede that the evidence supported the conspiracy convictions on count one, they assert that, as a matter of law, their conduct never crossed the elusive line which separates "mere preparation" from "attempt." ...

I.

The Government's evidence at trial consisted largely of the testimony of Vanessa Hodges, an unindicted co-conspirator, and of various FBI agents who surveilled the Manufacturers Hanover branch on June 21, 1976. Since the facts are of critical importance in any attempt case, we shall review the Government's proof in considerable detail.

On June 11, 1976, Vanessa Hodges was introduced to appellant Martin Allen by Pia Longhorne, another unindicted co-conspirator. Hodges wanted to meet someone who would help her carry out a plan to rob the Manufacturers Hanover branch located at 210 Flushing Avenue in Brooklyn, and she invited Allen to join her. Hodges proposed that the bank be robbed the next Monday, June 14th, at about 7:30 A.M. She hoped that they could enter with the bank manager at that time, grab the weekend deposits, and leave. Allen agreed to rob the bank with Hodges, and told her he had access to a car, two sawed-off shotguns, and a .38 caliber revolver.

The following Monday, June 14, Allen arrived at Longhorne's house about 7:30 A.M. in a car driven by appellant Robert Jackson. A suitcase in the back seat of the car contained a sawed-off shotgun, shells, materials intended as masks, and handcuffs to bind the bank manager. While Allen picked up Hodges at Longhorne's, Jackson filled the car with gas. The trio then left for the bank.

When they arrived, it was almost 8:00 A.M. It was thus too late to effect the first step of the plan, viz., entering the bank as the manager opened the door. They rode around for a while longer, and then went to a restaurant to get something to eat and discuss their next move. After eating, the trio drove back to the bank. Allen and Hodges left the car and walked over to the bank. They peered in and saw the bulky weekend deposits, but decided it was too risky to rob the bank without an extra man.

Consequently, Jackson, Hodges, and Allen drove to Coney Island in search of another accomplice. In front of a housing project on 33rd Street they found appellant William Scott, who promptly joined the team. Allen added to the arsenal another sawed-off shotgun obtained from one of the buildings in the project, and the group drove back to the bank. When they arrived again, Allen entered the bank to check the location of any surveillance cameras, while Jackson placed a piece of cardboard with a false license number over the authentic license plate of the car.[3] Allen reported back that a single surveillance camera was over the entrance door. After further discussion, Scott left the car and entered the bank. He came back and informed the group that the tellers were separating the weekend deposits and that a number of patrons were now in the bank. Hodges then suggested that they drop the plans for the robbery that day, and reschedule it for the following Monday, June 21. Accordingly, they left the vicinity of the bank and returned to Coney Island where, before splitting up, they purchased a pair of stockings for Hodges to wear over her head as a disguise and pairs of gloves for Hodges, Scott, and Allen to don before entering the bank.

Hodges was arrested on Friday, June 18, 1976 on an unrelated bank robbery charge, and immediately began cooperating with the Government. After relating the events of June 14, she told FBI agents that a robbery of the Manufacturers branch at 210 Flushing Avenue was now scheduled for the following Monday, June 21. The three black male robbers, according to Hodges, would be heavily armed with hand and shoulder weapons and expected to use a brown four-door sedan equipped with a cardboard license plate as the getaway car. She told the agents that Jackson, who would drive the car, was light-skinned with a moustache and a cut on his lip, and she described Allen as short, dark-skinned with facial hair, and Scott

---

3. Hodges' testimony indicates that, in order to avert suspicion, Jackson would first lift the trunk or hood of the car as though he were working under it before covering or uncovering the genuine license plates.

as 5 feet 9 inches, slim build, with an afro hair style and some sort of defect in his right eye.

At the request of the agents, Hodges called Allen on Saturday, June 19, and asked if he were still planning to do the job. He said that he was ready. On Sunday she called him again. This time Allen said that he was not going to rob the bank that Monday because he had learned that Hodges had been arrested and he feared that federal agents might be watching. Hodges nevertheless advised the agents that she thought the robbery might still take place as planned with the three men proceeding without her.

At about 7:00 A.M. on Monday, June 21, 1976, some ten FBI agents took various surveilling positions in the area of the bank. At about 7:39 A.M. the agents observed a brown four-door Lincoln, with a New York license plate on the front and a cardboard facsimile of a license plate on the rear, moving in an easterly direction on Flushing Avenue past the bank, which was located on the southeast corner of Flushing and Washington Avenues. The front seat of the Lincoln was occupied by a black male driver and a black male passenger with mutton-chop sideburns. The Lincoln circled the block and came to a stop at a fire hydrant situated at the side of the bank facing Washington Avenue, a short distance south of the corner of Flushing and Washington.

A third black male, who appeared to have an eye deformity, got out of the passenger side rear door of the Lincoln, walked to the corner of Flushing and Washington, and stood on the sidewalk in the vicinity of the bank's entrance. He then walked south on Washington Avenue, only to return a short time later with a container of coffee in his hand. He stood again on the corner of Washington and Flushing in front of the bank, drinking the coffee and looking around, before returning to the parked Lincoln.

The Lincoln pulled out, made a left turn onto Flushing, and proceeded in a westerly direction for one block to Waverly Avenue. It stopped, made a U-turn, and parked on the south side of Flushing between Waverly and Washington—a spot on the same side of the street as the bank entrance but separated from it by Washington Avenue. After remaining parked in this position for approximately five minutes, it pulled out and cruised east on Flushing past the bank again. The Lincoln then made a right onto Grand Avenue, the third street east of the bank, and headed south. It stopped halfway down the block, midway between Flushing and Park Avenues, and remained there for several minutes. During this time Jackson was seen working in the front of the car, which had its hood up.

The Lincoln was next sighted several minutes later in the same position it had previously occupied on the south side of Flushing Avenue between Waverly and Washington. The front license plate was now missing. The vehicle remained parked there for close to thirty minutes. Finally, it began moving east on Flushing Avenue once more, in the direction of the bank.

At some point near the bank as they passed down Flushing Avenue, the appellants detected the presence of the surveillance agents. The Lincoln accelerated down Flushing

Avenue and turned south on Grand Avenue again. It was overtaken by FBI agents who ordered the appellants out of the car and arrested them. The agents then observed a black and red plaid suitcase in the rear of the car. The zipper of the suitcase was partially open and exposed two loaded sawed-off shotguns,[4] a toy nickelplated revolver, a pair of handcuffs, and masks. A New York license plate was seen lying on the front floor of the car. All of these items were seized.

In his memorandum of decision, Chief Judge Mishler concluded that the evidence against Jackson, Scott, and Allen was "overwhelming" on counts one and four. In contrast, he characterized the question of whether the defendants had attempted a bank robbery as charged in counts two and three or were merely engaged in preparations as "a close one." After canvassing the authorities on what this court one month later called a "perplexing problem," Chief Judge Mishler applied the following two-tiered inquiry ...

First, the defendant must have been acting with the kind of culpability otherwise required for the commission of the crime which he is charged with attempting....

Second, the defendant must have engaged in conduct which constitutes a substantial step toward commission of the crime. A substantial step must be conduct strongly corroborative of the firmness of the defendant's criminal intent.

He concluded that on June 14 and again on June 21, the defendants took substantial steps, strongly corroborative of the firmness of their criminal intent, toward commission of the crime of bank robbery and found the defendants guilty on each of the two attempt counts. These appeals followed.

II.

"There is no comprehensive statutory definition of attempt in federal law." 18 U.S.C. § 2113(a)[5] specifically makes attempted bank robbery an offense.

---

4. One of the shotguns proved to be inoperative.

5. The subsection provides:

Whoever, by force and violence, or by intimidation, takes, or attempts to take, from the person or presence of another any property or money or any other thing of value belonging to, or in the care, custody, control, management, or possession of, any bank, credit union, or any savings and loan association; or

Whoever enters or attempts to enter any bank, credit union, or any savings and loan association, or any building used in whole or in part as a bank, credit union, or as a savings and loan association, with intent to commit in such bank, credit union, or in such savings and loan association, or building, or part thereof, so used, any felony affecting such bank or such savings and loan association and in violation of any statute of the United States, or any larceny—

Shall be fined not more than $5,000 or imprisoned not more than twenty years, or both.

Appellant Scott argues that the very wording of 18 U.S.C. §2113(a) precludes a finding that the actions charged in counts two and three reached the level of attempts. Relying on *United States v. Baker,* he contends that since the statute only mentions attempted taking and not attempted force, violence, or intimidation, it clearly contemplates that actual use of force, violence, or intimidation must precede an attempted taking in order to make out the offense of attempted bank robbery.

The *Stallworth* court faced a similar statutory construction argument which also relied heavily on *United States v. Baker.* In response to the assertion that the defendants in that case could not be convicted of attempted bank robbery because they neither entered the bank nor brandished weapons, Chief Judge Kaufman stated:

> We reject this wooden logic. Attempt is a subtle concept that requires a rational and logically sound definition, one that enables society to punish malefactors who have unequivocally set out upon a criminal course without requiring law enforcement officers to delay until innocent bystanders are imperiled.

Chief Judge Kaufman, writing for the court [in *Stallworth*], selected the two-tiered inquiry of *United States v. Mandujano,* "properly derived from the writings of many distinguished jurists," as stating the proper test for determining whether the foregoing conduct constituted an attempt. He observed that this analysis "conforms closely to the sensible definition of an attempt proffered by the American Law Institute's Model Penal Code."

The draftsmen of the Model Penal Code recognized the difficulty of arriving at a general standard for distinguishing acts of preparation from acts constituting an attempt. They found general agreement that when an actor committed the "last proximate act," i.e., when he had done all that he believed necessary to effect a particular result which is an element of the offense, he committed an attempt. They also concluded, however, that while the last proximate act is *sufficient* to constitute an attempt, it is not *necessary* to such a finding. The problem then was to devise a standard more inclusive than one requiring the last proximate act before attempt liability would attach, but less inclusive than one which would make every act done with the intent to commit a crime criminal....

The formulation upon which the draftsmen ultimately agreed required, in addition to criminal purpose, that an act be a substantial step in a course of conduct designed to accomplish a criminal result, and that it be strongly corroborative of criminal purpose in order for it to constitute such a substantial step. The following differences between this test and previous approaches to the preparation-attempt problem were noted:

> ... this formulation shifts the emphasis from what remains to be done—the chief concern of the proximity tests—to what the actor has already done. The fact that further major steps must be taken before the crime can be completed does not preclude a finding that the steps already undertaken are substantial. It is expected, in the normal case, that this approach will broaden the scope of attempt liability.

... the requirement of proving a substantial step generally will prove less of a hurdle for the prosecution than the res ipsa loquitur approach, which requires that the actor's conduct must itself manifest the criminal purpose. The difference will be illustrated in connection with the present section's requirement of corroboration. Here it should be noted that, in the present formulation, the two purposes to be served by the res ipsa loquitur test are, to a large extent, treated separately. Firmness of criminal purpose is intended to be shown by requiring a substantial step, while problems of proof are dealt with by the requirement of corroboration (although, under the reasoning previously expressed, the latter will also tend to establish firmness of purpose). Model Penal Code §5.01, Comment at 47 (Tent. Draft No. 10, 1960).

The draftsmen concluded that, in addition to assuring firmness of criminal design, the requirement of a substantial step would preclude attempt liability, with its accompanying harsh penalties, for relatively remote preparatory acts. At the same time, however, by not requiring a "last proximate act" or one of its various analogues it would permit the apprehension of dangerous persons at an earlier stage than the other approaches without immunizing them from attempt liability....

Chief Judge Mishler ... then found that on June 14 the appellants, already agreed upon a robbery plan, drove to the bank with loaded weapons. In order to carry the heavy weekend deposit sacks, they recruited another person. Cardboard was placed over the license, and the bank was entered and reconnoitered. Only then was the plan dropped for the moment and rescheduled for the following Monday. On that day, June 21, the defendants performed essentially the same acts. Since the cameras had already been located there was no need to enter the bank again, and since the appellants had arrived at the bank earlier, conditions were more favorable to their initial robbery plan than they had been on June 14. He concluded that on both occasions these men were seriously dedicated to the commission of a crime, had passed beyond the stage of preparation, and would have assaulted the bank had they not been dissuaded by certain external factors, viz., the breaking up of the weekend deposits and crowd of patrons in the bank on the afternoon of June 14 and the detection of the FBI surveillance on June 21.

We cannot say that these conclusions which Chief Judge Mishler reached as the trier of fact as to what the evidence before him established were erroneous. As in Stallworth, the criminal intent of the appellants was beyond dispute. The question remaining then is the substantiality of the steps taken on the dates in question, and how strongly this corroborates the firmness of their obvious criminal intent. This is a matter of degree.

On two separate occasions, appellants reconnoitered the place contemplated for the commission of the crime and possessed the paraphernalia to be employed in the commission of the crime—loaded sawed-off shotguns, extra shells, a toy revolver, handcuffs, and masks—which was specially designed for such unlawful use and which could serve no lawful purpose under the circumstances. Under the Model

Penal Code formulation, approved by the *Stallworth* court, either type of conduct, standing alone, was sufficient as a matter of law to constitute a "substantial step" if it strongly corroborated their criminal purpose. Here both types of conduct coincided on both June 14 and June 21, along with numerous other elements strongly corroborative of the firmness of appellants' criminal intent. The steps taken toward a successful bank robbery thus were not "insubstantial" as a matter of law, and Chief Judge Mishler found them "substantial" as a matter of fact. We are unwilling to substitute our assessment of the evidence for his, and thus affirm the convictions for attempted bank robbery on counts two and three.

The judgments of conviction are affirmed.

Problems

10.4 You are an Assistant United States Attorney assigned to work with the FBI bank robbery squad during the investigative phase of the *Jackson* case (i.e., before any arrests have been made). The FBI supervising agent on the case asks you to advise her when she should instruct the agents in the field to arrest Jackson and his partners. The FBI agents obviously do not want to wait until the robbery occurs, because someone might get hurt during the robbery and the perpetrators might escape. Also, the closer the perpetrators get to the actual robbery, the more likely it is that they will be armed and prepared to shoot, thus increasing the danger to the agents and other people in the area. The sooner the agents arrest them, the more likely it is that the would-be robbers will be surprised and less likely that they will harm anyone. But if the agents arrest the perpetrators too soon, you will not have sufficient evidence to support an attempt conviction. The agents need your advice on when and where to arrest the perpetrators for the crime of attempted bank robbery. At what point would you tell the surveilling agents to arrest Jackson and the others? In other words, what is the earliest point at which you feel confident that you will be able to convict Jackson and the others of attempted bank robbery?

10.5 Many states have modeled their attempt statutes on the Model Penal Code sections discussed in *Jackson*. Some of those states, though, have altered the Model Penal Code's language. How have the following three statutes modified the Model Penal Code's treatment of the conduct element in attempt? What is the significance of these modifications?

Arizona Revised Statutes

§ 13-1001

A. A person commits attempt if, acting with the kind of culpability otherwise required for commission of an offense, such person:

1. Intentionally engages in conduct which would constitute an offense if the attendant circumstances were as such person believes them to be; or

2. Intentionally does or omits to do anything which, under the circumstances as such person believes them to be, is any step in a course of conduct planned to culminate in commission of an offense; …

Tennessee Code Annotated

§ 39-12-101

(b) Conduct does not constitute a substantial step … unless the person's entire course of action is corroborative of the intent to commit the offense.

Kentucky Revised Statutes

§ 506.010

(2) Conduct shall not be held to constitute a substantial step … unless it is an act or omission which leaves no reasonable doubt as to the defendant's intention to commit the crime which he is charged with attempting.

Breaking Down the Model Penal Code

The Model Penal Code sets forth three different definitions for attempt in Subsections (a), (b), and (c) of Section 5.01(1), each of which is designed to apply to particular situations. They differ from one another in terms of the conduct each requires for liability.

Model Penal Code

§ 5.01. *Criminal Attempt.*

(1) Definition of Attempt. A person is guilty of an attempt to commit a crime if, acting with the kind of culpability otherwise required for commission of the crime, he:

(a) purposely engages in conduct that would constitute the crime if the attendant circumstances were as he believes them to be; or

(b) when causing a particular result is an element of the crime, does or omits to do anything with the purpose of causing or with the belief that it will cause such result without further conduct on his part; or

(c) purposely does or omits to do anything that, under the circumstances as he believes them to be, is an act or omission constituting a substantial step in a course of conduct planned to culminate in his commission of the crime.

* * *

Subsection (c) sets forth the substantial step test discussed earlier in this chapter and applied in the *Jackson* case, so we won't go over it here. It is the best-known and probably the most frequently applied conduct test for attempt under the MPC.

We focus here on Subsections (a) and (b). Students often struggle to figure out when these apply and precisely what each means. Let's look closely at these two Subsections to see when each is triggered.

Subsection (a)

Subsection (a) imposes attempt liability when the actor "purposely engages in *conduct that would constitute the crime* if the attendant circumstances were as *he believes them to be....*"

Consider the following factual scenario:

Bernard is suspected by the police of buying and reselling stolen electronics such as computers, televisions, and music equipment. The police set up a sting operation to catch Bernard. An informant introduces Peter, an undercover police officer, to Bernard and Peter tells Bernard that he has a truckload of stolen high-end flat-screen televisions that he needs to get rid of quickly. Bernard says he is interested in buying them, and he and Peter negotiate a price and a time and place for delivery. At the agreed-upon time and place, Peter shows up with a rental truck full of televisions and Bernard is there to meet him. Bernard inspects the merchandise, pays Peter the agreed-upon price and Peter hands the truck keys over to Bernard. After Bernard has driven just a few blocks, two police cars pull him over and Bernard is arrested. It turns out that Bernard cannot be charged with either receipt or possession of stolen property because the televisions were not stolen. They are the property of Huey's Electronics, a chain of electronics stores whose owner wanted to help the police put Bernard out of business. Huey's lent the truckload of televisions to the police to use in the sting operation.

Is Bernard liable for attempted receipt or attempted possession of stolen property in this scenario? The common law would have allowed him to raise a defense of impossibility because a circumstance element of the target offense—that the property be stolen—was not fulfilled. But the MPC did away with the impossibility defense for attempt in this situation. Bernard is liable under MPC 5.01(1)(a). Bernard engaged in the conduct—receipt and possession—that would constitute the target offense and he believed that the televisions were stolen even though they were not.

Subsection (b)

"When causing a particular result is an element of the crime," Subsection (b) imposes liability when the actor "*does or omits to do anything* with the purpose of causing or with the belief *that it will cause such result without further conduct on his part....*"

Assume that Gwen in Problem 10.2 fires her rifle several times at Albert with the objective of killing him but all the shots miss Albert. Is she liable for attempted murder? Clearly yes under MPC 5.01(1)(b). Her firing of the rifle several times are acts that she does with the purpose of causing Albert's death *without further conduct on her part.* There are no further steps for her to take in her assassination plan. In other words, she has done the *last act* of her plan. The "without further conduct" language essentially adopts a last act test. As previously noted, this is the Model Penal Code section that deals with what is sometimes called a "complete attempt."

Modern readers of the *McQuirter* case that follows find it troubling. The conduct of the police toward an African-American man walking in what was apparently a white neighborhood looks to have been what today would be called racial profiling. The *McQuirter* case was decided in Alabama in 1953. What else was going on in Alabama and other southern states during that era? In 1955, two years after the *McQuirter* opinion was written, Emmett Till, a 14-year old African American, was lynched in Mississippi for allegedly offending a white woman in a grocery store. The case raises important issues about the intersection of the criminal law of attempt and attitudes about race. As you read the case, think about how the Alabama law of attempt, reflected in *McQuirter*, might be reformulated to address these issues.

McQuirter v. State

36 Ala. App. 707 (1953)
Alabama Court of Appeals

Price, J.

Appellant, a Negro man, was found guilty of an attempt to commit an assault with intent to rape, under an indictment charging an assault with intent to rape. The jury assessed a fine of $500.

About 8:00 o'clock on the night of June 29, 1951, Mrs. Ted Allen, a white woman, with her two children and a neighbor's little girl, were drinking Coca-Cola at the "Tiny Diner" in Atmore. When they started in the direction of Mrs. Allen's home she noticed appellant sitting in the cab of a parked truck. As she passed the truck appellant said something unintelligible, opened the truck door and placed his foot on the running board.

Mrs. Allen testified appellant followed her down the street and when she reached Suell Lufkin's house she stopped. As she turned into the Lufkin house appellant was within two or three feet of her. She waited ten minutes for appellant to pass. When she proceeded on her way, appellant came toward her from behind a telephone pole. She told the children to run to Mr. Simmons' house and tell him to come and meet her. When appellant saw Mr. Simmons he turned and went back down the street to the intersection and leaned on a stop sign just across the street from Mrs. Allen's home. Mrs. Allen watched him at the sign from Mr. Simmons' porch for about thirty minutes, after which time he came back down the street and appellant went on home.

Mrs. Allen's testimony was corroborated by that of her young daughter. The daughter testified the appellant was within six feet of her mother as she approached the Lufkin house, and this witness said there was a while when she didn't see appellant at the intersection.

Mr. Lewis Simmons testified when the little girls ran up on his porch and said a Negro was after them, witness walked up the sidewalk to meet Mrs. Allen and saw appellant. Appellant went on down the street and stopped in front of Mrs. Allen's home and waited there approximately thirty minutes.

Mr. Clarence Bryars, a policeman in Atmore, testified that appellant stated after his arrest that he came to Atmore with the intention of getting him a white woman that night.

Mr. W. E. Strickland, Chief of Police of Atmore, testified that appellant stated in the Atmore jail he didn't know what was the matter with him; that he was drinking a little; that he and his partner had been to Pensacola; that his partner went to the "Front" to see a colored woman; that he didn't have any money and he sat in the truck and made up his mind he was going to get the first woman that came by and that this was the first woman that came by. He said he got out of the truck, came around the gas tank and watched the lady and when she started off he started off behind her; that he was going to carry her in the cotton patch and if she hollered he was going to kill her. He testified appellant made the same statement in the Brewton jail.

Mr. Norvelle Seals, Chief Deputy Sheriff, corroborated Mr. Strickland's testimony as to the statement by appellant at the Brewton jail.

Appellant, as a witness in his own behalf, testified he and Bill Page, another Negro, carried a load of junk-iron from Monroeville to Pensacola; on their way back to Monroeville they stopped in Atmore. They parked the truck near the "Tiny Diner" and rode to the "Front," the colored section, in a cab. Appellant came back to the truck around 8:00 o'clock and sat in the truck cab for about thirty minutes. He decided to go back to the "Front" to look for Bill Page. As he started up the street he saw prosecutrix and her children. He turned around and waited until he decided they had gone, then he walked up the street toward the "Front." When he reached the intersection at the telegraph pole he decided he didn't want to go to the "Front" and sat around there a few minutes, then went on to the "Front" and stayed about 25 or 30 minutes, and came back to the truck.

He denied that he followed Mrs. Allen or made any gesture toward molesting her or the children. He denied making the statements testified to by the officers.

He testified he had never been arrested before and introduced testimony by two residents of Monroeville as to his good reputation for peace and quiet and for truth and veracity.

Appellant insists the trial court erred in refusing the general affirmative charge and in denying the motion for a new trial on the ground the verdict was contrary to the evidence.

"'An attempt to commit an assault with intent to rape,' * * * means an attempt to rape which has not proceeded far enough to amount to an assault". Under the authorities in this state, to justify a conviction for an attempt to commit an assault with intent to rape the jury must be satisfied beyond a reasonable doubt that defendant intended to have sexual intercourse with prosecutrix against her will, by force or by putting her in fear.

Intent is a question to be determined by the jury from the facts and circumstances adduced on the trial, and if there is evidence from which it may be inferred that at the time of the attempt defendant intended to gratify his lustful desires against the resistance of the female a jury question is presented. In determining the question of intention the jury may consider social conditions and customs founded upon racial differences, such as that the prosecutrix was a white woman and defendant was a Negro man.

After considering the evidence in this case we are of the opinion it was sufficient to warrant the submission of the question of defendant's guilt to the jury, and was ample to sustain the judgment of conviction.

Defense counsel contends in brief that the testimony of the officers as to defendant's declarations of intent was inadmissible because no attempt or overt act toward carrying that intent into effect had been proven.

Defendant's grounds of objection to this evidence were that it was "irrelevant, incompetent and immaterial." Proper predicates were laid for the introduction of each of said statements. In the absence of a ground of objection calling the court's attention to the fact that the corpus delicti has not been sufficiently proven to authorize admission of a confession such question cannot be reviewed here.

Moreover, if any facts are proven from which the jury may reasonably infer that the crime has been committed proof of the confession is rendered admissible.

We find no reversible error in the record and the judgment of the trial court is affirmed.

Discussion Questions

1. What conduct was required in *McQuirter* for an attempt conviction? What mental state was required? What evidence of mental state did the prosecution rely on?

2. What role do you think the state of race relations in Alabama in 1953 may have played in the *McQuirter* case? What significance did the court attach to McQuirter's race and Allen's race? Would a court today attach the same significance? What about a modern jury?

3. An attempt to assault someone with intent to commit rape is a serious crime. If the trial judge truly believed that McQuirter was guilty of such a serious crime, why was he punished with only a fine? Might the police, the prosecutor and the judge have viewed McQuirter's "crime" as a black man walking in a white neighborhood or too close to a white woman?

Where does each conduct test found in the reading belong on this timeline?

Attempt
Conduct Plotting Exercise

Timeline

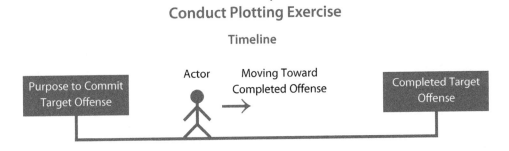

D. Mental States

Thinking clearly about the mental aspect of attempt liability requires analyzing separately an actor's mental states about conduct, result, and circumstance elements. In this section, we first address mental states regarding conduct and result elements. In the next section, we look at mental state about circumstance elements.

1. Mental States Regarding Conduct and Result Elements

Look back at Problem 10.3 in which minister Glenn forced his wife Darlene at gunpoint to place her hand into a rattlesnake cage. What mental state did Glenn have with respect to his conduct? What mental state did he have with regard to the death of Darlene? In your view, should Glenn's mental state qualify him for attempted murder? Does it qualify him for attempted murder under the statutes that follow? What if Glenn's objective had been only to scare Darlene but not to kill her? Would he be liable for attempted murder?

Problems

10.6 Late one summer evening a traveling carnival is operating in a public park in a major city. Some of the city's neighborhoods have recently experienced increased gang violence. Families with small children and lots of teenagers are walking around the carnival, playing games, and waiting in line for rides. In a parking area near the park about a dozen members of the local North gang, wearing the gang's colors, have gathered. Nearby are Charlie and Adam, two members of the rival South gang. Joe, a member of the Norths, calls Charlie and Adam derogatory names and challenges them to a fight. Charlie and Adam decline the invitation to fight and decide to leave the carnival in Adam's truck. As they walk away, several North members follow, continue to call them names, and strike Adam's truck as Charlie and Adam drive away.

Shortly thereafter, Charlie and Adam meet up with other South gang members. An older member of the gang, Nicholas, who is carrying a loaded handgun, asks Adam to drive him to the carnival parking area. When Adam does so, the Norths are still gathered in the parking lot. Adam drives his truck past the Norths three times and on the third pass stops the truck about 15 feet from the Norths. Nicholas, who is sitting in the front passenger seat of Adam's truck, makes a South gang sign with his left hand and then fires his gun out the window at the Norths.

Part (a) Assume for this part that Nicholas's shot hits and kills Joe and Nicholas is charged with murder. At trial there is conflicting testimony about whether Nicholas intended to kill Joe or anyone else or whether Nicholas shot with the intention only of scaring and intimidating the Norths. What jury instruction about mental state should the judge give the jury at the end of Nicholas's murder trial?

Part (b) Assume for this part that Nicholas's shot, although it came very close to hitting one of the Norths, did *not* hit or kill anyone and that Nicholas is charged with *attempted* murder. As in Part (a), at trial there is conflicting testimony about whether Nicholas intended to kill Joe or anyone else or whether Nicholas shot with the intention only of scaring and intimidating the Norths. What jury instruction about mental state should the judge give the jury at the end of Nicholas's *attempted* murder trial?

10.7 Julian is charged with one count of drug possession and one count of attempted sale of a drug. Julian drove his car to the parking lot of a local mall, where he approached several high school students. Three of these students testified at trial that Julian asked them "Do you want to buy a bag?" The students also testified that they understood Julian to mean a bag of marijuana and that they each declined Julian's offer. A security guard at the mall called police, who stopped Julian a few blocks from the mall and found multiple baggies of marijuana in his coat pocket. Assume Julian is liable for possession of marijuana. Is he also liable for attempt to sell marijuana? What jury instruction about mental state should the judge give the jury at the end of trial if Julian is charged with attempt to sell marijuana?

Kansas Statutes Annotated

§ 21-3301

(a) An attempt is any overt act toward the perpetration of a crime done by a person who intends to commit such crime but fails in the perpetration thereof or is prevented or intercepted in executing such crime.

Wisconsin Statutes

§ 939.32

(3) An attempt to commit a crime requires that the actor have an intent to perform acts and attain a result which, if accomplished, would constitute such crime and that the actor does acts toward the commission of the crime which demonstrate unequivocally, under all the circumstances, that the actor formed that intent and would commit the crime except for the intervention of another person or some other extraneous factor.

Model Penal Code

§ 5.01 Criminal Attempt

(1) **Definition of Attempt.** A person is guilty of an attempt to commit a crime if, acting with the kind of culpability otherwise required for commission of the crime, he:

    (a) purposely engages in conduct that would constitute the crime if the attendant circumstances were as he believes them to be; or

    (b) when causing a particular result is an element of the crime, does or omits to do anything with the purpose of causing or with the belief that it will cause such result without further conduct on his part; or

    (c) purposely does or omits to do anything that, under the circumstances as he believes them to be, is an act or omission constituting a substantial step in a course of conduct planned to culminate in his commission of the crime.

South Dakota v. Lyerla

424 N.W.2d 908 (1988)
Supreme Court of South Dakota

Koenkamp, J.

A jury convicted Gerald K. Lyerla (Lyerla) of second degree murder and two counts of attempted second degree murder. We affirm the second degree murder conviction, but reverse the convictions for attempted second degree murder.

On the night of January 18, 1986, while driving east on Interstate 90 in Haakon County, Lyerla fired three shots with his .357 magnum pistol at a pickup truck carrying three teenage girls. One was killed, the other two were injured. Only one bullet entered the pickup cab, the one that killed seventeen-year-old Tammy Jensen. Another bullet was recovered from the engine block; the third was never found. Lyerla fled the scene, but was later apprehended. He was charged in the alternative with first degree murder or second degree murder for the death of Tammy Jensen and two counts each of attempted first degree murder and alternatively two counts of attempted second degree murder of the two surviving girls.

Before the shooting, the teenagers and Lyerla were traveling in the same direction. The vehicles passed each other a few times. At one point when Lyerla tried to pass the girls, their truck accelerated so that he could not overtake them. Lyerla decided to leave the interstate. When he exited, the Jensen pickup pulled to the side of the road near the entry ramp. Lyerla loaded his pistol, reentered the interstate and passed the Jensen pickup. When the girls attempted to pass him, he fired at the passenger side of their truck.

At his trial, Lyerla told the jury that the teenagers were harassing him to such an extent that he feared for his life and fired the shots to disable their pickup. The two girls gave a different rendition of the events leading up to the shooting, but the prosecutor conceded in closing argument that Tammy Jensen was "trying to play games" with Lyerla by not letting him pass. Both Lyerla's version and that of the girls had a number of discrepancies. We view these inconsistencies to have been resolved by the jury's verdicts.

ATTEMPTED SECOND DEGREE MURDER

Lyerla argues that it is a legal impossibility to attempt to commit murder in the second degree and his two convictions for this offense should be reversed. Lyerla did not object to the court's instructions on attempted second degree murder. Ordinarily we will not consider questions on allegedly erroneous instructions unless the defendant made a timely objection to them.

Criminal offenses are created only by statute. If attempted second degree murder is not a crime in South Dakota, then a defendant's failure to object cannot establish that crime. Jurisdictional defects are not waived by failure to object.... To attempt second degree murder one must intend to have a criminally reckless state of mind,

i.e. perpetrating an imminently dangerous act while evincing a depraved mind, regardless of human life, but without a design to kill any particular person.

Whether there can be such a crime as attempted second degree murder has never
been determined in South Dakota. Interpreting a similar statute the Minnesota
Supreme Court ruled in *State v. Dahlstrom:*

> We do not conceive of any practical basis upon which the jury could have
> found defendant guilty of attempted murder in the third degree. Philosoph-
> ically, it might be possible to attempt to perpetrate an act imminently dan-
> gerous to others and evincing a depraved mind regardless of human life
> within the meaning of the phrase as used in 609.195, defining murder in the
> third degree.... But we cannot conceive of a factual situation which could
> make such conduct attempted murder in the third degree where the actor
> did not intend the death of anyone and where no death occurred.

Unlike the *Dahlstrom* case, a death occurred here, but the jury obviously decided
that Lyerla did not intend the death of the deceased since he was found guilty of the
lesser count of second degree murder. Nor did he intend to kill the other two girls
as the verdicts for attempted second degree murder confirm.

Other courts have likewise found attempted reckless homicide a logical impossibility. In *People v. Perez,* [a New York case] it was stated:

> However, murder in the second degree under PL 125.25 subdivision 2, in-
> volves no intent but instead requires a culpable mental state of recklessness.
> One may not intentionally attempt to cause the death of another by a reck-
> less act.

The Colorado Supreme Court [in *People v. Hernandez*] held:

> An attempt to commit criminal negligent homicide thus requires proof that
> the defendant intended to perpetrate an unintended killing—a logical im-
> possibility. The words "attempt" and "negligence" are at war with one another;
> they are internally inconsistent and cannot sensibly co-exist.

[Wisconsin courts have also] held under a statute similar to our own that the crime
of attempted second degree murder does not exist. We agree with the reasoning of
these courts. Stating the rule most succinctly:

> To commit murder, one need not intend to take life; but to be guilty of an
> attempt to murder, he must so intend. It is not sufficient that his act, had it
> proved fatal, would have been murder. [citing *Merritt v. Commonwealth,* a
> Virginia case].

... Defendant's convictions for attempted second degree murder are reversed. In
all other respects, the judgment of the trial court is affirmed.

Sabers, J., dissenting.

I dissent from the majority opinion on "attempted second degree murder." ... I
agree that "to attempt second degree murder one must intend to have a criminally
reckless state of mind, i.e. perpetrating an imminently dangerous act while evincing

a depraved mind, regardless of human life, but without a design to kill any particular person." However, the majority also cites the Minnesota Supreme Court case of *State v. Dahlstrom,* in part as follows:

> "... But we cannot conceive of a factual situation which could make such conduct attempted murder in the third degree where the actor did not intend the death of anyone and where no death occurred."

That concept is not that difficult:

> For example, knowing he is a bad shot, A attempts to shoot B's eyelashes off from fifty feet away
>
> —if A misses and kills B, it constitutes second-degree murder under South Dakota law;
>
> —if A misses and wounds B, it constitutes attempted second-degree murder under South Dakota law;
>
> —if A misses all together, it may constitute attempted second-degree murder under South Dakota law.

I agree with the majority that the jury obviously decided that Lyerla did not intend the death of the deceased since he was found guilty of the lesser count of second-degree murder. Nor did he intend to kill the other two girls as the verdicts for attempted second-degree murder confirm. However, had his acts resulted in their deaths, either directly as in the case of Tammy Jensen, or indirectly, through a resulting car accident, he would have been guilty of second-degree murder. Since deaths did not result he was guilty of attempted second-degree murder under South Dakota law.

SDCL 22-4-1 provides:

> "Any person who attempts to commit a crime and in the attempt does any act toward the commission of the crime, but fails or is prevented or intercepted in the perpetration thereof, is punishable where no provision is made by law for the punishment of such attempt[.]"

SDCL 22-16-7 provides:

> "Homicide is murder in the second degree when perpetrated by any act imminently dangerous to others and evincing a depraved mind, regardless of human life, although without any premeditated design to effect the death of any particular individual."

This statute deals with "homicide" which is named "murder in the second degree." Neither statute contains an element of specific intent. SDCL 22-16-7 simply requires an act. The act required must be dangerous to others (or stupid) under South Dakota law. If one attempts a "dangerous" or "stupid" act it is sufficient. The only "intent" or "attempt" necessary is a voluntary as opposed to a non-volitional or forced act. In this case, Lyerla clearly attempted the dangerous and stupid act of pulling the trigger and shooting the gun at or near the people or the car in which they were riding. This is sufficient for attempted second-degree murder under South Dakota law.

The cases from other jurisdictions cited by *Lyerla* have a common flaw. In each case the attempt statute contains an element of specific intent while the standard of culpability otherwise required for the commission of the underlying offense is something less than specific intent. In this respect, Instruction No. 20 (as set forth in footnote 4 of the majority opinion) was more favorable to Lyerla than the law required in that paragraph 1 implies that specific intent might also be required for second-degree murder.

The majority opinion cites *People v. Perez* and *People v. Hernandez* for the proposition that one cannot intentionally attempt to cause the death of another by a reckless act and for the proposition that the perpetration of an unintended killing is a logical impossibility. Further, these cases are cited to support the proposition that the words "attempt" and "negligence" are at war with one another; that they are internally inconsistent and cannot sensibly co-exist. These cases place emphasis on the word "intentional" contrary to the South Dakota statute on attempt. As previously indicated, the "intent" or "attempt" required under the South Dakota statute is simply to voluntarily act as opposed to an involuntary or forced action. In other words, an attempt to pull the trigger and shoot the gun is enough. This type of "attempt" and the "dangerous" or "stupid" act are not at war with one another; they are internally consistent and can sensibly co-exist.

Much of the confusion in this matter results from the use of the word murder, which implies an intent to take life. What we are really dealing with under South Dakota law is homicide, named second-degree murder. To intentionally pull the trigger and shoot a gun in this dangerous manner was not homicide because neither Gropper girl died, but it was attempted homicide, also known as attempted second-degree murder. Accordingly, attempted second-degree murder is a crime in South Dakota, and Lyerla's convictions for attempted second-degree murder should be affirmed.

Discussion Questions

1. Justice Koenkamp notes that "[c]riminal offenses are created only by statute." But does he refer to the South Dakota attempt statute in his analysis? Does the language of that statute support his position?

2. Which position do you think is better reasoned, the majority or the dissent? Do the purposes of punishment better support the majority or the dissent?

3. What would be the consequences in terms of the scope of attempt liability of adopting the dissent's position?

Diagramming *Lyerla*

Liability for attempting a crime such as homicide, in which the target offense has both a conduct element and a result element, requires that a defendant have more than one purpose—*both* purpose to engage in the conduct required by the target offense *and* purpose regarding the result required by the target offense. So, in Problem 10.2, if Gwen is arrested in her camouflage clothes with her rifle, the prosecution needs to prove that Gwen had *both* purpose to *fire* the rifle (the target offense conduct element) and purpose regarding Albert's *death* (the target offense result element).

The primary point of the *Lyerla* case is that even if the target offense may be satisfied with a mental state *less than purpose* regarding a result element, an attempt to commit that crime nonetheless *requires purpose*. In other words, the law of attempt ratchets up to purpose the mental state required for conviction of attempted murder beyond what is required for conviction of the target offense of murder. This is true not only in South Dakota, where Lyerla was prosecuted, but is generally true throughout American jurisdictions and under the Model Penal Code.

The following diagram illustrates this important point about the law of attempt. Look at the mental state box regarding death under the target offense of murder at the top of the diagram. You should remember from Chapter 6 that liability for murder can result when the defendant has purpose *or knowledge or extreme recklessness* regarding the death. Then look at and compare the mental state box regarding death under attempt at the bottom of the diagram. Only *purpose* regarding the death suffices for attempted murder. Neither knowledge nor extreme recklessness regarding the death are sufficient for attempted murder, even though each is sufficient for murder.

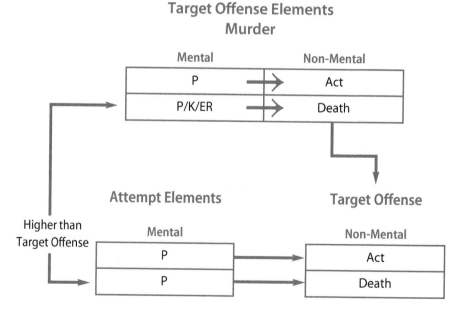

Diagramming the Purposes Required for Attempt

The following diagram illustrates an additional point about the mental states required for liability for an incomplete attempt, such as those governed by the Model Penal Code's substantial step test for a target offense that has a result element. It shows that with such incomplete attempts an actor must possess three different purposes in order to be liable: (1) purpose regarding the substantial step or steps; (2) purpose regarding the future conduct required by the target offense; and (3) purpose regarding the result required by the target offense.

Thus, in Problem 10.2, if Gwen is arrested in her camouflage clothes with her rifle when she takes up her position in the woods but *before* she takes a shot at her proposed victim, Albert, the prosecution needs to prove that Gwen had: (1) purpose to engage in the substantial steps she had already taken; (2) purpose to *fire* the rifle (the target offense conduct); and (3) purpose regarding Albert's *death* (the target offense result element).

Attempt Elements

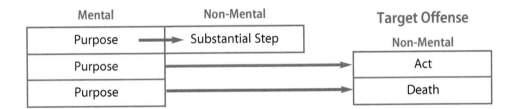

Montana v. Hembd

197 Mont. 438 (1982)
Montana Supreme Court

Sheehy, J.

John Hembd was charged by information in the District Court of the Thirteenth Judicial District, Yellowstone County, with the crime of negligent arson under section 45-6-102(1)(a), MCA. A jury found him guilty of "attempted misdemeanor negligent arson" and he appeals.

In the early evening of February 13, 1981, Hembd, who had been sitting in the lobby of the Billings Sheraton Hotel for two hours, was asked to leave by the hotel's security guard. Hotel employees watched Hembd after he left. They soon observed him in front of a hotel fire exit, with his back to certain doors that lead into the building. As he started to walk away, the employees entered the area in which he had been standing and discovered a styrofoam donut wrapper burning on top of a heater next to the wall. After extinguishing the flame the two employees seized Hembd who was a short distance away. Hembd allegedly stated, "You didn't see anything. You can't prove anything. You guys are crazy." Hembd admitted at trial that he was drunk at the time of the incident but denied setting the fire.

Hembd was charged with the crime of arson pursuant to section 45-6-102(1)(a), MCA. The jury was instructed on four alternate forms of verdict: felony negligent arson, "attempted felony negligent arson," misdemeanor negligent arson, and "attempted misdemeanor negligent arson." Hembd was found guilty of "attempted misdemeanor negligent arson."

This appeal raises two issues: (1) Is "attempted misdemeanor (or felony) negligent arson" a crime?; and (2) If Hembd was convicted of a nonexistent crime, did the purported conviction impliedly acquit him of misdemeanor or felony negligent arson?

We find that attempted misdemeanor negligent arson and attempted felony negligent arson are nonexistent crimes. Furthermore, we find that the jury's verdict, notwithstanding the fact that it convicted Hembd of a nonexistent crime, constituted an implied acquittal of the crimes of misdemeanor negligent arson and felony negligent arson, and therefore Hembd may not be retried for these offenses.

Hembd contends that there is no such crime as "attempted misdemeanor negligent arson." The State concedes this point in the following passage quoted from its brief:

"Attempt is defined by section 45-5-103, MCA, as follows:

1) A person commits the offense of attempt when with the purpose to commit a specific offense, he does any act toward the commission of such offense.

"The crime of misdemeanor negligent arson occurs when a person 'purposely or knowingly starts a fire or causes an explosion ... and thereby negligently' places property in danger of destruction, section 45-6-102, MCA. It is in combining these definitions that the problem becomes clear. It is possible to purposely attempt to start a fire. The crime of negligent arson, however, requires purposely or knowingly starting a fire and negligently placing property in danger. To purposely attempt to be negligent is a contradiction in terms. The trial court ruled that attempt modifies only the act of 'purposely or knowingly starting a fire.' That ruling ignores the definition of attempt. Attempt requires 'purpose to commit a specific offense' and, standing by itself, purposely starting a fire is not a punishable offense. The second requirement, negligently placing property in danger, is necessary to complete the crime of negligent arson. It is impossible to show one purposely was negligent."

Attempted negligent arson, be it misdemeanor or felony, is a nonexistent crime. The judgment is reversed and remanded with instructions to dismiss the action.

Discussion Questions

1. What are the elements of negligent arson under Montana law? Why do you think Hembd was not convicted of negligent arson? Lack of proof of a non-mental element? Lack of proof of a mental element? What mental state do you think Hembd had toward each of the non-mental elements of negligent arson?

2. Was Hembd blameworthy? Dangerous? Should he have been convicted of attempt? Of some other crime?

Problems

10.8 Is it ever possible to attempt a crime that has negligence as a required mental state? Can one, for example, be guilty of attempted negligent homicide? What about attempted negligent storage of a weapon?

10.9 Is it ever possible to attempt a crime that has recklessness as a required mental state? Can one, for example, be guilty of attempt to commit reckless vehicular homicide? What about attempted reckless driving?

10.10 Is it possible to commit attempted manslaughter?

10.11 Is it possible to commit attempted felony murder? Compare the following scenarios:

Part (a) Derek and Ben rob a bank. Derek threatens the tellers, bank guard, and customers with a gun while Ben goes from teller to teller collecting money. One of the customers is an elderly woman who has a heart attack and collapses due to the stress of being threatened at gunpoint. Derek and Ben flee with the money from the robbery. The bank manager calls 911 as soon as the robbers leave and responding EMS workers manage to save the elderly woman's life.

Part (b) Same facts as Part (a) except that one of the tellers hits a silent alarm when Derek and Ben enter the bank. A police cruiser happens to be nearby and responds to the silent alarm. Derek threatens the tellers, bank guard, and customers with a gun and an elderly customer has a heart attack and collapses due to the stress of being threatened at gunpoint. Before Ben can take any money from the tellers, Derek spots the police and he and Ben flee out a rear entrance without having taken any money. The bank manager calls 911 as soon as the robbers leave but responding EMS workers are not able to save the elderly customer's life.

2. Mental State Regarding a Circumstance Element

We have seen that purpose as to a required result is typically needed for an attempt conviction even if a reduced mental state as to that result suffices for conviction of the target offense. So, the law of attempt effectively raises any mental states lower than purpose regarding results in a target offense to the level of purpose. Should mental states regarding circumstance elements be treated similarly?

Problem

10.12 You are the law clerk to a judge before whom a criminal case is being tried. The defendant in the case, Jake, is charged with an *attempt* to violate the following statute:

> It is a felony punishable by 10 years imprisonment knowingly to sell crack cocaine within 1000 feet of any school.

For conviction under this statute, no mental state need be proven regarding the circumstance element "within 1,000 feet of any school." In other words, strict liability applies to that element. Assume that the defendant's conduct *was not* sufficient to warrant conviction of this target offense but *was* sufficient to qualify for an attempt to violate the statute. The defendant admits the conduct, but argues that he is not liable for attempt due to his alleged lack of knowledge that he was within 1000 feet of a school. The school in question was a preschool serving children of families with working parents and located in a light industrial building in a primarily commercial area. Jake was arrested by an undercover police officer in front of the building in which the preschool was located. Jake testified at trial and admitted engaging in conduct that would qualify as an attempt and that his conduct took place within 1000 feet of the preschool. But he testified that he was mistaken about whether the building in question contained a school. He believed the building and the surrounding area were strictly commercial. The judge is preparing the jury instructions for the attempt charge and wants to know the culpability required regarding the element of "within 1000 feet of any school." What is the required culpability regarding this circumstance element for attempt liability? What would it be under the MPC Comment below?

Comment to Model Penal Code § 5.01

The general principle is … that the actor must affirmatively desire to engage in the conduct or to cause the result that will constitute the principal offense.… The requirement of purpose extends to the conduct of the actor and to the results that his conduct causes, but his purpose need not encompass all of the circumstances included in the formal definition of the substantive offense. As to them, it is sufficient that he acts with the culpability that is required for commission of the completed crime.

Several illustrations may serve to clarify the point. Assume, for example, a statute that provides that sexual intercourse with a female under a prescribed age is an offense, and that a mistake as to age will not afford a defense no matter how reasonable its foundation. The policy of the substantive offense as to age, therefore, is one of strict liability, and if the actor has sexual intercourse with a female, he is guilty or not, depending upon her age and irrespective of his views as to her age. Suppose, however, that he is arrested before he engages in the proscribed conduct, and that the charge is an attempt to commit the offense. Should he then be entitled to rely on a mistake as to age as a defense?

Or should the policy of the substantive crime on this issue carry over to the attempt as well? Or, assume a statute that makes it a federal offense to murder an FBI agent and treats the agent's status as a member of the FBI as a jurisdictional ingredient, with no culpability required in respect to that element. The question again is whether the policy of the substantive crime should control the same issue when it arises on a charge of attempt, or whether there is a special policy that the law of attempt should embrace to change the result on this point.

Under the formulation ... [in the Model Penal Code], the proffered defense would not succeed in either case. In the statutory rape example, the actor must have a purpose to engage in sexual intercourse with a female in order to be charged with the attempt, and must engage in a substantial step in a course of conduct planned to culminate in his commission of that act. With respect to the age of the victim, however, it is sufficient if he acts "with the kind of culpability otherwise required for the commission of the crime," which in the case supposed is none at all. Since, therefore, mistake as to age is irrelevant with respect to the substantive offense, it is likewise irrelevant with respect to the attempt. The same result would obtain in the murder illustration. The actor must, in the case supposed, engage in a substantial step in a course of conduct planned to culminate in the death of his victim. But with respect to his awareness of the status of his victim as an FBI agent, a mistake would not be relevant since the policy of the substantive offense controls on such matters and that policy is one of strict liability.

The judgment is thus that if the defendant manifests a purpose to engage in the type of conduct or to cause the type of result that is forbidden by the criminal law, he has sufficiently exhibited his dangerousness to justify the imposition of criminal sanctions, so long as he otherwise acts with the kind of culpability that is sufficient for the completed offense. The objective is to select out those elements of the completed crime that, if the defendant desires to bring them about, indicate with clarity that he poses the type of danger to society that the substantive offense is designed to prevent. This objective is well served by the Code's approach ... of allowing the policy of the substantive offense to control with respect to circumstance elements.

E. Abandonment

Problems

10.13 Maria and Tim plan to rob Sam's camera shop. Maria visits the store, pretending to be a customer, and locates the wire for a surveillance camera that monitors Sam's store. On her way out, she surreptitiously cuts the wire. Maria and Tim buy disguises and purchase a toy gun that looks real. Tim joins Maria at the coffee shop next door to the camera shop. In the coffee shop's restrooms, both change into their disguises and Maria hides the toy gun in her handbag. Assume that Maria and Tim at this point are guilty of attempt under the applicable attempt statute in their state. In other words, assume they have met the conduct and mental state requirements for attempt liability in the jurisdiction where they live.

Part (a) Maria and Tim exit the coffee shop but just as they are about to enter Sam's store, Tim notices a police officer enter Sam's shop. Maria and Tim decide it's too risky to try the robbery that afternoon and decide to postpone the robbery until tomorrow. Each goes home. Does their decision to postpone the robbery extinguish their liability for attempted robbery?

Part (b) Assume the same facts except that as Maria and Tim leave the coffee shop, instead of observing a police officer, they encounter Tim's friend, Harry. Harry reminds Tim of Tim's dream of going to law school. Tim realizes that the robbery is a foolish idea and tells Maria that he has decided not to commit the robbery. Does Tim's change of heart extinguish Tim's attempt liability?

People v. Staples

6 Cal. App. 3d 61 (1970)
California Court of Appeals

Reppy, J.

Defendant was charged in an information with attempted burglary (Pen. Code, §§ 664, 459). Trial by jury was waived, and the matter submitted on the testimony contained in the transcript of the preliminary hearing together with exhibits. Defendant was found guilty....

I. The Facts

In October 1967, while his wife was away on a trip, defendant, a mathematician, under an assumed name, rented an office on the second floor of a building in Hollywood which was over the mezzanine of a bank. Directly below the mezzanine was the vault of the bank. Defendant was aware of the layout of the building, specifically of the relation of the office he rented to the bank vault. Defendant paid rent for the period from October 23 to November 23. The landlord had 10 days before commencement of the rental period within which to finish some interior repairs and painting. During this prerental period defendant brought into the office certain equipment. This included drilling tools, two acetylene gas tanks, a blow torch, a blanket, and a linoleum rug. The landlord observed these items when he came in from time to time to see how the repair work was progressing. Defendant learned from a custodian that no one was in the building on Saturdays. On Saturday, October 14, defendant drilled two groups of holes into the floor of the office above the mezzanine room. He stopped drilling before the holes went through the floor. He came back to the office several times thinking he might slowly drill down, covering the holes with the linoleum rug. At some point in time he installed a hasp lock on a closet, and planned to, or did, place his tools in it. However, he left the closet keys on the premises. Around the end of November, apparently after November 23, the landlord notified the police and turned the tools and equipment over to them. Defendant did not pay any more rent. It is not clear when he last entered the office, but it could have been after November 23, and even after the landlord had removed the equipment. On February 22, 1968, the police arrested defendant. After receiving advice as to his constitutional rights, defendant voluntarily made an oral statement which he reduced to writing.

Among other things which defendant wrote down were these:

> "Saturday, the 14th ... I drilled some small holes in the floor of the room. Because of tiredness, fear, and the implications of what I was doing, I stopped and went to sleep.

> "At this point I think my motives began to change. The actual [sic] commencement of my plan made me begin to realize that even if I were to succeed a fugitive life of living off of stolen money would not give the enjoyment of the life of a mathematician however humble a job I might have.
> "I still had not given up my plan however. I felt I had made a certain investment of time, money, effort and a certain pschological [sic] commitment to the concept.

> "I came back several times thinking I might store the tools in the closet and slowly drill down (covering the hole with a rug of linoleum square). As time went on (after two weeks or so). My wife came back and my life as bank robber seemed more and more absurd."

II. Discussion of Defendant's Contentions

Defendant's position in this appeal is that, as a matter of law, there was insufficient evidence upon which to convict him of a criminal attempt under Penal Code section 664. Defendant claims that his actions were all preparatory in nature and never reached a stage of advancement in relation to the substantive crime which he concededly intended to commit (burglary of the bank vault) so that criminal responsibility might attach....

The required specific intent was clearly established in the instant case. Defendant admitted in his written confession that he rented the office fully intending to burglarize the bank, that he brought in tools and equipment to accomplish this purpose, and that he began drilling into the floor with the intent of making an entry into the bank.

The question of whether defendant's conduct went beyond "mere preparation" raises some provocative problems. The briefs and the oral argument of counsel in this case point up a degree of ambiguity and uncertainty that permeates the law of attempts in this state. Each side has cited us to a different so-called "test" to determine whether this defendant's conduct went beyond the preparatory stage. Predictably each respective test in the eyes of its proponents yielded an opposite result....

None of the above statements of the law applicable to this category of attempts provide a litmus-like test, and perhaps no such test is achievable. Such precision is not required in this case, however. There was definitely substantial evidence entitling the trial judge to find that defendant's acts had gone beyond the preparation stage....

The instant case provides an out-of-the-ordinary factual situation.... Here, there was no direct proof of any actual interception. But it was clearly inferable by the trial judge that defendant became aware that the landlord had resumed control over the office and had turned defendant's equipment and tools over to the police. This was the equivalent of interception.

The inference of this nonvoluntary character of defendant's abandonment was a proper one for the trial judge to draw. However, it would seem that the character of the abandonment in situations of this type, whether it be voluntary (prompted by pangs of conscience or a change of heart) or nonvoluntary (established by inference in the instant case), is not controlling. The relevant factor is the determination of whether the acts of the perpetrator have reached such a stage of advancement that they can be classified as an attempt. Once that attempt is found there can be no exculpatory abandonment. "One of the purposes of the criminal law is to protect society from those who intend to injure it. When it is established that the defendant intended to commit a specific crime and that in carrying out this intention he committed an act that caused harm or sufficient danger of harm, it is immaterial that for some collateral reason he could not complete the intended crime."

The order is affirmed.

Model Penal Code

§ 5.01(4) Renunciation of Criminal Purpose

When the actor's conduct would otherwise constitute an attempt under Subsection (1)(b) or (1)(c) of this Section, it is an affirmative defense that he abandoned his effort to commit the crime or otherwise prevented its commission, under circumstances manifesting a complete and voluntary renunciation of his criminal purpose. The establishment of such defense does not, however, affect the liability of an accomplice who did not join in such abandonment or prevention.

Within the meaning of this Article, renunciation of criminal purpose is not voluntary if it is motivated, in whole or in part, by circumstances, not present or apparent at the inception of the actor's course of conduct, that increase the probability of detection or apprehension or that make more difficult the accomplishment of the criminal purpose. Renunciation is not complete if it is motivated by a decision to postpone the criminal conduct until a more advantageous time or to transfer the criminal effort to another but similar objective or victim.

Discussion Question

The *Staples* court states that "Once ... attempt is found there can be no exculpatory abandonment." The Model Penal Code, by contrast, recognizes abandonment as a defense. Which is the better view? Why? How are the purposes of punishment relevant in answering this question?

Review Problem

The following problem, inspired by two scenes from the HBO television series *The Wire*, provides an opportunity to review and apply the material on the law of attempt covered so far in this chapter.

10.14 Part (a) Otis makes his living "ripping and robbing"—stealing money from local drug dealers. In retaliation, a local drug kingpin, Stricker, has someone kidnap, torture, and kill one of Otis's close friends and crime partners. Otis becomes set on avenging his friend's death. Stricker leads Otis to believe that Monty was the hit man Stricker hired to kill his friend and that the torture was Monty's idea. Otis manages to get the jump on and shoot Monty. But while Monty lies bleeding, he convinces Otis that he had nothing to do with his friend's death and that Stricker has misled and set up both Monty and Otis. Otis then calls 911 and saves Monty's life. Is Otis liable under these facts for the attempted murder of Monty?

Part (b) Monty recovers from his wounds and decides to exact revenge on Stricker. But first he decides to track down and threaten Otis to get information and assistance from him. Monty's plan is to kill Otis if he refuses to cooperate but not to kill him if he cooperates and helps Monty track down Stricker and jointly seek revenge. Monty kidnaps another of Otis's compatriots and forces him to reveal Otis's hideout. Monty secretly follows and observes Otis for about a week to pick a good place to ambush him. Monty chooses an alley he knows Otis often walks down on his way home. He looks around the alley and finds a place where he can hide until Otis passes. On the night of the ambush, armed with a Walther handgun, Monty goes to his chosen hiding place. But Otis never shows up in the alley that night. Is Monty liable under these facts for attempt to murder Otis?

Part (c) Assume the facts are the same as in Part (b) except that Otis *does* show up and walks by the place where Monty is hiding. Monty walks up behind Otis with his handgun drawn and orders Otis to stop, drop the bag he is carrying, and turn around. Otis does so, but when he turns around Otis has drawn his own .45 caliber handgun. With both men pointing their guns at one another, Monty asks Otis if he will cooperate with him in tracking down and killing

Stricker so both can get their revenge. Otis agrees, Monty lowers his handgun, and he and Otis start planning their revenge on Stricker. Is Monty liable under these facts for attempting to murder Otis?

F. Impossibility

Should the fact that the target offense is "impossible" to commit exonerate? The *Dlugash* case, below, examines both the traditional and modern approaches to impossibility.

People v. Dlugash
41 N.Y.2d 725 (1977)
New York Court of Appeals

The criminal law is of ancient origin, but criminal liability for attempt to commit a crime is comparatively recent.... The ultimate issue is whether an individual's intentions and actions, though failing to achieve a manifest and malevolent criminal purpose, constitute a danger to organized society of sufficient magnitude to warrant the imposition of criminal sanctions.... Phrased somewhat differently, the concern centers on whether an individual should be liable for an attempt to commit a crime when, unknown to him, it was impossible to successfully complete the crime attempted. For years, serious studies have been made on the subject in an effort to resolve the continuing controversy when, if at all, the impossibility of successfully completing the criminal act should preclude liability for even making the futile attempt. The 1967 revision of the Penal Law approached the impossibility defense to the inchoate crime of attempt in a novel fashion. The statute provides that, if a person engages in conduct which would otherwise constitute an attempt to commit a crime, "it is no defense to a prosecution for such attempt that the crime charged to have been attempted was, under the attendant circumstances, factually or legally impossible of commission, if such crime could have been committed had the attendant circumstances been as such person believed them to be." (Penal Law, § 110.10.) This appeal presents to us, for the first time, a case involving the application of the modern statute. We hold that, under the proof presented by the People at trial, defendant Melvin Dlugash may be held for attempted murder, though the target of the attempt may have already been slain, by the hand of another, when Dlugash made his felonious attempt.

On December 22, 1973, Michael Geller, 25 years old, was found shot to death in the bedroom of his Brooklyn apartment. The body, which had literally been riddled by bullets, was found lying face up on the floor. An autopsy revealed that the victim had been shot in the face and head no less than seven times. Powder burns on the face indicated that the shots had been fired from within one foot of the victim. Four small caliber bullets were recovered from the victim's skull. The victim had also been critically wounded in the chest. One heavy caliber bullet passed through the left lung, penetrated the heart chamber, pierced the left ventricle of the heart upon entrance and again upon exit, and lodged in the victim's torso. A second bullet entered the left lung and passed through to the chest, but without reaching the heart area. Although the second bullet was damaged beyond identification, the bullet tracks indicated that these wounds were also inflicted by a bullet of heavy caliber. A tenth bullet, of unknown caliber, passed through the thumb of the victim's left hand. The autopsy report listed the cause of death as "[multiple] bullet wounds of head and chest with brain injury and massive bilateral hemothorax with penetration of [the] heart." Subsequent ballistics examination established that the four bullets recovered from the victim's head were .25 caliber bullets and that the heart-piercing bullet was of .38 caliber....

Defendant stated that, on the night of December 21, 1973, he, [Joe] Bush and Geller had been out drinking. Bush had been staying at Geller's apartment and, during the course of the evening, Geller several times demanded that Bush pay $ 100 towards the rent on the apartment. According to defendant, Bush rejected these demands, telling Geller that "you better shut up or you're going to get a bullet". All three returned to Geller's apartment at approximately midnight, took seats in the bedroom, and continued to drink until sometime between 3:00 and 3:30 in the morning. When Geller again pressed his demand for rent money, Bush drew his .38 caliber pistol, aimed it at Geller and fired three times. Geller fell to the floor. After the passage of a few minutes, perhaps two, perhaps as much as five, defendant walked over to the fallen Geller, drew his .25 caliber pistol, and fired approximately five shots in the victim's head and face. Defendant contended that, by the time he fired the shots, "it looked like Mike Geller was already dead". After the shots were fired, defendant and Bush walked to the apartment of a female acquaintance. Bush removed his shirt, wrapped the two guns and a knife in it, and left the apartment, telling Dlugash that he intended to dispose of the weapons. Bush returned 10 or 15 minutes later and stated that he had thrown the weapons down a sewer two or three blocks away.

For proof of defendant's culpability, the prosecution relied upon defendant's own admissions as related by the detective and the prosecutor. From the physicians, the prosecution sought to establish that Geller was still alive at the time defendant shot at him. Both physicians testified that each of the two chest wounds, for which defendant alleged Bush to be responsible, would have caused death without prompt medical attention. However, the victim would have remained alive until such time as his chest cavity became fully filled with blood. Depending on the circumstances, it might take 5 to 10 minutes for the chest cavity to fill. Neither prosecution witness could state, with medical certainty, that the victim was still alive when, perhaps five minutes after the initial chest wounds were inflicted, the defendant fired at the victim's head.

The defense produced but a single witness, the former Chief Medical Examiner of New York City. This expert stated that, in his view, Geller might have died of the chest wounds "very rapidly" since, in addition to the bleeding, a large bullet going through a lung and the heart would have other adverse medical effects. "Those wounds can be almost immediately or rapidly fatal or they may be delayed in there, in the time it would take for death to occur. But I would say that wounds like that which are described here as having gone through the lungs and the heart would be fatal wounds and in most cases they're rapidly fatal." ...

The jury found the defendant guilty of murder. The defendant then moved to set the verdict aside. He submitted an affidavit in which he contended that he "was absolutely, unequivocally and positively certain that Michael Geller was dead before [he] shot him." Further, the defendant averred that he was in fear for his life when he shot Geller. "This fear stemmed from the fact that Joseph Bush, the admitted killer of Geller, was holding a gun on me and telling me, in no uncertain terms, that if I didn't shoot the dead body I, too, would be killed." This motion was denied.[1]

On appeal, the Appellate Division reversed the judgment of conviction on the law and dismissed the indictment....

Preliminarily, we state our agreement with the Appellate Division that the evidence did not establish, beyond a reasonable doubt, that Geller was alive at the time defendant fired into his body. To sustain a homicide conviction, it must be established, beyond a reasonable doubt, that the defendant caused the death of another person. The People were required to establish that the shots fired by defendant Dlugash were a sufficiently direct cause of Geller's death. While the defendant admitted firing five shots at the victim approximately two to five minutes after Bush had fired three times, all three medical expert witnesses testified that they could not, with any degree of medical certainty, state whether the victim had been alive at the time the latter shots were fired by the defendant. Thus, the People failed to prove beyond a reasonable doubt that the victim had been alive at the time he was shot by the defendant. Whatever else it may be, it is not murder to shoot a dead body. Man dies but once....

[W]e must now decide whether, under the evidence presented, the defendant may be held for attempted murder, though someone else perhaps succeeded in killing the victim.

The concept that there could be criminal liability for an attempt, even if ultimately unsuccessful, to commit a crime is comparatively recent. The modern concept of attempt has been said to date from *Rex v Scofield* (Cald 397), decided in 1784.... The Revised Penal Law now provides that a person is guilty of an attempt to commit a crime when, with intent to commit a crime, he engages in conduct which tends to effect the commission of such crime. The most intriguing attempt cases are those where the attempt to commit a crime was unsuccessful due to mistakes of fact or law on the part of the would-be criminal. A general rule developed in most American jurisdictions that legal impossibility is a good defense but factual impossibility is not. Thus, for example, it was held that defendants who shot at a stuffed deer did not attempt to take a deer out of season, even though they believed the dummy to be a live animal. The court

---

1. It should be noted that Joe Bush pleaded guilty to a charge of manslaughter in the first degree....

stated that there was no criminal attempt because it was no crime to "take" a stuffed deer, and it is no crime to attempt to do that which is legal. On the other hand, factual impossibility was no defense. For example, a man was held liable for attempted murder when he shot into the room in which his target usually slept and, fortuitously, the target was sleeping elsewhere in the house that night. Although one bullet struck the target's customary pillow, attainment of the criminal objective was factually impossible....

As can be seen from even this abbreviated discussion, the distinction between "factual" and "legal" impossibility was a nice one indeed and the courts tended to place a greater value on legal form than on any substantive danger the defendant's actions posed for society. The approach of the draftsmen of the Model Penal Code was to eliminate the defense of impossibility in virtually all situations. Under the code provision, to constitute an attempt, it is still necessary that the result intended or desired by the actor constitute a crime. However, the code suggested a fundamental change to shift the locus of analysis to the actor's mental frame of reference and away from undue dependence upon external considerations. The basic premise of the code provision is that what was in the actor's own mind should be the standard for determining his dangerousness to society and, hence, his liability for attempted criminal conduct. In the belief that neither of the two branches of the traditional impossibility arguments detracts from the offender's moral culpability, the Legislature substantially carried the code's treatment of impossibility into the 1967 revision of the Penal Law. Thus, a person is guilty of an attempt when, with intent to commit a crime, he engages in conduct which tends to effect the commission of such crime. (Penal Law, § 110.00.) It is no defense that, under the attendant circumstances, the crime was factually or legally impossible of commission, "if such crime could have been committed had the attendant circumstances been as such person believed them to be." (Penal Law, § 110.10.) Thus, if defendant believed the victim to be alive at the time of the shooting, it is no defense to the charge of attempted murder that the victim may have been dead.

Turning to the facts of the case before us, we believe that there is sufficient evidence in the record from which the jury could conclude that the defendant believed Geller to be alive at the time defendant fired shots into Geller's head. Defendant admitted firing five shots at a most vital part of the victim's anatomy from virtually point blank range. Although defendant contended that the victim had already been grievously wounded by another, from the defendant's admitted actions, the jury could conclude that the defendant's purpose and intention was to administer the coup de grace.... Indeed, not only did defendant not come forward with his story immediately, but when the police arrived at his house, he related a false version designed to conceal his and Bush's complicity in the murder. All of these facts indicate a consciousness of guilt which defendant would not have had if he had truly believed that Geller was dead when he shot him ... In this case, there is ample other evidence to contradict the defendant's assertion that he believed Geller dead. There were five bullet wounds inflicted with stunning accuracy in a vital part of the victim's anatomy. The medical testimony indicated that Geller may have been alive at the time defendant fired at him. The defendant voluntarily left the jurisdiction immediately after the crime with his coperpetrator. Defendant did not report the crime to the police when left on his own by Bush. Instead, he attempted to conceal his and Bush's involvement with the homicide. In addition, the other portions of defendant's admissions make his contended belief that Geller was dead extremely improbable. Defendant, without a word of instruction from Bush, voluntarily got up from his seat after the passage of just a few minutes and fired five times point blank into the victim's face, snuffing out any remaining chance of life that Geller possessed. Certainly, this alone indicates a callous indifference to the taking of a human life. His admissions are barren of any claim of duress and reflect, instead, an unstinting cooperation in efforts to dispose of vital incriminating evidence. Indeed, defendant maintained a false version of the occurrence until such time as the police informed him that they had evidence that he lately possessed a gun of the same caliber as one of the weapons involved in the shooting. From all of this, the jury was certainly warranted in concluding that the defendant acted in the belief that Geller was yet alive when shot by defendant.

The jury convicted the defendant of murder. Necessarily, they found that defendant intended to kill a live human being. Subsumed within this finding is the conclusion that defendant acted in the belief that Geller was alive. Thus, there is no need for additional fact findings by a jury. Although it was not established beyond a reasonable doubt that Geller was, in fact, alive, such is no defense to attempted murder since a murder would have been committed "had the attendant circumstances been as [defendant] believed them to be." (Penal Law, § 110.10.) The jury necessarily found that defendant believed Geller to be alive when defendant shot at him....

The Model Penal Code Approach to Impossibility

As the *Dlugash* case indicates, the Model Penal Code represents the modern approach to impossibility.

Model Penal Code

§ 5.01 Criminal Attempt

(1) <u>Definition of Attempt</u>. A person is guilty of an attempt to commit a crime if, acting with the kind of culpability otherwise required for commission of the crime, he:

    (a) purposely engages in conduct that would constitute the crime if the attendant circumstances were as he believes them to be ...

* * *

The Model Penal Code drafters explained the MPC approach in the following Comment.

Model Penal Code Commentaries, Part 1, at 307

Subsection (1) is ... designed to reject the defense of impossibility, which has sometimes been successful in attempt prosecutions. It does so ... by providing that the defendant's conduct should be measured according to the circumstances as he believes them to be, rather than the circumstances as they may have existed in fact.

G. Synthesis and Review

Problem

10.15 Jerome is the leader of a group of anarchists who need money to fund a planned trip to Europe to demonstrate at an upcoming meeting of an organization devoted to developing world trade. Jerome decides to steal a famous painting from an art museum in a nearby city to fund the trip. Jerome confides his robbery plan to his fellow anarchists and asks for their assistance. The other anarchists are happy to use the proceeds of the theft to travel, but are unwilling to participate in the theft because any kind of organized, concerted action is against their principles. Jerome tells them he will steal the painting on his own. He visits the museum several times in order to be sure of its layout and plan his getaway route. He obtains a number of false identification documents, including a driver's license with a false name and address. On the day before the planned theft, Jerome rents a van to use in the robbery using a false name and the false identification documents. On the evening before the planned robbery, Jerome is reviewing a map of the bank and his getaway route when he hears a knock at the door. Jerome answers the door and police officers arrest him for attempted theft. It turns out that one of Jerome's fellow anarchists is an undercover agent who tape-recorded Jerome's statements about his plan to steal the painting. Is Jerome liable for attempted robbery?

Reconsider abandonment, also referred to as renunciation, in regard to anticipatory offenses in light of the following critique offered by Professor Evan Lee.

Canceling Crime

Evan Tsen Lee

30 Conn. L. Rev. 117–118, 125–26 (1997)

May one cancel liability for crimes already committed? In jurisdictions following the Model Penal Code ("MPC") on attempt, conspiracy, and solicitation, the answer is yes. The MPC provides a defense if the actor abandons the attempt, thwarts the conspiracy, or dissuades the person solicited under circumstances manifesting the actor's complete and voluntary renunciation of criminal purpose. The theory is not that the actor's desistance has left her short of liability for the attempt, conspiracy, or solicitation. The actor's renunciation relieves her of liability previously incurred.

The rather surprising proposition that one can erase existing criminal liability prompts [the following] question ... [I]f the MPC permits one to erase liability for attempts, conspiracies, and solicitations, why not for other crimes? Of course, no one should be able to reverse liability for a crime that necessarily entails a grave harm, such as a homicide or rape, because the harm cannot be undone. Harm is not an element of inchoate offenses. An attempted murder might involve harm, such as fright to the intended victim, but it might not, such as where the would-be killer breaks off the attempt before the intended victim learns of the plan. A conspiracy is nothing more than an agreement to commit an offense; it might culminate in the target offense, or it might die on the vine. The same is true of solicitation, which amounts to an attempted conspiracy. And yet there are many MPC offenses materially similar to attempts, conspiracies, and solicitations. A burglary requires only an unprivileged entry coupled with the purpose to commit a felony. No damage need be done to the structure, no person need be home, no underlying felony need be attempted. The burglary might result in no harm whatsoever. A larceny requires only the taking of property with the purpose of stealing. The item could be replaced undamaged without the victim ever learning of the taking. There are several other MPC offenses even more closely analogous to attempts and conspiracies than burglary and larceny. If the defense of renunciation is made available to attempt, conspiracy, and solicitation prosecutions, then why not for these analogous offenses? ...

The MPC burglary provision makes no mention of renunciation. But because MPC burglaries are a subspecies of MPC interruption-type attempts, it should not surprise us that the fact of renunciation has an identical moral impact on burglary and attempt liability. Consider the following hypotheticals:

1. A walks up to a sidewalk vendor with the intent to steal an item. While the vendor is occupied with a customer, A reaches toward the item. At the last moment, he has a complete change of heart and walks away;

2. B walks calmly into Bloomingdale's through an open door just after closing time with the intent to shoplift an item. Two steps into the store, he has a complete change of heart and calmly walks out undetected; or

3. C intends to kill D while his back is turned. C raises his gun and aims it. At the last moment, he has a complete change of heart and walks away.

4. E intends to kill F, whom he knows to be sleeping in the upstairs bedroom. E calmly walks into F's house through an unlocked back door and starts up the staircase. He then has a complete change of heart and calmly walks back out undetected.

In jurisdictions following the MPC on renunciation, A and C are not guilty of attempted theft and attempted murder, respectively. In jurisdictions following the MPC on burglary, B and E are guilty of burglary. This combination of results is untenable. A and B are in identical moral situations, as are C and E.

Discussion Questions

1. Should the law allow renunciation to cancel liability for anticipatory offenses in light of the disparity raised by Professor Lee's examples? If so, why? If not, why not?

2. If the law should allow such "cancellation," should renunciation be available to cancel liability for crimes like burglary and larceny? If so, to what other crimes should it extend?

Problems

10.16 Monty is a certified public accountant in the United States illegally "laundering" money for a Mexican drug cartel. For a variety of complicated reasons, Monty finds himself doing the laundering through a number of businesses, such as bars, resorts, and casinos located around a large lake in the state of Missouri that has long been a vacation spot for people from cities as far away as Chicago. Because of the work he does, Monty regularly finds himself with very large amounts of cash belonging to the head of the drug cartel and few places to effectively hide this cash until it can be laundered. Ruby is a young lady who works for Monty at several of his businesses and comes to know what Monty does in his work and where he has hidden the money to be laundered. Ruby and her family members all have criminal records and specialize in various types of theft. They convince Ruby to kill Monty so that the family can grab the money he has hidden. Monty has a house on the lake shore and a boat he keeps at a dock in front of the house that he sometimes uses to commute to the resort he owns. Ruby waits for Monty to leave for work one day. Shen then sneaks down onto the dock and runs electrical current from light fixtures near the dock to the steel ladder Monty will use to climb out of his boat when he comes home. Once Monty's hands make contact with the electrified steel ladder, Monty will be electrocuted and die.

Monty is under surveillance by FBI agents because they strongly suspect he is laundering drug money though they cannot yet prove it. Their ultimate goal is to catch Monty and then turn him as an informer, a witness, or both against the drug cartel. An FBI agent who has Monty's house and dock under surveillance sees Ruby fooling around with the lights on the dock. After she leaves, he sneaks down onto the dock and sees what she has done. Because he wants to keep Monty alive for possible future use as an informant or witness, the FBI agent undoes the wiring to the steel ladder and covers up Ruby' handiwork. Monty comes home, climbs out of his boat and walks safely up to his house.

Is Ruby liable for the attempted murder of Monty? If so, at what point?

10.17 Roger is a member of a white supremacist group that is, among other things, virulently racist and antisemitic. Over a period of months, he posts on Facebook statements, photos, and videos expressing his beliefs and goals. In particular, he mentions his desire to destroy a synagogue in the town where he lives.

An FBI agent posing as a female sympathizer contacts Roger through Facebook and expresses support for white supremacy ideology. Over the next few days, Roger sends the agent photos of himself wearing clothing adorned with swastikas and other symbols of white supremacy ideology. A few days later, the agent sends Roger a message saying, "I have friends who are kindred spirits in wanting to save the white race" and who would like to meet Roger. He agrees and the agent sets up a time and place and for the meeting.

A few days later, two other FBI agents working undercover meet Roger at a restaurant. They discuss, among other things, Roger's desire to destroy the synagogue. Roger tells them that he wants to do it with explosives and asks the agents if they can help him obtain some. The agents tell him that they can and Roger then drives with them to the synagogue. Sitting outside the synagogue in a car, Roger describes his plan to "blow up" the synagogue. One of the agents raises the possibility of someone being inside the synagogue when he sets off the explosives. In response, Roger states that he plans to do it late at night, so he doesn't think anyone will be there. But, if there are people present, Roger says he would "not care because they would be Jews." After this meeting, Roger asks two fellow members of his white supremacist group to help him carry out his plan and they agree.

Shortly thereafter, one of the agents contacts Roger, tells him he has the explosives, and asks Roger to meet him at a motel room. Roger arrives at the meeting displaying a Nazi armband and removes several items from his backpack, including a knife, a mask, and a copy of *Mein Kampf*. The agents display what appear to be several pipe bombs and packages of dynamite that are actually made with inert substances incapable of exploding. Roger thanks the agents for helping him to "make a move for our race." The agents hand the fake explosives to Roger, who puts them in a duffle bag and leaves the motel room.

Under the various tests you studied in this chapter, has Roger committed an attempt to destroy property? Attempted murder? Under those tests, what was the earliest point at which the FBI agents could have arrested him?

Chapter 11

Complicity

A. Introduction

We typically think of someone committing a crime by doing an act proscribed by a criminal statute, a person we will refer to in this chapter as a "principal actor" or simply a "principal." A bank robber intimidates and takes money from a bank teller. A drug dealer sells heroin. A hired killer shoots and kills a victim. But what about those who do not personally engage in the conduct proscribed by the statute, but assist or encourage those who do? Someone serves as a lookout and drives the getaway car for the bank robber. Another carries a gun to provide protection for the drug dealer. Someone pays the hired killer and chooses the victim. None of these people engaged in the conduct prohibited by the robbery, drug sale, or homicide statutes. In this chapter we refer to such people, whose liability is based on acts such as assistance or encouragement of a principal actor's crime, as accomplices. As with the crimes we have studied earlier in the course, an accomplice must fulfill both conduct and mental state requirements in order to be held liable.

The criminal law deals with accomplices through the doctrine of complicity, also known as accomplice or accessorial liability. Under that doctrine, those who assist or encourage another to commit a crime may be held liable for that crime even though they did not themselves perform the act specified in the statute defining the crime. This is described as *derivative* liability because the accomplice's liability derives from that of the principal, the person who engages in the prohibited conduct. To understand complicity, then, it is important to realize that complicity is not an independent crime, but a way of sharing in the liability for a crime. If accomplices satisfy the mental state requirements for accomplice liability, they can all—the lookout and getaway car driver, the bodyguard, and the person hiring the killer—be held fully liable for the crimes committed by those they assist or encourage.

The law of complicity has been a focal point in recent high-profile cases. On May 25, 2020, as the current edition of this book was being written, Minneapolis police officer Derek Chauvin killed George Floyd, a black man, by applying a choke hold to Mr. Floyd. As shown in a deeply disturbing and widely viewed cellphone video, Chauvin knelt on Mr. Floyd's neck for over eight minutes, during which Mr. Floyd repeatedly protested that he could not breathe. Following close to many other incidents of police brutalizing black people in cities across the country, the killing of Mr. Floyd fueled demands for racial justice and triggered mass protests across the United States and in other countries. After being fired by the police department, Chauvin was charged as the principal in the murder of Mr. Floyd. But three other police officers were also present at the scene of the killing and did nothing physically and little or nothing verbally to stop Chauvin from killing Mr. Floyd. Are these three officers criminally liable? If so, for what crime? Shortly after Chauvin was charged, the three officers were each charged under the law of complicity you will study in this chapter as accomplices to Chauvin's murder of Mr. Floyd. If the prosecution succeeds in proving that they were accomplices, each will be fully liable for murder and face the same potential punishment as Chauvin.

Another high-profile murder case that, as of this writing, is proceeding in Georgia involves the February 23, 2020, shooting death of Ahmaud Arbery. Mr.Arbery, a young black man, was out for a run in a neighborhood near his home when he was shot and killed. Three local men suspected that Mr. Arbery was a burglar, followed him in two trucks, and tried to seize him. At the time of death, one of the men, Travis McMichael, was struggling with Mr. Arbery for possession of the shotgun he had pointed at Mr. Arbery. He was charged with felony murder. At the time of the shooting, Gregory McMichael, Travis's father, was armed with a handgun and standing in the back of the pickup truck the two had used to follow Mr. Arbery. He was charged with murder and aggravated assault as an accomplice. A third man, William Bryan, joined the pursuit of Mr. Arbery, driving his own truck. Bryan was charged, again under the law of complicity, with felony murder based on the felony of "criminal attempt to commit false imprisonment."

Imposing liability on accomplices comports with the purposes of punishment. Accomplices are typically blameworthy and thus deserving of punishment from a retributive perspective. Without accomplices, crime is more difficult for the principal to commit; so, it seems logical to deter, incapacitate, and rehabilitate those who aid and encourage crime.

The common law developed a complex system for classifying various types of participation in crime. The common law categories included principals in the first and second degrees and accessories before and after the fact. Someone who committed a robbery by taking money from the person or presence of another person by threat of force was a principal in the first degree. A person who accompanied the robber to the scene of the crime to act as a lookout and help carry away the robbery proceeds was a principal in the second degree. One who, prior to the robbery and in return for a share of the proceeds, loaned the robber a gun to use in the robbery was an accessory before the fact. Someone who, after the robbery, provided the robber with a place to hide the robbery proceeds was an accessory after the fact. The significance of these classifications usually related to punishment and procedural issues.

Many jurisdictions still call someone who assists a criminal after the crime has been completed an accessory after the fact. Such a person is not typically held fully liable for the principal's crime. Rather, assisting a criminal after the fact is now usually treated as a separate crime with a lesser punishment. But the distinction between accessory before the fact and principal in the second degree has largely disappeared, along with the use of these terms. Those who would have fallen under the categories of accessory before the fact and principal in the second degree today are often referred to simply as accomplices and are "treated as principals" in the sense that they become liable for the same offense as the principal and are exposed to the same potential punishment.

As you will see in the cases and statutes that follow, judges and legislators often use an array of terms to describe the two categories we refer to simply as principal and accomplice. These variations in vocabulary can cause confusion and make the subject of complicity seem more complex at times than it actually is. This unfortunate practice stems in part from the continuing influence of common law terminology and in part from the failure of modern legislators to use clear, consistent, and well-defined terminology in writing statutes dealing with complicity. When you encounter such verbal variations, keep in mind that behind the motley assortment of terms lie just two primary categories: principal and accomplice.

Problem

11.1 Under the modern approach to complicity terminology described above, how should each of the participants below be classified? Is the participant a principal, an accomplice, or an accessory after the fact? Assume that theft is defined as taking the property of another with the intent to permanently deprive the owner of that property.

Part (a) A plans to steal B's mountain bike and sell it. In return for a share of the proceeds from the sale of the bike, C provides A with a skeleton key that will open the lock B uses on the bike. Using the skeleton key, A then steals B's bike. C is not present at the scene of A's theft of the bike.

Part (b) A plans to steal B's mountain bike and sell it. In return for a share of the proceeds from the sale of the bike, C accompanies A and acts as a lookout when A steals B's bike.

Part (c) A plans to steal B's mountain bike and sell it. C learns of A's plan. C, who dislikes B, says to A "go for it" as A sets off to steal the bike. A then steals B's bike.

Part (d) A steals B's bike. Afterward, A tells C what he has done and asks C to hide the bike and C does so.

In the rest of this chapter, we explore the conduct and mental state elements of complicity. We then turn to several special issues relating to accomplice liability.

B. Conduct

Problem

11.2 Modern statutes use an assortment of terms to describe acts that fulfill the conduct element for accomplice liability. Compare the conduct terminology found in the South Dakota and District of Columbia statutes that follow. Does the District of Columbia statute cover acts the South Dakota statute does not? Does the South Dakota statute cover acts the District of Columbia statute does not?

South Dakota Codified Laws

§ 22-3-3 Aiding, abetting or advising — Accountability as principal.

Any person who, with the intent to promote or facilitate the commission of a crime, aids, abets or advises another person in planning or committing the crime, is legally accountable, as a principal to the crime.

District of Columbia Code

§ 22-1805 Persons advising, inciting, or conniving at criminal offense to be charged as principals.

[I]n prosecutions for any criminal offense all persons advising, inciting, or conniving at the offense, or aiding or abetting the principal offender, shall be charged as principals and not as accessories....

1. Presence

Someone's presence at the scene of a crime can raise challenging issues in the context of complicity. Does presence necessarily signify participation in a crime? Does absence necessarily demonstrate lack of participation? How does the Nevada statute below deal with the presence issue?

Nevada Revised Statutes Annotated

§ 195.020 Principals

Every person concerned in the commission of a felony, gross misdemeanor or misdemeanor, whether he directly commits the act constituting the offense, or aids or abets in its commission, and whether present or absent; and every person who, directly or indirectly, counsels, encourages, hires, commands, induces or otherwise procures another to commit a felony, gross misdemeanor or misdemeanor is a principal, and shall be proceeded against and punished as such.

State v. V.T.

5 P.3d 1234 (2000)
Court of Appeals of Utah

Orme, J.

V.T. appeals the juvenile court's adjudication that by his continued presence during the crime, he was an accomplice to theft, a class A misdemeanor, in violation of Utah Code Ann. §76-6-404 (1999). We reverse.

On June 12, 1998, V.T. and two friends, "Moose" and Joey, went to a relative's apartment to avoid being picked up by police for curfew violations. The boys ended up spending the entire night at the apartment.

The next morning, the relative briefly left to run an errand, while the boys remained in her apartment. She returned about fifteen minutes later to find the boys gone, the door to her apartment wide open, and two of her guns missing. She immediately went in search of the group and found them hanging out together near her apartment complex. She confronted the boys about the theft of her guns and demanded that they return them to her. When they failed to do so, she reported the theft to the police.

Two days after the theft of her guns, she discovered that her camcorder, which had been in the apartment when the boys visited, was also missing, and she immediately reported its theft to the police. The police found the camcorder at a local pawn shop, where it had been pawned on the same day the guns were stolen.

Still inside the camcorder was a videotape featuring footage of V.T., Moose, and Joey. The tape included a segment where Moose telephoned a friend, in V.T.'s presence, and discussed pawning the stolen camcorder. V.T. never spoke or gestured during any of this footage.

V.T. was eventually picked up by the police, while riding in a car with Moose. V.T. was charged with two counts of theft of a firearm; one count of theft, relating to the camcorder; and, for having initially given the police a phony name, one count of giving false information to a peace officer, a violation of Utah Code Ann. §76-8-507 (1999)....

V.T. was tried under an accomplice theory on the three theft charges. The court found that V.T. had committed class A misdemeanor theft of the camcorder and had provided false information to a peace officer. The juvenile court summarized the basis for its adjudication concerning the camcorder theft as follows:

> I am going to find him guilty and I think the additional information that I
> have here that brings me peace of mind is that he was present a second time,
> he was shown on the camcorder when the camcorder was being handled at
> a time when he could've distanced himself from the activity. Not only do I
> have him there once with the group ... on the second incident ... there is

no gap on him being there when [the camcorder] is being handled and talked about and used in the confines of a room with a group of friends and those who were involved in this illegal activity.

V.T. appeals his adjudication concerning the theft of the camcorder.

The sole issue presented by V.T. is whether there was sufficient evidence to support the adjudication that he was an accomplice in the theft of the camcorder. When reviewing a juvenile court's decision for sufficiency of the evidence, we must consider all the facts, and all reasonable inferences which may be drawn therefrom, in a light most favorable to the juvenile court's determination, reversing only when it is "against the clear weight of the evidence, or if the appellate court otherwise reaches a definite and firm conviction that a mistake has been made."

Utah's accomplice liability statute, Utah Code Ann. § 76-2-202 (1999), provides:

> Every person, acting with the mental state required for the commission of an offense who directly commits the offense, who solicits, requests, commands, encourages, or intentionally aids another person to engage in conduct which constitutes an offense shall be criminally liable as a party for such conduct.

... The State argues that V.T.'s continued presence during the theft and subsequent phone conversation about selling the camcorder, coupled with his friendship with the other two boys, is enough evidence to support the inference that he had "encouraged" the other two in committing the theft and that he is therefore an accomplice to the crime. *Black's Law Dictionary* defines encourage as: "to instigate; to incite to action; to embolden; to help." *Black's Law Dictionary* 547 (7th ed. 1999). The plain meaning of the word confirms that to encourage others to take criminal action requires some form of active behavior, or at least verbalization, by a defendant. Passive behavior, such as mere presence—even continuous presence—absent evidence that the defendant affirmatively did something to instigate, incite, embolden, or help others in committing a crime is not enough to qualify as "encouragement" as that term is commonly used.

The case law in Utah is consistent with this definition: "'Mere presence, or even prior knowledge, does not make one an accomplice'" to a crime absent evidence showing—beyond a reasonable doubt—that defendant "advis[ed], instigat[ed], encourage[d], or assist[ed] in perpetration of the crime." ...

[S]omething more than a defendant's passive presence during the planning and commission of a crime is required to constitute "encouragement" so as to impose accomplice liability in Utah. There must be evidence showing that the defendant engaged in some active behavior, or at least speech or other expression, that served to assist or encourage the primary perpetrators in committing the crime.

The juvenile court's conclusion that V.T. was an accomplice to the camcorder theft was not supported by the evidence in this case. No evidence whatsoever was produced indicating V.T. had encouraged—much less that he solicited, requested, commanded or intentionally aided—the other two boys in the theft of the camcorder.

Instead, the evidence, read in the light most favorable to the juvenile court's decision, shows only that V.T. was present with the other two youths, albeit at multiple times: when the camcorder was stolen; when they were confronted about the theft of the guns; and when the plan to pawn the camcorder was being discussed by Moose.... [T]here is no indication in the record that V.T. had instigated, incited to action, emboldened, helped, or advised the other two boys in planning or committing the theft. The circumstantial evidence presented in this case, which only shows V.T.'s continuous presence during the events surrounding the theft, is sufficient for finding only that V.T. was a witness—not an accomplice—to the theft of the camcorder. And knowledge of a theft, without more, does not make one an accomplice.

The juvenile court's conclusion of accomplice liability was heavily influenced by the videotape footage of V.T., who at the time of the filming was necessarily in the presence of the camcorder, after it had been stolen. In fact, the court found that even though there was not enough evidence presented to find that V.T. was an accomplice in the theft of the guns, which were stolen at the same time and from the same apartment as the camcorder, the videotape footage was enough to find that V.T. was an accomplice to the camcorder theft. The juvenile court's heavy reliance on this footage shows that it made its conclusion of accomplice liability based not on any evidence that V.T. had encouraged the others to steal the camcorder, as required by section 76-2-202, but instead on the sole fact that V.T. allowed himself to remain in the company of Joey, Moose, and the stolen camcorder before, during, and immediately after the theft. As explained above, this "guilt by association" theory is not a basis on which accomplice liability can be premised under Utah law....

[W]e reverse....

Discussion Questions

1. On what resources did the court rely in its efforts to understand the accomplice liability statute?

2. Mere presence is not enough to satisfy the conduct element for accomplice liability. What if, in addition to his presence, V.T. had suggested, while Moose was on the phone discussing the pawning of the video camera, that they use the proceeds to buy new jackets? What if V.T.'s companions discussed taking the video camera with V.T. present and V.T. had given them a thumbs up sign?

3. Are criminals likely to commit a crime in the presence of someone who is not involved in the criminal scheme? Why? What inference might one draw from the fact that Joey and Moose allowed V.T. to witness their crimes?

4. The appellate court in the V.T. case states that "No evidence whatsoever was produced indicating that V.T. had encouraged—much less that he solicited, requested, commanded or intentionally aided—the other two boys in the theft of the camcorder." Is this assessment accurate?

Wilcox v. Jeffrey

1 All ER 464 (1951)
King's Bench Division

[A]t a court of summary jurisdiction ... the appellant, Herbert William Wilcox, owner and managing editor of a monthly magazine entitled "Jazz Illustrated," was charged with aiding and abetting one Coleman Hawkins, a citizen of the United States, in contravening art. 1 (4) of the Aliens Order, 1920, by failing to comply with a condition attached to a grant of leave to land in the United Kingdom, namely, that Hawkins should take no employment paid or unpaid during his stay, contrary to art. 18 (4) of the Order. It was proved or admitted that on Dec. 11, 1949, Hawkins arrived at a London airport and was met by, among others, the appellant. The appellant was present when an immigration officer interviewed two other persons who had previously applied for permission for Hawkins to perform at a concert in London, but had been told by the Ministry of Labour that their application had been refused. At that interview it was stated that Hawkins would attend the concert and would be "spotlighted" and introduced to the audience, but would not perform. The appellant said he was not connected with the persons responsible for organising the concert and that he had only gone to the airport to report Hawkins' arrival for his magazine. The immigration officer gave permission to Hawkins to remain for three days in this country, making it a condition that he should not take any paid or unpaid employment. The appellant was aware that such a condition had been imposed. Later the same day the appellant attended the concert, paying for admission. Hawkins was seated in a box, but after being "spotlighted" he went on the stage and played the saxophone. A description of the performance by Hawkins with several pages of photographs was later published in the appellant's magazine. The magistrate was of the opinion that the appellant aided and abetted the contravention of the Order by Hawkins and imposed a fine of £25 and £21 costs.

Lord Goddard, C.J.... Under the Aliens Order, art. 1 (1), it is provided that

> "... an alien coming ... by sea to a place in the United Kingdom—(a) shall not land in the United Kingdom without the leave of an immigration officer ..."

It is provided by art 1 (4) that

> "An immigration officer, in accordance with general or special directions of the Secretary of State, may, by general order or notice or otherwise, attach such conditions as he may think fit to the grant of leave to land, and the Secretary of State may at any time vary such conditions in such manner as he thinks fit, and the alien shall comply with the conditions so attached or varied...."

If the alien fails to comply, he is to be in the same position as if he has landed without permission, *i.e.*, he commits an offence.

The case is concerned with the visit of a celebrated professor of the saxophone, a gentleman by the name of Hawkins who was a citizen of the United States. He came here at the invitation of two gentlemen of the name of Curtis and Hughes, connected with a jazz club which enlivens the neighbourhood of Willesden. They, apparently, had applied for permission for Mr. Hawkins to land and it was refused, but, nevertheless, this professor of the saxophone arrived with four French musicians. When they came to the airport, among the people who were there to greet them was the appellant. He had not arranged their visit, but he knew they were coming and he was there to report the arrival of these important musicians for his magazine. So, evidently, he was regarding the visit of Mr. Hawkins as a matter which would be of interest to himself and the magazine which he was editing and selling for profit. Messrs. Curtis and Hughes arranged a concert at the Princes Theatre, London. The appellant attended that concert as a spectator. He paid for his ticket. Mr. Hawkins went on the stage and delighted the audience by playing the saxophone. The appellant did not get up and protest in the name of the musicians of England that Mr. Hawkins ought not to be here competing with them and taking the bread out of their mouths or the wind out of their instruments. It is not found that he actually applauded, but he was there having paid to go in, and, no doubt, enjoying the performance, and then, lo and behold, out comes his magazine with a most laudatory description, fully illustrated, of this concert. On those facts the magistrate has found that he aided and abetted....

The appellant paid to go to the concert and he went there because he wanted to report it. He must, therefore, be held to have been present, taking part, concurring, or encouraging, whichever word you like to use for expressing this conception. It was an illegal act on the part of Hawkins to play the saxophone or any other instrument at this concert. The appellant clearly knew that it was an unlawful act for him to play. He had gone there to hear him, and his presence and his payment to go there was an encouragement. He went there to make use of the performance, because he went there, as the magistrate finds and was justified in finding, to get "copy" for his newspaper. It might have been entirely different, as I say, if he had gone there and protested, saying: "The musicians' union do not like you foreigners coming here and playing and you ought to get off the stage." If he had booed, it might have been some evidence that he was not aiding and abetting. If he had gone as a member of a *claque* to try to drown the noise of the saxophone, he might very likely be found not guilty of aiding and abetting. In this case it seems clear that he was there, not only to approve and encourage what was done, but to take advantage of it by getting "copy" for his paper. In those circumstances there was evidence on which the magistrate could find that the appellant aided and abetted, and for these reasons I am of opinion that the appeal fails.

Appeal dismissed with costs.

Discussion Questions

1. What did Wilcox do to become an accomplice to a crime? What was the crime? Who was the principal?

2. What if Wilcox had not met Mr. Hawkins at the airport? What if Wilcox had not attended the performance? In either case, would he then have been shielded from accomplice liability?

3. What if Wilcox succeeded at trial in proving that Mr. Hawkins would have played regardless of anything Wilcox did or did not do. Would that affect Wilcox's liability as an accomplice?

4. What if Mr. Hawkins had no idea that Wilcox was at the airport or attended the concert? Should that affect Wilcox's liability for the crime?

Problem

11.3 Part (a) Sonny plans to rob a bank customer as the customer is walking away from the bank's ATM. He plans to demand money and threaten to hurt the person if his demand is not met. But because Sonny is small in stature and unintimidating in appearance, he fears his threat may not be taken seriously. Sonny asks his friend Al to accompany him. Al is tall and brawny with close cropped hair, multiple tattoos, and a prominent scar across his face. In short, Al looks very intimidating. Sonny tells Al that he will share the robbery proceeds equally with him if Al just comes with him and stands behind him. "All you have to do is stand there." Sonny tells him. On the evening of the robbery, Sonny approaches a young man as he leaves the ATM machine and steps into his path. Al stands about 20 feet behind Sonny. Sonny says "Give me all your money or the big guy will hurt you." The young man looks at Sonny, then at Al. He hands $200 to Sonny, turns, and flees. Is Al liable as an accomplice to Sonny's robbery?

Part (b) Same facts as in Part (a) but with the following variations. Al was recently released from prison where he served time for assault and robbery. He knows the police are likely to have his photo in the "mug book" they show robbery victims, so he doesn't want to be seen by Sonny's robbery victim. Al tells Sonny "Look, I'll come with you and I'll help you out if you need me. But I don't want to be seen unless you need my help." Al waits in the shadows of a doorway near the ATM machine where he cannot be seen. Sonny approaches the young man and says "Give me all your money or I'll hurt you." The young man hands $200 to Sonny, turns, and flees. Is Al liable as an accomplice to Sonny's robbery?

2. Causation

The following passage from a famous complicity case, *State ex. rel. Attorney Gen. v. Tally*, 102 Ala. 25, 69 (1893), makes an important point about accomplice liability:

> The assistance given, however, need not contribute to the criminal result in the sense that but for it the result would not have ensued. It is quite sufficient if it facilitated a result that would have transpired without it. It is quite enough if the aid merely renders it easier for the principal actor to accomplish the end intended by him and the aider and abettor, though in all human probability the end would have been attained without it.

In short, accomplice liability does not require "but for" causation between the accomplice's act and the principal's crime.

Problem

11.4 A plans to steal B's mountain bike and sell it. C learns of A's plan. C dislikes B and would like A to succeed in stealing B's bike, though C doesn't speak to A about A's plan. C spots B's bike in a bike rack outside B's apartment and notices that it is unlocked. C then leaves a text message for A telling him where the bike is located and that it is unlocked. A, though, spots B's unlocked bike on his own and proceeds to steal it. Assume A is arrested soon after the theft, his cell phone is seized by the police, and A never sees C's text message. Is C liable as an accomplice under the MPC?

3. Omissions

Problem

11.5 Dale is the night watchman at a warehouse used by a computer retailer to store its computers prior to shipping them around the country. Terry approaches Dale and offers him $500 to refrain from interfering with or reporting Terry's breaking into the warehouse and stealing some computers. Dale agrees, Terry pays him $500 and Terry steals the computers. Dale does nothing to stop Terry and does not report the theft. Does Dale have any criminal liability? If so, for what crimes?

State v. Walden

306 N.C. 466 (1982)
Supreme Court of North Carolina

Mitchell. J.

The principal question presented is whether a mother may be found guilty of assault on a theory of aiding and abetting solely on the basis that she was present when her child was assaulted but failed to take reasonable steps to prevent the assault. We answer this question in the affirmative and reverse the opinion of the Court of Appeals which held to the contrary and ordered a new trial.

On 28 April 1980, defendant was indicted under G.S. 14-32 as follows:

> THE JURORS FOR THE STATE UPON THEIR OATH PRESENT that on or about the 9th day of December, 1979, in Wake County Aleen Estes Walden did unlawfully and wilfully and feloniously assault Lamont Walden, age one year, with a certain deadly weapon, to wit: a leather belt with a metal buckle, inflicting serious bodily [sic] injuries, not resulting in death, upon the said Lamont Walden....

Lamont Walden is defendant's son. Defendant was convicted by a jury and sentenced to 5–10 years imprisonment.

The State offered evidence at trial tending to show that Mr. Jasper Billy Davis heard a child crying in the apartment next to his on Saturday evening, 8 December 1979. On Sunday morning, 9 December 1979, at approximately 10:00 a.m., Davis heard a small child screaming and hollering and heard a popping sound coming from the same apartment next door. The sound of the child screaming and hollering and the popping sound lasted for approximately one to one and one-half hours. Davis made a complaint to the Raleigh Police Department requesting that they investigate the noise that he was hearing.

Officer D. A. Weingarten of the Raleigh Police Department testified that he went to Davis' apartment on 9 December 1979. After speaking with Davis, the officer knocked on the door of the apartment next to the Davis apartment. A Miss Devine opened the door and allowed the officer to enter the apartment, where he stayed for a few minutes before leaving to obtain a search warrant. Officer Weingarten returned a short time later with a warrant to search the apartment in question. Upon entering the apartment, the officer saw Devine, the defendant Aleen Estes Walden and George Hoskins. The officer also saw five small children in a corner of the apartment and noticed cuts and bruises on the bodies of the children. One of the children the officer observed at this time was Lamont Walden, a small child in diapers. The officer observed red marks on the chest of Lamont Walden as well as a swollen lip, bruises on his legs and back and other bruises, scarring and cuts.

At trial three of these small children, Roderick Walden, ten years old, Stephen Walden, eight years old, and Derrick Walden, seven years old, testified that "Bishop" George Hoskins hit their brother Lamont Walden with a belt repeatedly over an extended period of time on Sunday, 9 December 1979. Each child testified that the defendant, their mother, was in the room with Hoskins and the baby (Lamont) at the time this beating occurred. Lamont Walden was crying and bleeding as a result of the beating Hoskins gave him. The children testified further that the defendant looked on the entire time the beating took place but did not say anything or do anything to stop the "Bishop" from beating Lamont or to otherwise deter such conduct.

Mrs. Annette McCullers, who is employed by Social Services of Wake County, testified that she observed the five children including Lamont on 9 December 1979.... McCullers talked with Lamont's brothers at this time, and each of them told her that Lamont had been beaten by "Bishop" George Hoskins....

The defendant offered evidence in the form of testimony of her father, Mr. Meredith Estes, tending to show that James Walden, the father of the Walden children, had whipped the children in the past when living with them. Estes testified that the defendant had never mistreated the children. He further testified that the children had told him that it was their father who beat them on the occasion in question, but that they had later changed their story and stated that George Hoskins beat them and also beat Lamont.

The defendant testified that she was living in an apartment with Miss Devine on 8 December 1979. Three of the defendant's sons had gone to the store with Devine and Hoskins. The defendant's two youngest children were with her. There was a knock on the door and the children's father entered. The father immediately began hitting Lamont Walden with a belt. The defendant tried to stop him but could not do so. The defendant testified that she was struck by the children's father on this occasion and received injuries to her face.

Based on the preceding evidence, the defendant was convicted of assault with a deadly weapon inflicting serious injury in violation of G.S. 14-32(b). During the trial, the State proceeded on the theory that the defendant aided and abetted George Hoskins in the commission of the assault on her child and was, therefore, guilty as a principal to the offense charged.

The defendant assigned as error the action of the trial court in denying her motion to dismiss and allowing the case against her for the felonious assault charge to go to the jury, when all of the evidence tended to show that the defendant did not perform any affirmative act of commission to encourage the perpetrator and did not herself administer the beating to her child. In support of this assignment, the defendant contends, among other things, that the trial court erred in instructing the jury as follows:

> It is the duty of a parent to protect their children and to do whatever may be reasonably necessary for their care and their safety. A parent has a duty to protect their children and cannot stand passively by and refuse to do so when it is reasonably within their power to protect their children. A parent is bound to provide such reasonable care as necessary, under the circum-

stances facing them at that particular time. However, a parent is not required to do the impossible or the unreasonable in caring for their children.

Now a person is not guilty of a crime merely because she is present at the scene. To be guilty she must aid or actively encourage the person committing the crime, or in some way communicate to this person her intention to assist in its commission; *or that she is present with the reasonable opportunity and duty to prevent the crime and fails to take reasonable steps to do so.*

So I charge that if you find from the evidence beyond a reasonable doubt, that on or about December 9th, 1979, Bishop Hoskins committed assault with a deadly weapon inflicting serious injury on Lamont Walden, that is that Bishop Hoskins intentionally hit Lamont Walden with a belt and that the belt was a deadly weapon, thereby inflicting serious injury upon Lamont Walden; and that the defendant was present at the time the crime was committed and did nothing and that in so doing the defendant knowingly advised, instigated, encouraged or aided Bishop Hoskins to commit that crime; *or that she was present with the reasonable opportunity and duty to prevent the crime and failed to take reasonable steps to do so*; it would be your duty to return a verdict of guilty of assault with a deadly weapon, inflicting serious injury. (Emphases added.)

The defendant contends that the quoted instructions of the trial court are erroneous in that they permitted the jury to convict her for failing to interfere with or attempt to prevent the commission of a felony. She argues that the law of this State does not allow a conviction in any case for aiding and abetting the commission of a crime absent some affirmative act of commission by the defendant assisting or encouraging the commission of the crime or indicating the defendant's approval and willingness to assist. We do not agree....

The mere presence of a person at the scene of a crime at the time of its commission does not make him a principal in the second degree; and this is so even though he makes no effort to prevent the crime, or even though he may silently approve of the crime, or even though he may secretly intend to assist the perpetrator in the commission of the crime in case his aid becomes necessary to its consummation. However, this general rule allows some exceptions. Where the common law has imposed affirmative duties upon persons standing in certain personal relationships to others, such as the duty of parents to care for their small children, one may be guilty of criminal conduct by failure to act or, stated otherwise, by an act of omission. Individuals also have been found criminally liable for failing to perform affirmative duties required by statute....

[W]e believe that to require a parent as a matter of law to take affirmative action to prevent harm to his or her child or be held criminally liable imposes a reasonable duty upon the parent. Further, we believe this duty is and has always been inherent in the duty of parents to provide for the safety and welfare of their children, which duty has long been recognized by the common law and by statute. This is not to say that parents have the legal duty to place themselves in danger of death or great bodily harm in coming to the aid of their children. To require such, would require every parent to exhibit courage and heroism which, although commendable in the extreme, cannot realistically be expected or required of all people. But parents do have the duty to take every step reasonably possible under the circumstances of a given situation to prevent harm to their children.

In some cases, depending upon the size and vitality of the parties involved, it might be reasonable to expect a parent to physically intervene and restrain the person attempting to injure the child. In other circumstances, it will be reasonable for a parent to go for help or to merely verbally protest an attack upon the child. What is reasonable in any given case will be a question for the jury after proper instructions from the trial court.

We think that the rule we announce today is compelled by our statutes and prior cases establishing the duty of parents to provide for the safety and welfare of their children. Further, we find our holding today to be consistent with our prior cases regarding the law of aiding and abetting. It remains the law that one may not be found to be an aider and abettor, and thus guilty as a principal, solely because he is present when a crime is committed. It will still be necessary, in order to have that effect, that it be shown that the defendant said or did something showing his consent to the criminal purpose and contribution to its execution. But we hold that the failure of a parent who is present to take all steps reasonably possible to protect the parent's child from an attack by another person constitutes an act of omission by the parent showing the parent's consent and contribution to the crime being committed.

Thus, we hold that the trial court properly allowed the jury in the present case to consider a verdict of guilty of assault with a deadly weapon inflicting serious injury, upon a theory of aiding and abetting, solely on the ground that the defendant was present when her child was brutally beaten by Hoskins but failed to take all steps reasonable to prevent the attack or otherwise protect the child from injury. Further, the jury having found that the defendant committed an act of omission constituting consent to and encouragement of the commission of the crime charged, the defendant would properly be found to have aided and abetted the principal. A person who so aids or abets another in the commission of a crime is equally guilty with that other person as a principal. Therefore, we find no error in the trial court's instructions, the verdict or the judgment on the charge of assault with a deadly weapon inflicting serious injury....

Reversed and remanded.

Discussion Questions

1. Would it have made a difference in *Walden* if the child's father had inflicted the injuries? Would the arguments for holding the mother as an accomplice be stronger or weaker?

2. Should it change the result if the jury believed that the defendant had tried to stop the assault but was herself assaulted? Why might a mother not intervene in violence against her children?

3. The *Walden* court states that "[a] person who so aids and abets another in the commission of a crime is equally guilty with that other person ..." Did Walden's blameworthiness equal that of George Hoskins? Was she as dangerous as George Hoskins?

4. Would it be preferable to treat Walden as a principal for the crime of child neglect or child endangerment? Or is it preferable to treat her as an accomplice to assault? If Hoskins had killed one of the children, should she have been held liable for homicide?

5. The court refers to Walden's "act of omission." Is this phrase self-contradictory?

6. Is a belt a "deadly weapon"? What interpretation arguments could you make as the prosecutor for an affirmative answer to this question? What interpretation arguments could you make as defense counsel for a negative answer?

7. The *Walden* court holds that "the failure of a parent who is present to take all steps reasonably possible to protect the parent's child from an attack by another person" shows "the parent's consent ... to the crime." Do you agree that failure to protect a child shows consent to harming the child?

* * *

The following excerpt is from a speech by Professor Sarah Buel, a former Assistant District Attorney and head of a Domestic Violence Unit. Professor Buel was herself a victim of domestic violence and a foster parent.[1]

> Probably the person that taught me most about the connection between domestic violence and child abuse was a foster child named Christopher, who came to me when he was three years old. When he first came to me he had two broken ribs and he had cigarette burns on the bottoms of his feet. And he stayed for about three months and then his father, who was the acknowledged perpetrator, said he was real sorry, and it would never happen again.

> And so the court allowed Christopher to go home, and within a few weeks I got a call, Christopher was in the hospital again. He had new cigarette burns on the bottoms of his feet and the palms of his hands and all of his ribs were broken. Those of you who know about early childhood development know

---

1. Violence Against Women: How to Improve the Legal Services' Response, Nov. 18, 1991 (cited in Defending Our Lives, Study and Resource Guide, 13, 19).

how resilient a child's ribs are. It's very hard to break them so it must have been a tremendous amount of force. So Christopher came home with me, and his mother was allowed to have visitation, as again his father acknowledged he was the one who had abused him.

But I was so righteous with her, because she was staying with the man who had done this to her child. What was wrong with this woman? She would come in, I would sort of notice that there were bruises on her, I didn't really let it register. My focus, my obsession, was with Christopher and keeping him safe.... And after a few months Christopher's father went back into court, and [said] he was real, real sorry, and it was never, never going to happen again. And the court allowed Christopher to go home with him.

The following August we buried Christopher, and we buried his mother right next to him. And as hard as it is for me to think and talk about Christopher even now, it is ten times harder, a hundred times harder for me to think about his mother. Because I did everything humanly possible to save Christopher. I went to every hearing, I went to every possible meeting, I called and wrote the mayor, the governor, the president, but I did nothing for his mother. Because I was so busy judging her, and so busy being righteous, and she could not have presented herself more clearly as a battered woman if she had a megaphone and a neon sign.

We learned at the murder trial that DSS [Department of Social Services], in writing, had told Christopher's mother that she needed to stay with his father if she ever wanted her child back.

4. The MPC Approach to Conduct for Complicity

Model Penal Code

§ 2.06 Liability for Conduct of Another; Complicity

(1) A person is guilty of an offense if it is committed by his own conduct or by the conduct of another person for which he is legally accountable, or both.

(2) A person is legally accountable for the conduct of another person when: ...

  (c) he is an accomplice of such other person in the commission of an offense.

(3) A person is an accomplice of another person in the commission of an offense if:

  (a) with the purpose of promoting or facilitating the commission of the offense, he

   (i)   solicits the other person to commit it, or

   (ii) aids or agrees or attempts to aid such other person in planning or committing it, or

   (iii) having a legal duty to prevent the commission of the offense, fails to make proper effort so to do; or

  (b) his conduct is expressly declared by law to establish his complicity.

* * *

1. How does the MPC differ from the statutes earlier in this section regarding conduct?

2. How would the defendants in the *V.T.* and *Walden* cases have fared under the MPC?

C. Mental States

The mental state aspect of complicity is at times expressed simply as intent or purpose regarding the principal's crime. Such a description results in ambiguity because it fails to state clearly what the actor's purpose must concern. Is purpose regarding the accomplice's own conduct of assisting or encouraging required? Is purpose regarding the principal's conduct required? What about a result element in the principal's crime, such as death or injury? Must the accomplice have purpose regarding such a result, even though a lesser mental state regarding the result, such as recklessness or negligence, is sufficient for the principal to be held liable? What about any circumstance elements required by the principal's crime? The following sections address these questions.

1. Mental State Regarding Conduct

What mental states do the following statutes require for accomplice liability? Which statute is clearer?

Utah Code Annotated
§ 76-2-202 Criminal responsibility for direct commission of offense or for conduct of another

Every person, acting with the mental state required for the commission of an offense who directly commits the offense, who solicits, requests, commands, encourages, or intentionally aids another person to engage in conduct which constitutes an offense shall be criminally liable as a party for such conduct.

Kansas Stat. Ann.
§ 21-3205 Liability for crimes of another

(1) A person is criminally responsible for a crime committed by another if such person intentionally aids, abets, advises, hires, counsels or procures the other to commit the crime.

People v. Beeman

35 Cal. 3d 547 (1984)
California Supreme Court

Reynoso, J.

Timothy Mark Beeman appeals from a judgment of conviction of robbery, burglary, false imprisonment, destruction of telephone equipment and assault with intent to commit a felony (Pen. Code, §§ 211, 459, 236, 591, 221). Appellant was not present during commission of the offenses. His conviction rested on the theory that he aided and abetted his acquaintances James Gray and Michael Burk.

The primary issue before us is whether the standard California Jury Instructions (CALJIC Nos. 3.00 and 3.01) adequately inform the jury of the criminal intent required to convict a defendant as an aider and abettor of the crime.

We hold that instruction No. 3.01 is erroneous. Sound law, embodied in a long line of California decisions, requires proof that an aider and abettor rendered aid with an intent or purpose of either committing, or of encouraging or facilitating commission of, the target offense. It was, therefore, error for the trial court to refuse the modified instruction requested by appellant. Our examination of the record convinces us that the error in this case was prejudicial and we therefore reverse appellant's convictions.

James Gray and Michael Burk drove from Oakland to Redding for the purpose of robbing appellant's sister-in-law, Mrs. Marjorie Beeman, of valuable jewelry, including a 3.5 carat diamond ring. They telephoned the residence to determine that she was home. Soon thereafter Burk knocked at the door of the victim's house, presented himself as a poll taker, and asked to be let in. When Mrs. Beeman asked for identification, he forced her into the hallway and entered. Gray, disguised in a ski mask, followed. The two subdued the victim, placed tape over her mouth and eyes and tied her to a bathroom fixture. Then they ransacked the house, taking numerous pieces of jewelry and a set of silverware. The jewelry included a 3.5 carat, heart-shaped diamond ring and a blue sapphire ring. The total value of these two rings was over $100,000. In the course of the robbery, telephone wires inside the house were cut.

Appellant was arrested six days later in Emeryville. He had in his possession several of the less valuable of the stolen rings. He supplied the police with information that led to the arrests of Burk and Gray. With Gray's cooperation appellant assisted police in recovering most of the stolen property.

Burk, Gray and appellant were jointly charged. After the trial court severed the trials, Burk and Gray pled guilty to robbery. At appellant's trial they testified that he had been extensively involved in planning the crime.

Burk testified that he had known appellant for two and one-half years. He had lived in appellant's apartment several times. Appellant had talked to him about rich relatives in Redding and had described a diamond ring worth $50,000. According to

Burk the feasibility of robbing appellant's relatives was first mentioned two and one-half months before the incident occurred. About one week before the robbery, the discussions became more specific. Appellant gave Burk the address and discussed the ruse of posing as a poll taker. It was decided that Gray and Burk would go to Redding because appellant wanted nothing to do with the actual robbery and because he feared being recognized. On the night before the offense appellant drew a floor plan of the victim's house and told Burk where the diamond ring was likely to be found. Appellant agreed to sell the jewelry for 20 percent of the proceeds.

After the robbery was completed, Burk telephoned appellant to report success. Appellant said that he would call the friend who might buy the jewelry. Burk and Gray drove to appellant's house and showed him the "loot." Appellant was angry that the others had taken so much jewelry, and demanded that his cut be increased from 20 percent to one-third.

Gray's testimony painted a similar picture. Gray also had known appellant for approximately two years prior to the incident. Gray said Burk had initially approached him about the robbery, supplied the victim's address, and described the diamond ring. Appellant had at some time described the layout of the house to Gray and Burk and had described to them the cars driven by various members of the victim's family. Gray and Burk, but not appellant, had discussed how to divide the proceeds. Both Gray and Burk owed money to appellant. In addition, Burk owed Gray $3,200.

According to Gray appellant had been present at a discussion three days before the robbery when it was mentioned that appellant could not go because his 6 foot 5 inch, 310-pound frame could be too easily recognized. Two days before the offense, however, appellant told Gray that he wanted nothing to do with the robbery of his relatives. On the day preceding the incident appellant and Gray spoke on the telephone. At that time appellant repeated he wanted nothing to do with the robbery, but confirmed that he had told Burk that he would not say anything if the others went ahead.

Gray confirmed that appellant was upset when he saw that his friends had gone through with the robbery and had taken all of the victim's jewelry. He was angered further when he discovered that Burk might easily be recognized because he had not disguised himself. Appellant then asked them to give him all of the stolen goods. Instead Burk and Gray gave appellant only a watch and some rings which they believed he could sell. Gray and Burk then traveled to San Jose where they sold the silverware for $900. Burk used this money to flee to Los Angeles. Sometime later appellant asked for Gray's cooperation in recovering and returning the property to the victim. On several occasions when Burk called them for more money, appellant stalled and avoided questions about the sale of the jewelry.

Appellant Beeman's testimony contradicted that of Burk and Gray as to nearly every material element of his own involvement. Appellant testified that he did not participate in the robbery or its planning. He confirmed that Burk had lived with him on several occasions, and that he had told Burk about Mrs. Beeman's jewelry, the valuable diamond ring, and the Beeman ranch, in the course of day-to-day conversations. He claimed that he had sketched a floor plan of the house some nine months prior to the robbery, only for the purpose of comparing it with the layout of a house belonging to another brother. He at first denied and then admitted describing the Beeman family cars, but insisted this never occurred in the context of planning a robbery.

Appellant stated that Burk first suggested that robbing Mrs. Beeman would be easy some five months before the incident. At that time, and on the five or six subsequent occasions when Burk raised the subject, appellant told Burk that his friends could do what they wanted but that he wanted no part of such a scheme.

Beeman admitted Burk had told him of the poll taker ruse within a week before the robbery, and that Burk told him they had bought a cap gun and handcuffs. He further admitted that he had allowed Burk to take some old clothes left at the apartment by a former roommate. At that time Beeman told Burk: "If you're going to do a robbery, you can't look like a bum." Nevertheless, appellant explained that he did not know Burk was then planning to commit this robbery. Further, although he knew there was a possibility Burk and Gray would try to rob Mrs. Beeman, appellant thought it very unlikely they would go through with it. He judged Burk capable of committing the crime but knew he had no car and no money to get to Redding. Appellant did not think Gray would cooperate.

Appellant agreed that he had talked with Gray on the phone two days before the robbery, and said he had then repeated he did not want to be involved. He claimed that Burk called him on the way back from Redding because he feared appellant would report him to the police, but knew appellant would want to protect Gray, who was his closer friend.

Appellant claimed he told the others to come to his house after the robbery and offered to sell the jewelry in order to buy time in which to figure out a way to collect and return the property. He took the most valuable piece to make sure it was not sold. Since Burk had a key to his apartment, appellant gave the diamond ring and a bracelet to a friend, Martinez, for safekeeping. After Burk fled to Los Angeles, appellant showed some of the jewelry to mutual acquaintances in order to lull Burk into believing he was attempting to sell it. During this time Burk called him on the phone several times asking for money and, when appellant told him of plans to return the property, threatened to have him killed.

When confronted with his prior statement to the police that he had given one of the rings to someone in exchange for a $50 loan, appellant admitted making the statement but denied that it was true. He also claimed that his statement on direct examination that "his [Burk's] face was seen. He didn't wear a mask. Didn't do anything he was supposed to do...." referred only to the reason Gray had given for wanting to return the victim's property.

Appellant requested that the jury be instructed in accord with *People v. Yarber* (1979) 90 Cal.App.3d 895 that aiding and abetting liability requires proof of intent to aid. The request was denied.

After three hours of deliberation, the jury submitted two written questions to the court: "We would like to hear again how one is determined to be an accessory and by what actions can he absolve himself"; and "Does inaction mean the party is guilty?" The jury was reinstructed in accord with the standard instructions, CALJIC Nos. 3.00 and 3.01. The court denied appellant's renewed request that the instructions be modified as suggested in *Yarber*, explaining that giving another, slightly different instruction at this point would further complicate matters. The jury returned its verdicts of guilty on all counts two hours later.

I

Penal Code section 31 provides in pertinent part: "All persons concerned in the commission of a crime, ... whether they directly commit the act constituting the offense, or aid and abet in its commission, or, not being present, have advised and encouraged its commission, ... are principals in any crime so committed." Thus, those persons who at common law would have been termed accessories before the fact and principals in the second degree as well as those who actually perpetrate the offense, are to be prosecuted, tried and punished as principals in California. The term "aider and abettor" is now often used to refer to principals other than the perpetrator, whether or not they are present at the commission of the offense.

CALJIC No. 3.00 defines principals to a crime to include "Those who, with knowledge of the unlawful purpose of the one who does directly and actively commit or attempt to commit the crime, aid and abet in its commission..., or ... Those who, whether present or not at the commission or attempted commission of the crime, advise and encourage its commission...." CALJIC No. 3.01 defines aiding and abetting as follows: "A person aids and abets the commission of a crime if, with knowledge of the unlawful purpose of the perpetrator of the crime, he aids, promotes, encourages or instigates by act or advice the commission of such crime."

Prior to 1974 CALJIC No. 3.01 read: "A person aids and abets the commission of a crime if he knowingly and with criminal intent aids, promotes, encourages or instigates by act or advice, or by act and advice, the commission of such crime."

Appellant asserts that the current instructions, in particular CALJIC No. 3.01, substitute an element of knowledge of the perpetrator's intent for the element of criminal intent of the accomplice, in contravention of common law principles and California case law. He argues that the instruction given permitted the jury to convict him of the same offenses as the perpetrators without finding that he harbored either the same criminal intent as they, or the specific intent to assist them, thus depriving him of his constitutional rights to due process and equal protection of the law. Appellant further urges that the error requires reversal because it removed a material issue from the jury and on this record it is impossible to conclude that the jury necessarily resolved the same factual question that would have been presented by the missing instruction.

The People argue that the standard instruction properly reflects California law, which requires no more than that the aider and abettor have knowledge of the perpetrator's criminal purpose and do a voluntary act which in fact aids the perpetrator.

The People further contend that defendants are adequately protected from conviction for acts committed under duress or which inadvertently aid a perpetrator by the limitation of the liability of an aider and abettor to those acts knowingly aided and their natural and reasonable consequences. Finally, the People argue that the modification proposed by *Yarber, supra,* is unnecessary because proof of intentional aiding in most cases can be inferred from aid with knowledge of the perpetrator's purpose. Thus, respondent argues, it is doubtful that the requested modification would bring about different results in the vast majority of cases.

II

… The essential conflict in current appellate opinions is between those cases which state that an aider and abettor must have an intent or purpose to commit or assist in the commission of the criminal offenses, and those finding it sufficient that the aider and abettor engage in the required acts with knowledge of the perpetrator's criminal purpose.[2] …

[W]e conclude that the weight of authority and sound law require proof that an aider and abettor act with knowledge of the criminal purpose of the perpetrator *and* with an intent or purpose either of committing, or of encouraging or facilitating commission of, the offense.…

When the definition of the offense includes the intent to do some act or achieve some consequence beyond the *actus reus* of the crime, the aider and abettor must share the specific intent of the perpetrator. By "share" we mean neither that the aider and abettor must be prepared to commit the offense by his or her own act should the perpetrator fail to do so, nor that the aider and abettor must seek to share the fruits of the crime. Rather, an aider and abettor will "share" the perpetrator's specific intent when he or she knows the full extent of the perpetrator's criminal purpose and gives aid or encouragement with the intent or purpose of facilitating the perpetrator's commission of the crime. The liability of an aider and abettor extends also to the natural and reasonable consequences of the acts he knowingly and intentionally aids and encourages.

CALJIC No. 3.01 inadequately defines aiding and abetting because it fails to insure that an aider and abettor will be found to have the required mental state with regard to his or her own act. While the instruction does include the word "abet," which encompasses the intent required by law, the word is arcane and its full import unlikely to be recognized by modern jurors. Moreover, even if jurors were made aware that "abet" means to encourage or facilitate, and implicitly to harbor an intent to further the crime encouraged, the instruction does not *require* them to find that intent because it defines an aider and abettor as one who "aids, promotes, encourages *or* instigates" (italics added). Thus, as one appellate court recently recognized, the instruction

---

2. Some cases which take the latter viewpoint intimate that the aider and abettor must also know that his acts will probably facilitate the perpetrator's commission of the offense.

would "technically allow a conviction if the defendant knowing of the perpetrator's unlawful purpose, negligently or accidentally aided the commission of the crime." ...

The convictions are reversed.

Discussion Questions

1. What mental state(s) does *Beeman* require regarding assistance in order to be liable as an accomplice? What language in Penal Code Section 31 supports the Court's reading of that statute?

2. What mental state(s) does *Beeman* require regarding the principal's crime? What language in Penal Code Section 31 supports the Court's reading of that statute?

3. Burk, Gray, and Beeman provided different versions of Beeman's role. As a juror, how would you have evaluated the credibility of each of these witnesses? What facts support the credibility of each witness? What facts undermine the credibility of each? Which version do you find most credible?

Problem

11.6 Part (a) P plans on killing V. A wants P to succeed in killing V. In other words, A has purpose regarding P's crime. A lends P a handgun to use in killing V and P uses it to kill V.

Part (b) B knows P plans to kill V, but is indifferent as to whether P does so. B lends P a handgun and P uses it to kill V.

Part (c) C is aware that there is a substantial risk that P may kill V but is indifferent as to whether P does so. C lends P a handgun and P uses it to kill V.

How would A, B, and C fare under the statutes and cases you have read so far in this section?

What mental state(s) should qualify an actor for accomplice liability? A, B, and C in Problem 11.6 are all blameworthy, aren't they? Don't the acts of all three in lending a handgun to P show that they are dangerous to society and thus in need of deterrence and incapacitation?

All agree that purposeful assistance of the sort illustrated in Problem 11.6(a) should qualify for liability. But there has been and continues to be debate about whether accomplice liability should encompass knowing assistance to crime, as in Problem 11.6 Part (b), or be limited to purposeful assistance, as in Part (a). Judge Learned Hand expressed what is now the prevailing view in favor of purpose and rejecting knowledge as a basis for complicity in his often-cited opinion in *United States v. Peoni*, 100 F.2d 401, 402 (2d Cir. 1938). After reviewing a series of definitions of accomplice liability, Judge Hand wrote:

[A]ll these definitions ... demand that he in some sort associate himself with the venture, that he participate in it as in something that he wishes to bring about, that he seek by his action to make it succeed. All the words used — even the most colorless, "abet" — carry an implication of purposive attitude towards it.

To capture this "purposive attitude," it is sometimes said that complicity requires that an accomplice have "a stake in the venture."

Two years later, the Fourth Circuit in *Backun v. United States*, 112 F.2d 635, 637 (4th Cir. 1940), staked out a different position in the following passage that is now the minority view, that knowledge of the principal's crime is enough for complicity even if purpose is lacking.

Guilt as an accessory depends, not on "having a stake" in the outcome of crime, ... but on aiding and assisting the perpetrators; and those who make a profit by furnishing to criminals, whether by sale or otherwise, the means to carry on their nefarious undertakings, aid them just as truly as if they were actual partners with them, having a stake in the fruits of their enterprise. To say that the sale of goods is a normally lawful transaction is beside the point. The seller may not ignore the purpose for which the purchase is made if he is advised of that purpose, or wash his hands of the aid that he has given the perpetrator of a felony by the plea that he has merely made a sale of merchandise. One who sells a gun to another knowing that he is buying it to commit a murder, would hardly escape conviction as an accessory to the murder by showing that he received full price for the gun; and no difference in principle can be drawn between such a case and any other case of a seller who knows that the purchaser intends to use the goods which he is purchasing in the commission of a felony. In any such case, not only does the act of the seller assist in the commission of the felony, but his will assents to its commission, since he could refuse to give assistance by refusing to make the sale.

The Model Penal Code considered adopting the *Backun* position, but, as the following statute indicates, it ultimately adopted Judge Hand's view.

Model Penal Code

§ 2.06 Liability for Conduct of Another; Complicity.

(3) A person is an accomplice of another person in the commission of the offense if:

  (a) with the purpose of promoting or facilitating the commission of the offense, he

    (i) solicits such other person to commit it, or

    (ii) aids or agrees or attempts to aid such other person in planning or committing it, or

    (iii) having a legal duty to prevent the commission of the offense, fails to make proper effort so to do; or

(b) his conduct is expressly declared by law to establish his complicity.

(4) When causing a particular result is an element of an offense, an accomplice in the conduct causing such result is an accomplice in the commission of that offense if he acts with the kind of culpability, if any, with respect to that result that is sufficient for the commission of the offense.

* * *

Some states, however, have used knowledge and even lower levels of culpability in dealing with those who provide a principal with assistance in committing a crime. What mental states do the following statutes use? What sort of liability does each impose?

Tennessee Code Annotated

§ 39-11-402 Criminal responsibility for conduct of another

A person is criminally responsible for an offense committed by the conduct of another if:

(1) Acting with the culpability required for the offense, the person causes or aids an innocent or irresponsible person to engage in conduct prohibited by the definition of the offense;

(2) Acting with intent to promote or assist the commission of the offense, or to benefit in the proceeds or results of the offense, the person solicits, directs, aids, or attempts to aid another person to commit the offense; or

(3) Having a duty imposed by law or voluntarily undertaken to prevent commission of the offense and acting with intent to benefit in the proceeds or results of the offense, or to promote or assist its commission, the person fails to make a reasonable effort to prevent commission of the offense.

§ 39-11-403 (2004) Criminal responsibility for facilitation of felony

(a) A person is criminally responsible for the facilitation of a felony if, knowing that another intends to commit a specific felony, but without the intent required for criminal responsibility under § 39-11-402(2), the person knowingly furnishes substantial assistance in the commission of the felony.

(b) The facilitation of the commission of a felony is an offense of the class next below the felony facilitated by the person so charged.

Connecticut General Statutes

§ 53a-8 Criminal liability for acts of another

(a) A person, acting with the mental state required for commission of an offense, who solicits, requests, commands, importunes or intentionally aids another person to engage in conduct which constitutes an offense shall be criminally liable for such conduct and may be prosecuted and punished as if he were the principal offender.

(b) A person who sells, delivers or provides any firearm ... to another person to engage in conduct which constitutes an offense knowing or under circumstances in which he should know that such other person intends to use such firearm in such conduct shall be criminally liable for such conduct and shall be prosecuted and punished as if he were the principal offender.

> ### Problem
>
> 11.7 Diagram the elements of complicity under each of the Tennessee statutes and the Connecticut statute above. How do these elements differ from the MPC?

2. Mental State Regarding a Result Element

Can one aid and abet a crime involving recklessness or negligence? Clearly one can aid and abet a crime involving reckless conduct, such as reckless driving. Imagine, for example, someone who aids and abets an illegal and dangerous drag race on a public street. But can one aid and abet a crime that involves recklessly or negligently causing a result? The following case deals with this question.

Washington v. Hopkins

147 Wash. 198 (1928)
Washington Supreme Court

Parker, J.

The defendant, Mrs. Hopkins, was by information filed in the superior court for King county jointly, with one John Doe, charged with the crime of manslaughter. The information charges, in substance, that John Doe, his true name being unknown, by his wilful, reckless and unlawful driving of an automobile on a public highway in King county, caused the death of Lois Ames. Mrs. Hopkins was, by the concluding language of the information, charged with aiding and abetting John Doe in the death of Lois Ames, as follows:

> "And she, said Christine Hopkins, being then and there present, and being then and there the owner of said Studebaker automobile and a passenger therein and knowing said John Doe to be intoxicated, wilfully and unlawfully entrusted the operation of said automobile to said John Doe and permitted him to drive the same upon said highway and did then and there wilfully, unlawfully and feloniously aid, encourage, assist, advise, counsel and abet him, the said John Doe, in said unlawful acts as hereinbefore set forth and in the said unlawful operation of said Studebaker automobile aforesaid."

Trial in the superior court sitting with a jury resulted in a verdict of guilty and a judgment thereon being rendered against Mrs. Hopkins, from which she has appealed to this court.

The principal question here presented is as to the sufficiency of the evidence to sustain the verdict and judgment. That question was presented to the trial court by appropriate timely motions which were overruled, and is here presented by appropriate assignments of error. At the time in question, Mrs. Hopkins was proprietor of, and lived at, a small hotel situated in the southerly portion of the main business district of Seattle. She was then, and had been for about three years, the owner of an enclosed Studebaker automobile which she was accustomed and well qualified to drive. Shortly before ten o'clock of the night in question, her friend "Jimmie Burns," as she called him, came to the hotel to see her. They then agreed to take an automobile ride northerly to a so-called "chicken dinner" resort beyond the city limits on the Bothell Highway. It was agreed that they would go in her automobile and that he would drive. Accordingly they proceeded northerly through the city some six or seven miles to a point very near and just inside the northerly city limits.

There is no direct evidence as to what occurred during this portion of their journey, nor is there any direct evidence as to the condition of either of them as to being intoxicated up to that time, other than she admitted to the police officers that she had taken two or three drinks of whiskey earlier in the evening. According to the evidence of a witness, who was driving north on the highway, just before reaching the city limits, the Hopkins' car passed close to the left of the car the witness was driving, going in the same direction. The witness noticed this particularly, because the car passed dangerously close and turned quickly to the right in front of the car of the witness, requiring some care on the part of the witness to avoid a collision at that time. The witness' car was going about twenty miles per hour; the Hopkins' car probably about twenty-five miles per hour. According to this witness and some other witnesses, the Hopkins' car was, upon and after passing that car, driven in a very erratic and apparently reckless manner. It proceeded in this manner so that, in going approximately a distance of two or three blocks farther, it, for the most part, proceeded on its left, the west, side of the somewhat wide pavement, its speed continuing at from twenty-five to thirty miles per hour.

While so proceeding for a distance of about two blocks to a short distance north of the city limits, it came in collision with the Ames car which was then being driven south on its right, the west, side of the pavement. When the driver of the Ames' car saw the approach of the Hopkins' car on its wrong side of the pavement, he checked his speed, which had previously been about twenty-five miles per hour, and finally seeing that he would have a head-on collision with the Hopkins' car, as it was proceeding on his side of the pavement, and there being a bank on that side preventing his turning off the pavement, to avoid the impending collision, if possible, he turned his car east to his left. The driver of the Hopkins' car, an instant later, turned his car east to its right, and struck the right side of the Ames' car back of the front wheel, forcing the Ames' car to the east side of the pavement and in some manner causing Mrs. Ames and her daughter Lois Ames to fall from their car to the pavement and come to rest partly under the Hopkins' car which was a much heavier car than the Ames' car. From the injuries so received Lois Ames died a few hours later.

There is practically no room for controversy over the facts we have thus far summarized. We think they leave no room for seriously arguing that they are not sufficient to warrant the jury in believing beyond a reasonable doubt that John Doe (Jimmie Burns), the driver of the Hopkins' car, was guilty of such reckless and unlawful acts on his part causing the death of Lois Ames as to make him guilty of manslaughter. This, of course, is but a part of our problem here.

We now notice facts, as the jury were warranted in believing them to exist, touching more particularly Mrs. Hopkins' relation to the reckless and unlawful acts of Jimmie Burns resulting in the death of Lois Ames. Jimmie Burns, as Mrs. Hopkins called the driver of her car, disappeared from the scene of the collision very soon after its occurrence, while others present were intent on and busily engaged in extricating Mrs. Ames and Lois Ames from the wreck. He has not been seen since then, hence the trial of Mrs. Hopkins alone. Mrs. Hopkins had been acquainted with Jimmie Burns some two or three months only. She did not know what his business or vocation was, or where he lived, only that he had come to her hotel occasionally....

Mrs. Hopkins sat in her car for some time immediately following the collision. One witness testified to talking to her there as follows:

"I informed her that she had been in a very bad wreck and had probably killed my little girl. Q. What did she say then? A. Well, she said—for a minute she didn't say anything, and then she said, 'I told him that he could not drive.'"

The jury could well believe from the evidence that Mrs. Hopkins was considerably under the influence of intoxicating liquor, though she apparently knew what she was doing and was conscious of her surroundings. That was apparently about an hour after she had the drinks of whiskey, as admitted by her.

As to the intoxication of the driver of Mrs. Hopkins' car, we have the testimony of a witness as to what he saw very soon after the collision, as follows:

"Q. Now, may I ask if, before you left, you saw any one else standing there? A. There was a man standing alongside of the car there. Q. Which car did you see him standing alongside? A. The Studebaker. Q. Which side was he standing on? A. He was standing on the right hand side of that car. Q. Did you have an opportunity to ascertain whether he was intoxicated or not? A. Yes, he was. Q. What was his posture or position? A. Just standing leaning against the car like that (indicating). Q. Did he render any assistance while you were lifting the car? A. None. Q. Did Mrs. Hopkins? A. None. Q. While you were there did Mrs. Hopkins get out of the Studebaker? A. Yes, she did after I came back, after I called the ambulance. Q. Where did she go to when she got out? A. In another lady's car; Mrs. Atkinson's car. Q. You say then you had some conversation with her? A. Yes. Q. Relate just exactly what was said. A. I went over to the car and I asked her what became of the driver, and she said she didn't know. I asked her who he was. She said 'Jimmie Burns.' I said, 'Where did he go to?' She said 'I don't know.'"

This witness judged of the man's intoxication by his actions and the strong smell of liquor on his breath. No witness actually saw a man sitting as a driver or otherwise in the Hopkins' car. While the identity of the drunk man leaning against the Hopkins' car as the driver of that car is not testified to directly, we have the additional circumstance of his sudden disappearance in the darkness and confusion.

We think, under all the circumstances shown, that the jury might well conclude that the intoxicated man leaning against Mrs. Hopkins' car, while she was sitting therein, very soon after the collision, was the driver of that car; that his intoxicated condition was such that he was unfit to drive a car; that it was not of sudden acquiring; that in time it extended back at least over the period of the approximately one half hour elapsing from the time that Mrs. Hopkins placed her car in his charge upon leaving her hotel; and that his intoxication was, or should have been, known to Mrs. Hopkins had she used due care in deciding whether or not she would entrust the driving of her car to him. Our opinion is that the evidence is sufficient to sustain the verdict and judgment.

It is contended in behalf of Mrs. Hopkins that the information does not state facts constituting the crime of manslaughter as against her. This, as we understand her counsel, is rested upon the theory that manslaughter is a crime of such nature as to preclude the possibility of there being an accessory before the fact to such crime. There does seem to be language of that purport in the decisions of this court in *State v. Robinson* 12 Wash. 349 and *State v. McFadden* 48 Wash. 259. However, Judge Hadley, speaking for the court in the latter case, said:

> "It is argued that such facts can in no event amount to other than a charge that appellant was an accessory before the fact, whereas the authorities hold that there cannot be such an accessory to the crime of manslaughter. This court so held in *State v. Robinson.* Our statute, Bal. Code, §6782, however, abolishes all distinctions between an accessory before the fact and a principal, and provides that 'all persons concerned in the commission of an offense, whether they directly counsel the act constituting the offense, or counsel, aid and abet in its commission, though not present, shall hereafter be indicted, tried, and punished as principals.' Under the said statute appellant may be, and is, charged here as a principal and not as an accessory." ...

> "Every person concerned in the commission of a felony, gross misdemeanor or misdemeanor, whether he directly commits the act constituting the offense, or aids or abets in its commission, and whether present or absent; and every person who directly or indirectly counsels, encourages, hires, commands, induces or otherwise procures another to commit a felony, gross misdemeanor or misdemeanor, is a principal, and shall be proceeded against and punished as such. The fact that the person aided, abetted, counseled, encouraged, hired, commanded, induced or procured, could not or did not entertain a criminal intent, shall not be a defense to any person aiding, abetting, counseling, encouraging, hiring, commanding, inducing or procuring him."

It is now the settled law in this state that intent to cause the death of another is not an element in the crime of manslaughter. This plainly does not mean that intent to do an unlawful or grossly negligent act resulting in the unintentional death of another is not an element of the crime of manslaughter. We think these are elements in the crime of manslaughter. So it seems to us that Mrs. Hopkins was by this information charged with negligence, in a criminal sense, in the placing of her car in the charge of John Doe, as driver, while he was intoxicated, she then knowing him to be intoxicated, and in then permitting him to drive it in the reckless, unlawful manner that resulted in the death of Lois Ames. So we conclude that the information sufficiently charged her, in contemplation of our law, as principal, though somewhat in form charging her as an accessory before the fact....

The judgment is affirmed.

French, J. (dissenting) In the case of *State v. Robinson* 12 Wash. 349, a prosecution under the aiding and abetting statute, this court laid down the rule:

"We think that § 1319 [Code Proc.] *supra*, contains but the usual provisions in force in all, or nearly all, of the states, and we have been cited to no case, nor have we found one in which a conviction for manslaughter has been sustained under circumstances similar to those disclosed by the record here. *The offense of manslaughter from its legal character excludes the possibility* of an accessory before the fact as an element in its composition." ...

The doctrine announced in the above cases is that the killing of a human being in order to constitute manslaughter must be involuntary and unintentional. I am unable to understand how a person can be aided and abetted in the doing of an unintentional and involuntary act by another person who has no intent.

Discussion Questions

1. Did Mrs. Hopkins's conduct satisfy the requirements for accessory liability? If so, what was that conduct?

2. What mental state do you think Mrs. Hopkins had with respect to the death of Lois Ames? With respect to Jimmie Burns driving her car?

3. Could Mrs. Hopkins be charged as a principal? Recall that as a principal Mrs. Hopkins' conduct would have had to cause the death. Would the prosecution encounter any problems proving that Mrs. Hopkins caused the death?

The Model Penal Code deals with mental state regarding result elements in the following provision.

Model Penal Code

§ 2.06 Liability for Conduct of Another; Complicity

(4) When causing a particular result is an element of an offense, an accomplice in the conduct causing such result is an accomplice in the commission of that offense if he acts with the kind of culpability, if any, with respect to that result that is sufficient for the commission of the offense.

Discussion Question

How would the *Hopkins* case be resolved under the MPC?

Breaking Down the MPC Complicity Mental States

We saw with the *Lyerla* case in Chapter 10 that when a target crime, such as homicide, has both a conduct element and a result element, attempt liability requires that an actor have both purpose to engage in the conduct required by the target offense *and* purpose regarding the result required by the target offense. The actor must have purpose regarding the result element even if the target offense may be satisfied with a mental state *less than purpose* regarding the result element.

The same is not true for complicity with regard to result elements in the principal's offense. Although complicity is often described as requiring purpose (or intent), that purpose requirement does not extend to result elements in the principal's offense. Instead, to be liable as an accomplice, the actor must simply have the mental state regarding a result element that is required for conviction of the principal.

The *Hopkins* case illustrates this point. The Model Penal Code adopts the same position. This is a critical point of contrast between attempt and complicity.

The following diagram illustrates this important point about the law of complicity using MPC reckless manslaughter. Look at the mental state box regarding death under the principal offense of manslaughter at the top of the diagram. Remember from Chapter 6 that recklessness regarding death qualifies an actor for manslaughter. Look at and compare the mental state box regarding death under complicity at the bottom of the diagram. It shows the same mental state of recklessness regarding the death element as the principal offense diagram.

Principal Offense Elements
Reckless Manslaughter

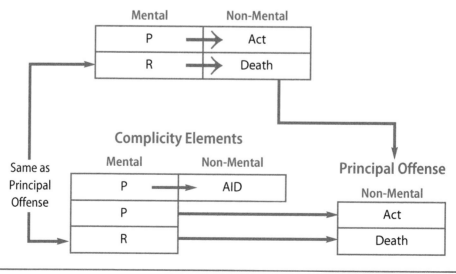

3. Mental State Regarding a Circumstance Element

Although the words *purpose* and *intent* are most often used to describe the mental state aspect of complicity, we saw in the previous section that such purpose does not necessarily extend to a result element in the principal's offense. What mental state does complicity require in relation to *circumstance* elements? Knowledge? Or, as with a result element, will a lower mental state regarding a circumstance suffice for accomplice liability if that is sufficient for conviction of the principal?

In the *Harris* case, below, the defendant was convicted of statutory rape on the basis of complicity. In Massachusetts, an accomplice is referred to as a "joint venturer."

Commonwealth v. Harris
74 Mass. App. Ct. 105 (2009)
Appeals Court of Massachusetts

McHugh, J.

… Before sentencing, [Harris] moved for a new trial on the ground that the evidence was insufficient to prove that he knew the victim's age, a fact he maintained was essential for conviction of statutory rape on a joint venture theory. That motion [was] … denied. On appeal, the defendant presses the same point.…

The facts of the case, viewed first in the light most favorable to the Commonwealth, are as follows. The defendant's friend, Carlos Johnson, met the thirteen year old victim, Jane Smith, on an eighteen and over telephone "chat line." After talking on the phone over the course of several days, Johnson and Smith arranged to meet in person at Smith's home. Although Johnson told Smith that he would meet her alone, he, the defendant, and two other men arrived at Smith's house at about 8:30 P.M. in a car the defendant was driving. As Smith left her house to meet Johnson, her father, standing about fifteen feet from the car, yelled that she should not get in because she was "underage." There was no direct evidence that anyone in the car heard what he said.

In response to her father's entreaties, Smith returned to her house, but quickly reemerged through a different door, met Johnson, and got into the car, positioning herself in the back seat between two unidentified men. Johnson sat in the front passenger seat and the defendant drove. The first stop was a liquor store, where the defendant got out to buy some potato chips and alcohol. While the defendant was gone, Smith told the occupants that she was thirteen years old.

When the defendant returned, Smith, who thought that she and Johnson were simply going to "hang out," asked to go to a nearby park and the men agreed. She also told the men that she had a curfew and could not stay out long. Instead of heading toward the park, however, the defendant drove toward a highway. Smith asked where they were going and Johnson said that they were headed for Seekonk. When she asked why, he told her, "We are just going to do a drive," and handed her the liquor, telling her to take "a couple of sips." She protested, but he ultimately persuaded her to take a drink and the car's other occupants had some drinks as well.

Eventually, the car arrived at a motel where the defendant got out and tried to get a room. He was unsuccessful because the motel required a credit card and he did not have one. Undeterred, he drove to another motel where he registered successfully and returned to the car with a room key. Although Smith was fearful of going into the room, Johnson persuaded her to go, saying that they were just going to stay there for a couple of minutes and "chill."

By this time, Smith, who had taken "a couple more sips" of the liquor during the drive between motels, was intoxicated to the point where she could not walk and her legs "were, like, buckling and everything." One or more of the men assisted her into the room where they sat her on a bed. Over the next hour, all but the defendant took turns having sexual intercourse with her while she drifted in and out of consciousness. The defendant, according to Smith, remained in the room throughout, sometimes watching television and sometimes watching what the others were doing to her.

After the men finished, they helped Smith back into the car. The defendant drove back to Smith's neighborhood, where he dropped her off somewhere in the vicinity of her house. Staggering, incoherent, and smelling of alcohol, she walked home sometime after 11 P.M. At home, she met her father, mother, and a police officer who had been dispatched to the house in response to a report of a missing juvenile. Upon observing Smith's condition, the officer suggested that her parents take her to a hospital. They did. Emergency room physicians determined that her blood-alcohol level was .131 and that she had suffered a number of painful vaginal injuries. Anal and vaginal swabs produced sperm, but none of the resulting extractions of deoxyribonucleic acid (DNA) could be traced to the defendant.

An investigation ensued and soon led to the defendant's arrest. He told the investigating officers that Johnson was about twenty-four years old. He said that he and Johnson lived in Providence, Rhode Island, and that, on the evening in question, Johnson had enlisted his help in obtaining a motel room because, unlike Johnson, the defendant had a credit card and Johnson thought that "hotels don't take cash anymore."

After the defendant agreed to assist, he drove Johnson, in Johnson's car, to an area with which the defendant was unfamiliar. They picked up "a girl," who turned out to be Smith, whom the defendant described as "kind of young and wearing white pants." As they picked her up, the defendant said, "you could hear someone yelling, 'You ain't going anywhere until I meet the person you're leaving with.'" At that point, Smith told the defendant and Johnson that she couldn't leave until her "dad [met] the person she was leaving with." Johnson and Smith got out of the car, apparently met her father, and then got back in.

The defendant said he first drove Johnson and Smith to a Ramada Inn hotel where, for some unexplained reason, he was unable to obtain a room. He then drove to a motel in Seekonk "where you only need an ID" as opposed to a credit card, and paid cash for a room. He escorted Smith and Johnson to the room where he "opened the door and showed them where they were supposed to go." Mission accomplished, the defendant then got back in the car and drove to Providence where he remained for about twenty to thirty minutes until Johnson telephoned and asked him to return. After driving back, he picked up Johnson and Smith and, once again, drove to Providence. Upon arrival, he got out as Johnson took his place at the wheel and, with Smith, drove off.

The defendant told the officers that he had not seen any alcohol that evening and that he had made no observations about Smith's condition when he returned to the Seekonk motel, though he noted that she "didn't say much" during the ride from Seekonk to Providence. Although the defendant did not testify at trial, he called two witnesses who said that they had seen him in Providence between approximately 9:30 P.M. and 10 P.M. on the relevant evening and corroborated other parts of his testimony.

Against that factual backdrop, the judge instructed the jury on the so-called presence and nonpresence theories of joint venture liability. The instruction did not address what the Commonwealth did or did not have to prove regarding the defendant's knowledge of the victim's age, but defense counsel neither sought an instruction on that subject nor objected to the instruction as given.

During the course of their two-day deliberations, however, the jury twice asked the judge about what the Commonwealth had to prove regarding the defendant's knowledge of Smith's age. On each occasion, the judge instructed, without objection, that conviction did not require proof that either Johnson or the defendant knew the victim's age.... Ultimately, the jury returned a verdict of guilty on the lesser included offense of statutory rape by joint venture.

The jury had not been asked to, and did not, indicate whether they reached their verdict on a presence or a nonpresence joint venture theory. Seizing on that omission, the defendant argues on appeal that conviction of statutory rape on a nonpresence joint venture theory requires proof that the defendant knew that sexual intercourse was planned for the room he procured for Smith and Johnson and that he knew Smith was under the age of sixteen. He argues that there was no evidence of the former and, on the latter, that the judge gave erroneous instructions in response to the jury's questions. Because there is no way to tell whether the jury convicted on a presence or on a nonpresence joint venture theory, he concludes, there is a substantial risk that the verdict represents a miscarriage of justice. We see things differently.

... Conviction of [statutory rape] as a principal does not require proof that the defendant knew the victim's age. On the contrary, "[i]t has long been the law of this Commonwealth that it is no defense that the defendant did not know that the victim was under the statutory age of consent. Further, it is immaterial that the defendant reasonably believed that the victim was sixteen years of age or older or that he may have attempted to ascertain her age."

Criminal liability as a joint venturer can be established either through a presence or through a nonpresence theory. Under the presence theory, liability arises if the defendant was "(1) present at the scene of the crime, (2) with knowledge that another intend[ed] to commit the crime or with intent to commit [the] crime, and (3) by agreement [was] willing and available to help the other if necessary." Elements (2) and (3) are often described as requiring the Commonwealth to prove that the defendant "'shared' the principal's criminal intent (i.e., 'mental state'), and may have merely stood by, but by agreement was ready to assist if necessary."

In contrast, liability under a nonpresence theory requires the Commonwealth to show that the defendant was an accessory before the fact, i.e., that he aided and abetted the principal before the crime took place. Conviction under this theory requires "'something more than mere acquiescence,' although not necessarily physical participation, 'if there is association with the criminal venture and any significant participation in it.' ... Therefore, it is clear that [conviction] as an accessory before the fact [requires] not only knowledge of the crime and a shared intent to bring it about, but also some sort of act that contributes to its happening."

"Under either theory[, however,] the critical question is whether the defendant acted with knowledge of the [crime] and with the intent to assist in the commission of that crime so as to accomplish its objective." Obviously, that question poses difficulties if, as here, an element of the crime does not require that the principal have any intent, or even knowledge, of one of the facts or circumstances that criminalizes what otherwise would be noncriminal activity. In those circumstances, the question becomes whether the joint venturer must have either knowledge or intent, in this case of Smith's age, that would not be required for conviction of the principal.

No Massachusetts case has directly addressed that question. Across the nation, only two decisions appear to have addressed it, and one of those has done so obliquely. In the first case, decided in 1922, the California District Court of Appeal affirmed the "aiding and abetting" conviction of an hotel owner who rented to an underage couple a room they used for sexual intercourse. *People v. Wood*, 56 Cal. App. 431, 205 P. 698 (1922). The court said that the defendant "knew the illegal purpose for which the room was to be used and knowingly both aided and abetted" the principal in commission of the crime. Accordingly, the court was not required to decide whether knowledge of the illegal purpose was always required for conviction and it offered no opinion on that issue.

In the second case, decided last year, the North Carolina Court of Appeals did express an opinion on the issue, holding that a defendant accused of "aiding and abetting" commission of the crime of statutory rape was entitled to an instruction that conviction required proof of "the defendant's intent to aid in the commission of a crime." *State v. Bowman*, 188 N.C. App. 635 (N.C. App. 2008). "[T]he question of defendant's intent," said the court, "is not limited to whether he aided the perpetrator but whether he aided with the specific intent to assist in the commission of the crime." In that case, the defendant had invited two adult male friends to his house with their female companions, one of whom was fourteen and the other fifteen. While in the house, the friends drank liquor and then had sexual intercourse in bedrooms while the defendant played computer games in the kitchen. Because of what it held was a specific intent requirement, the court reversed the defendant's conviction because the trial judge had refused the defendant's "request for an instruction that [he] had to know the age of the victims in order to be convicted of aiding and abetting statutory rape."

The North Carolina decision may have derived from the court's interpretation of the term "abetting" as used in North Carolina decisions.[4] We think that Massachusetts law requires a more nuanced approach and, in any event, believe that application of a specific intent requirement to all forms of statutory rape by joint venture would be both inconsistent with the public's legitimate needs and unnecessary to protect a defendant's significant interests.

More particularly, we do not think that knowledge of the child's age is required for conviction on a "presence" joint venture theory. When the joint venturer is "present," he or she has the same opportunity as the principal to make judgments about age from the child's appearance and other circumstances attending the encounter between the child and the principal. Accordingly, the joint venturer, like the principal "does not lack the ability to comply with the law; he must simply abstain from [facilitating] sexual intercourse when there is even the remotest possibility that [the principal's] partner is below the statutory age.... [The person] who contemplates [facilitating] intercourse with a partner of indeterminate age can resolve doubts in favor of compliance with the law without sacrificing behavior that society considers desirable."

To be sure, more difficult problems sometimes may arise when the Commonwealth proceeds under a joint venture theory that does not involve a "present" defendant. The nonpresence theory "is more at large, less contained," than the presence theory and "[w]e have found no Massachusetts appellate cases involving sex crimes where a defendant was convicted on a joint venture theory absent a common victim, physical presence at the immediate scene, or physical participation in the act." Therefore, if the Commonwealth proceeds on a "nonpresence" theory, avoidance of injustice may in some cases require proof that the joint venturer had more specific knowledge about the victim's age than would be required for conviction of the principal. Requiring greater knowledge in appropriate "nonpresence" cases would safeguard the defendant's right to due process of law and prevent realization of the fear expressed by the defendant in this case that "[f]amily planning professionals, pharmacists, or vendors of contraception could become rapists if the products they distribute were to 'aid' someone in achieving sexual intercourse with a person under" the age of sixteen.

However one might resolve the cases the defendant conjures, he surely was not in the family-planning profession and cannot invoke any special rules that might be applicable to family planners. More important, whether one looks at the evidence

---

4. "'[A]betting' serves to supply the mental state necessary to justify the imposition of criminal liability. This requirement looks for a criminal state of mind—specifically, it requires that the accomplice has both knowledge of the perpetrator's unlawful purpose to commit a crime, and the intent to facilitate the perpetrator's unlawful purpose." *Id.* at 648, quoting from Comment, *Developments*

in the light most favorable to the Commonwealth or in the light most favorable to the defendant, we are of the opinion that he was "present" during commission of the crime and had as much opportunity as the principal to make judgments about Smith's age. In the light most favorable to the Commonwealth, of course, the defendant was present at every single moment of the encounter and, while in the motel room, alternated between watching television and observing the principals' interactions with Smith.

The same result applies if one looks at the evidence in a light favoring the defendant. Presence is a functional concept and decided cases have never required presence throughout the venture, from beginning to end, for conviction on a presence theory.

Here, according to the defendant, the evening's activities began when the twenty-four year old Johnson enlisted his help in obtaining a hotel room. After agreeing to provide that help, the defendant drove Johnson to a rendezvous with Smith, who "looked kind of young." Smith told the pair that she could not leave with them until Johnson met her father, a restriction backed up by her father's voice in the background. Paternal clearance obtained, the defendant drove them directly to one motel and then to a second where he paid cash to obtain a room, escorted Johnson and Smith to the room, "opened the door and showed them where they were supposed to go." He then left, but returned shortly thereafter when summoned by Johnson and drove Johnson and Smith back to Providence.

In those circumstances, the defendant was sufficiently "present" to warrant conviction under a "presence" theory. His opportunity to make judgments about Smith's age was essentially the same as Johnson's. Despite his claim to the contrary, the defendant's association with Johnson fairly bristled with sexual adventure from beginning to end, and no one with an ounce of common sense could have doubted for an instant the nature of the activities Johnson planned for the motel room to which the defendant escorted him and Smith.

We recognize that the judge instructed the jury both on a presence and on a non-presence theory and that our analysis means that an instruction on the latter theory, though given without objection, was unwarranted. Whatever problems such an instruction might create in a different case, we think it created no substantial risk of a miscarriage of justice here. As just detailed, even if one concludes from the defendant's account of the evening's activities that he was not "present" for the crime because he was not in the room when it occurred, there was ample evidence to support a finding

---

in California Homicide Law: VII. Accomplice Liability: Derivative Responsibility, 36 Loy. L.A. L. Rev. 1524, 1526 (2003). Some Federal decisions have held that the same standard is applicable to prosecutions for violation of 18 U.S.C. §2, the Federal "aiding and abetting" statute. See *United States v. Sayetsitty*, 107 F.3d 1405, 1412 (9th Cir. 1997) ("[A]iding and abetting contains an additional element of specific intent, beyond the mental state required by the principal crime"); *United States v. Lawson*, 872 F.2d 179, 181 (6th Cir. 1989) (Conviction of "aiding and abetting" a strict liability firearms offense requires proof that the accomplice had a specific intent that the principal illegally possess the firearm).

that he aided and abetted the sexual contact between Johnson and Smith. Moreover, the defendant's extensive interaction with Johnson and Smith before and after they entered the motel room leads us to conclude that this is not among the cases where, even on a nonpresence theory, due process would require that he have greater knowledge than Johnson had about Smith's age. We say that because, even if we were to deem the defendant "not present" for purposes of the "nonpresence" joint venture theory, he nevertheless spent sufficient time in the company of Johnson and Smith to have had every opportunity Johnson had to make judgments about Smith's age. Due process is, therefore, afforded by holding him to the same knowledge requirements applicable to Johnson. . . .

In sum, the judge's answers to the jury's questions were correct and any error in giving an instruction regarding nonpresence joint venture liability did not create a substantial risk of a miscarriage of justice.

Judgment affirmed.

Discussion Questions

1. In the *Harris* case the court found that an accomplice to statutory rape need not know the victim's age to be convicted. The North Carolina court in the *Bowman* case, however, concluded that in the context of that case the prosecution did need to prove such knowledge. Which do you think is the better approach?

2. What level of culpability do you think Harris actually had in regard to the victim's age? Negligence? Recklessness? Knowledge?

3. What are the arguments for and against applying strict liability regarding age to an alleged accomplice to statutory rape?

4. Should the required culpability regarding age for accomplice liability in the context of statutory rape depend on whether an actor who assisted was present or not? Do you agree with the court's conclusion that, looking at the facts in the light most favorable to Harris, he was "sufficiently present" during the principal's crime?

5. Should the required culpability regarding age depend on whether the actor is a doctor or nurse providing family planning services?

4. Attempt to Aid and Abet

What is the relationship between attempt and complicity? Can one be an accessory to an attempt? Can one attempt to be an accessory?

Under the MPC provisions on complicity an attempt to aid a crime even if unsuccessful can render an actor liable for the principal's offense.

Model Penal Code

§ 2.06 Liability for Conduct of Another; Complicity

(3) A person is an accomplice of another person in the commission of an offense if:

    (a) with the purpose of promoting or facilitating the commission of the offense, he

        (i) solicits the other person to commit it, or

        (ii) aids or agrees or *attempts to aid* such other person in planning or committing it, or

        (iii) having a legal duty to prevent the commission of the offense, fails to make proper effort so to do; or

    (b) his conduct is expressly declared by law to establish his complicity.

(emphasis added).

* * *

What happens, though, if an actor attempts to aid a principal in committing a crime but the principal never commits the crime? The following provision from the attempt section of the MPC addresses this situation:

Model Penal Code

§ 5.01 Criminal Attempt.

(3) <u>Conduct Designed to Aid Another in Commission of a Crime.</u>

    A person who engages in conduct designed to aid another to commit a crime that would establish his complicity under Section 2.06 if the crime were committed by such other person, is guilty of an attempt to commit the crime, although the crime is not committed or attempted by such other person.

Problem

11.8 Cory stumbles upon Michelle's diary. From it, Cory learns that Michelle plans to rob a local video store. Cory detests the video store owner and is delighted that Michelle plans to rob him. Michelle has not yet acted on her plan. Unbeknownst to Michelle, Cory reconnoiters the video store and draws a map of the surveillance cameras. Cory leaves the map, a disguise, and burglar's tools on Michelle's back porch on the evening Michelle plans to commit the robbery. Michelle notices the package on the back porch, looks inside and sees the map, the disguise, and the tools. Just then, the police arrive. Someone else, it turns out, had also stumbled on Michelle's diary and warned the police of Michelle's plan. The police discover the package left by Cory and arrest Cory. Could a prosecutor in a jurisdiction that follows the MPC charge Cory with a crime? If so, what crime? Assume that Michelle has not gone far enough to be liable for attempt.

D. Abandonment and Other Limiting Principles

The common law provided a number of limitations on complicity liability and so does the Model Penal Code.

Model Penal Code

§ 2.06 Liability for Conduct of Another; Complicity

(6) Unless otherwise provided by the Code or by the law defining the offense, a person is not an accomplice in an offense committed by another person if:

(a) he is a victim of that offense; or

(b) the offense is so defined that his conduct is inevitably incident to its commission; or

(c) he terminates his complicity prior to the commission of the offense and

  (i) wholly deprives it of effectiveness in the commission of the offense; or

  (ii) gives timely warning to the law enforcement authorities or otherwise makes proper effort to prevent the commission of the offense.

Model Penal Code Commentators include as examples of the victim exclusion both a parent who pays ransom to a kidnapper of her child and a business person who yields to extortion by a racketeer.[2] With respect to conduct that is inevitably incident to a crime, the Commentators give as examples the purchaser in an unlawful sale and the previously unmarried party to a bigamous marriage.[3]

Problem

11.9 In the *Beeman* case, Beeman testified that "[t]wo days before the offense" he "told Gray that he wanted nothing to do with the robbery of his relatives." If Beeman's testimony is accepted as true, would MPC Section 2.06 (6) absolve Beeman of liability?

---

2. Model Penal Code Commentaries § 2.06, Art. 2, 323–324 (ALI 1985).

3. *Id.*

E. Special Issues

1. Conviction of the Principal

Indiana Code

§ 35-41-2-4 Aiding, inducing, or causing an offense

A person who knowingly or intentionally aids, induces, or causes another person to commit an offense commits that offense, even if the other person:

   (1) Has not been prosecuted for the offense;

   (2) Has not been convicted of the offense; or

   (3) Has been acquitted of the offense.

Kansas Stat. Ann.

§ 21-3205 Liability for crimes of another.

(1) A person is criminally responsible for a crime committed by another if such person intentionally aids, abets, advises, hires, counsels or procures the other to commit the crime.

…

(3) A person liable under this section may be charged with and convicted of the crime although the person alleged to have directly committed the act constituting the crime lacked criminal or legal capacity or has not been convicted or has been acquitted or has been convicted of some other degree of the crime or of some other crime based on the same act.

Problems

11.10 Alan and Rob meet in a bar one night while watching World Cup soccer matches on television. Both are fans of the Brazilian team playing Germany in the final match. While they are watching, boisterous German fans enter the bar and begin loudly insulting Alan, who replies in kind. One of the German fans invites Alan to step into an alleyway outside to settle their differences. Before Alan heads outside, Rob slips Alan a set of brass knuckles and says "beat the tar out of that jerk." Outside, Alan severely beats the German fan. Assume that self-defense is unavailable for Alan because he could have walked away from the challenge and that brass knuckles are a deadly weapon. Is Rob liable for assault with a deadly weapon under the following scenarios?

Part (a) Alan is a British citizen working at the British Embassy and therefore has diplomatic immunity and cannot be prosecuted.

Part (b) Alan is an American citizen but fled after the assault. Alan is a fugitive from justice at the time Rob is prosecuted.

Part (c) Alan was an American citizen but died in a high-speed chase when police attempted to arrest him.

Part (d) Alan suffers from a mental disease that did not render him insane at the time of the offense, but that makes it impossible for him to understand the charge against him and to assist his lawyer in his defense. Therefore, he is incompetent to be tried.

Part (e) Alan suffered from a mental disease that rendered him insane at the time of the offense.

2. Other Crimes Committed by the Principal

17-A Maine Revised Statutes

§ 57 Criminal liability for conduct of another; accomplices

3. A person is an accomplice of another person in the commission of a crime if:

A. With the intent of promoting or facilitating the commission of the crime, he solicits such other person to commit the crime, or aids or agrees to aid or attempts to aid such other person in planning or committing the crime. A person is an accomplice under this subsection to any crime the commission of which was a reasonably foreseeable consequence of his conduct....

Kansas Statutes Annotated

§ 21-3205 Liability for crimes of another

(1) A person is criminally responsible for a crime committed by another if such person intentionally aids, abets, advises, hires, counsels or procures the other to commit the crime.

(2) A person liable under subsection (1) hereof is also liable for any other crime committed in pursuance of the intended crime if reasonably foreseeable by such person as a probable consequence of committing or attempting to commit the crime intended.

Model Penal Code

§ 2.06 Liability for Conduct of Another; Complicity

(3) A person is an accomplice of another person in the commission of the offense if:

(a) with the purpose of promoting or facilitating the commission of the offense, he

(i) solicits such other person to commit it, or

  (ii) aids or agrees or attempts to aid such other person in planning or committing it, or

  (iii) having a legal duty to prevent the commission of the offense, fails to make proper effort so to do; or

 (b) his conduct is expressly declared by law to establish his complicity.

(4) When causing a particular result is an element of an offense, an accomplice in the conduct causing such result is an accomplice in the commission of that offense if he acts with the kind of culpability, if any, with respect to that result that is sufficient for the commission of the offense.

Problems

11.11 Samantha and Jared plan a burglary of Larry's home to steal his valuable stamp collection, which was mentioned in a recent newspaper article. Samantha shows Jared a pistol she is carrying in case of trouble. How would the following scenarios be resolved under the Kansas and Maine statutes, as well as the MPC provision?

Part (a) When Samantha and Jared arrive at Larry's house, his fierce dog is blocking the entrance to the backyard. Samantha and Jared had surveyed the house on several prior occasions and knew that the dog was sometimes left in the backyard. Samantha shoots the dog with her pistol. Samantha is later convicted under a statute that reads as follows:

> Any person who exhibits cruelty to animals in the form of physical assault causing injury or death is guilty of the crime of cruelty to animals.

Is Jared also liable for a cruelty to animals offense?

Part (b) When Samantha and Jared enter the house, they split up to search for the stamp collection. During his search, Jared finds $1,000 in cash hidden in a shoe box in Larry's bedroom closet. Jared puts the cash in his jacket pocket and does not tell Samantha about it. He then rejoins Samantha, who has found and taken the stamp collection. Jared is later arrested and convicted of theft of the $1,000 he took from Larry's closet. Is Samantha also liable for theft of the $1,000?

Part (c) What if Jared in Part (b) had found a stash of cocaine rather than cash and that Jared was later convicted of felony possession of cocaine. Is Samantha also liable for felony possession of cocaine?

Part (d) Assume in this part that when Samantha and Jared split up to search Larry's house, Samantha unexpectedly finds Larry and several friends playing cards in Larry's basement recreation room. One person there is Vince, an old enemy of Samantha's. Samantha shoots and injures Vince. Samantha is later convicted of assault based on her shooting of Vince. Is Jared also liable for assault based on Samantha's shooting of Vince?

11.12 Will and Virginia decide to rob a bank. Virginia enters the bank and obtains money from a teller using a threatening note. Will drives Virginia to and from the bank and acts as a lookout while Virginia is in the bank. They agreed beforehand that no one was to be injured during the robbery and Virginia does not carry a weapon during the robbery. The victim teller, however, suffers from a heart condition and dies of a heart attack brought about by the robbery. Assume Virginia is liable for felony murder. As her accomplice, is Will liable for felony murder as well?

3. Innocent Instrumentality

Reconsider a hypothetical you read in the mental state chapter about the political extremist who sends a letter containing anthrax to a government office and the mail carrier who delivers the letter. The extremist's purpose is to infect and kill a legislator whom the extremist has targeted because of the legislator's support for a particular policy. The mail carrier, by contrast, does not know the letter is contaminated. His only purpose is to deliver the mail. The legislator opens the letter, becomes infected, and dies.

This hypothetical is an example of what is known as the "innocent instrumentality" doctrine. Who should be held liable here for the homicide of the legislator? Who should the law recognize as the principal actor? The mailman lacks liability because he lacks any of the mental states required for homicide. And if no crime was committed by the mailman, how can the extremist be held as an accomplice? Remember that an accomplice shares in the principal's liability, that the accomplice's liability is said to derive from the principal's liability. To resolve this problem, the law treats the extremist as the principal, not as an accomplice. He is liable for murder having used the mailman as his innocent instrument.

4. The Feigning Accomplice

Richard believes that Josh has stolen Richard's watch. Josh denies the theft but does brag about having committed certain burglaries. Richard continues to believe that Josh is responsible for the missing watch. In the hopes of having the police catch Josh in the act of burglary, Richard pretends to agree to help Josh steal some liquor. After store hours, Richard boosts Josh up to a window, which Josh breaks; he then enters the liquor store through the broken window. As soon as Josh is inside, Richard phones 911 and reports a burglary in progress at the liquor store. Before the police arrive, Josh hands several bottles of alcohol out the window to Richard. When the police arrive, Richard tells them all about Josh's crimes. They ask Richard how Josh got into the store. Richard acknowledges helping Josh enter the store and taking the bottles of alcohol Josh handed out to him. The police arrest Richard and Josh.

This fact pattern, based on the facts of *Wilson v. People*, 103 Colo. 441 (1939), illustrates a "feigning accomplice." Is Richard liable as an accomplice? He certainly assisted Josh. But did Richard possess the mental state(s) required for accomplice liability? Assume Josh is charged with the following crimes:

- Breaking and entering the liquor store.

- Burglary, which requires breaking and entering the liquor store with intent to commit theft.

- Theft of the liquor bottles passed out to Richard. The crime of theft requires an intent to permanently deprive an owner of his or her property.

Is Richard liable as an accomplice for any of these crimes?

F. Synthesis and Review

Problems

11.13 A newspaper reported the following story. The Brazilian government is prosecuting Kube-i and Darrell Posey for violation of a criminal statute making it illegal for foreigners (i.e., non-Brazilian citizens) to interfere in Brazil's domestic affairs. Kube-i is a member of the Kaiapo Indian tribe, which inhabits the Amazon river basin in Brazil. Kube-i *is* a citizen of Brazil and the son of the chief of the Kaiapo tribe. Darrell Posey is an American anthropologist who has worked for the past 11 years among the Kaiapo and *is not* a citizen of Brazil. Posey has been active in recent years along with Kaiapo leaders in protesting the Brazilian government's destruction of the Amazon forest, pollution of the Amazon river and its tributaries, and general disregard of Indian rights. The criminal charge against Kube-i and Posey is based on a trip made by Kube-i and Posey to Washington, D.C., to meet with officers of the World Bank, which is considering approval of a $500 million loan to Brazil for a hydroelectric project entailing construction of two vast new dams in the Amazon basin, which would flood Kaiapo lands. The complaints of Kube-i and Posey have apparently delayed and complicated the loan approval, thus interfering in the eyes of the Brazilian prosecuting authorities with Brazil's domestic affairs. Assume that the activities of Kube-i and Posey do constitute "interfering with domestic affairs" for the purpose of the statute under which they have been charged. Lawyers have argued that the charging of a Brazilian citizen, Kube-i, with a crime limited by definition to persons who are not citizens of Brazil is a "legal anomaly."[4] How might one explain the supposed anomaly? In what other situations in our course have we encountered a similar apparent anomaly?

11.14 You are a lawyer working at a law firm in a large city. Your firm represents a shelter for runaway teenagers as a pro bono client. One day you are called by a doctor who provides free medical services on a volunteer basis for the teenagers at the shelter. The doctor tells you that a 15-year-old girl who has been staying at the shelter in recent weeks confided to the doctor that she has been engaging in prostitution to earn money for food and clothes. The doctor has tried unsuccessfully to talk the girl out of engaging in prostitution. Because the girl appears to be determined to continue to engage in prostitution, the doctor wants to provide her with protection against pregnancy. The doctor is considering prescribing a contraceptive for the girl, but is concerned about encountering legal problems for doing so. Under the law of complicity, would the doctor face potential criminal liability if the doctor prescribes the contraceptive? How would you advise the doctor to proceed?

11.15 As he often does, A goes for a run in a neighborhood near where he and his family live. A is a twenty-five year old black man. Partway through his run, A becomes thirsty and looks for a place to get a drink of water. He passes a lot on which a new house is in the early stages of construction. Its foundation is complete and the walls are partially framed, but no doors or windows have been installed. A walks onto the lot and into the shell of the house and finds a water faucet from which he takes a drink and then continues on his run.

G and his son, T, are residents of the neighborhood through which A runs. Both are white men. They see A running and observe him enter the house under construction. G and T are aware that there have been several burglaries in the neighborhood recently and think that A looks like the burglar. They decide to follow A in their pickup truck, seize him, then turn him over to the police.

T arms himself with a shotgun and G brings a handgun. With T driving and G in the truck's bed, they begin to search for A. Soon they start following him at a close distance. One of G's friends, W, sees G and T pursuing and joins their pursuit in his own truck. The men twice come close to trapping A between the trucks, but he manages to elude them. During their third attempt, W strikes A with the side of his truck. A, exhausted, stops and turns to confront the truck which T is driving. T gets out of the truck carrying his shotgun and pointing it at A. G remains in the truck bed pointing his handgun

---

4. *See* Marlise Simons, *Brazil Accuses Scholar of Aiding Indian Protest*, N.Y. Times, Aug. 14, 1988 at 14 and Marlise Simons, *Dams vs. Indians: The Battle Calls for War Paint*, N.Y. Times, Oct. 14, 1988 at 4.

in A's direction and W remains in his truck. G yells out to T "Don't shoot." As T nears him, A tries to defend himself by taking the shotgun from T. A struggle ensues over the shotgun during which the shotgun fires three times. Two of the shots strike A in the chest, killing him. After A collapses on the ground, T utters a racial slur. W remains in his truck and records the interaction between T and A on his cell phone.

Assume that the relevant jurisdiction has the following statutes:

Aggravated assault

(a) A person commits the offense of aggravated assault when he or she assaults:

…

(2) With a deadly weapon or with any object, device, or instrument which, when used offensively against a person, is likely to or actually does result in serious bodily injury; …

(b) … [A] person convicted of the offense of aggravated assault shall be punished by imprisonment for not less than one nor more than 20 years.

False imprisonment

(a) A person commits the offense of false imprisonment when, in violation of the personal liberty of another, he arrests, confines, or detains such person without legal authority.

(b) A person convicted of the offense of false imprisonment shall be punished by imprisonment for not less than one nor more than ten years.

Part (a) Is T liable for homicide? If so, for what category or categories of homicide? Is T a principal or an accomplice?

Part (b) Is G liable for homicide? If so, for what category or categories of homicide? Is G a principal or an accomplice?

Part (c) Is W liable for homicide? If so, for what category or categories of homicide? Is W a principal or an accomplice?

11.16 A grocery store employee calls police to report that a man used a counterfeit $20 bill to buy cigarettes. Four officers—A, B, C & D—respond to the call in two separate police cars. Officers B and C are the first to arrive on the scene. The merchant identifies Gordon, a forty-six year-old black man sitting in a car parked outside the store, as the man who used the counterfeit bill. Officer B walks over to the car, asks Gordon to get out, then pulls him out of the car. Officer B tells Gordon that he is under arrest for passing counterfeit currency and puts handcuffs on his wrists. Gordon walks with Officer B to the nearby sidewalk and, at Officer B's direction, sits down and, remaining calm, says "thank you." Shortly thereafter, Officers B and C stand Gordon up, walk him to their patrol car, and try to put Gordon into the back seat of the car. As they do so, Gordon stiffens and falls to the ground. He tells the officers "I'm not resisting, I'm claustrophobic."

At this point Officers A and D arrive in their patrol car. Together the officers try to force Gordon into the back seat. Again, Gordon stiffens and falls to the ground, repeatedly saying "I cannot breathe." Eventually the officers succeed in getting Gordon into the back seat. A few minutes later, Officer A pulls Gordon from the car. As he does so, Gordon falls to the ground face down. Officer A then places one of his knees on Gordon's neck and uses his body weight to restrict Gordon's breathing. This tactic, which falls within the broad category of a "choke hold," is extremely controversial. Some police officers apply force on the side of the neck to reduce blood flow and ideally induce unconsciousness, a technique known as a lateral neck restraint or "sleeper hold." Others apply the pressure directly to the windpipe or the back of the neck to provoke compliance. All of these tactics are dangerous, although some people believe sleeper holds are less likely to cause serious bodily injury or death.

Officer A continues to use the choke hold for approximately eight minutes, at the end of which Gordon is dead from asphyxiation. During the eight minutes, Gordon protests repeatedly "I can't breathe," calls out "Mama", and at one point says "I'm about to die." During the final minutes, Gordon is motionless and completely unresponsive. During the eight-minute period, people standing nearby shout to the officers to stop using the choke hold because of Gordon's obvious difficulty breathing. One person records the encounter on a cell phone.

Part (a) Officer A is a nineteen-year veteran of the police department. Among his duties is training cadets in the police academy and "rookie" (i.e., new and inexperienced) police officers. Is Officer A potentially liable for murder? If so, on what basis or bases?

Part (b) Officer B is a rookie police officer who has been on the police force for about a week. Officer A is one of the senior officers who trained Officer B. During the eight minutes Officer A applies the choke hold to Gordon, Officer B holds Gordon's back and asks Officer A "Should we roll him on his side?" and says "I'm worried about excited delirium or whatever." Officer A replies "That's why we have him on his stomach." Other than these statements, Officer B does nothing to assist Gordon, change his position, or reduce the force Officer A uses. Is Officer B potentially liable for murder?

Part (c) Officer C is also a rookie police officer who, like Officer B, has been on the police force for about a week. As with Officer B, Officer A is one of the senior officers who trained Officer C. During the eight minutes Officer A applies the choke hold to Gordon, Officer C holds Gordon's legs. He remains silent and does nothing to assist Gordon, change his position, or reduce the force Officer A uses. Is Officer C potentially liable for murder?

Part (d) Officer D is an experienced officer who has been on the police force for nine years. During the eight minutes Officer A applies the choke hold to Gordon, Officer D stands a few feet away from Officer A and Gordon, between them and the people on the nearby sidewalk protesting Officer A's conduct. He tells these people to keep their distance and not interfere. Officer B says nothing to Officer A and does nothing to assist Gordon, change his position, or reduce the force Officer A uses. Is Officer D potentially liable for murder?

Chapter 12

Conspiracy

A. Introduction

In this chapter, we turn to the crime of conspiracy. Like the crime of attempt, it is a form of anticipatory crime allowing the police to intervene and incapacitate criminals prior to the commission of the target offense. Unlike the crime of attempt, however, if the police are unable to intervene and prevent commission of the target crime, the prosecution in many jurisdictions can convict a defendant for both conspiracy *and* the target offense. Thus the penalty for conspiracy may be imposed as an addition to rather than a substitute for punishment for the target offense. Coconspirators in some jurisdictions can also be vicariously liable for crimes committed by other conspirators. In this way, conspiracy is similar to accomplice liability.

Prosecutors make frequent use of conspiracy because it offers several evidentiary and procedural advantages. Charging a particular act as an overt act in furtherance of a conspiracy opens the door to its admission at trial even if the rules of evidence might otherwise exclude it. Out-of-court statements made by any coconspirators during and in furtherance of a conspiracy are admissible at trial against other coconspirators despite the fact that these statements are hearsay and otherwise would be barred by the evidentiary rule against hearsay. A conspiracy charge helps justify the joint trial of coconspirators, resulting in a number of potential strategic disadvantages for defendants such as the risks of guilt by association and use of inconsistent defense strategies. A conspiracy charge gives prosecutors greater flexibility in choosing the place for trial. A conspiracy may be prosecuted either where the agreement was formed or in any place where an act in furtherance of the conspiracy took place. As a practical matter, conspiracy laws permit prosecutors to cast a wider net to sweep in low-level participants who might be willing to cooperate against "bigger fish" in the enterprise in exchange for leniency on their own charges.

Legislatures and courts also grant prosecutors and police additional leeway in the investigative techniques they may use against conspiracies. A federal case dealing with the use of wiretaps captures this idea:

> Like the Hydra of Greek mythology, the conspiracy may survive the destruction of its parts unless the conspiracy is completely destroyed. For even if some or many conspirators are imprisoned, others may remain at large, free to recruit others eager to break the law and to pursue the conspiracy's illegal

ends. Reflecting this concern, we have "consistently upheld findings of necessity where traditional investigative techniques lead only to apprehension and prosecution of the main conspirators, but not to apprehension and prosecution of ... other satellite conspirators." Because the government has a duty to extirpate conspiracy beyond its duty to prevent the mere commission of specific substantive offenses, we conclude that the government is entitled to more leeway in its investigative methods when it pursues a conspiracy. Just as the punishment should fit the crime, so too the rigor of the government's investigation should fit the threat posed to society by criminals' illicit and coordinated plans. The principle we announce here — that government has considerable latitude to wiretap suspected members of a criminal conspiracy (particularly when the conspirators are bent on the government's destruction) — reflects a larger principle of proportionality embodied in the wiretapping statute: the more grave the threat posed to our society, the greater the government's leeway in pursuing it.[1]

The crime of conspiracy is the focal point of considerable controversy. The classic justification offered for conspiracy is that by joining forces criminals pose increased danger to society. Such a combination is thought both to increase the likelihood of success and decrease the likelihood of repentance and desistance. As the quote above suggests, a conspiracy once started may live on despite the repentance of any particular conspirator.

Critics complain that the crime of conspiracy is vague and that its conduct requirement is too minimal to assure both danger and blameworthiness. Some claim that the crime of conspiracy is now unnecessary given the reach of modern attempt statutes and other anticipatory offenses. Others argue that the advantages it gives to police and prosecutors are simply unfair.

Our study of the elements of conspiracy begins with conduct. As the statutes below reflect, statutory conspiracy formulations routinely require some form of agreement to commit another crime. These statutes also reveal that jurisdictions vary on whether conspiracy requires any additional conduct beyond agreement. We then examine the mental states the government must prove to obtain a conspiracy conviction. The remainder of the chapter deals with an assortment of issues such as the scope of conspiracy and whether and how a coconspirator may terminate his association with a conspiracy.

Before turning to the individual elements of the crime of conspiracy and related issues, we consider first the highly publicized conspiracy case of Gilberto Valle. A New York City police officer, Valle went online to discuss with others his plans to kidnap, torture, kill, and cannibalize five women, including his wife. Valle was tried and convicted by a jury of conspiracy in 2013. His trial received nationwide press

---

1. *United States v. McGuire*, 307 F.3d 1192 (9th Cir. 2002).

coverage and was the subject of a documentary shown on HBO titled *Thought Crimes: The Case of the Cannibal Cop.*

The *Valle* case provides a preview of several issues you will study later in this chapter, such as the conduct and mental state elements of conspiracy and the distinction between unilateral and bilateral conspiracies. It also provides a good opportunity to review and examine in a particularly vivid context the purposes of punishment we studied in Chapter 2, *Punishment*, the line between thought and action we studied in Chapter 4, *Conduct*, and the appropriate use of and limits on anticipatory offenses we studied in Chapter 10, *Attempt*.

United States v. Valle

807 F.3d 508 (2015)
United States Court of Appeals for the Second Circuit

Parker, C.J.

This is a case about the line between fantasy and criminal intent. Although it is increasingly challenging to identify that line in the Internet age, it still exists and it must be rationally discernible in order to ensure that "a person's inclinations and fantasies are his own and beyond the reach of the government." We are loath to give the government the power to punish us for our thoughts and not our actions. That includes the power to criminalize an individual's expression of sexual fantasies, no matter how perverse or disturbing. Fantasizing about committing a crime, even a crime of violence against a real person whom you know, is not a crime.

This does not mean that fantasies are harmless. To the contrary, fantasies of violence against women are both a symptom of and a contributor to a culture of exploitation, a massive social harm that demeans women. Yet we must not forget that in a free and functioning society, not every harm is meant to be addressed with the federal criminal law. Because "[t]he link between fantasy and intent is too tenuous for fantasy [alone] to be probative," and because the remaining evidence is insufficient to prove the existence of an illegal agreement or Valle's specific intent to kidnap anyone, we affirm the district court's judgment of acquittal on the single count of conspiracy to kidnap....

Gilberto Valle is a native of Forest Hills, Queens. At the time of the events giving rise to his prosecution, he was an officer in the New York City Police Department living with his wife, Kathleen Mangan, and their infant daughter in Forest Hills. Valle has no prior criminal record and there is no evidence that he ever acted violently or threateningly towards anyone.

Valle was, however, an active member of an Internet sex fetish community called Dark Fetish Network ("DFN"). He connected with individuals around the world whom he knew only by screen names such as "Moody Blues" or "Aly Kahn," or by email addresses. Valle communicated with these individuals by email or web chat, usually in the late evening and early morning hours after his work shift. Many of his Internet communications involved the transmission of photographs of women he knew—including his wife, her colleagues from work, and some of his friends and acquaintances—to other DFN users with whom he discussed committing horrific acts of sexual violence. These "chats" consisted of gruesome and graphic descriptions of kidnapping, torturing, cooking, raping, murdering, and cannibalizing various women.

Valle's online fantasy life was, to say the least, extremely active during this period. However, there is no evidence that he ever learned the real identities of the individuals with whom he chatted, nor is there any evidence that he ever made concrete plans to meet in person or speak by telephone or web camera with any of them.

In September 2012, Mangan became concerned about Valle's late-night Internet activities after she found several disturbing images of dead women on a laptop that the couple shared. She installed spyware on the computer, which recorded each website entered by the computer's users and captured screen shots every five minutes. With the use of the spyware, Mangan found more disturbing pictures and records of websites that Valle visited. These included detailed emails and chats where Valle discussed butchering her and raping and torturing other women whom they knew. After confronting Valle about his computer use and moving out of the home with their daughter, Mangan contacted federal authorities.

Valle was subsequently arrested and charged with a single conspiracy to kidnap several of the women who were the subject of his chats. Although he had chatted with numerous individuals he met on DFN, the Government identified three alleged co-conspirators: Michael VanHise, a man from New Jersey who was known to Valle as "mikevanhise81@aol.com" and "michael19902135@yahoo.com"; an unidentified individual apparently located in Pakistan who used the screen name "Aly Khan"; and Dale Bolinger, a man in England who was known to Valle only by his screen name, "Moody Blues." And although Valle had discussed up to one hundred different women in his chats, the indictment alleged five targets of the kidnapping conspiracy: Kathleen Mangan, his wife; Alisa Friscia, Mangan's former co-worker; Andria Noble; Kristen Ponticelli; and Kimberly Sauer, a former college classmate of Valle's who was living in the Baltimore area.

... As an NYPD officer, Valle had access to the Omnixx Force Mobile ("OFM"), a computer program that allows officers to search various restricted databases, including the federal National Crime Information Center database, which contain sensitive information about individuals such as home addresses and dates of birth. It is undisputed that the NYPD's policy, known to Valle, was that these databases could only be accessed in the course of an officer's official duties and that accessing them for personal use violated Department rules. In May 2012, he accessed the OFM and searched for Maureen Hartigan, a woman he had known since high school and had discussed kidnapping with Aly Khan....

Following a 13-day trial, the jury returned a verdict of guilty.... Valle subsequently moved for a judgment of acquittal ... or, in the alternative, for a new trial....

In a thorough and thoughtful 118-page opinion, the district court (Gardephe, J.) granted Valle's Rule 29 motion with respect to the conspiracy charge.... Judge Gardephe ... concluded that, notwithstanding the jury's verdict to the contrary, the prosecutors had failed to prove beyond a reasonable doubt that Valle and his alleged co-conspirators had entered into a conspiracy to kidnap or that Valle had formed the requisite specific intent to kidnap. . . .

The Government has appealed the judgment of acquittal on the conspiracy count. . . .

To sustain a conspiracy conviction, the prosecution must prove beyond a reasonable doubt that the person charged with conspiracy knew of its existence and knowingly joined and participated in it. The Government must also prove, beyond a reasonable doubt, that the defendant possessed the specific intent to commit the offense that was the object of the conspiracy—here, kidnapping . . .

At trial, the prosecution built its case around Valle's chats and emails with his alleged co-conspirators. On appeal, it argues that these communications, "taken at face value, were fully sufficient to establish his intent to join a kidnapping conspiracy." We disagree.

. . . Valle's chats and emails with the three alleged co-conspirators were part of a much larger set of chats and emails with 24 individuals on DFN. According to the prosecution, the former were unique because they evinced "real" criminal intent while the rest did not. After reviewing the chats and emails introduced at trial, the district court concluded that the "real" and "fantasy" chats were indistinguishable.

Our review of the record yields the same conclusion. In both groups of chats, Valle transmits Facebook images of women and offers to kidnap and sell them on a "cash upon delivery" basis, and in both groups he expresses a desire to kidnap, rape, torture, and eat women whom he knows. In both groups Valle also claims to conduct surveillance of potential victims and discusses his intentions to kidnap them using chloroform and ropes. And in both groups he describes the various devices he "owns" that will assist in the process. Many of the "fantasy" chats also do not explicitly state that the participants are engaged in fantasy and are as graphic and detailed as the "real" chats. For example, the "real" chats and the "fantasy" chats both include haggling over the kidnapping fees that Valle "wanted to charge," although the prosecution argues that this haggling is unique to the "real" conspiracy with VanHise. The "real" chats thus contain the same core elements as the chats the Government concedes are "fantasy."[2]

Moreover, the "real" chats take place in the same time period as the admittedly "fantasy" chats. On the evening of July 12, 2012, for instance, Valle discusses kidnapping Andria Noble with Aly Khan in a "real" chat and, an hour later, discusses kidnapping Noble with someone else in a chat that was "fantasy." The prosecution thus proposed that Valle *simultaneously* agreed to kidnap Noble while also engaging

---

2. In a "fantasy" chat with "Tim Chase," for example, Valle and Chase agree to kidnap a woman on January 27, 2012. Valle supplies real pictures of the woman, they agree upon a price of $4,000 for Valle's services, and Valle states that the woman goes to the gym nightly and that he has kept a log of when she leaves and returns home. The two also agree upon a location "a hundred miles east of Erie" as the place of delivery. As Judge Gardephe found, there are no material differences between these chats with Chase, the fantasist, and Valle's chats with VanHise, the alleged co-conspirator.

in role-play about the same woman. This temporal proximity casts further doubt upon any rational distinction between the chats.

Even when "taken at face value," the "real" chats contain numerous other indicia of fantasy. For example, the prosecution alleged that Valle formed a genuine agreement with the specific intent to kidnap three different women in three different locations on the same day. First, Valle agreed with Aly Khan to lure Mangan to either India or Pakistan on February 20, 2012 and to slaughter her there. Second, he agreed with VanHise to kidnap Alisa Friscia in Manhattan on February 20, 2012 and deliver her to an unknown location in exchange for $4,000 in cash. Finally, Valle agreed with Aly Khan to kidnap Andria Noble on February 20, 2012 from her home in Columbus, Ohio. On appeal, the prosecution posits that the jury could have reasonably concluded that Valle seriously planned to kidnap Mangan, Friscia, *and* Noble on the same day and failed to go through with the kidnappings only because "an obstacle arose," or because he had a "fear of getting caught." We believe that no rational juror could reach this conclusion for the reason noted by Judge Gardephe: "The notion that Valle had resolved to lure Mangan to India or Pakistan [to slaughter with Aly Khan,] while at the same time kidnapping Andria Noble in Columbus, Ohio, and kidnapping Alisa Friscia from the Upper East Side of Manhattan, is simply outlandish."

In addition to plots that would put the same person in different places at the same time, the "real" chats are replete with references to fantastical elements such as a human-sized oven, a spit, and a remote cabin in the woods, none of which Valle owned or made any effort to acquire. The fantastical nature of the "real" chats is bolstered by the entirely virtual nature of the alleged conspirators' relationships. Valle had no pre-existing relationship with those with whom he chatted, and he formed no real life relationship with any of them. He did not know their real names and, indeed, could not be sure of their genders, ages, or locations. Neither he nor his alleged co-conspirators made any effort to communicate by telephone, text message, or web camera, much less meet in person. And weeks or months could go by between Valle's chats with any particular individual. While anonymity is not uncommon in Internet communications, the fantastical elements of the chats combined with the impersonal nature of the interactions provides pervasive and unmistakable indicia of deep fantasy.

Consequently, we need look no further than the prosecution's own work product to find reasonable doubt. The prosecution divided the exchanges into two groups and undertook to convince the jury to convict Valle on the theory that one group was fantasy and the other proved criminal intent. This exercise failed because the distinction the prosecution urged does not exist in this case. There is simply no material difference between the two groups of chats. We do not believe that the prosecution satisfies the proof beyond a reasonable doubt standard by relying upon a distinction that is untethered to reason or common sense....

The prosecution now urges that the distinction between "real" chats and "fantasy" role play was Valle's defense and that the district court applied the wrong standard by forcing the prosecution to disprove the defense theory of the case. As the exchanges above demonstrate, the distinction was introduced and relied on by the Government's case agent. In any event, intent is an essential element of the crime that the Government charged. The issue, therefore, is not whether the prosecution disproved *the defense*'s theory, but whether the prosecution proved *its* theory that Valle's "real" chats represented a departure from his otherwise entirely imaginary world.

Alternatively, the Government argues that even if it introduced the distinction, it did not rely on or concede the truth of the distinction because it "did not even introduce any of the 'fantasy' conversations at trial so that [a] comparison could be made" with the "real" chats. A sampling of the "fantasy" chats was introduced by the defense in its cross-examination of Agent Walsh. But regardless of how the exhibits were introduced, the Government's own investigation concluded that forty chats permitted the inference of conspiratorial intent, as compared to myriad other chats that did not. The Government claims that it does not have to prove a distinction between these two sets of chats because the jury could have rationally found that "defendants charged with attempting or conspiring to engage in criminal, deviant activity often contemporaneously engage in 'fantasy' behavior ... about activity ... that is similar to the charged conduct."

This contention proves too little. Once the Government constructs its case around the theory that a certain group of chats permits the inference of conspiratorial intent while another group of essentially similar chats is consistent with non-criminal behavior, some adequate explanation must be forthcoming. Where, as here, none is, the non-criminal chats are a powerful indicator that a reasonable juror must necessarily entertain reasonable doubt about the prosecution's case.

Unable to materially distinguish the "real" chats from the "fantasy" chats, the Government relies on evidence of "real world" steps that Valle took in order to "prepare" for the kidnappings. For example, the prosecution introduced evidence that Valle performed Internet searches for how to kidnap people, how to make chloroform, and how to restrain and cannibalize people. The prosecution also introduced evidence that Valle researched prior kidnappings, which it argues permitted the jury to infer that Valle was interested in how those kidnappers were caught so that he could learn from their experiences and avoid apprehension.

To be sure, Internet searches can provide some relevant proof of intent. However, an Internet search, in and of itself, is not criminal. Here, the searches on which the Government relies occurred in a context of deep fantasy. As with his chats and emails, Valle's Internet searches show that he was *interested* in committing acts of sexualized violence against women. Interest may be relevant evidence of intent, but it does not by itself prove intent. "No doubt some people commit sex crimes because they want to turn their fantasies into reality, but most people with criminal fantasies probably refrain from acting on them, because they know it would be wrong, or because they do not want to risk the penalties."

The Government also relies on at least two occasions when Valle engaged in acts of "surveillance" of his intended victims. First, the Government notes that Valle admitted in a post-arrest statement that he was on Friscia's block on March 1, 2012, two days after he allegedly agreed to kidnap her with VanHise. Valle told a government agent that he was on the block to drop off Mangan to have lunch with Friscia, but both Mangan and Friscia testified that they had not met for lunch that day. Valle indicated to the agent that he was on the block only very briefly, and there is no evidence to the contrary. There is also no evidence that he observed Friscia or her apartment building while he was on her block. Valle's false exculpatory explanation for being on the block is "insufficient proof on which to convict where other evidence of guilt is weak." As the district court found, no rational juror could conclude from this evidence alone that Valle was engaged in "surveillance."

Second, the prosecution and our dissenting colleague contend that the jury could convict Valle of a conspiracy to kidnap based on his communications with Moody Blues about Kimberly Sauer. This evidence is insufficient to show that Valle agreed or had the specific intent to kidnap Sauer and, in any event, it does not establish Moody Blues's intent.

Sauer is a former college classmate of Valle's who lives in Maryland. According to Sauer, she communicated with Valle by text message approximately ten to fifteen times a year. Mangan testified that she and Valle made three or four trips to Maryland during the course of their relationship (from 2009 through September 2012) and that each time she and Valle made an effort to see Sauer when in the area.

In January 2012, Valle asked Sauer for her address so that he could send her a Patrolmen's Benevolent Association card. The earliest chat between Valle and Moody Blues introduced at trial takes place seven months later, on July 9, 2012. During this conversation, Valle described several girls that he was "working on grabbing ... for thanksgiving," and told Moody Blues that "Kimberly [is] by far the easiest" to kidnap because he could "just show up at her home unannounced." After Valle suggested that "maybe you can make it here and help me with her, since you have experience," Moody Blues responded that he lives in England but it is "easy to get to the Big apple."

Valle also told Moody Blues that he was "single," had a "big gas oven," and that "no one is around [him] for about 3/4 of a mile." The two then discussed how they would truss up Sauer and cook her on an outdoor spit at Valle's mountain house. During this same chat, approximately one hour after Valle wrote that he wanted to kidnap someone for Thanksgiving, Valle told Moody Blues that he was "thinking of a Labor Day cookout ... with Kimberly as the main course." Valle noted that she had "been one of my favorite victims to fantasize about for almost 10 years now." Again during the same chat in early July, Valle sent Moody Blues a link to a video of Sauer on vacation and volunteered to make chloroform and buy rope. Moody Blues replied that "Labour day is the 3rd [of] September, not a lot of time to sort out plane tickets etc. Will see what cheap deals I can get."

One day later, on July 10, Valle sent Moody Blues "a word document, a blueprint of everything we will need to carry this out." The document, entitled "Abducting and Cooking Kimberly: A Blueprint," has a "target date" of September 2, 2012 for the abduction. It includes a photograph of Sauer, and accurately describes her age and marital status and that she is not a drug user, does not have tattoos, and drinks only occasionally. All of the other information in this document is false, including her last name, date of birth, birthplace, and educational history. The entire "plan" for abduction set out in the "Blueprint" is as follows: "I will arrive at some point Sunday night at her home to kidnap her. She lives in a quiet suburban neighborhood (Pictures of her house to be added)." The document also lists some materials that are needed, including a car, chloroform, rope, gag, tarp/plastic bags, gloves, and cheap sneakers. After receiving the "Blueprint," Moody Blues asked "[m]ay I have her address? For Googling using the Map app?" Valle lied that he was "not sure" of her exact address. There is no evidence in the record that Valle ever obtained any of the materials listed in the "Blueprint," or that the document was ever updated with pictures of Sauer's house or any additional information.

At some point prior to July 12, Valle called Sauer to tell her that he would be traveling to Maryland with his wife and daughter for a weekend. They made plans to meet for lunch on July 22. On July 17, Valle informed Moody Blues that he would be having lunch with Sauer. Later in this chat, Moody Blues asked Valle if he had a recipe for chloroform. Valle sent him a link. On July 19, Moody Blues again asked for Sauer's address, and Valle replied that he did not know it by heart. Valle never provided Moody Blues with Sauer's address.

On July 20, Valle conducted a number of Internet searches relating to kidnapping, including "how to kidnap someone," "how to chloroform a girl," and "kidnapped girl." On July 21, Valle traveled to Maryland with his wife and daughter. They visited several college friends, and had the scheduled lunch with Sauer on July 22. On July 21, Valle texted Sauer "[w]e drove by your pink building today," and she responded "Haha yay!" At trial, Sauer testified that she understood Valle to refer to her office building, which has pink-tinted windows, but that Valle had never visited her at work and she had never sent him photographs of the building. She described the lunch as "fine" and "pleasant."

On the evening of July 22, after Valle returned home, he emailed Moody Blues that Sauer "looked absolutely mouthwatering." Valle and Moody Blues said nothing more about the plot to kidnap Sauer and did not talk again for another month. On August 21, Valle and Moody Blues began to discuss Kristen Ponticelli, a recent graduate of Valle's high school whom he did not know. There is no evidence in the record that Valle and Moody Blues ever discussed Sauer or Ponticelli again after August 21.

As Judge Gardephe observed, the chats pertaining to Sauer are not materially different from the other fantasy chats. All of the elements of this alleged plot are equally fantastical, including the presence of the nonexistent mountain house, the human-sized oven, and the "Blueprint." The "plan" to kidnap Sauer in the "Blueprint" is no more detailed than is the "plan" in Valle's Internet chats with Moody Blues, nor does the list of materials required differ from the types of materials Valle discusses in his chats. And critically, Valle makes concerted efforts to conceal from Moody Blues any identifying information about Sauer that *could* be used in furtherance of a kidnapping such as her last name, date of birth, and the name of her alma mater. Although the prosecution speculates that Valle did not share accurate information about Sauer because he did not want Moody Blues to undertake the kidnapping without him, there is no evidence in the record to support such an inference.

Thus, the only meaningful difference between this alleged conspiracy and the "fantasy" chats is the occurrence of Valle's lunch with Sauer in Maryland during approximately the same time period as he discussed kidnapping her with Moody Blues. Although the Government characterizes Valle's communications with Sauer as "out of the blue," the record shows that they communicated by text message in the year prior to the alleged kidnapping plot on a regular basis and that they made an effort to see each other when Valle was in town. Valle did not have lunch with Sauer alone, but rather came with Mangan and their infant daughter. Moreover, the chats between Moody Blues and Valle leading up to and following the lunch make it impossible to conclude, without speculation, that the lunch was "surveillance" in furtherance of a genuine conspiracy. Moody Blues makes only a single reference to purchasing plane tickets in the July 9 chat, but that suggestion is never brought up again. Except for the e-mail recapping the lunch on July 22 and the August 24 conversation in which their focus moves to Ponticelli after a brief mention of Sauer, Moody Blues and Valle never again discuss Sauer or any plot to kidnap her. In fact, Moody Blues and Valle do not speak at all for the month after July 22, and the "target date" of September 2 passes with no discussion. And Valle never takes any step of any sort in furtherance of an alleged kidnapping.

We are in accord with the prosecution and our dissenting colleague that a jury might be able to distill some incriminating evidence from all of this. But "some" evidence is not the test. Because Valle's relationship with Moody Blues is essentially indistinguishable from his relationship with all of the others with whom he chatted, we agree with Judge Gardephe that a rational jury could not conclude that this evidence was sufficient to meet the "beyond any reasonable doubt" requirement....

Finally, on the basis of this evidence, it is impossible to determine beyond a reasonable doubt whether *Moody Blues*—or for that matter any of Valle's other alleged co-conspirators—ever had the specific intent to commit a kidnapping. We have taken a bilateral approach to the crime of conspiracy: at least two people must agree. "When one of two persons merely pretends to agree, the other party, whatever he may believe, is in fact not conspiring with anyone." The only evidence the Government offers to demonstrate Moody Blues's intent is the words he used in the chats. As we have explained, these chats of "real" criminal intent are rife with indicia of fantasy and contain the same substantive elements as the chats the Government concedes are "fantasy." The conclusion that the chats do not support a finding of Valle's conspiratorial intent applies with equal force to Moody Blues.

On this record, no reasonable juror could conclude beyond a reasonable doubt that Valle possessed the specific intent to kidnap anyone or that he and his alleged co-conspirators ever formed an agreement to actually carry out any of the purported kidnappings. The mere indulgence of fantasy, even of the repugnant and unsettling kind here, is not, without more, criminal. We therefore affirm the district court's judgment of acquittal as to the conspiracy count....

For these reasons, we affirm the judgment of acquittal as to the count of conspiracy to kidnap.

Discussion Questions

1. Based on the purposes of punishment you studied in Chapter 2, do you think Valle should have been subjected to conviction and punishment? Was he blameworthy? Was he dangerous? Are others such as him deterrable? Should he be incapacitated? If so, should that incapacitation take the form of a civil commitment procedure?

2. Could Valle have been held liable for attempt to kidnap? Attempt to conspire?

3. Judge Parker describes Valle's chats as having taken place in an "entirely imaginary world." Do you agree? What parts do you consider "imaginary" and what parts "real"?

4. Where and how should the line be drawn between "fantasy" and "real crime"? Between "thought" and "action"? Did Valle cross the line between fantasy and reality when he:

- Used real women as the subjects of his online conversations and planning?
- Transmitted photos of real women to others on the Internet?
- Conducted online searches on how to kidnap people and make chloroform?

What if Valle conducted actual surveillance of the women at issue? What if he had disclosed to others on the Internet their home and work addresses? The routes they followed to and from work? What if Valle told others on the Internet that his plans were real and not just fantasy? Would such statements prove that his plans were real? Or could such a statement be seen as simply another part of a fantasy?

5. After Valle's arrest, U.S. Attorney Preet Bharara, whose office prosecuted Valle, was quoted as saying "This case is all the more disturbing when you consider Valle's position as a New York City police officer and his sworn duty to serve and protect." Was Valle's status as a police officer significant in assessing his blameworthiness? His danger? Should someone who is a police officer be held to more demanding standards than other citizens when it comes to participation in disturbing Internet activity such as Valle's? Or should the stress of life as a police officer to some extent mitigate his culpability?

6. When there is conflicting evidence about whether a certain scheme is fantasy or real, what should trial and appellate judges do? Leave such cases to the jury to decide which inference is more credible because jurors are considered the ultimate arbiters of fact issues? Or take the issue away from the jury on the ground that the evidence is too weak to support a jury verdict of conviction?

Problem

12.1 What are the elements the government must prove to obtain a conspiracy conviction under the following statutes? What features do these statutes share with each other and with the elements of conspiracy applied in the *Valle* case? How do they differ?

Illinois Compiled Statutes

§ 720 ILCS 5/8-2 Conspiracy

(a) Elements of the offense. A person commits conspiracy when, with intent that an offense be committed, he agrees with another to the commission of that offense. No person may be convicted of conspiracy to commit an offense unless an act in furtherance of such agreement is alleged and proved to have been committed by him or by a co-conspirator.

Model Penal Code

§ 5.03 Criminal Conspiracy

(1) Definition of Conspiracy. A person is guilty of conspiracy with another person or persons to commit a crime if with the purpose of promoting or facilitating its commission he:

  (a) agrees with such other person or persons that they or one or more of them will engage in conduct that constitutes such crime or an attempt or solicitation to commit such crime; or

  (b) agrees to aid such other person or persons in the planning or commission of such crime or of an attempt or solicitation to commit such crime.

…

(5) Overt Act. No person may be convicted of conspiracy to commit a crime, other than a felony of the first or second degree, unless an overt act in pursuance of such conspiracy is alleged and proved to have been done by him or by a person with whom he conspired.

Ohio Revised Code

§ 2923.01 Conspiracy

(A) No person, with purpose to commit or to promote or facilitate the commission of [certain enumerated crimes] … shall do either of the following:

  (1) With another person or persons, plan or aid in planning the commission of any of the specified offenses;

  (2) Agree with another person or persons that one or more of them will engage in conduct that facilitates the commission of any of the specified offenses.

(B) No person shall be convicted of conspiracy unless a substantial overt act in furtherance of the conspiracy is alleged and proved to have been done by the accused or a person with whom the accused conspired, subsequent to the accused's entrance into the conspiracy. For purposes of this section, an overt act is substantial when it is of a character that manifests a purpose on the part of the actor that the object of the conspiracy should be completed.

North Dakota Code

§ 12.1-06-04 Criminal conspiracy

1. A person commits conspiracy if he agrees with one or more persons to engage in or cause conduct which, in fact, constitutes an offense or offenses, and any one or more of such persons does an overt act to effect an objective of the conspiracy. The agreement need not be explicit but may be implicit in the fact of collaboration or existence of other circumstances.

B. Conduct

1. Agreement

It is sometimes said that the essence of conspiracy, a word derived from a Latin verb meaning "to breathe together," is agreement. This seems simple enough. But what does it mean to *agree to commit a crime*? Need the agreement be explicit? Or will an implicit agreement suffice? As one might expect, agreements to commit crimes, unlike commercial contracts, are not typically committed to writing and usually are kept secret. How, then, do prosecutors prove and judges and juries decide whether an agreement existed? Such questions are not easily answered.

Problems

12.2 You are defense counsel representing Shawn, a young man charged with first degree murder. Your conversations with Shawn and the discovery provided by the prosecutor reveal the following. On the evening in question, Shawn was driving in his car with two friends, Terry and James. Terry, who was seated in the passenger's seat, recognized the driver of a nearby pickup truck as Marcus, a man with whom Terry had been feuding for the past several months over a woman each had dated. Terry told Shawn to follow the truck and Shawn did so. Shawn was aware of the feud between Terry and Marcus and also knew that Terry was usually armed. After several minutes of pursuit, the truck turned into an alley and Shawn pulled his car in behind it. Marcus stepped out of his truck and started walking toward Shawn's car. Terry in the meantime rolled down the passenger's window in Shawn's car. Terry pulled a 9-millimeter pistol out of his pocket, leaned out the window, and fired several shots at Marcus, striking him several times and killing him. Shawn then drove away from the scene of the shooting with both Terry and James still in the car. James, who was seated in the back seat throughout the incident, has agreed to testify for the prosecution.

The prosecution offers to dismiss the first degree murder charge in return for Shawn's guilty plea to a charge of conspiracy to commit murder. Is Shawn liable for conspiracy under the facts given? How would you advise him regarding the plea offer?

12.3 Part (a) Anna is married to Tim. Her brother, Frank, lives with Anna and Tim. Anna has two young children by her prior marriage to Lee. Anna divorced Lee several years ago and Lee was awarded primary physical custody of the children. Anna has visitation rights on alternate weekends. Custody and visitation have been ongoing sources of tension and conflict between Lee and Anna. Anna wants to see the children more often and is trying through her lawyer to obtain joint custody. Lee did not want a divorce from Anna and has been resisting her desire for greater access to the children. On several occasions, Lee has offered Anna greater access to the children in return for having sexual relations with him. Frank is close to Anna's children. He also knows of the attempts Lee has made to use access to the children to pressure Anna to have sexual relations with him. One evening after Anna and Lee argue on the phone about an upcoming visit with the children, Anna is visibly upset. She, Frank, and Tim are sitting in the kitchen of their house, when Frank says "I have an idea about how to take care of Lee." When Tim asks what his idea is, Frank says "Anna should call Lee on the phone, tell him that she has gotten separated from Tim, and that she wants Lee to come over. Then Anna should leave the house. When Lee gets here, I'll kill him." Neither Anna nor Tim says anything in response to Frank's proposal. Is either Anna or Tim liable for conspiracy to murder Lee?

Part (b) Would Anna or Tim's liability change given the following additional facts? If so, which do you find significant? About 10 days after Frank described his idea, Anna and Tim go away on an overnight camping trip. While they are away, Lee goes to their house, where Frank kills him. When Anna and Tim return, they help Frank place Lee's body in a 55-gallon steel drum and hide it in a ravine in a remote area. Police later determine that on the day before Anna and Tim left on their camping trip, someone made a phone call from their house to Lee's house. The police cannot determine who the caller was.

12.4 Members of two rival gangs, the Sharks and the Jets, attend a high school dance. At the dance, Tony, a member of the Jets, dances with Maria, the sister of the leader of the Sharks. The Sharks take offense and make insulting comments toward various Jets, who respond in kind. The confrontation quickly escalates and several members of the Jets draw knives and assault a number of Sharks, causing serious injuries. On these facts, can the Jets who attacked the Sharks be convicted of conspiracy to commit aggravated assault?

Martinez v. Wyoming

943 P.2d 1178 (1997)
Supreme Court of Wyoming

Macy, J.

Appellant Ben Martinez appeals from the judgment and sentence which the trial court entered after a jury found that he was guilty of conspiring to deliver a controlled substance and attempting to deliver a controlled substance....

At 5:00 a.m. on September 1, 1995, a confidential informant for the Division of Criminal Investigation (DCI) contacted Martinez, seeking to buy morphine. The informant was wearing a wire and was under surveillance at that time. Due to the early hour, Martinez told the informant that he would contact her between 8:30 and 9:00 a.m. and that he could get her five to ten vials of morphine for $200 each. When Martinez telephoned the informant at her home later that morning, DCI agents tape recorded the conversation.

After being again fitted with a wire monitor and being given $1,000 in recorded buy money, the informant drove to Martinez's home. Martinez got into the informant's vehicle, and they left to go meet Martinez's source. While they were en route, Martinez asked the informant to pull into a grocery store parking lot so that he could call his source to make sure that he was still at the agreed upon meeting place. When Martinez returned to the car, he told the informant that his source was "jittery" but that he thought he could still get five vials of morphine. The informant drove a short distance further before Martinez had her stop at a convenience store so that he could make another telephone call to his source. When Martinez returned to the car, he acted "jittery" and told the informant that he had to meet his source alone. He left in the informant's car with the buy money and returned approximately twenty minutes later. At that time, he told the informant that DCI agents had followed him and that he had decided not to go to his source's house. He went inside the convenience store where he again called his source. While Martinez was talking on the telephone, DCI agents entered the store and arrested him....

A jury found that Martinez was guilty of conspiring to deliver a controlled substance.... The trial court sentenced him to serve ... not less than four years nor more than eight years for the conspiracy conviction....

Martinez contends that the evidence which was produced at the trial was not sufficient to prove all the elements which were necessary to convict him of conspiring to deliver a controlled substance....

W.S. 35-7-1042 provides in part:

> Any person who attempts or conspires to commit any offense under this article within the state of Wyoming ... shall be punished by imprisonment or fine or both which may not exceed the maximum punishment prescribed

for the offense the commission of which was the object of the attempt or conspiracy ...

For a conspiracy-to-deliver-a-controlled-substance conviction to be sustained, the evidence must show beyond a reasonable doubt that the parties to the conspiracy voluntarily agreed to commit an offense under the Wyoming Controlled Substances Act of 1971. The existence of an agreement may be established in whole or in part by circumstantial evidence, and it is not necessary to demonstrate that the conspirators performed an overt act to complete the agreement's objective.

In *Smith v. State*, 902 P.2d 1271 (Wyo. 1995), we considered what type of agreement was necessary for a conspiracy to exist.

> "One might suppose that the agreement necessary for conspiracy is essentially like the agreement or 'meeting of the minds' which is critical to a contract, but this is not the case. Although there continues to exist some uncertainty as to the precise meaning of the word in the context of conspiracy, it is clear that the definition in this setting is somewhat more lax than elsewhere. A mere tacit understanding will suffice, and there need not be any written statement or even a speaking of words which expressly communicates agreement....

> "Because most conspiracies are clandestine in nature, the prosecution is seldom able to present direct evidence of the agreement. Courts have been sympathetic to this problem, and it is thus well established that the prosecution may 'rely on inferences drawn from the course of conduct of the alleged conspirators.'"

902 P.2d at 1281–82 (quoting Wayne R. LaFave & Austin W. Scott, Jr., Criminal Law at 460–61 (1972)).

The informant in this case testified that Martinez agreed to procure five to ten vials of morphine for her but that he had to get it from his source. She also explained in detail how Martinez called his source at different times while they were on their way to the source's house. Additionally, the jury heard a recording which had been made of the discussions that occurred between the informant and Martinez throughout the course of this transaction. The recording allowed the jury to hear Martinez making a deal with the informant to get morphine for her from another source. The deal specified the price for, as well as the amount of, morphine which was available. Furthermore, Martinez told DCI agents that he was on his way to get the morphine but that he changed his mind when he discovered he was being followed. He also informed them that he had received the buy money from the informant.

This evidence demonstrated that Martinez was planning to purchase morphine from his source and to deliver it to the informant. We hold, after reviewing the evidence in the light most favorable to the State, that the jury had sufficient evidence before it to conclude beyond a reasonable doubt that Martinez had an agreement with another person to violate the controlled substances act....

Affirmed.

Discussion Questions

1. With whom did Martinez agree? The informant? His source? Both?

2. Was the agreement in the *Martinez* case explicit or implicit? What evidence did the prosecution offer to prove the agreement?

3. How does the agreement needed for a conspiracy differ from the agreement needed for a contract?

4. Should it make a difference if one of the parties to the agreement on which a conspiracy charge is based is an informant working for the police? Can someone working for the government to foil a conspiracy's objective be considered a party to that conspiracy?

2. Bilateral versus Unilateral

Judge Parker in the *Valle* case stated that the Second Circuit uses a "bilateral" approach to conspiracy. In a bilateral conspiracy, at least two (and possibly more) people intend for the target offense to be committed. In *Valle*, then, the prosecution needed to prove that both Valle and at least one of the people with whom he "chatted" on the Internet intended to commit the target offense of kidnapping.

What if two people discuss the possibility of committing a crime and both say they agree to commit the crime, but only one sincerely commits to the criminal venture? The other person, perhaps a police officer or an informant working for the police, merely pretends to go along. Does this fall within the meaning of the word "agrees"? This factual scenario is referred to as a "unilateral" conspiracy because only one person intends for the target offense to be committed. Which approach gives the police greater power to interdict and incapacitate dangerous individuals?

Jurisdictions are split on whether they adopt a bilateral or unilateral approach to conspiracy. As exemplified in *Valle*, federal courts use a bilateral approach as did the common law. The Model Penal Code, though, uses the unilateral approach. Influenced by the Model Penal Code, a number of state legislatures have adopted the unilateral approach in drafting modern conspiracy statutes.

Problem

12.5 Does the following statute reflect use of a unilateral or bilateral approach to conspiracy?

13 Vermont Statutes Annotated

§ 1404 Conspiracy

(a) A person is guilty of conspiracy if, with the purpose that an offense ... be committed, that person agrees with one or more persons to commit or cause the commission of that offense, and at least two of the co-conspirators are persons who are neither law enforcement officials acting in official capacity nor persons acting in cooperation with a law enforcement official.

Problem

12.6 James approached Matthew in a bar one night and asked if he was interested in making some money. James proposed that together they rob an elderly man who keeps money and valuables at his home. Matthew told James he was interested but did so only to learn the details of James's plan so he could report him to the police. James then confided to Matthew the details of his plan for the robbery, which was to take place the following night. Immediately after they parted company, Matthew called the police and told them of James's plan. Following police instructions, Matthew met James the next evening and proceeded to the elderly gentleman's home. As they approached the home, James was arrested and charged with conspiracy to commit burglary and robbery. Is James liable for conspiracy?

Washington v. Pacheco

125 Wash. 2d 150 (1994)
Washington Supreme Court (en banc)

Johnson, J.

The Defendant, Herbert Pacheco, appeals his convictions for conspiracy to commit first degree murder and conspiracy to deliver a controlled substance. He contends he did not commit conspiracy within the meaning of RCW 9A.28.040 because no genuine agreement existed between him and his sole coconspirator, an undercover police agent. We hold RCW 9A.28.040 and RCW 69.50.407 require an actual agreement between two coconspirators, and, therefore, reverse his convictions for conspiracy to commit murder in the first degree and conspiracy to deliver a controlled substance.

Herbert Pacheco met Thomas Dillon in 1985, when Pacheco worked about 2 months for Dillon's private investigation firm. Pacheco bragged to Dillon about his involvement in illegal activities, including enforcement, collecting debts, procuring weapons, providing protection, and performing "hits."

In 1989, Dillon learned that Pacheco was a Clark County deputy sheriff. Dillon contacted the FBI and volunteered to inform on Pacheco. The FBI began an investigation of Pacheco. The Clark County Sheriff's office joined, and later directed the investigation.

The investigation involved the recording of conversations, face-to-face and over the telephone, between Dillon and Pacheco. During these conversations Dillon asked Pacheco to perform various jobs, including collections and information checks on individuals.

On March 26, 1990, according to a plan designed by the sheriff's office and the FBI, Dillon called Pacheco and told him he would like to meet to discuss a possible deal. Dillon and Pacheco met at a restaurant. Dillon said he had ties to the "Mafia" and offered Pacheco $500 in exchange for protection during a cocaine deal. Dillon told Pacheco that a buyer (an undercover FBI agent) would arrive shortly, and Pacheco was to protect Dillon during the transaction. Pacheco agreed. The undercover agent arrived and the purported drug transaction took place. Afterward, Dillon paid Pacheco $500.

The same scenario was replayed at a second purported drug transaction on April 2, 1990. Dillon again paid Pacheco $500. Later that night Dillon called Pacheco and pretended he had been shortchanged $40,000 in that afternoon's drug transaction. Dillon said he had been given $10,000 by his superiors to take care of the situation. Dillon agreed to meet Pacheco at a convenience store. At the store, Pacheco offered to kill the drug buyer for $10,000. Pacheco indicated if he had to kill anyone else, it would cost more. Pacheco proposed he go get his gun while Dillon located the drug buyer at his motel.

Dillon and Pacheco met at a lounge near the motel. They decided Pacheco would go to the lobby of the motel, call the buyer and convince him to come down to the lobby where Pacheco would then shoot him. Pacheco went to the lobby with a loaded gun, but he did not call the buyer's room. As Pacheco left the lobby, sheriff's deputies arrested him. Pacheco contended he was collecting evidence to build a case against Dillon and he thought he was following police procedures.

Pacheco was charged with conspiracy to commit first degree murder, attempted first degree murder, two counts of unlawful delivery of a controlled substance, two counts of conspiracy to deliver a controlled substance, and official misconduct. The official misconduct charge was dismissed. The jury found Pacheco not guilty of attempted first degree murder, but convicted him on all other counts.

The Court of Appeals affirmed the convictions. We accepted review of the conspiracy convictions, limited to the issue of whether a conspiracy exists when the sole coconspirator is an undercover agent.

The Defendant contends he did not commit conspiracy within the meaning of RCW 9A.28.040 because his sole coconspirator was an undercover police agent who never "agreed" to commit the crime of murder in the first degree.

The Defendant argues the statute retains the common law, bilateral approach to conspiracy, which requires an actual agreement to commit a crime between the defendant and at least one other. Therefore, a government agent feigning agreement with the defendant does not constitute a conspiracy under the common law approach because no genuine agreement is reached. The Defendant asserts Washington is among those states whose statutes are patterned after the Model Penal Code but have been interpreted as adopting only a limited form of the code's unilateral approach, and retaining the requirement of a bilateral underlying agreement.

The State contends RCW 9A.28.040 follows the code's purely unilateral approach. Under the code, actual agreement is not required as long as the defendant believes another is agreeing to commit the criminal act. Therefore, a purported agreement between a government agent and a defendant would satisfy the code's unilateral conspiratorial agreement approach.

Adopted in 1975, as a part of the overhaul of the criminal code § RCW 9A.28.040 provides in part:

> (1) A person is guilty of criminal conspiracy when, with intent that conduct constituting a crime be performed, he agrees with one or more persons to engage in or cause the performance of such conduct, and any one of them takes a substantial step in pursuance of such agreement.
>
> (2) It shall not be a defense to criminal conspiracy that the person or persons with whom the accused is alleged to have conspired:
>
> > (a) Has not been prosecuted or convicted; or
> >
> > (b) Has been convicted of a different offense; or
> >
> > (c) Is not amenable to justice; or
> >
> > (d) Has been acquitted; or
> >
> > (e) Lacked the capacity to commit an offense.

In construing a statute, our primary objective is to carry out the intent of the Legislature. When a term is not defined in a statute, the court may look to common law or a dictionary for the definition. As a general rule, we presume the Legislature intended undefined words to mean what they did at common law.

Subsection (1) of RCW 9A.28.040 expressly requires an agreement, but does not define the term. Black's Law Dictionary defines agreement as, "[a] meeting of two or more minds; a coming together in opinion or determination; the coming together in accord of two minds on a given proposition." Similarly, agreement is defined in Webster's as "1 a: the act of agreeing or coming to a mutual agreement ... b: oneness of opinion...." Webster's Third New International Dictionary 43 (1986). The dictionary definitions thus support the Defendant's argument.

Likewise, the common law definition of the agreement required for a conspiracy is defined not in unilateral terms but rather as a confederation or combination of minds. A conspiratorial agreement necessarily requires more than one to agree because it is impossible to conspire with oneself. We conclude that by requiring an agreement, the Legislature intended to retain the requirement of a genuine or bilateral agreement.

Subsection (2) provides the conspiratorial agreement may still be found even though the coconspirator cannot be convicted. In this sense, the statute incorporates a limited form of the code's unilateral conspiracy in that it is no longer necessary that agreement be proved against both conspirators. Thus, under subsection (2)'s unilateral approach, the failure to convict an accused's sole coconspirator will not prevent proof of the conspiratorial agreement against the accused. However, this does not indicate the Legislature intended to abandon the traditional requirement of two criminal participants reaching an underlying agreement.

Our case law supports this interpretation of RCW 9A.28.040. In *State v. Valladares*, two codefendants were charged with conspiracy to deliver cocaine. In a joint trial, one defendant was acquitted and the other, Valladares, was found guilty.

On appeal, the court held acquittal of Valladares' only alleged coconspirator mandated reversal of Valladares' conviction because the two outcomes were logically inconsistent. The inconsistent verdicts to the charge of conspiracy in the same trial nullified the possibility that the two coconspirators reached an agreement, a necessary element of the conspiracy. We said:

> RCW 9A.28.040(2)(d) provides that it shall not be a defense to a charge of criminal conspiracy that the person with whom the accused is alleged to have conspired has been acquitted. In this regard, the Washington Legislature appears to have adopted a unilateral approach to conspiracy by focusing on the culpability of the individual actor. At the same time, however, RCW 9A.28.040(1) makes an agreement with one or more persons a necessary element of the crime of conspiracy.

Valladares thus makes clear the Legislature adopted the unilateral approach to the limited extent set out in RCW 9A.28.040(2). However, the element of the "requisite corrupt agreement", or the bilateral agreement, is still necessary as set out in RCW 9A.28.040(1). Indeed, the essence of a conspiracy is the agreement to commit a crime. We will not presume the Legislature intended to overturn this long-established legal principle unless that intention is made very clear.

Additionally, the unilateral approach fails to carry out the primary purpose of the statute. The primary reason for making conspiracy a separate offense from the substantive crime is the increased danger to society posed by group criminal activity. However, the increased danger is nonexistent when a person "conspires" with a government agent who pretends agreement. In the feigned conspiracy there is no increased chance the criminal enterprise will succeed, no continuing criminal enterprise, no educating in criminal practices, and no greater difficulty of detection.

Indeed, it is questionable whether the unilateral conspiracy punishes criminal activity or merely criminal intentions. The "agreement" in a unilateral conspiracy is a legal fiction, a technical way of transforming nonconspiratorial conduct into a prohibited conspiracy. When one party merely pretends to agree, the other party, whatever he or she may believe about the pretender, is in fact not conspiring with anyone. Although the deluded party has the requisite criminal intent, there has been no criminal act.

The federal courts agree. In *Sears v. United States*, 343 F.2d 139, 142 (5th Cir. 1965), the Court of Appeals established the rule that "as it takes two to conspire, there can be no indictable conspiracy with a government informer who secretly intends to frustrate the conspiracy." Every federal court which has since considered the issue has adopted this approach.

Another concern with the unilateral approach is its potential for abuse. In a unilateral conspiracy, the State not only plays an active role in creating the offense, but also becomes the chief witness in proving the crime at trial. We agree with the Ninth Circuit this has the potential to put the State in the improper position of manufacturing crime. At the same time, such reaching is unnecessary because the punishable conduct in a unilateral conspiracy will almost always satisfy the elements of either solicitation or attempt. The State will still be able to thwart the activity and punish the defendant who attempts agreement with an undercover police officer....

In sum, the State has not persuaded us the Legislature intended to abandon the traditional requirement of an actual agreement. We hold RCW 9A.28.040 and RCW 69.50.407 require the defendant to reach a genuine agreement with at least one other coconspirator. The Defendant's convictions for conspiracy to commit murder in the first degree and conspiracy to deliver a controlled substance are reversed.

Durham, J. (dissenting). The jury found that Herbert Pacheco, an aspiring hit man, planned a murder for money. Moreover, he took a substantial step toward that objective. Yet the majority overturns his conviction for conspiracy to commit murder solely because he conspired with a government agent rather than with another hit man. The Washington conspiracy statute does not require a co-conspirator to be a nongovernment actor. In fact, the statute explicitly envisages so-called unilateral conspiracies, as the majority admits. Because neither our case law, the statute, nor the rationale of conspiracy crimes compel the result arrived at by the majority, I dissent.

We accepted review solely to determine whether Washington's conspiracy statute countenances unilateral conspiracies. Yet the majority fails to provide even a cursory analysis of the essential differences between the bilateral and unilateral approaches to conspiracy. The bilateral approach asks whether there is an agreement between two or more persons to commit a criminal act. Its focus is on the content of the agreement and whether there is a shared understanding between the conspirators. The unilateral approach is not concerned with the content of the agreement or whether there is a meeting of minds. Its sole concern is whether the agreement, shared or not, objectively manifests the criminal intent of at least one of the conspirators. The majority does not even mention this crucial difference, and instead merely assumes that all conspiracies must be bilateral. In other words, the majority assumes precisely what it is supposed to prove; it begs the question.

The result is a tangle of inaccuracies. First, the majority repeatedly contends that our decision in *State v. Valladares* either adopted or supports the bilateral theory of conspiracies. That is not true. In fact, *Valladares* explicitly reserved the question. ("We need not decide here what result might have been reached had" the defendant been charged with conspiring with two government agents.) *Valladares* decided only that, in a joint trial of co-conspirators, the jury verdict is inconsistent if one defendant is convicted of conspiracy while "his alleged coconspirator has been found not to have entered into any alleged agreement and no conspiracy with an unnamed coconspirator has been alleged." *Valladares* is about jury verdict consistency. The closest *Valladares* comes to commenting on the conspiracy statute itself is to note that "the Washington Legislature appears to have adopted a unilateral approach to conspiracy by focusing on the culpability of the individual actor."

Next, the majority portrays the unilateral approach to conspiracy as an outdated relic from a bygone era. The Model Penal Code endorses unilateral conspiracies, the majority admits, but "every federal court, which has since considered the issue" has adopted the bilateral approach. The majority neglects to mention that all the federal courts adopting bilateral conspiracy are construing a different statute, one whose language requires bilateral conspiracies. See 18 U.S.C. § 371 ("If two or more persons conspire ... to commit any offense against the United States"). In contrast, the Model Penal Code defines conspiracy "in terms of one person's agreeing with another, rather than in terms of an agreement among or between two or more people."

The code embodies a significant change in emphasis. In its view, the major basis of conspiratorial liability is not the group nature of the activity but the firm purpose of an individual to commit a crime which is objectively manifested in conspiring. *See* Model Penal Code § 5.03(1) cmt. at 104–05 (Tentative Draft No. 10, 1960). The Washington conspiracy statute tracks the Model Penal Code's language rather than the "two or more persons" language of the general federal conspiracy statute. In any event, far from being antiquated or obsolete, the "movement toward a unilateral theory of the crime is the modern trend in conspiracy law."

A comparison of the revised Washington conspiracy statute with its predecessor is far more revealing of legislative intent than the majority's simplistic and premature resort to dictionary definitions.[2] The predecessor statute used the phrase "whenever two or more persons shall conspire," which parallels the federal conspiracy statute and clearly requires bilateral conspiracy. Former RCW 9.22.010 (repealed in 1975). The revised statute, in contrast, tracks the definitional language of the Model Penal Code, which adopts unilateral conspiracy.[3]

---

2. The majority relies on a vague definition from Black's Law Dictionary of "agreement" as "[a] meeting of two or more minds" ... that is equally applicable to conspiracies and contracts. Not only does this ignore the far more relevant question of the actual changes in the sequence of statutes, it also disregards the crucial differences between a conspiracy and a contract. 2 Wayne R. LaFave & Austin W. Scott, Jr., Substantive Criminal Law § 6.4, at 71 (1986) ("One might suppose that the agreement necessary for conspiracy is essentially like the agreement or 'meeting of the minds' which is critical to a contract, but this is not the case.").

3. As the code's commentary states, the new definition "departs from the traditional view of conspiracy as an entirely bilateral or multilateral relationship, the view inherent in the standard formulation cast in terms of 'two or more persons' agreeing or combining to commit a crime. Attention is directed instead to each individual's culpability by framing the definition in terms of the conduct which suffices to establish the liability of any given actor, rather than the conduct of a group of which he is charged to be a part". Model Penal Code § 5.03(1) cmt. at 104–05 (Tentative Draft No. 10, 1960).

Under a unilateral formulation, the crime of conspiracy is committed when a person agrees to proceed in a prohibited manner; under a bilateral formulation, the crime of conspiracy is committed when two or more persons agree to proceed in such manner. The contrast between the prior and the present statute is clear, precise, and determinative.

Next, the majority constructs a straw man by claiming that the primary purpose of conspiracy is "the increased danger to society posed by group criminal activity." Preventing group criminal activity is the rationale behind bilateral conspiracy, but that rationale was decisively rejected by the Model Penal Code. At best, controlling group criminal activity is only one rationale for conspiracy statutes.

A bilateral theory of conspiracy and the rigid standard of mutuality that it demands … are inconsistent with the recognition of an independent rationale for conspiracy law based on a conspirator's firm expectation of committing a crime.

The majority compounds its own confusion by contending that unilateral conspiracies are factually impossible and therefore presumptively invalid. ("When one party merely pretends to agree, the other party, whatever he or she may believe about the pretender, is in fact not conspiring with anyone."). This argument amounts to the truism that it is factually impossible to have a "meeting of minds" on the commission of a future crime if one of the minds is a government agent who does not intend to commit the criminal act. However, a "meeting of minds" is not a prerequisite of unilateral conspiracy. In any event, factual impossibility is not a recognized defense. See 2 Wayne R. LaFave & Austin W. Scott, Jr., Substantive Criminal Law §6.3(2), at 42 (1986). The majority does nothing more than restate the discredited assumption that all conspiracies must be bilateral because conspiracy statutes attempt to target only group criminal activity.

Finally, I share the majority's concern about the potential for abuse of unilateral conspiracy. However, the majority fails to take into consideration the effect of the entrapment defense. The potential for abuse is further restricted by the statute itself, which requires not only an agreement to engage in criminal conduct but also "a substantial step in pursuance of such agreement." RCW 9A. 28.040(1). In the end, the majority succeeds only in providing a superfluous protection to criminal defendants at the price of hamstringing government attempts to nip criminal acts in the bud.

Problem

12.7 After the *Pacheco* case, the Washington legislature amended the Washington conspiracy statute. Here is the amended statute:

Revised Code of Washington § 9A.28.040 Criminal conspiracy

(1) A person is guilty of criminal conspiracy when, with intent that conduct constituting a crime be performed, he or she agrees with one or more persons to en-

gage in or cause the performance of such conduct, and any one of them takes a substantial step in pursuance of such agreement.

(2) It shall not be a defense to criminal conspiracy that the person or persons with whom the accused is alleged to have conspired:

    (a) Has not been prosecuted or convicted; or

    (b) Has been convicted of a different offense; or

    (c) Is not amenable to justice; or

    (d) Has been acquitted; or

    (e) Lacked the capacity to commit an offense; or

    (f) Is a law enforcement officer or other government agent who did not intend that a crime be committed.

Does the amended statute adopt a bilateral or unilateral approach? What language in the amended statute indicates which approach the legislature adopted?

Discussion Questions

1. Which is the better approach to conspiracy, unilateral or bilateral?

2. Which is more compatible with the word "agree"—the unilateral approach or the bilateral approach? Should legislatures use a word other than "agree" if they wish to penalize conduct such as Pacheco's?

3. Is it possible for someone to be criminally liable for an attempt to conspire?

3. Overt Act

Problem

12.8 What does each of the following conspiracy statutes require in terms of conduct? Do these statutes differ from the statutes that appear after Problem 12.1 in terms of conduct?

New Mexico Statutes Annotated

Section 30-28-2. Conspiracy

A. Conspiracy consists of knowingly combining with another for the purpose of committing a felony within or without this state.

Utah Code Annotated

Section 76-4-201. Conspiracy — Elements

For purposes of this part a person is guilty of conspiracy when he, intending that conduct constituting a crime be performed, agrees with one or more persons to engage in or cause the performance of the conduct and any one of them commits an overt act in pursuance of the conspiracy, except where the offense is a capital felony, a felony against the person, arson, burglary, or robbery, the overt act is not required for the commission of conspiracy.

Maine Criminal Code

§ 151 Conspiracy

1. A person is guilty of conspiracy if, with the intent that conduct be performed which, in fact, would constitute a crime or crimes, he agrees with one or more others to engage in or cause the performance of such conduct.

...

4. No person may be convicted of conspiracy to commit a crime unless it is alleged and proved that he, or one with whom he conspired, took a substantial step toward commission of the crime. A substantial step is any conduct which, under the circumstances in which it occurs, is strongly corroborative of the firmness of the actor's intent to complete commission of the crime; provided that speech alone may not constitute a substantial step.

State v. Dent

123 Wash. 2d 467 (1994)

Supreme Court of Washington (en banc)

Brachtenbach, J.

Defendants Dent and Balcinde were charged with conspiracy to commit first degree murder. Both defendants were convicted at a joint trial. [Both defendants raised the issue of] how the jury should be instructed as to the meaning of the "substantial step" element of a conspiracy....

Roland C. Dent and Carlos A. Balcinde were charged with conspiring to murder Dent's former girlfriend, Ann Powell. In late 1989 and early 1990, while on parole from an earlier conviction, Dent had a relationship with Powell. On February 22, 1990, Dent's parole was revoked based on an accusation made by Powell to Dent's parole officer that Dent had assaulted her. Following Powell's accusation, Dent was initially incarcerated in the King County Jail. Balcinde was also in the King County Jail at that time. It was during this time, when the codefendants were both in the King County Jail, that the conspiracy is alleged to have been formed. On February 23, 1990, Dent was transferred to the Shelton Corrections Center.

After his transfer, Dent contacted his then girlfriend, Joyful Tryon, to seek her help in communicating with Balcinde to advance the murder plan. Through numerous phone calls and letters, he asked her to (1) forward letters from Dent to Balcinde using a different or false return address; (2) give her handgun to Balcinde upon his release, after removing the serial number and reporting it stolen; (3) set aside $300 to $400 to pay Balcinde; (4) pick Balcinde up from the King County Jail upon his release; (5) show Balcinde a videotape from which he could identify Powell; and (6) show Balcinde where Powell was then residing. In one telephone conversation, Tryon asked what the gun was for, and Dent told her that "it was gonna [*sic*] be used for Ann [Powell]." During the time between Dent's transfer to the Shelton facility and Balcinde's release, Tryon and her sons also received phone calls from Balcinde.

During the time Tryon was receiving communications from codefendants, her sons became concerned that Dent was trying to involve her in some type of illegal activity. After they persuaded her to tell them what was being planned, they went to the police. After meeting with the police, Tryon agreed to cooperate with the police. With Tryon's cooperation, the investigating officers recorded a call from Dent to Tryon on March 15, 1990, pursuant to an order authorizing intercept. During the conversation, Tryon asked Dent if it was necessary to go through with "[p]utting [Powell] in the ground." Defendant Dent answered "I cannot allow the [Parole] Board to have the argument that there's someone who's afraid of me, someone who thinks I'm a threat to. As far as they're concerned, I should never get out of prison under those conditions."

The police also had Tryon write a letter to Balcinde telling him that she would pick him up on March 19, 1990, when he was scheduled to be released. A deputy posing as Tryon was sent to meet Balcinde, and, pursuant to a second order authorizing intercept, the conversation between the deputy and Balcinde was recorded. In response to questions asked by the deputy, Balcinde stated that he was "going to do what you write me before," that Tryon was supposed to pay him $300, and that he was supposed to view a picture or videotape relating to a person named Ann. In addition, Balcinde asked the deputy posing as Tryon whether she had been in contact with "RC."[1] Following this conversation, Balcinde entered the deputy's car and was placed under arrest as he reached for the money offered by the deputy....

Prior to the giving of the jury instructions, codefendants objected to the jury instruction defining the "substantial step" element of a conspiracy. The court rejected the instruction proposed by both defendants which defined "substantial step" as "more than mere preparation."...

The jury found both defendants guilty of conspiracy to commit first degree murder. Dent appealed his conviction.... The first issue presented on review is whether the trial court properly refused to give defendant's proposed instruction which provided that the "substantial step" element of a conspiracy requires "more than mere preparation." An individual commits conspiracy when with intent that conduct constituting a crime be performed, he [or she] agrees with one or more persons to engage in or

---

1. Defendant Dent's full name is Roland C. Dent.

cause the performance of such conduct, and any one of them takes a *substantial step in pursuance of such agreement.* (Italics ours.)

The trial court instructed the jury that a "substantial step" is "conduct which strongly indicates a criminal purpose." Defendants' proposed instruction ... defines the "substantial step" element of an *attempt* as "conduct which strongly indicates a criminal purpose and which is more than mere preparation."

The first difference between the two crimes is in the language describing the type of "substantial step" that is required for each. RCW 9A.28.020(1) provides:

> A person is guilty of an attempt to commit crime if, with intent to commit a specific crime, he does *any act which is a substantial step toward the commission of that crime.* (Italics ours.)

In contrast, RCW 9A.28.040(1) provides:

> A person is guilty of criminal conspiracy when, with intent that conduct constituting a crime be performed, he agrees with one or more persons to engage in or cause the performance of such conduct, and any one of them takes a *substantial step in pursuance of such agreement.* (Italics ours.)

The focus or end toward which a "substantial step" must be taken is described differently in each statute.

Additional differences between the two crimes can be found in the nature of the conduct sought to be prohibited and in the significance of the "substantial step" requirement (or overt act requirement in other jurisdictions), in each context, for determining whether the prohibited conduct has occurred. "In the case of attempt the act must go beyond preparation because the attempt is deemed a punishable segment of the crime intended." A "substantial step" is required in the attempt context to prevent the imposition of punishment based on intent alone.

The purpose of the "substantial step" or overt act requirement is different in the conspiracy context. A conspiracy has been defined as "a partnership in criminal purposes. The gist of the crime is the confederation or combination of minds." The purpose of the "substantial step" requirement is, therefore, to "manifest 'that the conspiracy is at work,' and is neither a project still resting solely in the minds of the conspirators nor a fully completed operation no longer in existence."

The different purposes underlying the act requirements of the two offenses are well recognized.

> [C]onspiracy focuses on the additional dangers inherent in group activity. In theory, once an individual reaches an agreement with one or more persons to perform an unlawful act, it becomes more likely that the individual will feel a greater commitment to carry out his original intent, providing a heightened group danger.
>
> *As an inchoate crime, conspiracy allows law-enforcement officials to intervene at a stage far earlier than attempt does.* To obtain an attempt conviction, the prosecutor must prove that the actor performed an act beyond mere prepa-

ration.... To obtain a conspiracy conviction, however, the prosecutor need only prove that the conspirators agreed to undertake a criminal scheme or, at most, that they took an overt step in pursuance of the conspiracy. *Even an insignificant act may suffice.* (Italics ours.)

Robbins, *Double Inchoate Crimes*, 26 Harv. J. on Legis 1, 27–29 (1989). *See* 2 W. LaFave & A. Scott, *Substantive Criminal Law* §6.5, at 95 (2d ed. 1986) (explaining that "[i]f the agreement has been established but the object has not been attained, virtually any act will satisfy the overt act requirement" of a conspiracy). Similarly, in distinguishing the crime of conspiracy from the crime of attempt, one court has explained that the essence of a conspiracy is the agreement to commit a crime. If an overt act is committed in furtherance of the conspiracy then, regardless of the act's importance to the overall scheme, there is no need to prove that the conspirators made a serious effort to carry out their agreement.

Other courts have implicitly recognized the distinction between the act requirements of the two crimes in discussing the type of acts which will support a conspiracy conviction. In Missouri, for an act to qualify as an overt act in furtherance of a conspiracy "there is no requirement that such act be a physical one or be a substantial step in the commission of the target offense." *State v. Madwell*, 846 S.W.2d 208, 209 (Mo.Ct.App.1993). For example, "[a] telephone conversation or even mere silence can be an overt act." *State v. Ray*, 768 S.W.2d 119, 121 (Mo.Ct.App. 1988). Other courts have held that telephone conversations and meetings during which planning is done are overt acts. *United States v. Lewis*, 676 F.2d 508, 511 (11th Cir.) (holding that a telephone call to arrange a meeting to plan the conspiracy was a sufficient overt act); *United States v. Civella*, 648 F.2d 1167, 1174 (8th Cir.) (holding that "[t]elephone conversations and meetings in which plans and arrangements are made in furtherance of the conspiracy are overt acts"); *United States v. Marable*, 574 F.2d 224, 230 (5th Cir.1978) (holding that the overt act requirement was met where the defendant, through phone conversations and meetings, participated in discussing and arranging the conspiracy). An attempt to collect compensation under the agreement might also serve as the necessary overt act for a conspiracy.

We agree that the conspiracy statute requires a lesser act than does the attempt statute. We are particularly persuaded by the fact that RCW 9A.28.040 requires only an act that is a "substantial step in pursuance of [the] agreement" as opposed to a "substantial step toward the commission of [the] crime." We hold that preparatory conduct which furthers the ability of the conspirators to carry out the agreement can be "a substantial step in pursuance of [the] agreement." Therefore, we hold that the trial court properly refused to instruct the jury that the "substantial step" element of a conspiracy requires more than mere preparation.... Defendants' convictions are affirmed.

Discussion Questions

1. If Joyful Tryon had not become an informant and instead had gone along with Dent's plan and performed the acts described in the third paragraph of the *Dent* opinion, when would she have committed a substantial step in pursuance of the conspiracy? In other words, when could the police have arrested Dent, Balcinde, *and* Tryon for the crime of conspiracy?

2. Does a substantial step under the Washington conspiracy statute as interpreted in *Dent* differ from a substantial step under the Maine conspiracy statute after Problem 12.8? Does it differ from a substantial overt act under the Ohio statute after Problem 12.1?

3. Is there a difference between an overt act and a substantial step?

4. Should what constitutes a substantial step for purposes of a conspiracy differ from what constitutes a substantial step for purposes of an attempt?

5. The *Dent* court states that "attempt is deemed a punishable segment of the crime intended." Do you agree with this description? Is conspiracy not "a punishable segment of the crime intended"?

Problem

12.9 Jules and Robert are baseball fans sitting in the back row of the bleachers at a baseball stadium. They learn that a homerun ball from a World Series game is being temporarily stored in a locker at the stadium. Two men claim ownership of the ball and are litigating their dispute. Experts estimate that the ball is worth $1,000,000. Jules is a locksmith and he proposes to Robert, who has actually seen the storage locker, that the two of them break into the locker and steal the ball. Jules assures Robert that Jules can pick the lock without any damage to the lock. Robert agrees and sketches a picture of the front of the storage locker to show Jules what the outside of the lock looks like. Unbeknownst to Jules and Robert, a police officer is working undercover posing as a hot dog vendor so she can scout the ballpark for possible terrorist activity. She overhears the conversation, sees Robert's sketch, and arrests Jules and Robert for conspiracy to commit grand theft. Are Jules and Robert liable for conspiracy?

C. Mental States

Problem

12.10 What mental state or states do the following statutes require for conspiracy liability? Is the *Lauria* case, below, consistent with these statutes?

Illinois Compiled Statutes

§ 720 ILCS 5/8-2 Conspiracy

(a) Elements of the offense. A person commits conspiracy when, with intent that an offense be committed, he agrees with another to the commission of that offense. No person may be convicted of conspiracy to commit an offense unless an act in furtherance of such agreement is alleged and proved to have been committed by him or by a co-conspirator.

Wyoming Statutes

§ 6-1-303 Conspiracy

(a) A person is guilty of conspiracy to commit a crime if he agrees with one (1) or more persons that they or one (1) or more of them will commit a crime and one (1) or more of them does an overt act to effect the objective of the agreement.

Tennessee Code

§ 39-12-103 Criminal conspiracy

(a) The offense of conspiracy is committed if two (2) or more people, each having the culpable mental state required for the offense which is the object of the conspiracy and each acting for the purpose of promoting or facilitating commission of an offense, agree that one (1) or more of them will engage in conduct which constitutes such offense.

Model Penal Code

§ 5.03 Criminal Conspiracy

(1) **Definition of Conspiracy.** A person is guilty of conspiracy with another person or persons to commit a crime if with the purpose of promoting or facilitating its commission he:

    (a) agrees with such other person or persons that they or one or more of them will engage in conduct that constitutes such crime or an attempt or solicitation to commit such crime; or

    (b) agrees to aid such other person or persons in the planning or commission of such crime or of an attempt or solicitation to commit such crime.

People v. Lauria

251 Cal. App. 2d 471 (1967)
California Court of Appeals

Fleming, J.

In an investigation of call-girl activity the police focused their attention on three prostitutes actively plying their trade on call, each of whom was using Lauria's telephone answering service, presumably for business purposes.

On January 8, 1965, Stella Weeks, a policewoman, signed up for telephone service with Lauria's answering service. Mrs. Weeks, in the course of her conversation with

Lauria's office manager, hinted broadly that she was a prostitute concerned with the secrecy of her activities and their concealment from the police. She was assured that the operation of the service was discreet and "about as safe as you can get." It was arranged that Mrs. Weeks need not leave her address with the answering service, but could pick up her calls and pay her bills in person.

On February 11, Mrs. Weeks talked to Lauria on the telephone and told him her business was modelling and she had been referred to the answering service by Terry, one of the three prostitutes under investigation. She complained that because of the operation of the service she had lost two valuable customers, referred to as tricks. Lauria defended his service and said that her friends had probably lied to her about having left calls for her. But he did not respond to Mrs. Weeks' hints that she needed customers in order to make money, other than to invite her to his house for a personal visit in order to get better acquainted. In the course of his talk he said "his business was taking messages." ...

On April 1 Lauria and the three prostitutes were arrested. Lauria complained to the police that this attention was undeserved, stating that Hollywood Call Board had 60 to 70 prostitutes on its board while his own service had only 9 or 10, that he kept separate records for known or suspected prostitutes for the convenience of himself and the police. When asked if his records were available to police who might come to the office to investigate call girls, Lauria replied that they were whenever the police had a specific name. However, his service didn't "arbitrarily tell the police about prostitutes on our board. As long as they pay their bills we tolerate them." In a subsequent voluntary appearance before the grand jury Lauria testified he had always cooperated with the police. But he admitted he knew some of his customers were prostitutes, and he knew Terry was a prostitute because he had personally used her services, and he knew she was paying for 500 calls a month.

Lauria and the three prostitutes were indicted for conspiracy to commit prostitution, and nine overt acts were specified. Subsequently the trial court set aside the indictment as having been brought without reasonable or probable cause. The People have appealed, claiming that a sufficient showing of an unlawful agreement to further prostitution was made.

To establish agreement, the People need show no more than a tacit, mutual understanding between coconspirators to accomplish an unlawful act. Here the People attempted to establish a conspiracy by showing that Lauria, well aware that his co-defendants were prostitutes who received business calls from customers through his telephone answering service, continued to furnish them with such service. This approach attempts to equate knowledge of another's criminal activity with conspiracy to further such criminal activity, and poses the question of the criminal responsibility of a furnisher of goods or services who knows his product is being used to assist the operation of an illegal business. Under what circumstances does a supplier become a part of a conspiracy to further an illegal enterprise by furnishing goods or services which he knows are to be used by the buyer for criminal purposes?

The two leading cases on this point face in opposite directions. In *United States v. Falcone*, the sellers of large quantities of sugar, yeast, and cans were absolved from participation in a moonshining conspiracy among distillers who bought from them, while in *Direct Sales Co. v. United States*, a wholesaler of drugs was convicted of conspiracy to violate the federal narcotic laws by selling drugs in quantity to a codefendant physician who was supplying them to addicts. The distinction between these two cases appears primarily based on the proposition that distributors of such dangerous products as drugs are required to exercise greater discrimination in the conduct of their business than are distributors of innocuous substances like sugar and yeast.

In the earlier case, *Falcone*, the sellers' knowledge of the illegal use of the goods was insufficient by itself to make the sellers participants in a conspiracy with the distillers who bought from them. Such knowledge fell short of proof of a conspiracy, and evidence on the volume of sales was too vague to support a jury finding that respondents knew of the conspiracy from the size of the sales alone.

In the later case of *Direct Sales*, the conviction of a drug wholesaler for conspiracy to violate federal narcotic laws was affirmed on a showing that it had actively promoted the sale of morphine sulphate in quantity and had sold codefendant physician, who practiced in a small town in South Carolina, more than 300 times his normal requirements of the drug, even though it had been repeatedly warned of the dangers of unrestricted sales of the drug. The court contrasted the restricted goods involved in *Direct Sales* with the articles of free commerce involved in *Falcone*: "All articles of commerce may be put to illegal ends," said the court. "But all do not have inherently the same susceptibility to harmful and illegal use.... This difference is important for two purposes. One is for making certain that the seller knows the buyer's intended illegal use. The other is to show that by the sale he intends to further, promote, and cooperate in it. This intent, when given effect by overt act, is the gist of conspiracy. While it is not identical with mere knowledge that another proposes unlawful action it is not unrelated to such knowledge.... The step from knowledge to intent and agreement may be taken. There is more than suspicion, more than knowledge, acquiescence, carelessness, indifference, lack of concern. There is informed and interested cooperation, stimulation, instigation. And there is also a 'stake in the venture' which, even if it may not be essential, is not irrelevant to the question of conspiracy."

While *Falcone* and *Direct Sales* may not be entirely consistent with each other in their full implications, they do provide us with a framework for the criminal liability of a supplier of lawful goods or services put to unlawful use. Both the element of knowledge of the illegal use of the goods or services and the element of intent to further that use must be present in order to make the supplier a participant in a criminal conspiracy.

Proof of knowledge is ordinarily a question of fact and requires no extended discussion in the present case. The knowledge of the supplier was sufficiently established when Lauria admitted he knew some of his customers were prostitutes and admitted he knew that Terry, an active subscriber to his service, was a prostitute. In the face of these admissions he could scarcely claim to have relied on the normal assumption an operator of a business or service is entitled to make, that his customers are behaving themselves in the eyes of the law. Because Lauria knew in fact that some of his customers were prostitutes, it is a legitimate inference he knew they were subscribing to his answering service for illegal business purposes and were using his service to make assignations for prostitution. On this record we think the prosecution is entitled to claim positive knowledge by Lauria of the use of his service to facilitate the business of prostitution.

The more perplexing issue in the case is the sufficiency of proof of intent to further the criminal enterprise. The element of intent may be proved either by direct evidence, or by evidence of circumstances from which an intent to further a criminal enterprise by supplying lawful goods or services may be inferred. Direct evidence of participation, such as advice from the supplier of legal goods or services to the user of those goods or services on their use for illegal purposes, ... provides the simplest case. When the intent to further and promote the criminal enterprise comes from the lips of the supplier himself, ambiguities of inference from circumstance need not trouble us. But in cases where direct proof of complicity is lacking, intent to further the conspiracy must be derived from the sale itself and its surrounding circumstances in order to establish the supplier's express or tacit agreement to join the conspiracy.

In the case at bench the prosecution argues that since Lauria knew his customers were using his service for illegal purposes but nevertheless continued to furnish it to them, he must have intended to assist them in carrying out their illegal activities. Thus through a union of knowledge and intent he became a participant in a criminal conspiracy. Essentially, the People argue that knowledge alone of the continuing use of his telephone facilities for criminal purposes provided a sufficient basis from which his intent to participate in those criminal activities could be inferred.

In examining precedents in this field we find that sometimes, but not always, the criminal intent of the supplier may be inferred from his knowledge of the unlawful use made of the product he supplies. Some consideration of characteristic patterns may be helpful.

1. Intent may be inferred from knowledge, when the purveyor of legal goods for illegal use has acquired a stake in the venture. For example, in *Regina v. Thomas*, a prosecution for living off the earnings of prostitution, the evidence showed that the accused ... rented a room at a grossly inflated rent to a prostitute for the purpose of carrying on her trade, a jury could find he was living on the earnings of prostitution.

In the present case, no proof was offered of inflated charges for the telephone answering services furnished the codefendants.

2. Intent may be inferred from knowledge, when no legitimate use for the goods or services exists. The leading California case is *People v. McLaughlin*, in which the court upheld a conviction of the suppliers of horse-racing information by wire for conspiracy to promote bookmaking, when it had been established that wire-service information had no other use than to supply information needed by bookmakers to conduct illegal gambling operations. ...

Other services of a comparable nature come to mind: the manufacturer of crooked dice and marked cards who sells his product to gambling casinos; the tipster who furnishes information on the movement of law enforcement officers to known law-breakers. In such cases the supplier must necessarily have an intent to further the illegal enterprise since there is no known honest use for his goods.

However, there is nothing in the furnishing of telephone answering service which would necessarily imply assistance in the performance of illegal activities. Nor is any inference to be derived from the use of an answering service by women, either in any particular volume of calls, or outside normal working hours. Night-club entertainers, registered nurses, faith healers, public stenographers, photographic models, and free lance substitute employees, provide examples of women in legitimate occupations whose employment might cause them to receive a volume of telephone calls at irregular hours.

3. Intent may be inferred from knowledge, when the volume of business with the buyer is grossly disproportionate to any legitimate demand, or when sales for illegal use amount to a high proportion of the seller's total business. In such cases an intent to participate in the illegal enterprise may be inferred from the quantity of the business done. For example, in *Direct Sales*, supra, the sale of narcotics to a rural physician in quantities 300 times greater than he would have normal use for provided potent evidence of an intent to further the illegal activity....

No evidence of any unusual volume of business with prostitutes was presented by the prosecution against Lauria.

Inflated charges, the sale of goods with no legitimate use, sales in inflated amounts, each may provide a fact of sufficient moment from which the intent of the seller to participate in the criminal enterprise may be inferred. In such instances participation by the supplier of legal goods to the illegal enterprise may be inferred because in one way or another the supplier has acquired a special interest in the operation of the illegal enterprise. His intent to participate in the crime of which he has knowledge may be inferred from the existence of his special interest.

Yet there are cases in which it cannot reasonably be said that the supplier has a stake in the venture or has acquired a special interest in the enterprise, but in which he has been held liable as a participant on the basis of knowledge alone. Some suggestion of this appears in *Direct Sales*, supra, where both the knowledge of the illegal use of the drugs and the intent of the supplier to aid that use were inferred.... It seems apparent from these cases that a supplier who furnishes equipment which he knows will be used to commit a serious crime may be deemed from that knowledge alone to have intended to produce the result. Such proof may justify an inference that the furnisher intended to aid the execution of the crime and that he thereby became a participant. For instance, we think the operator of a telephone answering service with positive knowledge that his service was being used to facilitate the extortion of ransom, the distribution of heroin, or the passing of counterfeit money who continued to furnish the service with knowledge of its use, might be chargeable on knowledge alone with participation in a scheme to extort money, to distribute narcotics, or to pass counterfeit money. The same result would follow the seller of gasoline who knew the buyer was using his product to make Molotov cocktails for terroristic use.

Logically, the same reasoning could be extended to crimes of every description. Yet we do not believe an inference of intent drawn from knowledge of criminal use properly applies to the less serious crimes classified as misdemeanors. The duty to take positive action to dissociate oneself from activities helpful to violations of the criminal law is far stronger and more compelling for felonies than it is for misdemeanors or petty offenses. In this respect, as in others, the distinction between felonies and misdemeanors, between more serious and less serious crime, retains continuing vitality.... We believe the distinction between the obligations arising from knowledge of a felony and those arising from knowledge of a misdemeanor continues to reflect basic human feelings about the duties owed by individuals to society....

With respect to misdemeanors, we conclude that positive knowledge of the supplier that his products or services are being used for criminal purposes does not, without more, establish an intent of the supplier to participate in the misdemeanors. With respect to felonies, we do not decide the converse, viz., that in all cases of felony knowledge of criminal use alone may justify an inference of the supplier's intent to participate in the crime. The implications of *Falcone* make the matter uncertain with respect to those felonies which are merely prohibited wrongs. But decision on this point is not compelled, and we leave the matter open.

From this analysis of precedent we deduce the following rule: the intent of a supplier who knows of the criminal use to which his supplies are put to participate in the criminal activity connected with the use of his supplies may be established by (1) direct evidence that he intends to participate, or (2) through an inference that he intends to participate based on, (a) his special interest in the activity, or (b) the aggravated nature of the crime itself.

When we review Lauria's activities in the light of this analysis, we find no proof that Lauria took any direct action to further, encourage, or direct the call-girl activities of his codefendants and we find an absence of circumstance from which his special interest in their activities could be inferred. Neither excessive charges for standardized services, nor the furnishing of services without a legitimate use, nor an unusual quantity of business with call girls, are present. The offense which he is charged with furthering is a misdemeanor, a category of crime which has never been made a required subject of positive disclosure to public authority. Under these circumstances, although proof of Lauria's knowledge of the criminal activities of his patrons was sufficient to charge him with that fact, there was insufficient evidence that he intended to further their criminal activities, and hence insufficient proof of his participation in a criminal conspiracy with his codefendants to further prostitution.

In absolving Lauria of complicity in a criminal conspiracy we do not wish to imply that the public authorities are without remedies to combat modern manifestations of the world's oldest profession.... The furnishing of telephone answering service in aid of prostitution could be made a crime. (Cf. Pen. Code, Section 316, which makes it a misdemeanor to let an apartment with knowledge of its use for prostitution.) Other solutions will doubtless occur to vigilant public authorities if the problem of call-girl activity needs further suppression.

The order is affirmed.

Discussion Questions

1. What is the holding of *Lauria*? Is it consistent with the statutes after Problem 12.10 that appear just before the *Lauria* case?

2. Should knowingly furnishing goods or services that will be used in criminal activity be sufficient for conspiracy?

3. Should the assurances by Lauria's office manager that the service was "about as safe as you can get" coupled with Lauria's knowledge of what the women who used his service were doing be enough to show Lauria's intent?

4. Does the distinction drawn in the *Lauria* case between misdemeanors and felonies make sense?

Problem

12.11 Part (a) Leo and Michael both enjoy racing cars. One day they agree that on the following Saturday night they will race each other on a stretch of highway outside town. They tell several of their friends and when the evening arrives a crowd of several dozen people gathers to see the race. Leo and Michael arrive at the scene of the race and are in their cars with the engines running at the starting line when a police cruiser pulls up and both are arrested for conspiracy to commit the crime of reckless driving. Are they liable?

Part (b) Assume that the race took place and that Leo's car spun out of control while trying to pass Michael and killed a bystander. Could Leo and Michael be convicted of conspiracy to commit manslaughter?

---

1. Mental State Regarding a Circumstance

Problem

12.12 Max is a part-time gun dealer who sells primarily at weekend gun shows. One weekend he is approached by Sid, who wants to buy a powerful handgun. Max doesn't typically carry the particular handgun Sid wants because it is more expensive and powerful than the sort of weapon buyers at weekend shows usually want to purchase. Sid is tall and husky and looks considerably older than his

17 years of age. Max tells Sid that he can introduce him to someone who can sell him the weapon if Sid is willing to pay Max a fee for doing so. Sid agrees to this arrangement. Max then contacts David, another gun dealer who maintains a supply of the handgun Sid is interested in, and proposes to introduce him to Sid if David will give him a 10 percent commission for arranging the sale. David agrees to this arrangement. Max then calls Sid and meets with him to set up a time and place for the sale and to collect a down payment on the weapon. Prior to the actual culmination of the sale, the police arrest both Max and David for conspiracy to violate a state law that makes it a felony to sell a handgun to anyone under the age of 18. This state law makes clear that strict liability applies to its age element. Is Max liable for the charged conspiracy? Is David liable for the charged conspiracy?

In the *Feola* case, below, the United States charged Feola with conspiracy under the following statute:

18 United States Code

§ 371

If two or more persons conspire either to commit any offense against the United States, or to defraud the United States, or any agency thereof in any manner or for any purpose, and one or more of such persons do any act to effect the object of the conspiracy, each shall be fined not more than $10,000 or imprisoned not more than five years, or both.

The object of the charged conspiracy in *Feola* was assault on a federal officer in violation of:

18 United States Code

§ 111. Assaulting, resisting, or impeding certain officers or employees.

Whoever forcibly assaults, resists, opposes, impedes, intimidates, or interferes with any person designated in section 1114 of this title while engaged in or on account of the performance of his official duties, shall be fined not more than $ 5,000 or imprisoned not more than three years, or both.

Whoever, in the commission of any such acts uses a deadly or dangerous weapon, shall be fined not more than $ 10,000 or imprisoned not more than ten years, or both.

* * *

Among the persons "designated in section 1114" of 18 U. S. C. is "any officer or employee ... of the Bureau of Narcotics and Dangerous Drugs."

United States v. Feola

420 U.S. 671 (1975)
United States Supreme Court

Blackmun, J.

This case presents the issue whether knowledge that the intended victim is a federal officer is a requisite for the crime of conspiracy, under 18 U.S.C. §371, to commit an offense violative of 18 U.S.C. §111, that is, an assault upon a federal officer while engaged in the performance of his official duties.

Respondent Feola and three others ... were indicted for violations of §§371 and 111. A jury found all four defendants guilty of both charges.... [T]he United States Court of Appeals for the Second Circuit ... affirmed the judgment of conviction on the substantive charges, but reversed the conspiracy convictions. Because of a conflict among the Federal Circuits on the scienter issue with respect to a conspiracy charge, we granted the Government's petition for a *writ of certiorari* in Feola's case.

The facts reveal a classic narcotics "rip-off." ... [T]he evidence shows that Feola and his confederates arranged for a sale of heroin to buyers who turned out to be undercover agents for the Bureau of Narcotics and Dangerous Drugs. The group planned to palm off on the purchasers, for a substantial sum, a form of sugar in place of heroin and, should that ruse fail, simply to surprise their unwitting buyers and relieve them of the cash they had brought along for payment. The plan failed when one agent, his suspicions being aroused, drew his revolver in time to counter an assault upon another agent from the rear.... Feola and his associates found themselves charged, to their undoubted surprise, with conspiring to assault, and with assaulting, federal officers.

At the trial, the District Court, without objection from the defense, charged the jurors that, in order to find any of the defendants guilty on either the conspiracy count or the substantive one, they were not required to conclude that the defendants were aware that their quarry were federal officers.

The Court of Appeals reversed the conspiracy convictions on a ground not advanced by any of the defendants. Although it approved the trial court's instructions to the jury on the substantive charge of assaulting a federal officer, it nonetheless concluded that the failure to charge that knowledge of the victim's official identity must be proved in order to convict on the conspiracy charge amounted to plain error. The court perceived itself bound by a line of cases, commencing with Judge Learned Hand's opinion in *United States v. Crimmins*, all holding that scienter of a factual element that confers federal jurisdiction, while unnecessary for conviction of the substantive offense, is required in order to sustain a conviction for conspiracy to commit the substantive offense....

The Government's plea is for symmetry. It urges that since criminal liability for the offense described in 18 U.S.C. §111 does not depend on whether the assailant harbored the specific intent to assault a federal officer, no greater scienter requirement can be engrafted upon the conspiracy offense, which is merely an agreement to commit the act proscribed by §111. Consideration of the Government's contention requires us preliminarily to pass upon its premise, the proposition that responsibility for assault upon a federal officer does not depend upon whether the assailant was aware of the official identity of his victim at the time he acted.

That the "federal officer" requirement is anything other than jurisdictional[9] is not seriously urged upon us; indeed, both Feola and the Court of Appeals, concede that scienter is not a necessary element of the substantive offense under §111....

This interpretation poses no risk of unfairness to defendants. It is no snare for the unsuspecting. Although the perpetrator of a narcotics "rip-off," such as the one involved here, may be surprised to find that his intended victim is a federal officer in civilian apparel, he nonetheless knows from the very outset that his planned course of conduct is wrongful. The situation is not one where legitimate conduct becomes unlawful solely because of the identity of the individual or agency affected. In a case of this kind the offender takes his victim as he finds him. The concept of criminal intent does not extend so far as to require that the actor understand not only the nature of his act but also its consequence for the choice of a judicial forum....

We hold, therefore, that in order to incur criminal liability under §111 an actor must entertain merely the criminal intent to do the acts therein specified. We now consider whether the rule should be different where persons conspire to commit those acts.

Our decisions establish that in order to sustain a judgment of conviction on a charge of conspiracy to violate a federal statute, the Government must prove at least the degree of criminal intent necessary for the substantive offense itself.... Respondent Feola urges upon us the proposition that the Government must show a degree of criminal intent in the conspiracy count greater than is necessary to convict for the substantive offense; he urges that even though it is not necessary to show that he was aware of the official identity of his assaulted victims in order to find him guilty of assaulting federal officers, in violation of 18 U. S. C. §111, the Government nonetheless must show that he was aware that his intended victims were undercover agents, if it is successfully to prosecute him for conspiring to assault federal agents. And the

---

9. We are content to state the issue this way despite its potential to mislead. Labeling a requirement "jurisdictional" does not necessarily mean, of course, that the requirement is not an element of the offense Congress intended to describe and to punish. Indeed, a requirement is sufficient to confer jurisdiction on the federal courts for what otherwise are state crimes precisely because it implicates factors that are an appropriate subject for federal concern. With respect to the present case, for example, a mere general policy of deterring assaults would probably prove to be an undesirable or insufficient basis for federal jurisdiction; but where Congress seeks to protect the integrity of federal functions and the safety of federal officers, the interest is sufficient to warrant federal involvement. The significance of labeling a statutory requirement as "jurisdictional" is not that the requirement is viewed as outside the scope of the evil Congress intended to forestall, but merely that the existence of the fact that confers federal jurisdiction need not be one in the mind of the actor at the time he perpetrates the act made criminal by the federal statute. The question, then, is not whether the requirement is jurisdictional, but whether it is jurisdictional only.

Court of Appeals held that the trial court's failure to charge the jury to this effect constituted plain error.

The general conspiracy statute, 18 U.S.C. §371, offers no textual support for the proposition that to be guilty of conspiracy a defendant in effect must have known that his conduct violated federal law. The statute makes it unlawful simply to "conspire ... to commit any offense against the United States." A natural reading of these words would be that since one can violate a criminal statute simply by engaging in the forbidden conduct, a conspiracy to commit that offense is nothing more than an agreement to engage in the prohibited conduct. Then where, as here, the substantive statute does not require that an assailant know the official status of his victim, there is nothing on the face of the conspiracy statute that would seem to require that those agreeing to the assault have a greater degree of knowledge....

With no support on the face of the general conspiracy statute ... respondent relies solely on the line of cases commencing with *United States v. Crimmins*, for the principle that the Government must prove "antifederal" intent in order to establish liability under §371. In *Crimmins*, the defendant had been found guilty of conspiring to receive stolen bonds that had been transported in interstate commerce. Upon review, the Court of Appeals pointed out that the evidence failed to establish that *Crimmins* actually knew the stolen bonds had moved into the State. Accepting for the sake of argument the assumption that such knowledge was not necessary to sustain a conviction on the substantive offense, Judge Learned Hand nevertheless concluded that to permit conspiratorial liability where the conspirators were ignorant of the federal implications of their acts would be to enlarge their agreement beyond its terms as they understood them. He capsulized the distinction in what has become well known as his "traffic light" analogy:

> While one may, for instance, be guilty of running past a traffic light of whose existence one is ignorant, one cannot be guilty of conspiring to run past such a light, for one cannot agree to run past a light unless one supposes that there is a light to run past.

Judge Hand's attractive, but perhaps seductive, analogy has received a mixed reception in the Courts of Appeals. The Second Circuit, of course, has followed it; others have rejected it. It appears that most have avoided it by the simple expedient of inferring the requisite knowledge from the scope of the conspiratorial venture. We conclude that the analogy, though effective prose, is, as applied to the facts before us, bad law.[24] ...

---

24. The Government rather effectively exposes the fallacy of the *Crimmins* traffic light analogy by recasting it in terms of a jurisdictional element. The suggested example is a traffic light on an Indian reservation. Surely, one may conspire with others to disobey the light but be ignorant of the fact that it is on the reservation. As applied to a jurisdictional element of this kind the formulation makes little sense.

One may run a traffic light "of whose existence one is ignorant," but assaulting another "of whose existence one is ignorant," probably would require unearthly intervention. Thus, the traffic light analogy, even if it were a correct statement of the law, is inapt, for the conduct proscribed by the substantive offense, here assault, is not of the type outlawed without regard to the intent of the actor to accomplish the result that is made criminal. If the analogy has any vitality at all, it is to conduct of the latter variety; that, however, is a question we save for another day. We hold here only that where a substantive offense embodies only a requirement of *mens rea* as to each of its elements, the general federal conspiracy statute requires no more....

Discussion Questions

1. Feola made no objection to the trial court's conspiracy instruction. Nor did he raise the issue on appeal. Why, then, did the Court of Appeals reverse Feola's conviction based on the conspiracy instruction? Should appellate courts consider questions not raised by a party?

2. Should there be symmetry between the mental states required for conspiracy and the mental states required for the target offense of the conspiracy, as the government argued before the Supreme Court in *Feola*? In other words, what mental state should the crime of conspiracy require regarding an attendant circumstance? What language would you add to the statutes after Problem 12.1 to implement your answer to the previous question?

3. How would the *Feola* case be resolved under the MPC statute that appears after Problem 12.1?

D. Scope of the Conspiracy

1. The *Pinkerton* Doctrine

Pinkerton v. United States
328 U.S. 640 (1946)
United States Supreme Court

Douglas, J.

[Daniel and Walter [Pinkerton], who were brothers living near each other, were charged in several counts with substantive offenses, and then a conspiracy count was added naming those offenses as overt acts. The proof showed that Walter alone committed the substantive crimes. There was none to establish that Daniel participated in them, aided and abetted Walter in committing them, or knew that he had done so. Daniel in fact was in the penitentiary, under sentence for other crimes, when some of Walter's crimes were done.

There was evidence, however, to show that over several years Daniel and Walter had confederated to commit similar crimes concerned with unlawful possession, transportation, and dealing in whiskey, in fraud of the federal revenues. On this evidence both were convicted of conspiracy. Walter also was convicted on the substantive counts on the proof of his committing the crimes charged....][3] ...

It is contended that there was insufficient evidence to implicate Daniel in the conspiracy. But we think there was enough evidence for submission of the issue to the jury.

There is, however, no evidence to show that Daniel participated directly in the commission of the substantive offenses on which his conviction has been sustained,[5] although there was evidence to show that these substantive offenses were in fact committed by Walter in furtherance of the unlawful agreement or conspiracy existing between the brothers. The question was submitted to the jury on the theory that each petitioner could be found guilty of the substantive offenses, if it was found at the time those offenses were committed petitioners were parties to an unlawful conspiracy and the substantive offenses charged were in fact committed in furtherance of it.[6] ... [The jury convicted Walter on nine of the substantive counts and on the conspiracy count. It found Daniel guilty on six of the substantive counts and the conspiracy count.]

... We have here a continuous conspiracy. There is here no evidence of the affirmative action on the part of Daniel which is necessary to establish his withdrawal from it.... "Having joined in an unlawful scheme, having constituted agents for its performance, scheme and agency to be continuous until full fruition be secured, until he does some act to disavow or defeat the purpose he is in no situation to claim the delay of the law. As the offense has not been terminated or accomplished he is still offending. And we think, consciously offending, offending as certainly, as we have said, as at the first moment of his confederation, and consciously through every moment of its existence." And so long as the partnership in crime continues, the partners act for each other in carrying it forward. It is settled that "an overt act of one partner may be the act of all without any new agreement specifically directed to that

---

3. These two paragraphs were relocated from the dissent to the majority opinion to enhance comprehensibility.

5. This question does not arise as to Walter. He was the direct actor in some of the substantive offenses on which his conviction rests. So the general sentence and fine are supportable under any one of those.

6. The trial court charged: "... after you gentlemen have considered all the evidence in this case, if you are satisfied from the evidence beyond a reasonable doubt that at the time these particular substantive offenses were committed, that is, the offenses charged in the first ten counts of this indictment if you are satisfied from the evidence beyond a reasonable doubt that the two defendants were in an unlawful conspiracy, as I have heretofore defined unlawful conspiracy to you, then you would have a right, if you found that to be true to your satisfaction beyond a reasonable doubt, to convict each of these defendants on all these substantive counts, provided the acts referred to in the substantive counts were acts in furtherance of the unlawful conspiracy or object of the unlawful conspiracy, which you have found from the evidence existed." Daniel was not indicted as an aider or abettor (see Criminal Code, §332, 18 U.S.C. 550), nor was his case submitted to the jury on that theory.

act." Motive or intent may be proved by the acts or declarations of some of the conspirators in furtherance of the common objective. A scheme to use the mails to defraud, which is joined in by more than one person, is a conspiracy. Yet all members are responsible, though only one did the mailing. The governing principle is the same when the substantive offense is committed by one of the conspirators in furtherance of the unlawful project. The criminal intent to do the act is established by the formation of the conspiracy. Each conspirator instigated the commission of the crime. The unlawful agreement contemplated precisely what was done. It was formed for the purpose. The act done was in execution of the enterprise. The rule which holds responsible one who counsels, procures, or commands another to commit a crime is founded on the same principle. That principle is recognized in the law of conspiracy when the overt act of one partner in crime is attributable to all. An overt act is an essential ingredient of the crime of conspiracy under § 37 of the Criminal Code, 18 U. S. C. § 88. If that can be supplied by the act of one conspirator, we fail to see why the same or other acts in furtherance of the conspiracy are likewise not attributable to the others for the purpose of holding them responsible for the substantive offense.

A different case would arise if the substantive offense committed by one of the conspirators was not in fact done in furtherance of the conspiracy, did not fall within the scope of the unlawful project, or was merely a part of the ramifications of the plan which could not be reasonably foreseen as a necessary or natural consequence of the unlawful agreement. But as we read this record, that is not this case.

Affirmed.

Rutledge, J. (dissenting in part) The judgment concerning Daniel Pinkerton should be reversed. In my opinion it is without precedent here and is a dangerous precedent to establish....

I think this ruling violates both the letter and the spirit of what Congress did when it separately defined the three classes of crime, namely, (1) completed substantive offenses;[1] (2) aiding, abetting or counseling another to commit them;[2] and (3) conspiracy to commit them.[3] Not only does this ignore the distinctions Congress has prescribed shall be observed. It either convicts one man for another's crime or punishes the man convicted twice for the same offense.

---

1. These of course comprehend the vast variety of offenses prescribed by federal law, conspiracies for accomplishing which may be charged under the catchall conspiracy statute, note 3.

2. "Whoever directly commits any act constituting an offense defined in any law of the United States, or aids, abets, counsels, commands, induces, or procures its commission, is a principal." 18 U.S.C. § 550.

3. "If two or more persons conspire either to commit any offense against the United States, or to defraud the United States in any manner or for any purpose, and one or more of such parties do any act to effect the object of the conspiracy, each of the parties to such conspiracy shall be fined not more than $ 10,000, or imprisoned not more than two years, or both." 18 U. S. C. § 88.

The three types of offense are not identical. Nor are their differences merely verbal. The gist of conspiracy is the agreement; that of aiding, abetting or counseling is in consciously advising or assisting another to commit particular offenses, and thus becoming a party to them; that of substantive crime, going a step beyond mere aiding, abetting, counseling to completion of the offense....

The Court's theory seems to be that Daniel and Walter became general partners in crime by virtue of their agreement and because of that agreement without more on his part Daniel became criminally responsible as a principal for everything Walter did thereafter in the nature of a criminal offense of the general sort the agreement contemplated, so long as there was not clear evidence that Daniel had withdrawn from or revoked the agreement. Whether or not his commitment to the penitentiary had that effect, the result is a vicarious criminal responsibility as broad as, or broader than, the vicarious civil liability of a partner for acts done by a copartner in the course of the firm's business.

Such analogies from private commercial law and the law of torts are dangerous, in my judgment, for transfer to the criminal field. Guilt there with us remains personal, not vicarious, for the more serious offenses. It should be kept so. The effect of Daniel's conviction in this case, to repeat, is either to attribute to him Walter's guilt or to punish him twice for the same offense, namely, agreeing with Walter to engage in crime. Without the agreement Daniel was guilty of no crime on this record. With it and no more, so far as his own conduct is concerned, he was guilty of two....

Discussion Questions

1. What are the criteria of the *Pinkerton* doctrine as explained in the majority opinion?

2. How does the doctrine affect the scope of liability of a conspirator?

2. Parties to a Conspiracy

Problem

12.13 Is the following MPC section consistent with the *McDermott* case below?

Model Penal Code

§ 5.03 Criminal Conspiracy

(2) Scope of Conspiratorial Relationship. If a person guilty of conspiracy, as defined by Subsection (1) of this Section, knows that a person with whom he conspires to commit a crime has conspired with another person or persons to commit the same crime, he is guilty of conspiring with such other person or persons, whether or not he knows their identity, to commit such crime.

United States v. McDermott

245 F.3d 133 (2d Cir. 2001)
United States Court of Appeals for the Second Circuit

Oakes, Senior Circuit Judge.

Defendant James J. McDermott appeals from a judgment entered against him in the United States District Court for the Southern District of New York following a jury trial ... convicting him of conspiracy to commit insider trading in violation of 18 U.S.C. §371 and of insider trading in violation of 15 U.S.C. §§78j(b) and 78ff and of 17 C.F.R. §240.10b-5. On appeal, McDermott contends ... that the evidence was insufficient as a matter of law to support his convictions.... We agree that there is insufficient evidence to support the conspiracy count, although sufficient evidence exists to support McDermott's conviction on the substantive offenses....

The present prosecution arose out of a triangulated love affair involving the president of a prominent investment bank, a pornographic film star and a New Jersey businessman.

Until May 1999, McDermott was the president, CEO and Chairman of Keefe Bruyette & Woods ("KBW"), an investment bank headquartered in New York City that specializes in mergers and acquisitions in the banking industry. Around 1996, McDermott began having an extramarital affair with Kathryn Gannon. Gannon was an adult film star and an alleged prostitute who performed using the stage name "Marylin Star." During the course of their affair, McDermott made numerous stock recommendations to Gannon. Unbeknownst to McDermott, Gannon was simultaneously having an affair with Anthony Pomponio and passing these recommendations to him. Although neither Gannon nor Pomponio had extensive training or expertise in securities trading, together they earned around $170,000 in profits during the period relevant to this case.

The government indicted McDermott, Gannon and Pomponio for conspiracy to commit insider trading and for insider trading on the theory that McDermott's recommendations to Gannon were based on non-public, material information. McDermott and Pomponio were tried together, but Gannon was not present.

The evidence at trial concerned primarily the relationship between McDermott and Gannon and the trading activities of Gannon and Pomponio. The Government built its case against McDermott almost entirely on circumstantial evidence linking records of telephone conversations between McDermott and Gannon with records of Gannon's and Pomponio's trading activities. Telephone records revealed that McDermott and Gannon engaged in approximately 800 telephone calls during the charged period, including up to 29 calls in one day. Trading records revealed correlations between the telephone calls and stock trades. In addition to these records, the sensational highlight of the government's evidence ... consisted of audiotape recordings of Pomponio's SEC deposition. These tapes undermined Pomponio's defense and credibility, as they recorded him poorly telling lies, evading questions and affecting incredulous reactions.[4] McDermott was sentenced to eight months' imprisonment, to be followed by a two-year term of supervised release, a $25,000 fine and $600 in special assessments.

Legal Sufficiency

McDermott challenges the sufficiency of the evidence to establish his convictions both for a single conspiracy to commit insider trading and for the related substantive offenses.

... Measured against this high standard, we find that the evidence was insufficient as a matter of law on the conspiracy count, but sufficient to establish McDermott's conviction for the substantive offenses.

The Conspiracy Count

"[I]n order to prove a single conspiracy, the government must show that each alleged member agreed to participate in what he knew to be a collective venture directed toward a common goal. The coconspirators need not have agreed on the details of the conspiracy, so long as they agreed on the essential nature of the plan." We have frequently noted that the "essence of conspiracy is the agreement and not the commission of the substantive offense." Additionally, it is a long-standing principle of this Court's law of conspiracy that "[n]obody is liable in conspiracy except for the fair import of the concerted purpose or agreement as he understands it; if later comers change that, he is not liable for the change; his liability is limited to the common purposes while he remains in it."

Despite this well-settled law, the government here asks us to redefine a conspiracy by its purpose, rather than by the agreement of its members to that purpose. The government argues that from the perspective of Gannon and Pomponio, albeit not from McDermott's perspective, there was a unitary purpose to commit insider trading based on information furnished by McDermott. According to the government, therefore, McDermott was part of the conspiracy even though he did not agree to pass information to both Gannon and Pomponio.

United States v. Carpenter forecloses the government's argument. In *Carpenter,* we reversed the conspiracy conviction of defendant Winans, a Wall Street Journal reporter who participated in a scheme with his friends Felis and Brant to misappropriate insider information and to use it for personal gain. Felis then passed the insider in-

---

4. The following is an excerpt from Pomponio's SEC audiotape testimony at the moment when the SEC lawyer confronted Pomponio with evidence that he and Gannon had purchased the same stocks within a short period of one another:

Q: Our records reflect that Ms. Gannon purchased her stock at 8:59 a.m. on August 26, 1997.
A: That's the same day you're saying?
Q: The same day, a half-hour before you did.
A: You're kidding? I'm serious. You really have that?
Q: Yes.
A: I can't believe that. I mean I believe you, I'm not saying I don't believe you but that is sheer coincidence. That's the kind of stuff that I don't like. That is sheer coincidence.

formation to Spratt, who was not part of the original agreement. We reversed Winans's conspiracy conviction to the extent that it involved Spratt's trades. Because Winans's original trading agreement with Felis and Brant was narrowly limited to specific persons not including Spratt, about whom Winans had no knowledge, we found that by passing the information to Spratt, Felis had "'used the information obtained from Winans beyond the scope of the original agreement.'"

In *Carpenter,* we left open three hypothetical avenues of liability against Winans. First, we emphasized that Winans "might have been liable for the Spratt trades had the scope of the trading agreement been broader, to include trading by or for persons other than the small group of conspirators herein." Second, we noted that Winans might have been liable for the Spratt trades had the trades been "'part of the ramifications of the plan which could ... be reasonably forseen [sic] as a necessary or natural consequence of the unlawful agreement.'" Third, we suggested that Winans might have been liable had he "at least known of the Felis-Spratt relationship."

Because none of these avenues of liability is applicable to this case, we find that McDermott is not liable for the trades made by Pomponio. There is no record evidence suggesting that McDermott's agreement with Gannon encompassed a broader scope than the two of them. McDermott and Gannon were having an affair, and it is not obvious that it was or should have been within McDermott's frame of reference that Gannon would share stock information with others similarly situated, or even that there existed others similarly situated. We decline to hold as a matter of law that a cheating heart must foresee a cheating heart. Indeed, the only evidence that McDermott did foresee or should have foreseen Gannon passing information to Pomponio consisted of evidence suggesting that Gannon was a prostitute—evidence that the district court explicitly prohibited. Moreover, the proof at trial established that McDermott had no knowledge of Pomponio's existence.

Accordingly, we hold that, as a matter of law, no rational jury could find McDermott guilty beyond a reasonable doubt of a single conspiracy with Pomponio to commit insider trading. The government has failed to show the most basic element of a single conspiracy, namely, an agreement to pass insider information to Gannon and possibly to another person, even if unknown. We therefore reverse the judgment of conviction on that count.

Discussion Questions

1. Should conspirator A's conspiracy liability be limited to the acts of other conspirators of whom A is aware? Or should conspiracy law treat A as assuming the risk that a coconspirator will involve an additional conspirator A is not aware of? In other words, is it fair to find that A has conspired with other people A never met and does not know are involved in the conspiracy?

2. McDermott did not apparently know about Pomponio. But Pomponio presumably knew about McDermott. From whose perspective should the scope of the conspiracy be measured? McDermott's? Gannon's? Pomponio's?

3. Even if McDermott did not know and should not have known of Gannon's intimate relationship with Pomponio, why isn't it reasonably foreseeable that Gannon might pass along stock tips to another person, such as a friend or family member? Consider the approach in Alabama:

> If a person knows or should know that one with whom he/she agrees has in turn agreed or will agree with another to effect the same criminal objective, he/she shall be deemed to have agreed with such other person, whether or not he/she knows the other's identity. Alabama Code § 13A-4-3.

4. Was it fair for the government to try McDermott and Pomponio together when the two had never met? What strategic advantages might there be for the prosecution in having such a joint trial?

3. Duration

United States v. Jimenez Recio

537 U.S. 270 (2003)
United States Supreme Court

Breyer, J.

We here consider the validity of a Ninth Circuit rule that a conspiracy ends automatically when the object of the conspiracy becomes impossible to achieve—when, for example, the Government frustrates a drug conspiracy's objective by seizing the drugs that its members have agreed to distribute. In our view, conspiracy law does not contain any such "automatic termination" rule.

In *United States v. Cruz*, the Ninth Circuit ... wrote that a conspiracy terminates when "there is affirmative evidence of abandonment, withdrawal, disavowal *or defeat of the object of the conspiracy*" (emphasis added). It considered the conviction of an individual who, the Government had charged, joined a conspiracy (to distribute drugs) after the Government had seized the drugs in question. The Circuit found that the Government's seizure of the drugs guaranteed the "defeat" of the conspiracy's objective, namely, drug distribution. The Circuit held that the conspiracy had terminated with that "defeat," *i.e.*, when the Government seized the drugs. Hence the individual, who had joined the conspiracy after that point, could not be convicted as a conspiracy member.

In this case the lower courts applied the *Cruz* rule to similar facts: On November 18, 1997, police stopped a truck in Nevada. They found, and seized, a large stash of illegal drugs. With the help of the truck's two drivers, they set up a sting. The Government took the truck to the drivers' destination, a mall in Idaho. The drivers paged a contact and described the truck's location. The contact said that he would call someone to get the truck. And three hours later, the two defendants, Francisco Jimenez Recio and Adrian Lopez-Meza, appeared in a car. Jimenez Recio drove away in the truck; Lopez-Meza drove the car away in a similar direction. Police stopped both vehicles and arrested both men.

A federal grand jury indicted Jimenez Recio, Lopez-Meza, and the two original truck drivers, charging them with having conspired, together and with others, to possess and to distribute unlawful drugs. A jury convicted all four. But the trial judge then decided that the jury instructions had been erroneous in respect to Jimenez Recio and Lopez-Meza. The judge noted that the Ninth Circuit, in *Cruz* had held that the Government could not prosecute drug conspiracy defendants unless they had joined the conspiracy before the Government seized the drugs. That holding, as applied here, meant that the jury could not convict Jimenez Recio and Lopez-Meza unless the jury believed they had joined the conspiracy before the Nevada police stopped the truck and seized the drugs. The judge ordered a new trial where the jury would be instructed to that effect. The new jury convicted the two men once again.

Jimenez Recio and Lopez-Meza appealed. They pointed out that, given *Cruz* the jury had to find that they had joined the conspiracy before the Nevada stop, and they claimed that the evidence was insufficient at both trials to warrant any such jury finding. The Ninth Circuit panel, by a vote of 2 to 1, agreed.... The Government sought certiorari. It noted that the Ninth Circuit's holding in this case was premised upon the legal rule enunciated in *Cruz*. And it asked us to decide the rule's validity, *i.e.,* to decide whether "a conspiracy ends as a matter of law when the government frustrates its objective." We agreed to consider that question.

In *Cruz,* the Ninth Circuit held that a conspiracy continues "until there is affirmative evidence of abandonment, withdrawal, disavowal or defeat of the object of the conspiracy." The critical portion of this statement is the last segment, that a conspiracy ends once there has been "defeat of [its] object." The Circuit's holdings make clear that the phrase means that the conspiracy ends through "defeat" when the Government intervenes, making the conspiracy's goals impossible to achieve, even if the conspirators do not know that the Government has intervened and are totally unaware that the conspiracy is bound to fail. In our view, this statement of the law is incorrect. A conspiracy does not automatically terminate simply because the Government, unbeknownst to some of the conspirators, has "defeat[ed]" the conspiracy's "object."

Two basic considerations convince us that this is the proper view of the law. First, the Ninth Circuit's rule is inconsistent with our own understanding of basic conspiracy law. The Court has repeatedly said that the essence of a conspiracy is "an agreement to commit an unlawful act." That agreement is "a distinct evil," which "may exist and be punished whether or not the substantive crime ensues." The conspiracy poses a "threat to the public" over and above the threat of the commission of the relevant substantive crime—both because the "[c]ombination in crime makes more likely the commission of [other] crimes" and because it "decreases the probability that the individuals involved will depart from their path of criminality." Where police have frustrated a conspiracy's specific objective but conspirators (unaware of that fact) have neither abandoned the conspiracy nor withdrawn, these special conspiracy-related dangers remain. So too remains the essence of the conspiracy—the agreement to commit the crime. That being so, the Government's defeat of the conspiracy's objective will not necessarily and automatically terminate the conspiracy.

Second, the view we endorse today is the view of almost all courts and commentators but for the Ninth Circuit. No other Federal Court of Appeals has adopted the Ninth Circuit's rule. Three have explicitly rejected it.... [T]he American Law Institute's Model Penal Code § 5.03 would find that a conspiracy "terminates when the crime or crimes that are its object are committed" or when the relevant "agreement ... is abandoned." It would not find "impossibility" a basis for termination.

The *Cruz* majority argued that the more traditional termination rule threatened "endless" potential liability. To illustrate the point, the majority posited a sting in which police instructed an arrested conspirator to go through the "telephone directory ... [and] call all of his acquaintances" to come and help him, with the Government obtaining convictions of those who did so. The problem with this example, however, is that, even though it is not necessarily an example of entrapment itself, it draws its persuasive force from the fact that it bears certain resemblances to entrapment. The law independently forbids convictions that rest upon entrapment. And the example fails to explain why a different branch of the law, conspiracy law, should be modified to forbid entrapment-like behavior that falls outside the bounds of current entrapment law. At the same time, the *Cruz* rule would reach well beyond arguable police misbehavior, potentially threatening the use of properly run law enforcement sting operations....

We conclude that the Ninth Circuit's conspiracy-termination law holding set forth in *Cruz* is erroneous in the manner discussed. We reverse the present judgment insofar as it relies upon that holding.

Discussion Questions

1. When should a conspiracy that fails to achieve its objective be treated as ending? When the objective of the conspiracy becomes impossible to achieve (e.g., when the government seizes drugs the conspiracy aims to distribute)? Or when the agreement underlying the conspiracy is abandoned? What are the arguments for and against each termination point?

2. When should a conspiracy that achieves its objective be treated as ending? When the target crime is committed? Or should the criminal law recognize that an agreement to commit a crime is likely to include an explicit or implicit agreement to conceal aspects of the crime extending well beyond the time of the crime's commission (e.g., to conceal the identity of the criminals, the means used to commit the crime, or even commission of the crime itself)? What are the arguments for and against recognizing such a concealment phase to conspiracies?

3. How does the doctrine regarding impossibility in the conspiracy context compare with that in the area of attempt liability?

4. The Wharton Rule

Another limitation on conspiracy liability is known as the Wharton Rule. It prevents prosecution for conspiracy "when the crime is of such a nature as to necessarily require the participation of two persons for its commission."[2] For example, assume that the crime of dueling requires the participation of two persons. Under such circumstances, even if Joe and Linda agree to duel against one another, and otherwise fulfill the jurisdiction's requirements for conspiracy, application of the Wharton Rule would prevent a successful conspiracy prosecution against them. According to Wharton, "the author whose name ... [the Rule] bears, ... conspiracy assumes ... a crime of such a nature that it is aggravated by a plurality of agents."[3] Because dueling already requires two people, dueling would not be a crime aggravated by having two people agree to duel. In 1975, the United States Supreme Court noted that "[t]he [Wharton] Rule ha[d] been applied by numerous courts, state and federal alike."[4]

In which of the following problems would the Wharton Rule prevent successful prosecution for conspiracy?

Problems

12.14 Claire agrees to sell narcotics to John and they commit a sufficient overt act to satisfy the applicable conspiracy statute. Can the prosecutor charge Claire with conspiracy to sell narcotics to John?

12.15 Travis and Hope agree to marry each other and then proceed to get married. Travis, however, is already married to Pam. Can the prosecution charge Travis with conspiracy to commit bigamy?

12.16 Yolanda and Nevil agree to and commit robbery. Can the prosecution charge Yolanda with conspiracy to commit robbery?

E. Abandonment

Problem

12.17 Part (a) Bill and Bob are driving in Bill's car one night when they notice a young woman alone and heading to her car in a remote corner of a parking lot. Bob and Bill quickly decide to rob the woman and use the money to go drinking at a local bar. Bill turns into the parking lot and pulls his car up next

---

2. *Ianelli v. United States*, 420 U.S. 770, 773 at n. 5 (1975) (quoting 1 R. ANDERSON, WHARTON'S CRIMINAL LAW AND PROCEDURE § 89, p. 191 (1957)).

3. MPC Commentaries § 5.04 p.482 (ALI 1985) (citing 2 F. WHARTON, CRIMINAL LAW § 1604 (12th ed. 1932)).

4. *Id.* at 774.

to the woman. Bob rolls down his window and, pretending to be lost, attempts to engage her in conversation. The woman is suspicious, though, and runs to her car. Bob yells "Let's get her!" Bill steps on the gas and pulls his car in front of the woman's car, attempting to prevent her escape. She then begins flashing her car's lights and honking its horn in an effort to draw attention to her plight. Bill abruptly pulls away and speeds out of the parking lot. Can Bill and Bob avoid liability for conspiracy by asserting they abandoned their conspiracy to rob the young woman?

Part (b) What if, after the woman runs to her car, instead of yelling "Let's get her!" Bob tells Bill he thinks it is not such a good idea to rob the woman, but Bill nonetheless continues with the plan and in fact robs the woman of her purse. Can Bob use an abandonment defense to a conspiracy charge?

Part (c) What if, after the woman runs to her car, Bill tells Bob he thinks it is not such a good idea to rob the woman, then turns the car around and leaves the parking lot. Can Bill use an abandonment defense to a conspiracy charge?

Model Penal Code

§ 5.06 Criminal Conspiracy

(6) **Renunciation of Criminal Purpose.** It is an affirmative defense that the actor, after conspiring to commit a crime, thwarted the success of the conspiracy, under circumstances manifesting a complete and voluntary renunciation of his criminal purpose.

Tennessee Code Annotated

§ 39-12-103 Criminal conspiracy

(e) (2) Abandonment of a conspiracy is presumed if neither the person nor anyone with whom the person conspired does any overt act in pursuance of the conspiracy during the applicable period of limitation.

(3) If an individual abandons the agreement, the conspiracy is terminated as to that person only if and when the person advises those with whom the person conspired of the abandonment, or the person informs law enforcement authorities of the existence of the conspiracy and of the person's participation therein.

Official Code of Georgia

§ 16-4-9 Withdrawal by coconspirator from agreement to commit crime

A coconspirator may be relieved from the effects of [the Georgia conspiracy statute] if he can show that before the overt act occurred he withdrew his agreement to commit a crime.

F. Synthesis and Review

1. Professor Phillip Johnson has argued that conspiracy is an "unnecessary crime" given the reach of modern attempt statutes.[5] Based on your study of these two anticipatory crimes, does the crime of conspiracy serve any function not served by the law of attempt?

2. If someone succeeds in committing the target offense, she cannot typically also be punished for an attempt to commit that offense although she will often have met all the requirements for an attempt. In other words, attempt liability evaporates upon completion of the target offense, a phenomenon traditionally described as the attempt *merging* with the completed offense. The same is not true for conspiracy. One who conspires to rob a bank and succeeds in robbing the bank may receive separate, cumulative punishment for both the bank robbery and the conspiracy. In traditional terminology, the crime of conspiracy does not merge with the completed target offense. When a defendant succeeds in committing the target offense, should separate punishment for anticipatory offenses be imposed? Why? Does it make sense to distinguish between attempt and conspiracy in answering these questions?

3. Should anticipatory offenses be combined? In other words, should we allow an anticipatory offense to be the target crime for another anticipatory offense? Consider the following possibilities:

   (a) conspiracy to attempt a crime?

   (b) conspiracy to solicit another to commit a crime?

   (c) attempt to conspire to commit a crime?

   (d) solicitation to conspire to commit a crime?

Problem

12.18 Part (a) Sherry Jones is a state court trial judge. The highest court in her state has issued an opinion indicating that state judges need not cooperate with federal immigration authorities seeking to enforce a civil immigration detainer against criminal suspects in the United States illegally. An immigration detainer is a formal request made by U.S. Immigration and Customs Enforcement (ICE) to another law enforcement agency, such as a local police department, to hold an individual whom ICE believes is deportable so that agents can take the person into custody. David Jimenez, an undocumented immigrant, has been charged

---

5. Phillip E. Johnson, *The Unnecessary Crime of Conspiracy*, 61 CAL. L. REV. 1137 (1973).

with a low-level theft crime. Judge Jones is handling his arraignment while federal ICE agents sit outside the courtroom waiting to apprehend Jimenez pursuant to a valid immigration detainer. Judge Jones, Jimenez's attorney, and the court bailiff hold a sidebar conference, during which the audiotape—ordinarily used by the court stenographer to record the proceedings—is turned off. Shortly thereafter, the bailiff takes Jimenez from the courtroom and allows him to leave the building through a side door, evading the ICE officials. Is Judge Jones guilty of violating the following statute?

> Whoever corruptly, or by threats or force, or by any threatening letter or communication influences, obstructs, or impedes or endeavors to influence, obstruct, or impede the due and proper administration of the law under which any pending proceeding is being had before any department or agency of the United States ... Shall be fined under this title, imprisoned not more than 5 years ... or both. 18 United States Code § 1505.

Part (b) Is Judge Jones guilty of *conspiring* to violate 18 United States Code § 1505 above?

Chapter 13

Theft

A. Introduction

Many crimes, such as homicide and rape, focus on physical harm or the risk of physical harm. But criminal law is also concerned with protecting property. The subject of this chapter, the law of theft, is one example.

This chapter examines four traditional theft offenses: larceny, larceny by trick, embezzlement, and false pretenses. We consider them through jury instructions, cases, and problems. Once we have developed an understanding of the components of these offenses, we turn to the historical development of theft to better understand why the distinctions among these types of theft arose. From there, we consider the fundamental and challenging issue of what types of property can be the subject of theft laws. Finally, we examine the Model Penal Code's consolidation of many previously distinct theft offenses into a single statutory scheme. Before turning to traditional theft offenses, though, we consider two recent appellate opinions that illustrate the challenges of applying statutes and traditional concepts found in the law of theft to the realities of the digital world.

The following two appellate opinions arose from federal and state prosecutions of Sergey Aleynikov, a computer programmer who, prior to leaving a job with one employer, surreptitiously made a digital copy of that employer's proprietary source code and then shared it with his new employer. What Aleynikov did certainly seems both blameworthy and something society would want to deter. His employer's source code was apparently quite valuable and thus one would think the criminal law should protect it. But is the law of theft, which is derived from common law created centuries ago, up to the task of protecting intellectual property in digital form? Have legislatures, through more modern statutes, provided protection for those such as Aleynikov's employer? You will see that the trial and appellate judges in the *Aleynikov* cases disagreed on how these questions should be answered.

The *Aleynikov* cases illustrate the challenges presented in applying statutes to the digital world and in setting the boundaries of concepts fundamental to the law of theft, such as what constitutes property, in modern contexts. In the federal case, the trial judge (and a jury) concluded that Aleynikov's source code copying fell within the federal theft statute under which he had been charged. On appeal, the Second Circuit disagreed, concluding that it did not fall within that statute. In the subsequent state prosecution, the trial judge found that Aleynikov had not violated a New York statute dealing with unlawful use of secret scientific material. As the Second Circuit did in the federal case, the New York appellate court disagreed with and reversed the trial judge. But, unlike the Second Circuit, the New York appellate court held that Aleynikov had violated the statute under which he had been tried and convicted.

These cases provide a preview of issues you will study later in this chapter, such as the types of conduct required by theft offenses and what constitutes the "property" that theft laws are meant to protect. Recall that in the *Barger* case in the section on possession in Chapter 4, *Conduct*, we saw the Oregon Supreme Court, as well as several state legislatures, grappling with a similar task—how to set the boundaries of traditional concepts of possession and control in the digital world of the Internet. The *Aleynikov* cases also provide a good opportunity to review in a new context issues you studied in Chapter 3, *Making Criminal Law*, such as various approaches to statutory interpretation and the role judges should or should not play in adapting statutes to new circumstances.

United States v. Aleynikov

676 F.3d 71 (2012)
United States Court of Appeals for the Second Circuit

Dennis, C.J.

Sergey Aleynikov was convicted, following a jury trial in the United States District Court for the Southern District of New York (Cote, J.), of stealing and transferring some of the proprietary computer source code used in his employer's high frequency trading system, in violation of the National Stolen Property Act, 18 U.S.C. § 2314 (the "NSPA").... On appeal, Aleynikov argues that his conduct did not constitute an offense under [the NSPA]. He argues that ... the source code was not a "stolen" "good" within the meaning of the NSPA.... We agree, and reverse the judgment of the district court.

Sergey Aleynikov, a computer programmer, was employed by Goldman Sachs & Co. ("Goldman") from May 2007 through June 2009, developing computer source code for the company's proprietary high-frequency trading ("HFT") system. An HFT system is a mechanism for making large volumes of trades in securities and commodities based on trading decisions effected in fractions of a second. Trades are executed on the basis of algorithms that incorporate rapid market developments and data from past trades. The computer programs used to operate Goldman's HFT system are of three kinds: [1] market connectivity programs that process real-time market data and execute trades; [2] programs that use algorithms to determine which trades to make; and [3] infrastructure programs that facilitate the flow of information throughout the trading system and monitor the system's performance. Aleynikov's work focused on developing code for this last category of infrastructure programs in Goldman's HFT system. High frequency trading is a competitive business that depends in large part on the speed with which information can be processed to seize fleeting market opportunities. Goldman closely guards the secrecy of each component of the system, and does not license the system to anyone. Goldman's confidentiality policies bound Aleynikov to keep in strict confidence all the firm's proprietary information, including any intellectual property created by Aleynikov. He was barred as well from taking it or using it when his employment ended.

By 2009, Aleynikov was earning $400,000, the highest-paid of the twenty-five programmers in his group. In April 2009, he accepted an offer to become an Executive Vice President at Teza Technologies LLC, a Chicago-based startup that was looking to develop its own HFT system. Aleynikov was hired, at over $1 million a year, to develop the market connectivity and infrastructure components of Teza's HFT system. Teza's founder (a former head of HFT at Chicago-based hedge fund Citadel Investment Group) emailed Aleynikov (and several other employees) in late May, conveying his expectation that they would develop a functional trading system within six months. It usually takes years for a team of programmers to develop an HFT system from scratch.

Aleynikov's last day at Goldman was June 5, 2009. At approximately 5:20 p.m., just before his going-away party, Aleynikov encrypted and uploaded to a server in Germany more than 500,000 lines of source code for Goldman's HFT system, including code for a substantial part of the infrastructure, and some of the algorithms and market data connectivity programs.

Some of the code pertained to programs that could operate independently of the rest of the Goldman system and could be integrated into a competitor's system. After uploading the source code, Aleynikov deleted the encryption program as well as the history of his computer commands. When he returned to his home in New Jersey, Aleynikov downloaded the source code from the server in Germany to his home computer, and copied some of the files to other computer devices he owned.

On July 2, 2009, Aleynikov flew from New Jersey to Chicago to attend meetings at Teza. He brought with him a flash drive and a laptop containing portions of the Goldman source code. When Aleynikov flew back the following day, he was arrested by the FBI at Newark Liberty International Airport.

The indictment charged him with violating ... the NSPA, which makes it a crime to "transport, transmit, or transfer in interstate or foreign commerce any goods, wares, merchandise, securities or money, of the value of $5,000 or more, knowing the same to have been stolen, converted or taken by fraud," 18 U.S.C. § 2314.... Aleynikov moved to dismiss the indictment for failure to state an offense. The district court ... denied Aleynikov's motion.

On appeal, Aleynikov renews his challenge to the sufficiency of the indictment [concerning violation of the NSPA].... Aleynikov argues that the source code—as purely intangible property—is not a "good" that was "stolen" within the meaning of the NSPA.

Aleynikov's challenge requires us to determine the scope of [the NSPA]. Statutory construction "must begin with the language employed by Congress and the assumption that the ordinary meaning of that language accurately expresses the legislative purpose." "Due respect for the prerogatives of Congress in defining federal crimes prompts restraint in this area, where we typically find a narrow interpretation appropriate."

We conclude that Aleynikov's conduct did not constitute an offense under ... the NSPA ... and that the indictment was therefore legally insufficient....

The NSPA makes it a crime to "transport, transmit, or transfer in interstate or foreign commerce any goods, wares, merchandise, securities or money, of the value of $5,000 or more, knowing the same to have been stolen, converted or taken by fraud." 18 U.S.C. § 2314. The statute does not define the terms "goods," "wares," or "merchandise." We have held that they provide "a general and comprehensive designation of such personal property or chattels as are ordinarily a subject of commerce." The decisive question is whether the source code that Aleynikov uploaded to a server in Germany, then downloaded to his computer devices in New Jersey, and later transferred to Illinois, constituted stolen "goods," "wares," or "merchandise" within the meaning of the NSPA. Based on the substantial weight of the case law, as well as the ordinary meaning of the words, we conclude that it did not.

We first considered the applicability of the NSPA to the theft of intellectual property in *United States v. Bottone*, 365 F.2d 389 (2d Cir. 1966) (Friendly, J.), in which photocopied documents outlining manufacturing procedures for certain pharmaceuticals were transported across state lines. Since the actual processes themselves (as opposed to photocopies) were never transported across state lines, the "serious question" (we explained) was whether "the papers showing [the] processes that were transported in interstate or foreign commerce were 'goods' which had been 'stolen, converted or taken by fraud' in view of the lack of proof that any of the physical materials so transported came from [the manufacturer's] possession." We held that the NSPA was violated there, observing that what was "stolen and transported" was, ultimately, "tangible goods," notwithstanding the "clever intermediate transcription [and] use of a photocopy machine." However, we suggested that a different result would obtain if there was no physical taking of tangible property whatsoever: "To be sure, where no tangible objects were ever taken or transported, a court would be hard pressed to conclude that 'goods' had been stolen and transported within the meaning of 2314." Hence, we observed, "the statute would presumably not extend to the case where a carefully guarded secret formula was memorized, carried away in the recesses of a thievish mind and placed in writing only after a boundary had been crossed." *Bottone* itself thus treats its holding as the furthest limit of a statute that is not endlessly elastic: Some tangible property must be taken from the owner for there to be deemed a "good" that is "stolen" for purposes of the NSPA.

Bottone's reading of the NSPA is confirmed by the Supreme Court's opinion in *Dowling v. United States*, 473 U.S. 207 (1985), which held that the NSPA did not apply to an interstate bootleg record operation. *Dowling* rejected the Government's argument that the unauthorized use of the musical compositions rendered them "stolen, converted or taken by fraud." Cases prosecuted under the NSPA "have always involved physical 'goods, wares, [or] merchandise' that have themselves been 'stolen, converted or taken by fraud' "—even if the stolen thing does not "remain in entirely unaltered form," and "owes a major portion of its value to an intangible component."

"This basic element"—the taking of a physical thing—"comports with the common-sense meaning of the statutory language: by requiring that the 'goods, wares [or] merchandise' be 'the same' as those 'stolen, converted or taken by fraud,' the provision seems clearly to contemplate a physical identity between the items unlawfully obtained and those eventually transported, and hence some prior physical taking of the subject goods."

We join other circuits in relying on *Dowling* for the proposition that the theft and subsequent interstate transmission of purely intangible property is beyond the scope of the NSPA.

In a close analog to the present case, the Tenth Circuit affirmed the dismissal of an indictment alleging that the defendant transported in interstate commerce a computer program containing source code that was taken from his employer. *United States v. Brown*, 925 F.2d 1301, 1305, 1309 (10th Cir. 1991). Citing *Dowling*, the court held that the NSPA "applies only to physical 'goods, wares or merchandise' " and that "[p]urely intellectual property is not within this category. It can be represented physically, such as through writing on a page, but the underlying, intellectual property itself, remains intangible." The Court concluded that "the computer program itself is an intangible intellectual property, and as such, it alone cannot constitute goods, wares, merchandise, securities or moneys which have been stolen, converted or taken" for purposes of the NSPA.

Similarly, the Seventh Circuit has held that numerical "Comdata codes" used by truckers to access money transfers at truck stops constitute intangible property the theft of which is not a violation of the NSPA. *United States v. Stafford*, 136 F.3d 1109 (7th Cir. 1998). The court reasoned that the codes themselves were not "goods, wares, or merchandise," but rather "information"; that the defendant had not been charged with transporting pieces of paper containing the codes; and that the only conduct charged was "transferring the codes themselves, which are simply sequences of digits."

The First Circuit has also concluded that the NSPA does not criminalize the theft of intangible things: The NSPA "does not apply to purely 'intangible information,' the theft of which is punishable under copyright law and other intellectual property statutes" but "*does apply* when there has been 'some tangible item taken, however insignificant or valueless it may be, absent the intangible component.' " *United States v. Martin*, 228 F.3d 1, 14–15 (1st Cir. 2000).

The Government argues that a tangibility requirement ignores a 1988 amendment, which added the words "transmit" and "transfer" to the terms: "transport, transmit, or transfer." The Government contends that the added words reflect an intent to cover generally transfers and transmissions of non-physical forms of stolen property. The evident purpose of the amendment, however, was to clarify that the statute applied to non-physical electronic transfers of *money*. Money, though it can be intangible, is specifically enumerated in § 2314 as a thing apart and distinct from "goods," "wares," or "merchandise." The addition to the possible means of transport does not bespeak an intent to alter or expand the ordinary meaning of "goods," "wares," or "merchandise" and therefore does not obviate the Government's need to identify a predicate good, ware, merchandise, security, or money that has been stolen.

By uploading Goldman's proprietary source code to a computer server in Germany, Aleynikov stole purely intangible property embodied in a purely intangible format. There was no allegation that he physically seized anything tangible from Goldman, such as a compact disc or thumb drive containing source code, so we need not decide whether that would suffice as a physical theft. Aleynikov later transported portions of the source code to Chicago, on his laptop and flash drive. However, there is no violation of the statute unless the good is transported with knowledge that "the same" has been stolen; the statute therefore presupposes that the thing stolen was a good or ware, etc., *at the time of the theft*. The wording "contemplate[s] a physical identity between the items unlawfully obtained and those eventually transported." The later storage of intangible property on a tangible medium does not transform the intangible property into a stolen good.

The infringement of copyright in *Dowling* parallels Aleynikov's theft of computer code. Although "[t]he infringer invades a statutorily defined province guaranteed to the copyright holder alone[,] ... he does not assume physical control over the copyright; nor does he wholly deprive its owner of its use." Because Aleynikov did not "assume physical control" over anything when he took the source code, and because he did not thereby "deprive [Goldman] of its use," Aleynikov did not violate the NSPA.

As the district court observed, Goldman's source code is highly valuable, and there is no doubt that in virtually every case involving proprietary computer code worth stealing, the value of the intangible code will vastly exceed the value of any physical item on which it might be stored. But federal crimes are "solely creatures of statute." We decline to stretch or update statutory words of plain and ordinary meaning in order to better accommodate the digital age.

For the foregoing reasons, the judgment of the district court is reversed.

People v. Aleynikov

148 A.D.3d 77 (2017)
Supreme Court of New York, Appellate Division, First Department

The People appeal from the order of the Supreme Court, New York County (Daniel P. Conviser, J.), ... which granted defendant's motion for a trial order of dismissal to the extent of setting aside the jury's verdict convicting him of unlawful use of secret scientific material.

Richter, J.... In September 2012, defendant was charged in a New York County indictment with two counts of unlawful use of secret scientific material (Penal Law § 165.07) (one count based on defendant's transfer of data on June 1, 2009, and the other based on his June 5, 2009 transfer), and one count of unlawful duplication of computer related material in the first degree (Penal Law § 156.30[1]). These state charges were based on the same conduct that led to his federal prosecution. On April 8, 2015, defendant proceeded to a trial before a jury. At the close of the People's case, defendant moved, pursuant to CPL 290.10, for a trial order of dismissal as to all counts of the indictment; the court reserved decision on the motion.

The jury returned a verdict of guilty on the count of the indictment charging unlawful use of secret scientific material arising from the June 5, 2009 transfer.... In a decision entered on or about July 6, 2015, as amended July 7, 2015, the trial court granted defendant's motion for a trial order of dismissal as to the two counts of unlawful use. The court concluded that the evidence was insufficient to show that: (i) defendant made a "tangible reproduction or representation" of the source code; and (ii) he acted with the "intent to appropriate ... the use of" the source code. The People appeal from the court's order to the extent it dismissed the unlawful use count related to the June 5, 2009 transfer. We now reverse.

... [W]e conclude that the evidence at trial was legally sufficient to establish defendant's guilt of unlawful use of secret scientific material. That statute, which became part of the Penal Law in 1967, provides:

> "A person is guilty of unlawful use of secret scientific material when, *with intent to appropriate to himself or another the use of secret scientific material*, and having no right to do so and no reasonable ground to believe that he has such right, he makes a *tangible reproduction or representation of such secret scientific material* by means of writing, photographing, drawing, mechanically or *electronically reproducing or recording* such secret scientific material"

(Penal Law § 165.07 [emphasis added]). In his motion for a trial order of dismissal, defendant did not challenge the People's proof that he electronically reproduced the source code. Nor did he claim that the source code did not constitute "secret scientific material," as that term is defined in Penal Law § 155.00(6). Rather, as relevant here, he argued that he did not make a tangible reproduction of the source code and that he lacked the requisite intent.

Although there is a dearth of case law interpreting this provision, the legislative history reveals why it was added to the Penal Law. The Temporary Commission on Revision of the Penal Law and Criminal Code explained that prior to the statute's enactment, "a person who [stole] the blueprints of a secret process, commit[ted] larceny[, but] one who surreptitiously [made] a photographic copy of such blueprint, leaving the original in its proper place, [did] not commit larceny because he [was] not stealing property'" (1967 NY Legis Ann at 21; *see* William C. Donnino, Practice Commentary, McKinney's Cons Laws of NY, Book 39, Penal Law § 165.07 at 200 ["In the absence of the unlawful use crime, the photographing [of a document containing a secret scientific formula] would not be a crime since it does not represent a traditional taking of the property'"]).

With this context in place, we turn to the arguments advanced by the People on this appeal. First, the People contend that, contrary to the trial court's conclusion, the evidence was sufficient to establish that defendant made a "tangible reproduction or representation" of the source code. The Penal Law does not define "tangible." ... As the clearest indicator of legislative intent is the statutory text, the starting point in any case of interpretation must always be the language itself, giving effect to the plain meaning thereof.'"

We must "presum[e] that lawmakers have used words as they are commonly or ordinarily employed, unless there is something in the context or purpose of the [statute] which shows a contrary intention." Further, Penal Law provisions "must be construed according to the fair import of their terms to promote justice and effect the objects of the law" (Penal Law § 5.00), and courts should "dispense with hypertechnical or strained interpretations" of penal provisions.

Where, as here, a word is not defined by statute, dictionary definitions serve as "useful guideposts" in determining the word's meaning. Black's Law Dictionary defines "tangible" as "[h]aving or possessing physical form; CORPOREAL[;] [c]apable of being touched and seen; perceptible to the touch; capable of being possessed or realized" (Black's Law Dictionary [9th ed 2009]). The People and defendant are in essential agreement that the term "tangible" means something having "physical form and characteristics." The heart of their dispute is whether defendant made a "tangible reproduction or representation" of Goldman's source code when he copied and saved the code onto the hard drive of the German server. We conclude that he did.

The testimony of the People's witnesses at trial established that defendant created a copy of the source code that physically resided on the server's hard drive, a physical medium. Mirko Manske, a German law enforcement officer, described how police removed "physical" hard drives from the German server. Other witnesses testified that computer data can be physically present on various storage media, including hard drives. FBI Agent Michael McSwain explained that source code that is stored on a computer's hard drive "takes up physical space" on the hard drive. Navin Kumar, a computer engineer at Goldman, testified that when computer files are stored on a hard drive or compact disk, they are "physically present on that hard drive or [compact disk]." In fact, Kumar stated that data can be "visible" in the "aggregate" when stored on a medium such as a compact disk. Kumar explained that although source code in its abstract sense as intellectual property does not have physical form, a "representation" of the source code is "concrete."

Despite this testimony, defendant argues that he did not make a "tangible reproduction or representation" of Goldman's source code because the source code remained in an intangible state even when defendant saved it onto the server's hard drive. The relevant question, however, is not whether the source code itself was tangible, but whether defendant made a tangible *reproduction* of it, which he unquestionably did when he copied it onto the server's "physical" hard drive where it took up "physical space" and was "physically present" (*see People v Barden*, 117 AD3d at 231 n 5 [although a credit card number is intangible, it can be reduced to a tangible medium in the form of an imprinted plastic credit card]; *United States v Zhang*, 995 F Supp 2d 340, 349 [ED Pa 2014] ["information stored in computer hardware has a physical manifestation"]; *see also* Penal Law §§ 156.00[2], [3] [both a "(c)omputer program" and "(c)omputer data" can exist "in any form, including magnetic storage media, punched cards, *or stored internally in the memory of the computer*" [emphasis added]).

There is no merit to defendant's argument that the unlawful use statute could not have been intended to criminalize his conduct because it was enacted in 1967, long before the advent of the technology used by defendant to copy Goldman's proprietary information. Whether the legislature envisioned the specific type of technology that exists today is not dispositive of this appeal. The statute was drafted with broad generalized language that fits squarely into today's digital world (*see People v Russo*, 131 Misc 2d 677, 681, 683, 501 N.Y.S.2d 276 [Suffolk County Court 1986] [concluding that in drafting the unlawful use statute, the legislature provided an "an elastic ... definition" for "secret scientific material" so as to include a "computer program" within its ambit]). It proscribes making tangible reproductions or representations of secret scientific material not only by means of "writing, photographing [and] drawing," but also by "mechanically or *electronically reproducing or recording* [the] material" (Penal Law § 165.07 [emphasis added]). There is no dispute that defendant's copying of the source code here was accomplished by "electronically reproducing" the code.

The trial court's apparent belief that the source code had to have been printed on paper in order to be tangible is at odds with the language of the statute. The statute merely requires a "tangible reproduction or representation" of the secret material, and is silent as to the medium upon which the reproduction or representation will reside. Thus, the fact that defendant made the reproduction onto a physical hard drive, rather than onto a piece of paper, is of no consequence. Both are tangible within the meaning of the unlawful use statute. It would be incongruous to allow defendant to escape criminal liability merely because he made a digital copy of the misappropriated source code instead of printing it onto a piece of paper (*see Thyroff v Nationwide Mut. Ins. Co.*, 8 NY3d 283, 292, 864 N.E.2d 1272, 832 N.Y.S.2d 873 [2007], quoting *Kremen v Cohen*, 337 F3d 1024, 1034 [9th Cir 2003] ["'It would be a curious jurisprudence that turned on the existence of a paper document rather than an electronic one'"]).

The natural extension of the trial court's position is that even if defendant had copied the source code onto a compact disk or a thumb drive, and walked out of Goldman's premises with that device, he still would not have violated the unlawful use statute because no paper was involved. Such a result makes little sense because a compact disk and a thumb drive are both unquestionably tangible. The trial court's position also ignores the trial evidence that a hard drive can be taken out of the server, and thus has a physical presence independent of the computer in which it was housed....

The Second Circuit's reversal of defendant's federal conviction under the National Stolen Property Act (18 USC § 2314) does not change the result. That federal statute makes it a crime, as relevant here, to "transmit, or transfer in ... foreign commerce any goods, ... knowing the same to have been stolen." The Second Circuit did not address the precise question presented here—whether defendant made a "tangible reproduction or representation" of the source code. Thus, the Second Circuit's interpretation of the federal statute, which has different elements from the unlawful use statute here, has no bearing on whether the trial evidence was sufficient to sustain the jury's verdict (*see Hartnett v New York City Tr. Auth.*, 200 AD2d 27, 32, [2d Dept 1994] ["A federal decision contrary in principle is not binding upon a State court in respect of a State statute."]).

Nor does the reasoning underlying the Second Circuit's decision call into question our conclusion here. In finding that defendant's conduct did not violate the National Stolen Property Act, the Second Circuit concluded that the source code transferred by defendant was "intangible property," and therefore was not a "stolen" "good" within the meaning of the federal statute. As discussed earlier, the relevant inquiry under the unlawful use statute is not whether the source code itself was tangible, but whether defendant made a tangible reproduction of it, which the evidence shows that he did....

Contrary to the trial court's conclusion, the evidence was legally sufficient to establish that defendant possessed the requisite mens rea. To sustain a conviction under the unlawful use statute, defendant must have acted with the "intent to appropriate to himself or another the use of" Goldman's source code (Penal Law § 165.07). Under Penal Law § 155.00[4], a person "appropriate[s]" property by exercising control over the property either (i) "permanently" or (ii) "for so extended a period or under such circumstances as to acquire the major portion of its economic value or benefit" (*see People v Jennings*, 69 NY2d 103, 118, 504 N.E.2d 1079, 512 N.Y.S.2d 652 [1983] [the concept of "appropriate" connotes a purpose to exert permanent or virtually permanent control]).

In finding the People's proof lacking, the trial court focused only on the second prong of the definition of "appropriate," and failed to appreciate the first prong, which refers to the intent to "permanently" exercise control. Here, the People's proof at trial permits a rational inference that defendant intended to exercise permanent control over the use of Goldman's source code, as opposed to a short-term borrowing. The People presented evidence that defendant surreptitiously uploaded the source code to the German server, downloaded it onto several personal computing devices, and then shared it with his new employer, a potential competitor of Goldman. The evidence further showed that defendant took multiple measures to cover up his illicit transfer of the data. Further, the record contains no evidence that defendant ever tried to return the misappropriated source code to Goldman, or to delete it from his or his new employer's devices.

Because the evidence was sufficient to show defendant's intent to exercise permanent control, the People correctly argue that they were not required to prove the second prong of the definition of "appropriate," i.e., that defendant intended to acquire the major portion of the economic value or benefit of the source code. Nor was it necessary for the People to prove that defendant intended to deprive Goldman of the use of the source code. The unlawful use statute only requires the intent to "appropriate" the use of the secret scientific material and does not require any intent to "deprive." Further, the statute does not require that defendant intend to appropriate the source code itself, but only the *use* of the code....

Accordingly, the order ... which ... granted defendant's motion for a trial order of dismissal to the extent of setting aside the jury's verdict convicting him of unlawful use of secret scientific material, should be reversed, on the law, the motion denied, the verdict reinstated, and the matter remanded for sentencing.

Discussion Questions

1. Aleynikov was first prosecuted in federal court. When the federal prosecution failed, New York state authorities prosecuted him in state court. Was it fair to require Aleynikov to defend himself twice for the same conduct? Given the language of the federal and state statutes at issue in the *Aleynikov* cases, would it have made sense to pursue the state case before pursuing the federal case? Why might the federal case have gone first?

2. Conducting two trials and briefing and arguing two appeals is time-consuming and costly. Should it have been this difficult to convict Aleynikov when the evidence of his misappropriation of valuable source code appeared to have been quite clear and largely uncontested by the defense?

3. What was the primary difficulty in convicting Aleynikov? The nature of his conduct? The nature of the property at issue? Or both?

4. Should the NSPA be amended to include conduct such as Aleynikov's? If so, how would you amend it?

5. Which court do you think does a better job of statutory interpretation? What approach or approaches to statutory interpretation does each opinion reflect?

6. The Second Circuit says that "a narrow interpretation" of the NSPA is appropriate. The New York appellate court states that it construes the New York statute "according to the fair import of [its] terms." What is the difference between these approaches to interpreting a statute?

7. The Second Circuit stated "We decline to stretch or update statutory words of plain and ordinary meaning in order to better accommodate the digital age." Is this the appropriate attitude for a court to take in applying an old statute in a new context? Does the New York appellate court reflect the same or a different attitude in interpreting the language of the New York statute?

8. The New York appellate court, in finding that Aleynikov's conduct fell within the New York statute, said "[i]t would be incongruous to allow defendant to escape criminal liability merely because he made a digital copy of the misappropriated source code instead of printing it onto a piece of paper." The Second Circuit appears to concede this incongruity, but nonetheless exempts Aleynikov from the reach of the federal statute. Which is the better approach?

B. Larceny

California Jury Instructions, Criminal, 6th ed.

14.02 Theft by Larceny — Defined (Pen. Code, § 487)

Defendant is accused of having committed the crime of grand theft, a violation of section 487 of the Penal Code.

Every person who steals, takes, carries, leads, or drives away the personal property of another with the specific intent to deprive the owner permanently of his property is guilty of the crime of theft by larceny. To constitute a "carrying away," the property need not be actually removed from the place or premises where it was kept, nor need it be retained by the perpetrator.

In order to prove this crime, each of the following elements must be proved:

1. A person took personal property of some value belonging to another;

2. When the person took the property she had the specific intent to deprive the alleged victim permanently of his property; and

3. The person carried the property away by obtaining physical possession and control for some period of time and by some movement of the property.

People v. Davis

19 Cal. 4th 301 (1998)
California Supreme Court

The elements of theft by larceny are well settled: the offense is committed by every person who (1) takes possession (2) of personal property (3) owned or possessed by another, (4) by means of trespass and (5) with intent to steal the property, and (6) carries the property away.

[Trespass here means without permission or consent.]

Problems

13.1 Rob heads out to remove the snow from the sidewalk in front of his home, only to discover that his snow blower is out of gasoline. Is Rob guilty of larceny in the following scenarios?

Part (a) Rob notices that the garage of his neighbor, Penelope, is open. He enters and takes her snow blower to clear his path. He intends to clear his path quickly and return the blower in less than an hour.

Part (b) Rob notices that the garage of his neighbor, Penelope, is open. He enters and siphons some of the gasoline from her snow blower into his so that his snow blower can run. When he siphons the gas, he makes a mental note to replace the gas that afternoon.

13.2 Terrance steals Jill's notebook computer, intending to sell it on eBay. On his way home from Jill's, Terrance stops at the grocery store. While Terrance is in the store, Hailey steals the computer from Terrance's car. Terrance discovers the computer missing and calls authorities, who discover the computer at Hailey's home. Can the prosecutor charge Hailey with larceny?

13.3 Sarah admires Bruce's new credit-card sized electronic organizer. Sarah asks to try it. Bruce hands it to her. Sarah takes off running with it and disappears into a waiting car. Can the prosecutor charge Sarah with larceny?

13.4 Delilah thinks that Samson's attachment to his long hair is silly. One evening, while he sleeps, Delilah cuts off Samson's ponytail. When Samson awakes, he is furious and calls the authorities requesting that Delilah be charged with larceny. Should the prosecutor charge Delilah with larceny under the jury instruction or the standard from the *Davis* case above in each of the fact patterns below?

Part (a) Delilah takes Samson's ponytail and auctions it in the local market for a substantial sum of money. She keeps the money.

Part (b) Delilah auctions the ponytail as in (a) above but gives the money to Samson.

Part (c) Delilah leaves the ponytail on the pillow next to Samson.

1. Conduct

State v. Carswell

296 N.C. 101, 249 S.E.2d 427 (1978)
Supreme Court of North Carolina

Upon a proper bill of indictment defendant was tried and convicted of felonious breaking and entering and felonious larceny. Respective consecutive sentences of ten and five years were imposed. He appealed both convictions to the Court of Appeals but they reversed as to the larceny conviction only and we allowed discretionary review thereon.

The State's evidence tended to show the following:

On the morning of 18 April 1976, Donald Ray Morgan was at the Day's Inn Motel where he was employed as a security guard. With him was Richard Strickland, a helper, and Mrs. Strickland, Richard's mother, who had brought her son some food. The motel was not in use at that time as it was still under construction. Upon inspection of the premises that morning, Mr. Morgan discovered that five or six rooms had been broken into during the night. In one of these, Room 158, the window air conditioner had been pried away from the base on which it rested in the bottom of the window, but it had not been removed.

Mr. Morgan asked Mrs. Strickland to stay at the motel while he called to report the incident to the Sheriff's Department. While he was gone, a pickup truck pulled into the motel with three people in it, one of them being the defendant. They wanted to get into the motel building and claimed that they were sent there by their boss. They left after Mrs. Strickland would not let them in.

Instead of relocking the doors that had been broken into, Mr. Morgan stayed at the motel and guarded the rooms from a point on the balcony of the second level some fifty to seventy-five feet away. Around 10:30 p.m. that night, the defendant and another man walked onto the premises of Day's Inn Motel from some nearby woods and entered Room 158. Through the window running across the entire front of the room, Mr. Morgan saw the two men take the air conditioner off its stand in the window and put it on the floor. The unit was moved approximately four to six inches toward the door.

After setting the air conditioner on the floor, the men left Room 158. Mr. Morgan stopped them as they appeared to be entering another room. The guard sent Mrs. Strickland, who again had come to the motel that night with food for her son, to the nearby Holiday Inn to call the Sheriff's Department.

Later that night, a pickup truck was seen driving up and down a road adjacent to the Day's Inn Motel. Mrs. Strickland testified that it was the same truck she had seen the defendant in that morning at the motel....

Copeland, J. The Court of Appeals held that the movement of the air conditioner in this case was an insufficient taking and asportation to constitute a case of larceny against the defendant. Because we believe that there was enough evidence to send the larceny charge to the jury, we reverse the Court of Appeals....

[T]he evidence [here] is considered in the light most favorable to the State, and the State is given the benefit of all reasonable inferences.

Larceny has been defined as "a wrongful taking and carrying away of the personal property of another without his consent, ... with intent to deprive the owner of his property and to appropriate it to the taker's use fraudulently." "A bare removal from the place in which he found the goods, though the thief does not quite make off with them, is a sufficient asportation, or carrying away." 4 W. Blackstone, Commentaries 231.

In *State v. Green*, 81 N.C. 560 (1879), the defendant unlocked his employer's safe and completely removed a drawer containing money. He was stopped before any of the money was taken from the drawer. This Court found these actions sufficient to constitute asportation of the money, and we upheld the larceny conviction.

The movement of the air conditioner in this case off its window base and four to six inches toward the door clearly is "a bare removal from the place in which the thief found [it]." The Court of Appeals apparently agreed; however, it correctly recognized that there is a taking element in larceny in addition to the asportation requirement. The Court of Appeals stated that "here the problem with the State's case is that the evidence of asportation does not also constitute sufficient evidence of taking."

This Court has defined "taking" in this context as the "severance of the goods from the possession of the owner." Thus, the accused must not only move the goods, but he must also have them in his possession, or under his control, even if only for an instant. This defendant picked the air conditioner up from its stand and laid it on the floor. This act was sufficient to put the object briefly under the control of the defendant, severed from the owner's possession.

In rare and somewhat comical situations, it is possible to have an asportation of an object without taking it, or gaining possession of it.

> "In a very famous case a rascal walking by a store lifted an overcoat from a dummy and endeavored to walk away with it. He soon discovered that the overcoat was secured by a chain and he did not succeed in breaking the chain. This was held not to be larceny because the rascal did not at any time have possession of the garment. He thought he did until he reached the end of the chain, but he was mistaken." R. Perkins, Criminal Law 222 (1957).

The air conditioner in question was not permanently connected to the premises of Day's Inn Motel at the time of the crime. It had previously been pried up from its base; therefore, when defendant and his companion moved it, they had possession of it for that moment. Thus, there was sufficient evidence to take the larceny charge to the jury.

The defendant's and the Court of Appeals' reliance on *State v. Jones*, 65 N.C. 395 (1871), is misplaced. In that case, the defendant merely turned a large barrel of turpentine, that was standing on its head, over on its side. This Court held that shifting the position of an object without moving it from where it was found is insufficient asportation to support a larceny conviction. The facts of this case show that there was an actual removal of the air conditioner from its base in the window to a point on the floor four to six inches toward the door. Thus, Jones is not controlling.

For the reasons stated above, the decision of the Court of Appeals is reversed, and the larceny judgment reinstated....

Discussion Questions

1. Why might courts have traditionally required both asportation and taking for a theft by larceny?

2. Should the "rascal" who "lifted the overcoat from a dummy" be guilty of a crime?

United States v. Mafnas

701 F.2d 83 (9th Cir. 1983)
Ninth Circuit Court of Appeals

Per Curiam.

Appellant (Mafnas) was convicted in the U.S. District Court of Guam of stealing money from two federally insured banks in violation of 18 U.S.C. §2113(b) which makes it a crime to " ... take ... with intent to steal ... any money belonging to ... any bank...."

Mafnas was employed by the Guam Armored Car Service (Service), which was hired by the Bank of Hawaii and the Bank of America to deliver bags of money. On three occasions Mafnas opened the bags and removed money. As a result he was convicted of three counts of stealing money from the banks.

This Circuit has held that §2113(b) applies only to common law larceny which requires a trespassory taking. Mafnas argues his taking was embezzlement rather than larceny as he had lawful possession of the bags, with the consent of the banks, when he took the money.

This problem arose centuries ago, and common law evolved to handle it. The law distinguishes between possession and custody.

> Ordinarily, ... if a person receives property for a limited or temporary purpose, he is only acquiring custody. Thus, if a person receives property from the owner with instructions to deliver it to the owner's house, he is only acquiring custody; therefore, his subsequent decision to keep the property for himself would constitute larceny.

3 Wharton's Criminal Law, at 353.

The District Court concluded that Mafnas was given temporary custody only, to deliver the money bags to their various destinations. The later decision to take the money was larceny, because it was beyond the consent of the owner, who retained constructive possession until the custodian's task was completed. This rationale was used in *United States v. Pruitt*, 446 F.2d 513, 515 (6th Cir. 1971). There, Pruitt was employed by a bank as a messenger. He devised a plan with another person to stage a fake robbery and split the money which Pruitt was delivering for the bank. The Sixth Circuit found that Pruitt had mere custody for the purpose of delivering the money, and that his wrongful conversion constituted larceny.

Mafnas distinguishes *Pruitt*, *supra*, because the common law sometimes differentiates between employees, who generally obtain custody only, and others (agents), who acquire possession. Although not spelled out, Mafnas essentially claims that he was a bailee, and that the contract between the banks and Service resulted in Service having lawful possession, and not mere custody over the bags.

The common law also found an answer to this situation. A bailee who "breaks bulk" commits larceny. Under this doctrine, the bailee-carrier was given possession of a bale, but not its contents. Therefore, when the bailee pilfered the entire bale, he was not guilty of larceny; but when he broke open the bale and took a portion or all of the contents, he was guilty of larceny because his taking was trespassory and it was from the constructive possession of another. 3 Wharton's Criminal Law 353–54.

Either way, Mafnas has committed the common law crime of larceny, replete with trespassory taking.

Mafnas also cannot profit from an argument that any theft on his part was from Service and not from the banks. Case law is clear that since what was taken was property belonging to the banks, it was property or money "in the care, custody, control, management, or possession of any bank" within the meaning of 18 U.S.C. §2113(b), notwithstanding the fact that it may have been in the possession of an armored car service serving as a bailee for hire.

Therefore, his conviction is affirmed.

Discussion Questions

1. Based upon the Court's opinion, how is possession distinguished from custody?

2. Should what Mafnas did be a crime or subject only to civil penalties?

Problem

13.5 David plays in a band that is in need of several guitar amps and other equipment. One day he drives to a town about 50 miles from the one in which he lives. There he uses a false identity and phony driver's license to rent the needed equipment from a music store. The time period specified in the rental agreement is three days. At the end of the three days, David keeps the equipment to use in his band. Is David liable for larceny?

2. Mental State

People v. Davis

19 Cal. 4th 301 (1998)
Supreme Court of California

Mosk, J.

We granted review to determine what crime is committed in the following circumstances: the defendant enters a store and picks up an item of merchandise displayed for sale, intending to claim that he owns it and to "return" it for cash or credit; he carries the item to a sales counter and asks the clerk for a "refund"; without the defendant's knowledge his conduct has been observed by a store security agent, who instructs the clerk to give him credit for the item; the clerk gives the defendant a credit voucher, and the agent detains him as he leaves the counter with the voucher;

he is charged with theft of the item. In the case at bar the Court of Appeal held the defendant is guilty of theft by trespassory larceny. We agree, and therefore affirm the judgment of the Court of Appeal.

Defendant entered a Mervyn's department store carrying a Mervyn's shopping bag. As he entered he was placed under camera surveillance by store security agent Carol German. While German both watched and filmed, defendant went to the men's department and took a shirt displayed for sale from its hanger; he then carried the shirt through the shoe department and into the women's department on the other side of the store. There he placed the shirt on a sales counter and told cashier Heather Smith that he had "bought it for his father" but it didn't fit and he wanted to "return" it. Smith asked him if he had the receipt, but he said he did not because "it was a gift." Smith informed him that if the value of a returned item is more than $20 and there is no receipt, the store policy is not to make a cash refund but to issue a Mervyn's credit voucher. At that point Smith was interrupted by a telephone call from German; German asked her if defendant was trying to "return" the shirt, and directed her to issue a credit voucher. Smith prepared the voucher and asked defendant to sign it; he did so, but used a false name. German detained him as he walked away from the counter with the voucher. Upon being questioned in the store security office, defendant gave a second false name and three different dates of birth; he also told German that he needed money to buy football cleats, asked her if they could "work something out," and offered to pay for the shirt.

Count 1 of the information charged defendant with the crime of petty theft with a prior theft-related conviction, a felony-misdemeanor alleging that defendant did "steal, take and carry away the personal property" of Mervyn's in violation of Penal Code section 484, subdivision (a)[1]. In a motion for judgment of acquittal filed after the People presented their case, defendant argued that on the facts shown he could be convicted of no more than an *attempt* to commit petty theft, and therefore sought dismissal of the petty theft charge. The court denied the motion.

The only theories of theft submitted to the jury in the instructions were theft by larceny and theft by trick and device. The jury found defendant guilty of petty theft as charged in the information. Defendant waived further jury trial, and the court found the allegation of a prior conviction to be true. The court denied defendant's motion to treat the petty theft as a misdemeanor and sentenced him to state prison.

The Court of Appeal deemed defendant's primary contention to be that the evidence was insufficient to support his conviction of petty theft on either theory submitted to the jury. The court held defendant could properly have been convicted of theft by larceny; the court therefore declined to reach the alternate theory of theft by trick and device, and affirmed the judgment. We granted review.

---

1. Insofar as it defines theft by larceny, Penal Code section 484, subdivision (a), provides simply that "Every person who shall feloniously steal, take, carry, lead, or drive away the personal property of another ... is guilty of theft." The statute is declaratory of the common law....

When the formerly distinct offenses of larceny, embezzlement, and obtaining property by false pretenses were consolidated in 1927 into the single crime of "theft" defined by Penal Code section 484, most of the procedural distinctions between those offenses were abolished. But their substantive distinctions were not: "The elements of the several types of theft included within section 484 have not been changed, however, and a judgment of conviction of theft, based on a general verdict of guilty, can be sustained only if the evidence discloses the elements of one of the consolidated offenses."

The elements of theft by larceny are well settled: the offense is committed by every person who (1) takes possession (2) of personal property (3) owned or possessed by another, (4) by means of trespass and (5) with intent to steal the property, and (6) carries the property away. The act of taking personal property from the possession of another is always a trespass[2] unless the owner consents to the taking freely and unconditionally[3] or the taker has a legal right to take the property. The intent to steal or *animus furandi* is the intent, without a good faith claim of right, to permanently deprive the owner of possession. And if the taking has begun, the slightest movement of the property constitutes a carrying away or asportation.

To begin with, the question is not whether Mervyn's consented to Smith's issuance of the voucher after defendant asked to "return" the shirt; rather, the question is whether Mervyn's consented to defendant's taking the shirt in the first instance. As the Court of Appeal correctly reasoned, a self-service store like Mervyn's impliedly consents to a customer's picking up and handling an item displayed for sale and carrying it from the display area to a sales counter with the intent of purchasing it; the store manifestly does not consent, however, to a customer's removing an item from a shelf or hanger if the customer's intent in taking possession of the item is to steal it.

Although we have found no California case addressing the precise question, a recent decision of the Ohio Court of Appeals is relevant. In *State v. Higgs* the defendant entered a Sears, Roebuck store and was observed on camera by store security agents as he removed a paper bag from his pocket, took a toy airplane from the merchandise display, and put it in the bag. He then carried the bag to a cashier and told her that the airplane had been a gift to his son but he was "returning" it because his son was too young for the toy. A security agent telephoned the cashier and instructed her to proceed with the transaction; the cashier gave the defendant a cash refund, and the security agents detained him. He was convicted of theft by larceny.

On appeal, the defendant contended *inter alia* that although the indictment charged theft of the toy airplane, the evidence showed the crime was, instead, theft of the

---

2. This is not traditional trespass onto real property, of course, but trespass *de bonis asportatis* or trespass "for goods carried away." (Perkins, *supra*, at p. 304.)

3. When the consent is procured by fraud it is invalid and the resulting offense is commonly called larceny by trick and device.

cash refund by means of false pretenses; that the store, acting through its agents, consented to the refund and thereby vitiated an element of the crime; and that in any event the store also consented to customers' carrying merchandise around the store without first paying for it.

Rejecting those claims and affirming the conviction, the appellate court reasoned:

> "The fact that a retail store permits customers to carry merchandise from one area of the store to another does not imply consent to conceal the merchandise in a bag and return the same for a cash refund. This act, not the act of taking the refund, constituted the criminal offense for which appellant was charged.... The fact that Sears consented to permitting a refund for the toy airplane was not relevant to the disposition of this case. The item unlawfully taken was the airplane, not the money. The record reveals neither Sears nor its authorized agents consented to the taking of that airplane."

In these circumstances the issue of consent—and therefore trespass—depends on the issue of intent to steal. We turn to that issue.

As noted earlier, the general rule is that the intent to steal required for conviction of larceny is an intent to deprive the owner *permanently* of possession of the property. For example, we have said it would not be larceny for a youth to take and hide another's bicycle to "get even" for being teased, if he intends to return it the following day. But the general rule is not inflexible: "The word 'permanently,' as used here is not to be taken literally." Our research discloses three relevant categories of cases holding that the requisite intent to steal may be found even though the defendant's primary purpose in taking the property is not to deprive the owner permanently of possession: i.e., (1) when the defendant intends to "sell" the property back to its owner, (2) when the defendant intends to claim a reward for "finding" the property, and (3) when, as here, the defendant intends to return the property to its owner for a "refund." There is thus ample authority for the *result* reached in the case at bar; the difficulty is in finding a rationale for so holding that is consistent with basic principles of the law of larceny. The cases in these three categories offer a variety of such rationales, some more relevant or more persuasive than others. We review them seriatim.[4]

---

4. Other categories of cases of temporary taking amounting to larceny have also been recognized. Thus the commentators agree there is an intent to steal when the *nature* of the property is such that even a temporary taking will deprive the owner of its primary economic value, e.g., when the property is dated material or perishable in nature or good for only seasonal use. (E.g., Perkins, *supra*, at p. 327 [taking cut flowers from a florist without consent, with intent to return them in a week]; Model Pen. Code & Commentaries, com. 6 to § 223.2, p. 175 [taking a neighbor's lawn mower without consent for the summer, with intent to return it in the fall].) Another such category is composed of cases in which the defendant takes property with intent to use it temporarily and then to *abandon* it in circumstances making it unlikely the owner will recover it. (E.g., *State v. Davis* (1875) 38 N.J.L. 176, 178 [horse and carriage abandoned on a public road "after many miles and hours of reckless driving"]; *State v. Ward* (1886) 19 Nev. 297 [10 P. 133, 135–136] [two horses abandoned on open road miles from ranch where taken]; *State v. Langis* (1968) 251 Or. 130 [444 P.2d 959, 960] [automobile taken with intent to leave it in city seventy miles away].)

A. *The "sale" cases*

The classic case of the first category is *Regina v. Hall* (1848) 169 Eng. Rep. 291. The defendant, an employee of a man named Atkin who made candles from tallow, took a quantity of tallow owned by Atkin and put it on Atkin's own scales, claiming it belonged to a butcher who was offering to sell it to Atkin. The jury were instructed that if they found the defendant took Atkin's property with the intent to sell it back to him as if it belonged to another and appropriate the proceeds, he was guilty of larceny. The jury so found, and the conviction was upheld on further review.

The defendant contended that his assertion of temporary ownership of the property for a particular purpose was not enough to constitute the required intent to permanently deprive. The justices expressed two rationales for holding to the contrary. First, one justice stressed that the deprivation would in fact have been permanent unless the owner had agreed to the condition imposed by the defendant, i.e., to "buy" the property. Baron Parke reasoned, "The intention was that the goods should never revert to the owner as his own property except by sale. They were therefore severed from the owner completely unless he chose to buy back what was in truth his own property."

The second rationale was that the defendant's claim of the right to sell the property was an assertion of a *right of ownership* and therefore evidence of an intent to permanently deprive. Chief Justice Denman reasoned, "The only question attempted to be raised here is as to the *animus furandi*, the intent to deprive the owner of his property. What better proof can there be of such intent, than the assertion of such a right of ownership by the prisoner as to entitle him to sell it." ...

Perkins offers yet another rationale for the rule that a defendant who takes property for the purpose of "selling" it back to its owner has the requisite intent to permanently deprive: by so doing the defendant creates a *substantial risk of permanent loss*, because if the owner does not buy back his property the defendant will have a powerful incentive to keep it in order to conceal the theft. As Perkins explains, "in the type of case suggested there is also a very considerable risk that [the owner] will not get back the property at all. If, for example, he should decide that his supply was ample and decline to pay the price, the trespasser would take away the property in order to conceal his own wrongdoing." (Perkins, *supra*, at p. 329.) As will appear, we find this rationale persuasive.

B. *The "reward" cases*

The cases in the second category hold that a defendant who takes property for the purpose of claiming a reward for "finding" it has the requisite intent to permanently deprive. Again the courts invoke differing rationales for this holding. One line of these cases is exemplified by *Commonwealth v. Mason* (1870) 105 Mass. 163. The defendant took possession of a horse that had strayed onto his property, with the intent to conceal it until the owner offered a reward and then to return it and claim the reward, or until the owner was induced to sell it to him for less than its worth. The court affirmed a conviction of larceny on the theory that the requisite felonious intent was shown because the defendant intended to deprive the owner of "a portion of the value of the property." The court did not explain this theory further, but later cases suggested that the "portion of the value" in question was the right to claim a reward—ordinarily less than the property's full value—for its return....

Another line of cases in this category also noted the taker's intent to appropriate "part of the value" of the property, but went on to emphasize a different rationale, i.e., that the taker had made the return of property *contingent* on the offer of a satisfactory reward, and if the contingency did not materialize the taker would keep the property....

The same rationale has been invoked when the defendant sought not a reward but a ransom. Thus in *State v. Hauptmann* (1935) 115 N.J.L. 412 [180 A. 809], the defendant kidnapped the infant son of Charles Lindbergh. The child was wearing a sleeping suit when he was abducted. In preliminary negotiations with Condon, Lindbergh's representative, the defendant agreed to send Condon the sleeping suit as evidence that Condon was dealing with "the right party"; the negotiations continued, the defendant sent the sleeping suit to Condon, and Condon thereupon accepted the defendant's ransom terms. The child was later found dead. The defendant was convicted of murder and of larceny of the sleeping suit, and the New Jersey high court affirmed.

On appeal, the defendant contended *inter alia* that there was no larceny because his intent was not to keep the sleeping suit permanently but to return it in order to advance the ransom negotiations. The court's rationale for rejecting the claim was the same as that of the "reward" cases discussed above: "the intent to return should be unconditional; and, where there is an element of coercion or of reward, as a condition of return, larceny is inferable." The court acknowledged that the sleeping suit "was surrendered without payment; but, on the other hand, it was an initial and probably essential step in the intended extortion of money, and it seems preposterous to suppose that it would ever have been surrendered except as a result of the first conversation between Condon and the holder of the suit, and as a guaranty that there was no mistake as to the 'right party.' It was well within the province of the jury to infer that, if Condon had refused to go on with the preliminaries, *the sleeping suit would never have been delivered.* In that situation, the larceny was established."...

Finally, Perkins again proposes the rationale of a substantial risk of permanent loss. He reasons that a taking with intent to hold for reward creates such a risk because "the intent will result in a permanent loss to the owner if he fails to offer or give a reward for the return of the property." Indeed, even the offer or payment of a reward may not eliminate the risk because the defendant still has an incentive to keep the property rather than expose himself to detection by returning it.

C. *The "refund" cases*

The third category comprises a substantial number of recent cases from our sister states affirming larceny convictions on facts identical or closely similar to those of the case at bar: in each, the defendant took an item of merchandise from a store display, carried it to a sales counter, claimed to own it, and asked for a "refund" of cash or credit. Although the cases are thus factually in point, the reasoning of their opinions is, ironically, of less assistance than the "sale" or "reward" cases in our search for a satisfactory rationale on the issue of the intent to permanently deprive....

... Several of the rationales articulated in the "sale" and "reward" cases, however, are also applicable to the "refund" cases. On close analysis, moreover, the relevant rationales may be reduced to a single line of reasoning that rests on both a principled and a practical basis.

First, as a matter of principle, a claim of the right to "return" an item taken from a store display is no less an assertion of a *right of ownership* than the claim of a right to "sell" stolen property back to its owner. And an intent to return such an item to the store only if the store pays a satisfactory "refund" is no less *conditional* than an intent to return stolen property to its owner only if the owner pays a satisfactory "reward." Just as in the latter case, it can be said in the former that "the purpose to return was founded wholly on the contingency that a [refund] would be offered, and unless the contingency happened the conversion was complete." It follows that a defendant who takes an item from a store display with the intent to claim its ownership and restore it only on condition that the store pay him a "refund" must be deemed to intend to permanently deprive the store of the item within the meaning of the law of larceny.

Second, as a practical matter, the risk that such a taking will be permanent is not a mere theoretical possibility; rather, by taking an item from a store display with the intent to demand a refund a defendant creates a substantial risk of permanent loss. This is so because if the defendant's attempt to obtain a refund for the item fails for any reason, he has a powerful incentive to keep the item in order to avoid drawing attention to the theft. A person who has taken an item from a store display and has claimed the right to "return" it at a sales counter, but has been rebuffed because, for example, he has no receipt, will not be inclined to run the risk of confirming the suspicions of the sales clerk or store security personnel by *putting the item back* in the display. Instead, just as in the case of a failed attempt to "sell" property back to its owner, "the trespasser would take away the property in order to conceal his own wrongdoing."

Applying the foregoing reasoning to the facts of the case at bar, we conclude that defendant's intent to claim ownership of the shirt and to return it to Mervyn's only on condition that the store pay him a "refund" constitutes an intent to permanently deprive Mervyn's of the shirt within the meaning of the law of larceny, and hence an intent to "feloniously steal" that property within the meaning of Penal Code section 484, subdivision (a) (fn. 1, *ante*). Because Mervyn's cannot be deemed to have consented to defendant's taking possession of the shirt with the intent to steal it, defendant's conduct also constituted a trespassory taking within the meaning of the law of larceny. It follows that the evidence supports the final two elements of the offense of theft by larceny, and the Court of Appeal was correct to affirm the judgment of conviction.

Problems

13.6 On November 3, 2002, the NEW YORK TIMES reported that after being caught by security guards outside the Saks Fifth Avenue department store with merchandise from the store worth $3,000 dollars for which she had not paid, Winona Ryder told the guards that she "had taken the items only because a director had told her to research a role in a forthcoming film."[5] Assume Ms. Ryder is charged with larceny. If true, would Ms. Ryder's explanation affect her liability?

As the *Davis* case illustrates, traditional larceny required an intent to permanently deprive the possessor or the owner of the property. Consider the following problems. Does the appropriate actor have the intent to permanently deprive?

13.7 On a hot summer day, Jorge gets ready to set up his snap-together backyard pool. He discovers, much to his dismay, that the filter is faulty. He knows that Wan has the same pool set and is away for a few weeks. Jorge hops the fence between their yards and disconnects Wan's pool filter. When Wan returns, Jorge tells Wan that Jorge has borrowed Wan's filter and will return it at the end of the summer. Does Jorge have the mental state required for larceny?

13.8 During property class, when Carol steps out during a break to hand in her moot court brief, Janette removes Carol's notebook computer from the classroom and hides it. When Carol returns, Janette offers to return Carol's computer if Carol pays Janette a finder's fee of $50. Does Janette have the mental state required for larceny?

How would you describe the mental state of the relevant actor in each of these problems? Reconsider footnote 4 in the *Davis* opinion. Does the analysis of that footnote affect your description?

3. Claim of Right

Problem

13.9 Chantal lends Paul her 10 and 20 pound free weights for a weekend workout. The next day, she sees Paul in the park working out. She notices that he often leaves the weights unattended. Chantal thinks that Paul is being careless with her property. She decides to retrieve the weights and take them back home where they will be safe. Paul, whose workout included a half-mile run between

---

5. Rick Lyman, *For the Ryder Trial, a Hollywood Script*, N.Y. TIMES, November 3, 2002 at 9:1.

two sets of free weights at opposite sides of the park, returns from the other side of the park to discover the weights missing. He calls the police to report the theft. When the police arrive, he explains that he was using two sets of weights, Chantal's, of which he is still in possession, and his own, which are now missing. The police track Paul's weights to Chantal's house. Is Chantal guilty of larceny?

Courts have often recognized the situation above, in which the actor presents a claim of right to the specific property he or she takes, as exonerating the actor from a charge of larceny. If we parse the actor's mental state carefully, we would likely conclude that she lacks the intent to permanently deprive the owner of the property as she believes she is the owner of the property. Although Chantal's belief that she owns the weights must be held in good faith, it need not be reasonable. The mental state in larceny associated with ownership of the property is a subjective one. In traditional common law parlance, larceny is a specific intent crime. Chantal lacks that required intent. Similar claims of right also arise when the accused is mistaken about whether he or she has permission to take the items or about whether the items have an owner.[6]

C. Larceny by Trick

California Jury Instruction, Criminal, 6th ed.

14.05 — Theft by Trick and Device — Defined ...

In order to prove this crime, each of the following elements must be proved:

1. A person obtained possession of personal property of some value belonging to the alleged victim;

2. That person obtained possession by making [a] false promise which [he] had no intention of performing, or by means of other fraud, artifice, trick, or device;

3. In surrendering possession of the property, the alleged victim did not intend to transfer the ownership; and

4. The person who obtained possession did so with the specific intent to deprive the alleged victim permanently of [his] property.

---

6. *See* Wayne LaFave, Criminal Law 811 (3d ed. 2000).

Discussion Question

How do larceny and larceny by trick differ?

Problems

13.10 Jethro approaches Karen, the manager of a local grocery store, and asks if he can buy one of the shopping carts. Jethro claims that he is homeless with no place to store and no means of transporting his belongings. Karen believes Jethro's claims and offers to sell Jethro the cart for $25.00, exactly the wholesale cost of the cart. Jethro promises to return later that afternoon with $25.00 worth of recyclables, which he will trade in for cash at the recycling center in the store's parking lot and then pay Karen the $25.00 for the cart. Jethro takes the cart and does not return to pay Karen. In fact, at the time that Jethro approached Karen, Jethro was not homeless. He planned to use the cart for an art project but did not believe that Karen would sell it to him for that purpose and certainly not at the wholesale price. Is Jethro guilty of the crime of larceny by trick under the jury instruction above?

13.11 Same as Problem 13.10, except that Jethro asked to borrow the cart for one week and promised to return to pay Karen $5.00 for the use of the cart. Karen agreed to the $5.00 fee for use of the cart for one week. Is Jethro guilty of the crime of larceny by trick under the jury instruction above?

D. Embezzlement

California Jury Instructions, Criminal, 6th ed.

14.07 Theft by Embezzlement Defined (Pen. Code, § 487)

Defendant is accused of having committed the crime of grand theft, a violation of section 487 of the Penal Code.

Every person to whom property has been entrusted who fraudulently appropriates that property to her own use or purpose, is guilty of the crime of theft by embezzlement.

In order to prove this crime, each of the following elements must be proved:

1. A relation of trust and confidence existed between two persons;

2. Pursuant to that relationship one of those persons accepted property entrusted to her by the other person; and

3. With the specific intent to deprive the other person of his property, the person appropriated or converted it to her own use or purpose.

Discussion Questions

1. How do larceny and larceny by trick differ from embezzlement?

2. Reconsider the *Mafnas* decision. Would the crime there be better characterized as embezzlement or larceny?

State v. Archie

123 N.M. 503 (1997)
Court of Appeals of New Mexico

Bosson, J.

Defendant appeals his conviction for embezzlement after a trial to the court without a jury. Defendant was on probation, confined by the conditions of his probation to stay within 150 feet of his telephone. As part of his probation, Defendant agreed to wear an electronic monitoring device (EMD) around his ankle which would communicate electronically with a computer connected to his telephone and thereby verify his presence as long as he continued to wear the EMD. Contrary to the conditions of probation, Defendant removed the EMD, damaging it, and threw it into a field. The value of the EMD was placed at over $250 and under $2500, thereby making this a fourth degree felony. On appeal, Defendant does not dispute that he violated his probation or that he may have committed the lesser crime of criminal damage to property. Defendant contends that his actions do not constitute the specific crime of embezzlement. We analyze Defendant's actions in light of the specific statutory elements of embezzlement and affirm.

The embezzlement statute, NMSA 1978, Section 30-16-8 (Cum. Supp. 1996), states: "Embezzlement consists of the embezzling or converting to his own use of anything of value, with which he has been entrusted, with fraudulent intent to deprive the owner thereof." The Uniform Jury Instruction 14-1641, further defines the elements of embezzlement:

> For you to find the defendant guilty of embezzlement..., the state must prove to your satisfaction beyond a reasonable doubt each of the following elements of the crime:
>
> 1. The defendant was entrusted with ___ ... ;
>
> 2. The defendant converted this ___ (property or money) to the defendant's own use. "Converting something to one's own use" means keeping another's property rather than returning it, or using another's property for one's own purpose [rather than] [even though the property is eventually used] for the purpose authorized by the owner;

3. At the time the defendant converted ___ (property or money), the defendant fraudulently intended to deprive the owner of the owner's property. "Fraudulently intended" means intended to deceive or cheat;

Defendant first argues that there was no showing of a traditional fiduciary relationship, without which he maintains an embezzlement conviction cannot stand. We disagree. Our earlier case of *State v. Moss* stands for the proposition that a specific or technical fiduciary relationship is not necessary to sustain an embezzlement conviction under New Mexico law. While some jurisdictions may require a special fiduciary relationship, such as employment or agency, as an element of the crime, New Mexico does not.

Defendant maintains there was no such evidence because Defendant, a convicted felon, was not holding the EMD under any assumption of trust or confidence on his part. We disagree. "Entrustment" occurs when property is committed or surrendered to another with a certain confidence regarding the care, use, or disposal of that property. As *Moss* states, the usual and ordinary meaning of "entrustment" is applicable unless an expression of legislative intent requires otherwise. In determining what is required by the element of entrustment, we are guided by legislative intent in enacting the embezzlement statute.

The crime of embezzlement did not exist at common law. Larceny, a common law crime, required that the thief take property from the victim's possession and that there be a "trespass in the taking." When the defendant is in lawful possession of the owner's property, which the defendant then fraudulently converts to his or her own use, the defendant cannot be convicted of larceny because there is no trespassory taking.

Statutes establishing embezzlement as an offense were passed to eliminate this loophole in the common law. We construe the term "entrusted" in New Mexico's embezzlement statute in accordance with this objective and in a manner to accomplish the legislative intent.

It is clear from the evidence that when the State turned over the EMD to Defendant, the State was relying on Defendant to act in a manner consistent with, and not adverse to, the State's interests with respect to the EMD. Defendant was after all on probation; he was free from incarceration on the strength of just such assurances that he would do what he was told and live up to his promises. Defendant even signed a written agreement with his probation officer by which he created these assurances with respect to his continued care and possession of the EMD. The agreement states:

EMD WEARER'S AGREEMENT

1. I, Andre Archie, understand that the electronic monitoring device (EMD) and all of its accessories are the property of the Adult Probation Parole Division of the Corrections Department with the State of New Mexico.

2. I accept full responsibility for the care of and return of the electronic monitoring device.

3. I understand that it is my responsibility to immediately notify the Adult Probation Parole Office if the monitor is damaged in any way or if the bracelet is purposely/accidentally removed from my leg.

4. I understand that if any part of the electronic monitoring device is damaged or lost while it is in my possession, I will be charged with Embezzlement, Theft, or Criminal Damage. The cost of the device is $1,950.00.

In addition, although Defendant argues that the transfer of possession was only for the State's benefit, Defendant received the benefit of being placed on probation, rather than being incarcerated. Therefore, assuming that Defendant is correct in arguing that he must receive a benefit, we are satisfied from the record that there was an entrustment of property sufficient to meet the requirements of the statute.

Defendant argues there was no evidence that he "converted" the EMD "to his own use"; instead, he disposed of the EMD or abandoned it but did not put it to "use" within the meaning of the statute. Again, we do not agree. When a person having possession of another's property treats the property as his own, whether he uses it, sells it, or discards it, he is using the property for his own purpose. Because Defendant threw away the EMD in an effort to end the State's ability to monitor his movements, there was evidence in this case that Defendant was using the EMD for his own purpose.

According to Professor LaFave, the gravamen of conversion is interfering with the rights of the owner, either to the property itself or to benefit from the manner in which the property was supposed to have been used. The details of the interference are less important than the interference itself. Professor LaFave describes the manner of the interference in broad terms: "using it up, selling it, pledging it, giving it away, delivering it to one not entitled to it, inflicting serious damage to it, claiming it against the owner ... each of these acts seriously interferes with the owner's rights and so constitutes a conversion" within the meaning of embezzlement. The statutory reference that the wrongdoer's conversion must be "to his own use" is more a reference to a "use" other than that authorized by the owner; or as LaFave states: "These words are not to be taken literally, however, for it is not a requirement for a conversion that the converter gain a personal benefit from his dealing with the property."

Defendant also claims there was no evidence of the kind of specific fraudulent intent that is necessary to support a conviction for embezzlement. Defendant protests that the district court had to infer intent, since it had not been specifically shown by the State. We do not see this as a basis for reversal. Defendant threw away the EMD after removing it, contrary to his promises in the EMD Wearer's Agreement. This gives rise to a reasonable inference that Defendant fraudulently intended to deprive the State of its property and the intended use thereof. Defendant knew that the EMD belonged to the State and not to him. Defendant also knew that he was not free to dispose of the EMD by throwing it away. Intent involves a defendant's state of mind and is seldom, if ever, susceptible to direct proof. Therefore, intent may be proved by circumstantial evidence. Under the circumstances of this case, it was reasonable for the fact finder to infer that Defendant threw away the State's property with the specific fraudulent intent "to deprive the owner thereof." Fraudulent intent is defined as an intent "to deceive or cheat." In light of Defendant's surreptitious actions, the evidence supports a reasonable inference to that effect....

The conviction is affirmed.

Discussion Questions

1. What does conversion mean in the context of embezzlement?

2. Historically, why might some jurisdictions have required a fiduciary relationship for the crime of embezzlement?

E. Theft by False Pretenses

California Jury Instructions, Criminal, 6th ed.

14.10 Theft by False Pretense — Defined and Elements (Pen. Code, § 487)

Defendant is accused of having committed the crime of grand theft, a violation of section 487 of the Penal Code. Every person who knowingly and designedly by any false or fraudulent representation or pretense, defrauds another person of money, labor, real or personal property, is guilty of the crime of theft by false pretense.

In order to prove this crime, each of the following elements must be proved:

1. A person made or caused to be made to the alleged victim by word or conduct, either (a) a promise without intent to perform it, or (b) a false pretense or representation of an existing or past fact known to the person to be false or made recklessly and without information which would justify a reasonable belief in its truth;

2. The person made the pretense, representation or promise with the specific intent to defraud;

3. The pretense, representation or promise was believed and relied upon by the alleged victim and was material in inducing her to part with her money or property even though the false pretense, representation or promise was not the sole cause; and

4. The theft was accomplished in that the alleged victim parted with her money or property intending to transfer ownership thereof.

Discussion Questions

1. How does theft by false pretenses differ from larceny and larceny by trick?

2. How does it differ from embezzlement?

Problems

13.12 Dan, who is perennially short of cash, noticed that his colleague, Jessie, liked to wear jewels. One day Dan bought a ring for $10 that a street seller said was cubic zirconium. Dan intended to trick Jessie into believing that the ring was a genuine diamond ring. Dan showed the shiny ring to Jessie and claimed it had a genuine half-carat diamond. Dan offered to sell Jessie the ring for $500. Jessie agreed and gave Dan the full $500 in cash. When Jessie had the ring appraised, it turned out that the ring did indeed have a genuine half-carat diamond. Is Dan guilty of the crime of theft by false pretenses?

13.13 Fred works as a private message courier in the port area of New York. He sees tourists from nations around the world arrive every day. Many are eager to spend their money to buy something to remember their New York experience. One day, Fred prints out a series of fancy and official-looking certificates on his home computer. Each states that the bearer has duly paid $50 and is now a 1/1,000,000 owner of the Brooklyn Bridge. Fred sets up a small booth near the docking area for ships. When tourists stop, Fred claims that he works for the Manhattan transportation department and that he raises money for the city by selling interests in Manhattan public works. With each certificate, Fred supplies a small metal replica of the Bridge, worth about $10. Has he committed theft in the circumstances described below?

Part (a) Nellie purchases a certificate and pays Fred $50. Fred is very convincing and she believes him. She asks Fred whether she will receive any distributions on her ownership interest from the tolls paid by those crossing the bridge. Fred assures her that, if she leaves her address, she will receive distributions.

Part (b) Ruby purchases a certificate and pays Fred $50. Ruby is skeptical that Fred can sell ownership shares in the Brooklyn Bridge but thinks the certificate is a great souvenir.

Part (c) Jeff purchases a certificate and pays Fred $50. Jeff is an undercover NYPD police officer. He is assigned to the fraud unit and was alerted by Nellie to Fred's activities. Jeff knows that Fred doesn't work for the city and wants evidence to prove that Fred's enterprise is a scam.

People v. Marsh

58 Cal. 2d 732 (1962)

Supreme Court of California

Defendants Marsh, Crane and Bateson were charged with attempted grand theft ... They were convicted....

The trial was a protracted one. The prosecution produced substantial evidence that defendants, none of whom possessed a medical license, worked together to obtain money from the sick and the neurotic on the false representation that the electric machines they possessed could cure almost any ailment. Most of the vital evidence was secured by undercover agents of the Food and Drug Administration, and is in the form of tape recordings of conversations between the defendants and the agents. This evidence, because of its nature, is uncontradicted. The prosecution evidence is overwhelming that such representations were made, that they were false, and that money was obtained from various persons based on such representations.... The amount secured from users of the machines varied between $175 to $2,000. It was usually exacted in the form of a "donation" to defendants' nonprofit organization for the "loan" of the machines. The evidence also shows that the $175 machine was identical in design with a device used commonly by radio and TV repairmen that retails for $49.95....

In each instance, obtaining money by false representations is the form of theft relied on by the prosecution, and the case was submitted to the jury on that theory. Under section 484 of the Penal Code an essential element of that offense is that defendant had the specific intent to defraud. Under this section, even if the defendants made false representations but made them in the bona fide belief, based upon reasonable grounds, that they were true, no offense was committed. In other words, a conviction of theft based on false representations cannot be sustained if the false representations were made in the actual and reasonable belief that they were true. The burden of proof on this issue is on the prosecution. It follows, as a matter of course, that a defendant is entitled, in such a case, to introduce proper evidence that tends to establish that he did not, in fact, possess the intent required by the code section. Such evidence may be introduced either to controvert the evidence produced by the prosecution, or to establish affirmatively the lack of the required criminal intent. It is elementary that if the prosecution can introduce evidence of a required specific intent, the defendant must be given the equal privilege of showing the lack of such intent.

In the instant case ... the making of the false representations, and the obtaining of money by the defendants was proved by overwhelming evidence. The defendants' defense was twofold: (1) that the representations were true in that the machines possessed the curative powers represented, and (2) that even if the representations made were false they were believed by defendants to be true; that they were based upon certain reports received from certain doctors and scientists; that reliance on such reports was reasonable. The first defense was clearly refuted by the prosecution. The evidence demonstrates that the representations were false. The main point involved on these appeals relates to the second defense—good faith reliance. In this connection, defendants properly produced some 15 witnesses who testified that the machines in question had in fact cured them of various ailments. The defendants were also permitted to testify that they relied on various reports of named scientists and doctors. But defendants were consistently prohibited from introducing into evidence the contents of the reports and conversations had with the doctors and scientists about the curative powers of the machines. In offering such evidence, defendants' counsel clearly stated to the trial court that he was not offering this evidence in the form of conversations, reports and letters to prove that the machines could cure, but was offering it solely to show the information the defendants relied upon in forming their belief that the machines could cure. While the trial court did permit defendants to testify that they had conversations with and had received communications from doctors and others commenting on the effectiveness of the machines, the trial court consistently excluded … the introduction of the contents of these conversations and communications.…

* * *

Ultimately the *Marsh* Court ruled that the contents of the conversations at issue were admissible. If jurors found that the defendants in the *Marsh* case actually and reasonably believed that the machines had curative powers, how should the jurors vote on the charge of theft by false pretenses?

Problems

What type of theft is involved in each of the following problems?

13.14 Erin and Matilda are college roommates. One morning, Erin tells Matilda that she is stopping at the bank on the way to class and asks Matilda if she needs anything dropped off. Matilda, who is always running late, asks Erin to take Matilda's ATM card and withdraw $100 from Matilda's account for her. Erin, who is desperately short of money, realizes that this is an opportunity to obtain some extra cash. Erin takes the ATM card, intending to keep it and withdraw an extra $250 for herself. When Erin and Matilda return to their apartment that evening, Erin gives Matilda $100 but claims to have lost the ATM card after withdrawing Matilda's $100. In fact, Erin has hidden the ATM card and kept an additional $250 that she withdrew.

13.15 Yolanda placed an ad in the local paper to sell her car. She receives a call and arranges to meet with Fallon, who expresses interest in the car. When they meet:

Part (a) Fallon asks to test-drive the car. Yolanda gives Fallon the keys. Fallon drives off into the sunset with the car, never to return.

Part (b) After Fallon test-drives the car, she returns and indicates that she would like to purchase it. Fallon gives Yolanda a false cashier's check for the full amount. Yolanda takes the check and signs over the pink slip, which transfers ownership of the car to Fallon.

This is the statute at issue in the *Cage* case, below:

Any person who, with intent to defraud or cheat, shall designedly, by color of any false token or writing or by any false or bogus check or other written, printed or engraved instrument, by spurious coin or metal in the similitude of coin, or by any other false pretense, cause any person to grant, convey, assign, demise, lease or mortgage any land or interest in land, or obtain the signature of any person to any written instrument, the making whereof would be punishable as forgery, or obtain from any person any money or personal property or the use of any instrument, facility or article or other valuable thing or service, or by means of any false weights or measures obtain a larger amount of quantity of property than was bargained for, or by means of any false weights or measures sell or dispose of a less amount of quantity of property than was bargained for, if such land or interest in land, money, personal property, use of such instrument, facility or article, valuable thing, service, larger amount obtained or less amount disposed of, shall be of the value of $100.00 or less, shall be guilty of a misdemeanor; and if such land, interest in land, money, personal property, use of such instrument, facility or article, valuable thing, service, larger amount obtained or less amount disposed of shall be of the value of more than $100.00, such person shall be guilty of a felony, punishable by imprisonment in the state prison not more than 10 years or by a fine of not more than $5,000.00.

People v. Cage

410 Mich. 401 (1981)
Supreme Court of Michigan

Per Curiam.

The issue presented is whether the crime of false pretenses may be predicated upon the misrepresentation of a present intent to do a future act. We conclude that it may not.

The defendant in the instant case pled guilty in Washtenaw Circuit Court to the charge of obtaining property having a value over $100 by false pretenses. During his plea, he admitted that he went to a Lincoln-Mercury dealer in Ypsilanti and obtained possession of a used car by telling a salesman that he would buy the car if he liked it after test driving it and having it "checked out" at a local service station. The defendant admitted that he had no such intention and made the statements in order to get possession of the car so that he could convert it to his own use.

On appeal, the defendant challenged the factual sufficiency of his plea, one of the grounds being that his misrepresentations related solely to future events or facts and not, as required for conviction of false pretenses under Michigan law, to past or present facts or circumstances.

The Court of Appeals affirmed defendant's conviction, holding in relevant part:

"While it might appear that defendant's misrepresentations were of a future fact, in reality what he misrepresented was his present intention which was clearly fraudulent. While there does not appear to be any Michigan case clearly on point we quote from a Texas court in *Kinder v. State*, 477 SW2d 584, 586 (Tex Crim App 1971), wherein the court stated:

> "The rule is that false promises or representations as to future happenings by which a person is induced to part with his property may form the basis of the offense of theft by false pretense so long as the proof shows that such promises are false *ab initio*."

"We find the foregoing rule enunciated by the Texas court to be sound and hereby adopt it. Defendant's contention is therefore without merit." *People v Cage*, 90 Mich App 497, 499; 282 NW2d 368 (1979).

The defendant has applied for leave to appeal to this Court.

We hold that the adoption of a rule construing false pretenses to incorporate misrepresentation of present mental state is at odds with Michigan law. The crime of false pretenses in Michigan, as in other jurisdictions, was created by statute. It is universally held, except where the statute specifically provides otherwise, that the pretense relied on to establish the offense must be a misrepresentation as to a present or existing fact, or a past fact or event, and may not be as to some event to take place in the future. Although it is quite possible to view a false statement of intention, such as a promise which the promisor intends not to keep, as a misrepresentation of existing mental state, the great weight of authority holds that a false promise will not suffice for false pretenses, however fraudulent it may be.

A minority of jurisdictions do recognize a false promise or intention as a false pretense and there does appear to be a modern trend in this direction....

Our review of Michigan precedent leaves us convinced that this jurisdiction early aligned itself with the majority rule that false statements of promise or intention may not form the basis for a conviction of false pretenses....

Although there may be valid arguments supporting an amendment of the false pretenses statute to incorporate misrepresentation of present mental state within the meaning of the crime of false pretenses, we are convinced that it should be done by legislative enactment.

… [W]e reverse the defendant's conviction and remand the case to the Washtenaw Circuit Court for further proceedings.

Discussion Questions

1. Why did the traditional approach limit conviction under a false pretenses theory to misrepresentations of past or existing facts rather than false statements of promise or intention?

2. What advantages did the traditional approach offer? What disadvantages?

Problem

13.16 Part (a) Priscilla attended a garage sale at which she found a used mountain bicycle for sale for $40.00. When she looked in her wallet, she realized that she didn't have enough cash with her to purchase the bike. Priscilla offered to pay the owner $20.00 and then to ride the bike home and bring back the remaining $20.00. Priscilla had every intention of returning promptly with the remaining $20.00. The owner agreed. After Priscilla rode off on the bike, she forgot about bringing the owner the remaining $20.00. Three days later, when she finally remembered that she owed the money to the owner, she was too embarrassed to go back to pay him. She kept the bike and never paid the remaining $20.00. Is Priscilla guilty of theft by false pretenses?

Part (b) Same as Part (a) except, at the time that Priscilla offered to return and pay the owner the additional $20, she had already decided that she would not return with the additional money. She believed that $20.00 for the bike was an appropriate price. Is Priscilla guilty of theft by false pretenses under *Cage*?

People v. Lorenzo

64 Cal. App. 3d Supp. 43 (1976)
Appellate Dept., Superior Court of California, Los Angeles

Opinion by Cole, Acting P. J.

Defendant appeals from his conviction of theft, in violation of Penal Code section 484, subdivision (a).

Defendant was observed by the manager of a Von's market to switch price tags from one kind of glove to another kind of glove and also to switch price tags placed on chickens. The manager of the store stood five or six feet behind defendant as the latter went through the check-out counter. Defendant paid for a number of chickens, a pair of gloves and other merchandise. Defendant had no conversation with the check-out clerk. Defendant then wheeled the shopping cart into the parking lot where he was arrested by the manager. Among the merchandise in the cart was a pair of gloves which bore a price tag lower than their regular and correct price. Testimony also established that two of the chickens in the cart had price tags on them which were for less than should have been the case. Two other chickens handled by defendant but left by him in the store, and not taken to the check-out counter bore loose price tags that should have been on the two chickens in question which defendant "purchased."

In other words, the evidence convincingly showed (although defendant denied it to be the case) that defendant switched price tags so as to buy merchandise for less than its correct price.

On this state of facts the question is whether defendant committed the offense for which he was convicted. The jury was instructed solely on the offense of theft by false pretenses. "[Obtaining] property by false pretenses is the fraudulent or deceitful acquisition of both title and possession of the property." It is clear that had defendant not been observed by the store manager he would have succeeded in acquiring title and possession.

"To support a conviction of theft for obtaining property by false pretenses, it must be shown that the defendant made a false pretense or representation with intent to defraud the owner of his property, and that the owner was in fact defrauded.... The false pretense or representation must have materially influenced the owner to part with his property...." In other words, as in any other case of fraud, the injured party must have been induced to part with his property in reliance on the false representation.

It is apparent to us that the crime of theft by false pretenses was not committed here. The victim of the crime was alleged to be Von's market. The manager of the market at all times was aware that defendant had switched the price labels and merely allowed defendant apparently to consummate his scheme in order to be able to arrest him in the parking lot. The manager at no time relied upon defendant's conduct. Since the manager is the agent of the victim-market owner and his knowledge is that of the victim (Civ. Code, § 2332) we cannot hold on these facts that theft by false pretenses was established.

The People argue, nevertheless, that another species of theft, larceny by trick, was established. Aside from the fact that the jury was never instructed on this theory, a considerable obstacle in the way of our adopting it, that crime is not established either for the same reason—lack of reliance. While our attention has not been called to any cases dealing with the element of reliance in the case of theft committed in the guise of larceny by trick, it is apparent that reliance is as much an element of this kind of theft as it is in the case of theft committed by the use of false pretenses. The only difference between larceny by trick and false pretenses is that in the latter both title and possession to the property in question are acquired by fraudulent means, whereas larceny by trick consists of the fraudulent acquisition of possession only and not title. It is basic law that reliance on a false representation is an element of fraud;

since fraudulent means are required in order for larceny by trick to be committed, a lack of such reliance must be equally fatal to the commission of that offense.

We are of the view, however, that the evidence amply establishes defendant's attempt to commit theft. Reliance is not an element of that offense. The successful consummation of the offense was prevented only by the manager's alertness. But for the manager's observations defendant would have carried the actual theft to its completion. Accordingly, pursuant to the authority vested in us by Penal Code section 1181, subdivision 6, we hold that the verdict and judgment must be modified to show that defendant is guilty of attempted theft only and not theft. Since we do not know what punishment the trial court would assess in light of this reduced offense it will be necessary for us to remand the matter to the trial court for resentencing....

Discussion Questions

1. Should theft by false pretenses require that the intended victim actually be deceived? Or should liability for that offense turn on the wrongful intention of the actor?

2. Why doesn't attempt require the same reliance as the completed crime?

Model Penal Code, *Comment* to § 223.1

Development of Traditional Theft Offenses. Distinctions among larceny, embezzlement, obtaining by false pretenses, extortion, and the other closely related theft offenses are explicable in terms of a long history of expansion of the role of the criminal law in protecting property. That history begins with a concern for crimes of violence–in the present context, the taking of property by force from the possession of another, *i.e.,* robbery. The criminal law then expanded, ... to cover all taking of another's property from his possession without his consent, even though no force was used. This misconduct was punished as larceny. The law then expanded once more, through some famous judicial manipulation of the concept of possession, to embrace misappropriation by a person who with the consent of the owner already had physical control over the property, as in the case of servants and even bailees in certain particularly defined situations.

At this point in the chronology of the law of theft, about the end of the 18th century, a combination of circumstances caused the initiative in the further development of the criminal law to pass from the courts to the legislature.... Perhaps the most direct influence of all was a revulsion against capital punishment, which was the penalty for all theft offenses except petty larceny during much of the 18th century. The severity of this penalty not only made the judges reluctant to enlarge felonious larceny but also may account for the host of artificial limitations that they engrafted on the offense, *e. g.,* the exclusion of growing crops, fixtures, deeds, and dogs.

Under legislative initiative, then, the law of theft continued to expand. The earliest statutes dealt with embezzlement by such narrowly defined groups as bank clerks. Subsequent laws extended coverage to agents, attorneys, bailees, fiduciaries, public officers, partners, mortgagors in possession, etc., until at last a few American legislatures enacted fraudulent-conversion statutes penalizing misappropriation by anyone who received or had in his possession or control the property of another or property which someone else "is entitled to receive and have." Indeed, some modern embezzlement statutes go so far as to penalize breach of faith without regard to whether anything is misappropriated. Thus, the fiduciary who makes forbidden investments, the official who deposits public funds in an unauthorized depository, the financial advisor who betrays his client into paying more for a property than the market value, may be designated an embezzler. Although this kind of coverage is relatively new for Anglo-American penal law, certain foreign codes have long recognized criminal "breach of trust" as a distinct entity.

The fraud aspects of theft, never regarded with such abhorrence as larceny, begin with the common-law misdemeanor of cheat. This offense required use of false weights or similar "tokens," thus limiting criminal deception to certain special techniques conceived as directed against the public generally.... A mere lie for the purpose of deceiving another in a business transaction did not become criminal until the Statute of 30 Geo. 2, ch. 24 (1757), created the misdemeanor of obtaining property by false pretenses. Even this statute was not at first believed to make mere misrepresentation criminal. Instead, it was thought to require some more elaborate swindling stratagem, such as French law to this day requires. Eventually it was settled in Anglo-American law that false representations of "fact," if "material," would suffice. Today's battleground is over such matters as misrepresentation of "opinion," "law," or "value," as well as "misleading omissions" and "false promises."

F. Property

In recent decades, substantial attention has focused on the types of property that can be the subject of theft. Consider the cases that follow.

Lund v. Commonwealth

217 Va. 688 (1977)
Supreme Court of Virginia

I'anson, C.J.

Defendant, Charles Walter Lund, was charged in an indictment with the theft of keys, computer cards, computer print-outs and using "without authority computer operation time and services of Computer Center Personnel at Virginia Polytechnic Institute and State University [V.P.I. or University] with intent to defraud, such property and services having a value of one hundred dollars or more." Code §§ 18.1-100 and 18.1-118 were referred to in the indictment as the applicable statutes. Defendant pleaded not guilty and waived trial by jury. He was found guilty of grand larceny and sentenced to two years in the State penitentiary. The sentence was suspended, and defendant was placed on probation for five years.

Defendant was a graduate student in statistics and a candidate for a Ph.D. degree at V.P.I. The preparation of his dissertation on the subject assigned to him by his faculty advisor required the use of computer operation time and services of the computer center personnel at the University. His faculty advisor neglected to arrange for defendant's use of the computer, but defendant used it without obtaining the proper authorization.

The computer used by the defendant was leased on an annual basis by V.P.I. from the IBM Corporation. The rental was paid by V.P.I. which allocates the cost of the computer center to various departments within the University by charging it to the budget of that department. This is a bookkeeping entry, and no money actually changes hands. The departments are allocated "computer credits [in dollars] back for their use [on] a proportional basis of their [budgetary] allotments." Each department manager receives a monthly statement showing the allotments used and the running balance in each account of his department.

An account is established when a duly authorized administrator or "department head" fills out a form allocating funds to a department of the University and an individual. When such form is received, the computer center assigns an account number to this allocation and provides a key to a locked post office box which is also numbered to the authorized individual and department. The account number and the post office box number are the access code which must be provided with each request before the computer will process a "deck of cards" prepared by the user and delivered to computer center personnel. The computer print-outs are usually returned to the locked post office box. When the product is too large for the box, a "check" is placed in the box, and it is used to receive the print-outs at the "computer center main window."

Defendant came under surveillance on October 12, 1974, because of complaints from various departments that unauthorized charges were being made to one or more of their accounts. When confronted by the University's investigator, defendant initially denied that he had used the computer service, but later admitted that he had. He gave to the investigator seven keys for boxes assigned to other persons. One of these keys was secreted in his sock. He told the investigating officer he had been given the keys by another student. A large number of computer cards and print-outs were taken from defendant's apartment.

The director of the computer center testified that the unauthorized sum spent out of the accounts associated with the seven post office box keys, amounted to $5,065. He estimated that on the basis of the computer cards and print-outs obtained from the defendant, as much as $26,384.16 in unauthorized computer time had been used by the defendant. He said, however, that the value of the cards and print-outs obtained from the defendant was "whatever scrap paper is worth."

Defendant testified that he used the computer without specific authority. He stated that he knew he was a large computer user, but, because he was doing work on his doctoral dissertation, he did not consider this use excessive or that "he was doing anything wrong."

Four faculty members testified in defendant's behalf. They all agreed that computer time "probably would have been" or "would have been" assigned to defendant if properly requested. Dr. Hinkleman, who replaced defendant's first advisor, testified that the computer time was essential for the defendant to carry out his assignment. He assumed that a sufficient number of computer hours had been arranged by Lund's prior faculty advisor.

The head of the statistics department, at the time of the trial, agreed with the testimony of the faculty members that Lund would have been assigned computer time if properly requested. He also testified that the committee, which recommended the awarding of degrees, was aware of the charges pending against defendant when he was awarded his doctorate by the University.

The defendant contends that his conviction of grand larceny of the keys, computer cards, and computer print-outs cannot be upheld under the provisions of Code § 18.1-100 because (1) there was no evidence that the articles were stolen, or that they had a value of $100 or more, and (2) computer time and services are not the subject of larceny under the provisions of Code §§ 18.1-100 or 18.1-118.

Code § 18.1-100 (now § 18.2-95) provides as follows:

> "Any person who:
>
> (1) Commits larceny from the person of another of money or other thing of value of five dollars or more, or
>
> (2) Commits simple larceny not from the person of another of goods and chattels of the value of one hundred dollars or more, shall be deemed guilty of grand larceny...."

Section 18.1-118 (now § 18.2-178) provides as follows:

> "If any person obtain, by any false pretense or token, from any person, with intent to defraud, money or other property which may be the subject of larceny, he shall be deemed guilty of larceny thereof;...."

The Commonwealth concedes that the defendant could not be convicted of grand larceny of the keys and computer cards because there was no evidence that those articles were stolen and that they had a market value of $100 or more. The Commonwealth argues, however, that the evidence shows the defendant violated the provisions of § 18.1-118 when he obtained by false pretense or token, with intent to defraud, the computer print-outs which had a value of over $5,000.

Under the provisions of Code § 18.1-118, for one to be guilty of the crime of larceny by false pretense, he must make a false representation of an existing fact with knowledge of its falsity and, on that basis, obtain from another person money or other property which may be the subject of larceny, with the intent to defraud.

At common law, larceny is the taking and carrying away of the goods and chattels of another with intent to deprive the owner of the possession thereof permanently. Code § 18.1-100 defines grand larceny as a taking from the person of another money or other thing of value of five dollars or more, or the taking not from the person of another goods and chattels of the value of $100 or more. The phrase "goods and chattels" cannot be interpreted to include computer time and services in light of the often repeated mandate that criminal statutes must be strictly construed.

At common law, labor or services could not be the subject of the crime of false pretense because neither time nor services may be taken and carried away. It has been generally held that, in the absence of a clearly expressed legislative intent, labor or services could not be the subject of the statutory crime of false pretense. Some jurisdictions have amended their criminal codes specifically to make it a crime to obtain labor or services by means of false pretense. We have no such provision in our statutes.

Furthermore, the unauthorized use of the computer is not the subject of larceny. Nowhere in Code § 18.1-100 or § 18.1-118 do we find the word "use." The language of the statutes connotes more than just the unauthorized use of the property of another. It refers to a taking and carrying away of a certain concrete article of personal property. There it was held that the unauthorized use of machinery and spinning facilities of another to process wool did not constitute larceny under New York's false pretense statute.

We hold that labor and services and the unauthorized use of the University's computer cannot be construed to be subjects of larceny under the provisions of Code §§ 18.1-100 and 18.1-118.

The Commonwealth argues that even though the computer print-outs had no market value, their value can be determined by the cost of the labor and services that produced them. We do not agree.

The cost of producing the print-outs is not the proper criterion of value for the purpose here. Where there is no market value of an article that has been stolen, the better rule is that its actual value should be proved. . . .

Here the evidence shows that the print-outs had no ascertainable monetary value to the University or the computer center. Indeed, the director of the computer center stated that the print-outs had no more value than scrap paper. Nor is there any evidence of their value to the defendant, and value to him could only be based on pure speculation and surmise. Hence, the evidence was insufficient to convict the defendant of grand larceny under either Code § 18.1-100 or § 18.1-118.

For the reasons stated, the judgment of the trial court is reversed, and the indictment is quashed.

Discussion Questions

1. In your view, should Lund's use of the computer have been treated as a crime? Should the prosecutor have charged him?

2. What factors do you think may have influenced the *Lund* court to rule as it did?

3. What challenges are presented in applying the law of theft you have studied so far in this chapter to fraudulent or unauthorized computer use?

4. Why do you suppose Lund waived his right to be tried by a jury?

5. *Lund* was decided in 1977. Do you think the *Lund* Court would reach a different conclusion today?

United States v. Farraj

142 F. Supp. 2d 484 (S.D.N.Y. 2001)
United States District Court, Southern District of New York

Marrero, J.

In summer of 2000, Said Farraj was a paralegal with the law firm of Orrick, Harrington & Sutcliffe LLP ("Orrick"). At the time, Orrick represented plaintiffs in a class action tobacco case: *Falise v. American Tobacco Co.*, ("*Falise*"). In preparation for the *Falise* trial, the attorneys and paralegals at Orrick created a trial plan (the "Trial Plan"), "exceeding 400 pages and including, among other things, trial strategy, deposition excerpts and summaries, and references to anticipated trial exhibits." Only Orrick employees assigned to *Falise* were permitted access to the Trial Plan. The Indictment does not reveal whether Said was included among such employees.

The Government charges that Said, using the moniker "FlyGuyNYt," e-mailed an 80-page excerpt of the Trial Plan to the *Falise* defendants' attorneys and offered to sell them the entire Plan. An FBI agent posing as one of the *Falise* defendants' attorneys negotiated with Said via e-mail and ultimately agreed to purchase the Trial Plan for $2 million. On July 21, 2000, Yeazid, Said's brother, met with a second undercover FBI agent at a McDonald's restaurant in lower Manhattan to receive payment. Yeazid was arrested then and gave a statement to the FBI implicating his brother.

The Government charges in count two that by e-mailing the Trial Plan excerpt across state lines, Said violated 18 U.S.C. §2314, which provides, in relevant part, that "whoever transports, transmits, or transfers in interstate or foreign commerce any goods, wares, merchandise, securities, or money, of the value of $5,000 or more, knowing the same to have been stolen, converted, or taken by fraud ... shall be fined under this title or imprisoned...." Said moves to dismiss, arguing that §2314 applies only to the physical asportation of tangible goods or currency, not to "information" stored and transmitted electronically, such as the Trial Plan excerpt e-mailed here. Neither the Supreme Court nor the Second Circuit has addressed this question directly, and this appears to be an issue of first impression in this District.

Interpretation of a criminal statute may be the judicial equivalent of juggling on a high wire. It demands a delicate balancing act, requiring the courts to walk a very fine line, hazards inherent in all directions. Read the law too broadly, and the court may overstep its bounds, treading on legislative prerogatives, and by judicial fiat extending the criminal law to conduct the lawmakers did not intend to proscribe, thereby infringing on the rights of individuals not meant to be prosecuted. Construing the law too narrowly, on the other hand, runs an equally grave risk. It could undermine the will of the legislators, allowing a potentially guilty offender to go free, and depriving the public of a measure of law enforcement and protection the statute contemplated. Either way, one misstep may plunge into misfortune, both violating the Constitution and offending common sense.

To manage these challenges, and somewhat complicate matters, the court's path is guided by competing doctrinal guidance. On the one hand is the long-standing stricture expressed by Chief Justice Marshall during the formative years of American constitutional jurisprudence:

> The rule that penal laws are to be construed strictly is perhaps not much less old than construction itself. It is founded on the tenderness of the laws for the rights of individuals; and on the plain principle that the power of punishment is vested in the legislative, not in the judicial department. It is the legislature, not the court, which is to define a crime, and ordain its punishment.

United States v. Wiltberger, 18 U.S. 76, 95, 5 L. Ed. 37 (1820).

Recognizing that the definition of federal crimes is solely a statutory function, the Supreme Court repeatedly has admonished that in assessing whether particular conduct is encompassed by criminal statutes the courts should be guided by a principle of narrow interpretation, demanding that Congress' intent be expressed in language that is clear and definite. When determining the reach of a federal criminal statute, a court "must pay close heed to language, legislative history, and purpose in order to strictly determine the scope of the conduct the enactment forbids." A criminal charge must be dismissed where the statute, as applied to the defendant's actions would not give "a person of ordinary intelligence fair notice that his contemplated conduct is forbidden."

At the same time, courts have been instructed to "free our minds from the notion that criminal statutes must be construed by some artificial and conventional rule." This seemingly contrasting guidance, however, does not reflect a true dichotomy, but only an adaptation of the general rule to fit the contours of a particular case.

The Second Circuit has held that the phrase "goods, wares, or merchandise" is " 'a general and comprehensive designation of such personal property or chattels as are ordinarily a subject of commerce.' " *In re Vericker*, 446 F.2d 244, 248 (2d Cir. 1971) (Friendly, J.). Said, relying on *Vericker*, argues that the Second Circuit has at times determined that documents fall outside the scope of § 2314. At other times, however, the Second Circuit and other courts have held that documents may be considered "goods, wares, [or] merchandise" under § 2314. See, e.g., *United States v. Greenwald*, 479 F.2d 320 (6th Cir. 1973) (documents containing secret chemical formulae); *United States v. Bottone*, 365 F.2d 389 (2d Cir. 1966)(drug manufacturing processes); *United*

States v. Seagraves, 265 F.2d 876 (geophysical maps); *United States v. Caparros*, 1987 U.S. Dist. LEXIS 2163, No. 85 Cr. 990, 1987 WL 8653 (S.D.N.Y. March 25, 1987) (secret business plans).

The FBI documents at issue in *Vericker* detailed the criminal activity of certain individuals. Judge Friendly reasoned that the FBI documents were not "goods, wares, [or] merchandise" within the meaning of the statute because the substance contained in the documents was not ordinarily the subject of commerce. The Trial Plan at issue here, however, as is true for trial plans generally, was the work product of a business relationship between client and attorney, and may thus be viewed as an ordinary subject of commerce, created for a commercial purpose and carrying inherent commercial value at least as to the persons directly interested in the matter.

Said argues that even if trial plans generally may be viewed as goods under §2314, he is accused of transmitting an "intangible," an electronic form of the document, and therefore that it was not a good, but merely "information."

The text of §2314 makes no distinction between tangible and intangible property, or between electronic and other manner of transfer across state lines. Indeed, in 1988, Congress amended §2314 to include the term "transmits" to reflect its agreement with the Second Circuit and other courts which had held that §2314 applied to money wire transfers, where the only interstate transportation took place electronically and where there was no transportation of any physical item. In *United States v. Gilboe*, the Second Circuit addressed the issue of electronic transfer for the first time and recognized that the manner in which funds were moved does not affect the ability to obtain tangible paper dollars or a bank check from the receiving account ... Indeed, we suspect that actual dollars rarely move between banks, particularly in international transactions.... The primary element of this offense, transportation, "does not require proof that any specific means of transporting were used." ...

Relying in part on the Second Circuit's decisions in *Gilboe* and *Bottone,* the court in *United States v. Riggs*, 739 F. Supp. 414 (N.D. Ill. 1990) held that the defendant violated §2314 when he downloaded a text file containing proprietary information onto a home computer, transferred it over a computer network to his co-defendant in another state, who then uploaded it onto a computer bulletin board. The court reasoned that just because the defendant stored the information on a computer, rather than printing it on paper, his acts were not removed from the purview of the statute:

In the instant case, if the information in Bell South's E911 text file had been affixed to a floppy disk, or printed out on a computer printer, then [the defendant's] transfer of that information across state lines would clearly constitute the transfer of "goods, wares, or merchandise" within the meaning of §2314. This court sees no reason to hold differently simply because [the defendant] stored the information inside a computer instead of printing it out on paper. In either case, the information is in a transferable, accessible, even salable form.

The court noted that "reading a tangibility requirement into the definition of 'goods, wares, or merchandise' might unduly restrict the scope of §2314, especially in this modern technological age," and recognized that although not tangible in a conventional sense, the stolen property was physically stored on a computer hard drive and could be viewed and printed out with the push of a button. "The accessibility of the information in readable form from a particular storage place also makes the information tangible, transferable, salable, and in this court's opinion, brings it within the definition of 'goods, wares, or merchandise' under §2314." ...

[T]he Court is persuaded that the view most closely analogous to Second Circuit doctrine is that which holds that the transfer of electronic documents via the internet across state lines does fall within the purview of §2314. The indictment is therefore upheld and the motion to dismiss count two is denied.

Discussion Questions

1. In light of the federal *Aleynikov* case you read at the outset of this chapter, how do you think the *Farraj* case would be resolved today?

2. Reconsider Samson's ponytail in Problem 13.4. Does the analysis in *Farraj* affect your answer?

3. In light of the *Farraj* court's opinion, if you access a website and view the contents on your screen, are you in possession of that information? If the website is password-protected and obtaining the password requires a fee, would you commit theft if you access the website without paying the fee?

G. Consolidation of Theft Offenses

With the proliferation of variations in theft offenses, successful prosecution of theft became quite complex. Consider Professor Louis Schwartz's comments on the need for consolidation of theft crimes:

> Penalizing thievish rascality by means of a variety of distinguishable offenses entailed a number of technical legal problems that led twentieth-century legislators to attempt to consolidate the historic array of theft offenses into a single comprehensive offense called theft or stealing. One of these problems was legislative, having to do with the propriety of prescribing different penalties for different forms of theft. More pressing was the prosecutor's problem of choosing the right offense to charge. From information provided by the police, [the prosecutor] might reasonably conclude that a case was larceny by trick, only to have that charge defeated by evidence that the culprit secured not merely possession but title; this would make the offense an obtaining by false pretenses rather than a larceny. If the prosecutor were foresighted enough, [the prosecutor] might have charged both offenses,

leaving it to the jury to select the proper one. But the vagaries of juries and the subtlety of the distinction might result in conviction on the wrong count and acquittal on the other. Upon appeal, the conviction on the wrong count would be reversed, and reprosecution on the right count would be barred by constitutional prohibition against retrying an accused on a charge upon which he has once been acquitted.[7]

As a result of these problems, the drafters of the MPC consolidated theft and related offenses into one set of crimes. Many jurisdictions have followed suit. Although the CALJIC instructions used in this chapter to define larceny, larceny by trick, embezzlement, and false pretenses furnished distinct definitions of the four types of theft, a separate instruction (CALJIC 14.47) explains that:

> If you are satisfied beyond a reasonable doubt and unanimously agree that defendant committed the crime of theft, you should find the defendant guilty. You are not required to agree as to which particular form of theft the defendant committed.[8]

Model Penal Code, *Theft and Related Offenses*

§ 223.0 Definitions

(1) "deprive" means: (a) to withhold property of another permanently or for so extended a period as to appropriate a major portion of its economic value, or with intent to restore only upon payment of reward or other compensation; or (b) to dispose of the property so as to make it unlikely that the owner will recover it....

(4) "movable property" means property the location of which can be changed, including things growing on, affixed to, or found in land, and documents although the rights represented thereby have no physical location; "immovable property" is all other property.

(5) "obtain" means: (a) in relation to property, to bring about a transfer or purported transfer of a legal interest in the property, whether to the obtainer or another; or (b) in relation to labor or service, to secure performance thereof.

(6) "property" means anything of value, including real estate, tangible and intangible personal property, contract rights, choses-in-action and other interests in or claims to wealth, admission or transportation tickets, captured or domestic animals, food and drink, electric or other power.

(7) "property of another" includes property in which any person other than the actor has an interest which the actor is not privileged to infringe, regardless of the fact that the actor also has an interest in the property and regardless of the fact that the other person might be precluded from civil recovery because the property was used in an unlawful transaction or was subject to forfeiture as contraband. Property

---

7. Louis B. Schwartz, *Theft*, 4 ENCYCLOPEDIA OF CRIME AND JUSTICE 1551 (1983).
8. California Jury Instructions—Criminal 14.47 (West 2004).

in possession of the actor shall not be deemed property of another who has only a security interest therein, even if legal title is in the creditor pursuant to a conditional sales contract or other security agreement.

§ 223.1. Consolidation of Theft Offenses; Grading; Provisions Applicable to Theft Generally.

(1) Consolidation of Theft Offenses. Conduct denominated theft in this Article constitutes a single offense. An accusation of theft may be supported by evidence that it was committed in any manner that would be theft under this Article, notwithstanding the specification of a different manner in the indictment or information, subject only to the power of the Court to ensure fair trial by granting a continuance or other appropriate relief where the conduct of the defense would be prejudiced by lack of fair notice or by surprise.

(2) Grading of Theft Offenses....

    (c) The amount involved in a theft shall be deemed to be the highest value, by any reasonable standard, of the property or services which the actor stole or attempted to steal. Amounts involved in thefts committed pursuant to one scheme or course of conduct, whether from the same person or several persons, may be aggregated in determining the grade of the offense.

(3) Claim of Right. It is an affirmative defense to prosecution for theft that the actor:

    (a) was unaware that the property or service was that of another; or

    (b) acted under an honest claim of right to the property or service involved or that he had a right to acquire or dispose of it as he did; or

    (c) took property exposed for sale, intending to purchase and pay for it promptly, or reasonably believing that the owner, if present, would have consented.

(4) Theft from Spouse. It is no defense that theft was from the actor's spouse, except that misappropriation of household and personal effects, or other property normally accessible to both spouses, is theft only if it occurs after the parties have ceased living together.

§ 223.2. Theft by Unlawful Taking or Disposition.

(1) Movable Property. A person is guilty of theft if he unlawfully takes, or exercises unlawful control over, movable property of another with purpose to deprive him thereof.

(2) Immovable Property. A person is guilty of theft if he unlawfully transfers immovable property of another or any interest therein with purpose to benefit himself or another not entitled thereto.

§ 223.3. Theft by Deception.

A person is guilty of theft if he purposely obtains property of another by deception. A person deceives if he purposely:

(1) creates or reinforces a false impression, including false impressions as to law, value, intention or other state of mind; but deception as to a person's intention to perform a promise shall not be inferred from the fact alone that he did not subsequently perform the promise; or

(2) prevents another from acquiring information which would affect his judgment of a transaction; or

(3) fails to correct a false impression which the deceiver previously created or reinforced, or which the deceiver knows to be influencing another to whom he stands in a fiduciary or confidential relationship; or

(4) fails to disclose a known lien, adverse claim or other legal impediment to the enjoyment of property which he transfers or encumbers in consideration for the property obtained, whether such impediment is or is not valid, or is or is not a matter of official record.

The term "deceive" does not, however, include falsity as to matters having no pecuniary significance, or puffing by statements unlikely to deceive ordinary persons in the group addressed.

Discussion Questions

1. How does the MPC deal with the issues raised by the common law term "permanently deprive"?

2. What position does the MPC take on the traditional common law approach limiting theft to tangible property?

Appendix

This Appendix includes Model Penal Code relevant to the topics covered in this book.

ARTICLE 1. PRELIMINARY

Section 1.02. Purposes; Principles of Construction.

(1) The general purposes of the provisions governing the definition of offenses are:

    (a) to forbid and prevent conduct that unjustifiably and inexcusably inflicts or threatens substantial harm to individual or public interests;

    (b) to subject to public control persons whose conduct indicates that they are disposed to commit crimes;

    (c) to safeguard conduct that is without fault from condemnation as criminal;

    (d) to give fair warning of the nature of the conduct declared to constitute an offense;

    (e) to differentiate on reasonable grounds between serious and minor offenses.

(2) The general purposes of the provisions governing the sentencing and treatment of offenders are:

    (a) to prevent the commission of offenses;

    (b) to promote the correction and rehabilitation of offenders;

    (c) to safeguard offenders against excessive, disproportionate or arbitrary punishment;

    (d) to give fair warning of the nature of the sentences that may be imposed on conviction of an offense;

    (e) to differentiate among offenders with a view to a just individualization in their treatment;

    (f) to define, coordinate and harmonize the powers, duties and functions of the courts and of administrative officers and agencies responsible for dealing with offenders;

    (g) to advance the use of generally accepted scientific methods and knowledge in the sentencing and treatment of offenders;

(h) to integrate responsibility for the administration of the correctional system in a State Department of Correction [or other single department or agency].

(3) The provisions of the Code shall be construed according to the fair import of their terms but when the language is susceptible of differing constructions it shall be interpreted to further the general purposes stated in this Section and the special purposes of the particular provision involved. The discretionary powers conferred by the Code shall be exercised in accordance with the criteria stated in the Code and, insofar as such criteria are not decisive, to further the general purposes stated in this Section.

...

Section 1.13. General Definitions.

In this Code, unless a different meaning plainly is required:

(1) "statute" includes the Constitution and a local law or ordinance of a political subdivision of the State;

(2) "act" or "action" means a bodily movement whether voluntary or involuntary;

(3) "voluntary" has the meaning specified in Section 2.01;

(4) "omission" means a failure to act;

(5) "conduct" means an action or omission and its accompanying state of mind, or, where relevant, a series of acts and omissions;

(6) "actor" includes, where relevant, a person guilty of an omission;

(7) "acted" includes, where relevant, "omitted to act";

(8) "person," "he" and "actor" include any natural person and, where relevant, a corporation or an unincorporated association;

(9) "element of an offense" means (i) such conduct or (ii) such attendant circumstances or (iii) such a result of conduct as

  (a) is included in the description of the forbidden conduct in the definition of the offense; or

  (b) establishes the required kind of culpability; or

  (c) negatives an excuse or justification for such conduct; or

  (d) negatives a defense under the statute of limitations; or

  (e) establishes jurisdiction or venue;

(10) "material element of an offense" means an element that does not relate exclusively to the statute of limitations, jurisdiction, venue, or to any other matter similarly unconnected with (i) the harm or evil, incident to conduct, sought to be prevented by the law defining the offense, or (ii) the existence of a justification or excuse for such conduct;

(11) "purposely" has the meaning specified in Section 2.02 and equivalent terms such as "with purpose," "designed" or "with design" have the same meaning;

(12) "intentionally" or "with intent" means purposely;

(13) "knowingly" has the meaning specified in Section 2.02 and equivalent terms such as "knowing" or "with knowledge" have the same meaning;

(14) "recklessly" has the meaning specified in Section 2.02 and equivalent terms such as "recklessness" or "with recklessness" have the same meaning;

(15) "negligently" has the meaning specified in Section 2.02 and equivalent terms such as "negligence" or "with negligence" have the same meaning;

(16) "reasonably believes" or "reasonable belief " designates a belief that the actor is not reckless or negligent in holding.

ARTICLE 2. GENERAL PRINCIPLES OF LIABILITY

Section 2.01. Requirement of Voluntary Act; Omission as Basis of Liability; Possession as an Act.

(1) A person is not guilty of an offense unless his liability is based on conduct that includes a voluntary act or the omission to perform an act of which he is physically capable.

(2) The following are not voluntary acts within the meaning of this Section:

   (a) a reflex or convulsion;

   (b) a bodily movement during unconsciousness or sleep;

   (c) conduct during hypnosis or resulting from hypnotic suggestion;

   (d) a bodily movement that otherwise is not a product of the effort or determination of the actor, either conscious or habitual.

(3) Liability for the commission of an offense may not be based on an omission unaccompanied by action unless:

   (a) the omission is expressly made sufficient by the law defining the offense; or

   (b) a duty to perform the omitted act is otherwise imposed by law.

(4) Possession is an act, within the meaning of this Section, if the possessor knowingly procured or received the thing possessed or was aware of his control thereof for a sufficient period to have been able to terminate his possession.

Section 2.02. General Requirements of Culpability.

(1) Minimum Requirements of Culpability. Except as provided in Section 2.05, a person is not guilty of an offense unless he acted purposely, knowingly, recklessly or negligently, as the law may require, with respect to each material element of the offense.

(2) Kinds of Culpability Defined.

   (a) Purposely.

   A person acts purposely with respect to a material element of an offense when:

(i)   if the element involves the nature of his conduct or a result thereof, it is his conscious object to engage in conduct of that nature or to cause such a result; and

(ii) if the element involves the attendant circumstances, he is aware of the existence of such circumstances or he believes or hopes that they exist.

(b) Knowingly.

A person acts knowingly with respect to a material element of an offense when:

(i)   if the element involves the nature of his conduct or the attendant circumstances, he is aware that his conduct is of that nature or that such circumstances exist; and

(ii) if the element involves a result of his conduct, he is aware that it is practically certain that his conduct will cause such a result.

(c) Recklessly.

A person acts recklessly with respect to a material element of an offense when he consciously disregards a substantial and unjustifiable risk that the material element exists or will result from his conduct. The risk must be of such a nature and degree that, considering the nature and purpose of the actor's conduct and the circumstances known to him, its disregard involves a gross deviation from the standard of conduct that a law-abiding person would observe in the actor's situation.

(d) Negligently.

A person acts negligently with respect to a material element of an offense when he should be aware of a substantial and unjustifiable risk that the material element exists or will result from his conduct. The risk must be of such a nature and degree that the actor's failure to perceive it, considering the nature and purpose of his conduct and the circumstances known to him, involves a gross deviation from the standard of care that a reasonable person would observe in the actor's situation.

(3) Culpability Required Unless Otherwise Provided. When the culpability sufficient to establish a material element of an offense is not prescribed by law, such element is established if a person acts purposely, knowingly or recklessly with respect thereto.

(4) Prescribed Culpability Requirement Applies to All Material Elements. When the law defining an offense prescribes the kind of culpability that is sufficient for the commission of an offense, without distinguishing among the material elements thereof, such provision shall apply to all the material elements of the offense, unless a contrary purpose plainly appears.

(5) Substitutes for Negligence, Recklessness and Knowledge. When the law provides that negligence suffices to establish an element of an offense, such element also is established if a person acts purposely, knowingly or recklessly. When recklessness suffices to establish an element, such element also is established if a person acts

purposely or knowingly. When acting knowingly suffices to establish an element, such element also is established if a person acts purposely.

(6) Requirement of Purpose Satisfied if Purpose Is Conditional. When a particular purpose is an element of an offense, the element is established although such purpose is conditional, unless the condition negatives the harm or evil sought to be prevented by the law defining the offense.

(7) Requirement of Knowledge Satisfied by Knowledge of High Probability. When knowledge of the existence of a particular fact is an element of an offense, such knowledge is established if a person is aware of a high probability of its existence, unless he actually believes that it does not exist.

(8) Requirement of Wilfulness Satisfied by Acting Knowingly. A requirement that an offense be committed wilfully is satisfied if a person acts knowingly with respect to the material elements of the offense, unless a purpose to impose further requirements appears.

(9) Culpability as to Illegality of Conduct. Neither knowledge nor recklessness or negligence as to whether conduct constitutes an offense or as to the existence, meaning or application of the law determining the elements of an offense is an element of such offense, unless the definition of the offense or the Code so provides.

(10) Culpability as Determinant of Grade of Offense. When the grade or degree of an offense depends on whether the offense is committed purposely, knowingly, recklessly or negligently, its grade or degree shall be the lowest for which the determinative kind of culpability is established with respect to any material element of the offense.

Section 2.03. Causal Relationship Between Conduct and Result; Divergence Between Result Designed or Contemplated and Actual Result or Between Probable and Actual Result.

(1) Conduct is the cause of a result when:

(a) it is an antecedent but for which the result in question would not have occurred; and

(b) the relationship between the conduct and result satisfies any additional causal requirements imposed by the Code or by the law defining the offense.

(2) When purposely or knowingly causing a particular result is an element of an offense, the element is not established if the actual result is not within the purpose or the contemplation of the actor unless:

(a) the actual result differs from that designed or contemplated, as the case may be, only in the respect that a different person or different property is injured or affected or that the injury or harm designed or contemplated would have been more serious or more extensive than that caused; or

(b) the actual result involves the same kind of injury or harm as that designed or contemplated and is not too remote or accidental in its occurrence to have a [just] bearing on the actor's liability or on the gravity of his offense.

(3) When recklessly or negligently causing a particular result is an element of an offense, the element is not established if the actual result is not within the risk of which the actor is aware or, in the case of negligence, of which he should be aware unless:

(a) the actual result differs from the probable result only in the respect that a different person or different property is injured or affected or that the probable injury or harm would have been more serious or more extensive than that caused; or

(b) the actual result involves the same kind of injury or harm as the probable result and is not too remote or accidental in its occurrence to have a [just] bearing on the actor's liability or on the gravity of his offense.

(4) When causing a particular result is a material element of an offense for which absolute liability is imposed by law, the element is not established unless the actual result is a probable consequence of the actor's conduct.

Section 2.04. Ignorance or Mistake.

(1) Ignorance or mistake as to a matter of fact or law is a defense if:

(a) the ignorance or mistake negatives the purpose, knowledge, belief, recklessness or negligence required to establish a material element of the offense; or

(b) the law provides that the state of mind established by such ignorance or mistake constitutes a defense.

(2) Although ignorance or mistake would otherwise afford a defense to the offense charged, the defense is not available if the defendant would be guilty of another offense had the situation been as he supposed. In such case, however, the ignorance or mistake of the defendant shall reduce the grade and degree of the offense of which he may be convicted to those of the offense of which he would be guilty had the situation been as he supposed.

(3) A belief that conduct does not legally constitute an offense is a defense to a prosecution for that offense based upon such conduct when:

(a) the statute or other enactment defining the offense is not known to the actor and has not been published or otherwise reasonably made available prior to the conduct alleged; or

(b) he acts in reasonable reliance upon an official statement of the law, afterward determined to be invalid or erroneous, contained in (i) a statute or other enactment; (ii) a judicial decision, opinion or judgment; (iii) an administrative order or grant of permission; or (iv) an official interpretation of the public officer or body charged by law with responsibility for the interpretation, administration or enforcement of the law defining the offense.

(4) The defendant must prove a defense arising under Subsection (3) of this Section by a preponderance of evidence.

Section 2.05. When Culpability Requirements Are Inapplicable to Violations and to Offenses Defined by Other Statutes; Effect of Absolute Liability in Reducing Grade of Offense to Violation.

(1) The requirements of culpability prescribed by Sections 2.01 and 2.02 do not apply to:

    (a) offenses that constitute violations, unless the requirement involved is included in the definition of the offense or the Court determines that its application is consistent with effective enforcement of the law defining the offense; or

    (b) offenses defined by statutes other than the Code, insofar as a legislative purpose to impose absolute liability for such offenses or with respect to any material element thereof plainly appears.

(2) Notwithstanding any other provision of existing law and unless a subsequent statute otherwise provides:

    (a) when absolute liability is imposed with respect to any material element of an offense defined by a statute other than the Code and a conviction is based upon such liability, the offense constitutes a violation; and

    (b) although absolute liability is imposed by law with respect to one or more of the material elements of an offense defined by a statute other than the Code, the culpable commission of the offense may be charged and proved, in which event negligence with respect to such elements constitutes sufficient culpability and the classification of the offense and the sentence that may be imposed therefor upon conviction are determined by Section 1.04 and Article 6 of the Code.

Section 2.06. Liability for Conduct of Another; Complicity.

(1) A person is guilty of an offense if it is committed by his own conduct or by the conduct of another person for which he is legally accountable, or both.

(2) A person is legally accountable for the conduct of another person when:

    (a) acting with the kind of culpability that is sufficient for the commission of the offense, he causes an innocent or irresponsible person to engage in such conduct; or

    (b) he is made accountable for the conduct of such other person by the Code or by the law defining the offense; or

    (c) he is an accomplice of such other person in the commission of the offense.

(3) A person is an accomplice of another person in the commission of an offense if:

    (a) with the purpose of promoting or facilitating the commission of the offense, he

    (i)   solicits such other person to commit it, or

    (ii) aids or agrees or attempts to aid such other person in planning or committing it, or

    (iii) having a legal duty to prevent the commission of the offense, fails to make proper effort so to do; or

(b) his conduct is expressly declared by law to establish his complicity.

(4) When causing a particular result is an element of an offense, an accomplice in the conduct causing such result is an accomplice in the commission of that offense if he acts with the kind of culpability, if any, with respect to that result that is sufficient for the commission of the offense.

(5) A person who is legally incapable of committing a particular offense himself may be guilty thereof if it is committed by the conduct of another person for which he is legally accountable, unless such liability is inconsistent with the purpose of the provision establishing his incapacity.

(6) Unless otherwise provided by the Code or by the law defining the offense, a person is not an accomplice in an offense committed by another person if:

(a) he is a victim of that offense; or

(b) the offense is so defined that his conduct is inevitably incident to its commission; or

(c) he terminates his complicity prior to the commission of the offense and

    (i)   wholly deprives it of effectiveness in the commission of the offense; or

    (ii) gives timely warning to the law enforcement authorities or otherwise makes proper effort to prevent the commission of the offense.

(7) An accomplice may be convicted on proof of the commission of the offense and of his complicity therein, though the person claimed to have committed the offense has not been prosecuted or convicted or has been convicted of a different offense or degree of offense or has an immunity to prosecution or conviction or has been acquitted.

...

Section 2.08. Intoxication.

(1) Except as provided in Subsection (4) of this Section, intoxication of the actor is not a defense unless it negatives an element of the offense.

(2) When recklessness establishes an element of the offense, if the actor, due to self-induced intoxication, is unaware of a risk of which he would have been aware had he been sober, such unawareness is immaterial.

(3) Intoxication does not, in itself, constitute mental disease within the meaning of Section 4.01.

(4) Intoxication that (a) is not self-induced or (b) is pathological is an affirmative defense if by reason of such intoxication the actor at the time of his conduct lacks substantial capacity either to appreciate its criminality [wrongfulness] or to conform his conduct to the requirements of law.

(5) Definitions. In this Section unless a different meaning plainly is required:

   (a) "intoxication" means a disturbance of mental or physical capacities resulting from the introduction of substances into the body;

   (b) "self-induced intoxication" means intoxication caused by substances that the actor knowingly introduces into his body, the tendency of which to cause intoxication he knows or ought to know, unless he introduces them pursuant to medical advice or under such circumstances as would afford a defense to a charge of crime;

   (c) "Pathological intoxication" means intoxication grossly excessive in degree, given the amount of the intoxicant, to which the actor does not know he is susceptible.

Section 2.09. Duress.

(1) It is an affirmative defense that the actor engaged in the conduct charged to constitute an offense because he was coerced to do so by the use of, or a threat to use, unlawful force against his person or the person of another, that a person of reasonable firmness in his situation would have been unable to resist.

(2) The defense provided by this Section is unavailable if the actor recklessly placed himself in a situation in which it was probable that he would be subjected to duress. The defense is also unavailable if he was negligent in placing himself in such a situation, whenever negligence suffices to establish culpability for the offense charged.

(3) It is not a defense that a woman acted on the command of her husband, unless she acted under such coercion as would establish a defense under this Section. [The presumption that a woman acting in the presence of her husband is coerced is abolished.]

(4) When the conduct of the actor would otherwise be justifiable under Section 3.02, this Section does not preclude such defense.

...

ARTICLE 3. GENERAL PRINCIPLES OF JUSTIFICATION

Section 3.01. Justification an Affirmative Defense; Civil Remedies Unaffected.

(1) In any prosecution based on conduct that is justifiable under this Article, justification is an affirmative defense.

(2) The fact that conduct is justifiable under this Article does not abolish or impair any remedy for such conduct that is available in any civil action.

Section 3.02. Justification Generally: Choice of Evils.

(1) Conduct that the actor believes to be necessary to avoid a harm or evil to himself or to another is justifiable, provided that:

    (a) the harm or evil sought to be avoided by such conduct is greater than that sought to be prevented by the law defining the offense charged; and

    (b) neither the Code nor other law defining the offense provides exceptions or defenses dealing with the specific situation involved; and

    (c) a legislative purpose to exclude the justification claimed does not otherwise plainly appear.

(2) When the actor was reckless or negligent in bringing about the situation requiring a choice of harms or evils or in appraising the necessity for his conduct, the justification afforded by this Section is unavailable in a prosecution for any offense for which recklessness or negligence, as the case may be, suffices to establish culpability.

…

Section 3.04. Use of Force in Self-Protection.

(1) <u>Use of Force Justifiable for Protection of the Person</u>. Subject to the provisions of this Section and of Section 3.09, the use of force upon or toward another person is justifiable when the actor believes that such force is immediately necessary for the purpose of protecting himself against the use of unlawful force by such other person on the present occasion.

(2) <u>Limitations on Justifying Necessity for Use of Force.</u>

    (a) The use of force is not justifiable under this Section:

        (i) to resist an arrest that the actor knows is being made by a peace officer, although the arrest is unlawful; or

        (ii) to resist force used by the occupier or possessor of property or by another person on his behalf, where the actor knows that the person using the force is doing so under a claim of right to protect the property, except that this limitation shall not apply if:

            (A) the actor is a public officer acting in the performance of his duties or a person lawfully assisting him therein or a person making or assisting in a lawful arrest; or

            (B) the actor has been unlawfully dispossessed of the property and is making a re-entry or recaption justified by Section 3.06; or

            (C) the actor believes that such force is necessary to protect himself against death or serious bodily injury.

    (b) The use of deadly force is not justifiable under this Section unless the actor believes that such force is necessary to protect himself against death, serious bodily injury, kidnapping or sexual intercourse compelled by force or threat; nor is it justifiable if:

(i) the actor, with the purpose of causing death or serious bodily injury, provoked the use of force against himself in the same encounter; or

(ii) the actor knows that he can avoid the necessity of using such force with complete safety by retreating or by surrendering possession of a thing to a person asserting a claim of right thereto or by complying with a demand that he abstain from any action that he has no duty to take, except that:

(A) the actor is not obliged to retreat from his dwelling or place of work, unless he was the initial aggressor or is assailed in his place of work by another person whose place of work the actor knows it to be; and

(B) a public officer justified in using force in the performance of his duties or a person justified in using force in his assistance or a person justified in using force in making an arrest or preventing an escape is not obliged to desist from efforts to perform such duty, effect such arrest or prevent such escape because of resistance or threatened resistance by or on behalf of the person against whom such action is directed.

(c) Except as required by paragraphs (a) and (b) of this Subsection, a person employing protective force may estimate the necessity thereof under the circumstances as he believes them to be when the force is used, without retreating, surrendering possession, doing any other act that he has no legal duty to do or abstaining from any lawful action.

(3) Use of Confinement as Protective Force. The justification afforded by this Section extends to the use of confinement as protective force only if the actor takes all reasonable measures to terminate the confinement as soon as he knows that he safely can, unless the person confined has been arrested on a charge of crime.

Section 3.05. Use of Force for the Protection of Other Persons.

(1) Subject to the provisions of this Section and of Section 3.09, the use of force upon or toward the person of another is justifiable to protect a third person when:

(a) the actor would be justified under Section 3.04 in using such force to protect himself against the injury he believes to be threatened to the person whom he seeks to protect; and

(b) under the circumstances as the actor believes them to be, the person whom he seeks to protect would be justified in using such protective force; and

(c) the actor believes that his intervention is necessary for the protection of such other person.

(2) Notwithstanding Subsection (1) of this Section:

(a) when the actor would be obliged under Section 3.04 to retreat, to surrender the possession of a thing or to comply with a demand before using force in self-protection, he is not obliged to do so before using force for the protection of another person, unless he knows that he can thereby secure the complete safety of such other person; and

(b) when the person whom the actor seeks to protect would be obliged under Section 3.04 to retreat, to surrender the possession of a thing or to comply with a demand if he knew that he could obtain complete safety by so doing, the actor is obliged to try to cause him to do so before using force in his protection if the actor knows that he can obtain complete safety in that way; and

(c) neither the actor nor the person whom he seeks to protect is obliged to retreat when in the other's dwelling or place of work to any greater extent than in his own.

Section 3.06. Use of Force for Protection of Property.

(1) Use of Force Justifiable for Protection of Property. Subject to the provisions of this Section and of Section 3.09, the use of force upon or toward the person of another is justifiable when the actor believes that such force is immediately necessary:

(a) to prevent or terminate an unlawful entry or other trespass upon land or a trespass against or the unlawful carrying away of tangible, movable property, provided that such land or movable property is, or is believed by the actor to be, in his possession or in the possession of another person for whose protection he acts; or

(b) to effect an entry or re-entry upon land or to retake tangible movable property, provided that the actor believes that he or the person by whose authority he acts or a person from whom he or such other person derives title was unlawfully dispossessed of such land or movable property and is entitled to possession, and provided, further, that:

(i)   the force is used immediately or on fresh pursuit after such dispossession; or

(ii) the actor believes that the person against whom he uses force has no claim of right to the possession of the property and, in the case of land, the circumstances, as the actor believes them to be, are of such urgency that it would be an exceptional hardship to postpone the entry or re-entry until a court order is obtained.

(2) Meaning of Possession. For the purposes of Subsection (1) of this Section:

(a) a person who has parted with the custody of property to another who refuses to restore it to him is no longer in possession, unless the property is movable and was and still is located on land in his possession;

(b) a person who has been dispossessed of land does not regain possession thereof merely by setting foot thereon;

(c) a person who has a license to use or occupy real property is deemed to be in possession thereof except against the licensor acting under claim of right.

(3) Limitations on Justifiable Use of Force.

(a) Request to Desist. The use of force is justifiable under this Section only if the actor first requests the person against whom such force is used to desist from his interference with the property, unless the actor believes that:

      (i)   such request would be useless; or

      (ii) it would be dangerous to himself or another person to make the request; or

      (iii) substantial harm will be done to the physical condition of the property that is sought to be protected before the request can effectively be made.

  (b) <u>Exclusion of Trespasser</u>. The use of force to prevent or terminate a trespass is not justifiable under this Section if the actor knows that the exclusion of the trespasser will expose him to substantial danger of serious bodily injury.

  (c) <u>Resistance of Lawful Re-entry or Recaption</u>. The use of force to prevent an entry or re-entry upon land or the recaption of movable property is not justifiable under this Section, although the actor believes that such re-entry or recaption is unlawful, if:

      (i)   the re-entry or recaption is made by or on behalf of a person who was actually dispossessed of the property; and

      (ii) it is otherwise justifiable under Subsection (1)(b) of this Section.

  (d) <u>Use of Deadly Force</u>. The use of deadly force is not justifiable under this Section unless the actor believes that:

      (i)   the person against whom the force is used is attempting to dispossess him of his dwelling otherwise than under a claim of right to its possession; or

      (ii) the person against whom the force is used is attempting to commit or consummate arson, burglary, robbery or other felonious theft or property destruction and either:

         (A) has employed or threatened deadly force against or in the presence of the actor; or

         (B) the use of force other than deadly force to prevent the commission or the consummation of the crime would expose the actor or another in his presence to substantial danger of serious bodily injury.

(4) <u>Use of Confinement as Protective Force</u>. The justification afforded by this Section extends to the use of confinement as protective force only if the actor takes all reasonable measures to terminate the confinement as soon as he knows that he can do so with safety to the property, unless the person confined has been arrested on a charge of crime.

(5) <u>Use of Device to Protect Property</u>. The justification afforded by this Section extends to the use of a device for the purpose of protecting property only if:

  (a) the device is not designed to cause or known to create a substantial risk of causing death or serious bodily injury; and

  (b) the use of the particular device to protect the property from entry or trespass is reasonable under the circumstances, as the actor believes them to be; and

  (c) the device is one customarily used for such a purpose or reasonable care is taken to make known to probable intruders the fact that it is used.

(6) <u>Use of Force to Pass Wrongful Obstructor</u>. The use of force to pass a person whom the actor believes to be purposely or knowingly and unjustifiably obstructing the actor from going to a place to which he may lawfully go is justifiable, provided that:

    (a) the actor believes that the person against whom he uses force has no claim of right to obstruct the actor; and

    (b) the actor is not being obstructed from entry or movement on land that he knows to be in the possession or custody of the person obstructing him, or in the possession or custody of another person by whose authority the obstructor acts, unless the circumstances, as the actor believes them to be, are of such urgency that it would not be reasonable to postpone the entry or movement on such land until a court order is obtained; and

    (c) the force used is not greater than would be justifiable if the person obstructing the actor were using force against him to prevent his passage.

    ...

Section 3.09. Mistake of Law as to Unlawfulness of Force or Legality of Arrest; Reckless or Negligent Use of Otherwise Justifiable Force; Reckless or Negligent Injury or Risk of Injury to Innocent Persons.

(1) The justification afforded by Sections 3.04 to 3.07, inclusive, is unavailable when:

    (a) the actor's belief in the unlawfulness of the force or conduct against which he employs protective force or his belief in the lawfulness of an arrest that he endeavors to effect by force is erroneous; and

    (b) his error is due to ignorance or mistake as to the provisions of the Code, any other provision of the criminal law or the law governing the legality of an arrest or search.

(2) When the actor believes that the use of force upon or toward the person of another is necessary for any of the purposes for which such belief would establish a justification under Sections 3.03 to 3.08 but the actor is reckless or negligent in having such belief or in acquiring or failing to acquire any knowledge or belief that is material to the justifiability of his use of force, the justification afforded by those Sections is unavailable in a prosecution for an offense for which recklessness or negligence, as the case may be, suffices to establish culpability.

(3) When the actor is justified under Sections 3.03 to 3.08 in using force upon or toward the person of another but he recklessly or negligently injures or creates a risk of injury to innocent persons, the justification afforded by those Sections is unavailable in a prosecution for such recklessness or negligence towards innocent persons.

    ...

ARTICLE 4. RESPONSIBILITY

Section 4.01. Mental Disease or Defect Excluding Responsibility.

(1) A person is not responsible for criminal conduct if at the time of such conduct as a result of mental disease or defect he lacks substantial capacity either to appreciate the criminality [wrongfulness] of his conduct or to conform his conduct to the requirements of law.

(2) As used in this Article, the terms "mental disease or defect" do not include an abnormality manifested only by repeated criminal or otherwise antisocial conduct.

Section 4.02. Evidence of Mental Disease or Defect Admissible When Relevant to Element of the Offense [; Mental Disease or Defect Impairing Capacity as Ground for Mitigation of Punishment in Capital Cases].

(1) Evidence that the defendant suffered from a mental disease or defect is admissible whenever it is relevant to prove that the defendant did or did not have a state of mind that is an element of the offense.

[(2) Whenever the jury or the Court is authorized to determine or to recommend whether or not the defendant shall be sentenced to death or imprisonment upon conviction, evidence that the capacity of the defendant to appreciate the criminality [wrongfulness] of his conduct or to conform his conduct to the requirements of law was impaired as a result of mental disease or defect is admissible in favor of sentence of imprisonment.]

Section 4.03. Mental Disease or Defect Excluding Responsibility Is Affirmative Defense; Requirement of Notice; Form of Verdict and Judgment When Finding of Irresponsibility Is Made.

(1) Mental disease or defect excluding responsibility is an affirmative defense.

(2) Evidence of mental disease or defect excluding responsibility is not admissible unless the defendant, at the time of entering his plea of not guilty or within ten days thereafter or at such later time as the Court may for good cause permit, files a written notice of his purpose to rely on such defense.

(3) When the defendant is acquitted on the ground of mental disease or defect excluding responsibility, the verdict and the judgment shall so state.

Section 4.04. Mental Disease or Defect Excluding Fitness to Proceed.

No person who as a result of mental disease or defect lacks capacity to understand the proceedings against him or to assist in his own defense shall be tried, convicted or sentenced for the commission of an offense so long as such incapacity endures.

Section 4.05. Psychiatric Examination of Defendant with Respect to Mental Disease or Defect.

(1) Whenever the defendant has filed a notice of intention to rely on the defense of mental disease or defect excluding responsibility, or there is reason to doubt his fitness to proceed, or reason to believe that mental disease or defect of the defendant will otherwise become an issue in the cause, the Court shall appoint at least one qualified psychiatrist or shall request the Superintendent of the Hospital to designate at least one qualified psychiatrist, which designation may be or include himself, to examine and report upon the mental condition of the defendant. The Court may order the defendant to be committed to a hospital or other suitable facility for the purpose of the examination for a period of not exceeding sixty days or such longer period as the Court determines to be necessary for the purpose and may direct that a qualified psychiatrist retained by the defendant be permitted to witness and participate in the examination.

(2) In such examination any method may be employed that is accepted by the medical profession for the examination of those alleged to be suffering from mental disease or defect.

(3) The report of the examination shall include the following: (a) a description of the nature of the examination; (b) a diagnosis of the mental condition of the defendant; (c) if the defendant suffers from a mental disease or defect, an opinion as to his capacity to understand the proceedings against him and to assist in his own defense; (d) when a notice of intention to rely on the defense of irresponsibility has been filed, an opinion as to the extent, if any, to which the capacity of the defendant to appreciate the criminality [wrongfulness] of his conduct or to conform his conduct to the requirements of law was impaired at the time of the criminal conduct charged; and (e) when directed by the Court, an opinion as to the capacity of the defendant to have a particular state of mind that is an element of the offense charged.

If the examination cannot be conducted by reason of the unwillingness of the defendant to participate therein, the report shall so state and shall include, if possible, an opinion as to whether such unwillingness of the defendant was the result of mental disease or defect.

The report of the examination shall be filed [in triplicate] with the clerk of the Court, who shall cause copies to be delivered to the district attorney and to counsel for the defendant.

Section 4.06. Determination of Fitness to Proceed; Effect of Finding of Unfitness; Proceedings if Fitness Is Regained [; Post-Commitment Hearing].

(1) When the defendant's fitness to proceed is drawn in question, the issue shall be determined by the Court. If neither the prosecuting attorney nor counsel for the defendant contests the finding of the report filed pursuant to Section 4.05, the Court may make the determination on the basis of such report. If the finding is contested, the Court shall hold a hearing on the issue. If the report is received in evidence upon

such hearing, the party who contests the finding thereof shall have the right to summon and to cross-examine the psychiatrists who joined in the report and to offer evidence upon the issue.

(2) If the Court determines that the defendant lacks fitness to proceed, the proceeding against him shall be suspended, except as provided in Subsection (3) [Subsections (3) and (4)] of this Section, and the Court shall commit him to the custody of the Commissioner of Mental Hygiene [Public Health or Correction] to be placed in an appropriate institution of the Department of Mental Hygiene [Public Health or Correction] for so long as such unfitness shall endure. When the Court, on its own motion or upon the application of the Commissioner of Mental Hygiene [Public Health or Correction] or the prosecuting attorney, determines, after a hearing if a hearing is requested, that the defendant has regained fitness to proceed, the proceeding shall be resumed. If, however, the Court is of the view that so much time has elapsed since the commitment of the defendant that it would be unjust to resume the criminal proceeding, the Court may dismiss the charge and may order the defendant to be discharged or, subject to the law governing the civil commitment of persons suffering from mental disease or defect, order the defendant to be committed to an appropriate institution of the Department of Mental Hygiene [Public Health].

(3) The fact that the defendant is unfit to proceed does not preclude any legal objection to the prosecution that is susceptible of fair determination prior to trial and without the personal participation of the defendant.

[Alternative: (3) At any time within ninety days after commitment as provided in Subsection (2) of this Section, or at any later time with permission of the Court granted for good cause, the defendant or his counsel or the Commissioner of Mental Hygiene [Public Health or Correction] may apply for a special post-commitment hearing. If the application is made by or on behalf of a defendant not represented by counsel, he shall be afforded a reasonable opportunity to obtain counsel, and if he lacks funds to do so, counsel shall be assigned by the Court. The application shall be granted only if counsel for the defendant satisfies the Court by affidavit or otherwise that as an attorney he has reasonable grounds for a good faith belief that his client has, on the facts and the law, a defense to the charge other than mental disease or defect excluding responsibility.

(4) If the motion for a special post-commitment hearing is granted, the hearing shall be by the Court without a jury. No evidence shall be offered at the hearing by either party on the issue of mental disease or defect as a defense to, or in mitigation of, the crime charged. After hearing, the Court may in an appropriate case quash the indictment or other charge, or find it to be defective or insufficient, or determine that it is not proved beyond a reasonable doubt by the evidence, or otherwise terminate the proceedings on the evidence or the law. In any such case, unless all defects in the proceedings are promptly cured, the Court shall terminate the commitment ordered under Subsection (2) of this Section and order the defendant to be discharged or, subject to the law governing the civil commitment of persons

suffering from mental disease or defect, order the defendant to be committed to an appropriate institution of the Department of Mental Hygiene [Public Health].]

Section 4.08. Legal Effect of Acquittal on the Ground of Mental Disease or Defect Excluding Responsibility; Commitment; Release or Discharge.

(1) When a defendant is acquitted on the ground of mental disease or defect excluding responsibility, the Court shall order him to be committed to the custody of the Commissioner of Mental Hygiene [Public Health] to be placed in an appropriate institution for custody, care and treatment.

(2) If the Commissioner of Mental Hygiene [Public Health] is of the view that a person committed to his custody, pursuant to Subsection (1) of this Section, may be discharged or released on condition without danger to himself or to others, he shall make application for the discharge or release of such person in a report to the Court by which such person was committed and shall transmit a copy of such application and report to the prosecuting attorney of the county [parish] from which the defendant was committed. The Court shall thereupon appoint at least two qualified psychiatrists to examine such person and to report within sixty days, or such longer period as the Court determines to be necessary for the purpose, their opinion as to his mental condition. To facilitate such examination and the proceedings thereon, the Court may cause such person to be confined in any institution located near the place where the Court sits, which may hereafter be designated by the Commissioner of Mental Hygiene [Public Health] as suitable for the temporary detention of irresponsible persons.

(3) If the Court is satisfied by the report filed pursuant to Subsection (2) of this Section and such testimony of the reporting psychiatrists as the Court deems necessary that the committed person may be discharged or released on condition without danger to himself or others, the Court shall order his discharge or his release on such conditions as the Court determines to be necessary. If the Court is not so satisfied, it shall promptly order a hearing to determine whether such person may safely be discharged or released. Any such hearing shall be deemed a civil proceeding and the burden shall be upon the committed person to prove that he may safely be discharged or released. According to the determination of the Court upon the hearing, the committed person shall thereupon be discharged or released on such conditions as the Court determines to be necessary, or shall be recommitted to the custody of the Commissioner of Mental Hygiene [Public Health], subject to discharge or release only in accordance with the procedure prescribed above for a first hearing.

(4) If, within [five] years after the conditional release of a committed person, the Court shall determine, after hearing evidence, that the conditions of release have not been fulfilled and that for the safety of such person or for the safety of others his conditional release should be revoked, the Court shall forthwith order him to be recommitted to the Commissioner of Mental Hygiene [Public Health], subject to discharge or release only in accordance with the procedure prescribed above for a first hearing.

(5) A committed person may make application for his discharge or release to the Court by which he was committed, and the procedure to be followed upon such application shall be the same as that prescribed above in the case of an application by the Commissioner of Mental Hygiene [Public Health]. However, no such application by a committed person need be considered until he has been confined for a period of not less than [six months] from the date of the order of commitment, and if the determination of the Court be adverse to the application, such person shall not be permitted to file a further application until [one year] has elapsed from the date of any preceding hearing on an application for his release or discharge.

ARTICLE 5. INCHOATE CRIMES

Section 5.01. Criminal Attempt.

(1) Definition of Attempt. A person is guilty of an attempt to commit a crime if, acting with the kind of culpability otherwise required for commission of the crime, he:

    (a) purposely engages in conduct that would constitute the crime if the attendant circumstances were as he believes them to be; or

    (b) when causing a particular result is an element of the crime, does or omits to do anything with the purpose of causing or with the belief that it will cause such result without further conduct on his part; or

    (c) purposely does or omits to do anything that, under the circumstances as he believes them to be, is an act or omission constituting a substantial step in a course of conduct planned to culminate in his commission of the crime.

(2) Conduct That May Be Held Substantial Step Under Subsection (1)(c). Conduct shall not be held to constitute a substantial step under Subsection (1)(c) of this Section unless it is strongly corroborative of the actor's criminal purpose. Without negativing the sufficiency of other conduct, the following, if strongly corroborative of the actor's criminal purpose, shall not be held insufficient as a matter of law:

    (a) lying in wait, searching for or following the contemplated victim of the crime;

    (b) enticing or seeking to entice the contemplated victim of the crime to go to the place contemplated for its commission;

    (c) reconnoitering the place contemplated for the commission of the crime;

    (d) unlawful entry of a structure, vehicle or enclosure in which it is contemplated that the crime will be committed;

    (e) possession of materials to be employed in the commission of the crime, that are specially designed for such unlawful use or that can serve no lawful purpose of the actor under the circumstances;

    (f) possession, collection or fabrication of materials to be employed in the commission of the crime, at or near the place contemplated for its commission, if such possession, collection or fabrication serves no lawful purpose of the actor under the circumstances;

(g) soliciting an innocent agent to engage in conduct constituting an element of the crime.

(3) <u>Conduct Designed to Aid Another in Commission of a Crime</u>. A person who engages in conduct designed to aid another to commit a crime that would establish his complicity under Section 2.06 if the crime were committed by such other person, is guilty of an attempt to commit the crime, although the crime is not committed or attempted by such other person.

(4) <u>Renunciation of Criminal Purpose</u>. When the actor's conduct would otherwise constitute an attempt under Subsection (1)(b) or (1)(c) of this Section, it is an affirmative defense that he abandoned his effort to commit the crime or otherwise prevented its commission, under circumstances manifesting a complete and voluntary renunciation of his criminal purpose. The establishment of such defense does not, however, affect the liability of an accomplice who did not join in such abandonment or prevention.

Within the meaning of this Article, renunciation of criminal purpose is not voluntary if it is motivated, in whole or in part, by circumstances, not present or apparent at the inception of the actor's course of conduct, that increase the probability of detection or apprehension or that make more difficult the accomplishment of the criminal purpose. Renunciation is not complete if it is motivated by a decision to postpone the criminal conduct until a more advantageous time or to transfer the criminal effort to another but similar objective or victim.

Section 5.02. Criminal Solicitation.

(1) <u>Definition of Solicitation</u>. A person is guilty of solicitation to commit a crime if with the purpose of promoting or facilitating its commission he commands, encourages or requests another person to engage in specific conduct that would constitute such crime or an attempt to commit such crime or would establish his complicity in its commission or attempted commission.

(2) <u>Uncommunicated Solicitation</u>. It is immaterial under Subsection (1) of this Section that the actor fails to communicate with the person he solicits to commit a crime if his conduct was designed to effect such communication.

(3) <u>Renunciation of Criminal Purpose</u>. It is an affirmative defense that the actor, after soliciting another person to commit a crime, persuaded him not to do so or otherwise prevented the commission of the crime, under circumstances manifesting a complete and voluntary renunciation of his criminal purpose.

Section 5.03. Criminal Conspiracy.

(1) <u>Definition of Conspiracy</u>. A person is guilty of conspiracy with another person or persons to commit a crime if with the purpose of promoting or facilitating its commission he:

(a) agrees with such other person or persons that they or one or more of them will engage in conduct that constitutes such crime or an attempt or solicitation to commit such crime; or

(b) agrees to aid such other person or persons in the planning or commission of such crime or of an attempt or solicitation to commit such crime.

(2) Scope of Conspiratorial Relationship. If a person guilty of conspiracy, as defined by Subsection (1) of this Section, knows that a person with whom he conspires to commit a crime has conspired with another person or persons to commit the same crime, he is guilty of conspiring with such other person or persons, whether or not he knows their identity, to commit such crime.

(3) Conspiracy with Multiple Criminal Objectives. If a person conspires to commit a number of crimes, he is guilty of only one conspiracy so long as such multiple crimes are the object of the same agreement or continuous conspiratorial relationship.

(4) Joinder and Venue in Conspiracy Prosecutions.

(a) Subject to the provisions of paragraph (b) of this Subsection, two or more persons charged with criminal conspiracy may be prosecuted jointly if:

(i) they are charged with conspiring with one another; or

(ii) the conspiracies alleged, whether they have the same or different parties, are so related that they constitute different aspects of a scheme of organized criminal conduct.

(b) In any joint prosecution under paragraph (a) of this Subsection:

(i) no defendant shall be charged with a conspiracy in any county [parish or district] other than one in which he entered into such conspiracy or in which an overt act pursuant to such conspiracy was done by him or by a person with whom he conspired; and

(ii) neither the liability of any defendant nor the admissibility against him of evidence of acts or declarations of another shall be enlarged by such joinder; and

(iii) the Court shall order a severance or take a special verdict as to any defendant who so requests, if it deems it necessary or appropriate to promote the fair determination of his guilt or innocence, and shall take any other proper measures to protect the fairness of the trial.

(5) Overt Act. No person may be convicted of conspiracy to commit a crime, other than a felony of the first or second degree, unless an overt act in pursuance of such conspiracy is alleged and proved to have been done by him or by a person with whom he conspired.

(6) Renunciation of Criminal Purpose. It is an affirmative defense that the actor, after conspiring to commit a crime, thwarted the success of the conspiracy, under circumstances manifesting a complete and voluntary renunciation of his criminal purpose.

(7) Duration of Conspiracy. For purposes of Section 1.06(4):

    (a) conspiracy is a continuing course of conduct that terminates when the crime or crimes that are its object are committed or the agreement that they be committed is abandoned by the defendant and by those with whom he conspired; and

    (b) such abandonment is presumed if neither the defendant nor anyone with whom he conspired does any overt act in pursuance of the conspiracy during the applicable period of limitation; and

    (c) if an individual abandons the agreement, the conspiracy is terminated as to him only if and when he advises those with whom he conspired of his abandonment or he informs the law enforcement authorities of the existence of the conspiracy and of his participation therein.

Section 5.04. Incapacity, Irresponsibility or Immunity of Party to Solicitation or Conspiracy.

(1) Except as provided in Subsection (2) of this Section, it is immaterial to the liability of a person who solicits or conspires with another to commit a crime that:

    (a) he or the person whom he solicits or with whom he conspires does not occupy a particular position or have a particular characteristic that is an element of such crime, if he believes that one of them does; or

    (b) the person whom he solicits or with whom he conspires is irresponsible or has an immunity to prosecution or conviction for the commission of the crime.

(2) It is a defense to a charge of solicitation or conspiracy to commit a crime that if the criminal object were achieved, the actor would not be guilty of a crime under the law defining the offense or as an accomplice under Section 2.06(5) or 2.06(6)(a) or (6)(b).

Section 5.05. Grading of Criminal Attempt, Solicitation and Conspiracy; Mitigation in Cases of Lesser Danger; Multiple Convictions Barred.

(1) Grading. Except as otherwise provided in this Section, attempt, solicitation and conspiracy are crimes of the same grade and degree as the most serious offense that is attempted or solicited or is an object of the conspiracy. An attempt, solicitation or conspiracy to commit a [capital crime or a] felony of the first degree is a felony of the second degree.

(2) Mitigation. If the particular conduct charged to constitute a criminal attempt, solicitation or conspiracy is so inherently unlikely to result or culminate in the commission of a crime that neither such conduct nor the actor presents a public danger warranting the grading of such offense under this Section, the Court shall exercise its power under Section 6.12 to enter judgment and impose sentence for a crime of lower grade or degree or, in extreme cases, may dismiss the prosecution.

    ...

ARTICLE 210. CRIMINAL HOMICIDE

Section 210.0. Definitions.

In Articles 210-213, unless a different meaning plainly is required:

(1) "human being" means a person who has been born and is alive;

(2) "bodily injury" means physical pain, illness or any impairment of physical condition;

(3) "serious bodily injury" means bodily injury which creates a substantial risk of death or which causes serious, permanent disfigurement, or protracted loss or impairment of the function of any bodily member or organ;

(4) "deadly weapon" means any firearm or other weapon, device, instrument, material or substance, whether animate or inanimate, which in the manner it is used or is intended to be used is known to be capable of producing death or serious bodily injury.

Section 210.1. Criminal Homicide.

(1) A person is guilty of criminal homicide if he purposely, knowingly, recklessly or negligently causes the death of another human being.

(2) Criminal homicide is murder, manslaughter or negligent homicide.

Section 210.2. Murder.

(1) Except as provided in Section 210.3(l)(b), criminal homicide constitutes murder when:

(a) it is committed purposely or knowingly; or

(b) it is committed recklessly under circumstances manifesting extreme indifference to the value of human life. Such recklessness and indifference are presumed if the actor is engaged or is an accomplice in the commission of, or an attempt to commit, or flight after committing or attempting to commit robbery, rape or deviate sexual intercourse by force or threat of force, arson, burglary, kidnapping or felonious escape.

(2) Murder is a felony of the first degree [but a person convicted of murder may be sentenced to death, as provided in Section 210.61].

Section 210.3. Manslaughter.

(1) Criminal homicide constitutes manslaughter when:

(a) it is committed recklessly; or

(b) a homicide which would otherwise be murder is committed under the influence of extreme mental or emotional disturbance for which there is reasonable explanation or excuse. The reasonableness of such explanation or excuse shall be determined from the viewpoint of a person in the actor's situation under the circumstances as he believes them to be.

(2) Manslaughter is a felony of the second degree.

Section 210.4. Negligent Homicide.

(1) Criminal homicide constitutes negligent homicide when it is committed negligently.

(2) Negligent homicide is a felony of the third degree.

Section 210.5. Causing or Aiding Suicide.

(1) <u>Causing Suicide as Criminal Homicide</u>. A person may be convicted of criminal homicide for causing another to commit suicide only if he purposely causes such suicide by force, duress or deception.

(2) <u>Aiding or Soliciting Suicide as an Independent Offense</u>. A person who purposely aids or solicits another to commit suicide is guilty of a felony of the second degree if his conduct causes such suicide or an attempted suicide, and otherwise of a misdemeanor.

...

ARTICLE 211. ASSAULT; RECKLESS ENDANGERING; THREATS

Section 211.0. Definitions.

In this Article, the definitions given in Section 210.0 apply unless a different meaning plainly is required.

Section 211.1. Assault.

(1) <u>Simple Assault</u>. A person is guilty of assault if he:
   (a) attempts to cause or purposely, knowingly or recklessly causes bodily injury to another; or
   (b) negligently causes bodily injury to another with a deadly weapon; or
   (c) attempts by physical menace to put another in fear of imminent serious bodily injury.

Simple assault is a misdemeanor unless committed in a fight or scuffle entered into by mutual consent, in which case it is a petty misdemeanor.

(2) <u>Aggravated Assault</u>. A person is guilty of aggravated assault if he:
   (a) attempts to cause serious bodily injury to another, or causes such injury purposely, knowingly or recklessly under circumstances manifesting extreme indifference to the value of human life; or
   (b) attempts to cause or purposely or knowingly causes bodily injury to another with a deadly weapon.

Aggravated assault under paragraph (a) is a felony of the second degree; aggravated assault under paragraph (b) is a felony of the third degree.

Section 211.2. Recklessly Endangering Another Person.

A person commits a misdemeanor if he recklessly engages in conduct which places or may place another person in danger of death or serious bodily injury. Recklessness and danger shall be presumed where a person knowingly points a firearm at or in the direction of another, whether or not the actor believed the firearm to be loaded.

...

ARTICLE 213. SEXUAL OFFENSES

Section 213.0. Definitions.

In this Article, unless a different meaning plainly is required:

(1) the definitions given in Section 210.0 apply;

(2) "Sexual intercourse" includes intercourse per os or per anum, with some penetration however slight; emission is not required;

(3) "Deviate sexual intercourse" means sexual intercourse per os or per anum between human beings who are not husband and wife, and any form of sexual intercourse with an animal.

Section 213.1. Rape and Related Offenses.

(1) <u>Rape</u>. A male who has sexual intercourse with a female not his wife is guilty of rape if:

  (a) he compels her to submit by force or by threat of imminent death, serious bodily injury, extreme pain or kidnapping, to be inflicted on anyone; or

  (b) he has substantially impaired her power to appraise or control her conduct by administering or employing without her knowledge drugs, intoxicants or other means for the purpose of preventing resistance; or

  (c) the female is unconscious; or

  (d) the female is less than 10 years old.

Rape is a felony of the second degree unless (i) in the course thereof the actor inflicts serious bodily injury upon anyone, or (ii) the victim was not a voluntary social companion of the actor upon the occasion of the crime and had not previously permitted him sexual liberties, in which cases the offense is a felony of the first degree.

(2) <u>Gross Sexual Imposition</u>. A male who has sexual intercourse with a female not his wife commits a felony of the third degree if:

  (a) he compels her to submit by any threat that would prevent resistance by a woman of ordinary resolution; or

  (b) he knows that she suffers from a mental disease or defect which renders her incapable of appraising the nature of her conduct; or

(c)   he knows that she is unaware that a sexual act is being committed upon her or that she submits because she mistakenly supposes that he is her husband.

Section 213.2. Deviate Sexual Intercourse by Force or Imposition.

(1)   <u>By Force or Its Equivalent</u>. A person who engages in deviate sexual intercourse with another person, or who causes another to engage in deviate sexual intercourse, commits a felony of the second degree if:

(a)   he compels the other person to participate by force or by threat of imminent death, serious bodily injury, extreme pain or kidnapping, to be inflicted on anyone; or

(b)   he has substantially impaired the other person's power to appraise or control his conduct, by administering or employing without the knowledge of the other person drugs, intoxicants or other means for the purpose of preventing resistance; or

(c)   the other person is unconscious; or

(d)   the other person is less than 10 years old.

(2)   <u>By Other Imposition</u>. A person who engages in deviate sexual intercourse with another person, or who causes another to engage in deviate sexual intercourse, commits a felony of the third degree if:

(a)   he compels the other person to participate by any threat that would prevent resistance by a person of ordinary resolution; or

(b)   he knows that the other person suffers from a mental disease or defect which renders him incapable of appraising the nature of his conduct; or

(c)   he knows that the other person submits because he is unaware that a sexual act is being committed upon him.

Section 213.3. Corruption of Minors and Seduction.

(1)   <u>Offense Defined</u>. A male who has sexual intercourse with a female not his wife, or any person who engages in deviate sexual intercourse or causes another to engage in deviate sexual intercourse, is guilty of an offense if:

(a)   the other person is less than [16] years old and the actor is at least [four] years older than the other person; or

(b)   the other person is less than 21 years old and the actor is his guardian or otherwise responsible for general supervision of his welfare; or

(c)   the other person is in custody of law or detained in a hospital or other institution and the actor has supervisory or disciplinary authority over him; or

(d)   the other person is a female who is induced to participate by a promise of marriage which the actor does not mean to perform.

(2)   <u>Grading</u>. An offense under paragraph (a) of Subsection (1) is a felony of the third degree. Otherwise an offense under this section is a misdemeanor.

Section 213.4. Sexual Assault.

A person who has sexual contact with another not his spouse, or causes such other to have sexual conduct with him, is guilty of sexual assault, a misdemeanor, if:

(1)   he knows that the contact is offensive to the other person; or

(2)   he knows that the other person suffers from a mental disease or defect which renders him or her incapable of appraising the nature of his or her conduct; or

(3)   he knows that the other person is unaware that a sexual act is being committed; or

(4)   the other person is less than 10 years old; or

(5)   he has substantially impaired the other person's power to appraise or control his or her conduct, by administering or employing without the other's knowledge drugs, intoxicants or other means for the purpose of preventing resistance; or

(6)   the other person is less than [16] years old and the actor is at least [four] years older than the other person; or

(7)   the other person is less than 21 years old and the actor is his guardian or otherwise responsible for general supervision of his welfare; or

(8)   the other person is in custody of law or detained in a hospital or other institution and the actor has supervisory or disciplinary authority over him.

Sexual contact is any touching of the sexual or other intimate parts of the person for the purpose of arousing or gratifying sexual desire.

...

ARTICLE 223. THEFT AND RELATED OFFENSES

Section 223.0. Definitions.

In this Article, unless a different meaning plainly is required:

(1)   "deprive" means: (a) to withhold property of another permanently or for so extended a period as to appropriate a major portion of its economic value, or with intent to restore only upon payment of reward or other compensation; or (b) to dispose of the property so as to make it unlikely that the owner will recover it.

(2)   "financial institution" means a bank, insurance company, credit union, building and loan association, investment trust or other organization held out to the public as a place of deposit of funds or medium of savings or collective investment.

(3)   "government" means the United States, any State, county, municipality, or other political unit, or any department, agency or subdivision of any of the foregoing, or any corporation or other association carrying out the functions of government.

(4)   "movable property" means property the location of which can be changed, including things growing on, affixed to, or found in land, and documents although the rights represented thereby have no physical location; "immovable property" is all other property.

(5) "obtain" means: (a) in relation to property, to bring about a transfer or purported transfer of a legal interest in the property, whether to the obtainer or another; or (b) in relation to labor or service, to secure performance thereof.

(6) "property" means anything of value, including real estate, tangible and intangible personal property, contract rights, choses-in-action and other interests in or claims to wealth, admission or transportation tickets, captured or domestic animals, food and drink, electric or other power.

(7) "property of another" includes property in which any person other than the actor has an interest which the actor is not privileged to infringe, regardless of the fact that the actor also has an interest in the property and regardless of the fact that the other person might be precluded from civil recovery because the property was used in an unlawful transaction or was subject to forfeiture as contraband. Property in possession of the actor shall not be deemed property of another who has only a security interest therein, even if legal title is in the creditor pursuant to a conditional sales contract or other security agreement.

Section 223.1. Consolidation of Theft Offenses; Grading; Provisions Applicable to Theft Generally.

(1) Consolidation of Theft Offenses. Conduct denominated theft in this Article constitutes a single offense. An accusation of theft may be supported by evidence that it was committed in any manner that would be theft under this Article, notwithstanding the specification of a different manner in the indictment or information, subject only to the power of the Court to ensure fair trial by granting a continuance or other appropriate relief where the conduct of the defense would be prejudiced by lack of fair notice or by surprise.

(2) Grading of Theft Offenses.

    (a) Theft constitutes a felony of the third degree if the amount involved exceeds $500, or if the property stolen is a firearm, automobile, airplane, motorcycle, motorboat, or other motor-propelled vehicle, or in the case of theft by receiving stolen property, if the receiver is in the business of buying or selling stolen property.

    (b) Theft not within the preceding paragraph constitutes a misdemeanor, except that if the property was not taken from the person or by threat, or in breach of a fiduciary obligation, and the actor proves by a preponderance of the evidence that the amount involved was less than $50, the offense constitutes a petty misdemeanor.

    (c) The amount involved in a theft shall be deemed to be the highest value, by any reasonable standard, of the property or services which the actor stole or attempted to steal. Amounts involved in thefts committed pursuant to one scheme or course of conduct, whether from the same person or several persons, may be aggregated in determining the grade of the offense.

(3) Claim of Right. It is an affirmative defense to prosecution for theft that the actor:

(a) was unaware that the property or service was that of another; or

(b) acted under an honest claim of right to the property or service involved or that he had a right to acquire or dispose of it as he did; or

(c) took property exposed for sale, intending to purchase and pay for it promptly, or reasonably believing that the owner, if present, would have consented.

(4) Theft from Spouse. It is no defense that theft was from the actor's spouse, except that misappropriation of household and personal effects, or other property normally accessible to both spouses, is theft only if it occurs after the parties have ceased living together.

Section 223.2. Theft by Unlawful Taking or Disposition.

(1) Movable Property. A person is guilty of theft if he unlawfully takes, or exercises unlawful control over, movable property of another with purpose to deprive him thereof.

(2) Immovable Property. A person is guilty of theft if he unlawfully transfers immovable property of another or any interest therein with purpose to benefit himself or another not entitled thereto.

Section 223.3. Theft by Deception.

A person is guilty of theft if he purposely obtains property of another by deception. A person deceives if he purposely:

(1) creates or reinforces a false impression, including false impressions as to law, value, intention or other state of mind; but deception as to a person's intention to perform a promise shall not be inferred from the fact alone that he did not subsequently perform the promise; or

(2) prevents another from acquiring information which would affect his judgment of a transaction; or

(3) fails to correct a false impression which the deceiver previously created or reinforced, or which the deceiver knows to be influencing another to whom he stands in a fiduciary or confidential relationship; or

(4) fails to disclose a known lien, adverse claim or other legal impediment to the enjoyment of property which he transfers or encumbers in consideration for the property obtained, whether such impediment is or is not valid, or is or is not a matter of official record.

The term "deceive" does not, however, include falsity as to matters having no pecuniary significance, or puffing by statements unlikely to deceive ordinary persons in the group addressed.

Section 223.4. Theft by Extortion.

A person is guilty of theft if he purposely obtains property of another by threatening to:

(1) inflict bodily injury on anyone or commit any other criminal offense; or

(2) accuse anyone of a criminal offense; or

(3) expose any secret tending to subject any person to hatred, contempt or ridicule, or to impair his credit or business repute;

(4) take or withhold action as an official, or cause an official to take or withhold action; or

(5) bring about or continue a strike, boycott or other collective unofficial action, if the property is not demanded or received for the benefit of the group in whose interest the actor purports to act; or

(6) testify or provide information or withhold testimony or information with respect to another's legal claim or defense; or

(7) inflict any other harm which would not benefit the actor.

It is an affirmative defense to prosecution based on paragraphs (2), (3) or (4) that the property obtained by threat of accusation, exposure, lawsuit or other invocation of official action was honestly claimed as restitution or indemnification for harm done in the circumstances to which such accusation, exposure, lawsuit or other official action relates, or as compensation for property or lawful services.

Section 223.5. Theft of Property Lost, Mislaid, or Delivered by Mistake.

A person who comes into control of property of another that he knows to have been lost, mislaid, or delivered under a mistake as to the nature or amount of the property or the identity of the recipient is guilty of theft if, with purpose to deprive the owner thereof, he fails to take reasonable measures to restore the property to a person entitled to have it.

Section 223.6. Receiving Stolen Property.

(1) Receiving. A person is guilty of theft if he purposely receives, retains, or disposes of movable property of another knowing that it has been stolen, or believing that it has probably been stolen, unless the property is received, retained, or disposed with purpose to restore it to the owner. "Receiving" means acquiring possession, control or title, or lending on the security of the property.

(2) Presumption of Knowledge. The requisite knowledge or belief is presumed in the case of a dealer who:

(a) is found in possession or control of property stolen from two or more persons on separate occasions; or

(b) has received stolen property in another transaction within the year preceding the transaction charged; or

(c) being a dealer in property of the sort received, acquires it for a consideration which he knows is far below its reasonable value.

"Dealer" means a person in the business of buying or selling goods including a pawnbroker.

Index